Methodological Issues & Strategies in Clinical Research

Third Edition

Methodological Issues & Strategies in Clinical Research

Third Edition

Edited by
Alan E. Kazdin

American Psychological Association
Washington, DC

Published by
American Psychological Association
750 First Street, NE
Washington, DC 20002
www.apa.org

To order
APA Order Department
P.O. Box 92984
Washington, DC 20090-2984
Tel: (800) 374-2721; Direct: (202) 336-5510
Fax: (202) 336-5502; TDD/TTY: (202) 336-6123
On-line: www.apa.org/books/
E-mail: order@apa.org

In the U.K., Europe, Africa, and the Middle East, copies may be ordered from
American Psychological Association
3 Henrietta Street
Covent Garden, London
WC2E 8LU England

Typeset in Goudy by G & S Typesetters, Inc., Austin, TX

Printer: United Book Press, Inc., Baltimore, MD
Cover Designer: Minker Design, Bethesda, MD
Technical/Production Editor: Rosemary Moulton

The opinions and statements published are the responsibility of the authors, and such opinions and statements do not necessarily represent the policies of the American Psychological Association.

Library of Congress Cataloging-in-Publication Data

Methodological issues & strategies in clinical research / edited by Alan E. Kazdin.—3rd ed.
    p.   cm.
  Includes bibliographical references and index.
  ISBN 1-55798-958-3
  1. Clinical psychology—Research—Methodology. I. Kazdin, Alan E. II. Title:
Methodological issues and strategies in clinical research.
  RC467.8.M48 2002
  616.89'007'2—dc21

                                                                        2002011069

British Library Cataloguing-in-Publication Data
A CIP record is available from the British Library.

Printed in the United States of America
First Edition

CONTENTS

CONTRIBUTORS

David H. Barlow, Center for Anxiety and Related Disorders, Boston University

Daryl J. Bem, Department of Psychology, Cornell University, New York

Leslie Case, Department of Psychology, University of South Dakota, Vermillion

Lee Anna Clark, Department of Psychology, University of Iowa, Iowa City

Gregory N. Clarke, Kaiser Permanente Center for Health Research, Portland, OR

Jacob Cohen, Department of Psychology, New York University (deceased)

Michael Cowles, Department of Psychology, York University, Toronto

Betsy Davis, School of Psychology, University of Oregon, Eugene

Caroline Davis, Department of Psychology, York University, Toronto

Robert R. Dies, New Port Richey, FL

Sara L. Dolan, Department of Psychology, University of Iowa, Iowa City

Elena J. Eisman, Massachusetts Psychological Association, Boston

Lorraine D. Eyde, U.S. Office of Personnel Management, Washington, DC

Arthur E. Finch, Department of Psychology, Brigham Young University, Provo, UT

Mark A. Fine, Department of Human Development and Family Studies, University of Missouri, Columbia

Stephen E. Finn, Center for Therapeutic Assessment, Austin, TX

Kevin J. Fleming, Department of Psychology, University of Notre Dame, Notre Dame, IN

Barbara J. Fly, Colorado Springs, CO

Roland H. Good III, School of Psychology, University of Oregon, Eugene

Elena L. Grigorenko, Child Study Center, Yale University School of Medicine and Moscow State University, New Haven, CT

Stephen N. Haynes, Department of Psychology, University of Hawaii, Honolulu

Grayson N. Holmbeck, Department of Psychology, Loyola University of Chicago

George S. Howard, Department of Psychology, University of Notre Dame, Notre Dame, IN

Louis M. Hsu, Department of Psychology, Fairleigh Dickinson University, Teaneck, NJ

Lynn D. Johnson, Brief Therapy Center, Salt Lake City, UT

Gary G. Kay, Georgetown University Medical Center, Washington, DC

Alan E. Kazdin, Child Study Center, Yale University School of Medicine, New Haven, CT

Karen Strohm Kitchener, College of Education, University of Denver

Tom W. Kubiszyn, American Psychological Association, Washington, DC

Lawrence A. Kurdek, Department of Psychology, Wright State University, Dayton, OH

Michael J. Lambert, Department of Psychology, Brigham Young University, Provo, UT

Patrick R. Lang, Child and Family Studies Program, University of Denver

Mark W. Lipsey, Department of Psychology and Human Development, Vanderbilt University, Nashville, TN

Brendan A. Maher, Department of Psychology, Harvard University, Cambridge, MA

Scott E. Maxwell, Department of Psychology, University of Notre Dame, Notre Dame, IN

Gregory J. Meyer, Department of Psychology, University of Alaska–Anchorage

Dale T. Miller, Department of Psychology, Princeton University, Princeton, NJ

Douglas G. Mook, Department of Psychology, University of Virginia, Charlottesville

Karla Moras, Department of Psychiatry, University of Pennsylvania School of Medicine, Philadelphia

Kevin L. Moreland, Fort Walton Beach, FL (deceased)

David L. Morgan, Department of Psychology, Spalding University, Louisville, KY

Robin K. Morgan, Department of Psychology, Indiana University Southeast, New Albany

Peter E. Nathan, Department of Psychology, University of Iowa, Iowa City

Sumie Okazaki, Department of Psychology, University of Wisconsin, Madison

John C. Okiishi, Department of Psychology, Brigham Young University, Provo, UT

Jacqueline B. Persons, Center for Cognitive Therapy, Oakland, CA

Deborah A. Prentice, Department of Psychology, Princeton University, Princeton, NJ

Geoffrey M. Reed, Department of Psychiatry and Behavioral Science, University of California at Los Angeles

Frank L. Schmidt, Department of Management and Organizations, University of Iowa, Iowa City

George Silberschatz, Department of Psychiatry, University of California, San Francisco

M. Brewster Smith, Professor Emeritus of Psychology, University of California at Santa Cruz

Timothy B. Smith, Department of Counseling Psychology and Special Education, Brigham Young University, Provo, UT

Robert J. Sternberg, Department of Psychology, Yale University, New Haven, CT

Scott P. Stuart, Department of Psychology, University of Iowa, Iowa City

Stanley Sue, Department of Psychology, University of California at Davis

Leslie A. Telfer, Veterans Administration Center, Palo Alto, CA

William P. van Bark, Littleton, CO

Howard Wainer, Educational Testing Service, Princeton, NJ

Bruce E. Wampold, Division of Counseling Psychology, University of Wisconsin, Madison

David Watson, Department of Psychology, University of Iowa, Iowa City

Laura Weinman, Counseling Psychology Program, University of Denver

Allan W. Wicker, Department of Psychology, Claremont Graduate School, Claremont, CA

Leland Wilkinson, SPSS Incorporated, Chicago

David B. Wilson, Administration of Justice Program, George Mason University, Fairfax, VA

Brian T. Yates, Department of Psychology, American University, Washington, DC

PREFACE

ALAN E. KAZDIN

This book of readings is designed to improve understanding of methodology and research practices in clinical psychology. Students and professionals in training or actively involved in research are the intended audience. Although the primary focus is on clinical psychology, many of the chapters address issues that span the field of psychology more generally. The issues and methods raised in the readings are particularly relevant to areas of research within psychology (e.g., clinical, counseling, educational, and school psychology) and to other disciplines (e.g., psychiatry, nursing, and social work). These areas span theory, research, and application and, hence, share many methodological challenges and opportunities.

The emphasis of this book is on the dominant paradigm that characterizes contemporary scientific research. Among the salient characteristics of this paradigm are the focus on theory, systematic assessment, null hypothesis testing, and quantitative analyses of results. Just as scientific knowledge is not the only way of knowing (e.g., deduction, intuitionism), the current paradigm is not the only way of studying phenomena empirically (e.g., qualitative research, nonstatistical methods of data evaluation). Nevertheless, it is central that students and professionals master and keep abreast of the dominant paradigm, understand the many methodological options and advances, and be alert to the many obstacles and shoals when designing their studies. The goal of the book is to foster greater understanding of the strengths, limitations, and options of methodology in the context of contemporary research practices.

ORGANIZATION OF THIS BOOK AND CHAPTER SELECTION

The contents of the book include experimental design, principles, procedures, and practices that govern research, assessment, sources of artifact and bias, methods of data analyses and interpretation, ethical issues, and publication and communication of the results of research. The organization of the book conveys features of research that follow in approximate logical and often temporal order as they arise in the flow of an investigation. Thus, underpinnings of research, development of the research idea, and procedures within the study obviously precede data analyses and the writeup of the study. The parts of the book include

1. Introduction: Overview and Background
2. Beginning the Research Process
3. Methods: Principles and Practices
4. Assessment
5. Data Analysis, Evaluation, and Interpretation
6. Special Topics in Clinical Research
7. Ethics in Research
8. Publication and Communication of Research
9. Perspectives on Methodology.

Although there is a flow and sequence of the research process, underlying this book and the selection of articles is the view that diverse facets of design are integrally related and many emerge when the study is conceived. For example, in the planning stage of a study, the theory and rationale at the very outset are, or at least should be, related to the plans for the data analyses and anticipated interpretations of the results. Typically, at this point investigators are not too concerned with analyses of the results or, of course, with the critical issues that will form the basis of the discussion in a writeup or report of the study. Yet, critical thought about how one is likely to analyze the data and the specific conclusions one wishes to draw from the study greatly influence core features of the design, such as the experimental conditions, the plan for their administration between or within subjects, sample size and composition, and the type and range of measures.

Similarly, limitations of a study are usually discussed at the end of the journal article that describes the study. This is clearly the place to discuss them, and many limitations can be identified only when the study is completed. For example, we may only learn *during* the study that 90% of participants in the control group went on a group vacation and missed the posttest. Yet, many of the questions that are converted later to limitations can be identified and considered before the first participant is run. For example, if no effects or no differences are obtained, will this investigation be regarded as a strong and careful test of the hypotheses? Do the conditions of the investigation represent a sample of the conditions to which the investigator wishes to generalize? Do the control or comparison groups permit the investigator to comment specifically on what was responsible for group differences? These, of course, are all questions about methodology.

The quality of a study is usually related to the coherence of its conceptualization (hypotheses, predictions), the procedures to test that conceptualization (sample, measures, conditions, data evaluation), and the interpretations the author makes based on these procedures. Methodology is not just a set of practices, such as random assignment and use of control groups, but more fundamentally pertains to correspondence between what the investigator wishes to say about the findings and what he or she is entitled to say based on how the study was designed and conducted. Although the topics of the present book reflect and are organized according to the flow of research, chapters were selected that transcend and blur boundaries and discrete steps of research. Indeed, some chapters placed in one section may have a title that suggests they could be placed in another sections. The placements are quite deliberate of course. But all of the chapters help to convey the interdependence of all phases of research.

Research design is dynamic and cumulative; methods of design, assessment, and evaluation continually evolve and emerge. Thus, the book can only sample the available articles to address relevant domains to aid the researcher. Chapters were selected to address core topics, including generating and testing hypotheses, selecting the sample, developing or selecting measures, designing studies that are statistically powerful, presenting the data, and communicating the results. Some chapters from prior editions were retained because they still reflect classic statements on key topics. In the third edition, chapters were added to expand on core concepts, to reflect contemporary issues in research, and to elaborate ethical responsibilities in relation to research participants and to science more generally. Examples include chapters on mediators and moderators; sampling issues including investigation of underrepresented groups, methods for studying efficacy, and effectiveness of psychotherapy; making research relevant to clinical practice, introducing facets of research (systematic observation and evaluation) in clinical practice, the ways in which methodology influences the conclusions of studies, and ethical practices in research; and key features of preparing empirical and review papers for publication.

In this edition, I have added sections to introduce the book and to provide a closing perspective on methodology. These convey why we use and need methodology at all and some of the broader lessons that methodology teaches for researchers. As in prior editions of the book, I have written material to introduce each section of book to convey the rationale for the readings and how they relate to the overall themes of that section.

A book of readings on methodology has a great potential for missing the bestseller list. (Related, I regret to report that as I prepare this preface, the movie rights for this book have *still* not been decided, and hence my acting career continues to be on hold.) Chapters in edited volumes are notoriously uneven in quality and level. The topic of methodology adds to the risk by being viewed as dry, technical, and difficult competition against alternatives for Saturday night entertainment. However, an effort was made to steer sharply away from the shoals of checkered quality and tedium.

To that end, three considerations guided the selection of articles for the chapters. First, chapters were designed to cover several steps or stages that emerge in planning and executing research. Key stages in the research process include developing the research idea; selecting methods, procedures, and assessment devices; analyzing and interpreting the data; and preparing a written report to communicate what was accomplished and why. Second, chapters were selected not only to improve the understanding of research methods but also to provide concrete recommendations and practices to guide the design, execution, and writeup of an investigation. Thus, many of the chapters include suggestions that can be readily applied to improve an investigator's research. Finally, an effort was made to identify highly readable articles. Hundreds of articles within the past several years were identified and evaluated, given their thrust and focus. From these, articles were selected that eschewed technical jargon and related features that might engender insomnia among the most vigilant. When possible, I have tried to provide chapters that give contrasting positions on a topic to convey that many methodological practices we take for granted are debatable and debated.

Apart from the material I have added here and there, each of the chapters has been published previously. An advantage is they have traversed the review and publication process and hence their merit already has been favorably evaluated in advance of inclusion in this volume. In many cases as well, these articles are recognized to be among the classics because of the message and clarity of presentation.

The rationale for selecting readable articles extends beyond the obvious. Technical writings and coverage of individual topics are critical to the development of research acumen. At the same time, such writings often require detailed discussion and dialogue to establish the core concepts and to cull their implications. The process of selection in the present book was designed to identify articles whose critical points could be readily gleaned from the articles themselves. In terms of technical level, the book includes many fascinating and deep topics but is relatively free from formulae or mathematical equations. I am not against formulae, and indeed as an infant I recall drinking it on a regular basis. However, methodology for a book of this sort ought to be very accessible—pithy but not technical. Given the coverage and readable style, the book can be readily used on its own, particularly for graduate and advanced undergraduate courses, or as a supplement to other texts (e.g., Kazdin, 2003; Rosenthal & Rosnow, 1991; Shadish, Cook, & Campbell, 2002).

ACKNOWLEDGMENTS

Several people have contributed to the development of the book. The contributors whose articles are included are gratefully acknowledged, not only for their articles but also for the special contribution their work makes to psychology. I am grateful for the assistance and support of Lansing Hays, acquisitions editor at the American Psychological Association. Colleagues (faculty and students) in the Department of Psychology and the Child Study Center at Yale University provided in an ongoing way a very special environment for deliberating, discussing, and dissecting research issues and hence served as an important impetus for the present book. In addition, many students have commented on the chapters that are included in the book and hence helped to screen their final selection. Raquelle Kaye helped in numerous ways with many technical features of preparing materials for the book.

While this book was prepared, I received support from William T. Grant Foundation (98-1872-98), the State of Connecticut Department of Social Services, and the National Institute of Mental Health (MH59029). I am extremely grateful for the support and the learning opportunities these grants provide.

REFERENCES

Kazdin, A. E. (2003). *Research design in clinical psychology* (3rd ed.). Needham Heights, MA: Allyn & Bacon.

Rosenthal, R., & Rosnow, R. L. (1991). *Essentials of behavioral research: Methods and data analysis* (2nd ed.). New York: McGraw-Hill.

Shadish, W. R., Cook, T. D., & Campbell, D. T. (2002). *Experimental and quasi-experimental designs for generalized causal inference*. Boston: Houghton-Mifflin.

Methodological Issues & Strategies in Clinical Research

Third Edition

I

INTRODUCTION: OVERVIEW AND BACKGROUND

This part is designed to provide the context for methodology and research design in general and in relation to psychological research in particular. The two chapters that begin the book delineate the scope of methodology, the domains of psychology, and their interrelation. Both call for the importance of multiple ways of studying a phenomenon because how something is studied very much influences what the findings are and what one learns.

In chapter 1, I provide an overview of what methodology is and why we learn, teach, and draw on many specific research practices. Basic tenets of science and how we proceed to accumulate knowledge require that we address a host of concerns or impediments to knowledge. Methodology provides a way of codifying these concerns and strategies to deal with them. The chapter describes the rationale for using methodology and the important contributions that methodology makes to knowledge. As the book unfolds, it will be clear that methodology is not merely a tool to acquire knowledge but shapes, contributes to, and partially dictates the knowledge we obtain.

In chapter 2, Robert J. Sternberg and Elena L. Grigorenko discuss an approach to psychology that they call *unified psychology*. A key theme is to consider a different way of conducting research and organizing the discipline of psychology. Currently, the focus is on specialty areas or subdisciplines, such as behavioral neuroscience and cognitive, clinical, developmental, and social psychology, to mention a few. Research in these areas may focus on a particular topic (e.g., learning, memory, stereotyping, attachment, response to stress) from a small set of methodological approaches and from one or a few conceptual views. Sternberg and Grigorenko suggest focusing on a substantive topic (e.g., learning) and studying that from multiple theoretical perspectives and with multiple methods. This unifies psychology by bringing together those who are interested in the phenomenon without the traditional and somewhat artificial subdivisions of psychology.

This chapter previews many issues in later parts of the book. A major theme is that adherence to a single conceptual view (e.g., cognitive–behavioral, social learning, psychoanalytic) and narrow range of methods of investigating phenomena (e.g., a narrow set of measures, research designs, and data-analytic techniques) greatly limits what we learn. The yield from research is directly influenced by methods of investigation, and this alone ought to encourage studying phenomena in different ways. The significance of these points becomes more explicit in later chapters, as we see that restricted methods lead to a restricted knowledge base. That is, methodology makes an active contribution to what we learn.

1

METHODOLOGY: WHAT IT IS AND WHY IT IS SO IMPORTANT

ALAN E. KAZDIN

Scientific knowledge is very special; it is knowledge that is based on the accumulation of empirical evidence. Empirical evidence is a rich concept that includes systematic and careful observation of the phenomenon of interest. Although I will say more about this, methodology encompasses the many ways in which these observations are made, the arrangements of situations to obtain the observations, and the means of evaluating the findings and drawing inferences. The rationale and underpinnings of methodology follow directly from key tenets of science. Consider some of the salient tenets and how they relate to the research methods.

KEY CHARACTERISTICS OF SCIENTIFIC KNOWLEDGE

First, scientific knowledge is based on *parsimony*, or the practice of providing the simplest version or account of the data among alternatives that are available. This does not in any way mean that explanations are simple. Rather, this refers to the practice of not adding all sorts of complex constructs, views, relationships among variables, and explanations if an equally plausible account can be provided that is simpler. We add complexity to our explanations as needed. If two or more competing views can explain why individuals behave in a particular way, we adopt the simpler of the two until the more complex one is shown to be superior in some way.

A well-known illustration of competing interpretations is from cosmology and pertains to the orbiting of planets in our solar system. Nicolas Copernicus (1473–1543), a Polish scientist and astronomer, advocated the view that the planets orbited around the sun (heliocentric view) rather than around the earth (geocentric view). This latter view had been advanced by Claudius Ptolemy (ca. 85–165), a Greek astronomer and mathematician. Ptolemy's view had dominated for hundreds of years. The superiority of Copernicus's view was not determined by public opinion surveys or the fact that Ptolemy was no longer alive to defend his position. Rather, the account could better explain the orbits of the planets as well as other phenomena and could do so more simply, that is, parsimoniously.

Parsimony relates to methodology in concrete ways. When an investigation is completed we ask how to explain the findings or lack of findings. The investigator may have all sorts of explanations of why the results came out the way they did. Methodology has a whole set of explanations that may be as or more parsimonious than the one the investigator promotes. These explanations, illustrated later in this chapter, are usually more parsimonious because they can account for findings across a wide range of studies and areas of research. That is, we may not need the investigator's interpretation of the findings; some flagrant design flaw may leave open the possibility of a much more parsimonious interpretation than the one he or she provides. The task of research is to design a study so that the account or explanation we wish to support will be a parsimonious account among the available explanations.

Second, *plausible rival hypothesis* is another key concept of science (Campbell & Stanley, 1966; Cook & Campbell, 1979). A plausible rival hypothesis refers to an interpretation of the results of an investigation on the basis of some other influence than the one the investigator has studied or wishes to discuss. The question to ask at the completion of a study is whether other interpretations are plausible to explain the findings. This sounds so much like parsimony that the distinction is worth making explicit. Parsimony refers to adopting the simpler of two or more explanations that account equally well for the data. The concept is quite useful in reducing the number and complexity of concepts that are added to explain a particular finding.

Plausible rival hypothesis as a concept is related to parsimony but has a slightly different thrust. At the end of the investigation, can other plausible interpretations be made of the finding than one advanced by the investigator? Simplicity of the interpretation (parsimony) may or may not be relevant. At the end of the study could be 2 or 10 equally complex interpretations of the results, so parsimony is not the issue. For example, let us say we have an amazing hypothesis that people who take cough drops during a cold get better faster than those who do not. We do a massive survey of students and identify two groups — those who take cough drops when ill and those who do not. We keep track of participants and closely monitor all those who get colds in the next few months. Then we call them every day and find out when their cold is over. Alas, we find that those individuals who take cough drops get better in half the time compared with those who did not take cough drops. We are all ready to conclude that as predicted, taking cough drops is helpful in limiting the duration of colds.

Plausible rival hypotheses come in here by raising the question, Are there other plausible explanations of the results? The answer is a resounding yes! It may be that people in the cough drop group are just healthier in general. Perhaps those who take cough drops tend to take better care of themselves in general (maybe better eating habits, more exercise) or take care of themselves during a cold more (a little more bed rest and chicken soup), or have a history that indicates they are healthier to begin with. Perhaps they would have colds of shorter duration because of these reasons, and cough drops are not needed at all. We could multiply these explanations of the findings. The explanations do not have to be more or less parsimonious than the cough drop interpretation. They are all plausible, and one cannot decide from the study whether cough drops make any difference. Methodology is all about plausible rival hypotheses and making some hypotheses or interpretations more plausible than others. We engage in various methodological practices (e.g., random assignment, use of comparison and control groups, keeping experimenters naive with regard to the hypotheses) to make some hypotheses (interpretations) implausible. In the example, we might control for some of the interpretations I added to give a better test of the cough drop hypothesis.

Third, *replication* is central to science. Replication refers to repetition or repeatability and is important in two ways. First, the procedures used in research must be repeatable. If one were to ask another scientist, "How did you get that finding?" the unacceptable and inaappropriate answers (drawn from childhood) are "I'm not telling!" or "For me to know and you to find out." Science operates so that what investigators do in a study, how they do it, and all of the circumstances are described. Others must be able to repeat the study. One might refer to this as replicability of the procedures. Second, can the findings be reproduced? A question about the results of any study is whether the findings can be repeated or obtained again by someone using identical or similar procedures.

Replication relates to parsimony and plausible rival hypotheses. Were the results evident in this one study due to a chance effect or to some odd circumstance in the situation of which the investigator may be unaware? Could there be a simple (parsimonious) explanation or one that is equally plausible (rival hypothesis)? Replication is needed to establish the credibility and genuineness of the finding. It would be unthinkable for a researcher to say he or she demonstrated a cure for a type of cancer but that other scientists could not replicate the results. One study might excite the news media and the public who reads the story. Yet, the scientific community might be very skeptical until other investigators replicated this finding. Only through repeated demonstration does one gain confidence in a finding. The initial investigation that obtained the result is tantalizing, promising, and may be true, but we need more. Skepticism for a finding is not suspicion directed toward the original investigator but rather comes form the realization that many influences might explain the results. For example, a finding might emerge due to "chance," an artifact that is embedded in statistical testing. That is, sometimes the data will show a statistically significant effect even if there is no real effect in the world.

Fourth, science encourages *caution and precision in thinking*. This does not mean that scientists (humans) are invariably cautious and precise. Rather the scientific community, to which we belong, demands of us as investigators that we are careful in not going beyond the data, or at least not too far. The demands mean we can say only what was demonstrated and that any other part remains to be determined by further research. For example, in research we distinguish key concepts such as a correlation, risk factor, and cause. A *correlation* indicates that two variables are related to each other at a particular point in time. A *risk factor* means that two variables are correlated with each other, but one clearly comes before the other. For example, having a parent with a history of depression increases the risk of depression in the offspring. Risk means an increase in probability and not in inevitable result. A *cause* means that one variable leads to, produces, and is responsible for a particular outcome. For example, animal research shows that various experiences early in development (e.g., physical contact with a parent, ingestion of toxins such as lead) influence brain development. The studies can show a causal relation because presenting or withholding experiences dictates the outcome. Other relations exist among variables, including many types of causal relations; I have only mentioned a few to convey the point (see Haynes, 1992; Kazdin, 2003; Kraemer et al., 1997). When a study only shows a correlation, the scientific community and the investigators themselves are cautioned not to go beyond the data and to assume or to state something more.

The caution and precision of scientific statements and inferences stand in contrast with inferences drawn in everyday life. The public at large and the media freely use such terms as *because*, *due to*, and *cause* in connecting concepts. Are children aggressive because they were abused, will using this cosmetic cream make me younger, and so on? The question itself is simplistic by suggesting that one variable leads to a particular outcome and that the relation is causal. Information in daily life moves seamlessly from *casual* to *causal* inferences. Science encourages greater care. For example, we know that having a cigarette smoker in the home increases the likelihood that an infant in that home will die from sudden infant death syndrome (SIDS; Shadish, Cook, and Campbell, 2002). (SIDS refers to the death of an infant, usually between the ages of 2 weeks and 2 years that cannot be traced to disease, physical abuse, or other disorders. Many more children die of SIDS in a year than all who die of cancer, heart disease, pneumonia, child abuse, AIDS, cystic fibrosis, and muscular dystrophy combined.) Hearing the relationship I mentioned (smoking as a risk factor) in casual thinking almost naturally leads one to assume smoking is the culprit (cause). Moreover it is even more tempting to move to interventions—we ought to stop smoking to decrease SIDS. Scientific thinking is a bit more cautious. Smoking as a cause has not been established. Could it be one of many causes? Perhaps it is not a cause at all but correlated with something that is more likely to play a causal role? These questions and, of course, the very process of questioning are science.

I have mentioned key characteristics of scientific knowledge. The underpinnings, tenets, and assumptions of science serve as topic for books and academic courses. I have highlighted these concepts to provide the rationale for methodology. Methodology provides a way to obtain scientific knowledge and to operationalize many of the key concepts in the context of empirical research.

WHAT IS METHODOLOGY?

Methodology is the overarching term that encompasses diverse principles, procedures, and practices related to the conduct of research. Conducting research includes planning, executing, and evaluating the results of an investigation. Research involves a process that moves from an idea, planning and executing an investigation, evaluating the results, and communicating the findings. Methodology includes the entire process. At each stage are specific procedures and concrete practices. They are familiar to researchers and include selecting the sample, assigning participants to conditions, manipulating an independent variable, assessing the effects, and analyzing the results. The different facets of methodology are specialty areas that constitute their own set of books, courses, and areas of expertise. For example, *research design* refers to the many ways on which studies can be arranged and conducted; *assessment* refers to all facets of measurement and measurement validation, and *data evaluation* refers to the many options and methods of evaluating results quantitatively and qualitatively. This book discusses and integrates each of these areas.

Conducting research raises many issues, and these become part of methodology as well. A prime example is the protection of the rights of the participants and the ethical issues raised by investigator–participant interaction. For example, the execution of research involves ways of interacting with participants (e.g., humans and animals) and administering various procedures (e.g., experimental manipulations, assessments) to them as part of the investigation. Experimental research with humans requires special informed-consent procedures as part of the ways of protecting participant rights. Research with "infrahuman subjects," as nonhuman animals are often called, involves many protections as well, including animal care facilities, the procedures permitted in the name of research, and how animals are cared for after the research is completed. The ethics of research is a major and critically important area of methodology and involves several principles, practices, and procedures.

Research design, assessment, data evaluation, and ethics of research include many specific practices and procedures. When we first learn methodology, we often want to focus on the procedures. Some of this is essential, of course. For example, at some point we must learn how to evaluate our data and precisely what statistics to use. There are many concrete practices to learn, and these are central to methodology, but it is a disservice to reduce methodology to these practices.

Methodology also refers to a way of thinking about phenomena of interest. That way of thinking is captured by concepts already mentioned including parsimony, plausible rival hypotheses, the importance of replication, and cautious and conservative statements about what is known. Methodology refers to a *problem-solving approach* to obtain the answers we wish. If our hypothesis is that x leads to y, what needs to be done to test that? Will the research design, sample, and ways of implementing the idea permit the conclusions we wish to make?

Consider an example. Let us say you have a friend who believes in horoscopes and wonders whether these are valid (accurate) or reasonably accurate enough to help guide one's daily life. Your friend knows that you have read this far in this book and are an expert methodologist. Your friend asks if you could do a quick empirical test of the accuracy of horoscopes. Eager to apply your amazing skills, you answer, "Yes, of course." The next thoughts you have are the problem solving part of methodology. No, I do not mean the thoughts as you reflect on how to extract yourself from this situation to which you so impulsively agreed. Rather I mean the part when you move from the general idea to the study.

The question raised by your friends ("Are or to what extent are horoscopes accurate?") must to be translated, converted, operationalized, and so on into an empirical investigation. The thought processes have you thinking along several dimensions. How will accuracy of a horoscope be defined? What observations, measures, and data need to be collected to answer this question? If the data suggest that horoscopes *are* accurate, will the study show that it is horoscopes, or could something else interfere with drawing this conclusion? Researchers who conduct many studies move to these questions and answers without making the process explicit.

The thought processes begin with questions and then their answers. In this example, it would not be very difficult to evaluate the question of whether horoscopes are accurate. There are unlimited ways in which this might be studied, but let me describe a few options. First, we need to have a way of measuring the "accuracy of horoscopes." Let us say that we read 100 horoscopes and list all the events or processes that are mentioned. We use these to develop a checklist of things that can happen during the week. The items encompass all things that horoscopes are apt to conclude that could be evaluated as happening or not happening. Then we need some research participants. Let us say we select 24 participants for this study. We select 2 participants for each of the 12 astrological signs, so, for example, in our study we have two people who share the same sign (e.g., Sagittarius). (I hope one of my old advisors is not reading this or does not learn about how I am misusing the expensive education graduate school provided.) At the end of each day (perhaps before bedtime), we ask each participant to fill out our checklist of events that happened to him or her during the day. Let us say we gather three weeks of data. Each day, we also have two or three research assistants go through two newspapers or sources and look at each horoscope for each sign and fill out a checklist regarding what that sign says for that day. That is, the research assistants, who do not know the purpose of the study, are asking what a given astrological sign (e.g., Aquarius) says in Newspaper 1 and Newspaper 2 for that day and does this with all the signs. At the end of the three weeks (or some time frame), we look at the descriptions of the participants and the research assistants and test for convergence.

Convergence can mean many different things, and it would be good merely to mention two options rather than devote this book to working out the details of this study. First, for a given day, week, or three-week period, is there agreement between the events identified that happened to each person and those events predicted from his or her sign? For example, if my sign is Aquarius, is there any agreement between the horoscopes for my sign and events that I say have happened to me? This is quantifiable. Second, is the agreement higher for events that happened to each person and his or her horoscope than the agreement for events that happened for a randomly selected sign that did not belong to that person? It may be that such general platitudes are given in any given horoscope, that anyone's sign is equally applicable and "accurate" as my own. All of this can continue. The point is not to describe my dissertation—I mean this hypothetical study—but rather to convey that one moves from an idea to the test. I have not elaborated many of the details. Even so, the movement from idea to empirical test and some of the key steps, problem-solving steps so to speak, make this translation evident.

GOALS AND ROLES OF METHODOLOGY

The overall purpose of methodology is to permit one to draw sound or valid inferences. This means that one wants to reach conclusions that are as free as possible from competing interpretations (plausible rival hypotheses). We engage in the practices and procedures of methodology not for their own sake but to help with interpretation and to bring clarity or relative clarity to our findings. In this process, methodology has two major roles.

First, methodology *codifies the sources of problems* that emerge in drawing inferences. Essentially, methodology provides a list of most of the problems to be wary of, what might go wrong, or what the investigator ought to think about before the first participant is ever seen in the study. In everyday life, we develop fears and worries based on experience; some biological predisposition; information from relatives, peers, and the media; and no doubt many other sources. We have some friends who worry about exams, elevators, catching a disease, being struck by lightning, and so on—wouldn't it be better if there were a master list somewhere from which we could select? In the context of science, methodology provides a master list of sources of worry or concern.

What to worry about is not a very sophisticated term. Understandably, other terms are used in methodology to identify these and include *sources of artifact and bias* and *threats to experimental validity* (see Cook & Campbell, 1979; Kazdin, 2003; Shadish, Cook, & Campbell, 2002). Table 1.1 lists several of these sources of artifact and bias that interfere with drawing sound inferences. I have listed many of the main problems, but many more exist. One never has to memorize the list, because some are more salient in a given area of research than others and become well known (e.g., placebo effects). Also, the citations noted previously provide extensive lists and descriptions of the various problems.

Some of the problems are so pervasive in research that one can almost always be sure to point them out. For example, when a student comes into my office to discuss a study, I usually start the conversation by rubbing my fingers through my toupee and shaking my head back and forth as if I were saying "no" to convey signs of deep frustration and despair. I usually have my student's riveted attention (not counting the time my toupee fell to the floor). Then, before he or she speaks, I begin the back-and-forth head shaking; continue that for at least two seconds of silence; and then say, "Oh—no, no, no—your sample is *much* too small." (I have been wrong on a few occasions, such as the time the student entered my office merely to ask where the bathroom was.)

We have learned from years of reviews from the 1960s up to the present that many studies do not provide very good tests of their hypotheses because the sample has too few participants (for one review of reviews, see Sedlmeier & Gigerenzer, 1989). In general, it is wise to know well in advance

TABLE 1.1
Examples of the Problems in Drawing Valid Inferences and Solutions to Address Them

Problem	Defined	Possible Solutions
History and maturation	Changes that occur over time due to events (history) or processes within the individual (maturation). Perhaps the results of the study are due to such changes rather than to the manipulation, intervention, or independent variable.	Include a control group that does not receive treatment. If the groups are composed by random assignment, the historical and maturational influences will be controlled. It is likely that such influences will apply to both (all) groups, and group differences are likely to be due to the experimental manipulation.
Testing	Taking any test on more than one occasion often leads to changes in performance (e.g., improvement). Studies that assess participants on multiple occasions (e.g., pretest and posttest) might show change just because of repeated testing.	A control group that receives the same assessments but does not receive the intervention or experimental manipulation makes repeated testing implausible as an explanation of any group differences.
Selection biases	The groups (e.g., treatment, control) are different to begin because of how they were selected or formed. Any differences between groups at the end of the study may be due to these differences rather than to anything the investigator does.	Assign participants randomly to conditions. With reasonably large samples, this is likely to produce groups that are equivalent before the manipulation is provided. Alternatively, participants can be matched on variables (e.g., level of anxiety) and randomly assigned to groups in matched sets so groups are equivalent on key variables.
Attrition (dropping out)	Loss of participants over the course of the study can make groups different. The random composition of the	Try to minimize the loss of participantts. Also, evaluate characteristics of participants who did versus those who did

(continued)

TABLE 1.1 (*continued*)

Problem	Defined	Possible Solutions
	groups has changed because participants selectively excluded themselves. The groups may be different from each other, leading to a selection bias, as noted previously.	not drop out. Complete statistical tests designed to control for the impact of loss of participants (e.g., intent-to-treat analyses).
Cues of the experimental situation	It may be that incidental cues of the experiment (what participants believe, what they are told, the expectations unwittingly conveyed about how they ought to perform) explain the group differences rather than the experimental manipulation. Cues may foster a way of responding that accounts for the results.	Use a control group that receives all but the special part of the intervention, so almost all cues are identical across groups. Interview participants in the study or in pilot work to ask how they are likely to behave to see if cues would lead to a systematic way of responding. Use measures that are not so transparent that participants can readily discern what is being measured.
Sample characteristics	The findings may be restricted to the special sample that was used; the finding is genuine but may not apply to others (e.g., of different ages, sex, ethnicity, culture).	Include different types of participants (e.g., men, women; more than one ethnic group). Analyze the results in a way that permits one to see if a characteristic of the sample in fact relates to the finding; replicate results with other samples.
Sample size (low power)	No differences were obtained in the study because the power (ability to detect a true difference when one exists) was too low.	Use a larger sample. Use a within-subjects design (pre- and post-measures on the same participants). Also, make directional statistical predictions and use directional (one-tailed) statistical tests. Use other statistics (such as effect size) than those that focus on statistical significance.

TABLE 1.1 (*continued*)

Problem	Defined	Possible Solutions
Questionable reliability and validity of the measure	No statistically significant differences were obtained because the measure has considerable error variability (unreliability), or it is not clear that this measure is a very good measure of the construct of interest.	Use measures that have validity and reliability data pertinent to the focus of the investigation. Use multiple measures and combine them statistically (e.g., by factor analysis) for a better index of the construct of interest. Use multiple measures that rely on different methods (e.g., self-report, direct observation). Conduct analyses on the measures to assess directly within the study whether measurement issues might explain the findings (e.g., internal consistency, test–retest reliability).

Note: This table illustrates how methodology codifies *problems* to which researchers must be sensitive in their demonstrations and *solutions* to rule out or address these problems. The list of problems or solutions presented here is not exhaustive (see Cook & Campbell, 1979; Kazdin, 2003; Shadish et al., 2002).

of beginning the study if one could obtain the desired effect based on such issues as statistical power. I mentioned that methodology codifies many of the problems that can emerge in conducting and interpreting research, and sample size is just one of them.

Second, methodology also codifies many of the *solutions to the problems* and practices that can help draw valid inferences. Here, too, in everyday life and outside of the context of methodology, it would be useful to have a list of solutions to the problems we worry about. On the back of the sheet that says, worry about lightning, ebola virus, mad cow disease, and germs from friends, how great it would be to have a long list of solutions. In the context of research, methodology provides a long list of solutions and strategies. In Table 1.1, I have listed some of the solutions that methodology encourages. I sample only some of the major solutions to some of the major problems. One can see that we engage in research methodological practices (solutions) to address specific problems (sources of artifact, bias, or threats to validity).

If methodology were merely a list of problems and solutions, then one might not need a course or a book. One could just master the lists and go on to other topics. The problem is that designing a study involves many decision points, and each of these has some implications for drawing conclusions.

Consider that I want to study new treatment for depression. Who will be the participants, and how will I select them? The answers to these questions can determine whether treatment works and, if it does work, whether this effect can be shown statistically. For example, if I recruit individuals of any age who are depressed (e.g., ages 15–60 years) and individuals who are depressed for whatever reason (e.g., clinical depression, bereavement), I may be less likely to find an effect because of the variability or individual differences in participants and types of depression. Also, if I include only college students who seem depressed on a self-report measure, this may be fine but limit the extent to which the results might apply to patients with clinical depression.

One can see from this point that one cannot just use methodology to go to a problem and then move to a solution. Research situations require consideration of what problems will emerge, what solutions are possible, and the trade-offs of one solution versus another. Like in many other aspects of life, sometimes electing one solution or course of action limits other courses of action. Methodology requires a deeper understanding of practices so that these trade-offs can be thoughtfully considered in relation to the specific hypothesis the investigator wishes to test.

WHY IS METHODOLOGY IMPORTANT

Methodology is the basis for accumulation of scientific knowledge. Advances in theory and research depend on a means of addressing (asking and answering) questions (hypotheses and predictions) that guide research. Methodology is the common language among the sciences that adheres to the tenets outlined previously and that provides the means of accumulating knowledge. Through scientific research one can describe and explain phenomena of interest and do so in ways that are cumulative. Scientific advances are emerging weekly and across scores of disciplines. These can be traced to all of the principles, practices, and procedures that are central to research.

That methodology is pivotal to scientific advances is true but also sounds too abstract and cerebral. Methodological issues also affect decisions in everyday life and indeed decisions about life and death. For example, we all are keenly interested in the development of treatments for life-threatening illnesses. How could methodology figure into this? Well, studies of treatments for cancer occasionally have been unable to demonstrate differences due to weak statistical power (see Freiman, Chalmers, Smith, & Kuebler, 1978). A more recent review of medical research for a variety of diseases and conditions revealed that more than 25 percent of the published studies (from 1975 to 1990) surveyed revealed no differences among the treatments that were studied (Moher, Dulberg, & Wells, 1994). In the majority of these studies, statistical power was weak.

Of course, I personally am not pleased to learn that viable treatments might be available, but one could not tell because the studies were not well designed. That is, the sample size was too small to demonstrate a real effect, if there is one. Forget about the tax dollars likely to be wasted (from federal- and state-funded research), the enormous inconvenience and perhaps pain (physical and psychological) of many of the participants run in such trials, and the ethical issues all of this raises by exposing participants to any condition when the research might not be able to obtain an answer. We want all investigators who design studies, who review proposals for research, or who are involved in the research process in some way to understand methodology to minimize delays in accumulating knowledge that can affect people in everyday life.

METHODOLOGY IN CLINICAL PSYCHOLOGY

Although methodology is central to all science in general, there are special reasons to focus on issues related to research in clinical psychology. Clinical psychology embraces all of the usual features of scientific research, such as defining the research idea, generating hypotheses, designing investigations, and collecting and analyzing data. Yet, in clinical psychology research is conducted in laboratory and clinical settings and addresses theoretical and applied issues. Other areas of psychology such as counseling, educational, and school psychology and other disciplines such as psychiatry, nursing, and social work also engage in research that spans quite diverse settings, participants, and goals. Research in these areas often presents novel challenges to the investigator. Consider the diversity of topics, samples, and settings in which clinical psychological research is conducted.

The scope of research in clinical psychology is enormous. Among the *topics* addressed are the assessment, diagnosis, course, treatment, and prevention of social, emotional, and behavioral problems; personality; family processes and peer relationships; the interface of mental and physical health; and cross-cultural differences. The *populations* studied include children, adolescents, adults, and elderly people and people with special experiences (e.g., homelessness, divorce, prisoners of prior wars); medical impairment and disease (e.g., cancer, AIDS, spinal cord injury, diabetes); or psychological disorder or dysfunction (e.g., depression, anxiety, posttraumatic stress disorder, autism). People in contact with special populations, that is, who are exposed to someone with a special condition, themselves are often studied (e.g., children of alcoholics, spouses of depressed patients, siblings of children with physical disabilities). Research in clinical psychology is conducted in diverse *settings* (e.g., laboratory, clinics, hospitals, prisons, schools, industry) and in the absence of structured settings (e.g., runaway children, homeless families).

Finally, research in clinical psychology is also conducted *in conjunction with many other areas of research and different disciplines* (e.g., criminology, health psychology, neurology, pediatrics, psychiatry, public health).

Understandably, diverse methods of study are required to meet the varied conditions in which clinical psychologists work and the special challenges in drawing valid scientific inferences from these situations. The methodological diversity of clinical research, as the substantive diversity, can be illustrated in many ways. Studies vary in the extent to which the investigator can exert control over the assignment of cases to conditions or administration of the intervention (e.g., true experiments and quasi-experiments) and the selection of preexisting groups and how they are followed and evaluated. Occasionally, clinical psychologists conduct research with college students recruited from introductory psychology classes at a university. Participants are seen for a session or two and complete a laboratory task. If one looks at the premier journals in clinical psychology (e.g., *Journal of Abnormal Psychology*, *Journal of Consulting and Clinical Psychology*), this is not the usual paradigm for research. Clinical samples may be studied and evaluated over a period of time, even if only a month or two. Recruiting participants, retaining them if the study lasts weeks or months, ensuring that their care is fine if they are in a clinical sample, and obtaining enough participants to test the hypotheses are a few of the salient challenges. How these challenges are met has major implications for the conclusions that can be reached and whether the conclusions can be generalized to other investigators, samples, and settings. The challenges also mean that quite different methodological approaches often are used, including diverse designs (e.g., group and single case) and methods of data evaluation (e.g., statistical and clinical significance and nonstatistical data evaluation; Kazdin, 2003).

The purpose in highlighting the diversity of clinical psychology is to underscore the importance of facility with the methods of research. Special demands or constraints are frequently placed on the clinical researcher. Ideal methodological practices (e.g., random assignment) are not always available, but they are not always necessary. Also, restrictions may limit the researcher's options (e.g., a control group might not be feasible, only small sample sizes are available). The task of the scientist is to draw valid inferences from the situation and to use methodology, design, and statistics toward that end. In clinical psychology and related areas of research, the options in methodology, design, and statistics must be greater than in more basic research areas to permit the investigator to select and identify creative solutions. Clinical research is not in any way "soft" science; indeed, the processes involved in clinical research reflect science at its best precisely because of the thinking and methodological ingenuity required to force nature to reveal its secrets. Deploying strategies to accomplish this requires an appreciation of the purposes of research and the underpinnings of research strategies.

GOAL AND FOCUS OF THIS BOOK

The goal of this book is to help readers design, conduct, recognize, and appreciate high-quality research. High-quality research encompasses several distinguishable components. First, of course, is *the idea, theory, or prediction that underlies the study* and its contribution to knowledge. There is no substitute for a novel conceptualization or clever hypothesis that allows us a new way to study and understand a phenomenon of interest. Second, *how that idea is translated into an investigation* is critical. Many options exist for evaluating or testing the idea. The quality of the study is determined by the options selected and the extent to which they reveal the phenomenon and rule out plausible rival interpretations. Third, *communication of the findings* is critically important. Communication of findings is not only describing the creative idea and the methods that were used; in addition, the investigator must place the research in the context of what is known and what needs to be known. It is valuable and praiseworthy to be skilled at any one of these three components. High-quality research stems from being skilled in each of the components and putting them together in an investigation.

This book addresses each of the components of research and is intended to augment skills in their conceptualization and execution. The chapters are organized into parts that are designed to reflect the flow of research issues and processes.

In this "Introduction: Overview and Background" (Part I) to the book, beginning with the present chapter, I have conveyed what methodology is and the roles it plays in scientific knowledge. Perhaps the most critical point is to conceive methodology not only as a set of practices but as a way of approaching the subject matter of interest. The goal of research is to draw valid inferences, and methodology (design, assessment, data evaluation methods) provides the means to accomplish this. Chapter 2 discusses psychology as a field, how it is organized, and the implications for understanding psychological processes. This chapter begins a theme that will pervade other sections, namely, it is valuable to encourage diverse approaches, both conceptual and methodological, in studying a topic of interest because the approach can influence precisely what one learns.

Part II, "Beginning the Research Process," begins with a major challenge of research, namely, developing the idea for the study. Chapters are included that encompass the process of generating ideas. Also, one way to consider the focus of the study is the type of relation one is trying to demonstrate. Evaluation of mediators and moderators is discussed to convey the impact of conceptualization of the independent variables on design and data evaluation issues. We can see even at this early stage that conceptualization of the study (e.g., hypothesized relations among independent and dependent variables) has direct implications for how the data might be analyzed.

Part III, "Methods: Principles and Practices," includes chapters that address procedures, practices, and design options. Chapters cover sampling of participants, which is familiar, and sampling of stimulus conditions to which participants are exposed, which is less familiar. Sampling biases and sampling of underrepresented groups also are discussed.

Part IV, "Assessment," presents scale evaluation and development. Although most of our work does not involve development of scales, selecting measures for research is a critical step. Chapters on scale development and measurement reliability and validity convey key issues that influence or ought to influence the measures we select and the interpretation of results of research. Issues raised in the assessment of underrepresented groups are also included in this part. Ethnic and minority issues, of interest in their own right, raise broader points about sampling, measurement validation, and generality of results.

Part V, "Data Analysis, Evaluation, and Interpretation," includes several chapters that relate data evaluation to other facets of research. Major attention is given to statistical significance testing, including its origins, strengths, and limitations. There is deep concern among many methodologists and statisticians regarding the uses and misuses of statistical significance and null hypothesis testing. The chapters convey the manifold issues involved and options for data presentation and analysis.

Part VI, "Special Topics in Clinical Research," addresses diverse topics of special interest in areas of clinical research and practice. Chapters discuss the issues raised in studying psychotherapy in the controlled settings and the implications for extending findings to clinical practice. The broader issue these chapters convey is that the way in which something (e.g., psychotherapy) is studied contributes to the results. Clinical work is often seen as a place where systematic evaluation cannot be done or is done quite loosely. This is changing. Indeed, to optimize the benefits of treatment to patients, evaluation of client progress in clinical practice is essential. Chapters also discuss and illustrate evaluation in clinical work. Finally, chapters discuss outcome assessment and how to expand on the usual measures to evaluate interventions.

Part VII, "Ethics in Research," presents multiple ethical issues and practices to guide research. This part begins with the ethical principles and codes developed by the American Psychological Association. Chapters convey the strengths, limitations, and challenges that ethical codes and issues present for research. Special topics are illustrated with chapters on ethical transgressions that emerge in graduate training. Also, a chapter related to the ethics of authorship and allocation of credit (e.g., deciding who is an author, who is first author) is included because of the sensitivity of the issues in collaborative research and particularly in collaborations of students and faculty.

Part VIII, "Publication and Communication of Research," addresses the preparation of manuscripts designed to communicate research. Communication is a logical conclusion to completion of research. From the standpoint of methodology, the rationale for research processes and practices is critically important to convey in the written report of research. Chapters are designed to convey the thought processes prompted by methodology that deserves attention in preparing reports on one's own research, reviewing the literature within an area, conducting meta-analyses, and preparing grant applications. One chapter focuses on how the design issues are incorporated into article preparation; other chapters provide recommendations for writing empirical and review articles.

In Part IX, "Perspectives on Methodology," I provide closing comments to convey some of the broader lessons that methodology teaches. Among the recommendations is to encourage the use of novel and diverse methods of investigation. The purpose is not diversity and novelty for their own sake; rather, methods of studying a phenomenon often influence what can be learned and what specifically is learned. Complementary methods of study can elaborate the phenomenon in new ways. Researchers are encouraged to study phenomena in diverse ways and in their careers to develop collaborations that facilitate this. Novel findings come from novel methods. Such findings also come from novel ideas, but even novel ideas studied with the usual participants, usual measures, and usual data analyses can be constrained.

The chapters within each part raise points central to the respective aspect or phase of the study. At the same time, many chapters connect the research process by spanning different phases of research and hence serve a valuable role in conveying how theory, research design, assessment, and statistical evaluation act in concert. There is a flow to research and a seamless process. A given study is in a sequence and historical tradition in the area of investigation; within the study itself is a process that does not quite have a clear beginning and end. For example, the write-up of a study is not the end of a sequence of tasks in research. The well-described and presented write-up ought to point rather clearly to the next studies, and hence it constitutes a new beginning. Chapters have been selected to magnify facets of the research process, to identify components of high-quality research, and to delineate practices we can adopt to improve our own investigations.

One caveat is related to the seamless processes and interconnected steps of research that warrants mention. The titles of many of the chapters might suggest that they are misplaced in the parts in which I have put them. Although one could quibble with the placement of a chapter, the titles did not determine chapter selection, placement, or use. For example, in "Publication and Communication of Research" is a chapter whose title clearly suggests it is devoted to statistical evaluation. No so. The chapter is an excellent statement of many considerations that enter into the design of a study and that are central to cover in writing up the results. Similarly, in "Assessment" is a chapter on analogue behavioral observations. What is that about? As it turns out, among the chapter's many accomplishments is a remarkable presentation of different types of validity that are pivotal to understand. There are many other examples. They do not reflect problems in placing chapters but rather the interconnectedness of the different facets of methodology. I have divided the book into parts, but the research process is continuous, and considerations (assessment, design, data) emerge at multiple places (before the study is begun, when the write-up is under way).

REFERENCES

Campbell, D. T., & Stanley, J. C. (1966). *Experimental and quasi-experimental designs for research*. Chicago: Rand McNally.

Cook, T. D., & Campbell, D. T. (1979). *Quasi-experimentation: Design and analysis issues for field settings*. Chicago: Rand McNally.

Freiman, J. A., Chalmers, T. C., Smith, H., & Kuebler, R. R. (1978). The importance of beta, the Type II error, and sample size in the design and interpretation of the randomized control trial. *New England Journal of Medicine, 299,* 690–694.

Haynes, S. N. (1992). *Models of causality in psychopathology: Toward dynamic, synthetic, and nonlinear models of behavior disorders.* Needham Heights, MA: Allyn & Bacon.

Kazdin, A. E. (2003). *Research design in clinical psychology* (4th ed.). Needham Heights, MA: Allyn & Bacon.

Kraemer, H. C., Kazdin, A. E., Offord, D. R., Kessler, R. C., Jensen, P. S., & Kupfer, D. J. (1997). Coming to terms with the terms of risk. *Archives of General Psychiatry, 54,* 337–343.

Moher, D., Dulberg, C. S., & Wells, G. A. (1994). Statistical power, sample size, and their reporting in randomized controlled trials. *Journal of the American Medical Association, 272,* 122–124.

Sedlmeier, P., & Gigerenzer, G. (1989). Do studies of statistical power have an effect on the power of studies? *Psychological Bulletin, 105,* 309–316.

Shadish, W. R., Cook, T. D., & Campbell, D. T. (2002). *Experimental and quasi-experimental designs for generalized causal inference.* Boston: Houghton-Mifflin. http://sids-network.org

2

UNIFIED PSYCHOLOGY

ROBERT J. STERNBERG AND ELENA L. GRIGORENKO

Unified psychology is the multiparadigmatic, multidisciplinary, and inte-grated study of psychological phenomena through converging operations. In this article, we propose that unified psychology can and should supplement traditional approaches to psychology. Some readers might even find it a suit-able replacement for several traditional approaches. To unpack our definition, we need to look at each of its aspects. But before we do, we must summarize a major contention of our article.

Unified psychology, as we conceive of it, involves giving up or, at least, putting aside what we believe to be three bad habits that are commonplace among some psychologists. The bad habits are (a) exclusive or almost exclu-

Reprinted from the *American Psychologist*, 56, 1069–1079. Copyright 2001 by the American Psycholog-ical Association.

Preparation of this chapter was supported by Grant REC-9979843 from the National Science Foundation and by Grant R206R000001 awarded under the Javits Act Program, as administered by the Office of Educational Research and Improvement, U.S. Department of Education.

Grantees undertaking such projects are encouraged to freely express their professional judgment. Therefore, this chapter does not necessarily represent the positions or the policies of the U.S. govern-ment, and no official endorsement should be inferred.

This chapter represents a substantial expansion of ideas first presented in Sternberg and Grigorenko (2001), on which the third major section of the chapter is based.

sive reliance on a single methodology (e.g., response time measurements or fMRI measurements) rather than multiple converging methodologies for studying psychological phenomena; (b) identification of scholars in psychology in terms of psychological subdisciplines (e.g., social psychology or clinical psychology) rather than in terms of the psychological phenomena they study; and (c) adherence to single underlying paradigms for the investigation of psychological phenomena (e.g., behaviorism, cognitivism, psychoanalysis).

Before we elaborate on our view of the good habits that can replace these bad ones, we discuss some previous proposals regarding the notion of a unified psychology. We also consider objections that have been raised to such proposals.

PREVIOUS PROPOSALS REGARDING THE UNIFICATION OF PSYCHOLOGY

Perhaps the whole issue of unity versus disunity—in psychology or any other science—was best framed by Berlin (1953), who argued that there are different sorts of people: *hedgehogs,* who try to relate everything to a single system or vision, and *foxes,* who pursue many different paths without trying to fit them together. (A third class of person is a fox who sees him- or herself as a hedgehog.) The distinction is based on the words of the Greek poet Archilochus, who said, "The fox knows many things, but the hedgehog knows one big thing." Therefore, those who seek unification are the hedgehogs.

Although the distinction may be too sharp, it seems roughly to apply to the literature that has grown up around the issue of unification in psychology. Consider the views of both hedgehogs and foxes.

Attempts by hedgehogs to unify psychology go back a long way, in part because psychology has a long history as a "house divided" (Kimble, 1989, p. 491). For example, Baldwin (1902) went about integrating the study of development with that of evolution; Baldwin (1897/1906) also combined social–psychological and developmental techniques in studying mental development. But many attempts at unification are much more recent.

One of the most ambitious and more recent efforts at unifying psychology was undertaken by Staats (1991), who proposed what he referred to as a "unified positivism and unification psychology" (p. 899; see also Staats, 1983, 1993). Staats suggested that psychology has suffered from a crisis of disunity and that the crisis has needed, for some time, to be resolved. He further suggested that unification could be achieved not by the old "grand theories" of psychology but through interlevel and interfield theories. An interlevel theory would seek to bridge different levels of analysis of a phenomenon, such as the application of basic learning principles to language learning. The idea here is to form connections between one level of analysis that calls on more elementary principles—in this case, presumably, learning theory—and a second level of analysis that presumably is more molar—in this case, presumably, language learning. An interfield theory would seek to bridge different fields of analysis of the same phenomenon, such as biological and psychological approaches to a problem. The idea here is to form connections between fields that may have members studying the same problem with different methods and different perspectives.

Staats (1999) further suggested that part of the reason that psychology may have failed to become unified is because it lacks an infrastructure for unification. For example, in unified sciences, there are single terms corresponding to particular theoretical constructs, such as the quark in physics. In psychology, particular theoretical constructs are often associated with multiple terms, with the distinctions among them unclear. Staats gave "self-concept," "self-image," "self-perception," "self-esteem," "self-confidence," "self," and "self-efficacy" as examples of concepts whose differences are, in his opinion, at best, ill-defined. Further problems discouraging unification are that (a) there are many theories in psychology but few attempts to interrelate them and (b) each theory must be discussed using a different language, so conversations in which theories are being compared or contrasted sometimes are virtually unintelligible.

A somewhat different approach has been taken by systems theorists (e.g., Kuo, 1967, 1976; Magnusson, 2000; Sameroff, 1983; Schneirla, 1957; Thelen, 1992; Thelen & Smith, 1994, 1998). For example, Magnusson (2000) has proposed that a holistic approach to psychological inquiry and to the individual can provide a basis for integrating and unifying many diverse outlooks on human development. Sameroff and Bartko (1998) have applied a political-systems metaphor to child development. Lerner (1998) has also taken a systems approach, arguing that the multiple levels of organization that constitute human life—from the biological to the individual to the social and beyond—all need to be understood within a common framework. Cairns (1998) has made a similar suggestion. Bronfenbrenner (1979; Bronenbrenner & Morris, 1998) has actually proposed such a framework, with interlocking systems of development, such as the microsystem, which encompasses the individual; the mesosystem, which encompasses the family, school, peers, religious institutions, and so forth; the exosystem, which includes the extended family, neighbors, mass media, social welfare and legal services, and so forth; and the macrosystem, which includes the attitudes and ideologies of the culture.

Other investigators, although not necessarily proposing such comprehensive frameworks, have also argued in favor of the unification of psychology and have made related suggestions regarding the need for some kind of effort at unification. For example, Royce (1970) suggested that psychology was fragmenting and needed more organization and more unity. Bevan (1991, 1994) argued that specialization can give rise to "regressive fragmentation" (Bevan, 1994, p. 505) and "self-limiting specialization" (Bevan, 1982,

p. 1311), which alienate psychology from larger human concerns. Maher (1985) also spoke of the fragmentation and chaotic diversity in psychology. MacIntyre (1985) suggested that such chaos gives rise to the view that psychology is prescientific rather than scientific. Rychlak (1988) saw the problem of fragmentation as having three aspects: theoretical, methodological, and scholarly. He believed that a first step toward unification would be the development of a greater tolerance by psychologists of differences among psychologists. DeGroot (1989) suggested that for psychologists to achieve unification, they would need to reach some kind of greater consensus both as to the mission of psychology and as to what constituted its methods. Kimble (1994) suggested that unification was desirable and could be achieved by a set of principles, which he proposed in his article. Fowler (1990) also called for unification, in his case, of science and practice. Wapner and Demick (1989) argued that the unification of psychology was overdue, whereas Anastasi (1990) suggested that psychology already was making large steps toward unification.

Not everyone has believed the unification of psychology to be a good idea. Some of the foxes' critiques of unification have been in direct response to Staats's (1991) call for unification. McNally (1992) suggested, on the basis of his analysis of Kuhn (1991), that the diversity and disunity present in psychology might be a sign of health rather than of illness. Kukla (1992) proposed that the whole goal of unification is questionable: Psychologists should concentrate on producing the best theories possible and then let the chips fall where they may. And Green (1992), although not taking issue with the notion of unity, suggested that Staats's positivistic program is not the optimal way to achieve unity.

Other researchers also have questioned the prospects for unification. For example, Koch (1981) suggested that psychology, by its nature, may not be unifiable. (See Leary, 2001, for a detailed analysis of Koch's point of view.) Krech (1970) also believed that psychology, by its nature, could not be unified. Wertheimer (1988) suggested that at best, unification would face many obstacles. Kendler (1987) suggested that a natural division exists between psychology as a natural science and as a social science and that this division would continue to express itself in psychological theory and research. In a separate article, Kendler (1970) suggested that unifying psychology requires reducing any two of the three subject matters of behavior, neurophysiological events, and phenomenal experience to the third. Messer (1988) argued that even clinical psychology, a part of the social science side of psychology, would be difficult to unify. Viney (1989) noted that unity has both pros and cons and that both must be considered before psychology moves toward unification. And Scott (1991) observed that as psychology branches out and becomes more specialized, divisions are to be expected as a natural outcome.

Clearly, then, there have been diverse points of view regarding whether unification is possible and, if so, what form it should take. In this article, we propose one such form that the unification of psychology might take, which we refer to here as *unified psychology*.

CONVERGING OPERATIONS

Converging operations refers to the use of multiple methodologies for studying a single psychological phenomenon or problem. The term was first introduced by Garner, Hake, and Erikson (1956) in a groundbreaking article on psychological methodology. The basic idea is that any one operation is, in all likelihood, inadequate for the comprehensive study of any psychological phenomenon. The reason is that any methodology introduces biases of one kind or another, often of multiple kinds. By using multiple converging methodologies (i.e., converging operations) for the study of a single psychological phenomenon or problem, one averages over sources of bias.

There are many examples of how converging operations can illuminate phenomena in a way that no one operation can. (See the original Garner et al., 1956, article for examples.) Often new constructs are especially well served by such operations.

Consider, for a first example, the construct of prejudice. Prejudice traditionally has been measured in one of two ways: either by a questionnaire asking participants to characterize their feelings toward groups of people (Allport, 1929; Dovidio & Gaertner, 2000) or by observations of behavior (Sherif, Harvey, White, Hood, & Sherif, 1961/1988). Many studies have shown that attitudes are often not particularly good predictors of behavior (e.g., Dovidio, Kawakami, Johnson, Johnson, & Howard, 1997). If one wished to understand prejudices, one would have to study both participants' verbally expressed attitudes and participants' actual behavior.

Of course, one could say that the crucial measure is behavior and that the attitudes are only interesting to the extent that they predict behavior. We disagree. Behavior is as interesting a predictor of attitudes, as are attitudes of behavior. There is no ultimate dependent variable. Consider an example of this notion as it applies to attitudes and prejudices.

Recently, Greenwald, Banaji, and their colleagues (Greenwald & Banaji, 1995; Greenwald et al., 2000) have developed measures of implicit attitudes that examine a wholly different aspect of how people feel about certain groups of individuals. These measures each are referred to as an Implicit Association Test or IAT (Greenwald, McGhee, & Schwartz, 1998). The IAT is a computer-based reaction time measure that estimates the degree of association between target concepts, such as attitudes toward African Americans and attitudes toward White Americans, and an evaluative dimension, such as pleasant–unpleasant. For example, African American faces are paired with the words *good* or *bad*, as are White American faces. On half the trials, one pushes the same response key for White and *good*, and on the other half, one presses the same key for White and *bad*. The same holds for Black and *good* and Black and *bad*. One can then compare the time it takes to associate *good* or *bad* with White or Black. The test provides a relative measure. In other words, a target concept (attitudes toward African Americans) must have a contrasting domain (attitudes toward White Americans). A participant's responses will indicate an implicit attitude toward African Americans relative to his or her implicit attitude toward White Americans.

Using such measures, these investigators have found consistently prejudiced implicit attitudes of White Americans toward African Americans and even often of African Americans toward African Americans. They have uncovered other negative implicit attitudes as well. Their measures of implicit attitudes correlate only poorly with the traditional measures of explicit attitudes, in which one simply asks individuals to state or rate their attitudes toward members of various groups. Thus, what result one gets depends on the dependent variable one uses.

The data suggest converging operations are needed if one wishes to fully understand people's attitudes toward various groups. One may wish to look at, for example, indicators of implicit attitudes, which usually involve timed decision tasks; measures of explicit attitudes, which typically take the form of questionnaires; or assessments of behavior. Ideally, one looks at all three.

Of course, there are many other examples of attitudes failing to predict behavior. Most people would agree that drunken driving is irresponsible, but a number of these people do it anyway. Many people who know that condom use may literally save their lives by preventing transmission of the HIV virus nevertheless fail to use condoms when they know they should. People who know that smoking is killing them continue to smoke. The examples are endless.

Another example of the need for converging operations can be seen in the study and measurement of intelligence and related intellectual abilities. Sternberg, Grigorenko, Ferrari, and Clinkenbeard (1999) used both multiple-choice and essay items to assess analytical, creative, and practical intellectual abilities. One of their analyses involved the use of confirmatory factor analysis by which they investigated, among other things, how effective the two item types (multiple choice and essay) were in assessing the three different kinds of abilities. They found that the multiple-choice items were the more effective in assessing analytical abilities—the types of abilities assessed by traditional tests of intellectual skills—whereas the essay items were more effective in assessing creative and practical abilities. Using just one type of item (e.g., all multiple choice or all essay) would have resulted in inferior measurements.

The principle of converging operations applies beyond the particular kinds of test items to the kinds of investigative operations used as well. The study of intelligence traditionally has drawn heavily on factor analysis. For example, Carroll (1993) followed in a long line of investigators who have developed and tested theories of intelligence largely or exclusively on the basis of factor analysis (e.g., Guilford, 1967; Spearman, 1927; Thurstone, 1938; see reviews in Brody, 2000; Carroll, 1982; Mackintosh, 1998; Sternberg, 1990). Nothing is wrong with factor analysis per se, but any single method has advantages and drawbacks. For example, factor analysis as typically used in the study of intelligence relies solely on the use of individual differences as sources of data. But many other useful sources of information can be drawn on to study intelligence, such as cultural analysis (Laboratory of Comparative Human Cognition, 1983; Serpell, 2000), cognitive analysis (Cooper & Regan, 1982; Deary, 2000; Estes, 1982; Lohman, 2000; Sternberg, 1982), and biological analysis (e.g., Larson, Haier, LaCasse, & Hazen, 1995; MacLullich, Seckl, Starr, & Deary, 1998; Vernon, 1997; Vernon, Wickett, Bazana, & Stelmack, 2000). These other methods of investigation can yield findings simply not susceptible to discovery by factor analysis and, in some cases, may call into question some of the results of factor analysis (e.g., Gardner, 1983, 1999; Sternberg, 1985, 1997). Our goal here is not to take a position on whether the results of factor analysis or any other single method in particular are right or wrong. It is simply to point out that converging operations can yield insights about psychological phenomena that are opaque to any single methodology.

If, as Garner et al. (1956) claimed, converging operations are so superior to single operations, why do some and perhaps many psychologists rely largely or even exclusively on a single method of analysis (or, for that matter, only two methods of analysis)? We believe there are three main reasons, none of them really acceptable from a research standpoint.

Training

Psychologists may have been trained largely in the use of a single methodology. They may have subsequently invested heavily in that methodology in their work. Learning how to do structural equation modeling, neural imaging, or qualitative analysis, for example, can require a large amount of work, especially if one wishes to perfect each of the set of techniques. Researchers may seek to maximize the return on their time investment and to use what they have learned as much as possible. Even if they come to see the flaws of their preferred methodology, they may come to view the time invested as a sunken cost and seek to justify or even redeem the investment anyway. They thereby can become fixed in their use of a single method of analysis.

Panaceas

Researchers can come to view a single methodology as representing a kind of panacea for the study of a certain problem or set of problems. At one time, exploratory factor analysis was seen in this way by some psychometric investigators, until its limitations became increasingly apparent (e.g., the existence of an infinite number of rotations of axes, all representing equally legitimate solutions statistically). To some of the same investigators, as well as to other investigators, confirmatory factor analysis or structural equation modeling may have come to seem to be a panacea, although these methods, too, have their limitations, such as reliance on individual differences. Today, some scientists view neural imaging methods as a panacea. Some psychologists are busy compiling mental atlases that link certain areas of the brain to certain aspects of cognitive processing, although they are often oblivious to the functional relations between the two and are sometimes making these links in the absence of an adequate theoretical foundation (see Sternberg, 2000). The truth is that no method will provide a panacea: Different methods have different advantages and disadvantages, and by using multiple methods, one capitalizes on the strengths of the methods while helping to minimize the effects of their weaknesses.

Norms

Norms of a field may also lead to methodological fixation. Some years ago, Robert J. Sternberg submitted an article to one of the most prestigious psychological journals available. He was asked to revise the article, replacing regression analyses of the phenomenon under investigation with analyses of variance. The request was odd because the two methods of analysis gave equivalent information (see Cohen & Cohen, 1983). But the norm of the journal was use of analysis of variance reporting. Fields, journals, and other collectivities develop norms that to the members of those collectivities may seem perfectly reasonable and even beyond question. These norms may become presuppositions of behavior that are accepted in a rather mindless way (Langer, 1997). The norms may lead investigators to do things in a certain way, not because it is the best way, but, rather, because it comes to be perceived as the only way or the only way worth pursuing.

In Sum

Unified psychology, then, means giving up on single operations in favor of multiple converging operations. Such work requires either that individuals be trained in a wider variety of methodologies than they currently are trained in or else that they work in teams having members with various kinds of expertise (see Sternberg & Grigorenko, 1999).

Ultimately, the converging operations and perspectives that are brought to bear on a problem can and generally should go even beyond those of psychology. Investigations of many psychological phenomena can be enriched by the ideas of other disciplines, such as biology, anthropology, and neuroscience (Woodward & Devonis, 1993). For example, psychologists can enrich their perspectives of child rearing by understanding how people in other cultures rear children, or they can broaden their perspectives on aggressive behavior by taking into account what is considered to be aggressive in the first place in one culture versus another.

MULTIDISCIPLINARY, INTEGRATED STUDY OF PSYCHOLOGICAL PHENOMENA

Field fixation can be as damaging to the understanding of psychological phenomena as is methodological fixation. Psychology is divided into areas such as biological psychology, clinical psychology, cognitive psychology, developmental psychology, industrial and organizational psychology, social psychology, and personality psychology. Departments often organize the specializations of their professors in this way; graduate programs are usually structured in this way; jobs are typically advertised in this way. This organization of the field, departments, graduate programs, and jobs represents a suboptimal organization of the field. It encourages division rather than unification.

Preserving the Status Quo

Several factors play a role in maintaining the current suboptimal organization of psychology.

Tradition

First and foremost, this method of organization is the way things have been done for a long time. When a system of organization is entrenched, people tend to accept it as a given. For example, most psychology departments have chairpersons, but members of those departments probably do not spend a lot of time questioning whether they should have chairpersons — they just accept this system of organization. Of course, new fields within psychology come and go. For example, the fields of evolutionary psychology and health psychology are relative newcomers to the roster of fields of psychology. They will either become part of the standard organization of the field or slowly disappear.

Vested Interest

Second, once a discipline such as psychology has been organized in a certain way, people in the discipline acquire a vested interest in maintaining that organization, much as people gain a vested interest in maintaining any system that seemingly has worked for them in the past. For example, most cognitive psychologists were trained as cognitive psychologists, and personality psychologists as personality psychologists. Were the field suddenly to reorganize, current scholars and practitioners might find themselves without the kind of knowledge base and even the socially organized field of inquiry that would allow them to continue to function successfully.

The Need to Specialize

Third, no one can specialize in everything. Students of psychology need to specialize in some way, and structuring psychology in terms of fields has been viewed as a sensible way to define specializations. Thus, someone who specializes in social psychology will be expected to know about a series of related phenomena such as impression formation, attribution, and stereotyping. Someone who specializes in cognitive psychology will be expected to know about a set of related phenomena such as perception, memory, and thinking. Successively greater levels of specialization ultimately may be encouraged; for example, a cognitive psychologist may pursue a very specific line of inquiry, such as cognitive approaches to memory, to implicit memory, or to the use of priming methodology in studying implicit memory.

Reasons to Change

We believe that the current organization of the field is distinctly suboptimal and even maladaptive. We have several reasons for this belief.

The Field Could Be Organized Better to Understand Psychological Phenomena

Examples of psychological phenomena include memory, intelligence, dyslexia, attachment, creativity, prejudice, and amnesia, among others. None of these phenomena are best studied within a specialized field of psychology.

For example, although memory can be investigated as a cognitive phenomenon, it can and should be studied through the techniques of a number of other fields. These fields include biological psychology and cognitive neuroscience (e.g., in attempts to find out where in the brain memories are stored), clinical psychology (e.g., in the conflict over repressed memories), social psychology (e.g., in preferential memory for self-referential memories), and behavioral genetics (e.g., in the heritability of memory characteristics), to name just some of the relevant fields. Someone studying memory through only one approach or set of techniques will understand only part of the phenomenon.

Similarly, extraversion can be and has been studied from personality, differential, biological, cognitive, social, cultural, and other points of view. Someone studying extraversion from only one of these points of view—for example, personality—almost certainly will understand the phenomenon only in a narrow way, in terms of, say, extraversion as a trait, without fully appreciating the role of biological or cognitive processes or of culture, for that matter.

The same argument can be applied to virtually any psychological phenomenon. By subsuming psychological phenomena under fields of psychology, the discipline encourages a narrow view rather than a broad approach to understanding psychological phenomena.

Organizing by Fields Can Isolate Individuals Who Study the Same Phenomena

For example, two individuals within a psychology department may both study attachment, but if one is in personality psychology and another in developmental psychology, they may have little interaction. This is because in a typical department, students and professors are located next to—and attend the same meetings and read the same journals as—others in their field regardless of the phenomena being studied.

The Current Organization May Create False Oppositions Between Individuals or Groups Studying Phenomena From Different Vantage Points

Here is an example: Individuals studying memory from a cognitive perspective may never quite understand the work of those studying memory from a clinical standpoint. This can lead to a sense of hostility toward the viewpoints of those who do not understand their (preferred) way of studying memory. Or individuals studying love from social psychological versus clinical points of view may (and sometimes do) see themselves in opposition, as though there were a uniquely correct approach to studying a psychological phenomenon.

The Current System Tends to Marginalize Psychological Phenomena That Fall Outside the Boundaries of a Specific Field

For example, psychological phenomena such as imagination, motivation, or emotion may tend to be ignored in a department if they are not seen as part of the core of a field. This also extends to the people studying such phenomena, who may have difficulty getting hired because hiring is often done by area, and the people studying phenomena at the interface of fields of psychology may be perceived as not fitting neatly into any one area. In turn, faculty in a given area may not want to hire such people if they feel that their area will not get the full benefit of a slot or that such individuals will not contribute adequately to graduate (or even undergraduate) training in that so-called core field.

Research May Tilt Toward Issues to Which a Limited Set of Tools May Be Applied

The current system essentially equips students with a set of tools (e.g., the methods of developmental psychology, or cognitive neuroscience, or social psychology, or mathematical psychology). Instead of allowing students to be driven by substantive issues, the system encourages students to search for a phenomenon for which they can use their tools, much in the way a carpenter might seek objects for which he or she can use a hammer.

The Current System Can Discourage New Ways of Studying Problems

If someone wishes to educate students in terms of the existing boundaries of fields, he or she will encounter few problems. But if he or she wants to cross those boundaries, other faculty may worry that the individual students will not be properly trained in a field, may have trouble getting a job, or may not fit into the departmental structure. In truth, they may be justified in all these concerns.

The Traditional Disciplinary Approach of Largely Subsuming Psychological Phenomena Under Fields of Study Rather Than the Other Way Around Leads Psychologists to Confuse Aspects of Phenomena With the Phenomena as a Whole

This confusion is analogous to the use of synecdoche in speech, where one substitutes a part for a whole (e.g., *crown* for *kingdom*). However, unlike poets or other writers, psychologists are unaware of their use of this device. The psychologists believe they are studying the whole phenomenon when, in fact, they are studying only a small part of it.

Consider the well-worn parable of the blind men each touching a different part of the elephant and each being convinced that he is touching a different animal. In psychology, the situation is like always studying the same part of a phenomenon and thinking that this part tells you all you need to know to understand the whole phenomenon. Consider two examples.

In the study of human intelligence, psychometricians may keep discovering a "general factor" and thus become convinced that the general factor largely explains intelligence. Biological psychologists may find a spot or two in the brain that light up during the fMRI or PET scan analysis of the commission of cognitive tasks and become convinced that these parts of the brain fully explain intelligence. Cultural psychologists may find wide cultural differences in notions of the nature of intelligence and become convinced that intelligence is best explained simply as a cultural invention. Each psychologist touches a different part of the metaphorical elephant and becomes convinced that part represents the whole (and fairly simple) animal.

As a second example, attention deficit hyperactivity disorder (ADHD) has genetic, neuropsychological, cognitive, educational, social, and cultural aspects. Some of the debate in the field of ADHD has come to be over whether the origins of ADHD are genetic, neuropsychological, cognitive, educational, social, or cultural. This ongoing, fruitless debate is unlikely to end until scientists are trained in each other's fields and paradigms so that they will understand that learning disabilities, like other psychological phenomena, need to be understood from all of these perspectives, not just one. Of course, the same argument applies to many other psychological phenomena, such as emotions, consciousness, motivation, mental disorders, perception, memory, and creativity.

A Phenomenon-Based Proposal

In general, scientists who are not well trained in one another's techniques are likely to be suspicious of others' techniques and of the conclusions drawn from them. These scientists probably will continue to do research within their own paradigm, which keeps supporting their views and thereby reinforces their confidence that they are right and that those who adhere to a paradigm from some other field are misguided.

We believe that a more sensible and psychologically justifiable way of organizing psychology as a discipline and in departments and graduate study is in terms of psychological phenomena—which are not arbitrary—rather than so-called fields of psychology—which largely are arbitrary. Under this approach, an individual might choose to specialize in a set of related phenomena, such as learning and memory, stereotyping and prejudice, or motivation and emotion, and then study the phenomena of interest from multiple points of view. The individual thus would reach a fuller understanding of the phenomena being studied because he or she would not be limited by a set of assumptions or methods drawn from only one field of psychology.

Our proposal carries with it a number of advantages that are largely complementary to the disadvantages of the field-based approach that currently dominates the discipline. People might very well end up specializing in several related psychological phenomena, but they would understand these phenomena broadly rather than narrowly, which is certainly an advantage if their goal is comprehensive psychological understanding. Psychology would be less susceptible to tendencies that field-based organization encourages: narrowness, isolation, false oppositions, marginalization, largely method-driven rather than phenomenon-driven approaches to research, discouragement of new ways of approaching psychological phenomena, and confusion of the part with the whole.

In Sum

Unified psychology, then, means giving up a single disciplinary approach in favor of an integrated multidisciplinary approach in which problems rather than subdisciplines become the key basis for the study of psychology. One chooses a particular disciplinary approach because it is useful in studying a psychological phenomenon rather than choosing a particular psychological problem because it happens to fall within the subdiscipline in terms of which one defines oneself.

THE APPROACH OF UNIFIED PSYCHOLOGY

The history of psychology may be viewed as the history of a sequence of failed paradigms. The paradigms failed not because they were wrong—paradigms are not right or wrong (Kuhn, 1970)—but rather because they provided only incomplete perspectives on the problems to which they were applied. Almost every introductory psychology student learns how structuralism gained in popularity, only eventually to fall when its weaknesses were appreciated. The student learns as well how functionalism, associationism, and a host of other "–isms" have come and gone, with each generation of researchers hoping that their –ism will somehow be the last. At best, the sequence of paradigms has represented a dialectical progression (Hegel, 1807/1931; see discussion in Sternberg, 1999), with new paradigms synthesizing the best aspects of older ones. At worst, one failed –ism has simply replaced another without any signs of learning on the part of its adherents that this paradigm, too, shall pass. Of course, in each of these generations, many scholars have believed that they have at last found the answer, oblivious to the fact that they have merely repeated a pattern of the past.

When Robert J. Sternberg was in graduate school, he asked his graduate advisor about work the advisor had done previously on mathematical models of learning theory. The advisor, Gordon Bower, remarked that he had trouble remembering why he thought earlier that the questions the models addressed were so important. Such is how paradigms come and go. They go not when they are proven wrong but when they run out of steam, fail to account for new empirical results, or fail to provide the means to answer the questions that investigators in a given period of time most want to answer (see Kuhn, 1970, for a detailed discussion of the evolution of paradigms).

If one considers a basic psychological phenomenon, such as learning, one realizes that it can be studied in terms of an evolutionary paradigm, a brain-based biological paradigm, a cognitive paradigm, a behaviorist paradigm, a psychoanalytic paradigm, a genetic–epistemological paradigm, and so forth. There is no one correct perspective. Each perspective presents a different way of understanding the problem of learning.

SOME POTENTIAL OBJECTIONS TO
THE ENDEAVOR OF UNIFIED PSYCHOLOGY

Of course, there are potential objections to the concept of unified psychology. Consider some of them as well as possible responses.

The Discipline of Psychology Already Is Unified; the Call for a Unified Psychology Attacks a Straw Person

We see relatively little unification in the field at the present. The large majority of journals are specialized. Some that are not in theory are in practice accepting only articles in which the authors use certain accepted paradigms or methodologies. Granting panels often accept grant proposals in much the same way, although, of course, there are exceptions. Conventions or sections of conventions often are specialized. Courses often are taught in a disunified way, with topics presented in isolation from each other. For the most part, jobs are advertised in terms of fields of specialization, and promotions may depend on convincing referees within a narrow field of specialization that one is truly a member of the in-group of that field and that one is an important contributor to it. Even within broad-based organizations, such as the American Psychological Association, it has proven difficult to unify special interests, and many groups have split off precisely because of the difficulty of keeping the field unified and the view of some that such unification is not important.

The Discipline Already Has a Field of General Psychology, Which Is the Same as Unified Psychology

In today's world, general psychology is not the same as unified psychology. General psychology encompasses various fields of psychology but does not necessarily unify them. General psychology texts often cover a variety of topics in psychology without unifying them at all. For example, learning and memory typically are covered in separate chapters, despite their obvious relationship. General psychology is embracing but not necessarily unifying. But to the extent one wishes to redefine general psychology as unifying and not just embracing the many aspects that constitute psychology, we would be happy to view this form of general psychology as being the same as our proposed unified psychology.

Even if Unified Psychology Is Not the Same as General Psychology, There Is Nothing New in the Concept

At some level, we agree. Unified psychology represents a goal toward which many people have strived ever since psychology's earliest days. But not so many people have achieved it, and we suspect that as the field becomes more specialized, fewer and fewer people will. The term *unified psychology*, at worst, may help provide a rubric for a pretheoretical stance that many scientists and practitioners will find fits them better than rubrics that force adherence to paradigms or methodologies that are in themselves incomplete. To the extent that psychologists use a term to motivate what they do, we believe the term serves a valuable purpose. Thinking of oneself as, say, a social psychologist or a personality psychologist may guide what one studies and how one studies it. Thinking of oneself as a unified psychologist may do the same.

The Term *Unified Psychology* Is a Misnomer, Because One Has Substituted Divisions by Phenomena for Divisions by Fields

One perhaps could argue that the term *unified* never would apply unless one looked at something solely as a gestalt—as a single, indivisible entity. We disagree with this point of view, because even that indivisible entity would be a part of some greater whole, which in turn would be a part of some greater whole, and soon one would lapse into infinite regress. Unification is always with respect to something. When we use the term *unified*, we use it with respect to what currently constitutes the subdisciplines of psychology. We make no claim that our proposal is unified with respect to everything, a claim we believe, in any case, would be meaningless.

The Direction of the Discipline Is Toward Specialization, Not Integration: Needed in Training Are Specialists Who Can Do Precise Scientific Work, Not Generalists or Even Dilettantes Who, However Useful They Might Have Been in Psychology's Prescientific Days, No Longer Advance the Discipline

We have argued elsewhere (Sternberg & Grigorenko, 1999) that dilettantism is and always has been useful to the discipline of psychology. But unified psychology goes beyond dilettantism and is not contrary to specialization. Today, people of course need some kind of specialization. However, there is a narrow form of specialization and a broad form. Narrow specialization is where one looks at a problem with tunnel vision and knows only a narrow range of techniques to apply in solving that problem. In broad specialization, one may look at a fairly specific problem but do so with open eyes and with the benefit of the many problem-solving techniques a multi-disciplinary approach leaves at one's disposal. Any phenomenon, no matter how specialized, can be studied in such a way. The value of such study is the message that unified psychology conveys.

The Proposal Is Inconvenient and Even Impractical

In the near term, our proposal would be inconvenient because it is inconsistent with an entrenched system that extends to departmental organization, graduate and even undergraduate education, job offerings, and the like. It also is inconvenient simply because this is not the way people currently in the field have been trained, and people tend to value systems that have worked for them in the past and are likely to work for them in the future without disturbing their world. We believe or, at least, hope that the inconvenience of a new system would be outweighed by the ultimate benefit to the field that the proposed system would offer.

Training Under the New System Would Take Too Long

Some might view the kind of training we propose as taking longer than traditional training, but we see no reason to believe this is so. What would change is not so much how long one spends in training but how one spends the time one is in training. Truly, training in psychology is lifelong, and no matter what kind of graduate training one receives, one always needs to be learning in order to stay on top of a field, however that field is defined. Good training does not end with a diploma but, in some respects, merely changes in form with the diploma.

In Solving One Kind of Problem of Suboptimal Divisions, the New System Introduces Others

One could argue that the new system introduces new problems that are not so different from the ones it is supposed to solve. For example, psychological phenomena are mutually interdependent. Thus, studying such phenomena in depth still would give one only a limited picture of them. For example, interpersonal attraction may depend on personality, attitudes, early experience, and so forth. We believe this objection is mistaken, however. The comprehensive study of any phenomenon, such as interpersonal attraction, always has brought and always will bring to bear multiple perspectives on the multiple factors that contribute to the phenomenon. We view such interdependence not as a problem for but as an advantage of our approach.

In Sum

Unified psychology, then, means giving up a single paradigm in favor of the use of whatever paradigm may help shed light on a problem. Multiple paradigms can contribute to the understanding of a single psychological phenomenon, whereas locking oneself into any single paradigm reduces one's ability to fully grasp the phenomenon of interest.

SOME IMPLICATIONS OF THE UNIFIED-PSYCHOLOGY VIEW

The unified-psychology perspective has several implications for modern-day work in psychology. Here are a few of them.

Psychology Will Only Fragment if Psychologists Wish It To

Gardner (1992) argued that psychology is undergoing a process of fragmentation and that eventually it may become a much smaller field, with much of what is currently classified as psychology being subsumed by disciplines such as cognitive science or cognitive neuroscience. Not everyone agrees with this assessment. However, psychology is more likely to fragment if people accept new fields as somehow providing the final questions or answers that old ones lacked. For example, researchers in the field of cognitive science have much to gain from studying the contexts of behavior, the social psychology of cognitive processes, links between cognition and emotion (or personality), and so forth. The new panaceas are no better than the old ones. Psychology needs all its parts—integrated in a unified way.

Students of psychology need to be trained in general psychology as well as in specializations and other fields of inquiry (e.g., biology, philosophy, anthropology, sociology, and statistics). However, general psychology is not tantamount to unified psychology. It is not enough to have all the disciplines of psychology under one big roof. The disciplines need to be synthesized with respect to paradigms, theories, and methods (see also Kalmar & Sternberg, 1988).

New Movements Will Soon Fail if They Are Not Unified

In our view, current thinking often inadvertently repeats the mistakes of prior thinking. For example, we are very optimistic about the development of positive psychology (Seligman & Csikszentmihalyi, 2000). But looking only at the positive side of phenomena is likely to be as restrictive as looking only at the negative side. Ultimately, psychologists have to learn, as they have in the past, that a synthesis is needed to integrate a thesis and its antithesis. Neuroscientific approaches to cognition are proving to be quite useful, and the overwhelming number of jobs being offered in the cognitive neuroscience area suggests that this trend has taken hold across many departments of psychology. But cognitive neuroscience, like any other approach, answers some questions but not others. It is probably less useful than traditional cognitive approaches, for example, in suggesting to teachers how they can improve student learning. Teachers can benefit from knowing about the hazards of massed versus distributed practice or of retroactive and proactive interference. It is less clear how they can benefit, at this time, from knowing the part of the brain in which performance on a particular cognitive task is localized. Eventually, they may well be able to benefit. In the meantime, new approaches will continue to emerge, and they will have in common with current and past approaches that they answer some questions well, other questions poorly, and still other questions not at all.

We must admit to one fact: Unified movements will eventually fail too, in a sense. No movement lasts forever. However, what a unified movement is in the best position to do is to plant the seeds for its successors. For example, a unified approach to prejudice will reveal what questions cannot be answered with any available paradigms or methods and will help force psychologists to think of new ways to answer the questions that are recalcitrant under any available approach.

The Field of Psychology Is Not Well Set Up for the Propagation of Unified Psychology

Psychology departments are typically organized by fields. Graduate study is typically organized by fields. Often, many members of a given field within a given department share a common paradigm or methodological approach. Many awards and prizes within the field of psychology are organized by fields. Journals and granting organizations often divide themselves up by fields. Even divisions of the American Psychological Association are organized, to a large extent, by fields. There inevitably will be substantial vested interest in maintaining current systems for organizing old knowledge, discovering new knowledge, and propagating both kinds of knowledge. Therefore, we do not expect many immediate converts and suspect we will hear in the near future many reasons why the current system is the best system. People who profit from a system rarely wish to give it up! Eventually, of course, we hope that there will be many converts to the notion of unified psychology and that they, too, will wish to maintain their views. They will have one advantage, perhaps, over some others: They may be flexible enough to synthesize the new views with their existing old ones.

One of the Biggest Problems Is That People May Think
They Practice Unified Psychology When in Fact They Do Not

Virtually everyone wishes to see him- or herself as open-minded and, moreover, as someone who is not locked into any one stifling way of doing things. Therefore, many people may believe they already practice unified psychology. But the organizational issues described above with respect to the field of psychology make it unlikely that this is the case. The field of psychology currently is organized, as we have discussed, to promote the individual disciplines much more than the unified study of phenomena. Indeed, examples abound of how work that falls or people who fall between the cracks can suffer. The people without a specialization recognized in the current system of psychology may find themselves locked out of jobs, journals, grants, prizes, and other aspects of the meager reward system psychology has to offer. Some people may well be termed *eclectic* for their use of a variety of ideas or techniques, but they may not sufficiently synthesize them to truly be unified psychologists. At the same time, some scholars may well practice unified psychology, and, of course, we hope they will diffuse their perspective to many others as well.

It is easy to become a unified psychologist. One need adhere to no particular set of methods, to no particular field, and to no particular paradigm. Indeed, the first step is precisely adhering to none of the above. We hope that many psychologists might find such a nonrestrictive way of thinking attractive. If any or all wish to view unified psychology as old wine in new bottles, we remind them that so often old wines are the best of all but old bottles — sometimes with lead in their foil or corks that have rotted — usually are not the best. So we will be very happy if, after all, some decide that unified psychology is a vintage old wine in a new and better bottle. And we will be even happier if people drink of it.

REFERENCES

Allport, G. W. (1929). The composition of political attitudes. *American Journal of Sociology, 35,* 220–238.

Anastasi, A. (1990, August). *Are there unifying trends in the psychologies of 1990?* Invited address presented at the 98th Annual Convention of the American Psychological Association, Boston, MA.

Baldwin, J. M. (1902). *Development and evolution.* New York: Macmillan.

Baldwin, J. M. (1906). *Social and ethical interpretations in mental development: A study in social psychology.* New York: Macmillan. (Original work published 1897)

Berlin, I. (1953). *The hedgehog and the fox.* New York: Simon & Schuster.

Bevan, W. (1982). A sermon of sorts in three plus parts. *American Psychologist, 37*, 1303–1322.

Bevan, W. (1991). Contemporary psychology: A tour inside the onion. *American Psychologist, 46*, 475–483.

Bevan, W. (1994). Plain truths and home cooking: Thoughts on the making and re-making of psychology. *American Psychologist, 49*, 505–509.

Brody, N. (2000). History of theories and measurements of intelligence. In R. J. Sternberg (Ed.), *Handbook of intelligence* (16–33). New York: Cambridge University Press.

Bronfenbrenner, U. (1979). *The ecology of human development.* Cambridge, MA: Harvard University Press.

Bronfenbrenner, U., & Morris, P. A. (1998). The ecology of developmental processes. In W. Damon (Series Ed.) & R. M. Lerner (Vol. Ed.), *Handbook of child psychology* (5th ed., Vol. 1, pp. 993–1028). New York: Wiley.

Cairns, R. B. (1998). The making of developmental psychology. In W. Damon (Series Ed.) & R. B. Lerner (Vol. Ed.), *Handbook of child psychology* (5th ed., Vol. 1, pp. 25–105). New York: Wiley.

Carroll, J. B. (1982). The measurement of intelligence. In R. J. Sternberg (Ed.), *Handbook of human intelligence* (pp. 29–120). New York: Cambridge University Press.

Carroll, J. B. (1993). *Human cognitive abilities: A survey of factor-analytic studies.* New York: Cambridge University Press.

Cohen, J., & Cohen, P. (1983). *Applied multiple regression/correlation analysis for the behavioral sciences* (2nd ed.). Hillsdale, NJ: Erlbaum.

Cooper, L. A., & Regan, D. T. (1982). Attention, perception, and intelligence. In R. J. Sternberg (Ed.), *Handbook of human intelligence* (pp. 123–169). New York: Cambridge University Press.

Deary, I. J. (2000). Simple information processing. In R. J. Sternberg (Ed.), *Handbook of intelligence* (267–284). New York: Cambridge University Press.

DeGroot, A. D. (1989, April). *Unifying psychology: Its preconditions.* Address presented at the Fourth International Congress of the International Association of Theoretical Psychology, Amsterdam, The Netherlands.

Dovidio, J. F., & Gaertner, S. L. (2000). Aversive racism and selection decisions: 1989 and 1999. *Psychological Science, 11*, 315–319.

Dovidio, J. F., Kawakami, K., Johnson, C., Johnson, B., & Howard, A. (1997). On the nature of prejudice: Automatic and controlled processes. *Journal of Experimental Social Psychology, 33*, 510–540.

Estes, W. K. (1982). Learning, memory, and intelligence. In R. J. Sternberg (Ed.), *Handbook of intelligence* (pp. 170–224). New York: Cambridge University Press.

Fowler, R. D. (1990). The core discipline. *American Psychologist, 45*, 1–6.

Gardner, H. (1983). *Frames of mind: The theory of multiple intelligences.* New York: Basic Books.

Gardner, H. (1992). Scientific psychology: Should we bury it or praise it? *New Ideas in Psychology, 10,* 179–190.

Gardner, H. (1999). *Intelligence reframed: Multiple intelligences for the 21st century.* New York: Basic Books.

Garner, W. R., Hake, H. W., & Erikson, C. W. (1956). Operationism and the concept of perception. *Psychological Review, 63,* 149–159.

Green, C. D. (1992). Is unified positivism the answer to psychology's disunity? *American Psychologist, 47,* 1057–1058.

Greenwald, A. G, & Banaji, M. R. (1995). Implicit social cognition: Attitudes, self-esteem, and stereotypes. *Psychological Review, 102,* 4–27.

Greenwald, A. G., Banaji, M. R., Rudman, L. A., Farnham, S. D., Nosek, B. A., & Rosier, M. (2000). Prologue to a unified theory of attitudes, stereotypes, and self-concept. In J. P. Forgas (Ed.), *Feeling and thinking: The role of affect in social cognition* (pp. 308–330). New York: Cambridge University Press.

Greenwald, A. G., McGhee, D. E., & Schwartz, J. L. K. (1998). Measuring individual differences in implicit cognition: The implicit association test. *Journal of Personality and Social Psychology, 74,* 1464–1480.

Guilford, J. P. (1967). *The nature of human intelligence.* New York: McGraw-Hill.

Hegel, G. W. F. (1931). *The phenomenology of the mind* (J. D. Baillie, Trans.; 2nd ed.). London: Allen & Unwin. (Original work published 1807)

Kalmar, D. A., & Sternberg, R. J. (1988). Theory knitting: An integrative approach to theory development. *Philosophical Psychology, 1,* 153–170.

Kendler, H. H. (1970). The unity of psychology. *The Canadian Psychologist, 11,* 30–47.

Kendler, H. H. (1987). A good divorce is better than a bad marriage. In A. W. Staats & L. P. Mos (Eds.), *Annals of theoretical psychology* (Vol. 5, pp. 55–89). New York: Plenum.

Kimble, G. A. (1989). Psychology from the standpoint of a generalist. *American Psychologist, 44,* 491–499.

Kimble, G. A. (1994). A frame of reference for psychology. *American Psychologist, 49,* 510–519.

Koch, S. (1981). The nature and limits of psychological knowledge: Lessons of a century qua "science." *American Psychologist, 36,* 257–269.

Krech, (1970). Epilogue. In J. R. Royce (Ed.), *Toward unification in psychology: The first Banff Conference on Theoretical Psychology* (297–301). Toronto, Ontario, Canada: University of Toronto Press.

Kuhn, T. S. (1970). *The structure of scientific revolutions* (2nd ed.). Chicago: University of Chicago Press.

Kuhn, T. S. (1991, November). *The problem with the historical philosophy of science* [The Robert and Maurine Rothschild Distinguished Lecture]. Address presented to a meeting of the History of Science Department, Harvard University, Cambridge, MA.

Kukla, A. (1992). Unification as a goal for psychology. *American Psychologist, 47,* 1054–1055.

Kuo, Z.-Y. (1967). *The dynamics of behavior development.* New York: Random House.

Kuo, Z.-Y. (1976). *The dynamics of behavior development: An epigenetic view.* New York: Plenum.

Laboratory of Comparative Human Cognition. (1983). Culture and cognitive development. In P. Mussen (Series Ed.) & W. Kessen (Vol. Ed.), *Handbook of child psychology* (4th ed., Vol. 1, pp. 295–356). New York: Wiley.

Langer, E. J. (1997). *The power of mindful learning.* Needham Heights, MA: Addison-Wesley.

Larson, G. E., Haier, R. J., LaCasse, L., & Hazen, K. (1995). Evaluation of a "mental effort" hypothesis for correlations between cortical metabolism and intelligence. *Intelligence, 21,* 267–278.

Leary, D. E. (2001). One big idea, one ultimate concern: Sigmund Koch's critique of psychology and hope for the future. *American Psychologist, 56,* 425–432.

Lerner, R. M. (1998). Theories of human development: Contemporary perspectives. In W. Damon (Series Ed.) & R. M. Lerner (Vol. Ed.), *Handbook of child psychology* (5th ed., Vol. 1, pp. 1–24). New York: Wiley.

Lohman, D. F. (2000). Complex information processing and intelligence. In R. J. Sternberg (Ed.), *Handbook of intelligence* (pp. 285–340). New York: Cambridge University Press.

MacIntyre, R. B. (1985). Psychology's fragmentation and suggested remedies. *International Newsletter of Paradigmatic Psychology, 1,* 20–21.

Mackintosh, N. J. (1998). *IQ and human intelligence.* Oxford, England: Oxford University Press.

MacLullich, A. M. J., Seckl, J. R., Starr, J. M., & Deary, I. J. (1998). The biology of intelligence: From association to mechanism. *Intelligence, 26,* 63–73.

Magnusson, D. (2000). The individual as the organizing principle in psychological inquiry: A holistic approach. In L. R. Bergman, R. B. Cairns, L.-G. Nilsson, & L. Nystedt (Eds.), *Developmental science and the holistic approach* (33–47). Mahwah, NJ: Erlbaum.

Maher, B. A. (1985). Underpinnings of today's chaotic diversity. *International Newsletter of Paradigmatic Psychology, 1,* 17–19.

McNally, R. J. (1992). Disunity in psychology: Chaos or speciation? *American Psychologist, 47,* 1054.

Messer, S. B. (1988). Philosophical obstacles to unification of psychology. *International Newsletter of Uninomic Psychology, 5,* 22–24.

Royce, J. R. (Ed.). (1970). *Toward unification in psychology: The first Banff Conference on Theoretical Psychology.* Toronto, Ontario, Canada: University of Toronto Press.

Rychlak, J. F. (1988). Unification through understanding and tolerance of opposition. *International Newsletter of Uninomic Psychology, 5,* 113–115.

Sameroff, A. J. (1983). Developmental systems: Contexts and evolution. In P. H. Mussen (Ed.) & W. Kessen (Vol. Ed.), *Handbook of child psychology* (4th ed., Vol. 1, pp. 237–294). New York: Wiley.

Sameroff, A. J., Bartko, W. T. (1998). Political and scientific models of development. In D. Pushkar, W. M. Bukowski, A. E. Schwartzman, D. M. Stack, & D. R. White (Eds.), *Improving competence across the lifespan* (177–192). New York: Plenum.

Schneirla, T. C. (1957). The concept of development in comparative psychology. In D. B. Harris (Ed.), *The concept of development* (pp. 78–108). Minneapolis: University of Minnesota Press.

Scott, T. R. (1991). A personal view of the future of psychology departments. *American Psychologist, 46,* 975–976.

Seligman, M. E. P., & Csikszentmihalyi, M. (2000). Positive psychology: An introduction. *American Psychologist, 55,* 5–14.

Serpell, R. (2000). Intelligence and culture. In R. J. Sternberg (Ed.), *Handbook of intelligence* (pp. 549–580). New York: Cambridge University Press.

Sherif, M., Harvey, L. J., White, B. J., Hood, W. R., & Sherif, C. W. (1988). *The Robber's Cave experiment: Intergroup conflict and cooperation.* Middletown, CT: Wesleyan University Press. (Original work published 1961)

Spearman, C. (1927). *The abilities of man.* London: Macmillan.

Staats, A. W. (1983). *Psychology's crisis of disunity: Philosophy and method for a unified science.* New York: Praeger.

Staats, A. W. (1991). Unified positivism and unification psychology: Fad or new field? *American Psychologist, 46,* 899–912.

Staats, A. W. (1993). Separatism with unification. In H. V. Rappard, P. J. Van Strien, L. P. Mos, & W. J. Baker (Eds.), *Annals of theoretical psychology* (Vol. 9, pp. 155–164). New York: Plenum.

Staats, A. W. (1999). Unifying psychology requires new infrastructure, theory, method, and a research agenda. *Review of General Psychology, 3,* 3–13.

Sternberg, R. J. (Ed.). (1982). *Handbook of human intelligence.* New York: Cambridge University Press.

Sternberg, R. J. (1985). *Beyond IQ: A triarchic theory of human intelligence.* New York: Cambridge University Press.

Sternberg, R. J. (1990). *Metaphors of mind: Conceptions of the nature of intelligence.* New York: Cambridge University Press.

Sternberg, R. J. (1997). *Successful intelligence.* New York: Plume.

Sternberg, R. J. (1999). A dialectical basis for understanding the study of cognition. In R. J. Sternberg (Ed.), *The nature of cognition* (pp. 51–78). Cambridge, MA: MIT Press.

Sternberg, R. J. (2000). *Handbook of intelligence.* New York: Cambridge University Press.

Sternberg, R. J., & Grigorenko, E. L. (1999). In praise of dilettantism. *APS Observer, 12*(5), 37–38.

Sternberg, R. J., & Grigorenko, E. L. (2001). The misorganization of psychology. *APS Observer*, *14*(1), 1, 20.

Sternberg, R. J., Grigorenko, E. L., Ferrari, M., & Clinkenbeard, P. (1999). A triarchic analysis of an aptitude–treatment interaction. *European Journal of Psychological Assessment*, *15*, 1–11.

Thelen, E. (1992). Development as a dynamic system. *Current Directions in Psychological Science*, *1*, 189–193.

Thelen, E., & Smith, L. B. (1994). *A dynamic systems approach to the development of cognition and action*. Cambridge, MA: MIT Press.

Thelen, E., & Smith, L. B. (1998). Dynamic systems theories. In W. Damon (Series Ed.) & R. M. Lerner (Vol. Ed.), *Handbook of child psychology* (5th ed., Vol. 1, pp. 563–634). New York: Wiley.

Thurstone, L. L. (1938). *Primary mental abilities*. Chicago: University of Chicago Press.

Vernon, P. A. (1997). Behavioral genetic and biological approaches to intelligence. In H. Nyborg (Ed.), *The scientific study of human nature: Tribute to Hans J. Eysenck at eighty* (pp. 240–258). Oxford, England: Pergamon/Elsevier Science.

Vernon, P. A., Wickett, J. C., Bazana, P. G., & Stelmack, R. M. (2000). The neuropsychology and psychophysiology of human intelligence. In R. J. Sternberg (Ed.), *Handbook of intelligence* (pp. 245–264). New York: Cambridge University Press.

Viney, W. (1989). The cyclops and the twelve-eyed toad: William James and the unity–disunity problem in psychology. *American Psychologist*, *44*, 1261–1265.

Wapner, S., Demick, J. (1989). A holistic, developmental systems approach to person–environment functioning. *International Newsletter of Uninomic Psychology*, *8*, 15–30.

Wertheimer, M. (1988). Obstacles to the integration of competing theories in psychology. *Philosophical Psychology*, *1*, 131–137.

Woodward, W. R., Devonis, D. (1993). Toward a new understanding of scientific change: Applying interfield theory to the history of psychology. In H. V. Rappard, P. J. Van Strien, L. P. Mos, & W. J. Baker (Eds.), *Annals of theoretical psychology* (Vol. 9, pp. 87–123). New York: Plenum.

II

BEGINNING
THE RESEARCH PROCESS

Research begins with the idea or question for investigation. For investigators beginning their research careers, identifying and generating the idea for a study is the most difficult part of the research. This is understandable because of the vague mandate, expectation, and challenge presented to us as researchers to investigate something new and important or to be creative. Of course there is never a substitute for inspiration, intuition, brilliance, and creativity (but see my dissertation for an example of how to avoid all of these). There are systematic ways one can pursue to generate ideas for research, and these have been nicely detailed elsewhere (McGuire, 1997). In clinical psychology, the idea for an investigation often emerges from considering

- special populations (e.g., characteristics of patients with a particular disorder, their parents or offspring);
- individuals who appear to be exceptions (e.g., individuals at risk for delinquency or depression who do not show the problem or outcome);
- subtypes (e.g., different attachment patterns, different types of anxiety disorder);

- resolving a specific issue from prior research (e.g., including better or different control conditions to resolve an ambiguity about why change occurred or what the critical ingredient is);
- interventions (e.g., ways of treating or preventing a particular problem or promoting development);
- moderators (e.g., any characteristic such as age, sex, or culture that may interact with or alter the relation of two other variables, the extent to which an intervention works with one type of individual vs. another);
- mediators (e.g., the mechanisms or processes that explain how change comes about); and
- theory (e.g., a test of predictions derived from a conceptual model or describing a phenomena in ways that may generate theory).

These sources do not exhaust the bases for individual investigations, nor are they mutually exclusive (Kazdin, 2003). Even so, they do convey that one can consider the type of study or question at a more abstract level of analysis. That is, what does this study hope to accomplish? Many design issues will follow from clarifying the broad goal as well as the specific hypotheses. The chapters in this part provide more concrete illustrations of developing the research idea.

RESEARCH IDEAS

Looking at a phenomenon in news ways is a useful way to generate novel ideas for research. Of course, that is more easily said than done. In chapter 3 by Allan W. Wicker, several strategies are presented to generate novel ideas, including alternative ways of selecting, developing, and playing with ideas; examining the contexts in which phenomena occur; challenging central assumptions; and scrutinizing key concepts. What is particularly novel about this chapter is the broad range of strategies that are presented and illustrated.

Another strategy for developing ideas for the study is to consider different ways in which the variables of interest may relate to each other or to another phenomenon. Several authors have discussed different types of relations, including correlation, risk factors, and causal relations, each of which includes many variations (see Haynes, 1992; Kraemer et al., 1997). To develop a study, one can identify the topic of interest and ask what are the correlates, risk factors, and causes? Of the relations demonstrated (e.g., correlation), can one move to cause by studying the phenomenon in a different way?

A key distinction that represents two of the many ways in which variables can relate to the phenomenon of interest is between mediators and moderators (Baron & Kenny, 1986). *Mediators* refer to the reasons, processes, or mechanisms that are responsible for the effect of an intervention or experimental manipulation; *moderators* refer to those variables with which a particular relation interacts (e.g., sex, race, context). In developing the idea, the investigator might identify domains of interest (e.g., depression and marital functioning, peer popularity and grades) and whether studying mediators or moderators of the relations might lead to new insights.

For example, if one were interested in the relation of depression and marital satisfaction, one might test a mediation hypothesis to see whether one leads to or contributes to another, whether the relation is bidirectional (each can lead to the other), and whether changing one leads to a change in the other. In addition or alternatively, one might test for moderation, that is, whether the relationship depends on a third variable. Does depression lead to marital dissatisfaction for some individuals but not others, and can one predict what variables distinguish (moderate) the relation? Perhaps, marital dissatisfaction is greater (or less) among depressed individuals who have been married a few (or very many) years or with several (or no) children.

A particular relation in any area of science is not likely to hold for all cases for all time. Moderators focus on those conditions in which the relation may vary. As a guide to research one can begin by asking what is the relation of variable x and y, and does this relation vary as a function of variable z (e.g., characteristics of the individual or context)?

Chapter 4 by Grayson N. Holmbeck elaborates the distinction between mediator and moderator and gives examples of their use. The examples not only clarify the distinction but also are useful when viewed from a broader perspective. Different pathways, mechanisms, and relations exist among variables, and the task for the researcher is to think about these in advance of the study and to ensure that the design, conditions, and data analyses can address these relations. Statistical approaches to evaluation of mediation and moderation are also discussed and underscore the importance of considering data-analytic issues early in the research process. The early data-analytic questions are not only the usual one of "How can these data be analyzed" but also "If the data *are* analyzed in this way, will this yield the answer?" Much more is said in subsequent chapters about these questions.

FOCI OF RESEARCH

Along with the research idea is the way in which the idea will be studied. The ways could mean the sample, design, setting, and other conditions of the study. For example, will the demonstration be in a laboratory, clinical, or community setting and with students, patients, or random individuals walking the streets (not likely to be a very random group)? Is the goal to test a hypothesis or to describe a phenomenon in ways that might be useful to generate a hypothesis or to understand the phenomenon or test its applications? These are some of the questions that relate to the focus of research.

This section begins with chapter 5 by Douglas G. Mook, who discusses the purposes and importance of laboratory research. A central point is that research in the laboratory is often designed to convey what *can* happen and in so doing contributes significantly to understanding of human functioning, that is, to theory. Generality or applicability of the results is not always important or relevant. Mook elaborates the role of laboratory research and its unique contribution to understanding.

Laboratory and basic research is critically important in clinical psychology. For example, in the context of psychotherapy, there is a bandwagon movement (which I call a "BM") among funding agencies, blue (but also pink) ribbon panels, task forces, and organizations. The movement argues for tests of treatment in clinics rather than in research settings. Generality of treatment from research to clinical practice is critically important, and the call for increased relevance of research to practice is welcome. At the same time, few, if any, programs of research are devoted to understanding *why* treatment works (see Kazdin, 2000). In the short and long run, the best clinical work will come from knowing what goes on in therapy to make it effective. This may require work well outside of the context of clinical settings. One need not pit basic (laboratory) versus applied (clinical) research — they are both needed and address different issues. Yet in the example of therapy, there is so little effort to understand treatment that strong pressures for application may not speed progress toward effective clinical work.

In a different context from clinical work, Mook underscores the importance of understanding psychological processes. I add to his excellent points that when the goal of research is to apply findings, to help people, to build things, and so on, basic research is as, if not more, important than application. Understanding how something works, when something works, and why something works is the best guarantee to making it work in new applications.

When we conduct research, it is obviously important to select an experimental manipulation or condition that will produce a strong effect. A strong effect is one that is likely to be detected in our tests of statistical significance or show a relatively large effect size. Indeed, when the results of an investigation show no differences between conditions, one interpretation is that the manipulation was not sufficiently potent. For example, perhaps the investigator compared people with a small amount of characteristic x versus those a lot more of characteristic x and found no difference. It might have been better to search for a stronger effect and compare those with none of the characteristic (no x) versus those with high levels or a lot of x. In general, this type of thinking is prudent. However, more of a variable (higher dose, more extreme scores) does not invariably lead to more of an effect because not all relations are linear. Also, and rarely discussed, sometimes demonstrating a little effect is a wise strategy.

Deborah A. Prentice and Dale T. Miller discuss in chapter 6 the importance of demonstrating small effects. They begin with a discussion of effect size and hence might give the impression that this chapter may belong in the part on data analysis later in the book. Yet, it is very important for the researcher to have the concept of effect size in mind at the stage that he or she is designing the investigation, because it influences all sorts of decisions (e.g., what conditions or groups ought to be included that would maximize an effect size, how many participants should be included). The chapter conveys that small effects may have important implications both for theory and application. Indeed, in applied work we know that small effects summed over time for an individual (e.g., Abelson, 1985) or spread across many individuals (e.g., aspirin for treatment of heart disease) can have major applied consequences, even though the magnitude of their effects (e.g., effect size) may be small (Meyer et al., chapter 13, in this volume; Rosnow & Rosenthal, 1989). This chapter raises conceptual as well as methodological issues by prompting us to think about the conditions that could show an experimental effect, about whether the magnitude of the effect is important for what we are trying to accomplish, and the relation between the design and hypotheses of the study and the results.

REFERENCES

Abelson, R. (1985). A variance explanation paradox: When a little is a lot. *Psychological Bulletin, 97*, 129–133.

Baron, R. M., & Kenny, D. A. (1986). The moderator–mediator variable distinction in social psychological research: Conceptual, strategic, and statistical considerations. *Journal of Personality and Social Psychology, 51*, 1173–1182.

Haynes, S. N. (1992). *Models of causality in psychopathology: Toward dynamic, synthetic, and nonlinear models of behavior disorders.* Needham Heights, MA: Allyn & Bacon.

Kazdin, A. E. (2000). *Psychotherapy for children and adolescents: Directions for research and practice.* New York: Oxford University Press.

Kazdin, A. E. (2003). *Research design in clinical psychology* (3rd ed.). Needham Heights, MA: Allyn & Bacon.

Kraemer, H. C., Kazdin, A. E., Offord, D. R., Kessler, R. C., Jensen, P. S., & Kupfer, D. J. (1997). Coming to terms with the terms of risk. *Archives of General Psychiatry, 54*, 337–343.

McGuire, W. J. (1997). Creative hypothesis generating in psychology: Some useful heuristics. *Annual Review of Psychology, 48*, 1–30.

Rosnow, R. L., & Rosenthal, R. (1989). Statistical procedures and the justification of knowledge in psychological science. *American Psychologist, 44*, 1276–1284.

RESEARCH IDEAS

3

GETTING OUT OF OUR CONCEPTUAL RUTS: STRATEGIES FOR EXPANDING CONCEPTUAL FRAMEWORKS

ALLAN W. WICKER

In 1879, Sir Francis Galton published an article describing a leisurely stroll he took in the interests of science—specifically to explore how the mind works. In the article, Galton told of walking down a London street and scrutinizing every object that came into his view. He recorded the first thought or two that occurred to him as he focused on each of about 300 objects. Galton reported that this method produced a great variety of associations, including memories of events that had occurred years earlier.

After several days, Galton repeated the walk and the recording procedure and again found a variety of associations. He also discovered a great deal of repetition or overlap in his thoughts on the two occasions. Galton likened his thoughts to actors in theater processions in which the players march off one side of the stage and reappear on the other. This recurrence of ideas

Reprinted from the *American Psychologist, 40,* 1094–1103. Copyright 1985 by the American Psychological Association.

piqued Galton's curiosity. He next devised some word association tasks that led him to the same conclusion as his walks, namely, that "the roadways of our minds are worn into very deep ruts" (Galton, 1879, cited by Crovitz, 1970, p. 35).

Although Galton's methods may have been faulty by present standards, he seems to have discovered a stable psychological principle: the recurrence of ideas (Crovitz, 1970). My comments here assume that Galton was right — that our thoughts flow in a limited number of channels and that our research efforts are thereby constrained.

This article sketches a variety of approaches for stimulating new insights on familiar research problems. Four sets of strategies, phrased as advice to researchers, are discussed as follows:

1. Researchers should play with ideas through a process of selecting and applying metaphors, representing ideas graphically, changing the scale, and attending to the process.
2. Researchers should consider contexts. They can place specific problems in a larger domain, make comparisons outside the problem domain, examine processes in the settings in which they naturally occur, consider the practical implications of research, and probe library resources.
3. It is important for researchers to probe and tinker with assumptions through such techniques as exposing hidden assumptions, making the opposite assumption, and simultaneously trusting and doubting the same assumption.
4. Finally, it is vital that researchers clarify and systematize their conceptual frameworks. They should scrutinize the meanings of key concepts, specify relationships among concepts, and write a concept paper.

The need for psychologists to attend to conceptual framing processes has been widely acknowledged (see, for example, Brinberg & McGrath, 1985; Campbell, Daft, & Hulin, 1982; Caplan & Nelson, 1973; Gergen, 1978, 1982; Jones, 1983; McGuire, 1973, in press; Tyler, 1983; Wachtel, 1980; Weick, 1979).

Several caveats are in order before we proceed:

1. Some readers may already be familiar with certain strategies and find them obvious. I have tried to include a diversity of heuristics in the hope that even seasoned investigators will find something of value.
2. Given the goal of presenting a range of strategies, only limited space is available for describing and illustrating each procedure. There is a risk that important and complex topics have been oversimplified — possibly even trivialized. I strongly rec-

ommend further reading on any strategy that seems promising; references are provided in the text.

3. These strategies are offered as heuristics. Most have not been systematically evaluated, although they have been useful to the scholars who proposed them and to others who have used them.

4. The substantial and important psychological literature on problem solving and critical and creative thinking has not been reviewed or even cited here. Much of that research addresses problems for which there are consensual solutions derived from mathematical or other logical systems. And some of that literature presumes that thinking habits developed from work on abstract puzzles or exercises are readily transferable to a wide range of other problems. The present concern is how to generate useful ideas whose "accuracy" cannot immediately be assessed. The following strategies draw upon, and in some cases expand, the researcher's existing knowledge structures (cf. Glaser, 1984). They are directly applicable to research problems in all areas of psychology.

PLAY WITH IDEAS

A playful, even whimsical, attitude toward exploring ideas is appropriate for the first set of strategies. These strategies include working with metaphors, drawing sketches, imagining extremes, and recasting entities as processes.

Select and Apply Metaphors

Playing with metaphors can evoke new perspectives on a problem. One strategy for exploiting metaphors is to identify some features from the research domain that are also discernible in another domain—perhaps another discipline or area of activity. Attention is shifted to this new area (the metaphor), which is then closely examined. From this examination, the researcher may discover some variables, relationships, or patterns that can usefully be translated back to the research problem.

A productive metaphor in social psychology is McGuire's inoculation theory of resistance to persuasion. The metaphor used was the medical procedure of stimulating bodily defenses against massive viral attacks by inoculating individuals with weakened forms of the virus. This procedure suggested the possibility of increasing resistance to persuasion by presenting weak arguments before strong arguments are encountered (McGuire, 1964). (The heuristic value of metaphors is discussed in Gowin, 1981b; Smith, 1981; and Weick, 1979. Leary, 1983, has analyzed the role of metaphor in the history of psychology. See Lakoff & Johnson, 1980, for a readable philosophical / linguistic analysis of metaphors.)

Exploring multiple, unusual metaphors may lead researchers to a greater awareness of the complexities and subtleties inherent in their domains (Weick, 1979). For example, likening interpersonal attraction to magnetic fields, a performance of Swan Lake, symbiosis, and hypnotism may reveal significant aspects of personal relationships that are not considered by such established perspectives as social exchange and equity theories.

Represent Ideas Graphically

A casual scan of such journals as *Science, American Scientist,* and *Scientific American* suggests that researchers in the physical and biological sciences make greater use of graphic presentations than do psychologists. We may be overlooking a powerful tool. In the development stages of a research problem, a pad of large drawing paper and a set of multicolored pens may be more useful than a typewriter. Visual images and sketches of problems can be liberating to researchers accustomed to representing their ideas only in linear arrangements of words, sentences, and paragraphs. Kurt Lewin, who used diagrams extensively, reportedly was ecstatic upon discovering a three-colored automatic pencil, which he carried everywhere to sketch his ideas (R. G. Barker, personal communications, April 10, 1983).

Many kinds of graphic schemes can be used to explore ideas and communicate them to others. Tabular grids, organization charts, flow diagrams, topological regions, and schematics are examples of abstract graphic languages. They have their own grammar and syntax and can be used to portray a variety of contents (McKim, 1972; Nelms, 1981). Figure 3.1 illustrates the flow diagram; it simply and clearly presents the three main approaches re-

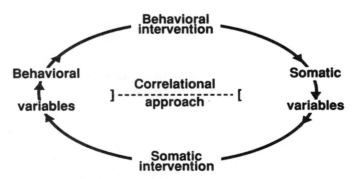

Figure 3.1. A graphic representation of three approaches to research on the relation between behavioral and somatic variables. *Note:* From "Experience, Memory, and the Brain" by M. R. Rosenzweig, 1983, *American Psychologist, 39,* p. 366. Copyright 1984 by the American Psychological Association. Reprinted with permission of the author.

searchers have taken in studying relations between behavioral and somatic variables.

In freehand idea sketching, there are no rules to be followed. With practice, researchers can fluently represent and explore their ideas and boldly experiment with relationships just as artists, composers, and urban planners have profitably done (McKim, 1972).

Change the Scale

Imagining extreme changes in proportion can stimulate our thinking. Mills (1959) gave this advice: "If something seems very minute, imagine it to be simply enormous, and ask yourself: What difference might that make? And vice versa, for gigantic phenomena" (p. 215). He then asked readers to imagine what preliterate villages might have been like with 30 million inhabitants. Or, to take another example, consider how childrearing would be different if at birth children had the motor ability and strength of adults. And if there were no memory loss, how would human information processing be different?

A variation of this procedure is to imagine what would be required for a perfect relationship to exist between two variables presumed to be linked. For example, psychologists have often assumed that a person's expressed attitudes determine how he or she will behave in daily affairs (Cohen, 1964). However, for people to act in complete accordance with their attitudes, they would have to be independently wealthy, to have unlimited time at their disposal, to have no regard for the opinions of others, to be unaffected by unforseen chance occurrences, to have a wide range of high-level skills, and even to be in several places at once (Wicker, 1969). Reflections on such factors can lead to more realistic theories and expectations.

Attend to Process

Research psychologists typically favor concepts that represent stable entities, perhaps because such concepts are easier to measure and to incorporate into theories than are processes. Yet it can be fruitful to view presumably stable concepts in dynamic terms. One systematic approach that can help us focus on process is the tagmemic method from the field of rhetoric: The same unit of experience is regarded alternatively as a "particle" (a thing in itself), a "wave" (a thing changing over time), and as part of a field (a thing in context; Young, Becker, & Pike, 1970).

A related strategy is changing nouns into verbs, or as Weick (1979) advised, "think'ing.'" Many concepts in our research vocabularies are nouns: perception, organization, social norm. Weick suggested imagining such concepts not as stable entities but as dynamic processes, constantly in flux, continually being reconstructed through accretion and erosion. Changing nouns to verbs may promote process imagery. Thus, one would speak of perceiving, organizing, and "norming."

In a recent application of this strategy, Wicker (in press) has recast the behavior setting concept from a relatively stable "given" to a more dynamic entity that develops over a series of life stages and in response to changing internal and external conditions.

CONSIDER CONTEXTS

The strategies in this section direct researchers' attention to the extended social world in which psychological events occur. These strategies are not theoretically neutral. They advance a viewpoint that has been expressed in ecological and environmental psychology (e.g., Barker, 1968; Stokols, 1982; Wicker, in press) and that has been stated more generally in terms of the implications for psychology of the new "realist" philosophy of science (e.g., Georgoudi & Rosnow, 1985; Manicas & Secord, 1983). The style of thought promoted here contrasts with much that is typical in psychology, but it can broaden our perspectives and suggest alternatives to traditional practices and ways of thinking.

Place Specific Problems in a Larger Domain

Researchers can use this strategy to decide where to begin work in a new area and to plan new research directions. The goal is to map out the broader domain of which an existing or contemplated study is only a part. Once the boundaries and features of a conceptual territory have been charted, judgments can be made about which areas are most promising for further exploration.

Such mapping of a research problem depends upon the researcher's current conceptual frame and upon a variety of information sources, such as intuition, theory, and research findings. An early step is to specify the boundaries of the broader domain at an appropriate level of abstraction. For example, in one of the several case studies cited by McGrath (1968) to illustrate this strategy, the domain was bounded by criteria for the mental health of emotionally disturbed patients.

Once the domain has been defined, the next step is to identify the major factors or influences that bear on the topic. Each of the major factors can then be analyzed into its components or attributes, and a systematic classification scheme can be developed. By examining all logical combinations of attributes, investigators can plan research to cover appropriate—perhaps neglected—aspects of the problem. In McGrath's (1968) example, three main factors were identified and analyzed into components: (a) sources of data on patients' mental health, whose components included self-reports, ratings by staff, and observations in standard and uncontrived situations; (b) modes of behavior, including motor, cognitive, emotional, and social; and (c) temporal frame of measurement, including measures of immediate treatments, overall hospital stay, and posthospital adjustment. This conceptual framework helped guide a study of how patients were affected by their move to a new hospital building.

A set of components applicable to most research domains consists of actors, behaviors, and contexts (Runkel & McGrath, 1972). Actors may be individuals, groups, organizations, or entire communities. Behaviors are actions that actors undertake toward objects. Contexts are immediate surroundings of actors and their behaviors, including time, place, and condition. Each component would be further subdivided into aspects appropriate to the research domain. Laying out the components and their subdivisions in a grid produces a domain "map" on which any particular investigation can be located. For example, the following factors could be used in a classification scheme for group problem solving: members' abilities and motives, type of tasks performed, relationships among members, group staffing levels, and type of settings in which groups perform.

Developing a comprehensive framework for a research domain contrasts with the more prevalent "up and out" strategy, in which investigators link their work on relatively narrow, focused topics with events outside their domain and then transpose their framework and findings to this new area. For example, research on students' verbal reactions to brief intervals of crowding has been extrapolated to prisons, homes, and transportation systems. An analysis of crowding using the three components metioned above would reveal many additional factors that could be considered and incorporated into subsequent research. Actors could be expanded to include prisoners and homemakers; behaviors could include social interaction and task performance; contexts could include living quarters, worksites, recreational settings, and time frames of months or years. Some research on crowding reflects these broader considerations (e.g., Cox, Paulus, & McCain, 1984).

Make Comparisons Outside the Problem Domain

We are familiar with the principle that knowledge is an awareness of differences—it is our rationale for using control groups. This principle can be invoked to generate new ideas: Comparisons can be made with actors, behaviors, or settings outside one's current problem domain. For example, Piotrkowski (1978) has provided insights into family interaction patterns by examining the nature of the work that family members perform both inside and outside the home. The emotional availability of family members to one another may depend less on their personalities than on the quality and timing of their work experiences, such as how stressful and fatiguing the work is and whether overtime and late shift work is involved.

More remote comparisons may also be fruitful. What we regard as basic social and cognitive processes are conditioned by cultural and historical factors (Gergen, 1982; Mills, 1959; Segall, Campbell, & Herskovitz, 1966). Researchers who focus on contemporary events in Western culture can profitably examine similar events in other periods and cultures. Guttentag and Secord's (1983) recent elaboration of social exchange theory to include social structural variables provides an illustration: Social exchange theorists have regarded participants in dyadic interactions as free agents capable of negotiating the most favorable outcomes for themselves. Using data from several cultures and historical periods, the investigators demonstrated that the demographic condition of disproportionate sex ratios (substantially more men than women in a particular population, or vice versa) directly affected the exchange process between man and women. For example, when men outnumbered women, men were less likely to enter or stay in a monogamous heterosexual relationship. Women might either cater to men or withdraw from them to express female independence (Guttentag & Secord, 1983; Secord, 1984). (More general treatments of theoretical and methodological issues in historical and cross-cultural research are found in Gergen & Gergen, 1984, and Malpass, 1977.)

We can also probe the structure of contemporary society for subtle influences on how we frame research topics. Sampson (1981) was concerned that psychologists interpret and present socially and historically limited events as fundamental properties of the human mind. He argued that the predominant psychological world view portrays people as independent agents whose primary functions are ruminations—cognitive activities such as planning, wishing, thinking, organizing, and problem solving—with little regard for the objective social world. Furthermore, he contended that such a view may not only be time bound, but may also serve to reaffirm present societal arrangements and values. Sampson's advocacy of a "critical study or psychology and society, a study that is self-conscious about its context, its values, and its relationship to human freedom (p. 741)" has numerous and profound implications for many specific research domains. Theories of work motivation, for example, may need to consider the worker's psychological state *and* the organizational, legal, economic, cultural, and even nutritional conditions under which work is performed (cf. Barrett & Bass, 1976).

Parenthetically, it is worth noting that academic disciplines and research specialties may also benefit from "outside" influences; for example, requirements in graduate programs for coursework outside the major field (Lawson, 1984), cross-disciplinary collaboration, and serious efforts to include perspectives of women, ethnic minorities, gays, and scholars from developing countries.

Examine Processes in the Settings in Which They Naturally Occur

Most psychological and behavioral processes unfold in behavior settings (taken-for-granted configurations of time, place, and objects where routine patterns of behavior occur) such as offices, workshops, hospital waiting rooms, parks, and worship services (Barker, 1968). These small-scale, commonsense units of social organization variously promote, afford, permit, encourage, and require behaviors that are part of or are compatible with the main activity, and they discourage or prohibit behaviors that interfere with it.

By contrast, much psychological research is conducted in contrived environments that lack the characteristics of behavior settings. Table 3.1 illustrates some differences between features of a typical laboratory study of small groups (see Miller, 1971) and a behavior setting.

In some psychological specialties, theories are formulated and may be revised on the basis of generations of studies conducted exclusively in the laboratory. Recognized experts may lack firsthand experience with the events and subjects that produce their data (cf. Jones, 1983). Yet the work of such seminal figures as Piaget and Lewin illustrates the benefits of direct observation of behaviors in context. (Observational strategies are discussed by Lofland, 1976, and Weick, 1968.)

Ideally, researchers who wish to consider contextual factors would first identify and then representatively sample settings where the behaviors of

TABLE 3.1
Contrast Between a Typical Small Group Study
and Behavior Setting Features

Typical small group study	Behavior setting features
Fixed duration, 1 hour or less	Indefinite duration, typically months or years
Group composed of college students	Staff composed of community members
No prior interaction among group members	Extensive prior interaction among staff members
Imposed task, often an intellectual problem to be solved	Endogenous tasks, typically involving behavior objects such as equipment and supplies
Casual interactions	Meaningful interactions
No enduring local culture	Established local culture
No hierarchical relationships among members	Hierarchical relationships among members
Closed system: no personnel changes, not part of a system network including suppliers, external information sources, and recipients of products	Open system: changes in personnel, part of a system network that includes suppliers, external information sources, and recipients of products.

interest regularly occur (cf. Brunswik, 1947; Petrinovich, 1979). But such an extensive effort may not be necessary to gain insights from behavioral contexts. Investigators might observe people in a few settings where the behaviors or processes of interest are a significant part of the program. For example, workers' adjustments to stress can be studied in police dispatcher worksites (Kirmeyer, 1984).

Ventures out of the laboratory can reveal neglected but significant influences on a behavior or process. For example, an environmental psychologist interested in personal space might, by observing people in medical office waiting rooms, discover that people's sense of what is a comfortable distance from others depends on how ill they feel, on whether the others may have contagious diseases, and on furniture arrangements and design, including whether chairs have armrests.

Consider Practical Implications of Research

Reflections on how research might be applied also can lead to expanded views of basic psychological processes. For example, theories and findings on human learning and memory can be used to design instructional materials. Though such efforts, previously unseen gaps in existing frameworks might become evident and could lead to broadened research procedures. Stimulus materials could be made more complex and more natural, response alternatives increased and made more meaningful, time frames expanded, and tasks and environments made more realistic (Mackie, 1974). Designed applications could be discussed with practitioners and then be implemented and evaluated.

Probe Library Resources

One of the most accessible vehicles for transcending narrow conceptual frames is the research library, whose extensive resources are scarcely considered by many researchers. As psychologists, we may limit our literature searches to work listed in the *Psychological Abstracts* or even to a few select journals. If so, we are ignoring enormous amounts of potentially useful information and sources of ideas from the larger social world.

The resources include both quantitative and qualitative data. Baseline data and other statistics relevant to most research topics can usually be found. For example, the *Statistical Abstract of the United States* (1985), published annually by the Bureau of the Census, includes national data on health, education, housing, social services, the labor force, energy, transportation, and many other topics. It also contains a guide to other statistical publications.

Statistics such as these can provide perspectives not generally available in the psychological literature. They can, for example, show trends in the frequency and distribution of events. Such data can suggest new research directions: A research might choose to give greater emphasis to cases that are more frequent, use more resources, have more beneficial or detrimental consequences, affect more people, or are on the leading edge of an important trend or development. Researchers of legal decision making might, for example, be influenced by the following facts: (a) In each of the past several years, less than 7% of civil cases before U.S. District Courts came to trial, and (b) from 1965 to 1983, the percentage of cases (civil and criminal cases combined) tried by jury in these courts declined from 51% to 40% (*Statistical Abstract of the United States*, 1985, pp. 178–179). Researchers of mock juries might profitably expand their work to include other aspects of legal decision making such as pretrial negotiations and the ways that judges consider and weigh evidence. (Bibliographies of useful statistical sources are found in Bart & Frankel, 1981; and Cottam & Pelton, 1977.)

Libraries are also a bountiful source of qualitative information on the range of human experience and behavior. These data take many forms: newspapers and magazines, popular nonfiction, oral histories, legal cases, ethnographies, diaries and letters, atlases, novels, and photographs, as well as the scholarly literature. Such materials can be sampled and analyzed much as a sociological field worker selects and studies people and events in a community. Qualitative information in libraries can be perused at the researcher's convenience, and it often covers extended time periods, allowing for analysis of trends. (The use of library data in theory building is discussed by Glaser & Strauss, 1967, chapter 7.)

The benefits of consulting a broad range of sources are evident in Heider's (1958/1983) influential book, *The Psychology of Interpersonal Relations*. In an attempt to document and systematize the layperson's knowledge of social relationships, Heider drew upon the works of philosophers, economists, novelists, humorists—and social scientists. For example, he credited the 17th century philosopher Spinoza for the insights that led to his statement of cognitive balance.

An illustration of the creative use of qualitative data in a psychological specialty where laboratory investigations predominate is Neisser's (1981) study of the memory of former presidential counsel John Dean. Neiser compared Dean's testimony before the Senate Watergate Investigating Committee with subsequently revealed manuscripts of the conversations Dean had testified about. Neisser's analysis drew upon memory theories and recent laboratory-based research to suggest a new term (*repisodic*) for memories that are accurate in the general substance but inaccurate in their detail (Neisser, 1981).

PROBE AND TINKER WITH ASSUMPTIONS

Virtually any conceptual framework, methodology, or perspective on a problem incorporates judgments that are accepted as true, even though they may not have been confirmed. Probing and tinkering with these assumptions can stimulate thinking in productive directions. Strategies considered here include making hidden assumptions explicit, making opposing assumptions, and simultaneously trusting and discrediting the same assumption.

Expose Hidden Assumptions

The task of revealing our own implicit assumptions is inherently difficult and can never be fully accomplished. Some assumptions may be imbedded in everyday or technical language, and others may be tied into our sensory and nervous systems. About all we can hope for is an increased awareness of a small portion of the assumptive network. And to probe any assumption, we must trust many others (Campbell, 1974).

The contrastive strategy—juxtaposing dissimilar elements from alternative or competing perspectives—is one way to uncover hidden assumptions. The juxtaposition can also lead to more precise statements of one or both conceptual frameworks. The conditions under which the alternative perspectives are most applicable may thus be clarified (McGuire, in press). To illustrate, two theories make contradictory predictions about how staff members respond when service settings such as child day care facilities and emergency medical services are understaffed. One theory (Barker, 1968) predicted a positive response: The staff will work harder, will assume additional responsibilities, and will have increased feelings of self-worth and competence. Another theory (Milgram, 1970) predicted such negative responses as disaffection with the work and disregard for clients' individual needs and low-priority claims for attention. Both theories are likely to be correct in certain circumstances. Positive responses may occur in settings where understaffing is infrequent and known to be temporary, whereas negative responses may characterize settings where there is a chronic shortage of staff members (Wicker, 1979/1983). In this case, the theorists apparently made different implicit assumptions about the frequency and duration of understaffing.

Allison's (1971) analysis of governmental decision making during the 1962 Cuban Missile Crisis illustrates the benefits of applying different conceptual perspectives to the same set of events. He demonstrated that certain actions were best explained by assuming that the various branches of the American and Soviet governments (such as the U.S. Navy and the Soviet KGB) followed their standard operating procedures. Other actions were better understood as "resultants" of pulling and hauling by political players within the governments. Both perspectives were contrasted with the more commonly accepted "rational actor model," which presumes that governmental actions are chosen after reviews of the costs and benefits of alternatives (Allison, 1971).

Make the Opposite Assumption

A more playful strategy is to recast an explicit assumption into its opposite and then to explore the implications of the reversal. A general procedure for recasting theoretical assumptions has been suggested by Davis (1971), who contended that theories are judged interesting when they challenge the assumption ground of an audience. He identified 12 general ways of recasting theoretical statements (see Table 3.2).

The following example illustrates the general–local contrast from Davis's list. Many research psychologists assume that if they empirically test a hypothesized relationship and the predicted result is obtained, they confirm not only that particular relationship but also the higher level conceptual hypothesis and general theory from which it was derived. An opposing assumption is that demonstrated effects are conceptually local, that is, limited to a subset of populations and/or conditions similar to those in the investigation. Researchers who seriously consider this latter assumption may become more sensitive to differences in populations and conditions and may even become interested in developing taxonomies that would be useful for specifying limits of generality.

An argument along these lines has been advanced by McKelvey (1982). He stated that management theorists and academic social scientists (notably social psychologists and sociologists) routinely advance principles that they assume are applicable to organizations in general. In a provocative challenge to this assumption, McKelvey drew upon evolutionary theory to

TABLE 3.2
Ways of Recasting Theoretical Statements

What something seems to be	What it is in reality (or vice versa)
Disorganized	Organized
Heterogeneous	Composed of a single element
A property of persons	A property of a larger social system
Local	General
Stable and unchanging	Unstable and changing
Ineffective	Effective
Bad	Good
Unrelated	Correlated
Coexisting	Incompatible
Positively correlated	Negatively correlated
Similar	Opposite
Cause	Effect

Note: Adapted from "That's Interesting: Toward a Phenomenology of Sociology and Sociology of Phenomenology" by M. S. Davis, 1971, *Philosophy of the Social Sciences, 1,* pp. 309–314. Copyright 1971 by Wilfred Laurier University Press. Adapted with permission.

propose an "organizational species" concept, "dominant competence," that he believed could be used to build a taxonomy of organizations.

Numerous recognized theoretical contributions in psychology can be viewed as articulated denials of existing assumptions. For example, Barker's (1963) classic article introducing behavior settings was essentially a rejection of the view that human environments are disordered, unstable, and without obvious boundaries. And Zajonc's (1965) analysis of social facilitation was a demonstration that seemingly incompatible research findings can coexist in a framework that distinguishes between responses that are high and low in the subject's response hierarchy.

Simultaneously Trust and Doubt the Same Assumption

Our thinking becomes more complicated when we devalue what we believe:

> Any person who has a view of the world and who also discredits part of that view winds up with two ways to examine a situation. Discrediting is a way to enhance a requisite variety and a way to register more of the variety that's present in the world. (Weick, 1979, p. 228)

Researchers can use this device to introduce flexibility and ambivalence into their conceptual framework—they can trust an assumption for some purposes and distrust it for others. The strategy has both theoretical and methodological applications. For example, when attempting to explain the behavior of people over their life span, a personality theorist might presume that actions are guided by a few enduring behavioral dispositions (traits), but when considering how people act on a specific occasion the theorist might doubt that traits are useful. Or a researcher might devise and administer a questionnaire or interview schedule on the assumption that people respond openly and freely, but interpret the responses in a way that assumes people respond primarily in guarded and self-serving ways.

CLARIFY AND SYSTEMATIZE THE CONCEPTUAL FRAMEWORK

Most of the above strategies will expand the researcher's conceptual framework. At some point the enlarged set of ideas should be reviewed to select the most provocative thoughts for further, more intensive analysis. The following procedures can be helpful in this sifting process as well as earlier in the conceptual framing process.

Scrutinize the Meanings of Key Concepts

Researchers should have and communicate a clear understanding of the concepts they use. One way to clarify meanings of key terms is to explore their roots, synonyms, and earliest known uses. Numerous sources are available, including dictionaries (etymological, unabridged, reverse, technical), technical books, handbooks, and encyclopedias. The nuances in meaning revealed by these sources can help researchers choose terms that precisely express their ideas. Consider, for example, the nuances implicit in the root meanings of these related words: *educate* (to rear or bring up), *instruct* (to construct or arrange), *teach* (to show, guide, or direct), and *train* (to pull, draw, or drag) (*Webster's Third New International Dictionary of the English Language, Unabridged*, 1969).

Theorists need to be sensitive to the different levels of generality that are implied by their concepts. Often it is advisable to examine terms at more than one level. Abstract terms can often be broken into components whose various meanings are worth exploring. For example, *health-promoting behavior* may include several types of actions, including habits like tooth brushing and infrequent voluntary activities like scheduling and taking a physical examination. More general terms may be sought for theoretical concepts currently defined in a limited domain. More abstract terms also may suggest other domains where the theory might be applied (Mills, 1959, pp. 212–213). For example, the concept "social loss of dying patients" can be expanded to "the social value of people" (Glaser & Strauss, 1967).

Concept analysis, a procedure developed by philosophers, can be used to clarify our thinking about terms we use in research. The first step is to identify cases or examples that clearly fit the intended meaning of the concept being analyzed. To illustrate, a clear example of my concept of job involvement might be working extra hours without pay when there is no external pressure to do so. Other examples—ones that are clearly outside the intended meaning and others that are borderline—are then evoked. From a careful review of such cases, the researcher can draw out the essential properties of the concept as he or she uses it. (Concept analysis is described and illustrated in Wilson, 1963, and in Gowin, 1981b, pp. 199–205.)

Specify Relationships Among Concepts

The most rigorous ways of expressing relationships among concepts, such as mathematical modeling and hypothetico-deductive systems, are well known to psychologists. Other procedures such as concept mapping can also be used to simplify and clarify a research domain. Figure 3.2 illustrates a concept map; it represents Gowin's (1981a) theory of educating. The first step in producing such a map is to list the major concepts that are part of a developing framework or theory. The concepts are then ranked in order of importance. This order is preserved in the concept map, with the most important concept at the top, and so on. Concepts are placed in boxes, and relationships among concepts are indicated by lines and brief verbal descriptions (Gowin, 1981a, pp. 93–95).

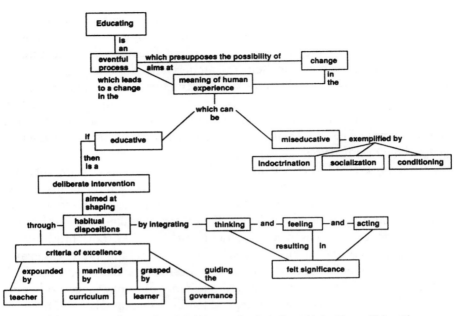

Figure 3.2. Concept map of Gowin's theory of educating. *Note:* From *Educating* (p. 94) by D. B. Gowin, 1981, Ithaca, NY: Cornell University Press. Copyright 1981 by Cornell University Press. Reprinted with permission.

In another variation of concept mapping, arrows are used to show a presumed direction of causality, and signs ($+$, $-$) are used to show whether the influence is positive or negative. From the pattern of such relationships, inferences can be drawn about the domain being considered; for example, whether a system is amenable to change, and if so, where change efforts might be directed (Maruyama, 1963; Weick, 1979, pp. 68–88).

Write a Concept Paper

Perhaps the most powerful tool for ordering and clarifying thinking is putting one's ideas into words. Writing is so familiar and often so burdensome that we often overlook or avoid it until we feel ready to communicate with an audience. Writing should be brought into play much earlier; it is an excellent medium for experimenting with conceptual meanings and relationships. Working papers can help researchers explore their thoughts and reveal gaps, inconsistencies, and faulty reasoning (Flower, 1981). In such papers researchers should address questions such as these: What is the core issue or question here? Why is it so important? What key concepts are imbedded in this topic and how are they related? What alternative methods can be used to answer the central question? What types of answers are desirable and feasible? (cf. Gowin, 1981a, pp. 86–107).

HOW TO BEGIN

Researchers who wish to explore these techniques should choose several strategies that seem appropriate to their problem and then consult the cited references for further details on each strategy. Any strategy explored should be given at least several hours of the researcher's "best time"—a period when he or she is alert, relaxed, and free from distractions and interruptions. Not every strategy attempted will prove fruitful for a given person or problem.

Devoting time to expanding and ordering one's conceptual frame can seem like a frivolous diversion from more pressing tasks. Yet the potential payoffs are substantial. A single new insight can go a long way, particularly in specialties in which theoretical and methodological traditions are strong and in which most published contributions are variations on familiar themes. Properly developed, a fresh idea can have a lasting impact.

REFERENCES

Allison, G. T. (1971). *Essence of decision*. Boston: Little, Brown.

Barker, R. G. (1963). On the nature of the environment. *Journal of Social Issues*, *19*(4), 17–38.

Barker, R. G. (1968). *Ecological psychology: Concepts and methods for studying the environment of human behavior*. Stanford, CA: Stanford University Press.

Barrett, G. V., & Bass, B. M. (1976). Cross-cultural issues in industrial and organizational psychology. In M. D. Dunnette (Ed.), *Handbook of industrial and organizational psychology* (pp. 1639–1686). Chicago: Rand McNally.

Bart, P., & Frankel, L. (1981). *The student sociologist's handbook* (3rd ed.). Glenview, IL: Scott, Foresman.

Brinberg, D., & McGrath, J. E. (1985). *Validity and the research process*. Beverly Hills, CA: Sage.

Brunswik, E. (1947). *Systematic and representative design on psychological experiments*. Berkeley: University of California Press.

Campbell, D. T. (1974, September). *Qualitative knowing in action research*. Paper presented at the 82nd Annual Convention of the American Psychological Association, New Orleans.

Campbell, J. P., Daft, R. L., & Hulin, C. L. (1982). *What to study: Generating and developing research questions*. Beverly Hills, CA: Sage.

Caplan, N., & Nelson, S. D. (1973). On being useful: The nature and consequences of psychological research on social problems. *American Psychologist*, *28*, 199–211.

Cohen, A. R. (1964). *Attitude change and social influence*. New York: Basic Books.

Cottam, K. M., & Pelton, R. W. (1977). *Writer's research handbook*. New York: Barnes & Noble.

Cox, V. C., Paulus, P. B., & McCain, G. (1984). Prison crowding research: The relevance for prison housing standards and a general approach regarding crowding phenomena. *American Psychologist, 39*, 1148–1160.

Crovitz, H. F. (1970). *Galton's walk*. New York: Harper & Row.

Davis, M. S. (1971). That's interesting: Toward a phenomenology of sociology and a sociology of phenomenology. *Philosophy of the Social Sciences, 1*, 309–314.

Flower, L. (1981). *Problem-solving strategies for writing*. New York: Harcourt Brace Jovanovich.

Galton, F. (1879). Psychometric experiments. *Brain, 2*, 148–162.

Georgoudi, M., & Rosnow, R. L. (1985). Notes toward a contextualist understanding of social psychology. *Personality and Social Psychology Bulletin, 11*, 5–22.

Gergen, K. J. (1978). Toward generative theory. *Journal of Personality and Social Psychology, 36*, 1344–1360.

Gergen, K. J. (1982). *Toward transformation in social knowledge*. New York: Springer.

Gergen, K. J., & Gergen, M. M. (Eds.). (1984). *Historical social psychology*. Hillsdale, NJ: Erlbaum.

Glaser, B. G., & Strauss, A. L. (1967). *The discovery of grounded theory*. Hawthorne, NY: Aldine.

Glaser, R. (1984). Education and thinking: The role of knowledge. *American Psychologist, 39*, 93–104.

Gowin, D. B. (1981a). *Educating*. Ithaca, NY: Cornell University Press.

Gowin, D. B. (1981b). Philosophy. In N. L. Smith (Ed.), *Metaphors for evaluation* (pp. 181–209). Beverly Hills, CA: Sage.

Guttentag, M., & Secord, P. F. (1983). *Too many women? The sex ratio question*. Beverly Hills, CA: Sage.

Heider, F. (1983). *The psychology of interpersonal relations*. Hillsdale, NJ: Erlbaum. (Original work published 1958)

Jones, R. A. (1983, December). Academic insularity and the failure to integrate social and clinical psychology. *Society for the Advancement of Social Psychology Newsletter*, pp. 10–13.

Kirmeyer, S. L. (1984). Observing the work of police dispatchers: Work overload in service organizations. In S. Oskamp (Ed.), *Applied social psychology annual* (Vol. 5, pp. 45–66). Beverly Hills, CA: Sage.

Lakoff, G., & Johnson, M. (1980). *Metaphors we live by*. Chicago: University of Chicago Press.

Lawson, R. B. (1984). The graduate curriculum. *Science, 225*, 675.

Leary, D. E. (1983, April). *Psyche's muse: The role of metaphor in psychology*. Paper presented at the meeting of the Western Psychological Association, San Francisco.

Lofland, J. (1976). *Doing social life: The qualitative study of human interaction in natural settings.* New York: Wiley.

Mackie, R. R. (1974, September). *Chuckholes in the bumpy road from research to application.* Paper presented at the 82nd Annual Convention of the American Psychological Association, New Orleans.

Malpass, R. S. (1977). Theory and method in cross-cultural psychology. *American Psychologist, 32,* 1069–1079.

Manicas, P. T., & Secord, P. F. (1983). Implications for psychology of the new philosophy of science. *American Psychologist, 38,* 399–413.

Maruyama, A. J. (1963). The second cybernetics: Deviation-amplifying mutual casual processes. *American Scientist, 51,* 164–179.

McGrath, J. E. (1968). A multifacet approach to classification of individual group, and organization concepts. in B. P. Indik & F. K. Berrien (Eds.), *People, groups, and organizations* (pp. 192–215). New York: Teachers College Press.

McGuire, W. J. (1964). Inducing resistance to persuasion. In L. Berkowitz (Ed.), *Advances in experimental social psychology* (Vol. 1, pp. 192–229). New York: Academic Press.

McGuire, W. J. (1973). The yin and yang of progress in social psychology: Seven koan. *Journal of Personality and Social Psychology, 26,* 446–456.

McGuire, W. J. (in press). Toward psychology's second century. In S. Koch & D. E. Leary (Eds.), *A century of psychology as science.* New York: McGraw-Hill.

McKelvey, B. (1982). *Organizational systematics.* Berkeley: University of California Press.

McKim, R. H. (1972). *Experiences in visual thinking.* Monterey, CA: Brooks/Cole.

Milgram, S. (1970). The experience of living in cities. *Science, 167,* 1461–1468.

Miller, J. G. (1971). Living systems: The Group. *Behavioral Science, 16,* 302–398.

Mills, C. W. (1959). *The sociological imagination.* New York: Oxford University Press.

Neisser, U. (1981). John Dean's memory: A case study. *Cognition, 9,* 1–22.

Nelms, N. (1981). *Thinking with a pencil.* Berkeley: Ten Speed Press.

Petrinovich, L. (1979). Probabilistic functionalism: A conception of research method. *American Psychologist, 34,* 373–390.

Piotrkowski, C. S. (1978). *Work and the family system.* New York: Free Press.

Rosenzweig, M. R. (1984). Experience, memory, and the brain. *American Psychologist, 39,* 365–376.

Runkel, P. J., & McGrath, J. E. (1972). *Research on human behavior: A systematic guide to method.* New York: Holt, Rinehart & Winston.

Sampson, E. E. (1981). Cognitive psychology as ideology. *American Psychologist, 36,* 730–743.

Secord, P. F. (1984). Love misogyny, and feminism in selected historical periods. In K. J. Gergen & M. M. Gergen (Eds.), *Historical social psychology* (pp. 259–280). Hillsdale, NJ: Erlbaum.

Segall, M. H., Campbell, D. T., & Herskovitz, M. J. (1966). *The influence of culture on visual perception*. Indianapolis, IN: Bobbs-Merrill.

Smith, N. L. (1981). Metaphors for evaluation. In N. L. Smith (Ed.), *Metaphors for evaluation* (pp. 51–65). Beverly Hills, CA: Sage.

Statistical abstract of the United States. (1985). Washington, DC: U.S. Government Printing Office.

Stokols, D. (1982). Environmental psychology: A coming of age. In A. Kraut (Ed.), *G. Stanley Hall lecture series* (Vol. 2, pp. 155–205). Washington, DC: American Psychological Association.

Tyler, L. E. (1983). *Thinking creatively*. San Francisco: Jossey-Bass.

Wachtel, P. L. (1980). Investigation and its discontents: Some constraints on progress in psychological research. *American Psychologist, 35*, 399–408.

Webster's third new international dictionary of the English language, unabridged. (1969). Springfield, MA: Merriam-Webster.

Weick, K. E. (1968). Systematic observational methods. In G. Lindzey & E. Aronson (Eds.), *The handbook of social psychology* (2nd ed., pp. 357–451). Reading, MA: Addison-Wesley.

Weick, K. E. (1979). *The social psychology of organizing* (2nd ed.). Reading, MA: Addison-Wesley.

Wicker, A. W. (1969). Attitudes versus actions: The relationship of verbal and overt behavioral responses to attitude objects. *Journal of Social Issues, 25*(4), 41–78.

Wicker, A. W. (1983). *An introduction to ecological psychology*. New York: Cambridge University Press. (Original work published 1979)

Wicker, A. W. (in press). Behavior settings reconsidered: Temporal stages, resources, internal dynamics, context. In D. Stokols & I. Altman (Eds.), *Handbook of environmental psychology*. New York: Wiley.

Wilson, J. B. (1963). *Thinking with concepts*. Cambridge, England: Cambridge University Press.

Young, R. E., Becker, A. L., & Pike, K. L. (1970). *Rhetoric: Discovery and change*. New York: Harcourt Brace Jovanovich.

Zajonc, R. B. (1965). Social facilitation. *Science, 149*, 269–274.

4

TOWARD TERMINOLOGICAL, CONCEPTUAL, AND STATISTICAL CLARITY IN THE STUDY OF MEDIATORS AND MODERATORS: EXAMPLES FROM THE CHILD–CLINICAL AND PEDIATRIC PSYCHOLOGY LITERATURES

GRAYSON N. HOLMBECK

Despite the appearance of several useful discussions of differences between mediated and moderated effects (e.g., Aldwin, 1994; Baron & Kenny, 1986; James & Brett, 1984), there continue to be inconsistencies in the use of these terms. More specifically, several types of problems occur with some regularity: (a) vague or interchangeable use of the terms, (b) inconsistencies

Reprinted from the *Journal of Consulting and Clinical Psychology, 65,* 599–610. Copyright 1997 by the American Psychological Association.

Completion of this article was suported in part by Social and Behavioral Sciences Research Grants 12-FY93-0621 and 12-FY95-0496 from the March of Dimes Birth Defects Foundation and by Grant R01-MH50423 from the National Institute of Mental Health.

between terminology and the underlying conceptualization of the variables used, (c) use of data-analytic procedures that fail to test for mediated and moderated effects, and (d) a mismatch between written text and diagrammatic figures.

Frequently, terminological, conceptual, and statistical inconsistencies are all present in the same study, such as when investigators conceptualize a variable as a moderator (e.g., coping strategies are hypothesized to serve a protective or buffering function), use the term *mediator* (rather than *moderator*) to describe the impact of the variable, provide a figure where the variable is presented as a mediator (rather than a moderator), and conduct statistical analyses that test neither mediation nor moderation. When such mismatches among terminology, theory, figures, and statistical analyses exist, findings become particularly difficult to interpret.

A lack of conceptual and statistical clarity in the study of mediated and moderated effects has become particularly prevalent in mental health literatures where investigators seek to examine factors that mediate or moderate associations between selected predictors and adjustment outcomes. In the child-clinical and pediatric psychology literatures, for example, models of predictor – adjustment relationships have become quite complex (e.g., Grych & Fincham, 1990; Thompson, Gil, Burbach, Keith, & Kinny, 1993). Investigators working in these areas have found it necessary to invoke conceptual models that include mediated and moderated effects.

The purpose of this discussion is threefold: (a) the terms "mediator" and "moderator" are defined and differentiated, (b) statistical strategies for testing mediated and moderated effects are reviewed, and (c) examples of troublesome and appropriate uses of these terms in the child-clinical and pediatric psychology literatures are presented. Although examples have been drawn from only two literatures, the points made apply to any research area where mediated or moderated effects are of interest.

DEFINITION OF MEDIATED AND MODERATED EFFECTS

According to Baron and Kenny, a moderator specifies the conditions under which a given effect occurs, as well as the conditions under which the direction or strength of an effect vary. They describe a moderator variable as the following:

> a qualitative (e.g., sex, race, class) or quantitative . . . variable that affects the direction and/or strength of a relation between an independent or predictor variable and a dependent or criterion variable . . . a basic moderator effect can be represented as an interaction between a focal independent variable and a factor (the moderator) that specifies the appropriate conditions for its operation . . . Moderator variables are typically introduced when there is an unexpectedly weak or inconsistent

relation between a predictor and a criterion variable. (Baron & Kenny, 1986, pp. 1174, 1178)

In other words, a moderator variable is one that affects the relationship between two variables, so that the nature of the impact of the predictor on the criterion varies according to the level or value of the moderator (also see Saunders, 1956; Zedeck, 1971). A moderator interacts with a predictor variable in such a way as to have an impact on the level of a dependent variable.

A mediator, on the other hand, specifies how (or the mechanism by which) a given effect occurs (Baron & Kenny, 1986; James & Brett, 1984). More specifically, Baron and Kenny (1986) describe a mediator variable as the following:

> the generative mechanism through which the focal independent variable is able to influence the dependent variable of interest . . . (and) Mediation . . . is best done in the case of a strong relation between the predictor and the criterion variable. (pp. 1173, 1178)

Stated more simply, "the independent variable causes the mediator which then causes the outcome" (Shadish & Sweeney, 1991, p. 883). Although one may argue that the relationships among independent variable, mediator, and outcome may not necessarily be "causal," the nature of the mediated relationship is such that the independent variable influences the mediator which, in turn, influences the outcome. Also critical is the prerequisite that there be a significant association between the independent variable and the dependent variable before testing for a mediated effect.

Mediators and moderators can also be differentiated diagrammatically (see Figure 4.1; see also Baron & Kenny, 1986; Cohen & Cohen, 1983). A

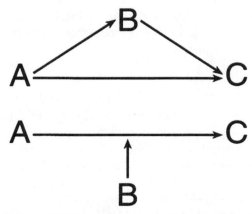

Figure 4.1. Models of mediated and moderated effects. In the top model, B mediates the relationship between A and C. In the bottom model, B moderates the relationship between A and C.

mediator (B in the top model in Figure 4.1) falls in the causal pathway between two variables (A and C in the top model in Figure 4.1; James & Brett, 1984); that is, if A is significantly associated with C, and if A influences B and B influences C, then B is a mediating variable between A and C (more detailed criteria are discussed later). On the other hand, if A is expected to be related to C, but only under certain conditions of B, then B is a moderator variable (see bottom model in Figure 4.1). The moderator (B) can be drawn to indicate that it has an impact on the relationship between A and C. Although some variables are more likely to be moderators than mediators (e.g., gender), some variables could serve either function, depending on the conceptual model under investigation (although not in the same analysis; see Lewis & Kliewer, 1996; Quittner, Glueckauf & Jackson, 1990; Sandler, Tein, & West, 1994, for examples where coping strategies or social support were tested as both mediators and moderators in competing models). Moreover, both moderators and mediators can be specified within the same model (e.g., moderated mediation; James & Brett, 1984; for examples of this strategy, see Harnish, Dodge, & Valente, 1995; Holmbeck, 1996; Simons, Lorenz, Wu, & Conger, 1993).

An example illustrates the distinction between moderated and mediated effects. This example is based on Fauber, Forehand, Thomas, and Wierson's (1990) study of marital conflict and adolescent adjustment in intact and divorced families. To examine the processes by which marital conflict has a negative influence on child adjustment, Fauber and his colleagues hypothesized that marital conflict has a negative impact on the quality of parenting to which a child is exposed which, in turn, has an impact on child adjustment. In this case, parenting quality is a potential mediator of the conflict → adjustment relationship and is predicted to account (at least partially) for this relationship. Alternatively, if one sought to test the hypothesis that the conflict → adjustment relationship would hold only for divorced families and would not hold for intact families, then one would be studying whether family structure (i.e., intact vs. divorced) moderates associations between marital conflict and child adjustment.

STATISTICAL STRATEGIES FOR TESTING MODERATED EFFECTS

For both moderated and mediated effects, two types of statistical strategies are discussed: multiple regression (as reviewed by Baron & Kenny, 1986, and as used by several investigators) and structural equation modeling (SEM; see Tabachnick & Fidell, 1996, for a relatively straightforward discussion; also see Bollen, 1989; Byrne, 1994; Hoyle, 1995; Jaccard & Wan, 1996; Mueller, 1996). Although SEM is often considered the preferred method because of the information that it provides on the degree of "fit" for the entire model after controlling for measurement error (Peyrot, 1996), proper use of regression techniques can also provide meaningful tests of hypotheses. Moreover, for investigators working in the area of pediatric psychology, where sample Ns are often relatively small, use of regression techniques (as opposed to SEM) may be necessary because of power considerations (see Tabachnick & Fidell, 1996, for a discussion of sample size and SEM). Although regression strategies may be more familiar to many readers of this journal, user-friendly versions of SEM software are now available (e.g., EQS; Bentler, 1995; although Jaccard & Wan, 1996, argue that LISREL 8, Jöreskog & Sörbom, 1993, is currently the preferred software when attempting to analyze the significance of interaction effects because EQS does not permit nonlinear constraints among parameters).

Regression Approach to Testing Moderated Effects

Although the manner in which moderators are tested statistically varies somewhat depending on whether the predictor and moderator are continuous or dichotomous (Baron & Kenny, 1986; Mason, Tu, & Cauce, 1996), the general strategy is the same regardless of the nature of the variables involved. As noted earlier, a moderator effect is an interaction effect. The preferred strategy is to use the variables in their continuous form (if they are not dichotomies) and to use multiple regression techniques (Cohen & Cohen, 1983; Cohen & Wills, 1985; Jaccard, Turrisi, & Wan, 1990; James & Brett, 1984; Mason et al., 1996).

The predictor and moderator main effects (and any covariates, if applicable) are entered into the regression equation first, followed by the interaction of the predictor and the moderator (e.g., Fuhrman & Holmbeck, 1995). Depending on the investigator's conceptual framework, the main effects can be entered in a hierarchical, stepwise, or simultaneous fashion (Cohen & Cohen, 1983). For example, in analyses involving marital conflict as a predictor and family structure as a moderator, marital conflict and family structure could be entered in any order or simultaneously. The interaction term is represented by the product of the two main effects (e.g., Marital Conflict × Family Structure) and "only becomes the interaction when its constituent elements are partialled" (Cohen & Cohen, 1983, p. 305; see also Aiken & West, 1991; Evans, 1991; Friedrich, 1982; Holmbeck, 1989). Thus, although the main effects may be entered in any order, they must be entered before the interaction term for the product of these two terms to represent the interaction when it enters the equation.

Given the manner in which the interaction is computed, the main effects (i.e., the predictor and the moderator) will be highly correlated with the interaction term, which can produce "ill-conditioning" error messages when using some statistical software packages. To eliminate problematic multicollinearity effects between first-order terms (i.e., the independent variable and the moderator) and the higher order terms (i.e., the interaction terms), Aiken and West (1991) have recommended that the independent variable and the moderator be "centered" before testing the significance of the interaction term. To center a variable, scores are put into the deviation score form by simply subtracting the sample mean from all individuals' scores on the variable, thus producing a revised sample mean of zero. Such transformations have no impact on the level of significance of the interaction terms or the simple slopes of any plotted regression lines.

Statistically significant interactions are interpreted by plotting simple regression lines for high and low values of the moderator variable (Aiken & West, 1991; Cohen & Cohen, 1983; James & Brett, 1984; for recent examples with data tables or figures, see Brody, Stoneman, & Gauger, 1996; Colder, Lochman, & Wells, in press; Fuhrman & Holmbeck, 1995; Silverberg, Marczak, & Gondoli, 1996; Wagner, Cohen, & Brook, 1996). To plot regression lines, an equation is used that includes terms for the covariates (if applicable), the two main effects (e.g., marital conflict and family structure), and the interaction term (e.g., Marital Conflict × Family Structure), along with the corresponding unstandardized regression coefficients and the y intercept (Aiken & West, 1991; Cohen & Cohen, 1983; Holmbeck, 1989). By substituting into this equation all possible combinations of high (e.g., M + 1 SD) and low (e.g., M − 1 SD) values of the predictor and the moderator (i.e., high-high, low-low, high-low, and low-high), two regression lines can be generated where predicted values of the dependent variable are plotted (e.g., Fuhrman & Holmbeck, 1995). Also, as carefully explained by Aiken and West (1991), investigators can test the significance of the slopes for these simple regression lines (e.g., Colder, Lochman, & Wells, in press; Silverberg et al., 1996; Wagner et al., 1996; although, in some cases, associations between the predictor and the dependent variable may be curvilinear; Molina & Chassin, 1996). In the case of categorical moderator variables, high and low values are represented by the two dichotomous dummy values for this variable. With respect to covariates, the means can be substituted for these terms in the equation (which are multiplied by their corresponding regression weights). This strategy for including covariates should only be used, however, if the investigator has tested for the presence of significant interaction effects between the covariates and independent variables and found them to be nonsignificant.

As a caution to the reader, it is worth noting that significant moderator effects may be difficult to detect statistically. This difficulty is most likely to occur in studies where samples are relatively homogeneous because all high and low values of the moderator and predictor may not be adequately represented (see McClelland & Judd, 1993, for a complete discussion of this issue). Also, unreliability of measurement in the main effects is compounded once a multiplicative term is computed (see Jaccard & Wan, 1995, for suggestions on how to examine and take into account such unreliability when conducting statistical analyses).

SEM Approach to Testing Moderated Effects

Because of the problem of compounding of measurement error when computing interaction terms, several authors have maintained that SEM strategies provide a less biased assessment of the significance of moderator effects (e.g., Jaccard & Wan, 1996; Peyrot, 1996; Ping, 1996). In fact, regression strategies tend to underestimate the effect size of the interaction term, particularly as measurement error in the predictor and moderator variable increases (Jaccard & Wan, 1996; Peyrot, 1996). The SEM strategy is also preferred when the investigator has more than one measured variable for each of the constructs (or latent variables) assessed.

The logic behind testing the significance of interaction effects with SEM designs is relatively straightforward, particularly when the moderator is a dichotomous variable (Jaccard & Wan, 1996; Ping, 1996). Suppose that one is interested in whether the association between a latent predictor variable (which is assessed with more than one measured variable) and a latent criterion variable (which is also assessed with more than one measured variable) vary as a function of gender. To test for the presence of moderation, one assesses the overall fit of the model under two conditions: (a) when there are no constraints on the solution (i.e., when the relationship between the predictor and criterion variables can vary as a function of gender) and (b) when the association between the predictor and criterion variables is constrained to be equal (i.e., an equality constraint) for the two genders (see Farrell, 1994; Jaccard & Wan, 1996, for more in-depth treatments of this data-analytic technique; see Simons et al., 1993, for an empirical example). The effect of this constraint is to test a model where no Predictor × Gender interaction is present. One can then calculate and test the significance of the difference between the goodness-of-fit chi-square values for the two models. Unlike other data-analytic strategies, nonsignificant (i.e., lower) chi-square values are indicative of a better fit. The magnitude of the difference between chi-square values determines the degree to which an interaction effect is present; that is, if there is a significant deterioration in model fit when evaluating the model under the constraint of the second condition (an assumption of no interaction), this would indicate that a significant interaction is present.

When the predictor, criterion, and moderator are continuous, the analyses are more complex. On initial inspection, one may assume that all possible products of the measured indicators could be computed as indicators of a latent interaction variable (e.g., there would be 25 such interaction indicators if the moderator and predictor latent variables were each assessed with 5 indicators). On the other hand, Jöreskog and Yang (1996) and Jaccard and Wan (1996) have maintained that fewer terms are needed but that several constraints must be imposed to test the significance of the interaction effect (a complete discussion of interactions involving continuous variables is beyond the scope of this article; see Jaccard and Wan, 1996, for a discussion of these issues, as well as programming examples using LISREL 8).

STATISTICAL STRATEGIES FOR TESTING MEDIATED EFFECTS

As was done for moderated effects, both regression and SEM strategies for testing mediated effects are discussed here.

Regression Approach to Testing Mediated Effects

According to Baron and Kenny (1986), four conditions must be met for a variable to be considered a mediator: (a) the predictor, A, must be significantly associated with the hypothesized mediator, B (letters refer to variables in Figure 1), (b) the predictor, A, must be significantly associated with the dependent measure, C, (c) the mediator, B, must be significantly associated with the dependent variable, C, and (d) the impact of the predictor, A, on the dependent measure, C, is less after controlling for the mediator, B.[1] A corollary of the second condition is that there first has to be a significant relationship between the predictor and the dependent variable for a mediator to serve its mediating role. In other words, if A and C are not significantly associated, there is no significant effect to mediate. Such a bivariate association between A and C is not required in the case of moderated effects (nor is it required in the case on an indirect effect, as discussed later).

The four conditions can be tested with three multiple regression analyses (see Eckenrode, Rowe, Laird, & Brathwaite, 1995, for an example that includes figures as well as a complete explanation of this data-analytic strategy). This strategy is similar to that used when conducting a path analysis (Cohen & Cohen, 1983; Nie, Hull, Jenkins, Steinbrenner, & Bent, 1975). The significance of the A → B path (in the direction predicted; Condition 1 above) is examined in the first regression, after controlling for any covariates. The significance of the A → C path (Condition 2) is examined in the second regression. Finally, A and B are used as predictors in the third equation where C is the dependent variable. Baron and Kenny (1986) have recommended using simultaneous entry (rather than hierarchical entry) in this

---

[1] Although Baron and Kenny (1986) list three conditions of mediation (rather than four), their third condition actually contains two subconditions; the predictor (A) must be significantly associated with the outcome (C), and this association must be less after controlling for the mediator (B).

third equation, so that the effect of B on C is examined after A is controlled and the effect of A on C is examined after B is controlled (borrowing from path-analytic methodology; Nie et al., 1975). The significance of the B → C path in this third equation is a test of Condition 3. The relative effect of A on C in this equation (when B is controlled), in comparison with the effect of A on C in the second equation (when B is controlled), is the test of Condition 4. Specifically, A should be less highly associated with C in the third equation than was the case in the second equation. As Baron and Kenny (1986) discussed, it would be unusual in psychology for this A → C effect to be reduced from significance to zero. Thus, the degree to which the effect is reduced (e.g., the change in regression coefficients) is an indicator of the potency of the mediator. Moveover, significance of the indirect effect can be tested (Baron & Kenny, 1986). The reader should note, however, that Baron and Kenny's (1986) discussion of Sobel's (1982) significance test only includes an equation that determines the estimated standard error of the indirect effect. A recent article by Sobel (1988, p. 56) includes a more complete explanation of how to apply the significance test and compute confidence intervals for the indirect effect (see also Colder, Chassin, Stice, & Curran, in press; Ireys, Werthamer-Larsson, Kolodner, & Gross, 1994; Lustig, Ireys, Sills, & Walsh, 1996, for empirical examples).

SEM Approach to Testing Mediated Effects

The logic for using SEM to test for mediated effects is similar to that discussed earlier for moderated effects involving a dichotomous moderator. Again, the SEM strategy is particularly useful when one has multiple indicators for the latent variables under investigation.

Assuming that there is a latent predictor variable (A), an hypothesized latent mediator variable (B), and a latent outcome variable (C), one would first assess the fit of the direct effect (A → C) model (Hoyle & Smith, 1994). Assuming an adequate fit, the investigator than tests the fit of the overall A → B → C model. Assuming that the overall model provides an adequate fit, the A → B and B → C path coefficients are examined. At this point, the A → C, A → B, and B → C paths (as well as the A → B → C model) should all be significant in the directions predicted (which is analogous to the regression strategy discussed above).

The final step in assessing whether there is a mediational effect is to assess the fit of the A → B → C model under two conditions: (a) when the A → C path is constrained to zero, and (b) when the A → C path is not constrained. One then examines whether the second model provides a significant improvement in fit over the first model. As noted earlier, improvement in fit is assessed with a significance test on the basis of the difference between the two model chi-squares. If there is a mediational effect, the addition of the

A → C path to the constrained model should not improve the fit. In other words, the previously significant A → C path is reduced to nonsignificance (i.e., it does not improve the fit of the model) when the mediator is taken into account (which is, again, analogous to the regression approach). It is also useful at this point to report and compare the A → C path coefficients for when B is, versus when B is not, included in the model.

An additional consideration of using SEM to test for mediational effects is the important distinction between indirect and mediated effects. An example is used to highlight this distinction. Capaldi, Crosby, and Clark (1996) recently conducted an EQS-based longitudinal study, where they concluded that the effect of aggression in the family of origin on aggression in young adult intimate relationships was mediated by the level of boys' antisocial behaviors during adolescence. On the other hand, Capaldi and her colleagues appear to have found that the direct path between the predictor and criterion was not significant (i.e., all eight correlations between the measured variables for the predictor and the measured variables for the criterion were nonsignificant), despite the fact that the predictor → mediator and mediator → criterion paths were significant. Although there is evidence for an indirect effect between predictor and criterion, the findings suggest that the mediator does not (and cannot) significantly "account" for the predictor → criterion relationship (because there was not a significant relationship between predictor and criterion in the first place; Hoyle & Smith, 1994). Thus, Capaldi et al.'s (1996) findings fit the criteria for an indirect effect but do not fit the criteria for a mediated effect (as defined here). In the case of such an indirect effect, one must be conservative when discussing interpretations of links between predictor and criterion because one cannot claim that the predictor and criterion are significantly associated.

It is relatively commonplace for investigators who use SEM to claim support for a mediational model, when they have only tested the significance of and found support for an indirect pathway. Statistical textbooks (e.g., Tabachnick & Fidell, 1996) also use "mediational pathway" and "indirect pathway" interchangeably. As noted earlier, it is critical to test whether the direct path between predictor and criterion is significant (Holye & Smith, 1994) and, if so, whether this previously significant direct pathway fails to improve the fit of the mediational model.

INCONSISTENCIES IN THE TESTING OF MEDIATION AND MODERATION: EXAMPLES FROM THE PEDIATRIC AND CHILD-CLINICAL PSYCHOLOGY LITERATURES

Researchers in the area of pediatric psychology have noted that most chronic illnesses and physical disabilities require ongoing medical management and place considerable physical, psychological, and social demands on the individuals and families involved (e.g., Quittner, 1992). It is also the case, however, that there is considerable variability in the degree to which children and their families exhibit higher levels of adjustment difficulties (Thompson et al., 1993). The fact that there is such variability has led several investigators to suggest mechanisms that buffer (or exacerbate) the impact of illness on adjustment outcomes (e.g., coping resources, family functioning, illness appraisal; Thompson et al., 1993; Thompson & Gustafson, 1996; Wallander & Thompson, 1995). Similarly, child-clinical psychologists have long been interested in the child adjustment outcomes of various stressors as well as factors which account for such stressor → outcome associations. One such stressor, marital conflict, has received considerable theoretical and empirical attention (e.g., Cummings, Davies, & Simpson, 1994; Grych & Fincham, 1990; O'Brien, Margolin, & John, 1995).

Although the literatures on adjustment to illness and adjustment to marital conflict during childhood have advanced to the point where model development is now possible, several recent attempts to identify factors which are associated with adjustment have not taken full advantage of the terminological, conceptual, or statistical advances that would facilitate progress in the field. Many of these conceptual and statistical issues relate to use of the terms "mediating" and moderating." This section will highlight the following types of problems that have begun to emerge in these literatures as investigators have embarked on the study of moderated and mediated effects (see Appendix): (a) terminological inconsistencies, (b) inconsistencies between terminology and conceptualization, (c) inconsistencies between terminology and statistical analyses, (d) lack of diagrammatic clarity, and (e) lack of conceptual clarity when a proposed mediator represents a "response" to a predictor.

Terminological Inconsistencies

In this section, the following types of terminological inconsistencies will be discussed: (a) idiosyncratic definitions of terms, (b) lack of clarity in the labeling of variables, and (c) interchangeable use of terms.

An example of an idiosyncratic definition of the term mediator comes from the work of Thompson and his colleagues (Thompson, Kronenberger, Johnson, & Whiting, 1989), who have recently presented a transactional stress and coping model of psychological adjustment in children with chronic illness (e.g., Thompson et al., 1993; Thompson & Gustafson, 1996). In an earlier report on the role of central nervous system functioning and family relationships in the adjustment of children with myelodysplasia, Thompson et al. (1989) hypothesized the following:

> illness factors (e.g., type, age of onset, and severity), demographic factors (e.g., socioeconomic status), cognitive processes, and social support

mediate the relationship between the stress of chronic illness and psychosocial outcome. "Mediate" means that these factors and processes contribute to the variability in psychosocial outcome. In particular, there is theoretical and empirical evidence that family functioning is one type of social support that can lower the risk of poor psychosocial outcome in the face of the stress associated with chronic illness. (p. 243)

Thompson's definition of mediation is clearly at odds with that offered by several authors (e.g., Baron & Kenny, 1986; James & Brett, 1984), as well as standard dictionary definitions (e.g., to mediate is "to serve as a vehicle for bringing about a result . . . to occupy an intermediate or middle position"; *The American Heritage Dictionary of the American Language*, 1969, p. 814). Specifically, there is no specification of an A → B → C relationship. Although it is not the case that all investigators must adhere to the same definitions of all terms, it is likely that progress in the field will be hampered if the same term is used in different ways by different scholars.

The quote from Thompson et al. (1989) also demonstrates the second form of terminological inconsistency: a lack of clarity in the labeling of variables. Some of the variables that Thompson et al. (1989) list as potential mediators in the quote (e.g., age of onset, socioeconomic status) should probably have been listed as moderators. "Moderation" (rather than "mediation") appears to be what Thompson and his colleagues had in mind, given the last sentence in the quote (which is a clear description of a moderated effect). Variables such as age of onset and socioeconomic status presumably dictate conditions under which the stress of a chronic illness is (or is not) associated with problematic outcomes (i.e., these variables are more likely to serve a moderational than a mediational role; see Hackworth & McMahon, 1991, for a similar lack of clarity in the use of the term "mediating").

Finally, some investigators have, inappropriately, used the terms "mediating" and "moderating" interchangeably. Baron and Kenny (1986) provide some examples of this problem from the social psychology literature. More recently, Davies and Cummings (1995) appear to be using the terms interchangeably when discussing Grych and Fincham's (1990) model of child adjustment to marital conflict. On the one hand, Davies and Cummings (1995) maintain that Grych and Fincham (1990) "have proposed that intraindividual factors, including cognitive processes . . . and emotional states, interact with the characteristics of marital conflict to shape its impact" (p. 677), which implies that Grych and Fincham have proposed a moderational model. Later in the same article, Davies and Cummings (1995) argued that Grych and Fincham have emphasized "the delineation of cognitive processes mediating the impact of marital conflict on children . . ." (p. 678). Thus, Davies and Cummings have identified the same process as both a moderated effect and a mediated effect (see Hanson, Henggeler, & Burghen, 1987, and Mullins et al., 1991, for similar examples).

Inconsistencies Between Terminology and Conceptualization

Two types of inconsistencies are highlighted in this section: (a) the term "mediator" is used, but the variable in question is not conceptualized as a mediator or a moderator, and (b) the term "mediator" is used, but the variable is conceptualized as a moderator.

As an example of the first type of inconsistency, Thompson and colleagues present a diagrammatic model that includes "mediational processes" (e.g., cognitive processes, methods of coping, family functioning; Thompson, Gil, Abrams, & Phillips, 1992; Thompson et al., 1993; Thompson, Gustafson, & Gil, 1995; Thompson, Gustafson, Hamlett, & Spock, 1992), but the variables contained within these components of the model are not conceptualized as mediators, at least as the authors have described them in their published work.[2] Instead, Thompson et al. (1993) argued that "child cognitive processes, child pain-coping strategies, and maternal psychological adjustment will account for independent and significant increments in the variance in child adjustment over and above that accounted for by illness and demographic parameters" (p. 469). This is a statement of neither mediation nor moderation; rather, this hypothesis is a statement of relative predictive utility. In an example from the child-clinical literature, Cummings et al. (1994) used children's appraisals of marital conflict and perceived coping efficacy as mediators between marital conflict and child adjustment. Despite the use of the term "mediation," these investigators have not made a clear case for how their variables could serve a mediational function (i.e., they do not present a model in the $A \rightarrow B \rightarrow C$ format, either in written or diagrammatic form).

As an example of the second type of inconsistency (i.e., the term "mediation" is used but the variable appears to be conceptualized as a moderator), Ireys et al. (1994) examined "perceived impact" as a variable that mediates associations between several illness parameters and psychological symptoms. Although the analyses appear to provide accurate tests of mediational effects, Ireys et al. (1994) have implied that perceived impact may serve a moderating function:

> Some young adults with a chronic health condition, for example, view their disorder as negatively affecting most aspects of their lives and may therefore report high levels of psychological symptomatology; others, with similar conditions, may view their condition in a less burdensome light . . . How a young adult perceives that a condition has influenced a

---

[2] Thompson and his colleagues have not used the phrase "mediational processes" in recent diagrammatic versions of their model (e.g., Thompson, Gil, Gustafson, et al., 1994; Thompson & Gustafson, 1996; Thompson, Gustafson, George, & Spock, 1994; Wallander & Thompson, 1995). On the other hand, the figure that they use continues to represent a mediational model, and they continue to use the term *mediate* in their writings (e.g., Thompson & Gustafson, 1996).

developmentally important task . . . appears to alter significantly some of the associations between specific condition characteristics and mental health status. (pp. 206, 219)

These statements appear to describe a moderated effect (rather than the intended mediational effect); an individual's condition is more likely to have a negative effect on outcome when the illness is perceived in a certain way (see Barakat & Linney, 1992, for a similar example).

In an example from the child-clinical literature, Grych and Fincham (1990) have provided a cognitive-contextual framework for understanding children's responses to marital conflict and emphasize "the role of cognitive factors in mediating the relationship between marital conflict and maladjustment" (p. 277). On the other hand, the examples they provide suggest that they are discussing a moderated effect. For example, in discussing causal attributions, they suggest that "a child who views him or herself as a cause of parental conflict is likely to experience more distress than a child who attributes the cause of conflict to one or both parents or to outside circumstances" (p. 282). This statement implies that the effect of marital conflict on adjustment is moderated by the child's attributions insofar as marital conflict is expected to have an impact on adjustment only under certain conditions (see O'Brien et al., 1995; Rudolph, Dennig, & Weisz, 1995, for similar examples).

Inconsistencies Between Terminology and Statistical Analyses

Three types of inconsistencies are highlighted in this section: (a) The term "mediation" is used, but the analyses test neither mediation nor moderation, (b) the term "moderation" is used, but the analyses test neither mediation nor moderation, and (c) a lack of clarity in discussing implications of statistical results.

Although Thompson and his colleagues use the term "mediator," their data analyses do not test for the presence of mediational effects (see also Varni, Wilcox, & Hanson, 1988). Consistent with the predictive utility hypothesis discussed above, Thompson et al. typically use hierarchical regression strategies to assess differential predictive utility rather than mediational effects (e.g., Thompson et al., 1993). On the other hand, Thompson et al. would probably not advance mediational hypotheses (as defined here), given their a priori expectation that disease parameters are not likely to be significantly associated with adjustment outcomes (Thompson et al., 1993). Similar inconsistencies have emerged in the child-clinical literature (Cummings et al., 1994; O'Brien et al., 1995).

A related statistical concern is that some investigators have not provided complete tests of moderated effects. To explain variability in the adjustment levels of children (and the parents of children) with chronic illnesses and handicapping conditions, Wallander proposed a disability – stress – coping model (Wallander & Varni, 1992). Risk factors are differentiated from resistance factors; the latter "are thought to influence the risk-adjustment relationship, both through a moderation process and via direct influence on adjustment" (Wallander & Varni, 1992, p. 282). Despite the clarity of this conceptualization, Wallander and Varni (1992) apparently have not examined whether their "resistance" factors serve a moderating function, even though it appears that they have the data to test this aspect of their model (although see Wallander & Bachanas, 1997, for an unpublished report). Wallander's strategy to date has been to examine direct (main) effects with hierarchical regressions (e.g., Wallander, Varni, Babani, Banis, & Wilcox, 1989; Wallander, Varni, Babani, DeHaan, et al., 1989), which is similar to Thompson's predictive utility approach (see Barakat & Linney, 1992; Hamlett, Pellegrini, & Katz, 1992; Mullins et al., 1991; for other examples of this approach).

Finally, some investigators demonstrate a lack of clarity when discussing the implications of statistical findings. In Wallander, Pitt, and Mellins's (1990) study of the relationship between child functional independence and maternal adaptation, they argue that "the lack of even a weak relationship in this study suggests there is relatively little to be *moderated* [emphasis added] in this sample" (p. 823). Contrary to this statement, the strongest moderation effects occur (in a statistical sense) when there are no main effects present (i.e., when both independent variables are not associated with the dependent measure; see Baron & Kenny, 1986, Footnote 1). When no main effects are present, a significant interaction would indicate that a pure moderated effect had emerged (i.e., a crossover interaction; Baron & Kenny, 1986).

Lack of Diagrammatic Clarity

Although moderational hypotheses are discussed in the text of Wallander's articles, it is not clear from his figures that moderated effects are proposed. Referring to the diagram of the model (which appears in several of Wallander's articles; Wallander & Varni, 1992; Wallander, Varni, Babani, Banis, & Wilcox, 1989; Wallander, Varni, Babani, DeHaan, et al., 1989), most variable clusters appear to have direct effects on other variable clusters. Moreover, some of the hypothesized moderating variable clusters (i.e., resistance factors) directly affect the predictors (e.g., psychosocial stressors) and the outcomes (e.g., adaptation). The connection between psychosocial stressors and adaptation appears to "pass through" the resistance factors, which appears to be Wallander's diagrammatic strategy for indicating a moderated effect. As it is, however, the model appears to be more mediational than moderational; the figure obscures the "moderating" aspects of the model.[3] As evidence of this lack of clarity, other investigators have had differing interpretations of this model. Lustig et al. (1996), for example, maintain that Wallander, Varni, Babani, DeHaan, et al.'s (1989) model suggests that associations between the functional severity of a child's medical condition and maternal adaptation are "mediated" by maternal appraisals and coping. Contrary to this statement, Wallander, Varni, Babani, DeHaan et al. (1989) suggest that "the impact of these risk factors on adaptation is . . . hypothesized to be moderated by social-ecological factors, intrapersonal factors, and coping" (p. 372; see Brown, Ievers, & Donegan, 1997; Mullins et al., 1991, for similar examples).

Lack of Conceptual Clarity When a Proposed Mediator (e.g., Coping) Represents a "Response" to a Predictor (e.g., Marital Conflict)

In many of the examples discussed thus far, a variable is included in a model that represents a response to another variable in the model. Variables such as coping strategies, cognitive appraisals, and causal attributions cannot exist in isolation; they only exist in relation to variables that have preceded them (e.g., marital conflict, a chronic illness). One cannot exhibit a coping strategy in response to marital conflict, for example, if there is no marital conflict in the first place. Some have also argued that such "response" variables are the mechanism through which the independent variable influences the dependent variable and are, therefore, best thought of as mediators (e.g., Folkman & Lazarus, 1991). In many investigations, such variables are included in a "box" that is placed, connected by arrows, between antecedent (e.g., stress) and outcome (e.g., adjustment) variables (e.g., Barakat & Linney, 1992; Thompson et al., 1993).

On the other hand, investigators who use variables such as coping strategies and cognitive appraisals as mediators rarely provide a complete rationale for how these variables could serve a mediational function (as defined in this article). For example, Thompson and his colleagues (e.g., Thompson & Gustafson, 1996) have not articulated how a child's illness parameters could influence the coping strategies used by the mother (the A → B portion of the model; top of Figure 1). To do so, they would need to select a specific coping strategy (e.g., denial) and propose how such a coping strategy is expected to be used with greater (or lesser) frequency when there are higher (or lower) levels of some illness parameter (e.g., severity of illness; Frese, 1986).

---

[3] To their credit, Wallander and his colleagues have recently provided a revised model that more clearly represents the hypothesized moderated effects (see Wallander & Thompson, 1995; Wallander & Varni, 1995). On the other hand, the moderational effects of the intrapersonal factors and social-ecological factors are still not clearly indicated. It appears that the moderational influence of these two factors is mediated by "stress processing," despite Wallander, Varni, Babani, DeHaan, et al.'s (1989) statements that all three of these resistance factors serve a moderational role.

They would also need to propose that higher (or lower) rates of certain maternal adjustment outcomes are expected when this particular coping strategy is used with greater (or lesser) frequency (B → C in Figure 1). Finally, they would need to propose that the illness parameters are expected to be associated with the maternal adjustment outcomes (A → C in Figure 1). Although Thompson and his colleagues do not provide this type of conceptualization (nor is such a conceptualization consistent with the types of predictions that are typically advanced by these investigators), it is possible to advance such hypotheses. One might predict, for example, that the higher the severity of childhood illness, the smaller a parent's family support network, which would, in turn, be associated with higher levels of maladjustment. Several investigators have conceptualized variables such as coping, appraisal, and social support as "mediational," although the degree to which a conceptual rationale is provided varies considerably (e.g., Blankfield & Holahan, 1996; Holahan, Valentiner, & Moos, 1995; Jose, Cafasso, & D'Anna, 1994; Lewis & Kliewer, 1996; Quittner, 1992; Quittner et al., 1990; Sandler et al., 1994).

Contrary to this "mediational" perspective, coping strategies and other "response" variables) can also be viewed as buffers or protective factors (i.e., moderators) of the stress → adjustment relationship (Aldwin, 1994; Cohen & Wills, 1985; Conrad & Hammen, 1993; Holmbeck, 1996; Jessor, Van Den Bos, Vanderryn, Costa, & Turbin, 1995; Rutter, 1990; see Frese, 1986, for a discussion of the mediational vs. moderational roles of coping strategies). From this perspective, high levels of stress are expected to produce poor outcomes only when the level of the protective factor is low. To examine such protective effects, one would test the significance of Stress × Protective Factor interactions after entering the main effects.

Why are variables such as coping and appraisal so frequently referred to as mediators and so often represented as mediators in diagrammatic versions of prediction or causal models, without the requisite rationale? Although it is probably impossible to trace the actual roots of this practice, some of the early work on coping and appraisal has been influential (see Thompson & Gustafson, 1996, for a review). Lazarus and Folkman (1984), for example, maintain the following:

> Under comparable conditions . . . one person responds with anger, another with depression, yet another with anxiety or guilt; and still others feel challenged rather than threatened . . . In order to understand variations among individuals under comparable conditions, we must take into account the cognitive processes that intervene between the encounter and the reaction, and the factors that affect the nature of this mediation. (pp. 22–23)

Although they use the term "mediation," Lazarus and Folkman (1984) appear to be describing a moderational process. In fact, they clearly endorse an individual differences perspective on coping and appraisal when they argue that there is considerable variability across individuals with respect to how they cope with and appraise stressors and that these individual differences influence the impact of the stressor on the outcome. Despite this perspective, their use of the term "mediation" and diagrams that include mediational causal pathways (e.g., Folkman & Lazarus, 1991) appear to have been more influential than the conceptualization, as is evidenced by the frequent references to Lazarus and Folkman's (1984) theory as an example of a mediational model (e.g., Thompson et al., 1993).

A key distinction in this lack of clarity seems to involve the difference between temporal antecedents and causal antecedents. From a temporal perspective, many of the diagrammatic versions of mediational models make sense. In a recent article by La Greca and her colleagues (La Greca, Vernberg, Silverman, & Prinstein, 1996), for example, a diagram of a mediational model is presented where "exposure to traumatic events" precedes "efforts to process and cope with events," which precedes "posttraumatic stress disorder symptomatology." From a temporal perspective, this figure is understandable insofar as the traumatic event precedes (temporally) the coping efforts which precede (temporally) the adjustment outcome.

On the other hand, a figure such as this lacks clarity as a causal model (also see Barakat & Linney, 1992; Folkman & Lazarus, 1991; Thompson et al., 1993; Thompson & Gustafson, 1996). Although the occurrence of a traumatic event will precede coping temporally and may (or may not) stimulate the individual to begin coping, whether the level of a stressor is high or low does not necessarily dictate what specific coping strategy will be chosen by a given individual or the degree to which this specific coping strategy will be used (i.e., coping strategies are individual differences variables; Lazarus & Folkman, 1984). As discussed above, a "response variable" model only becomes mediational when the investigator provides predictions that certain specific mediational "responses" (e.g., coping strategies) are expected to be more (or less) likely to be used when the level of a stressor is higher (or lower; see Quittner et al., 1990, for an example of such predictions where social support is used as a mediator). A corollary of this statement is that such models also require that the level of the stressor (e.g., marital conflict, severity of illness) vary across individuals in the study (i.e., one cannot assess the impact of a mediator when the predictor has no variability). Moreover, all individuals in the study should have been exposed to the stressor to some degree (otherwise coping and appraisal strategies are not necessary and become irrelevant for those individuals not exposed to the stressor; Rogers & Holmbeck, 1997).

It is my contention that many of the diagrammatic versions of these "response variable" models should probably be drawn as moderator models (see Figure 4.1) and should be analyzed as such. "Moderator" modeling and data-analytic strategies would probably be more consistent with the conceptualizations provided by most investigators (e.g., Aldwin, 1994). Moreover, those who advance predictive utility hypotheses should probably not provide figures that include mediated or moderated causal pathways. On the other hand, it is not my contention that variables such as coping, social support, and cognitive processes can never serve a mediational function (although, as discussed above, it is incumbent on the investigator to explain carefully how such mediation can occur; see Lewis & Kliewer, 1996; Quittner et al., 1990).

EXEMPLARY USES OF MEDIATION AND MODERATION

There are several instances in the pediatric and child-clinical literatures in which moderating or mediating effects have been hypothesized and tested in a manner consistent with the recommendations provided in this review.

Pediatric Psychology

Murch and Cohen (1989) were interested in buffers and exacerbators (i.e., moderators) of the relationship between life stress and psychological distress in adolescents with spina bifida. In this study, the conceptualization and statistical strategy are appropriate and clearly presented (also see Kager & Holden, 1992; Walker, Garber, & Greene, 1994; for other examples of moderator analyses with a pediatric sample). Varni and Setoguchi (1996) conducted a study of associations between perceived physical appearance and adjustment as mediated by general self-esteem in adolescents with congenital or acquired limb deficiencies. Their analyses were conducted in line with Baron and Kenny's (1986) recommendations and their mediational model was supported. Although their figure was useful, it may have been helpful for the reader if the results of the mediational analyses had been tabled (see Melnyk, 1995, for another example of mediator analyses with a pediatric example).

Finally, Quittner (1992; Quittner et al., 1990) tested for the presence of moderated and mediated effects within the same study. Mediated effects of social support in a study of families with deaf offspring, are presented diagrammatically and are fully tested. Similarly, moderated effects are discussed and tested as well. In another study that tested the significance of both mediated and moderated effects, Lewis and Kliewer (1996) examined associations between hope and adjustment as mediated or moderated by coping strategies in children with sickle cell disease. These investigators found support for the moderational model but not the mediational model. This study serves as a model for maintaining consistency between figures, written text, and tabled data. The tabled data for moderated effects (i.e., Lewis & Kliewer, 1996, Table 3) are particularly informative and well organized.

Child-Clinical Psychology

Allen, Leadbeater, and Aber (1994) examined moderators of associations between psychological factors (as well as other predictors) and problem behaviors in at-risk adolescents. In addition to testing for significance of interaction terms in their data analyses, they also tested for the significance of multiple moderated effects within a longitudinal design. By first controlling for earlier levels of the outcome when predicting later levels of the outcome, they were able to determine whether moderated effects were predictive of stability in the outcome (see Sandler et al., 1994, for another study of moderated effects within a longitudinal context; also see Colder, Lochman, & Wells, in press; Frank & Jackson, 1996; Fuhrman & Holmbeck, 1995; Jessor et al., 1995; Molina & Chassin, 1996; Rogers & Holmbeck, 1997; Silverberg et al., 1996; Wagner et al., 1996, for other examples of moderated effects within the child and adolescent adjustment literature).

Several studies of mediated effects in the literature on child adjustment have used the multiple regression strategy (e.g., Boivin, Hymel, & Bukowski, 1995; Campbell, Pierce, Moore, Marakovitz, & Newby, 1996; Eckenrode et al., 1995; Feldman & Weinberger, 1994; Felner et al., 1995; Lenhart & Rabiner, 1995; Taylor, 1996; Taylor, Casten, & Flickinger, 1993; Taylor & Roberts, 1995). Feldman and Weinberger (1994), for example, examined whether child self-restraint was a mediator of associations between parenting behaviors and child delinquent behavior. Baron and Kenny's (1986) strategy for assessing mediated effects was used. As was the case in the Allen et al. (1994) study, Feldman and Weinberger (1994) used a longitudinal design to assess associations among their variables. Although the study of mediated relationships has received relatively little attention in the child treatment literature (see Treadwell & Kendall, 1996, for an exception), some have suggested that such relationships could be incorporated into meta-analyses of treatment studies (Shadish & Sweeney, 1991).

Other mediational studies have used SEM (e.g., Blankfeld & Holahan, 1996; Colder, Chassin, et al., in press; Conger, Patterson, & Ge, 1995; Harnish et al., 1995; Holahan et al., 1995; Reynolds, Mavrogenes, Bezruczko, & Hagemann, 1996; Simons et al., 1993). Additionally, the Harnish et al. (1995) and Simons et al. (1993) studies examined both moderated and mediated effects, with Harnish et al. (1995) clearly assessing whether there was a mediational effect by examining the degree to which the direct effect between predictor and criterion was reduced after accounting for the mediator.

CONCLUSION

This discussion highlighted the need for consistency in the use of the terms "mediating" and "moderating" in the child-clinical and pediatric psychology literatures. It was recommended that care be taken in discussing these processes and that investigators be clear about what statistical approaches are appropriate for a given hypothesis. Because research in pediatric and child-clinical psychology has important treatment, prevention, and public policy implications, and given that the relationship between stress and adjustment is a complex one, appropriate modeling and statistical techniques are needed to move the field toward greater understanding.

APPENDIX 4.A.

Examples of Terminological, Conceptual, and Statistical Inconsistencies in the Research Literature

A. Terminological inconsistencies

    1. Idiosyncratic definitions of terms
    2. Lack of clarity in the labeling of variables
    3. Interchangeable use of terms

B. Inconsistencies between terminology and conceptualization

    1. The term *mediator* is used, but the variable in question is not conceptualized as a mediator or a moderator
    2. The term *mediator* is used, but the variable is conceptualized as a moderator

C. Inconsistencies between terminology and statistical analyses

    1. The term *mediation* is used, but the analyses test neither mediation nor moderation
    2. The term *moderation* is used, but the analyses test neither mediation nor moderation
    3. Lack of clarity in discussing implications of statistical results

D. Lack of diagrammatic clarity
E. Lack of conceptual clarity when a proposed mediator (e.g., coping) represents a "response" to a predictor (e.g., marital conflict)

REFERENCES

Aiken, L. S. & West, S. G. (1991), *Multiple regression: Testing and interpreting interactions*. Newbury Park, CA: Sage.

Aldwin, C. M. (1994). *Stress, coping, and development: An integrative perspective*. New York: Guilford.

Allen, J. P., Leadbeater, B. J., & Aber, J. L. (1994). The development of problem behavior syndromes in at-risk adolescents. *Development and Psychopathology, 6,* 323–342.

The American Heritage Dictionary of the English Language. (1969). New York: Houghton Mifflin.

Barakat, L. P., & Linney, J. A. (1992). Children with physical handicaps and their mothers: The interrelation of social support, maternal adjustment, and child adjustment. *Journal of Pediatric Psychology, 17,* 725–739.

Baron, R. M., & Kenny, D. A. (1986). The moderator–mediator variable distinction in social psychology research: Conceptual, strategic, and statistical considerations. *Journal of Personality and Social Psychology, 51,* 1173–1182.

Bentler, P. M. (1995). *EQS: Structural equations program manual.* Encino, CA: Multivariate Software.

Blankfeld, D. F., & Holahan, C. J. (1996). Family support, coping strategies, and depressive symptoms among mothers of children with diabetes. *Family Psychology, 10,* 174–179.

Boivin, M., Hymel, S., & Bukowski, W. M. (1995). The roles of social withdrawal, peer rejection, and victimization by peers in predicting loneliness and depressed mood in childhood. *Development and Psychopathology, 7,* 765–785.

Bollen, K. A. (1989). *Structural equations with latent variables.* New York: Wiley.

Brody, G. H., Stoneman, Z., & Gauger, K. (1996). Parent–child relationships, family problem-solving behavior, and sibling relationship quality: The moderating role of sibling temperament. *Child Development, 67,* 1289–1300.

Brown, R. T., Ievers, C. E., & Donegan, J. E. (1997, April). *Risk-resistance adaptation model for children with sickle cell syndromes.* Paper presented at the Florida Conference on Child Health Psychology, Gainesville, FL.

Byrne, B. M. (1994). *Structural equation modeling with EQS and EQS/Windows: Basic concepts, applications, and programming.* Thousand Oaks, CA: Sage.

Campbell, S. B., Pierce, E. W., Moore, G., Marakovitz, S., & Newby, K. (1996). Boys' externalizing problems at elementary school age: Pathways from early behavior problems, maternal control, and family stress. *Development and Psychopathology, 8,* 701–719.

Capaldi, D. M., Crosby, L., & Clark, S. (1996, March). *The prediction of aggression in young adult intimate relationships from aggression in the family of origin: A mediational model.* Paper presented at the sixth annual meeting of the Society for Research on Adolescence, Boston.

Cohen, J., & Cohen, P. (1983). *Applied multiple regression/correlation analysis for the behavior sciences* (2nd ed.). Hillsdale, NJ: Erlbaum.

Cohen, S., & Wills, T. A. (1985). Stress, social support, and the buffering hypothesis. *Psychological Bulletin, 98,* 310–357.

Colder, C. R., Chassin, L., Stice, E. M., & Curran, P. J. (in press). Alcohol expectancies as potential mediators of parent alcoholism effects on the development of adolescent heavy drinking. *Journal of Research on Adolescence.*

Colder, C. R., Lochman, J. E., & Wells, K. C. (in press). The moderating effects of children's fear and activity level on relations between parenting practices and childhood symptomatology. *Journal of Abnormal Child Psychology*.

Conger, R. D., Patterson, G. R., & Ge, X. (1995). It takes two to replicate: A mediational model for the impact of parents' stress on adolescent adjustment. *Child Development, 66*, 80–97.

Conrad, M., & Hammen, C. (1993). Protective and resource factors in high- and low-risk children: A comparison of children with unipolar, bipolar, medically ill, and normal mothers. *Developmental Psychopathology, 5*, 593–607.

Cummings, E. M., Davies, P. T., and Simpson, K. S. (1994). Marital conflict, gender, and children's appraisals and coping efficacy as mediators of child adjustment. *Journal of Family Psychology, 8*, 141–149.

Davies, P. T., & Cummings, E. M. (1995). Children's emotions as organizers of their reactions to interadult anger: A functionalist perspective. *Developmental Psychology, 31*, 677–684.

Eckenrode, J., Rowe, E., Laird, M., & Brathwaite, J. (1995). Mobility as a mediator of the effects of child maltreatment on academic performance. *Child Development, 66*, 1130–1142.

Evans, M. G. (1991). The problem of analyzing multiplicative composites: Interactions revisited. *American Psychologist, 46*, 6–15.

Farrell, A. D., (1994). Structural equation modeling with longitudinal data: Strategies for examining group differences and reciprocal relationships. *Journal of Consulting and Clinical Psychology, 62*, 477–487.

Fauber, R., Forehand, R., Thomas, A. M., & Wierson, M. (1990). A mediational model of the impact of marital conflict on adolescent adjustment in intact and divorced families: The role of disrupted parenting. *Child Development, 61*, 1112–1123.

Feldman, S. S., & Weinberger, D. A. (1994). Self-restraint as a mediator of family influences on boys' delinquent behavior: A longitudinal study. *Child Development, 65*, 195–211.

Felner, R. D., Brand, S., DuBois, D. L., Adan, A. M., Mulhall, P. F., & Evans, E. G. (1995). Socioeconomic disadvantage, proximal environmental experiences, and socioeconomic and academic adjustment in early adolescence: Investigation of a mediated effects model. *Child Development, 66*, 774–792.

Folkman, S., & Lazarus, R. S. (1991). Coping and emotion. In A. Monat & R. S. Lazarus (Eds.), *Stress and coping: An anthology* (3rd ed., pp. 207–227). New York: Columbia University Press.

Frank, S., & Jackson, S. (1996). Family experiences as moderators of the relationship between eating symptoms and personality disturbance. *Journal of Youth and Adolescence, 25*, 55–72.

Frese, M. (1986). Coping as a moderator and mediator between stress and work and psychosomatic complaints. In M. H. Appley & R. Trumball (Eds.), *Dynamics of stress: Physiological, psychological, and social perspectives* (pp. 183–206). New York: Plenum.

Friedrich, R. J. (1982). In defense of multiplicative terms in multiple regression equations. *American Journal of Political Science, 26,* 797–833.

Fuhrman, T., & Holmbeck, G. N. (1995). A contextual moderator analysis of emotional autonomy and adjustment in adolescence. *Child Development, 66,* 793–811.

Grych, J. H., & Finchman, F. D. (1990). Marital conflict and children's adjustment: A cognitive-contextual framework. *Psychological Bulletin, 108,* 267–290.

Hackworth, S. R., & McMahon, R. J. (1991). Factors mediating children's health care attitudes. *Journal of Pediatric Psychology, 16,* 69–85.

Hamlett, K. W., Pellegrini, D. S., & Katz, K. S. (1992). Childhood chronic illness as a family stressor. *Journal of Pediatric Psychology, 17,* 33–47.

Hanson, C. L., Henggeler, S. W., & Burghen, G. A. (1987). Social competence and parental support as mediators of the link between stress and metabolic control in adolescents with insulin-dependent diabetes mellitus. *Journal of Consulting and Clinical Psychology, 55,* 529–533.

Harnish, J. D., Dodge, K. A., & Valente, E. (1995). Mother–child interaction quality as a partial mediator of the roles of maternal depressive symptomatology and socioeconomic status in the development of child behavior problems. *Child Development, 66,* 739–753.

Holahan, C. J., Valentiner, D. P., & Moos, R. H. (1995). Parental support, coping strategies, and psychological adjustment: An integrative model with late adolescents. *Journal of Youth and Adolescence, 24,* 633–648.

Holmbeck, G. N. (1989). Masculinity, femininity, and multiple regression: Comment on Zeldow, Daugherty, and Clark's "Masculinity, femininity, and psychosocial adjustment in medical students: A 2-year follow-up." *Journal of Personality Assessment, 53,* 583–599.

Holmbeck, G. N. (1996). A model of family relational transformations during the transition to adolescence: Parent–adolescent conflict and adaptation. In J. A. Graber, J. Brooks-Gunn, & A. C. Petersen (Eds.), *Transitions through adolescence: Interpersonal domains and context* (pp. 167–199). Mahwah, NJ: Erlbaum.

Holye, R. H. (Ed.). (1995). *Structural equation modeling: Concepts, issues, and applications.* Thousand Oaks, CA: Sage.

Holye, R. H., & Smith, G. T. (1994). Formulating clinical research hypotheses as structural equation models: A conceptual overview. *Journal of Consulting and Clinical Psychology, 62,* 429–440.

Ireys, H. T., Werthamer-Larsson, Kolodner, K. B., & Gross, S. S. (1994). Mental health of young adults with chronic illness: The mediating effect of perceived impact. *Journal of Pediatric Psychology, 19,* 205–222.

Jaccard, J., Turrisi, R., & Wan, C. K. (1990). *Interaction effects in multiple regression.* Newbury Park, CA: Sage.

Jaccard, J., & Wan, C. K. (1995). Measurement error in the analysis of interaction effects between continuous predictors using multiple regression: Multiple indicator and structural equation approaches. *Psychological Bulletin, 17,* 348–357.

Jaccard, J., & Wan, C. K. (1996). *LISREL approaches to interaction effects in multiple regression*. Thousand Oaks, CA: Sage.

James, L. R., & Brett, J. M. (1984). Mediators, moderators, and tests for mediation. *Journal of Applied Psycholgy, 69*, 307–321.

Jessor, R., Van Den Bos, J., Vanderryn, J., Costa, F. M., & Turbin, M. S. (1995). Protective factors in adolescent problem behavior: Moderator effects and developmental change. *Developmental Psychology, 31*, 923–933.

Jöreskog, K., & Sörbom, D. (1993). *LISREL VIII*. Chicago: Scientific Software.

Jöreskog, K., & Yang, F. (1996). Nonlinear structural equation models: The Kenny–Judd model with interaction effects. In G. Marcoulides & R. Schumacker (Eds.), *Advanced structural equation modeling* (pp. 57–88). Hillsdale, NJ: Erlbaum.

Jose, P. E., Cafasso, L. L., & D'Anna, C. A. (1994). Ethnic group differences in children's coping strategies. *Sociological Studies of Children, 6*, 25–53.

Kager, V. A., & Holden, E. W. (1992). Preliminary investigation of the direct and moderating effects of family and individual variables on the adjustment of children and adolescents with diabetes. *Journal of Pediatric Psychology, 17*, 491–502.

La Greca, A. M., Vernberg, E. M., Silverman, W. K., & Prinstein, M. J. (1996). Symptoms of posttraumatic stress in children after Hurricane Andrew: A prospective study. *Journal of Consulting and Clinical Psychology, 64*, 712–723.

Lazarus, R. S., & Folkman, S. (1984). *Stress, appraisal, and coping*. New York: Springer.

Lenhart, L. A., & Rabiner, D. L. (1995). An integrative approach to the study of social competence in adolescence. *Development and Psychopathology, 7*, 543–561.

Lewis, H. A., & Kliewer, W. (1996). Hope, coping, and adjustment among children with sickle cell disease: Tests of mediator and moderator models. *Journal of Pediatric Psychology, 21*, 25-41.

Lustig, J. L., Ireys, H. T., Sills, E. M., & Walsh, B. B. (1996). Mental health of mothers of children with juvenile rheumatoid arthritis: Appraisal as a mediator. *Journal of Pediatric Psychology, 21*, 719–733.

Mason, C. A., Tu, S., & Cauce, A. M. (1996). Assessing moderator variables: Two computer simulation studies. *Educational and Psychological Measurement, 56*, 45–62.

McClelland, G. H., & Judd, C. M. (1993). Statistical difficulties of detecting interactions and moderator effects. *Psychological Bulletin, 114*, 376–390.

Melnyk, B. M. (1995). Coping with unplanned childhood hospitalization: The mediating functions of parental beliefs. *Journal of Pediatric Psychology, 20*, 299–312.

Molina, B. S. G., & Chassin, L. (1996). The parent–adolescent relationship at puberty: Hispanic ethnicity and parent alcoholism as moderators. *Developmental Psychology, 32*, 675–686.

Mueller, R. O. (1996). *Basic principles of structural equation modeling: An introduction to LISREL and EQS*. New York: Springer.

Mullins, L. L., Olson, R. A., Reyes, S., Bernardy, N., Huszti, H. C., & Volk, R. J. (1991). Risk and resistance factors in the adaptation of mothers of children with cystic fibrosis. *Journal of Pediatric Psychology, 16,* 701–715.

Murch, R. L., & Cohen, L. H. (1989). Relationships among life stress, perceived family environment, and the psychological distress of spina bifida adolescents. *Journal of Pediatric Psychology, 14,* 193–214.

Nie, N. M., Hull, C. H., Jenkins, J. G., Steinbrenner, K., & Bent, D. H. (1975). *SPSS: Statistical package for the social sciences* (2nd ed.). New York: McGraw-Hill.

O'Brien, M., Margolin, G., & John, R. S. (1995). Relation among marital conflict, child coping, and child adjustment. *Journal of Clinical Child Psychology, 24,* 346–361.

Peyrot, M. (1996). Causal analysis: Theory and application. *Journal of Pediatric Psychology, 21,* 3–24.

Ping, R. A. (1996). Latent variable interaction and quadratic effect estimation: A two-step technique using structural equation analysis. *Psychological Bulletin, 119,* 166–175.

Quittner, A. L. (1992). Re-examining research on stress and social support: The importance of contextual factors. In A. M. La Greca, L. J. Siegel, J. L. Wallander, & C. E. Walker (Eds.), *Stress and coping in child health* (pp. 85–115). New York: Guilford.

Quittner, A. L., Glueckauf, R. L., & Jackson, D. N. (1990). Chronic parenting stress: Moderating versus mediating effects of social support. *Journal of Personality and Social Psychology, 59,* 1266–1278.

Reynolds, A. J., Mavrogenes, N. A., Bezruczko, N., & Hagemann, M. (1996). Cognitive and family support mediators of preschool effectiveness: A confirmatory analysis. *Child Development, 67,* 1119–1140.

Rogers, M. J., & Holmbeck, G. N. (1997). Effects of interparental aggression on children's adjustment: The moderating role of cognitive appraisal and coping. *Journal of Family Psychology, 11,* 125–130.

Rudolph, K. D., Dennig, M. D., & Weisz, J. R. (1995). Determinants and consequences of children's coping in the medical setting: Conceptualization, review, and critique. *Psychological Bulletin, 118,* 328–357.

Rutter, M. (1990). Psychosocial resilience and protective mechanisms. In J. Rolf, A. S. Masten, D. Cicchetti, K. H. Nuechterlein, & S. Weintraub (Eds.), *Risk and protective factors in the development of psychopathology* (pp. 181–214). New York: Cambridge University Press.

Sandler, I. N., Tein, J. Y., & West, S. G. (1994). Coping, stress, and the psychological symptoms of children of divorce: A cross-sectional and longitudinal study. *Child Development, 65,* 1744–1763.

Saunders, D. R. (1956). Moderator variables in prediction. *Educational and Psychological Measurement, 16,* 209–222.

Shadish, W. R., & Sweeney, R. B. (1991). Mediators and moderators in meta-analysis: There's a reason we don't let dodo birds tell us which psychotherapies should have prizes. *Journal of Consulting and Clinical Psychology, 59,* 883–893.

Silverberg, S. B., Marczak, M. S., & Gondoli, D. M. (1996). Maternal depressive symptoms and achievement-related outcomes among adolescent daughters: Variations by family structure. *Journal of Early Adolescence, 16,* 90–109.

Simons, R. L., Lorenz, F. O., Wu, C. I., & Conger, R. D. (1993). Social network and marital support as mediators and moderators of the impact of stress and depression on parental behavior. *Developmental Psychology, 29,* 368–381.

Sobel, M. E. (1982). Asymptotic confidence intervals for indirect effects in structural equations models. In S. Leinhart (Ed.), *Sociological methodology 1982* (pp. 290–312). San Francisco: Jossey-Bass.

Sobel, M. E. (1988). Direct and indirect effects in linear structural equation models. In J. S. Long (Ed.), *Common problems/proper solutions: Avoiding error in quantitative research* (pp. 46–64). Beverly Hills, CA: Sage.

Tabachnick, B. G., & Fidell, L. S. (1996). *Using multivariate statistics* (3rd ed.). New York: Harper Collins.

Taylor, R. D., (1996). Adolescents' perceptions of kinship support and family management practices: Association with adolescent adjustment in African American families. *Developmental Psychology, 32,* 687–695.

Taylor, R. D., Casten R., & Flickinger, S. M. (1993). Influence of kinship support on the parenting experiences and psychosocial adjustment of African American adolescents. *Developmental Psychology, 29,* 382–388.

Taylor, R. D., & Roberts, D. (1995). Kinship support and maternal and adolescent well-being in economically disadvantaged African American families. *Child Development, 66,* 1585–1597.

Thompson, R. J., Gil, K. M., Abrams, M. R., & Phillips, G. (1992). Stress, coping, and psychosocial adjustment of adults with sickle cell disease. *Journal of Consulting and Clinical Psychology, 80,* 433–440.

Thompson, R. J., Gil, K. M., Burbach, D. J., Keith, B. R., & Kinney, T. R. (1993). Role of child and maternal processes in the psychological adjustment of children with sickle cell disease. *Journal of Consulting and Clinical Psychology, 61,* 468–474.

Thompson, R. J., Gil, K. M., Gustafson, K. E., George, L. K., Keith, B. R., Spock, A., & Kinney, T. R. (1994). Stability and change in the psychological adjustment of mothers of children and adolescents with cystic fibrosis and sickle cell disease. *Journal of Pediatric Psychology, 19,* 171–188.

Thompson, R. J., & Gustafson, K. E. (1996). *Adaptation to chronic childhood illness.* Washington, DC: American Psychological Association.

Thompson, R. J., Gustafson, K. E., George, L. K., & Spock, A. (1994). Change over a 12-month period in the psychological adjustment of children and adolescents with cystic fibrosis. *Journal of Pediatric Psychology, 19,* 189–203.

Thompson, R. J., Gustafson, K. E., & Gil, K. M. (1995). Psychological adjustment of adolescents with cystic fibrosis or sickle cell disease and their mothers. In J. L.

Wallander & L. J. Siegel (Eds.), *Adolescent health problems: Behavioral perspectives* (pp. 232–247). New York: Guilford.

Thompson, R. J., Gustafson, K. E., Hamlett, K. W., & Spock, A. (1992). Psychological adjustment of children with cystic fibrosis: The role of child cognitive processes and maternal adjustment. *Journal of Pediatric Psychology, 17,* 741–755.

Thompson, R. J., Kronenberger, W. G., Johnson, D. F., & Whiting, K. (1989). The role of central nervous system functioning and family functioning in behavioral problems of children with myelodysplasia. *Developmental and Behavioral Pediatrics, 10,* 242–248.

Treadwell, K. R. H., & Kendall, P. C. (1996). Self-talk in youth with anxiety disorders: States of mind, content specificity, and treatment outcome. *Journal of Consulting and Clinical Psychology, 64,* 941–950.

Varni, J. W., & Setogouchi, Y. (1996). Perceived physical appearance and adjustment of adolescent with congenital/acquired limb deficiencies: A path-analytic model. *Journal of Clinical Child Psychology, 25,* 201–208.

Varni, J. W., Wilcox, K. T., & Hanson, V. (1988). Mediating effects of family social support on child psychological adjustment in juvenile rheumatoid arthritis. *Health Psychology, 7,* 421–431.

Wagner, B. M., Cohen, P., & Brook, J. S. (1996). Parent/adolescent relationships: Moderators of the effects of stressful life events. *Journal of Adolescent Research, 11,* 347–374.

Walker, L. S., Garber, J., & Green, J. W. (1994). Somatic complaints in pediatric patients: A prospective study of the role of negative life events, child social and academic competence, and parental somatic symptoms. *Journal of Consulting and Clinical Psychology, 62,* 1213–1221.

Wallander, J. L., & Bachanas, P. (1997). *A longitudinal investigation of stress as a risk factor for maladjustment in children with chronic physical conditions: Moderation or mediation by family variables.* Unpublished manuscript, University of Alabama at Birmingham.

Wallandar, J. L., Pitt, L. C., & Mellins, C. A. (1990). Child functional independence and maternal psychosocial stress as risk factors threatening adaptation in mother of physically or sensorially handicapped children. *Journal of Consulting and Clinical Psychology, 58,* 818–824.

Wallander, J. L., & Thompson R. J. (1995). Psychosocial adjustment of children with chronic physical conditions. In M. C. Roberts (Ed.), *Handbook of pediatric psychology* (pp. 124–141). New York: Guilford Press.

Wallander, J. L., & Varni, J. W. (1992). Adjustment in children with chronic physical disorders: Programmatic research on a disability-stress-coping model. In A. M. La Greca, L. J. Siegel, J. L. Wallander, & C. E. Walker (Eds.), *Stress and coping in child health* (pp. 279–298). New York: Guilford Press.

Wallandar, J. L., & Varni, J. W. (1995). Appraisal, coping, and adjustment in adolescents with a physical disability. In J. L. Wallandar & L. J. Siegel (Eds.), *Adolescent health problems: Behavioral perspectives* (pp. 209–231). New York: Guilford Press.

Wallander, J. L., Varni, J. W., Babani, L., DeHann, C. B., Wilcox, K. T., & Banis, H. T. (1989). The social environment and the adaptation of mothers of physically handicapped children. *Journal of Pediatric Psychology, 14*, 371–387.

Zedeck, S. (1971). Problems with the use of "moderator" variables. *Psychological Bulletin, 76*, 295–310.

FOCI OF RESEARCH

5

IN DEFENSE OF
EXTERNAL INVALIDITY

DOUGLAS G. MOOK

The greatest weakness of laboratory experiments lies in their artificiality. Social processes observed to occur within a laboratory setting might not necessarily occur within more natural social settings.
    —Babbie, 1975, p. 254

In order to behave like scientists we must construct situations in which our subjects . . . can behave as little like human beings as possible and we do this in order to allow ourselves to make statements about the nature of their humanity.
    —Bannister, 1966, p. 24

Experimental psychologists frequently have to listen to remarks like these. And one who has taught courses in research methods and experimental psychology, as I have for the past several years, has probably had no problem in alerting students to the "artificiality" of research settings. Students, like laypersons (and not a few social scientists for that matter), come to us quite prepared to point out the remoteness of our experimental chambers, our preoccupation with rats and college sophomores, and the comic-opera "reactivity" of our shock generators, electrode paste, and judgments of lengths of line segments on white paper.

They see all this. My problem has been not to alert them to these considerations, but to break their habit of dismissing well-done, meaningful, informative research on grounds of "artificiality."

The task has become a bit harder over the last few years because a full-fledged "purr" word has gained currency: *external validity*. Articles and mono-

Reprinted from the *American Psychologist, 38,* 379–387. Copyright 1983 by the American Psychological Association.

graphs have been written about its proper nurture, and checklists of specific threats to its well-being are now appearing in textbooks. Studies unescorted by it are afflicted by—what else?—*external invalidity*. That phrase has a lovely mouth-filling resonance to it, and there is, to be sure, a certain poetic justice in our being attacked with our own jargon.

WARM FUZZIES AND COLD CREEPIES

The trouble is that, like most "purr" and "snarl" words, the phrases *external validity* and *external invalidity* can serve as serious barriers to thought. Obviously, any kind of validity is a warm, fuzzy Good Thing; and just as obviously, any kind of invalidity must be a cold, creepy Bad Thing. Who could doubt it?

It seems to me that these phrases trapped even their originators, in just that way. Campbell and Stanley (1967) introduce the concept thus: "*External validity* asks the question of *generalizability*: To what populations, settings, treatment variables, and measurement variables can this effect be generalized?" (p. 5). Fair enough. External validity is not an automatic desideratum; it *asks a question*. It invites us to think about the prior questions: To what populations, settings, and so on, do we *want* the effect to be generalized? Do we want to generalize it at all?

But their next sentence is: "Both types of criteria are obviously important . . ." And ". . . the selection of designs strong in both types of validity is obviously our ideal" (Campbell & Stanley, 1967, p. 5).

I intend to argue that this is simply wrong. If it sounds plausible, it is because the word *validity* has given it a warm coat of downy fuzz. Who wants to be invalid—internally, externally, or in any other way? One might as well ask for acne. In a way, I wish the authors had stayed with the term *generalizability*, precisely because it does not sound nearly so good. It would then be easier to remember that we are not dealing with a criterion, like clear skin, but with a question, like "How can we get this sofa down the stairs?" One asks that question if, and only if, moving the sofa is what one wants to do.

But *generalizability* is not quite right either. The question of external validity is not the same as the question of generalizability. Even an experiment that is clearly "applicable to the real world," perhaps because it was conducted there (e.g., Bickman's, 1974, studies of obedience on the street corner), will have *some* limits to its generalizability. Cultural, historical, and age-group limits will surely be present; but these are unknown and no single study can discover them all. Their determination is empirical.

The external-validity question is a special case. It comes to this: Are the sample, the setting, and the manipulation so artificial that the class of "target" real-life situations to which the results can be generalized is likely to be trivially small? If so, the experiment lacks external validity. But that argument still begs the question I wish to raise here: Is such generalization our intent? Is it what we want to do? Not always.

THE AGRICULTURAL MODEL

These baleful remarks about external validity (EV) are not quite fair to its originators. In defining the concept, they had a particular kind of research in mind, and it was the kind in which the problem of EV is meaningful and important.

These are the applied experiments. Campbell and Stanley (1967) had in mind the kind of investigation that is designed to evaluate a new teaching procedure or the effects of an "enrichment" program on the culturally deprived. For that matter, the research context in which sampling theory was developed in its modern form—agricultural research—has a similar purpose. The experimental setting resembles, or is a special case of, a real-life setting in which one wants to know what to do. Does this fertilizer (or this pedagogical device) promote growth in this kind of crop (or this kind of child)? If one finds a significant improvement in the experimental subjects as compared with the controls, one predicts that implementation of a similar manipulation, in a similar setting with similar subjects, will be of benefit on a larger scale.

That kind of argument does assume that one's experimental manipulation represents the broader-scale implementation and that one's subjects and settings represent their target populations. Indeed, part of the thrust of the EV concept is that we have been concerned only with subject representativeness and not enough with representativeness of the settings and manipulations we have sampled in doing experiments.

Deese (1972), for example, has taken us to task for this neglect:

> Some particular set of conditions in an experiment is generally taken to be representative of all possible conditions of a similar type. . . . In the investigation of altruism, situations are devised to permit people to make altruistic choices. Usually a single situation provides the setting for the experimental testing. . . . [the experimenter] will allow that one particular situation to stand for the unspecified circumstances in which an individual could be altruistic. . . . the social psychologist as experimenter is content to let a particular situation stand for an indefinite range of possible testing situations in a vague and unspecified way. (pp. 59–60)

It comes down to this: The experimenter is generalizing on the basis of a small and biased sample, not of subjects (though probably those too), but of settings and manipulations.[1]

---

[1] In fairness, Deese goes on to make a distinction much like the one I intend here. "If the theory and observations are explicitly related to one another through some rigorous logical process, then the

The entire argument rests, however, on an applied, or what I call an "agricultural," conception of the aims of research. The assumption is that the experiment is *intended* to be generalized to similar subjects, manipulations, and settings. If this is so, then the broader the generalizations one can make, the more real-world occurrences one can predict from one's findings and the more one has learned about the real world from them. However, it may not be so. There are experiments—very many of them—that do not have such generalization as their aim.

This is not to deny that we have talked nonsense on occasion. We have. Sweeping generalizations about "altruism," or "anxiety," or "honesty" have been made on evidence that does not begin to support them, and for the reasons Deese gives. But let it also be said that in many such cases, we have seemed to talk nonsense only because our critics, or we ourselves, have assumed that the "agricultural" goal of generalization is part of our intent.

But in many (perhaps most) of the experiments Deese has in mind, the logic goes in a different direction. We are not *making* generalizations, but *testing* them. To show what a difference this makes, let me turn to an example.

A CASE STUDY OF A FLAT FLUNK

Surely one of the experiments that has had permanent impact on our thinking is the study of "mother love" in rhesus monkeys, elegantly conducted by Harlow. His wire mothers and terry-cloth mothers are permanent additions to our vocabulary of classic manipulations. And his finding that contact comfort was a powerful determinant of "attachment," whereas nutrition was small potatoes, was a massive spike in the coffin of the moribund, but still wriggling, drive-reduction theories of the 1950s.

As a case study, let us see how the Harlow wire- and cloth-mother experiment stands up to the criteria of EV.

The original discussion of EV by Campbell and Stanley (1967) reveals that the experimental investigation they had in mind was a rather complex mixed design with pretests, a treatment imposed or withheld (the independent variable), and a posttest. Since Harlow's experiment does not fit this mold, the first two of their "threats to external validity" do not arise at all: pretest effects on responsiveness and multiple-treatment interference.

The other two threats on their list do arise in Harlow's case. First, "there remains the possibility that the effects . . . hold only for that unique population from which the . . . [subjects were] selected" (Campbell & Stanley, 1967, p. 19). More generally, this is the problem of sampling bias, and it raises the

sampling of conditions may become completely unnecessary" (p. 60). I agree. "But a theory having such power is almost never found in psychology" (p. 61). I disagree, not because I think our theories are all that powerful, but because I do not think all that much power is required for what we are usually trying to do.

spectre of an unrepresentative sample. Of course, as every student knows, the way to combat the problem (and never mind that nobody does it) is to select a random sample from the population of interest.

Were Harlow's baby monkeys representative of the population of monkeys in general? Obviously not; they were born in captivity and then orphaned besides. Well, were they a representative sample of the population of lab-born, orphaned monkeys? There was no attempt at all to make them so. It must be concluded that Harlow's sampling procedures fell far short of the ideal.

Second, we have the undeniable fact of the "patent artificiality of the experimental setting" (Campbell & Stanley, 1967, p. 20). Campbell and Stanley go on to discuss the problems posed by the subjects' knowledge that they are in an experiment and by what we now call "demand characteristics." But the problem can be generalized again: How do we know that what the subjects do in this artificial setting is what they would do in a more natural one? Solutions have involved hiding from the subjects the fact that they are subjects; moving from a laboratory to a field setting; and, going further, trying for a "representative sample" of the field settings themselves (e.g., Brunswik, 1955).

What then of Harlow's work? One does not know whether his subjects knew they were in an experiment; certainly there is every chance that they experienced "expectations of the unusual, with wonder and active puzzling" (Campbell & Stanley, 1967, p. 21). In short, they must have been cautious, bewildered, reactive baby monkeys indeed. And what of the representatives of the setting? Real monkeys do not live within walls. They do not encounter mother figures made of wire mesh, with rubber nipples; nor is the advent of a terry-cloth cylinder, warmed by a light bulb, a part of their natural lifestyle. What can this contrived situation possibly tell us about how monkeys with natural upbringing would behave in a natural setting?

On the face of it, the verdict must be a flat flunk. On every criterion of EV that applies at all, we find Harlow's experiment either manifestly deficient or simply unevaluable. And yet our tendency is to respond to this critique with a resounding "So what?" And I think we are quite right to so respond.

Why? Because using the lab results to make generalizations about real-world behavior was no part of Harlow's intention. It was not what he was trying to do. That being the case, the concept of EV simply does not arise—except in an indirect and remote sense to be clarified shortly.

Harlow did not conclude, "Wild monkeys in the jungle probably would choose terry-cloth over wire mothers, too, if offered the choice." First, it would be a moot conclusion, since that simply is not going to happen. Second, who cares whether they would or not? The generalization would be trivial even if true. What Harlow did conclude was that the hunger-reduction interpretation of mother love would not work. If anything about his experiment has external validity, it is this theoretical point, not the findings themselves. And to see whether the theoretical conclusion is valid, we extend the experiments or test predictions based on theory.[2] We do not dismiss the findings and go back to do the experiment "properly," in the jungle with a random sample of baby monkeys.

The distinction between generality of findings and generality of theoretical conclusions underscores what seems to me the most important source of confusion in all this, which is the assumption that the purpose of collecting data in the laboratory is to *predict real-life behavior in the real world*. Of course, there are times when that is what we are trying to do, and there are times when it is not. When it is, then the problem of EV confronts us, full force. When it is not, then the problem of EV is either meaningless or trivial, and a misplaced preoccupation with it can seriously distort our evaluation of the research.

But if we are not using our experiments to predict real-life behavior, what are we using them for? Why else do an experiment?

There are a number of other things we may be doing. First, we may be asking whether something *can* happen, rather than whether it typically *does* happen. Second, our prediction may be in the other direction; it may specify something that ought to happen *in the lab*, and so we go to the lab to see whether it does. Third, we may demonstrate the power of a phenomenon by showing what happens even under unnatural conditions that ought to preclude it. Finally, we may use the lab to produce conditions that have no counterpart in real life at all, so that the concept of "generalizing to the real world" has no meaning. But even where findings cannot possibly generalize and are not supposed to, they can contribute to an understanding of the processes going on. Once again, it is that understanding which has external validity (if it does)—not the findings themselves, much less the setting and the sample. And this implies in turn that we cannot assess that kind of validity by examining the experiment itself.

ALTERNATIVES TO GENERALIZATION

"What Can" Versus "What Does"

"Person perception studies using photographs or brief exposure of the stimulus person have commonly found that spectacles, lipstick and untidy hair have a great effect on judgments of intelligence and other traits. It is suggested . . . that these results are probably exaggerations of any effect that

---

[2] The term *theory* is used loosely to mean, not a strict deductive system, but a conclusion on which different findings converge. Harlow's demonstration draws much of its force from the context of other findings (by Ainsworth, Bowlby, Spitz, and others) with which it articulates.

might occur when more information about a person is available" (Argyle, 1969, p. 19). Later in the same text, Argyle gives a specific example: "Argyle and McHenry found that targeted persons were judged as 13 points of IQ more intelligent when wearing spectacles and when seen for 15 seconds; however, if they were seen during 5 minutes of conversation spectacles made no difference" (p. 135).

Argyle (1969) offers these data as an example of how "the results [of an independent variable studied in isolation] may be exaggerated" (p. 19). Exaggerated with respect to what? With respect to what "really" goes on in the world of affairs. It is clear that on these grounds, Argyle takes the 5-minute study, in which glasses made no difference, more seriously than the 15-second study, in which they did.

Now from an "applied" perspective, there is no question that Argyle is right. Suppose that only the 15-second results were known; and suppose that on the basis of them, employment counselors began advising their students to wear glasses or sales executives began requiring their salespeople to do so. The result would be a great deal of wasted time, and all because of an "exaggerated effect," or what I have called an "inflated variable" (Mook, 1982). Powerful in the laboratory (13 IQ points are a lot!), eyeglasses are a trivial guide to a person's intelligence and are treated as such when more information is available.

On the other hand, is it not worth knowing that such a bias *can* occur, even under restricted conditions? Does it imply an implicit "theory" or set of "heuristics" that we carry about with us? If so, where do they come from?

There are some intriguing issues here. Why should the person's wearing eyeglasses affect our judgments of his or her intelligence under any conditions whatever? As a pure guess, I would hazard the following: Maybe we believe that (a) intelligent people read more than less intelligent ones, and (b) that reading leads to visual problems, wherefore (c) the more intelligent are more likely to need glasses. If that is how the argument runs, then it is an instance of how our person perceptions are influenced by causal "schemata" (Nisbett & Ross, 1980)—even where at least one step in the theoretical sequence ([b] above) is, as far as we know, simply false.

Looked at in that way, the difference between the 15-second and the 5-minute condition is itself worth investigating further (as it would not be if the latter simply "invalidated" the former). If we are so ready to abandon a rather silly causal theory in the light of more data, why are some other causal theories, many of them even sillier, so fiercely resistant to change?

The point is that in thinking about the matter this way, we are taking the results strictly as we find them. The fact that eyeglasses *can* influence our judgments of intelligence, though it may be quite devoid of real-world application, surely says something about us as judges. If we look just at that, then the issue of external validity does not arise. We are no longer concerned with generalizing from the lab to the real world. The lab (qua lab) has led us to ask questions that might not otherwise occur to us. Surely that alone makes the research more than a sterile intellectual exercise.

Predicting From and Predicting To

The next case study has a special place in my heart. It is one of the things that led directly to this article, which I wrote fresh from a delightful roaring argument with my students about the issues at hand.

The study is a test of the tension-reduction view of alcohol consumption, conducted by Higgins and Marlatt (1973). Briefly, the subjects were made either highly anxious or not so anxious by the threat of electric shock, and were permitted access to alcohol as desired. If alcohol reduces tension and if people drink it because it does so (Cappell & Herman, 1972), then the anxious subjects should have drunk more. They did not.

Writing about this experiment, one of my better students gave it short shrift: "Surely not many alcoholics are presented with such a threat under normal conditions."

Indeed. The threat of electric shock can hardly be "representative" of the dangers faced by anyone except electricians, hi-fi builders, and Psychology 101 students. What then? It depends! It depends on what kind of conclusion one draws and what one's purpose is in doing the study.

Higgins and Marlatt could have drawn this conclusion: "Threat of shock did not cause our subjects to drink in these circumstances. Therefore, it probably would not cause similar subjects to drink in similar circumstances either." A properly cautious conclusion, and manifestly trivial.

Or they could have drawn this conclusion: "Threat of shock did not cause our subjects to drink in these circumstances. Therefore, tension or anxiety probably does not cause people to drink in normal, real-world situations." That conclusion would be manifestly risky, not to say foolish; and it is that kind of conclusion which raises the issue of EV. Such a conclusion does assume that we can generalize from the simple and protected lab setting to the complex and dangerous real-life one and that the fear of shock can represent the general case of tension and anxiety. And let me admit again that we have been guilty of just this kind of foolishness on more than one occasion.

But that is not the conclusion Higgins and Marlatt drew. Their argument had an entirely different shape, one that changes everything. Paraphrased, it went thus: "Threat of shock did not cause our subjects to drink in these circumstances. Therefore, the tension-reduction hypothesis, which predicts that it should have done so, either is false or is in need of qualification." This is our old friend, the hypothetico-deductive method, in action. The important point to see is that the generalizability of the results, from lab to real life, is not claimed. It plays no part in the argument at all.

Of course, these findings may not require *much* modification of the tension-reduction hypothesis. It is possible—indeed it is highly likely—that there are tensions and tensions; and perhaps the nagging fears and self-doubts of the everyday have a quite different status from the acute fear of electric shock. Maybe alcohol does reduce these chronic fears and is taken, sometimes abusively, because it does so.[3] If these possibilities can be shown to be true, then we could sharpen the tension-reduction hypothesis, restricting it (as it is not restricted now) to certain kinds of tension and, perhaps, to certain settings. In short, we could advance our understanding. And the "artificial" laboratory findings would have contributed to that advance. Surely we cannot reasonably ask for more.

It seems to me that this kind of argument characterizes much of our research—much more of it than our critics recognize. In very many cases, we are not using what happens in the laboratory to "predict" the real world. Prediction goes the other way: Our theory specifies what subjects should do *in the laboratory*. Then we go to the laboratory to ask, Do they do it? And we modify our theory, or hang onto it for the time being, as results dictate. Thus we improve our theories, and—to say it again—it is these that generalize to the real world if anything does.

Let me turn to an example of another kind. To this point, it is artificiality of *setting* that has been the focus. Analogous considerations can arise, however, when one thinks through the implications of artificiality of, or bias in, the *sample*. Consider a case study.

A great deal of folklore, supported by some powerful psychological theories, would have it that children acquire speech of the forms approved by their culture—that is, grammatical speech—through the impact of parents' reactions to what they say. If a child emits a properly formed sentence (so the argument goes), the parent responds with approval or attention. If the utterance is ungrammatical, the parent corrects it or, at the least, withholds approval.

Direct observation of parent–child interactions, however, reveals that this need not happen. Brown and Hanlon (1970) report that parents react to the content of a child's speech, not to its form. If the sentence emitted is factually correct, it is likely to be approved by the parent; if false, disapproved. But whether the utterance embodies correct grammatical form has surprisingly little to do with the parent's reaction to it.

What kind of sample were Brown and Hanlon dealing with here? Families that (a) lived in Boston, (b) were well educated, and (c) were willing to have squadrons of psychologists camped in their living rooms, taping their

---

[3] I should note, however, that there is considerable doubt about that as a statement of the general case. Like Harlow's experiment, the Higgins and Marlatt (1973) study articulates with a growing body of data from very different sources and settings, but all, in this case, calling the tension-reduction theory into question (cf. Mello & Mendelson, 1978).

conversations. It is virtually certain that the sample was biased even with respect to the already limited "population" of upper-class-Bostonian-parents-of-young-children.

Surely a sample like that is a poor basis from which to generalize to any interesting population. But what if we turn it around? We start with the theoretical proposition: Parents respond to the grammar of their children's utterances (as by making approval contingent or by correcting mistakes). Now we make the prediction: Therefore, the *parents we observe* ought to do that. And the prediction is disconfirmed.

Going further, if we find that the children Brown and Hanlon studied went on to acquire Bostonian-approved syntax, as seems likely, then we can draw a further prediction and see it disconfirmed. If the theory is true, and if *these* parents do not react to grammaticality or its absence, then *these* children should not pick up grammatical speech. If they do so anyway, then parental approval is not necessary for the acquisition of grammar. And that is shown not by generalizing from sample to population, but by what happened *in the sample*.

It is of course legitimate to wonder whether the same contingencies would appear in Kansas City working-class families or in slum dwellers in the Argentine. Maybe parental approval/disapproval is a much more potent influence on children's speech in some cultures or subcultures than in others. Nevertheless, the fact would remain that the parental approval theory holds only in some instances and must be qualified appropriately. Again, that would be well worth knowing, and *this* sample of families would have played a part in establishing it.

The confusion here may reflect simple historical accident. Considerations of sampling from populations were brought to our attention largely by survey researchers, for whom the procedure of "generalizing to a population" is of vital concern. If we want to estimate the proportion of the electorate intending to vote for Candidate X, and if $Y\%$ of our sample intends to do so, then we want to be able to say something like this: "We can be 95% confident that $Y\%$ of the voters, plus or minus Z, intend to vote for X." Then the issue of representativeness is squarely before us, and the horror stories of biased sampling and wildly wrong predictions, from the *Literary Digest* poll on down, have every right to keep us awake at night.

But what has to be thought through, case by case, is whether that is the kind of conclusion we intend to draw. In the Brown and Hanlon (1970) case, nothing could be more unjustified than a statement of the kind, "We can be $W\%$ certain that $X\%$ of the utterances of Boston children, plus or minus Y, are true and are approved." The biased sample rules such a conclusion out of court at the outset. But it was never intended. The intended conclusion was not about a population but about a theory. That parental approval tracks content rather than form, in *these children*, means that the parental approval theory of grammar acquisition either is simply false or interacts in unsuspected ways with some attribute(s) of the home.

In yet other cases, the subjects are of interest precisely because of their unrepresentativeness. Washoe, Sarah, and our other special students are of interest because they are not representative of a language-using species. And with all the quarrels their accomplishments have given rise to, I have not seen them challenged as "unrepresentative chimps," except by students on examinations (I am not making that up). The achievements of mnemonists (which show us what *can* happen, rather than what typically *does*) are of interest because mnemonists are not representative of the rest of us. And when one comes across a mnemonist one studies that mnemonist, without much concern for his or her representativeness even as a mnemonist.

But what do students read? "Samples should always be as representative as possible of the population under study." "[A] major concern of the behavioral scientist is to ensure that the sample itself is a good representative [sic] of the population." (The sources of these quotations do not matter; they come from an accidental sample of books on my shelf.)

The trouble with these remarks is not that they are false — sometimes they are true — but that they are unqualified. Representativeness of sample is of vital importance for certain purposes, such as survey research. For other purposes it is a trivial issue.[4] Therefore, one must evaluate the sampling procedure in light of the purpose — separately, case by case.

Taking the Package Apart

Everyone knows that we make experimental settings artificial for a reason. We do it to control for extraneous variables and to permit separation of factors that do not come separately in Nature-as-you-find-it. But that leaves us wondering how, having stepped out of Nature, we get back in again. How do our findings apply to the real-life setting in all its complexity?

I think there are times when the answer has to be, "They don't." But we then may add, "Something else does. It is called understanding."

As an example, consider dark adaptation. Psychophysical experiments,

---

[4] There is another sense in which "generalizing to a population" attends most psychological research: One usually tests the significance of one's findings, and in doing so one speaks of sample values as estimates of population parameters. In this connection, though, the students are usually reassured that they can always define the population in terms of the sample and take it from there — which effectively leaves them wondering what all the flap was about in the first place.

Perhaps this is the place to note that some of the case studies I have presented may raise questions in the reader's mind that are not dealt with here. Some raise the problem of interpreting null conclusions; adequacy of controls for confounding variables may be worrisome; and the Brown and Hanlon (1970) study faced the problem of observer effects (adequately dealt with, I think; see Mook, 1982). Except perhaps for the last one, however, these issues are separate from the problem of external validity, which is the only concern here.

conducted in restricted, simplified, ecologically invalid settings, have taught us these things among others:

1. Dark adaptation occurs in two phases. There is a rapid and rather small increase in sensitivity, followed by a delayed but greater increase.
2. The first of these phases reflects dark adaptation by the cones; the second, by the rods.

Hecht (1934) demonstrated the second of these conclusions by taking advantage of some facts about cones (themselves established in ecologically invalid photochemical and histological laboratories). Cones are densely packed near the fovea; and they are much less sensitive than the rods to the shorter visible wavelengths. Thus, Hecht was able to tease out the cone component of the dark-adaptation curve by making his stimuli small, restricting them to the center of the visual field, and turning them red.

Now let us contemplate the manifest ecological invalidity of this setting. We have a human subject in a dark room, staring at a place where a tiny red light may appear. Who on earth spends time doing that, in the world of affairs? And on each trial, the subject simply makes a "yes, I see it /no, I don't" response. Surely we have subjects who "behave as little like human beings as possible" (Bannister, 1966)—We might be calibrating a photocell for all the difference it would make.

How then do the findings apply to the real world? They do not. The task, variables, and setting have no real-world counterparts. What does apply, and in spades, is the understanding of how the visual system works that such experiments have given us. That is what we apply to the real-world setting—to flying planes at night, to the problem of reading X-ray prints on the spot, to effective treatment of night blindness produced by vitamin deficiency, and much besides.

Such experiments, I say, give us understanding of real-world phenomena. Why? Because the *processes* we dissect in the laboratory also operate in the real world. The dark-adaptation data are of interest because they show us a process that does occur in many real-world situations. Thus we could, it is true, look at the laboratory as a member of a class of "target" settings to which the results apply, but it certainly is not a "representative" member of that set. We might think of it as a limiting, or even *defining*, member of that set. To what settings do the results apply? The shortest answer is: to any setting in which it is relevant that (for instance) as the illumination dims, sensitivity to longer visible wavelengths drops out before sensitivity to short ones does. The findings do not represent a class of real-world phenomena; they define one.

Alternatively, one might use the lab not to explore a known phenomenon, but to determine whether such and such a phenomenon exists or can be made to occur. (Here again the emphasis is on what can happen, not what usually does.) Henshel (1980) has noted that some intriguing and important phenomena, such as biofeedback, could never have been discovered by sampling or mimicking natural settings. He points out, too, that if a desirable phenomenon occurs under laboratory conditions, one may seek to make natural settings mimic the laboratory rather than the other way around. Engineers are familiar with this approach. So, for instance, are many behavior therapists.

(I part company with Henshel's excellent discussion only when he writes, "The requirement of 'realism,' or a faithful mimicking of the outside world in the laboratory experiment, applies only to . . . hypothesis testing within the logico-deductive model of research" [p. 470]. For reasons given earlier, I do not think it need apply even there.)

THE DRAMA OF THE ARTIFICIAL

To this point, I have considered alternatives to the "analogue" model of research and have pointed out that we need not intend to generalize our results from sample to population, or from lab to life. There are cases in which we do want to do that, of course. Where we do, we meet another temptation: We may assume that in order to *generalize* to "real life," the laboratory setting should *resemble* the real-life one as much as possible. This assumption is the force behind the cry for "representative settings."

The assumption is false. There are cases in which the generalization from research setting to real-life settings is made all the stronger by the lack of resemblance between the two. Consider an example.

A research project that comes in for criticism along these lines is the well-known work on obedience by Milgram (1974). In his work, the difference between a laboratory and a real-life setting is brought sharply into focus. Soldiers in the jungles of Viet Nam, concentration camp guards on the fields of Eastern Europe—what resemblance do their environments bear to a sterile room with a shock generator and an intercom, presided over by a white-coated scientist? As a setting, Milgram's surely is a prototype of an "unnatural" one.

One possible reaction to that fact is to dismiss the work bag and baggage, as Argyle (1969) seems to do: "When a subject steps inside a psychological laboratory he steps out of culture, and all the normal rules and conventions are temporarily discarded and replaced by the single rule of laboratory culture—'do what the experimenter says, no matter how absurd or unethical it may be'" (p. 20). He goes on to cite Milgram's work as an example.

All of this—which is perfectly true—comes in a discussion of how "laboratory research can produce the wrong results" (Argyle, 1969, p. 19). The wrong results! But that is the whole point of the results. What Milgram has shown is how easily we can "step out of culture" in just the way Argyle describes—and how, once out of culture, we proceed to violate its "normal rules and conventions" in ways that are a revelation to us when they occur. Remember, by the way, that most of the people Milgram interviewed grossly underestimated the amount of compliance that would occur *in that laboratory setting*.

Another reaction, just as wrong but unfortunately even more tempting, is to start listing similarities and differences between the lab setting and the natural one. The temptation here is to get involved in count-'em mechanics: The more differences there are, the greater the external invalidity. Thus:

> One element lacking in Milgram's situation that typically obtains in similar naturalistic situations is that the experimenter had no real power to harm the subject if the subject failed to obey orders. The subject could always simply get up and walk out of the experiment, never to see the experimenter again. So when considering Milgram's results, it should be borne in mind that a powerful source of obedience in the real world was lacking in this situation. (Kantowitz & Roediger, 1978, pp. 387–388)

"Borne in mind" to what conclusion? Since the next sentence is "Nonetheless, Milgram's results are truly remarkable" (p. 388), we must suppose that the remarks were meant in criticism.

Now the lack of threat of punishment is, to be sure, a major difference between Milgram's lab and the jungle war or concentration camp setting. But what happened? An astonishing two thirds obeyed anyway. The force of the experimenter's authority was sufficient to induce normal decent adults to inflict pain on another human being, even though they could have refused without risk. Surely the absence of power to punish, though a distinct difference between Milgram's setting and the others, only adds to the drama of what he saw.

There are other threats to the external validity of Milgram's findings, and some of them must be taken more seriously. There is the possibility that the orders he gave were "legitimized by the laboratory setting" (Orne & Evans, 1969, p. 199). Perhaps his subjects said in effect, "This is a scientific experiment run by a responsible investigator, so maybe the whole business isn't as dangerous as it looks." This possibility (which is quite distinct from the last one, though the checklist approach often confuses the two) does leave us with nagging doubts about the generalizability of Milgram's findings. Camp guards and jungle fighters do not have this cognitive escape hatch available to them. If Milgram's subjects did say "It must not be dangerous," then his conclusion—people are surprisingly willing to inflict danger under orders—is in fact weakened.

The important thing to see is that the checklist approach will not serve us. Here we have two differences between lab and life—the absence of punishment and the possibility of discounting the danger of obedience. The latter difference weakens the impact of Milgram's findings; the former strengthens it. Obviously we must move beyond a simple count of differences and think through what the effect of each one is likely to be.

VALIDITY OF WHAT?

Ultimately, what makes research findings of interest is that they help us understand everyday life. That understanding, however, comes from theory or the analysis of mechanism; it is not a matter of "generalizing" the findings themselves. This kind of validity applies (if it does) to statements like "The hunger-reduction interpretation of infant attachment will not do," or "Theory-driven inferences may bias first impressions," or "The Purkinje shift occurs because rod vision has *these* characteristics and cone vision has *those*." The validity of these generalizations is tested by their success at prediction and has nothing to do with the naturalness, representativeness, or even non-reactivity of the investigations on which they rest.

Of course there are also those cases in which one does want to predict real-life behavior directly from research findings. Survey research, and most experiments in applied settings such as factory or classroom, have that end in view. Predicting real-life behavior is a perfectly legitimate and honorable way to use research. When we engage in it, we do confront the problem of EV, and Babbie's (1975) comment about the artificiality of experiments has force.

What I have argued here is that Babbie's comment has force *only* then. If this is so, then external validity, far from being "obviously our ideal" (Campbell & Stanley, 1967), is a concept that applies only to a rather limited subset of the research we do.

A CHECKLIST OF DECISIONS

I am afraid that there is no alternative to thinking through, case by case, (a) what conclusion we want to draw and (b) whether the specifics of our sample or setting will prevent us from drawing it. Of course there are seldom any fixed rules about how to "think through" anything interesting. But here is a sample of questions one might ask in deciding whether the usual criteria of external validity should even be considered:

As to the sample: Am I (or is he or she whose work I am evaluating) trying to estimate from sample characteristics the characteristics of some population? Or am I trying to draw conclusions not about a population, but about a theory that specifies what *these* subjects ought to do? Or (as in linguistic apes) would it be important if *any* subject does, or can be made to do, this or that?

As to the setting: Is it my intention to predict what would happen in a real-life setting or "target" class of such settings? Our "thinking through" divides depending on the answer.

The answer may be no. Once again, we may be testing a prediction rather than making one; our theory may specify what ought to happen in *this* setting. Then the question is whether the setting gives the theory a fair hearing, and the external-validity question vanishes altogether.

Or the answer may be yes. Then we must ask, Is it therefore necessary that the setting be "representative" of the class of target settings? Is it enough that it be *a* member of that class, if it captures processes that must operate in all such settings? If the latter, perhaps it should be a "limiting case" of the settings in which the processes operate — the simplest possible one, as a psychophysics lab is intended to be. In that case, the stripped-down setting may actually *define* the class of target settings to which the findings apply, as in the dark-adaptation story. The question is only whether the setting actually preserves the processes of interest,[5] and again the issue of external validity disappears.

We may push our thinking through a set further. Suppose there are distinct differences between the research setting and the real-life target ones. We should remember to ask: So what? Will they weaken or restrict our conclusions? Or might they actually strengthen and extend them (as does the absence of power to punish in Milgram's experiments)?

Thinking through is of course another warm, fuzzy phrase, I quite agree. But I mean it to contrast with the cold creepies with which my students assault research findings: knee-jerk reactions to "artificiality"; finger-jerk pointing to "biased samples" and "unnatural settings"; and now, tongue-jerk imprecations about "external invalidity." People are already far too eager to dismiss what we have learned (even that biased sample who come to college and elect our courses!). If they do so, let it be for the right reasons.

REFERENCES

Argyle, M. (1969). *Social interaction*. Chicago: Atherton Press.

Babbie, E. R. (1975). *The practice of social research*. Belmont, CA: Wadsworth.

Bannister, D. (1966). Psychology as an exercise in paradox. *Bulletin of the British Psychological Society, 19*, 21–26.

---

[5] Of course, whether an artificial setting does preserve the process can be a very real question. Much controversy centers on such questions as whether the operant-conditioning chamber really captures the processes that operate in, say, the marketplace. If resolution of that issue comes, however, it will depend on whether the one setting permits successful predictions about the other. It will not come from pointing to the "unnaturalness" of the one and the "naturalness" of the other. There is no dispute about that.

Bickman, L. (1974, July). Social roles and uniforms: Clothes make the person. *Psychology Today*, pp. 49–51.

Brown, R., & Hanlon, C. (1970). Derivational complexity and order of acquisition in child speech. In J. R. Hayes (Ed.), *Cognition and the development of language*. New York: Wiley.

Brunswik, E. (1955). Representative design and probabilistic theory in a functional psychology. *Psychological Review, 62*, 193–217.

Campbell, D. T., & Stanley, J. C. (1967). *Experimental and quasi-experimental designs for research*. Chicago: Rand McNally.

Cappell, H., & Herman, C. P. (1972). Alcohol and tension reduction: A review. *Quarterly Journal of Studies on Alcohol, 33*, 33–64.

Deese, J. (1972). *Psychology as science and art*. New York: Harcourt Brace Jovanovich.

Hecht, S. (1934). Vision II: The nature of the photoreceptor process. In C. Murchison (Ed.), *Handbook of general experimental psychology*. Worcester, MA: Clark University Press.

Henshel, R. L. (1980). The purposes of laboratory experimentation and the virtues of deliberate artificiality. *Journal of Experimental Social Psychology, 16*, 466–478.

Higgins, R. L., & Marlatt, G. A. (1973). Effects of anxiety arousal on the consumption of alcohol by alcoholics and social drinkers. *Journal of Consulting and Clinical Psychology, 41*, 426–433.

Kantowitz, B. H., & Roediger, H. L., III. (1978). *Experimental psychology*. Chicago: Rand McNally.

Mello, N. K., & Mendelson, J. H. (1978). Alcohol and human behavior. In L. L. Iverson, S. D. Iverson, & S. H. Snyder (Eds.), *Handbook of psychopharmacology: Vol. 12. Drugs of abuse*. New York: Plenum Press.

Milgram, S. (1974). *Obedience to authority*. New York: Harper & Row.

Mook, D. G. (1982). *Psychological research: Strategy and tactics*. New York: Harper & Row.

Nisbett, R. E., & Ross, L. (1980). *Human inference: Strategies and shortcomings in social judgment*. New York: Century.

Orne, M. T., & Evans, T. J. (1965). Social control in the psychological experiment: Anti-social behavior and hypnosis. *Journal of Personality and Social Psychology, 1*, 189–200.

6

WHEN SMALL EFFECTS
ARE IMPRESSIVE

DEBORAH A. PRENTICE AND DALE T. MILLER

Psychologists are increasingly interested in statistical techniques that allow them to say something about the importance of their effects. This growing interest stems in large part from the realization that conventional significance-testing procedures provide an impoverished and possibly even misleading view of how seriously to take any particular result. Current wisdom regarding the use of statistics in psychological research holds that (a) the size of an effect is at least as informative as its statistical significance, if not more informative and (b) meta-analysis provides an important tool for assessing the reliability and magnitude of an effect across multiple studies (see, e.g., Cohen, 1990; Rosnow & Rosenthal, 1989). Underlying these points is the general argument that one should pay attention to size, as well as significance level, in deciding how impressed to be with an effect.

Whereas the use of effect size and other statistical measures of strength is relatively new in psychology, the goal of demonstrating the importance of an effect is not new at all. In this article, we examine the alternative ways in

Reprinted from *Psychological Bulletin, 112*, 160–164. Copyright 1992 by the American Psychological Association.

which psychologists have approached this task and the implications of these approaches for questions of how much variance is accounted for. We argue that what makes some effects seem important is not their magnitude but rather the methodologies of the studies that produced them. The statistical size of an effect is heavily dependent on the operationalization of the independent variables and the choice of a dependent variable in a particular study. Thus, with sufficient ingenuity, a researcher can design an experiment so that even a small effect is impressive.

Our purpose here is to document these methodological strategies for demonstrating important effects. We consider effects to be important to the extent that they have had a major impact on thinking in the field (e.g., findings that are frequently cited, those that are featured in survey textbooks). Thus, our analysis is retrospective; we focus on examples of studies that have provided convincing demonstrations of the importance of certain psychological variables or processes, despite the fact that many of them have yielded small effects. Moreover, we make no assumptions about the motivations or intentions of the researchers whose work we cite but simply seek to make explicit the methodological approaches that they have used so successfully. We begin with a brief review of the rationale for using measures of effect size as an index of importance and then describe two alternative methodological strategies for demonstrating an important effect.

STATISTICAL STRENGTH OF AN EFFECT

One reasonable way to determine the importance of an effect is to compute it, using one of a family of effect-size measures (Cohen, 1977). The two most commonly used measures of effect size are the standardized mean difference (d) and the correlation coefficient (r), although there is an effect size index appropriate to any statistical test. These measures have many beneficial properties: (a) They indicate the degree to which a phenomenon is present in a population on a continuous scale, with zero always indicating that the phenomenon is absent (i.e., that the null hypothesis is true), (b) they come with conventions for what values constitute a small, medium, and large effect, (c) they provide some indication of the practical significance of an effect (which significance tests do not), (d) they can be used to compare quantitatively the results of two or more studies, and (e) they can be used in power analyses to guide decisions about how many subjects are needed in a study (see Cohen, 1977, 1990; Rosnow & Rosenthal, 1989). In short, effect size is a simple, easy-to-understand quantitative measure that provides one useful index of the importance of an effect.

An additional argument in favor of using effect size as a measure of importance is that effect sizes can be collected across studies. Most contemporary approaches to meta-analysis involve estimating effect sizes for each of a set of relevant studies or findings and then analyzing the mean and variability of these estimates (see Bangert-Drowns, 1986). Thus, effect size can serve as a measure of the importance of an effect not only in the context of a single study but also in a review of multiple studies conducted within a similar paradigm. For this reason, many researchers have suggested that effect sizes should be reported routinely for all significant and nonsignificant results (see Rosnow & Rosenthal, 1989).

ALTERNATIVE METHODS OF DEMONSTRATING THE IMPORTANCE OF AN EFFECT

Effect size and other measures of variance accounted for are unquestionably useful for assessing the magnitude of an effect and serve as an important supplement to conventional significance tests. One might question, in fact, why it has taken psychologists so long to discover these procedures (Cohen, 1990). One possible answer to this question is that in some areas of psychology, researchers have relied on alternative conceptions of what makes an effect seem important. Whether intentionally or unintentionally, these researchers have approached the problem of how to demonstrate the importance of an effect with more attention to design than to analysis: They have adopted methodological strategies that create impressive demonstrations, even though the studies often yield effects that are statistically small. We consider two of these strategies, along with their implications for statistical measures of strength.

Minimal Manipulations of the Independent Variable

One strategy for demonstrating important effects involves showing that even the most minimal manipulation of the independent variable still accounts for some variance in the dependent variable. A classic example of this approach is the so-called minimal group experiments of Tajfel and his colleagues (e.g., Billig & Tajfel, 1973; Tajfel, Billig, Bundy, & Flament, 1971). At the time these experiments were conducted, much research had already demonstrated that people favor members of their own group over members of other groups. But these investigators were interested in identifying the minimal conditions necessary to produce this ethnocentrism effect and thus conducted a series of studies using increasingly minimal manipulations of group membership. In one of the early studies in this series, boys were told that they tended either to overestimate or to underestimate the number of dots on briefly presented slides (Tajfel et al., 1971). When later given the opportunity to allocate points in a game, overestimators consistently allocated more points to other overestimators and underestimators to other underestimators. This effect was taken as strong evidence of ethnocentrism:

Even though the groups were based on a meaningless classification and members had no contact with each other, they still showed a preference for the in group.

Subsequent minimal group experiments provided still more convincing evidence of the importance of ethnocentrism without yielding effects of any greater magnitude. In the most minimal of the experiments, subjects were told that they were being assigned to groups at random and were even shown the lottery ticket that determined whether they were a member of the Phi group or the Gamma group (Locksley, Ortiz, & Hepburn, 1980). Even with explicit random assignment, subjects still showed a preference for members of their own group. The minimal group experiments, and this last study in particular, are impressive demonstrations of ethnocentrism, regardless of the size of the effects they produce. Indeed, the strength of these demonstrations derives not from the proportion of variance in allocations that group membership can account for but instead from the fact that such a slight manipulation of group membership can account for any variance in allocations at all.

Another example of this methodological tradition is provided by research on the effects of mere exposure on liking (see Harrison, 1977, for a review). Studies have demonstrated that exposure increases liking for stimuli as diverse as musical selections, Chinese-like characters, photographs of men's faces, and nonsense words, both in laboratory (Zajonc, 1968) and field (Zajonc & Rajecki, 1969) experiments. But just how mere an exposure is necessary to show increased liking? Additional investigations have focused on exploring the limits of this mere exposure effect. In one study, subjects listened to an audiotape of a prose passage in one ear while musical melodies played in their other, unattended ear. Even though they could not recognize the melodies later, subjects still liked them better than melodies to which they had not been exposed (Wilson, 1979). In another study, subjects were shown slides of geometric figures for durations too brief to permit recognition and still preferred these figures to those they had not previously seen (Kunst-Wilson & Zajonc, 1980). The minimal manipulations used in these studies did more than just provide yet another demonstration of the exposure–liking effect; they also showed how simply and subtly this effect could be produced.

The psychological literature (particularly the social psychological literature) offers many more examples of the minimalist approach to demonstrating an important effect. In these studies, the use of a minimal manipulation serves to demonstrate that even under the most inauspicious circumstances, the independent variable still has an effect. Consider, for example, a study by Isen and Levin (1972) that showed that putting people in a good mood leads them to be more helpful. They manipulated mood by giving some subjects cookies while they studied in the library (good mood) and giving other subjects nothing (control). There are clearly many stronger manipulations of mood that they might have used. They could, perhaps, have given good-mood subjects a free meal in a fancy restaurant or good grades in their courses or even a winning ticket in the lottery. These manipulations may very well have shown a stronger effect of mood on helping in terms of variance accounted for.[1] But Isen and Levin's cookie study still provides a convincing and memorable demonstration of the effect; the power of this demonstration derives in large part from the subtlety of the instigating stimulus. Indeed, this demonstration would become no less impressive if a meta-analysis on cookie studies showed that the manipulation accounted for little variance. Furthermore, although mood effects might be interesting however heavy-handed the manipulation that produced them, the cookie study was perhaps made more interesting by its reliance on the minimalist approach.

Choice of a Difficult-to-Influence Dependent Variable

A second approach to demonstrating important effects involves choosing a dependent variable that seems especially unlikely to yield to influence from the independent variable. A good example of this strategy comes from the literature on physical attractiveness. Many studies have shown that physically attractive people are seen as more intelligent, successful, sociable, kind, sensitive, and so on (see Berscheid & Walster, 1974, for a review). These findings suggest that physical attractiveness has a powerful effect on social perception. Even more convincing evidence of the importance of this effect comes from studies showing that physically attractive people receive more positive job recommendations, even when attractiveness could not possibly influence job performance (Cash, Gillen, & Burns, 1977). But could we imagine a still more impressive demonstration of the importance of physical attractiveness in social perception? Efran (1974) examined the effect of the physical attractiveness of a defendant on judgments of guilt and severity of punishment by a simulated jury. Even though legal judgments are supposed to be unaffected by such extraneous factors as attractiveness, in fact, Efran found that attractive defendants were judged less likely to be guilty and received less punishment than unattractive defendants (see also Sigall & Ostrove, 1975). This demonstration that physical attractiveness matters in the courtroom is impressive, despite the fact that it matters much less here than in other domains of interpersonal judgment. One is inclined to conclude from this study that if attractiveness can even affect legal judgments, then there is no domain of social perception that is immune to its influence.[2]

---

[1] We do not imply here that when a small manipulation produces a small effect, a large manipulation will always produce a large effect. Indeed, a linear relationship between the size of the manipulation and the size of the effect is not necessary to our claims about the importance of small effects. We argue that a result can be important regardless of its magnitude if it changes the way people think about a psychological variable or process.

[2] Sudnow (1967) has suggested that physical attractiveness may even influence the speed with which people are pronounced dead on arrival in emergency rooms. An empirical demonstration of this effect might well be the most impressive evidence for the importance of physical attractiveness yet!

Another example of achieving a convincing demonstration through selection of a resistant dependent variable is Asch's (1951) classic studies of conformity to group pressure. At the time that Asch undertook these studies, much research had already demonstrated the influence of group pressure on perceptual judgments when reality was ambiguous (e.g., Sherif, 1936). Asch believed that a truer test of the power of group pressure would require individuals to yield to a group judgment that they "perceived to be contrary to fact" (Asch, 1951, p. 177). In a prototypical study, a naive subject was asked to judge the length of a line after observing each of 8 other subjects (who were actually experimental confederates) give the same objectively incorrect answer. In this situation, one third of the judgments of naive subjects conformed with the erroneous judgment of the majority. This finding provides a striking demonstration of the importance of group pressure, regardless of whether one considers one third a large effect or a small effect. The fact that any subjects conformed to an obviously incorrect judgment is impressive.[3]

This strategy of showing that a psychological variable or process is important by demonstrating that it operates even in domains you would think were immune to its effects goes beyond the experimental tradition. For example, Durkheim's (1897/1951) finding of a relationship between social structure and suicide rates was impressive despite the fact that these macro variables surely cannot account for much of the variance. But the strength of the finding derives from the implication that if a behavior as individualistic and atomistic as suicide is correlated with social structure, we cannot assume that there is any microbehavior that is independent of it. Similarly, Freud's (1901/1971) analysis of the psychopathology of everyday life strongly suggested a pervasive influence of unconscious motives even though the incidence of slips of the tongue and lapses of memory is quite low. Again, the argument is that if the unconscious intrudes even in ordinary speech and memory, it must be quite powerful indeed.

Before leaving this section, we should note that judgments of the importance of an effect are, of course, highly subjective. Moreover, our arguments for the impressiveness of the demonstrations we have described apply primarily to researchers who focus on the independent variables or psychological processes under investigation, not to those who focus on the dependent variables. We would not, for example, expect a legal scholar to be impressed with the Efran study, nor would we necessarily expect a suicidologist to consider Durkheim's finding important. For investigators who define their research area in terms of a particular dependent variable or empirical relation-

---

[3] The Asch experiments also demonstrated how minimal a manipulation of group pressure was required to produce the effect by using an ad hoc group composed entirely of individuals unknown to the subject and by showing that even with only 3 members of the majority group (compared with 8 in the prototypical case), the effect still held.

ship (i.e., convergent researchers; see McGuire, 1983), variance accounted for may very well be the critical measure of the importance of an effect.

STATISTICAL VERSUS METHODOLOGICAL ROUTES TO AN IMPRESSIVE DEMONSTRATION

As we have suggested, statistical measures of variance accounted for are not the only tools researchers have to show that an effect is important. Despite the many virtues of these measures, in the context of particular studies, they can prove to be quite limited for conveying the importance of a finding. Declaring an effect to be important in effect-size terms is saying that a particular operationalization of the independent variable accounted for a lot of the variance in a particular dependent variable. This conception of importance makes sense if the experimenter is committed to the operations that were used to generate the data. If, however, the experimenter could easily have operationalized the independent variable differently or chosen a different dependent variable, the argument for using effect size, or more generally variance accounted for, as a measure of importance breaks down (see Mayo, 1978, for a similar argument).

In psychology, the utility of statistical versus methodological strategies for demonstrating the importance of an effect tends to divide along area lines. Statistical approaches are most useful in areas of psychology in which the operationalization of the independent variable and the choice of a dependent variable are clearly defined by the problem itself. For example, investigators interested in comparing the effectiveness of different methods of classroom teaching, the outcomes of different psychotherapeutic techniques, or the validity of different aptitude tests are typically committed to their operationalizations of these variables and to their choice of outcome measures. In these cases, effect size is a perfectly appropriate measure of importance, and indeed, meta-analyses have proven very useful for reviewing studies in these areas (see Bangert-Drowns, 1986).

By contrast, the problems addressed in other areas of psychology afford the investigator a great deal more latitude in decisions regarding experimental design. Investigators of the effects of ethnocentrism, stimulus exposure, or mood have many possible operationalizations of these variables at their disposal. Similarly, those interested in demonstrating the importance of physical attractiveness or group pressure can choose among a multitude of dependent measures. Social psychologists who study these problems often design their studies so as to explore the limits of the effects. Studies in this tradition are likely to result in some number of small effect sizes and skeptical meta-analyses. But although these effect sizes may force us to reconsider the strength of an operationalization or the choice of a dependent variable (both of which were, in fact, designed to yield small effects), they do not force us to reconsider the importance of an independent variable or a psychological process.

One difficulty raised by these methodological approaches to demonstrating an important effect is how to quantify them.[4] That is, how does one measure just how minimal a manipulation is or how unlikely a dependent variable is to yield to influence? Although we know of no simple metric on which to rely, one possible strategy is to argue, using Bayesian reasoning, that an effect is important to the extent that it increases the odds that a hypothesis is true compared with its alternatives (Abelson, 1990). For example, consider the hypothesis that a good mood increases helping. The odds that this hypothesis is true might be enhanced to a greater extent by an experiment showing that cookie recipients help more than by an experiment showing that lottery winners help more. Similarly, the hypothesis that physical attractiveness affects social perception might become relatively more likely given a demonstration that attractiveness affects judgments in the courtroom than that it affects judgments in the personnel office. This strategy works well in principle, but unfortunately, the practical difficulties of applying Bayes's theorem (e.g., estimating prior probabilities; see Abelson, 1990) limit its utility. Still, this Bayesian approach highlights the fact that the amount of variance an effect accounts for is just one of many ways to think about its importance and further suggests the possibility that alternative conceptions of importance can be quantified.

We are not the first to argue that small effects can, in fact, be important. Three major defenses of their potential importance have been offered previously: (a) Small effects may have enormous implications in a practical context, (b) small effects in ongoing processes may accumulate over time to become large effects, and (c) small effects may be quite important theoretically (see, e.g., Abelson, 1985; Mook, 1983; Rosenthal & Rubin, 1983; Yeaton & Sechrest, 1981). These arguments are well-taken, but they differ in both spirit and substance from what we are asserting here. In the types of studies we have described, small effects are important not because they have practical consequences nor because they accrue into large effects, nor because they lead to theory revision (indeed, in most of these cases, the effect or process under investigation was well established prior to the studies described). Instead, they are important because they show that an effect is so pervasive, it holds even under the most inauspicious circumstances.[5] More-

---

[4] In the examples in this article, we have set the criteria for a minimal manipulation of an independent variable and a difficult-to-influence dependent variable relative to other studies in the research area. For example, the minimal group studies use a minimal manipulation of group membership relative to other studies of ethnocentrism. However, one can conceive of these criteria more broadly in terms of people's expectations about whether a particular operationalization of an independent variable should have an effect or whether a particular dependent variable should be influenceable.

[5] Investigators have used a similar logic of showing that an effect holds even under inauspicious conditions by demonstrating an established effect on a population that seems very unlikely to be affected.

over, these methodological strategies for demonstrating importance underscore the fact that the size of an effect depends not just on the relationship between the independent and dependent variables but also on the operations used to generate the data. Many studies are not designed to account for a lot of variance and are no less impressive for the statistical size of the effects they produce.

SUMMARY AND CONCLUSIONS

In summary, we have argued here that although effect size can be a very useful measure of the strength of an effect, there are alternative ways to demonstrate that an effect is important. We have focused on two methodological approaches, in which importance is a function of how minor a manipulation of the independent variable or how resistant a dependent variable will still produce an effect. Our purpose has been to make explicit what experimenters who have used these methodologies have perhaps known implicitly: Showing that an effect holds even under the most unlikely circumstances possible can be as impressive as (or, in some cases, perhaps even more impressive than) showing that it accounts for a great deal of variance. Indeed, researchers might do well to consider these alternative goals (e.g., accounting for maximal variance, using the most minimal manipulation) when designing and reporting their studies.

The arguments we have made against the exclusive use of effect size as a means for evaluating the importance of empirical results apply equally well to regression analysis, path analysis, and all other techniques that are based on calculation of the proportion of variance accounted for. These techniques can tell us a lot about the strength of a particular operationalization, but their utility as measures of importance is limited by the relation of that operationalization to the independent variable or psychological process under investigation. In the studies we have described, investigators have minimized the power of an operationalization and, in so doing, have succeeded in demonstrating the power of the underlying process. Thus, a small effect size, low multiple correlation, or negligible path value will not lead these investigators to question their conclusions. On the contrary, they will be pleased that their effect survived the toughest test they could give it and will be more convinced than ever of its importance.

For example, showing that even physicians are overconfident about their diagnoses (Christensen-Szalanski & Bushyhead, 1981) or that even divinity students will not stop to help an emergency victim (Darley & Batson, 1973) provides impressive evidence for these psychological phenomena.

REFERENCES

Abelson, R. P. (1985). A variance explanation paradox: When a little is a lot. *Psychological Bulletin, 97*, 128–132.

Abelson, R. P. (1990). *Thinking about statistics*. Unpublished manuscript, Yale University.

Asch, S. (1951). Effects of group pressure upon the modification and distortion of judgments. In H. Guetzkow (Ed.), *Groups, leadership and men* (pp. 177–190). Pittsburgh, PA: Carnegie Press.

Bangert-Drowns, R. L. (1986). Review of developments in meta-analytic method. *Psychological Bulletin, 99*, 388–399.

Berscheid, E., & Walster, E. (1974). Physical attractiveness. In L. Berkowitz (Ed.), *Advances in experimental social psychology* (Vol. 7, pp. 157–215). San Diego, CA: Academic Press.

Billig, M., & Tajfel, H. (1973). Social categorization and similarity in intergroup behavior. *European Journal of Social Psychology, 3*, 27–52.

Cash, T., Gillen, B., & Burns, D. (1977). Sexism and "beautyism" in personnel consultant decision making. *Journal of Applied Psychology, 62*, 301–310.

Christensen-Szalanski, J., & Bushyhead, J. (1981). Physicians' use of probabilistic information in a real clinical setting. *Journal of Experimental Psychology: Human Perception and Performance, 7*, 928–935.

Cohen, J. (1977). *Statistical power analysis for the behavioral sciences*. San Diego, CA: Academic Press.

Cohen, J. (1990). Things I have learned (so far). *American Psychologist, 45*, 1304–1312.

Darley, J., & Batson, C. (1973). From Jerusalem to Jericho: A study of situational and dispositional variables in helping behavior. *Journal of Personality and Social Psychology, 27*, 100–108.

Durkheim, E. (1951). *Suicide* (J. Spaulding & G. Simpson, Trans.). Glencoe, IL: Free Press. (Original work published 1897)

Efran, M. (1974). The effect of physical appearance on the judgment of guilt, interpersonal attractiveness, and severity of recommended punishment in a simulated jury task. *Journal of Research in Personality, 8*, 45–54.

Freud, S. (1971). *The psychopathology of everyday life* (A. Tyson, Trans.). New York: Norton. (Original work published 1901)

Harrison, A. (1977). Mere exposure. In L. Berkowitz (Ed.), *Advances in experimental social psychology* (Vol. 10, pp. 39–83). San Diego, CA: Academic Press.

Isen, A. M., & Levin, P. F. (1972). The effect of feeling good on helping: Cookies and kindness. *Journal of Personality and Social Psychology, 21*, 384–388.

Kunst-Wilson, W., & Zajonc, R. (1980). Affective discrimination of stimuli that cannot be recognized. *Science, 207*, 557–558.

Locksley, A., Ortiz, V., & Hepburn, C. (1980). Social categorization and discriminatory behavior: Extinguishing the minimal intergroup discrimination effect. *Journal of Personality and Social Psychology, 39*, 773–783.

Mayo, R. J. (1978). Statistical considerations in analyzing the results of a collection of experiments. *Behavioral and Brain Sciences, 1*, 400–401.

McGuire, W. J. (1983). A contextualist theory of knowledge: Its implications for innovation and reform in psychological research. In L. Berkowitz (Ed.), *Advances in experimental social psychology* (Vol. 16, pp. 1–47). San Diego, CA: Academic Press.

Mook, D. G. (1983). In defense of external invalidity. *American Psychologist, 38*, 379–387.

Rosenthal, R., & Rubin, D. (1983). A note on percent of variance explained as a measure of the importance of effects. *Journal of Applied Social Psychology, 9*, 395–396.

Rosnow, R., & Rosenthal, R. (1989). Statistical procedures and the justification of knowledge in psychological science. *American Psychologist, 44*, 1276–1284.

Sherif, M. (1936). *The psychology of group norms.* New York: Harper & Row.

Sigall, H., & Ostrove, N. (1975). Beautiful but dangerous: Effects of offender attractiveness and nature of the crime on juridic judgments. *Journal of Personality and Social Psychology, 31*, 410–414.

Sudnow, D. (1967). Dead on arrival. *Transaction, 5*, 36–44.

Tajfel, H., Billig, M., Bundy, R., & Flament, C. (1971). Social categorization and intergroup behavior. *European Journal of Social Psychology, 1*, 149–178.

Wilson, W. (1979). Feeling more than we can know: Exposure effects without learning. *Journal of Personality and Social Psychology, 37*, 811–821.

Yeaton, W., & Sechrest, L. (1981). Meaningful measures of effect. *Journal of Consulting and Clinical Psychology, 49*, 766–767.

Zajonc, R. (1968). Attitudinal effects of mere exposure. *Journal of Personality and Social Psychology, Monograph Supplement, 9*(2, Pt. 2).

Zajonc, R., & Rajecki, D. (1969). Exposure and affect: A field experiment. *Psychonomic Science, 17*, 216–217.

III

METHODS: PRINCIPLES AND PRACTICES

Methodological issues emerge early in the development of a study. Indeed, they are often merged with or immediately follow the idea, hypothesis, or prediction that is the impetus for the study. Almost immediately one must consider how to move from the idea to the test of that idea, with what participants, measures, interventions, conditions of the study, and so on. These considerations are quite important and will affect the inferences that can be drawn once the study is completed.

Students and professionals alike are often concerned with publishing the findings from a study. A common view is that whether the findings of a study can be published depends largely on "how the results come out." To some extent this is true. But it is also false. A study can be designed so the results are fairly meaningful or important no matter how they come out. Yet let us leave aside the results or findings of a study. There is insufficient appreciation of the fact that publication of an article, whether it can be published and the prestige value of the journal in which it might be published, is heavily determined before the first participant is seen. How the study is conducted and the quality of the inferences that can be drawn play a central role in what the investigator can conclude and whether the conclusion is really an advance. These components of a study depend equally on the idea and the methodology used to test it.

The chapters in this part address several conditions of research that emerge when moving from the idea to implementation of research. They directly relate to conditions that influence the conclusions that can be reached from a study. Subsequent chapters and parts of this book will continue to build on facets of methodology that contribute to the quality of a study and the strength of inferences that can be drawn.

SAMPLING PARTICIPANTS AND CONDITIONS

The selection and assignment of research participants to conditions are central to experimentation. Among the many issues is the concern over biases that can emerge when participants are assigned to groups or conditions. In an *experiment*, the investigator is going to manipulate conditions in some way or provide conditions to some participants but not to others. This is distinguished from an *observational study*, in which the investigator may select participants because they are different (e.g., depressed vs. not depressed) in some ways already or have been subjected to an "intervention" not under experimental control (e.g., history of abuse vs. no history of abuse). In an experiment, an initial goal is to form groups (e.g., experimental and control) with no preexisting differences. We would like the groups to be equivalent before they are exposed to the different conditions. If the groups are equivalent when assigned to conditions but differ at the end of the experiment after the manipulation has been administered, we are in a much stronger position to argue that the manipulation may have been responsible for any group differences. Investigators often believe that an unbiased method (e.g., random) of selecting cases from an available subject pool and assigning these cases to conditions produces equivalent groups. *Equivalence* means that no differences exist on a host of "nuisance variables," that is, those variables that are not of interest to the investigator (e.g., social class, intelligence, various personality traits) but that might explain the presence or absence of group differences at the end of the experiment.

Chapter 7 by Louis M. Hsu discusses how groups may differ if small samples are used, even when participants are assigned randomly to conditions. Among the problems is that real group differences before the intervention or experimental manipulation is provided may not be easily detectable and may distort the results. Hsu elaborates the concept of randomization and identifies situations in which misleading conclusions about the intervention might be drawn. Psychotherapy research is used as a basis to illustrate several of the points and to make recommendations for minimal sample sizes in research. Small sample sizes (e.g., ns < 20 per group) characterize a great deal of psychological research, well beyond the confines of psychotherapy. Consequently, points raised in this chapter warrant careful consideration in the design of studies.

Researchers are concerned with the generality of results from one set of participants (e.g., college students) to another (e.g., clinic cases). Indeed, when one raises the notion of "sampling" or the "sample" of a study, invariably attention is drawn to the participants. A neglected feature of generality pertains to the stimulus conditions included in the investigation and how they are sampled. The conditions presented to the participant reflect such features as the range, number, and characteristics of the experimenters, therapists, vignettes, stories, or other stimulus materials. Experimenters often include a narrow range of stimulus conditions (e.g., one therapist, one vignette) with the idea that this controls or holds constant the stimuli presented to the participant. Yet a restricted range of stimulus conditions can greatly restrict the conclusions of the study.

Chapter 8 by Brendan A. Maher notes the importance of representing a broader range of stimulus conditions within an experiment. He discusses the concept of *representative design*, which refers to sampling the range of stimulus conditions to which the investigator wishes to generalize. Sampling of stimulus conditions is critically important as the basis for deciding the generality of results of a study and more fundamentally for separating the influence of the intervention or experimental manipulation from a restricted or single stimulus condition with which it may be confounded.

The notion of sampling stimulus conditions also can be used to help generate ideas for research, going back to an earlier part in the book. As one reads the write-up of a study, one can consider if there might be something about the stimulus conditions that the investigator viewed as ancillary but was likely to contribute to the results in important ways. Another study showing that the finding is restricted to very specific conditions (i.e., is moderated by stimulus conditions) often can contribute to understanding how the phenomenon operates.

ETHNICITY AND UNDERREPRESENTED GROUPS

The inclusion of underrepresented and often neglected samples is important in research for all sorts of reasons. In referring to these samples, the usual and sometimes exclusive focus is on racial or ethnic groups and women. It is worth emphasizing these, but other underrepresented groups exist, and from a methodological perspective raise similar issues. For example, findings obtained with college students are rarely tested with community samples, with individuals who have mental retardation or histories of delinquency, with individuals from diverse cultures, and so on. Sampling of ethnic groups is important in its own right but also raises fundamental issues that have broader generality.

First and perhaps foremost, findings may vary as a function of (be moderated by) characteristics of the sample. If research is restricted primarily to one sample, the generality of the findings remain open as a question. Consider ethnicity as the focus. It may be that ethnic differences would be expected in some areas more than others. For example, if family attachments or extended family attachments vary as a function of ethnic group or culture, this could have far-reaching implications for all sorts of areas in which such attachments may be relevant (e.g., marital relations, child adjustment, bereavement). In any case, it is critical to sample across ethnicity and cultural groups and to ensure their representation in research and that the findings considered to be "true" apply beyond the narrow context in which they may have been demonstrated.

Second, assessment and use of various assessment tools across ethnic, cultural, or other groups can raise special issues. Often psychological measures are devised, developed, and validated with one group (e.g., college students or European American community samples). Extending measures to another group does not mean merely administering that measure to others. The meaning of the test items and how the test items organize themselves (e.g., through factor analysis) may readily vary as a function of characteristics of the group. Research is needed in many areas to develop the tools to elaborate phenomena in ways that capture or are sensitive to group differences. Alternatively, validation research is needed to establish that a test "behaves" in the same or similar way across a range of groups. When the evidence does not show that, new or different variations of the measure may be needed.

Finally, and perhaps most critically, including underrepresented groups is not merely adding another ethnic group to the sample or analyzing the data by ethnicity. This is often required in grant applications and may deter rather than foster scientific advances. The issue is not merely including some samples but predicting and explaining any differences that emerge or indeed why such differences are worth searching for. Merely extending a finding to another sample is not a very inspired study unless an interesting reason exists to expect that the results may not generalize and then testing that reason.

The challenge comes from the impossible task of testing findings across all different groups. On the one hand, all groups ought to have equal access to research. Moreover, clinical research often has direct benefits (e.g., free treatment, free screening, novel treatments for incurable conditions), and these too ought not to be withheld. On the other hand, we do not wish to test every finding with every group that can be delineated. Indeed, this is not very practical. For example, the most recent U.S. census recognizes 126 different racial and ethnic identities.[1] We could go very far with one hypothesis and do the uninspired tests with each of these groups. Why stop in the United States? A little excursion beyond our borders adds to this. For example, some African countries can distinguish more than 200 ethnic groups (see www.infoplease.com/ipa/A0855617.html). All psychological, biological, health, and other findings could not be tested among these different groups.

Apart from the practical issues, the scientific agenda is broader than merely testing findings with different groups. We are interested in many peoples of the world, in many cultures, and in many subgroups within a culture. We wish to know the extent to which findings extend to different peoples and the principles or processes that can explain how culture affects affect, cognition, behavior, development, the family, and so on. Understanding different groups requires more than their inclusion in research; it requires evaluation of processes that account differences.

For example, if differences are expected as a function of sex, ethnicity, social class, country of origin, or type of personality style, it is advisable for the investigator to specify *why* this would be expected and to measure the processes or hypothesized bases for group differences in the investigation. This type of study is a much more significant contribution than merely assessing whether effects of prior research generalize to a new set of participants who vary in some way from the original sample. As these comments suggest, sampling and generality of findings across participants not only are topics of methodology but also raise important substantive questions about research findings and the factors that may influence them.

The chapters in this section articulate many of the issues related to the study of underrepresented groups. In chapter 9, Stanley Sue discusses the paucity of work on ethnic minority groups. This includes studies that omit different groups and studies that include various groups but do not conduct data analyses to evaluate whether the findings are moderated by ethnicity. Sue discusses external validity, that is, the generality of findings and the need for greater attention to generality across ethnic groups. He discusses how generality of findings needs to be demonstrated rather than

---

[1] The 2000 U.S. Census recognized more than 60 different racial options, including 6 single races (White, Black, Asian, American Indian or Alaska Native, Native Hawaiian or Other Pacific Islander, and Some Other), 15 possible combinations of 2 races, 20 combinations of 3 races, 15 combinations of 4 races, 6 combinations of 5 races, and one grand combination of all 6. Moreover, these racial categories were further combined with two ethnic categories (Hispanic or non-Hispanic), which lead ultimately to 126 combinations of race and ethnicity. Even at that it is obvious that many of the groupings (e.g., the 6 single races) gloss over important distinctions. The number (e.g., 126 combinations) itself is not significant for present purposes except to convey the point that it would not be possible or I believe desirable to evaluate whether particular findings extended across each of the recognized populations. Of course, race and ethnicity leave out many other grouping variables (e.g., age, gender identity and preference, country of origin) that delineate us and can make a difference in psychological and biological domains.

assumed, obstacles to ethnic minority research, and recommendations to expand on the range of methodologies used to elaborate group differences.

In chapter 10, Leslie Case and Timothy B. Smith examine the extent to which research actually recruits and studies participants from diverse ethnic backgrounds. Several journals and research areas were evaluated to determine the extent to which participants of different ethnicities are included. The results indicated that African Americans are included in research in a greater proportion than their representation in the U.S. population; Hispanic Americans are underrepresented in relation to their proportion in the population. We also learn from this chapter that many studies (approximately 40 percent) do not even report ethnicity of participants. Even though many studies include various ethnic groups, we do not have an understanding of how and why ethnicity influences or moderates phenomena of interest in the research. This is why I have said that merely including more and different people in a study is not very inspired and by itself may not necessarily improve our understanding. Clearly much basic work needs to be done.

SAMPLING PARTICIPANTS
AND CONDITIONS

7

RANDOM SAMPLING, RANDOMIZATION, AND EQUIVALENCE OF CONTRASTED GROUPS IN PSYCHOTHERAPY OUTCOME RESEARCH

LOUIS M. HSU

Simple random sampling and random assignment (randomization) are some of the best and most popular methods of attaining the pretreatment equivalence of contrasted groups in psychological research (see Cook & Campbell, 1979), in medical research (see O'Fallon et al., 1978), and in the specialized area of psychotherapy efficacy studies (Huesmann, 1982; Kendall & Norton-Ford, 1982; D. A. Shapiro & Shapiro, 1983). In fact, in a recent meta-analysis of comparative psychotherapy outcome research that focused on some of the best studies in this area, D. A. Shapiro and Shapiro (1982, 1983) noted that unconstrained randomization was used in 57% of the client groups.

Reprinted from the *Journal of Consulting and Clinical Psychology, 57*, 131–137. Copyright 1989 by the American Psychological Association.

One of the most appealing characteristics of random sampling and randomization is that these methods can equate groups on several nuisance variables simultaneously and that these methods do not require the researcher to be aware of (a) how the important nuisance variables are related to the response measure, (b) the identities of the important nuisance variables, or even (c) the number of important nuisance variables (see Efron, 1971). These are, perhaps, the principal advantages of simple randomization and random sampling over alternative methods of controlling the effects of nuisance variables such as matching, stratification, analysis of covariance, analysis of covariance with reliability corrections, change score analysis, and standardized change score analysis. In all of these alternatives, the efficacy of control of the nuisance variables is contingent on the researcher's ability to identify the important nuisance variables or to develop a realistic model of how the contrasted groups would differ in the absence of different treatment effects (see Boruch, 1976; Kenny, 1975, 1979; Lord, 1967, 1969; McKinlay, 1977). Several authors have noted that, when sufficient information is available, these as well as other alternatives may be clearly preferable to simple random sampling and randomization (e.g., Fleiss, 1981, 1986; Pocock & Simon, 1975; Simon, 1979). Unfortunately, this information is often not available. (See Boruch, 1976, for an excellent discussion of this topic and for numerous real-world illustrations of problems associated with various alternatives to randomization.) Simple random sampling and randomization appear to be the methods of choice for controlling the effects of nuisance variables, especially the internal validity threats of maturation and selection and the selection–maturation interaction (see Cook & Campbell, 1979; Kirk, 1982), when information about the importance, the identities, and the number of variables is lacking.

However, as noted by Efron (1971), "complete randomization . . . suffers from the disadvantage that in experiments which are limited to a small number of subjects, the final distributions of treatments and controls [on the nuisance variables] can be very unbalanced" (p. 403). Similarly, Cook and Campbell (1979) warned that the "equivalence achieved by random assignment is probabilistic" (p. 341) and that it may not work with small samples. A related point was made by Keppel (1973): "Random assignment of subjects to treatments will ensure in the long run that there will be an equivalence of subjects across the different treatments" (p. 24). All of these statements indicate that random sampling and randomization can be expected to result in the equivalence of large samples but need not result in the equivalence of small samples.

It is generally recognized that clinical studies often involve small samples. Kraemer (1981), for example, pointed out that "a minority of clinical research studies report [as many as] 30–40 subjects" (p. 311). She further noted that "in recent psychiatric clinical research, 20 seems a generally acceptable sample size" (p. 311) but that "many studies with fewer than 20 subjects are published" (p. 311). The situation appears to be even worse in the specialized area of comparative therapy outcome studies (see Kazdin, 1986). More specifically, D. A. Shapiro and Shapiro (1983), whose meta-analysis focused on "an unbiased sample relatively well-designed, recently published comparative outcome studies" (p. 43) in this area, reported that "the 414 treated groups in our meta-analysis contained a mean of 11.98 ($SD = 7.12$) clients; the 143 control groups contained a mean of 12.12 ($SD = 6.64$) clients" (p. 44). They further indicated (a) that "forty-two (10%) of the treated groups contained six or fewer clients" (p. 44), (b) that 109 (26%) of these groups contained 7 to 9 clients, (c) that 148 (36%) contained between 10 and 12 clients, and (d) that only 115 (28%) contained 13 or more clients.

This article has five objectives related to the equivalence of contrasted groups in psychotherapy efficacy studies. The first objective is to investigate the relation of sample size and number of nuisance variables to the equivalence of groups in two popular models, a simple randomization model and a simple random sampling model. The second objective is to discuss the specific implications of these relations concerning the equivalence of groups described in D. A. Shapiro and Shapiro's (1982, 1983) recent meta-analyses of psychotherapy efficacy studies. The third objective is to illustrate how nonequivalence of contrasted groups can result in Simpson's paradox: The less beneficial treatment is estimated to be more beneficial. The fourth objective is to discuss the implications of Tversky and Kahneman's findings (1971) about belief in the law of small numbers concerning the interpretation of estimates of the relative efficacy of treatments in small psychotherapy efficacy studies. And the fifth objective is to compare the minimum sample sizes required for equivalence with the minimum sample sizes that have been recommended by Kraemer (1981) on the basis of other criteria.

FACTORS DETERMINING THE EQUIVALENCE OF GROUPS

Randomization

The efficacy of randomization as a method of equating groups on nuisance variables can be investigated in a variety of research designs. The single-factor independent-groups design was selected here because of the popularity of this design in comparative psychotherapy outcome research (see D. A. Shapiro & Shapiro, 1982). More specifically, this section focuses on a randomization (also called random assignment or permutation) version of this design. The next section focuses on a random sampling version of the same design.

Consider that N subjects are available for an experiment in which a treatment is to be contrasted with a control condition. Half of the subjects are randomly selected from the pool of N and are assigned to the treatment condition, whereas the remaining half are assigned to the control condition (the term *control* is a convenient term used, in this note, to refer to any condition other than the treatment condition, including other forms of treatment). Consider that the N subjects differ on K independent dichotomous variables and that the same fraction of the N subjects fall in one category of the dichotomy as in the other. It should be noted that this last characteristic does not exclude studies in which nuisance variables are continuous because continuous nuisance variables can be dichotomized at the median of the combined groups. For example, if a pool of 60 subjects is available for a study, we may think of 30 as scoring above (and 30 as scoring below) the median of the combined groups on a social desirability scale. In this example, we might define the treatment and control groups as non-equivalent in social desirability if the proportion of subjects who exceed the combined groups' median is at least twice as large in one group (say the treatment group) as it is in the other (the control group). More generally, in this section we will define the groups as nonequivalent on any nuisance variable (including pretreatment values of the dependent variable) if the proportion of subjects who fall in one category of the dichotomous nuisance variable in one group is at least twice that of the other group.[1]

The general term of the hypergeometric distribution was used to determine, for the class of experiments described previously, the probability of the nonequivalence of groups on any one nuisance variable for subject pool sizes ranging from 8 to 100. (see Table 7.1). The general term of binomial expansion was then used to estimate the probability that the groups would be nonequivalent on at least one of the K nuisance variables (for K = 2 and K = 3) for the same subject pool sizes.

Table 7.1 shows that the probability the equal-sized treatment and control groups will be nonequivalent (a) increases with an increase in the number of nuisance variables and (b) generally decreases, with one exception, with an increase in the size of the total subject pool. The exception reflects the fact that the minimum imbalance for the presence of nonequivalence, as defined in this article, cannot be obtained for all Ns: Note, more specifically, that when the total pool size is 12, it is possible for the proportion of above-median subjects (on the nuisance variable) in the treatment group (viz., 4/6)

---

[1] An anonymous reviewer noted that my definition of nonequivalence does not take into account nonequivalence with respect to interactions of nuisance variables. I acknowledge that this is an important limitation of my definition. It should be noted that a definition that takes interactions of nuisance variables into account would generally imply that larger sample sizes would be required for equivalence than the sample sizes implied by my definition. This makes sense, in the context of this article, if we conceive of interactions as additional dichotomous nuisance variables defined in terms of combinations of levels of the original nuisance variables. The same reviewer suggested that nonequivalence for interactions could be defined in terms of imbalance across treatment and control groups, within any combination of levels of the original dichotomous nuisance variables. This is a very interesting idea but, in my opinion, it would typically result in a very conservative view of equivalence because it would require labeling entire groups as nonequivalent if imbalance occurred in what would typically be a small fraction (related to the number of combinations of levels of the original dichotomous variables) of these groups.

TABLE 7.1
Estimated Probabilities That Groups Constructed by Random Assignment Will be Nonequivalent on at Least One Nuisance Variable as a Function of the Number of Nuisance Variables and the Total Sample Size (N)

	Number of nuisance variables		
N	1	2	3
8	.4857	.7355	.8640
12	.5671	.8126	.9189
18	.3469	.5735	.7214
24	.2203	.3921	.5260
32	.0756	.1455	.2101
40	.0256	.0505	.0749
64	.0055	.0110	.0164
80	.0034	.0068	.0102
100	.0006	.0012	.0018

Note: Nonequivalence was considered to occur for one nuisance variable in the randomization model if the proportion of subjects who belonged to one category of the dichotomous variable was at least twice as large in one group as in the other.

to be exactly twice that of the control group (2/4). But if $N = 8$, the smallest imbalance that fits the definition of nonequivalence is 3/4 for one group and 1/4 for the other. In that case, the ratio of the proportions is not 2.0 but rather 3.0.

The following example may be used to illustrate the meaning of the entries in Table 7.1. Suppose that a pool of 18 subjects is available for a comparative outcome study. Nine subjects randomly drawn from this pool are assigned to the treatment condition, whereas the remaining 9 are assigned to the control condition. Now consider that these 18 subjects are evenly split on two independent dichotomous nuisance variables. Note that it is necessary to have measurements of these nuisance variables, nor is it necessary even to know what these variables are, in order to use Table 7.1. The entry of .5735 corresponding to a row entry of 18 (the total pool size) and a column entry of 2 (the number of nuisance variables) indicates a probability of about .57 that the two groups are nonequivalent (as previously defined) on at least one of the two nuisance variables. Thus, in this situation, it is likely that randomization will not result in groups that can be considered equivalent on the nuisance variables.

Random Sampling

The random sampling version of the two independent groups design, considered in this article, differs from the randomization version in the following way. Instead of having a fixed number of subjects available for the study, the researcher has a very large pool of potential subjects. A random sample of $(N/2)$ subjects is drawn from this pool and exposed to the treatment condition; another independent random sample of $(N/2)$ subjects is drawn from the same pool and is exposed to the control condition. Thus, in the random sampling model, the samples used in the study are viewed as independent random samples drawn from a very large pool of subjects. In the randomization model, all available subjects are used, and the two samples are not viewed as random samples from a large population. As in the case of the randomization model, we will assume in the random sampling model that subjects can be dichotomized into two equal-sized categories on each of K independent nuisance variables.[2] These categories may once more be defined in terms of median splits, but these splits are made in the population rather than in the combined samples. Nonequivalence in the random sampling model will be defined in a manner that is comparable to the definition of nonequivalence adopted in the randomization model: The groups will be viewed as nonequivalent on one nuisance variable if the proportion of one group falling in one category of the dichotomized variable differs from the corresponding proportion in the second group by at least .33333. For example, if 68% of one group is above the population median and only 33% of the second group is above the population median, then the groups would differ by $.68 - .33 = .35$ and, therefore, would be viewed as nonequivalent.

The exact probabilities of nonequivalence on at least one nuisance variable were determined for similar combinations of total sample sizes as those considered in the randomization model and for 1–10 nuisance variables. The algorithms used to determine these probabilities were similar to the algorithms that may be used to calculate exact probabilities in ridit analysis (see Fleiss, 1981, 1986). Figure 7.1 summarizes the findings for total sample sizes ranging from 6 to 84 and for numbers of nuisance variables ranging from 1 to 10. It is clear that these results, for the random sampling model, are very similar to the results obtained for the randomization model.

EQUIVALENCE OF GROUPS IN PSYCHOTHERAPY EFFICACY STUDIES

It may be recalled that in D.A. Shapiro and Shapiro's (1982, 1983) meta-analysis, (a) 10% of the treated groups contained 6 or fewer clients, (b) 26%

---

[2] An anonymous reviewer noted that the possible lack of independence of nuisance variables and the implications of nonindependence of nuisance variables should be mentioned. This reviewer indicated that if nuisance variables are nonindependent, then "the number of nuisance variables one has to worry about may not be as large as one thinks, because control of one variable may indirectly result in control of another." Consistent with this reviewer's comment, it should be noted that certain types of dependence between nuisance variables would imply that, as the number of nuisance variables increases, the probability of nonequivalence on at least one will not be as large as expected if these variables were independent. It should also be noted that other types of dependence imply the opposite: That is, that increasing the number of these nuisance variables would result in a greater increase in the probability of nonequivalence on at least one nuisance variable than would be expected if these variables were independent.

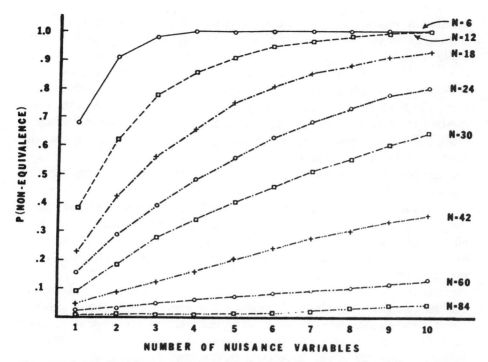

Figure 7.1. The probability of nonequivalence of randomly selected groups on at least one nuisance variable as a function of number of nuisance variables and total sample size.

contained 7–9 clients, (c) 36% contained 10–12 clients, and (d) only 28% contained 13 or more clients. An examination of the Table 7.1 entries relevant to groups with 6 or fewer clients indicates that if two contrasted groups in a design involving randomization each contained 6 clients, the probability would be greater than .5 that the groups would be nonequivalent following random assignment, even if the clients differed on only one nuisance variable. Figure 7.1 yields comparable findings if the clients differed on two nuisance variables. Similarly, entries relevant to groups with 7 to 9 clients suggest that groups containing 9 clients would probably be nonequivalent (i.e., the probability of nonequivalence would be greater than .5) if subjects in the pool differed on as few as two independent nuisance variables for the randomization model and on three nuisance variables for the sampling model. Entries relevant to groups with 10 to 12 clients indicate a better than even chance of nonequivalence of two randomly assigned groups containing 12 subjects each if subjects in the pool of 24 subjects differed on as few as three independent nuisance variables in the randomization model and on four or more independent nuisance variables in the random sampling model. It should be recalled, in relation to this finding, that the average sizes of client and control groups in D.A. Shapiro and Shapiro's (1982, 1983) meta-analyses were 11.98 and 12.12, respectively, and that only 28% of client groups were larger than 12. (The realism of considering that several important nuisance variables may be present in a variety of research settings has been clearly demonstrated by Boruch, 1976.) Thus, it appears that in more than half of the comparitive therapy outcome studies examined by D.A. Shapiro and Shapiro (1983), the samples were of small enough size to suggest (assuming that the models used in this article are realistic) a better than even chance of nonequivalence of the contrasted groups constructed by random assignment or random sampling.

It must be emphasized that the object of this article is not to argue against the use of simple randomization or random sampling in psychotherapy efficacy studies. Nor is the object to argue against the use of these methods for the purpose of creating equivalent contrasted groups (for that argument, see Luborsky, Singer, & Luborsky, 1975). Instead, the object is to draw attention to specific conditions under which it may be unrealistic (and to other conditions under which it may be realistic) to expect that these methods will result in the equivalence of contrasted groups and to point out some possible harmful consequences of nonequivalence on the estimation of the relative efficacy of different psychotherapeutic treatments.

CONSEQUENCES OF NONEQUIVALENCE: SIMPSON'S PARADOX

The major consequence of any specific degree of nonequivalence between contrasted groups is bias in the estimates of relative efficacy of treatment effects: That is, the difference in the effects of the treatments (or of the treatment versus the control condition) on the therapy outcome measure may be either overestimated or underestimated because of the nonequivalence of the contrasted groups on the nuisance variables (see Pocock & Simon, 1975, for a more detailed discussion of this topic).

Only the most serious type of bias will be described in this section: In the presence of nonequivalence on a dichotomous nuisance variable, it is possible that the control condition will result in a greater mean on the outcome measure than will the treatment condition, even though the treatment mean is greater than the control mean within each level of the nuisance variable. That is, the efficacy of the treatment is underestimated to the point that it is wrongly estimated to be less effective than the control condition. It is, of course, also possible for the opposite to happen—that the treatment mean will be greater than the control mean even though the control mean is greater than the treatment mean within each of the two levels of the nui-

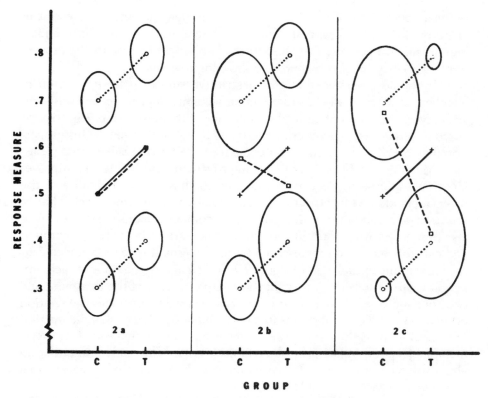

Figure 7.2. The biasing effects of three degrees of nonequivalence of groups (Figures 2a, 2b, 2c) on the estimate of differences between group means.

sance variable. Occurrences of this type may be viewed as manifestations of what has been described, in somewhat different contexts, as the reversal paradox (e.g., S. H. Shapiro, 1982; Simpson, 1951; Wagner, 1982). (See Messick and van de Geer, 1981, for an excellent discussion of the potential universality of the reversal paradox.)

Graphic methods proposed by Paik (1985) may be used to illustrate how the reversal paradox can be caused by the nonequivalence of the psychotherapy treatment and control groups on a dichotomous nuisance variable (see Figure 7.2). Figure 7.2 is divided into three parts (2a, 2b, and 2c). Each part represents a different degree of nonequivalence.

Each ellipse in each part corresponds to a subgroup of patients defined by a level of the dichotomous nuisance variable (e.g., say, the presence or absence of some condition) and a level of the independent variable (i.e., treatment or control). The sizes of the ellipses are proportional to subgroup sizes. The six ellipses in the upper portion of Figure 7.2 correspond to the presence of the nuisance variable, and the six ellipses in the lower portion correspond to the absence of the nuisance variable. Let us view the outcome measure as dichotomous for each patient: The patient manifests or does not manifest improvement. Each circle at the center of an ellipse represents the proportion of patients in the subgroup who show improvement.

It should be noted that this descriptive statistic (the proportion of members of a group who manifest improvement) appears to be consistent with several measures of clinical significance of the results of psychotherapy outcome studies (see Jacobson, Follette, & Revenstorf, 1984). This proportion may be viewed as a mean outcome measure for that subgroup if we assign a dummy variable value of 1 for improvement and of 0 for no improvement. We choose to do this in order to emphasize the generality of the reversal paradox with respect to psychotherapy response measures: That is, the reversal paradox is not limited to dichotomous response measures but is also observable with continuous response measures. Group (i.e., treatment and control) means are represented by the two small squares connected by the broken line in each part of Figure 7.2. It is clear that the slope of each broken line carries information about the relative efficacy of the treatment and control conditions. The solid straight lines are used to represent the relation of treatment and control means in a balanced design (i.e., the same fraction of control subjects show the presence of the nuisance variable as of the treatment subjects). Similarly, the slope of each dotted line carries information about the relative efficacy of the treatment and control conditions within a level of the nuisance variable.

It is apparent that only when the slope of the broken line is identical to the slope of both dotted lines in a part of Figure 7.2 is the estimate of the relative efficacy of the treatment and control conditions the same within levels of the nuisance variable as it is when we ignore the nuisance variable. Note that this happens only in 2a, where the proportion of the control group that manifests the presence of the nuisance variable is equal to that of the treatment group (as reflected in the sizes of the ellipses). 2b shows the effect of the minimum degree of imbalance that was considered to yield nonequivalence in both the randomization and the random sampling models discussed previously: The proportion of control subjects who show the presence of the nuisance variables (.67) is more than twice that of treatment subjects, or the difference between these proportions is at least .33. Note the influence of relative sizes of subgroups (reflected in the relative sizes of corresponding ellipses) within each group on the position of the group mean: In 2a, the group mean is halfway between the subgroup means, reflecting the fact that these subgroups are of equal size. In 2c, the group mean is 95% of the distance between the two subgroup means, reflecting the fact that one subgroup is 95% of the size of the group. In 2b, the group mean is two thirds of the distance between subgroup means, reflecting the fact that one subgroup is twice as large as the other within that group.

An examination of 2b indicates that even when this minimum degree of imbalance is present, estimates of the relative efficacy of treatment and control not only will be different from the estimates obtained within levels of the nuisance variable but also will be reversed. That is, the mean outcome score (viz., 0 = *no improvement*, 1 = *improvement*) of all control subjects is greater than that of all treatment subjects even though the treatment mean is greater than the control mean within each level of the nuisance variable.

Figure 2c shows the effect of increasing the degree of imbalance: Now we consider that 95% of the control subjects and only 5% of the treatment subjects show the presence of the nuisance variable. The difference in the slopes of the dotted and broken lines illustrate a very large reversal: The means of outcome measures of treatment subjects are greater than those of control subjects within each level of the nuisance variable, whereas the mean of all control subjects is much larger than that of all treatment subjects. Note more specifically that 68% of control patients show improvement, whereas only 42% of treatment patients show improvement but that, within each level of the nuisance variable, a greater proportion of treatment patients show improvement than of control patients (80% vs. 70% for the presence of the nuisance variable and 40% vs. 30% for absence of that variable). There are two principal reasons for the large reversal in 2c: First, the nuisance variable has a strong effect on the response measure, and, second, the degree of imbalance (or nonequivalence) is large. Researchers typically have little control over the first reason but can control the second reason by using sufficiently large samples.

NONEQUIVALENCE AND NONSIGNIFICANCE

Tversky and Kahneman (1971) found that both naive subjects and trained scientists tend to "view a sample randomly drawn from a population as highly representative, that is, similar to the population in all essential characteristics. Consequently, they expect any two samples drawn from a particular population to be more similar to one another . . . than sampling theory would predict, at least for small samples" (p. 105). Tversky and Kahneman (1971) described this expectation as a belief in the law of small numbers.

This belief, which is an unrealistic expectation of the equivalence of small groups constructed by random sampling, can result in misinterpretations of estimates of treatment efficacy obtained in individual studies. As was observed in 2a, the equivalence of groups implies a lack of bias of the estimate of the relative efficacy of treatments. Consequently, one who believes in the law of small numbers is likely to consider the observed difference between group means a valid index of the relative efficacy of the treatments. As noted by Tversky and Kahneman (1971), "if [a scientist] believes in the law of small numbers, [he or she] will have exaggerated confidence in the validity of conclusions based on small samples" (p. 106).

Those who believe in the law of small numbers tend to ignore or downplay the influence of sampling error on estimates of treatment effects and, therefore, tend to downplay the importance of statistical significance tests, which evaluate estimates of treatment effects in relation to estimates of sampling error (see Tversky and Kahneman, 1971). However, these tests yield valid significance levels when groups have been constructed by randomization (see Efron, 1971, p. 404) or random sampling (Winer, 1971). The failure to obtain a statistically significant difference should be interpreted to mean that the difference can be conservatively explained in terms of sampling error rather than in terms of the effects of treatments.[3] As noted by Tversky and Kahneman (1971), "the computation of significance levels . . . forces the scientist to evaluate the obtained effect in terms of a valid estimate of sampling variance rather than in terms of his subjective biased estimate" (p. 106).

Tversky and Kahneman's (1971) points appear worth repeating because of the numerous criticisms of significance tests that have recently appeared in psychological journals (see Kupfersmid, 1988, for a summary). Cohen and Hyman (1979), for example, stated that "even if . . . results are not statistically significant, the magnitude or direction of the effect is often (more than just occasionally) most significant" (p. 14). Cohen and Hyman (1979) illustrated their point by noting that a statistically nonsignificant sample effect size of 1 (in a situation in which the predicted effect size was .5) obtained from small samples is a "dramatically significant difference" (p. 14). They also noted that "a researcher can not find that difference and then not accept it because of high alpha" (p. 14). Similarly, Carver (1978) argued that estimates of treatment effects "should be interpreted with respect to the research hypothesis regardless of its statistical significance" (p. 394). It is clear that following Cohen and Hyman's (1979) and Carver's (1978) advice, in the area of psychotherapy efficacy studies in which samples are small and nonequivalence is therefore highly probable (see Table 7.1 and Figure 7.1), could easily result in the misinterpretation of biased and misleading estimates of treatment efficacy. Clearly, the worst situations of this type occur when the reversal paradox in which the wrong treatment could be estimated to yield the better outcome.

---

[3] An anonymous reviewer noted that randomization and random sampling are sufficient to ensure the validity of statistical significance tests and that failure to use these methods raises questions about the validity of these tests. This reviewer also noted that "the probability of a significant result includes the probability of a false positive result arising from random variation (nonequivalence) between the two groups." An important implication of this statement is that the nonsignificance of a statistical test should be interpreted to mean that the observed difference between group means can reasonably be attributed to sampling error (which includes nonequivalence of groups).

MINIMUM SAMPLE SIZES:
AGREEMENT OF DIFFERENT CRITERIA

That there are certain combinations of total subject pool sizes and numbers of nuisance variables for which random sampling and randomization should not be expected to result in the equivalence of treatment and control groups is clearly demonstrated in Table 7.1 (for the randomization model) and Figure 7.1 (for the random sampling model). Also demonstrated in Table 7.1 and Figure 7.1 is the fact that when samples are large (40 per group), randomization and random sampling appear to be effective methods of creating groups that are equivalent on the maximum number of nuisance variables examined in this article. Even when samples are of moderate size (20–40 per group), randomization and random sampling appear to work well provided the number of nuisance variables is small.

Kraemer (1981) noted that "a sample size of 20 [per group] which seems acceptable and feasible and which yields reasonable power in well-designed research (based on our own experience as well as evidence in published research . . .) . . . seems a reasonable base level for sample size" (p. 312). She also argued against using sample sizes less than 10 (p. 311). Her recommendations are based on criteria of "acceptability, feasibility, [statistical] power, and cost" (p. 311). The information in Table 7.1 and Figure 7.1 clearly supports her argument against using samples smaller than 10 and conditionally supports her recommendation of sample sizes of 20. The condition for recommendation of samples as small as 20, based on Table 7.1 and Figure 7.1 information, is that the number of important nuisance variables be small. Recommendations that sample size equal 20 or more, based on Kraemer's criteria and on the criteria of equivalence of this note, appear to be relevant to research in the area of comparative psychotherapy outcome studies because sample sizes of past studies in this area have generally been below 20 (Kazdin, 1986; D. A. Shapiro & Shapiro, 1982, 1983). It is an interesting coincidence that sample sizes that appear to be consistent with the criteria of acceptability, feasibility, statistical power, and cost (Kraemer's criteria) are about the same as the minimum sample sizes that appear to be consistent with the criteria of equivalence (as defined in this article) of contrasted groups on nuisance variables and on preexisting values of the psychotherapy response variable.

REFERENCES

Boruch, R. F. (1976). On common contentions about randomized field experiments. In G. Glass (Ed.), *Evaluation studies: Review annual* (Vol. 1, pp. 158–194). Beverly Hills, CA: Sage.

Carver, R. P. (1978). The case against statistical significance testing. *Harvard Educational Review, 48*, 378–399.

Cohen, S. A., & Hyman, J. S. (1979). How come so many hypotheses in educational research are supported? *Educational Researcher, 8*, 12–16.

Cook, T. D., & Campbell, D. T. (1979). *Quasi-experimentation: Design and analysis issues for field settings.* Chicago: Rand McNally.

Efron, B. (1971). Forcing a sequential experiment to be balanced. *Biometrics, 58*, 403–417.

Fleiss, J. L. (1981). *Statistical analysis for rates and proportions.* New York: Wiley.

Fleiss, J. L. (1986). *The design and analysis of clinical experiments.* New York: Wiley.

Huesmann, L. R. (1982). Experimental methods in research in psychopathology. In P. C. Kendall & J. N. Butcher (Eds.), *Handbook of research methods in clinical psychology* (pp. 223–248). New York: Wiley.

Jacobson, N. S., Follette, W. C., & Revenstorf, D. (1984). Psychotherapy outcome research: Methods for reporting variability and evaluating clinical significance. *Behavior Therapy, 15*, 336–352.

Kazdin, A. E. (1986). Comparative outcome studies in psychotherapy: Methodological issues and strategies. *Journal of Consulting and Clinical Psychology, 54*, 95–105.

Kendall, P. C., & Norton-Ford, J. D. (1982). Therapy outcome research methods. In P. C. Kendall & J. N. Butcher (Eds.), *Handbook of research methods in clinical psychology* (pp. 429–460). New York: Wiley.

Kenny, D. A. (1975). A quasi-experimental approach to assessing treatment effects in the nonequivalent control group design. *Psychological Bulletin, 82*, 887–903.

Kenny, D. A. (1979). *Correlation and causality.* New York: Wiley.

Keppel, G. (1973). *Design and analysis: A researcher's handbook.* Englewood Cliffs, NJ: Prentice-Hall.

Kirk, R. (1982). *Experimental design* (2nd ed.). Belmont, CA: Brooks/Cole.

Kraemer, H. C. (1981). Coping strategies in psychiatric clinical research. *Journal of Consulting and Clinical Psychology, 49*, 309–319.

Kupfersmid, J. (1988). Improving what is published. *American Psychologist, 43*, 635–642.

Lord, F. M. (1967). A paradox in the interpretation of group comparisons. *Psychological Bulletin, 68*, 304–305.

Lord, F. M. (1969). Statistical adjustments when comparing pre-existing groups. *Psychological Bulletin, 72*, 336–337.

Luborsky, L., Singer, B., & Luborsky, L. (1975). Comparative studies of psychotherapies. *Archives of General Psychiatry, 32*, 995–1008.

McKinlay, S. (1977). Pair-matching—A reappraisal of a popular technique. *Biometrics, 33*, 725–735.

Messick, D. A., & van de Geer, J. P. (1981). A reversal paradox. *Psychological Bulletin, 90*, 582–593.

O'Fallon, J. R., Dubey, S. D., Salsburg, D. S., Edmonson, J. H., Soffer, A., & Colton, T. (1978). Should there be statistical guidelines for medical research papers? *Biometrics, 34,* 687–695.

Paik, M. (1985). A graphic representation of a three-way contingency table: Simpson's paradox and correlation. *American Statistician, 39,* 53–54.

Pocock, S. J., & Simon, R. (1975). Sequential treatment assignment with balancing for prognostic vactors in the controlled clinical trial. *Biometrics, 31,* 103–115.

Shapiro, D. A., & Shapiro, D. (1982). Meta-analysis of comparative therapy outcome studies: A replication and refinement. *Psychological Bulletin, 92,* 581–604.

Shapiro, D. A., & Shapiro, D. (1983). Comparative therapy outcome research: Methodological implications of meta-analysis. *Journal of Consulting and Clinical Psychology, 51,* 42–53.

Shapiro, S. H. (1982). Collapsing contingency tables—A geometric approach. *American Statistician, 36,* 43–46.

Simon, R. (1979). Restricted randomization designs in clinical trials. *Biometrics, 35,* 503–512.

Simpson, E. H. (1951). The interpretation of interaction in contingency tables. *Journal of the Royal Statistical Society, 13,* 238–241.

Strube, M. J., & Hartmann, D. P. (1982). A critical appraisal of meta-analysis. *British Journal of Psychology, 21,* 129–139.

Tversky, A., & Kahneman, D. (1971). Belief in the law of small numbers. *Psychological Bulletin, 76,* 105–110.

Wagner, C. H. (1982). Simpson's paradox in real life. *American Statistician, 36,* 46–48.

Winer, B. J. (1971). *Statistical principles in experimental design.* New York: McGraw-Hill.

8

STIMULUS SAMPLING IN CLINICAL RESEARCH: REPRESENTATIVE DESIGN REVIEWED

BRENDAN A. MAHER

More than 30 years ago, Egon Brunswik (1947) pointed out that if we wish to generalize the results of a psychological experiment to populations of subjects and to populations of stimuli, we must sample from both populations. This argument was elaborated by him in other articles and was summarized cogently in a short article by Hammond (1948). The purpose of this article is to review the issues that Brunswik raised and to examine some of their implications for contemporary research in clinical psychology.

Brunswik's thesis is very simple. When we conduct an experiment intended to investigate the effect of different values of an independent variable on a population, we always take care to draw a sample of subjects that is representative of the population in question. We do so, naturally, because we recognize the range of variation that exists in populations of individuals. We wish to make sure that deviant individual values do not distort our estimate

Reprinted from the *Journal of Consulting and Clinical Psychology, 46*, 643–647. Copyright 1978 by the American Psychological Association.

of the parameters of the population. If the stimuli that we use are defined in physical units, we are (or should be) careful to confine our generalizations to the range of values actually included in the study. When physical units are involved, we have relative confidence that the stimulus can be replicated by another investigator, provided that the detailed description of the stimulus is followed carefully. Should a subsequent investigator change one or more of these attributes, we are not surprised if there is a concomitant change in the responses that are made to the stimulus.

When the stimuli to which the subjects respond cannot be defined in physical units and are likely to vary within a population, a different situation arises. Outstanding examples are to be seen in research directed to the investigation of the effects of human beings as stimuli that elicit behavior from other human beings. Consider some instances drawn from recent volumes of this journal. Acosta and Sheehan (1976) reported that Mexican American subjects viewed an Anglo American professional therapist as more competent than a Mexican American professional when all other variables were matched. Babad, Mann, and Mar-Hayim (1975) reported that trainee clinicians who were told that a testee was a high-achieving upper-middle class child assigned higher scores to Wechsler Intelligence Scale for Children (WISC) responses than did another sample of clinicians who were led to believe that the same responses had been made by an underachieving deprived child. Research of this kind is generally cast in terms of a hypothesis that members of a specified population respond in discriminatory fashion to members of certain other populations. Thus, for example, we encounter such questions as, Do physicians give less adequate medical care to ex-mental patients than they do to normal medical patients? (Farina, Hagelauer, & Holzberg, 1976) and Are therapists with a behavioral orientation less affected by the label *patient* when evaluating observed behavior than are therapists of psychodynamic persuasion? (Langer & Abelson, 1974).

SINGLE-STIMULUS DESIGN

Human attributes are generally distributed in such a fashion that any one of them is likely to be found in conjunction with a wide variety of others. Let us consider an investigation of bias toward ex-mental patients. To belabor the obvious a little, we can note that the attribute *ex-mental patient* can be associated with any measure of intelligence, age, sex, education, socioeconomic status, physical attractiveness, and so forth. It is true that some of these attributes may have significant correlations with each other; a patient of upper socioeconomic status is quite likely to have had substantial education, for example. Nonetheless, even the largest of these correlations is quite modest, and the population of ex-mental patients to which we wish to generalize have a wide range of values on these attributes.

When we employ only one person as a stimulus, we are faced with the fact that the specific values of some of the other attributes possessed by this person will also have stimulus value that will be unknown and uncontrolled. Responses made by a sample of the normal population to an ex-mental patient who is female, young, attractive, articulate, and intelligent may well be different from those made to a normal control who is male, old, ugly, incoherent, and dull. These differences cannot be assigned to the patient/nonpatient status of the two stimulus persons, as many other unidentified differences were uncontrolled. At first sight it may appear that this problem is solved by the simple expedient of matching the patient and the control on all variables other than that of patient status. Unfortunately, this can only be achieved at the cost of further difficulties. We do not know the full range of variables that should be matched, and hence this solution necessarily involves resort to an actor and a script, barring the unlikely availability of discordant monozygotic twins for research purposes! Scripts bring with them some special problems, of which more will be said later. The main point to note here is that the use of a *single* human stimulus acting as his or her own control fails to deal with the problem of the *interaction* of the attribute under investigation with those that have been controlled by matching. Pursuing for a moment the example of responses to the label *ex-mental patient*, let us consider a hypothetical study using a male actor with athletic physique and vigorous movements. The willingness of a normal subject to accept this individual as a fellow worker, neighbor, or friend may well be influenced by the perception that the ex-patient, if violent, could be dangerous. Had the actor been older and visibly frail, the reaction might well be different. Under the first set of circumstances, the bias hypothesis would probably be confirmed, and under the second set, the null hypothesis might fail to be rejected.

An additional difficulty is incurred by the single-stimulus own-control strategy. We cannot determine whether a finding of no difference between group means is due to the weakness of the hypothesis, errors of method, or the inadvertent selection of an atypical stimulus person to represent one or both conditions. An example of the complexities of interpretation with this design can be found in Farina et al. (1976). These investigators hypothesized that physicians would provide less adequate medical care to former mental patients than to normal medical students. To test this hypothesis one stimulus person, a 23-year-old male graduate student, approached 32 medical practitioners. In each case he entered the doctor's office

> carrying a motorcycle helmet and a small knapsack. . . . The same symptoms were reported to all doctors. Stomach pains suggestive of ulcers were selected to be neither clearly psychiatric nor unrelated to the mind. . . . Every other practitioner was told the pains had first occurred 9 months earlier while the patient was traveling around the country. The remaining 16 doctors were also informed that the pain had appeared

9 months earlier, but at that time the patient reported being in a mental hospital. (Farina et al., 1976, p. 499)

No significant difference of any relevance was found in the kind of medical care given by the practitioners under either condition. In conclusion, the authors stated that "a former mental patient seems to receive the same medical treatment as anyone else" (p. 499).

Logically, several conclusions are compatible with this finding. One obviously valid conclusion is that a young male motorcyclist with the symptoms of ulcers receives a certain class of treatment whether or not he describes himself as a former mental patient. We cannot tell whether this treatment is the same, better, or worse than that typically given to a random sample of the normal population of patients who seek treatment for stomach pains, as no such sample was obtained. A substantial number of physicians may have had opinions about motorcyclists as unfavorable as those that they were hypothesized to have about former mental patients, and hence both conditions produced equally inadequate medical care. Alternatively, the physicians may have felt the necessity to be unusually careful in providing care to individuals who might be assumed to be irresponsible (such as motorcyclists and mental patients), and hence they provided better than average care. Finally, medical practice may be sufficiently precise about the adequate procedures to follow with patients who complain of stomach pains that no real room for bias exists, the treatment provided being the same as would be given to any sample of patients.

We can summarize the limitations of the single-stimulus design as follows:

1. Obtained differences may be due to the validity of the tested hypothesis or to the effect of uncontrolled stimulus variables in critical interaction with the intended independent variable. No method of distinguishing between these two explanations is possible.

2. Lack of difference may be due to the invalidity of the hypothesis, undiscovered methodological factors such as subject sampling error, or the presence of an uncontrolled stimulus variable operating to either counteract the effect of the intended independent variable or to raise this effect to a ceiling value in both experimental and control situations.

It is readily apparent that the problem of uncontrolled attributes occurring in a single stimulus person can only be solved by the provision of an adequate sample of stimulus persons, since they will tend to cancel each other out. No satisfactory solution is possible within the single-stimulus design.

SCRIPTS AND MANTICORES

Some investigators have attempted to solve the problems of the single-subject stimulus by fabricating scripts without the use of a human actor to present them. Case histories, dossiers, vignettes, audiotapes, or other devices have been used to reduce the effects of the uncontrolled aspects of a human stimulus. Thus, in a study by Babad et al. (1975), the trainee clinicians were given only the WISC protocol and did not see the child who was alleged to have been tested. These manufactured materials may be termed *scripts*. Scripts may be taken from existing sources of genuine material, such as clinical files; they may be created de novo in accordance with prior theoretical guidelines or in an attempt to present an ideal "typical" case.

When the script is drawn from original clinical files, the investigator is assured that at least one such case exists in nature. The limitations on the results obtained from such scripts are, in principle, the same as those that plague any single-stimulus design. Some minor advantage accrues to the method, however, in that the number of uncontrolled accidental attributes has been reduced by the elimination of those attributes associated with physical appearance, dress, and so forth. When the script is fabricated for research purposes, a new problem develops—namely that in devising material according to theoretical guidelines, a case is created that like the manticore, may never have existed in nature. We can imagine a hypothetical investigation of the attitudes of males toward females of varying degrees of power. Varying naval ranks with male and female gender of the occupant of each rank, we create the dossier of an imaginary female Fleet Admiral. Whatever our male subject's response to this dossier may be, we have no way of knowing whether it is due to the theoretically important combination of high rank with female gender or to the singularity of a combination that is, as yet, unknown to human experience.

For a recent illustration of this problem, we can turn to Acosta and Sheehan (1976). They presented groups of Mexican American and Anglo American undergraduates with a videotaped excerpt of enacted psychotherapy. Each group saw an identical tape, except that in one version the therapist spoke English with a slight Spanish accent and in the other version the accent was standard American English. Some subjects were told that the therapist was a highly trained professional; the others were told that the therapist was a para-professional of limited experience. There were thus four experimental conditions and two kinds of subjects. The Spanish-accent tape of a trained professional was introduced with a background vignette describing the therapist as American born of Mexican parentage and as having a Harvard doctorate in his field and a distinguished professional record. For the American-English-accent tape, the therapist was introduced with the same vignette but with an Anglo-Saxon name and parentage identified as

Northern European. Anglo American ratings of the therapist's competence were uninfluenced by the ethnic identification, whereas Mexican Americans rated the Mexican American therapist less favorably than the Anglo American therapist.

In their discussion of this somewhat surprising result, the authors noted that the number of Mexican American therapists actually in practice in the United States shortly before the study was done was 48 (28 psychologists and 20 psychiatrists). We do not know what characteristics would be typical of this population, and no attempt seems to have been made to ascertain them before preparing the script. There is, therefore, no way to be sure that the therapeutic style, choice of words, gesture, and so forth, were authentically typical of actual Mexican American therapists. Given that essentially the same script was used for both ethnic conditions, we must conclude that either one or the other version of the script was ethnically inaccurate or, less likely, that the only actual difference that would be seen in the comparative behaviors of Mexican American and Anglo American therapists would be their accent. In brief, we cannot ignore the possibility that the Mexican American subjects disapproved of the Mexican American therapist not because he was Mexican American but because his behavior was not representative of that of actual Mexican Americans. Like the woman admiral, he may have presented a combination of characteristics that is theoretically possible but unknown in the experience of the subjects responding to it. The only guarantee that a script is free from impossible or improbable combinations of variables is when it is directly drawn from an actual clinical case or other human transaction. We cannot produce a fictional script of a psychotherapeutic session with any confidence that it is as representative as a transcript of an actual session. The ideal or typical therapeutic interview may be as rare as the perfect textbook case of conversion hysteria or as a stereotypical Mexican American. This rarity or implausibility may well determine a subject's response far more than the attributes that were planned to make it appear typical. Our hesitation in generalizing from a single stimulus case to a population of cases is increased substantially by the prospect of generalizing from a case that is not known to have existed at all.

REPRESENTATIVE DESIGN

The moral to the foregoing review is simple. If we wish to generalize to populations of stimuli, we must sample from them. Only in this way can we be confident that the various attributes that are found in the population will be properly represented in the sample. Those attributes that are significantly correlated with membership in the population will appear in appropriate and better-than-chance proportions; those attributes that are uncorrelated with population membership will appear in chance proportions but will not affect the outcomes. If we intend to draw conclusions about the way in which physicians treat former mental patients, we must sample physicians and former mental patients. If we wish to know what Mexican American students think of Mexican American therapists, we must sample students and therapists. This is the essence of Brunswik's (1947) concept of representative design. There is no satisfactory alternative to it. Nonetheless, the use of representative design is rarely, if ever, seen in reported research. There are, in my opinion, three reasons for this. First, many clinical psychologists are unaware of Brunswik's work. The remedy for this is obvious and easy to apply. Second, there is a common failure to understand that the replication of single-stimulus studies with additional single-stimulus studies cannot create accumulated representative design unless the selection of single-stimulus persons was achieved by sampling.

Let us consider a hypothetical series of studies of the effect of examiner gender on children's test responses. In the population of examiners, there are likely to be attributes that distinguish males from females in addition to those that are inseparable from gender. Thus the proportions of married and single persons, prior experience with children, knowledge of various hobbies, mean age, prior locale of undergraduate education, and so forth, may differ between the two groups. In the first study we use one male examiner and one female examiner, each with 1 year of experience. Using samples of male and female children, we find differences in test responses attributable to examiner gender. Conscious of the fact that we included inexperienced examiners, we replicate the study with one male examiner and one female examiner each with 3 years of experience. Now we find no difference. Our series ends when we have made gender comparisons for examiners with 1, 3, 5, 7, 9, 11, 13, 15, 17, and 19 years of experience. We found significant examiner effects at every level of experience except 3 and 5 years. As 8 of our 10 students have found significant difference due to gender, we conclude that there is a generalizable finding. We might even treat the entire series as a single experiment comparing the group of 10 male examiners with the group of 10 female examiners and find a statistically significant difference between the mean test responses elicited by one group versus the other.

To accept this conclusion it is first necessary to know what the true proportion of the total population of examiners at each level of experience is. If the experience range of 3 to 5 years includes 65% of all examiners, our best conclusion is that gender differences have not been established. The reason is, of course, that the "sample" of examiners was not representative of the population to which it is intended to generalize, being underrepresented in the 3- to 5-year experience range. Note that we cannot handle this by some proportional weighing of the data obtained from the examiners with 3 to 5 years of experience, as the results obtained from those comparisons suffer from the limitations of single-stimulus design and might well be due to the effects of uncontrolled differences between examiners other than gender.

A third reason for the failure to use representative design is that it is laborious and expensive. Providing an adequate sample of stimulus persons, each of whom is to be observed by an adequate sample of subjects, necessarily involves large numbers and long hours. For some investigators it is, as one of my correspondents put it, "too hard to do it right."

There is however, no satisfactory alternative to doing it right. Clinical psychology is concerned with real people and not with hypothetical collections of attributes. Our research into the behavior of patients, therapists, diagnosticians, normal persons, and the like, must produce generalizations that are valid for actual populations of these people. Conclusions based on inadequate sampling may be worse than no conclusions at all if we decide to base our clinical decisions on them. If the patience and time that it takes to do it right create better science, our gratitude should not be diminished by the probability that fewer publications will be produced.

REFERENCES

Acosta, F. X., & Sheehan, J. G. (1976). Preferences toward Mexican American and Anglo American psychotherapists. *Journal of Consulting and Clinical Psychology*, 44, 272–279.

Babad, E. Y., Mann, M., & Mar-Hayim, M. (1975). Bias in scoring WISC subtests. *Journal of Consulting and Clinical Psychology*, 43, 268.

Brunswik, E. (1947). *Systematic and representative design of psychological experiments.* Berkeley: University of California Press.

Farina, A., Hagelauer, H. D., & Holzberg, J. D. (1976). Influence of psychiatric history on physician's response to a new patient. *Journal of Consulting and Clinical Psychology*, 44, 499.

Hammond, K. (1948). Subject and object sampling—A note. *Psychological Bulletin*, 45, 530–533.

Langer, E. J., & Abelson, R. P. (1974). A patient by any other name . . . : Clinician group of differences in labeling bias. *Journal of Consulting and Clinical Psychology*, 42, 4–9.

ETHNICITY AND UNDERREPRESENTED GROUPS

9

SCIENCE, ETHNICITY, AND BIAS: WHERE HAVE WE GONE WRONG?

STANLEY SUE

One issue has bedeviled psychology for many decades — namely, the relationship between racial and ethnic bias and the practice of psychological science. In 1972, Thomas and Sillen discussed "scientific racism" and the ways in which theories and empirical research perpetuated a biased view of African Americans and other ethnic minority groups (Thomas & Sillen, 1972). Indeed, in the foreword to their book, Kenneth B. Clark, past president of the American Psychological Association, noted that

> Probably the most disturbing insight obtained from the relentless clarity
> with which this book documents the case of racism . . . is the ironic
> fact that the students, research workers, and professionals in the behav-
> ioral sciences — like members of the clergy and educators — are no more

Reprinted from the *American Psychologist, 54,* 1070–1077. Copyright 1999 by the American Psychological Association.

An earlier version of this chapter was presented as a keynote address at the National Multicultural Conference and Summit, Newport Beach, CA, January 1999. The chapter is supported in part by Grant RO1-MH44331 from the National Institute of Mental Health.

I am indebted to Sumie Okazaki, Rick Robins, and David Takeuchi for their comments on this chapter.

immune by virtue of their values and training to the disease and superstition of American racism than is the average man. (p. xii)

Most of the controversies presented in the book are still being debated in the field. For example, issues over race and intelligence, test bias, equivalence of measures (conceptual, translation, and scalar equivalence) across different ethnic groups, deficit model theories, the design and interpretation of research on ethnic minority groups, stereotyping, focus on social structure versus the individual, and the influence of culture continue to be prominent and contentious themes in American psychology (Herrnstein & Murray, 1994; Ivey, Ivey, & Simek-Morgan, 1997; Jones, 1997; Ponterotto & Pedersen, 1993; Sandoval, Frisby, Geisinger, Scheuneman, & Greiner, 1998; Segall, Lonner, & Berry, 1998; Steele, 1997; D. W. Sue & Sue, 1999; Triandis & Brislin, 1984).

The questions I address are these: Is science biased against ethnic minority research? Are ethnic minority researchers simply playing, as some believe, a "White man's game"? Should ethnic minority researchers turn to alternatives rather than traditional experimental and empirical methods? Why is there a relative lack of ethnic minority research and high-quality ethnic research? How can we promote and encourage good ethnic minority research?

Let me state from the outset my position: I believe that there is a lack of psychological research on ethnic minority populations; that research on ethnic minority groups is uneven, with much of it at a relatively low level; and that funding for ethnic minority research has been woefully inadequate. The reasons for these problems are subtle and systemic. Science and scientific methods are not the culprit. Rather, the culprit is how science has been practiced—an effect caused by the selective enforcement of the principles of science. This selective enforcement of the principles of science emphasizes internal validity over external validity, which discourages the growth and development of ethnic minority research. As a consequence, steps must be taken in psychology to rectify the situation, not only in the interest of ethnic minority populations but also in the promotion of better science. (Incidentally, I realize terms such as *Whites*, *Asian Americans*, and *ethnic minority group* are often offensive, stereotypic referents. My use of the terms refers to the aggregate group rather than to individuals.)

ETHNIC RESEARCH

Having served on editorial boards and grant review panels, I have often encountered colleagues who criticize much of ethnic minority research as being descriptive in nature, simple in design, and lacking in grounding in sophisticated and mature psychological theory. These are, of course, sufficient justification for not accepting a paper for publication or for rejecting proposals for funding. Even in my own research, I have often resorted to basic demographic and descriptive studies. For example, I examined the kinds of problems encountered by Asian Americans, who are often perceived as a model minority group, and the correlates of their utilization of mental health services (S. Sue, Sue, Sue, & Takeuchi, 1995). I felt it was important to point to ethnic differences in behaviors, and these studies added new knowledge to the field. However, the nature of the knowledge was basic and descriptive about Asian Americans. From the data, it was difficult to draw inferences concerning the reasons for the utilization rates or the implications for other populations. Therefore, the work had value in understanding one particular ethnic minority group but unclear value in generalizing beyond that group. The discrepancy in values also meant that research of this kind could engender different reactions from reviewers. One reviewer might view the research positively because of an understanding of the nature of the ethnic field and an ability to place the value of the contribution in context. Another reviewer might negatively evaluate the same work because of a lack of understanding of the field, a desire to have the work demonstrate greater generality than the targeted group, or uncertainty as to the theoretical rationale for the research. In cases where reviewers disagree about the merit of a research paper submitted for publication, the typical practice is to not accept the paper for publication.

There is evidence that the journal literature contains relatively few articles on ethnic minority groups. For example, Graham (1992) examined the number of empirical research articles on African Americans in several psychology journals. She identified articles in which African Americans were the population of interest or in which data were analyzed by race and included African Americans. These articles constituted only 3.6% of the total published between 1970 and 1989. Surprisingly, there was actually a decline in the number of such articles over time. After conducting a content analysis of three behavioral psychology journals for empirical or theoretical and treatment-oriented or assessment-oriented articles, Iwamasa and Smith (1996) found only 1.3% of the articles focused on U.S. ethnic minority groups. Padilla and Lindholm (1995) also noted a paucity of publications on topics devoted to race, ethnicity, and culture in major psychology journals.

One parsimonious explanation for the state of ethnic minority research is that there are few researchers interested in the topic and that the ethnic field is relatively underdeveloped. In this view, it will take time before culturally appropriate research measures, tools, and methodologies can be established. I do not believe that the notion of underdevelopment can fully explain the disparity in research sophistication and publication rates. Rather, the current practices in psychological science have contributed to the problem. To understand how this is possible, we need to examine the philosophy of science, epistemology, and research principles.

SCIENCE

There are many ways of knowing. Widely recognized philosophers from Descartes to Kant to Wittgenstein have tried to identify how one knows, what one knows, and what it means to know. Science is a way to know things. There are other ways of knowing, such as having spiritual awareness or personal intuition (a form of knowledge or of cognition independent of experience or reason). These ways of knowing cannot be distinguished from each other simply on the basis of being correct or incorrect. Knowledge generated from science as well as spiritual and intuitive means can be wrong. For example, in science, we can draw invalid conclusions not only because of methodological and conceptual problems but also because of scientific convention. When alpha levels are specified in testing hypotheses, Type I and Type II errors will inevitably occur in the long run.

Science is used to describe, explain, predict, and modify phenomena. There are several basic guiding principles in the philosophy of science, including convincingness (credibility) and skepticism. The principle of convincingness refers to the direct relationship between the use of rigorous scientific methodology and the likelihood of convincing or persuading a fairminded, critically thinking person of the findings or conclusions. Through the elegance and soundness of scientific methodology and theoretical coherence, one gains confidence that the findings are valid (Abelson, 1995); the more rigorous the study, the better. The continuing efforts to refine science and to design rigorous studies have led to the use of operational definitions, replication, matching, manipulation checks, control groups, random assignments, experimental procedures, blind studies, sampling techniques, theory building, methods of controlling confounding variables, follow-ups, statistical power, clinical significance, sophisticated statistical procedures, and the like.

Another important principle is skepticism. Under this principle, one must question, doubt, or suspend judgment until sufficient information is available. Skeptics demand that evidence and proof be offered before conclusions can be drawn (Marken, 1981). Scientific skepticism is considered good. One must thoughtfully gather evidence and be persuaded by the evidence rather than by prejudice, bias, or uncritical thinking. The basis for the principle comes from philosophers and scientists who embrace logical positivism and logical empiricism.

In psychological science, one of the most critical tasks to master is the ability to draw causal inferences from research. We want to understand why something occurs, that is, the causal factors. To do this, the research must have internal and external validity. Internal validity concerns the extent to which conclusions can be drawn about the causal effects of one variable on another (i.e., the effect of the independent variable on the dependent variable). The interest in making causal inferences goes beyond quantitative research. Even in qualitative research, a variety of strategies are used to strengthen internal validity so causal inferences can be drawn, such as the use of prolonged substantial engagement, persistent observations, peer debriefing, negative case analysis, progressive subjectivity, member checks, and triangulation (Mertens, 1998).

External validity is the extent to which one can generalize the results of the research to the populations and settings of interest. One tries to study the population of interest. If sampling is necessary, a variety of strategies can be used to generate a sample that is representative of the population. There are some limited circumstances in which generality of findings is not always relevant or necessary (Kazdin, 1999). However, more typically, both internal validity and external validity are important and should be equal partners in the scientific endeavor. The lack of internal validity does not allow causal inferences to be made without some degree of convincingness or credibility. The lack of external validity may render findings meaningless with the actual population of interest. A natural tension always exists between internal and external validity. For experimenters to achieve perfect internal validity, a laboratory is often the perfect setting. For experimenters to achieve perfect external validity, research is conducted in the actual environment with the accompanying noise and extraneous variables that normally exist.

SELECTIVE ENFORCEMENT OF SCIENTIFIC PRINCIPLES

It is my belief that internal validity and external validity are not equal partners and that if we have erred, it is in the direction of attention to internal rather than external validity in psychological science. Far more papers submitted for publication are probably rejected because of design flaws, inability to control for confounding or extraneous variables, and so on than for possible external validity problems. Because one must first obtain an unambiguous finding before one can generalize about it, internal validity often takes precedence over external validity (Alloy, Abramson, Raniere, & Dyller, 1999). Indeed, one could argue that the demand for rigor in internal validity far exceeds that for external validity. Consider the fact that college student samples are used extensively in psychological research without much attention to the representativeness or generality of the sample. Kazdin (1999) noted that students are typically enrolled in undergraduate psychology courses and receive monetary rewards or course credit for participation. Is this sample representative of human beings in general or college students in particular?

Sears (1986) found that the use of college sophomores as participants has resulted in a biased view of human beings that reflects the idiosyncrasies of college students. Even the widely used practice of selecting (self-reported) distressed college students to study depression has been criticized as being inappropriate (Coyne, 1994). When college students are used, ethnicity or race is typically ignored as a variable of interest, and the underrepresentation of certain minority groups and persons from different cultures as research participants is of concern (Kazdin, 1999).

Another fact should be considered. Americans are the largest producers of psychological research. The overwhelming subject of the research is Americans. The United States constitutes less than 5% of the world's population. Therefore, on the basis of a sample of less than 5% of the world, theories and principles are developed that are mistakenly assumed to apply to human beings in general; that is, they are assumed to be universal. Seldom are researchers only interested in whether an independent variable affects the dependent variable for the particular participants used in the investigation. They usually want to make a general statement about some larger population (Robinson, 1976). They then make the mistake of discussing human beings without much reference to the particular sample on which the research was based.

Interestingly, Korchin (1980) noted that researchers tend to question the generality of findings only when the research involves ethnic minority populations. Korchin mentioned that once he and his colleague had conducted research on why some African American youths had made extraordinary achievements. A paper from the research was submitted for publication and rejected. One reviewer had indicated that the research was grievously flawed because it lacked a White control group. Why was a White control group necessary if the interest was in African Americans? More critically, Korchin asked why we do not require studies of Whites to have an African American control group. In other words, we ask that ethnic minority research show its pertinence to other groups or more general phenomena, but we fail to make the same requests when the research involves White populations. The answer to the question of when a control group is needed depends on the research question being asked.

To further illustrate the tendency to assume generality, let me describe my experiences as a member of the APA Division 12 Task Force on Psychological Interventions. The charge of the task force was to determine which psychotherapeutic interventions had met rigorous criteria (including replication) for being designated an empirically validated treatment. During the course of the investigation, the task force (Chambless et al., 1996) found that no rigorous studies had ever been conducted on the effectiveness of treatment for members of ethnic minority groups. How, then, can treatments be designated as validated, where validity is attributed to the treatment itself, when cross-cultural validity has never been established? The dilemma was recognized by researchers, and the phrase "empirically supported treatment" rather than "empirically validated treatment" was subsequently adopted (Chambless & Hollon, 1998). Therefore, this situation shows that the practice in research has often been to assume generality of findings when it is not warranted, an external validity problem. Abelson (1995) indicated that generality of effects is often limited by cultural factors and that universals are rare among human beings.

The tendency to ignore external validity problems (which can also impact internal validity) is also illustrated by contrasts made by Padilla and Lindholm (1995) in their analysis of descriptions of participant populations in research studies. For example, these extracts were in two different research reports Padilla and Lindholm cited:

> Subjects were 32 children from the Berkeley area. Subjects included 15 boys and girls. Children came from a variety of socioeconomic backgrounds, though most were Caucasian and middle class. (p. 100)
>
> In all, 423 sixth- and seventh-grade students . . . participated in the study. The school was in a predominantly working-class . . . community. The average student age was 11.87 and 13. 08 for sixth and seventh graders, respectively. The sample was equally representative of males (52%) and females (48%), with 68% of the sample being Caucasian, 23% Black, 5% Hispanic, and 7% other minority status. (p. 100)

Padilla and Lindholm noted that in these two descriptions there was basic demographic information, but it was too general to be meaningful and not cross-tabulated. For example, in the second study, how many sixth graders were girls? How many of the boys were members of various ethnic groups? Without such information, it would be difficult to replicate the study. In contrast, the following description was made of an experimental study involving primates:

> The subjects were 28 pigtailed macaque infants. Of these, 17 were classified as normal or at low risk for developmental deficits (i.e., normal birth weight, no history of clinical problems), and 11 were classified as high risk. Of the high-risk animals, 6 had experienced significant trauma at birth or during the early neonatal period (e.g., breech delivery with respiratory complications). Three high-risk subjects were part of an ongoing study examining the effects of parental reproductive history and maternal stress on growth and development. . . . The infants were separated from their mothers at birth. . . . All animals were socialized in play groups daily. (as quoted in Padilla & Lindholm, 1995, p. 101)

The detailed information reflects the importance that the researchers placed on the sample. As mentioned earlier, in psychological research with human beings, we seem to deemphasize background characteristics and to draw broad conclusions about human beings in general rather than about the particular human beings in the study. In other words, our modus operandi is to assume that the work is universally applicable; the burden of proof is placed on researchers concerned about race, ethnicity, and bias to show that there are ethnic differences. Whatever happened to the scientific notion of skepticism, where little is taken for granted, where conclusions are drawn from evidence and not from assumptions? We have not followed good scientific principles in assuming that findings from research on one population can be generalized to other populations. At a recent meeting of psychology journal editors, the need for better demographic descriptions of study participants, including more precise definitions of race and ethnicity, was emphasized (Azar, 1999).

The phenomenon of selective enforcement of scientific criteria is apparent. We criticize research for problems in internal validity. Yet, we pay relatively little attention to external validity. Whether in research papers submitted for publication or research grant proposals submitted for funding, ethnic minority research is primarily scrutinized for internal validity problems. This is appropriate. Yet, much of research, whether or not it is focused on ethnics, is not criticized for external validity problems. In experimental studies, the discrepancies between internal and external validity are brought into bold relief. Rigorous and sometimes elegant experimental designs allow us to make causal inferences. However, because of their rigor and need to control for extraneous variables, they frequently involve small numbers of participants, forgoing issues of sampling and representativeness. The ultimate example of this is the single-participant experimental design. In dealing with a single-participant experiment, such as an ABAB time-series design, extraneous variables like maturation and reactivity can be controlled, and in the process, alternative explanations can be eliminated. The generality of findings from such a design is unclear.

A similar situation occurs in the mental health field, where a distinction is made between efficacy and effectiveness research. On the one hand, in the past, efficacy studies were considered the gold-standard methodology in evaluating the outcome of mental health treatments. These studies were important in demonstrating the causal effects of a particular intervention on mental health symptoms. However, experimenters tended to use highly restrictive exclusion criteria that enhanced internal validity in their designs. For example, in an efficacy study of a psychotherapeutic treatment for schizophrenia, exclusionary criteria might include comorbidity, current use of psychotropic medication, and non-White race. Such a practice would limit the applicability or generality of the findings. On the other hand, effectiveness research is gaining appreciation because it examines treatment outcomes in more typical real-life situations, where patients may have multiple disorders, be taking medication, and be members of various racial groups.

CONSEQUENCES OF THE SELECTIVE
ENFORCEMENT OF SCIENTIFIC PRINCIPLES

Focus on internal validity has had the effect of discouraging ethnic minority research. Because much psychological research is not based on ethnic minority populations, it is unclear whether a particular theory or principle is applicable to all racial groups, whether an intervention has the same phenomenological meaning for different cultural groups, or whether measures or questionnaires are valid for these populations. Ethnic minority research has a weaker substantive base on which to demonstrate internal validity. Consequently, much effort has to be expended in discovering basic relationships between variables, developing measures, and so on. For example, ethnic researchers cannot simply assume that the Minnesota Multiphasic Personality Inventory−2 is a valid instrument for, say, Cambodian Americans. Much effort must be expended in translating, back-translating, and testing the instrument. Ironically, in some cases, by the time an instrument originally designed for White Americans has been found to be valid for an ethnic minority population, a new, revised version is available for White Americans, and another round of validation must be initiated for the ethnic minority population.

The greater the demands for internal validity, the more the mainstream research will dominate. To be sure, the demand for rigor in internal validity will improve ethnic minority research, but the gap will widen between ethnic minority and mainstream research. A vicious cycle is created in which demands for rigorous internal validity result in relatively few minority research projects and less funding; the reduction in research and funding makes it difficult to develop appropriate measures, designs, and research tools; training opportunities in ethnic minority research are difficult to find; it is then a problem to meet demands for rigor. Note that I am not trying to characterize all ethnic minority research as lacking rigor and internal validity. There are many examples of outstanding, rigorously designed studies conducted on ethnic minority populations. My main point is there are systemic forces that discourage the development of ethnic minority research. Unfortunately, these forces are not well recognized, and much ethnic minority research has been negatively viewed.

Another factor that discourages ethnic minority research is that such research is difficult to conduct. Researchers may avoid ethnic minority research for a variety of reasons, including difficulties in recruiting ethnic participants, not having validated measures to use, the unknown validity of mainstream theories, and the often controversial nature of ethnic minority research (e.g., the heated debates over race and intelligence). As a case in point, several of us at our National Institute of Mental Health−funded research center were interested in conducting the first large-scale study of the rate, distribution, and correlates of mental disorders among Chinese Americans. In previous national surveys of the mental health of Americans (Kessler et al., 1994; Robins & Regier, 1991), Chinese Americans and Asian Americans were not analyzed, presumably because of their small sample sizes in the studies. Because of the problems in finding a representative sample of a relatively small minority group, devising valid measures and translating instruments into Chinese, training bilingual and bicultural interviewers, and so on, it cost $1.5 million to conduct a two-wave study (see Takeuchi et al., 1998). Nearly 20,000 households were approached to find 1,700 Chinese respondents. Thus, ethnic minority research can be very costly and difficult to initiate. Given the difficulties in conducting research, the field's emphasis on internal validity, and the paucity of ethnic minority studies, it is not surprising that ethnic minority research continues to lag behind that of the mainstream.

My position is not that psychological principles or theories cannot be generalized from one population to another. Many principles can be applied to different populations. Problems occur when the assumption of generality is made. Generality is a phenomenon that should be empirically tested. It is in the best interest of science, and it is certainly consistent with the tradition of scientific skepticism, to avoid drawing premature and untested assumptions. Moreover, when theories and models applied to different populations are examined, important ethnic and cultural differences are often found.

ETHNIC AND CULTURAL DIFFERENCES: TWO EXAMPLES

Research on ethnic differences has yielded important insights about the applicability of theories and models. For example, my colleagues and I have examined ethnic differences in sexual aggression (Hall, Sue, Narang, & Lilly, in press). Theoretical models of men's sexual aggression have emphasized intrapersonal factors (Hall & Barongan, 1997): the physiological, cognitive, affective, and developmental variables that may motivate them to become sexually aggressive. Such perpetrator characteristics are more strongly associated with sexual aggression than are victim characteristics. After removing the effects of social desirability, intrapersonal variables (rape myth acceptance, hostility toward women, and the belief that rape is morally wrong) accounted for a significant increment in the amount of variance observed in sexual aggression. Situational variables (number of consenting sex partners, drinking before or during sex, being drunk before or during sex) did not account for a significant amount of variance in sexual aggression.

Whereas the motivation for behavior in many Western cultures tends to be individually based or independent in nature, motivation for behavior in collectivist cultures tends to depend on social context or be interdependent (Markus & Kitayama, 1991). Unlike the emphasis on individualism in mainstream American culture, American cultures having non-Western origins often emphasize collectivist values. Collectivist cultures emphasize attending to others, fitting within the community, role relationships, and interpersonal harmony.

We hypothesized that specific aspects of collectivist cultures may serve as protective factors against sexually aggressive behavior. The importance of fitting in with the group may cause group norms to be more influential in collectivist than in individualist cultures. We conducted two studies in which we assessed self-reported sexual aggression, intrapersonal factors (rape myth acceptance and hostility toward women), and interpersonal factors (concerns over loss of face and effects of sexual aggression on relationships with parents) among Asian American and White male university students. The results of the two studies supported the hypothesis that interpersonal variables would be more relevant in a model of sexual aggression for Asian American men than in a model for White men. Although intrapersonal variables were important for both groups, interpersonal variables were a predictor of sexual aggression only for Asian Americans. The preliminary findings on sexual aggression may well imply fundamental differences in explanatory models for individualistic and collectivist cultures.

In another study, we were interested in possible ethnic differences in predictors of academic achievement. Past research has demonstrated the importance of high school grades and Scholastic Aptitude Test (SAT) scores (particularly the verbal portion of the SAT) in predicting subsequent grades in college. Because little research had been conducted on Asian Americans, we wanted to examine the predictors for this population (S. Sue & Abe, 1988).

From a total freshman student population of 22,105 who enrolled in any of the eight University of California campuses, the records of the 4,113 domestic Asian (nonforeign) students were examined and compared with those of 1,000 randomly selected White students. Asian American students were also divided into two groups by presumed English proficiency: those for whom English was probably the best language and those for whom English was probably not the best language. The criterion variable was university freshman grade point average (GPA), which was the average of all grades received by a student during the academic year. Six predictor variables were used for the GPA: high school GPA, SAT–Verbal (SAT–V) score, SAT–Mathematical (SAT–M) score, English composition score from the College Board Achievement Test (CBAT) series, and Level I or Level II mathematics test (MI or MII) score from the CBAT series. Because the overall results with the SAT scores were similar to those using the English composition and the MI and MII CBAT scores, only the results for high school GPA and SAT scores are presented.

Very different regression formulas best predicted university GPA for Whites and Asian Americans. For Whites, high school GPA and SAT–V were the best predictors of university GPA, with SAT–M adding virtually nothing to the prediction equation. For Asian Americans, high school GPA and SAT–M were the best predictors, with SAT–V adding very little insight.

The results were consistent regardless of declared academic major, gender, or acculturation level of the students. Interestingly, important differences within the Asian American sample were found, depending on precise ethnicity. The results are important because in test bias research, one indicator of bias is whether regression slopes for predicting behaviors differ for different groups. We have evidence that they do—culture and ethnicity do make a difference.

As noted by Kazdin (1999) and Lin, Poland, and Nakasaki (1993), even biological responses to psychotropic medication (e.g., for depression and anxiety) can vary greatly as a function of racial and ethnic differences. "Such findings underscore the need to sample broadly, to evaluate the moderating role of sample differences, and to pursue mechanisms through which moderating factors may operate" (Kazdin, 1999, p. 20). These findings provide convergent evidence for the importance of testing the validity of models and theories with different populations. The findings inevitably raise the question of whether all theories must be tested with every population, surely an impossible task. My response is "yes." We cannot assume a priori that explanatory models apply to different populations in the absence of evidence or logical reasoning. My position is consistent with the principle of scientific skepticism.

SOME SOLUTIONS

How do we go about increasing the quality and quantity of research on ethnic minority populations? Interestingly, the National Institute of Mental Health has attempted to encourage researchers to include female and ethnic minority research participants (Hohmann & Parron, 1996) by issuing several research guidelines:

1. Women and members of minorities and their subpopulations must be included in all human participant research.
2. Cost is not an acceptable reason for excluding these groups.
3. Programs and support for outreach efforts should be initiated to recruit these groups into clinical studies.

Because of the guidelines, many researchers complained that they were often being compelled to modify their projects. They had to justify why they did not include women and minorities in their studies. Some attributed the policy to "political correctness." Hohmann and Parron argued that the policy reflected scientific, not political, concerns. The scientific principle was based on the heterogeneity of the population of the United States, which necessitated research that would reflect the population's diversity.

Both the research complainants and Hohmann and Parron (1996) were correct to some degree. On the one hand, of course there were political considerations. The policy would not have been adopted if there were not political considerations and pressures. On the other hand, critics of the policy failed to see the scientific merit of inclusion. The fact that the nation is heterogeneous makes the inclusion policy important. However, heterogeneity per se is not a scientific matter. It is when we generalize from one sample to other populations that a scientific principle is pertinent. This is the external validity issue. If we want to draw conclusions about human beings, we must study human beings in all their diversity and not particular samples.

It should be noted that engaging in ethnic minority research does not magically induce external validity. A focus on different populations can be used to discover how universal research findings or theories are. Ethnicity should not be treated as a nuisance variable. Understanding ethnic differences is not only helpful to ethnic groups, it is good for science. The United States is one of the most diverse societies in the world. Why not take advantage of that fact by promoting external validity and by testing the generality of theories?

Interestingly, psychologists in the testing and assessment field have taken several major steps to emphasize the importance of the external validity of instruments. The principles they propose researchers follow (see Sandoval et al., 1998) include an explicit statement of the nature of the sample on which tests have been standardized and the population(s) for which a test is appropriate. They also note that it is incorrect to consider a test valid for all populations because no test is valid for all purposes or in all situations.

I believe that progress in the development of ethnic minority research in particular and research in general will be well served by engaging in several tasks. First, ethnic minority research will be improved if demands are made for greater external validity while strong internal validity standards are maintained in all research studies. There should also be a true desire to include many different populations in research in order to find out if phenomena are universal or particularistic. Those who construct theories and principles in psychology ought to explicitly detail the population on which the theories and principles are built. In cases where those theories and principles are built on limited populations, they should be viewed as local theories until they are cross-validated. The intent of this recommendation is not to imply that theories and principles lack generality: They may or may not. The point is that they require evidence, in the best tradition of science and the principle of skepticism, and cross-validation. The burden of proof is to show that results are universally applicable. By explicitly delineating the limitations in generality, researchers may be motivated to study other populations to establish the applicability of principles and theories. Similarly, in ethnic minority research, it is important to not only gain knowledge of the particular targeted ethnic group but also contribute to the understanding of more general processes, principles, or limitations in these principles.

Second, a wide range of research methodologies should be used, particularly in ethnic minority research. Traditional psychological scientists tend to prefer experimental methods in the study of cause and effect. As mentioned previously, experimenters conducting ethnic minority research often cannot assume that existing theories or propositions developed on other populations are strictly applicable to the population they are studying. Therefore, a variety of research methods, including qualitative and ethnographic strategies, should be used to create a more substantial knowledge base. Sears (1986) has suggested that very different kinds of people in very different behavioral settings using different research methodologies should be recruited as participants to avoid the study of "college sophomores in the laboratory."

Third, ethnicity is a distal and largely demographic concept in explaining observed differences. Ethnic and cross-cultural researchers should try to go beyond comparisons of different populations. If ethnic differences are found, researchers should explain what aspects of ethnicity are responsible for the differences. For example, as noted before, we found differences between Asians and White Americans in predictors of sexual aggression. Ethnicity (Asian or White) is a distal concept in explaining the differences. A more proximal explanatory concept is that Asians and Whites differ in interpersonal–intrapersonal orientation. Therefore, the meaning of ethnicity is frequently the most important variable to study.

In conclusion, science is not biased against ethnic minority groups. Rather, the problem is that criteria used to judge the suitability of research for publication and for funding are selectively enforced so that internal validity is elevated over external validity. In addition, because ethnic minority research is not as well developed as mainstream research and is more difficult to conduct, internal validity criteria suppress research progress. This in turn keeps ethnic minority research from becoming better developed. Ethnic minority researchers should not turn away from science; rather, demands should be made that all research show relevance for different groups. The issue of internal and external validity may also explain why psychology has been so reluctant to recognize culture. Segall et al. (1998) believe that culture is too encompassing, so it is ignored or taken for granted. Another explanation is that the very tools we use as psychological scientists—research methodologies and emphases—steer us away from culture. In practice, internal validity takes precedence over the generality or specificity of findings.

REFERENCES

Abelson, R. P. (1995). *Statistics as principled argument*. Hillsdale, NJ: Erlbaum.

Azar, B. (1999, February). Journal editors find consortium helps researchers shape goals. *APA Monitor*, 20.

Chambless, D. L., & Hollon, S. D. (1998). Defining empirically supported therapies. *Journal of Consulting and Clinical Psychology, 66,* 7–18.

Chambless, D. L., Sandersom, W. C., Shoham, V., Bennett-Johnson, S., Pope, K. S., Crits-Christoph, P., Baker, M., Johnson, B., Woody, S. R., Sue, S., Beutler, L., Williams, D. A., & McCurry, S. (1996). An update on empirically validated therapies. *Clinical Psychologist, 49,* 5–18.

Coyne, J. C. (1994). Self-reported distress: Analog or ersatz depression? *Psychological Bulletin, 116,* 29–45.

Graham, S. (1992). "Most of the subjects were White and middle class": Trends in published research on African Americans in selected APA journals, 1970–1989. *American Psychologist, 47,* 629–639.

Hall, G. N., & Barongan, C. (1997). Prevention of sexual aggression: Sociocultural risk and protective factors. *American Psychologist, 52,* 5–14.

Hall, G. N., Sue, S., Narang, D. S., & Lilly, R. S. (2000). Culture-specific models of men's sexual aggression: Intra- and interpersonal determinants. *Cultural Diversity and Ethnic Minority Psychology, 6,* 252–268.

Herrnstein, R. E., & Murray, C. A. (1994). *The bell curve.* New York: Free Press.

Hohmann, A. A., & Parron, D. L. (1996). How the new NIH guidelines on inclusion of women and minorities apply: Efficacy trials, effectiveness trials, and validity. *Journal of Consulting and Clinical Psychology, 64,* 851–855.

Ivey, A. E., Ivey, M. B., & Simek-Morgan, L. (1997). *Counseling and psychotherapy: A multicultural perspective.* Boston: Allyn & Bacon.

Iwamasa, G. Y., & Smith, S. K. (1996). Ethnic diversity in behavioral psychology: A review of the literature. *Behavior Modification, 20,* 45–59.

Jones, J. M. (1997). *Prejudice and racism.* San Francisco: McGraw-Hill.

Kazdin, A. E. (1999). Overview of research design issues in clinical psychology. In P. C. Kendall, J. N. Butcher, & G. N. Holmbeck (Eds.) *Handbook of research methods in clinical psychology* (pp. 3–30). New York: Wiley.

Kessler, R. C., McGonagle, K. A., Zhao, S., Nelson, C. B., Hughes, M., Eshleman, S., Wittchen, H., & Kendler, K. S. (1994). Lifetime and 12-month prevalence of DSM–III–R psychiatric disorders in the United States. *Archives of General Psychiatry, 51,* 8–19.

Korchin, S. J. (1980). Clinical psychology and minority problems. *American Psychologist, 35,* 262–269.

Lin, K. M., Poland, R., & Nakasaki, G. (Eds.). (1993). *Psychopharmacology and the psychobiology of ethnicity.* Washington, DC: American Psychiatric Press.

Marken, R. (1981). *Methods in experimental psychology.* Monterey, CA: Brooks/Cole.

Markus, H. R., & Kitayama, S. (1991). Culture and self: Implications for cognition, emotion, and motivation. *Psychological Review, 98,* 224–253.

Mertens, D. M. (1998). *Research methods in education and psychology.* Thousand Oaks, CA: Sage.

Padilla, A. M., & Lindholm, K. J. (1995). Quantitative educational research with ethnic minorities. In J. A. Banks & C. A. McGee-Banks (Eds.), *Handbook of research on multicultural education* (pp. 97–113). New York: Macmillan.

Ponterotto, J. G., & Pedersen, P. B. (1993). *Preventing prejudice: A guide for counselors and educators*. Newbury Park, CA: Sage.

Robins, L. N., & Regier, D. A. (1991). *Psychiatric disorders in America: The epidemiologic catchment area study*. New York: Free Press.

Robinson, P. W. (1976). *Fundamentals of experimental psychology: A comparative approach*. Englewood Cliffs, NJ: Prentice Hall.

Sandoval, J., Frisby, C. L., Geisinger, K. F., Scheuneman, J. D., & Grenier, J. R. (1998). *Test interpretation and diversity: Achieving equity in assessment*. Washington, DC: American Psychological Association.

Sears, D. O. (1986). College Sophomores in the laboratory: Influences of a narrow data base on social psychology's view of human nature. *Journal of Personality and Social Psychology, 51*, 515–530.

Segall, M. H., Lonner, W. J., & Berry, J. W. (1998). Cross-cultural psychology as a scholarly discipline: On the flowering of culture in behavioral research. *American Psychologist, 53*, 1101–1110.

Steele, C. M. (1997). A threat in the air: How stereotypes shape intellectual identity and performance. *American Psychologist, 52*, 613–629.

Sue, D. W., & Sue, D. (1999). *Counseling the culturally different*. New York: Wiley.

Sue, S., & Abe, J. (1988). *Predictors of academic achievement among Asian American and White students*. New York: College Board.

Sue, S., Sue, D. W., Sue, L., & Takeuchi, D. T. (1995). Psychopathology among Asian Americans. *Cultural Diversity and Mental Health, 1*, 39–54.

Takeuchi, D. T., Chung, R. C., Lin, K. M., Shen, H., Kurasaki, K., Chun, C., & Sue, S. (1998). Lifetime and twelve-month prevalence rates of major depressive episodes and dysthymia among Chinese Americans in Los Angeles. *American Journal of Psychiatry, 155*, 1407–1414.

Thomas, A., & Sillen, A. (1972). *Racism and psychiatry*. New York: Brunner/Mazel.

Triandis, H. C., & Brislin, R. W. (1984). Cross-cultural psychology. *American Psychologist, 39*, 1006–1016.

10

ETHNIC REPRESENTATION IN A SAMPLE OF THE LITERATURE OF APPLIED PSYCHOLOGY

LESLIE CASE AND TIMOTHY B. SMITH

In his parting editorial, former *Journal of Consulting and Clinical Psychology* editor Larry Beutler (1996) emphasized the importance of detailed reporting of demographic information of human participants. He encouraged efforts to reliably measure and analyze demographic constructs, and he cited a statement developed by the National Institute of Mental Health's Editor's Consortium that clearly spells out the need to do so:

> Not only is the complete description of a study sample central to the scientific goals of sound and replicable research, but also these variables may affect the generalizability of the research findings. This information is necessary for the meaningful interpretation of findings from a particular study. Moreover, the availability of this information provides the methodological basis for determining the extent to which findings depend upon individual and sociodemographic characteristics of the sample. (pp. 846–847)

Reporting and analyzing sample composition are "good science," a standard to be met in the interest of external validity. Of course, representative sampling is essential to external validity (Babbie, 1998). Because psychological research must be relevant and appropriate for individuals from diverse ethnic backgrounds (S. Sue, 1999), researchers must use samples that adequately represent diverse populations. Published research often determines what is taught and which mental health interventions are used. However, if the results of research are not examined in relation to the ethnic composition of the participants, the value of such research is limited, and what it advocates may even prove harmful (D. W. Sue & Sue, 1999).

The majority of psychotherapy research has been conducted with predominantly middle-class White Americans (Alvidrez, Azocar, & Miranda, 1996; Graham, 1992). As a result, limited data are available to help researchers and practitioners ensure that appropriate services are provided to clients from different backgrounds (Miranda, 1996). Few psychotherapy studies include representative numbers of people of color in their samples, despite the fact that the proportion of people of color is increasing in the United States (Alvidrez et al., 1996). Such traditional patterns reflect cultural biases within the field, and some observers imply that underrepresentation of people of color in psychological research may be a product of institutionalized racism (D. W. Sue & Sue, 1999). Although likely unintentional, such misrepresentation clearly compromises the quality of the field.

MULTICULTURAL PUBLICATION CONTENT

Previous studies on the inclusiveness of psychological research have noted the lack of journal articles focused specifically on people of color. For example, Graham (1992) found that only 3.6% of the articles in 6 journals published by the American Psychological Association (APA) between 1970 and 1989 had content specific to African Americans. Furthermore, she noted a decline in such articles over time, from 5.2% during the period 1970–1974 to 2.0% during the period 1985–1989. Similarly, Santos de Barona (1993) reported an average annual decline of 1.5 articles on people of color in 11 APA journals over 21 years. Proportions of journal content specific to people of color as low as 1.3% have been reported by reviewers (Iwamasa & Smith, 1996).

Because a disproportionately small percentage of the research literature focuses on concerns specific to people of color, an implicit (albeit incorrect) assumption may be that such a focus is not necessary: As long as people of color are adequately represented in the research samples, then the results should generalize to those populations. However, although several studies have examined the content of research with respect to its focus on people of color, no examination has scrutinized the degree to which people of color are actually represented in research samples.

DIFFICULTIES ACHIEVING REPRESENTATIVE SAMPLES

Researchers have given varied reasons for not including people of color in their studies. For some, the unwillingness to investigate topics that are socially relevant but not "politically correct" is problematic (Beutler, Brown, Crothers, Booker, & Seabrook, 1996). For others, the practical difficulties and higher expenses incurred in gaining access to certain populations serve as deterrents (S. Sue, 1999), because people of color are underrepresented in the university and mental health settings from which researchers typically recruit participants (Hough et al., 1987; Santos de Barona, 1993; Snowden & Cheung, 1990; Wells, Hough, Golding, Burnam, & Karno, 1987).

Distrust of research among some people of color is another factor to consider, because research has often been misused in regard to these groups (Maultsby, 1982; D. W. Sue & Sue, 1999). For example, research has historically been used as a justification for slavery, as a "scientific" rationale for segregation, and as support for the concept of racial inferiority and superiority (Williams, 1986). Additionally, the stigma that some people of color attach to concepts of mental health and illness may reduce their willingness to become involved in psychological research (Griffith & Baker, 1993).

Despite the number of reasons given for noninclusive research, strategies to overcome these difficulties have also been detailed in the literature. For example, techniques that have been used to successfully recruit participants of Hispanic origin for psychological research include incorporating social networking strategies, using face-to-face recruitment, forming professional relationships with community agencies and offering free training to agency personnel, advertising in both English and Spanish, providing transportation and child care, and placing reminder phone calls (e.g., Hooks, Tsong, Henske, Baranowski, & Levin, 1986). Furthermore, retention can be enhanced through culturally sensitive treatment and by incorporating family members, assessing level of acculturation, and using bilingual staff (Mezzich, Ruiz, & Munoz, 1999; Miranda, Azocar, Organista, Munoz, & Lieberman, 1996).

RECENT MULTICULTURAL EMPHASES

The recommendations for inclusive recruitment strategies we have just listed are part of the larger context of the contemporary emphasis on multiculturalism. For example, APA's training standards have been revised to include provisions for integrating multicultural themes into the curricula of psychology training programs (e.g., Yutrzenka, 1995). Similarly, revisions of ethical codes of APA (1992), the National Association of School Psychologists (NASP, 1997), and the American Counseling Association (ACA, 1995) address multicultural issues for researchers and practitioners.

Concerns over the issue of adequate sample representation have also led to changes in the policies of research-funding institutions. For example, the National Institutes of Health (NIH) have mandated that women and minority group members be included in all NIH-supported research (NIH, 1994). Neither the cost of including diverse populations nor the geographic area of the investigator can be used to rationalize inadequate representation. Such changes are being adopted throughout the field to correct the underrepresentation of minorities in clinical research and to aid the scientific community in producing generalizable research (Miranda, 1996).

A NEEDED SELF-EXAMINATION: SCRUTINIZING PSYCHOLOGY

Although the field of psychology is certainly "talking the talk" about multiculturalism, is it also "walking the walk"? It is hoped that the recent discourse on multiculturalism in the literature of psychology has initiated action. To determine whether efforts have been made to adequately represent people of color in empirical research samples, this study examines a sample of literature produced over a recent 5-year period. We then compare data from a recent census of the United States with the percentages of people of color included in the research samples. On the basis of the research cited previously in this article, we hypothesized that the overall percentage of people of color among research participants would be less than the percentage represented in census population estimates and that this underrepresentation would be found for all ethnic minority groups.

METHOD

We chose journals from 1993 to 1997 to represent the applied subdisciplines of clinical, counseling, and school psychology on the basis of their classification in the most recent edition of APA's *Journals in Psychology* (APA, 1997). Journals were not included in this study if they did not focus on service provision, if they had an explicitly international focus, if they represented specific subspecialties, if they were explicitly theoretical, or if they specifically focused on people of color. Table 10.1 lists the resulting 14 journals selected by subdiscipline.

TABLE 10.1
Reporting Rates of Psychology Journals Reviewed

Journal	%
Clinical psychology	
Journal of Abnormal Psychology	60.0
Journal of Clinical Child Psychology	78.6
Journal of Clinical Psychology	59.8
Journal of Consulting and Clinical Psychology	69.4
Professional Psychology: Research and Practice	37.0
Counseling psychology	
Counseling Psychologist	65.0
Counselor Education and Supervision	54.0
Journal of Counseling and Development	56.8
Journal of Counseling Psychology	82.1
School psychology	
Journal of Instructional Psychology	33.3
Journal of School Psychology	59.8
Psychology in the Schools	61.9
School Psychology Review	57.6
The School Counselor	37.0

Note: % = percentage of research articles reporting participant ethnicity.

Within the selected journals, we reviewed each empirical article with human participants. Theoretical articles, program descriptions, book reviews, rebuttals, editorial statements, literature reviews, meta-analyses, film reviews, commemorative award speeches, tributes, and brief reports of 2 pages or less were not considered in the analyses.

For each article, we recorded the ethnic composition of the research sample reported by the authors. Researchers used various descriptions of the ethnicity of their sample, with most being compatible with the categories of the U. S. Bureau of the Census (1996). However, some authors used a nondescriptive "other," and some studies involved participants from outside the United States. Thus, eight categories of participants were coded in this study: African American, Hispanic American, Asian American or Pacific Islander, Native American, European American, international, other, and not reported. Studies in which content focused on a specific ethnic group were also noted following examination of the abstract and the *Method* section of the article.

RESULTS

After the data were coded, a reliability check of the articles was performed by an independent, trained coder. The number of agreements divided by the number of agreements and disagreements yielded a reliability estimate

TABLE 10.2
Percentages of Ethnic Groups in Psychology
Research Samples Compared With U.S. Census Data

Ethnic group	Research samples (%)	U.S. Census (%)
People of color	25.9	26.3
African American	16.4	12.0
Hispanic origin	5.7	10.3
Asian American or Pacific Islander	2.8	3.3
American Indian	1.1	0.7
European American (White)	74.1	73.6

Note: Percentages for research sample composition are those with "other" and "international" participants eliminated from analyses. Census data are from the the U.S. Bureau of Census (1996).

of 99.7%. Of the 2,536 empirical articles coded, 1,552 (61.2%) reported the ethnicity of their participant pools. The average reporting rates differed substantially between the individual journals, ranging from 82% to 33% (see Table 10.1).

Across all articles, 54.4% of the research participants were European American, 12.3% were African American, 4.4% were Hispanic American, 2.1% were Asian American, 0.8% were Native American, 22.5% were international, and 3.4% were other. To facilitate accurate comparison with U.S. census data, we subsequently removed the other and international categories from the analyses (Table 10.2). When the resulting percentages from all studies were compared with those of the 1996 U.S. census data, significant differences were found, $\chi^2(N = 1,180) = 46.91, p < .001$. Specifically, the research samples typically overrepresented African Americans ($z = 4.68$, $p < .001$) but underrepresented Hispanic Americans ($z = 5.21, p < .001$) in comparison with their representation in the general population.

We also examined the content of the research studies to see how many of the studies focused specifically on issues pertinent to people of color. Overall, 7.2% of the articles focused on a specific racial or ethnic group, with 5.2% focused solely on one group of interest, and 2.0% comparing that group with a Caucasian sample.

DISCUSSION

In light of recent concerns about the external validity of psychotherapy research (e.g., D. W. Sue & Sue, 1999; S. Sue, 1999), the purpose of this study is to investigate the current state of participation of people of color in psychological research. Although previous critiques have focused on content relevant to specific ethnic groups (Alvidrez et al., 1996) or on the report rates of demographic variables (Beutler et al., 1996), this article is the first to examine a broad range of applied research to determine ethnic-specific content, reporting rates, and representation of ethnic groups compared with population estimates.

Contrary to expectations (Graham, 1992), African American participants were actually overrepresented in comparison with population estimates. This finding seems to indicate that some researchers emphasize recruitment among this group. Research samples also included Asian Americans and Native Americans in proportions similar to population estimates. However, research samples underrepresented Hispanic Americans by about 44% in comparison with population estimates.

Although these data do not identify causative factors, the related estimate that about 39% of the people of Hispanic origin living in the United States are not fluent in English (U.S. Bureau of the Census, 1996) may indicate that researchers fail to use the Spanish language in their recruitment procedures. The field of psychology seems to be talking the talk about multiculturalism, but apparently in English only. Because Hispanic Americans constitute the fastest growing ethnic group in the nation (U.S. Bureau of the Census, 1996) and because monolingual Spanish speakers may have greater needs for clinical services than English speakers do (Schur & Albers, 1996), the results of this study should serve as a wake-up call (or *llamada urgente*) to the field. Recommendations for adaptations of mental health care (e.g., Mezzich et al., 1999) and for successful research recruitment and retention (Hooks et al., 1986) should be seriously considered.

Because we recognize the need for enhanced external validity in psychological research (S. Sue, 1999), it is encouraging to note that 7.2% of the studies had content specific to an ethnic group. This estimate is notably higher than the proportions found in previous studies, which have ranged between 1% and 5% (Graham, 1992; Iwamasa & Smith, 1996). Support for increasing the quantity of such emic research comes from Triandis (1996), who has argued that work with specific groups is the key to a universal psychology, wherein cultural variants to theory are identified and cultural biases are appropriately minimized.

It should be recognized, however, that the results of this study are subject to a major limitation. Similar to the findings of Beutler et al. (1996), we found that nearly 40% of the studies we reviewed failed to report the ethnicity of the participants. Hence, the results of this study suffer from problems related to external validity (we note the irony of this). It is possible that ethnicity was not reported in many studies because the samples were predominantly or exclusively Caucasian. However, because so many data are missing, this interpretation is speculative.

Given the wide variability across the journals in the reporting of ethnic information (see Table 10.1), efforts to enhance external validity are perhaps best made at the level of manuscript review. Although it is encouraging that the editors of APA journals have begun to address this issue (Azar, 1999), the discourse must initiate widespread change in editorial practice. In this regard, Beutler et al.'s (1996) recommendations remain the standard to which the field should adhere: If we are to substantially increase our knowledge about "what works with whom," ethnicity should consistently be treated like any other construct in the social sciences. To report detailed information regarding ethnicity is therefore only the bare minimum standard. Strength of ethnic identification and variables that have been found to mediate the effects of ethnicity, such as individualism–collectivism (Triandis, 1996), can be analyzed in relation to the results of a study. The burden of proof of external validity therefore shifts from those conducting ethnic minority research to all professionals publishing their work (S. Sue, 1999). Such burden is not a politically correct subjugation of scientific practice to the tenets of multiculturalism; it is simply "walking the talk" of good science.

REFERENCES

Alvidrez, J., Azocar, F., & Miranda, J. (1996). Demystifying the concept of ethnicity for psychotherapy researchers. *Journal of Consulting and Clinical Psychology, 64,* 903–908.

American Counseling Association. (1995). ACA *code of ethics and standards of practice.* Baltimore, MD: Author.

American Psychological Association. (1992). Ethical principles of psychologists and code of conduct. *American Psychologist, 47,* 1597–1611.

American Psychological Association. (1997). *Journals in psychology: A resource listing for authors.* Washington, DC: Author.

Azar, B. (1999, February). Journal editors find consortium helps researchers shape goals. *APA Monitor,* p. 20.

Babbie, E. (1998). *The practice of social research* (8th ed.). Boston: Wadsworth.

Beutler, L. E. (1996). The view from the rear: An editorial. *Journal of Consulting and Clinical Psychology, 64,* 845–847.

Beutler, L. E., Brown, M. T., Crothers, L., Booker, K., & Seabrook, M. K. (1996). The dilemma of factitious demographic distinctions in psychological research. *Journal of Consulting and Clinical Psychology, 64,* 892–902.

Graham, S. (1992). "Most of the subjects were White and middle class": Trends in published research on African Americans in selected APA journals, 1970–1989. *American Psychologist, 47,* 629–639.

Griffith, E. H., & Baker, F. M. (1993). Psychiatric care of African Americans. In A. C. Gaw (Ed.), *Culture, ethnicity and mental illness* (pp. 147–173). Washington, DC: American Psychiatric Press.

Hooks, P. C., Tsong, Y., Henske, J. C., Baranowski, T., Levin, J. S. (1986). Social networking as a recruitment strategy for Mexican American families in community health research. *Hispanic Journal of Behavioral Sciences, 8,* 345–355.

Hough, R. L., Landsverk, J. A., Karno, M., Burnam, M. A., Timbers, D. M., Escobar, J. I., et al. (1987). Utilization of health and mental health services by Los Angeles Mexican Americans and non-Hispanic Whites. *Archives of General Psychiatry, 44,* 702–709.

Iwamasa, G. Y., & Smith, S. K. (1996). Ethnic diversity in behavioral psychology: A review of the literature. *Behavior Modification, 20,* 45–59.

Maultsby, M. C. (1982). A historical view of Blacks' distrust of psychiatry. In S. M. Turner & R. T. Jones (Eds.), *Behavior modification in Black populations: Psychosocial issues and empirical findings.* New York: Plenum.

Mezzich, J. E., Ruiz, P., & Munoz, R. A. (1999). Mental health care for Hispanic Americans: A current perspective. *Cultural Diversity and Ethnic Minority Psychology, 5,* 91–102.

Miranda, J. (1996). Introduction to the special section on recruiting and retaining minorities in psychotherapy research. *Journal of Consulting and Clinical Psychology, 64,* 848–850.

Miranda, J., Azocar, F., Organista, K. C., Munoz, R. F., & Lieberman, A. (1996). Recruiting and retaining low-income Latinos in psychotherapy research. *Journal of Consulting and Clinical Psychology, 64,* 868–874.

National Association of School Psychologists. (1997). *Principles for professional ethics.* Bethesda, MD: NASP Publications.

National Institutes of Health. (1994). *NIH guidelines on the inclusion of women and minorities as subjects in clinical research.* 59, Fed. Reg. 14, 508 (Document No. 94–5435, National Archives and Records Administration, Washington, DC).

Santos de Barona, M. (1993). The availability of ethnic materials in psychology journals: A review of 20 years of journal publication. *Contemporary Educational Psychology, 18,* 391–400.

Schur, C. L., & Albers, L. A. (1996). Language, sociodemographics, and health care use of Hispanic adults. *Journal of Health Care for the Poor and Underserved, 7,* 140–158.

Snowden, L. R., & Cheung, F. K. (1990). Use of inpatient mental health services by members of ethnic minority groups. *American Psychologist, 45,* 347–355.

Sue, D. W., & Sue, D. (1999). *Counseling the culturally different: Theory and practice* (3rd ed.). New York: Wiley.

Sue, S. (1999). Science, ethnicity, and bias: Where have we gone wrong? *American Psychologist, 54,* 1070–1077.

Triandis, H. C. (1996). The psychological measurement of cultural syndromes. *American Psychologist, 51,* 407–415.

U.S. Bureau of the Census. (1996). *Statistical abstracts of the United States* (116th ed.). Washington, DC: U.S. Government Printing Office.

Wells, K. B., Hough, R. L., Golding, J. M., Burnam, M. A., & Karno, M. (1987). Which Mexican Americans underutilize health services? *American Journal of Psychiatry, 144,* 918–922.

Williams, D. H. (1986). The epidemiology of mental illness in Afro-Americans. *Hospital and Community Psychiatry, 37,* 42–49.

Yutrzenka, B. A. (1995). Making a case for training in ethnic and cultural diversity in increasing treatment efficacy. *Journal of Consulting and Clinical Psychology, 63,* 197–206.

IV

ASSESSMENT

A critical distinction is between constructs we wish to assess and the measures we use to assess them. The *constructs* refer to the characteristics we are interested in studying such as attachment, extraversion, aggression, withdrawal, and depression. The *measures* are the ways of operationalizing these constructs. As we design and conduct an investigation, we are usually interested in constructs rather than in the measures. The exception, of course, is where we are focusing specifically on a particular measure we are evaluating or developing.

As a more concrete way of noting this distinction, if we were writing a proposal or article, the "Introduction" to the study is where we focus on concepts, how they relate to each other, causes, mechanisms, and so on. When we move into the "Method" section, we describe the specific ways of measuring those concepts. We retain the focus on the measures as we analyze the data and report them in the "Results." Finally, in the "Discussion" section, we usually move back to the level of the construct. That is, we are drawing inferences about relations among constructs that the measures were useful in helping us assess.

To assess the constructs of interest and the hypothesized relations in the study, usually one can select from many measures, including those available and those that could be developed. For example, to assess anxiety of adults there are all sorts of self-report scales, other report scales, clinical ratings, direct observational measures, and psychophysiological measures. Not all of the measures that reflect the construct would be expected to show the effects we predict. We already know that multiple measures of the "same" construct (e.g., multiple measures of psychopathology or of therapeutic change) are not perfectly correlated, in part because of imperfect reliability of the individual measures but also because different measures often assess different facets of a construct.

A recommendation that is useful to follow whenever possible is to use multiple measures of a given construct in any study. That is, if one is interested in depression or happiness as a construct in the study, it is advantageous to assess that construct in more than one way. Ideally, the measures would use different methods of assessment (e.g., self-report, direct observations, psychophysiological responses). We want more than one index of the construct, in part to ensure that our conclusions are not restricted to one measure and method of assessing the construct.

The recommendation can be expanded to a broader statement. As a guideline for research, it is useful to include in a study few constructs and multiple measures of a given construct rather than multiple constructs and only one measure per construct. Of course, exceptions exist. Sometimes in once-in-a-lifetime longitudinal studies, an extensive assessment battery and many constructs are included. The rationale may in part be practical, leaving aside the specific research questions. That is, the study is not easy to do, and one wants to maximize the information one can obtain. Even so, if some constructs are a high priority or key to the main goals of the study, one would want to represent them with more than one psychological measure.

Selecting measures for research is a critical step. How ought one select measures, and what are the criteria for using a measure? Often researchers select a measure for their research because it has been used previously. Wading through the literature to see if the measure has been used before is important, but this is not the main, major, or most informed criterion for deciding whether to include the measure in one's own study. It is important to understand psychological measures, how they are developed, and criteria for their use and selection. These topics are addressed by the chapters in this part.

DEVELOPING MEASURES

It is important to be aware of how scales are developed and the criteria that can and ought to be used to determine whether the measure actually addresses the construct we wish to investigate. All else being equal, we wish to select a measure that has gone through careful development, but what does that mean? Careful development is not a matter of using the measure and computing a few correlations that are consistent with what one might predict.

Chapter 11 by Lee Anna Clark and David Watson discusses scale development and relates this explicitly to construct validity and the role of theory. Key topics include conceptualization of the construct and its boundary conditions, item development, selection of the response format or scaling method, pilot testing, and criteria to select the final items based on the initial data. The chapter conveys the importance of the investigator's conceptualization of the measure in the decision-making process of item selection and scale validation. Perhaps as valuable is the notion that even when the investigator may not have an explicit model of the scale and the relation of the scale to the construct, the data analyses used (e.g., solution used in factor analysis) to evaluate the measure may embrace a particular model. The model, whether or not explicit, can influence interpretation of the results. The chapter nicely integrates scale development, theory, and data analyses.

RELIABILITY, VALIDITY, AND UTILITY

The *psychometric properties* of an instrument refer to those indices of the quality, consistency, and meaning of the measure. Key concepts are reliability and validity of the measure. *Reliability* generally refers to consistency of the measure. This encompasses consistency within the measure (i.e., how the items relate to each other), consistency between different parts or alternate forms of the same measure, and consistency of participant performance on the measure over time (test–retest reliability for a given group of participants). *Validity* refers to the content and whether the measure assesses the domain of interest. We could easily call the measure the Lipshitz (name of scale developer) Anger Scale, but what evidence is there that this is measuring anger? Perhaps the scale is really getting at obnoxiousness or being mildly miffed but not really anger. Validity pertains to the accumulation of evidence that the scale measures what it purports to. Validity research encompasses the relation of performance on the measure to performance on other measures at the same time or in the future and to other criteria (e.g., real-world expressions of anger, anger level of the individual as rated by others, direct observations of how the person responds when provoked in role-play interactions).

Any single definition of reliability and validity is hazardous because each is a broad concept with several subtypes and meanings. Thus, when someone asks, "What is the reliability of the scale?" it is safe to assume the person does understand reliability. There is no *the* reliability of the scale. There are multiple reliabilities and validities. It is important to know what these are, their meaning, and their relevance to the study one is considering.

In chapter 12, Stephen N. Haynes discusses analogue behavioral observations, a type of assessment in which the investigator samples overt behavior to assess a construct of interest. The behavior is studied in the context of a laboratory setting (e.g., via role-play or contrived activities) rather than through direct observations in the home or everyday life. Analogue assessments are important in their own right as an assessment modality. The chapter is included here for its additional strengths; it discusses dimensions that are useful to evaluate any type of psychological measure. Table 12.1 provides a superb summary of the types of reliability and validity that are pertinent for evaluation of virtually all psychological measures. There are few places where a list of key concepts is so well presented and explained. (I have asked all my students to carry a photocopy of this table with them at all times and whenever they are contemplating use of a measure in their research to ask themselves what of the information in the table is known about the measure.) The chapter includes many examples of useful measures as well.

In chapter 13 by Gregory J. Meyer and his colleagues, psychological assessment is discussed more broadly. What are the purposes of assessment, and how do psychological measures fare in what they accomplish. The chapter raises key issues related to the evaluation and utility of various measures. It includes many tables that convey the strength of relations (correlations) of various sorts of measures, whether or not they are psychological measures. The tables do not have to be read in detail to grasp the important points. An overriding issue of the tables and discussion is the magnitude of the relation between variables (e.g., treatment and outcome). As researchers, we learn about correlations between variables and often expect medium-to-high product–moment correlations (e.g., $r > .5$). This chapter conveys that important relations may be evident at much lower levels and places psychological measures in a broader context to illustrate the points. Other assessment issues are also addressed, including the relation of psychological tests and clinical interviews and agreement or correspondence of different methods. Although I indicate that readers might speed up the reading of this chapter by reading the tables very lightly, I hasten to add I was not able to do that on my reading and rereading. There are many intriguing empirical relations that the tables elaborate, and the information can generate ideas for further research.

MEASUREMENT AMONG DIFFERENT SAMPLES

When we discuss measures, we often refer to them as if they had unvarying properties and that the properties inhere in the measure itself. This is evident when one asks, what is the test–retest reliability or internal consistency of this or that measure? Actually, the evidence in behalf of a measure is dependent on conditions of administration, that is, all those facets with which the validation evidence has been associated. These conditions may include characteristics of the participants (e.g., age, ethnic group, culture, context such as college class or field setting) and others.

Measures are often extended beyond the conditions in which they were originally developed. One of the common extensions is use of a measure with new populations, including people of different ages, socioeconomic status, and culture. Such extensions are not inherently problematic. Indeed, in principle one could argue that any sample could be conceived as drawing from a "new" population, because some characteristics of the new sample are not the same as the original validation sample. For example, one could say, even though the measure was validated with young adults, it was not used with *these* young adults in my study or in *this* part of the country. These young adults were born later than those of the original sample and might, by growing up at a different time, behave differently. This concern may or may not be trivial, depending on the focus of the measure (e.g., on views of sex roles, politics, substances such as alcohol or marijuana, which may change over time).

Whether the application of the measure to a different sample or new contexts warrants supplementary validity information to aid in interpreting the findings is somewhat of a judgment call. Obviously, if a new use of the scale departs markedly from the circumstances in which the test was validated, then the case becomes clearer. For example, a measure of social and emotional problems might be well validated with adults (e.g., > 20 years old). Use of the measure with high school students (ages 16–8 years) might well be questionable and warrant validation evidence within the study that reports this. Use of the measure with even younger youths (e.g., ages 12–16 years) is likely to be challenged without stronger evidence that the scale still applies to this group and behaves the same way. As a general guideline, if the existing validation evidence does not include sampling data from the pertinent population, then use of the measure ought to include information (some data) to support the meaning and interpretation of the measure in this new application. One need not begin a long list of reliability and validity studies with each new application. Yet, data are needed to suggest that a measure behaves in the way we expect and can be interpreted to reflect the construct of interest.

Chapter 14 by Sumie Okazaki and Stanley Sue discusses assessment issues that emerge in extending measures to diverse ethnic groups. The chapter examines methodological issues, beyond assessment considerations, including what comparisons ought to be made to draw influences about ethnicity, what variables might be controlled, and what defines a population or subpopulation, that is, at what level of generality ought a particular group be studied (e.g., is it meaningful to study Asian Americans or American Indians as a group, given the many subdivisions and different cultures that can be distinguished within each group?). Apart from these critical issues, broader conceptual and methodological issues are raised about sampling, the importance of cross-validation of measures among samples, and the use of college students versus community samples. The equivalence of measures across samples is also raised and reflects the extent to which the underlying construct holds the same meaning among different samples and whether the measure reveals similar psychometric properties (e.g., reliability and validity) for these populations. These issues foster greater care in conceptualizing use of measurement techniques and underscore the importance of including within a study evidence that the measure behaves in a way that is consistent with prior uses or supports the construct and conceptualization the investigator has in mind. Also, studying constructs among different populations, groups, or cultures represents an important line of work. One can theorize about population differences and in the process raise important substantive questions about culture, development, and values.

DEVELOPING MEASURES

11

CONSTRUCTING VALIDITY:
BASIC ISSUES IN OBJECTIVE
SCALE DEVELOPMENT

LEE ANNA CLARK AND DAVID WATSON

Scale development remains a growth industry within psychology. A PsycLIT database survey of articles published in the 6-year period from 1989 through 1994 revealed 1,726 articles with the key words "test construction" or "scale development" published in English-language journals, 270 in other-language journals, and 552 doctoral dissertations. During this same period (i.e., beginning with its inception), 50 articles addressing scale development or test construction were published in *Psychological Assessment* alone. The majority of these articles reported the development of one or more new measures (82%); most of the rest presented new scales derived from an existing instrument (10%). We use these 41 scale-development articles as a reference set for our discussion. Clearly, despite the criticism leveled at psychological testing in recent years, assessment retains a central role within the field.

Given that test construction remains a thriving activity, it is worthwhile

Reprinted from *Psychological Assessment, 7,* 309–319. Copyright 1995 by the American Psychological Association.

to reconsider the scale development process periodically to maintain and enhance the quality of this enterprise. The goal of this article is to articulate some basic principles that we believe anyone developing a scale should know and follow. Many of these principles have been stated before, but we repeat them here both because they are sufficiently important to bear repetition and because a review of the recent literature indicates that they are still not universally honored.

We focus on verbally mediated measures; thus, for example, we do not address the development of behavioral observation scales. Moreover, our primary focus is on self-report measures, because these constitute the majority (67%) of our reference sample. Nonetheless, most of the basic principles we articulate are applicable to interview-based measures and rating scales designed to be completed by clinicians, parents, teachers, spouses, peers, and so forth.

Before proceeding further, it is interesting to examine the new measures comprising our *Psychological Assessment* sample. This examination sample offers a glimpse at why scale development continues unabated, as well as the nature of the unmet needs these scale developers are seeking to fill. First, not surprisingly given this journal's focus, more than half (61%) of the scales assess some aspect of psychopathology, personality, or adjustment. The next most common categories are measures of attitudes and interpersonal relations (20% and 15%, respectively). The remaining scales assess a miscellany of behaviors, abilities, response validity, trauma experience, and so forth. In all categories, most new scales apparently tap relatively narrow constructs, such as suicidality, fear of intimacy, postpartum adjustment, drug-use expectancies, or parent–teenager relations, that have a focused range of utility. However, the extent to which the score variance of such scales is, in fact, attributable to the named target construct is an important issue that we will consider.

THE CENTRALITY OF PSYCHOLOGICAL MEASUREMENT

It has become axiomatic that (publishable) assessment instruments are supposed to be reliable and valid; indeed, every article in the *Psychological Assessment* set addresses these qualities. However, it appears that many test developers do not fully appreciate the complexity of these concepts. As this article is being prepared, the *Standards for Educational and Psychological Testing* (American Psychological Association, 1985) are undergoing intensive review and revision for the first time in a decade. Strong and conflicting pressures regarding the *Standards'* revision are being brought to bear on the Joint Committee on the Standards for Educational and Psychological Testing by diverse groups, and major changes in the *Standards* are expected. Whatever else it may do, however, the Joint Committee intends to emphasize the centrality of construct validity in testing even more than in previous versions, according to Cochair C. D. Spielberger (personal communication, February 15, 1995). And yet, widespread misunderstanding remains regarding precisely what construct validity is and what establishing construct validity entails.

Cronbach and Meehl (1955) argued that investigating the construct validity of a measure necessarily involves at least the following three steps: (a) articulating a set of theoretical concepts and their interrelations, (b) developing ways to measure the hypothetical constructs proposed by the theory, and (c) empirically testing the hypothesized relations among constructs and their observable manifestations. This means that without an articulated theory (which Cronbach and Meehl termed "the nomological net"), there is no construct validity. The Joint Committee's emphasis on the centrality of construct validity is therefore highly appropriate because the process of establishing construct validity represents a key element in differentiating psychology as a science from other, nonscientific approaches to the analysis of human behavior.

Construct validity cannot be inferred from a single set of observations, whether these pertain to a measure's factor structure, correlations with other measures, differentiation between selected groups, or hypothesized changes over time or in response to an experimental manipulation. Clearly, a series of investigations is required even to begin the process of identifying the psychological construct that underlies a measure. Nonetheless, Cronbach and Meehl's (1955) dictum that "One does not validate a test, but only a principle for making inferences" (p. 297) is often ignored, as scale developers speak lightly — sometimes in a single sentence — of establishing the construct validity of a scale. Even the more straightforward concept of reliability is widely mistreated, as we discuss in a later section.

It also should be noted that construct validity is important from the standpoint of practical utility as well as science. That is, for economic reasons, practitioners increasingly are being asked to justify the use of specific assessment procedures to third-party payers. Clear documentation of the precision and efficiency of psychological measures will be required in the near future. The most precise and efficient measures are those with established construct validity; they are manifestations of constructs in an articulated theory that is well supported by empirical data. Thus, construct validity lies at the heart of the clinical utility of assessment and should be respected by scale developers and users alike.

A THEORETICAL MODEL FOR SCALE DEVELOPMENT

Loevinger's (1957) monograph arguably remains the most complete exposition of theoretically based psychological test construction. Like any great work, however, her monograph requires exegesis, and in this article we assume this role. Specifically, we offer practical guidance for applying Loevinger's theoretical approach to the actual process of scale development. We limit ourselves to that portion of her article that details the "three components of construct validity," which she labels *substantive, structural,* and *external.* More specifically, because our topic is initial scale development, we focus primarily on the first two of these components, which together address a measure's "internal validity" (Loevinger, 1957, p. 654). Smith and McCarthy's (1995) article in this special issue addresses the external component more thoroughly.

SUBSTANTIVE VALIDITY: CONCEPTUALIZATION AND DEVELOPMENT OF AN INITIAL ITEM POOL

Conceptualization

Our PsycLIT database search suggests that human psychology is sufficiently complex that there is no limit to the number of psychological constructs that can be operationalized as scales. One now widely recognized reason for this is that psychological constructs are ordered hierarchically at different levels of abstraction or breadth (see Comrey, 1988; John, 1990; Watson, Clark, & Harkness, 1994). In the area of personality, for example, one can conceive of the narrow traits of talkativeness and physical expressiveness, the somewhat broader concepts of gregariousness and assertiveness, and the still more general disposition of extraversion. Scales can be developed to assess constructs at each of many levels of abstraction. Consequently, a key issue to be resolved in the initial developmental stage is the scope or generality of the target construct.

As mentioned, our *Psychological Assessment* sample consists primarily of scales that assess narrow-band (e.g., Cocaine Expectancy Questionnaire; Jaffe & Kilbey, 1994) or midlevel (Social Phobia and Anxiety Inventory; Turner, Beidel, Dancu, & Stanley, 1989) constructs. It is noteworthy, therefore, that Loevinger (1957) argued that, even when relatively narrow measurements are desired, those scales based on a "deeper knowledge of psychological theory" (p. 641) will be more helpful in making specific pragmatic decisions than those developed using a purely "answer-based" technology. Accordingly, even narrow-band measures should be embedded in a theoretical framework, and even measures of the same basic phenomenon will vary with the theoretical perspective of the developer.

A critical first step is to develop a precise and detailed conception of the target construct and its theoretical context. We have found that writing out a brief, formal description of the construct is very useful in crystallizing one's conceptual model. For example, in developing the Exhibitionism scale of the Schedule for Nonadaptive and Adaptive Personality (SNAP; Clark, 1993), the initial target construct was defined as a continuum ranging from normal adaptive functioning to potentially pathological behavior of which the high end was defined by overly dramatic, reactive, and intensely expressed behavior; an exaggerated expression of emotions; excessive attention-seeking behavior; an inordinate need for admiration; vanity; and a demanding interpersonal style.

This emphasis on theory is not meant to be intimidating. That is, we do not mean to imply that one must have a fully articulated set of interrelated theoretical concepts before embarking on scale development. Our point, rather, is that thinking about these theoretical issues prior to the actual process of scale construction increases the likelihood that the resulting scale will make a substantial contribution to the psychological literature.

Literature Review

To articulate the basic construct as clearly and thoroughly as possible, it is necessary to review the relevant literature to see how others have approached the same problem. Initially, the review should include previous attempts to conceptualize and assess both the same construct and closely related constructs. For instance, in developing a new measure of hopelessness, a thorough literature search would encompass measures of related constructs at various levels of the hierarchy in which the target construct is embedded—for example, depression and optimism–pessimism—in addition to existing measures of hopelessness.

Subsequently, the review should be broadened to encompass what may appear to be less immediately related constructs to articulate the conceptual boundaries of the target construct. That is, in the initial stages one investigates existing scales and concepts to which the target is expected to be related. Then, one also must examine entities from which the target is to be distinguished. In other words, a good theory articulates not only what a construct is, but also what it is not. Continuing with the hopelessness example, a thorough review would reveal that various measures of negative affect (depression, anxiety, hostility, guilt and shame, dissatisfaction, etc.) are strongly intercorrelated, so that it is important to articulate the hypothesized relation of hopelessness to other negative affects. Similarly, a good measure will have a predicted convergent and discriminant correlational pattern (Smith & McCarthy, 1995), and it is important to consider this aspect of measurement at the initial as well as later stages of development.

The importance of a comprehensive literature review cannot be overstated. First, such a review will serve to clarify the nature and range of the content of the target construct. Second, a literature review may help to identify problems with existing measures (e.g., unclear instructions or problematic response formats) that then can be avoided in one's own scale. Finally, and perhaps most importantly, a thorough review will indicate whether the proposed scale is actually needed. If reasonably good measures of the target construct already exist, why create another? Unless the prospective test developer can clearly articulate ways in which the proposed scale will represent either a theoretical or an empirical improvement over existing measures, it is preferable to avoid contributing to the needless proliferation of assessment instruments.

Creation of an Item Pool

Once the scope and range of the content domain have been tentatively identified, the actual task of item writing can begin. No existing data-analytic technique can remedy serious deficiencies in an item pool. Accordingly, the creation of the initial pool is a crucial stage in scale construction. The fundamental goal at this stage is to sample systematically all content that is potentially relevant to the target construct. Loevinger (1957) offered the classic articulation of this principle: *"The items of the pool should be chosen so as to sample all possible contents which might comprise the putative trait according to all known alternative theories of the trait"* (p. 659, emphasis in original).

Two key implications of this principle are that the initial pool (a) should be broader and more comprehensive than one's own theoretical view of the target construct and (b) should include content that ultimately will be shown to be tangential or even unrelated to the core construct. The logic underlying this principle is simple: Subsequent psychometric analyses can identify weak, unrelated items that should be dropped from the emerging scale but are powerless to detect content that should have been included but was not. Accordingly, in creating the item pool one always should err on the side of overinclusiveness. The importance of the initial literature review becomes quite obvious in this connection.

In addition to sampling a sufficient breadth of content, the scale developer must ensure that there is an adequate sample of items within each of the major content areas comprising the broadly conceptualized domain; failure to do so may mean that one or more of these areas will be underrepresented in the final scale. To ensure that each important aspect of the construct is assessed adequately, some test developers have recommended that formal subscales be created to assess each major content area. Hogan (1983), for instance, identified 10 content areas (e.g., anxiety, guilt, and somatic complaints) that make up the more general dimension of Adjustment versus Maladjustment and created 4- to 10-item "homogeneous item composites" to assess each of them. Similarly, Comrey (1988) has championed the use of "factored homogeneous item dimensions" to assess individual content areas within a specified domain.

The important point here is not that a particular procedure must be followed, but that scale developers need to ensure that each content area is well represented in the initial item pool. If only one or two items are written to cover a particular content area, then the chances of that content being represented in the final scale are much reduced. Loevinger (1957) recommended that the proportion of items devoted to each content area be proportional to the importance of that content in the target construct. This is a worthy goal, although in most cases the theoretically ideal proportions will be unknown. However, broader content areas should probably be represented by more items than narrower content areas.

Many of the procedures that we are discussing are traditionally described as the *theoretical–rational* or *deductive* method of scale development. We consider this approach to be an important initial step in a more extensive process rather than a scale development method to be used by itself. Similarly, Loevinger (1957) affirmed that content issues must always be considered in defining the domain, but emphasized that alone they are insufficient. That is, empirical validation of content (as distinguished from "blind empiricism") is important: "If theory is fully to profit from test construction . . . every item [on a scale] must be accounted for" (Loevinger, 1957, p. 657). This obviously is a very lofty goal and clearly is articulated as an ideal to be striven for rather than an absolute requirement (for a very similar view, see Comrey, 1988). For further discussion of content validity issues, see Haynes, Richard, and Kubany (1995) in this special issue.

In this context, we emphasize that good scale construction typically is an iterative process involving several periods of item writing, followed in each case by conceptual and psychometric analysis. These analyses serve to sharpen one's understanding of the nature and structure of the target domain as well as to identify deficiencies in the initial item pool. For instance, a factor analysis might establish that the items can be subdivided into several subscales but that the initial pool does not contain enough items to assess each of these content domains reliably. Accordingly, new items need to be written and again subjected to psychometric analyses. Alternatively, analyses may suggest that conceptualization of the target construct as, for example, a single bipolar dimension is countermanded by evidence that the two poles actually represent separate and distinct entities. In this case, revision of one's theoretical model may be in order.

An examination of the *Psychological Assessment* sample of scale development articles indicates that most test developers did start with a large item pool that was reduced to a smaller final set. However, it is not clear whether this finding reflects the broad and systematic domain sampling that we advocate or, alternatively, the mere elimination of items that were psychometrically weak for any number of reasons. That is, we saw little evidence of an iterative process through which the conceptualization of the target construct was itself affected by the process of scale development (see Smith & McCarthy, 1995, and Tellegen & Waller, in press, for discussions of this issue).

In addition to sampling well, it also is essential to write "good" items. When developing a scale it is worth the time to consult the available literature on item writing (e.g., Angleitner & Wiggins, 1985; Comrey, 1988; Kline, 1986). What constitutes a good item? First, the language should be simple, straightforward, and appropriate for the reading level of the scale's target population. For instance, scales intended for use in general clinical samples need to be readily understandable by respondents with only a modest education. In addition, one should avoid using trendy expressions that quickly may become dated, as well as colloquialisms and other language for which the familiarity (and thus utility) will vary widely with age, ethnicity, region, gender, and so forth. Finally, there is little point in writing items that virtually everyone (e.g., "Sometimes I am happier than at other times") or no one (e.g., "I am always furious") will endorse, unless they are intended to assess invalid responding. For this and other reasons we discuss later, items should be written to ensure variability in responding.

Item writers also should be careful to avoid complex or "double-barreled" items that actually assess more than one characteristic. At best, such items are ambiguous; at worst, they may leave respondents with no viable response alternative. Consider, for example, the true–false item, "I would never drink and drive for fear that I might be stopped by the police," which confounds the occurrence versus nonoccurrence of a behavior (drinking and driving) with a putative motive for that behavior (fear of legal complications). As such, it may leave respondents who avoid drinking and driving—but who do so for other reasons (e.g., because it is dangerous or morally wrong)—puzzled as to how they should respond. Of equal or greater concern is the fact that respondents will interpret complex items in different ways; accordingly, their responses will reflect the heterogeneity of their interpretations, and the item likely will show very poor psychometric properties as a result.

Furthermore, the exact phrasing of items can exert a profound influence on the construct that is actually measured. This is well illustrated by the example of the general personality trait of neuroticism (negative affectivity; Watson & Clark 1984). Over the years, it has been demonstrated repeatedly that attempts to assess a specific construct (such as hardiness or pessimism) have yielded instead yet another measure that is strongly saturated with this pervasive dimension. Indeed, items must be worded very carefully to avoid tapping into the broad individual differences in affect and cognition that characterize neuroticism. For instance, our own experience has shown that the inclusion of almost any negative mood term (e.g., "I worry about . . . ," or "I am upset [or bothered or troubled] by . . .") virtually guarantees that an item will have a substantial neuroticism component; the inclusion of several such affect-laden items, in turn, ensures that the resulting scale — regardless of its intended construct — will be primarily a marker of neuroticism.

Choice of Format

Finally, in creating the initial item pool, the test developer also must decide on the response format to be used. Clearly, the two dominant response formats in contemporary personality assessment are dichotomous responding (e.g., true–false and yes–no) and Likert-type rating scales with three or more options. Checklists, forced-choice, and visual analog measures also have been used over the years, but for various reasons have fallen out of favor. *Checklists* — scales that permit respondents to scan a list and check only the applicable items — proved to be problematic because they are more prone to response biases than formats that require a response to every item (Bentler, 1969; D. P. Green, Goldman, & Salovey, 1993). Most *forced-choice* formats, in which respondents must choose between alternatives that represent different constructs, are limited in that the resulting scores are ipsative; that is, they reflect only the relative intraindividual strength of the assessed constructs and do not provide normative, interindividual information. Finally, *visual analog* scales provide a free range of response options along a defined continuum, usually anchored at the two endpoints (e.g., *No pain at all* vs. *Excruciating pain; worst I can imagine*). This scale type is rarely used for multi-item scales because they are extremely laborious to score, although this may change with increased use of computer administration. Thus, they are most useful when a single (or few) measurements are desired and the target construct is either very simple (e.g., a single mood term) or represents a summary judgment (e.g., bodily pain).[1]

There are several considerations in choosing between dichotomous and Likert-type formats; furthermore, in the latter case, one also has to decide the number of response options to offer and how to label the response options. Comrey (1988) has criticized dichotomous response formats extensively, arguing that "multiple-choice item formats are more reliable, give more stable results, and produce better scales" (p. 758). Comrey's points are cogent and should be taken very seriously, especially his valid assertion that dichotomous items with extremely unbalanced response distributions (i.e., those in which virtually everyone answers either true or false) can lead to distorted correlational results. However, this problem can be avoided by carefully inspecting individual item frequencies during scale development and eliminating items with extreme response rates (one often-used cutoff is any item on which more than 95% of all respondents give the same response). Furthermore, dichotomous response formats offer an important advantage over rating scales:

---

[1] We are grateful to an anonymous reviewer for providing additional information regarding visual analog scales.

Other things being equal, respondents can answer many more items in the same amount of time. Consequently, if assessment time is limited, dichotomous formats can yield significantly more information. Moreover, Loevinger (1957) has argued that response biases are more problematic with Likert-type scales and that the assumption of equal-interval scaling often is not justified.

Likert-type scales are used with a number of different response formats: among the most popular are the frequency (*never* to *always*), degree or extent (*not at all* to *very much*), similarity (*like me* or *not like me*), and agreement (*strongly agree* to *strongly disagree*) formats. Obviously, the nature of the response option constrains item content in an important way (see Comrey, 1988). For example, the item "I often lose my temper" would be inappropriate if used with a frequency format. Note also that with an odd number of response options (typically, five or seven), the label for the middle option must be considered carefully; for example, *cannot say* confounds possible uncertainty about item meaning with a midrange rating of the attribute. An even number of response options (typically, four or six) eliminates this problem but forces respondents to "fall on one side of the fence or the other," which some may find objectionable. In a related vein, it must be emphasized also that providing more response alternatives (e.g., a 9-point rather than a 5-point scale) does not necessarily enhance reliability or validity. In fact, increasing the number of alternatives actually may reduce validity if respondents are unable to make the more subtle distinctions that are required. That is, having too many alternatives can introduce an element of random responding that renders scores less valid.

Finally, we emphasize that dichotomous and rating scale formats typically yield very similar results. For example, neuroticism scales using various formats (including true–false, yes–no, and rating scales) are all highly intercorrelated and clearly define a single common factor (Watson, Clark, & Harkness, 1994). In light of these considerations, we cannot conclude that one type of format is generally preferable to the other. Used intelligently, both formats can yield highly reliable and valid scales. To ensure such intelligent usage, we strongly recommend that a proposed format be pilot-tested on a moderately sized sample to obtain preliminary information about both respondent reactions and response option distributions.

STRUCTURAL VALIDITY: ITEM SELECTION
AND PSYCHOMETRIC EVALUATION

Test Construction Strategies

The choice of a primary test construction or item selection strategy is as important as the compilation of the initial item pool. In particular, the item selection strategy should be matched to the goal of scale development and to the theoretical conceptualization of the target construct. In this regard, Loevinger (1957) described three main conceptual models: (a) quantitative (dimensional) models that differentiate individuals with respect to degree or level of the target construct, (b) class models that seek to categorize individuals into qualitatively different groups, and (c) more complex dynamic models.

It is beyond the scope of this article to discuss either dynamic or class models; however, we note with concern that some of the articles in the *Psychological Assessment* sample applied methods more appropriate for quantitative models (e.g., factor analysis) to constructs that appeared to reflect class models (such as diagnoses). Of course, some theoreticians have argued that the empirical data do not strongly support class models even in the case of psychiatric diagnoses (e.g., Clark, Watson, & Reynolds, 1995) and, therefore, that dimensional or quantitative models are more appropriate. Thus, these aforementioned *Psychological Assessment* scale developers may have implicitly accepted this stance in selecting their test construction method. In any case, analytic methods appropriate for class model constructs do exist and should be used to develop measures of such constructs (e.g., Gangestad & Snyder, 1991; Meehl & Golden, 1982).

Loevinger (1957) advanced the concept of structural validity, that is, the extent to which a scale's internal structure (i.e., the interitem correlations) parallels the external structure of the target trait (i.e., correlations among nontest manifestations of the trait). She also emphasized that items should reflect the underlying (latent) trait variance. These three concerns parallel the three main item selection strategies in use for quantitative model constructs: empirical (primarily reflecting concern with nontest manifestations), internal consistency (concerned with the interitem structure), and item response theory (focused on the latent trait). The fact that structural validity encompasses all three concerns demonstrates that these methods may be used in conjunction with one another and that exclusive reliance on a single method is neither required nor necessarily desirable.

Criterion-Based Methods

Meehl's (1945) "empirical manifesto" ushered in the heyday of empirically keyed test construction. Backed by Meehl's cogent arguments that a test response could be considered verbal behavior in its own right—with nontest correlates to be discovered empirically—test developers embraced criterion keying as a method that permitted a wide range of practical problems to be addressed in an apparently straightforward manner. With widespread use, however, the limitations of this approach quickly became evident. From a technical viewpoint, major difficulties arose in cross-validating and generalizing instruments to new settings and different populations. More fundamentally, the relative inability of the method to advance psychological theory was a severe disappointment. With the advent of construct validity (Cronbach & Meehl, 1955), it became difficult to advocate exclusive reliance on pure "blind empiricism" in test construction. Yet, empirical approaches are still in use; in fact, 17% of the *Psychological Assessment* sample relied primarily on criterion groups for item selection.

Certainly, it is important not to throw the baby out with the bathwater. Correlations of a test with theoretically relevant criteria still constitute crucial evidence of validity, and there is no reason to avoid examining these correlations even in the early stages of scale development. One very strong approach would be to administer the initial item pool to a large heterogeneous sample (e.g., one encompassing both normal range and clinical levels of the target construct). Then, one basis (among several) for selecting items would be the power of the items to differentiate appropriately between subgroups in the sample (e.g., normal vs. clinical, or between individuals with different behavioral patterns or diagnoses within the clinical range).

Internal Consistency Methods

Currently, the single most widely used method for item selection in scale development is some form of internal consistency analysis. For example, 32% of the *Psychological Assessment* sample used factor analysis, and an additional 17% used another variant of the internal consistency method. These non–factor-analytic analyses typically used corrected item–total correlations to eliminate items that did not correlate strongly with the assessed construct. Appropriately, factor analytic methods were used most frequently when the target construct was conceptualized as multidimensional and, therefore, subscales were desired. Indeed, whenever factor analysis was used, the resulting instrument had subscales, although subscales sometimes were developed without benefit of factor analysis, usually through some combination of rational and internal consistency analyses. Because Floyd and Widaman's (1995) article in this special issue examines the role of factor analysis in scale development in detail, we focus here on only a few basic issues.

First, put simply, factor analytic results provide information, not answers or solutions. That is, factor analysis is a tool that can be used wisely or foolishly. Naturally, the better one understands the tool the more likely it is to be used wisely, so we strongly recommend that scale developers either educate themselves about the technique or consult with a psychometrician at each stage of the development process. The power of the technique is such that blind adherence to a few simple rules is not likely to result in a terrible scale, but neither is it likely to be optimal.

Second, there is no substitute for good theory and careful thought when using these techniques. To a considerable extent, internal consistency is always had at the expense of breadth, so simply retaining the 10 or 20 "top" items may not yield the scale that best represents the target construct. That is, the few items correlating most strongly with the assessed or (in the case of factor analysis) latent construct may be highly redundant with one another; consequently, including them all will increase internal consistency estimates but also will create an overly narrow scale that likely will not assess the construct optimally. We consider this "attenuation paradox" (Loevinger, 1954) in more detail later.

Similarly, if items that reflect the theoretical core of the construct do not correlate strongly with it in preliminary analyses, it is not wise simply to eliminate them without consideration of why they did not behave as expected. Other explanations (e.g., Is the theory inadequate? Is the item poorly worded? Is the sample nonrepresentative in some important way? Is the item's base rate too extreme? Are there too few items representing the core construct?) should be considered before such items are eliminated.

Item Response Theory (IRT)

Although IRT is by no means new, it has only recently begun to capture general attention. IRT is based on the assumption that test responses reflect an underlying trait (or set of traits, although most users assume that a single dominant trait can explain most of the response variance) and, moreover, that the relation between response and trait can be described for each test item by a monotonically increasing function called an *item characteristic curve* (ICC). Individuals with higher levels of the trait have higher expected probabilities for answering an item correctly (in the case of an ability) or in the keyed direction (for traits related to personality or psychopathology), and the ICC provides the precise value of these probabilities for each level of the trait.

Once the item parameters have been established (actually, estimated) by testing on a suitably large and heterogeneous group, IRT methods offer several advantages to scale developers. First, the methods provide a statistic indicating the precision with which an individual respondent's trait level is estimated. Thus, for example, the user can know whether the scale provides more precise estimates of the trait at the lower, middle, or upper end of the distribution. Second, trait-level estimates can be made independent of the particular set of items administered, thus providing greater flexibility and efficiency of assessment than is afforded by tests in which the ICCs are unknown. This property permits the development of computer-adaptive tests, in which assessment is focused primarily on those items for which maximum discriminative ability lies close to the respondent's trait level.

Standard intelligence tests make use of this IRT feature in a basic way. That is, older individuals are not administered the first, very easy items for each subtest unless they fail on the first few items tested. Rather, it is assumed that they would pass these items and they are given credit for them. Similarly, when examinees fail a sufficient number of items on a subtest, they are not administered the remaining, more difficult items under the assumption that they would fail them also. Scales developed using IRT simply apply these same features in a more comprehensive and precise manner. Interested readers are referred to Hambleton, Swaminathan, and Rogers (1991) for a relatively nontechnical presentation of IRT principles and applications and to King, King, Fairbank, Schlenger, and Surface (1993), Reise and Waller (1993), and Reise, Widaman, and Pugh (1993) for recent discussions.

Initial Data Collection

Inclusion of Comparison (Anchor) Scales

In the initial round of data collection, it is common practice to administer the preliminary item pool without any additional items or scales. This practice is regrettable, however, because it does not permit examination of the boundaries of the target construct; as we discussed earlier, exploring these boundaries is absolutely critical to understanding the construct from both theoretical and empirical viewpoints. Just as the literature was reviewed initially to discover existing scales and concepts to which the target is expected to be related and from which it must be differentiated, marker scales assessing these other constructs should be included in the initial data collection. Too often test developers discover late in the process that their new scale correlates .85 with an existing measure.

Sample Considerations

It can be very helpful to do some preliminary pilot-testing on moderately sized samples of convenience (e.g., 100–200 college students for testing item formats) before launching a major scale development project. However, it is likely that some basic item content decisions will be made after the first full round of data collection, decisions that will shape the future empirical and conceptual development of the scale. Therefore, after initial pilot-testing, it is very important to use a large and appropriately heterogeneous sample for the first major stage of scale development. On the basis of existing evidence regarding the stability and replicability of structural analyses (Guadagnoli & Velicer, 1988), we recommend that a minimum of 300 respondents be assessed at this stage. Moreover, if the scale is to be used in a clinical setting it is critical to obtain data on patient samples early on, rather than rely solely on college students until relatively late in the development process. One reason for obtaining data on patient samples early on is because the target construct may have rather different properties in different samples. If this fact is not discovered until late in the development process, the utility of the scale may be seriously compromised.

Psychometric Evaluation

Analysis of Item Distributions

Before conducting more complex structural analyses, scale developers should examine the response distributions of the individual items. In inspecting these distributions, two considerations are paramount. First, it is important to identify and eliminate items that have highly skewed and unbalanced distributions. In a true–false format, these are items that virtually everyone (e.g., 95% or more) either endorses or denies: with a Likert rating format, these are items to which almost all respondents respond similarly (e.g., "slightly agree"). Highly unbalanced items are undesirable for several reasons. First, when most respondents answer similarly, items convey little information. Second, owing to their limited variability, these items are likely to correlate weakly with other items in the pool and therefore will fare poorly in subsequent structural analyses. Third, as noted earlier, items with extremely unbalanced distributions can produce highly unstable correlational results. Comrey (1988), for instance, pointed out that if one individual answers false to two items, whereas the remaining 199 all answer true, the items will correlate 1.0 with one another. With a more normal distribution, a high correlation would indicate that the items are redundant and that one of them probably should be eliminated. However, in this case, if that one individual changed just one of those responses to true, the 1.0 correlation would disappear. Clearly, the normal decision-making rules cannot be applied in this situation.

However, before excluding an item on the basis of an unbalanced distribution, it is essential to examine data from diverse samples representing the entire range of the scale's target population. Most notably, many items will show very different response distributions across clinical and nonclinical samples. For instance, the item "I have things in my possession that I can't explain how I got" likely would be endorsed by very few undergraduates and, therefore, would show a markedly unbalanced distribution in a student sample. In an appropriate patient sample, however, this item may be useful in assessing clinically significant levels of dissociative pathology. Thus, it may be desirable to retain items that assess important construct-relevant information in one type of sample, even if they have extremely unbalanced distributions (and relatively poor psychometric properties) in others.

This brings us to the second consideration, namely, that it is desirable to retain items showing a broad range of distributions. In the case of true–false items, this means keeping items with widely varying endorsement percentages. The reason for this is that most constructs are conceived to be—and, in fact, are empirically shown to be—continuously distributed dimensions, and scores can occur anywhere along the entire dimension.

Consequently, it is important to retain items that discriminate at different points along the continuum. For example, in assessing the broad personality dimension of extraversion, it clearly would be undesirable to retain only those items that discriminated extreme introverts from everyone else; rather, one should include at least some items that differentiate extreme introverts from mild introverts, mild introverts from mild extraverts, and mild extraverts from extreme extraverts. Similarly, returning to an earlier example, the item "I have things in my possession that I can't explain how I got" may be useful precisely because it serves to define the extreme upper end of the dissociative continuum (i.e., those who suffer from dissociative identity disorder).

This is, in fact, one of the key advantages offered by IRT (King et al., 1993; Reise & Waller, 1993; Reise et al., 1993). As noted earlier, IRT yields parameter estimates that specify the point in a continuum at which a given item is maximally informative. These estimates, then, can be used as a basis for choosing an efficient set of items that yield precise assessment across the entire range of the continuum. Naturally, this almost invariably leads to the retention of items with widely varying distributions.

Unidimensionality, Internal Consistency, and Coefficient Alpha

The next crucial stage is to conduct structural analyses to determine which items are to be eliminated from or retained in the item pool. This stage is most critical when the test developer is seeking to create a theoretically based measure of a target construct, so that the goal is to measure one thing (i.e., the target construct)—and only this thing—as precisely as possible. This goal may seem relatively straightforward, but it is readily apparent from the recent literature that it remains poorly understood by test developers and users. The most obvious problem is the widespread misapprehension that the attainment of this goal can be established simply by demonstrating that a scale shows an acceptable level of internal consistency reliability, as estimated by an index such as coefficient alpha (Cronbach, 1951) or K-R 20 (Kuder & Richardson, 1937). A further complication is the fact that there are no longer any clear standards regarding what level of reliability is considered acceptable. For instance, although Nunnally (1978) recommended minimum standards of .80 and .90 for basic and applied research, respectively, it is not uncommon for contemporary researchers to characterize reliabilities in the .60s and .70s as good or adequate (e.g., Dekovic, Janssens, & Gerris, 1991; Holden, Fekken, & Cotton, 1991).

More fundamentally, psychometricians long have disavowed the practice of using reliability indices to establish the homogeneity of a scale (see Boyle, 1991; Cortina, 1993; S. B. Green, Lissitz, & Mulaik, 1977). To understand why this is so, it is necessary to distinguish between internal consistency on the one hand and homogeneity or unidimensionality on the other. *Internal consistency* refers to the overall degree to which the items that make up a scale are intercorrelated, whereas *homogeneity* and *unidimensionality* indicate whether the scale items assess a single underlying factor or construct (Briggs & Cheek, 1986; Cortina, 1993; S. B. Green et al., 1977). As such, internal consistency is a necessary but not sufficient condition for homogeneity or unidimensionality. In other words, a scale cannot be homogeneous unless all of its items are interrelated, but as we illustrate later, a scale can contain many interrelated items and still not be unidimensional. Because theory-driven assessment seeks to measure a single construct systematically, the test developer ultimately is pursuing the goal of homogeneity or unidimensionality rather than internal consistency per se.

Unfortunately, K-R 20 and coefficient alpha are measures of internal consistency rather than homogeneity and so are of limited utility in establishing the unidimensionality of a scale. Furthermore, they are ambiguous and imperfect indicators of internal consistency because they essentially are a function of two parameters: the number of test items and the average intercorrelation among the items (Cortina, 1993; Cronbach, 1951). That is, one can achieve a high internal consistency reliability estimate by having either many items or highly intercorrelated items (or some combination of the two). Whereas the degree of item intercorrelation is a straightforward indicator of internal consistency, the number of items is entirely irrelevant. In practical terms, this means that as the number of items becomes quite large, it is exceedingly difficult to avoid achieving a high reliability estimate. Cortina (1993), in fact, suggested that coefficient alpha is virtually useless as an index of internal consistency for scales containing 40 or more items.

Accordingly, the average interitem correlation (which is a straightforward measure of internal consistency) is a much more useful index than coefficient alpha per se (which is not). Thus, test developers should work toward a target mean interitem correlation rather than try to achieve a particular level of alpha. As a more specific guideline, we recommend that the average interitem correlation fall in the range of .15–.50 (see Briggs & Cheek, 1986). This rather wide range is suggested because the optimal value necessarily will vary with the generality versus specificity of the target construct. If one is measuring a broad higher order construct such as extraversion, a mean correlation as low as .15–.20 probably is desirable; by contrast, for a valid measure of a narrower construct such as talkativeness, a much higher mean intercorrelation (perhaps in the .40–.50 range) is needed.

As suggested earlier, however, the average interitem correlation alone cannot establish the unidimensionality of a scale; in fact, a multidimensional scale actually can have an acceptable level of internal consistency. Cortina (1993, Table 2), for instance, reported the example of an artificially constructed 18-item scale composed of two distinct 9-item groups. The items that made up each cluster were highly homogeneous and in each case had an average interitem correlation of .50. However, the two groups were made to be orthogonal, such that items in different clusters correlated zero with one another. Obviously, the scale was not unidimensional, but instead reflected two distinct dimensions; nevertheless, it had a coefficient alpha of .85 and a moderate mean interitem correlation of approximately .24.

This example clearly illustrates that one can achieve a seemingly satisfactory mean interitem correlation by averaging many high coefficients with many low ones. Thus, unidimensionality cannot be ensured simply by focusing on the mean interitem correlation; rather, it is necessary to examine the range and distribution of these correlations as well. Consequently, we must amend our earlier guideline to state that virtually all of the individual interitem correlations should fall somewhere in the range of .15 to .50. Put another way, to ensure unidimensionality, almost all of the interitem correlations should be moderate in magnitude and should cluster narrowly around the mean value. B. F. Green (1978) articulated this principle most eloquently, stating that the item intercorrelation matrix should appear as "a calm but insistent sea of small, highly similar correlations" (pp. 665–666).

The "Attenuation Paradox"

Some readers may be puzzled by our assertion that all of the interitem correlations should be moderate in magnitude. As we have seen, estimates of internal consistency will increase as the average interitem correlation increases; obviously, therefore, one can maximize internal consistency estimates by retaining items that are very highly correlated with others in the pool. It is not desirable, therefore, to retain highly intercorrelated items in the final scale?

No, it is not. This is the essence of the classic attenuation paradox in psychometric theory (see Boyle, 1991; Briggs & Cheek, 1986; Loevinger, 1954, 1957). Simply put, the paradox is that increasing the internal consistency of a test beyond a certain point will not enhance its construct validity and, in fact, may occur at the expense of validity. One reason for this is that strongly intercorrelated items are highly redundant: Once one of them is included in the scale, the other(s) contribute virtually no incremental information. For instance, it is well known that a test developer can achieve a highly reliable scale simply by writing several slightly reworded versions of the same basic item. Consider, for example, the three items "I often feel uncomfortable at parties," "Large social gatherings make me uneasy," and "I usually feel anxious at big social events." Because virtually everyone will respond to these variants in the same way (e.g., they either will endorse or deny them all), the items together will yield little more construct-relevant information than any one item individually. Accordingly, a scale will yield far more information—and, hence, be a more valid measure of a construct—if it contains more differentiated items that are only moderately intercorrelated.

Note, moreover, that maximizing internal consistency almost invariably produces a scale that is quite narrow in content; if the scale is narrower than the target construct, its validity is compromised. For instance, imagine two investigators each developing measures of general negative affect. The first chooses terms reflecting a wide array of negative mood states (scared, angry, guilty, sad, and scornful), whereas the second selects various indicators of fear and anxiety (scared, fearful, anxious, worried, and nervous). The latter scale will yield a higher reliability estimate, in that it consists of more semantically similar (and, therefore, more strongly intercorrelated) items; clearly, however, the former scale is a more valid measure of the broad construct of general negative affect.

In light of this paradox, it becomes clear that the goal of scale construction is to maximize validity rather than reliability. This is not to say that internal consistency estimates are useless or inappropriate. Indeed, coefficient alpha and other indices of internal consistency convey very important information regarding the proportion of error variance contained in the scale (see Cortina, 1993), and it is always desirable to demonstrate that a scale possesses an adequate level of reliability. Following the general guidelines of Nunnally (1978), we recommend that scale developers always strive for a coefficient alpha of at least .80; if a new scale or subscale falls below this mark, then revision should be undertaken to try to raise reliability to an acceptable level. This may involve writing additional items for a too-brief scale or eliminating weaker items from a longer one. Nevertheless, an overconcern with internal consistency per se can be counterproductive: Once this benchmark of .80 has been secured with an appropriate number of items (as low as 4 or 5 items for very narrow constructs up to about 35 items for broad dimensions), there is no need to strive for any substantial increases in reliability.

Structural Analyses in Scale Construction

Given that internal consistency estimates are untrustworthy guides, how can one achieve the desired goal of a unidimensional scale? How does one produce a "calm sea of highly similar correlations?" It is conceivable that this could be accomplished through a careful inspection of the item intercorrelation matrix, perhaps in conjunction with a standard reliability program (such as those contained in SAS and SPSS). However, as the pool of candidate items increases, this process becomes unwieldy. Note, for instance, that a pool of only 30 items generates 435 individual intercorrelations to be inspected and evaluated, and that a pool of 40 items produces nearly 800 item intercorrelations.

Consequently, psychometricians strongly recommend that the test developer begin by factor-analyzing the items (Briggs & Cheek, 1986; Comrey, 1988; Cortina, 1993; Floyd & Widaman, 1995). Unfortunately, many test developers are hesitant to use factor analysis, either because it requires a relatively large number of respondents or because it involves several perplexing decisions. Both these concerns are unwarranted. First, it is true that factor analysis requires a minimum of 200–300 respondents (Comrey, 1988; Guadagnoli & Velicer, 1988), but this ultimately is no more than is needed for any good correlational or reliability analysis. Second, although the factor analyst must make a number of tactical decisions (e.g., methods of factor extraction and rotation), these decisions typically have much less effect on the resulting factor structures than is commonly believed; in fact, factor structures have been shown to be highly robust across different methods of factor extraction and rotation (see Guadagnoli & Velicer, 1988; Snook & Gorsuch, 1989; Watson et al., 1994). Hence, there is no reason to avoid using factor techniques in the initial stages of item selection. Nevertheless, as we stated earlier, the more one knows about this technique, the greater the probability that it will be used wisely; therefore, it is important that test developers either learn about the technique or consult with a psychometrician during the scale development process.

A thorough discussion of factor analysis is beyond the scope of this article (see especially Floyd & Widaman, 1995), but we will offer a very brief sketch of how it can be used in item selection. For the sake of simplicity, we consider the case of constructing a single unidimensional measure. First, subject the items to either a principal factor analysis (strongly preferred by Comrey, 1988) or a principal components analysis (recommended by Cortina, 1993) and extract the first few factors (say, four or five); in this simplified case, there is no need to be concerned with rotation. Next, examine the loadings of items on the first unrotated factor or component, which can be viewed as a direct measure of the common construct defined by the item pool. Items that load weakly on this first factor (below .35 in a principal factor analysis or below .40 in a principal components analysis) tend to be modestly correlated with the others and are leading candidates for removal from the scale. Similarly, items that have stronger loadings on later factors also are likely candidates for deletion. Conversely, items that load relatively strongly on the first factor and relatively weakly on subsequent factors are excellent candidates for retention. Thus, factor analysis quickly enables one to generate testable hypotheses regarding which items are good indicators of the construct and which are not. These predictions then can be evaluated in subsequent correlational and reliability analyses, which also can be used to identify pairs of redundant, highly correlated items.

A well-designed factor analysis also can play a crucial role in enhancing the discriminant validity of a new measure. For instance, we noted earlier that many new scales are not clearly differentiable from the broad trait of neuroticism (negative affectivity), thereby lacking discriminant validity. The easiest way to avoid creating yet another neuroticism measure is to subject the items of the provisional scale—together with a roughly equal number of neuroticism items—to a joint factor analysis. In this instance, one would extract two factors and rotate them to "simple structure" (e.g., using varimax or promax). Ideally, the target scale items (but often only a subset thereof) will load strongly on one factor, whereas the neuroticism items will load highly on the other. If not, then the new scale apparently is indistinguishable from neuroticism and the situation is likely to be hopeless. If so, then items that load strongly on the provisional scale factor—but quite weakly on the neuroticism factor—are excellent candidates for retention; conversely, items with relatively high loadings on the neuroticism factor have poor discriminant validity and probably should be dropped. This procedure can be followed for any construct that needs to be differentiated from the target scale, as long as marker items assessing the construct have been included in the initial data collection. At this stage of development, confirmatory factor analytic techniques also can be used to evaluate interrelations among scale items and their discriminant validity in comparison with related measures (see Floyd & Widaman, 1995, for an expanded discussion of the role of confirmatory factor analytic techniques in scale construction).

Creating Subscales

We conclude this section with a brief consideration of subscales. In using the term *subscales*, we are referring to a situation in which a set of related measures are designed both to be assessed and analyzed separately and also to be combined into a single overall score. In other words, subscales are hypothesized to be specific manifestations of a more general construct. Defined in this way, subscales are a popular and important feature of test construction, as illustrated by the fact that approximately 70% of the *Psychological Assessment* sample included subscale development.

Creating valid subscales is an exceptionally tricky process, so much so that it is difficult to believe that it can be accomplished without some variant of factor analysis.[2] Indeed, the test constructor resembles the legendary hero Odysseus, who had to steer a narrow course between the twin terrors of Scylla and Charybdis. On the one hand, it makes no psychometric sense to combine unrelated items or subscales into a single overall score (although many scales developed by criterion keying do, in fact, show this property; see Carver, 1989). Accordingly, the scale developer must establish that all of the items—regardless of how they are placed in the various subscales—define a single general factor. If they do not, then the items need to be split off into separate, distinct scales. On the other hand, it also makes no psychometric sense to take a homogeneous pool of substantially intercorrelated items and arbitrarily divide it into separate subscales (e.g., on the basis of apparent differences in content). Accordingly, the scale developer must demonstrate

---

[2] We acknowledge that this statement reflects a modern prejudice. Loevinger, Gleser, and DuBois (1953) developed a technique for "maximizing the discriminating power of a multiple-score test" (p. 309) that achieves the same end. This technique also has the practical advantage of treating items as all-or-none units, thereby paralleling the way they typically are used in scoring scales; by contrast, factor analysis apportions the item variance among the extracted factors, which necessitates decisions regarding factor-loading cutoffs to retain or eliminate items.

that the intrasubscale item correlations (i.e., among the items that make up each subscale) are systematically higher than the intersubscale item correlations (i.e., between the items of different subscales). If this condition cannot be met, then the subscales should be abandoned in favor of a single overall score.

To illustrate the test developer's dilemma, consider the example of a test composed of two 10-item subscales. Let us further assume that the average intercorrelation of the items that make up Subscale A is .40, whereas that for Subscale B is .35. If, on the one hand, the average correlation between the A items and the B items is near zero — such that the two subscales also are essentially uncorrelated — then there is no justification for combining them into a single overall score; rather, they simply should be analyzed as two distinct constructs. On the other hand, if the average correlation between the A items and the B items is much above .30, there is no justification for dividing the items into two arbitrary subscales; instead, they simply should be summed into a single 20-item score. In this hypothetical case, the test developer's task is to have the mean correlation between the A items and B items be significantly greater than zero but substantially less than the average within-subscale values (say, .20). Without the assistance of a sophisticated structural technique such as factor analysis, this truly is a formidable task. Finally, we emphasize again that in making the decision of whether subscales are warranted, both theoretical and empirical considerations should be brought to bear, and data from diverse samples representing the entire range of the scale's target population should be considered.

EXTERNAL VALIDITY: THE ONGOING PROCESS

Just as graduation is properly called *commencement* to emphasize that it signals a beginning as well as an end, the process that we have described represents the initial rather than the final steps in scale development, refinement, and validation. However, the quality of the initial stages has clear ramifications for those stages that follow. For example, if the target concept is clearly conceptualized and delineated initially, then the resulting scale more likely will represent a novel contribution to the assessment armamentarium. If a widely relevant range of content is included in the original item pool, then the scale's range of clinical utility will be more clearly defined. Similarly, if the scale has been constructed with a focus on unidimensionality and not just internal consistency, then the scale will identify a more homogeneous clinical group, rather than a heterogeneous group requiring further demarcation. Finally, if issues of convergent and discriminant validity have been considered from the outset, then it will be far easier to delineate the construct boundaries precisely and to achieve the important goal of knowing exactly what the scale measures and what it does not.

Previously, Jackson (1970) has written extensively about the role of external validity in scale development. Moreover, in this issue, Smith and McCarthy (1995) describe the later refinement stages in some detail, so we conclude by noting simply that both the target of measurement and measurement of the target are important for optimal scale development. That is, later stages will proceed more smoothly if the earlier stages have been marked by both theoretical clarity (i.e., careful definition of the construct) and empirical precision (i.e., careful consideration of psychometric principles and procedures). Thus, we leave the aspiring scale developer well begun but far less than half done.

REFERENCES

American Psychological Association. (1985). *Standards for educational and psychological testing*. Washington, DC: Author.

Angleitner, A., & Wiggins, J. S. (1985). *Personality assessment via questionnaires*. New York: Springer-Verlag.

Bentler, P. M. (1969). Semantic space is (approximately) bipolar. *Journal of Psychology, 71*, 33–40.

Boyle, G. J. (1991). Does item homogeneity indicate internal consistency or item redundancy in psychometric scales? *Personality and Individual Differences, 3*, 291–294.

Briggs, S. R., & Cheek, J. M. (1986). The role of factor analysis in the development and evaluation of personality scales. *Journal of Personality, 54*, 106–148.

Carver, C. S. (1989). How should multifaceted personality constructs be tested? Issues illustrated by self-monitoring, attributional style, and hardiness. *Journal of Personality and Social Psychology, 56*, 577–585.

Clark, L. A. (1993). *Schedule for Nonadaptive and Adaptive Personality (SNAP)*. Minneapolis: University of Minnesota Press.

Clark, L. A., Watson, D., & Reynolds, S. (1995). Diagnosis and classification in psychopathology: Challenges to the current system and future directions. *Annual Review of Psychology, 46*, 121–153.

Comrey, A. L. (1988). Factor-analytic methods of scale development in personality and clinical psychology. *Journal of Consulting and Clinical Psychology, 56*, 754–761.

Cortina, J. M. (1993). What is coefficient alpha? An examination of theory and applications. *Journal of Applied Psychology, 78*, 98–104.

Cronbach, L. J. (1951). Coefficient alpha and the internal structure of tests. *Psychometrika, 16*, 297–334.

Cronbach, L. J., & Meehl, P. E. (1955). Construct validity in psychological test. *Psychological Bulletin, 52*, 281–302.

Dekovic, M., Janssens, J. M. A. M., & Gerris, J. R. M. (1991). Factor structure and construct validity of the Block Child Rearing Practices Report (CRPR). *Psychological Assessment, 3*, 182–187.

Floyd, F. J., & Widaman, K. F. (1995). Factor analysis in the development and refinement of clinical assessment instruments. *Psychological Assessment, 7*, 286–299.

Gangestad, S. W., & Snyder, M. (1991). Taxonomic analysis redux: Some statistical considerations for testing a latent class model. *Journal of Personality and Social Psychology, 61*, 141–161.

Green, B. F., Jr. (1978). In defense of measurement. *American Psychologist, 33*, 664–670.

Green, D. P., Goldman, S. L., & Salovey, P. (1993). Measurement error masks bipolarity in affect ratings. *Journal of Personality and Social Psychology, 64*, 1029–1041.

Green, S. B., Lissitz, R. W., & Mulaik, S. A. (1977). Limitations of coefficient alpha as an index of test unidimensionality. *Educational and Psychological Measurement, 37*, 827–838.

Guadagnoli, E., & Velicer, W. F. (1988). Relation of sample size to the stability of component patterns. *Psychological Bulletin, 103*, 265–275.

Hambleton, R. K., Swaminathan, H., & Rogers, H. J. (1991). *Fundamentals of item response theory*. Newbury Park, CA: Sage.

Haynes, S. N., Richard, D. C. S., & Kubany, E. S. (1995). Content validity in psychological assessment. A functional approach to concepts and methods. *Psychological Assessment, 7*, 238–247.

Hogan, R. T. (1983). A socioanalytic theory of personality. In M. Page (Ed.), *1982 Nebraska Symposium on Motivation* (pp. 55–89). Lincoln: University of Nebraska Press.

Holden, R. R., Fekken, G. C., & Cotton, D. H. G. (1991). Assessing psychopathology using structured test-item response latencies. *Psychological Assessment, 3*, 111–118.

Jackson, D. N. (1970). A sequential system for personality scale development. In C. D. Spielberger (Ed.), *Current topics in clinical and community psychology* (Vol. 2, pp. 61–96). New York: Academic Press.

Jaffe, A., & Kilbey, M. M. (1994). The Cocaine Expectancy Questionnaire (CEQ): Construction and predictive utility. *Psychological Assessment, 6*, 18–26.

John, O. P. (1990). The "Big Five" factor taxonomy: Dimensions of personality in the natural language and in questionnaires. In L. A. Pervin (Ed.), *Handbook of personality: Theory and research* (pp. 66–100). New York: Guilford Press.

King, D. W., King, L. A., Fairbank, J. A., Schlenger, W. E., & Surface, C. R. (1993). Enhancing the precision of the Mississippi Scale for Combat-Related Posttraumatic Stress Disorder: An application of item response theory. *Psychological Assessment, 5*, 457–471.

Kline, P. (1986). *A handbook of test construction: Introduction to psychometric design*. New York: Methuen.

Kuder, G. F., & Richardson, M. W. (1937). The theory of the estimation of test reliability. *Psychometrika, 2*, 151–160.

Loevinger, J. (1954). The attenuation paradox in test theory. *Psychological Bulletin, 51*, 493–504.

Loevinger, J. (1957). Objective tests as instruments of psychological theory. *Psychological Reports, 3*, 635–694.

Loevinger, J., Gleser, G. C., & DuBois, P. H. (1953). Maximizing the discriminating power of a multiple-score test. *Psychometrika, 18*, 309–317.

Meehl, P. E. (1945). The dynamics of structured personality tests. *Journal of Clinical Psychology, 1*, 296–303.

Meehl, P. E., & Golden, R. R. (1982). Taxometric methods. In P. C. Kendall & J. N. Butcher (Eds.), *Handbook of research methods in clinical psychology* (pp. 127–181). New York: Wiley.

Nunnally, J. C. (1978). *Psychometric theory* (2nd ed.). New York: McGraw-Hill.

Reise, S. P., & Waller, N. G. (1993). Traitedness and the assessment of response pattern scalability. *Journal of Personality and Social Psychology, 65*, 143–151.

Reise, S. P., Widaman, K. F., & Pugh, R. H. (1993). Confirmatory factor analysis and item response theory: Two approaches for exploring measurement invariance. *Psychological Bulletin, 114*, 552–566.

Smith, G. T., & McCarthy, D. M. (1995). Methodological considerations in the refinement of clinical assessment instruments. *Psychological Assessment, 7*, 300–308.

Snook, S. C., & Gorsuch, R. L. (1989). Component analysis versus common factor analysis: A Monte Carlo study. *Psychological Bulletin, 106*, 148–154.

Tellegen, A., & Waller, N. G. (in press). Exploring personality through test construction: Development of the Multidimensional Personality Questionnaire. In S. R. Briggs & J. M. Cheek (Eds.), *Personality measures: Development and evaluation* (Vol. 1). Greenwich, CT: JAI Press.

Turner, S., Beidel, D. C., Dancu, C. V., & Stanley, M. A. (1989). An empirically derived inventory to measure social fears and anxiety: The Social Phobia and Anxiety Inventory. *Psychological Assessment, 1*, 35–40.

Watson, D., & Clark, L. A. (1984). Negative affectivity: The disposition to experience aversive emotional states. *Psychological Bulletin, 96*, 465–490.

Watson, D., Clark, L. A., & Harkness, A. R. (1994). Structures of personality and their relevance to psychopathology. *Journal of Abnormal Psychology, 103*, 18–31.

RELIABILITY, VALIDITY, AND UTILITY

12

CLINICAL APPLICATIONS OF ANALOGUE BEHAVIORAL OBSERVATION: DIMENSIONS OF PSYCHOMETRIC EVALUATION

STEPHEN N. HAYNES

Analogue psychological assessment involves measurement in a contrived environment. The goal of this assessment strategy is to derive valid and cost-effective estimates of a client's behavior, thoughts and cognitive processes, emotions, and physiological functioning, and of interactions between the client and others, in the environment in which the client normally functions. Analogue psychological assessment is also used to help a clinician generate hypotheses about factors that maintain a client's behavior problems and factors that affect treatment outcome. Measures of behaviors and events derived in analogue assessment are presumed to be valid estimates of similar behaviors and events in the client's natural environment (Barkley, 1991). Most psychological assessment methods, such as questionnaires, interviews, and psychophysiological laboratory assessment, are analogue, in that

Reprinted from *Psychological Assessment, 13,* 73–85. Copyright 2001 by the American Psychological Association.

inferences about a client are derived in an environment different from the environment of primary interest.

This chapter and the Special Section in *Psychological Assessment* (2001, pp. 3–98) focus on a subset of applications of a particular type of analogue psychological assessment—clinical assessment applications of analogue behavioral observation. These articles address the use of analogue behavioral observation to aid clinicians' judgments about a client's behavior problems (e.g., their type, magnitude, frequency), to identify factors that affect the client's behavior problems, to formulate treatment strategies, and to evaluate treatment outcome.

There are several classes of analogue behavioral observation methods. These include role-plays, experimental functional analysis, enactment analogues, contrived situation tests, think-aloud procedures, family and marital interaction tasks, response generation tasks, and behavioral avoidance tests. Typologies of analogue behavioral observation methods have been discussed in Haynes (1978), Haynes and O'Brien (2000), McFall (1977), Nay (1986), Shapiro and Kratochwill (1988), and Torgrud and Holborn (1992). Within each class of analogue behavioral observation methods, there are many instruments, which often differ in their elements, such as instructions to participants, stimuli presented to participants and their method of presentation, the use and behavior of confederates, and the response modes measured and units of measurement.[1]

Analogue behavioral observation methods have several characteristics in common: (a) the measurement of a client's overt behavior (and sometimes the measurement of subjective, cognitive, and physiological events), (b) measurement in a contrived situation that is analogous to situations that the client is likely to encounter in his or her natural environment or measurement in situations that are likely to elicit client behaviors that help the clinician in forming judgments about the client (e.g., measurement of the client's response to potential future stressors), and (c) the use of contrived settings, instructions, and stimuli that increase the probability that clinically important behaviors and functional relations will occur.

In clinical assessment applications, the goal of analogue behavioral observation is to derive valid inferences about how the client will behave in a current or future natural environment. Many specific examples of analogue

---

[1] An *assessment method* is a class of procedures for deriving data on the behavior of a client or clients (e.g., behavioral observation in the natural environment and self-report questionnaires are "methods" of assessment). An *assessment instrument* is a specific procedure for deriving data on the behavior of a client or clients on a specific assessment occasion (e.g., a specific behavioral avoidance test; a specific self-report depression questionnaire). A *measure* refers to a number that represents the variable being measured (e.g., the observed rate of behavior or a blood pressure reading during a measurement session). *Measurement* is the process of assigning a numerical value to a variable dimension (e.g., rate, duration, magnitude), so that relations of the numbers reflect relations among the measured variables (Haynes & O'Brien, 2000; Sederer & Dickey, 1996).

behavioral observation instruments are provided in articles by Heyman (2001), Mori and Armendariz (2001), Norton and Hope (2001), and Roberts (2001; see also overview by Mash and Foster, 2001).

In this article, I discuss the *psychometry* of analogue behavioral observation: principles and methods of psychometry that guide the validation of analogue behavioral observation instruments, the evaluation of research on analogue behavioral observation, and clinical judgments from analogue behavioral observation. I discuss content and convergent validity, generalizability and ecological validity, cost-effectiveness, clinical utility, and incremental validity. Sources of variance in the measures and contingent clinical judgments, such as instructions to participants, the behavior of confederates, temporal aspects of the assessment process, and observers, are also presented. This article addresses principles of psychometry from classical test theory that are relevant to researchers who are developing analogue behavioral observation instruments and to clinicians who are using them in clinical assessment settings. Alternative approaches to psychometry, such as item response and generalizability theory, delineated in Anastasi and Urbina (1997) and Nunnally and Bernstein (1994), are not discussed.

I focus on principles, rather than results, of psychometric evaluation. Studies on the validity and clinical utility of specific analogue behavioral observation instruments are presented in other articles in the Special Section in *Psychological Assessment* (2001, pp. 3–98). Although analogue behavioral observation methods can be applied in the client's natural environment (e.g., Schill, Kratochwill, & Gardner, 1996), the focus of this article is on analogue behavioral observation of clients in clinic settings.

I emphasize several aspects of the psychometry of analogue behavioral observation:

1. Analogue behavioral observation instruments are often developed with insufficient attention to their psychometric properties and with insufficient adherence to well-established principles of assessment instrument development.
2. Content validity is particularly important in the evaluation of analogue behavioral observation instruments.
3. The importance of each dimension of psychometric evaluation varies across analogue behavioral observation assessment instruments and as a function of the type of judgments that are to be drawn.
4. The validity of measures and inferences from an analogue behavioral observation assessment instrument can erode over time as ideas about the targeted construct evolve.
5. Because they are often idiographic, analogue behavioral observation instruments may provide sensitive measures of immediate treatment effects.

6. Analogue behavioral observation assessment may be especially useful in detecting important functional relations associated with clients' behavior problems and in planning treatment strategies.
7. There are multiple sources of variance in analogue behavioral observation measures; these sources of variance can differ across instruments and applications.

PRINCIPLES OF VALIDATION APPLIED TO ANALOGUE BEHAVIORAL OBSERVATION

Modern psychometry evolved from efforts to measure presumably stable latent variables such as intelligence and personality traits (Anastasi & Urbina, 1997; Nunnally & Bernstein, 1994) in stable assessment environments. In these applications, psychometry addressed the degree to which an assessment instrument provided a precise measure of the targeted construct (i.e., construct validity), methods of constructing valid assessment instruments, and methods of estimating the sources and magnitude of measurement variance.

The application of psychometry to behavioral assessment methods introduces complexities: (a) The assessment stimuli presented to the client and the setting in which assessment occurs can change across assessment occasions; (b) measured behaviors can be unstable across time, situations, and assessment occasions; (c) measures are often considered to be direct samples of behavior rather than markers of higher order constructs; and (d) inferences from obtained data are often idiographically, rather than nomothetically, based. Because of these assumptions of the behavioral assessment paradigm, the applicability of psychometric principles has been a frequent topic of discussion (Cone, 1998; Foster & Cone, 1995; Haynes, Nelson, & Blaine, 1999; Haynes & O'Brien, 2000; Silva, 1993).

Table 12.1 presents an overview of psychometric principles and their application to analogue behavioral observation. The sections below emphasize selected components of this table: content validity, clinical utility, incremental validity, and cost-effectiveness and treatment utility. The conditional and unstable nature of validity and the implications of the idiographic nature of analogue behavioral observation are also considered. Although all principles and methods of psychometric evaluation are applicable to all behavioral observation methods, I focus on several that are particularly relevant to analogue behavioral observation. Dimensions such as interrater reliability, observer accuracy, and time and event sampling are covered in other sources (Cone, 1998; Haynes et al., 1999; Haynes & O'Brien, 2000; Silva, 1993; Suen & Ary, 1989).

One important dimension of psychometric evaluation is *content validity*—the degree to which elements of an assessment instrument are relevant

TABLE 12.1
The Application of Validity, Reliability, and Clinical
Utility Concepts to Analogue Observation Instruments

Evaluative Dimension	Definition	Examples of Application to Analogue Observation
Construct Validity	Comprises the evidence and rationales indicating the degree to which data from an assessment instrument measures the targeted construct; includes all evidence bearing on the measure and encompasses all types of validity	The degree to which measures of content validity, convergent validity, temporal stability, and discriminant validity of an analogue behavioral observation measure of social anxiety and skills tap the construct of social anxiety
Content Validity	The degree to which elements of an assessment instrument are relevant to and representative of the targeted construct, for a particular assessment purpose	The degree to which the instructions, scenarios and tasks, scenario duration and time samples, scenarios/situations sampled, measures obtained (e.g., behaviors coded, ratings) are representative and relevant to the assessment of a client with trauma, fear, or anxiety problems
Convergent Validity	The degree to which the data from the assessment instrument are coherently related to other measures of the same construct as well as to other variables that they are expected, on theoretical grounds, to be related to the construct	The degree to which social skills measures from a role-play assessment are correlated with measures from self- or participant reports; the degree to which parenting skills measures from parent–child analogue observation are correlated with self-reported parenting skills
Cost-Effectiveness	The cost (e.g., time, financial) of deriving information with an assessment instrument relative to the contribution of that information to a clinical judgment	The degree to which the information derived from observing parent–child interactions helps the clinician make treatment decisions relative to the time required to obtain the information
Discriminant Validity	The degree to which data from an assessment instrument are not related unduly to exemplars of other constructs	The degree to which an analogue observation measure of parent–adolescent communication does not reflect ethnic, intelligence, or social desirability variables
Discriminative Validity	The degree to which measures from an assessment instrument can differentiate individuals in groups, formed from independent criteria, known to vary on the measured construct	The magnitudes of differences between distressed vs. nondistressed marital couples in their problem solving or angry behaviors during an analogue communication task
Ecological Validity	Similar to "external" validity; the degree to which findings from an assessment instrument are generalizable across settings	The degree to which findings from an analogue observation assessment of a psychiatric inpatient's social behaviors are indicative of those behaviors for the patient while on the unit or at home

(continued)

TABLE 12.1 (*continued*)

Evaluative Dimension	Definition	Examples of Application to Analogue Observation
Exportability	The degree to which an assessment instrument developed in one setting can be used in another setting	The degree to which an analogue observation measure of childhood social anxiety developed at a university research clinic can be adopted by clinicians at a community-based clinic
Incremental Validity	The degree to which data from an assessment instrument/process increase the validity of judgments beyond that associated with alternative assessment instruments	The degree to which analogue behavioral observation of a child's self-injurious behaviors identifies maintaining factors, beyond reports from the child's parents or teachers
Internal Consistency	The degree of consistency of the items or elements within an assessment instrument	The degree to which several behaviors that are added together to form a "hostile communication" score in analogue assessment of family interaction are correlated; the degree to which several role-play scenarios in an analogue social skills assessment instrument yield similar measures
Internal Validity	The degree to which observed changes in a dependent variable are attributable to changes in the independent variable	The degree to which changes in a child's self-injurious behavior are a function of the changes in response contingencies implemented in an ABAB reversal design
Interobserver Agreement	The extent of agreement between scores obtained from different assessors	The degree to which two observers agree on the skill level or rate of discreet social behaviors of a hospitalized psychiatric patient during a role-play test of assertiveness skills
Temporal Stability	The degree of agreement between measures of the same variable acquired at different times; it is an index of reliability and validity only when no changes would be expected in the measured variable within the measurement interval	The degree of agreement of measures of parent–child interactions in two free-play situations, one week apart
Treatment Validity/ Utility	The degree to which data from an assessment instrument can affect treatment decisions and outcome	The degree to which information from an analogue assessment of the problem-solving skills of a distressed married couple helps in planning treatment for that couple

Note: Definitions are drawn from the Glossary of Haynes and O'Brien (2000).

to, and representative of, the targeted construct for a particular assessment purpose (Haynes, Richard, & Kubany, 1995). Content validity applies to all aspects of an assessment instrument that affect the instrument's relevance and representativeness (Goldfried & Kent, 1972). For example, if one goal of analogue behavioral observation assessment is to identify important parent–child interactions that maintain a child's oppositional behavior at home, a free-play situation in the clinic, in which the parent delivers few commands to the child, would not be a *relevant* situation. That is, the situation may have low content validity for that assessment goal. However, the same situation would be more relevant if the goal of assessment were to observe the parent's ability to engage in free play and talk positively with the child (see review in Roberts, 2001). Similarly, observing a married couple in an unstructured discussion would be less relevant for the assessment of their problem-solving communication patterns that would observing the couple trying to resolve an issue about which they disagree (see review in Heyman, 2001).

The *representativeness* of an analogue behavioral observation instrument is the degree to which its elements sample all elements that affect the behavior problem in the natural environment. For example, an analogue behavioral observation assessment instrument designed to identify the conditions that promote or maintain self-injurious behaviors by a child would be representative to the degree that the situations in the assessment sampled situations (e.g., high task demands, response contingent social attention and withdrawal) that potentially affect the self-injurious behavior in the natural environment. Analogue behavioral observation of a child who was self-injurious that used a single condition, such as manipulation of the level of task demands for the child, would be relevant but probably not representative of the array of possible controlling conditions (see reviews in Repp & Horner, 2000). Commenting on this issue in the analogue assessment of fear, McGlynn and Rose (1998) noted that given the many stimuli that most anxious clients find fearful, a single situation in a behavior avoidance test is unlikely to represent the array of feared situations faced by a client in the natural environment.

Content validity of analogue behavioral observation instruments is also affected by other elements of the instrument. For example, the relevance of the assessment instrument can be affected by *instructions* to participants (e.g., instructions to a distressed couple to "try to resolve" vs. "discuss as usual" a conflictual topic), *temporal aspects* of the assessment (e.g., the length of time that a client with social anxiety or a client with delusional thoughts is observed in social interactions), and the *events coded and measures obtained* (e.g., which behaviors are observed and whether frequency, duration, or functional relations are measured in analogue parent–child interactions).[2]

---

[2] In behavioral assessment, a functional relation is a relation between two events that can be expressed as an equation (Haynes & O'Brien, 2000; Vogt, 1993). It does not imply a causal relation. Examples of functional relations include the conditional probability of one event (e.g., verbal reprimand by a

Content validity of analogue behavioral observation instruments affects the ecological, convergent, criterion, discriminative, and discriminant validity and the clinical utility of measures and inferences (Gettinger, 1988). In the examples above, measures derived from free-play parent–child interactions and nonproblem marital discussion situations may be temporally consistent but limited in the degree to which they (a) discriminate between distressed and nondistressed dyads (i.e., *discriminative validity*), (b) correlate with other measures of the same phenomena (i.e., *convergent validity*), and (c) help in the identification of treatment targets (i.e., *treatment utility*).

As the examples above indicate, content validity also affects the degree to which measures derived from an analogue behavioral observation instrument serve as markers for the same phenomena in the natural environment. An analogue behavioral observation of parent–child interaction that does not include problematic situations will probably not provide valid indices of problematic parent–child interactions at home. The congruence between measures derived from clinic and natural environment settings is sometimes called the *ecological validity* of a measure (Barkley, 1991; see Table 12.1).

Inspection of articles that involve assessment with analogue behavioral observation methods suggest that *the development of analogue behavioral observation instruments has not been congruent with standard psychometric principles of content validation* (e.g., principles outlined in Anastasi & Urbina, 1997; Bennett, 1982; DeVellis, 1991; Haynes et al., 1995; Nunnally & Bernstein, 1994; Shapiro & Kratochwill, 1988). A principled and sequential approach to the development of analogue behavioral observation instruments, an approach designed to maximize content validity, would involve the following:

1. Specification of the *goals* of the assessment instrument, the clinical judgments that are to be affected by the obtained measures. The goals might include the identification and specification of problem behaviors, the identification of functional or causal relations, and/or treatment outcome evaluation. The behaviors, response modes, and scenarios included in an analogue behavioral observation instrument should be congruent with the goals of the assessment (see 2–5 below).

2. Specification of the *behaviors, functional relations*, and *constructs* and their *facets*, to be measured. For example, the assessor should identify those aspects of "positive parental discipline" practices that are to be measured by an analogue behavioral observation instrument. Without specification of the targets of measurement, the degree to which the measures tap that target

---

parent) given another event (e.g., noncompliance of a child to a parent request), covariation between two events (e.g., the correlation between self-reported distress and observed behaviors in analogue assessment of pain), and (with stronger causal inferences) the identification of controlling variables for a behavior problem through experimental manipulation (Repp & Horner, 2000).

cannot be determined (see Heyman, 2001, for additional discussion of construct development).

3. Specification of the *response modes* and *dimensions* that are to be measured. Targeted response modes could include overt behavioral, cognitive, and emotional; targeted dimensions of observed behavior could include frequency, magnitude, and duration.

4. Specification of the *methods of data acquisition*. Data could be collected through observation, psychophysiological instrmentation, and self-report.

5. Selection of *scenarios, situations,* and *instructions*. For example, the assessor should identify those types of social situations that are most problematic for clients with social skills deficits.

6. As suggested in Item 1 in this list, *matching dimensions, modes, facets, scenarios,* and *goals of assessment* to ensure that targeted phenomena are adequately measured and inferences can be drawn that are relevant to the goals of assessment. Marital problem-solving interactions can be measured by observer ratings, observer-recorded time-sampled behaviors, self-reports of subjective distress, psychophysiological measures of arousal, and ratings of one spouse by the other, with different instructions. The inferences that are to be drawn from the assessment instrument should guide decisions about the elements of an analogue behavioral observation instrument. (See also the discussion of mode – method match by Cone, 1979.)

7. Sensitivity to *dimensions of individual differences,* such as gender, religion, age, ethnicity, and sexual orientation. For example, what would be considered as "positive problem solving" by a family might differ as a function of ethnicity or culture (Paniagua, 1994).

8. *Multiple sources for the development of the instrument*. Decisions about the elements of the analogue behavioral observation instrument should be based on multiple sources, such as the clinical experience of the assessor, research on causal variables associated with the targeted behavior problem, and previously validated elements from other analogue behavioral observation instruments. It is particularly important that decisions about the elements of an analogue behavioral observation instrument be based on systematic input and evaluation by experts and persons from the targeted population. For an example of commendable instrument development procedures, see Gaffney and McFall (1981), who used population sampling to develop a role-play social skills assessment instrument, the Problem Inventory for Adolescent Girls.

9. *Pilot tests* of the initial version of the instrument to select the situations and measures that are the most valid and clinically useful.

In sum, analogue behavioral observation instruments should be developed with the same degree of scholarly rigor characteristic of widely used self-report and cognitive assessment instruments (e.g., MMPI, WAIS, BDI; Goldstein & Hersen, 2000). Developers should select situations, instructions, manipulations, confederates, events to be measured, units of measurement, and temporal parameters of the assessment instruments that are relevant to and representative of the targeted phenomena for a particular assessment goal. Although these development principles are especially applicable to nomothetically derived (i.e., standardized) analogue behavioral observation instruments, most are applicable to idiographically developed instruments, those constructed by a clinician for an individual client.

THE CONDITIONAL NATURE OF VALIDITY

The previous example of how a free-play situation in an analogue parent–child observation instrument can have differential content validity, depending on the goal of the assessment, introduced an important tenet of psychometry: *The psychometric properties of an assessment instrument are conditional;* Messick, 1993; Nay, 1986). Validity is not an unconditional property of an assessment instrument. The validity of an assessment instrument (more specifically, of measures derived from an assessment instrument) can vary as a function of the assessment occasion. Table 12.2 outlines sources of variance in analogue behavioral observation and, consequently, lists variables that affect the validity of measures.

Validity is a *multidimensional construct* and is often used to mean "construct validity"—the sum of inferences from multiple validity indices, such as those listed in Table 12.1. As I noted, the indices of validity of an assessment instrument are conditional: The validity of an analogue behavioral observation instrument can vary, depending on characteristics of the participants (e.g., age and developmental–cognitive level, ethnicity, sex) and the participants' behavior problems. For example, Bellack, Mueser, Gingerich, and Agresta (1997), in their discussion of analogue behavioral observation of the social skills of patients with schizophrenic symptoms, suggested that brief assessments are less useful with patients with recent onset symptoms: Longer procedures are needed to evaluate these patients' ability to stay on task and sustain social interactions.

Validity can also be affected by the type and specificity of derived measures (e.g., global ratings of social skill vs. measures of specific social behaviors) and the dimensions of measures (e.g., rate vs. duration of a behavior

TABLE 12.2
Sources of True and Error Variance in Measures
Obtained From Analogue Behavioral Observation

Source of Variance	Description
Behavior Sampling	Which behaviors are measured and how data are aggregated (e.g., measuring irrelevant behaviors can lead to erroneous inferences about clients)
Client Variables	The client's ability to act in a role-play; motivation to participate; ability to understand the assessment task; cooperation with assessment task
Construct Precision Specification	The degree to which the targeted construct, its domain and facets, has been specified (e.g., how well "positive communication" has been specified)
Contrast and Context Effects	The degree to which measures are affected by previously measures and the assessment context in which the analogue behavioral observation occurs
Duration of Observation	The length of time that a client is observed or exposed to a particular scenario
Instructions	Instructions to clients about the purpose of the assessment (e.g., whether family members are told to discuss a problem area as they would at home or to solve the problem as best they can)
Methods of Recording and Data Acquisition	For example, data can be acquired from video or audio recordings, direct observation during the assessment, written responses from participants, and psychophysiological recordings
Observers/Raters	
Bias	When measures are affected by ethnic-, gender-, age-, disability-, or disorder-based biases of the observers
Drift	Systematic changes in observer behavior over time
Errors	Observer errors due to poor training, inattention, cognitive impairments
Reactive Effects	The degree to which the behavior of clients is modified by the assessment process
Stimuli/Scenarios/Tasks	The situations and scenarios within which data are acquired. For example, the trauma scenarios to which a client with PTSD is exposed and how they are presented (e.g., audiotaped or videotaped presentation or imaginal instructions); the social stimuli presented to a client in an ABAB design; background sounds; degree of congruence with salient events and stimuli in the natural environment
Time Samples	The duration of periods into which an observation period is divided. Usually, the duration time samples covary directly with the frequency and inversely with the duration of the observed behavior

Note: Definitions are drawn from the Glossary of Haynes and O'Brien (2000).

problem). The manner in which data are aggregated and small changes in the elements of an assessment instrument, such as instructions to participants and duration of scenarios, can also affect the validity of an instrument. For example, Heyman (2001) noted that 10–15 min of interaction in a clinic setting may be sufficient to derive reliable measures of couple interactions (based on Heyman's Rapid Marital Interaction Coding System). However, it is likely that this observation duration is sufficient for some couples and not for others, as a function of variables such as topic of the discussion, emotional state of the participants before the discussion, and characteristics of the communication patterns.

Given the conditional nature of validity, the elements of an analogue behavioral observation instrument that are most likely to result in valid and useful measures for a client will differ across the dimensions noted above and across clients. For example, the instructions, settings, and behavior codes that are most likely to provide valid and clinically useful measures of parent–child interactions are likely to be different for families with a child with severe self-injurious behaviors who has developmental disabilities than for families with a child with oppositional behaviors who is developmentally advanced. Similarly, the instructions, topics, and behavior codes that are most likely to provide valid and clinically useful measures of marital interaction are likely to be different for couples with domestic violence problems than for couples where one spouse has schizophrenic symptoms.

As suggested in the discussion of content validity, the goals of the assessment, the inferences that are to be drawn from the assessment, also affect the validity of the analogue behavioral observation instrument. For example, an analogue behavioral observation assessment instrument may provide valid measures for the identification and description of a child's problem behaviors but not for the identification of antecedent and contingent factors maintaining those problem behaviors. Congruent with this tenet, Bellack et al. (1997) noted that the role-play assessment of social skills (e.g., their Response Generation Task) with patients with schizophrenic symptoms is more likely to provide valid information about the patient's social skills capacity or knowledge than about the patient's typical social interactions. Similarly, the Family Interaction Task used by Patterson and Forgatch (1995), in which families discuss "hot" problems, may more likely be a valid measure of family problem-solving abilities than of typical ways in which a family tries to solve problems at home.

As I discuss later in this article, analogue behavioral observation instruments may provide more valid and useful estimates of *functional relations* (see discussions of functional analysis and functional assessment by Haynes & O'Brien, 2000; O'Neill, Horner, Albin, Storey, & Sprague, 1990; Repp & Horner, 2000) relevant to a behavior problem than of the rates of behaviors in the client's natural environment. For example, an analogue observation of a married couple discussing conflicts in a clinic setting (Heyman, 2001) may not accurately estimate the rates at which disagreements, interruptions, or compliments occur in their home because the couple may avoid discussing conflicts at home or may modify communication styles in the presence of their children. Consequently, measures of behavior rates obtained in the analogue observation situation would not be *generalizable* to the home environment. That is, the analogue behavioral observation instrument may have low ecological validity for behavior rates. Low magnitudes of *convergent validity*, an index of ecological validity when convergent measures are obtained in the natural environment, would be obtained when comparing behavior rates observed in the analogue clinic setting with the rates of the same behaviors observed in the home.

However, the same analogue behavioral observation instrument may provide ecologically valid estimates of other phenomena, such as how each spouse responds to the other's positive or negative behaviors, the emotional tone accompanying problem discussions, and the problem-solving skills of each spouse. Thus, estimates of the ecological, and other forms of convergent, validity of an analogue behavioral observation instrument depend on the targets of assessment and the measures derived from the analogue and validation instruments.[3]

This example illustrates another tenet of psychometric evaluation: *Inferences about the validity of an assessment instrument can differ across psychometric evaluative dimensions*. An analogue behavioral observation instrument can demonstrate strong discriminative validity and temporal stability and concurrently demonstrate weak convergent or ecological validity, depending on the validation measures used and other characteristics of the assessment occasions (e.g., duration, setting, instructions).

The goals of the analogue behavioral observation affect the relevance of each dimension of psychometric validation (Gettinger, 1988). For example, if the goal of the assessment is to estimate the client's social skills or knowledge, the degree to which the measures of social behaviors obtained from the analogue behavioral observation correlate with the client's social behaviors at home is not an important indicator of validity of the analogue measures. In this case, analogue and home measures target different constructs (e.g., skills vs. performance). Similarly, some analogue behavioral observation instruments may provide better measures of immediate treatment outcomes than of ultimate treatment outcomes or better measures of discriminative validity than of convergent validity.

Measures and inferences from analogue behavioral observation may be valid for some participants and not others. Many studies have noted differ-

---

[3] In studies of the ecological validity of analogue behavioral observation instruments, sources of variance, outlined in Table 12.2, should be matched in analogue and natural environments. Covariance between measures derived from the analogue and natural environments could reflect the degree of similarity in client characteristics, settings, response parameters, and temporal aspects of the assessment (e.g., duration), among other factors (see Barkley, 1991, for additional discussion).

ences in typical patterns of social interactions and cognition across participants as a function of dimensions of individual difference, such as ethnicity, sex, and age (Sue, Kurasaki, & Srinivasan, 1999; Vazquez Nuttall, Sanchez, Borras Osorio, Nuttall, & Varvogli, 1996). Bellack et al. (1997), in their discussion of analogue behavioral observation of the social skills of schizophrenic patients, suggested that brief assessments are less useful with patients with recent onset symptoms: Longer procedures are needed to evaluate these patients' ability to stay on task and sustain social interactions. Consequently, *interaction effects* between participants and elements of the specific analogue behavioral observation instrument should be considered when drawing inferences from prior validity studies: Are validity inferences from prior studies relevant to the client in the current assessment occasion? Dimensions of individual differences should also be considered when constructing new analogue behavioral observation instruments, to increase the chance that the elements are relevant and representative for the clients with which the instrument will be applied.

Validity markers and correction formulas, similar to those used with some personality assessment instruments (see discussions in Rogers, 1997; Stone et al., 2000), have not been developed for analogue behavioral observation instruments. In these strategies, validity checks are imbedded within the assessment instrument and resultant indices are used to modify obtained measures or to suggest that obtained measures may be invalid.

It may be possible to derive markers of validity of measures obtained from an analogue behavioral observation instrument by using self-reports (e.g., self-reports of how typical the client's behavior was during the analogue assessment) and by examining the relation between the patterns of behavior (e.g., rate, stability) in analogue and natural environments. For example, Derby et al. (1992) suggested that analogue behavioral observation may provide a more valid measure of child problem behaviors when the behaviors are emitted at a high rate in an analogue assessment setting than when they are emitted at a low rate. Such markers could help the assessor estimate the confidence that should be placed in inferences derived from the analogue behavioral observation.

As suggested earlier, the validity of analogue behavioral observation also depends on the measures derived. For example, just because a social anxiety or social skills role-play results in valid ratings by judges of social skills and anxiety (e.g., Bellack et al., 1997; Kadden, Litt, Cooney, & Busher, 1992), this does not mean that other measures, such as discrete verbal or paralinguistic behaviors, would also be valid. Similarly, the validity of an analogue assessment instrument can vary across *response modes*. That is, an analogue behavioral observation instrument may result in valid subjective reports of distress and observed behavior rates but not of psychophysiological measures, and vice versa. For example, Kadden et al. (1992) found that measures of "urges to drink" were more valid than observed drinking patterns, in a role-play assessment of the degree to which alcoholics could cope with situations that often provoke drinking, in predicting treatment outcome.

Validity may also depend on levels of *data aggregation*. An analogue behavioral observation instrument may provide valid and useful measures of a behavior when data are aggregated across many minutes but not when data are derived from shorter time frames, and vice versa. For example, Barkley (1991) suggested that data aggregated over more or longer intervals may be associated with more valid measures of attention of children diagnosed with attention deficit hyperactivity disorder.

The conditional nature of validity is congruent with a previous recommendation: Research on the psychometric properties of analogue behavioral observation should focus on interaction effects. For example, it may be useful to find that a clinic marital communication assessment instrument has good convergent validity with measures of typical marital satisfaction and communication in the home. However, it is more useful for clinical assessment purposes to find that indices of convergent validity are significantly higher for couples who report problem-solving difficulties than for couples who do not (or for older couples than for younger couples, or for couples who have been married for a longer time). Information on interaction effects in validation research helps the clinician make decisions about the applicability of an analogue behavioral observation instrument for individual clients.

The conditional and multidimensional aspects of psychometric indices have several implications for the interpretation of validation research:

1. Descriptions of validation research (e.g., in an introduction section of an article) should include the specific dimension of reliability and validity evaluated, the measures derived, and the characteristics of the assessment occasion and participants.
2. The results of validation research are not necessarily generalizable across assessment settings, goals, and participants.
3. Inferences about the validity of an assessment instrument depend on the judgments that will be affected by obtained measures (e.g., functional analysis, treatment focus, estimates of behavior rates).
4. Validity inferences are not generalizable across dimensions of psychometric evaluation.

THE UNSTABLE NATURE OF VALIDITY

Because it is the degree to which an assessment instrument taps a targeted construct, validity, especially content validity, can diminish over time as ideas about the construct evolve. The representativeness and relevance of elements of an analogue behavioral observation instrument are evaluated in the context of contemporaneous but evolving ideas about the targeted construct. Thus, the elements of an assessment instrument may become less relevant and representative as new data are acquired and ideas about the construct domain and facets are modified.

For example, current models of "marital communication and problem solving" include paralinguistic, psychophysiological and emotional, and other elements of dyadic communication that were not included in models developed in the 1960s and 1970s. Analogue behavioral observation instruments for the assessment of marital communication and problem solving that were developed at that time may fail to capture properties of contemporaneous models (see review of marital observation systems by Weiss & Heyman, 1997, and review of marital assessment in Sayers & Sarwer, 1998).

The dynamic nature of an assessment instrument's validity has several implications for the interpretation of validation studies:

1. The validity of an assessment instrument can diminish over time, and past validity indices should not be presumed to be generalizable to contemporaneous applications of the instrument.
2. Findings from previous validation studies should be considered in the context of the domain and facets of the targeted construct as originally measured.
3. The validity, particularly content validity, of assessment instruments should be periodically reevaluated in the context of contemporaneous models of the targeted constructs.
4. Assessment instruments should be revised and reevaluated as their targeted constructs evolve (see Special Section on the Methods and Implications of Revising Assessment Instruments, *Psychological Assessment*, 2000, 235–303).
5. Inferences based on data from an outdated assessment instrument, one that targets constructs that have evolved since the instrument was developed, may be erroneous.

PRINCIPLES OF VALIDATION AND THE IDIOGRAPHIC NATURE OF ANALOGUE BEHAVIORAL OBSERVATION

Analogue behavioral observation is often used as an idiographic assessment strategy (see discussions of idiographic and nomothetic assessment in Cone, 1986; Haynes & O'Brien, 2000; Nelson-Gray, 1996; Silva, 1993). That is, elements of the assessment instrument, such as the specific role-play scenario presented to a client and the discussion topics for a family, can differ across clients and across studies that used the same method and instrument.

Analogue behavioral observation instruments are often idiographically constructed to increase their ecological validity, the degree to which measures obtained reflect the client's behavior in the natural environment (Meier & Hope, 1998). For example, Chiauzzi, Heimberg, Becker, and Gansler (1985) found that measures from personalized role-plays, in which the content of the role-play was based on interviews with each participant, were more strongly correlated with self-reported depression than were measures from standardized role-plays.

Inferences from idiographic measures are often based on the degree of approximation to the clients' goals or level of functioning rather than on normative comparisons. For example, in an idiographic approach to analogue behavioral observation of a child's self-injurious behavior, inferences about the variables that affect those behaviors are more likely to be based on the relative conditional probabilities of the child's behavior across situations or as a function of different response contingencies rather than on comparisons of the child's behavior in the analogue situation with the behavior of other children in the same situation.

The relative utility of an idiographic, compared with a nomothetic, approach to analogue behavioral observation depends on the clinical judgments that are to be made. Standardized analogue behavioral observation instruments might be preferred if the inferences involve comparisons of a client with other clients. Idiographic analogue observation instruments might be preferred if the inferences involve the identification of functional relations relevant to a client's behavior problems.

As Kern (1991) and Torgrud and Holborn (1992) noted, analogue behavioral observation often involves a combination of nomothetic and idiographic strategies. Usually, a standardized method is used to develop individually tailored assessment instruments. The elements of the instrument may vary across clients, but the elements are selected by methods standardized across clients. For example, the same semistructured interview might be used for all clients with social anxiety disorders to determine which individualized sets of social situations are presented during an analogue behavioral observation assessment.

The idiographic nature of analogue behavioral observation does not diminish the importance of psychometric evaluation. Important clinical judgments and decisions are based on measures from idiographic analogue behavioral observation. However, the applicability and utility of various psychometric evaluative dimensions are affected by its idiographic nature. In particular, there are implications for the generalizability of inferences across clients and for the importance of content validation strategies.

First, the degree to which measures can be aggregated and the *generalizability of inferences* across clients are limited to the higher order construct that is common across clients in idiographic assessment. For example, each client in the study by Shalev, Orr, and Pittman (1993) was exposed, in a clinic setting, to audiotaped descriptions of his or her personal traumatic life events. Although the stimuli differed, all clients were exposed to scenes depicting their personal "traumatic life events," which were constructed from each client's description of those events. Thus, with this assessment strategy one could draw idiographic inferences, such as the magnitude of changes across therapy sessions in the magnitude of each client's response to depictions of their personal traumatic life events. One could also draw nomothetic inferences, such as changes across therapy sessions in the magnitude of clients' responses to "depictions of traumatic life events."

Because procedural variations can affect measures and inferences, small differences across studies in the format of an analogue behavioral observation measure can complicate the integration of their results. For example, Mori and Armendariz (2001) noted that Behavioral Avoidance Tests used to study the fears of children have varied in the method of instructions, number of steps, and information presented to clients about the feared stimulus. Further, any modification of procedures, temporal parameters, or behavioral codes (see Heyman, 2001, regarding idiosyncratic uses of marital interaction coding systems) used in an analogue behavioral observation instrument annuls the psychometric foundation for that instrument.

Content validity is a particularly important evaluative dimension of idiographic assessment instruments because it addresses ecological validity. Content validity addresses questions such as, "To what degree are the situations in an assertiveness role-play assessment relevant to those situations that are most problematic for the client?" and "Do the situations in an assertiveness role-play assessment adequately sample the situations that are the most problematic for the client?"

As I noted earlier, the goal of analogue behavioral observation is to measure behaviors that are analogous and relevant to a client's behavior problems, in settings analogous to those in which the client's behavior problems occur, and in response to stimuli analogous to those most strongly associated with the client's behavior problems. Consequently, the relevance and representativeness of the analogue behavioral observation measures, settings, and stimuli (i.e., its content validity) for each client affect confidence in inferences about the client's behavior problems, the functional relations associated with the client's behavior problems, and the effects of treatment.

Measures from every assessment instrument, including those from analogue behavioral observation, reflect true variance in the targeted construct and systematic and unsystematic error variance (Anastasi & Urbina, 1997; Nunnally & Bernstein, 1994). The degree of confidence that we can place in judgments from analogue behavioral observation depends on estimates of the relative contribution of true and error sources to obtained measures. These estimates are guided by indices of temporal stability and internal consistency, but particularly of convergent validity. Because the validity of measures is conditional and imperfect, clinical judgments informed by analogue behavioral observation are strengthened if they are consistent with additional measures derived in multimethod and multisource assessment.[4]

In summary, clinicians who use idiographic analogue behavioral observation instruments should carefully attend to elements of the instrument that affect the validity, particularly the ecological validity, of the measures. Elements should be selected that are relevant for the client and for the goals of the assessment, to increase ecological validity. Clinicians who adopt previously validated analogue behavioral observation instruments should attend to the relevance of the original elements for the characteristics of the client and for the goals of the assessment and recognize that modifications from the original structure can affect obtained measures.

CLINICAL UTILITY OF ANALOGUE BEHAVIORAL OBSERVATION

Information from analogue behavioral observation can be used to guide judgments about clients' psychiatric diagnoses, the relative importance and characteristics of clients' behavior problems, factors that may trigger and maintain those behavior problems, the best treatment foci for a client, treatment prognosis and outcome, and clients' ability to cope effectively with future stressors (see discussion of clinical judgment in Garb, 1998). The *clinical utility* of an analogue behavioral observation instrument is the degree to which obtained information enhances the validity of clinical judgments.

Three interrelated aspects of the clinical utility of analogue behavioral observation are discussed below: (a) cost-effectiveness and incremental utility and validity, (b) treatment utility and the identification of functional relations, and (c) sensitivity to change.

Cost-Effectiveness and Incremental Utility and Validity

Incremental validity is the degree to which information from an assessment instrument increases the validity of clinical judgments beyond that associated with other measures (Cohen, Swerdlik, & Phillips, 1996; Garb, 1984; Haynes & O'Brien, 2000). *Cost-effectiveness* is the cost (e.g., assessor and client time, financial cost, degree of treatment delay) of deriving information from an assessment instrument, relative to the contribution of that information to clinical judgments: the ratio of incremental validity to cost. Cost-effectiveness and incremental validity are important and interrelated

---

[4]Incremental validity would not be expected with additional measures when they incorporate more error than extant measures and when the additional measures have a high degree of shared variance with extant measures (i.e., when they exhibit multicolinearity).

facets of clinical utility of analogue behavioral observation and are addressed in several contributions to the Special Section on analogue behavioral observation in *Psychological Assessment* (2001, pp. 3–98).

As are all psychometric evaluative dimensions, cost-effectiveness and incremental validity of analogue behavioral observation methods, and of specific analogue behavioral observation instruments, are conditional. Cost-effectiveness and incremental validity depend on many aspects of the assessment occasion, such as the goals of assessment, the availability of other, less-costly assessment instruments that provide valid measures of the targeted constructs, the characteristics of the client and of the targeted behaviors (such as the client's cognitive abilities and the rate of the targeted behavior problems), the ease of administration, and the difficulty in deriving measures (such as the complexity of the coding system; Shapiro & Kratochwill, 1988).

Analogue behavioral observation is based on the assumption that the validity of clinicians' judgments is strengthened by direct observation of clients in clinically important interactions and situations—that to understand a behavior problem, we have to see it (Haynes & O'Brien, 2000; Kendall & Braswell, 1985; Torgrud & Holborn, 1992). Direct observation has been assumed by behavioral assessors to be essential to the assessment of problem behaviors, and analogue methods were assumed to be more cost-effective than observation in the client's natural environment (Cone, 1979; Haynes, 1978; Nay, 1986; Shapiro & Kratochwill, 1988). The initial catalyst for the development of analogue behavioral observation methods was its presumed cost-effectiveness relative to observation in the natural environment. Although most assessment scholars champion the cost-effectiveness of analogue behavioral observation, relative to observation in the natural environment, cost-effectiveness and incremental validity evaluations of analogue behavioral observation must be based on comparisons with all methods of measuring the targeted phenomenon, such as self-report questionnaires and informant ratings.[5]

Analogue behavioral observation is more likely to be incrementally useful and cost-effective when valid and less costly alternative methods of assessment are unavailable (Nay, 1986; Silverman & Serafini, 1998). Reports from informants, such as reports of the functions of a child's self-injurious behaviors by parents and teachers using the Motivation Assessment Scale (Du-

---

[5] Incremental validity and cost-effectiveness evaluations of assessment instrument are complex, frequently discussed, and rarely conducted with clinical case formulation and treatment design. They involve predictive validity estimates, such as estimates of functional relations (e.g., in the form of correlations; y) for a behavior problem from a standard set of measures (x_1) and a standard set of measures plus the additional measure (x_2); calculations of changes in y as a function of the additional measure, in a stepwise manner, are made with the following equation: $y_{incr} = (x_1 + x_2) - x_1$. Cost-effectiveness is the ratio of y_{incr} to the cost of x_2. Thus, incremental validity and cost-effectiveness indices of an instrument can only be interpreted in comparison with the same indices for other instruments used for the same clinical judgment purpose.

rand & Crimmins, 1988), can be valid. However, they can also be affected by respondent biases, inattention, limitations in respondents' ability to detect functional relations, and insufficient exposure to the client (Repp & Horner, 2000).

Cost-effectiveness of analogue behavioral observation also depends on the clinical judgments that are to be drawn and the phenomena about which they are drawn. An analogue behavioral observation instrument can vary in its relative cost-effectiveness, depending on the goals of the assessment, the assessment setting (e.g., outpatient vs. inpatient settings), the targeted behavior, and characteristics of the client. For example, Roberts (2001) reviewed several studies that suggested that analogue behavioral observation with children may be more cost-effective when the focus is on oppositional behavior problems than when the focus is on mood or anxiety disorders.

Because analogue behavioral observation is carried out to facilitate the direct observation of behavior problems and the identification of important functional relations relevant to those behavior problems, it is most likely to be cost-effective and useful when behavior problems are difficult to observe in the natural environment and when they occur at a high rate in the analogue environment. It can be particularly difficult to directly observe low-rate and socially sensitive behavior problems, such as severe oppositional, panic, and verbally aggressive behaviors, in the natural environment (see discussions of behavioral observation by Cone, 1999, and Tryon, 1998). Analogue settings can sometimes be constructed to increase the chance that these low-rate and socially sensitive behaviors can be observed and functional relations can be identified.

For example, if parents and their oppositional adolescent have stopped talking about their family conflicts, home observations and self-reports may not provide useful information about their conflict resolution abilities. In this case, important communication abilities and dialogue patterns may be more easily observed in a structured clinic situation in which families are instructed to discuss a topic about which they disagree.

Similarly, functional relations relevant to a child's self-injurious behaviors can be established more easily, using single-subject designs, if those behaviors occur at a high rate in the clinic setting (Repp & Horner, 2000). Because many occurrences of a problem behavior may be necessary to confidently identify maintaining, triggering, and relevant setting variables, the duration and number of observation sessions necessary to provide valid measures of functional relations are inversely related to the rate of the behavior. Behaviors that occur at a low rate in analogue settings may not be amenable to cost-effective analogue behavioral observation, and alternative methods, such as self-monitoring (see Special Section on self-monitoring in *Psychological Assessment*, 1999, pp. 411–497) or informant reports (Achenbach, McConaughy, & Howell, 1987), may be more valid and useful. However, there is an extensive literature documenting the multiple sources of error in self- and informant-report assessment methods (see discussions in Stone et al., 2000), and observing even a few occurrences of a problem behavior can be a rich source of clinical hypotheses.

Research on the incremental validity of analogue behavioral obser- vation has rarely been conducted (see discussion of incremental validity in Garb, 1984, and Foster & Cone, 1995). Consequently, the incremental va- lidity and utility of analogue behavioral observation methods, although ad- vocated by many behavioral assessment scholar, require further study.

Treatment Utility and the Identification of Functional Relations

Many treatment strategies are designed to modify variables and func- tional relations presumed to trigger or maintain behavior problems (i.e., hy- pothesized causal variables; Haynes, 1992). For example, behavioral manage- ment programs for oppositional children often change the parent or teacher response contingencies presumed to maintain the oppositional behavior (Webster-Stratton, 2000). Cognitive interventions with depressed adults of- ten attempt to modify the clients' beliefs and automatic thoughts in response to life stressors, which are presumed to maintain or trigger depressed mood (Persons & Fresco, 1998).

The identification of functional relations, particularly causal relations relevant to a behavior problem, may be one of the most useful contributions of analogue behavioral observation. Analogue behavioral observation often includes estimating, through manipulation of time-series analyses, the co- variance between the clients' behavior problems and hypothesized controll- ing events. Consequently, analogue behavioral observation can often help identify functional relations for behavior problems, which can become the target of treatment.

Causal hypotheses from analogue behavioral observation can be de- rived in several ways. They can be derived from qualitative observation, such as watching a parent and adolescent attempt to solve a family problem, from examining the interactive sequences of behaviors, such as sequential analy- ses of husband and wife interactions, and through experimental manipula- tions, in which the effect of systematic manipulation of hypothesized causal variables on behavior is examined.[6]

---

[6] The terms "functional analysis" and "functional assessment" are used inconsistently across disciplines and authors. Functional analysis is used by many authors in developmental disabilities research to refer to the experimental manipulation of hypothesized controlling factors. It was used by Haynes and others (Haynes & O'Brien, 2000), more broadly, to refer to the identification of functional relations though a variety of assessment methods. Cone (1999) discussed functional analysis and functional assessment concepts and terms and recommended that functional analysis be restricted to assessment involving experimental manipulation.

The validity of inferences about functional and causal relations depends on the data-analytic and experimental manipulation strategies used in the analogue behavioral observation. Confidence in causal inferences is strengthened with the use of interrupted time-series designs (i.e., experimental manipulation, ABAB reversal and withdrawal designs; Kazdin, 1998). Without showing that a behavior problem can reliably be affected by systematic manipulation of antecedent and/or consequent events, causal inferences can only be derived from indices of covariance. Covariance between two events is a marker for causality but can also occur when both events are similarly affected by other variables. Additionally, precedence of the hypothesized controlling variables is often difficult to establish. Methods of experimental manipulation in analogue behavioral observation, primarily with severe behaviors, were illustrated in many chapters in a book edited by Repp and Horner (2000).[7]

Given the importance of information on functional relations for treatment planning, the cost-effectiveness of analogue behavioral observation as a method of functional analysis is decreased to the degree that the same information can be obtained from self- and informant reports. Although there are notable exceptions, such as the Alcohol Use Inventory (Horn, Wanberg, & Foster, 1990), the West Haven–Yale Multidimensional Pain Inventory (Kerns, Turk, & Rudy, 1985), the Culturally Informed Functional Assessment Interview: A Strategy for Cross-Cultural Behavioral Practice (Tanaka-Matsumi, Seiden, Nei, & Lam, 1996), and the Alcohol Expectancy Questionnaire (Allen & Litten, 1993), most structured and semistructured interviews and questionnaires provide information on the characteristics and relative magnitude of behavior problems but not on relevant functional relations.

The identification of functional relations is only one facet of clinical utility. Analogue behavioral observation can also be evaluated on the degree to which it can be used to specify clients' skills and abilities (e.g., social skills, Bellack et al., 1997; academic abilities, Gettinger, 1988), to identify feared stimuli and the magnitude of fear responses (McGlynn & Rose, 1998), and to measure immediate and intermediate responses to treatment (e.g., Chaney, O'Leary, & Marlatt, 1978).

As with all dimensions of evaluation, the incremental utility of analogue behavioral observation for treatment planning and evaluation is conditional. For example, the degree to which information on functional relations (from analogue behavioral observation and other strategies for functional analysis)

---

[7] With analogue behavioral observation instruments that involve systematic manipulations (interrupted time-series designs), *internal validity* becomes an important evaluative dimension. With this assessment strategy, internal validity is the degree to which observed changes in the targeted behaviors are a function of changes in the manipulated variables.

is useful in the design of intervention programs depends on the following: (a) the degree to which a client's behavior problems are affected by modifiable variables, as opposed to unmodifiable variables, such as neurological injury; (b) the degree to which important functional relations are not associated with the client's diagnosis (if diagnosis is sufficient to identify the causes of a behavior problem for a client, it can be the primary basis for treatment decisions); (c) the degree to which the analogue behavioral observation instrument provides valid measures of functional relations for a particular client and behavior problem; (d) the power of intervention strategies to modify the identified functional relations; and (e) the degree to which a standardized intervention program can cost-effectively address the important functional relations across clients with the same behavior problem (Haynes, Leisen, & Blaine, 1997).

Sensitivity to Change

A potential advantage of analogue behavioral observation, a partial function of its idiographic nature, is *sensitivity to change*. Sensitivity to change is the degree to which a measure reflects true changes in the targeted construct over time. In idiographically constructed analogue behavioral observation instruments, the situations and scenarios, stimuli, response contingencies presented to the client, and behaviors sampled should all be relevant to the client. If all elements of an instrument are relevant, then variance in the measures should be minimally influenced by irrelevant sources. For example, the degree to which a multisituational analogue assessment of social anxiety is sensitive to change for a client would be a function of the proportion of situations presented in the analogue that were relevant to the anxiety-provoking situations for the client; irrelevant situations would diminish the sensitivity of the instrument to true changes in the client's social anxiety.

Because of its sensitivity to change, analogue behavioral observation may provide a useful measure of *immediate and intermediate treatment effects* (Mash & Hunsley, 1993). In conditions in which analogue behavioral observation provides a measure of skills or knowledge, the frequent application of an analogue behavioral observation instrument (Gaynor, Baird, & Nelson-Gray, 1999) may provide early indications of treatment effects (see also discussion by Norton & Hope, 2001). For this purpose, and in the context of ecological validity discussed earlier, analogue behavioral observation may have high *negative predictive power* (i.e., the probability that a client who does not manifest a skill or knowledge in the assessment will also not manifest the skill or knowledge in the natural environment). However, it may not necessarily have high *positive predictive power* (the probability that a client who manifests a skill or knowledge in the analogue behavioral observation assessment will also manifest that skill or knowledge in the natural environment). Thus, analogue behavioral observation may provide more powerful measures of immediate and intermediate treatment failure than of treatment success.

In summary, analogue behavioral observation methods have the potential to be cost-effective for many goals of clinical assessment. They may prove to be particularly useful (a) for identifying functional relations relevant to a clients' behavior problems, (b) for the early identification of treatment failure, (c) as an observational component of a multimethod and multisource assessment strategy, (d) when respondents cannot validly report important information, and (e) for increasing the probability of difficult-to-observe problem behaviors.

SUMMARY AND RECOMMENDATIONS

In this chapter, I reviewed principles of psychometric evaluation as applied to analogue behavioral observation in research and clinical contexts. Researchers who are developing analogue behavioral observation instruments, and clinicians who are applying them, should (a) specify the judgments that are to be based on measures from instruments, (b) specify the behaviors, functional relations, dimensions, response modes, and constructs that are to be measured with the instrument, (c) select scenarios, situations, and instructions to maximize ecological validity, and (d) be sensitive to the fact that validity can vary across dimensions of individual differences.

The conditional nature of validity means that descriptions of validation research should include the specific descriptions of the dimension of reliability and validity evaluated, the measures and judgments that were the object of validation, the samples involved in the validation, the assessment setting, and the elements of assessment instrument.

In selecting an analogue behavioral observation instrument for clinical assessment, the clinician should also be cognizant of the dynamic nature of validity. Past indices of validity may not be applicable to contemporaneous ideas about the targeted construct. Assessment researchers should also periodically reevaluate the validity of an analogue assessment instrument in the context of contemporaneous models of the targeted constructs.

Clinical assessment applications of analogue behavioral observation often involve a combination of nomothetic and idiographic strategies, to increase the ecological validity of measures. Although generalizations across persons may be constrained, well-constructed idiographic analogue behavioral observation instruments can aid clinicians in making judgments about functional relations, approximations to treatment goals, and immediate treatment effects. Because they have not been subjected to prior validation research, idiographic instruments may be susceptible to error, and the clinician should attend closely to the content validity of their elements.

Because they can assist in the identification of functional relations, analogue behavioral observation methods may be incrementally useful and cost-effective in selecting intervention targets. Because of its sensitivity to change, analogue behavioral observation may assist in the early identification of treatment failure. Analogue behavioral observation may also be useful in the assessment of difficult-to-observe problem behaviors and functional relations.

REFERENCES

Achenbach, T. M., McConaughy, S. H., & Howell, (1987). Child/adolescent behavioral and emotional problems: Implications of crossinformant correlations for situational specificity. *Psychological Bulletin, 101*, 213–232.

Allen, J. P., & Litten, R. Z. (1993). Psychometric and laboratory measures to assist in the treatment of alcoholism. *Clinical Psychology Review, 13*, 223–239.

Anastasi, A., & Urbina, S. (1997). *Psychological testing*. Englewood Cliffs, NJ: Prentice Hall.

Barkley, R. A. (1991). The ecological validity of laboratory and analog assessment of ADHD symptoms. *Journal of Abnormal Child Psychology, 19*, 149–178.

Bellack, A. S., Mueser, K. T., Gingerich, S., & Agresta, J. (1997). *Social skills training for schizophrenia: A step-by-step guide*. New York: Guilford Press.

Bennett, R. E. (1982). Cautions for the use of informal measures in the educational assessment of exceptional children. *Journal of Learning Disabilities, 15*, 337–339.

Chaney, E. F., O'Leary, M. R., & Marlatt, G. A. (1978). Skill training with problem drinkers. *Journal of Consulting and Clinical Psychology, 46*, 1092–1104.

Chiauzzi, E. J., Heimberg, R. G., Becker, R. E., & Gansler, D. (1985). Personalized versus standard role plays in the assessment of depressed patients' social skill. *Journal of Psychopathology and Behavioral Assessment, 7*, 121–133.

Cohen, R. J., Swerdlik, M. E., & Phillips, S. M. (1996). *Psychological testing and measurement: An introduction to tests and measurement* (3rd ed.). Mountain View, CA: Mayfield.

Cone, J. D. (1979). Confounded comparisons in triple response mode assessment research. *Behavioral Assessment, 11*, 85–95.

Cone, J. D. (1986). Idiographic, nomothetic, and related perspectives in behavioral assessment. In R. O. Nelson & S. C. Hayes (Eds.), *Conceptual foundations of behavioral assessment* (pp. 111–128). New York: Guilford Press.

Cone, J. D. (1998). Psychometric considerations: Concepts, contents, and methods. In A. S. Bellack & M. Hersen (Eds.), *Behavioral assessment: A practical handbook* (4th ed., pp. 22–46). Boston: Allyn & Bacon.

Cone, J. (1999). Observational assessment: Measure development and research issues. In P. C. Kendall, J. N. Butcher, & G. N. Holmbeck (Eds.), *Handbook of research methods in clinical psychology* (2nd ed., pp. 183–223). New York: Wiley.

Derby, K. M., Wacker, D. P., Sasso, G., Steege, M., Northup, J., Cigrand, K., et al. (1992). Brief functional analysis techniques to evaluate aberrant behavior in an outpatient setting: A summary of 79 cases. *Journal of Applied Behavior Analysis, 25*, 713–721.

DeVellis, R. F. (1991). *Scale development: Theory and applications*. Newbury Park, CA: Sage.

Durand, V. M., & Crimmins, D. M. (1988). Identifying the variables maintaining self-injurious behaviors. *Journal of Autism and Developmental Disorders, 18*, 99–117.

Foster, S. L., & Cone, J. D. (1995). Validity issues in clinical assessment. *Psychological Assessment, 7*, 248–260.

Gaffney, L. R., & McFall, R. M. (1981). A comparison of social skills in delinquent and nondelinquent adolescent girls using a behavioral role-playing inventory. *Journal of Consulting and Clinical Psychology, 49*, 959–967.

Garb, H. N. (1984). The incremental validity of information used in personality assessment. *Clinical Psychology Review, 4*, 641–655.

Garb, H. N. (1998). *Studying the clinician: Judgment research and psychological assessment*. Washington, DC: American Psychological Association.

Gaynor, S. T., Baird, S. C., & Nelson-Gray, R. O. (1999). Application of time-series (single-subject) designs in clinical psychology. In P. C. Kendall, J. N. Butcher, & G. N. Holmbeck (Eds.), *Handbook of research methods in clinical psychology* (2nd ed., pp. 297–329). New York: Wiley.

Gettinger, M. (1988). Analogue assessment: Evaluating academic abilities. In E. S. Shapiro & T. R. Kratochwill (Eds.), *Behavioral assessment in schools: Conceptual foundations and practical applications* (pp. 247–289). New York: Guilford Press.

Goldfried, M. R., & Kent, R. N. (1972). Traditional versus behavioral assessment: A comparison of methodological and theoretical assumptions. *Psychological Bulletin, 77*, 409–420.

Goldstein, G., & Hersen, M. (Eds.). (2000). *Handbook of psychological assessment* (3rd ed.). New York: Pergamon-Elsevier Science.

Haynes, S. N. (1978). *Principles of behavior assessment*. New York: Gardner Press.

Haynes, S. N. (1992). *Models of causality in psychopathology: Toward synthetic, dynamic, and nonlinear models of causality in psychopathology*. Boston: Allyn & Bacon.

Haynes, S. N., Leisen, M. B., & Blaine, D. D. (1997). Design of individualized behavior treatment programs using functional analytic clinical case models. *Psychological Assessment, 9*, 334–348.

Haynes, S. N., Nelson, K., & Blaine, D. C. (1999). Psychometric foundations of assessment research. In P. C. Kendall, J. N. Butcher, & G. N. Holmbeck (Eds.), *Handbook of research methods in clinical psychology* (2nd ed., pp. 125–154). New York: Wiley.

Haynes, S. N., & O'Brien, W. O. (2000). *Principles of behavioral assessment: A functional approach to psychological assessment*. New York: Plenum/Kluwer Press.

Haynes, S. N., Richard, D. C. S., & Kubany, E. (1995). Content validity in psychological assessment. A functional approach to concepts and methods. *Psychological Assessment, 7*, 238–247.

Heyman, R. E. (2001). Observation of couple conflicts: Clinical assessment applications, stubborn truths, and shaky foundations. *Psychological Assessment, 13*, 5–35.

Horn, J. L., Wanberg, K. H., & Foster, F. M. (1990). *Guide to the Alcohol Use Inventory (AUI)*. Minneapolis, MN: National Computer Systems.

Kadden, R. M., Litt, M. D., Cooney, N. L., & Busher, D. A. (1992). Relationship between role-play measures of coping skills and alcoholism treatment outcome. *Addictive Behaviors, 17*, 425–437.

Kazdin, A. (1998). *Research design in clinical psychology*. Boston: Allyn & Bacon.

Kendall, P. C., & Braswell, L. (1985). *Cognitive–behavioral therapy for impulsive children*. New York: Guilford Press.

Kern, J. M. (1991). An evaluation of a novel role-play methodology: The standardized idiographic approach. *Behavior Therapy, 22*, 13–29.

Kerns, R. D., Turk, D. C., & Rudy, T. E. (1985). The West Haven–Yale Multidimensional Pain Inventory (WHYMPI). *Pain, 23*, 345–356.

Mash, E. J., & Foster, S. (2001). Exporting analogue behavioral observation from research to clinical practice: Useful or cost-defective? *Psychological Assessment, 13*, 86–98.

Mash, E. J., & Hunsley, J. (1993). Assessment considerations in the identification of failing psychotherapy: Bringing the negatives out of the darkroom. *Psychological Assessment, 5*, 292–301.

McFall, R. M. (1977). Analogue methods in behavioral assessment: Issues and prospects. In J. D. Cone & R. P. Hawkins (Eds.), *Behavioral assessment: New directions* (pp. 152–177). New York: Brunner/Mazel.

McGlynn, F. D., & Rose, M. P. (1998). Assessment of anxiety and fear. In A. S. Bellack & M. Hersen (Eds.), *Behavioral assessment: A practical handbook* (4th ed., pp. 179–209). Boston: Allyn & Bacon.

Meier, V. J., & Hope, D. A. (1998). Assessment of social skills. In A. S. Bellack & M. Hersen (Eds.), *Behavioral assessment: A practical handbook* (4th ed., pp. 232–255). Boston: Allyn & Bacon.

Messick, S. (1993). Validity. In R. L. Linn (Ed.), *Educational measurement* (3rd ed., pp. 13–103). Phoenix, AZ: Oryx Press.

Mori, L. T., & Armendariz, G. M. (2001). Observational assessment of child behavior problems. *Psychological Assessment, 13*, 36–45.

Nay, W. R. (1986). Analogue measures. In A. R. Ciminero, C. S. Calhoun, & H. E. Adams (Eds.), *Handbook of behavioral assessment* (pp. 223–252). New York: Wiley.

Nelson-Gray, R. O. (1996). Treatment outcome measures: Nomothetic or idiographic? *Clinical Psychology: Science and Practice, 3*, 164–167.

Norton, P. J., Hope, D. A. (2001). Analogue observational methods in the assessment of social functioning. *Psychological Assessment, 13,* 59–72.

Nunnally, J. C., & Bernstein, I. H. (1994). *Psychometric theory.* New York: McGraw-Hill.

O'Neill, R. E., Horner, R. H., Albin, R. W., Storey, K., & Sprague, J. R. (1990). *Functional analysis of problem behavior: A practical assessment guide.* Sycamore, IL: Sycamore.

Paniagua, F. A. (1994). *Assessing and treating culturally diverse clients: A practical guide.* Thousand Oaks, CA: Sage.

Patterson, G. R., & Forgatch, M. S. (1995). Predicting future clinical adjustment from treatment outcome and process variables. *Psychological Assessment, 7,* 275–285.

Persons, J. B., & Fresco, D. M. (1998). Assessment of depression. In A. S. Bellack & M. Hersen (Eds.), *Behavioral assessment: A practical handbook* (4th ed., pp. 210–231). Boston: Allyn & Bacon.

Repp, A. C., & Horner, R. H. (2000). *Functional analysis of problem behavior: From effective assessment to effective support.* Belmont, CA: Wadsworth.

Roberts, M. W. (2001). Clinic observations of structured parent–child interaction. *Psychological Assessment, 12.*

Rogers, R. (Ed.). (1997). *Clinical assessment of malingering and deception* (2nd ed.). New York: Guilford Press.

Sayers, S. L., & Sarwer, D. B. (1998). Assessment of marital dysfunction. In A. S. Bellack & M. Hersen (Eds.), *Behavioral assessment: A practical handbook* (4th ed., pp. 293–314). Boston: Allyn & Bacon.

Schill, M. T., Kratochwill, T. R., & Gardner, W. I. (1996). Conducting a functional analysis of behavior. In M. J. Breen & C. R. Fiedler (Eds.), *Behavioral approach to assessment of youth with emotional/behavioral disorders: A handbook for school-based practitioners* (pp. 83–180). Austin, TX: PRO-ED.

Sederer, L. L., & Dickey, B. (Eds.). (1996). *Outcomes assessment in clinical practice.* Baltimore: Williams & Wilkins.

Shalev, A. Y., Orr, S. P., & Pittman, R. K. (1993). Psychophysiologic assessment of traumatic imagery in Israeli civilian patients with post-traumatic stress disorder. *American Journal of Psychiatry, 150,* 620–624.

Shapiro, E. S., & Kratochwill, T. R. (1988). Analogue assessment: Methods for assessing emotional and behavioral problems. In E. S. Shapiro & T. R. Kratochwill (Eds.), *Behavioral assessment in schools: Conceptual foundations and practical applications* (pp. 290–322). New York: Guilford Press.

Silva, F. (1993). *Psychometric foundations and behavioral assessment.* Newbury Park, CA: Sage.

Silverman, W. K., & Serafini, L. T. (1998). Assessment of child behavior problems: Internalizing disorders. In A. S. Bellack & M. Hersen (Eds.), *Behavioral assessment: A practical handbook* (4th ed., pp. 342–360). Boston: Allyn & Bacon.

Stone, A. A., Turkkan, J. S., Bachrach, C. A., Jobe, J. B., Kurtzman, H. S., & Cain, V. S. (Eds.). (2000). *The science of self-report: Implications for research and practice*. Mahwah, NJ: Erlbaum.

Sue, S., Kurasaki, K. S., & Srinivasan, S. (1999). Ethnicity, gender, and cross-cultural issues in clinical research. In P. C. Kendall, J. N. Butcher, & G. N. Holmbeck (Eds.), *Handbook of research methods in clinical psychology* (2nd ed., pp. 54–71). New York: Wiley.

Suen, H. K., & Ary, D. (1989). *Analyzing quantitative behavioral data*. Hillsdale, NJ: Erlbaum.

Tanaka-Matsumi, J., Seiden, D. Y., Nei, K., & Lam, N. K. (1996). The Culturally Informed Functional Assessment (CIFA) Interview: A strategy for cross-cultural behavioral practice. *Cognitive and Behavioral Practice, 3*, 215–233.

Torgrud, L. J., & Holborn, S. W. (1992). Developing externally valid role-play for assessment of social skills: A behavior analytic perspective. *Behavioral Assessment, 14*, 245–277.

Tryon, W. W. (1998). Behavioral observation. In M. Hersen & A. S. Bellack (Eds.), *Behavioral assessment: A practical handbook* (4th ed., pp. 79–103). Boston: Allyn & Bacon.

Vazquez Nuttall, E., Sanchez, W., Borras Osorio, L., Nuttall, R. L., & Varvogli, L. (1996). Assessing the culturally and linguistically different child with emotional and behavioral problems. In M. J. Breen & C. R. Fiedler (Eds.), *Behavioral approach to assessment of youth with emotional/behavioral disorders: A handbook for school-based practitioners* (pp. 451–502). Austin, TX: PRO-ED.

Vogt, W. P. (1993). *Dictionary of statistics and methodology: A nontechnical guide for the social sciences*. Thousand Oaks, CA: Sage.

Webster-Stratton, C. (2000). Oppositional-defiant and conduct-disordered children. In M. Hersen & R. T. Ammerman (Eds.), *Advanced abnormal child psychology* (2nd ed., pp. 387–412). Mahwah, NJ: Erlbaum.

Weiss, R. L., & Heyman, R. E. (1997). A clinical-research overview of couples interactions. In W. K. Halford & H. J. Markman (Eds.), *Clinical handbook of marriage and couples intervention* (pp. 13–41). West Sussex, England: Wiley.

13

PSYCHOLOGICAL TESTING AND PSYCHOLOGICAL ASSESSMENT: A REVIEW OF EVIDENCE AND ISSUES

GREGORY J. MEYER, STEPHEN E. FINN, LORRAINE D. EYDE,
GARY G. KAY, KEVIN L. MORELAND, ROBERT R. DIES, ELENA J. EISMAN,
TOM W. KUBISZYN, AND GEOFFREY M. REED

For clinical psychologists, assessment is second only to psychotherapy in terms of its professional importance (Greenberg, Smith, & Muenzen, 1995; Norcross, Karg, & Prochaska, 1997; Phelps, Eisman, & Kohout, 1998). However, unlike psychotherapy, formal assessment is a distinctive and unique aspect of psychological practice relative to the activities performed by other health care providers. Unfortunately, with dramatic health care changes over the past decade, the utility of psychological assessment has been increasingly challenged (Eisman et al., 1998, 2000), and there has been declining use of the time-intensive, clinician-administered instruments that have historically defined professional practice (Piotrowski, 1999; Piotrowski, Belter, &

Reprinted from the *American Psychologist*, 56, 128–165. Copyright 2001 by the American Psychological Association. We thank the Society for Personality Assessment for supporting Gregory J. Meyer's organization of the literature summarized in this chapter.

Keller, 1998). In response, the American Psychological Association's (APA) Board of Professional Affairs (BPA) established a Psychological Assessment Work Group (PAWG) in 1996 and commissioned it (a) to evaluate contemporary threats to psychological and neuropsychological assessment services and (b) to assemble evidence on the efficacy of assessment in clinical practice. The PAWG's findings and recommendations were released in two reports to the BPA (Eisman et al., 1998; Meyer et al., 1998; also see Eisman et al., 2000; Kubiszyn et al., 2000). This chapter extends Meyer et al. (1998) by providing a large and systematic summary of evidence on testing and assessment.[1]

Our goals are sixfold. First, we briefly describe the purposes and appropriate applications of psychological assessment. Second, we provide a broad overview of testing and assessment validity. Although we present a great deal of data, by necessity, we paint in broad strokes and rely heavily on evidence gathered through meta-analytic reviews. Third, to help readers understand the strength of the assessment evidence, we highlight findings in two comparative contexts. To ensure a general understanding of what constitutes a small or large correlation (our effect size measure), we review a variety of nontest correlations culled from psychology, medicine, and everyday life. Next, to more specifically appreciate the test findings, we consider psychological test validity alongside medical test validity. On the basis of these data, we conclude that there is substantial evidence to support psychological testing and assessment. Fourth, we describe features that make testing a valuable source of clinical information and present an extensive overview of evidence that documents how distinct methods of assessment provide unique perspectives. We use the latter to illustrate the clinical value of a multimethod test battery and to highlight the limitations that emerge when using an interview as the sole basis for understanding patients. Fifth, we discuss the distinction between testing and assessment and highlight vital issues that are often overlooked in the research literature. Finally, we identify productive avenues for future research.

THE PURPOSES AND APPROPRIATE USES OF PSYCHOLOGICAL ASSESSMENT

Some of the primary purposes of assessment are to (a) describe current functioning, including cognitive abilities, severity of disturbance, and capacity for independent living; (b) confirm, refute, or modify the impressions formed by clinicians through their less structured interactions with patients;

---

[1] The PAWG reports can be obtained free of charge from Christopher J. McLaughlin, Assistant Director, Practice Directorate, American Psychological Association, 750 First Street NE, Washington, DC 20002-4242: cmclaughlin@apa.org. Because of space limitations, this chapter does not cover some important issues detailed in Meyer et al. (1998).

(c) identify therapeutic needs, highlight issues likely to emerge in treatment, recommend forms of intervention, and offer guidance about likely outcomes; (d) aid in the differential diagnosis of emotional, behavioral, and cognitive disorders; (e) monitor treatment over time to evaluate the success of interventions or to identify new issues that may require attention as original concerns are resolved; (f) manage risk, including minimization of potential legal liabilities and identification of untoward treatment reactions; and (g) provide skilled, empathic assessment feedback as a therapeutic intervention in itself.

APA ethical principles dictate that psychologists provide services that are in the best interests of their patients (American Psychological Association, 1992). Thus, all assessors should be able to furnish a sound rationale for their work and explain the expected benefits of an assessment, as well as the anticipated costs. Although it is valuable to understand the benefits of a test relative to its general costs, it is important to realize how cost–benefit ratios ultimately can be determined only for individual patients when working in a clinical context (Cronbach & Gleser, 1965; Finn, 1982). Tests expected to have more benefits than costs for one patient may have different or even reversed cost–benefit ratios for another. For instance, memory tests may have an excellent cost–benefit ratio for an elderly patient with memory complaints but a decidedly unfavorable ratio for a young adult for whom there is no reason to suspect memory problems. This implies that general bureaucratic rules about appropriate test protocols are highly suspect. A test that is too long or costly for general use may be essential for clarifying the clinical picture with particular patients. In addition, certain assessment practices that may have been common in some settings can now be seen as questionable, including (a) mandated testing of patients on a fixed schedule regardless of whether the repeat assessment is clinically indicated, (b) administrative guidelines specifying that all patients or no patients are to receive psychological evaluations, and (c) habitual testing of all patients using large fixed batteries (Griffith, 1997; Meier, 1994).

Finally, although specific rules cannot be developed, provisional guidelines for when assessments are likely to have the greatest utility in general clinical practice can be offered (Finn & Tonsager, 1997; Haynes, Leisen, & Blaine, 1997).[2]

In *pretreatment evaluation*, when the goal is to describe current functioning, confirm or refute clinical impressions, identify treatment needs, suggest appropriate interventions, or aid in differential diagnosis, assessment is likely to yield the greatest overall utility when (a) the treating clinician or patient has salient questions, (b) there are a variety of treatment approaches

---

[2] Different issues are likely to come to the forefront during forensic evaluations, although they are not considered here.

from which to choose and a body of knowledge linking treatment methods to patient characteristics, (c) the patient has had little success in prior treatment, or (d) the patient has complex problems and treatment goals must be prioritized. The *therapeutic impact* of assessment on patients and their interpersonal systems (i.e., family, teachers, and involved health service providers) is likely to be greatest when (a) initial treatment efforts have failed, (b) patients are curious about themselves and motivated to participate, (c) collaborative procedures are used to engage the patient, (d) family and allied health service providers are invited to furnish input, and (e) patients and relevant others are given detailed feedback about results.

Identifying several circumstances when assessments are likely to be particularly useful does not mean that assessments under other circumstances are questionable. Rather, the key that determines when assessment is appropriate is the rationale for using specific instruments with a particular patient under a unique set of circumstances to address a distinctive set of referral questions. An assessment should not be performed if this information cannot be offered to patients, referring clinicians, and third-party payers.

A FOUNDATION FOR UNDERSTANDING
TESTING AND ASSESSMENT VALIDITY EVIDENCE

To summarize the validity literature on psychological testing and assessment, we use the correlation coefficient as our effect size index. In this context, the effect size quantifies the strength of association between a predictor test scale and a relevant criterion variable. To judge whether the test validity findings are poor, moderate, or substantial, it helps to be clear on the circumstances when one is likely to see a correlation of .10, .20, .30, and so on. Therefore, before delving into the literature on testing and assessment, we present an overview of some non-test-related correlational values.[3]

We believe this is important for several reasons. Because psychology has historically emphasized statistical significance over effect size magnitudes and because it is very hard to recognize effect magnitudes from many univariate statistics (e.g., t, F, χ^2) or multivariate analyses, it is often difficult to appreciate the size of the associations that are studied in psychology or encountered in daily life.

In addition, three readily accessible but inappropriate benchmarks can lead to unrealistically high expectations about effect magnitudes. First, it is easy to recall a perfect association (i.e., $r = 1.00$). However, perfect associations are never encountered in applied psychological research, making this

---

[3] J. Cohen (1988) suggested helpful rules of thumb to characterize the size of correlations (wherein $r \sim \pm .10$ is *small*, $r \sim \pm .30$ is *medium*, and $r \sim \pm .50$ is *large*). However, following Rosenthal (1990, 1995), we believe it is most optimal to let actual relationships serve as mental benchmarks.

benchmark unrealistic. Second, it is easy to implicitly compare validity correlations with reliability coefficients because the latter are frequently reported in the literature. However, reliability coefficients (which are often in the range of $r = .70$ or higher) evaluate only the correspondence between a variable and itself. As a result, they cannot provide a reasonable standard for evaluating the association between two distinct real-world variables.

A final class of coefficients may often come to mind, although again they do not provide a reasonable standard of comparison. These are monomethod validity coefficients. Such coefficients (often in the range of $r \geq .50$) are ubiquitous in the psychological literature. They are obtained whenever numerical values on a predictor and criterion are completely or largely derived from the same source of information. Examples include (a) a self-report scale (e.g., of depression) that is validated by correlating it with a conceptually similar scale that is also derived from self-report (i.e., another questionnaire or a structured interview) or (b) an individually administered performance task (e.g., of verbal intelligence) that is correlated with a second performance task thought to measure the same construct. Because the systematic error of method variance is aligned in such studies, the results are artificially inflated and do not provide a reasonable benchmark for considering the real-world associations between two independently measured variables.

With the foregoing in mind, Table 13.1 contains a range of illustrative correlations. When considering these results (and those in the next table), several points should be noted. First, all examples make use of coefficients that have not been corrected for unreliability, range restriction, or the imperfect construct validity of criterion measures. Second, the coefficients do not all come from equivalent designs. Some studies select extreme groups of participants (e.g., patients with severe Alzheimer's disease vs. nonpatients with normal cognitive functioning); examine rare, low-base-rate events; artificially dichotomize truly continuous variables; use relatively small samples; or use procedures not typically found in clinical practice (e.g., consensus reading of electrocardiograms by two physicians). All of these methodological factors can influence validity coefficients and make them fluctuate or systematically differ in magnitude (Hunter & Schmidt, 1990). Consequently, even though table entries are organized by their magnitude, differences between one entry and another should be interpreted cautiously.

In terms of the data in Table 13.1, one of the first examples indicates how taking aspirin on a regular basis helps to reduce the risk of dying from a heart attack ($r = .02$; Table 13.1, Entry 2), even though the effect would be considered quite small. Other small effects include the impact of chemotherapy on breast cancer survival ($r = .03$; Table 13.1, Entry 4), the association between a major league baseball player's batting average and his success in obtaining a hit in a particular instance at bat ($r = .06$; Table 13.1, Entry 7), and the value of antihistamines for reducing sneezes and a runny nose ($r = .11$; Table 13.1, Entry 16). Correlations are somewhat higher for the extent

TABLE 13.1
Examples of the Strength of Relationship Between
Two Variables in Terms of the Correlation Coefficient *(r)*

Predictor and criterion (study and notes)	r	N
1. Effect of sugar consumption on the behavior and cognitive processes of children (Wolraich, Wilson, & White, 1995; the sample-size weighted effect across the 14 measurement categories reported in their Table 2 was $r = .01$. However, none of the individual outcomes produced effect sizes that were significantly different from zero. Thus, $r = 0.0$ is reported as the most accurate estimate of the true effect).	.00	560
2. Aspirin and reduced risk of death by heart attack (Steering Committee of the Physicians' Health Study Research Group, 1988).	.02	22,071
3. Antihypertensive medication and reduced risk of stroke (Psaty et al., 1997; the effect of treatment was actually smaller for all other disease end points studied [i.e., coronary heart disease, congestive heart failure, cardiovascular mortality, and total mortality]).	.03	59,086
4. Chemotherapy and surviving breast cancer (Early Breast Cancer Trialists' Collaborative Group, 1988).	.03	9,069
5. Post-MI cardiac rehabilitation and reduced death from cardiovascular complications (Oldridge, Guyatt, Fischer, & Rimm, 1988; weighted effect calculated from data in their Table 3. Cardiac rehabilitation was not effective in reducing the risk for a second nonfatal MI [$r = -.03$; effect in direction opposite of expectation]).	.04	4,044
6. Alendronate and reduction in fractures in postmenopausal women with osteoporosis (Karpf et al., 1997; weighted effect calculated from data in their Table 3).	.05	1,602
7. General batting skill as a Major League baseball player and hit success on a given instance at bat (Abelson, 1985; results were mathematically estimated by the author, and thus, no *N* is given).	.06	—
8. Aspirin and heparin (vs. aspirin alone) for unstable angina and reduced MI or death (Oler, Whooley, Oler, & Grady, 1996; weighted effect calculated from data in their Table 2).	.07	1,353
9. Antibiotic treatment of acute middle ear pain in children and improvement at 2 to 7 days (Del Mar, Glasziou, & Hayem, 1997; coefficient derived from z value reported in their Figure 1. All other outcomes were smaller).	.08	1,843
10. Calcium intake and bone mass in premenopausal women (Welten, Kemper, Post, & Van Staveren, 1995).	.08	2,493
11. Coronary artery bypass surgery for stable heart disease and survival at 5 years (Yusuf et al., 1994).	.08	2,649
12. Ever smoking and subsequent incidence of lung cancer within 25 years (Islam & Schottenfeld, 1994).	.08	3,956
13. Gender and observed risk-taking behavior (males are higher; Byrnes, Miller, & Schafer, 1999).	.09	($k = 94$)
14. Impact of parental divorce on problems with child well-being and functioning (Amato & Keith, 1991).	.09	($k = 238$)

TABLE 13.1 (*continued*)

Predictor and criterion (study and notes)	r	N
15. Alcohol use during pregnancy and subsequent premature birth (data combined from Kliegman, Madura, Kiwi, Eisenberg, & Yamashita, 1994, and Jacobson et al., 1994).	.09	741
16. Antihistamine use and reduced runny nose and sneezing (D'Agostino et al., 1998; these results were averaged across criteria and days of assessment. The largest independent *N* is reported).	.11	1,023
17. Combat exposure in Vietnam and subsequent PTSD within18 years (Centers for Disease Control, Vietnam Experience Study, 1988).	.11	2,490
18. Extent of low-level lead exposure and reduced childhood IQ (Needleman & Gatsonis, 1990; effect size reflects a partial correlation correcting for other baseline characteristics that affect IQ scores [e.g., parental IQ], derived as the weighted effect across blood and tooth lead measurements reported in their Table 5).	.12	3,210
19. Extent of familial social support and lower blood pressure (Uchino, Cacioppo, & Kiecolt-Glaser, 1996).	.12	(*K* = 12)
20. Impact of media violence on subsequent naturally occurring interpersonal aggression (Wood, Wong, & Chachere, 1991).	.13	(*k* = 12)
21. Effect of relapse prevention on improvement in substance abusers (Irvin, Bowers, Dunn, & Wang, 1999).	.14	(*K* = 26)
22. Effect of nonsteroidal anti-inflammatory drugs (e.g., ibuprofen) on pain reduction (results were combined from Ahmad et al., 1997; Eisenberg, Berkey, Carr, Mosteller, & Chalmers, 1994; and Po & Zhang, 1998; effect sizes were obtained from mean differences in the treatment vs. control conditions in conjunction with the standard error of the difference and the appropriate *n*s. The meta-analyses by Po and Zhang [*N* = 3,390] and by Ahmad et al. [*N* = 4,302] appeared to use the same data for up to 458 patients.Thus, the total *N* reported here was reduced by this number. Across meta-analyses, multiple outcomes were averaged, and, because *n*s fluctuated across dependent variables, the largest value was used to represent the study. Finally, Po and Zhang reported that codeine added to ibuprofen enhanced pain reduction, though results from the other two studies did not support this conclusion).	.14	8,488
23. Self-disclosure and likability (Collins & Miller, 1994).	.14	(*k* = 94)
24. Post–high school grades and job performance (Roth, BeVier, Switzer, & Schippmann, 1996).	.16	13,984
25. Prominent movie critics' ratings of 1998 films and U.S. box office success (data combined from Lewin, 1999, and the Movie Times, 1999; the reported result is the average correlation computed across the ratings given by 15 movie critics. For each critic, ratings for up to 100 movies were correlated with the adjusted box office total gross income [adjusted gross = gross income/maximum number of theaters that showed the film]).	.17	(*k* = 15)
26. Relating material to oneself (vs. general "others") and improved memory (Symons & Johnson, 1997; coefficient-derived from their Table 3).	.17	(*k* = 69)

(*continued*)

TABLE 13.1 (*continued*)

Predictor and criterion (study and notes)	r	N
27. Extent of brain tissue destruction on impaired learning behavior in monkeys (Irle, 1990; the average effect was derived from Spearman correlations and combined results across all eight dependent variables analyzed. As indicated by the author, similar findings have been obtained for humans).	.17	(K = 283)
28. Nicotine patch (vs. placebo) and smoking abstinence at outcome (Fiore, Smith, Jorenby, & Baker, 1994; sample weighted effect calculated from data in their Table 4. Effect was equivalent for abstinence at end of treatment and at 6-month follow-up).	.18	5,098
29. Adult criminal history and subsequent recidivism among mentally disordered offenders (Bonta, Law, & Hanson, 1998; data from their Table 8 were combined for criminal and violent recidivism and the average Zr [mean effect size] was transformed to r).	.18	6,475
30. Clozapine (vs. conventional neuroleptics) and clinical improvement in schizophrenia (Wahlbeck, Cheine, Essali, & Adams, 1999).	.20	1,850
31. Validity of employment interviews for predicting job success (McDaniel, Whetzel, Schmidt, & Maurer, 1994).	.20	25,244
32. Extent of social support and enhanced immune functioning (Uchino, Cacioppo, & Kiecolt-Glaser, 1996).	.21	(K = 9)
33. Quality of parents' marital relationship and quality of parent–child relationship (Erel & Burman, 1995).	.22	(k = 253)
34. Family/couples therapy vs. alternative interventions and outcome of drug abuse treatment (Stanton & Shadish, 1997; data drawn from their Table 3).	.23	(K = 13)
35. General effectiveness of psychological, educational, and behavioral treatments (Lipsey & Wilson, 1993).	.23	(K ≈ 9,400)
36. Effect of alcohol on aggressive behavior (Ito, Miller, & Pollock, 1996; data drawn from their p. 67).	.23	(K = 47)
37. Positive parenting behavior and lower rates of child externalizing behavior problems (Rothbaum & Weisz, 1995).	.24	(K = 47)
38. Viagra (oral sildenafil) and side effects of headache and flushing (Goldstein et al., 1998; coefficient is the weighted effect from their Table 3 comparing Viagra with placebo in both the DR and DE trials).	.25	861
39. Gender and weight for U.S. adults (men are heavier; U.S. Department of Health and Human Services, National Center for Health Statistics, 1996;[a] analysis used only weights that were actually measured).	.26	16,950
40. General validity of screening procedures for selecting job personnel: 1964–1992 (Russell et al., 1994; coefficient reflects the unweighted average validity coefficient from studies published in *Personnel Psychology* and *Journal of Applied Psychology*).	.27	(K = 138)
41. Effect of psychological therapy under clinically representative conditions (Shadish et al., 1997).[b]	.27	(K = 56)
42. ECT for depression (vs. simulated ECT) and subsequent improvement (Janick et al., 1985).	.29	205
43. Sleeping pills (benzodiazapines or zolpidem) and short-term improvement in chronic insomnia (Nowell et al.,	.30	680

TABLE 13.1 (*continued*)

Predictor and criterion (study and notes)	r	N
1997; effect size of treatment relative to placebo, averaged across outcomes of sleep-onset latency, total sleep time, number of awakenings, and sleep quality, as reported in their Table 5. *N* derived from their text, not from their Table 1).		
44. Clinical depression and suppressed immune functioning (Herbert & Cohen, 1993; weighted effect derived from all parameters in their Table 1 using the "restricted" methodologically superior studies. Average *N* is reported).	.32	438
45. Psychotherapy and subsequent well-being (M. L. Smith & Glass, 1977).	.32	($K = 375$)
46. Gender and self-reported assertiveness (males are higher; Feingold, 1994; coefficient derived from the "general adult" row of Feingold's Table 6).	.32	19,546
47. Test reliability and the magnitude of construct validity coefficients (Peter & Churchill, 1986; the authors used the term *nomological validity* rather than construct validity).	.33	($k = 129$)
48. Elevation above sea level and lower daily temperatures in the U.S.A. (National Oceanic and Atmospheric Administration, 1999; data reflect the average of the daily correlations of altitude with maximum temperature and altitude with minimum temperature across 187 U.S. recording stations for the time period from January 1, 1970, to December 31, 1996).	.34	($k = 19,724$)
49. Viagra (oral sildenafil) and improved male sexual functioning (Goldstein et al., 1998; coefficient is the weighted effect comparing Viagra with placebo from both the DR and DE trials. The authors did not report univariate effect size statistics, so effects were derived from all outcomes that allowed for these calculations: (a) frequency of penetration [DR, DE], (b) maintenance after penetration [DR, DE], (c) percentage of men reporting global improvement [DR, DE], and (d) percentage of men with Grade 3 or 4 erections [DR]. For (a) and (b) in the DE trial, the pooled *SD* was estimated from the more differentiated subgroup standard errors presented in their Table 2. *N* varied across analyses, and the average is reported).	.38	779
50. Observer ratings of attractiveness for each member of a romantic partnership (Feingold, 1988).	.39	1,299
51. Past behavior as a predictor of future behavior (Ouellette & Wood, 1998; data drawn from their Table 1).	.39	($k = 16$)
52. Loss in habitat size and population decline for interior-dwelling species[c] (Bender, Contreras, & Fahrig, 1998; the *N* in this analysis refers to the number of landscape patches examined).	.40	2,406
53. Social conformity under the Asch line judgment task (Bond & Smith, 1996).	.42	4,627
54. Gender and self-reported empathy and nurturance (females are higher; Feingold, 1994; coefficient is derived from the "general adult" row of Feingold's Table 6).	.42	19,546
55. Weight and height for U.S. adults (U.S. Department of Health and Human Services, National Center for Health	.44	16,948

(*continued*)

TABLE 13.1 (*continued*)

Predictor and criterion (study and notes)	r	N
Statistics, 1996; analysis used only weights and heights that were actually measured).		
56. Parental reports of attachment to their parents and quality of their child's attachment (Van Ijzendoorn, 1995).	.47	854
57. Increasing age and declining speed of information processing in adults (Verhaeghen & Salthouse, 1997).	.52	11,044
58. Gender and arm strength for adults (men are stronger; Blakley, Quinones, Crawford & Jago, 1994;[a] effect size was computed from the means and standard deviations for arm lift strength reported in their Table 6).	.55	12,392
59. Nearness to the equator and daily temperature in the U.S.A. (National Oceanic and Atmospheric Administration, 1999; data reflect the average of the daily correlations for latitude with maximum temperature and latitude with minimum temperature across 187 U.S. recording stations for the time period from January 1, 1970, to December 31, 1996).	.60	($k = 19,724$)
60. Gender and height for U.S. adults (men are taller; U.S. Department of Health and Human Services, National Center for Health Statistics, 1996,[a] analysis used only heights that were actually measured).	.67	16,962

Note: DE = dose escalation; DR = dose response; ECT= electroconvulsive therapy; IQ = intelligence quotient; k = number of effect sizes contributing to the mean estimate; K = number of studies contributing to the mean estimate; MI = myocardial infarction; PTSD = posttraumatic stress disorder.
[a]These values differ from those reported Meyer and Handler (1997) and Meyer et al. (1998) because they are based on larger samples. [b]Treatment was conducted outside a university, patients were referred through usual clinical channels, and treatment was conducted by experienced therapists with regular caseloads. For a subgroup of 15 studies in which therapists also did not use a treatment manual and did not have their treatment techniques monitored, the average r was .25. [c]Interior-dwelling species are those that are live within the central portion of a habitat as opposed to its border.

of damaged brain tissue and impaired learning in nonhuman primates ($r =$ .17; Table 13.1, Entry 27), the link between prominent movie critics' reviews and box office success ($r = .17$; Table 13.1, Entry 25), and the ability of employment interviews to predict job success ($r = .20$; Table 13.1, Entry 31). In the middle range of the values listed in Table 13.1 are the association of gender and weight ($r = .26$; Table 13.1, Entry 39), the effect of psychotherapy under clinically representative conditions ($r = .27$; Table 13.1, Entry 41), the effect of sleeping pills for short-term treatment of insomnia ($r = .30$; Table 13.1, Entry 43), the impact of elevation on daily temperatures in the United States ($r = .34$; Table 13.1, Entry 48), and the effect of contiguous natural environments on the population density of species that prefer the center of those habitats ($r = .40$; Table 13.1, Entry 52). Recently, the medication Viagra has received extensive media attention. As Table 13.1 indicates, the initial large-scale clinical trial on this drug found that its impact on improved sexual functioning was $r = .38$ (Table 13.1, Entry 49), whereas its influence on unwanted side effects was $r = .25$ (Table 13.1, Entry 38). At the high end of the spectrum is the relationship between gender and arm strength ($r = .55$; Table 13.1, Entry 58) or height ($r = .67$; Table 13.1, Entry 60), with male adults being stronger and taller than female adults. One also sees a strong connection between physical distance from the equator (and thus the sun) and daily temperature recordings in the United States ($r = .60$; Table 13.1, Entry 59), so that in the northern hemisphere, more northern locations have cooler temperatures than southern ones.

By and large, the examples in Table 13.1 illustrate how many medical and psychological interventions (e.g., antihypertensive medication, nicotine patches, sleeping pills, psychotherapy), as well as many constructs that interest psychologists (e.g., the impact of divorce, parenting strategies, memorization techniques, alcohol, psychometric reliability), produce correlations in the range of approximately .15 to .30. Even the axiom that past behavior is the best predictor of future behavior produces a correlation of only $r = .39$ (Table 13.1, Entry 51; see Ouellette & Wood, 1998, for moderators).

In many respects, these findings highlight how challenging it is to consistently achieve uncorrected univariate correlations that are much above .30. Given psychologists' frequent desire to square correlational values and discuss findings using proportion of variance terminology, some may feel disappointed by the magnitudes in Table 13.1 because many variables account for only about 2% to 9% of the variance in a criterion.[4]

Indeed, even the extent of brain damaged tissue accounts for only 3% of the variance in primate learning behavior, the degree of landscape fragmentation accounts for only 16% of the variance in the population density of central habitat species, and the distance from the sun accounts for only 37% of the variance in daily U.S. temperature. For those who may be inclined to square the values in Table 13.1 and feel discouraged, we recommend an alternative, which is to reconceptualize effect size magnitudes.

Instead of relying on unrealistic benchmarks to evaluate the findings in Table 13.1, it seems that psychologists studying highly complex human behavior should be rather satisfied when they can identify replicated univariate correlations among independently measured constructs that are of the magnitude observed for antihistamine effectiveness ($r = .11$; Table 13.1, Entry 16), college grades and job performance ($r = .16$; Table 13.1, Entry 24), or criminal history and recidivism ($r = .18$; Table 13.1, Entry 29). Furthermore, it appears that psychologists generally should be pleased when they can attain replicated univariate correlations among independently measured constructs that approximate the magnitude seen for gender and weight ($r = .26$; Table 13.1, Entry 39), reliability and validity ($r = .33$; Table 13.1, Entry 47), or elevation above sea level and daily temperature ($r = .34$; Table 13.1, Entry

---

[4] For a general criticism of squared correlations and reasons to avoid them, see D'Andrade and Dart (1990) and Ozer (1985). For a discussion of why r would be preferred to r^2 as an effect size measure, see J. Cohen (1988), Hunter and Schmidt (1990), and Rosenthal (1991).

48). Finally, psychologists probably should rejoice when they find replicated evidence that uncorrected univariate correlations are of the same magnitude as those observed for gender and arm strength ($r = .55$; Table 13.1, Entry 58) or for latitude and daily temperature ($r = .60$; Table 13.1, Entry 59).

EXAMPLES OF EVIDENCE SUPPORTING THE GOALS OF PSYCHOLOGICAL TESTING AND ASSESSMENT

The PAWG report provided a narrative review of data on the utility of testing for various clinical purposes (Meyer et al., 1998; also see Kubiszyn et al., 2000), including (a) the description of clinical symptomatology and differential diagnosis, (b) the description and prediction of functional capacities in everyday behavior, (c) the prediction of subsequent functioning and differential treatment needs for medical and mental health conditions, (d) the monitoring of treatment over time, and (e) the use of psychological assessment as a treatment in itself. Our current goal is to provide a more systematic overview of the psychological testing and assessment evidence.

To provide a reasonable overview of the evidence, we present data from meta-analytic reviews and several large-scale studies (the latter are noted in our table). To identify relevant meta-analyses, we searched PsycINFO for English language articles using the term *meta-analy** combined with the terms *test* or *validity* or *neuropsych** or *personality* or *cognitive*.[5]

When the search was last run (December 1999), it produced 1,352 articles, to which we added 5 studies uncovered during a search of the medical literature (see below) and 5 that were known to us but had not been indexed. After deleting irrelevant articles, 241 studies remained. From these, we selected examples that either reviewed commonly used instruments or illustrated a wide range of testing and assessment applications. Specifically, from the pool of 241 meta-analyses, we obtained and reviewed 107 articles and present results from 69.[6] No studies were excluded because of the results they obtained.

---

[5] A complete list of all search results and decisions can be obtained from Gregory J. Meyer.

[6] Irrelevant articles included comments or letters and meta-analyses that dealt with (a) psychotherapy, (b) medical tests or procedures, (c) the reliability or internal structure of a test, (d) methodological issues, (e) gender differences in personality or cognitive functioning, (f) nonapplied topics (e.g., extrasensory perception), and (g) instances when meta-analysis was used only to summarize several samples gathered by the author(s). The 38 studies that we obtained but did not use were excluded because they did not allow us to calculate a univariate correlational effect size ($n = 13$), presented results without clear hypotheses or that were difficult to characterize as validity coefficients (e.g., sensitivity to change from various treatments; lack of ethnic differences; $n = 7$), did not use traditional psychological tests or mixed test and nontest predictors ($n = 7$), overlapped with results from a larger or more recent meta-analysis($n = 4$), presented clearly confounded predictors and criteria ($n = 4$), examined a literature that the original authors believed was unsuitable for meta-analysis ($n = 1$), were not genuine meta-analyses ($n = 1$), or summarized only statistically significant findings from the primary studies ($n = 1$). When necessary, we translated original research findings into a correlation using standard formulas

To provide a reasonable overview of the evidence on medical testing, we used PubMed to search the English language MEDLINE literature with three strategies. The first search combined the MeSH terms *meta-analysis* and *Diagnostic Techniques and Procedures*. The second strategy was an unrestricted field search that combined the term *meta-analysis* with *MRI* or *CT* or *ultrasound* or *x-ray* or *sensitivity* or *specificity*. These searches produced 776 unique references, which were combined with 12 medical test citations found in our PsycINFO search and 3 additional citations from a recent review (Lijmer et al., 1999). After deleting irrelevant articles, we were left with a final pool of 203 articles. From these, we again selected examples that reviewed commonly used instruments or illustrated a wide range of applications. From the pool of 203 meta-analyses, we obtained and reviewed 99 and present results for 57.[7]

No studies were excluded due to the results they obtained. Our final search examined medically focused, multidisciplinary geriatric assessment teams. Because many controlled trials have examined the value of these teams on subsequent survival, we extended a 1991 meta-analysis on this topic through July 1999. Post-1989 studies were identified by combining the following text words: (*assessment* or *evaluation* or *consultation*) and geriatric and (*control** or *random**) and (*mortality* or *survival*). This search produced 109 studies, for which 18 provided relevant data. In conjunction with the earlier meta-analysis, results from a total of 32 samples were summarized.

Table 13.2 contains the findings from our review, with validity coefficients for psychological tests interspersed with validity coefficients for medical tests. Because this table contains a large amount of information, we urge readers to closely examine the results before reading further.

A thorough inspection of Table 13.2 suggests four observations. First, both psychological and medical tests have varying degrees of validity, ranging from tests that are essentially uninformative for a given criterion (e.g., the Minnesota Multiphasic Personality Inventory [MMPI] Ego Strength scale [Table 13.2, Entry 5] or the dexamethasone suppression test [Table 13.2, Entry 1] for predicting response to treatment) to tests that are strongly predictive of appropriate criteria (e.g., neuropsychological tests for differentiating

---

(see, e.g., Rosenthal, 1991). Because some studies included variables with unequal variances, skewed distributions, or very high specificity rates, we did not use the procedures detailed by Hasselblad and Hedges (1995).

[7] Irrelevant articles included comments and letters as well as meta-analyses that (a) dealt with treatment, (b) addressed methodology, (c) focused on incidence or prevalence, (d) did not have an abstract, (e) dealt with psychological tests, (f) focused solely on estimating cost effectiveness, or (g) dealt with animals. The 42 studies that we obtained but did not use were excluded because they did not allow us to calculate a univariate correlational effect size ($n = 29$), overlapped with results reported elsewhere or from a more recent meta-analysis ($n = 6$), were not a genuine meta-analysis or estimated only normative test values ($n = 3$), did not use traditional definitions for statistics or the accepted gold standard criterion ($n = 2$), relied heavily on data from abstracts rather than complete reports ($n = 1$), or were considered by the original authors to be a tentative pilot investigation ($n = 1$).

TABLE 13.2
Examples of Testing and Assessment Validity
Coefficients With an Emphasis on Meta-Analytic Results

Predictor and criterion (study and notes)	r	N
1. Dexamethasone suppression test scores and response to depression treatment (Ribeiro, Tandon, Grunhaus, & Greden, 1993).[a]	.00	2,068
2. Fecal occult blood test screening and reduced death from colorectal cancer (Towler et al., 1998).	.01	329,642
3. Routine umbilical artery Doppler ultrasound and reduced perinatal deaths in low-risk women (Goffinet, Paris-Llado, Nisand, & Bréart, 1997; the authors also examined the impact of routine umbilical artery ultrasound on 13 other measures of successful outcome. The average effect size across these other criteria was $r = -.0036$ [ns from 6,373 to 11,375], with the largest correlation in the expected direction being .0097 [for Apgar scores at 5 minutes]).	.01	11,375
4. Routine ultrasound examinations and successful pregnancy outcomes (Bucher & Schmidt, 1993; outcomes considered were live births [$r = .0009$], no induced labor [$r = .0176$], no low Apgar scores [$r = -.0067$], no miscarriages [$r = .0054$], and no perinatal mortality [$r = .0168$]).	.01	16,227
5. MMPI Ego Strength scores and subsequent psychotherapy outcome (Meyer & Handler, 1997; this meta-analysis considered only studies in which the Ego Strength scale was used along with the Rorschach PRS).	.02	280
6. Routine umbilical artery Doppler ultrasound and reduced perinatal deaths in high-risk women (Alfirevic & Neilson, 1995; the authors also examined the impact of routine umbilical artery ultrasound on 19 other measures of successful outcome. The average effect size across these other criteria was .018 [ns from 476 to 7,474]).	.03	7,474
7. Denial–repressive coping style and development of breast cancer (McKenna, Zevon, Corn, & Rounds, 1999; weighted effect size computed from the study data in their Table 1).	.03	12,908
8. Triple marker[b] prenatal screening of maternal serum and identification of Trisomy 18 (Yankowitz, Fulton, Williamson, Grant, & Budelier, 1998).[c]	.03	40,748
9. Impact of geriatric medical assessment teams on reduced deaths (data combined from the meta-analysis by Rubenstein, Stuck, Siu, & Wieland, 1991, and the following more recent studies: Boult et al., 1994; Büla et al., 1999; Burns, Nichols, Graney, & Cloar, 1995; Engelhardt et al., 1996; Fabacher et al., 1994; Fretwell et al., 1990; Germain, Knoeffel, Wieland, & Rubenstein, 1995; Hansen, Poulsen, & Sørensen, 1995; Harris et el., 1991; Karppi & Tilvis, 1995; Naughton, Moran, Feinglass, Falconer, & Williams, 1994; Reuben et al., 1995; Rubenstein, Josephson, Harker, Miller, & Wieland, 1995; Rubin, Sizemore, Loftis, & de Mola, 1993; Silverman et al., 1995; Siu et al., 1996; Thomas, Brahan, & Haywood, 1993; and Trentini et al., 1995; only the latest available outcome data were used for each sample).	.04	10,065

TABLE 13.2 (*continued*)

Predictor and criterion (study and notes)	r	N
10. MMPI depression profile scores and subsequent cancer within 20 years (Persky, Kempthorne-Rawson, & Shekelle, 1987).[c]	.05	2,018
11. Ventilatory lung function test scores and subsequent lung cancer within 25 years (Islam & Schottenfeld, 1994).[c]	.06	3,956
12. Rorschach Interaction Scale scores and subsequent cancer within 30 years (Graves, Phil, Mead, & Pearson, 1986; scores remained significant predictors after controlling for baseline smoking, serum cholesterol, systolic blood pressure, weight, and age).[c]	.07	1,027
13. Unique contribution of an MMPI high-point code (vs. other codes) to conceptually relevant criteria (McGrath & Ingersoll, 1999a, 1999b).	.07	8,614
14. MMPI scores and subsequent prison misconduct (Gendreau, Goggin, & Law, 1997).	.07	17,636
15. Beck Hopelessness Scale scores and subsequent suicide (data combined from Beck, Brown, Berchick, Stewart, & Steer, 1990; and Beck, Steer, Kovacs, & Garrison, 1985).[c]	.08	2,123
16. MMPI elevations on Scales F, 6, or 8 and criminal defendant incompetency (Nicholson & Kugler, 1991).	.08	1,461
17. Extraversion test scores and success in sales (concurrent and predictive; data combined from Barrick & Mount, 1991, Table 2; Salgado, 1997, Table 3; and Vinchur, Schippman, Switzer, & Roth, 1998 [coefficients from their Tables 2 and 3 were averaged, and the largest n was used for the overall sample size]).	.08	6,004
18. Attention and concentration test scores and residual mild head trauma (Binder, Rohling, & Larrabee, 1997).	.09	622
19. In cervical cancer, lack of glandular differentiation on tissue biopsy and survival past 5 years (Heatley, 1999; this study reported two meta-analyses. The other one found that nuclear DNA content was of no value for predicting cancer progression in initially low-grade cervical intraepithelial neoplasia).	.11	685
20. Negative emotionality test scores and subsequent heart disease (Booth-Kewley & Friedman, 1987; data were derived from their Table 7, with negative emotionality defined by the weighted effect for anger/hostility/ aggression, depression, and anxiety).	.11	(k = 11)
21. Triple marker[b] prenatal screening of maternal serum and identification of Down's syndrome (Conde-Agudelo & Kafury-Goeta, 1998; results were reported across all ages).	.11	194,326
22. General cognitive ability and involvement in automobile accidents (Arthur, Barrett, & Alexander, 1991).	.12	1,020
23. Conscientiousness test scores and job proficiency (concurrent and predictive; data combined from Barrick & Mount, 1991, Table 3; Mount, Barrick, & Stewart, 1998; Salgado, 1998, Table 1; and Vinchur et al., 1998 [coefficients from their Tables 2 and 3 were averaged, and the largest n was used for the overall sample size]).	.12	21,650

(*continued*)

TABLE 13.2 (*continued*)

Predictor and criterion (study and notes)	r	N
24. Platform posturography and detection of balance deficits due to vestibular impairment (Di Fabio, 1996).	.13	1,477
25. General intelligence and success in military pilot training (Martinussen, 1996).	.13	15,403
26. Self-report scores of achievement motivation and spontaneous achievement behavior (Spangler, 1992; coefficient derived from the weighted average of the semioperant and operant criterion data reported in Spangler's Table 2).	.15	(k = 104)
27. Graduate Record Exam Verbal or Quantitative scores and subsequent graduate GPA in psychology (E. L. Goldberg & Alliger, 1992).	.15	963
28. Low serotonin metabolites in cerebrospinal fluid (5-HIAA) and subsequent suicide attempts (Lester, 1995).	.16	140
29. Personality tests and conceptually meaningful job performance criteria (data combined from Robertson & Kinder, 1993; Tett, Jackson, & Rothstein, 1991; and Tett, Jackson, Rothstein, & Reddon, 1994; we used the single scale predictors from Robertson & Kinder [their Table 3] and the confirmatory results from Table1 in Tett et al., 1994).	.16	11, 101
30. Implicit memory tests and differentiation of normal cognitive ability from dementia (Meiran & Jelicic, 1995).	.16	1, 156
31. MMPI Cook–Medley Hostility Scale elevations and subsequent death from all causes (T. Q. Miller, Smith, Turner, Guijarro, & Hallet, 1996; data were drawn from their Table 6).	.16	4,747
32. Motivation to manage from the Miner Sentence Completion Test and managerial effectiveness (Carson & Gilliard, 1993; results were averaged across the three performance criterion measures of managerial success. Because the three criterion measures were not independent across studies, the N reported is the largest n used for any single criterion).	.17	2, 151
33. Extraversion and subjective well-being (DeNeve & Cooper, 1998).	.17	10,364
34. MRI T_2 hyperintensities and differentiation of affective disorder patients from healthy controls (Videbech, 1997; data from Videbech's Tables 1 and 2 were combined, but only those statistics used by the original author are included here).	.17	1,575
35. Test anxiety scales and lower school grades (Hembree, 1988; reported effect is the average effect size for the course grade and GPA data from Hembree's Table1. Participants were assumed to be independent across studies).	.17	5,750
36. High trait anger assessed in an interpersonal analogue and elevated blood pressure (Jorgensen, Johnson, Kolodziej, & Schreer, 1996; data come from the "Overall" column of their Table 4).	.18	(k = 34)
37. Reduced blood flow and subsequent thrombosis or failure of synthetic hemodialysis graft (Paulson, Ram, Birk, & Work, 1999).	.18	4,569
38. MMPI Validity Scales and detection of known or suspected underreported psychopathology (Baer, Wetter, & Berry,	.18	328

TABLE 13.2 (*continued*)

Predictor and criterion (study and notes)	r	N
1992; weighted average effect size was calculated from data reported in their Table 1 for all studies using participants presumed to be underreporting).		
39. Dexamethasone suppression test scores and subsequent suicide (Lester, 1992).	.19	626
40. Short-term memory tests and subsequent job performance (Verive & McDaniel, 1996).	.19	17,741
41. Depression test scores and subsequent recurrence of herpes simplex virus symptoms (Zorrilla, McKay, Luborsky, & Schmidt, 1996; effect size is for prospective studies).	.20	333
42. Four preoperative cardiac tests and prediction of death or MI within 1 week of vascular surgery (Mantha et al., 1994; the four tests considered were dipyridamole-thallium scintigraphy, ejection fraction estimation by radionuclide ventriculography, ambulatory ECG, and dobutamine stress ECG. The authors concluded no test was conclusively superior to the others).	.20	1,991
43. Scholastic Aptitude Test scores and subsequent college GPA (Baron & Norman, 1992).[c]	.20	3,816
44. Self-reported dependency test scores and physical illness (Bornstein, 1998; weighted effect size was calculated from the retrospective studies reported in Bornstein's Table 1 [Studies 3, 5, 7, 8, 13, and 19] and the prospective studies listed in Bornstein's Table 2 [Studies 1–4]).	.21	1,034
45. Dexamethasone suppression test scores and psychotic vs. nonpsychotic major depression (Nelson & Davis, 1997; effect size calculated from the weighted effects for the individual studies in their Table 1).	.22	984
46. Traditional ECG stress test results and coronary artery disease (Fleischmann, Hunink, Kuntz, & Douglas, 1998; results were estimated from the reported sensitivity and specificity in conjunction with the base rate of coronary artery disease and the total independent N across studies).	.22	5,431
47. Graduate Record Exam Quantitative scores and subsequent graduate GPA (Morrison & Morrison, 1995).	.22	5, 186
48. TAT scores of achievement motivation and spontaneous achievement behavior (Spangler, 1992; coefficient was derived from the weighted average of the semioperant and operant criterion data in Spangler's Table 2).	.22	(k = 82)
49. Isometric strength test scores and job ratings of physical ability (Blakley, Quinones, & Crawford, 1994).	.23	1,364
50. Single serum progesterone testing and diagnosis of ectopic pregnancy (Mol, Lijmer, Ankum, van der Veen, & Bossuyt, 1998; following the original authors, we used only the 18 prospective or retrospective cohort studies listed in their Table III).	.23	6,742
51. Cognitive multitask performance test scores and subsequent pilot proficiency (Damos, 1993).	.23	6,920
52. WISC distractibility subscales and learning disability diagnoses (Kavale & Forness, 1984; the effect sizes from	.24	(K = 54)

(*continued*)

TABLE 13.2 (*continued*)

Predictor and criterion (study and notes)	r	N
this meta-analysis are likely to be underestimates because the authors computed the average effect for individual test scales rather than the effect for a composite pattern).		
53. Fetal fibronectin testing and prediction of preterm delivery (Faron, Boulvain, Irion, Bernard, & Fraser, 1998; data were aggregated across low- and high-risk populations and across designs with single or repeated testing for all studies using delivery before 37 weeks as the criterion).	.24	7,900
54. Decreased bone mineral density and lifetime risk of hip fracture in women (Marshall, Johnell, & Wedel, 1996; the results were restricted to those from absorptiometry using single or dual energy, photon, or X-ray; quantitative CT; quantitative MRI; or ultrasound scanning. The overall effect was estimated from their Table 3 using a total lifetime incidence of 15%; the effect would be smaller if the lifetime risk incidence was lower [e.g., if the incidence were 3%, the effect would be $r = .13$]. Total N was derived from the n for each study in their Table 1 reporting the incidence of hip fractures).	.25	20,849
55. General intelligence test scores and functional effectiveness across jobs (Schmitt, Gooding, Noe, & Kirsch, 1984; data were obtained from their Table 4).	.25	40,230
56. Internal locus of control and subjective well-being (DeNeve & Cooper, 1998).	.25	8,481
57. Integrity test scores and subsequent supervisory ratings of job performance (Ones, Viswesvaran, & Schmidt, 1993; effect size was taken from the "predictive-applicant" cell of their Table 8).	.25	7,550
58. Self-reported dependency test scores and dependent behavior (Bornstein, 1999; coefficient was derived from all results listed in Bornstein's Table 1 as reported in his footnote 8).	.26	3,013
59. Self-efficacy appraisals and health-related treatment outcomes (Holden, 1991).	.26	3,527
60. Elevated Jenkins Activity Survey scores and heart rate and blood pressure reactivity (Lyness, 1993; the effect size reflects the average reactivity for heart rate, systolic blood pressure, and diastolic blood pressure as reported in Lyness's Table 6. It was assumed that overlapping studies contributed to each of these criterion estimates, so k was estimated as the largest number of effect sizes contributing to a single criterion measure).	.26	($k = 44$)
61. Combined internal, stable, and global attributions for negative event outcomes and depression (Sweeney, Anderson, & Bailey, 1986; only the finding that dealt with the composite measure of attributions and negative outcome was included. Coefficients were lower for positive outcomes and for single types of attributions [e.g., internal]).	.27	5,788
62. Neuroticism and decreased subjective well-being (DeNeve & Cooper, 1998).	.27	9,777

TABLE 13.2 (*continued*)

Predictor and criterion (study and notes)	*r*	*N*
63. Screening mammogram results and detection of breast cancer within 2 years (Mushlin, Kouides, & Shapiro, 1998).	.27	192,009
64. Microbiologic blood culture tests to detect bloodstream infection from vascular catheters (Siegman-Igra et al., 1997; only results from studies without criterion contamination were summarized [see Siegman-Igra et al., 1997, pp. 933–934]).	.28	1,354
65. C-reactive protein test results and diagnosis of acute appendicitis (Hallan & Åsberg, 1997; mean weighted effect size was derived from data in their Table 1, excluding two studies that did not use histology as the validating criteria and one study that did not report the prevalence of appendicitis).	.28	3,338
66. Graduate Record Exam Verbal scores and subsequent graduate GPA (Morrison & Morrison, 1995).	.28	5, 186
67. Hare Psychopathy Checklist scores and subsequent criminal recidivism (Salekin, Rogers, & Sewell, 1996; only effects for predictive studies were summarized).	.28	1,605
68. Short-term memory tests and subsequent performance on job training (Verive & McDaniel, 1996).	.28	16,521
69. Cranial ultrasound results in preterm infants and subsequent developmental disabilities (Ng & Dear, 1990).	.29	1,604
70. Serum CA-125 testing and detection of endometriosis (Mol, Bayram, et al., 1998).	.29	2,811
71. Neuropsychological test scores and differentiation of patients with multiple sclerosis (Wishart & Sharpe, 1997).	.29	($k = 322$)
72. For women, ECG stress test results and detection of coronary artery disease (Kwok, Kim, Grady, Segal, & Redberg, 1999; our *N* was obtained from their Table 1. It differs from the *N* reported by the authors [3,872 vs. 3,721], though it is not clear what would account for this difference. Although the article also examined the thallium stress test and the exercise ECG, there were not sufficient data for us to generate effect sizes for these measures).	.30	3,872
73. YASR total problems and psychiatric referral status (receiving treatment vs. not; Achenbach, 1997; effect size was estimated from data in Part 1 of Achenbach's Table 7.5. Because the percentages listed in this table were too imprecise to accurately generate effect size estimates, all possible 2 × 2 tables that would match the given percentages were generated. Subsequently, the effect size was obtained from those 2 × 2 tables that also produced odds ratios that exactly matched the odds ratios reported in the text. When rounded to two decimal places, all appropriate 2 × 2 tables produced the same effect size. The effect size compares the self-reports of young adults in treatment with the self-reports of demographically matched controls who were not receiving treatment).[c]	.30	1, 142
74. Fecal leukocyte results and detection of acute infectious diarrhea (Huicho, Campos, Rivera, & Guerrant, 1996;	.30	7, 132

(*continued*)

TABLE 13.2 (*continued*)

Predictor and criterion (study and notes)	r	N
results are reported for the most studied test [$K = 19$]. For the remaining tests, effect sizes could be generated for only two small studies of fecal lactoferrin, and the average results for occult blood tests were lower [$r = .26$; $K = 7$]).		
75. Neuropsychological test scores and differentiation of learning disabilities (Kavale & Nye, 1985; we report the results for neuropsychological functioning because it was studied most frequently).	.30	($K = 394$)
76. Continuous performance test scores and differentiation of ADHD and control children (Losier, McGrath, & Klein, 1996; overall sample weighted effect was derived by combining the omission and commission data reported in their Tables 7 and 8).	.31	720
77. Effects of psychological assessment feedback on subsequent patient well-being (coefficient combined the follow-up data reported in Finn & Tonsager, 1992; and Newman & Greenway, 1997).[c]	.31	120
78. Expressed emotion on the CFI and subsequent relapse in schizophrenia and mood disorders (Butzlaff & Hooley, 1998).	.32	1,737
79. CT results and detection of aortic injury (Mirvis, Shanmuganathan, Miller, White, & Turney, 1996; from the information provided, an effect size could not be computed for two studies included in this meta-analysis).	.32	3,579
80. Screening mammogram results and detection of breast cancer within 1 year (Mushlin, Kouides, & Shapiro, 1998; overall effect size includes studies that combined mammography with clinical breast examination).	.32	263,359
81. Halstead–Reitan Neuropsychological Tests and differentiation of impaired vs. control children (Forster & Leckliter, 1994; the reported weighted effect size is slightly inflated because some observations were based on group differences relative to the control group standard deviation [rather than the pooled standard deviation]. When possible, effect sizes were computed directly from the data reported in their Tables 1 and 2. The reported N indicates the total number of independent observations across studies).	.33	858
82. CT results for enlarged ventricular volume and differentiation of schizophrenia from controls (Raz & Raz, 1990).	.33	($k = 53$)
83. Long-term memory test scores and diagnosis of multiple sclerosis (Thornton & Raz, 1997; effect size was obtained from their Table 2 with the outlier study excluded).	.33	($K = 33$)
84. Hare Psychopathy Checklist scores and subsequent violent behavior (Salekin, Rogers, & Sewell, 1996; only effects for predictive studies were summarized).	.33	1,567
85. Alanine aminotransferase results and detection of improved liver function in hepatitis C patients (Bonis, Ioannidis, Cappelleri, Kaplan, & Lau, 1997; data reflect the criterion of any histologically identified improvement).	.34	480
86. Rorschach scores and conceptually meaningful criterion measures (data combined from Atkinson, 1986, Table 1 [$K = 79$]; Hiller, Rosenthal, Bornstein, Berry, & Brunell-	.35	($K = 122$)

TABLE 13.2 (continued)

Predictor and criterion (study and notes)	r	N
Neuleib, 1999, Table 4 [K = 30]; and K. P. Parker, Hanson, & Hunsley, 1988, Table 2 [K = 14]. Hiller et al. expressed concern that Atkinson's and K. P. Parker et al.'s effect size estimates may have been inflated by some results derived from unfocused F tests [i.e., with > df in the numerator]. However, Atkinson excluded effects based on F, and K. P. Parker et al.'s average effect size actually increased when F test results were excluded. Recently, Garb, Florio, & Grove, 1998, conducted reanalyses of K. P. Parker et al.'s data. Although these reanalyses have been criticized [see K. P. Parker, Hunsley, & Hanson, 1999], if the results from Garb et al.'s first, second, or third analysis were used in lieu of those from K. P. Parker et al., the synthesized results reported here would change by −.0096, −.0036, or −.0007, respectively, for the Rorschach and by .0203, .0288, or .0288, respectively, for the MMPI [see Entry 100, this table]).		
87. Papanicolaou test (Pap smear) and detection of cervical abnormalities (Fahey, Irwig, & Macaskill, 1995; overall weighted effect calculated from data reported in their Appendix 1).	.36	17,421
88. Conventional dental X rays and diagnosis of biting surface cavities (occlusal caries; Ie & Verdonschot, 1994; the overall weighted effect was derived from all the studies listed in their Table 1. In each case, the original citations were obtained, and raw effect sizes were calculated from the initial study).	.36	5,466
89. Incremental contribution of Rorschach PRS scores over IQ to predict psychotherapy outcome (Meyer, 2000).	.36	290
90. Rorschach or Apperceptive Test Dependency scores and physical illness (Bornstein, 1998; weighted effect size was calculated from the retrospective studies reported in Bornstein's Table 1 [Studies 1, 11, 14–16, and 18]. No prospective studies used these types of scales as predictors).	.36	325
91. Assessment center evaluations and job success (data combined from Schmitt, Gooding, Noe, & Kirsch, 1984; and Gaugler, Rosenthal, Thornton, & Bentson, 1987; the overall effect size was derived from the sample weighted average reported in each study. Although Schmitt et al.'s study was conducted earlier than Gaugler et al.'s, they relied on a larger N. Because each meta-analysis undoubtedly relied on some common studies, the N reported here is from Schmitt et al.).	.37	15,345
92. Competency screening sentence-completion test scores and defendant competency (Nicholson & Kugler, 1991).	.37	627
93. MCMI–II scale score and averageability to detect depressive or psychotic disorders (Ganellen, 1996; each study contributed one effect size averaged across diagnostic criteria and type of predictor scales [single vs. multiple scales]. Results were averaged across analyses reported in different publications using the same sample. Although	.37	575

(continued)

TABLE 13.2 (*continued*)

Predictor and criterion (study and notes)	r	N
Ganellen reported larger effect sizes for studies that used multiscale predictors, these studies relied on unreplicated multivariate predictor equations. As such, multiscale predictors were averaged with hypothesized, single-scale predictors).[c]		
94. MMPI scale scores and average ability to detect depressive or psychotic disorders (Ganellen, 1996; see Entry 93, this table).[c]	.37	927
95. Rorschach Apperceptive Test Dependency scores and dependent behavior (Bornstein, 1999; coefficient was derived from all results listed in Bornstein's Table 1 as reported in his footnote 8).	.37	1,808
96. Accuracy of home pregnancy test kits in patients conducting testing at home (Bastian, Nanda, Hasselblad, & Simel, 1998; results derived from the pooled "effectiveness score," which was described and thus treated as equivalent to Cohen's *d*. Also, findings were very different when tests were evaluated using researcher-assisted volunteers rather than actual patients [*r* = .81; *N* = 465]).	.38	155
97. Sperm penetration assay results and success with in vitro fertilization (Mol, Meijer, et al., 1998).	.39	1,335
98. Endovaginal ultrasound in postmenopausal women and detection of endometrial cancer (Smith-Bindman et al., 1998; effect size was derived from the authors' pooled results [their Table 2] using their recommended cutoff of 5 mm to define endometrial thickening).	.39	3,443
99. MMPI Validity Scales and detection of underreported psychopathology (primarily analogue studies; Baer, Wetter, & Berry, 1992; weighted average effect size calculated from data in their Table 1).	.39	2,297
100. MMPI scores and conceptually meaningful criterion measures (data combined from Atkinson, 1986, Table 1; Hiller, Rosenthal, Bornstein, Berry, & Brunell-Neuleib, 1999, Table 4; and K. P. Parker, Hanson, & Hunsley, 1988, Table 2. See also Entry 86, this table).	.39	(*K* = 138)
101. Neuropsychologists' test-based judgments and presence/absence of impairment (Garb & Schramke, 1996; coefficient was calculated from the accuracy of judgments relative to base rates [see Garb & Schramke, 1996, pp. 143, 144–145]).	.40	2,235
102. Prostate-specific antigen and estimated detection of prostate cancer for men age 60–70 (Aziz & Barathur, 1993).	.40	4,200
103. Short-term verbal learning and differentiation of major depression from controls (Veiel, 1997; although the author reported many effect sizes, we report the variable that was studied most often).	.41	(*K* = 10)
104. CT results and detection of lymph node metastases in cervical cancer (Scheidler, Hricak, Yu, Subak, & Segal, 1997; an effect size could not be computed for one study included in this meta-analysis).	.41	1,022
105. Dissociative Experiences Scale scores and detection of MPD or PTSD vs. controls (Van Ijzendoorn & Schuengel,	.41	1,705

TABLE 13.2 (continued)

Predictor and criterion (study and notes)	r	N
1996; we assumed the Ns for both criterion diagnoses were not independent, so the reported N is that for the largest analysis).		
106. Colposcopy and detection of normal/low-grade SIL vs. high-grade SIL/cancer of the cervix (Mitchell, Schotten-feld, Tortolero-Luna, Cantor, & Richards-Kortum, 1998; effect sizes were calculated from data reported in their Table 3).	.42	2,249
107. Cortical tuber count on MRI and degree of impaired cognitive development in tuberous sclerosis (M. Goodman et al., 1997).	.43	157
108. Conventional dental X-rays and diagnosis of between-tooth cavities (approximal caries; Van Rijkom & Verdon-schot, 1995; this is an unweighted effect size for all studies that used a "strong" validity criterion [i.e., micro-radiography, histology, or cavity preparation]).	.43	(K = 8)
109. Cardiac fluoroscopy and diagnosis of coronary artery disease (Gianrossi, Detrano, Colombo, & Froelicher, 1990).	.43	3,765
110. Serum chlamydia antibody levels and detection of fertility problems due to tubal pathology (Mol et al., 1997; only the results for the optimal predictor assays and optimal criterion measures are presented).	.44	2, 131
111. Rorschach PRS scores and subsequent psychotherapy outcome (Meyer & Handler, 1997, 2000).	.44	783
112. Digitally enhanced dental X-rays and diagnosis of biting surfaces cavities (Ie & Verdonschot, 1994; the overall weighted effect size was derived from all the studies listed in their Table 1. In each case, the original citations were obtained, and raw effect sizes were calculated from the initial study).	.44	2,870
113. WAIS IQ and obtained level of education (Hanson, Hunsley, & Parker, 1988).	.44	(k = 9)
114. MMPI Validity Scales and detection of known or sus-pected malingered psychopathology (data combined from Berry, Baer, & Harris, 1991; and Rogers, Sewell, & Sale-kin, 1994; the average weighted effect size was calcu-lated from data presented in Tables 1 and 2 of Berry et al. and Table 1 of Rogers et al. for participants presumed or judged to be malingering disturbance).	.45	771
115. D-dimer blood test results and detection of deep vein thrombosis or pulmonary embolism (Becker, Philbrick, Bachhuber, & Humphries, 1996; results are reported for only the 13 [of 29] studies with stronger methodology).	.45	1,652
116. Exercise SPECT imaging and identification of coronary artery disease (Fleischmann, Hunink, Kuntz, & Douglas, 1998; results were estimated from the reported sensitivity and specificity in conjunction with the base rate of coro-nary artery disease and the total independent N across studies).	.46	3,237
117. Antineutrophil cytoplasmic antibody testing and detection of Wegener's granulomatosis (Rao et al., 1995; sensitivity for each study was estimated from their Figure 1).	.47	13,562

(continued)

TABLE 13.2 (*continued*)

Predictor and criterion (study and notes)	r	N
118. Technetium bone scanning results and detection of osteomyelitis (bone infection; Littenberg, Mushlin, & the Diagnostic Technology Assessment Consortium, 1992).	.48	255
119. Clinical examination with routine lab tests and detection of metastatic lung cancer (Silvestri, Littenberg, & Colice, 1995).	.48	1,593
120. Lecithin/sphingomyelin ratio and prediction of neonatal respiratory distress syndrome (Petersen, Smith, Okoro-dudu, & Bissell, 1996; the most frequently studied predictor test was reported).	.50	1, 170
121. Sensitivity of total serum cholesterol levels to changes in dietary cholesterol (Howell, McNamara, Tosca, Smith, & Gaines, 1997).	.50	($k = 307$)
122. Memory recall tests and differentiation of schizophrenia from controls (Aleman, Hijman, de Haan, & Kahn, 1999; effect size is for studies with demographically matched comparison participants).	.50	2,290
123. CBCL parent report of total problems and psychiatric referral status (receiving treatment vs. not; Achenbach, 1991b; raw data to generate this effect size were obtained from Thomas M. Achenbach [personal communication, February 5, 1999]. Coefficient compares parent ratings of children in treatment with parent ratings of demographically matched control children not receiving treatment).[c]	.51	4,220
124. WAIS IQ subtests and differentiation of dementia from controls (H. Christensen & Mackinnon, 1992; effect computed from data presented in their Tables 1 and 2. The reported N is for the largest sample across the individual subtest comparisons).	.52	516
125. Single serum progesterone testing and diagnosis of any nonviable pregnancy (Mol, Lijmer, et al., 1998; following the original authors, we used only the 10 prospective cohort studies listed in their Table II).	.52	3,804
126. MRI results and detection of ruptured silicone gel breast implants (C. M. Goodman, Cohen, Thornby, & Netscher, 1998; these authors found that mammography [$r = .21$, $N = 381$] and ultrasound [$r = .42$, $N = 541$] were less effective than MRI).	.53	382
127. Association of Hachinski ischemic scores with post-mortem classification of dementia type (Moroney et al., 1997; effect size computed from their Figure 1 using continuous scores and the Alzheimer's, mixed, and multiinfarct group classifications on a continuum).	.55	312
128. MRI results and detection of lymph node metastases in cervical cancer (Scheidler, Hricak, Yu, Subak, & Segal, 1997; an effect size could not be computed for one study included in this meta-analysis).	.55	817
129. Cognitive tests of information-processing speed and reasoning ability (Verhaeghen & Salthouse, 1997).	.55	4,026
130. MRI results and differentiation of dementia from controls (Zakzanis, 1998; PET and SPECT findings from this meta-analysis were slightly less valid or based on smaller samples, so are not reported. Neuropsychological findings	.57	374

TABLE 13.2 (*continued*)

Predictor and criterion (study and notes)	r	N
were not used because D. Christensen, Hadzi-Pavlovic, & Jacomb, 1991, reported a more extensive meta-analysis).		
131. WAIS IQ scores and conceptually meaningful criterion measures (K. P. Parker, Hanson, & Hunsley, 1988, Table 2; Hiller, Rosenthal, Bornstein, Berry, & Brunell-Neuleib, 1999, expressed concern about K. P. Parker et al.'s results because some effect sizes came from unfocused F tests [i.e., >1 *df* in the numerator], although the overall effect increases when these results are excluded).	.57	(K = 39)
132. Exercise ECG results and identification of coronary artery disease (Fleischmann, Hunink, Kuntz, & Douglas, 1998; results were estimated from the reported sensitivity and specificity in conjunction with the base rate of coronary artery disease and the total independent N across studies).	.58	2,637
133. Ultrasound results and identification of deep venous thrombosis (Wells, Lensing, Davidson, Prins, & Hirsh, 1995).	.60	1,616
134. Neuropsychologists' test-based judgments and presence/localization of impairment (Garb & Schramke, 1996; effect size calculated from the accuracy of judgments relative to base rates [see Garb & Schramke, 1996, pp. 143, 144–145]).	.60	1,606
135. Long-term verbal memory tests and differentiation of dementia from depression (H. Christensen, Griffiths, MacKinnon, & Jacomb, 1997; effect data taken from their Table 4).	.61	(K = 32)
136. CT results and detection of metastases from head and neck cancer (Merrit, Williams, James, & Porubsky, 1997; N was obtained from the original studies).	.64	517
137. Neuropsychological tests and differentiation of dementia from controls (D. Christensen, Hadzi-Pavlovic, & Jacomb, 1991; the effect size was derived from studies explicitly stating that dementia had been diagnosed independent of the neuropsychological test results [see D. Christensen et al., 1991, p. 150]).	.68	(k = 94)
138. Immunoglobulin-G antiperinuclear factor scores and detection of rheumatoid arthritis (Berthelot, Garnier, Glémarec, & Flipo, 1998).	.68	2,541
139. MMPI Validity Scales and detection of malingered psychopathology (primarily analogue studies; data combined from Berry, Baer, & Harris, 1991; and Rogers, Sewell, & Salekin, 1994; average weighted effect size calculated from Tables 1 and 2 of Berry et al. and Table 1 of Rogers et al.).	.74	11,204
140. MMPI basic scales: booklet vs. computerized form (Finger & Ones, 1999; the alternate forms reliability coefficients for each scale were weighted by sample size [*n*s from 508 to 872], and the average N is reported).	.78	732
141. Thoracic impedance scores and criterion measures of cardiac stroke volume and output (Fuller, 1992; only data from methodologically "adequate" studies were included.	.81	(K = 24)

(*continued*)

TABLE 13.2 (*continued*)

Predictor and criterion (study and notes)	r	N
The mean weighted correlation for each criterion measure was weighted by the number of studies contributing to the mean and then averaged across all criterion measures. Because Fuller [1992, p. 105] cryptically stated that studies were excluded unless there was "concurrence of measurement between the two instruments being compared," it is possible that relevant studies were omitted when the findings did not support the hypothesis).		
142. Creatinine clearance test results and kidney function (glomerual filtration rate; Campens & Buntinx, 1997; results for measured and estimated [by the Cockroft–Gault formula] creatinine clearance were pooled. The N reported in our table is slightly inflated because it was impossible to identify the specific n for two of the studies that used both measures).	.83	2,459
143. Duplex ultrasonography results and identification of peripheral artery disease (de Vries, Hunink, & Polak, 1996; weighted effect size derived from data in their Table 2 using patient samples. The reported N refers to the number of observations; some patients were tested multiple times).	.83	4,906
144. Finger or ear pulse oximetry readings in patients and arterial oxygen saturation (L. A. Jensen, Onyskiw, & Prasad, 1998).	.84	4,354

Note: ADHD = attention-deficit hyperactivity disorder; CBCL = Child Behavior Checklist; CFI = Camberwell Family Interview; CT = computed tomography; ECG = electrocardiogram; GPA = grade point average; IQ = intelligence quotient; k = number of effect sizes contributing to the mean estimate; K = number of studies contributing to the mean estimates; MCMI–II = Millon Clinical Multiaxial Inventory—2nd Edition; MMPI = Minnesota Multiphasic Personality Inventory; MPD = multiple personality disorder; MRI = magnetic resonance imaging; PET = positron emission tomography; PRS = Prognostic Rating Scale; PTSD = posttraumatic stress disorder; SIL = squamous intraepithelial lesions; SPECT = single photon emission computed tomography; TAT = Thematic Apperception Test; WAIS = Wechsler Adult Intelligence Scale; WISC = Wechsler Intelligence Scale for Children; YASR = Young Adult Self-Report.
[a]The actual effect was a statistically nonsignificant value of −.013 (i.e., in the direction of opposite of prediction). [b]Triple marker refers to the joint use of alpha-fetoprotein, human chorionic gonadotropin, and unconjugated estriol. [c]These results are not from meta-analyses and were not identified through our systematic literature search.

dementia from normal cognitive functioning [Table 13.2, Entry 137], computed tomography [CT] for detecting metastases from head and neck cancer [Table 13.2, Entry 136]).

Second, validity coefficients for many psychological tests are indistinguishable from those observed for many medical tests. For instance, when considering validity coefficients in the .30 to .50 range, one finds results from the MMPI (Table 13.2, Entries 94, 99, 100, & 114), Millon Clinical Multiaxial Inventory (Table 13.2, Entry 93), Thematic Apperception Test (TAT; Table 13.2, Entries 90 & 95), Rorschach (Table 13.2, Entries 86, 89, 90, 95, & 111), Hare Psychopathy Checklist (Table 13.2, Entry 84), various neuropsychological and cognitive tests (Table 13.2, Entries 75, 76, 81, 83, 101, 103, 113, & 122), and the impact of psychological assessment feedback on the subsequent well-being of patients (Table 13.2, Entry 77). One also finds results from electrocardiograms (Table 13.2, Entry 72), CT (Table 13.2, Entries 79, 82, & 104), mammography (Table 13.2, Entry 80), magnetic resonance imaging (MRI; Table 13.2, Entry 107), ultrasound (Table 13.2, Entry 98), dental radiographs (Table 13.2, Entries 88, 108, & 112), Papanicolaou (Pap) smears (Table 13.2, Entry 87), cardiac fluoroscopy (Table 13.2, Entry 109), single photon emission computed tomography (Table 13.2, Entry 116), technetium bone scanning (Table 13.2, Entry 118), and serum cholesterol levels (Table 13.2, Entry 121).

At the upper end of Table 13.2, one generally sees results from studies in which the experimental design helped to increase effect size magnitudes. Of the 22 coefficients above .50, 19 are larger than the effects likely to be found in applied clinical practice. Most often (in 17 cases), this was because the condition to be detected by the test (e.g., peripheral artery disease, impaired kidney function, malingering) occurred much more often in the research studies than it would in actual practice (Finn & Kamphuis, 1995; Lijmer et al., 1999). In another instance, tests from the same method family as the predictor were used occasionally as validation criteria (Table 13.2, Entry 131), and in a final instance, it appears the author may have excluded studies when results were not as expected (Table 13.2, Entry 141). Despite these factors, what is most salient for our purpose is the difficulty one has in distinguishing psychological test validity from medical test validity. For instance, the ability to detect dementia is at least as good with neuropsychological tests ($r = .68$; Table 13.2, Entry 137) as it is with MRI ($r = .57$; Table 13.2, Entry 130).

At the low end of the validity range, one generally sees results from studies that should produce low associations. These include studies that (a) evaluate the impact of testing on a subsequent outcome variable (e.g., ultrasound on pregnancy outcome, Table 13.2, Entries 3, 4, & 6; geriatric medical assessment on reduced deaths, Table 13.2, Entry 9), (b) use tests to screen for rare conditions (e.g., triple marker screening for Trisomy 18, Table 13.2, Entry 8), or (c) use tests to predict rare outcome events (e.g., hopelessness for predicting suicide, Table 13.2, Entry 15). Once again, however, even at these lower values, psychological test validity is difficult to distinguish from medical test validity. For instance, the MMPI, Rorschach, and ventilatory lung function test all have roughly equal validity coefficients ($rs = .05-07$; Table 13.2, Entries 10–12) for the difficult task of predicting cancer 2 to 3 decades later.

As a third general observation, our review does not reveal uniformly superior or uniformly inferior methods of psychological assessment. Despite the perceptions held by some, assessments with the Rorschach and TAT do not produce consistently lower validity coefficients than alternative personality tests. Instead, performance tests of cognitive ability, performance tests of personality (e.g., Rorschach, TAT), and self-report tests of personality all produce a range of validity coefficients that vary largely as a function of the criterion under consideration.[8]

Fourth, the findings indicate that psychological tests often generate substantial effect sizes. In particular, the validity coefficients found for psychological tests frequently exceed the coefficients found for many of the medical and psychological interventions listed in Table 13.1.

Taken together, the extensive array of findings in Table 13.2 offers compelling support for the value of psychological testing and assessment. To the extent that health care administrators differentially limit reimbursement for psychological tests relative to medical tests, such actions are not justifiable on the basis of a broad overview of the empirical evidence.

DISTINCTIONS BETWEEN PSYCHOLOGICAL TESTING AND PSYCHOLOGICAL ASSESSMENT

Psychological testing is a relatively straightforward process wherein a particular scale is administered to obtain a specific score. Subsequently, a descriptive meaning can be applied to the score on the basis of normative, nomothetic[9] findings. In contrast, psychological assessment is concerned with the clinician who takes a variety of test scores, generally obtained from multiple test methods, and considers the data in the context of history, referral information, and observed behavior to understand the person being evaluated, to answer the referral questions, and then to communicate findings to the patient, his or her significant others, and referral sources.

In psychological testing, the nomothetic meaning associated with a scaled score of 10 on the Arithmetic subtest from the Wechsler Adult Intelligence Scale–Third Edition (Wechsler, 1997) is that a person possesses av-

---

[8]Technically, it is not appropriate to compare validity coefficients across the types of tests presented in Table 13.2. As our notes to the table indicate, we did not report every coefficient obtained from each meta-analysis, some meta-analyses contributed more than one coefficient to the table, and at times, results from more than one meta-analysis were combined into a single value for the table. Furthermore, we made no effort to correct for design features that may have caused effect sizes to vary, and the table contains a vast array of nonequivalent criterion measures and validation tasks. Nonetheless, we realize that some readers may still wonder if differences exist within Table 13.2. Keeping in mind how the analysis is not strictly warranted, we used a random effects model and looked for differences across types of tests using the studies that were identified in our meta-analytic search. There were no significant differences at a global level, $F(4, 128) = 1.96, p \geq .05$, or when pairwise differences were examined with post hoc Scheffé tests. The unweighted means rs were as follows: Self-report personality tests = .24 ($SD = .18, n = 24$), performance personality tests (i.e., Rorschach, apperceptive storytelling tasks, sentence completion) = .33 ($SD = .09, n = 8$), cognitive or neuropsychological tests = .34 ($SD = .17$, $n = 26$), other psychological tests (e.g., observer ratings) = .30 ($SD = .08, n = 7$), and medical tests = .36 ($SD = .21, n = 63$).

[9]Nomothetic refers to general laws or principles. Nomothetic research typically studies the relationship among a limited number of characteristics across a large number of people. Idiographic refers to the intensive study of a single individual. Here, the focus is on how a large number of characteristics fit together uniquely within one person or in the context of a single life.

erage skills in mental calculations. In an idiographic assessment, the same score may have very different meanings. After considering all relevant information, this score may mean a patient with a recent head injury has had a precipitous decline in auditory attention span and the capacity to mentally manipulate information. In a patient undergoing cognitive remediation for attentional problems secondary to a head injury, the same score may mean there has been a substantial recovery of cognitive functioning. In a third, otherwise very intelligent patient, a score of 10 may mean pronounced symptoms of anxiety and depression are impairing skills in active concentration. Thus, and consistent with Shea's (1985) observation that no clinical question can be answered solely by a test score, many different conditions can lead to an identical score on a particular test. The assessment task is to use test-derived sources of information in combination with historical data, presenting complaints, observations, interview results, and information from third parties to disentangle the competing possibilities (Eyde et al., 1993). The process is far from simple and requires a high degree of skill and sophistication to be implemented properly.

DISTINCTIONS BETWEEN FORMAL ASSESSMENT AND OTHER SOURCES OF CLINICAL INFORMATION

All mental health professionals assess patient problems. Almost universally, such evaluations rely on unstructured interviews and informal observations as the key sources of information about the patient. Although these methods can be efficient and effective ways to obtain data, they are also limited. When interviews are unstructured, clinicians may overlook certain areas of functioning and focus more exclusively on presenting complaints. When interviews are highly structured, clinicians can lose the forest for the trees and make precise but errant judgments (Hammond, 1996; Tucker, 1998). Such mistakes may occur when the clinician focuses on responses to specific interview questions (e.g., diagnostic criteria) without fully considering the salience of these responses in the patient's broader life context or without adequately recognizing how the individual responses fit together into a symptomatically coherent pattern (Arkes, 1981; Klein, Ouimette, Kelly, Ferro, & Riso, 1994; Perry, 1992).

Additional confounds derive from patients, who are often poor historians and/or biased presenters of information (see, e.g., John & Robins, 1994; Moffitt et al., 1997; Rogler, Malgady, & Tryon, 1992; Widom & Morris, 1997). For instance, neurologically impaired patients frequently lack awareness of their deficits or personality changes (Lezak, 1995), and response styles such as defensiveness or exaggeration affect the way patients are viewed by clinical interviewers or observers (see, e.g., Alterman et al., 1996; Pogge,

Stokes, Frank, Wong, & Harvey, 1997). Defensive patients are seen as more healthy, whereas patients who exaggerate their distress are seen as more impaired. In contrast to less formal clinical methods, psychological testing can identify such biased self-presentation styles (see Entries 38, 99, 114, & 139 in Table 13.2), leading to a more accurate understanding of the patient's genuine difficulties.

There are several other ways that formal psychological assessment can circumvent problems associated with typical clinical interviews. First, psychological assessments generally measure a large number of personality, cognitive, or neuropsychological characteristics simultaneously. As a result, they are inclusive and often cover a range of functional domains, many of which might be overlooked during less formal evaluation procedures.

Second, psychological tests provide empirically quantified information, allowing for more precise measurement of patient characteristics than is usually obtained from interviews.

Third, psychological tests have standardized administration and scoring procedures. Because each patient is presented with a uniform stimulus that serves as a common yardstick to measure his or her characteristics, an experienced clinician has enhanced ability to detect subtle behavioral cues that may indicate psychological or neuropsychological complications (see, e.g., Lezak, 1995). Standardization also can reduce legal and ethical problems because it minimizes the prospect that unintended bias may adversely affect the patient. In less formal assessments, standardization is lacking, and the interaction between clinician and patient can vary considerably as a function of many factors.

Fourth, psychological tests are normed, permitting each patient to be compared with a relevant group of peers, which in turn allows the clinician to formulate refined inferences about strengths and limitations. Although clinicians using informal evaluation procedures generate their own internal standards over time, these are less systematic and are more likely to be skewed by the type of patients seen in a particular setting. Moreover, normed information accurately conveys how typical or unusual the patient is on a given characteristic, which helps clinicians to more adequately consider base rates — the frequency with which certain conditions occur in a setting (see, e.g., Finn & Kamphuis, 1995).

Fifth, research on the reliability and validity of individual test scales sets formal assessment apart from other sources of clinical information. These data allow the astute clinician to understand the strengths or limitations of various scores. Without this, practitioners have little ability to gauge the accuracy of the data they process when making judgments.

The use of test batteries is a final distinguishing feature of formal psychological assessment. In a battery, psychologists generally use a range of methods to obtain information and cross-check hypotheses. These methods include self-reports, performance tasks, observations, and information derived from behavioral or functional assessment strategies (see Haynes et al., 1997). By incorporating multiple methods, the assessment psychologist is able to efficiently gather a wide range of information to facilitate understanding the patient.

CROSS-METHOD AGREEMENT

Our last point raises a critical issue about the extent to which distinct assessment methods provide unique versus redundant information. To evaluate this issue, Table 13.3 presents a broad survey of examples. As before, we attempted to draw on meta-analytic reviews or large-scale studies for this table, though this information was not often available. Consequently, many of the entries represent a new synthesis of relevant literature.[10]

To highlight independent methods, we excluded studies that used aggregation strategies to maximize associations (e.g., self-reports correlated with a composite of spouse and peer reports; see Cheek, 1982; Epstein, 1983; Tsujimoto, Hamilton, & Berger, 1990) and ignored moderators of agreement that may have been identified in the literature. We also excluded studies in which cross-method comparisons were not reasonably independent. For instance, we omitted studies in which patients completed a written self-report instrument that was then correlated with the results from a structured interview that asked comparable questions in an oral format (see, e.g., Richter, Werner, Heerlein, Kraus, & Sauer, 1998). However, to provide a wide array of contrasts across different sources, we at times report results that are inflated by criterion contamination.

A review of Table 13.3 indicates that distinct assessment methods provide unique information. This is evident from the relatively low to moderate associations between independent methods of assessing similar constructs. The findings hold for children and adults and when various types of knowledgeable informants (e.g., self, clinician, parent, peer) are compared with each other or with observed behaviors and task performance. For instance, child and adolescent self-ratings have only moderate correspondence with the ratings of parents (Table 13.3, Entries 1–4), teachers (Table 13.3, Entries 8–10), clinicians (Table 13.3, Entries 5 & 6), or observers (Table 13.3, Entry 7), and the ratings from each of these sources have only moderate associations with each other (Table 3, Entries 12–18, 20–21). For adults, self-reports of personality and mood have small to moderate associations with the

---

[10]For Table 13.3, we searched PsycINFO using a variety of strategies. We also relied on bibliographic citations from contemporary articles and reviews. Although we undoubtedly overlooked pertinent studies, our search was extensive. The 55 entries in Table 13.3 integrate data from more than 800 samples and 190,000 participants, and we included all studies that fit within our search parameters. Thus, we are confident the findings are robust and generalizable.

TABLE 13.3
A Sample of Cross-Method Convergent Associations
Across Single, Independent Sources of Information

Sources of data and constructs (study and notes)	r	κ	N
Children and Adolescents			
1. Self vs. parent: behavioral and emotional problems (data combined from Achenbach, 1991a, Achenbach, McConaughy, & Howell, 1987; Cole, Peeke, Martin, Truglio, & Seroczynski, 1998 [average correlation estimated from ranges reported in Cole et al., 1998, p. 452, with *N* determined by the number of participants (288) multiplied by the number of data collection waves (6)]; Cole,Truglio, & Peeke, 1997; Epkins & Meyers, 1994; Forehand, Frame, Wierson, Armistead, & Kempton, 1991; Handwerk, Larzelere, Soper, & Friman, 1999; Henry, Moffitt, Caspi, Langley, & Silva, 1994; Lee, Elliott, & Barbour, 1994; McConaughy, Stanger, & Achenbach, 1992 [concurrent results only]; Meyer, 1996b [average associations between MMPI–A scales and conceptually matched parent ratings derived from the MMPI–A restandardization sample]; Pastorelli, Barbaranelli, Cermak, Rozsa, & Caprara, 1997; Phares & Compas, 1990; Phares, Compas, & Howell, 1989; Reynolds & Kamphaus, 1998 [using only scales with the same name]; Treiber & Mabe, 1987; Verhulst & van der Ende, 1991, 1992).	.29		14,102
2. Self vs. parent: behavioral and emotional problems— *Q* correlations of profile similarity (Achenbach, 1991a; the *Q* correlations were averaged across boys and girls and across 89 common items and eight syndrome scales).	.29		1,829
3. Self vs. parent: symptom change in treatment (Lambert, Salzer, & Bickman, 1998).	.19		199
4. Self vs. parent: *DSM* Axis I disorder (data combined from Frick, Silverthorn, & Evans, 1994; Puura et al., 1998; Rapee, Barrett, Dadds, & Evans, 1994; Reich, Herjanic, Welner, & Gandhy, 1982; Rubio-Stipec et al., 1994; and Vitiello, Malone, Buschle, Delaney, & Behar, 1990).		.24	1, 136
5. Self vs. clinician: behavioral and emotional problems (data combined from Achenbach, McConaughy, & Howell, 1987; and Meyer, 1996b [average associations between MMPI–A scales and conceptually matched clinician ratings derived from the MMPI–A restandardization sample]).	.14		1,079
6. Self vs. clinician: *DSM* Axis I disorder (data summarize associations between diagnoses from fully structured interviews [i.e., self-report] and clinician-assigned diagnoses; data combined from Aronen, Noam, & Weinstein, 1993; Ezpeleta, de la Osa, Doménech, Navarro, & Losilla, 1997; Piacentini et al., 1993; Rubio-Stipec et al., 1994; Schwab-Stone et al., 1996 [excluding predictor and criterion data generated by the same clinician during the same interview]; Vitiello, Malone, Buschle, Delaney, & Behar, 1990; and Weinstein, Stone, Noam, Grives, & Schwab-Stone, 1989).		.23[a]	998

TABLE 13.3 (*continued*)

Sources of data and constructs (study and notes)	r	κ	N
7. Self vs. clinical observer: change in treatment (Lambert, Salzer, & Bickman, 1998).	.28		199
8. Self vs. teacher: Behavioral and emotional problems (data combined with Achenbach, 1991a; Achenbach, McConaughy, & Howell, 1987; Cole, Truglio, & Peeke, 1997; Crowley, Worchel, & Ash, 1992; Epkins & Meyers, 1994; Forehand, Frame, Wierson, Armistead, & Kempton, 1991; Henry, Moffitt, Caspi, Langley, & Silva, 1994; Lee, Elliott, & Barbour, 1994; Malloy, Yarlas, Montvilo, & Sugarman, 1996; Phares, Compas, & Howell, 1989; Reynolds & Kamphaus, 1998 [using only scales with the same name]; Verhulst & van der Ende, 1991; and Wolfe et al., 1987).	.21		9,814
9. Self vs. teacher: behavioral and emotional problems— Q correlations of profile similarity (Achenbach, 1991a; the Q correlations were averaged across boys and girls and across 89 common items and eight syndrome scales).	.17		1,222
10. Self vs. teacher: test anxiety (Hembree, 1988; reported effect is the average for the lower and intermediate grade levels given in Table 4 of the article).	.23		3,099
11. Self vs. aggregated peer ratings: behavioral and emotional problems (data combined from Achenbach, McConaughy, & Howell, 1987; Cole, Truglio, & Peeke, 1997; Crowley, Worchel, & Ash, 1992; Epkins & Meyers, 1994; Malloy, Yarlas, Montvilo, & Sugarman, 1996; and Pastorelli, Barbaranelli, Cermak, Rozsa, & Caprara, 1997).[b]	.26		8,821
12. Parent vs. teacher: summed behavioral and emotional problems (data combined from Achenbach, 1991a; Achenbach, McConaughy, & Howell, 1987; Carter, Grigorenko, & Pauls, 1995; M. Cohen, Becker, & Campbell, 1990; Cole,Truglio, & Peeke, 1997; Epkins & Meyers, 1994; Forehand, Frame, Wierson, Armistead, & Kempton, 1991; Garrison & Earls, 1985; Henry, Moffitt, Caspi, Laugley, & Silva, 1994; P. S. Jensen, Traylor, Xanakis, & Davis, 1987; Kline & Lachar, 1992 [results limited to obvious correspondence in their Table 2]; Kumpulainen et al., 1999 [matched factor constructs only]; Lee, Elliott, & Barbour, 1994; McConaughy, Stanger, & Achenbach, 1992 [concurrent results only]; Phares, Compas, & Howell, 1989; Reynolds & Kamphaus, 1998 [using only scales with the same name]; Spiker, Kraemer, Constantine, & Bryant, 1992; Verhulst & Akkerhuis, 1989; and Verhulst & van der Ende, 1991).	.29		29,163
13. Parent vs. teacher: specific behavioral and emotional problems (Verhulst & Akkerhuis, 1989).	.16		1,161
14. Parent vs. teacher: behavioral and emotional problems—Q correlations of profile similarity (Achenbach, 1991a; the Q correlations were averaged across boys and girls and across 89 common items and eight syndrome scales).	.22		2,274

(*continued*)

TABLE 13.3 (*continued*)

Sources of data and constructs (study and notes)	*r*	*κ*	*N*
15. Parent vs. teacher: *DSM* Axis I disorder (data combined from Frick, Silverthorn, & Evans, 1994; and Offord et al., 1996).		.13	1,229
16. Parent vs. clinician: behavioral and emotional problems (data combined from Achenbach, McConaughy, & Howell, 1987; and Kline & Lachar, 1992 [results limited to obvious correspondence in their Table 2]).	.34		1,725
17. Parent vs. clinician: *DSM* Axis I disorder (data summarize associations between diagnoses from fully structured interviews [i.e., parent report] or diagnostic questionnaires and clinician-assigned diagnoses; data combined from Ezpeleta, de la Osa, Doménech, Navarro, & Losilla, 1997; Morita, Suzuki, & Kamoshita, 1990; Piacentini et al., 1993; Rubio-Stipec et al., 1994; Schwab-Stone et al., 1996 [excluding predictor and criterion data generated by the same clinician during the same interview]; and Vitiello, Malone, Buschle, Delaney, & Behar, 1990).		.39[a]	786
18. Parent vs. direct observer of child behavior: behavioral and emotional problems (Achenbach, McConaughy, & Howell, 1987).	.27		279
19. Parent vs. cognitive test: attentional problems (effect summarizes the association between parent ratings of inattention and the WISC–R/III Freedom From Distractibility Index; data combined from M. Cohen, Becker, & Campbell, 1990; Reinecke, Beebe, & Stein, 1999; and Riccio, Cohen, Hall, & Ross, 1997).	.03		451
20. Teacher vs. clinician: behavioral and emotional problems (Achenbach, McConaughy, & Howell, 1987).	.34		1,325
21. Teacher vs. direct observer of child behavior: behavioral and emotional problems (Achenbach, McConaughy, & Howell, 1987).	.42		732
22. Teacher vs. cognitive test: attentional problems (effect summarizes the association between teacher ratings of inattention and the WISC–R/III Freedom From Distractibility Index; data combined from Anastopoulos, Spisto, & Maher, 1994; M. Cohen, Becker, & Campbell, 1990; Lowman, Schwanz, & Kamphaus, 1996; Reinecke, Beebe, & Stein, 1999; and Riccio, Cohen, Hall, & Ross, 1997).	.10		483
Adults			
23. Self vs. spouse/partner: personality and mood (data combined from A. L. Edwards & Klockars, 1981; and Meyer, 1996b [average association between MMPI–2 scales and conceptually matched spouse ratings derived from the MMPI–2 restandardization sample]).	.29		2,011
24. Self vs. spouse/partner: Big Five personality traits— domains and facets (data combined from Bagby et al., 1998 [included friend and spouse ratings]; Borkenau & Liebler, 1993; Conley, 1985 [concurrent ratings only]; Costa & McCrae, 1988 [only concurrent correlations were used], 1992; Foltz, Morse, Calvo, & Barber, 1997;	.44		1,774

TABLE 13.3 (*continued*)

Sources of data and constructs (study and notes)	r	κ	N
McCrae, 1982; McCrae, Stone, Fagan, & Costa, 1998; Mutén, 1991; and Yang et al., 1999).			
25. Self vs. parent: personality characteristics (including the Big Five; data combined from Caldwell-Andrews, Baer, & Berry, 2000; Funder, Kolar, & Blackman, 1995; Harkness, Tellegen, & Waller, 1995; and Harlan & Clark, 1999; if results for both mothers and fathers were reported for the same participants, they were treated as independent findings. The median correlation for self–father ratings was used from Harlan & Clark because this was all that was reported).	.33		828
26. Self vs. peer: personality and mood (data combined from Funder & Colvin, 1988; Funder, Kolar, & Blackman, 1995; Harkness, Tellegen, & Waller, 1995; A. F. Hayes & Dunning, 1997; Hill, Zrull, & McIntire, 1998; Kurokawa & Weed, 1998; Oltmanns, Turkheimer, & Strauss, 1998; Paunonen, 1989 [estimates derived from unpartialed correlations reported in Paunonen's Figures 2 and 3 using only degree of acquaintanceship rated 6–9]; Watson & Clark, 1991; and Zuckerman et al., 1988. Funder and Colvin reported correlations between self-ratings and the composite of two informants. Because the average interinformant correlation was also reported, an estimate of the correlation between self-ratings and the ratings of a single informant was generated using the formula provided by Tsujimoto, Hamilton, & Berger, 1990. The same formula was used with data in Oltmanns et al. to estimate the correlation between self-ratings and the ratings of a single peer).	.27		2,119
27. Self vs. peer: Big Five personality traits—domains and facets (data combined from Cheek, 1982; Costa & McCrae, 1992; Funder, Kolar, & Blackman, 1995 [the two sets of self–peer associations in their Table 1 were treated as independent samples]; John & Robins, 1993; Koestner, Bernieri, & Zuckerman, 1994; McCrae & Costa, 1987; Paulhus & Reynolds, 1995; Piedmont, 1994; Zuckerman, Bernieri, Koestner, & Rosenthal, 1989; and Zuckerman, Miyake, Koestner, Baldwin, & Osborne, 1991. For Paulhus & Reynolds, the Wave 2 validity coefficients from their Table 4 were adjusted to reflect the validity of a single rater. This was done by assuming the initial findings were generated from four-rater composites and using the formula presented in Tsujimoto, Hamilton, & Berger, 1990. The same formula was used to estimate validity for a single rater from Piedmont's data, although it could not be used with Koestner et al.).	.31		1,967
28. Self vs. peer: job performance (Conway & Huffcutt, 1997).	.19		6,359
29. Self vs. significant other: attentional problems and impulsivity (Ryan, 1998).	.22		202
30. Self vs. significant other: *DSM* Axis II personality disorder diagnosis (data combined from Bernstein		.12	768

(*continued*)

TABLE 13.3 (*continued*)

Sources of data and constructs (study and notes)	r	κ	N
et al., 1997; Dowson, 1992 [kappa estimated to be 0.0 when values were not reported but said to be non-significant]; Dreessen, Hildebrand, & Arntz, 1998; Ferro & Klein, 1997; Riso, Klein, Anderson, Ouimette, & Lizardi, 1994; and Zimmerman, Pfohl, Coryell, Stangl, & Corenthal, 1988).			
31. Self vs. clinician: treatment-related functioning, symptomatology, and outcome (data combined from Cribbs & Niva, 2000, and Nebeker, Lambert, & Huefner, 1995).	.29		7,903
32. Self vs. clinician: *DSM* Axis II personality disorder characteristics (findings examine the correspondence between self-report scales of personality disorders and clinician ratings on the same dimensions; data were combined from Barber & Morse, 1994 [using only the dimensional scores reported in their Table 5]; Burgess, 1991; de Ruiter & Greeven, 2000; Ekselius, Lindström, von Knorring, Bodlund, & Kullgren, 1994 [coefficients were Spearman correlations]; Fossati et al., 1998; Hart, Forth, & Hare, 1991; Hunt & Andrews, 1992 [intraclass correlations were used in this study]; Kennedy et al., 1995; Marlowe, Husband, Bonieskie, Kirby, & Platt, 1997; Millon, 1994; Overholser, 1994 [Studies 1, 5, 8, 9, 12, and 13 from Overholser's Table III were used]; Rogers, Salekin, & Sewell, 1999 [Studies 12, 19, 20, and 22 from their Table 3 were used]; Soldz, Budman, Demby, & Merry, 1993; and Trull & Larson, 1994).	.33[a]		2,778
33. Self vs. clinician: *DSM* Axis II personality disorder diagnosis (findings examine the correspondence between diagnostic cutoff criteria from self-report scales and clinician-assigned diagnoses; data were combined from de Ruiter & Greeven, 2000; Ekselius, Lindström, von Knorring, Bodlund, & Kullgren, 1994 [kappa was calculated from their Tables 1 and 2]; Fossati et al., 1998; Jacobsberg, Perry, & Frances, 1995 [kappa was calculated from their Table 1]; Kennedy et al., 1995; Marlowe, Husband, Bonieskie, Kirby, & Platt, 1997 [kappa was calculated from their Table 3 using BR > 84 data; BR > 74 data led to a smaller average kappa]; Nussbaum & Rogers, 1992; Perry, 1992; Renneberg, Chambless, Dowdall, Fauerbach, & Gracely, 1992 [kappa coefficients were available for all disorders using BR > 74 as the cutoff, so they were used here]; Rogers, Salekin, & Sewell, 1999 [Studies 2 and 11 were used]; Soldz, Budman, Demby, & Merry, 1993; and Trull & Larson, 1994).	.18[a]		2,859
34. Self vs. clinician: *DSM* Axis I disorders (Meyer, 2002; coefficient summarizes the association between diagnoses from a fully structured interview [i.e., self-report] and clinician-assigned diagnoses, excluding designs in which both diagnoses were derived from the same interview).	.34[a]		5,990
35. Self vs. clinician: Big Five personality traits (domains only; Piedmont & Ciarrocchi, 1999).	.32		132

TABLE 13.3 (*continued*)

Sources of data and constructs (study and notes)	r	κ	N
36. Self vs. supervisor: job performance (Conway & Huff-cutt, 1997).	.22		10,359
37. Self vs. subordinate: job performance (Conway & Huffcutt, 1997).	.14		5,925
38. Self vs. cognitive test or grades: general intelligence (data combined from Borkenau & Liebler, 1993; Mabe & West, 1982 [using the *n*s reported in their Table 1]; and Paulhus, Lysy, & Yik, 1998).	.24		904
39. Self vs. cognitive test or grades: scholastic ability (Mabe & West, 1982; the reported *N* was derived from their Table 1 using studies that reported on the strength of association).[c]	.38		8,745
40. Self vs. cognitive test: memory problems (data combined from Branca, Giordani, Lutz, & Saper, 1995; Brown, Dodrill, Clark, & Zych, 1991; Gagnon et al., 1994; Gass, Russell, & Hamilton, 1990 [using only the memory-specific self-report scale]; Herzog & Rodgers, 1989; Johansson, Allen-Burge, & Zarit, 1997; Olsson & Juslin, 1999; Seidenberg, Haltiner, Taylor, Hermann, & Wyler, 1994; G. E. Smith, Petersen, Ivnik, Malec, & Tangalos, 1996; J. L.Taylor, Miller, & Tinklenberg, 1992; and Zelinski, Gilewski, & Anthony-Bergstone, 1990).	.13		5,717
41. Self vs. cognitive test: attentional problems (data combined from Meyer, 1996b; Paulhus, Aks, & Coren, 1990; Ryan, 1998; Seidenberg, Haltiner, Taylor, Hermann, & Wyler, 1994; and Turner & Gilliland, 1997 [unreported but nonsignificant correlations were considered to be zero]).	.06		522
42. Self vs. Thematic Apperception Test: achievement motivation (Spangler, 1992).[c]	.09		2,785
43. Self vs. Thematic Apperception Test: problem solving (Ronan, Colavito, & Hammontree, 1993).	.13		199
44. Self vs. Rorschach: emotional distress, psychosis, and interpersonal wariness (data combined from Meyer, 1997; and Meyer, Riethmiller, Brooks, Benoit, & Handler, 2000).	.04		689
45. Self vs. observed behavior: personality characteristics (data combined from Gosling, John, Craik, & Robins, 1998; Kolar, Funder, & Colvin, 1996; and Moskowitz, 1990. Kolar et al. used the aggregated ratings of six observers on average, whereas Moskowitz relied on the aggregated ratings of four observers; thus, the overall coefficient reported here is larger than it would be if each study had relied on behavior ratings from a single observer).	.16		274
46. Self vs. observed behavior: attitudes (Kraus, 1995; the reported *N* was derived from the total number of studies times the average *n* per study. Kim & Hunter, 1993, also conducted a meta-analysis of attitude–behavior relations. However, in their criterion measures, they did not distinguish between self-reported behavior and observed behavior).	.32		15,624

(*continued*)

TABLE 13.3. (*continued*)

Sources of data and constructs (study and notes)	r	κ	N
47. Peers vs. observed behavior: personality characteristics (Kolar, Funder, & Colvin, 1996; coefficient reflects the average of two sets of single-peer ratings correlated with observed behavior. Ratings of observed behavior were aggregated from six observers on average, so the reported correlation is larger than would be found if behavior was rated by a single observer).	.15		264
48. Clinician vs. consensus best estimate: *DSM* Axis II personality disorder diagnosis (data combined from Perry, 1992 [using only the Skodol et al. data]; Pilkonis et al., 1995 [all diagnostic data in their Table 1 were averaged]); and Pilkonis, Heape, Ruddy, & Serrao, 1991 [excluding PAF data but including baseline and follow-up kappa for "any personality disorder"].		.28	218
49. Significant other vs. significant other: target patient's *DSM* personality disorder diagnosis (Ferro & Klein, 1997).		.32	386
50. Significant other vs. clinician: target patient's depressive signs and symptoms (G. Parker et al., 1992; average agreement computed from their Tables 1 and 2).		.13	141
51. Judgments from one source of test data vs. another: personality, needs, and IQ (data combined from L. R. Goldberg & Werts, 1966; Howard, 1962 [total *N* was determined by multiplying the 10 patients by the seven raters]; and Little & Shneidman, 1959. For Little and Shneidman, congruence across judgments from the Rorschach, Thematic Apperception Test, MMPI, and Make a Picture Story Test was estimated by subtracting the average coefficient in their Table 10 from the average test coefficient reported in their Table 9).[d]	.12		158
52. Supervisor vs. peers: job performance (Conway & Huffcutt, 1997).	.34		7,101
53. Supervisor vs. subordinate: job performance (Conway & Huffcutt, 1997).	.22		4,815
54. Peers vs. subordinate: job performance (Conway & Huffcutt, 1997).	.22		3,938
55. Objective criteria vs. managerial ratings: job success (Bommer, Johnson, Rich, Podsakoff, & MacKenzie, 1995).	.32		8,341

Note: BR = base rate; *DSM* = *Diagnostic and Statistical Manual of Mental Disorders;* IQ = intelligence quotient; MMPI = Minnesota Multiphasic Personality Inventory; MMPI–A = adolescent version of MMPI; PAF = Personality Assessment Form; WISC–R/III = Wechsler Intelligence Scale for Children—Revised & Third Edition.

[a] These coefficients are inflated by criterion contamination. For instance, in an effort to maximize cross-observer correspondence, one study (Ekselius, Lindstrom, von Knorring, Bodlund, & Kullgren, 1994) went so far as to exclude the inferences that clinicians developed from their direct observations of the patient as a way to increase diagnostic agreement between patients and clinicians. [b] Because much of this data reflects the correlation between aggregated peer ratings and self-ratings, the coefficient is larger than would be obtained between self-ratings and the ratings of a single peer. [c] Result combines some data from children and adolescents with adults. [d] These studies were from the late 1950s and early 1960s. It is unclear whether the data may be different using more contemporary scoring and interpretive practices.

same characteristics measured by those who are close to the target person (Table 13.3, Entries 23–25, 29–30), peers (Table 13.3, Entries 26–28), clinicians (Table 13.3, Entries 31–34), performance tasks (Table 13.3, Entries 38–44), or observed behavior (Table 13.3, Entries 45–47).

The substantial independence between methods clearly extends into the clinical arena. Not only do patients, clinicians, parents, and observers have different views about psychotherapy progress or functioning in treatment (see Table 13.3, Entries 3, 7, & 31) but diagnoses have only moderate associations when they are derived from self-reports or the reports of parents, significant others and clinicians (see Table 13.3, Entries 4, 6, 15, 17, 30, 33, 34, 48, & 49).[11]

The data in Table 13.3 have numerous implications, both for the science of psychology and for applied clinical practice. We emphasize just two points. First, at best, any single assessment method provides a partial or incomplete representation of the characteristics it intends to measure. Second, in the world of applied clinical practice, it is not easy to obtain accurate or consensually agreed on information about patients. Both issues are considered in more detail below.

Distinct Methods and the Assessment Battery

A number of authors have described several key features that distinguish assessment methods (see, e.g., Achenbach, 1995; Achenbach, McConaughy, & Howell, 1987; Finn, 1996; McClelland, Koestner, & Weinberger, 1989; Meyer, 1996b; S. B. Miller, 1987; Moskowitz, 1986; Winter, John, Stewart, Klohnen, & Duncan, 1998). Under optimal conditions, (a) unstructured interviews elicit information relevant to thematic life narratives, although they are constrained by the range of topics considered and ambiguities inherent when interpreting this information; (b) structured interviews and self-report instruments elicit details concerning patients' conscious understanding of themselves and overtly experienced symptomatology, although they are limited by the patients' motivation to communicate frankly and their ability to make accurate judgments; (c) performance-based personality tests (e.g., Rorschach, TAT) elicit data about behavior in unstructured settings or implicit dynamics and underlying templates of perception and motivation, although they are constrained by task engagement and the nature of the stimulus materials; (d) performance-based cognitive tasks elicit findings about problem solving and functional capacities, although they are limited by motivation, task engagement, and setting; and (e) observer rating scales

---

[11] Methodologically, agreement between diagnoses derived from self-reports and clinicians is inflated by criterion contamination because clinicians must ground their diagnostic conclusions in the information reported by patients. Similar confounds also likely affect the associations between self-ratings and significant-other ratings.

elicit an informant's perception of the patient, although they are constrained by the parameters of a particular type of relationship (e.g., spouse, coworker, therapist) and the setting in which the observations transpire. These distinctions provide each method with particular strengths for measuring certain qualities, as well as inherent restrictions for measuring the full scope of human functioning.

More than 40 years ago, Campbell and Fiske (1959) noted how relative independence among psychological methods can point to unappreciated complexity in the phenomena under investigation. Thus, although low cross-method correspondence can potentially indicate problems with one or both methods under consideration, correlations can document only what is shared between two variables. As such, cross-method correlations cannot reveal what makes a test distinctive or unique, and they also cannot reveal how good a test is in any specific sense. Given the intricacy of human functioning and the method distinctions outlined above, psychologists should anticipate disagreements when similarly named scales are compared across diverse assessment methods. Furthermore, given the validity data provided in Table 13.2, psychologists should view the results in Table 13.3 as indicating that each assessment method identifies useful data not available from other sources. As is done in other scientific disciplines (Meyer, 1996b), clinicians and researchers should recognize the unique strengths and limitations of various assessment methods and harness these qualities to select methods that help them more fully understand the complexity of the individual being evaluated.[12]

Test batteries, particularly in the area of personality assessment, have been criticized at times because evidence for the incremental validity of each test within the battery has not been consistently demonstrated (see, e.g., Garb, 1984). However, several logical and empirical considerations support the multimethod battery as a means to maximize assessment validity.

In particular, we believe that there is a direct parallel between empirical research and applied clinical practice on this issue. In research, *monomethod* bias and *monooperation* bias are critical threats to the validity of any investigation (Cook & Campbell, 1979). Thus, research validity is compromised when information is derived from a single method of measurement (e.g., self-report) and when a construct has been operationally defined in a single way (e.g., depression delineated by emotional rather than physiological, interpersonal, or cognitive symptoms).

---

[12]Unlike other scientific disciplines, a factor that contributes to divergence across psychological methods undoubtedly emerges from a discipline-wide propensity to ignore the fundamental measurement question, which is whether the objects or attributes psychologists aspire to measure actually have quantitative properties (Michell, 1997). In part, this question is ignored because test results can have practical utility even without this knowledge. Utility does not demand cross-method convergence. However, precise convergence would be required for any two methods that purported to measure the same quantitative attribute.

The optimal methodology to enhance the construct validity of nomothetic research consists of combining data from multiple methods and multiple operational definitions (see, e.g., Cole, Martin, Powers, & Truglio, 1996; Cook & Campbell, 1979; Epstein, 1980, 1983). To our knowledge, the same standards have not been directly linked to principles for guiding the idiographic clinical assessments that are designed to understand the full complexity of a single individual. We believe the parallels should be explicit.

Just as optimal research recognizes that any method of measurement and any single operational definition of a construct are incomplete, optimal clinical assessment should recognize that the same constraints exist when measuring phenomena in the life of a single person. Furthermore, just as effective nomothetic research recognizes how validity is maximized when variables are measured by multiple methods, particularly when the methods produce meaningful discrepancies (Cheek, 1982; Cole et al., 1996; Tsujimoto et al., 1990), the quality of idiographic assessment can be enhanced by clinicians who integrate the data from multiple methods of assessment (Achenbach, 1995; Colvin, Block, & Funder, 1995; Ganellen, 1994; McClelland et al., 1989; Meyer, 1996b, 1997; S. B. Miller, 1987; Shedler, Mayman, & Manis, 1993; Winter et al., 1998).

It is well known that lapses in reasoning often may accompany clinical judgment (see, e.g., Arkes, 1981; Borum, Otto, & Golding, 1993; Garb, 1994; Hammond, 1996; Holt, 1986). Although these pitfalls also can affect assessments, the evaluation process incorporates some inherent checks on clinical reasoning. An assessment battery is likely to generate findings that, at least superficially, appear conflicting or contradictory. When assessors systematically integrate this information, they are forced to consider questions, symptoms, dynamics, and behaviors from multiple perspectives — simply because everything does not fit together in a neat and uncomplicated package. Clinicians must consider the nature of the information provided by each testing method, the peculiarities associated with the specific way different scales define a construct, the reliability and validity of different scales, and the motivational and environmental circumstances that were present during the testing. Assuming no data can be deemed invalid and ignored, then the assessment clinician must conceptualize the patient in a way that synthesizes all of the test scores. Next, these test-based conceptualizations must be reconciled with what is known from history, referral information, and observation. Finally, all of this information must be integrated with the clinician's understanding of the complex condition(s) being assessed (e.g., narcissistic personality disorder, learning disability, transference reactions, contingencies that maintain obsessive behaviors) and the many other complex conditions that need to be considered and then ruled out as unimportant or irrelevant. Although there are many places in this process for errors to develop, the careful consideration of multimethod assessment data can provide a powerful antidote to the normal judgment biases that are inherent in clinical work (see also Borum et al., 1993; Spengler, Strohmer, Dixon, & Shivy, 1995). This line of reasoning also suggests that by relying on a multimethod assessment battery, practitioners have historically used the most efficient means at their disposal to maximize the validity of their judgments about individual clients.

Method Disparities and Errors in Practice

Current knowledge about the substantial disagreements between methods of information gathering has important implications for health care. The data indicate that even though it may be less expensive at the outset, a single clinician using a single method (e.g., interview) to obtain information from a patient will develop an incomplete or biased understanding of that patient. To the extent that such impressions guide diagnostic and treatment decisions, patients will be misunderstood, mischaracterized, misdiagnosed, and less than optimally treated. Over the long term, this should increase health care costs.

These issues are not trivial. The evidence indicates that clinicians who use a single method to obtain patient information regularly draw faulty conclusions. For instance, Fennig, Craig, Tanenberg-Karant, and Bromet (1994) reviewed the diagnoses assigned to 223 patients as part of usual hospital practice. Clinical diagnoses were then compared with diagnoses derived from a comprehensive multimethod assessment that consisted of a semistructured patient interview, a review of the patient's medical record, a semistructured interview with the treating clinician, and an interview with the patient's significant other, all of which were then reviewed and synthesized by two clinicians to derive final diagnoses from the multimethod assessment.

Even though Fennig, Craig, Tanenberg-Karant, and Bromet (1994) used very liberal criteria to define diagnostic agreement (e.g., major depression with psychotic features was treated as equivalent to dysthymia), the diagnoses assigned during the course of typical clinical practice had poor agreement with the diagnostic formulations derived from the more extensive synthesis of multiple assessment methods. Overall, after discounting chance agreement, the clinical diagnoses agreed with the multimethod conclusions only about 45% to 50% of the time.[13]

This was true for a range of disorders on the schizophrenic, bipolar, and depressive spectrums. Because these conditions are treated in decidedly different ways, such frequent misdiagnoses in typical practice suggest that many patients erroneously receive antipsychotic, antimanic, and antidepressant medications.

---

[13] In a separate study with the same population, Fennig, Craig, Lavelle, Kovasznay, and Bromet (1994) demonstrated how clinicians who derived psychiatric diagnoses after synthesizing information from multiple sources had much higher correspondence with the gold standard criterion diagnoses.

Another example involves fully structured interviews like the Composite International Diagnostic Interview (CIDI), which have a format that makes them essentially equivalent to an oral self-report instrument. A salient question concerns the extent to which diagnoses from CIDI-type scales agree with those derived from clinicians who also rely on their impression of the patient (e.g., from semistructured interviews, from clinical consensus after following the patient over time). Although diagnoses from the CIDI and diagnoses derived from semistructured interviews suffer from criterion contamination because both the predictor and criterion rely on the patient's report as a primary source of information (see, e.g., Malgady, Rogler, & Tryon, 1992), Table 13.3 indicates that across 33 samples and 5,990 patients, the correspondence between CIDI-type diagnoses and clinician diagnoses was quite modest ($\kappa = .34$; Table 13.3, Entry 34; see Meyer, 2002). Similar findings have been observed when Axis I diagnoses from the Structured Clinical Interview for the *Diagnostic and Statistical Manual of Mental Disorders* were compared with clinician diagnoses (mean $\kappa = .26$, $N = 100$; Steiner, Tebes, Sledge, & Walker, 1995), suggesting again that the source of information for diagnostic inferences exerts a prominent influence over final classifications (see, e.g., Offord et al., 1996).

Although the above disagreements are pronounced, even more drastic errors have been found for personality disorders. Perry (1992) and Pilkonis et al. (1995) compared diagnoses derived from a semistructured clinical interview with diagnoses based on more extensive and complex assessments using multiple methods of gathering patient information. Across studies, there was a meager correspondence between the diagnoses derived from a single clinician using the single method of assessment and the diagnoses derived from the multimethod evaluations ($\kappa = .28$; $N = 218$; see Entry 48 in Table 13.3). In fact, after correcting for agreements due to chance, about 70% of the interview-based diagnoses were in error.

The evidence also indicates that personality disorder diagnoses diverge substantially across other sources of information. For instance, Table 13.3 shows that diagnoses derived from self-report bear little resemblance to those derived from clinicians ($\kappa = .18$, $N = 2,859$; Table 13.3, Entry 33) and that diagnoses from semistructured patient interviews bear little resemblance to those based on semistructured interviews with significant others in the patient's life ($\kappa = .12$, $N = 768$; Table 13.3, Entry 30).

Although the latter results are sobering, they are open to interpretation about which perspective is more correct. The most relevant evidence is that which compared interviews with the multimethod synthesis of information. These data clearly demonstrate how conclusions derived from a typical evaluation using a single method of assessment had little correspondence with those derived from a more comprehensive evaluation. By necessity then, the research findings indicate that many patients may be misunderstood or improperly treated when they do not receive thorough assessments. Errors of misappraisal and mistreatment are most likely when administrative efforts to save money restrict clinicians to very brief and circumscribed evaluations.

ISSUES AT THE INTERFACE OF
ASSESSMENT RESEARCH AND PRACTICE

Virtually all research with purported relevance to assessment has examined the nomothetic association between isolated test scores and equally isolated criterion measures (e.g., MMPI Depression scores in patients with depression vs. patients without that diagnosis). In such an approach, the scores from one scale are evaluated out of context from other test scores and sources of information. This strategy is ideal for scale validation because it allows for an understanding of the strengths and limitations of a single scale, divorced from the array of other factors that impinge on any assessment (Cronbach & Meehl, 1955). However, this research strategy does very little for the assessment clinician, who is almost never concerned with a single scale but rather with one scale in the context of other scales and other sources of information.

Because the nomothetic association between different methods is generally small to moderate, if the results from most testing research are considered in isolation, the observed validity coefficients suggest that psychologists have a limited capacity to make sound, individualized judgments from test scales alone. This is true even for the substantial coefficients presented in Table 13.2. In fact, if the value of clinical assessment could be supported only by testing the evidence that documents the validity of test scales divorced from contextual factors (i.e., Tables 12.2 and 12.3), then, as a profession, psychologists might be forced to abandon assessment as a justifiable activity. When one considers the errors associated with measurement and the infrequent occurrence of most clinical conditions, validity coefficients are too small to justify testing-based decisions for individuals (Hummel, 1999) Thus, someone with a high score on the Depression scale of the MMPI cannot be assigned a depressive diagnosis with conviction, just as someone with a low score on the Wechsler Memory Scale (WMS) cannot be assigned a diagnosis of Alzheimer's disease with confidence. This is true even when scores deviate substantially from normal.[14]

---

[14] Psychologists can of course still use testing data (i.e., scores derived from a single scale or a single prediction equation) if the data are applied in a selection context, such as with employment screening tests, the Graduate Record Examination, and the Scholastic Aptitude Test. This is because one can choose a small number of applicants from a large pool as a way to maximize validity (H.C. Taylor & Russell, 1939). However, this strategy reflects an application of nomothetically derived validity coefficients in an appropriate nomothetic context. Such procedures are not helpful when applying nomothetic validity coefficients to the idiographic practice of psychological assessment.

The fact that one cannot derive unequivocal clinical conclusions from test scores considered in isolation should not be a surprise, as sophisticated clinicians would never expect to make a diagnosis from just a single test or scale. However, failure to appreciate the testing-versus-assessment distinction has led some to seriously question the utility of psychological tests in clinical contexts (see, e.g., Hummel, 1999; Rogers, Salekin, & Sewell, 1999). When this important difference is not recognized or fully appreciated, the testing literature may lead to pessimism about psychological assessment, even though they are quite different activities.

Because most research studies do not use the same type of data that clinicians do when performing an individualized assessment, the validity coefficients from testing research may underestimate the validity of test findings when they are integrated into a systematic and individualized psychological assessment. To illustrate, when conducting an idiographic assessment using an MMPI, the clinician begins by examining the validity scales to understand the patient's test-taking approach. This analysis is completed first because all other scale elevations need to be interpreted in this light. The same elevation on the MMPI Depression scale means something very different when the validity scales indicate the patient was open and straightforward during the evaluation, rather than guarded and defensive. Other contextual factors must also be considered. A T score of 100 on the F Scale (Infrequency) may have very different implications if the patient is tested on an acute inpatient ward rather than in an outpatient clinic. In the latter setting, this elevation is more likely to indicate that the MMPI–2 data are invalid because the patient responded to items in an inconsistent manner or magnified the extent of his or her disturbance. However, in an inpatient setting, the very same score is more likely to be an accurate reflection of the patient's acute distress and genuine disturbance. Competently trained clinicians recognize these contextual factors and interpret scale scores accordingly.

The same type of reasoning is used when evaluating data from other assessment methods. For example, neuropsychological test scores are considered in light of the patient's level of fatigue, attention, cooperation, estimated premorbid level of functioning, and so forth because all of these factors can influence performance and the proper interpretation of obtained scores.

The important point here is that contextual factors play a very large role in determining the final scores obtained on psychological tests. In methodological terms, when test scores are studied across large groups of people, the contextual factors associated with each person contribute to what is known as *method variance* (see, e.g., Campbell & Fiske, 1959; L. K. Edwards & Edwards, 1991; Glutting, Oakland, & Konold, 1994; Jackson, Fraboni, & Helmes, 1997; Meyer, 1997; Oakland & Glutting, 1990). Tests used in other scientific disciplines are less affected by these factors, as results from an X ray, blood chemistry panel, seismograph, or carbon-14 dating test never depend on the motivation, rapport, or drowsiness of the object under study. However, these are all critical factors that influence the scores obtained on any psychological test.

Although skilled clinicians appear to recognize the contextual factors described above, it is much more difficult to make such individualized adjustments when conducting research. This is because scale scores are not given differential trustworthiness weights to reflect the fact that some are obtained from patients who are exaggerating, some from patients who are unmotivated, some from patients who are open and frank, some from patients who are highly guarded and defended, and so on. Rather, every test score is identically weighted and regarded as if it were equally valid. (Of course, every criterion score is treated in the same fashion.)

The salience of these individualized contextual factors may be easier to recognize with two specific examples. First, consider a clinician who is asked to determine if a man is depressed given (a) an MMPI–2 Depression score that is unusually low, (b) a mild elevation on MMPI–2 Scale 3 (Hysteria), (c) an elevated Rorschach Depression Index, (d) clinical observations on the Brief Psychiatric Rating Scale (BPRS) that yield somewhat elevated scores for emotional withdrawal and guilt feelings but a suppressed score for depressive mood, (e) the patient's report that he recently lost a loved one and now has sleeping difficulties, and (f) a report from the patient's sister that since childhood he has successfully coped with problems by "looking on the bright side of things." With these data, the clinician could conclude the man is struggling with an underlying depressive condition (as evident on portions of the BPRS, Rorschach, and history) brought about by his recent loss (from the history), even though his generally upbeat coping strategy (from his sister's description and MMPI–2 Scale 3) prevents him from acknowledging his troubles (as evident from the MMPI–2 Depression scale and part of the BPRS). One might also infer that his defenses serve an important function and that treatment that abruptly confronted his underlying emotions could leave him in a psychologically unbalanced state.

Note how in this individualized context, the MMPI–2 Depression score supports the valid conclusion that the patient is struggling with depression despite the fact that it indicates less depression than would be found in an average person without psychiatric difficulties. The MMPI–2 score is low for this man because it accurately reflects his efforts to cope by keeping depressive experiences at bay (cf. Finn, 1996; Meyer, 1997). Unfortunately, the clinical accuracy of a score like this is lost in a typical statistical analysis because correlations, t tests, F tests, and so on do not take into account the complex array of unique contextual variables associated with individual patients. In fact, in a typical study, the clinical accuracy of this man's MMPI–2 score would be treated as error, and including his score in research would serve only to reduce the size of a correlation, t value, or F value that quantified the validity of the MMPI–2. Thus, even though this man's MMPI–2 would provide valid information for an idiographic assessment, it would actually make the MMPI–2 scale appear less valid in nomothetic research.

As another example, early stage dementia is more likely when an elderly person's memory is poor yet other cognitive abilities are intact. Thus, the diagnosis is more probable if assessment data reveal low memory test performance (e.g., on the WMS) in combination with high scores on a test like the National Adult Reading Test (NART), which estimates premorbid intelligence on the basis of the pronunciation of irregularly spelled words. This idiographic contrast quantifies a key feature of the disorder. Dementia is also more likely if the patient minimizes memory problems even though his or her spouse reports instances of poor memory, if the family history is positive for Alzheimer's disease, if there is no evidence of localized dysfunction on other neuropsychological tests, and if recent MRI or CT scans do not show localized signs of stroke.

In a large meta-analysis, D. Christensen, Hadzi-Pavlovic, and Jacomb (1991) found scores from the WMS and similar tests had a strong ability to differentiate patients with dementia from normal controls (see Entry 137 in Table 13.2). However, NART scores had a minimal ability to make this kind of discrimination ($r = .14$). Thus, the testing results indicated NART scores were not very useful for diagnosis. In clinical practice, however, an assessment clinician would be most inclined to diagnose dementia when test scores indicated high premorbid cognitive functioning (i.e., high NART scores) in the presence of currently compromised memory (e.g., low WMS scores). Thus, because the NART is not only a valid measure of preexisting cognitive abilities (Spreen & Strauss, 1998) but also relatively insensitive to dementia symptoms, it can be a critical asset for diagnosing dementia on an individual-by-individual basis. If one had relied on just the nomothetic effect size, one would have concluded that the NART was of little value to the diagnosis of dementia, even though its applied clinical value is actually much higher because it allows the clinician to estimate an individual's memory decline relative to his or her premorbid cognitive abilities.

More generally, to the extent that clinicians view all test data in a contextually differentiated fashion, the practical value of tests used in clinical assessment is likely greater than what is suggested by the research on their nomothetic associations.[15] However, trying to document the validity of

---

[15] Our argument is not that clinical judgment will consistently surpass statistical decision rules in a head-to-head comparison (Meyer et al., 1998; see Grove, Zald, Lebow, Snitz, & Nelson, 2000, for a meta-analytic review). Rather, it is that the practical validity of psychological assessment (i.e., the sophisticated integration of data from multiple tests and sources of contextual information) is probably greater than what is suggested by the validity coefficients found in the testing literature (i.e., scale data in which the many contextual factors affecting all observed scores are treated as error variance). Also, if this line of reasoning is extended, one should expect nomothetic validity coefficients for testing data to increase when researchers begin to differentially weight scores to reflect individualized contextual influences. As a simple example that builds on the text discussion, if researchers attend to premorbid intelligence as an important contextual variable, dementia studies should produce larger effect sizes

individualized, contextually embedded inferences is incredibly complex—and virtually impossible if one hopes to find a relatively large sample of people with the same pattern of test and extratest information (i.e., history, observed behavior, motivational context, etc.). Research cannot realistically hope to approximate such an ideal. Nevertheless, using just test scores, a growing body of findings supports the value of combining data from more than one type of assessment method, even when these methods disagree within or across individuals (see, e.g., Colvin et al., 1995; Davidson, 1996; Ganellen, 1994; Klein et al., 1994; McClelland et al., 1989; Meyer, 1997; Meyer, Riethmiller, Brooks, Benoit, & Handler, 2000; Power et al., 1998; Robertson & Kinder, 1993; Shedler et al., 1993; Winter et al., 1998).

FUTURE RESEARCH

Assessment is a complicated activity that requires (a) sophisticated understanding of personality, psychopathology, or the many ways in which neurological disorders are manifested in cognition and behavior; (b) knowledge of psychological measurement, statistics, and research methods; (c) recognition that different assessment methods produce qualitatively distinct kinds of information; (d) understanding of the particular strengths and limitations of each method and of different scales within each method; (e) a capacity to conceptualize the diverse real-world conditions that could give rise to a particular pattern of test data; (f) the ability to challenge one's judgment by systematically linking the presence and absence of test indicators to the psychological characteristics under consideration; and (g) the interpersonal skill and emotional sensitivity to effectively communicate findings to patients, significant others, and referral sources.

Although psychological tests can assist clinicians with case formulation and treatment recommendations, they are only tools. Tests do not think for themselves, nor do they directly communicate with patients. Like a stethoscope, a blood pressure gauge, or an MRI scan, a psychological test is a dumb tool, and the worth of the tool cannot be separated from the sophistication of the clinician who draws inferences from it and then communicates with patients and other professionals. Because assessment competence requires a considerable investment of time and effort, further documenting the worth of this investment is our final consideration.

More than 20 years ago, psychologists with an interest in treatment took the lead in demonstrating how clinicians have practical utility for enhancing patient outcome (M. L. Smith & Glass, 1977). Today, the beneficial

---

when the NART–WMS discrepancy is the dependent variable than when WMS and NART scores are considered in isolation.

impact of treatment continues to be documented (see, e.g., Lipsey & Wilson, 1993; Seligman, 1995; Shadish et al., 1997). Assessment research—in both psychology and medicine—has generally followed a path that differs from treatment research. Although notable exceptions exist (see Entries 77 & 91 in Table 13.2), researchers have historically focused at a micro level to evaluate the psychometric reliability and validity of test scales that are divorced from an individualized context. This focus is certainly important. However, researchers should also focus at a macro level to evaluate the practical value of clinicians who use tests as tools that help them provide professional consultation and benefit to patients and allied health care providers.

We are not the first to recognize this imbalance in the literature. It has been noted regularly over the years (see, e.g., Finn & Tonsager, 1997; S. C. Hayes, Nelson, & Jarrett, 1987; Korchin & Schuldberg, 1981; McReynolds, 1985; Meehl, 1959; Moreland, Fowler, & Honaker, 1994; Persons, 1991). Unfortunately, recognizing the imbalance has not yet been sufficient to correct it.

Research designs for evaluating assessment utility have been proposed by S. C. Hayes et al. (1987) and recently discussed again by Finn and Tonsager (1997). Even a relatively simple design addressing the utility of psychological assessment for affecting referral sources, patient care, and patient well-being would be of considerable value. For example, a group of patients deemed to be in need of psychological assessment could be provided with (a) a flexible, multimethod assessment battery using tests typically used in practice and selected on the basis of idiographic referral questions by a clinician competent in the relevant domain, (b) personal feedback from the assessment, and (c) feedback to their treating and referring clinicians. These patients could then be contrasted with an appropriate control group, such as patients who also were deemed to be in need of a psychological assessment but received a comparable amount of therapy rather than any of the above.[16] Given that the main purpose of assessment is to provide useful information to patients and referral sources, key outcomes would directly address these issues (e.g., resolution of patient and therapist referral questions, congruence over treatment goals, confidence that treatment is moving in a helpful direction).[17] Conducting this type of research would complement the very strong findings in

---

[16]The experimental and control groups should consist of patients deemed to be in need of an assessment according to some reasonable clinical criteria. Just as every patient does not need a CT scan, every patient does not need a psychological assessment. Randomly assigning all patients to experimental and control conditions would serve only to drastically reduce the statistical power of the design and the size of any observed effect. Also, in the current health care climate, it should be possible to find providers who refuse to authorize psychological assessments regardless of need (Eisman et al., 1998, 2000). Thus, the design could provide anew assessment service rather than withhold appropriate care from patients otherwise eligible for it.

[17]Previously, we said it may be valuable to measure the impact of assessment on outcomes like length, cost, or speed of improvement in treatment (Meyer et al., 1998). However, these are distal outcomes that do not have direct relationships to the reasons that prompt an assessment referral. Thus, although

Table 13.2 by documenting the extent to which the test-informed assessment clinician is useful and effective in everyday clinical practice.

A second important issue concerns the accuracy of judgments made by assessment clinicians. This could be addressed by building on the basic design mentioned above to have clinicians describe the patients in the experimental and control groups using standard measures of symptomatology and functioning. The accuracy of the ratings given to patients who received a flexible, multimethod assessment battery would then be compared with those generated for patients who did not receive an assessment but were deemed to be in need of one. This comparison would quantify the value of assessment for the accurate understanding of patients.

The key to the latter type of study—and what would set it apart from prior research in this area—is ensuring that the criterion judgments that determine accuracy are as systematic, comprehensive, and true as possible. Particularly for personality assessment, there is no ready gold standard that allows psychologists to know a patient with certainty. Table 13.3 reveals unequivocally that psychologists cannot use self-, clinician, teacher, spouse, or peer ratings as a criterion because judgments from these different perspectives agree only modestly. Thus, every single source of information diverges substantially from every other potential source, and it is impossible to say that one (e.g., clinician) is more true than any other (e.g., spouse). Yet if one wants to evaluate the accuracy of judgments derived from a psychological assessment, one must have excellent criteria available first. Thus, following Meehl (1959), criterion ratings should be obtained by the consensus of experts after patients have been followed over time, after interviews have been conducted with significant others, after interviews have been conducted with mental health and medical personnel who have encountered the patients, and after systematic consideration has been given to all the available data for each person (see Klein et al., 1994, and Pilkonis et al., 1995, for examples applied to diagnostic criteria; see Faraone & Tsuang, 1994, Meyer, 1996a, and Tsujimoto et al., 1990, for alternative ways to maximize criterion validity). Ensuring that the criterion measures are sufficient gold standards will require a considerable investment of time and resources. However, if psychologists wish to clearly document whether judgments and inferences are more accurate when they are derived from a multimethod psychological assessment, it is necessary to spend the time and resources on a design that can actually answer the question.

_____

it may be interesting to learn about these derivative effects, the sample sizes required to detect differences of this sort are likely to be huge (Sturm, Unützer, & Katon, 1999) and tangential to the core purpose of assessment. (In many respects, the mismatch in this design would be analogous to a situation where researchers tried to evaluate the effectiveness of treatment by determining how much an intervention aided differential diagnosis.)

CONCLUSIONS

Formal assessment is a vital element in psychology's professional heritage and a central part of professional practice today. This review has documented the very strong and positive evidence that already exists on the value of psychological testing and assessment for clinical practice. We have demonstrated that the validity of psychological tests is comparable to the validity of medical tests and indicated that differential limits on reimbursement for psychological and medical tests cannot be justified on the basis of the empirical evidence. We have also demonstrated that distinct assessment methods provide unique sources of data and have documented how sole reliance on a clinical interview often leads to an incomplete understanding of patients. On the basis of a large array of evidence, we have argued that optimal knowledge in clinical practice (as in research) is obtained from the sophisticated integration of information derived from a multimethod assessment battery. Finally, to advance research, we have identified critical implications that flow from the distinction between testing and assessment and have called for future investigations to focus on the practical value of assessment clinicians who provide test-informed services to patients and referral sources. We hope this review simultaneously clarifies the strong evidence that supports testing while helping to initiate new research that can further demonstrate the unique value of well-trained psychologists providing formal assessments in applied health care settings. We invite all psychologists to join us in advancing the utility of this core and distinctive aspect of our profession.

REFERENCES

Abelson, R. P. (1985). A variance explanation paradox: When a little is a lot. *Psychological Bulletin, 97*, 129–133.

Achenbach, T. M. (1991a). *Integrative guide for the 1991 CBCL/4–18, YSR, and TRF profiles*. Burlington: University of Vermont, Department of Psychiatry.

Achenbach, T. M. (1991b). *Manual for the Child Behavior Checklist and 1991 Profile*. Burlington: University of Vermont, Department of Psychiatry.

Achenbach, T. M. (1995). Empirically based assessment and taxonomy: Applications to clinical research. *Psychological Assessment, 7*, 261–274.

Achenbach, T. M. (1997). *Manual for the Young Adult Self-Report and Young Adult Behavior Checklist*. Burlington: University of Vermont, Department of Psychiatry.

Achenbach, T. M., McConaughy, S. H., & Howell, C. T. (1987). Child/adolescent behavioral and emotional problems: Implications of cross-informant correlations for situational specificity. *Psychological Bulletin, 101*, 213–232.

Ahmad, N., Grad, H. A., Haas, D. A., Aronson, K. J., Jokovic, A., & Locker, D.

(1997). The efficacy of nonopioid analgesics for postoperative dental pain: A meta-analysis. *Anesthesia Progress, 44,* 119–126.

Aleman, A., Hijman, R., de Haan, E. H. F., & Kahn, R. S. (1999). Memory impairment in schizophrenia: A meta-analysis. *American Journal of Psychiatry, 156,* 1358–1366.

Alfirevic, Z., & Neilson, J. P. (1995). Doppler ultrasonography in high-risk pregnancies: Systematic review with meta-analysis. *American Journal of Obstetrics and Gynecology, 172,* 1379–1387.

Alterman, A. I., Snider, E. C., Cacciola, J. S., Brown, L. S., Jr., Zaballero, A., & Siddiqui, N. (1996). Evidence for response set effects in structured research interviews. *Journal of Nervous and Mental Disease, 184,* 403–410.

Amato, P. R., & Keith, B. (1991). Parental divorce and the well-being of children: A meta-analysis. *Psychological Bulletin, 110,* 26–46.

American Psychological Association. (1992). Ethical principles of psychologists and code of conduct. *American Psychologist, 47,* 1597–1611.

Anastopoulos, A. D., Spisto, M. A., & Maher, M. C. (1994). The WISC–III Freedom From Distractibility factor: Its utility in identifying children with attention deficit hyperactivity disorder. *Psychological Assessment, 6,* 368–371.

Arkes, H. R. (1981). Impediments to accurate clinical judgment and possible ways to minimize their impact. *Journal of Consulting and Clinical Psychology, 49,* 323–330.

Aronen, E. T., Noam, G. G., & Weinstein, S. R. (1993). Structured diagnostic interviews and clinicians' discharge diagnoses in hospitalized adolescents. *Journal of the American Academy of Child and Adolescent Psychiatry, 32,* 674–681.

Arthur, W., Barrett, G. V., & Alexander, R. A. (1991). Prediction of vehicular accident involvement: A meta-analysis. *Human Performance, 4,* 89–105.

Atkinson, L. (1986). The comparative validities of the Rorschach and MMPI: A meta-analysis. *Canadian Psychology, 27,* 238–247.

Aziz, D. C., & Barathur, R. B. (1993). Prostate-specific antigen and prostate volume: A meta-analysis of prostate cancer screening criteria. *Journal of Clinical Laboratory Analysis, 7,* 283–292.

Baer, R. A., Wetter, M. W., & Berry, D. T. R. (1992). Detection of underreporting of psychopathology on the MMPI: A meta-analysis. *Clinical Psychology Review, 12,* 509–525.

Bagby, R. M., Rector, N. A., Bindseil, K., Dickens, S. E., Levitan, R. D., & Kennedy, S. H. (1998). Self-report ratings and informants' ratings of personalities of depressed outpatients. *American Journal of Psychiatry, 155,* 437–438.

Barber, J. P., & Morse, J. Q. (1994). Validation of the Wisconsin Personality Disorders Inventory with the SCID–II and PDE. *Journal of Personality Disorders, 8,* 307–319.

Baron, J., & Norman, M. F., (1992). SATs, achievement tests, and high-school class rank as predictors of college performance. *Educational and Psychological Measurement, 52,* 1047–1055.

Barrick, M. R., & Mount, M. K. (1991). The Big Five personality dimensions and job performance: A meta-analysis. *Personnel Psychology, 44,* 1–26.

Bastian, L. A., Nanda, K., Hasselblad, V., & Simel, D. L. (1998). Diagnostic efficiency of home pregnancy test kits: A meta-analysis. *Archives of Family Medicine, 7,* 465–469.

Beck, A. T., Brown, G., Berchick, R. J., Stewart, B. L., & Steer, R. A. (1990). Relationship between hopelessness and ultimate suicide: A replication with psychiatric outpatients. *American Journal of Psychiatry, 147,* 190–195.

Beck, A. T., Steer, R. A., Kovacs, M., & Garrison, B. (1985). Hopelessness and eventual suicide: A 10-year prospective study of patients hospitalized with suicidal ideation. *American Journal of Psychiatry, 142,* 559–563.

Becker, D. M., Philbrick, J. T., Bachhuber, T. L., & Humphries, J. E. (1996). D-dimer testing and acute venous thromboembolism: A shortcut to accurate diagnosis? *Archives of Internal Medicine, 156,* 939–946.

Bender, D. J., Contreras, T. A., & Fahrig, L., (1998). Habitat loss and population decline: A meta-analysis of the patch size effect. *Ecology, 79,* 517–533.

Bernstein, D. P., Kasapis, C., Bergman A., Weld, E., Mitropoulou, V., Horvath, T., et al. (1997). Assessing Axis II disorders by informant interview. *Journal of Personality Disorders. 11,* 158–167.

Berry, D. T. R., Baer, R. A., & Harris M. J. (1991). Detection of malingering on the MMPI: A meta-analysis. *Clinical Psychology Review, 11,* 585–598.

Berthelot, J.-M., Garnier, P., Glémarec, J., & Flipo, R.-M. (1998). Diagnostic value for rheumatoid arthritis of antiperinuclear factor at the 1:100 threshold: Study of 600 patients and meta-analysis of the literature. *Revue du Rhumatisme, 65,* 9–14.

Binder, L. M., Rohling, M. L., & Larrabee, G. J. (1997). A review of mild head trauma: Part I. Meta-analytic review of neuropsychological studies. *Journal of Clinical and Experimental Neuropsychology, 19,* 421–431.

Blakley, B. R., Quinones, M. A., Crawford, M. S., & Jago, I. A. (1994). The validity of isometric strength tests. *Personnel Psychology, 47,* 247–274.

Bommer, W. H., Johnson J. L., Rich, G., Podsakoff, P. M., & MacKenzie, S. B. (1995). On the interchangeability of objective and subjective measures of employee performance: A meta-analysis. *Personnel Psychology, 48,* 587–605.

Bond, R., & Smith P. B. (1996). Culture and conformity: A meta-analysis of studies using Asch's (1952b, 1956) line judgment task. *Psychological Bulletin, 119,* 111–137.

Bonis, P. A., Ioannidis, J. P., Cappelleri, J. C. Kaplan, M. M., & Lau, J. (1997). Correlation of biochemical response to interferon alfa with histological improvement in hepatitis C: A meta-analysis of diagnostic test characteristics. *Hepatology, 26,* 1035–1044.

Bonta, J., Law, M., & Hanson K. (1998). The prediction of criminal and violent recidivism among mentally disordered offenders: A meta-analysis. *Psychological Bulletin, 123,* 123–142.

Booth-Kewley, S., & Friedman, H. S. (1987). Psychological predictors of heart disease: A quantitative review. *Psychological Bulletin 101*, 343–362.

Borkenau, P., & Liebler, A. (1993). Convergence of stranger ratings of personality and intelligence with self-ratings, partner ratings, and measured intelligence. *Journal of Personality and Social Psychology, 65*, 546–553.

Bornstein, R. F. (1998). Interpersonal dependency and physical illness: A meta-analytic review of retrospective and prospective studies. *Journal of Research in Personality, 32*, 480–497.

Bornstein R. F. (1999). Criterion validity of objective and projective dependency tests: A meta-analytic assessment of behavioral prediction. *Psychological Assessment, 11*, 48–57.

Borum, R., Otto R., & Golding S. (1993). Improving clinical judgment and decision making in forensic evaluation. *Journal of Psychiatry and Law, 21*, 35–76.

Boult, C., Boult, L., Murphy, C., Ebbitt, B., Luptak, M., & Kane R. L. (1994). A controlled trial of outpatient geriatric evaluation and management. *Journal of the American Geriatrics Society, 42*, 465–470.

Branca, B., Giordani, B., Lutz, T. & Saper J. R. (1995). Self-report of cognition and objective test performance in posttraumatic headache. *Headache, 36*, 300–306.

Brown, F. H., Jr., Dodrill, C. B., Clark, T., & Zych K. (1991). An investigation of the relationship between self-report of memory functioning and memory test performance. *Journal of Clinical Psychology, 47*, 772–777.

Bucher, H. C., & Schmidt J. G. (1993). Does routine ultrasound scanning improve outcome in pregnancy? Meta-analysis of various outcome measures. *British Medical Journal, 307*, 13–17.

Büla, C. J., Bérod, A. C., Stuck, A. E., Alessi, C. A., Aronow H. U., Santos-Eggimann, B., et al. (1999). Effectiveness of preventive in-home geriatric assessment in well functioning, community-dwelling older people: Secondary analysis of a randomized trial. *Journal of the American Geriatrics Society, 47*, 389–395.

Burgess, J. W. (1991). The Personality Inventory Scales: A self-rating clinical instrument for diagnosis of personality disorder. *Psychological Reports, 69*, 1235–1246.

Burns, R., Nichols, L. O., Graney, M. J., & Cloar, F. T. (1995). Impact of continued geriatric outpatient management on health outcomes of older veterans. *Archives of Internal Medicine, 155*, 1313–1318.

Butzlaff, R. L., & Hooley J. M. (1998). Expressed emotion and psychiatric relapse: A meta-analysis. *Archives of General Psychiatry, 55*, 547–552.

Byrnes, J. P., Miller, D. C., & Schafer W. D. (1999). Gender differences in risk taking: A meta-analysis. *Psychological Bulletin, 125*, 367–383.

Caldwell-Andrews, A., Baer, R. A., & Berry D. T. R. (2000). Effects of response set on NEO–PI–R scores and their relations to external criteria. *Journal of Personality Assessment, 74*, 472–488.

Campbell, D. T., & Fiske D. W. (1959). Convergent and discriminant validation by the multitrait–multimethod matrix. *Psychological Bulletin, 56*, 81–105.

Campens, D., & Buntinx, F. (1997). Selecting the best renal function tests: A meta-analysis of diagnostic studies. *International Journal of Technology Assessment in Health Care, 13*, 343–356.

Carson, K. P., & Gilliard D. J. (1993). Construct validity of the Miner Sentence Completion Scale. *Journal of Occupational and Organizational Psychology, 66*, 171–175.

Carter, A. S., Grigorenko, E. L., & Pauls D. L. (1995). A Russian adaption of the Child Behavior Checklist: Psychometric properties and associations with child and maternal affective symptomatology and family functioning. *Journal of Abnormal Child Psychology, 23*, 661–684.

Centers for Disease Control, Vietnam Experience Study. (1988). Health status of Vietnam veterans: I. Psychosocial characteristics. *JAMA, 259*, 2701–2707.

Cheek, J. M. (1982). Aggregation, moderator variables, and the validity of personality tests: A peer-rating study. *Journal of Personality and Social Psychology, 43*, 1254–1269.

Christensen, D., Hadzi-Pavlovic, D., & Jacomb, P. (1991). The psychometric differentiation of dementia from normal aging: A meta-analysis. *Psychological Assessment, 3*, 147–155.

Christensen, H., Griffiths, K., MacKinnon, A., & Jacomb P. (1997). A quantitative review of cognitive deficits in depression and Alzheimer-type dementia. *Journal of the International Neuropsychological Society, 3*, 631–651.

Christensen, H., & Mackinnon, A. (1992). Wechsler Intelligence Scale profiles in Alzheimer type dementia and healthy ageing. *International Journal of Geriatric Psychiatry, 7*, 241–246.

Cohen, J. (1988). *Statistical power for the behavioral sciences* (2nd ed.). Hillsdale, NJ: Erlbaum.

Cohen, M., Becker, M. G., & Campbell, R. (1990). Relationships among four methods of assessment of children with attention deficit–hyperactivity disorder. *Journal of School Psychology, 28*, 189–202.

Cole, D. A., Martin, J. M., Powers, B., & Truglio, R. (1996). Modeling causal relations between academic and social competence and depression: A multitrait–multimethod longitudinal study of children. *Journal of Abnormal Psychology, 105*, 258–270.

Cole, D. A., Peeke, L. G., Martin, J. M., Truglio, R., & Seroczynski, A. D. (1998). A longitudinal look at the relation between depression and anxiety in children and adolescents. *Journal of Consulting and Clinical Psychology, 66*, 451–460.

Cole, D. A., Truglio, R., & Peeke, L. (1997). Relation between symptoms of anxiety and depression in children: A multitrait–multimethod–multigroup assessment. *Journal of Consulting and Clinical Psychology, 65*, 110–119.

Collins, N. L., & Miller L. C. (1994). Self-disclosure and liking: A meta-analytic review. *Psychological Bulletin, 116*, 457–475.

Colvin, C. R., Block, J., & Funder, D. C. (1995). Overly positive self-evaluations and personality: Negative implications for mental health. *Journal of Personality and Social Psychology, 68,* 1152–1162.

Conde-Agudelo, A., & Kafury-Goeta, A. C. (1998). Triple-marker test as screening for Down syndrome: A meta-analysis. *Obstetrical and Gynecological Survey, 53,* 369–376.

Conley, J. J. (1985). Longitudinal stability of personality traits: A multitrait–multimethod–multioccasion analysis. *Journal of Personality and Social Psychology, 49,* 1266–1282.

Conway, J. M., & Huffcutt, A. I. (1997). Psychometric properties of multisource performance ratings: A meta-analysis of subordinate, supervisor, peer, and self-ratings. *Human Performance, 10,* 331–360.

Cook, T. D., & Campbell, D. T. (1979). *Quasi-experimentation: Design and analysis issues for field settings.* Boston: Houghton-Mifflin.

Costa P. T., Jr., & McCrae, R. R. (1988). Personality in adulthood: A six-year longitudinal study of self-reports and spouse ratings on the NEO Personality Inventory. *Journal of Personality and Social Psychology, 54,* 853–863.

Costa, P. T., Jr., & McCrae, R. R. (1992). *Revised NEO Personality Inventory: Professional manual.* Odessa, FL: Psychological Assessment Resources.

Cribbs, J. B., & Niva E. J. (2000, April). *The extent of client and therapist agreement on therapeutic constructs: A meta-analysis.* Poster session presented at the annual meeting of the Western Psychological Association, Portland, OR.

Cronbach, L. J., & Gleser, G. C. (1965). *Psychological tests and personnel decisions.* Urbana: University of Illinois Press.

Cronbach, L. J., & Meehl, P. E. (1955). Construct validity in psychological tests. *Psychological Bulletin, 52,* 281–302.

Crowley, S. L., Worchel, F. F., & Ash, M. J. (1992). Self-report, peer-report, and teacher-report measures of childhood depression: An analysis by item. *Journal of Personality Assessment, 59,* 189–203.

D'Agostino R. B., Sr., Weintraub, M., Russell, H. K., Stepanians, M., D'Agostino, R. B., Jr., Cantilena, L. R., et al. (1998). The effectiveness of antihistamines in reducing the severity of runny nose and sneezing: A meta-analysis. *Clinical Pharmacology and Therapeutics, 64,* 579–596.

Damos, D. L. (1993). Using meta-analysis to compare the predictive validity of single- and multiple-task measures to flight performance. *Human Factors, 35,* 615–628.

D'Andrade, R., & Dart, J. (1990). The interpretation of r versus r² or why percent of variance accounted for is a poor measure of size of effect. *Journal of Quantitative Anthropology, 2,* 47–59.

Davidson, K. W. (1996). Self- and expert-reported emotion inhibition: On the utility of both data sources. *Journal of Research in Personality, 30,* 535–549.

Del Mar, C., Glasziou, P., & Hayem, M. (1997). Are antibiotics indicated as initial treatment for children with acute otitis media? A meta-analysis. *British Medical Journal, 314*, 1526–1529.

DeNeve, K. M., & Cooper H. (1998). The happy personality: A meta-analysis of 137 personality traits and subjective well-being. *Psychological Bulletin, 124*, 197–229.

de Ruiter, C., & Greeven, P. G. J. (2000). Personality disorders in a Dutch forensic psychiatric sample: Convergence of interview and self-report measures. *Journal of Personality Disorders, 14*, 162–170.

de Vries. S. O., Hunink, M. G. M., & Polak, J. F. (1996). Summary receiver operating characteristic curves as a technique for meta-analysis of the diagnostic performance of duplex ultrasonography in peripheral arterial disease. *Academic Radiology, 3*, 361–369.

Di Fabio, R. P. (1996). Meta-analysis of the sensitivity and specificity of platform posturography. *Archives of Otolaryngology—Head and Neck Surgery, 122*, 150–156.

Dowson, J. H. (1992). Assessment of *DSM–III–R* personality disorders by self-report questionnaire: The role of informants and a screening test for co-morbid personality disorders (STCPD). *British Journal of Psychiatry, 161*, 344–352.

Dreessen, L., Hildebrand, M., & Arntz A. (1998). Patient–informant concordance on the Structured Clinical Interview for *DSM–III–R* Personality Disorders (SCID–II). *Journal of Personality Disorders, 12*, 149–161.

Early Breast Cancer Trialists' Collaborative Group. (1988). Effects of adjuvant tamoxifen and of cytotoxic therapy on mortality in early breast cancer. *New England Journal of Medicine, 319*, 1681–1692.

Edwards, A. L., & Klockars, A. J. (1981). Significant others and self-evaluation: Relationships between perceived and actual evaluations. *Personality and Social Psychology Bulletin, 7*, 244–251.

Edwards. L. K., & Edwards, A. L. (1991). A principal-components analysis of the Minnesota Multiphasic Personality Inventory factor scales. *Journal of Personality and Social Psychology, 60*, 766–772.

Eisenberg, E., Berkey, C. S., Carr, D. B., Mosteller, F., & Chalmers T. C. (1994). Efficacy and safety of nonsteroidal antiinflammatory drugs for cancer pain: A meta-analysis. *Journal of Clinical Oncology, 12*, 2756–2765.

Eisman, E., Dies, R., Finn, S. E., Eyde, L., Kay, G. G., Kubiszyn, T., et al. (1998). *Problems and limitations in the use of psychological assessment in contemporary health-care delivery: Report of the Board of Professional Affairs Psychological Assessment Work Group, Part II.* Washington, DC: American Psychological Association.

Eisman, E. J., Dies, R. R., Finn, S. E., Eyde, L. D., Kay, G. G., Kubiszyn, T. W., et al. (2000). Problems and limitations in the use of psychological assessment in the contemporary health care delivery system. *Professional Psychology: Research and Practice, 31*, 131–140.

Ekselius, L., Lindström, E., von Knorring, L., Bodlund, O., & Kullgren, G. (1994). SCID II interviews and the SCID Screen questionnaire as diagnostic tools for personality disorders in *DSM–III–R*. *Acta Psychiatrica Scandinavica, 90*, 120–123.

Engelhardt, J. B., Toseland, R. W., O'Donnell, J. C., Richie, J. T., Jue, D., & Banks, S. (1996). The effectiveness and efficiency of outpatient geriatric evaluation and management. *Journal of the American Geriatrics Society, 44*, 847–856.

Epkins, C. C., & Meyers, A. W. (1994). Assessment of childhood depression, anxiety, and aggression: Convergent and discriminant validity of self-, parent-, teacher-, and peer-report measures. *Journal of Personality Assessment, 62*, 364–381.

Epstein, S. (1980). The stability of behavior: II. Implications for psychological research. *American Psychologist, 35*, 790–806.

Epstein, S. (1983). Aggregation and beyond: Some basic issues on the prediction of behavior. *Journal of Personality, 51*, 360–392.

Erel, O., & Burman, B. (1995). Interrelatedness of marital relations and parent–child relations: A meta-analytic review. *Psychological Bulletin, 118*, 108–132.

Eyde, L. D., Robertson, G. J., Krug, S. E., Moreland, K. L., Robertson, A. G., Shewan, C., et al. (1993). *Responsible test use: Case studies for assessing human behavior.* Washington, DC: American Psychological Association.

Ezpeleta, L., de la Osa, N., Doménech, J. M., Navarro J. B., & Losilla, J. M. (1997). Diagnostic agreement between clinicians and the Diagnostic Interview for Children and Adolescents (DICA–R) in an outpatient sample. *Journal of Child Psychology and Psychiatry, 38*, 431–440.

Fabacher, D., Josephson, K., Pietruszka, F., Linderborn, K., Morley, J. E. & Rubenstein, L. Z. (1994). An in-home preventive assessment program for independent older adults: A randomized controlled trial. *Journal of the American Geriatrics Society, 42*, 630–638.

Fahey, M. T., Irwig, L., & Macaskill, P. (1995). Meta-analysis of Pap test accuracy. *American Journal of Epidemiology, 141*, 680–689.

Faraone, S. V., & Tsuang, M. T. (1994). Measuring diagnostic accuracy in the absence of a "gold standard." *American Journal of Psychiatry, 151*, 650–657.

Faron, G., Boulvain, M., Irion, O., Bernard, P.-M., & Fraser, W. D. (1998). Prediction of preterm delivery by fetal fibronectin: A meta-analysis. *Obstetrics and Gynecology, 92*, 153–158.

Feingold, A. (1988). Matching for attractiveness in romantic partners and same-sex friends: A meta-analysis and theoretical critique. *Psychological Bulletin, 104*, 226–235.

Feingold, A. (1994). Gender differences in personality: A meta-analysis. *Psychological Bulletin, 116*, 429–456.

Fennig, S., Craig, T. J., Lavelle, J., Kovasznay, B., & Bromet, E. J. (1994). Best-estimate versus structured interview-based diagnosis in first-admission psychosis. *Comprehensive Psychiatry, 35*, 341–348.

Fennig, S., Craig, T. J., Tanenberg-Karant, M., & Bromet, E. J. (1994). Comparison of facility and research diagnoses in first-admission psychotic patients. *American Journal of Psychiatry, 151*, 1423–1429.

Ferro, T., & Klein, D. N. (1997). Family history assessment of personality disorders: I. Concordance with direct interview and between pairs of informants. *Journal of Personality Disorders, 11*, 123–136.

Finger, M. S., & Ones, D. S. (1999). Psychometric equivalence of the computer and booklet forms of the MMPI: A meta-analysis. *Psychological Assessment, 11*, 58–66.

Finn, S. E. (1982). Base rates, utilities, and *DSM–III*: Shortcomings of fixed-rule systems of psychodiagnosis. *Journal of Abnormal Psychology, 91*, 294–302.

Finn, S. E. (1996). Assessment feedback integrating MMPI–2 and Rorschach findings. *Journal of Personality Assessment, 67*, 543–557.

Finn, S. E., & Kamphuis, J. H. (1995). What a clinician needs to know about base rates. In J. N. Butcher (Ed.), *Clinical personality assessment: Practical approaches* (pp. 224–235). New York: Oxford University Press.

Finn S. E., & Tonsager, M. E. (1992). The therapeutic effects of providing MMPI–2 test feedback to college students awaiting psychotherapy. *Psychological Assessment, 4*, 278–287.

Finn, S. E., & Tonsager, M. E. (1997). Information-gathering and therapeutic models of assessment: Complementary paradigms. *Psychological Assessment, 9*, 374–385.

Fiore, M. C., Smith, S. S., Jorenby, D. E., & Baker, T. B. (1994). The effectiveness of the nicotine patch for smoking cessation: A meta-analysis. *JAMA, 271*, 1940–1947.

Fleischmann, K. E., Hunink, M. G. M., Kuntz, K. M., & Douglas, P. S. (1998). Exercise echocardiography or exercise SPECT imaging? A meta-analysis of diagnostic test performance. *JAMA, 280*, 913–920.

Foltz, C., Morse, J. Q., Calvo, N., & Barber, J. P. (1997). Self- and observer ratings on the NEO–FFI in couples: Initial evidence of the psychometric properties of an observer form. *Assessment, 4*, 287–295.

Forehand, R., Frame, C. L., Wierson, M., Armistead, L., & Kempton, T. (1991). Assessment of incarcerated juvenile delinquents: Agreement across raters and approaches to psychopathology. *Journal of Psychopathology and Behavioral Assessment, 13*, 17–25.

Forster, A. A., & Leckliter, I. N. (1994). The Halstead–Reitan Neuropsychological Test Battery for older children: The effects of age versus clinical status on test performance. *Developmental Neuropsychology, 10*, 299–312.

Fossati, A., Maffei, C., Bagnato, M., Donati, D., Donini, M., Fiorilli, M., et al. (1998). Brief communication: Criterion validity of the Personality Diagnostic Questionnaire—4+ (PDQ–4+) in a mixed psychiatric sample. *Journal of Personality Disorders, 12*, 172–178.

Fretwell, M. D., Raymond, P. M., McGarvey, S. T., Owens, N., Traines, M., Silliman, R. A., et al. (1990). The Senior Care Study: A controlled trial of a consultative/unit-based geriatric assessment program in acute care. *Journal of the American Geriatrics Society, 38*, 1073–1081.

Frick, P. J., Silverthorn, P., & Evans, C. (1994). Assessment of childhood anxiety using structured interviews: Patterns of agreement among informants and association with maternal anxiety. *Psychological Assessment, 6*, 372–379.

Fuller, H. D. (1992). The validity of cardiac output measurement by thoracic impedance: A meta-analysis. *Clinical and Investigative Medicine, 15*, 103–112.

Funder, D. C., & Colvin, C. R. (1988). Friends and strangers: Acquaintanceship, agreement, and the accuracy of personality judgment. *Journal of Personality and Social Psychology, 55*, 149–158.

Funder, D. C., Kolar, D. C., & Blackman, M. C. (1995). Agreement among judges of personality: Interpersonal relations, similarity, and acquaintanceship. *Journal of Personality and Social Psychology, 69*, 656–672.

Gagnon, M., Dartigues, J. F., Mazaux, J. M., Dequae, L., Letenneur L., Giroire, J. M., et al. (1994). Self-reported memory complaints and memory performance in elderly French community residents: Results of the PAQUID research program. *Neuroepidemiology, 13*, 145–154.

Ganellen, R. J. (1994). Attempting to conceal psychological disturbance: MMPI defensive response sets and the Rorschach. *Journal of Personality Assessment, 63*, 423–437.

Ganellen, R. J. (1996). Comparing the diagnostic efficiency of the MMPI, MCMI–II, and Rorschach: A review. *Journal of Personality Assessment, 67*, 219–243.

Garb, H. N. (1984). The incremental validity of information used in personality assessment. *Clinical Psychology Review, 4*, 641–655.

Garb, H. N. (1994). Cognitive heuristics and biases in personality assessment. In L. Heath, R. S. Tindale, J. Edwards, E. Posavac, F. Bryant, E. Henderson, et al. (Eds.), *Applications of heuristics and biases to social issues* (pp. 73–90). New York: Plenum.

Garb, H. N., Florio, C. M., & Grove, W. M. (1998). The validity of the Rorschach and the Minnesota Multiphasic Personality Inventory: Results from meta-analyses. *Psychological Science, 9*, 402–404.

Garb, H. N., & Schramke C. J. (1996). Judgment research and neuropsychological assessment: A narrative review and meta-analyses. *Psychological Bulletin, 120*, 140–153.

Garrison, W. T., & Earls, F. (1985). The Child Behavior Checklist as a screening instrument for young children. *Journal of the American Academy of Child Psychiatry, 24*, 76–80.

Gass, C. S., Russell, E. W., & Hamilton, R. A. (1990). Accuracy of MMPI-based inferences regarding memory and concentration in closed-head-trauma patients. *Psychological Assessment, 2*, 175–178.

Gaugler, B. B., Rosenthal, D. B., Thornton, G. C., III, & Bentson, C. (1987). Meta-analysis of assessment center validity. *Journal of Applied Psychology, 72*, 493–511.

Gendreau, P., Goggin, C. E., & Law, M. A. (1997). Predicting prison misconduct. *Criminal Justice and Behavior, 24*, 414–431.

Germain, M., Knoeffel, F., Wieland, D., & Rubenstein, L. Z. (1995). A geriatric assessment and intervention team for hospital inpatients awaiting transfer to a geriatric unit: A randomized trial. *Aging: Clinical and Experimental Research, 7*, 55–60.

Gianrossi, R., Detrano, R., Colombo, A., & Froelicher, V. (1990). Cardiac fluoroscopy for the diagnosis of coronary artery disease: A meta analytic review. *American Heart Journal, 120*, 1179–1188.

Glutting, J. J., Oakland, T., & Konold, T. R. (1994). Criterion-related bias with the Guide to the Assessment of Test-Session Behavior for the WISC–III and WIAT: Possible race/ethnicity, gender, and SES effects. *Journal of School Psychology, 32*, 355–369.

Goffinet, F., Paris-Llado, J., Nisand, I., & Bréart, G. (1997). Umbilical artery Doppler velocimetry in unselected and low risk pregnancies: A review of randomized controlled trials. *British Journal of Obstetrics and Gynaecology, 104*, 425–430.

Goldberg. E. L., & Alliger, G. M. (1992). Assessing the validity of the GRE for students in psychology: A validity generalization approach. *Educational and Psychological Measurement, 52*, 1019–1027.

Goldberg, L. R., & Werts, C. E. (1966). The reliability of clinicians' judgments: A multitrait–multimethod approach. *Journal of Consulting Psychology, 30*, 199–206.

Goldstein, I., Lue, T. F., Padma-Nathan, H., Rosen, R. C., Steers, W. D., & Wicker, P. A. (1998). Oral Sildenafil in the treatment of erectile dysfunction: Sildenafil Study Group. *New England Journal of Medicine, 338*, 1397–1404.

Goodman, C. M., Cohen, V., Thornby, J., & Netscher, D. (1998). The life span of silicone gel breast implants and a comparison of mammography, ultrasonography, and magnetic resonance imaging in detecting implant rupture: A meta-analysis. *Annals of Plastic Surgery, 41*, 577–586.

Goodman, M., Lamm, S. H., Engel, A., Shepherd, C. W., Houser, O. W., & Gomez, M. R. (1997). Cortical tuber count: A biomarker indicating neurologic severity of tuberous sclerosis complex. *Journal of Child Neurology, 12*, 85–90.

Gosling, S. D., John, O. P., Craik, K. H., & Robins, R. W. (1998). Do people know how they behave? Self-reported act frequencies compared with on-line coding of observers. *Journal of Personality and Social Psychology, 74*, 1337–1349.

Graves, P. L., Phil, M., Mead, L. A., & Pearson, T. A. (1986). The Rorschach Interaction Scale as a potential predictor of cancer. *Psychosomatic Medicine, 48*, 549–563.

Greenberg, S., Smith, I. L., & Muenzen, P. M. (1995). *Executive summary: Study of the practice of licensed psychologists in the United States and Canada.* New York: Professional Examination Service.

Griffith, L. F. (1997). Surviving no-frills mental healthcare: The future of psychological assessment. *Journal of Practical Psychiatry and Behavioral Health, 3*, 255–258.

Grove, W. M., Zald, D. H., Lebow, B. S., Snitz, B. E., & Nelson C. (2000). Clinical versus mechanical prediction: A meta-analysis. *Psychological Assessment, 12*, 19–30.

Hallan, S., & Åsberg, A. (1997). The accuracy of C-reactive protein in diagnosing acute appendicitis: A meta-analysis. *Scandinavian Journal of Clinical and Laboratory Investigation, 57*, 373–380.

Hammond, K. R. (1996). *Human judgment and social policy: Irreducible uncertainty, inevitable error, unavoidable injustice*. New York: Oxford University Press.

Handwerk, M. L., Larzelere, R. E., Soper, S. H., & Friman, P. C. (1999). Parent and child discrepancies in reporting severity of problem behaviors in three out-of-home settings. *Psychological Assessment, 11*, 14–23.

Hansen, F. R., Poulsen, H., & Sørensen, K. H. (1995). A model of regular geriatric follow-up by home visits to selected patients discharged from a geriatric ward: A randomized control trial. *Aging: Clinical and Experimental Research, 7*, 202–206.

Hanson, R. K., Hunsley, J., & Parker, K. C. H. (1988). The relationship between WAIS subtest reliability, "g" loadings, and meta-analytically derived validity estimates. *Journal of Clinical Psychology, 44*, 557–563.

Harkness, A. R., Tellegen, A., & Waller, N. (1995). Differential convergence of self-report and informant data for Multidimensional Personality Questionnaire traits: Implications for the construct of negative emotionality. *Journal of Personality Assessment, 64*, 185–204.

Harlan E., & Clark, L. A. (1999). Short forms of the Schedule for Nonadaptive and Adaptive Personality (SNAP) for self- and collateral ratings: Development, reliability, and validity. *Assessment, 6*, 131–145.

Harris, R. D., Chalmers, J. P., Henschke, P. J., Tonkin, A., Popplewell, P. Y., Stewart, A. M., et al. (1991). A randomized study of outcomes in a defined group of acutely ill elderly patients managed in a geriatric assessment unit or a general medical unit. *Australian and New Zealand Journal of Medicine, 21*, 230–234.

Hart, S. D., Forth, A. E., & Hare, R. D. (1991). The MCMI–II and psychopathy. *Journal of Personality Disorders, 5*, 318–327.

Hasselblad, V., & Hedges, L. V. (1995). Meta-analysis of screening and diagnostic tests. *Psychological Bulletin, 117*, 167–178.

Hayes, A. F., & Dunning, D. (1997). Construal processes and trait ambiguity: Implications for self–peer agreement in personality judgment. *Journal of Personality and Social Psychology, 72*, 664–677.

Hayes, S. C., Nelson, R. O., & Jarrett, R. B. (1987). The treatment utility of assessment. *American Psychologist, 42*, 963–974.

Haynes, S. N., Leisen, M. B., & Blaine, D. (1997). The design of individualized behavioral treatment programs using functional analytic clinical case models. *Psychological Assessment, 9*, 334–348.

Heatley, M. K. (1999). Systematic review and meta-analysis in anatomic pathology: The value of nuclear DNA content in predicting progression in low grade CIN, the significance of the histological subtype on prognosis in cervical carcinoma. *Histology and Histopathology, 14,* 203–215.

Hembree, R. (1988). Correlates, causes, effects, and treatment of test anxiety. *Review of Educational Research, 58,* 47–77.

Henry, B., Moffitt, T. E., Caspi, A., Langley, J., & Silva, P. A. (1994). On the "remembrance of things past": A longitudinal evaluation of the retrospective method. *Psychological Assessment, 6,* 92–101.

Herbert, T. B., & Cohen, S. (1993). Depression and immunity: A meta-analytic review. *Psychological Bulletin, 113,* 472–486.

Herzog, A. R., & Rodgers, W. L. (1989). Age differences in memory performance and memory ratings as measured in a sample survey. *Psychology and Aging, 4,* 173–182.

Hill, R. W., Zrull, M. C., & McIntire, K. (1998). Differences between self- and peer ratings of interpersonal problems. *Assessment, 5,* 67–83.

Hiller, J. B., Rosenthal, R., Bornstein, R. F., Berry, D. T. R., & Brunell-Neuleib, S. (1999). A comparative meta-analysis of Rorschach and MMPI validity. *Psychological Assessment, 11,* 278–296.

Holden, G. (1991). The relationship of self-efficacy appraisals to subsequent health related outcomes: A meta-analysis. *Social Work in Health Care, 16,* 53–93.

Holt, R. R. (1986). Clinical and statistical prediction: A retrospective and would-be integrative perspective. *Journal of Personality Assessment, 50,* 376–386.

Howard, K. I. (1962). The convergent and discriminant validation of ipsative ratings from three projective instruments. *Journal of Clinical Psychology, 18,* 183–188.

Howell, W. H., McNamara, D. J., Tosca, M. A., Smith, B. T., & Gaines, J. A. (1997). Plasma lipid and lipoprotein responses to dietary fat and cholesterol: A meta-analysis. *American Journal of Clinical Nutrition, 65,* 1747–1764.

Huicho, L., Campos, M., Rivera, J., & Guerrant, R. L. (1996). Fecal screening tests in the approach to acute infectious diarrhea: A scientific overview. *Pediatric Infectious Disease Journal 15,* 486–494.

Hummel, T. J. (1999). The usefulness of tests in clinical decisions. In J. W. Lichtenberg & R. K. Goodyear (Eds.), *Scientist–practitioner perspectives on test interpretation.* Boston: Allyn & Bacon.

Hunt, C., & Andrews, G. (1992). Measuring personality disorders: The use of self-report questionnaires. *Journal of Personality Disorders, 6,* 125–133.

Hunter, J. E., & Schmidt, F. L. (1990). *Methods of meta-analysis: Correcting error and bias in research findings.* Newbury Park, CA: Sage.

Ie, Y. L., & Verdonschot, E. H. (1994). Performance of diagnostic systems in occlusal caries detection compared. *Community Dentistry and Oral Epidemiology, 22,* 187–191.

Irle, E. (1990). An analysis of the correlation of lesion size, localization and behavioral effects in 283 published studies of cortical and subcortical lesions in old-world monkeys. *Brain Research Reviews, 15*, 181–213.

Irvin, J. E., Bowers, C. A., Dunn, M. E., & Wang, M. C. (1999). Efficacy of relapse prevention: A meta-analytic review. *Journal of Consulting and Clinical Psychology, 67*, 563–570.

Islam, S. S., & Schottenfeld, D. (1994) Declining FEV_1 and chronic productive cough in cigarette smokers: A 25-year prospective study of lung cancer incidence in Tecumseh, Michigan. *Cancer Epidemiology, Biomarkers and Prevention, 3*, 289–298.

Ito, T. A., Miller, N., & Pollock, V. E. (1996). Alcohol and aggression: A meta-analysis on the moderating effects of inhibitory cues, triggering events, and self-focused attention. *Psychological Bulletin, 120*, 60–82.

Jackson, D. N., Fraboni, M., & Helmes, E. (1997). MMPI–2 content scales: How much content do they measure? *Assessment, 4*, 111–117.

Jacobsberg, L., Perry, S., & Frances, A. (1995). Diagnostic agreement between the SCID–II Screening Questionnaire and the Personality Disorder Examination. *Journal of Personality Assessment, 65*, 428–433.

Jacobson, J. L., Jacobson, S. W., Sokal, R. J., Martier, S. S., Ager, J. W., & Shankaran, S. (1994). Effects of alcohol use, smoking, and illicit drug use on fetal growth in Black infants. *Journal of Pediatrics, 124*, 757–764.

Janick, P. G., Davis, J. M., Gibbons, R. D., Ericksen, S., Chang, S., & Gallagher, P. (1985). Efficacy of ECT: A meta-analysis. *American Journal of Psychiatry, 142*, 297–302.

Jensen, L. A., Onyskiw, J. E., & Prasad, N. G. N. (1998). Meta-analysis of arterial oxygen saturation monitoring by pulse oximetry in adults. *Heart and Lung, 27*, 387–408.

Jensen, P. S., Traylor, J., Xanakis, S. N., & Davis, H. (1987). Child psychopathology rating scales and interrater agreement: I. Parents' gender and psychiatric symptoms. *Journal of the American Academy of Child and Adolescent Psychiatry, 27*, 442–450.

Johansson, B., Allen-Burge, R., & Zarit, S. H. (1997). Self-reports on memory functioning in a longitudinal study of the oldest old: Relation to current, prospective, and retrospective performance. *Journal of Gerontology: Psychological Sciences, 52B*, P139–P146.

John, O. P., & Robins R. W. (1993). Determinants of interjudge agreement on personality traits: The Big Five domains, observability, evaluativeness, and the unique perspective of the self. *Journal of Personality, 61*, 521–551.

John, O. P., & Robins R. W. (1994). Accuracy and bias in self-perception: Individual differences in self-enhancement and the role of narcissism. *Journal of Personality and Social Psychology, 66*, 206–219.

Jorgensen, R. S., Johnson, B. T., Kolodziej, M. E., & Schreer, G. E. (1996). Elevated blood pressure and personality: A meta-analytic review. *Psychological Bulletin, 120*, 293–320.

Karpf, D. B., Shapiro, D. R., Seeman, E., Ensrud, K. E., Johnston, C. C., Adami, S., et al. (1997). Prevention of nonvertebral fractures by alendronate: A meta-analysis. *JAMA, 277*, 1159–1164.

Karppi, P., & Tilvis, R. (1995). Effectiveness of a Finnish geriatric inpatient assessment: Two-year follow up of a randomized clinical trial on community-dwelling patients. *Scandinavian Journal of Primary Health, 13*, 93–98.

Kavale, K. A., & Forness, S. R. (1984). A meta-analysis of the validity of Wechsler scale profiles and recategorizations: Patterns or parodies? *Learning Disability Quarterly, 7*, 136–156.

Kavale, K. A., & Nye, C. (1985). Parameters of learning disabilities in achievement, linguistic, neuropsychological, and social/behavioral domains. *Journal of Special Education, 19*, 443–458.

Kennedy, S. H., Katz, R., Rockert, W., Mendlowitz, S., Ralevski, E., & Clewes, J. (1995). Assessment of personality disorders in anorexia nervosa and bulimia nervosa: A comparison of self-report and structured interview methods. *Journal of Nervous and Mental Disease, 183*, 358–364.

Kim, M.-S., & Hunter, J. E. (1993). Attitude–behavior relations: A meta-analysis of attitudinal relevance and topic. *Journal of Communication, 43*, 101–142.

Klein, D. N., Ouimette, P. C., Kelly, H. S., Ferro, T., & Riso, L. P. (1994). Test–retest reliability of team consensus best-estimate diagnoses of Axis I and II disorders in a family study. *American Journal of Psychiatry, 151*, 1043–1047.

Kliegman, R. M., Madura, D., Kiwi, R., Eisenberg, I., & Yamashita, T. (1994). Relation of maternal cocaine use to the risks of prematurity and low birth weight. *Journal of Pediatrics, 124*, 751–756.

Kline, R. B., & Lachar, D. (1992). Evaluation of age, sex, and race bias in the Personality Inventory for Children (PIC). *Psychological Assessment, 4*, 333–339.

Koestner, R., Bernieri, F., & Zuckerman, M. (1994). Self–peer agreement as a function of two kinds of trait relevance: Personal and social. *Social Behavior and Personality, 22*, 17–30.

Kolar, D. W., Funder D. C., & Colvin, C. R. (1996). Comparing the accuracy of personality judgments by the self and knowledgeable others. *Journal of Personality, 64*, 311–337.

Korchin, S. J., & Schuldberg, D. (1981). The future of clinical assessment. *American Psychologist, 36*, 1147–1158.

Kraus, S. J. (1995). Attitudes and the prediction of behavior: A meta-analysis of the empirical literature. *Personality and Social Psychology Bulletin, 21*, 58–75.

Kubiszyn, T. W., Meyer, G. J., Finn, S. E., Eyde, L. D., Kay, G. G., Moreland, K. L., et al. (2000). Empirical support for psychological assessment in clinical health care settings. *Professional Psychology: Research and Practice, 31*, 119–130.

Kumpulainen, K., Räsänen, E., Heuttonen, L., Moilanen, I., Piha, J., Puura, K., et al. (1999). Children's behavioral/emotional problems: A comparison of parents' and teachers' reports for elementary school-aged children. *European Child and Adolescent Psychiatry, 8*(Suppl. 4), IV/41–IV/47.

Kurokawa, N. K. S., & Weed, N. C. (1998). Interrater agreement on the Coping Inventory for Stressful Situations (CISS). *Assessment, 5,* 93–100.

Kwok, Y., Kim, C., Grady, D., Segal, M., & Redberg, R. (1999). Meta-analysis of exercise testing to detect coronary artery disease in women. *American Journal of Cardiology, 83,* 660–666.

Lambert, W., Salzer, M. S., & Bickman, L. (1998). Clinical outcome, consumer satisfaction, and ad hoc ratings of improvement in children's mental health. *Journal of Consulting and Clinical Psychology, 66,* 270–279.

Lee, S. W., Elliott, J., & Barbour, J. D. (1994). A comparison of cross-informant behavior ratings in school-based diagnosis. *Behavioral Disorders, 19,* 87–97.

Lester, D. (1992). The dexamethasone suppression test as an indicator of suicide: A meta-analysis. *Pharmacopsychiatry, 25,* 265–270.

Lester, D. (1995). The concentration of neurotransmitter metabolites in the cerebrospinal fluid of suicidal individuals: A meta-analysis. *Pharmacopsychiatry, 28,* 45–50.

Lewin, A. (1999, April). Critics' choice: The nation's top critics rate the 100 most noteworthy films of 1998. *Premiere, 12,* 86–87.

Lezak, M. D. (1995). *Neuropsychological assessment* (3rd ed.). New York: Oxford University Press.

Lijmer, J. C., Mol, B. W., Heisterkamp, S., Bonsel, G. J., Prins, M. H., van der Meulen, J. H. P., et al. (1999). Empirical evidence of design-related bias in studies of diagnostic tests. *JAMA, 282,* 1061–1066.

Lipsey, M. W., & Wilson, D. B. (1993). The efficacy of psychological, educational, and behavioral treatment: Confirmation from meta-analysis. *American Psychologist, 48,* 1181–1209.

Littenberg, B., Mushlin, A. I., & the Diagnostic Technology Assessment Consortium. (1992). Technetium bone scanning in the diagnosis of osteomyelitis: A meta-analysis of test performance. *Journal of General Internal Medicine, 7,* 158–163.

Little, K. B., & Shneidman, E. S. (1959). Congruencies among interpretations of psychological test and anamnestic data. *Psychological Monographs: General and Applied, 73,* 1–42.

Losier, B. J., McGrath, P. J., & Klein, R. M. (1996). Error patterns of the Continuous Performance Test in non-medicated and medicated samples of children with and without ADHD: A meta-analytic review. *Journal of Child Psychology and Psychiatry and Allied Disciplines, 37,* 971–987.

Lowman, M. G., Schwanz, K. A., & Kamphaus, R. W. (1996). WISC–III third factor: Critical measurement issues. *Canadian Journal of School Psychology, 12,* 15–22.

Lyness, S. A. (1993). Predictors of differences between Type A and B individuals in heart rate and blood pressure reactivity. *Psychological Bulletin, 114,* 266–295.

Mabe, P. A., III, & West, S. G. (1982). Validity of self-evaluation of ability: A review and meta-analysis. *Journal of Applied Psychology, 67,* 434–452.

Malgady, R. G., Rogler, L. H., & Tryon W. W. (1992). Issues of validity in the Diagnostic Interview Schedule. *Journal of Psychiatric Research, 26,* 59–67.

Malloy, T. E., Yarlas, A., Montvilo, R. K., & Sugarman, D. B. (1996). Agreement and accuracy in children's interpersonal perceptions: A social relations analysis. *Journal of Personality and Social Psychology, 71,* 692–702.

Mantha, S., Roizen, M. F., Barnard, J., Thisted, R. A., Ellis, J. E., & Foss, J. (1994). Relative effectiveness of four preoperative tests for predicting adverse cardiac outcomes after vascular surgery: A meta-analysis. *Anesthesia and Analgesia, 79,* 422–433.

Marlowe, D. B., Husband, S. D., Bonieskie, L. M., Kirby, K. C., & Platt, J. J. (1997). Structured interview versus self-report test vantages for the assessment of personality pathology in cocaine dependence. *Journal of Personality Disorders, 11,* 177–190.

Marshall, D., Johnell, O., & Wedel, H. (1996). Meta-analysis of how well measures of bone mineral density predict occurrence of osteoporotic fractures. *British Medical Journal, 312,* 1254–1259.

Martinussen, M. (1996). Psychological measures as predictors of pilot performance: A meta-analysis. *International Journal of Aviation Psychology, 6,* 1–20.

McClelland, D. C., Koestner, R., & Weinberger, J. (1989). How do self-attributed and implicit motives differ? *Psychological Review, 96,* 690–702.

McConaughy, S. H., Stanger, C., & Achenbach, T. M. (1992). Three-year course of behavioral/emotional problems in a national sample of 4- to 16-year-olds: I. Agreement among informants. *Journal of the American Academy of Child and Adolescent Psychiatry, 31,* 932–940.

McCrae, R. R. (1982). Consensual validation of personality traits: Evidence from self-reports and ratings. *Journal of Personality and Social Psychology, 43,* 293–303.

McCrae, R. R., & Costa, P. T., Jr. (1987). Validation of the five-factor model of personality across instruments and observers. *Journal of Personality and Social Psychology, 52,* 81–90.

McCrae, R. R., Stone, S. V., Fagan, P. J., & Costa, P. T., Jr. (1998). Identifying causes of disagreement between self-reports and spouse ratings of personality. *Journal of Personality, 66,* 285–313.

McDaniel, M. A., Whetzel, D. L., Schmidt, F. L., & Maurer, S. D. (1994). The validity of employment interviews: A comprehensive review and meta-analysis. *Journal of Applied Psychology, 79,* 599–616.

McGrath, R. E., & Ingersoll J. (1999a). Writing a good cookbook: I. A review of MMPI high-point code system studies. *Journal of Personality Assessment, 73,* 149–178.

McGrath, R. E., & Ingersoll, J. (1999b). Writing a good cookbook: II. A synthesis of MMPI high-point code system study effect sizes. *Journal of Personality Assessment, 73,* 179–198.

McKenna, M. C., Zevon, M. A., Corn, B., & Rounds, J. (1999). Psychosocial factors and the development of breast cancer: A meta-analysis. *Health Psychology, 18,* 520–531.

McReynolds, P. (1985). Psychological assessment and clinical practice: Problems and prospects. In J. N. Butcher & C. D. Spielberger (Eds.), *Advances in personality assessment* (Vol. 4, pp. 1–30). Hillsdale, NJ: Erlbaum.

Meehl P. E., (1959). Some ruminations on the validation of clinical procedures. *Canadian Journal of Psychology, 13,* 102–128.

Meier, S. T. (1994). *The chronic crisis in psychological measurement and assessment.* San Diego, CA: Academic Press.

Meiran N., & Jelicic, M. (1995). Implicit memory in Alzheimer's disease: A meta-analysis. *Neuropsychology, 9,* 291–303.

Merrit, R. M., Williams, M. F., James, T. H., & Porubsky, E. S. (1997). Detection of cervical metastasis: A meta-analysis comparing computed tomography with physical examination. *Archives of Otolaryngology and Head and Neck Surgery, 123,* 149–152.

Meyer, G. J. (1996a). Construct validation of scales derived from the Rorschach method: A review of issues and introduction to the Rorschach Rating Scale. *Journal of Personality Assessment, 67,* 598–628.

Meyer, G. J. (1996b). The Rorschach and MMPI: Toward a more scientifically differentiated understanding of cross-method assessment. *Journal of Personality Assessment, 67,* 558–578.

Meyer, G. J. (1997). On the integration of personality assessment methods: The Rorschach and MMPI–2. *Journal of Personality Assessment, 68,* 297–330.

Meyer, G. J. (2000). Incremental validity of the Rorschach Prognostic Rating Scale over the MMPI Ego Strength Scale and IQ. *Journal of Personality Assessment, 74,* 356–370.

Meyer G. J. (2002). Distinctions among information gathering methods and implications for a refined taxonomy of psychopathology. In L. E. Beutler & M. L. Malik (Eds.), *Rethinking the DSM: A psychological perspective. Decade of behavior.* Washington, DC: American Psychological Association.

Meyer, G. J., Finn, S. E., Eyde, L. D., Kay, G. G., Kubiszyn, T. W., Moreland, K. L., et al. (1998). *Benefits and costs of psychological assessment in healthcare delivery: Report of the Board of Professional Affairs Psychological Assessment Work Group, Part 1.* Washington, DC: American Psychological Association.

Meyer, G. J., & Handler, L. (1997). The ability of the Rorschach to predict subsequent outcome: A meta-analysis of the Rorschach Prognostic Rating Scale. *Journal of Personality Assessment, 69,* 1–38.

Meyer, G. J., & Handler L. (2000). "The ability of the Rorschach to predict subsequent outcome: A meta-analysis of the Rorschach Prognostic Rating Scale": Correction. *Journal of Personality Assessment, 74,* 504–506.

Meyer, G. J., Riethmiller, R. J., Brooks, G. D., Benoit, W. A., & Handler, L. (2000). A replication of Rorschach and MMPI–2 convergent validity. *Journal of Personality Assessment, 74,* 175–215.

Michell, J. (1997). Quantitative science and the definition of *measurement* in psychology. *British Journal of Psychology, 88*, 355–383.

Miller, S. B. (1987). A comparison of methods of inquiry. *Bulletin of the Menninger Clinic, 51*, 505–518.

Miller, T. Q., Smith, T. W., Turner, C. W., Guijarro, M. L., & Hallet, A. J. (1996). A meta-analytic review of research on hostility and physical health. *Psychological Bulletin, 119*, 322–348.

Millon, T. (1994). *Millon Clinical Multiaxial Inventory–III manual*. Minneapolis, MN: National Computer Systems.

Mirvis, S. E., Shanmuganathan, K., Miller, B. H., White, C. S., & Turney, S. Z. (1996). Traumatic aortic injury: Diagnosis with contrast-enhanced thoracic CT: Five-year experience at a major trauma center. *Radiology, 200*, 413–422.

Mitchell, M. F., Schottenfeld, D., Tortolero-Luna, G., Cantor, S. B., & Richards-Kortum, R. (1998). Colposcopy for the diagnosis of squamous intraepithelial lesions: A meta-analysis. *Obstetrics and Gynecology, 91*, 626–631.

Moffitt, T. E., Caspi, A., Krueger, R. F., Magdol, L., Margolin, G., Silva, P. A., et al. (1997). Do partners agree about abuse in their relationship? A psychometric evaluation of interpartner agreement. *Psychological Assessment, 9*, 47–56.

Mol, B. W. J., Bayram, N., Lijmer, J. G., Wiegerinck, M. A. H. M., Bongers, M. Y., van der Veen, F., et al. (1998). The performance of CA-125 measurement in the detection of endometriosis: A meta-analysis. *Fertility and Sterility, 70*, 1101–1108.

Mol, B. W. J., Lijmer, J. G., Ankum, W. M., van der Veen, F., & Bossuyt, P. M. M. (1998). The accuracy of single serum progesterone measurement in the diagnosis of ectopic pregnancy: A meta-analysis. *Human Reproduction, 13*, 3220–3227.

Mol, B. W. J., Lijmer, J., Dijkman, B., van der Veen, F., Wertheim, P., & Bossuyt, P. M. M. (1997). The accuracy of serum chlamydial antibodies in the diagnosis of tubal pathology: A meta-analysis. *Fertility and Sterility, 67*, 1031–1037.

Mol, B. W. J., Meijer, S., Yuppa, S., Tan, E., de Vries, J., Bossuyt, P. M. M., et al. (1998). Sperm penetration assay in predicting successful in vitro fertilization. *Journal of Reproductive Medicine, 43*, 503–508.

Moreland, K. L., Fowler, R. D., & Honaker, L. M. (1994). Future directions in the use of psychological assessment for treatment planning and outcome assessment: Predictions and recommendations. In M. E. Maruish (Ed.), *The use of psychological testing for treatment planning and outcome assessment* (pp. 581–602). Hillsdale, NJ: Erlbaum.

Morita, H., Suzuki, M., & Kamoshita, S. (1990). Screening measures for detecting psychiatric disorders in Japanese secondary school children. *Journal of Child Psychology and Psychiatry, 31*, 603–617.

Moroney, J. T., Bagiella, E., Desmond, D. W., Hachinski, V. C., Mölsä, P. K., Gustafson, L., et al. (1997). Meta-analysis of the Hachinski Ischemic Score in pathologically verified dementias. *Neurology, 49*, 1096–1105.

Morrison, T., & Morrison, M. (1995). A meta-analytic assessment of the predictive validity of the quantitative and verbal components of the Graduate Record Examination with graduate grade point average representing the criterion of success. *Educational and Psychological Measurement, 55*, 309–316.

Moskowitz, D. S. (1986). Comparison of self-reports, reports by knowledgeable informants, and behavioral observation data. *Journal of Personality, 54*, 294–317.

Moskowitz, D. S. (1990). Convergence of self-reports and independent observers: Dominance and friendliness. *Journal of Personality and Social Psychology, 58*, 1096–1106.

Mount, M. K., Barrick, M. R., & Stewart, G. L. (1998). Five-factor model of personality and performance in jobs involving interpersonal interactions. *Human Performance, 11*, 145–165.

The Movie Times. (1999). *Movies of 1998 box office totals*. No place of publication given: Author. Retrieved December 27, 2000, from http://www.the-movie-times .com/thrsdir/moviesof98.html

Mushlin, A. I., Kouides, R. W., & Shapiro, D. E. (1998). Estimating the accuracy of screening mammography: A meta-analysis. *American Journal of Preventive Medicine, 14*, 143–153.

Mutén, E. (1991). Self-reports, spouse ratings, and psychophysiological assessment in a behavioral medicine program: An application of the five-factor model. *Journal of Personality Assessment, 57*, 449–464.

National Oceanic and Atmospheric Administration. (1999). *Climate research data: The daily historical climatology network*. Raw data retrieved December 9, 1999, from http://www.ncdc.noaa.gov/ol/climate/research/ushen/daily.html

Naughton, B. J., Moran, M. B., Feinglass, J., Falconer, J., & Williams, M. E. (1994). Reducing hospital costs for the geriatric patient admitted from the emergency department: A randomized trial. *Journal of the American Geriatrics Society, 42*, 1045–1049.

Nebeker, R. S., Lambert, M. J., & Huefner, J. C. (1995). Ethnic differences on the Outcome Questionnaire. *Psychological Reports, 77*, 875–879.

Needleman, H. L., & Gatsonis, C. A. (1990). Low-level lead exposure and the IQ of children: A meta-analysis of modern studies. *JAMA, 263*, 673–678.

Nelson, J. C., & Davis, J. M. (1997). DST studies in psychotic depression: A meta-analysis. *American Journal of Psychiatry, 154*, 1497–1503.

Newman, M. L., & Greenway, P. (1997). Therapeutic effects of providing MMPI–2 test feedback to clients at a university counseling service: A collaborative approach. *Psychological Assessment, 9*, 122–131.

Ng, P. C., & Dear, P. R. F. (1990). The predictive value of a normal ultrasound scan in the preterm baby: A meta-analysis. *Acta Paediatrica Scandinavica, 79*, 286–291.

Nicholson, R. A., & Kugler, K. E. (1991). Competent and incompetent criminal defendants: A quantitative review of the comparative research. *Psychological Bulletin, 109*, 355–370.

Norcross, J. C., Karg, R. S., & Prochaska, J. O. (1997). Clinical psychologists in the 1990s: Part II. *Clinical Psychologist, 50*, 4–11.

Nowell, P. D., Mazumdar, S., Buysse, D. J., Dew, M. A., Reynolds, C. F., III, & Kupfer, D. F. (1997). Benzodiazepines and zolpidem for chronic insomnia: A meta-analysis of treatment efficacy. *JAMA, 278*, 2170–2177.

Nussbaum, D., & Rogers, R. (1992). Screening psychiatric patients for Axis II disorders. *Canadian Journal of Psychiatry, 37*, 658–660.

Oakland, T., & Glutting, J. J. (1990). Examiner observations of children's WISC–R test-related behaviors: Possible socioeconomic status, race, and gender effects. *Psychological Assessment, 2*, 86–90.

Offord, D. R., Boyle, M. H., Racine, Y., Szatmari, P., Fleming, J. E., Sanford, M., et al. (1996). Integrating data from multiple informants. *Journal of the American Academy of Child and Adolescent Psychiatry, 35*, 1078–1085.

Oldridge, N. B., Guyatt, G. H., Fischer, M. E., & Rimm, A. A. (1988). Cardiac rehabilitation after myocardial infarction: Combined experience of randomized clinical trials. *JAMA, 260*, 945–950.

Oler, A., Whooley, M. A., Oler, J., & Grady, D. (1996). Adding heparin to aspirin reduces the incidence of myocardial infarction and death in patients with unstable angina. *JAMA, 276*, 811–815.

Olsson, N., & Juslin, P. (1999). Can self-reported encoding strategy and recognition skill be diagnostic of performance in eyewitness identifications? *Journal of Applied Psychology, 84*, 42–49.

Oltmanns, T. F., Turkheimer, E., & Strauss M. E. (1998). Peer assessment of personality traits and pathology in female college students. *Assessment, 5*, 53–65.

Ones, D. S., Viswesvaran, C., & Schmidt, F. L. (1993). Comprehensive meta-analysis of integrity test validities: Findings and implications for personnel selection and theories of job performance. *Journal of Applied Psychology, 78*, 679–703.

Ouellette, J. A., & Wood, W. (1998). Habit and intention in everyday life: The multiple processes by which past behavior predicts future behavior. *Psychological Bulletin, 124*, 54–74.

Overholser, J. C. (1994). The personality disorders: A review and critique of contemporary assessment strategies. *Journal of Contemporary Psychotherapy, 24*, 223–243.

Ozer, D. J. (1985). Correlation and the coefficient of determination. *Psychological Bulletin, 97*, 307–315.

Parker, G., Boyce, P., Mitchell, P., Hadzi-Pavlovic, D., Wilhelm, K., Hickie, I., et al. (1992). Comparison of clinician rated and family corrobative witness data for depressed patients. *Journal of Affective Disorders, 24*, 25–34.

Parker, K. P., Hanson, R. K., & Hunsley, J. (1988). MMPI, Rorschach, and WAIS: A meta-analytic comparison of reliability, stability, and validity. *Psychological Bulletin, 103*, 367–373.

Parker, K. P., Hunsley, J., & Hanson, R. K. (1999). Old wine from old skins sometimes tastes like vinegar: A response to Garb, Florio, and Grove. *Psychological Science, 10,* 291–292.

Pastorelli, C., Barbaranelli, C., Cermak, I., Rozsa, S., & Caprara, G. V. (1997). Measuring emotional instability, prosocial behavior and aggression in pre-adolescents: A cross-national study. *Personality and Individual Differences, 23,* 691–703.

Paulhus, D. L., Aks, D. J., & Coren, S. (1990). Independence of performance and self-report measures of distractibility. *Journal of Social Psychology, 130,* 781–787.

Paulhus, D. L., Lysy, D. C., & Yik, M. S. M. (1998). Self-report measures of intelligence: Are they useful as proxy IQ tests? *Journal of Personality, 64,* 525–554.

Paulhus, D. L., & Reynolds, S. (1995). Enhancing target variance in personality impressions: Highlighting the person in person perception. *Journal of Personality and Social Psychology, 69,* 1233–1242.

Paulson, W. D., Ram, S. J., Birk, C. G., & Work, J. (1999). Does blood flow accurately predict thrombosis or failure of hemodialysis synthetic grafts? A meta-analysis. *American Journal of Kidney Diseases, 34,* 478–485.

Paunonen, S. V. (1989). Consensus in personality judgments: Moderating effects of target–rater acquaintanceship and behavior observability. *Journal of Personality and Social Psychology, 56,* 823–833.

Perry, J. C. (1992). Problems and considerations in the valid assessment of personality disorders. *American Journal of Psychiatry, 149,* 1645–1653.

Persky, V. W., Kempthorne-Rawson, J., & Shekelle, R. B. (1987). Personality and risk of cancer: 20-year follow-up of the Western Electric study. *Psychosomatic Medicine, 49,* 435–449.

Persons, J. B. (1991). Psychotherapy outcome studies do not accurately represent current models of psychotherapy: A proposed remedy. *American Psychologist, 46,* 99–106.

Peter, J. P., & Churchill, G. A., Jr. (1986). Relationships among research design choices and psychometric properties of rating scales: A meta-analysis. *Journal of Marketing Research, 23,* 1–10.

Petersen, J. R., Smith, E., Okorodudu, A. O., & Bissell, M. G. (1996). Comparison of four methods (L/S ratio, TDx FLM, lamellar bodies, PG) for fetal lung maturity using meta-analysis. *Clinical Laboratory Management Review, 10,* 169–175.

Phares, V., & Compas, B. E. (1990). Adolescents' subjective distress over their emotional/behavioral problems. *Journal of Consulting and Clinical Psychology, 58,* 596–603.

Phares, V., Compas, B. E., & Howell, D. C. (1989). Perspectives on child behavior problems: Comparisons of children's self-reports with parent and teacher reports. *Psychological Assessment, 1,* 68–71.

Phelps, R., Eisman, E. J., & Kohout, J. (1998). Psychological practice and managed care: Results of the CAPP practitioner survey. *Professional Psychology: Research and Practice, 29,* 31–36.

Piacentini, J., Shaffer, D., Fisher, P., Schwab-Stone, M., Davies, M., & Gioia, P. (1993). The Diagnostic Interview Schedule for Children–Revised Version (DISC–R): III. Concurrent criterion validity. *Journal of the American Academy of Child and Adolescent Psychiatry, 32,* 658–665

Piedmont, R. L. (1994). Validation of the NEO–PI–R observer form for college students: Toward a paradigm for studying personality development. *Assessment, 1,* 259–268.

Piedmont, R. L., & Ciarrocchi, J. W. (1999). The utility of the Revised NEO Personality Inventory in an outpatient, drug rehabilitation context. *Psychology of Addictive Behaviors, 13,* 213–226.

Pilkonis, P. A., Heape, C. L., Proietti, J. M., Clark, S. W., McDavid, J. D., & Pitts, T. E. (1995). The reliability and validity of two structured diagnostic interviews for personality disorders. *Archives of General Psychiatry, 52,* 1025–1033.

Pilkonis, P. A., Heape, C. L., Ruddy, J., & Serrao, P. (1991). Validity in the diagnosis of personality disorders: The use of the LEAD standard. *Psychological Assessment, 3,* 46–54.

Piotrowski, C. (1999). Assessment practices in the era of managed care: Current status and future directions. *Journal of Clinical Psychology, 55,* 787–796.

Piotrowski, C., Belter, R. W., & Keller, J. W. (1998). The impact of "managed care" on the practice of psychological testing: Preliminary findings. *Journal of Personality Assessment, 70,* 441–447.

Po, A. L., & Zhang, W. Y. (1998). Analgesic efficacy of ibuprofen alone and in combination with codeine or caffeine in post-surgical pain: A meta-analysis. *European Journal of Clinical Pharmacology, 53,* 303–311.

Pogge, D. L., Stokes, J. M., Frank, J., Wong, H., & Harvey, P. D. (1997). Association of MMPI validity scales and therapist ratings of psychopathology in adolescent psychiatric inpatients. *Assessment, 4,* 17–27.

Power, T. J., Andrews, T. J., Eiraldi, R. B., Doherty, B. J., Ikeda, M. J., DuPaul, G. J., et al. (1998). Evaluating attention deficit hyperactivity disorder using multiple informants: The incremental utility of combining teacher with parent reports. *Psychological Assessment, 10,* 250–260.

Psaty, B. M., Smith, N. L., Siscovick, D. S., Koepsell, T. D., Weiss, N. S., Heckbert, S. R., et al. (1997). Health outcomes associated with antihypertensive therapies used as first-line agents: A systematic review and meta-analysis. *JAMA, 277,* 739–745.

Puura, K., Almqvist, F., Tamminen, T., Piha, J., Räsänen, E., Kumpulainen, K., et al. (1998). Psychiatric disturbances among prepubertal children in Southern Finland. *Social Psychiatry and Psychiatric Epidemiology, 33,* 310–318.

Rao, J. K., Weinberger, M., Oddone, E. Z., Allen, N. B., Landsman, P., & Feussner, J. R. (1995). The role of antineutrophil cytoplasmic antibody (c-ANCA) testing in the diagnosis of Wegener granulomatosis: A literature review and meta-analysis. *Annals of Internal Medicine, 123,* 925–932.

Rapee, R. M., Barrett, P. M., Dadds, M. R., & Evans, L. E. (1994). Reliability of the

DSM–III–R childhood anxiety disorders using structured interview: Interrater and parent–child agreement. *Journal of the American Academy of Child and Adolescent Psychiatry, 33,* 984–992.

Raz, S., & Raz, N. (1990). Structural brain abnormalities in the major psychoses: A quantitative review of the evidence from computerized imaging. *Psychological Bulletin, 108,* 93–108.

Reich, W., Herjanic, B., Welner, Z., & Gandhy, P. R. (1982). Development of a structured psychiatric interview for children: Agreement on diagnoses comparing child and parent interviews. *Journal of Abnormal Child Psychology, 10,* 325–336.

Reinecke, M. A., Beebe, D. W., & Stein, M. A. (1999). The third factor of the WISC–III: It's (probably) not Freedom From Distractibility. *Journal of the American Academy of Child and Adolescent Psychiatry, 38,* 322–328.

Renneberg, B., Chambless, D. L., Dowdall, D. J., Fauerbach, J. A., & Gracely, E. J. (1992). The Structured Clinical Interview for *DSM–III–R,* Axis II and the Millon Clinical Multiaxial Inventory: A concurrent validity study of personality disorders among anxious outpatients. *Journal of Personality Disorders, 6,* 117–124.

Reuben, D. B., Borok, G. M., Wolde-Tsadik, G., Ershoff, D. H., Fishman, L. K., Ambrosini, V. L., et al. (1995). A randomized trial of comprehensive geriatric assessment in the care of hospitalized patients. *New England Journal of Medicine, 332,* 1345–1350.

Reynolds, C. R., & Kamphaus, R. W. (1998). *BASC: Behavioral Assessment for Children manual.* Circle Pines, MN: American Guidance Service.

Ribeiro, S. C. M., Tandon, R., Grunhaus, L., & Greden, J. F. (1993). The DST as a predictor of outcome in depression: A meta-analysis. *American Journal of Psychiatry, 150,* 1618–1629.

Riccio, C. A., Cohen, M. J., Hall, J., & Ross, C. M. (1997). The third and fourth factors of the WISC–III: What they don't measure. *Journal of Psychoeducational Assessment, 15,* 27–39.

Richter, P., Werner, J., Heerlein, A., Kraus, A., & Sauer, H. (1998). On the validity of the Beck Depression Inventory: A review. *Psychopathology, 31,* 160–168.

Riso, L. P., Klein, D. N., Anderson, R. L., Ouimette, P. C., & Lizardi, H. (1994). Concordance between patients and informants on the Personality Disorder Examination. *American Journal of Psychiatry, 151,* 568–573.

Robertson, I. T., & Kinder, A. (1993). Personality and job competences: The criterion-related validity of some personality variables. *Journal of Occupational and Organizational Psychology, 66,* 225–244.

Rogers, R., Salekin, R. T., & Sewell, K. W. (1999). Validation of the Millon Clinical Multiaxial Inventory for Axis II disorders: Does it meet the *Daubert* standard? *Law and Human Behavior, 23,* 425–443.

Rogers, R., Sewell, K. W., & Salekin, R. T. (1994). A meta-analysis of malingering on the MMPI–2. *Assessment, 1,* 227–237.

Rogler, L. H., Malgady, R. G., & Tryon, W. W. (1992). Evaluation of mental health:

Issues of memory in the Diagnostic Interview Schedule. *Journal of Nervous and Mental Disease, 180*, 215–222.

Ronan, G. F., Colavito, V. A., & Hammontree, S. R. (1993). Personal Problem-Solving System for scoring TAT responses: Preliminary validity and reliability data. *Journal of Personality Assessment, 61*, 28–40.

Rosenthal, R. (1990). How are we doing in soft psychology? *American Psychologist, 45*, 775–777.

Rosenthal, R. (1991). *Meta-analytic procedures for social research* (Rev. ed.). Newbury Park, CA: Sage.

Rosenthal, R. (1995). Progress in clinical psychology: Is there any? *Clinical Psychology: Science and Practice, 2*, 133–150.

Roth, P. L., BeVier, C. A., Switzer, F. S., & Schippmann, J. S. (1996). Meta-analyzing the relationship between grades and job performance. *Journal of Applied Psychology, 81*, 548–556.

Rothbaum, F., & Weisz, J. R. (1995). Parental caregiving and child externalizing behavior in nonclinical samples: A meta-analysis. *Psychological Bulletin, 116*, 55–74.

Rubenstein, L. Z., Josephson, K. R., Harker, J. O., Miller, D. K., & Wieland, D. (1995). The Sepulveda GEU Study revisited: Long-term outcomes, use of services, and costs. *Aging (Milano), 7*, 212–217.

Rubenstein, L. Z., Stuck, A. E., Siu, A. L., & Wieland, D. (1991). Impacts of geriatric evaluation and management programs on defined outcomes: Overview of the evidence. *Journal of the American Geriatrics Society, 39*, 8S–16S.

Rubin, C. D., Sizemore, M. T., Loftis, P. A., & de Mola, N. L. (1993). A randomized, controlled trial of outpatient geriatric evaluation and management in a large public hospital. *Journal of the American Geriatrics Society, 41*, 1023–1028.

Rubio-Stipec, M., Canino, G. J., Shrout, P., Dulcan, M., Freeman, D., & Bravo, M. (1994). Psychometric properties of parents and children as informants in child psychiatry epidemiology with the Spanish Diagnostic Interview Schedule for Children (DISC–2). *Journal of Abnormal Child Psychology, 22*, 703–720.

Russell, C. J., Settoon, R. P., McGrath, R. N., Blanton, A. E., Kidwell, R. E., Lohrke, F. T., et al. (1994). Investigator characteristics as moderators of personnel selection research: A meta-analysis. *Journal of Applied Psychology, 79*, 163–170.

Ryan, K. J. (1998). *Heteromethod validity of self-reports, observational scales, and performance measures in the assessment of attention and impulsivity.* Unpublished master's thesis, University of Alaska Anchorage.

Salekin, R. T., Rogers, R., & Sewell, K. W. (1996). A review and meta-analysis of the Psychopathy Checklist and Psychopathy Checklist–Revised: Predictive validity of dangerousness. *Clinical Psychology: Science and Practice, 3*, 203–215.

Salgado, J. S. (1997). The five-factor model of personality and job performance in the European Community. *Journal of Applied Psychology, 82*, 30–43.

Salgado, J. S. (1998). Big Five personality dimensions and job performance in army and civil occupations: A European perspective. *Human Performance, 11,* 271–288.

Scheidler, J., Hricak, H., Yu, K. K., Subak, L., & Segal, M. R. (1997). Radiological evaluation of lymph node metastases in patients with cervical cancer: A meta-analysis. *JAMA, 278,* 1096–1101.

Schmitt, N., Gooding, R. Z., Noe, R. A., & Kirsch, M. (1984). Metaanalyses of validity studies published between 1964 and 1982 and the investigation of study characteristics. *Personnel Psychology, 37,* 407–422.

Schwab-Stone, M. E., Shaffer, D., Dulcan, M. K., Jensen, P. S., Fisher, P., Bird, H. R., et al. (1996). Criterion validity of the NIMH Diagnostic Interview Schedule for Children Version 2.3 (DISC–2.3). *Journal of the American Academy of Child and Adolescent Psychiatry, 35,* 878–888.

Seidenberg, M., Haltiner, A., Taylor, M. A., Hermann, B. B., & Wyler, A. (1994). Development and validation of a multiple ability self-report questionnaire. *Journal of Clinical and Experimental Neuropsychology, 16,* 93–104.

Seligman, M. E. (1995). The effectiveness of psychotherapy: The *Consumer Reports* study. *American Psychologist, 50,* 965–974.

Shadish, W. R., Matt, G. E., Navarro, A. M., Siegle, G., Crits-Christoph, P., Hazel-rigg, M. D., et al. (1997). Evidence that therapy works in clinically representative conditions. *Journal of Consulting and Clinical Psychology, 65,* 355–365.

Shea, V. (1985). Overview of the assessment process. In C. S. Newmark (Ed.), *Major psychological assessment instruments* (pp. 1–10). Boston: Allyn & Bacon.

Shedler, J., Mayman, M., & Manis, M. (1993). The illusion of mental health. *American Psychologist, 48,* 1117–1131.

Siegman-Igra, Y., Anglim, A. M., Shapiro, D. E., Adal, K. A., Strain, B. A., & Farr, B. M. (1997). Diagnosis of vascular catheter-related bloodstream infection: A meta-analysis. *Journal of Clinical Microbiology, 35,* 928–936.

Silverman, M., Musa, D., Martin, D. C., Lave, J. R., Adams, J., & Ricci, E. M. (1995). Evaluation of outpatient geriatric assessment: A randomized multi-site trial. *Journal of the American Geriatrics Society, 43,* 733–740.

Silvestri, G. A., Littenberg, B., & Colice, G. L. (1995). The clinical evaluation for detecting metastic lung cancer: A meta-analysis. *American Journal of Respiratory and Critical Care Medicine, 152,* 225–230.

Siu, A. L., Kravitz, R. L., Keeler, E., Hemmerling, K., Kington, R., Davis. J. W., et al. (1996). Postdischarge geriatric assessment of hospitalized frail elderly patients. *Archives of Internal Medicine, 156,* 76–81.

Smith, G. E., Petersen, R. C., Ivnik, R. J., Malec, J. F., & Tangalos, E. G. (1996). Subjective memory complaints, psychological distress, and longitudinal change in objective memory performance. *Psychology and Aging, 11,* 272–279.

Smith, M. L., & Glass, G. V. (1977). Meta-analysis of psychotherapy outcome studies. *American Psychologist, 32,* 752–760.

Smith-Bindman, R., Kerlikowske, K., Feldstein, V. A., Subak, L., Scheidler, J., Segal,

M., et al. (1998). Endovaginal ultrasound to exclude endometrial cancer and other abnormalities. *JAMA, 280*, 1510–1517.

Soldz, S., Budman, S., Demby, A., & Merry, J. (1993). Diagnostic agreement between the Personality Disorder Examination and the MCMI–II. *Journal of Personality Assessment, 60*, 486–499.

Spangler, W. D. (1992). Validity of questionnaire and TAT measures of need for achievement: Two meta-analyses. *Psychological Bulletin, 112*, 140–154.

Spengler, P. M., Strohmer, D. C., Dixon, D. N., & Shivy, V. A. (1995). A scientist–practitioner model of psychological assessment: Implications for training, practice and research. *Counseling Psychologist, 23*, 506–534.

Spiker, D., Kraemer, H. C., Constantine, N. A., & Bryant, D. (1992). Reliability and validity of behavior problem checklists as measures of stable traits in low birth weight, premature preschoolers. *Child Development, 63*, 1481–1496.

Spreen, O., & Strauss, E. (1998). *A compendium of neuropsychological tests: Administration, norms, and commentary* (2nd ed.). New York: Oxford University Press.

Stanton, M. D., & Shadish, W. R. (1997). Outcome, attrition, and family–couples treatment for drug abuse: A meta-analysis and review of the controlled, comparative studies. *Psychological Bulletin, 122*, 170–191.

Steering Committee of the Physicians' Health Study Research Group. (1988). Preliminary report: Findings from the aspirin component of the ongoing physicians' health study. *New England Journal of Medicine, 318*, 262–264.

Steiner, J. L., Tebes, J. K., Sledge, W. H., & Walker, M. L. (1995). A comparison of the Structured Clinical Interview for *DSM–III–R* and clinical diagnoses. *Journal of Nervous and Mental Disease, 183*, 365–369.

Sturm, R., Unützer, J., & Katon, W. (1999). Effectiveness research and implications for study design: Sample size and statistical power. *General Hospital Psychiatry, 21*, 274–283.

Sweeney, P. D., Anderson, K., & Bailey, S. (1986). Attributional style in depression: A meta-analytic review. *Journal of Personality and Social Psychology, 50*, 974–991.

Symons, C. S., & Johnson, B. T. (1997). The self-reference effect in memory: A meta-analysis. *Psychological Bulletin, 121*, 371–394.

Taylor, H. C., & Russell, J. T. (1939). The relationship of validity coefficients to the practical effectiveness of tests in selection: Discussion and tables. *Journal of Applied Psychology, 23*, 565–578.

Taylor, J. L., Miller, T. P., & Tinklenberg, J. R. (1992). Correlates of memory decline: A 4-year longitudinal study of older adults with memory complaints. *Psychology and Aging, 7*, 185–193.

Tett, R. P., Jackson, D. N., & Rothstein, M. (1991). Personality measures as predictors of job performance: A meta-analytic review. *Personnel Psychology, 44*, 703–742.

Tett, R. P., Jackson, D. N., Rothstein, M., & Reddon, J. R. (1994). Meta-analysis of personality–job performance relations: A reply to Ones, Mount, Barrick, and Hunter (1994). *Personnel Psychology, 47,* 157–172.

Thomas, D. R., Brahan, R., & Haywood, B. P. (1993). Inpatient community-based geriatric assessment reduces subsequent mortality. *Journal of the American Geriatrics Society, 41,* 101–104.

Thornton, A. E., & Raz, N. (1997). Memory impairment in multiple sclerosis: A quantitative review. *Neuropsychology, 11,* 357–366.

Towler, B., Irwig, L., Glasziou, P., Kewenter, J., Weller, D., & Silagy, C. (1998). A systematic review of the effects of screening for colorectal cancer using the faecal occult blood test, Hemoccult. *British Medical Journal, 317,* 559–565.

Treiber, F. A., & Mabe, P. A., III (1987). Child and parent perceptions of children's psychopathology in psychiatric outpatient children. *Journal of Abnormal Child Psychology, 15,* 115–124.

Trentini, M., Semeraro, S., Rossi, E., Giannandrea, E., Vanelli, M., Pandiani, G., et al. (1995). A multicenter randomized trial of comprehensive geriatric assessment and management: Experimental design, baseline data, and six-month preliminary results. *Aging (Milano), 7,* 224–233.

Trull, T. J., & Larson, S. L. (1994). External validity of two personality disorder inventories. *Journal of Personality Disorders, 8,* 96–103.

Tsujimoto, R. N., Hamilton, M., & Berger, D. E. (1990). Averaging multiple judges to improve validity: Aid to planning cost-effective clinical research. *Psychological Assessment, 2,* 432–437,

Tucker, G. J. (1998). Putting *DSM–IV* in perspective. *American Journal of Psychiatry, 155,* 159–161.

Turner, R. G., & Gilliland, L. (1977). Comparison of self-report and performance measures of attention. *Perceptual and Motor Skills, 45,* 409–410.

Uchino, B. N., Cacioppo, J. T., & Kiecolt-Glaser, J. K. (1996). The relationship between social support and physiological processes: A review with emphasis on underlying mechanisms and implications for health. *Psychological Bulletin, 119,* 488–531.

Van Ijzendoorn, M. H. (1995). Adult attachment representations, parental responsiveness, and infant attachment: A meta-analysis on the predictive validity of the adult attachment interview. *Psychological Bulletin, 117,* 387–403.

U.S. Department of Health and Human Services, National Center for Health Statistics. (1996). *Third National Health and Nutrition Examination Survey, 1988–1994.* Hyattsville, MD: Center for Disease Control and Prevention. Retrieved from NHANES III Laboratory data file (CD-ROM, No. 76200).

Van Ijzendoorn, M. H., & Schuengel, C. (1996). The measurement of dissociation in normal and clinical populations: Meta-analytic validation of the Dissociative Experiences Scale (DES). *Clinical Psychology Review, 16,* 365–382.

Van Rijkom, H. M., & Verdonschot, E. H. (1995). Factors involved in validity measurements of diagnostic tests for approximal caries: A meta-analysis. *Caries Research, 29,* 364–370.

Veiel, H. O. F. (1997). A preliminary profile of neuropsychological deficits associated with major depression. *Journal of Clinical and Experimental Neuropsychology, 19*, 587–603.

Verhaeghen, P., & Salthouse, T. A. (1997). Meta-analysis of age–cognition relations in adulthood: Estimates of linear and nonlinear age effects and structural models. *Psychological Bulletin, 122*, 231–249.

Verhulst, F. C., & Akkerhuis, G. W. (1989). Agreement between parents' and teachers' ratings of behavioral/emotional problems of children aged 4–12. *Journal of Child Psychology and Psychiatry, 30*, 123–136.

Verhulst, F. C., & van der Ende, J. (1991). Assessment of child psychopathology: Relationships between different methods, different informants and clinical judgment of severity. *Acta Psychiatrica Scandinavica, 84*, 155–159.

Verhulst, F. C., & van der Ende, J. (1992). Agreement between parents' reports and adolescents' self-reports of problem behavior. *Journal of Child Psychology and Psychiatry, 33*, 1011–1023.

Verive, J. M., & McDaniel, M. A. (1996). Short-term memory tests in personnel selection: Low adverse impact and high validity. *Intelligence, 23*, 15–32.

Videbech, P. (1997). MRI findings in patients with affective disorder: A meta-analysis. *Acta Psychiatrica Scandinavica, 96*, 157–168.

Vinchur, A. J., Schippman, J. S., Switzer, F. S., III, & Roth, P. L. (1998). A meta-analytic review of predictors of job performance for salespeople. *Journal of Applied Psychology, 83*, 586–597.

Vitiello, B., Malone, R., Buschle, P. R., Delaney, M. A., & Behar, D. (1990). Reliability of *DSM–III* diagnoses of hospitalized children. *Hospital and Community Psychiatry, 41*, 63–67.

Wahlbeck, K., Cheine, M., Essali, A., & Adams, C. (1999). Evidence of clozapine's effectiveness in schizophrenia: A systematic review and meta-analysis of randomized trials. *American Journal of Psychiatry, 156*, 990–999.

Watson, D., & Clark, L. A. (1991). Self-versus peer ratings of specific emotional traits: Evidence of convergent and discriminant validity. *Journal of Personality and Social Psychology, 60*, 927–940.

Wechsler, D. (1997). *WAIS–III: Wechsler Adult Intelligence Scale–Third Edition.* San Antonio, TX: Psychological Corporation.

Weinstein, S. R., Stone, K., Noam, G. G., Grives, K., & Schwab-Stone, M. (1989). Comparison of DISC with clinicians' *DSM–III* diagnoses in psychiatric patients. *Journal of the American Academy of Child and Adolescent Psychiatry, 28*, 53–60.

Wells, P. S., Lensing, A. W. A., Davidson, B. L., Prins, M. H., & Hirsh, J. (1995). Accuracy of ultrasound for the diagnosis of deep venous thrombosis in asymptomatic patients after orthopedic surgery: A meta-analysis. *Annals of Internal Medicine, 122*, 47–53.

Welten, D. C., Kemper, H. C. G., Post, G. B., & Van Staveren, W. A. (1995). A meta-analysis of the effect of calcium intake on bone mass in young and middle-aged females and males. *Journal of Nutrition, 125,* 2802–2813.

Widom, C. S., & Morris, S. (1997). Accuracy of adult recollections of childhood victimization: Part 2. Childhood sexual abuse. *Psychological Assessment, 9,* 34–46.

Winter, D. G., John, O. P., Stewart, A. J., Klohnen, E. C., & Duncan, L. E. (1998). Traits and motives: Toward an integration of two traditions in personality research. *Psychological Review, 105,* 230–250.

Wishart, H., & Sharpe, D. (1997). Neuropsychological aspects of multiple sclerosis: A quantitative review. *Journal of Clinical and Experimental Neuropsychology, 19,* 810–824.

Wolfe, V. V., Finch, A. J., Saylor, C. F., Blount, R. L., Pallmeyer, T. P., & Carek, D. J. (1987). Negative affectivity in children: A multitrait–multimethod investigation. *Journal of Consulting and Clinical Psychology, 55,* 245–250.

Wolraich, M. L., Wilson, D. B., & White, J. W. (1995). The effect of sugar on behavior or cognition in children. *JAMA, 274,* 1617–1621.

Wood, W., Wong, F. Y., & Chachere, J. G. (1991). Effects of media violence on viewers' aggression in unconstrained social interaction. *Psychological Bulletin, 109,* 371–383.

Yang, J., McCrae, R. R., Costa, P. T., Jr., Dai, X., Yao, S., Cai, T., et al. (1999). Cross-cultural personality assessment in psychiatric populations: The NEO–PI–R in the People's Republic of China. *Psychological Assessment, 11,* 359–368.

Yankowitz, J., Fulton, A., Williamson, R., Grant, S. S., & Budelier, W. T. (1998). Prospective evaluation of prenatal maternal serum screening for Trisomy 18. *American Journal of Obstetrics and Gynecology, 178,* 446–450.

Yusuf, S., Zucker, D., Peduzzi, P., Fisher, L. D., Takaro, T., Kennedy, J. W., et al (1994). Effect of coronary artery bypass graft surgery on survival: Overview of 10-year results from the randomized trials by the Coronary Artery Bypass Graft Surgery Trialists Collaboration. *Lancet, 344,* 563–570.

Zakzanis, K. K. (1998). Quantitative evidence for neuroanatomic and neuropsychological markers in dementia of the Alzheimer type. *Journal of Clinical and Experimental Neuropsychology, 20,* 259–269.

Zelinski, E. M., Gilewski, M. J., & Anthony-Bergstone, C. R. (1990). Memory Functioning Questionnaire: Concurrent validity with memory performance and self-reported memory failures. *Psychology and Aging, 5,* 388–399.

Zimmerman, M., Pfohl, B., Coryell, W., Stangl, D., & Corenthal, C. (1988). Diagnosing personality disorder in depressed patients: A comparison of patient and informant interviews. *Archives of General Psychiatry, 45,* 733–737.

Zorrilla, E. P., McKay, J. R., Luborsky, L., & Schmidt, K. (1996). Relation of stressor and depressive symptoms to clinical progression of viral illness. *American Journal of Psychiatry, 153,* 626–635.

Zuckerman, M., Bernieri, F., Koestner, R., & Rosenthal, R. (1989). To predict some of the people some of the time: In search of moderators. *Journal of Personality and Social Psychology, 57,* 279–293.

Zuckerman, M., Koestner, R., DeBoy, T., Garcia, T., Maresca, B. C., & Sartoris, J. M. (1988). To predict some of the people some of the time: A reexamination of the moderator variable approach in personality theory. *Journal of Personality and Social Psychology, 54,* 1006–1019.

Zuckerman, M., Miyake, K., Koestner, R., Baldwin, C. H., & Osborne, J. W. (1991). Uniqueness as a moderator of self–peer agreement. *Personality and Social Psychology Bulletin, 17,* 385–391.

MEASUREMENT AMONG
DIFFERENT SAMPLES

14

METHODOLOGICAL ISSUES IN ASSESSMENT RESEARCH WITH ETHNIC MINORITIES

SUMIE OKAZAKI AND STANLEY SUE

Assessment research on ethnic minority groups has had a controversial history. For example, comparisons of intellectual abilities and cognitive skills, of self-esteem and self-hatred, of personality patterns, and of prevalence rates and degrees of psychopathology among different ethnic and racial groups have generated considerable controversy regarding the validity of findings. It is our belief that conducting valid assessment research with ethnic minority groups is particularly problematic because of methodological, conceptual, and practical difficulties that arise in such research. This article addresses common methodological problems that have plagued assessment research on ethnic minorities. Our intent here is not to provide definitive solutions to methodological problems but rather to raise issues that many researchers may not have otherwise considered, so that informed decisions can be made about how to handle variables related to ethnicity. We also pose

Reprinted from *Psychological Assessment, 7*, 367–375. Copyright 1995 by the American Psychological Association.

some guidelines for future assessment research with ethnic minorities to improve the knowledge base not only for ethnic minorities but also for the field of psychological assessment. In doing so, we will closely examine fundamental problems such as sample heterogeneity, measurement of culture, and underlying assumptions about ethnicity, all of which make assessment research with ethnic minorities inherently challenging. Because our work involves Asian Americans, many of the cited examples deal with this population, although the point behind the examples may apply to other ethnic groups.

We refer to assessment research in a broad sense and use examples from extant literature on cognitive, personality, and clinical psychodiagnostic assessment with various ethnic minority groups. The focus is not on particular assessment instruments but on underlying conceptual and methodological issues with respect to ethnicity.

ETHNICITY AND RACE

Use of Terms

From the outset, let us address some definitional issues. It must be noted that the notions of race and ethnic minority status are highly charged with potential political ramifications. A prevailing example of a classification system with vast political consequences is the use of the terms race and Hispanic origin by the U.S. Bureau of the Census, whose population count influences each region's allotment of federal funds as well as possible district realignment for voting purposes. The U.S. Bureau of the Census uses the following categories: White; Black; American Indian, Eskimo, or Aleut; Asian or Pacific Islanders; Hispanic origin (of any race); and Other. The use of the term "race" appears to imply biological factors, as races are typically defined by observable physiognomic features such as skin color, hair type and color, eye color, stature, facial features, and so forth. However, some researchers have argued that designation of race is often arbitrary and that within-race differences in even the physiognomic features are greater than between-race differences (Zuckerman, 1990), and this topic continues to be hotly debated (e.g., Yee, Fairchild, Weizmann, & Wyatt, 1993).

There is no one definition of ethnicity, race, and culture that is agreed on by all. Indeed, it is common for both researchers and others to refer to ethnicity, culture, and race interchangeably when identifying and categorizing people by background (Betancourt & Lopez, 1993). Granted, these terms are closely related, as illustrated by a definition of ethnic status provided by Eaton (1980, p. 160):

> Ethnic status is defined as an easily identifiable characteristic that implies a common cultural history with others possessing the same charac-

teristic. The most common ethnic "identifiers" are race, religion, country of origin, language, and/or cultural background.

It is quite obvious that various characteristics serving as ethnic identifiers do not usually occur as independent features but appear in interrelated patterns and configurations (Dahlstrom, 1986), thus the common practice of interchanging the terms is understandable to a degree. However, confusion or a lack of differentiation among race, ethnicity, and culture at the terminology level likely reflects confusion at the conceptual level. That is, is the research concerned with race as a biological variable, ethnicity as a demographic variable, or some aspect of subjective cultural experience as a psychological variable?

Often, the implicit rationale behind grouping together individuals of the same racial or ethnic background and conducting assessment research using ethnicity as an independent or predictor variable is based on the assumptions that (a) these individuals share some common psychological characteristics associated with culture and (b) such shared cultural – psychological characteristics are related to personality or psychopathology. However, ethnicity is a demographic variable that is relatively distal to the variable of psychological or clinical interest. In many research studies, the participants' ethnicity may be serving as a proxy for psychological variables such as cultural values, self-concept, minority status, and so forth. Nonetheless, communications of findings (in the form of journal reports) often fail to clarify what assumptions were made about psychological characteristics of the particular sample in research studies. We believe that imprecisely using race and ethnicity to categorize individuals and then conducting studies on such population groups have contributed to the problems in assessment research with ethnic minorities. In the absence of each research study explicating the assumptions underlying the use of such categorical variables, we cannot assume that researchers are studying and communicating about the same constructs. Therefore, we echo the assertions made by Clark (1987) and by Betancourt and Lopez (1993) that research involving individuals from different ethnic and cultural backgrounds must specify and directly measure the underlying psychological variables associated with culture that are hypothesized to produce cultural or ethnic group differences.

Individual Differences Versus Group Characteristics

Some have argued that grouping together individuals based on ethnicity or race perpetuates unnecessary stereotyping or useless categorizations. Although we will, in the next section, point to the pitfalls of underestimating within-group heterogeneity, we still uphold the value of conducting research on broad groups of individuals classified into ethnic minority groups to the extent that as previously discussed, certain sets of characteristics covary with racial, ethnic, or cultural groups. After all, what is culture, if not a set of values and attitudes, a world view, and so forth that are shared by a large number of people who also share, to a greater or lesser extent, other demographic and physical characteristics? One caveat in examining characteristics of a broad group rests on a basic principle, namely, the greater the heterogeneity, the less precise the prediction is apt to be. Thus, although we may conclude that in general, White Americans are more individualistic than are Mexican Americans, we cannot predict with any certainty the level of individualism of a particular person. It is obvious that the confounding of an individual with the individual's culture results in stereotyping. Furthermore, an awkwardness exists when terms such as *Asian Americans* or *African Americans* are used because within-group heterogeneity cannot be conveyed by such terms. By making explicit the meaning of the terms and the context in which they are used, one can reduce some of the awkwardness.

COMMON METHODOLOGICAL PROBLEMS

Methodological problems with respect to ethnic minorities can occur at all stages of assessment research. We will examine salient issues in the stages of design (with respect to the population focus), sampling, measure selection and establishing equivalence of measures, method of assessment, and interpretation of data.

Population Focus

Selecting Participants

In the initial design of assessment research, a salient dilemma confronting researchers may be which ethnic groups to include in the design and for what purpose. Let us examine two scenarios, one case in which the primary research question does not involve ethnicity or culture and another case in which the research question does concern ethnic minorities. In the scenario in which the main investigation does not involve ethnicity, a researcher must decide which ethnic minority group(s), if any, to include in the design. If ethnic minority individuals comprise a subsample that is too small with which to run separate or comparative analyses with the majority ethnic group, a researcher may choose to exclude them from analyses altogether. This certainly simplifies the problem, but it does not contribute to the much needed knowledge of whether the findings may be generalized to ethnic minorities. If a subsample of ethnic minorities is too small for meaningful analyses but large enough not to be discarded, a researcher must contend with the knowledge that observed variance in the variables of interest may contain some unmeasured or unanalyzed factors related to ethnicity. On the other hand, a well-intentioned researcher may collect data from sizable ethnic minority groups but without a sound conceptual basis or a planned course of analyses for handling the ethnicity variable. A common outcome in such a case may be that ethnicity is relegated to the status of an extraneous variable, to be dealt with as an afterthought in the analysis.

In the second scenario, where the primary research question is concerned with ethnic minorities (e.g., establishing psychometric properties of an established assessment measure for an ethnic minority group), a frequent dilemma involves deciding whether to collect data solely from the target ethnic minority group or to compare the ethnic minorities with a control group. It is a common practice to compare one or more ethnic minority groups with Whites on a psychological characteristic of empirical interest. A part of this practice is rooted in the existing research paradigm that emphasizes differences (with "statistical significance") across groups. And because many assessment measures and methods have been developed and normed on largely, if not exclusively, White populations (e.g., the original Minnesota Multiphasic Personality Inventory; MMPI), researchers are taken to task to assess whether these measures and methods are psychometrically and practically valid with ethnic minorities. However, the rare comparison paradigm should not go unquestioned. The comparative approach has been criticized for potentially reinforcing racial stereotypes or the interpretation of non-White behavior as deviant as well as underestimating or overlooking within-ethnic group variations (Azibo, 1988; Campbell, 1967; Graham, 1992). The question often posed is, Are within-group differences as important or as valid as between-group differences? An example of the dilemma was presented by Korchin (1980). Korchin wanted to assess the determinants of personality competence among two groups of African American men — those demonstrating exceptional and average competence. Results of the study were analyzed, and a paper on the study was submitted to a major journal. One of the paper's reviewers criticized the study as being "grievously flawed," because no White control group was employed. Korchin raised several questions. Why should a White control group have been employed when the purpose of the study was to analyze within-group differences? What would happen if someone submitted a study identical in all respects except that all participants were White? Would it be criticized because it lacked an African American control group? There are no easy answers to these questions. As suggested by Korchin, assumptions concerning the appropriateness of comparisons should be guided by the purpose of a particular study.

Ethnic Comparisons

Once the question of population focus (i.e., inclusion or exclusion of specific ethnic minority groups) has been resolved, the next issue to consider is "matching" two or more ethnic groups for comparison purposes. Group comparisons are commonly achieved through two methods: (a) matching the participants a priori on the relevant but secondary variables or (b) controlling for those variables post hoc in analyses. With respect to matching, ethnic groups are typically matched on demographic characteristics such as age, sex, and possibly socioeconomic status, as well as defining characteristics such as psychiatric diagnoses. However, it may be difficult to match two or more ethnic groups on all relevant characteristics, as it has been well documented that various sectors of ethnic minority populations differ in the nature and distribution of characteristics. For example, American Indians have a much higher rate of unemployment, a larger number of individuals living under the poverty level, a higher school dropout rate, and a shorter life expectancy than other ethnic groups (LaFromboise, 1988). Graham (1992) noted the paramount importance of controlling for group differences in socioeconomic status when comparing African Americans and Whites, given overrepresentation of African Americans in economically disadvantaged segments of the population.

In deciding which variables need to be controlled for in the ethnic group comparisons, again, there is no agreed list of variables that are considered as essential control variables for each ethnic group. It is advised that variability in social and demographic characteristics (e.g., educational attainment, income level, language fluency, etc.) be statistically controlled in the analysis when ethnic differences exist on such variables and when the researcher has a reason to believe such differences may moderate the relationship between the variables of interest. A potential problem that remains in matching participants or controlling for differences in social characteristics is that a researcher may assume, given similar demographics of two ethnic groups, that individuals constituting the study are similar on a number of other unmeasured variables. Some have argued that similar demographics may have different effects for ethnic minorities, such as the interactive effect of ethnicity and social class on stress and distress (Cervantes & Castro, 1985; Kessler & Neighbors, 1986). A more sophisticated understanding of psychological correlates of demographic characteristics, including ethnicity, is needed.

Sampling

The design problem over inclusion or exclusion of ethnic minorities in assessment research is closely tied to problems in sampling. In this section we review specific sampling techniques used to identify and solicit participation of ethnic minority participants. Some of the examples for obtaining ethnic minority samples are not from personality assessment research but from epidemiological and community studies targeting subclinical or nonclinical ethnic minority populations. They are used here as illustrations of methods for obtaining difficult-to-reach samples.

Identifying Participants

Foremost in the sampling problem is identifying the ethnicity of participants. Self-identification of ethnicity by participants' self-report is the most common method, and this is most often accomplished by a limited categorical listing of ethnic groups, as defined by the investigator. Ethnicity may be defined at a broad level (e.g., Latino or Hispanic) or at a more specific level (e.g., Puerto Rican, Mexican American, etc.). Researchers are also faced with the decision of how to classify persons of mixed racial or ethnic backgrounds (see Hall, 1992; Root, 1992). Another method for identifying potential participants' ethnicity is through the surname identification method. Some ethnic groups such as Asians and Hispanics have unequivocally ethnic surnames (e.g., "Kim" for Koreans, "Nguyen" for Vietnamese, and "Gutierrez" for Latino), which enables surname-based community sampling methodology. Indeed some studies have used surnames or other key characteristics as the sole basis for determining participants' ethnicity (e.g., Dion & Giordano, 1990; Dion & Toner, 1988). This method for ascertaining the ethnicity of participants (i.e., without cross-validation from the participants) is sometimes the only option, particularly when working with archival data, but this obviously limits the certainty with which the results may be interpreted. There are further issues with respect to identification of ethnicity. Sasao and Sue (1993) pointed to the faulty but commonly made assumption that once individuals are identified as belonging to a certain ethnic–cultural group, they share a common understanding of their own ethnicity or culture and identify with the ethnic–cultural group. To illustrate, in a high school drug abuse survey conducted in multicultural communities in Southern California (Sasao, 1992), approximately 20% of the Chinese American students indicated their primary cultural identification was Mexican, though the self-perceived ethnicity of these Chinese students was Chinese.

Small Sample Size

Collecting data from a large enough sample of ethnic minorities has long posed a challenge, partly because of the small overall population size. Let us take the example of American Indians (technically categorized as American Indians, Eskimo, or Aleut by the U.S. Bureau of the Census), who comprised only 0.8% of the total U.S. population according to the 1990 U.S. Census (U.S. Bureau of the Census, 1991). American Indian populations tend to be geographically much more concentrated than does the general U.S. population, as the majority of American Indians lived in just six states in 1990. The American Indian population was highest in Alaska, where it comprised about 16% of that state's total population, but there were 35 states in which American Indians represented less than 1% of the total population of each state in 1990 (U.S. Bureau of the Census, 1991). About half of the

American Indian population lives in urban areas and about half lives in rural areas or areas on or adjacent to reservations that are located in the Plains States (Bureau of Indian Affairs, 1991). Thus, locating an adequate sample size of American Indian participants is difficult, if not impractical, in many states and regions.

The problem of small sample size often results in researchers combining the data from a number of ethnic–cultural groups with some common origin (e.g., combining Chinese Americans, Japanese Americans, and Korean Americans into one group), or in the case of American Indians, across tribal groups (e.g., combining Hopis, Lakotas, and Navahos into one group). However, broadening the ethnic grouping increases heterogeneity. Again, taking the case of American Indians, there are over 510 federally recognized tribes, including more than 200 Alaskan Native villages (Bureau of Indian Affairs, 1991). American Indian tribes vary enormously in customs, language, and type of family structure, so much so that Tefft (1967) argued that differences between certain tribal groups are greater than those between Indians and Whites on some variables. American Indian individuals also vary in their degree of acculturation and exposure to tribal or White American cultures, whether they live on or off a reservation, ethnic or tribal identification, experience with racism, and so forth. Given such a list of even the most basic sources of sample heterogeneity, a researcher is inevitably faced with the decision of which sources of variability can or cannot be overlooked in aggregating individuals into an ethnic group classification. This discussion is not to underestimate the cultural diversity within the White American population; in fact, it is intended to stimulate a more refined treatment of ethnicity and culture in psychological research.

Recruiting Participants

In efforts to recruit ethnic minority participants, researchers must consider possible ethnic and cultural differences in participants' likelihood to participate in psychological assessment research. Are ethnic minorities less likely to cooperate with research? Are the rates of attrition from research studies equal across ethnic groups? For some ethnic groups, cultural values may influence their participation or response patterns in research. Ying (1989) analyzed the cases of nonresponse to Center for Epidemiological Studies-Depression scale (CES-D) items in a community sample of Chinese Americans. The original study was conducted as a telephone interview study with randomly selected Chinese-surnamed households listed in the San Francisco public telephone directory. Ying found that demographic factors such as age, sex, and education as well as item content were related to the rates of nonresponse to CES-D items. Ying explained that older Chinese women were less likely to be familiar with telephone surveys, the methodology which, in and of itself, may reflect a middle-class American lifestyle and set of values. Older Chinese women may experience being questioned by a stranger about mood and somatic symptoms as foreign and intrusive yet refrain from directly refusing to participate because such behavior would be too assertive and impolite. For other Chinese community cohorts such as middle-aged Chinese men, endorsement of positive feelings (e.g., feeling good about self or feeling happy and enjoying life) may be regarded as indicative of immodesty and frivolousness in Chinese culture, thus such values may also contribute to nonresponse. This type of in-depth analysis of nonresponse illustrates the importance of considering the potential influence of cultural and social norms in responding to and participating in psychological research.

Use of College Samples

For ethnic minority groups for which it is extremely difficult to obtain a large community sample of participants, sampling from college populations is a particularly attractive and viable option because of the ease of access to a relatively large captive pool of potential participants. For example, a significant portion of Asian American personality and psychopathology literature has been conducted with college students (Leong, 1986; Uba, 1994). This sampling strategy clearly impacts the question of representativeness of the sample. Sears (1985) argued that a significant portion of psychological research is conducted with college sophomores, and he pointed to the hazards of basing much of what we know about human processes on a sample not representative of the larger population. Sears named a number of differences between American college undergraduates and the general population, such as education, test-taking experience, and restricted age range, which in turn are associated with intrapsychic characteristics such as a less than fully formulated sense of self, less crystallized social and political attitudes, highly unstable peer relationships, and so forth. The same criticisms apply to assessment research with ethnic minorities, and the representativeness of ethnic minority college students must be carefully assessed, not only with respect to socioeconomic and educational attainment of student participants in relation to their age cohorts who do not attend college but also with respect to a correspondent set of values and attitudes, a limited range of political awareness of self-identification, and an American education. For language minority groups such as some American Indians, immigrant Asian Americans, and immigrant Latinos (and some would argue African Americans; see Helms, 1992), good or adequate English language skills are necessary to gain entrance into colleges and universities. However, those with university-level English skills may not be representative of a significant portion of immigrant ethnic minorities. Ethnic minority college samples tend to underestimate both the demographic and the psychosocial diversity of the larger ethnic minority populations. Consequently, sample heterogeneity, as high as it may be in college samples, may still be an underestimate of true population heterogeneity.

Use of Community Samples

Given the questionable generalizability of research studies with ethnic minority college students to the ethnic community population at large, it is often desirable, although also extremely challenging, to sample from ethnic minority communities. Many research studies conducted with ethnic minorities in the community rely on systematic or captive sampling or snowball sampling (a method in which one starts with a known group of participants, and recruits more participants through contacts) in intact ethnic groups or organizations such as churches, temples, professional associations, political organizations, social clubs, kinship associations, and so forth. It is clear that each of these organizations attracts a subsample of the target ethnic community, and the results cannot be easily generalized to the entire group. Sasao and Sue (1993) criticized psychological research with ethnic minorities for its lack of ecological and contextual considerations. Specifically, Sasao and Sue argued that too often, research ignores the societal context in relation to other relevant ethnic – cultural community groups. Many psychological characteristics of clinical interest may be greatly influenced by the target community group's geographical and political context in which ethnic minority individuals function, such that psychological research on African Americans in South Central Los Angeles must take into account the community's relation to Korean Americans and the contemporary political climate. When the research question involves the assessment of psychopathology, studies may be conducted with those ethnic minority participants who utilize clinical services. There is some evidence to indicate differential patterns of mental health services utilization among different ethnic minority groups (Sue, Fujino, Hu, Takeuchi, & Zane, 1991), thereby making it difficult to assess the generalizability of the findings. Clearly, the procurement of representative and adequately sized samples of ethnic minorities poses a considerable methodological challenge.

Establishing Equivalence of Measures

One goal of assessment research with ethnic minorities is to conduct reliable and valid assessment while minimizing cultural or ethnic bias. Use of assessment measures in research with ethnic minorities presents several problems, primarily with respect to equivalence. Brislin (1993) discussed three types of equivalence (translation, conceptual, and metric) as being of foremost concern in cross-cultural research methodology. To the extent that assessment research is concerned with effects of culture on assessed psychological characteristics among ethnic minorities, the cross-cultural principles apply to research with ethnic minorities.

Although some of the frequently used assessment instruments such as the Wechsler scales, the SCL-90-R, the Zung Self-Rating Depression Scale, and the MMPI have been translated into languages such as Spanish, Japanese, and Chinese, researchers and clinicians are often faced with the sheer lack of relevant assessment measures in the language of the target ethnic minority populations that also have established translation equivalence. Importantly, linguistic equivalence issues also cannot be ignored for ethnic minority participants who are functionally English-speaking. For example, Helms (1992) argued that most African Americans in the United States are probably exposed to some versions of both Black and White English, yet commonly used standardized tests are in White standard English. A recent study examining Spanish–English bilingualism among Hispanic immigrants (Bahrick, Hall, Goggin, Bahrick, & Berger, 1994) indicated a complex interaction among language dominance, the assessment task (e.g., oral comprehension, vocabulary recognition, category generation, etc.), age at immigration, and other factors. Such findings suggest that the type of language skills used to assess bilingual participants in either English or their first language may influence some results.

In the absence of appropriate assessment measures for which the translated versions' psychometric properties have been established, a researcher may choose to translate and adopt the instrument to the ethnic minority group of research interest. In order to ensure that a newly translated measure has achieved translation equivalence, a multistep method has been recommended, in which translation (e.g., from English to Spanish) is followed by back translation (from Spanish to English), comparison of the two versions (e.g., English and English), revisions in the translation, and so forth (Brislin, 1993). Geisinger (1994) has outlined a set of rigorous methodological steps for translating an assessment instrument and adopting it to a new culture. However, it must be acknowledged that carefully following the methodological steps suggested by Geisinger and performing psychometric analyses would require multiple, adequately sized samples of ethnic minorities, leaving the researcher once again with dilemmas in obtaining large sample sizes.

Conceptual equivalence is concerned with whether the psychological construct under investigation (e.g., depression, intelligence, or assertiveness) holds the same meanings in two or more cultural groups. Conceptual equivalence of a construct may be highly dependent on the context in which the assessment takes place. Although this may be true for any participant population, researchers must be aware that for ethnic minorities, variability of and sensitivity to contextual factors may be increased as they move between a traditional cultural setting (e.g., family and ethnic communities) and a more mainstream American cultural setting (e.g., work, school, etc.). For example, in assessing the meaning of aggressiveness in youths, an assessment may be conducted in a school setting, in which Latinos, Asians, and Whites share the same environmental space, and to a large extent, the same ecological context. If the construct is found to be equivalent in this setting, it may not necessarily translate into conceptual equivalence in other settings, such as the family or the street culture.

Metric equivalence refers to the assumption that the same metric can be used to measure the same concept in two or more cultures. For example, the test score of 100 for a White participant is assumed to be interpretable in the same manner as the test score of 100 for a Mexican American participant. Metric equivalence is often overlooked or assumed without empirical validation in research with ethnic minorities, particularly if the measure does not involve translation. The danger of assuming equivalence of translated measures was illustrated by an analysis comparing the Wechsler Adult Intelligence Scale (WAIS) and its Spanish adaptation, Escala de Inteligencia Wechsler para Adultos (EIWA; Lopez & Romero, 1988), in which major differences between the two instruments were found with respect to the conversion of raw scores to scale scores, administration, and content. Lopez and Romero pointed to the importance of noting the rural, less educated characteristics of the Puerto Rican sample on which the EIWA was normed, and concluded that "psychologists should not expect the scores of the EIWA to be comparable with those of the WAIS, and perhaps even with the scores of the WAIS-R" (Lopez & Romero, 1988, p. 269). It is also critical to note here the heterogeneity within an ethnic minority group (e.g., rural Puerto Rican vs. urban Mexican American), which may be underestimated or overlooked because of a common language (in this case, Spanish) when a translated version is available.

In research, psychometric statistical analyses are often performed in order to address equivalence problems of a measure across ethnic groups. For example, Ben-Porath (1990) advocated the use of replicatory factor analysis (i.e., using the same factor analytic method to examine the factor structure of a newly translated or adopted instrument that was used in the original measure) to establish cross-cultural validity of the instrument. Ben-Porath also suggested that prior to conducting factor analyses, it is important to examine the distribution of the scale items across ethnic and cultural groups in order to detect possible range restrictions and outliers. This is particularly vital to the assessment studies involving ethnic minorities, as Helms (1992) cautioned that cultural and interethnic factors may compromise the basic assumptions underlying statistics, such as independence of ethnic groups with respect to culture or equal range and variance between ethnic groups. Regression analyses have also been used to study instrument or test bias, specifically to examine whether tests make predictions that are similar, and similarly accurate, to those of a criterion measure. If, for example, regression slopes for a test or evaluation procedure and a criterion differ for different groups, test bias exists. Such studies require that fairly clear-cut criteria can be found on which to judge the adequacy of predictors. An example of this approach was provided by Timbrook and Graham (1994), who examined ethnic differences between African Americans and Whites in the restandardization sample of the MMPI-2. The researchers used ratings of interpersonal behavior and personality characteristics of the participants made by their partners as external criteria against which the accuracy of predictions of five MMPI-2 clinical scales could be examined. Regression equations were developed to predict the partner rating scale scores, and no ethnic differences were found on the accuracy of the MMPI-2 scale predictions.

Methods of Assessment

Thus far, our discussion of methodological issues in measure selection for use with ethnic minorities has been primarily focused on standardized objective personality assessment measures (with the exception of the Wechsler scales), most often of the self-report variety. However, it is debatable whether some methods of assessment may be more likely to result in cultural or ethnic bias than others. There are at least three approaches to assessment that have been understudied with respect to ethnic minorities: (a) behavioral observations, (b) qualitative assessment, and (c) projective tests. One may question for ethnic minorities whether behavioral observation methods are more prone to bias than self-report instruments, whether qualitative assessment is more prone to bias than quantitative data, or whether projective tests are more prone to bias than objective tests.

Surveying the assessment research on ethnic minorities, there is a shortage of assessment methodology using observational data. Behavioral observation methodologies often involve in-depth, microlevel analysis of behavior. Although largescale surveys are necessary in order to obtain some normative information on ethnic minorities, the field is ripe for a contribution in microlevel analysis as well. The behavioral observation methods also have the advantage of requiring relatively small sample sizes that are necessary to conduct analyses, although generalizability to the larger population is likely to be compromised with potential self-selection of ethnic or cultural minority participants who are willing to participate in such in-depth assessment research.

Psychological assessment research, which is heavily rooted in psychometric tradition, has favored quantitative research. Although the limitations of qualitative methodologies must be acknowledged, little empirical work has examined the relative advantages and disadvantages of collecting qualitative data from ethnic minorities. Brink (1994) argued that purely quantitative measurement methodologies used to assess ethnic minority populations (e.g., elderly Hispanics) are insufficiently sensitive to cultural factors and recommended integrating psychometric data with qualitative methodologies (e.g., in-depth interviews and life histories).

Finally, some have argued that cross-cultural (and by extension, ethnic minority) research may have prematurely dismissed the usefulness of projective measures of assessment because of the assumption that such instruments are too rooted in Western culture (Draguns, 1990). The problem here is the lack of empirical evidence to argue for or against the notion that ambiguous stimuli used in projective tests are less culturally bound but that clinical interpretations are more prone to bias by the interpreter's cultural background. Research on the use of projective tests with Asian Americans is notably absent (Okazaki & Sue, 1995), but a body of research exists on the use of the Rorschach and picture-story tests (e.g., the Thematic Apperception Test) with African Americans, Latinos, and several American Indian tribes (see Gray-Little, 1995; Rogler, Malgady, & Rodriguez, 1989; Velasquez, 1995). Increased attention in ethnic minority assessment research to various methods of assessment is consistent with recommendations made by cross-cultural methodologists to use multiple assessment measures to establish convergent validity of cultural constructs.

Interpretation of Data

A common problem in conducting ethnic comparison research is that differences tend to be evaluated in disfavor of ethnic minorities. For example, Rogler, Malgady, and Rodriguez (1989) argued that ethnic differences on personality measures are often interpreted negatively from the Western perspective. In the case of Latinos, their scores on personality measures are often interpreted as indicating low verbal fluency, less emotional responsiveness, and more pathology, all of which are considered as undesirable characteristics in American society. However, the same scores may be interpreted as reflecting appropriate restraint and respect for authority. In a study comparing clinical evaluations by Chinese American and White therapists of the same clients (either Chinese American or White), therapists' ratings of client functioning have been found to vary as a function of the interaction of therapist and client ethnicity (Li-Repac, 1980), which suggests interpretive bias. At the same time, one must also be aware of the danger of underestimating pathology for culturally different clients through overattribution of bizarre behavior or thought patterns to that person's culture (Lopez, 1989). It is essential to be aware of possible cultural bias, either in overpathologizing or underpathologizing ethnic minorities when interpreting ethnic differences on assessment measures.

GUIDELINES

Based on the various methodological issues we have raised with respect to assessment research with ethnic minorities, we summarize several guidelines for considering ethnicity and related variables below.

1. Assumptions underlying the use of ethnicity should be made explicit. A researcher must ask, Is the research concerned with ethnicity as a demographic variable, or is it being used as a proxy for a psychological construct hypothesized to covary with ethnicity?

2. Research reports should contain more elaborated, fuller discussions of the sample and the sampling methodology used. That is, rather than merely indicating the number of African Americans, Asian Americans, Latinos, and American Indians included in the sample, details should be made explicit on variables such as generalized status, acculturation, self-identification, ethnic and cultural composition of the neighborhoods or communities, and so forth. Such discussions will help promote better communication among researchers and focus future research efforts by identifying what we know about whom.

3. Given inherent problems with small sample size in ethnic minority research, we suggest the following strategies to maximize the significance of each study: (a) For studies examining ethnic differences on various assessment instruments, enough details regarding the sampling methodology, data analyses, and statistical findings should be reported to allow meta-analyses and cross-study comparisons and (b) individual studies with small samples of ethnic minorities should test specific cultural hypotheses that may contribute to ethnic variance on assessment processes or instruments, with increased attention on whether statistically significant ethnic differences are also clinically significant (see Timbrook and Graham, 1994, for an example of this approach).

4. Individual studies should consider using multiple measures and multiple methods of assessments. Given that many assessment tools and instruments have not been widely used or cross-culturally validated with ethnic minority groups, it is advisable to use several different measures in order to test convergent validity. To the extent that results converge, there is incremental validity.

5. Expert cultural or ethnic consultants should be involved in evaluating the translation and conceptual equivalence of the measures prior to data collection or in interpreting the results of studies. These consultants can often provide the cultural context for anticipating and interpreting the responses of ethnic minorities.

6. Findings from assessment tools pertinent to ethnic and cultural variables should generate hypotheses for further testing or con-

firmation rather than routine assumptions that the findings are valid.

CONCLUSION

Little attention in the past has been paid to the relevance of ethnicity and cultural issues in psychological research. Graham (1992) recently conducted a content analysis of empirical articles concerned with African Americans that were published in six top psychology journals between 1970 and 1989. The results, which indicated a decline in the amount of African American research over the years and a relative lack of methodological rigor of existing research, were a sobering indictment of the scientific psychological community's level of sophistication in examining ethnic and cultural factors. Lack of research, training, or both in cross-cultural assessment often leads to misdiagnosis, overestimation, underestimation, or neglect of psychopathology, which in turn has grave consequences, such as treatment failure, at individual levels (Westermeyer, 1987).

However, assessment research with ethnic minorities should not be encouraged merely because of a potential for negative consequences in neglecting ethnic minorities. As noted by proponents of cross-cultural psychology, studies of cultural variations are good for both psychology and science (Triandis & Brislin, 1984). For one, the inclusion of ethnicity and culture-related variables increases the range of human behavior variables to explore and understand. For instance, an examination of the collectivism-individualism dimension of interpersonal orientation within the middle-class White American college student population will yield a fairly narrow and skewed range. By including ethnic minorities and individuals from other cultures, the full range of this construct as well as its relationship to other personality and clinical variables can be fruitfully examined. Another advantage to including ethnic and cultural variables in research is that it provides a better test of theories. Establishing the generalizability or limitations of personality theories and of assessment tools through systematic testing with a broad range of individuals benefits the field (Ben-Porath, 1990). And lastly, the American Psychological Association (APA) Board of Ethnic Minority Affairs in 1991 developed a set of guidelines for providers of psychological services to ethnically, linguistically, and culturally diverse populations (APA, 1933), which parallels the APA Ethical Standards guidelines. It is clearly stated in this guideline (APA, 1993, p. 46) that:

> Psychologists consider the validity of a given instrument or procedure and interpret resulting data, keeping in mind the cultural and linguistic characteristics of the person being assessed. Psychologists are aware of

the test's reference population and possible limitations of such instruments with other populations.

Hence, it is crucial that research on the validity of various assessment tools and procedures for ethnic minority population continue to add to the necessary database in order for the psychological community to responsibly carry out these guidelines.

There are many methodological challenges to conducting assessment research with ethnic minorities, but this is not a cause for throwing out the baby with the bath water. By making explicit the assumptions underlying the use of ethnicity as a predictor variable, the collective scientific community will begin to differentiate between racial stereotypes and legitimate uses of ethnic or cultural generalizations.

REFERENCES

American Psychological Association (1993). Guidelines for providers of psychological services to ethnic, linguistic, and culturally diverse populations. *American Psychologist, 48,* 45–48.

Azibo, D. A. (1988). Understanding the proper and improper usage of the comparative research framework. *Journal of Black Psychology, 15,* 81–91.

Bahrick, H. P., Hall, L. K., Goggin, J. P., Bahrick, L. E., & Berger, S. A. (1994). Fifty years of language maintenance and language dominance in bilingual Hispanic immigrants. *Journal of Experimental Psychology: General, 123,* 264–283.

Ben-Porath, Y. S. (1990). Cross-cultural assessment of personality: The case for replicatory factor analysis. In J. N. Butcher & C. D. Spielberger (Eds.), *Advances in personality assessment* (Vol. 8, pp. 27–48). Hillsdale, NJ: Erlbaum.

Betancourt, H., & Lopez, S. R. (1993). The study of culture, ethnicity, and race in American psychology. *American Psychologist, 48,* 629–637.

Brink, T. L. (1994). The need for qualitative research on mental health elderly Hispanics. *International Journal of Aging and Human Development, 38,* 279–291.

Brislin, R. W. (1993). *Understanding culture's influence on behavior.* New York: Harcourt Brace Jovanovich.

Bureau of Indian Affairs. (1991). *American Indians today* (3rd ed.). Washington, DC: U.S. Department of the Interior.

Campbell, D. T. (1967). Stereotypes and the perception of group differences. *American Psychologist, 22,* 817–829.

Cervantes, R. C., & Castro, F. G. (1985). Stress, coping, and Mexican American mental health: A systematic review. *Hispanic Journal of Behavioral Sciences, 7,* 1–73.

Clark, L. A. (1987). Mutual relevance of mainstream and cross-cultural psychology. *Journal of Consulting and Clinical Psychology, 55,* 461–470.

Dahlstrom, W. G. (1986). Ethnic status and personality measurement. In W. G. Dahlstrom, D. Lacher, & L. E. Dahlstrom (Eds.), *MMPI patterns of American minorities* (pp. 3 – 23). Minneapolis: University of Minnesota Press.

Dion, K. L., & Giordano, C. (1990). Ethnicity and sex as correlates of depression symptoms in a Canadian university sample. *International Journal of Social Psychiatry, 36*, 30 – 41.

Dion, K. L., & Toner, B. B. (1988). Ethnic differences in test anxiety. *Journal of Social Psychology, 128*, 165 – 172.

Draguns, J. G. (1990). Applications of cross-cultural psychology in the field of mental health. In R. W. Brislin (Ed.), *Applied cross-cultural psychology* (pp. 302 – 324). Newbury Park, CA: Sage.

Eaton, W. W. (1980). *The sociology of mental illness*. New York: Praeger.

Geisinger, K. F. (1994). Cross-cultural normative assessment: Translation and adaptation issues influencing the normative interpretation of assessment instruments. *Psychological Assessment, 6*, 304 – 312.

Graham, S. (1992). "Most of the subjects were White and middle class": Trends in published research on African Americans in selected APA journals, 1970 – 1989. *American Psychologist, 47*, 629 – 639.

Gray-Little, B. (1995). The assessment of psychopathology in racial and ethnic minorities. In J. N. Butcher (Ed.), *Clinical personality assessment: Practical approaches* (pp. 140 – 157). New York: Oxford University Press.

Hall, C. C. I. (1992). Please choose one: Ethnic identity choices for biracial individuals. In M. P. P. Root (Ed.), *Racially mixed people in America* (pp. 250 – 264). Newbury Park, CA: Sage.

Helms, J. E. (1992). Why is there no study of cultural equivalence in standardized cognitive ability testing? *American Psychologist, 47*, 1083 – 1101.

Kessler, R. C., & Neighbors, H. W. (1986). A new perspective on the relationships among race, social class and psychological distress. *Journal of Health and Social Behavior, 27*, 107 – 115.

Korchin, S. J. (1980). Clinical psychology and minority problems. *American Psychologist, 35*, 262 – 269.

LaFromboise, T. D. (1988). American Indian mental health policy. *American Psychologist, 43*, 388 – 397.

Leong, F. T. L. (1986). Counseling and psychotherapy with Asian-Americans: Review of the literature. *Journal of Counseling Psychology, 33*, 196 – 206.

Li-Repac, D. (1980). Cultural influences on clinical perception: A comparison between Caucasian and Chinese-American therapists. *Journal of Cross-Cultural Psychology, 11*, 327 – 342.

Lopez, S. R. (1989). Patient variable biases in clinical judgment: Conceptual overview and methodological considerations. *Psychological Bulletin, 106*, 184 – 204.

Lopez, S., & Romero, A. (1988). Assessing the intellectual functioning of Spanish-speaking adults: Comparison of the EIWA and the WAIS. *Professional Psychology: Research and Practice, 19*, 263 – 270.

Okazaki, S., & Sue, S. (1995). Cultural considerations in psychological assessment of Asian Americans. In J. N. Butcher (Ed.), *Clinical personality assessment: Practical approaches* (pp. 107–119). New York: Oxford University Press.

Rogler, L. H., Malgady, R. G., & Rodriguez, O. (1989). *Hispanics and mental health: A framework for research*. Malabalar, FL: Krieger.

Root, M. P. P. (1992). Back to the drawing board: Methodological issues in research on multiracial people. In M. P. P. Root (Ed.), *Racially mixed people in America* (pp. 181–189). Newbury Park, CA: Sage.

Sasao, T. (1992). *Correlates of substance use and problem behaviors in multiethnic high school settings*. Unpublished manuscript, University of California, Los Angeles.

Sasao, T., & Sue, S. (1993). Toward a culturally anchored ecological framework of research in ethnic-cultural communities. *American Journal of Community Psychology, 21*, 705–727.

Sears, D. O. (1985). College sophomores in the laboratory: Influences of a narrow data base on psychology's view of human nature. *Journal of Personality and Social Psychology, 51*, 515–530.

Sue, S., Fujino, D. C., Hu, L., Takeuchi, D., & Zane, N. W. S. (1991). Community mental health services for ethnic minority groups: A test of cultural responsive hypothesis. *Journal of Consulting and Clinical Psychology, 59*, 533–540.

Tefft, S. K. (1967). Anomie, values, and culture change among teen-age Indians: An exploratory study. *Sociology of Education, 40*, 145–157.

Timbrook, R. E., & Graham, J. R. (1994). Ethnic differences on the MMPI-2? *Psychological Assessment, 6*, 212–217.

Triandis, H. C., & Brislin, R. W. (1984). Cross-cultural psychology. *American Psychologist, 39*, 1006–1016.

Uba, L. (1994). *Asian Americans: Personality patterns, identity, and mental health*. New York: Guilford.

U.S. Bureau of the Census. (1991). Race and Hispanic origin. *1990 Census Profile (No. 2)*. Washington, DC: U.S. Department of Commerce.

Velasquez, R. J. (1995). Personality assessment of Hispanic clients. In J. N. Butcher (Ed.), *Clinical personality assessment: Practical approaches* (pp. 120–139). New York: Oxford University Press.

Westermeyer, J. (1987). Cultural factors in clinical assessment. *Journal of Consulting and Clinical Psychology, 55*, 471–478.

Yee, A. H., Fairchild, H. H., Weizmann, F., & Wyatt, G. E. (1993). Addressing psychology's problems with race. *American Psychologist, 48*, 1132–1140.

Ying, Y. (1989). Nonresponse on the Center for Epidemiological Studies-Depression scale in Chinese Americans. *International Journal of Social Psychiatry, 35*, 156–163.

Zuckerman, M. (1990). Some dubious premises in research and theory on racial differences: Scientific, social, and ethical issues. *American Psychologist, 45*, 1297–1303.

V

DATA ANALYSIS, EVALUATION, AND INTERPRETATION

Data analysis refers to systematic evaluation of the information that has been collected, usually to describe what has been found (summarize or codify the information) and to draw inferences about the relations between the independent and dependent variables. For most researchers, data analysis is considered to be synonymous with *quantitative evaluation of the results*, that is, application of statistical tests. Clearly, in contemporary scientific research quantitative evaluation and in particular statistical significance testing dominates. There are many other data options such as graphical methods to present and describe the data, qualitative evaluations of data that systematize narrative descriptions, and the use of visual inspection to draw inferences about change (Kazdin, 2003). The different methods are useful to mention, if only to convey that what we often take as a given or the essence of data evaluation in research is, in the scheme of scientific research, one approach to identify whether effects are reliable, important, and likely to be replicable. This part focuses on statistical evaluation because it is central in contemporary research. Also, it is pivotal for students to master issues of quantitative evaluation because this is the starting point for most of us as researchers.

The nightmare of methodologists and statisticians is having a colleague or student convene a meeting that begins with the statement, "I have finished collecting the data and was wondering what analyses I ought to do." (I have had a "friend" about my age, weight, and height who, on more than one occasion, has jumped out of his basement window after a meeting that began with this question.) A general view we inadvertently foster in training is that statistics are merely a tool to evaluate the results and as such are not really part of the design. Yet the methods to analyze the data are central to the design of the study and to the conceptualization of the phenomenon that is studied. The need to address questions about the data analysis begins at the point that the hypothesis or prediction is first formulated. With that hypothesis or prediction, one can ask, "How will the data be analyzed to test this hypothesis?" "What are the chances that the results would support the prediction, if in fact the prediction were true?" and "If there are potential confounding influences, can suitable controls (experimental or statistical) be used?"

The data-analytic strategies are not at all trivial in the design and execution of a study. How well, and indeed whether, the hypotheses are well tested depend on strategies and the plan for the data analyses. Decisions about the data analyses depend on how many different measures will be combined or evaluated; the relation of independent variables (predictors) and outcomes (criteria) to each other; whether the hypotheses focus on mediators, moderators, and direct or indirect causal paths; and other issues, many of which emerge before the first participant of the study is seen.

It is critical to begin the study with a clear idea of how the data will be analyzed and the likelihood that if there is an effect, it can be readily detected. This does not mean that all data analyses that eventually will be completed need to be specified in advance. Many data analyses will elaborate specific findings and pursue interesting tributaries that flow from the main findings; some of these can be determined only once the pattern of data is revealed. Yet, the primary hypotheses and predictions are not of this form, and how they will be tested statistically ought to be specified in advance.

Chapters in this part emphasize fundamental issues about statistical evaluation that emerge both in the planning and data-analytic stages of the study. They discuss the meaning of referring to a finding as "statistically significant." Key concepts are raised, including alpha (α) or the probability level used to decide whether an effect is statistically significant, sample size (N), the magnitude of an effect (effect size), and statistical power (the extent to which a study can detect a difference when one truly exists). Although the interrelations of these concepts are often discussed and well known, the knowledge is rarely translated into the design of a study by individual investigators, a point to which I return shortly.

BACKGROUND AND UNDERPINNINGS OF DATA ANALYSES

The vast majority of psychological research focuses on null hypothesis testing and statistical significance. *Statistical significance* refers to conventions regarding when to consider a particular finding or difference as reliable or unlikely to be due to "chance." Most statisticians within psychology probably would say that as a criterion for knowledge, statistical significance is relied on too heavily. Statistical significance and the p level on which it is based are not a magical threshold for calling an effect veridical. Unfortunately researchers tend to consider a finding that meets the criterion of $p < .05$ as real and that effects above this level are likely to be due to chance (Rosenthal & Gaito, 1963), although whatever criterion (p level) was adopted, there would always be cases that just missed. Perhaps a criterion will always have the problem of seeming or being arbitrary at the cutoff point. The problem is not only in specifying a criterion but also in the use of that criterion for binary decisions, namely, to reject or accept the null hypothesis. Thus, the null hypothesis is rejected at $p = .04$ or .05 but not at .059 or .06. This does not sound very reasonable. Indeed, as Rosnow and Rosenthal (1989) noted, "surely, God loves the .06 nearly as much as the .05" (p. 1277).

Any particular level of significance is a useful guideline and may provide a screening device or filter for making some decisions about variables and effects to pursue, study, and elaborate, but it is hardly a level to be worshipped. Chapter 15 by Michael Cowles and Caroline Davis discusses the origins of the use of $p < .05$ as a criterion for deciding statistical significance. The foundations of the criterion for statistical significance are important to understand because of the marked influence of this convention. Also, the use, abuse, and misinterpretation of findings that meet the criterion of $p < .05$ are elaborated in subsequent chapters. A very useful beginning is to see what the founding mothers and fathers of statistical significance had in mind. As researchers we often rigidly invoke the .05, especially when we review the findings of others. The fact that this p level has no strong or firmly defensible basis is an important step in building the flexibility and humility about how and why we use statistical tests. Also, occasions exist in which researchers might be encouraged to be more lenient than $p < .05$ or avoid a test of significance altogether. This sounds like heresy, but consideration of this view begins by seeing the basis for our adoption of a specific p level.

In the planning of research, investigators often focus on the rationale for the study and several procedural decisions. For example, in graduate student training, master's degree or doctoral research proposals may consist of "Introduction" and "Method" sections without further material regarding the methods of statistical evaluation. However, as I mentioned previously, the quality of the study and the strength of the inferences that can be drawn can be enhanced by considering statistical evaluation *before* the design of the study is finalized. Among the questions one might ask are, "What analyses will be completed"; "If the data are analyzed exactly as I plan, will the results really answer or address the hypotheses"; and "Are there special characteristics of the sample or data that will influence the analyses (e.g., dropping out by some participants)"? Such considerations often change the hypotheses, the design (e.g., sample, number of groups), and range of measures that are used.

Occasionally in life and methodology, the difference between brilliance and dullness has to do with the timing. It is brilliant to decide to wear a parachute before jumping out of an airplane; the same decision after one leaps is, well, much less brilliant. Similarly, the considerations I have mentioned previously are praiseworthy before a study is begun and often punishment worthy after a study is done. Sometimes investigators mention "limitations" in the "Discussion" section that pertain to considerations that one could have easily considered before jumping out of the airplane.

The importance of considering statistical evaluation in planning the study is recognized in many contexts outside of graduate training. For example, in preparing grant applications, a key section in the research plan is a description of what data analyses will be conducted, how the hypotheses will be tested in relation to these analyses, and whether the key statistical tests are sufficiently powerful to detect differences. At another level, developing a clear plan of the strategies for data analyses at the design stage also conveys how much and how carefully the investigator has thought about the study.

Whether in a proposal or final article, the connection between the hypotheses or predictions and statistical analyses ought to be explicit. That is, it ought to be clear to readers of the article at all times why a particular statistical analysis was conducted; what it is designed to accomplish; and how the analysis reflects a prediction, hypothesis, or critical issue. Chapter 16 by Bruce E. Wampold, Betsy Davis, and Roland H. Good III introduce the notion of *hypothesis validity* to refer to the connections among the theory, hypotheses, and statistical evaluation. With examples from clinical research, the authors note the importance of specifying predictions and hypotheses and the relation of the specific analyses to these predictions. Several statistical evaluation issues are raised, including the use of multiple statistical tests within a given study and the use and limits of omnibus tests.

In chapter 17, Jacob Cohen discusses in an informal and highly engaging style critical issues related to conducting research and data analyses. Among the key points are the importance of keeping research "simple" in the sense of limiting the number of independent and dependent variables; emphasizing few variables and many participants rather than the reverse; looking closely at the data; and simplifying the data analyses and reporting when possible. Also, the chapter begins the discussion on null hypothesis testing and power that we take up further in this book.

NULL HYPOTHESES AND STATISTICAL SIGNIFICANCE TESTING

In this section, fundamental issues about statistical significance tests are confronted directly. The section begins with chapter 18 by Jacob Cohen that focuses more specifically on power and its relation to of α, N, and effect size. *Power*, of course, refers to the likelihood of detecting a difference in an investigation when in fact a genuine difference exists between conditions or, stated another way, the likelihood of rejecting the null hypothesis (no difference) when that hypothesis is false.

More than 40 years ago, Cohen (1962) published an article that evaluated the extent to which studies in abnormal and social psychology had sufficient power to detect differences if such differences existed. The main conclusion was that power is very weak in most studies. Since that time, many evaluations of research have been completed, spanning areas within clinical psychology (Kazantzis, 2000; Kazdin & Bass, 1989; Rossi, 1990), other areas of psychology, and other disciplines (e.g., Sedlmeier & Gigerenzer, 1989). Alas, the conclusions are quite similar to those reached by Cohen in 1962, namely, that the power of most studies is rather weak, except when there are very strong effects (effect sizes). Studies continue to be designed and reported with weak power, and there are no genuine signs that things are getting better. In this chapter, Cohen provides useful tables for estimating power and sample sizes needed for an investigation. Because significance testing continues to dominate contemporary research, it is essential to master key concepts such as power and effect size on which such testing depends.

Statistical significance testing has been challenged. When statistical tests and null hypothesis testing first emerged (Fisher, 1925; Neyman & Pearson, 1928), there were significant objections regarding their use (Berkson, 1938). At the most extreme level, the objection is that the use of significant tests retards the development of knowledge and actually harms our science (see Meehl, 1978; Shrout, 1997). Chapter 19 by Frank L. Schmidt elaborates the bases of the objections and the uses and misinterpretations of statistical significance testing. The chapter calls for abandoning statistical significance testing. Much of the confusion in the literature and seeming inconsistencies among the findings of related studies is the direct result of the way we analyze the data and draw inferences from these analyses rather than differences obtained in the studies themselves. Schmidt argues for estimates of effect size and confidence intervals as a way to make our research literature less confusing and contradictory than it seems. He discusses the role of meta-analysis as a means of developing cumulative knowledge. Among the strengths of meta-analysis is the ability to integrate findings from multiple studies. He shows with a detailed example how conclusions from multiple studies are much more likely to converge using meta-analysis and effect size rather than using tests of statistical significance. There has been a long tradition of challenging significance testing; Schmidt underscores positive alternatives and what they could mean for our science more generally.

It is clear that many statisticians are against current statistical significance and null hypothesis testing and are frustrated at the widespread misuse and misinterpretation of the results from such tests. Another side places the role of such tests in perspective in terms of what such tests can and cannot do. Rather than abandoning such tests, the argument focuses on more appropriate and restricted uses. Chapter 20 by Howard Wainer conveys situations in which significance testing is particularly useful. Examples are drawn from diverse topics and with rather dramatic questions (e.g., "Is there a God?") to rivet our attention. I mentioned previously that the data analyses to be used in a study ought to be connected closely to the hypotheses, and chapter 16 by Wampold et al. elaborates this point concretely. The chapters by Schmidt and Wainer address related points, namely, we ought to consider in advance of a study whether null hypothesis testing and statistical evaluation are the most suitable ways of addressing the question that drives the study. The challenge is not so simple as taking a position of whether statistical tests are good or bad and misguided or well advised but rather whether they will address the question to which we seek answers.

In chapter 21, George S. Howard, Scott E. Maxwell, and Kevin J. Fleming present three ways to analyze a given data set: statistical significance testing, meta-analysis, and Bayesian analysis. It is rare that one can see a given data set analyzed in different ways. A discussion of the issues and strengths and limits of each type of analysis is valuable. If readers are mildly intimidated by some of the graphs, the key points and arguments can be culled from the text without mastery of these. The key points are that multiple options exist for evaluating results, they address different facets of the data, and they do so in different ways. I have noted before that not all measures of a given construct may show the same results in a study; not all of the ways of analyzing the data will show the same finding either. This does not mean that everything is relative and depends on everything else but conveys that what one does methodologically speaking can have quite important implications for the findings.

For the researcher designing a study, these chapters point to a few common questions. How will you analyze your data? Why will you use *those* analyses? Will the study be powerful enough to detect the likely effects you would obtain? There are a bunch of wrong answers to these questions (e.g., "My advisor suggested this," "This is the only statistical analysis I know," 'I read a study sort of like mine that used these analyses"). I am not advocating that you, the readers, give great answers. It is merely essential at this point to encourage you to ask yourself the questions. So much can be done to strengthen a study with little changes in measurement strategies, use of repeated testing, and other strategies (Kazdin, 2003) that a few queries at the outset can have important implications for the results.

REFERENCES

Berkson, J. (1938). Some difficulties of interpretation encountered in the application of the chi-square test. *Journal of the American Statistical Association, 33*, 526–542.

Cohen, J. (1962). The statistical power of abnormal–social psychological research: A review. *Journal of Abnormal and Social Psychology, 65*, 145–153.

Fisher, R. A. (1925). *Statistical methods for research workers*. London: Oliver & Boyd.

Kazantzis, N. (2000). Power to detect homework effects in psychotherapy outcome research. *Journal of Consulting and Clinical Psychology, 68*, 166–170.

Kazdin, A. E. (2003). *Research design in clinical psychology* (3rd ed.). Needham Heights, MA: Allyn & Bacon.

Kazdin, A. E., & Bass, D. (1989). Power to detect differences between alternative treatments in comparative psychotherapy outcome research. *Journal of Consulting and Clinical Psychology, 57*, 138–147.

Meehl, P. (1978). Theoretical risks and tabular asterisks: Sir Karl, Sir Ronald, and the slow progress of soft psychology. *Journal of Consulting and Clinical Psychology, 46*, 806–834.

Neyman, J., & Pearson, E. S. (1928). On the use and interpretation of certain test criteria for purposes of statistical inference. *Biometrika, 294*, 175–240 (Part 1), 263–294 (Part 2).

Rosenthal, R., & Gaito, J. (1963). The interpretation of levels of significance by psychological researchers. *Journal of Psychology, 55*, 33–38.

Rosnow, R. L., & Rosenthal, R. (1989). Statistical procedures and the justification of knowledge in psychological science. *American Psychologist, 44*, 1276–1284.

Rossi, J. S. (1990). Statistical power of psychological research: What have we gained in 20 years? *Journal of Consulting and Clinical Psychology, 58*, 646–656.

Sedlmeier, P., & Gigerenzer, G. (1989). Do studies of statistical power have an effect on the power of studies? *Psychological Bulletin, 105*, 309–316.

Shrout, P. E. (Ed.). (1997). Should significance tests be banned? Introduction to a special series exploring the pros and cons. *Psychological Science, 8*, 1–20.

BACKGROUND AND UNDERPINNINGS OF DATA ANALYSES

15

ON THE ORIGINS OF THE .05 LEVEL
OF STATISTICAL SIGNIFICANCE

MICHAEL COWLES AND CAROLINE DAVIS

It is generally understood that the conventional use of the 5% level as the maximum acceptable probability for determining statistical significance was established, somewhat arbitrarily, by Sir Ronald Fisher when he developed his procedures for the analysis of variance.

Fisher's (1925) statement in his book, *Statistical Methods for Research Workers*, seems to be the first specific mention of the $p = .05$ level as determining statistical significance.

> It is convenient to take this point as a limit in judging whether a deviation is to be considered significant or not. Deviations exceeding twice the standard deviation are thus formally regarded as significant. (p. 47)

Cochran (1976), commenting on a slightly later, but essentially similar, statement by Fisher (1926), says that, "Students sometimes ask, 'how

Reprinted from the *American Psychologist, 37*, 553–558. Copyright 1982 by the American Psychological Association.

did the 5 per cent significance level or Type I error come to be used as a standard?' . . . I am not sure but this is the first comment known to me on the choice of 5 per cent" (p. 15).

In the 1926 article Fisher acknowledges that other levels may be used:

> If one in twenty does not seem high enough odds, we may, if we prefer it, draw the line at one in fifty (the 2 per cent point), or one in a hundred (the one per cent point). Personally, the writer prefers to set a low standard of significance at the 5 per cent point, and ignore entirely all results which fail to reach this level. A significant fact should be regarded as experimentally established only if a properly designed experiment *rarely fails* to give this level of significance. (p. 504)

Cochran feels that Fisher was fairly casual about the choice, "as the words *convenient* and *prefers* have indicated" (p. 16). However, the statement quoted above leaves no doubt about Fisher's acceptance of the level as the critical cutoff point, once he had decided upon it.

Other writers, well-versed in the history and development of probability, have also fostered the attitude that the level is an arbitrary one. Yule and Kendall (1950), in the 14th edition of a book first published by Yule in 1911, state,

> In the examples we have given . . . our judgment whether P was small enough to justify us in suspecting a significant difference . . . has been more or less intuitive. Most people would agree . . . that a probability of .0001 is so small that the evidence is very much in favour . . . Suppose we had obtained $P = 0.1$. . . . Where, if anywhere, can we draw the line? The odds against the observed event which influence a decision one way or the other depend to some extent on the caution of the investigator. Some people (not necessarily statisticians) would regard odds of ten to one as sufficient. Others would be more conservative and reserve judgment until the odds were much greater. It is a matter of personal taste. (pp. 471–472)

Cramer (1955), in a completely rewritten version of a Swedish text first published in 1926, tells his readers,

> a value of t . . . will be denoted as *almost significant* if t exceeds the 5% value, but falls short of the 1% . . . called *significant* if t lies between the 1% and 0.1% values and *highly significant* if t exceeds the 0.1% value. This is, of course, a purely conventional terminology. (p. 202)

The issue to be considered is whether the choice of the 5% value was as arbitrary and casual as is so often implied. An examination of the history of probability and statistical theory, however, indicates that the choice was far from arbitrary and was influenced by previous scientific conventions that themselves were based on the notion of "chance" and the unlikelihood of an event occurring.

ORIGINS

As David (1962) has so articulately and elegantly described, the first glimmerings of an appreciation of long-run relative frequencies, randomness, and the unlikelihood of rare events being merely fortuitous go back at least to the Greek mathematicians and the Roman philosophers. Later, however, the spread of Christianity and the collapse of the Roman Empire made the Church the sole haven for scholars. This religious philosophy that accepted a universe in which every event, no matter how trivial, as being caused by an omnipotent God left no place for the investigation of random events. This is very likely the reason why the seeds of mathematical probability theory were not sown until late in 17th-century France. The opportunities had always been there: Because both the archaelogical and the written records show that gambling has been an ever-popular pastime, informal and relatively unsystematic "systems" for calculating "odds" were undoubtedly developed.

The questions posed by Antoine Gombauld, the Chevalier de Méré, related to certain gaming problems, sparked off the correspondence between Blaise Pascal and Pierre Fermat in 1654. Here are the beginnings of combinatorial algebra and mathematical probability theory (again see David, 1962).

In a slightly later (1662) development, John Graunt, a London haberdasher, constructed tables from the Bills of Mortality, parish accounts regularly recorded from early in the 17th century and, most importantly, used these tables for a series of statistical, actuarial inferences.

Graunt was, for example, able to reassure readers of his quite remarkable, unassuming, and refreshing work that,

> This *casualty* [Lunacy] being so uncertain, I shall not force myself to make any inference from the numbers, and proportions we finde in our Bills concerning it: onely I dare ensure any man at this present, well in his Wits, for one in the thousand, that he shall not die a *Lunatick* in *Bedlam*, within these seven years, because I finde not above one in about one thousand five hundred have do so. (Graunt, 1662/1956, p. 1430)

Here is a statement based on numerical data and couched in terms not so very far removed from those in reports in the modern literature.

In 1657, Huygens (1657/1970) published a tract, *On Reasoning in Games of Dice*, that was based upon the exchanges between Pascal and Fermat, and in 1713 Jacques Bernoulli's (1713/1970) book, *The Art of Conjecture*, developed a theory of games of chance. De Moivre's (1756/1967) *The Doctrine of Chances* was the most important of the gambling manuals; it appeared in three editions in 1718, 1738, and 1756. In the two later editions De Moivre presents a method, which he had first published in 1733, of approximating the sum of a very large number of binomial terms. It is safe to say that no other theoretical mathematical abstraction has had such an important influence on psychology and the social sciences as that method, for it generates the bell-shaped curve now commonly known by the name Karl Pearson gave it: the normal distribution.

The law of frequency of errors is often attributed to Laplace (1749 – 1827) and Gauss (1777 – 1855). Both men developed the use of the distribution outside of gaming and in particular demonstrated its utility in evaluating the variable results of measurements and observations in astronomy and in geodetic surveying. With the introduction of this distribution into the field of the biological and social sciences, we may start to trace the path that leads to the $p = .05$ level.

THE NORMAL DISTRIBUTION

The credit for the extension of the use of calculations used to assess observational error or gaming expectancies into the organization of human characteristics goes to Lambert Adolphe Quetelet (1796 – 1874), a Belgian astronomer.

Quetelet (1849) found, for example, that the frequency distribution of the chest girths of 5,738 Scottish soldiers closely approximated the normal curve. Moreover, he used the curve to infer what he took to be a non-chance occurrence. In examining the distribution of the heights of 100,000 French army conscripts, he observed a discrepancy between the calculated and reported frequencies of men falling at the minimum height for military service. "Is it not a fair presumption that the . . . men who constitute the difference of these numbers have been fraudulently rejected?" (p. 97).

Sir Francis Galton (1822 – 1911) eagerly adopted the curve in the organization of the anthropometric data that he collected and introduced the concept of percentiles.

> All persons conversant with statistics are aware that this supposition brings Variability within the grasp of the laws of Chance, with the result that the relative frequency of Deviations of different amounts admits of being calculated, when these amounts are measured in terms of any self-contained unit of variability, such as our Q. (Galton, 1889, pp. 54 – 55)

Q is the symbol for the semi-interquartile range, defined as one half of the difference between the score at the 75th percentile (the third quartile) and the 25th percentile (the first quartile). This means that in a distribution of scores, one half of the deviations fall within $\pm$ Q of the mean, which in the normal distribution falls at the 50th percentile (the second quartile). This measure of variability is equivalent to the *probable error*.

PROBABLE ERROR

The unit of measure of the abscissa of the normal distribution has had many forms. Today the *standard deviation* is the unit of choice, but for many years the probable error (*PE*) was in common use, and it is still used occasionally in the physical sciences. Fundamentally, probable error defines the deviation from a central measure between whose positive and negative values one half of the cases may be expected to fall by chance.

The term appeared in the early 19th century among German mathematical astronomers. Although De Moivre refers to the concept on which *PE* is based, Bessel used the term (*der wahrscheinliche Fehler*) for the first time in 1818. It was subsequently adopted by Gauss, who developed several methods of computing it (Walker, 1929). It was first used with the normal distribution in instances where it was necessary to determine the best possible value of the true position of a point from a series of measurements or observations all of which involved an element of error.

It remained for Karl Pearson (1894) to coin the term *standard deviation*, but the calculation of an equivalent value had existed since De Moivre. Simple calculation shows that the *PE* is equivalent to 0.674560, or roughly ⅔ of a standard deviation.

It was apparently normal practice for Quetelet and Galton to express values in a normal distribution as a function of *PE*, and it seems reasonable to assume that their preference was the overriding influence in its being used in subsequent statistical practice. It should be noted in passing that Galton (1889) objected to the name probable error, calling it a "cumbrous, slipshod, and misleading phrase."

The probable error is, quite clearly, not the most probable of all errors, and the use of the term *error* in describing the variation of human characteristics perhaps carries the analogy with measurement error distribution a shade too far.

STATISTICAL TESTS

In 1893 Pearson began his investigations into the general problem of fitting observed distributions to theoretical curves. The work led eventually to the formulation of the χ^2 test of "goodness of fit" in 1900, one of the most important developments in the history of statistics.

Weldon, the co-founder with Pearson of the biometric school (both men, of course, being much influenced by Galton), approached the problem of discrepancies between theory and observation in a much more empirical way, tossing coins and dice and comparing the outcomes with the binomial model.

In a letter written to Galton in 1894, Weldon asks for a comment on the results of some 7,000 throws of 12 dice collected for him by a clerk at University College, London.

> A day or two ago Pearson wanted some records of the kind in a hurry, in order to illustrate a lecture, and I gave him the record of the clerk's 7,000 tosses . . . on examination he rejects them because he thinks the deviation from the theoretically most probable result is so great as to make the record intrinsically incredible. (E. S. Pearson, 1965/1970, p. 331)

This incident set off a good deal of correspondence and discussion among the biometricians. These interchanges contain various references to odds and probabilities beyond which one would be ready to assert that the outcome was unlikely to be chance. Certainly it seems to have been agreed that what we now call the alpha level should have a relatively low value.

But only with the publication of the χ^2 test, the first test that enabled us to determine the probability of occurrence of discrepancies between expected and measured frequencies in a distribution, are indications of specific criteria to be found. Here we see the beginnings of standard rejection levels (i.e., points at which the probability of occurrence is so small as to make it difficult, perhaps impossible, for one to regard the observed distribution as a random variation on the theoretical distribution).

Pearson did not choose one particular value as the point of rejection. However, from an examination of the various examples of χ^2 calculations presented, with their corresponding probability values, one can see the range within which what might be described as a mixture of intuitive and statistical rejection occurred. The following remarks are from Pearson's paper: $p =$ .5586 ("thus we may consider the fit remarkably good" [p. 170]); $p = .28$ ("fairly represented" [p. 174]); $p = .1$ ("not very improbable that the observed frequencies are compatible with a random sampling" [p. 171]); $p = .01$ ("this very improbable result" [p. 172]).

From Pearson's comments, it appears that he began to have some doubts about the goodness of fit at the .1 level ("not very improbable" implies that the results were perhaps a *little* improbable); however, he was convinced of the unlikelihood of the fit at the .01 level. The midpoint between the two is, of course, the .05 level.

William Gosset (who wrote under the pen name of "Student") began his employment with the Guinness Brewery in Dublin in 1899. Scientific methods were just starting to be applied to the brewing industry. Among Gossett's tasks was the supervision of what were essentially quality control experiments. The necessity of using small samples meant that his results were, at best, only approximations to the probability values derived from the normal curve. Therefore the circumstances of his work led Gosset to formulate the small-sample distribution that is called the *t* distribution.

With respect to the determination of a level of significance, Student's

(1908) article, in which he published his derivation of the t test, stated that "three times the probable error in the normal curve, for most purposes, would be considered significant" (p. 13).

A few years later, another important article was published under the joint authorship of an agronomist and an astronomer (Wood & Stratton, 1910). This paper was essentially to provide direction in the use of probability in interpreting experimental results. These authors endorse the use of PE as a measure: "The astronomer . . . has devised a method of estimating the accuracy of his averages . . . the agriculturist cannot do better than follow his example" (p. 425). They recommend "taking 30 to 1 as the lowest odds which can be accepted as giving practical certainty that a difference is significant" (p. 433). Such odds applied to the normal probability curve correspond to a difference from the mean of 3.2 PE (for practical purposes this was probably rounded to 3 PE).

What specifically determined the adoption of this convention is largely a matter of speculation. Perhaps it was a combination of the preferred use of the PE as a measure by early statisticians like Galton and the influence of Pearson and his statements about the unlikelihood of particular results. In any case, it is clear that as early as 1908 $X \pm 3\ PE$ was accepted as a useful rule of thumb for rejecting differences occurring as the result of chance fluctuations.

Certainly by the time Fisher published his first book on statistical methods 17 years later, 3PE was a frequently used convention for determining statistical significance in a variety of sciences that employed statistical tests as experimental tools. For example, an article in the 1925 volume of the *British Journal of Psychology* reports that the chance occurrence of all calculated correlations is "greater than 3 times the PE" (Flugel, 1925).

McGaughy (1924) uses the term *critical ratio* for the expression $X/3PE$, where X represents a difference. This, he says, is "the accepted standard for the undoubted significance of an obtained difference between averages" and cites Jones (1921).

Having examined the events preceding Fisher's 1925 publication and remembering the context of his discussion, consideration of his first reference to $p = .05$ quite clearly indicates nothing startling or new, or for that matter arbitrary, about what he was suggesting.

A fact that would have been no surprise to most of those reading his book (and which, indeed, Fisher pointed out) is that "a deviation of three times the probable error is effectively equivalent to one of twice the standard error" (Fisher, 1925, pp. 47 – 48).

Fisher then cannot be credited with establishing the value of the significance level. What he can perhaps be credited with is the beginning of a trend to express a value in a distribution in terms of its own standard deviation instead of its probable error. Fisher was apparently convinced of the advantages of using standard deviation (SD), as evidenced by his remark that "The common use of the probable error is its only recommendation" (p. 48).

Fisher provided calculations for a "probability integral table," from which for any value (described as a function of its *SD*), one could find what proportion of the total population had a larger deviation. Therefore, when conducting any critical test, use of this table necessitated expressing the deviation of a value in terms of its *SD*.

Although, strictly speaking, the conventional rejection level of 3*PE* is equivalent to two times the *SD* (in modern terminology, a z score of 2), which expressed as a percentage is about 4.56%, one may hazard a guess that Fisher simply rounded off this value to 5% for ease of explanation. Furthermore, it seems reasonable to assume that as the use of statistical analysis was extended to the social sciences, the tendency to report experimental results in terms of their associated probability values rather than transforming them to z score values provided a broader base for general understanding by those not thoroughly grounded in statistical theory. In other words, the statement that the probability of obtaining a particular result by chance was less than 5% could be more easily digested by the uninitiated than the report that the result represented a z score of approximately 2.

SUBJECTIVE PROBABILITY

How the 5% significance level came to be adopted as a standard has been considered. However, *why* this level seemed appropriate to early statisticians, or why it has continued to prevail in statistical analysis for so long, must be approached not so much from a historical point of view, but from a consideration of the concept of *probability*.

Definitions of the term are most frequently based on expositions of the formal mathematical theory of probability. This may reflect the need to bridge the reality of events in everyday life and the philosophy of logic. Probability in this sense is an objective exercise that uses numerical calculations based on the mathematical theories of arrangements and frequency for the purpose of estimation and prediction.

What often eludes precise definition is the idea that, fundamentally, probability refers to the personal cognition of individuals whereby their knowledge of past experience aids in the formation of a system of expectations with which they face future events. This has been called *subjective probability* to distinguish this notion from its more formal mathematical counterpart.

Alberoni (1962a, 1962b) has conceptualized the intellectual processes that underlie the operation of subjective probability. When individuals cannot find a cause or a regular pattern to explain some differences or variation in the real world, they arrive at the idea of *chance*. This, in turn, forms their expectations for future events. If, however, at some point the events begin to contradict the expectations they have formed, they introduce *cause* and abandon the idea of chance. The point at which this rejection occurs depends largely on the degree of discrepancy and how it is interpreted by each individual. Alberoni refers to this point as the "threshold of dismissal of the idea of chance."

The fundamental questions that remain are straightforward and simple: Do people, scientists and nonscientists, generally feel that an event which occurs 5% of the time or less is a rare event? Are they prepared to ascribe a cause other than mere chance to such infrequent events?

If the answer to both these questions is "Yes," or even "Generally speaking, yes," then the adoption of the level as a criterion for judging outcomes is justifiable.

There is no doubt that the "threshold of dismissal of the idea of chance" depends on a complex set of factors specific to each individual, and therefore varies among individuals.[1] As a formal statement, however, the level has a longer history than is generally appreciated.

REFERENCES

Alberoni, F. (1962a). Contribution to the study of subjective probability. Part I. *Journal of General Psychology, 66,* 241–264.

Alberoni, F. (1962b). Contribution to the study of subjective probability. Prediction. Part II. *Journal of General Psychology, 66,* 265–285.

Bernoulli, J. (1970). *The art of conjecture* (F. Maseres, Ed. & Trans.). New York: Redex Microprint. (Original work published 1795)

Bessel, F. W. (1818). *Ueber den Ort des Polarsterns.* Berlin: Berliner Astronomische Jahrbuch für 1818.

Cochran, W. G. (1976). Early development of techniques in comparative experimentation. In D. B. Owen (Ed.), *On the history of statistics and probability.* New York: Dekker.

Cramer, H. (1955). *The elements of probability theory.* New York: Wiley.

David, F. N. (1962). *Games, gods and gambling.* New York: Hafner.

De Moivre, A. (1967). *The doctrine of chances* (3rd ed.). New York: Chelsea. (Original work published 1756)

Fisher, R. A. (1925). *Statistical methods for research workers.* Edinburgh: Oliver & Boyd.

Fisher, R. A. (1926). The arrangement of field experiments. *Journal of the Ministry of Agriculture, 33,* 503–513.

Flugel, J. C. (1925). A quantitative study of feeling and emotion in everyday life. *British Journal of Psychology, 15,* 318–355.

---

[1]We have some evidence, based on both formal and informal data, that people, on average, do indeed approach this threshold when the odds reach about 1 in 10 and are pretty well convinced when the odds are 1 in 100. The midpoint of the two values is close to .05, or odds of 1 in 20. One is reminded that these subjective probability norms are congruent with the ideas expressed in Pearson's 1900 publication.

Galton, F. (1889). *Natural inheritance*. London: Macmillan.

Graunt, J. (1956). Natural and political observations made upon the bills of mortality, 1662. In J. R. Newman (Ed.), *The world of mathematics*. New York: Simon & Schuster. (Original work published 1662)

Huygens, C. (1970). On reasoning in games. In J. Bernoulli (F. Maseres, Ed. & Trans.), *The art of conjecture*. New York: Redex Microprint. (Original work published 1657)

Jones, D. C. (1921). *A first course in statistics*. London: Bell.

McGaughy, J. R. (1924). *The fiscal administration of city school systems*. New York: Macmillan.

Pearson, E. S. (1970). Some incidents in the early history of biometry and statistics, 1890 – 94. In E. S. Pearson & M. G. Kendall (Eds.), *Studies in the history of statistics and probability*. London: Griffin. (Original work published 1965)

Pearson, K. (1894). Contributions to the mathematical theory of evolution: I. On the dissection of asymmetrical frequency curves. *Philosophical Transactions*, Part I, pp. 71–110.

Pearson, K. (1990). On the criterion that a given system of deviations from the probable in the case of a correlated system of variables is such that it can be reasonably supposed to have arisen from random sampling. *Philosophical Magazine, 50*, 150 –175.

Quetelet, L. A. (1849). *Letters on the theory of probabilities* (O. G. Downes, Trans). London: Layton.

Student [W. S. Gossett]. (1908) The probable error of a mean. *Biometrika, 6*, 1 – 25.

Walker, H. M. (1929). *Studies in the history of statistical method*. Baltimore, MD: Williams & Wilkins.

Wood, T. B., & Stratton, F. J. M. (1910). The interpretation of experimental results. *Journal of Agricultural Science, 3*, 417 – 440.

Yule, G. U., & Kendall, M. G. (1950). *An introduction to the theory of statistics* (14th ed.). London: Griffin.

16

HYPOTHESIS VALIDITY OF
CLINICAL RESEARCH

BRUCE E. WAMPOLD, BETSY DAVIS, AND ROLAND H. GOOD III

Clinical research spans a wide range of applied areas. To varying degrees, the basis of this research emanates from principles of behavior and behavior change. On the more technological side are treatment studies that answer the questions of whether a treatment works or which treatment is more effective (Kazdin, 1980, 1986), and status studies, which are designed to identify differences between populations. Yet certainly even these studies rely heavily on principles of behavior and behavior change to design the treatments, select measures, and interpret the results. For example, it is important to know whether maternal depression is associated with childhood problems; however, the curious investigator will soon seek to understand the nature of the relation between these two constructs (e.g., Dumas, Gibson, & Albin, 1989; Forehand, Lautenschlager, Faust, & Graziano, 1986; Hops et al., 1987). The link between theory and constructs in applied research is discussed by Cook and Campbell (1979):

Reprinted from the *Journal of Consulting and Clinical Psychology*, 58, 360 – 367. Copyright 1990 by the American Psychological Association.

Researchers would like to be able to give their presumed cause and effect operations names which refer to theoretical constructs. The need for this is most explicit in theory-testing research where the operations are explicitly derived to represent theoretical notions. But applied researchers also like to give generalized abstract names to their variables, for it is hardly useful to assume that the relationship between the two variables is causal if one cannot summarize these variables other than by describing them in exhaustive operational detail. (p. 38)

Although the importance of theory for the design of interpretation of clinical research is apparent, the mechanics of designing research in such a way that the results will be theoretically interesting are far from clear. The purpose of our article is to explore some of the aspects of clinical research that relate to theory. We have designated the term *hypothesis validity* to refer to the extent to which research results reflect theoretically derived predictions about the relations between or among constructs. If a study has adequate hypothesis validity, the results will be informative about the nature of the relation between constructs; that is, the study will inform theory. If a study has inadequate hypothesis validity, ambiguity about the relation between constructs will result, and indeed less certainty about the relation may exist than before the research was conducted. Hypothesis validity involves the development and statement of research hypotheses, the match of statistical hypotheses to research hypotheses, and the focus of statistical tests.

THE ROLE OF HYPOTHESES IN THEORY TESTING

Some important points from the philosophy of science as it relates to hypotheses supply the language to discuss and the base from which to develop hypothesis validity. Adopting the notation of Chow (1988), the crucial concepts needed for this discussion are illustrated in Table 16.1 and discussed below. Consider a theory T_1. Implication I_{11} of theory T_1 specifies an outcome that should occur given the mechanisms of the theory. $A.I_{11}$ represents the implication plus the auxiliary assumptions (e.g., normality of scores). X is an experimental expectation given $A.I_{11}$ (under the proper experimental conditions). Deductively, if the theory implies that X will occur (given the implication and the auxiliary assumptions, i.e., $A.I_{11}$) and if an experimental outcome D that is dissimilar to X is obtained, then the theory T_1 must be false. This approach to testing theory, which has been labeled the *falsificationist approach* (Popper, 1968), has bothered many philosophers of science, especially when used in conjunction with statistical tests (Folger, 1989; Mahoney, 1978; Meehl, 1978; Serlin, 1987; Serlin & Lapsley, 1985).

In the context of statistical hypothesis testing, falsification occurs when the null hypothesis is not rejected because the obtained result D is contrary to the expected result X. However, there are many ways that failure to reject

TABLE 16.1
Deductive Logic of Hypothesis Testing

Theory Implication	T_1 I_{11} Falsification	T_1 I_{11} Corroboration
Major premise	If $A.I_{11}$ then X under EFG	If $A.I_{11}$ then X under EFG
Minor premise	D is dissimilar to X.	D is similar to X.
Experimental conclusion	$A.I_{11}$ is false.	$A.I_{11}$ could be true.
Theoretical conclusion	T_1 is false.	T_1 could be true.

Note: T_1 = theory of interest; I_{11} = one implication of T_1; EFG = control and independent variables of the experiment; X = experimental expectation; A = set of auxiliary assumptions underlying the experiment; D = experimental outcomes (i.e., the pattern shown by the dependent variable in various conditions of the experiment). From "Significance Test or Effect Size?" by S. L. Chow, 1988, *Psychological Bulletin, 103*, p. 107. Copyright 1988 by the American Psychological Association. Adapted by permission. See also Folger, 1989.

the null hypothesis can result other than the fact that the theory is false, ruining the clean deductive nature of falsification (Folger, 1989). The obtained findings may be due to chance (Type II error), incorrect formulation of the implication of the theory, misspecification of the expected outcome X, low power, poor experimental methods, unreliable variables, or violated assumptions (Cook & Campbell, 1979; Folger, 1989).

Besides being epistemologically troublesome, falsification is not the modus operandi of research in the social sciences. If anything, there is a prejudice against research that fails to reject the null hypothesis, especially in clinically related areas (Atkinson, Furlong, & Wampold, 1982; Fagley, 1985; Greenwald, 1975; Mahoney, 1977). The alternative hypothesis holds the upper hand in psychological research; that is, researchers usually hope to reject the null hypothesis and lend support to a particular point of view. Furthermore, journal editors and reviewers look to significant results to inform the field (Atkinson et al., 1982). However, there are epistemological problems with this approach as well. The fact that the obtained pattern of results D is similar to the predicted pattern X does not imply that the theory T_1 is true, because other theories may also imply a predicted pattern X. Claiming the truth of a theory on the basis of the appearance of the expected pattern of results is a deductive error called *affirming the consequent*. The problems with affirming the consequent in psychological research have been acknowledged previously (e.g., Folger, 1989; Mahoney, 1978). Nevertheless, an experiment that produces the theoretically expected pattern of results has survived an attempt at falsification. In such a case, the theory is said to be *corroborated*; corroboration implies that the theory has been tested and has survived, which is quite different from implying that it has been confirmed (see Mahoney, 1978).

There is another problem with statistical testing and theory that is more subtle, and yet more troublesome, than the deductive problems we have discussed. In the hard sciences, as methods are refined (e.g., better measurement of phenomena), theories are winnowed, leaving fewer theories that are as-cribed to with more confidence. Just the opposite is true in many areas of so-cial science research. It is reasonable to believe that the null hypothesis is not literally true; that is, all constructs are related, even if to some small de-gree. As methods are refined, error variance will be reduced and statistical tests will be more powerful. As a consequence, it will be more likely that theories will be corroborated and less likely that they will be falsified and re-jected. Instead of winnowing, theories will proliferate (Serlin, 1987; Serlin & Lapsley, 1985).

Several remedies to the philosophical problems of hypothesis testing have been suggested. An omnipresent suggestion involves the use of effect-size measures, confidence intervals, statements about power, measures of clinical significance, or other measures that reflect the degree to which the obtained results differ from that hypothesized under the null hypothesis (e.g., Cohen, 1988; Cook & Campbell, 1979; Fagley, 1985; Folger, 1989; Haase, Waechter, & Solomon, 1982; Jacobson, Follette, & Revenstorf, 1984; Ros-now & Rosenthal, 1988; Wampold, Furlong, & Atkinson, 1983). These mea-sures are useful because they provide information in addition to the binary decision of whether the null hypothesis is rejected, although their use is controversial logically and statistically (Chow, 1988, 1989; Hollon & Flick, 1988; Mitchell & Hartmann, 1981; Murray & Dosser, 1987; O'Grady, 1982).

Another remedy to the traditional hypothesis-testing strategy is to use alternative statistical paradigms or to use no statistics at all. The Bayesian ap-proach readjusts prior estimates of the probabilities of events with informa-tion provided by new samples (Schmitt, 1969). Serlin and Lapsley (1985) have promulgated the *good-enough principle,* which embodies a hypothesis-testing strategy in which, instead of hypothesizing a null effect, the researcher hypothesizes the magnitude of the effect that is sufficient to corroborate the theory or that is clinically significant. Of course, the researcher may eschew the use of statistical tests entirely; a significant body of knowledge has been accumulated in experimental and applied areas by the visual analysis of data generated by single-subject designs (Barlow & Hersen, 1984).

Hypothesis validity addresses the interrelations of theory, research hy-potheses, and statistical hypotheses. Research hypotheses are derived from theory and can be characterized as statements about the presumed relations among constructs. In Chow's (1988) framework, the research hypotheses represent an implication of the theory. Research hypotheses should be stated in such a way that a theory is falsifiable and that competing theories can be winnowed. Clarity of a research hypothesis is vital to determine whether an obtained outcome is similar or dissimilar to the outcome predicted by theory.

Certain properties of statistical hypotheses are needed in order to assure adequate hypothesis validity. First, statistical hypotheses should be congru-ent with the research hypotheses. If the research hypotheses posit a relation between constructs on the basis of means, then the statistical hypotheses should be phrased in terms of μ, the population mean. However, a statistical hypothesis regarding μ would be inappropriate if the implication of the theory was phrased in terms of differences in variances. Second, statistical hypotheses must be sufficiently specific to determine whether the obtained result is similar or dissimilar to the predicted experimental outcome.

The relations among theory, research hypotheses, statistical hypotheses, and results are presented in Figure 16.1. The design of experiments involves deriving research hypotheses from theory, matching statistical hypotheses to research hypotheses, and creating the experiment in order to obtain the results. It is interesting to note that design texts and courses often focus on the last operation (i.e., design of the experiment rather than design of the research). Inference proceeds in the opposite direction. The results are used to make decisions about the statistical hypotheses (e.g., reject the null hypothesis), and these decisions indicate whether the predicted patterns stipulated in the research hypotheses have been verified, determining whether the theory is corroborated or falsified. Traditional statistics texts concentrate on making inferences from sample data (i.e., the results) to statements about population parameters (i.e., statistical hypotheses). Hypothesis

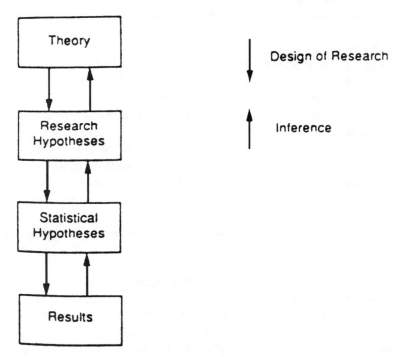

Figure 16.1. Design and inference in theory testing.

validity involves both the design of research and the inferences made from the results of studies.

In the spirit of Campbell and Stanley (1966), Bracht and Glass (1968), and Cook and Campbell (1979), we discuss hypothesis validity in more detail by posing threats to hypothesis validity.

THREATS TO HYPOTHESIS VALIDITY

Inconsequential Research Hypotheses

In Chow's (1988) framework, I_{11} was an implication of theory T_1. There are many other implications from theory T_1 that could be made (i.e., I_{12}, I_{13}, etc.). An important question is whether I_{11} represents a crucial issue. That is, from the set of possible implications (some of which may not have been entertained by the researcher), is I_{11} central to determining the veridicality of the theory T_1 in comparison with T_2, T_3, and so forth? Implication I_{11} is suboptimal to the extent that competing theories would have implications similar to I_{11}. For example, if theory T_2 implied I_{21}, which was identical to I_{11}, then any experimental result corroborating T_1 would also corroborate T_2. The hypothesis validity of a study is strengthened when the number of tenable theories that have implications similar to I_{11} is small. Ideally, corroborating T_1 should simultaneously falsify a large number of competing theories.

In his discussion of strong inference, Platt (1964) discussed the importance of determining the crucial question and devising research so that various explanations for observed phenomena can be ruled out. Implication I_{11} is superior to other implications to the extent that research that is based on this implication will result in a clearer understanding of the relation between constructs than would research that is based on other implications, and to the extent that this understanding is important to understanding the psychological phenomena of interest. Thus, strong inference is based, in part, on inductive reasoning about the implications of the theory under scrutiny.

Framing the discussion of research questions notationally should not be construed to indicate that this process is necessarily formal or deductive. Essentially the researcher surveys existing knowledge relating to his or her problems and attempts to pose the important unanswered question. Examining crucial hypotheses leads to the extension of knowledge, the winnowing of theories, the clarification of discrepancies, the identification of active ingredients of treatments, and so on. Inconsequential research hypotheses, on the other hand, do not produce resolution because they do not lead to a convergence of knowledge.

Platt (1964) addressed the issue of inconsequential research hypotheses by advocating multiple hypotheses. He has claimed that sciences that progress rapidly are characterized by experimentation that tests one theory against another. In that way, the results simultaneously corroborate one theory while falsifying another. For example, in particle physics, two models might be postulated; one model cannot explain the appearance of a certain particle in an experiment, whereas the other can explain it. If the particle appears (reliably), the first model is abandoned, and the second is tentatively adopted until a competing model is developed and tested against the tentatively adopted model.

This multiple hypothesis idea has implications for the manner in which models are tested in psychological research, especially with the advent of modeling techniques such as LISREL (Jöreskog & Sörbom, 1988). Typically, a model is proposed (one that is based on theory, it is hoped), and its compatibility with sample data is assessed. If the sample data are not consistent with the model proposed, the model is rejected (e.g., a significant chi-square goodness-of-fit test is obtained). On the other hand, if the goodness of fit is not significant, the model is retained. However, it is not proved, because this conclusion would be affirming the consequent (Cliff, 1983); there may be other models that fit the data as well (or better) than the model proposed. According to the multiple-hypothesis concept, stronger inferences can be made by contrasting competing models. For example, using a LISREL analysis of attitudes, Kerlinger (1980) demonstrated that a model with separate conservative and liberal dimensions was superior to a model with conservatism and liberalism as poles on a single dimension.

Ambiguous Research Hypotheses

Ambiguous research hypotheses make it difficult to ascertain how the results of a study influence our theoretical understanding. If the experimental expectation (X in Chow's [1988] notation) is not specified sufficiently, it may well be impossible to determine whether the obtained results D are similar or dissimilar to what was expected. Ambiguity with regard to research hypotheses results in the inability to falsify a theory, a particularly troublesome state of affairs from a philosophy of science perspective (Mahoney, 1978; Platt, 1964; Popper, 1968).

Ambiguous research hypotheses are often stated in journal articles with phrases such as "the purpose of the present study is to explore the relation between . . ." or "the purpose is to determine the relation between. . . ." In one sense, such research cannot fail, because some relation between variables will be "discovered," even if the relation is null (i.e., no relation). In another sense, the research will always fail because the results do not falsify or corroborate any theory about the true state of affairs.

As an example of ambiguous research hypotheses, consider the following purpose of a study (Webster-Stratton, 1988) on parents' perceptions of child deviance:

> The present study attempted to determine (a) the relation of parental adjustment measures of such variables as depression, marital satisfaction, parenting stress, and other negative life stressors to mothers' and fathers' perceptions of their children's deviant behaviors; (b) the relation of teachers' independent perceptions of the children's behaviors to mothers' and fathers' perceptions; (c) the relation of mother, father, and teacher perceptions of child behaviors to observed mother, father, and child behaviors; and (d) the relation of parent measures to observed mother, father, and child behaviors. (pp. 909–910)

Interpretation of the results of this study was problematic because there was no predicted experimental outcome of result with which to compare the obtained pattern of results. It is not surprising that this research discovered some patterns that confirmed previous research (e.g., mothers' perceptions of their children's deviant behaviors were affected by mothers' personal adjustment) and some patterns that contradicted other previous research (e.g., that teacher reports were better than maternal depression for the prediction of mothers' reports of child deviance).

Although careful observation is an important step in the development of hypotheses in any science, reliance on exploratory research can result only in confusion, if for no other reason than that some of the observed patterns are due to chance. A preponderance of studies with ambiguous research hypotheses will tend not to converge on important principles of behavior but will result in post hoc attempts to reconcile discrepant findings. As a result, weak theories will proliferate.

An example of clear hypotheses is provided by Borkovec and Mathews (1988) in a study of nonphobic anxiety disorders: "Clients with predominantly cognitive symptoms might be expected to respond better to techniques addressing this symptom domain, whereas clients with predominantly somatic symptoms might improve more under coping desensitization" (p. 878). This hypothesis is specific enough that, if other aspects of the study are valid (including other aspects of hypothesis validity discussed later), the results can clearly corroborate or fail to support the Borkovec and Mathews prediction.

As a hypothetical example to illustrate research hypotheses (and later statistical tests), consider a treatment study contrasting a behavioral intervention and a cognitive intervention. To answer Paul's (1967) question about which treatments work with which type of clients, further suppose the differential effects of the treatment on two types of persons—cognitively oriented and noncognitively oriented. Suppose five dependent variables were used to operationally define the construct targeted for change (e.g., marital satisfaction). A reasonable and specific hypothesis would be that the behav-

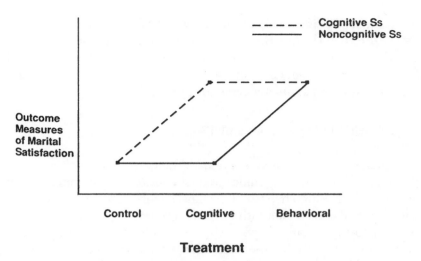

Treatment

Figure 16.2. Predicted pattern for outcome variables for Type of Subject × Treatment. (Higher scores indicate more satisfaction.)

ior therapy would be effective with both types of subjects (i.e., cognitively oriented and noncognitively oriented), whereas the cognitive therapy would be effective only with the cognitively oriented subjects. The anticipated pattern of results is presented in Figure 16.2.

The argument for specificity in research hypotheses has been made in the context of traditional hypothesis testing. However, our points are as pertinent, if not more so, for many alternative strategies. For example, in the Bayesian approach, specificity is important because one has to stipulate prior probabilities. According to the good-enough principle, the minimal effect size that represents importance must be specified (Serlin & Lapsley, 1985).

Noncongruence of Research Hypotheses and Statistical Hypotheses

To determine whether the obtained outcome *D* is similar or dissimilar to the experimental expectation X, the statistical hypothesis must correspond to the research hypothesis. When the research and statistical hypotheses are incongruent, even persuasive statistical evidence (small alpha levels, high power, large effect sizes) will not allow valid inferences to be made about the research hypotheses.

Although the problems of noncongruence seem obvious, consider the case in which the research hypothesis addresses differences in variances; that is, a treatment is expected to increase the variance (and quite possibly leave the mean unchanged). For example, a treatment for autoimmune deficiency syndrome could possibly prolong the lives of one half of the subjects and hasten the death of the other half. In such a case, it would be inappropriate to hypothesize mean differences à la an analysis of variance (ANOVA; $viz.$, $\mu_1 = \mu_2 = \ldots \mu_j$) when the question of interest is whether the variances are equal (viz., $\sigma^2_1 = \sigma^2_2 = \ldots = \sigma^2_j$). A perusal of the statistical tests used in clinical research convincingly demonstrates, we believe, that differences among groups are expressed as differences among means by default.

Diffuse Statistical Hypotheses and Tests

Statistical tests are used to evaluate the extent to which an observed experimental outcome D is similar or dissimilar to the experimental expectation X. If the research hypothesis is translated into one set of statistical hypotheses (a null and an alternative), then, if the statistical test is valid and is congruent to the research hypothesis, the results of the statistical test will provide information so that the researcher can decide whether D is similar to X. If the null hypothesis for this test is rejected in favor of an alternative hypothesis that is consistent with X, then the conclusion is made that D is similar to X. If the null hypothesis is not rejected, then the conclusion is made that D is dissimilar to X (Chow, 1988). Of course, the decisions made could be incorrect (viz., Type I and Type II error).

Diffusion of statistical tests is created in one of three ways: First, a specific research hypothesis can be (and often is) translated into many statistical hypotheses and tests. Second, the statistical test used may be an omnibus test that does not focus on a specific research question. Third, extraneous independent variables may be included.

Multiple Statistical Tests

When more than one set of statistical hypotheses is tested per research hypothesis, theoretical ambiguity can result because it is not clear what pattern of results will corroborate or falsify the conjecture embodied in the research hypothesis. Specifically, many statistical tests per research hypothesis are problematic for two reasons. First, there is uncertainty with regard to the interpretation of many statistical tests because the results may not be consistent. Suppose that the researcher conducts two statistical tests. One yields a result consistent with the theory, and the other yields a result that is inconsistent with the theory, as might be the case when two dependent variables are used. Is this evidence for or against the theory?

The interpretation of multiple statistical tests is further compounded by the fact that some of the statistically significant results will have occurred by chance when there was no effect (Type I error), and some of the nonsignificant results will have occurred even though the expected effect was present (Type II error). Control of experimentwise Type I error will minimize the Type I errors but will lead to greater experimentwise Type II error. In any event, the question remains, "Which results were due to Type I and Type II errors?"

TABLE 16.2
Pattern of Predicted Significant *T* Tests

Test	Significant
Control/cognitive Ss vs. control/noncognitive Ss	No
Cognitive Tx/cognitive Ss vs. cognitive Tx/noncognitive Ss	Yes
Behavioral Tx/cognitive Ss vs. behavioral Tx/noncognitive Ss	No
Control/cognitive Ss vs. cognitive Tx/cognitive Ss	Yes
Control/cognitive Ss vs. behavioral Tx/cognitive Ss	Yes
Control/noncognitive Ss vs. cognitive Tx/noncognitive Ss	No
Control/noncognitive Ss vs. behavioral Tx/noncognitive Ss	Yes
Cognitive Tx/cognitive Ss vs. behavioral Tx/cognitive Ss	No
Cognitive Tx/noncognitive Ss vs. behavioral Tx/noncognitive Ss	Yes

Note: S = subject. Tx = treatment.

The problem with many statistical tests is illustrated by the Borkovec and Mathews (1988) study of nonphobic anxiety. For the specific hypothesis with regard to clients with cognitive and with somatic symptoms, several statistical tests were used. Predictably the outcome was ambiguous, giving rise to difficulties in interpretation: "Such an ambiguous outcome is open to a variety of interpretations" (Borkovec & Mathews, 1988, p. 882).

To further illustrate the ambiguity created by many statistical tests, consider the example presented earlier with regard to the behavioral and cognitive treatments for cognitively and noncognitively oriented subjects. To test the research hypothesis embodied in Figure 16.2, a series of *t* tests for each dependent variable could be conducted in which several tests would be expected to be significant and others nonsignificant. These *t* tests are presented in Table 16.2; 45 tests would be needed (9 for each dependent variable). Clearly such an approach is questionable because it is unclear what degree of correspondence with the expected pattern of results in Table 16.2 would be required to corroborate the research hypothesis. Suppose that 1 of the *t*-test outcomes was not as expected; would that still be strong enough evidence to decide that the results were consistent with the prediction? What about 2 or 3, 35 or 40? As mentioned previously, this question is complicated by the fact that the probability of a Type I error has escalated dramatically. One could, of course, control the experimentwise Type I error rate with a Bonferroni type procedure, although this would be a very conservative approach, resulting in unacceptable experimentwise Type II error rates (Hays, 1988; Rosenthal & Rubin, 1984).

Omnibus Tests

Omnibus tests are problematic because they contain effects, contrasts, or combinations that do not reflect solely the research hypothesis. Hence, several different research hypotheses can lead to a significant omnibus test. For example, an omnibus *F* test in an ANOVA for a treatment study with several treatments may be due to the treatments' being superior to the control group, or may be due to one treatment's being superior to the other treatments and to the control group. Although differences may be explored post hoc, planned comparisons are advantageous for theory testing. The interpretation given to the results of a planned comparison (or any other focused test[1]) is a direct test of a specific hypothesis. On the other hand, if the omnibus F test is significant at a given level, then some possible post hoc comparison must be significant at that level (Hays, 1988; Wampold & Drew, 1990); however, there is no assurance that this comparison will be interpretable. Even if the comparison is interpretable, the interpretation is made post hoc, and correspondence to a predicted pattern is precluded.

There are problems with omnibus tests other than their questionable relation to theory. Omnibus tests (and post hoc follow-up tests) are statistically less powerful means to detect effects than are focused tests (Hays, 1988; Rosnow & Rosenthal, 1988). Furthermore, calculation and interpretation of effect sizes for omnibus tests are problematic (Rosnow & Rosenthal, 1988).

Returning to the marital satisfaction example, we could conduct a 3 (two treatments plus control group) × 2 (type of subject) ANOVA for each dependent variable, a less diffuse choice than conducting the 45 t tests. However, this approach also suffers from multiple tests because it yields 15 F tests, 2 tests of main effects, and 1 test of the interaction effect for each of the five dependent variables. However, the omnibus F test for the ANOVA is particularly pernicious because it does not directly address the pattern of expected results. The research hypothesis embodied in Figure 1 combines a main effect and an interaction effect.

The expected pattern of results for this problem can be neatly expressed as a planned comparison (see display below). However, even though this comparison tests the research hypothesis directly, testing this comparison for each dependent variable maintains the multiple statistical test problem.

Tx:	Control	Control	Cognitive	Cognitive	Behavioral	Behavioral
Ss:	Cognitive	Noncognitive	Cognitive	Noncognitive	Cognitive	Noncognitive
Comparison:	−1	−1	+1	−1	+1	+1

The most focused test would be a multivariate planned comparison. This one test would answer the question of whether the expected pattern of means was reflected in the sample data and thus would avoid multiple statistical tests as well as omnibus tests. There would be no need to conduct follow-up tests because the research hypothesis did not specify differential

---

[1] Focused tests have been defined by Rosnow and Rosenthal (1988) to be "significance tests that address precise questions, such as any t test, any F test with 1 df in the numerator, and any $1-df \chi^2$ test" (p. 204). However, there are tests with more than 1 df that answer specific questions. For example, a general linear model F test that all higher order interaction effects are zero could be used to show that a number of independent variables do not interact with a treatment variable.

effects for individual outcome variables; presumably the variables were measuring the same construct.

In this example, the focused test was one multivariate test. However, this example should not be taken to indicate that multivariate tests are necessarily less diffuse than univariate tests. A common practice is to conduct omnibus multivariate analyses of variance (MANOVAs) followed by omnibus univariate ANOVAs. This practice is diffuse because of the omnibus nature of the tests and because it is not clear which pattern of the univariate tests corroborates the research hypothesis. In fact, it is possible to reject the multivariate null hypothesis while not being able to reject any of the univariate null hypotheses (Huberty & Morris, 1989). It has been recommended that significant multivariate tests be followed by discriminant analyses so that the linear combination of variables that best differentiate the groups can be examined (e.g., Bray & Maxwell, 1982). Although this may be an improvement over univariate Fs, without hypothesizing linear combinations, it remains difficult to link the statistical results to the research hypotheses.

The choice of a multivariate test should depend on the research hypothesis. Multivariate tests often are advocated for the express purpose of controlling experimentwise Type I error (e.g., Leary & Altmaier, 1980). Although controlling Type I error is beneficial, consideration of hypothesis validity of the study should be the primary criterion in the choice of a statistical procedure. For example, when the dependent variables are conceptually independent and result in multiple research questions, multiple ANOVAs may be the appropriate procedures to answer specific research questions (Huberty & Morris, 1989).

Generally, the less diffuse the statistical tests (and hence statistical hypotheses), the greater the hypothesis validity of the study. To the extent possible, one statistical test should be focused on one research hypothesis. Accordingly, planned comparisons would be preferable to omnibus F tests in the ANOVA context, a test of a hypothesized curvilinear relation would treat other curvilinear relations as residual, higher order interactions with no theoretical relevance would not be tested, parameters would be contrasted rather than tested individually (e.g., tests of differences between correlations), and so forth.

The importance of focusing a few specific tests on research questions rather than using diffuse tests has long been emphasized. Serlin (1987) has succinctly summarized the theoretical problems associated with omnibus tests:

> But one still sees omnibus F tests performed in analysis of variance, even though almost all the contrasts subsumed by the omnibus null hypothesis have *no possibility of interpretation* [italics added]. In a similar fashion, the omnibus null hypothesis in multivariate analysis of variance subsumes

an even larger set of mostly *uninterpretable* [italics added] contrasts performed on mostly *uninterpretable* [italics added] linear combinations of the dependent variables. Finally, the omnibus null hypothesis in regression analysis examines whether any of an infinite set of linear combinations of the predictor variables is related to the dependent variable. In each of these cases, *a consideration of the theoretically derived research questions under examination in the experiment would obviate the use of the omnibus hypothesis test* [italics added]. (p. 370)

Extraneous Independent Variables

Often independent variables are included in a study to increase the external validity of a study, that is, to increase the generalizability of the results across persons, settings, or time (Cook & Campbell, 1979). For example, to determine whether the results apply equally to men and women, gender may be added to a design as an independent variable. Of course, the set of possible independent variables related to persons, settings, or time is very large. With regard to persons, the most widely used variables include gender, ethnicity, socioeconomic status, and intelligence, although there are many other variables that could be included. Furthermore, each of these variables very likely glosses over other important distinctions. For example, gender ignores sex role orientation, and ethnicity ignores level of acculturation.

The choice of independent variables related to generalizability is difficult. We contend that this choice should be driven by theory to the extent possible. If there is good reason to believe that the results of a study will differ for men and women, then there is a good rationale to include gender in the study. However, if the theory implies that sex role orientation is the critical variable, then sex role orientation should be included.

Inclusion of extraneous variables inflates the number of hypotheses tested, increasing the diffusion of the statistical tests. In the typical factorial design, each independent variable added to the design introduces another main effect as well as interaction effects with the other independent variables. Additional independent variables also increase the likelihood that omnibus tests will be used because it becomes more difficult and less appropriate (without theory) to make specific predictions with regard to the main and, particularly, the interaction effects.

One could suggest another caution about additional independent variables. If an additional independent variable is important enough to be included in the study, it should be treated as a legitimate part of the design, and predictions should be made about the outcome for this variable. The irrelevance of independent variables is demonstrated when researchers conduct a preliminary test for differences on a variable such as gender and then collapse over this factor when no significant differences are found. This process rules out the possibility of detecting an interaction effect as well, which is often the most interesting of results from an external validity point of view.

CONCLUSIONS

The purpose of our article is to call attention to the connection between theory and results of individual studies. The concept of hypothesis validity has been introduced to emphasize the importance of drawing crucial implications from theory, stating clear research hypotheses, matching statistical hypotheses with research hypotheses, and focusing the statistical tests on the research hypotheses. We hope that the presentation of hypothesis validity provides a framework that is useful for the design and critique of clinical research.

Any conceptual framework is somewhat arbitrary; hypothesis validity is no exception. Hypothesis validity borders on both construct validity of putative causes and effects and statistical conclusion validity, as discussed by Cook and Campbell (1979). Construct validity of putative causes and effects involves determining the degree to which the variables included in a study reflect theoretical constructs. Clearly, construct validity plays an important role in the theoretical relevance of studies. However, hypothesis validity differs from construct validity by focusing on the relation between the constructs; construct validity focuses on the operationalization of the constructs.

Hypothesis validity is also related to statistical conclusion validity. Multiple statistical tests pose threats to statistical conclusion validity because of fishing and error rate problems (Cook & Campbell, 1979). However, even if these problems are attenuated by statistical means (e.g., using the Bonferroni inequality), ambiguity is present because of the difficulty in comparing the obtained pattern of results with the predicted pattern of results. Focused tests are advantageous primarily because they provide an explicit test of a specific hypothesis, although they are also desirable from a statistical point of view (e.g., increased power under certain circumstances).

Hypothesis validity applies most directly to theoretically driven clinical research. What about purely exploratory research or technological research? In any field of empirical inquiry, exploration is important. Most researchers enjoy searching through data to discover unanticipated relations among variables. Nevertheless, the search is guided by knowledge and understanding of theory, and interpretation of the discoveries is made within a theoretical context. Although the tenets of hypothesis validity do not apply as directly to purely exploratory research, they are critical to testing the conjectures that emanate from the exploratory phase.

Examples of purely technological research in clinical psychology are difficult to find. At first glance, comparative treatment studies may appear to answer the atheoretical question about the relative efficacy of two or more treatments (Kazdin, 1980, 1986). However, development of the treatment will most likely rely on principles of behavior change, selection of the dependent measures will be based on the intended outcome, and interpretation of the results will be explained within a theoretical context. Regardless of the degree to which such studies rely on theory, the principles of hypothesis validity are valuable. One still wants to conduct a study crucial to establishing the relative efficacy of a treatment, to state clearly the research hypotheses about relative efficacy, to match the statistical hypotheses to the research hypotheses, and so on.

We hope that describing the threats to hypothesis validity will result in more thought about the research hypotheses and how they can be tested elegantly. If a researcher uses a strong rope to lower himself or herself from theory to research hypotheses to statistical hypotheses and finally to the results of a study, then he or she will be able to climb back with the results so that a valid statement about theory can be made. If the rope is fatally frayed at some point, the results picked up at the bottom will be of little value (and may become burdensome weight) for the return journey.

REFERENCES

Atkinson, D. R., Furlong, M. J., & Wampold, B. E. (1982). Statistical significance, reviewer evaluations, and the scientific process: Is there a (statistically) significant relationship? *Journal of Counseling Psychology, 29,* 189–194.

Barlow, D. H., & Hersen, M. (1984). *Single case experimental designs: Strategies for studying behavior change* (2nd ed.). New York: Pergamon Press.

Borkovec, T. D., & Mathews, A. M. (1988). Treatment of nonphobic anxiety disorders: A comparison of nondirective, cognitive, and coping desensitization. *Journal of Consulting and Clinical Psychology, 56,* 877–884.

Bracht, G. H., & Glass, G. V. (1968). The external validity of experiments. *American Educational Research Journal, 5,* 437–474.

Bray, H. J., & Maxwell, S. E. (1982). Analyzing and interpreting significant MANOVAS. *Review of Educational Research, 52,* 340–367.

Campbell, D. T., & Stanley, J. C. (1966). *Experimental and quasi-experimental designs for research.* Chicago: Rand McNally.

Chow, S. L. (1988). Significance test or effect size? *Psychological Bulletin, 103,* 105–110.

Chow, S. L. (1989). Significance tests and deduction: Reply to Folger. (1989). *Psychological Bulletin, 106,* 161–165, 778.

Cliff, N. (1983). Some cautions concerning the application of causal modeling methods. *Multivariate Behavioral Research, 18,* 115–126.

Cohen, J. (1988). *Statistical power analysis for the behavioral sciences* (2nd ed.). Hillsdale, NJ: Erlbaum.

Cook, T. D., & Campbell, D. T. (1979). *Quasi-experimentation: Design and analysis for field settings.* Chicago: Rand McNally.

Dumas, J. E., Gibson, J. A., & Albin, J. B. (1989). Behavioral correlates of maternal depressive symptomatology in conduct-disordered children. *Journal of Consulting and Clinical Psychology, 57,* 516–521.

Fagley, N. S. (1985). Applied statistical power analysis and the interpretation of nonsignificant results by research consumers. *Journal of Counseling Psychology, 32,* 391–396.

Folger, R. (1989). Significance tests and the duplicity of binary decisions. *Psychological Bulletin, 106,* 155–160.

Forehand, R., Lautenschlager, G. J., Faust, J., & Graziano, W. G. (1986). Parent perceptions and parent – child interaction in clinic-referred children: A preliminary investigation of the effects of maternal depressive moods. *Behaviour Research and Therapy, 24,* 73–75.

Greenwald, A. G. (1975). Consequences of prejudice against the null hypothesis. *Psychological Bulletin, 82,* 1–20.

Haase, R. F., Waechter, D. M., & Solomon, G. S. (1982). How significant is a significant difference? Average effect size of research in counseling psychology. *Journal of Counseling Psychology, 29,* 58–65.

Hays, W. L. (1988). *Statistics* (4th ed.). New York: Holt, Rinehart & Winston.

Hollon, S. D., & Flick, S. N. (1988). On the meaning and methods of clinical significance. *Behavioral Assessment, 10,* 197–206.

Hops, H., Biglan, A., Sherman, L., Arthur, J., Friedman, L., & Osteen, V. (1987). Home observations of family interactions of depressed women. *Journal of Consulting and Clinical Psychology, 55,* 341–346.

Huberty, C. J., & Morris, J. D. (1989). Multivariate analysis versus multiple univariate analyses. *Psychological Bulletin, 105,* 302–308.

Jacobson, N. S., Follette, W. C., & Revenstorf, D. (1984). Psychotherapy outcome research: Methods for reporting variability and evaluating clinical significance. *Behavior Therapy, 17,* 336 – 352.

Jöreskog, K. G., & Sörbom, D. (1988). LISREL VII: *A guide to the program and applications* [Computer program manual]. Chicago: SPSS.

Kazdin, A. E. (1980). *Research design in clinical psychology.* New York: Harper & Row.

Kazdin, A. E. (1986). The evaluation of psychotherapy: Research design and methodology. In S. L. Garfield & A. E. Bergin (Eds.), *Handbook of psychotherapy and behavior change* (3rd ed., pp. 23–68). New York: Wiley.

Kerlinger, F. N. (1980). Analysis of covariance structures test of a criterial referents theory of attitudes. *Multivariate Behavioral Research, 15,* 403 – 422.

Leary, M. R., & Altmaier, E. M. (1980). Type I error in counseling research: A plea for multivariate analyses. *Journal of Counseling Psychology, 27,* 611–615.

Mahoney, M. J. (1977). Publication prejudices: An experimental study of confirmatory bias in the peer review system. *Cognitive Therapy and Research, 1,* 161–175.

Mahoney, M. J. (1978). Experimental methods and outcome evaluation. *Journal of Consulting and Clinical Psychology, 46,* 660 – 672.

Meehl, P. (1978). Theoretical risks and tabular asterisks: Sir Karl, Sir Ronald, and the slow progress of soft psychology. *Journal of Consulting and Clinical Psychology, 46,* 806–834.

Mitchell, C., & Hartmann, D. P. (1981). A cautionary note on the use of omega squared to evaluate the effectiveness of behavioral treatments. *Behavioral Assessment, 3,* 93–100.

Murray, L. W., & Dosser, D. A., Jr. (1987). How significant is a significant difference? Problems with the measurement of magnitude of effect. *Journal of Counseling Psychology, 34,* 68–72.

O'Grady, K. E. (1982). Measures of explained variance: Caution and limitations. *Psychological Bulletin, 92,* 766–777.

Paul, G. L. (1967). Strategy of outcome research in psychotherapy. *Journal of Consulting Psychology, 31,* 104–118.

Platt, J. R. (1964). Strong inference. *Science, 146,* 347–353.

Popper, K. (1968). *Conjectures and refutations.* London: Routledge & Kegan Paul.

Rosenthal, R., & Rubin, D. B. (1984). Multiple contrasts and ordered Bonferroni procedures. *Journal of Educational Psychology, 76,* 1028–1034.

Rosnow, R. L., & Rosenthal, R. (1988). Focused tests of significance and effect size estimation in counseling psychology. *Journal of Counseling Psychology, 35,* 203–208.

Schmitt, S. A. (1969). *Measuring uncertainty: An elementary introduction to Bayesian statistics.* Reading, MA: Addison-Wesley.

Serlin, R. C. (1987). Hypothesis testing, theory building, and the philosophy of science. *Journal of Counseling Psychology, 34,* 365–371.

Serlin, R. C., & Lapsley, D. K. (1985). Rationality in psychological research: The good-enough principle. *American Psychologist, 40,* 73–83.

Wampold, B. E., Furlong, M. J., & Atkinson, D. R. (1983). Statistical significance, power, and effect size: A response to the reexamination of reviewer bias. *Journal of Counseling Psychology, 30,* 459–463.

Wampold, B. E., & Drew, C. J. (1990). *Theory and application of statistics.* New York: McGraw-Hill.

Webster-Stratton, C. (1988). Mothers' and fathers' perceptions of child deviance: Roles of parent and child behaviors and parent adjustment. *Journal of Consulting and Clinical Psychology, 56,* 909–915.

17

THINGS I HAVE LEARNED (SO FAR)

JACOB COHEN

What I have learned (so far) has come from working with students and colleagues, from experience (sometimes bitter) with journal editors and review committees, and from the writings of, among others, Paul Meehl, David Bakan, William Rozeboom, Robyn Dawes, Howard Wainer, Robert Rosenthal, and more recently, Gerd Gigerenzer, Michael Oakes, and Leland Wilkinson. Although they are not always explicitly referenced, many of you will be able to detect their footprints in what follows.

SOME THINGS YOU LEARN AREN'T SO

One of the things I learned early on was that some things you learn aren't so. In graduate school, right after World War II, I learned that for doctoral dissertations and most other purposes, when comparing groups, the proper sample size is 30 cases per group. The number 30 seems to have arisen from the understanding that with fewer than 30 cases, you were dealing with "small" samples that required specialized handling with "small-sample

Reprinted from the *American Psychologist, 45,* 1304 – 1312. Copyright 1990 by the American Psychological Association.

statistics" instead of the critical-ratio approach we had been taught. Some of us knew about these exotic small-sample statistics—in fact, one of my fellow doctoral candidates undertook a dissertation, the distinguishing feature of which was a sample of only 20 cases per group, so that he could demonstrate his prowess with small-sample statistics. It wasn't until some years later that I discovered (mind you, not invented) power analysis, one of whose fruits was the revelation that for a two-independent-group-mean comparison with $n = 30$ per group at the sanctified two-tailed .05 level, the probability that a medium-sized effect would be labeled as significant by the most modern methods (a t test) was only .47. Thus, it was approximately a coin flip whether one would get a significant result, even though, in reality, the effect size was meaningful. My $n = 20$ friend's power was rather worse (.33), but of course he couldn't know that, and he ended up with nonsignificant results— with which he proceeded to demolish an important branch of psychoanalytic theory.

LESS IS MORE

One thing I learned over a long period of time that *is* so is the validity of the general principle that *less is more*, except of course for sample size (Cohen & Cohen, 1983, pp. 169–171). I have encountered too many studies with prodigious numbers of dependent variables, or with what seemed to me far too many independent variables, or (heaven help us) both.

In any given investigation that isn't explicitly exploratory, we should be studying few independent variables and even fewer dependent variables, for a variety of reasons.

If all of the dependent variables are to be related to all of the independent variables by simple bivariate analyses or multiple regression, the number of hypothesis tests that will be performed willy-nilly is at least the product of the sizes of the two sets. Using the .05 level for many tests escalates the experimentwise Type 1 error rate—or in plain English, greatly increases the chances of discovering things that aren't so. If, for example, you study 6 dependent and 10 independent variables and should find that your harvest yields 6 asterisks, you know full well that if there were no real associations in any of the 60 tests, the chance of getting one or more "significant" results is quite high (something like $1 - .95^{60}$, which equals, coincidentally, .95), and that you would expect three spuriously significant results on the average. You then must ask yourself some embarrassing questions, such as, Well, which three are real?, or even, Is six significant *significantly* more than the chance-expected three? (It so happens that it isn't.)

And of course, as you've probably discovered, you're not likely to solve your multiple tests problem with the Bonferroni maneuver. Dividing .05 by

60 sets a per-test significance criterion of $.05/60 = 0.00083$, and therefore a critical two-sided t value of about 3.5. The effects you're dealing with may not be large enough to produce any interesting ts that high, unless you're lucky.

Nor can you find salvation by doing six stepwise multiple regressions on the 10 independent variables. The amount of capitalization on chance that this entails is more than I know how to compute, but certainly more than would a simple harvest of asterisks for 60 regression coefficients (Wilkinson, 1990, p. 481).

In short, the results of this humongous study are a muddle. There is no solution to your problem. You wouldn't, of course, write up the study for publication as if the unproductive three quarters of your variables never existed. . . .

The irony is that people who do studies like this often start off with some useful central idea that, if pursued modestly by means of a few highly targeted variables and hypotheses, would likely produce significant results. These could, if propriety or the consequences of early toilet training deemed it necessary, successfully withstand the challenge of a Bonferroni or other experimentwise-adjusted alpha procedure.

A special case of the too-many-variables problem arises in multiple regression-correlation analysis with large numbers of independent variables. As the number of independent variables increases, the chances are that their redundancy in regard to criterion relevance also increases. Because redundancy increases the standard errors of partial regression and correlation coefficients and thus reduces their statistical significance, the results are likely to be zilch.

I have so heavily emphasized the desirability of working with few variables and large sample sizes that some of my students have spread the rumor that my idea of the perfect study is one with 10,000 cases and no variables. They go too far.

A less profound application of the less-is-more principle is to our habits of reporting numerical results. There are computer programs that report by default four, five, or even more decimal places for all numerical results. Their authors might well be excused because, for all the programmer knows, they may be used by atomic scientists. But we social scientists should know better than to repeat our results to so many places. What, pray, does an $r = .12345$ mean? or, for an IQ distribution, a mean of 105.6345? For $N = 100$, the standard error of the r is about .1 and the standard error of the IQ mean about 1.5. Thus, the *345* part of $r = .12345$ is only 3% of its standard error, and the *345* part of the IQ mean of 105.6345 is only 2% of its standard error. These superfluous decimal places are no better than random numbers. They are actually worse than useless because the clutter they create, particularly in tables, serves to distract the eye and mind from the necessary comparisons among the meaningful leading digits. Less is indeed more here.

SIMPLE IS BETTER

I've also learned that simple is better, which is a kind of loose generalization of less is more. The simple-is-better idea is widely applicable to the representation, analysis, and reporting of data.

If, as the old cliché has it, a picture is worth a thousand words, in describing a distribution, a frequency polygon or, better still, a Tukey (1977, pp. 1–26) stem and leaf diagram is usually worth more than the first four moments, that is, the mean, standard deviation, skewness, and kurtosis. I do not question that the moments efficiently summarize the distribution or that they are useful in some analytic contexts. Statistics packages eagerly give them to us and we dutifully publish them, but they do not usually make it possible for most of us or most of the consumers of our products to see the distribution. They don't tell us, for example, that there are no cases between scores of 72 and 90, or that this score of 24 is somewhere in left field, or that there is a pile-up of scores of 9. These are the kinds of features of our data that we surely need to know about, and they become immediately evident with simple graphic representation.

Graphic display is even more important in the case of bivariate data. Underlying each product – moment correlation coefficient in an acre of such coefficients there lies a simple scatter diagram that the r presumes to summarize, and well it might. That is, it does so if the joint distribution is more-or-less bivariate normal—which means, among other things, that the relationship must be linear and that there are no wild outlying points. We know that least squares measures, like means and standard deviations, are sensitive to outliers. Well, Pearson correlations are even more so. About 15 years ago, Wainer and Thissen (1976) published a data set made up of the heights in inches and weights in pounds of 25 subjects, for which the r was a perfectly reasonable .83. But if an error in transcription were made so that the height and weight values for one of the 25 subjects were switched, the r would become −.26, a rather large and costly error!

There is hardly any excuse for gaps, outliers, curvilinearity, or other pathology to exist in our data unbeknownst to us. The same computer statistics package with which we can do very complicated analyses like quasi-Newtonian nonlinear estimation and multidimensional scaling with Guttman's coefficient of alienation also can give us simple scatter plots and stem and leaf diagrams with which we can see our data. A proper multiple regression/correlation analysis does not begin with a matrix of correlation coefficients, means, and standard deviations, but rather with a set of stem and leaf diagrams and scatter plots. We sometimes learn more from what we see than from what we compute; sometimes what we learn from what we see is that we shouldn't compute, at least not on those data as they stand.

Computers are a blessing, but another of the things I have learned is that they are not an unmixed blessing. Forty years ago, before computers

(B.C., that is), for my doctoral dissertation, I did three factor analyses on the 11 subtests of the Wechsler-Bellevue, with samples of 100 cases each of psychoneurotic, schizophrenic, and brain-damaged patients. Working with a pad and pencil, 10-to-the-inch graph paper, a table of products of two-digit numbers, and a Friden electromechanical desk calculator that did square roots "automatically," the whole process took the better part of a year. Nowadays, on a desktop computer, the job is done virtually in microseconds (or at least lickety-split). But another important difference between then and now is that the sheer laboriousness of the task assured that throughout the entire process I was in intimate contact with the data and their analysis. There was no chance that there were funny things about my data or intermediate results that I didn't know about, things that could vitiate my conclusions.

I know that I sound my age, but don't get me wrong—I love computers and revel in the ease with which data analysis is accomplished with a good interactive statistics package like SYSTAT and SYGRAPH (Wilkinson, 1990). I am, however, appalled by the fact that some publishers of statistics packages successfully hawk their wares with the pitch that it isn't necessary to understand statistics to use them. But the same package that makes it possible for an ignoramus to do a factor analysis with a pull-down menu and the click of a mouse also can greatly facilitate with awesome speed and efficiency the performance of simple and informative analyses.

A prime example of the simple-is-better principle is found in the compositing of values. We are taught and teach our students that for purposes of predicting a criterion from a set of predictor variables, assuming for simplicity (and as the mathematicians say, "with no loss of generality"), that all variables are standardized, we achieve maximum linear prediction by doing a multiple regression analysis and forming a composite by weighting the predictor z scores by their betas. It can be shown as a mathematical necessity that with these betas as weights, the resulting composite generates a higher correlation with the criterion in the sample at hand than does a linear composite formed using any other weights.

Yet as a practical matter, most of the time, we are better off using unit weights: $+1$ for positively related predictors, -1 for negatively related predictors, and 0, that is, throw away poorly related predictors (Dawes, 1979; Wainer, 1976). The catch is that the betas come with guarantees to be better than the unit weights only for the sample on which they were determined. (It's almost like a TV set being guaranteed to work only in the store.) But the investigator is not interested in making predictions for that sample—he or she *knows* the criterion values for those cases. The idea is to combine the predictors for maximal prediction for *future* samples. The reason the betas are not likely to be optimal for future samples is that they are likely to have large standard errors. For the typical 100 or 200 cases and 5 or 10 correlated predictors, the unit weights will work as well or better.

Let me offer a concrete illustration to help make the point clear. A running example in our regression text (Cohen & Cohen, 1983) has for a sample of college faculty their salary estimated from four independent variables: years since PhD, sex (coded in the modern manner—1 for female and 0 for male), number of publications, and number of citations. The sample multiple correlation computes to .70. What we want to estimate is the correlation we would get if we used the sample beta weights in the population, the cross-validated multiple correlation, which unfortunately shrinks to a value smaller than the shrunken multiple correlation. For $N = 100$ cases, using Rozeboom's (1978) formula, that comes to .67. Not bad. But using unit weights, we do better: .69. With 300 or 400 cases, the increased sampling stability pushes up the cross-validated correlation, but it remains slightly smaller than the .69 value for unit weights. Increasing sample size to 500 or 600 will increase the cross-validated correlation in this example to the point at which it is larger than the unit-weighted .69, but only trivially, by a couple of points in the *third* decimal! When sample size is only 50, the cross-validated multiple correlation is only .63, whereas the unit weighted correlation remains at .69. The sample size doesn't affect the unit weighted correlation because we don't estimate unstable regression coefficients. It is, of course, subject to sampling error, but so is the cross-validated multiple correlation.

Now, unit weights will not always be as good or better than beta weights. For some relatively rare patterns of correlation (suppression is one), or when the betas vary greatly relative to their mean, or when the ratio of sample size to the number of predictors is as much as 30 to 1 and the multiple correlation is as large as .75, the beta weights may be better, but even in these rare circumstances, probably not much better.

Furthermore, the unit weights work well outside the context of multiple regression where we have criterion data—that is, in a situation in which we wish to measure some concept by combining indicators, or some abstract factor generated in a factor analysis. Unit weights on standardized scores are likely to be better for our purposes than the factor scores generated by the computer program, which are, after all, the fruits of a regression analysis for that sample of the variables on the factor as criterion.

Consider that when we go to predict freshman grade point average from a 30-item test, we don't do a regression analysis to get the "optimal" weights with which to combine the item scores—we just add them up, like Galton did. Simple is better.

We are, however, *not* applying the simple-is-better principle when we "simplify" a multivalued graduated variable (like IQ, or number of children, or symptom severity) by cutting it somewhere along its span and making it into a dichotomy. This is sometimes done with a profession of modesty about the quality or accuracy of the variable, or to "simplify" the analysis. This is not an application, but rather a perversion of simple is better, because this practice is one of willful discarding of information. It has been shown that when you so mutilate a variable, you typically reduce its squared correlation with other variables by about 36% (Cohen, 1983). Don't do it. This kind of simplification is of a piece with the practice of "simplifying" a factorial design ANOVA by reducing all cell sizes to the size of the smallest by dropping cases. They are both ways of throwing away the most precious commodity we deal with: information.

Rather more generally, I think I have begun to learn how to use statistics in the social sciences.

The atmosphere that characterizes statistics as applied in the social and biomedical sciences is that of a secular religion (Salsburg, 1985), apparently of Judeo–Christian derivation, as it employs as its most powerful icon a six-pointed cross, often presented multiply for enhanced authority. I confess that I am an agnostic.

THE FISHERIAN LEGACY

When I began studying statistical inference, I was met with a surprise shared by many neophytes. I found that if, for example, I wanted to see whether poor kids estimated the size of coins to be bigger than did rich kids, after I gathered the data, I couldn't test this research hypothesis, but rather the null hypothesis that poor kids perceived coins to be the same size as did rich kids. This seemed kind of strange and backward to me, but I was rather quickly acculturated (or, if you like, converted, or perhaps brainwashed) to the Fisherian faith that science proceeds only through inductive inference and that inductive inference is achieved chiefly by rejecting null hypotheses, usually at the .05 level. (It wasn't until much later that I learned that the philosopher of science, Karl Popper, 1959, advocated the formulation of falsifiable *research* hypotheses and designing research that could falsify *them*.)

The fact that Fisher's ideas quickly became *the* basis for statistical inference in the behavioral sciences is not surprising — they were very attractive. They offered a deterministic scheme, mechanical and objective, independent of content, and led to clear-cut yes–no decisions. For years, nurtured on the psychological statistics text books of the 1940s and 1950s, I never dreamed that they were the source of bitter controversies (Gigerenzer & Murray, 1987).

Take, for example, the yes–no decision feature. It was quite appropriate to agronomy, which was where Fisher came from. The outcome of an experiment can quite properly be the decision to use this rather than that amount of manure or to plant this or that variety of wheat. But we do not deal in manure, at least not knowingly. Similarly, in other technologies — for example, engineering quality control or education — research is frequently designed to produce decisions. However, things are not quite so clearly decision-oriented in the development of scientific theories.

Next, consider the sanctified (and sanctifying) magic .05 level. This basis for decision has played a remarkable role in the social sciences and in the lives of social scientists. In governing decisions about the status of null hypotheses, it came to determine decisions about the acceptance of doctoral dissertations and the granting of research funding, and about publication, promotion, and whether to have a baby just now. Its arbitrary unreasonable tyranny has led to data fudging of varying degrees of subtlety from grossly altering data to dropping cases where there "must have been" errors.

THE NULL HYPOTHESIS TESTS US

We cannot charge R. A. Fisher with all of the sins of the last half century that have been committed in his name (or more often anonymously but as part of his legacy), but they deserve cataloging (Gigerenzer & Murray, 1987; Oakes, 1986). Over the years, I have learned not to make errors of the following kinds:

When a Fisherian null hypothesis is rejected with an associated probability of, for example, .026, it is *not* the case that the probability that the null hypothesis is true is .026 (or less than .05, or any other value we can specify). Given our framework of probability as long-run relative frequency—as much as we might wish it to be otherwise—this result does not tell us about the truth of the null hypothesis, given the data. (For this we have to go to Bayesian or likelihood statistics, in which probability is not relative frequency but degree of belief.) What it tells us is the probability of the data, given the truth of the null hypothesis—which is not the same thing, as much as it may sound like it.

If the p value with which we reject the Fisherian null hypothesis does not tell us the probability that the null hypothesis is true, it certainly cannot tell us anything about the probability that the *research* or alternate hypothesis is true. In fact, there *is* no alternate hypothesis in Fisher's scheme: Indeed, he violently opposed its inclusion by Neyman and Pearson.

Despite widespread misconceptions to the contrary, the rejection of a given null hypothesis gives us no basis for estimating the probability that a replication of the research will again result in rejecting that null hypothesis.

Of course, everyone knows that failure to reject the Fisherian null hypothesis does not warrant the conclusion that it is true. Fisher certainly knew and emphasized it, and our textbooks duly so instruct us. Yet how often do we read in the discussion and conclusions of articles now appearing in our most prestigious journals that "there is no difference" or "no relationship"? (This is 40 years after my $N = 20$ friend used a nonsignificant result to demolish psychoanalytic theory.)

The other side of this coin is the interpretation that accompanies results that surmount the .05 barrier and achieve the state of grace of "statistical significance." "Everyone" knows that all this means is that the effect is not nil, and nothing more. Yet how often do we see such a result to be taken to mean, at least implicitly, that the effect is *significant,* that is, *important, large.* If a result is *highly* significant, say $p < .001$, the temptation to make this misinterpretation becomes all but irresistible.

Let's take a close look at this null hypothesis—the fulcrum of the Fisherian scheme—that we so earnestly seek to negate. A null hypothesis is any precise statement about a state of affairs in a population, usually the value of a parameter, frequently zero. It is called a "null" hypothesis because the strategy is to nullify it or because it means "nothing doing." Thus, "the difference in the mean scores of U.S. men and women on an Attitude Toward the U.N. scale is zero" is a null hypothesis. "The product–moment r between height and IQ in high school students is zero" is another. "The proportion of men in a population of adult dyslexics is .50" is yet another. Each is a precise statement—for example, if the population r between height and IQ is in fact .03, the null hypothesis that it is zero is false. It is also false if the r is .01, .001, or .000001!

A little thought reveals a fact widely understood among statisticians: The null hypothesis, taken literally (and that's the only way you can take it in formal hypothesis testing), is *always* false in the real world. It can only be true in the bowels of a computer processor running a Monte Carlo study (and even then a stray electron may make it false). If it is false, even to a tiny degree, it must be the case that a large enough sample will produce a significant result and lead to its rejection. So if the null hypothesis is always false, what's the big deal about rejecting it?

Another problem that bothered me was the asymmetry of the Fisherian scheme: If your test exceeded a critical value, you could conclude, subject to the alpha risk, that your null was false, but if you fell short of that critical value, you couldn't conclude that the null was true. In fact, all you could conclude is that you *couldn't* conclude that the null was false. In other words, you could hardly conclude anything.

And yet another problem I had was that if the null were false, it had to be false to some degree. It had to make a difference whether the population mean difference was 5 or 50, or whether the population correlation was .10 or .30, and this was not taken into account in the prevailing method. I had stumbled onto something that I learned after awhile was one of the bases of the Neyman–Pearson critique of Fisher's system of statistical induction.

In 1928 (when I was in kindergarten), Jerzy Neyman and Karl Pearson's boy Egon began publishing papers that offered a rather different perspective on statistical inference (Neyman & Pearson, 1928a, 1928b). Among other things, they argued that rather than having a single hypothesis that one either rejected or not, things could be so organized that one could choose between two hypotheses, one of which could be the null hypothesis and the other an alternate hypothesis. One could attach to the precisely defined null an alpha risk, and to the equally precisely defined alternate hypothesis a beta risk. The rejection of the null hypotheses when it was true was an error of the first kind, controlled by the alpha criterion, but the failure to reject it when the alternate hypothesis was true was also an error, an error of the second kind, which could be controlled to occur at a rate beta. Thus, given the magnitude of the difference between the null and the alternate (that is, given the hypothetical population effect size), and setting values for alpha and beta, one could determine the sample size necessary to meet these conditions. Or, with the effect size, alpha, and the sample size set, one could determine the beta, or its complement, the probability of rejecting the null hypothesis, the power of the test.

Now, R. A. Fisher was undoubtedly the greatest statistician of this century, rightly called "the father of modern statistics," but he had a blind spot. Moreover, he was a stubborn and frequently vicious intellectual opponent. A feud with Karl Pearson had kept Fisher's papers out of *Biometrika*, which Karl Pearson edited. After old-man Pearson retired, efforts by Egon Pearson and Neyman to avoid battling with Fisher were to no avail. Fisher wrote that they were like Russians who thought that "pure science" should be "geared to technological performance" as "in a five-year plan." He once led off the discussion on a paper by Neyman at the Royal Statistical Society by saying that Neyman should have chosen a topic "on which he could speak with authority" (Gigerenzer & Murray, 1987, p. 17). Fisher fiercely condemned the Neyman–Pearson heresy.

I was of course aware of none of this. The statistics texts on which I was raised and their later editions to which I repeatedly turned in the 1950s and 1960s presented null hypothesis testing à la Fisher as a done deal, as *the* way to do statistical inference. The ideas of Neyman and Pearson were barely or not at all mentioned, or dismissed as too complicated.

When I finally stumbled onto power analysis, and managed to overcome the handicap of a background with no working math beyond high school algebra (to say nothing of mathematical statistics), it was as if I had died and gone to heaven. After I learned what noncentral distributions were and figured out that it was important to decompose noncentrality parameters into their constituents of effect size and sample size, I realized that I had a framework for hypothesis testing that had four parameters: the alpha significance criterion, the sample size, the population effect size, and the power of the test. For any statistical test, any one of these was a function of the other three. This meant, for example, that for a significance test of a product–moment correlation, using a two-sided .05 alpha criterion and a sample size of 50 cases, if the population correlation is .30, my long-run probability of rejecting the null hypothesis and finding the sample correlation to be significant was .57, a coin flip. As another example, for the same $\alpha = .05$ and population $r = .30$, if I want to have .80 power, I could determine that I needed a sample size of 85.

Playing with this new toy (and with a small grant from the National Institute of Mental Health) I did what came to be called a meta-analysis of the articles in the 1960 volume of the *Journal of Abnormal and Social Psychology* (Cohen, 1962). I found, among other things, that using the nondirectional .05 criterion, the median power to detect a medium effect was .46—a rather abysmal result. Of course, investigators could not have known how underpowered their research was, as their training had not prepared them to know anything about power, let alone how to use it in research planning. One might think that after 1969, when I published my power handbook that made power analysis as easy as falling off a log, the concepts and methods of power analysis would be taken to the hearts of null hypothesis testers. So one might think. (Stay tuned.)

Among the less obvious benefits of power analysis was that it made it possible to "prove" null hypotheses. Of course, as I've already noted, everyone knows that one can't actually prove null hypotheses. But when an investigator means to prove a null hypothesis, the point is not to demonstrate that the population effect size is, say, zero to a million or more decimal places, but rather to show that it is of no more than negligible or trivial size (Cohen, 1988, pp. 16 – 17). Then, from a power analysis at, say, $\alpha = .05$, with power set at, say, .95, so that $\beta = .05$, also, the sample size necessary to detect this negligible effect with .95 probability can be determined. Now if the research is carried out using that sample size, and the result is *not* significant, as there had been a .95 chance of detecting this negligible effect, and the effect was *not* detected, the conclusion is justified that no nontrivial effect exists, at the $\beta = .05$ level. This does, in fact, probabilistically prove the intended null hypothesis of no more than a trivially small effect. The reasoning is impeccable, but when you go to apply it, you discover that it takes enormous sample sizes to do so. For example, if we adopt the above parameters for a significance test of a correlation coefficient and $r = .10$ is taken as a negligible effect size, it requires a sample of almost 1,300 cases. More modest but still reasonable demands for power of course require smaller sample sizes, but not sufficiently smaller to matter for most investigators—even .80 power to detect a population correlation of .10 requires almost 800 cases. So it generally takes an impractically large sample size to prove the null hypothesis as I've redefined it; however, the procedure makes clear what it takes to say or imply from the failure to reject the null hypothesis that there is no nontrivial effect.

A salutary effect of power analysis is that it draws one forcibly to consider the magnitude of effects. In psychology, and especially in soft psychology, under the sway of the Fisherian scheme, there has been little consciousness of how big things are. The very popular ANOVA designs yield F ratios, and it is these whose size is of concern. First off is the question of whether they made the sanctifying .05 cut-off and are thus significant, and then how far they fell below this cut-off: Were they perhaps *highly significant* (*p* less than .01) or *very highly significant* (less than .001)? Because science is inevitably about magnitudes, it is not surprising how frequently *p* values are treated as surrogates for effect sizes.

One of the things that drew me early to correlation analysis was that it yielded an *r*, a measure of effect size, which was then translated into a *t* or *F* and assessed for significance, whereas the analysis of variance or covariance yielded only an *F* and told me nothing about effect size. As many of the variables with which we worked were expressed in arbitrary units (points on a scale, trials to learn a maze), and the Fisherian scheme seemed quite complete by itself and made no demands on us to think about effect sizes, we simply had no language with which to address them.

In retrospect, it seems to me simultaneously quite understandable yet also ridiculous to try to develop theories about human behavior with *p* values from Fisherian hypothesis testing and no more than a primitive sense of effect size. And I wish I were talking about the long, long ago. In 1986, there appeared in the *New York Times* a UPI dispatch under the headline "Children's Height Linked to Test Scores." The article described a study that involved nearly 14,000 children 6 to 17 years of age that reported a *definite* link between height (age- and sex-adjusted) and scores on tests of both intelligence and achievement. The relationship was described as significant, and persisting, even after controlling for other factors, including socioeconomic status, birth order, family size, and physical maturity. The authors noted that the effect was small, but *significant,* and that it didn't warrant giving children growth hormone to make them taller and thus brighter. They speculated that the effect might be due to treating shorter children as less mature, but that there were alternative biological explanations.

Now this was a newspaper story, the fruit of the ever-inquiring mind of a science reporter, not a journal article, so perhaps it is understandable that there was no effort to deal with the actual size of this small effect. But it got me to wondering about how small this significant relationship might be. Well, if we take significant to mean $p < .001$ (in the interest of scientific tough-mindedness), it turns out that a correlation of .0278 is significant for 14,000 cases. But I've found that when dealing with variables expressed in units whose magnitude we understand, the effect size in linear relationships is better comprehended with regression than with correlation coefficients. So, accepting the authors' implicit causal model, it works out that raising a child's IQ from 100 to 130 would require giving the child enough growth hormone to increase his or her height by 14 ft (more or less). If the causality goes the other way, and one wanted to create basketball players, a 4-in. increase in height would require raising the IQ about 900 points. Well, they said it was a small effect. (When I later checked the journal article that described this research, it turned out that the correlation was much larger than .0278. It was actually about .11, so that for a 30-point increase in IQ it would take only enough growth hormone to produce a 3.5-ft increase in height, or with the causality reversed, a 4-in. increase in height would require an increase of only 233 IQ points.)

I am happy to say that the long neglect of attention to effect size seems to be coming to a close. The clumsy and fundamentally invalid box-score method of literature review based on p values is being replaced by effect-size-based meta-analysis as formulated by Gene Glass (1977). The effect size measure most often used is the standardized mean difference d of power analysis. Several book-length treatments of meta-analysis have been published, and applications to various fields of psychology are appearing in substantial numbers in the *Psychological Bulletin* and other prestigious publications. In the typical meta-analysis, the research literature on some issue is surveyed and the effect sizes that were found in the relevant studies are gathered. Note that the observational unit is the study. These data do not only provide an estimate of the level and variability of the effect size in a domain based on multiple studies and therefore on many observations, but by relating effect size to various substantive and methodological characteristics over the studies, much can be learned about the issue under investigation and how best to investigate it. One hopes that this ferment may persuade researchers to explicitly report effect sizes and thus reduce the burden on meta-analysts and others of having to make assumptions to dig them out of their inadequately reported research results. In a field as scattered (not to say anarchic) as ours, meta-analysis constitutes a welcome force toward the cumulation of knowledge. Meta-analysis makes me very happy.

Despite my career-long identification with statistical inference, I believe, together with such luminaries as Meehl (1978), Tukey (1977), and Gigerenzer (Gigerenzer & Murray, 1987), that hypothesis testing has been greatly overemphasized in psychology and in the other disciplines that use it. It has diverted our attention from crucial issues. Mesmerized by a single all-purpose, mechanized, "objective" ritual in which we convert numbers into other numbers and get a yes—no answer, we have come to neglect close scrutiny of where the numbers came from. Recall that in his delightful parable about averaging the numbers of football jerseys, Lord (1953) pointed out that "the numbers don't know where they came from." But surely *we* must know where they came from and should be far more concerned with why and what and how well we are measuring, manipulating conditions, and selecting our samples.

We have also lost sight of the fact that the error variance in our observations should challenge us to efforts to reduce it and not simply to thoughtlessly tuck it into the denominator of an F or t test.

HOW TO USE STATISTICS

So, how would I use statistics in psychological research? First of all, descriptively. John Tukey's (1977) *Exploratory Data Analysis* is an inspiring account of how to effect graphic and numerical analyses of the data at hand so as to understand *them*. The techniques, although subtle in conception, are simple in application, requiring no more than pencil and paper (Tukey says if you have a hand-held calculator, fine). Although he recognizes the importance of what he calls confirmation (statistical inference), he manages to fill 700 pages with techniques of "mere" description, pointing out in the preface that the emphasis on inference in modern statistics has resulted in a loss of flexibility in data analysis.

Then, in planning research, I think it wise to *plan* the research. This means making tentative informed judgments about, among many other things, the size of the population effect or effects you're chasing, the level of alpha risk you want to take (conveniently, but not necessarily .05), and the power you want (usually some relatively large value like .80). These specified, it is a simple matter to determine the sample size you need. It is then a good idea to rethink your specifications. If, as is often the case, this sample size is beyond your resources, consider the possibility of reducing your power demand or, perhaps the effect size, or even (heaven help us) increasing your alpha level. Or, the required sample may be smaller than you can comfortably manage, which also should lead you to rethink and possibly revise your original specifications. This process ends when you have a credible and viable set of specifications, or when you discover that no practicable set is possible and the research as originally conceived must be abandoned. Although you would hardly expect it from reading the current literature, failure to subject your research plans to power analysis is simply irrational.

Next, I have learned and taught that the primary product of a research inquiry is one or more measures of effect size, not *p* values (Cohen, 1965). Effect-size measures include mean differences (raw or standardized), correlations and squared correlation of all kinds, odds ratios, kappas—whatever conveys the magnitude of the phenomenon of interest appropriate to the research context. If, for example, you are comparing groups on a variable measured in units that are well understood by your readers (IQ points, or dollars, or number of children, or months of survival), mean differences are excellent measures of effect size. When this isn't the case, and it isn't the case more often than it is, the results can be translated into standardized mean differences (*d* values) or some measure of correlation or association (Cohen, 1988). (Not that we understand as well as we should the meaning of a given level of correlation [Oakes, 1986, pp. 88–92]. It has been shown that psychologists typically overestimate how much relationship a given correlation represents, thinking of a correlation of .50 not as its square of .25 that its proportion of

420 *JACOB COHEN*

variance represents, but more like its cube root of about .80, which represents only wishful thinking! But that's another story.)

Then, having found the sample effect size, you can attach a p value to it, but it is far more informative to provide a confidence interval. As you know, a confidence interval gives the range of values of the effect-size index that includes the population value with a given probability. It tells you incidentally whether the effect is significant, but much more—it provides an estimate of the range of values it might have, surely a useful piece of knowledge in a science that presumes to be quantitative. (By the way, I don't think that we should routinely use 95% intervals: Our interests are often better served by more tolerant 80% intervals.)

Remember that throughout the process in which you conceive, plan, execute, and write up a research, it is on your informed judgment as a scientist that you must rely, and this holds as much for the statistical aspects of the work as it does for all the others. This means that your informed judgment governs the setting of the parameters involved in the planning (alpha, beta, population effect size, sample size, confidence interval), and that informed judgment also governs the conclusions you will draw.

In his brilliant analysis of what he called the "inference revolution" in psychology, Gerd Gigerenzer showed how and why no single royal road of drawing conclusions from data is possible, and particularly not one that does not strongly depend on the substantive issues concerned—that is, on everything that went into the research besides the number crunching. An essential ingredient in the research process is the judgment of the scientist. He or she must decide by how much a theoretical proposition has been advanced by the data, just as he or she decided what to study, what data to get, and how to get it. I believe that statistical inference applied with informed judgment is a useful tool in this process, but it isn't the most important tool: It is not as important as everything that came before it. Some scientists, physicists for example, manage without the statistics, although to be sure not without the informed judgment. Indeed, some pretty good psychologists have managed without statistical inference: There come to mind Wundt, Kohler, Piaget, Lewin, Bartlett, Stevens, and if you'll permit me, Freud, among others. Indeed, Skinner (1957) thought of dedicating his book *Verbal Behavior* (and I quote) "to the statisticians and scientific methodologists with whose help this book would never have been completed" (p. 111). I submit that the proper application of statistics by sensible statistical methodologists (Tukey, for example) would not have hurt Skinner's work. It might even have done it some good.

The implications of the things I have learned (so far) are not consonant with much of what I see about me as standard statistical practice. The prevailing yes–no decision at the magic .05 level from a single research is a far cry from the use of informed judgment. Science simply doesn't work that way.

A successful piece of research doesn't conclusively settle an issue, it just makes some theoretical propositions to some degree more likely. Only successful future replication in the same and different settings (as might be found through meta-analysis) provides an approach to settling the issue. How much more likely this single research makes the proposition depends on many things, but not on whether p is equal to or greater than .05; .05 is not a cliff but a convenient reference point along the possibility–probability continuum. There is no ontological basis for dichotomous decision making in psychological inquiry. The point was neatly made by Rosnow and Rosenthal (1989) last year in the *American Psychologist*. They wrote "surely, God loves the .06 nearly as much as the .05" (p. 1277). To which I say amen!

Finally, I have learned, but not easily, that things take time. As I've already mentioned, almost three decades ago, I published a power survey of the articles in the 1960 volume of the *Journal of Abnormal and Social Psychology* (Cohen, 1962) in which I found that the median power to detect a medium effect size under representative conditions was only .46. The first edition of my power handbook came out in 1969. Since then, more than two dozen power and effect-size surveys have been published in psychology and related fields (Cohen, 1988, pp. xi–xii). There have also been a slew of articles on power-analytic methodology. Statistics textbooks, even some undergraduate ones, give some space to power analysis, and several computer programs for power analysis are available (e.g., Borenstein & Cohen, 1988). They tell me that some major funding entities require that their grant applications contain power analyses, and that in one of those agencies my power book can be found in every office.

The problem is that, as practiced, current research hardly reflects much attention to power. How often have you seen any mention of power in the journals you read, let alone an actual power analysis in the methods sections of the articles? Last year in *Psychological Bulletin*, Sedlmeier and Gigerenzer (1989) published an article entitled "Do Studies of Statistical Power Have an Effect on the Power of Studies?". The answer was no. Using the same methods I had used on the articles in the 1960 *Journal of Abnormal and Social Psychology* (Cohen, 1962), they performed a power analysis on the 1984 *Journal of Abnormal Psychology* and found that the median power under the same conditions was .44, a little worse than the .46 I had found 24 years earlier. It was worse still (.37) when they took into account the occasional use of an experimentwise alpha criterion. Even worse than that, in some 11% of the studies, research hypotheses were framed as null hypotheses and their nonsignificance interpreted as confirmation. The median power of these studies to detect a medium effect at the two-tailed .05 level was .25! These are not isolated results: Rossi, Rossi, and Cottrill (in press), using the same methods, did a power survey of the 142 articles in the 1982 volumes of the *Journal of Personality and Social Psychology* and the *Journal of Abnormal Psychology* and found essentially the same results.

A less egregious example of the inertia of methodological advance is set correlation, which is a highly flexible realization of the multivariate general linear model. I published it in an article in 1982, and we included it in an appendix in the 1983 edition of our regression text (Cohen, 1982; Cohen & Cohen, 1983). Set correlation can be viewed as a generalization of multiple correlation to the multivariate case, and with it you can study the relationship between anything and anything else, controlling for whatever you want in either the anything or the anything else, or both. I think it's a great method; at least, my usually critical colleagues haven't complained. Yet, as far as I'm aware, it has hardly been used outside the family. (The publication of a program as a SYSTAT supplementary module [Cohen, 1989] may make a difference.)

But I do not despair. I remember that W. S. Gosset, the fellow who worked in a brewery and appeared in print modestly as "Student," published the t test a decade before we entered World War I, and the test didn't get into the psychological statistics textbooks until after World War II.

These things take time. So, if you publish something that you think is really good, and a year or a decade or two go by and hardly anyone seems to have taken notice, remember the t test, and take heart.

REFERENCES

Borenstein, M., & Cohen, J. (1988). *Statistical power analysis: A computer program*. Hillsdale, NJ: Erlbaum.

Children's height linked to test scores. (1986, October 7). *New York Times*, p. C4.

Cohen, J. (1962). The statistical power of abnormal-social psychological research: A review. *Journal of Abnormal and Social Psychology, 65*, 145–153.

Cohen, J. (1965). Some statistical issues in psychological research. In B. B. Wolman (Ed.), *Handbook of clinical psychology* (pp. 95–121). New York: McGraw-Hill.

Cohen, J. (1982). Set correlation as a general multivariate data-analytic method. *Multivariate Behavioral Research, 17*, 301–341.

Cohen, J. (1983). The cost of dichotomization. *Applied Psychological Measurement, 7*, 249–253.

Cohen, J. (1988). *Statistical power analysis for the behavioral sciences* (2nd ed.). Hillsdale, NJ: Erlbaum.

Cohen, J. (1989). *SETCOR: Set correlation analysis, a supplementary module for SYSTAT and SYGRAPH*. Evanston, IL: SYSTAT.

Cohen, J., & Cohen, P. (1983). *Applied multiple regression/correlation analysis for the behavioral sciences* (2nd ed.). Hillsdale, NJ: Erlbaum.

Dawes, R. M. (1979). The robust beauty of improper linear models in decision making. *American Psychologist, 34*, 571–582.

Gigerenzer, G., & Murray, D. J. (1987). *Cognition as intuitive statistics*. Hillsdale, NJ: Erlbaum.

Glass, G. V. (1977). Integrating findings: The meta-analysis of research. In L. Shulman (Ed.), *Review of research in education* (Vol. 5, pp. 351–379). Itasca, IL: Peacock.

Lord, F. M. (1953). On the statistical treatment of football numbers. *American Psychologist, 8*, 750–751.

Meehl, P. E. (1978). Theoretical risks and tabular asterisks: Sir Karl, Sir Ronald, and the slow progress of soft psychology. *Journal of Consulting and Clinical Psychology, 46*, 806–834.

Neyman, J., & Pearson, E. (1928a). On the use and interpretation of certain test criteria for purposes of statistical inference: Part I. *Biometrika, 20A*, 175–240.

Neyman, J., & Pearson, E. (1928b). On the use and interpretation of certain test criteria for purposes of statistical inference: Part II. *Biometrika, 20A*, 263–294.

Oakes, M. (1986). *Statistical inference: A commentary for the social and behavioral sciences*. New York: Wiley.

Popper, K. (1959). *The logic of scientific discovery*. New York: Basic Books.

Rosnow, R. L., & Rosenthal, R. (1989). Statistical procedures and the justification of knowledge in psychological science. *American Psychologist, 44*, 1276–1284.

Rossi, J. S., Rossi, S. R., & Cottrill, S. D. (in press). Statistical power in research in social and abnormal psychology. *Journal of Consulting and Clinical Psychology*.

Rozeboom, W. W. (1978). Estimation of cross-validated multiple correlation: A clarification. *Psychological Bulletin, 85*, 1348–1351.

Salsburg, D. S. (1985). The religion of statistics as practiced in medical journals. *American Statistician, 39*, 220–223.

Sedlmeier, P., & Gigerenzer, G. (1989). Do studies of statistical power have an effect on the power of studies? *Psychological Bulletin, 105*, 309–316.

Skinner, B. F. (1957). *Verbal behavior*. New York: Appleton-Century-Crofts.

Tukey, J. W. (1977). *Exploratory data analysis*. Reading, MA: Addison-Wesley.

Wainer, H. (1976). Estimating coefficients in linear models: It don't make no nevermind. *Psychological Bulletin, 83*, 213–217.

Wainer, H., & Thissen, D. (1976). When jackknifing fails (or does it?). *Psychometrika, 41*, 9–34.

Wilkinson, L. (1990). *SYSTAT: The system for statistics*. Evanston, IL: SYSTAT.

NULL HYPOTHESES
AND STATISTICAL
SIGNIFICANCE TESTING

18

A POWER PRIMER

JACOB COHEN

The preface to the first edition of my power handbook (Cohen, 1969) begins:

> During my first dozen years of teaching and consulting on applied statistics with behavioral scientists, I became increasingly impressed with the importance of statistical power analysis, an importance which was increased an order of magnitude by its neglect in our textbooks and curricula. The case for its importance is easily made: What behavioral scientist would view with equanimity the question of the probability that his investigation would lead to statistically significant results, i.e., its power? (p. vii)

This neglect was obvious through casual observation and had been confirmed by a power review of the 1960 volume of the *Journal of Abnormal and Social Psychology*, which found the mean power to detect medium effect sizes to be .48 (Cohen, 1962). Thus, the chance of obtaining a significant result was about that of tossing a head with a fair coin. I attributed this disregard of

Reprinted from *Psychological Bulletin, 112*, 155–159. Copyright 1992 by the American Psychological Association.

power to the inaccessibility of a meager and mathematically difficult literature, beginning with its origin in the work of Neyman and Pearson (1928, 1933).

The power handbook was supposed to solve the problem. It required no more background than an introductory psychological statistics course that included significance testing. The exposition was verbal–intuitive and carried largely by many worked examples drawn from across the spectrum of behavioral science.

In the ensuing two decades, the book has been through revised (1977) and second (1988) editions and has inspired dozens of power and effect-size surveys in many areas of the social and life sciences (Cohen, 1988, pp. xi–xii). During this period, there has been a spate of articles on power analysis in the social science literature, a baker's dozen of computer programs (reviewed in Goldstein, 1989), and a breakthrough into popular statistics textbooks (Cohen, 1988, pp. xii–xiii).

Sedlmeier and Gigerenzer (1989) reported a power review of the 1984 volume of the *Journal of Abnormal Psychology* (some 24 years after mine) under the title, "Do Studies of Statistical Power Have an Effect on the Power of Studies?" The answer was no. Neither their study nor the dozen other power reviews they cite (excepting those fields in which large sample sizes are used, e.g., sociology, market research) showed any material improvement in power. Thus, a quarter century has brought no increase in the probability of obtaining a significant result.

Why is this? There is no controversy among methodologists about the importance of power analysis, and there are ample accessible resources for estimating sample sizes in research planning using power analysis. My 2-decades-long expectation that methods sections in research articles in psychological journals would invariably include power analyses has not been realized. Indeed, they almost invariably do not. Of the 54 articles Sedlmeier and Gigerenzer (1989) reviewed, only 2 mentioned power, and none estimated power or necessary sample size or the population effect size they posited. In 7 of the studies, null hypotheses served as research hypotheses that were confirmed when the results were nonsignificant. Assuming a medium effect size, the median power for these tests was .25! Thus, these authors concluded that their research hypotheses of no effect were supported when they had only a .25 chance of rejecting these null hypotheses in the presence of substantial population effects.

It is not at all clear why researchers continue to ignore power analysis. The passive acceptance of this state of affairs by editors and reviewers is even more of a mystery. At least part of the reason may be the low level of consciousness about effect size: It is as if the only concern about magnitude in much psychological research is with regard to the statistical test result and its accompanying p value, not with regard to the psychological phenomenon under study. Sedlmeier and Gigerenzer (1989) attribute this to the accident of the historical precedence of Fisherian theory, its hybridization with the contradictory Neyman–Pearson theory, and the apparent completeness of Fisherian null hypothesis testing: objective, mechanical, and a clear-cut go–no-go decision straddled over $p = .05$. I have suggested that the neglect of power analysis simply exemplifies the slow movement of methodological advance (Cohen, 1988, p. xiv), noting that it took some 40 years from Student's publication of the t test to its inclusion of psychological statistics textbooks (Cohen, 1990, p. 1311).

An associate editor of this journal suggests another reason: Researchers find too complicated, or do not have at hand, either my book or other reference material for power analysis. He suggests that a short rule-of-thumb treatment of necessary sample size might make a difference. Hence this article.

In this bare bones treatment, I cover only the simplest cases, the most common designs and tests, and only three levels of effect size. For readers who find this inadequate, I unhesitatingly recommend *Statistic Power Analysis for the Behavioral Sciences* (Cohen, 1988; hereafter SPABS). It covers special cases, one-sided tests, unequal sample sizes, other null hypotheses, set correlation and multivariate methods and gives substantive examples of small, medium, and large effect sizes for the various tests. It offers well over 100 worked illustrative examples and is as user friendly as I know how to make it, the technical material being relegated to an appendix.

METHOD

Statistical power analysis exploits the relationships among the four variables involved in statistical inference: sample size (N), significance criterion (α), population effect size (ES), and statistical power. For any statistical model, these relationships are such that each is a function of the other three. For example, in power reviews, for any given statistical test, we can determine power for given α, N, and ES. For research planning, however, it is most useful to determine the N necessary to have a specified power for given α and ES; this article addresses this use.

The Significance Criterion, α

The risk of mistakenly rejecting the null hypothesis (H_o) and thus of committing a Type I error, α, represents a policy: the maximum risk attending such a rejection. Unless otherwise stated (and it rarely is), it is taken to equal .05 (part of the Fisherian legacy; Cohen, 1990). Other values may of course be selected. For example, in studies testing several H_0s, it is recommended that $\alpha = .01$ per hypothesis in order that the experimentwise risk (i.e., the risk of any false rejections) not become too large. Also, for tests whose parameters may be either positive or negative, the α risk may be defined as two sided or one sided. The many tables in SPABS provide for both kinds, but the sample sizes provided in this note are all for two-sided tests at $\alpha = .01$, $.05$, and $.10$, the last for circumstances in which a less rigorous standard for rejection is desired, as, for example, in exploratory studies. For unreconstructed one tailers (see Cohen, 1965), the tabled sample sizes provide close approximations for one-sided tests at $\frac{1}{2}\alpha$ (e.g., the sample sizes tabled under $\alpha = .10$ may be used for one-sided tests at $\alpha = .05$).

Power

The statistical power of a significance test is the long-term probability, given the population ES, α, and N of rejecting H_0. When the ES is not equal to zero, H_0 is false, so failure to reject it also incurs an error. This is a Type II error, and for any given ES, α, and N, its probability of occurring is β. Power is thus $1 - \beta$, the probability of rejecting a false H_0.

In this treatment, the only specification for power is .80 (so $\beta = .20$), a convention proposed for general use. (SPABS provides for 11 levels of power in most of its N tables.) A materially smaller value than .80 would incur too great a risk of a Type II error. A materially larger value would result in a demand for N that is likely to exceed the investigator's resources. Taken with the conventional $\alpha = .05$, power of .80 results in a $\beta:\alpha$ ratio of $4:1$ (.20 to .05) of the two kinds of risks. (See SPABS, pp. 53–56.)

Sample Size

In research planning, the investigator needs to know the N necessary to attain the desired power for the specified α and hypothesized ES. N increases with an increase in power desired, a decrease in the ES, and a decrease in α. For statistical tests involving two or more groups, N as here defined is the necessary sample size for *each* group.

Effect Size

Researchers find specifying the ES the most difficult part of power analysis. As suggested above, the difficulty is at least partly due to the generally low level of consciousness of the magnitude of phenomena that characterizes much of psychology. This in turn may help explain why, despite the stricture of methodologists, significance testing is so heavily preferred to confidence interval estimation, although the wide intervals that usually result may also play a role (Cohen, 1990). However, neither the determination of power or necessary sample size can proceed without the investigator having some idea about the degree to which the H_0 is believed to be false (i.e., the ES).

In the Neyman–Pearson method of statistical inference, in addition to the specification of H_0, an alternate hypothesis (H_1) is counterpoised against H_0. The degree to which H_0 is false is indexed by the discrepancy between H_0 and H_1 and is called the ES. Each statistical test has its own ES index. All the indexes are scale free and continuous, ranging upward from zero, and for all, the H_0 is that ES = 0. For example, for testing the product–moment correlation of a sample for significance, the ES is simply the population r, so H_0 posits that $r = 0$. As another example, for testing the significance of the departure of a population proportion (P) from .50, the ES index is $g = P - .50$, so the H_0 is that $g = 0$. For the tests of the significance of the difference between independent means, correlation coefficients, and proportions, the H_0 is that the difference equals zero. Table 18.1 gives for each of the tests the definition of its ES index.

To convey the meaning of any given ES index, it is necessary to have some idea of its scale. To this end, I have proposed as conventions or operational definitions small, medium, and large values for each that are at least approximately consistent across the different ES indexes. My intent was that medium ES represent an effect likely to be visible to the naked eye of a careful observer. (It has since been noted in effect-size surveys that it approxi-

TABLE 18.1
ES Indexes and Their Values for Small, Medium,
and Large Effects

Test	ES Index	Effect size		
		Small	Medium	Large
1. m_A vs. m_B for independent means	$d = \dfrac{m_A - m_B}{\sigma}$	.20	.50	.80
2. Significance of product-moment r	r	.10	.30	.50
3. r_A vs. r_B for independent rs	$q = z_A - z_B$ where z = Fisher's z	.10	.30	.50
4. $P = .5$ and the sign test	$g = P - .50$	.05	.15	.25
5. P_A vs. P_B for independent proportions	$h\ \phi_A - \phi_B$ where ϕ = arcsine transformation	.20	.50	.80
6. Chi-square for goodness of fit and contingency	$w = \sqrt{\sum\limits_{j=1}^{k} \dfrac{(P_{1i} - P_{0i})^2}{P_{0i}}}$	.10	.30	.50
7. One-way analysis of variance	$f = \dfrac{\sigma_m}{\sigma}$	.10	.25	.40
8. Multiple and multiple partial correlation	$f^2 = \dfrac{R^2}{1 - R^2}$	.02	.15	.35

Note: ES = population effect size.

mates the average size of observed effects in various fields.) I set small ES to be noticeably smaller than medium but not so small as to be trivial, and I set large ES to be the same distance above medium as small was below it. Although the definitions were made subjectively, with some early minor adjustments, these conventions have been fixed since the 1977 edition of SPABS and have come into general use. Table 18.1 contains these values for the tests considered here.

In the present treatment, the H_1s are the ESs that operationally define small, medium, and large effects as given in Table 18.1. For the test of the significance of a sample r, for example, because the ES for this test is simply the alternate-hypothetical population r, small, medium, and large ESs are respectively .10, .30, and .50. The ES index for the t test of the difference between independent means is d, the difference expressed in units of (i.e., divided by) the within-population standard deviation. For this test, the H_0 is that $d = 0$ and the small, medium, and large ESs (or H_1s) are $d = .20, .50$, and .80. Thus, an operationally defined medium difference between means is half a standard deviation; concretely, for IQ scores in which the population standard deviation is 15, a medium difference between means is 7.5 IQ points.

STATISTICAL TESTS

The tests covered here are the most common tests used in psychological research:

1. The t test for the difference between two independent means, with $df = 2(N - 1)$.
2. The t test for the significance of a product-moment correlation coefficient r, with $df = N - 2$.
3. The test for the difference between two independent rs, accomplished as a normal curve test through the Fisher z transformation of r (tabled in many statistical texts).
4. The binomial distribution or, for large samples, the normal curve (or equivalent chi-square, 1 df) test that a population proportion $(P) = .50$. This test is also used in the nonparametric sign test for differences between paired observations.
5. The normal curve test for the difference between two independent proportions, accomplished through the arcsine transformation ϕ (tabled in many statistical texts). The results are effectively the same when the test is made using the chi-square test with 1 degree of freedom.
6. The chi-square test for goodness of fit (one way) or association in two-way contingency tables. In Table 18.1, k is the number

TABLE 18.2
N For Small, Medium, and Large ES at Power = .80
for α = .01, .05, and .10

| | α | | | | | | | | |
| | .01 | | | .05 | | | .10 | | |
Test	Sm	Med	Lg	Sm	Med	Lg	Sm	Med	Lg
1. Mean dif	586	95	38	393	64	26	310	50	20
2. Sig r	1,163	125	41	783	85	28	617	68	22
3. r dif	2,339	263	96	1,573	177	66	1,240	140	52
4. P = .5	1,165	127	44	783	85	30	616	67	23
5. P dif	584	93	36	392	63	25	309	49	19
6. χ^2									
1df	1,168	130	38	785	87	26	618	69	25
2df	1,388	154	56	964	107	39	771	86	31
3df	1,546	172	62	1,090	121	44	880	98	35
4df	1,675	186	67	1,194	133	48	968	108	39
5df	1,787	199	71	1,293	143	51	1,045	116	42
6df	1,887	210	75	1,362	151	54	1,113	124	45
7. ANOVA									
2g[a]	586	95	38	393	64	26	310	50	20
3g[a]	464	76	30	322	52	21	258	41	17
4g[a]	388	63	25	274	45	18	221	36	15
5g[a]	336	55	22	240	39	16	193	32	13
6g[a]	299	49	20	215	35	14	174	28	12
7g[a]	271	44	18	195	32	13	159	26	11
8. Mult R									
2k[b]	698	97	45	481	67	30			
3k[b]	780	108	50	547	76	34			
4k[b]	841	118	55	599	84	38			
5k[b]	901	126	59	645	91	42			
6k[b]	953	134	63	686	97	45			
7k[b]	998	141	66	726	102	48			
8k[b]	1,039	147	69	757	107	50			

Note: ES = population effect size, Sm = small, Med = medium, Lg = large, diff = difference, ANOVA = analysis of variance. Tests numbered as in Table 1.
[a] Number of groups.   [b] Number of independent variables.

of cells and P_{0i} and P_{1i} are the null hypothetical and alternate hypothetical population proportions in cell i. (Note that w's structure is the same as chi-square's for cell sample frequencies.) For goodness-of-fit tests, the $df = k - 1$, and for contingency tables, $df = (a - 1)(b - 1)$, where a and b are the number of levels in the two variables. Table 18.2 provides (total) sample sizes for 1 through 6 degrees of freedom.

7. One-way analysis of variance. Assuming equal sample sizes (as we do throughout), for g groups, the F test has $df = g - 1$, $g(N - 1)$. The ES index is the standard deviation of the g population means divided by the common within-population standard deviation. Provision is made in Table 18.2 for 2 through 7 groups.

8. Multiple and multiple partial correlation. For k independent variables, the significance test is the standard F test for $df = k$, $N - k - 1$. The ES index, f^2, is defined for either squared multiple or squared multiple partial correlations (R^2). Table 18.2 provides for 2 through 8 independent variables.

Note that because all tests of population parameters that can be either positive or negative (Tests 1–5) are two-sided, their ES indexes here are absolute values.

In using the material that follows, keep in mind that the ES posited by the investigator is what he or she believes holds for the population and that the sample size that is found is conditional on the ES. Thus, if a study is planned in which the investigator believes that a population r is of medium size (ES $= r = .30$ from Table 18.1) and the t test is to be performed with two-sided $\alpha = .05$, then the power of this test is .80 if the sample size is 85 (from Table 18.2). If, using 85 cases, t is not significant, then either r is smaller than .30 or the investigator has been the victim of the .20 (β) risk of making a Type II error.

EXAMPLES

The necessary N for power of .80 for the following examples are found in Table 18.2.

1. To detect a medium difference between two independent sample means ($d = .50$ in Table 18.1) at $\alpha = .05$ requires $N = 64$ in each group. (A d of .50 is equivalent to a point-biserial correlation of .243; see SPABS, pp. 22–24.)
2. For a significance test of a sample r at $\alpha = .01$, when the population r is large (.50 in Table 18.2), a sample size $= 41$ is required. At $\alpha = .05$, the necessary sample size $= 28$.
3. To detect a medium-sized difference between two population rs ($q = .30$ in Table 18.1) at $\alpha = .05$ requires $N = 177$ in each group. (The following pairs of rs yield $q = .30$: .00, .29; .20, .46; .40, .62; .60, .76; .80, .89; .90, .94; see SPABS, pp. 113–116.)
4. The sign test tests the H_0 that .50 of a population of paired differences are positive. If the population proportion's departure from .50 is medium ($q = .15$ in Table 18.1), at $\alpha = .10$, the necessary $N = 67$; at $\alpha = .05$, it is 85.
5. To detect a small difference between two independent population proportions ($h = .20$ in Table 18.1) at $\alpha = .05$ requires $N = 392$ cases in each group. (The following pairs of Ps yield approximate values of $h = .20$: .05, .10; .20, .29; .40, .50; .60, .70; .80, .87; .90, .95; see SPABS, p. 184f.)

6. A 3×4 contingency table has 6 degrees of freedom. To detect a medium degree of association in the population ($w = .30$ in Table 18.1) at $\alpha = .05$ required $N = 151$. ($w = .30$ corresponds to a contingency coefficient of .287, and for 6 degrees of freedom, a Cramèr ϕ of .212; see SPABS, pp. 220–227).

7. A psychologist considers alternate research plans involving comparisons of the means of either three or four groups in both of which she believes that the ES is medium ($f = .25$ in Table 18.1). She finds that at $\alpha = .05$, the necessary sample size per group is 52 cases for the three-group plan and 45 cases for the four-group plan, thus, total sample sizes of 156 and 180. (When $f = .25$, the proportion of variance accounted for by group membership is .0588; see SPABS, pp. 280–284.)

8. A psychologist plans a research in which he will do a multiple regression/correlation analysis and perform all the significance tests at $\alpha = .01$. For the F test of the multiple R^2, he expects a medium ES, that is, $f^2 = .15$ (from Table 18.1). He has a candidate set of eight independent variables for which Table 18.2 indicates that the required sample size is 147, which exceeds his resources. However, from his knowledge of the research area, he believes that the information in the eight variables can be effectively summarized in three. For three variables, the necessary sample size is only 108. (Given the relationship between f^2 and R^2, the values for small, medium, and large R^2 are respectively .0196, .1304, and .2592, and for R, .14, .36, and .51; see SPABS, pp. 410–414.)

REFERENCES

Cohen, J. (1962). The statistical power of abnormal–social psychological research: A review. *Journal of Abnormal and Social Psychology*, 65, 145–153.

Cohen, J. (1965). Some statistical issues in psychological research. In B. B. Wolman (Ed.), *Handbook of clinical psychology* (pp. 95–121). New York: McGraw-Hill.

Cohen, J. (1969). *Statistical power analysis for the behavioral sciences*. San Diego, CA: Academic Press.

Cohen, J. (1988). *Statistical power analysis for the behavioral sciences* (2nd ed.). Hillsdale, NJ: Erlbaum.

Cohen, J. (1990). Things I have learned (so far). *American Psychologist*, 45, 1304–1312.

Goldstein, R. (1989). Power and sample size via MS/PC-DOS computers. *American Statistician*, 43, 253–260.

Neyman, J., & Pearson, E. S. (1928). On the use and interpretation of certain test criteria for purposes of statistical inference. *Biometrika, 20A,* 175–240, 263–294.

Neyman, J., & Pearson, E. S. (1933). On the problem of the most efficient tests of statistical hypotheses. *Transactions of the Royal Society of London Series A, 231,* 289–337.

Sedlmeier, P., & Gigerenzer, G. (1989). Do studies of statistical power have an effect on the power of studies? *Psychological Bulletin, 105,* 309–316.

19

STATISTICAL SIGNIFICANCE TESTING AND CUMULATIVE KNOWLEDGE IN PSYCHOLOGY: IMPLICATIONS FOR TRAINING OF RESEARCHERS

FRANK L. SCHMIDT

In 1990, Aiken, West, Sechrest, and Reno published an important article surveying the teaching of quantitative methods in graduate psychology programs. They were concerned about what was not being taught or was being inadequately taught to future researchers and the harm this might cause to research progress in psychology. For example, they found that new and important quantitative methods such as causal modeling, confirmatory factor analysis, and meta-analysis were not being taught in the majority of graduate programs. This is indeed a legitimate cause for concern. But in this article, I am concerned about the opposite: what is being taught and the harm that this is doing. Aiken et al. found that the vast majority of programs were

Reprinted from *Psychological Methods*, 1, 115–129. Copyright 1996 by the American Psychological Association.

teaching, on a rather thorough basis, what they referred to as "the old standards of statistics"; traditional inferential statistics. This includes the *t* test, the *F* test, the chi-square test, analysis of variance (ANOVA), and other methods of statistical significance testing. Hypothesis testing based on the statistical significance test has been the main feature of graduate training in statistics in psychology for over 40 years, and the Aiken et al. study showed that it still is.

Methods of data analysis and interpretation have a major effect on the development of cumulative knowledge. I demonstrate in this article that reliance on statistical significance testing in the analysis and interpretation of research data has systematically retarded the growth of cumulative knowledge in psychology (Hunter & Schmidt, 1990b; Schmidt, 1992). This conclusion is not new. It has been articulated in different ways by Rozeboom (1960), Meehl (1967), Carver (1978), Guttman (1985), Oakes (1986), Loftus (1991, 1994), and others, and most recently by Cohen (1994). Jack Hunter and I have used meta-analysis methods to show that these traditional data analysis methods militate against the discovery of the underlying regularities and relationships that are the foundation for scientific progress (Hunter & Schmidt, 1990b). Those of us who are the keepers of the methodological and quantitative flame for the field of psychology bear the major responsibility for this failure because we have continued to emphasize significance testing in the training of graduate students despite clear demonstrations of the deficiencies of this approach to data analysis. We correctly decry the fact that quantitative methods are given inadequate attention in graduate programs, and we worry that this signals a future decline in research quality. Yet it was our excessive emphasis on so-called inferential statistical methods that caused a much more serious problem. And we ignore this fact.

My conclusion is that we must abandon the statistical significance test. In our graduate programs we must teach that for analysis of data from individual studies, the appropriate statistics are point estimates of effect sizes and confidence intervals around these point estimates. We must teach that for analysis of data from multiple studies, the appropriate method is meta-analysis. I am not the first to reach the conclusion that significance testing should be replaced by point estimates and confidence intervals. Jones stated this conclusion as early as 1955, and Kish in 1959. Rozeboom reached this conclusion in 1960. Carver stated this conclusion in 1978, as did Hunter in 1979 in an invited American Psychological Association (APA) address, and Oakes in his excellent 1986 book. So far, these individuals (and others) have all been voices crying in the wilderness.

Why then is the situation any different today? If the closely reasoned and logically flawless arguments of Kish, Rozeboom, Carver, and Hunter have been ignored all these years — and they have — what reason is there to believe that this will not continue to be the case? There is in fact a reason to be optimistic that in the future we will see reform of data analysis methods in psychology. That reason is the development and widespread use of meta-analysis methods. These methods have revealed more clearly than ever before the extent to which reliance on significance testing has retarded the growth of cumulative knowledge in psychology. These demonstrations based on meta-analysis methods are what is new. As conclusions from research literature come more and more to be based on findings from meta-analysis (Cooper & Hedges, 1994; Lipsey & Wilson, 1993; Schmidt, 1992), the significance test necessarily becomes less and less important. At worst, significance tests will become progressively deemphasized. At best, their use will be discontinued and replaced in individual studies by point estimation of effect sizes and confidence intervals.

The reader's reaction to this might be that this is just one opinion and that there are defenses of statistical significance testing that are as convincing as the arguments and demonstrations I present in this article. This is not true. As Oakes (1986) stated, it is "extraordinarily difficult to find a statistician who argues explicitly in favor of the retention of significance tests" (p. 71). A few psychologists have so argued. But Oakes (1986) and Carver (1978) have carefully considered all such arguments and shown them to be logically flawed and hence false. Also, even these few defenders of significance testing (e.g., Winch & Campbell, 1969) agree that the dominant usages of such tests in data analysis in psychology are misuses, and they hold that the role of significance tests in data analysis should be greatly reduced. As you read this article, I want you to consider this challenge: Can you articulate even one legitimate contribution that significance testing has made (or makes) to the research enterprise (i.e., any way in which it contributes to the development of cumulative scientific knowledge?) I believe you will not be able to do so.

TRADITIONAL METHODS VERSUS META-ANALYSIS

Psychology and the other social sciences have traditionally relied heavily on the statistical significance test in interpreting the meaning of data, both in individual studies and in research literature. Following the fateful lead of Fisher (1932), null hypothesis significance testing has been the dominant data analysis procedure. The prevailing decision rule, as Oakes (1986) has demonstrated empirically, has been this: If the statistic (t, F, etc.) is significant, there is an effect (or a relation); if it is not significant, then there is no effect (or relation). These prevailing interpretational procedures have focused heavily on the control of Type I errors, with little attention being paid to the control of Type II errors. A Type I error (alpha error) consists of concluding that there is a relation or an effect when there is not. A Type II error (beta error) consists of the opposite, concluding that there is no relation or effect when there is. Alpha levels have been controlled at the .05 or

.01 levels, but beta levels have by default been allowed to climb to high levels, often in the 50% to 80% range (Cohen, 1962, 1988, 1990, 1994; Schmidt, Hunter, & Urry, 1976). To illustrate this, let us look at an example from a hypothetical but statistically typical area of experimental psychology.

Suppose the research question is the effect of a certain drug on learning, and suppose the actual effect of a particular dosage is an increase of one half of a standard deviation in the amount learned. An effect size of .50 is considered medium-sized by Cohen (1988) and corresponds to the difference between the 50th and 69th percentiles in a normal distribution. With an effect size of this magnitude, 69% of the experimental group would exceed the mean of the control group, if both were normally distributed. Many reviews of various literatures have found relations of this general magnitude (Hunter & Schmidt, 1990b). Now suppose that a large number of studies are conducted on this dosage, each with 15 rats in the experimental group and 15 in the control group.

Figure 19.1 shows the distribution of effect sizes (d values) expected under the null hypothesis. All variability around the mean value of zero is due to sampling error. To be significant at the .05 level (with a one-tailed test), the effect size must be .62 or larger. If the null hypothesis is true, only 5% will be that large or larger. In analyzing their data, researchers in psychology typically focus only on the information in Figure 19.1. Most believe that their significance test limits the probability of an error to 5%.

Actually, in this example the probability of a Type I error is zero, not 5%. Because the actual effect size is always .50, the null hypothesis is always false, and therefore there is no possibility of a Type I error. One cannot falsely conclude that there is an effect when in fact there is an effect. When the null hypothesis is false, the only kind of error that can occur is a Type II error: failure to detect the effect that is present (and the total error rate for the study

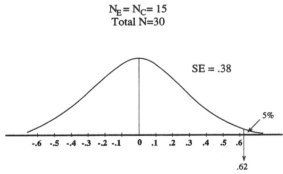

Figure 19.1. Null distribution of d values in a series of experiments. Required for significance: $d_c = 0.62$; $d_c = [1.645(0.38)] = 0.62$ (one-tailed test, $\alpha = .05$).

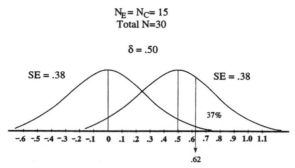

$N_E = N_C = 15$
Total N=30

$\delta = .50$

SE = .38   SE = .38

37%

-.6 -.5 -.4 -.3 -.2 -.1 0 .1 .2 .3 .4 .5 .6 .7 .8 .9 1.0 1.1

.62

Figure 19.2. Statistical power in a series of experiments. Required for significance: d_c = 0.62 (one-tailed test, α = .05); statistical power = 0.37; Type II error rate = 63%; Type I error rate = 0%.

is therefore the Type II error rate). The only type of error that can occur is the type that is not controlled.

Figure 19.2 shows not only the irrelevant null distribution but also the actual distribution of effect sizes across these studies. The mean of this distribution is the true value of .50, but because of sampling error, there is substantial variation in observed effect sizes. Again, to be significant, the effect size must be .62 or larger. Only 37% of studies conducted will obtain a significant effect size; thus statistical power for each of these studies is only .37. That is, the true (population) effect size of the drug is always .50; it is never zero. Yet it is only detected as significant in 37% of the studies. The error rate in this research literature is 63%, not 5%, as many would mistakenly believe.

In actuality, the error rate would be even higher. Most researchers in experimental psychology would traditionally have used F tests from an ANOVA to analyze these data. This means the significance test would be two-tailed rather than one-tailed as in our example. With a two-tailed test (i.e., one-way ANOVA), statistical power is even lower: .26 instead of .37. The Type II error rate (and hence the overall error rate) would be 74%. Also, this example assumes use of a z test; any researchers not using an ANOVA would probably use a t test. For a one-tailed t test with α = .05 and df = 28, the effect size (d value) must be .65 to be significant. (The t value must be at least 1.70, instead of the 1.645 required for the z test.) With the t test, statistical power would also be lower: .35 instead of .37. Thus both commonly used alternative significance tests would yield even lower statistical power and produce even higher error rates.

Also, note in Figure 19.2 that the studies that are significant yield distorted estimates of effect sizes. The true effect size is always .50; all departures from .50 are due solely to sampling error. But the minimum value required for significance is .62. The obtained d value must be .12 above its true value—24% larger than its real value—to be significant. The average of the significant d values is .89, which is 78% larger than the true value of .50.

In any study in this research literature that by chance yields the correct value of .50, the conclusion under the prevailing decision rule is that there is no relationship. That is, it is only the studies that by chance are quite inaccurate that lead to the correct conclusion that a relationship exists.

How would this body of studies be interpreted as a research literature? There are two interpretations that would have traditionally been accepted. The first is based on the traditional voting method (critiqued by Light & Smith, 1971, and by Hedges & Olkin, 1980). Using this method, one would note that 63% of the studies found "no relationship." Since this is a majority of the studies, the conclusion would be that no relation exists. This conclusion is completely false, yet many reviews in the past have been conducted in just this manner (Hedges & Olkin, 1980).

The second interpretation is as follows: In 63% of the studies, the drug had no effect. However, in 37% of the studies, the drug did have an effect. (Moreover, when the drug did have an effect, the effect was quite large, averaging .89.) Research is needed to identify the moderator variables (interactions) that cause the drug to have an effect in some studies but not in others. For example, perhaps the strain of rat used or the mode of injecting the drug affects study outcomes. This interpretation is also completely erroneous. In addition, it leads to wasted research efforts to identify nonexistent moderator variables.

Both traditional interpretations fail to reveal the true meaning of the studies and hence fail to lead to cumulative knowledge. In fact, the traditional methods based on significance testing make it impossible to reach correct conclusions about the meaning of these studies. This is what is meant by the statement that traditional data analysis methods militate against the development of cumulative knowledge.

How would meta-analysis interpret these studies? Different approaches to meta-analysis use somewhat different quantitative procedures (Bangert-Drowns, 1986; Glass, McGaw, & Smith, 1981; Hedges & Olkin, 1985; Hunter, Schmidt, & Jackson, 1982; Hunter & Schmidt, 1990b; Rosenthal, 1984, 1991). I illustrate this example using the methods presented by Hunter, Schmidt, and Jackson (1982) and Hunter and Schmidt (1990b). Figure 19.3 shows that meta-analysis reaches the correct conclusion. Meta-analysis first computes the variance of the observed d values (using the ordinary formula for the variance of any set of numbers). Next, it uses the standard formula for the sampling error variance of d values (e.g., see Hunter & Schmidt, 1990b, chap. 7) to determine how much variance would be expected in observed d values from sampling error alone. The amount of real variance in population d values (δ values) is estimated as the difference between the two. In our example, this difference is zero, indicating correctly that there is only one

I. **Compute Actual Variance of Effect Sizes**

    1. $S_d^2 = .1444$ (Observed Variance of d Values)

    2. $S_e^2 = .1444$ (Variance Predicted from Sampling Error)

    3. $S_\delta^2 = S_d^2 - S_e^2$

    4. $S_\delta^2 = .1444 - .1444 = 0$ (True Variance of δ Values)

II. **Compute Mean Effect Size**

    1. $\overline{d} = .50$ (Mean Observed d Value)

    2. $\delta = .50$

    3. $SD_\delta = 0$

III. **Conclusion:**   There is only one effect size, and its value is .50 standard deviation.

Figure 19.3. Meta-analysis of drug studies.

population value. This single population value is estimated as the average observed value, which is .50 here, the correct value. If the number of studies is large, the average d value will be close to the true (population) value, because sampling errors are random and hence average out to zero.[1]

Note that these meta-analysis methods do not rely on statistical significance tests. Only effect sizes are used, and significance tests are not used in analyzing the effect sizes. Unlike traditional methods based on significance tests, meta-analysis leads to correct conclusions and hence leads to cumulative knowledge.

The data in this example are hypothetical. However, if one accepts the validity of basic statistical formulas for sampling error, one will have no reservations about this example. But the same principles do apply to real data, as shown next by an example from research in personnel selection. Table 19.1 shows observed validity coefficients (correlations) from 21 studies of a single clerical test and a single measure of job performance. Each study has $n = 68$ (the median n in the literature in personnel psychology), and every study is a random draw (without replacement) from a single larger

---

[1]Actually the d statistic has a slight positive (upward) bias as the estimator of δ, the population value. Formulas are available to correct observed d values for this bias and are given in Hedges and Olkin (1985, p. 81) and Hunter and Schmidt (1990b, p. 262). This example assumes that this correction has been made. This bias is trivial if the sample size is 10 or greater in both the experimental and control groups.

TABLE 19.1
21 Validity Studies,
$N = 68$ for Each

Study	Observed validity correlation
1	.04
2	.14
3	.31*
4	.12
5	.38*
6	.27*
7	.15
8	.36*
9	.20
10	.02
11	.23
12	.11
13	.21
14	.37*
15	.14
16	.29*
17	.26*
18	.17
19	.39*
20	.22
21	.21

*$p < .05$ (two tailed).

validity study with 1,428 subjects. The correlation in the large study (uncorrected for measurement error, range restriction, or other artifacts) is .22 (Schmidt, Ocasio, Hillery, & Hunter, 1985).

The validity is significant in 8 (or 38%) of these studies, for an error rate of 62%. The traditional conclusion would be that this test is valid in 38% of the organizations, and invalid in the rest, and that in organizations in which it is valid, its mean observed validity is .33 (which is 50% larger than its real value). Meta-analysis of these validities indicates that the mean is .22 and that all variance in the coefficients is due solely to sampling error. The meta-analysis conclusions are correct; the traditional conclusions are false.

In these examples, the only type of error that is controlled—Type I error—is the type that cannot occur. In most areas of research, as time goes by, researchers gain a better and better understanding of the processes they are studying; as a result, it is less and less frequently the case that the null hypothesis is "true" and more and more likely that the null hypothesis is false. Thus Type I error decreases in importance, and Type II error increases in importance. This means that as time goes by, researchers should be paying increasing attention to Type II error and to statistical power and increasingly less attention to Type I error. However, a recent review in *Psychological Bul-*

letin (Sedlmeier & Gigerenzer, 1989) concluded that the average statistical power of studies in one APA journal had declined from 46% to 37% over a 22-year period (despite the earlier appeal in that journal by Cohen in 1962 for attention to statistical power). Only 2 of the 64 experiments reviewed even mentioned statistical power, and none computed estimates of power. The review concluded that the decline in power was due to increased use of alpha-adjusted procedures (such as the Newman–Keuls, Duncan, and Scheffé procedures). That is, instead of attempting to reduce the Type II error rate, researchers had been imposing increasingly stringent controls on Type I errors, which probably cannot occur in most studies. The result is a further increase in the Type II error rate, an average increase of 17%. This trend illustrates the deep illogic embedded in the use of significance tests.

These examples have examined only the effects of sampling error. There are other statistical and measurement artifacts that cause artifactual variation in effect sizes and correlations across studies, for example, differences between studies in amount of measurement error, in degree of range restriction, and in dichotomization of measures. Also, in meta-analysis, d values and correlations must be corrected for downward bias due to such research artifacts as measurement error and dichotomization of measures. These artifacts are beyond the scope of this presentation but are covered in detail elsewhere (Hunter & Schmidt, 1990a, 1990b; Schmidt & Hunter, 1996). My purpose here is to demonstrate only that traditional data analysis and interpretation methods logically lead to erroneous conclusions and to demonstrate that meta-analysis solves these problems at the level of aggregate research literatures.

For almost 50 years, reliance on statistical significance testing in psychology and the other social sciences has led to frequent serious errors in interpreting the meaning of data (Hunter & Schmidt, 1990b, pp. 29–42 and 483–484), errors that have systematically retarded the growth of cumulative knowledge. Despite the best efforts of such individuals as Kish (1959), Rozeboom (1960), Meehl (1967), Carver (1978), Hunter (1979), Guttman (1985), and Oakes (1986), it has not been possible to wean researchers away from their entrancement with significance testing. Can we now at least hope that the lessons from meta-analysis will finally stimulate change? I would like to answer in the affirmative, but later in this article I present reasons why I do not believe these demonstrations alone will be sufficient to bring about reform. Other steps are also needed.

In my introduction, I state that the appropriate method for analyzing data from multiple studies is meta-analysis. These two examples illustrate that point dramatically. I also state that the appropriate way to analyze data in a single study is by means of point estimation of the effect size and use of a confidence interval around this point estimate. If this had been done in the studies in these two examples, what would these two research literatures have looked like prior to application of meta-analysis?

In the first example, from the experimental psychology literature, the traditional practice would have been to report only the F statistic values and their associated significance levels. Anyone looking at this literature would see that 26% of these F ratios are significant and 74% are nonsignificant. This would create at best the impression of a contradictory set of studies. With appropriate data analysis methods, the observed d value is computed in each study; this is the point estimate of the effect size. Anyone looking at this literature would quickly see that the vast majority of these effect sizes— 91%—are positive. This gives a very different and much more accurate impression than does the observation that 74% of the effects are nonsignificant. Next, the confidence interval around each effect size is computed and presented. A glance at these confidence intervals would reveal that almost all of them overlap with almost all of the other confidence intervals. This again correctly suggests that the studies are in substantial agreement, contrary to the false impression given by the traditional information that 26% are significant and 74% are nonsignificant. (These studies use simple one-way ANOVA designs; however, d values and confidence intervals can also be computed when factorial ANOVA designs or repeated measures designs are used.)

To see this point more clearly, let us consider again the observed correlations in Table 19.1. The observed correlation is an index of effect size, and therefore in a truly traditional analysis it would not be reported; only significance levels would be reported. So all we would know is that in 62% of the studies there was "no significant relationship," and in 38% of the studies there was a significant relationship. Table 19.2 shows the information that would be provided by use of point estimates of effect size and confidence intervals. In Table 19.2, the observed correlations are arranged in order of size with their 95% confidence intervals.

The first thing that is obvious is that all the correlations are positive. It can also be seen that every confidence interval overlaps every other confidence interval, indicating that these studies could all be estimating the same population parameter, which indeed they are. This is true for even the largest and smallest correlations. The confidence interval for the largest correlation (.39) is .19 to .59. The confidence interval for the smallest correlation (.02) is −.22 to .26. These confidence intervals have an overlap of .07. Thus in contrast to the picture provided by null hypothesis significance testing, point estimates and confidence intervals provide a much more correct picture, a picture that correctly indicates substantial agreement among the studies.[2]

---

[2] The confidence intervals in Table 19.2 have been computed using the usual formula for the standard error of the sample correlation: $SE = (1 - r^2)/\sqrt{N - 1}$. Hence these confidence intervals are symmetrical. Some would advocate the use of Fisher's Z transformation of r in computing confidence intervals for r. This position is typically based on the belief that the sampling distribution of Fisher's Z transformation of r is normally distributed, while r itself is skewed. Actually, both are skewed and both approach normality as N increases, and the Fisher's Z transformation approaches normality only marginally faster than r as N increases. For a population correlation of .22 and sample sizes in the ranges considered here, the differences are trivial.

TABLE 19.2

95% Confidence Intervals
for Correlations From Table 1,
$N = 68$ for Each

Study	Observed correlation	95% confidence interval	
		Lower	Upper
1	.39	.19	.59
2	.38	.18	.58
3	.37	.16	.58
4	.36	.15	.57
5	.31	.09	.53
6	.29	.07	.51
7	.27	.05	.49
8	.26	.04	.48
9	.23	.00	.46
10	.22	−.01	.45
11	.21	−.02	.44
12	.21	−.02	.44
13	.20	−.03	.43
14	.17	−.06	.40
15	.15	−.08	.38
16	.14	−.09	.37
17	.14	−.09	.37
18	.12	−.12	.36
19	.11	−.13	.35
20	.04	−.20	.28
21	.02	−.22	.26

There are also other reasons for preferring confidence intervals (see Carver, 1978; Hunter & Schmidt, 1990b, pp. 29–33; Kish, 1959; Oakes, 1986, p. 67; and Rozeboom, 1960). One important reason is that, unlike the significance test, the confidence interval does hold the overall error rate to the desired level. In the example from experimental psychology, we saw that many researchers believed that the error rate for the significance test was held to 5% because the alpha level used was .05, when in fact the error rate was really 63% (74% if F tests from an ANOVA are used). However, if the 95% confidence interval is used, the overall error rate is in fact held to 5%. Only 5% of such computed confidence intervals will be expected to not include the population (true) effect size and 95% will.

To many researchers today, the idea of substituting point estimates and confidence intervals for significance tests might seem radical. Therefore it is important to remember that prior to the appearance of Fisher's 1932 and 1935 texts, data analysis in individual studies was typically conducted using point estimates and confidence intervals (Oakes, 1986). The point estimates were usually accompanied by estimates of the "probable error," the 50% confidence interval. Significance tests were rarely used (and confidence intervals were not interpreted in terms of statistical significance). Most of us rarely look at the psychological journals of the 1920s and early 1930s, but if we did, this is what we would see. As can be seen both in the psychology research journals and in psychology statistics textbooks, during the latter half of the 1930s and during the 1940s, under the influence of Fisher, psychological researchers adopted en masse Fisher's null hypothesis significance testing approach to analysis of data in individual studies (Huberty, 1993). This was a major mistake. It was Sir Ronald Fisher who led psychological researchers down the primrose path of significance testing. All the other social sciences were similarly deceived, as were researchers in medicine, finance, marketing, and other areas.

Fisher's influence not only explains this unfortunate change, it also suggests one reason why psychologists for so long gave virtually no attention to the question of statistical power. The concept of statistical power does not exist in Fisherian statistics. In Fisherian statistics, the focus of attention is solely on the null hypothesis. No alternative hypothesis is introduced. Without an alternative hypothesis, there can be no concept of statistical power. When Neyman and Pearson (1932, 1933) later introduced the concepts of the alternate hypothesis and statistical power, Fisher argued that statistical power was irrelevant to statistical significance testing as used in scientific inference (Oakes, 1986). We have seen in our two examples how untrue that statement is.

Thus it is clear that even if meta-analysis had never been developed, use of point estimates of effect size and confidence intervals in interpreting data in individual studies would have made our research literatures far less confusing, far less apparently contradictory, and far more informative than those that have been produced by the dominant practice of reliance on significance tests. Indeed, the fact of almost universal reliance on significance tests in data analysis in individual studies is a major factor in making meta-analysis absolutely essential to making sense of research literatures (Hunter & Schmidt, 1990b, chap. 1).

However, it is important to understand that meta-analysis would still be useful even had researchers always relied only on point estimates and confidence intervals, because the very large numbers of studies characteristic of many of today's literatures create information overload even if each study has been appropriately analyzed. Indeed, we saw earlier that applying meta-analysis to the studies in Table 19.1 produces an even clearer and more accurate picture of the meaning of these studies than the application of point estimates and confidence intervals shown in Table 19.2. In our example, meta-analysis tells us that there is only one population correlation and that that value is .22. Confidence intervals tell us only that there may be only one population value; they do not specify what that value might be. In addition, in more complex applications, meta-analysis makes possible corrections for the effects of other artifacts—both systematic and unsystematic—that bias effect size estimates and cause false variation in such estimates across studies (Hunter & Schmidt, 1990b).

CONSEQUENCES OF TRADITIONAL SIGNIFICANCE TESTING

As we have seen, traditional reliance on statistical significance testing leads to the false appearance of conflicting and internally contradictory research literatures. This has a debilitating effect on the general research effort to develop cumulative theoretical knowledge and understanding. However, it is also important to note that it destroys the usefulness of psychological research as a means for solving practical problems in society.

The sequence of events has been much the same in one applied research area after another. First, there is initial optimism about using social science research to answer socially important questions that arise. Do government-sponsored job-training programs work? One will do studies to find out. Does integration increase the school achievement of Black children? Research will provide the answer. Next, several studies on the question are conducted, but the results are conflicting. There is some disappointment that the question has not been answered, but policymakers—and people in general—are still optimistic. They, along with the researchers, conclude that more research is needed to identify the interactions (moderators) that have caused the conflicting findings. For example, perhaps whether job training works depends on the age and education of the trainees. Maybe smaller classes in the schools are beneficial only for lower IQ children. Researchers may hypothesize that psychotherapy works for middle-class patients but not lower-class patients.

In the third phase, a large number of research studies are funded and conducted to test these moderator hypotheses. When they are completed, there is now a large body of studies, but instead of being resolved, the number of conflicts increases. The moderator hypotheses from the initial studies are not borne out. No one can make much sense out of the conflicting findings. Researchers conclude that the phenomenon that was selected for study in this particular case has turned out to be hopelessly complex, and so they turn to the investigation of another question, hoping that this time the question will turn out to be more tractable. Research sponsors, government officials, and the public become disenchanted and cynical. Research funding agencies cut money for research in this area and in related areas. After this cycle has been repeated enough times, social and behavioral scientists themselves become cynical about the value of their own work, and they begin to express doubts about whether behavioral and social science research is capable in principle of developing cumulative knowledge and providing general answers to socially important questions (e.g., see Cronbach, 1975; Gergen, 1982; Meehl, 1978). Cronbach's (1975) article "The Two Disciplines of Scientific Psychology Revisited" is a clear statement of this sense of hopelessness.

Clearly, at this point the need is not for more primary research studies but for some means of making sense of the vast number of accumulated study findings. This is the purpose of meta-analysis. Applications of meta-analysis to accumulated research literatures have generally shown that research findings are not nearly as conflicting as we had thought and that useful general conclusions can be drawn from past research. I have summarized some of these findings in a recent article (Schmidt, 1992; see also Hunter & Schmidt, in press). Thus, socially important applied questions can be answered.

Even more important, it means that scientific progress is possible. It means that cumulative understanding and progress in theory development is possible after all. It means that the behavioral and social sciences can attain the status of true sciences; they are not doomed forever to the status of quasi-sciences or pseudosciences. One result of this is that the gloom, cynicism, and nihilism that have enveloped many in the behavioral and social sciences is lifting. Young people starting out in the behavioral and social sciences today can hope for a much brighter future.

These are among the considerable benefits of abandoning statistical significance testing in favor of point estimates of effect sizes and confidence intervals in individual studies and meta-analysis for combining findings across multiple studies.

IS STATISTICAL POWER THE SOLUTION?

So far in this article, the deficiencies of significance testing that I have emphasized are those stemming from low statistical power in typical studies. Significance testing has other important problems, and I discuss some of these later. However, in our work on meta-analysis methods, John Hunter and I have repeatedly been confronted by researchers who state that the only problem with significance testing is low power and that if this problem could be solved, there would be no problems with reliance on significance testing in data analysis and interpretation. Almost invariably, these individuals see the solution as larger sample sizes. They believe that the problem would be solved if every researcher before conducting each study would calculate the number of subjects needed for "adequate" power (usually taken as power of .80), given the expected effect size and the desired alpha level, and then use that sample size.

What this position overlooks is that this requirement would make it impossible for most studies ever to be conducted. At the inception of research in a given area, the questions are often of the form, "Does Treatment

A have an effect?" If Treatment A indeed has a substantial effect, the sample size needed for adequate power may not be prohibitively large. But as research develops, subsequent questions tend to take the form, "Does Treatment A have a larger effect than does Treatment B?" The effect size then becomes the difference between the two effects. A similar progression occurs in correlational research. Such effect sizes will often be much smaller, and the required sample sizes are therefore often quite large, often 1,000 or more (Schmidt & Hunter, 1978). This is just to attain power of .80, which still allows a 20% Type II error rate when the null hypothesis is false. Many researchers cannot obtain that many subjects, no matter how hard they try; either it is beyond their resources or the subjects are just unavailable at any cost. Thus the upshot of this position would be that many — perhaps most — studies would not be conducted at all.

People advocating the position being critiqued here would say this would be no loss at all. They argue that a study with inadequate power contributes nothing and therefore should not be conducted. But such studies do contain valuable information when combined with others like them in a meta-analysis. In fact, very precise meta-analysis results can be obtained on the basis of studies that all have inadequate statistical power individually. The information in these studies is lost if these studies are never conducted.

The belief that such studies are worthless is based on two false assumptions: (a) the assumption that each individual study must be able to support and justify a conclusion, and (b) the assumption that every study should be analyzed with significance tests. In fact, meta-analysis has made clear that any single study is rarely adequate by itself to answer a scientific question. Therefore each study should be considered as a data point to be contributed to a later meta-analysis, and individual studies should be analyzed using not significance tests but point estimates of effect sizes and confidence intervals.

How, then, can we solve the problem of statistical power in individual studies? Actually, this problem is a pseudoproblem. It can be "solved" by discontinuing the significance test. As Oakes (1986, p. 68) noted, statistical power is a legitimate concept only within the context of statistical significance testing. If significance testing is no longer used, then the concept of statistical power has no place and is not meaningful. In particular, there need be no concern with statistical power when point estimates and confidence intervals are used to analyze data in studies and when meta-analysis is used to integrate findings across studies.[3] Thus when there is no significance testing, there are no statistical power problems.

---

[3] Some state that confidence intervals are the same as significance tests, because if the lower bound of the confidence interval does not include zero, that fact indicates that the effect size estimate is statistically significant. But the fact that the confidence interval can be interpreted as a significance test does not mean that it must be so interpreted. There is no necessity for such an interpretation, and as noted earlier, the probable errors (50% confidence intervals) popularly used in the literature up until the mid 1930s were never interpreted as significance tests.

WHY ARE RESEARCHERS ADDICTED
TO SIGNIFICANCE TESTING?

Time after time, even in recent years, I have seen researchers who have learned to understand the deceptiveness of significance testing sink back into the habit of reliance on significance testing. I have occasionally done it myself. Why is it so hard for us to break our addiction to significance testing? Methodologists such as Bakan (1966), Meehl (1967), Rozeboom (1960), Oakes (1986), Carver (1978), and others have explored the various possible reasons why researchers seem to be unable to give up significance testing.

Significance testing creates an illusion of objectivity, and objectivity is a critical value in science. But objectivity makes a negative contribution when it sabotages the research enterprise by making it impossible to reach correct conclusions about the meaning of data.

Researchers conform to the dominant practice of reliance on significance testing because they fear that failure to follow these conventional practices would cause their studies to be rejected by journal editors. But the solution to this problem is not conformity to counterproductive practices but education of editors and reviewers.

There is also a feeling that, as bad as significance testing is, there is no satisfactory alternative; just looking at the data and making interpretations will not do. But as we have seen, there is a good statistical alternative: point estimates and confidence intervals.

However, I do not believe that these and similar reasons are the whole story. An important part of the explanation is that researchers hold false beliefs about significance testing, beliefs that tell them that significance testing offers important benefits to researchers that it in fact does not. Three of these beliefs are particularly important.

The first is the false belief that the significance level of a study indicates the probability of successful replication of the study. Oakes (1986, pp. 79–82) empirically studied the beliefs about the meaning of significance tests of 70 research psychologists and advanced graduate students. They were presented with the following scenario:

> Suppose you have a treatment which you suspect may alter performance on a certain task. You compare the means of your control and experimental groups (20 subjects in each). Further, suppose you use a simple independent means t test and your result is $t = 2.7$, d.f. $= 38$, p $= .01$. (Oakes, 1986, p. 79)

He then asked them to indicate whether each of several statements were true or false. One of these statements was this:

> You have a reliable experimental finding in the sense that if, hypothetically, the experiment were repeated a great number of times, you would obtain a significant result in 99% of such studies. (Oakes, 1986, p. 79)

Sixty percent of the researchers indicated that this false statement is true. The significance level gives no information about the probability of replication. This statement confuses significance level with power. The probability of replication is the power of the study; the power of this study is not .99, but rather .43.[4] If this study is repeated many times, the best estimate is that less than half of all such studies will be significant at the chosen alpha level of .01. Yet 60% of the researchers endorsed the belief that 99% of such studies would be significant. This false belief may help to explain the traditional indifference to power among researchers. Many researchers believe a power analysis does not provide any information not already given by the significance level. Furthermore, this belief leads to the false conclusion that statistical power for every statistically significant finding is very high, at least .95.

That many researchers hold this false belief has been known for decades. Bakan criticized this error in 1966, and Lykken discussed it at some length in 1968. The following statement from an introductory statistics textbook by Nunnally (1975) is a clear statement of this belief:

> If the statistical significance is at the .05 level, it is more informative to talk about the *statistical confidence* as being at the .95 level. This means that the investigator can be confident with odds of 95 out of 100 that the observed difference will hold up in future investigations. (p. 195)

Most researchers, however, do not usually explicitly state this belief. The fact that they hold it is revealed by their description of statistically significant findings. Researchers obtaining a statistically significant result often refer to it as "a reliable difference," meaning one that is replicable. In fact, a false argument frequently heard in favor of significance testing is that we must have significance tests in order to know whether our findings are reliable or not. As Carver (1978) pointed out, the popularity of statistical significance testing would be greatly reduced if researchers could be made to realize that the statistical significance level does not indicate the replicability of research data. So it is critical that this false belief be eradicated from the minds of researchers.

A second false belief widely held by researchers is that statistical significance level provides an index of the importance or size of a difference or relation (Bakan, 1966). A difference significant at the .001 level is regarded as theoretically (or practically) more important or larger than a difference significant at only the .05 level. In research reports in the literature, one sees statements such as the following: "Moreover, this difference is

---

[4] The statistical power for future replications of this study is estimated as follows. The best estimate of the population effect size is the effect size (d value) observed in this study. This observed d value is $2t/\sqrt{N}$ (Hunter & Schmidt, 1990b, p. 272), which is .85 here. With 20 subjects each in the experimental and control groups, an alpha level of .01 (two tailed), and a population d value of .85, the power of the t test is .43.

highly significant ($p < .001$)," implying that the difference is therefore large or important. This belief ignores the fact that significance level depends on sample size; highly significant differences in large sample studies may be smaller than even nonsignificant differences in smaller sample studies. This belief also ignores the fact that even if sample sizes were equal across studies compared, the p values would still provide no index of the actual size of the difference or effect. Only effect size indices can do that.

Because of the influence of meta-analysis, the practice of computing effect sizes has become more frequent in some research literatures, thus mitigating the pernicious effects of this false belief. But in other areas, especially in many areas of experimental psychology, effect sizes are rarely computed, and it remains the practice to infer size or importance of obtained findings from statistical significance levels. In an empirical study, Oakes (1986, pp. 86–88) found that psychological researchers infer grossly overestimated effect sizes from significance levels. When the study p values were .01, they estimated effect sizes as five times as large as they actually were.

The size or importance of findings is information important to researchers. Researchers who continue to believe that statistical significance levels reveal the size or importance of differences or relations will continue to refuse to abandon significance testing in favor of point estimates and confidence intervals. So this is a second false belief that must be eradicated.

The third false belief held by many researchers is the most devastating of all to the research enterprise. This is the belief that if a difference or relation is not statistically significant, then it is zero, or at least so small that it can safely be considered to be zero. This is the belief that if the null hypothesis is not rejected, then it is to be accepted. This is the belief that a major benefit from significance tests is that they tell us whether a difference or effect is real or "probably just occurred by chance." If a difference is not significant, then we know that it is probably just due to chance. The two examples discussed earlier show how detrimental this false operational decision rule is to the attainment of cumulative knowledge in psychology. This belief makes it impossible to discern the real meaning of research literatures.

Although some of his writings are ambiguous on this point, Fisher himself probably did not advocate this decision rule. In his 1935 book he stated,

> It should be noted that this null hypothesis is never proved or established, but is possibly disproved in the course of experimentation. Every experiment may be said to exist only in order to give the facts a chance of disproving the null hypothesis. (p. 19)

If the null hypothesis is not rejected, Fisher's position was that nothing could be concluded. But researchers find it hard to go to all the trouble of conducting a study only to conclude that nothing can be concluded. Oakes (1986) has shown empirically that the operational decision rule used by researchers is indeed "if it is not significant, it is zero." Use of this decision rule amounts to an implicit belief on the part of researchers that the power of significance tests is perfect or nearly perfect. Such a belief would account for the surprise typically expressed by researchers when informed of the low level of statistical power in most studies.

The confidence of researchers in a research finding is not a linear function of its significance level. Rosenthal and Gaito (1963) studied the confidence that researchers have that a difference is real as a function of the p value of the significance test. They found a precipitous decline in confidence as the p value increased from .05 to .06 or .07. There was no similar "cliff effect" as the p value increased from .01 to .05. This finding suggests that researchers believe that any finding significant at the .05 level or beyond is real and that any finding with a larger p value—even one only marginally larger—is zero.

Researchers must be disabused of the false belief that if a finding is not significant, it is zero. This belief has probably done more than any of the other false beliefs about significance testing to retard the growth of cumulative knowledge in psychology. Those of us concerned with the development of meta-analysis methods hope that demonstrations of the sort given earlier in this article will effectively eliminate this false belief.

I believe that these false beliefs are a major cause of the addiction of researchers to significance tests. Many researchers believe that statistical significance testing confers important benefits that are in fact completely imaginary. If we were clairvoyant and could enter the mind of a typical researcher, we might eavesdrop on the following thoughts:

> Significance tests have been repeatedly criticized by methodological specialists, but I find them very useful in interpreting my research data, and I have no intention of giving them up. If my findings are not significant, then I know that they probably just occurred by chance and that the true difference is probably zero. If the result is significant, then I know I have a reliable finding. The p values from the significance tests tell me whether the relationships in my data are large enough to be important or not. I can also determine from the p value what the chances are that these findings would replicate if I conducted a new study. These are very valuable things for a researcher to know. I wish the critics of significance testing would recognize this fact.

Every one of these thoughts about the benefits of significance testing is false. I ask the reader to ponder this question: Does this describe your thoughts about the significance test?

ANALYSIS OF COSTS AND BENEFITS

We saw earlier that meta-analysis reveals clearly the horrendous costs in failure to attain cumulative knowledge that psychology pays as the price for its addiction to significance testing. I expressed the hope that the appreciation of these massive costs will do what 40 years of logical demonstrations of the deficiencies of significance testing have failed to do: convince researchers to abandon the significance test in favor of point estimates of effect sizes and confidence intervals. But it seems unlikely to me that even these graphic demonstrations of costs will alone lead researchers to give up statistical significance testing. We must also consider the perceived benefits of significance testing. Researchers believe that significance testing confers important imaginary benefits. Many researchers may believe that these "benefits" are important enough to outweigh even the terrible costs that significance testing extracts from the research enterprise. It is unlikely that researchers will abandon significance testing unless and until they are educated to see that they are not getting the benefits they believe they are getting from significance testing. This means that quantitative psychologists and teachers of statistics and other methodological courses have the responsibility to teach researchers not only the high costs of significance testing but also the fact that the benefits typically ascribed to them are illusory. The failure to do the latter has been a major oversight for almost 50 years.

CURRENT SITUATION IN DATA ANALYSIS IN PSYCHOLOGY

There is a fundamental contradiction in the current situation with respect to quantitative methods. The research literatures and conclusions in our journals are now being shaped by the results and findings of meta-analyses, and this development is solving many of the problems created by reliance on significance testing (Cooper & Hedges, 1994; Hunter & Schmidt, 1990b). Yet the content of our basic graduate statistics courses has not changed (Aiken et al., 1990); we are training our young researchers in the discredited practices and methods of the past. Let us examine this anomaly in more detail.

Meta-analysis has explicated the critical role of sampling error, measurement error, and other artifacts in determining the observed findings and the statistical power of individual studies. In doing so, it has revealed how little information there typically is in any single study. It has shown that, contrary to widespread belief, a single primary study can rarely resolve an issue or answer a question. Any individual study must be considered a data point to be contributed to a future meta-analysis. Thus the scientific status and value of the individual study is necessarily lower than has typically been imagined in the past.

As a result, there has been a shift of the focus of scientific discovery in our research literatures from the individual primary study to the meta-analysis, creating a major change in the relative status of reviews. Journals that formerly published only primary studies and refused to publish reviews are now publishing meta-analytic reviews in large numbers. Today, many discoveries and advances in cumulative knowledge are being made not by those who do primary research studies but by those who use meta-analysis to discover the latent meaning of existing research literatures. This is apparent not only in the number of meta-analyses being published but also—and perhaps more important—in the shifting pattern of citations in the literature and in textbooks from primary studies to meta-analyses. The same is true in education, social psychology, medicine, finance, accounting, marketing, and other areas (Hunter & Schmidt, 1990a, chap. 1).

In my own substantive area of industrial/organizational psychology there is even some evidence of reduced reliance on significance testing in analyses of data within individual studies. Studies are much more likely today than in the past to report effect sizes and more likely to report confidence intervals. Results of significance tests are usually still reported, but they are now often sandwiched into parentheses almost as an afterthought and are often given appropriately minimal attention. It is rare today in industrial/organizational psychology for a finding to be touted as important solely on the basis of its p value.

Thus when we look at the research enterprise being conducted by the established researchers of our field, we see major improvements over the situation that prevailed even 10 years ago. However—and this is the worrisome part—there have been no similar improvements in the teaching of quantitative methods in graduate and undergraduate programs. Our younger generations of upcoming researchers are still being inculcated with the old, discredited methods of reliance on statistical significance testing. When we teach students how to analyze and interpret data in individual studies, we are still teaching them to apply t tests, F tests, chi-square tests, and ANOVAS. We are teaching them the same methods that for over 40 years made it impossible to discern the real meaning of data and research literatures and have therefore retarded the development of cumulative knowledge in psychology and the social sciences. We must introduce the reforms needed to solve this serious problem.

It will not be easy. At Michigan State University, John Hunter and Ralph Levine reformed the graduate statistics course sequence in psychology over the last 2 years along the general lines indicated in this article. The result was protests from significance testing traditionalists among the faculty. These faculty did not contend that the new methods were erroneous; rather, they were concerned that their graduate students might not be able to get their research published unless they used traditional significance testing-based methods of data analysis. They did not succeed in derailing the reform, but it has not been easy for these two pioneers. But this must be done and done everywhere. We can no longer tolerate a situation in which our upcoming generation of researchers are being trained to use discredited data analysis methods while the broader research enterprise of which they are to become a part has moved toward improved methods.

REFERENCES

Aiken, L. S., West, S. G., Sechrest, L., & Reno, R. R. (1990). Graduate training in statistics, methodology, and measurement in psychology: A survey of PhD programs in North America. *American Psychologist, 45*, 721–734.

Bakan, D. (1966). The test of significance in psychological research. *Psychological Bulletin, 66*, 423–437.

Bangert-Drowns, R. L. (1986). Review of developments in meta-analytic method. *Psychological Bulletin, 99*, 388–399.

Carver, R. P. (1978). The case against statistical significance testing. *Harvard Educational Review, 48*, 378–399.

Cohen, J. (1962). The statistical power of abnormal-social psychological research: A review. *Journal of Abnormal and Social Psychology, 65*, 145–153.

Cohen, J. (1988). *Statistical power analysis for the behavioral sciences* (2nd ed.) Hillsdale, NJ: Erlbaum.

Cohen, J. (1990). Things I have learned (so far). *American Psychologist, 45*, 1304–1312.

Cohen, J. (1994). The earth is round ($p < .05$). *American Psychologist, 49*, 997–1003.

Cooper, H. M., & Hedges, L. V. (1994). *Handbook of research synthesis*. New York: Russell Sage Foundation.

Cronbach, L. J. (1975). The two disciplines of scientific psychology revisited. *American Psychologist, 30*, 116–127.

Fisher, R. A. (1932). *Statistical methods for research workers* (4th ed.). Edinburgh, Scotland: Oliver & Boyd.

Fisher, R. A. (1935). *The design of experiments*. Edinburgh, Scotland: Oliver & Boyd.

Gergen, K. J. (1982). *Toward transformation in social knowledge*. New York: Springer-Verlag.

Glass, G. V., McGaw, B., & Smith, M. L. (1981). *Meta-analysis in social research*. Beverly Hills, CA: Sage.

Guttman, L. (1985). The illogic of statistical inference for cumulative science. *Applied Stochastic Models and Data Analysis, 1*, 3–10.

Hedges, L. V., & Olkin, I. (1980). Vote counting methods in research synthesis. *Psychological Bulletin, 88*, 359–369.

Hedges, L. V., & Olkin, I. (1985). *Statistical methods for meta-analysis*. Orlando, FL: Academic Press.

Huberty, C. J. (1993). Historical origins of statistical testing practices. *Journal of Experimental Education, 61*, 317–333.

Hunter, J. E. (1979, September). *Cumulating results across studies: A critique of factor analysis, canonical correlation, MANOVA, and statistical significance testing.* Invited address presented at the 86th Annual Convention of the American Psychological Association, New York, NY.

Hunter, J. E., & Schmidt, F. L. (1990a). Dichotomization of continuous variables: The implications for meta-analysis. *Journal of Applied Psychology, 75*, 334–349.

Hunter, J. E., & Schmidt, F. L. (1990b). *Methods of meta-analysis: Correcting error and bias in research findings.* Newbury Park, CA: Sage.

Hunter, J. E., & Schmidt, F. L. (in press). Cumulative research knowledge and social policy formulation: The critical role of meta-analysis. *Psychology, Public Policy, and Law.*

Hunter, J. E., Schmidt, F. L., & Jackson, G. B. (1982). *Meta-analysis: Cumulating research findings across studies.* Beverly Hills, CA: Sage.

Jones, L. V. (1955). Statistics and research design. *Annual Review of Psychology, 6*, 405–430.

Kish, L. (1959). Some statistical problems in research design. *American Sociological Review, 24*, 328–338.

Light, R. J., & Smith, P. V. (1971). Accumulating evidence: Procedures for resolving contradictions among different research studies. *Harvard Educational Review, 41*, 429–471.

Lipsey, M. W., & Wilson, D. B. (1993). The efficacy of psychological, educational, and behavioral treatment. *American Psychologist, 48*, 1181–1209.

Loftus, G. R. (1991). On the tyranny of hypothesis testing in the social sciences. *Contemporary Psychology, 36*, 102–105.

Loftus, G. R. (1994, August). *Why psychology will never be a real science until we change the way we analyze data.* Address presented at the American Psychological Association 102nd Annual Convention, Los Angeles, CA.

Lykken, D. (1968). Statistical significance in psychological research. *Psychological Bulletin, 70*, 151–159.

Meehl, P. E. (1967). Theory testing in psychology and physics: A methodological paradox. *Philosophy of Science, 34*, 103–115.

Meehl, P. E. (1978). Theoretical risks and tabular asterisks: Sir Karl, Sir Ronald and the slow process of soft psychology. *Journal of Consulting and Clinical Psychology, 46*, 806–834.

Neyman, J., & Pearson, E. S. (1932). The testing of statistical hypotheses in relation to probabilities a priori. *Proceedings of the Cambridge Philosophical Society, 29*, 492–516.

Neyman, J., & Pearson, E. S. (1933). On the problem of the most efficient tests of statistical hypotheses. *Philosophical Transactions of the Royal Society of London, A231*, 289–337.

Nunnally, J. C. (1975). *Introduction to statistics for psychology and education*. New York: McGraw-Hill.

Oakes, M. L. (1986). *Statistical inference: A commentary for the social and behavioral sciences*. New York: Wiley.

Rosenthal, R. (1984). *Meta-analytic procedures for social research*. Beverly Hills, CA: Sage.

Rosenthal, R. (1991). *Meta-analytic procedures for social research* (2nd ed.). Newbury Park, CA: Sage.

Rosenthal, R., & Gaito, J. (1963). The interpretation of levels of significance by psychological researchers. *Journal of Psychology, 55*, 33–38.

Rozeboom, W. W. (1960). The fallacy of the null hypothesis significance test. *Psychological Bulletin, 57*, 416–428.

Schmidt, F. L. (1992). What do data really mean? Research findings, meta-analysis, and cumulative knowledge in psychology. *American Psychologist, 47*, 1173–1181.

Schmidt, F. L., & Hunter, J. E. (1978). Moderator research and the law of small numbers. *Personnel Psychology, 31*, 215–232.

Schmidt, F. L., & Hunter, J. E. (1996). Measurement error in psychological research; Lessons from 26 research scenarios. *Psychological Methods, 1*, 199–223.

Schmidt, F. L., Hunter, J. E., & Urry, V. E. (1976). Statistical power in criterion-related validation studies. *Journal of Applied Psychology, 61*, 473–485.

Schmidt, F. L., Ocasio, B. P., Hillery, J. M., & Hunter, J. E. (1985). Further within-setting empirical tests of the situational specificity hypothesis in personnel selection. *Personnel Psychology, 38*, 509–524.

Sedlmeier, P., & Gigerenzer, G. (1989). Do studies of statistical power have an effect on the power of studies? *Psychological Bulletin, 105*, 309–316.

Winch, R. F., & Campbell, D. T. (1969). Proof? No. Evidence? Yes. The significance of tests of significance. *American Sociologist, 4*, 140–143.

20

ONE CHEER FOR NULL HYPOTHESIS SIGNIFICANCE TESTING

HOWARD WAINER

A major consideration for the American Psychological Association (APA) Task Force on Statistical Inference deliberations is the extent to which traditional null hypothesis significance testing (NHT) should be discouraged or even disallowed in the descriptions of research contained within the confines of APA journals. Members of the task force regularly receive substantial collections of comments and suggestions from APA members.

A large number of these comments and suggestions are surprisingly adamant in their opposition to NHT. The lack of appreciation of the potential value of NHT in the appropriate circumstances suggested that it might be useful to offer at least one cheer for NHT, a procedure that I believe can be a powerful and useful weapon in our methodological armorata.

Reprinted from *Psychological Methods*, 4, 212–213. Copyright 1999 by the American Psychological Association.

The time spent in writing this chapter was supported by the Educational Testing Service research allocation. I would like to thank my friends and colleagues Erich Lehmann, George Miller, Bob Mislevy, Don Rubin, and Spencer Swinton for helpful discussions about null hypothesis testing that clarified my own thinking.

To be perfectly honest, I am a little at a loss to understand fully the vehemence and vindictiveness that have recently greeted NHT. These criticisms seem to focus primarily on the misuse of NHT. This focus on the technique rather than on those who misuse it seems to be misplaced. (Don't ask me to be consistent here, because I find the National Rifle Association's similar defense of handguns completely specious.)

All would agree that "6:00 p.m." is a pretty stupid answer to most questions. But, because it is precisely the correct answer to some questions, it would be shortsighted to ban forever the use of "6:00 p.m."

Thus, it seems to me that the issue is to specify more clearly the kinds of questions for which NHT is suitable. To do this I do two things. First I take a broader view of its use than simply within scientific psychology. Second I go a little overboard and specify six different questions for which a reliable reject−not reject decision would be generally welcomed as a major breakthrough. I do not mean to imply that doing more (e.g., estimating the direction or size of the effect) might not have improved matters further; rather, only that when such further elaborations are not possible a simple, trustworthy reject−not reject decision can still be worthwhile.

How worthwhile? The canny reader will note that someone who could have done the appropriate studies to yield a reliable reject−not reject decision in some of the situations listed subsequently might have been rewarded with a Nobel Prize or even canonization. It is of some historical interest to note that the earliest example (Example 6) of NHT was aiming at the latter.

EXAMPLE 1: PHYSICS

H_0: $c_i = c_j$ for all i and j
H_1: $c_i \neq c_j$

Here c_i is the speed of light in reference frame i. Note that if, after credible effort when reference frames i and j are moving away from each other at great speeds, we were still unable to reject the null hypothesis, we would have gone a long way toward providing the basis for the theory of relativity. Einstein would have been pleased.

EXAMPLE 2: COSMOLOGY (A ONE-TAILED TEST)

H_0: $V_U \leq 0$
H_1: $V_U > 0$

V_U is the speed of expansion of the universe. Of course, solving the estimation problem $V_U = r$ for r would be a bigger contribution still, but rejecting H_0 is still a pretty impressive piece of work.

EXAMPLE 3: GEOPHYSICS

$H_0: D_{T\text{-}NY}(t) = k$
$H_1: D_{T\text{-}NY}(t) \neq k$

$D_{T\text{-}NY}(t)$ is the distance between Tokyo and New York City at some time t. The null hypothesis is simply that this distance is constant over time; the alternative is that it changes. Rejecting H_0 provides powerful evidence of continental drift and thus supports the theory of plate tectonics. Lacking such evidence, Vine and Matthews, in their definitive 1963 article, needed to use more indirect magnetic evidence to support their claim of the movement of the Earth's surface on giant plates. I suspect their task would have been much easier if they could have simply said, "Reject H_0 at $p < .001$."

EXAMPLE 4: CAREER COUNSELING

$H_0: E_s = T$
$H_1: E_s \neq T$

E_s is one's employment status at the end of next year; T is tenured. I suspect that there are a very large number of assistant professors who would find "Reject H_0 at $p < .001$" an enormously informative result.

EXAMPLE 5: PSYCHOLOGY

$H_0: \geq_I(t) = \geq_I(t + 1)$
$H_1: \geq_I(t) \neq \geq_I(t + 1)$

Here $_I(t)$ is the mean human intelligence at time t. Rejecting the null hypothesis suggests that the intelligence of the human race is changing. Once again, it would be more valuable to estimate the direction and rate of change, but just being able to state that intelligence is changing would be an important contribution. Early in this century, eugenicists warned of the dangers of differential reproduction rates, and shadows of this warning have shown up even in more recent work (Herrnstein & Murray, 1994). Rejecting H_0 must lie at the start of any credible eugenic theory.

EXAMPLE 6: THEOLOGY

$H_0: N_G = 0$
$H_1: N_G > 0$

N_G is the "number of supreme beings." I believe that a valid study that could conclude $P(\text{data} \mid H_0) < .0001$ would be greeted with enormous approbation. It is of more than passing interest to note that the earliest study I know of to use NHT (Arbuthnot, 1710) was concerned with exactly this hypothesis. Arbuthnot rejected H_0.

In this note, I have attempted to illustrate circumstances in which science is advanced with only a binary result. Sometimes such an advance is primitive, and if we can do better, we ought to. Sometimes it is the best we can do, and in doing so we have made a real advance. Scientific investigations only rarely must end with a simple reject – not reject decision, although they often include such decisions as part of their beginnings. The real test of relativity used the assumption that the speed of light was a constant to derive other observational equations, but having evidence to support that assumption was an important start. Providing a test of fit for a complex model (i.e., likelihood ratio tests for nested models) may be the most powerful use of NHT.

NHT, when used in its proper place, can provide us with valuable help. It is surely not the most powerful weapon we have, but neither is factor analysis, and no one is advocating a ban on that. So let me offer up one cheer for NHT with the hope that it can continue to be used when it can be of help and that instructors will more clearly indicate those circumstances.

REFERENCES

Arbuthnot, J. (1710). An argument for divine providence taken from the constant regularity in the births of both sexes. *Philosophical Transactions of the Royal Society, London, 27.*

Herrnstein, R., & Murray, C. (1994). *The bell curve: Intelligence and class structure in American life*. New York: Free Press.

Vine, F. J., & Matthews, D. H. (1963). Magnetic anomalies over oceanic ridges. *Nature, 199*, 947–949.

21

THE PROOF OF THE PUDDING: AN ILLUSTRATION OF THE RELATIVE STRENGTHS OF NULL HYPOTHESIS, META-ANALYSIS, AND BAYESIAN ANALYSIS

GEORGE S. HOWARD, SCOTT E. MAXWELL, AND KEVIN J. FLEMING

When Sancho Panza announced to Don Quixote that "the proof of the pudding is in the eating of it" (Cervantes, 1615/1986, p. 305), he was making an epistemological claim. People can always argue the relative merits of chocolate versus vanilla pudding, or the merits of pudding made from cows' milk versus goats' milk. However, because pudding is not an end in itself, but a means to other ends (e.g., bodily nourishment, pleasurable taste), rational argument will eventually cede to more pragmatic considerations. Statistical techniques are scientists' tools, which in combination with other tools (e.g., theories, methodologies) can sometimes produce tasty and nourishing knowledge. How effective are psychologists' statistical tools?

Reprinted from *Psychological Methods*, 5, 315–332. Copyright 2000 by the American Psychological Association.

Null hypothesis statistical tests (NHST) have been attacked in the psychology literature for many years. Despite numerous critiques of psychology's overreliance on NHST (Cohen, 1994; Kirk, 1996; McGrath, 1998; Meehl, 1978; Schmidt, 1996) and a number of spirited defenses (Abelson, 1997; Baril & Cannon, 1995; Frick, 1996; Hagan, 1997; Mulaik, Raju, & Harshman, 1997), many readers remain perplexed as to the exact nature of the problems with NHST and the value of alternatives to NHST (e.g., meta-analysis [Schmidt, 1992]; confidence intervals [Borenstein, 1994; Loftus & Masson, 1996]; parameter estimation [Cohen, 1988]; Bayesian statistics [Berry, 1996; Lee, 1997; Pruzek, 1997]). This chapter analyzes a series of three studies designed to measure the effectiveness of a program to reduce alcohol consumption in college students. These primary analyses will be conducted with three different statistical tools: NHST, meta-analysis, and Bayesian techniques.

Although the problems with NHST have been well documented, their use still dominates the research literature in psychology. Cohen (1994) has claimed that "after four decades of severe criticism, the ritual of null hypothesis significance testing—mechanical dichotomous decisions around a sacred .05 criterion—still persists" (p. 997). Some critics are shockingly extreme in their criticism of NHST: "Null hypothesis significance testing is surely the most bone-headedly misguided procedure ever institutionalized in the rote training of science students" (Rozeboom, 1997, p. 335). Or consider Tryon's (1998) depressing summary:

> Regardless of the technical merits or demerits of NHST, the fact that statistical experts and investigators publishing in the best journals cannot consistently interpret the results of these analyses is extremely disturbing. Seventy-two years of education have resulted in minuscule, if any, progress toward correcting this situation. It is difficult to estimate the handicap that widespread, incorrect, and intractable use of a primary data analytic method has on a scientific discipline, but the deleterious effects are undoubtedly substantial and may be the strongest reason for adopting other data analytic methods. (p. 796)

Why have psychological researchers been so slow in moving to analytic alternatives to NHST? Few researchers actually possess the technical expertise to render a judgment of the relative superiority of, for example, NHST approaches versus Bayesian approaches. However, one need not be a gourmet to render an opinion of the taste of different recipes for pudding. Similarly, observing several analytic techniques at work on the same sets of data might give psychologists the "flavor" of each approach's unique strengths and weaknesses.

First, it is important to be clear on exactly what aspect of NHST is being objected to, and how many of the "alternative" analytic techniques are already in use in the psychological literature. As Cohen (1994) suggested, the pervasive practice of focusing on a dichotomous acceptance/rejection of a null hypothesis can be problematic in programs of scientific research. This is especially true if achieving statistical significance becomes an important factor in the determination of whether an article is accepted for publication (Rosnow & Rosenthal, 1989; Sterling, 1959; Sterling, Rosenbaum, & Weinkam, 1995). This is because the null hypothesis is (arguably) never literally true, and thus, with a sufficiently large sample size, any nondirectional experimental hypothesis will be accepted. Of course, the sample size necessary to achieve reasonable statistical power to detect minuscule effects may be astronomical, so that all other things being equal, larger effects are more likely to appear in the literature than are smaller effects. Furthermore, one possible defense of hypothesis testing is that it reveals the directions of effects, whether they be small or large. Nevertheless, by focusing on the rejection of a null hypothesis as a criterion for scientific acceptance, a discipline adopts a stance where (in theory) every empirical proposition can be found to be statistically significant, even if the effect in question is minuscule (this problem is less severe when a one-tailed test is used). On the other hand, when researchers design studies with low power, the natural (and unfortunate) inclination when confronted with a statistically nonsignificant result is often to interpret the result as also being scientifically insignificant. Designing studies with low power also tends to lead to a body of literature in which results appear to contradict one another. For example, a group of researchers investigating a common set of potential correlates of depression may each provide empirical support for a unique predictor in a single study, simply because the probability of finding at least one statistically significant correlate may be reasonably high, even though the statistical power to detect any specific correlate is deficient.

Critics of NHST in psychology often recommend the use of graphical presentations, confidence intervals, effect sizes, and parameter estimation as methods that will partially remedy some of problems produced by overreliance on NHST techniques (Wilkinson et al., 1999). As we demonstrate, these approaches are completely consistent with NHST and will greatly enhance the scientific value of the data we report. All of the approaches recommended above are applicable, whether one analyzes the results from a single study or a series of replications (both literal and conceptual) of a study.

Suppose one wondered whether taking a particular course could reduce students' alcohol consumption more than taking a different course. It is a straightforward task to conduct an NHST analysis (along with graphs, confidence intervals, effect sizes, etc.) of the data that would test this proposition. Note that the analysis of the study's findings would be identical whether it was the first time the study was conducted or whether it was the hundredth time. At the level of data analysis, the use of NHST in psychological research seems to have fostered the isolation of studies within a programmatic series of investigations. Even when the results of a series of studies on a particular research question are published, the data from each study are usually analyzed separately. Rosnow and Rosenthal (1989) present an example of how the isolation of studies in the NHST approach (combined with power issues) can wreak havoc in psychological science.

> Smith conducts an experiment (with $N = 80$) to show the effects of leadership style on productivity and finds that style A is better than B. Jones is skeptical (because he invented style B) and replicates (with $N = 20$). Jones reports a failure to replicate; his t was 1.06, $df = 18$, $p > .30$, whereas Smith's t had been 2.21, $df = 78$, $p < .05$. It is true that Jones did not replicate Smith's p value. However, the magnitude of the effect obtained by Jones ($r = .24$ or $d = 50$) was identical to the effect obtained by Smith. Jones had found exactly what Smith had found even though the p values of the two studies were not very close. Because of the smaller sample size of 20, Jones's power to reject at .05 was .18, whereas Smith's power (N of 80) was .60 —more than three times greater. (pp. 1277–1278)

However, there are two categories of recommended alternatives to NHST that we believe are especially valuable for research in psychology: meta-analysis and Bayesian approaches. A unique strength of these two approaches lies in their ability to quantify the results of prior studies on a particular research hypothesis and to allow those data to enter into the primary analysis of the findings of any new study in examining the question of interest. To dramatize this important virtue, the primary data analysis from three studies on a topic is conducted by meta-analysis, and then by Bayesian techniques. These two approaches are then contrasted with an NHST approach that focuses on the separate analysis of the data from each study.

Numerous critics of NHST have recommended such approaches as replication and presentation of confidence intervals as alternatives to NHST in a single study. Reluctance to replicate may stem in part from the perceived need to achieve statistical significance at the .05 level in each and every study. For example, if multiple independent studies are conducted, each with a power of .70, the probability of two successive studies both attaining statistical significance is only .49, and the probability for three successive studies drops to .34. However, we show that meta-analysis and Bayesian approaches offer researchers the opportunity to demonstrate that additional studies increase the precision of estimated effects, even when results may not replicate from the perspective of NHST. In particular, meta-analysis and Bayesian approaches typically yield narrower confidence intervals when data are combined over multiple studies, thus encouraging researchers to present their results in terms of confidence intervals over multiple studies.

AN ILLUSTRATION OF THREE STATISTICAL APPROACHES

Three evaluations of the Psychology of Healthy Lifestyles (PHL) course were conducted. Study 1 was conducted in the fall of 1996 on 18 freshmen (13 furnished complete data) who were randomly assigned to PHL, out of 77 students who enrolled for psychology sections in a required university seminar. Students who were randomly assigned to university seminars in either social psychology or the history of psychology (36 out of 49 students furnished complete data) served as control participants. All missing data were due to students who were absent from class the day the survey was administered.

Eighty-nine treatment participants (out of 98 students in PHL) furnished complete data for Study 2 (fall 1997), and 50 treatment participants (out of 63 students) took part in Study 3 (spring 1998). There were 179 control participants in Study 2 and 85 control participants in Study 3. The assignment of participants to control conditions in Studies 2 and 3 was nonrandom, as freshmen taking an introduction to psychology course served as controls. Participation was voluntary, and all students received course credit. One can see that Studies 2 and 3 are replications of Study 1, even though a few minor aspects of the studies changed from study to study.

The topic of alcohol use and abuse by young adults actually consumes less than 6 hr of class time in PHL. It was also considered in all control courses except the history of psychology seminar in Study 1. This article focuses on the course's impact on the typical student's increase in alcohol consumption from senior year of high school to freshman year of college.

A question from the CORE substance abuse survey (Pressley, Harrold, Scouten, Lyerla, & Wmeilman, 1994) was used as a "Pre" measure ("Think back to your senior year of high school. About how many alcoholic drinks did you consume in a typical week?") and "Post" measure ("What is the average number of drinks you consume a week?") of alcohol consumption. The data of interest (Post mean number of drinks/week minus Pre mean number of drinks/week) considered changes from high school until the completion of the PHL or control courses in the college freshman year.

RESULTS AND ANALYSES

The data on mean change for treatment and control subjects from high school to completion of PHL and control courses in the three studies are presented in Table 21.1. A measure of the practical impact of the treatment was constructed to compare the statistical significance to the practical importance of the treatment (Kirk, 1996). The final column of Table 21.1 reflects how much less (expressed in percentages) the treatment participants in-

TABLE 21.1
Means and Standard Deviations for Increases From Pre to Post on Number of Drinks per Week for Treatment and Control Participants in the Three Studies

Study	Treatment			Control			Mean difference	Practical impact
	n	M	SD	n	M	SD		
1	13	1.58	2.19	36	2.21	2.98	0.63	29%
2	89	1.26	4.18	179	2.69	4.87	1.43	53%
3	50	0.80	5.47	85	2.95	6.20	2.15	73%

Note: Individuals in the treatment condition were students in a Psychology of Healthy Lifestyles course. Students enrolled in other courses served as controls. Practical impact reflects how much less treatment participants increased their alcohol consumption relative to changes in the control group.

creased their alcohol consumption relative to changes in their control group counterparts (i.e., mean difference between change in treatment and control groups divided by control mean change).

Is the Course Effective? An NHST Approach

Our interpretation of these data sets, as a doctrinaire NHST theorist would interpret them, borders on caricature. This is done for two reasons. First, we believe there is nothing intrinsically wrong with NHST. If we were to sensitively interpret these data, the critiques of Cohen (1994), Meehl (1978), Schmidt (1996), and others might ring hollow. The critics are not rejecting all of NHST, rather they are decrying a set of scientific shortcomings that they witness in the research literature, which are due to our overreliance on NHST approaches. Second, our ability to now properly interpret NHST results has been enriched by the discipline's response to the earlier critiques of NHST. Therefore, a doctrinaire interpretation helps readers to appreciate the improvements in our research practices that critics have achieved thus far.

Our only departure from a narrow doctrinaire presentation of NHST is that we supplement significance tests with confidence intervals. We do so not only to illustrate one example of how significance tests can be combined with other approaches to yield a better understanding of one's data but also because we form confidence intervals in each of the other approaches. Thus, by forming confidence intervals, we can more directly compare the NHST approach with meta-analytic and Bayesian approaches. We should hasten to point out that forming confidence intervals is only one of many suggested methods for supplementing NHST. The interested reader is referred to such sources as Harlow (1997), Steiger and Fouladi (1997), and Wilkinson and Task Force on Statistical Inference (1999) for further discussion of these issues and suggestions for specific alternatives.

An independent groups t test comparing mean change scores for treatment and control participants in Study 1 was nonsignificant, $t(47) = .70$, $p = .48$. This result is not surprising given the small sample size. Because the null hypothesis could not be rejected, one cannot assert that the treatment was effective beyond chance. Presumably, researchers in these circumstances would consider giving up on the PHL course and returning to their other university commitments.

A t test for independent groups on the same measure in Study 2 revealed that treatment participants reported increasing their drinking significantly less than controls, $t(266) = 2.37$, $p = .018$. A doctrinaire NHST advocate might see the results of Study 2 as a failure to replicate the findings of Study 1. Thus, at this point in the program of research, one would be confused—the course first appeared unsuccessful, then successful.

Finally, a similar analysis of the data in Study 3 revealed that treatment participants again reported increasing their drinking significantly less, $t(133) = 2.03$, $p = .042$, than control group participants from high school to college. In the face of these data, even a doctrinaire NHST psychologist might conclude that the PHL class significantly constrained drinking increases in these research participants, as two out of three rejections of the null hypothesis is rather encouraging. However, consider the NHST advocate's dilemma if Study 3 had obtained the same results as Study 1. Technically, the null hypothesis would only have been rejected once in three attempts, but intuitively, the data from this package of three studies would look rather promising.

We believe that in many respects the most serious limitation of NHST is that it has led researchers to focus their efforts on designing a single study to address scientific hypotheses. Although it might seem that the direct ability to test a statistical hypothesis would translate into a direct benefit for testing a scientific hypothesis, it is rarely the case in psychology that a single study can be viewed as providing a definitive test of a scientific hypothesis. Instead, multiple studies are almost always necessary. However, a serious limitation of the doctrinaire NHST approach is that it does not provide a useful foundation for accumulating evidence over multiple studies. For example, a narrow but traditional NHST interpretation of a single study is that either the null hypothesis is rejected or it is not. Thus, from this perspective, a series of studies yields a series of dichotomous "yes-or-no" outcomes. Historically, "vote-counting" methods have been used to accumulate these dichotomous outcomes over studies. However, Hedges and Olkin (1980) have convincingly shown that vote counting is ineffective as a method of accumulating results over studies. Somewhat less problematic is synthesis based on p values (see Winer, 1971, for further details). However, the fundamental problem with both of these approaches is that they fail to provide information about the parameters of direct interest (e.g., magnitude of treatment effect) in the original studies. We will see that both meta-analysis and Bayesian

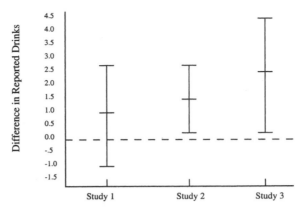

Figure 21.1. Mean difference between groups and 95% confidence interval, presented separately for each study. Dashed line represents the null hypothesis.

analysis provide a remedy to this problem by focusing attention on and accumulating evidence about parameters of direct interest to the investigator. Ironically, hypothesis testing often has a role to play even in meta-analysis and Bayesian analysis, but the hypotheses to be tested are different because they continue to pertain to the parameters of original interest. Thus, in our view, the advantage of meta-analysis and Bayesian analysis is not so much that they avoid significance testing, but instead that they provide methods for accumulating information over multiple studies in a manner that still focuses on the parameters of scientific interest, such as the magnitude of a treatment effect.

As a way of combating a simplistic overreliance on the results of NHST, several critics recommend graphic presentations of results along with confidence intervals. Figure 21.1 depicts the findings of the three studies analyzed separately.

Because the confidence interval around the mean for Study 1 includes no difference (i.e., the zero value), the null hypothesis could not be rejected at an alpha level of .05. The confidence intervals for all three studies are quite large. Cohen (1994) believed that such large confidence intervals represent a prime reason why psychologists have been slow to include confidence intervals in reporting their results.

Is the Course Effective? A Meta-Analytic Approach

Meta-analysis is frequently used as a secondary data analysis strategy (Cooper, 1998; Cooper & Hedges, 1994). In this article, meta-analysis is offered as a primary analysis strategy that represents an improvement over doctrinaire NHST because it allows one to accumulate data over studies to obtain a summary evaluation of the hypotheses of interest. Figure 21.2 presents

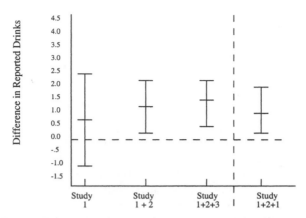

Figure 21.2. Mean difference between treatment and control groups and 95% confidence interval meta-analysis of various groupings of studies. The final column depicts the result that would have been obtained if the results of Study 3 had been exactly like those of Study 1. The horizontal dashed line represents the null hypothesis.

the meta-analytic mean treatment size and 95% confidence interval after the first study, after the first two studies, and after the three studies. The mean treatment effect (and confidence interval) after Study 1 is identical to the NHST analysis of Study 1 shown in Figure 21.1.[1] However, when the results from Study 2 are added to the meta-analysis, the mean treatment effect is clearly statistically significant (i.e., the confidence interval does not include zero), and the width of the confidence interval shrinks dramatically. Adding the results of Study 3 to the meta-analysis provides stronger evidence against the null hypothesis (the lower limit of the confidence interval rises from .1995 to .4721), even though the estimate of the mean treatment effect after three studies (1.36) is close to the effect size estimate after two studies (1.18). Once again, the addition of the third study further reduces the width of the confidence interval (see Figure 21.2, third column). One can see that the meta-analytic approach yields dramatically clearer results of the findings of the three studies than does an NHST approach that treats the data from these studies separately.

The fourth column in Figure 21.2 represents an explicit analysis of the hypothetical example suggested earlier. What would one conclude if the results of Study 3 had been identical to those found in Study 1 (i.e., same effect size, same N, etc.)? Having found nonsignificant results once and

---

[1] Because Studies 2 and 3 are not literal replications, a random-effects meta-analysis model might be deemed more appropriate than a fixed-effects model. However, a homogeneity analysis reveals that mean effects are not statistically different from one another, $\chi^2(2) = 1.22$, $p > .05$. Similarly, both the unweighted and weighted estimates of the between-studies variance component are negative. Thus, the random-effects model reduces to the fixed-effects model for these data.

significant results in another study from an NHST perspective, this "rubber match" would have made the score two nonsignificant findings and one significant finding. This would be a troubling occurrence for an NHST theorist who would be unable to conclude that the treatment was effective. But the fourth column of Figure 21.2 demonstrates that meta-analysis still can reject the null hypothesis, even with data from one "positive" study and two studies that failed to reject the null hypothesis.

Recall that in the real, three-study situation, the doctrinaire NHST scientist believes there is reasonable evidence to reject the null hypothesis — as two rejections out of three studies is promising indeed, given the conservative nature of $\alpha = .05$. The meta-analysis advocate clearly rejects the null hypothesis after Study 2, and then does so even more forcefully after Study 3 (the lower limit after three studies is .47, vs. .20 after two studies). However, scientifically, there is an even more important finding emerging. With the addition of each study's data, we obtain a more precise estimate of the PHL course's impact on students' drinking. After three studies, we can say with 95% confidence that PHL participants' reported increases (from high school to the completion of the course) in alcohol consumption will be from half a drink to two and a quarter drinks per week less than students who take some other course (e.g., Introduction to Psychology) instead. Our meta-analysis of Studies 1–3 now allows us to predict that treatment participants' increases in alcohol consumption will be 1.36 drinks/week less than those of control participants. Scientifically speaking, this strategy is superior to merely taking a fourth swing at a questionable null hypothesis.

The analysis thus far dramatizes two points. First, when analyzing data from a series of studies individually, as a doctrinaire NHST advocate might recommend, a researcher places the interpretation of her or his findings at serious risk with each replication, because the discipline recommends a rather conservative criterion ($\alpha = .05$). Of course, this conservative criterion is chosen to minimize the chance of Type I error. Perhaps researchers' tacit understanding of this sad reality has led them to be reluctant to replicate positive findings; instead, many publish without replication and move on to new research questions. Meta-analytic approaches (and Bayesian techniques) reverse this scientifically imprudent state of affairs. Second, one of Cohen's (1994) recommendations for change in reporting results was that

> as researchers, we routinely report effect sizes in the form of confidence limits. "Everyone knows" that confidence intervals contain all the information to be found in significance tests and much more . . . yet they are rarely to be found in the literature. I suspect that the reason they are not reported is that they are so embarrassingly large! (p. 1002)

Figure 21.2 depicts how a series of replications analyzed with meta-analysis can be relied on to solve the problem of "embarrassingly large" confidence intervals.

Before moving to Bayesian analyses, we reiterate that the NHST theorist depicted herein is largely a caricature. We still see value in null hypothesis testing, as was evident in our interpretation of the statistical significance of the results of the meta-analysis.

Is the Course Effective? A Bayesian Approach

Most readers of this journal are familiar with NHST and meta-analysis, so we could simply demonstrate the use of these procedures on our data. Because few psychologists are familiar with Bayesian analysis, a bit more explanation behind the decisions made in analyzing these data with Bayes's theorem is required. Further, Appendix 21.A contains a detailed Bayesian analysis of a very simple data set for the benefit of readers completely unfamiliar with this approach.

Traditional NHST as well as most examples of meta-analysis in the psychological literature is based on a frequentist interpretation of probability. From this perspective, the probability of an event is defined as its long-run relative frequency. For example, if a coin is tossed repeatedly, what proportion of tosses will result in heads in the long run? As has often been pointed out, an important implication of this perspective is that the null hypothesis is either true or false, and it is presumed to remain so over repeated trials. Even though the magnitude of the treatment effect is unknown, and its estimate would certainly vary from sample to sample, in the long run the population parameter value is regarded as a fixed constant. Because this value is fixed, with enough trials, the effect becomes either zero or nonzero. The treatment either has an effect or it does not. Thus, the probability that the null hypothesis is true (or false) is either 0 or 1. No other values are possible, so it becomes meaningless to talk about the probability that the null hypothesis is true or false, much less to attempt to quantify the probability. The primary distinction of the Bayesian approach is that it becomes permissible to interpret data as altering the truth or falsity of the null hypothesis. Thus, the purpose of collecting data is to allow empirical observations to alter an individual's beliefs about the phenomenon in question. This represents an important philosophical departure from the Fisherian and Neyman–Pearson NHST models, in which data are collected in order to choose between null and experimental hypotheses or between two alternative hypotheses.

A Bayesian analysis of data from these studies could proceed in any number of ways. For example, one possibility is to perform a test of the null hypothesis that the treatment and control group means are equal to one another. This test would then differ from standard NHST primarily in that it would incorporate information about the prior distribution. Another popular approach from the Bayesian perspective is to calculate the probability that the treatment has a beneficial effect relative to the control. In addition, when multiple studies are available, Louis and Zelterman (1994) describe a

Bayesian approach to meta-analysis. Further, Hedges (1998) shows how Bayesian meta-analysis can be implemented through hierarchical linear modeling. Such models provide parameters at multiple levels (e.g., a single study or a collection of studies) and allow uncertainty to be incorporated into models at multiple levels. For example, as in our presentation of meta-analysis, one issue that must be confronted is whether to regard effects as fixed or random. For simplicity, we continue to regard effects as fixed in our presentation of the Bayesian approach, but interested readers are encouraged to consult Hedges for further consideration of this issue. In our example, we have chosen to present yet another possibility for quantifying prior beliefs, namely, forming a 95% confidence interval for the mean difference between treatment and control. Our principal reason for emphasizing this approach is that it provides the clearest comparison with our NHST and meta-analysis findings, but readers should realize that this is far from the only way a Bayesian analysis might proceed.

The heart of Bayesian approaches lies in researchers precisely stating their beliefs (called *a priori* probabilities) about the outcome of the study before conducting the study. A priori beliefs are a lot like planned comparisons, but they are stated even more precisely and are more like point predictions (e.g., effect sizes, actual differences between group means, the exact size of a correlation coefficient). Priors can represent the researcher's own beliefs about a study's likely outcome, or they can be an expectation obtained from a review of the extant empirical literature. In addition to specifying an expected parameter value, strength of prior conviction is represented through some measure of variability of a prior probability distribution. The researcher then conducts the experiment and, using Bayes's theorem, calculates a new probability distribution (a posteriori) that is a reflection of the researcher's prior beliefs about the study's outcome, properly modified by the study's data. One of the most difficult aspects of Bayesian approaches lies in the specification of one's initial set of prior beliefs (i.e., precise beliefs about a study's outcome before any study on the topic is conducted).

Although usually viewed as less than optimal by most Bayesians, one can opt for a "noninformative" prior, which claims that in the researcher's opinion, all possible outcomes would be equally unsurprising. Although over 70 years of experience with null hypothesis testing might seduce researchers into believing that we have no prior expectations regarding our studies, a study's design often actually suggests our prior expectations.

Table 21.2 contains the initial prior (explained below) and the posterior means and standard deviations after each of the three studies. Posterior means and standard deviations from each study become the prior means and standard deviations for the next study in the series. The first column of data represents a Bayesian analysis of our three studies with no prior information supplied. Thus, the posterior probabilities in the "After Study 1" row are equal to the treatment and control means in Study 1 found in Table 21.1. The

TABLE 21.2
Means and Standard Deviations for Changes From High School to College in the Number of Alcoholic Drinks per Week for Treatment and Control Participants for Initial Prior Beliefs and Posterior Probabilities After Each of Three Studies

Sequence and Group	Noninformative prior		Confident pessimist		Confident optimist	
	M	SD	M	SD	M	SD
Initial prior						
Treatment	—	∞	5.5	.500	1.5	.500
Control	—	∞	5.5	.500	5.5	.500
After Study 1						
Treatment	1.58	.653	4.05	.397	1.53	.397
Control	2.21	.497	3.85	.353	3.85	.353
After Study 2						
Treatment	1.36	.366	2.80	.295	1.41	.290
Control	2.52	.293	3.29	.253	3.29	.253
After Study 3						
Treatment	1.25	.331	2.55	.276	1.33	.276
Control	2.59	.269	3.24	.237	3.24	.237

data presented in the "After Study 2" row represent the combination of prior probabilities ("After Study 1") with the data from Study 2 by means of Bayes's theorem, in the manner specified in Appendix 21.A. Because noninformative initial beliefs in themselves add nothing to an analysis of the data, this Bayesian analysis is mathematically equivalent (although not carrying the same technical interpretation) to the meta-analysis results reported in Figure 21.2.

A number of methods have been developed for eliciting prior probabilities in Bayesian analyses. Most of these methods focus on helping an individual generate a prior probability distribution that satisfies his or her intuitive feelings about the parameter(s) in question. Our approach in this article has a somewhat different focus. We chose to elicit prior probabilities from a group of 16 advanced graduate students and faculty because they had sufficient knowledge of both probability distributions and the alcohol consumption patterns of students on campus. Our goal was to develop general evidence about the range of prior beliefs in the efficacy of an alcohol intervention program such as the one assessed in our three studies.

We began with an assumption that each person's prior distribution about the increase in number of drinks per week in both the control and treatment conditions could be represented by a normal distribution. We made this assumption because (a) it seemed reasonable, (b) it led to relatively straightforward mathematics, and (c) it was the most frequent choice of prior distribution. Kadane and Wolfson (1996) provided further discussion and examples of methods for eliciting prior distributions, especially in the context of studies examining mean differences between groups. Thus, a mean and standard deviation must be specified to identify the parameters of a normal prior distribution. We asked each person to give us three pieces of information: (a) the mean increase in number of drinks per week they would expect to occur in the absence of an intervention, (b) the mean increase they would expect if individuals received a brief intervention as part of a course during a semester, and (c) a 95% confidence interval reflecting how certain they were about the estimate they provided in answer to the first question. The first two responses provided the mean of each person's prior distributions for the control and treatment conditions, respectively. The standard deviation (assumed for simplicity to be the same for both distributions) was obtained by dividing the width of the 95% confidence interval by 4, because the distance between the 5th and 95th percentiles equaled approximately 4 standard deviations in a normal distribution.

The preceding process produced 16 prior distributions. Instead of presenting the Bayesian approach for all 16 individuals, we have chosen three scenarios: (a) a noninformative prior, (b) a "confident" optimist, and (c) a "confident" pessimist. The noninformative prior scenario is simply one in which the prior receives no weight in calculating the posterior distribution after the first study. The prior distribution for the confident optimist was obtained in the following manner. The 16 respondents were rank ordered with respect to the mean difference they specified between the treatment and control groups. The mean for the prior of the confident optimist was then taken to be the median of the top quartile of respondents. The mean for the confident pessimist was derived in the same manner, except that it was based on the bottom quartile of respondents. The standard deviation of the prior distribution in both cases was taken to be the median standard deviation across all 16 respondents. By using the same standard deviation for both optimistic and pessimistic prior distributions, we essentially assumed that the optimist and the pessimist had the same degree of confidence in their prior beliefs.

The end result of this process produced two normal distributions with very little overlap. Our prototype optimist's prior distribution has a mean of 4.0 and a standard deviation of 0.5. Thus, the optimist is 95% confident that the true treatment effect corresponds to a reduction of between three and five drinks a week. As it turned out, 4 of our 16 respondents expressed a belief that the treatment would have no effect whatsoever, and thus the prototype pessimist's prior distribution has a mean of 0.0, once again with a standard deviation of 0.5. Such an individual is 95% confident that the true treatment effect lies somewhere between a reduction of one drink a week and an increase of one drink a week.

Keep in mind that the prototypic optimist and pessimist distributions shown here are intended to represent polar extremes of prior belief. Al-

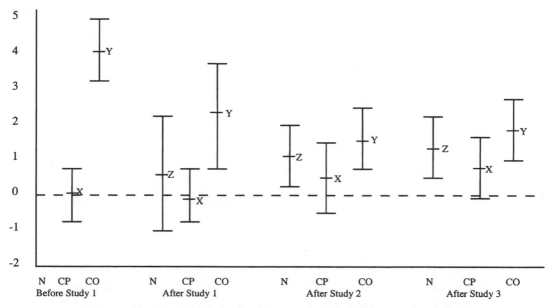

Figure 21.3. Mean difference between groups and 95% confidence interval for Bayesian analysis using noninformative (N), "confident" pessimist (CP), and "confident" optimist (CO) prior probabilities. Dashed line represents the null hypothesis. Before Study 1, the distribution of the N prior theoretically ranges from $-\infty$ to ∞; thus, it is not shown. X, Y, and Z refer to the centers of the CP, CO, and N intervals, respectively.

though we have left out the "silent majority" (the middle 50%), a comparison of posterior beliefs of the optimists and the pessimists reveals the extent to which the accumulation of data across additional studies should compel very different initial beliefs to converge.

Figure 21.3 graphically presents the results of our three studies using different initial prior distributions (noninformative, confident optimist, and confident pessimist). The far left of Figure 21.3 graphically depicts the initial 95% confidence interval of the confident optimist and confident pessimist. (No interval is shown for noninformative before Study 1, because the interval theoretically stretches from $-\infty$ to ∞.) By reading related confidence intervals from left to right in Figure 21.3, one can trace the development of our estimate of the treatment's mean effectiveness (and changes in the confidence interval around those means) as the data from each study are added to the analysis. Inspection of the confidence intervals from left to right for confident optimists shown in Figure 21.3 suggests that the optimists' initial prior beliefs were inappropriately high (i.e., treatment participants were to drink 4 drinks/week fewer than controls). These beliefs gradually became more realistic (i.e., 2.32 after Study 1, 1.88 after Study 2, 1.91 after Study 3) but still retained some evidence of the higher initial expectations, when contrasted with the 1.33 value found in both the Bayesian analysis with non-informed prior beliefs and the meta-analysis.

An interesting pattern of results was found with the addition of the studies' data to the prior beliefs of the confident pessimist. The confident pessimist's initial beliefs are anchored at zero difference between treatment and control participants in mean change scores from high school to freshman year of college. Then, after the first study, this type of rater actually expects control participants to perform better than treatment participants ($M = -.20$) on high school-to-college changes in reported alcohol consumption (see Appendix 21.B). However, after two ($M = .48$) and then three ($M = .70$) studies, the confident pessimist expects superior performance by treatment participants. However, even after three positive studies, confident pessimists' confidence interval still includes the null value (two-tailed). Apparently, it would require a fourth positive study ($p < .05$, two-tailed) to convince the confident pessimist of the value of the PHL course.

The confident optimist rejects the null hypothesis at each stage in this series of studies. Similarly, after both Studies 2 and 3, the analysis with non-informative initial priors also rejects the null hypothesis. However, with noninformative priors and the data from Study 1 alone, the null hypothesis cannot be rejected. At one level this is unsurprising, as this analysis is mathematically identical (albeit conceptually different) to the NHST analysis of Study 1 alone, which also was unable to reject the null hypothesis (see Figure 21.1, Study 1). More generally, all intervals associated with the noninformative prior are mathematically identical to the corresponding meta-analysis intervals shown in Figure 21.2. Although they differ conceptually, such matters as whether an interval does or does not contain zero will necessarily be the same in these two approaches.

Finally, inspection of the size of all confidence intervals shown in Figure 21.3 reveals once again that as the data from more replications are included, the width of the confidence intervals grows narrower for Bayesian analyses, as was the case with meta-analysis.

At this point in the exercise, researchers steeped in the frequentist tradition might (incorrectly) see Bayesian approaches as nothing more than meta-analysis with the addition of initial prior probabilities. However, the interpretation of our findings is fundamentally different, which allows researchers to make some additional claims that are not coherent from a frequentist perspective. For example, a reasonable question might be, "What is the probability that the treatment has some beneficial effect on reports of average number of drinks consumed?" In a more general sense, after having conducted this series of studies, researchers might ask how likely is it that the treatment "works?" The irony is that this question is meaningless from a frequentist NHST framework because, as we have already discussed, from this perspective the probability is either 0 or 1. Because no other values are even

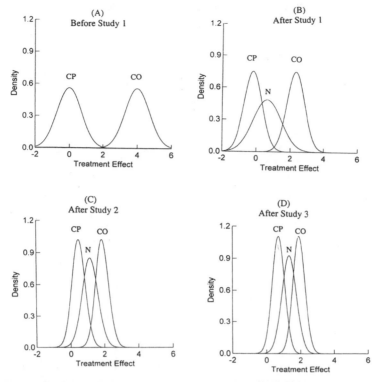

Figure 21.4. Probability distributions of the magnitude of the treatment effect using noninformative (N), "confident" pessimist (CP), and "confident" optimist (CO) prior probabilities. For Panel A, the distribution of the N prior theoretically ranges from $-\infty$ to ∞; thus, it is not shown.

theoretically possible in this framework, it becomes meaningless to discuss the probability that the treatment works from the viewpoint of traditional NHST. The irony is that this question cannot be answered from a frequentist NHST framework, because it is meaningless from that perspective. The frequentist definition of probability is long-run, relative frequency. However, the magnitude of the treatment effect is assumed to be a constant. Even though it is unknown, the value of this parameter is fixed. Because it never varies, the probability that the effect is nonzero is either 0 or 1—either the treatment has an effect or it does not. Thus, in traditional NHST, it is meaningless to discuss the probability that the treatment works.

However, the Bayesian perspective views the treatment effect in terms of a researcher's beliefs. From this perspective, it makes eminent sense to ask how likely it is that the treatment effect exceeds zero.

Figures 21.4 and 21.5 illustrate how the Bayesian method can address this question, as well as other potentially interesting related questions. Notice that both figures consist of four panels. In both cases, Panel A represents

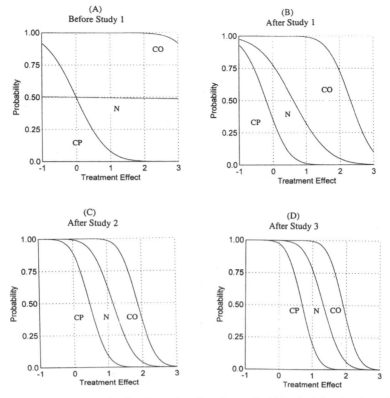

Figure 21.5. Cumulative distributions showing the probability that the treatment effect is at least as large as the value on the *x*-axis, for noninformative (N), "confident" pessimist (CP), and "confident" optimist (CO) prior probabilities.

beliefs before any data collection, whereas Panels B, C, and D represent cumulative beliefs after Studies 1, 2, and 3, respectively. Each panel depicts three curves, one for the confident pessimist, a second for the confident optimist, and a third for a noninformative prior. In all cases, the *x*-axis indicates the magnitude of the treatment effect, that is, the difference between the mean of the difference score in the control group minus the mean of the difference score in the treatment group. The difference between the two figures is that Figure 21.4 shows the density function corresponding to each belief distribution, whereas Figure 21.5 shows the corresponding cumulative distribution functions. With one exception (to be discussed momentarily), the distributions shown in Figure 21.4 all have a familiar bell shape, which is a consequence of our normality assumption. For example, in Panel A, we see two normal distributions, one with a mean of 0 and another with a mean of 4. These two distributions correspond to the treatment effect values shown previously in Table 21.2 for the confident pessimist and the confident optimist, respectively. Although it is less obvious, the standard deviations of the distributions in Figure 21.4 also are a direct reflection of the standard deviations shown in Table 21.2. This explains the apparent absence of a distribution for the noninformative prior. As shown in Table 21.2, the standard deviation of the distribution for the noninformative prior is theoretically infinitely large, so the corresponding distribution is theoretically flat across the entire width of the x-axis, all the way from $-\infty$ to ∞. The other three panels in Figure 21.4 show each person's distribution for the treatment effect after Study 1, after Studies 1 and 2, and after Studies 1–3, respectively. The most dramatic pattern here is the convergence of the three distributions. As more data are obtained, initial differences reflected in the prior probabilities carry increasingly less weight.

Figure 21.5 is mathematically equivalent to Figure 21.4 but conveys different information by presenting the distributions as cumulative functions. Although less familiar to most readers than the density functions of Figure 21.4, in many respects these cumulative functions are ultimately more informative for interpreting the results of a Bayesian analysis. Each curve in Figure 21.5 shows the probability that for the person in question (i.e., the confident pessimist, the confident optimist, or the individual with a noninformative prior) the treatment effect is at least as large as the value on the x-axis. A couple of examples may be useful to explain how to interpret these graphs. First, notice that the prior curve for the pessimist (in Panel A) shows a probability of .50 for an x value of 0. Recall that the mean of the prior pessimist distribution was zero, because a negative treatment effect was judged by the pessimist to be just as likely as a positive treatment effect. The curve in Panel A confirms that in the pessimist view, the probability is .50 that the treatment effect is at least as large as zero. Further notice that in the pessimist view, the prior probability that the treatment effect exceeds 2 is virtually zero. Second, the prior curve for the optimist (still in Panel A) shows that from this viewpoint, the treatment effect almost certainly exceeds 2 and is even likely to exceed 3. One clear implication of Panel A is that the three types of individuals have widely discrepant prior beliefs about the magnitude of the treatment effect. However, an equally clear pattern emerges in moving from Panel A to Panel D. By necessity, as more data become available, the three perspectives become increasingly similar. Notice in particular that by the end of the third study, even the pessimist believes that the treatment effect is almost certainly greater than zero. The optimist's beliefs have also been altered by the data. After initially believing that the treatment effect was almost certainly above 2, and probably even above 3, Panel D shows that after Study 3, the optimist view is now that the effect is almost certainly above 1 but is very unlikely to exceed 3. Graphs such as those shown in Figure 21.4 can be a useful tool for interpreting group differences, either from a single study or a succession of studies. We would encourage researchers to consider the possible benefits of presenting their data on group mean differences (or other types of parameter values) in this manner (see Berry, 1996, for more details).

GENERAL DISCUSSION

Our focus in this article has been solely on the statistical issues associated with NHST, meta-analysis, and Bayesian analysis as applied to our illustrative set of three studies. Our presentation has addressed what Cook and Campbell (1979) termed "statistical conclusion validity," the form of validity that lies at the heart of the debate about NHST. The full substantive evaluation of the results, particularly with respect to inferences about the effectiveness of the program, would also include consideration of other tools such as measurement, methodology, theory, and prior empirical research. As with many field studies, the likely effects of other threats to internal and construct validity such as nonrandom assignment to treatment and control programs in Studies 2 and 3, attrition, and the validity of the retrospective pretests would need to be critically considered and debated (Cook & Campbell, 1979). Improved statistical procedures do not obviate the necessity for careful attention to basic design and measurement considerations.

Numerous arguments supporting the continued use of NHST approaches (Frick, 1996; Hagan, 1997) have competed with calls for change in the status quo (Cohen, 1994; Kirk, 1996; McGrath, 1998; Meehl, 1978; Schmidt, 1996), leaving many psychologists confused and uncertain as to how best to analyze data and present their results. This study approached these issues from a completely different perspective. The results from a series of three studies were analyzed three different ways to give readers a concrete experience with the relative strengths and weaknesses of the three approaches.

The authors believe that psychology is in the middle of a profound shift in the statistical tools that it uses. Because of the brilliance of Sir Ronald Fisher's NHST approach and his explicit rejection of Bayesian approaches (based on a now-discredited view of the role of subjectivity in the philosophy of science), psychology became overreliant on NHST for about a 60-year period. Although much good work was accomplished during this period, the discipline's failure to fully use alternative statistical tools eventually created problems. Over the past 20 years, a revolution in the analytic approaches (beyond null hypothesis testing) available to psychologists has begun. Graphical presentation techniques, parameter estimation, confidence intervals, and meta-analysis are among the tools now accepted into widespread use. We believe that the near future will witness the widespread use of a broader range of statistical prosthetic devices. Bayesian approaches should be among the innovations that psychologists consider.

Because this article urges psychologists to create a better future, in part by considering additional statistical procedures, one hesitates to give too much attention to the history of NHST in psychology. The outcome of our discipline's problematic set of decisions over time has been characterized as follows: "I believe that the almost universal reliance on merely refuting the null hypothesis [is] one of the worst things [that] ever happened in the history of psychology" (Meehl, 1978, p. 817). There are several excellent historical treatments of the personalities involved (e.g., R. A. Fisher, E. S. Pearson, J. Neyman, T. Bayes; see Gigerenzer, 1993; Gigerenzer et al., 1989) and the issues at stake (e.g., p[hypothesis/data] vs. p[data/hypothesis]; exact level of significance as a property of data [Fisher] vs. alpha as a property of a test [Neyman and Pearson]). The eventual impact of this series of historical statistical controversies on research in psychology is now clear. A frequentist, hybrid form of hypothesis testing (Gigerenzer, 1993) came to dominate psychological research between 1940 and 1980. Positive results became synonymous with rejecting a null hypothesis.

> The figures are telling. Before 1940, null hypothesis testing using analysis of variance or t test was practically nonexistent: Rucci and Tweney (1980) found only 17 articles in all from 1934 through 1940. By 1955, more than 80% of the empirical articles in four leading journals used null hypothesis testing (Sterling, 1959). Today, the figure is close to 100%. By the early 1950s, half of the psychology departments in leading U.S. universities had made inferential statistics a graduate program requirement (Rucci & Tweney, 1980). Editors and experimenters began to measure the quality of research by the level of significance obtained. For instance, in 1962, the editor of the *Journal of Experimental Psychology*, A. W. Melton (1962, pp. 553–554), stated his criteria for accepting articles. In brief, if the null hypothesis was rejected at the .05 level but not at the .01 level, there was a "strong reluctance" to publish the results, whereas findings significant at the .01 level deserved a place in the journal. The *Publication Manual of the American Psychological Association* (1974) prescribed how to report the results of significance tests (but did not mention other statistical methods) and used, as Melton did, the label *negative* results synonymously with "not having rejected the null" and the label *positive* results with "having rejected the null." (Gigerenzer, 1993, p. 313)

At this point in history (ca. 1950), textbook authors also began to imply (incorrectly) that given data, the results of frequentist statistical tests could yield information about the probabilities of hypotheses, which has always been the researcher's desire, but which can only be properly ascertained by Bayesian approaches.

Perhaps our most fundamental point is that NHST, confidence intervals, meta-analysis, and Bayesian analysis are in no sense mutually exclusive. Instead, we believe that they complement one another, whether applied to individual studies or syntheses of multiple studies. Psychologists will continue to use statistical data analyses to describe empirical relationships and support inductive inferences. We have demonstrated some of the problems that have developed over a 60-year period as a result of the myopic use of NHST in psychological science. Because of some unintended negative consequences of the institutionalization of the classical NHST procedure, we demonstrated ways of analyzing data (meta-analysis, Bayesian approaches) that enhance hypothesis testing and offer more useful and scientifically meaningful information than does NHST alone. Much of what we have demonstrated has been said before in the context of theoretical arguments made elsewhere. However, it is often important for researchers in the field to see analyses in action for them to be able to take the next step of analyzing their data with these newer approaches. Finally, showing our graduate students a better way to analyze data than is typically found in psychological journals is important so that the next generation might be able to avoid the pitfalls that handicapped their forebearers.

APPENDIX 21.A.
ILLUSTRATION OF LOGIC
UNDERLYING BAYESIAN APPROACH

To illustrate the logic and the mechanics of the Bayesian approach, we present an example similar in spirit to the alcohol intervention studies discussed in the body of the chapter. Suppose an educational researcher is interested in estimating the mean Wechsler Intelligence Scale for Children (WISC) score of first-grade students in a large school district. A Bayesian analysis would capitalize on the researcher's prior knowledge, which might come from data collected in previous years, from any information about students in this district, or from normative information about the test itself.

In particular, the first step of a Bayesian analysis typically involves translating this prior knowledge into a probabilistic form, known as the *prior distribution*. In our examples, the prior distribution represents an individual's initial beliefs about the likely values of the population mean WISC score of first graders in this school district. The beliefs represented by this prior distribution are then altered to some extent by the observed data, resulting in a posterior distribution. The following example illustrates how the prior distribution and the data are combined to produce the posterior distribution.

For simplicity, we will suppose that the investigator knows that the WISC is normed to have a mean of 100. Furthermore, with no further information, we will assume that the researcher is comfortable with a mean of 100 for his or her prior distribution. The shape of the prior distribution is also important. For continuous data, a normal prior has many advantages, so that is what we will assume for the researcher. Having specified a mean of 100 for the normal prior, the one remaining parameter that must be specified is the standard deviation. Suppose the researcher is 95% confident that the true population mean WISC score of first graders in this district is between 90 and 110. Such a spread is consistent with a standard deviation of approximately 5, so we will assume a normal prior distribution with a mean of 100 and a standard deviation of 5 for our researcher.

The next step is obviously to collect some data. Suppose a random sample of 49 students yields a mean of 108 and a standard deviation of 14. The Bayesian analysis proceeds by using the information in the sample to alter the beliefs expressed in the prior distribution.

When the prior distribution of the mean is normal, the posterior distribution will also be normal if either (a) the parent population distribution underlying the observation is normal, or (b) the sample is moderately large, in which case the central limit theorem assures at least approximate normality. In theory, the procedure we present also requires that the population standard deviation be known. In practice, however, large-sample approximations justify this procedure even when the standard deviation is unknown, as long as the sample is not too small. For example, Berry (1996) recommends adjustments or alternate procedures only when sample size is below 30.

The fact that the posterior distribution is normal implies that all information about the distribution is captured in two parameters: the mean and the standard deviation. Thus, the remaining question is how to calculate the mean and the standard deviation of the posterior distribution.

The mean of the posterior distribution can be shown through Bayes's theorem to be a weighted average of the mean of the prior distribution and the sample mean observed in the data. Thus, in our example, the posterior mean will be somewhere between 100 and 108. The relative weights for the prior and the sample are proportional to the precision associated with each source of information. As the word suggests, *precision* simply reflects the degree of certainty reflected in a particular source.

When a normal distribution is assumed, the calculation of weights for means is very straightforward. To show how the weights are derived, we must introduce some notation. Let μ_0 and σ_0 represent the mean and standard deviation, respectively, of the prior distribution. Similarly, let $\bar{Y}$ and $\hat{s}$ represent the mean and the standard deviation, respectively, observed in the sample. The prior precision, denoted p_0, is then given by $p_0 = 1/\sigma_0^2$. In our example, $p_0 = 1/(5)^2$, or 0.04. Notice that smaller values of σ_0^2 correspond to tighter prior distributions and, hence, more precision. The sample precision p is similarly given by $p = n/\hat{s}^2$, which is the reciprocal of the squared standard error of the mean. In our WISC data, $p = 49/(14)^2$, or 0.25.

At first glance, it might seem unfair that the numerator for p is n but the numerator for p_0 is only 1. However, this comparison is misleading, because the corresponding denominator terms, $\hat{s}^2$ and σ_0^2, are not directly comparable. Instead, $\hat{s}^2$ estimates the variance of a single observation, whereas σ_0^2 reflects the perceived variance of the mean. As a result, σ_0^2 and $\hat{s}^2/n$ are comparable to one another, and these two terms form the basis for prior precision and precision based on the data.

The relative weights of the prior and the sample for calculating the posterior mean come from the respective precisions. Specifically, the mean of the posterior distribution is given by

$$\mu_1 = \left(\frac{p_0}{p_0 + p}\right)\mu_0 + \left(\frac{p}{p_0 + p}\right).$$

In our data, $p_0/(p_0 + p) = .04/(.04 + .25)$, and $p_0/(p_0 + p) = .25/(.04 + .25)$, implying weights of .14 for the prior and .86 for the sample. The resultant posterior mean is 106.90 in this example. Notice that this value is of necessity between the prior and sample means of 100 and 108, but for this example it is substantially closer to the sample mean because the sample value is considerably more precise in this instance.

It may also be of interest to calculate the standard deviation of the posterior distribution, which in the case of means is given by $\sigma_1 = 1/\sqrt{p_0 + p}$. In our example, $\sigma_1 = 1/\sqrt{0.04 + 0.25} = 1.86$.

Thus, before collecting data, our researcher believed that the mean was most likely to be 100, but the mean could (with 95% confidence) be anywhere from 90 to 110. However, observing data has altered the researcher's beliefs. Now he or she believes that the most likely value of the mean is 106.90. Uncertainty has also been substantially reduced, because he or she now believes (with 95% confidence) that the mean is between 103.25 and 110.55.

Several additional points deserve mention here. First, it is important to realize that the relative weights of the prior distribution and the sample data (.14 and .86, respectively, in our example) depend on three values: the standard deviation of the prior distribution, the sample size, and the observed standard deviation of scores in the sample. A researcher with a great deal of prior confidence will have a prior distribution with a small standard deviation, in which case the prior will receive relatively more weight. As a result, this person's prior beliefs will be less altered than those of someone else who had the same prior mean but expressed less initial certainty about his or her beliefs.

Second, the prior distribution can be thought of as contributing additional data points to the observed sample. In the case of estimating a mean from a normal population, the effective sample size of the prior distribution is given by $n_0 = s^2/\sigma_0^2$, which is approximately equal to 8 in our example. Thus, the researcher's prior beliefs about the population mean are equivalent to having observed 8 scores with a mean of 100 (recall that 100 was the prior mean). In addition to these 8 hypothetical scores, the researcher obtains a sample of 49 scores with a mean of 108. The mean of all 57 scores is

106.88, which agrees within rounding error with the mean of the posterior distribution.

Third, the standard deviation of the posterior distribution can be found by using the same logic just described for the mean. Substituting $n^0 = \hat{s}^2/\sigma_0^2$ into the expression for σ_1 shows that the posterior standard deviation can be written as $\sigma_1 = \hat{s}/\sqrt{n_0 + n}$. In our example, $\hat{s} = 14$, $n = 49$, and n_0 is approximately 8, yielding a value of 1.85 for σ_1, within rounding error of the actual value of 1.86. Thus, once again, it is as if 57 children's WISC scores had been calculated and their standard deviation was 14, thus producing a standard error of the mean equal to 1.85 (i.e., $14/\sqrt{57}$). Notice also that the standard deviation of the posterior distribution is necessarily smaller than the standard deviation of the prior distribution or the standard deviation of the sample mean (except for a noninformative prior, in which case they are equal). Both sources of information contribute to increased precision and certainty about the parameter in question.

Fourth, a common criticism of the Bayesian approach has been the subjectivity introduced by the prior distribution. However, implicit in the previous discussion is the fact that as sample size increases, the relative weight of the prior decreases. Thus, given enough data, individuals with very different prior beliefs will discover that their posterior distributions have essentially become identical. On the other hand, discrepant posterior distributions simply suggest the need for additional data before researchers can be expected to agree.

Fifth, the example included here is intended to illustrate the basic logic whereby the Bayesian approach combines prior knowledge with observed data to produce a posterior distribution. Although the logic illustrated here is applicable well beyond the case of a mean in a normal distribution, the actual calculations can become much more daunting. Interested readers may want to consult such sources as Albert (1996), Berry (1996), Lee (1997), and Gelman, Carlin, Stern, and Rubin (1995) for further information about applying Bayesian methods to more complicated problems. In addition, software for performing Bayesian analyses is becoming much more widely available. For example, as of this writing, Bayesian software is beginning to become available free of charge through the Internet, at such sites as FIRST BAYES (http://www.shef.ac.uk/&sim§lao/lb.html) and BUGS (http://www.mrcbsu .cam.ac.uk/bugs/Welcome.html).

APPENDIX 21.B. EXPLANATION OF APPARENT
PARADOX IN BAYESIAN ANALYSIS OF STUDY 1

This scenario represents a somewhat paradoxical finding, given that the confident pessimist initially believes that drinking will increase by equal mounts for treatment and control participants (i.e., by 4 drinks per person), and the data show control participants actually increasing by 2.21drinks/person, whereas treatment participants increased by only 1.58 drinks/person! How could this scenario lead to posterior probabilities in which control participants were actually expected to increase their drinking over time .20 drinks/week less than treatment participants?

The paradox dissolves when one recalls that in Study 1 there were only 13 persons in the treatment group but 36 persons in the control group. Like NHST and meta-analysis, Bayesian statistics are dependent on sample size, as the data adjust prior expectations for each group (treatment or control) separately. Confident pessimists expected both treatment and control participants' drinking to increase by 5 drinks/person from high school to college. Thus a mean of zero is found for the initial prior beliefs of confident pessimists in Figure 21.3. After Study 1, the control group's posterior change from high school to college was 3.85, whereas the treatment group's posterior change was 4.05—in spite of the fact that treatment participants increased their drinking less than did control participants in Study 1. Because Study 1 data corrected the initially too-high change score estimates, a larger correction was made for control participants than for treatment participants because the control group was almost three times as large as the treatment group in the study.

Stated slightly differently, had the treatment group been of the same size ($n = 36$) as the control group in Study 1, the posterior treatment mean (after Study 1) would have been adjusted to 3.22 (rather than .05) and the difference between treatment and controls in posterior means in that case would have maintained the .63 treatment group superiority found in the data. Such anomalous findings, due to differences in sample sizes, are also found with NHST and meta-analytic approaches. Mathematically, Bayesian approaches seem to be no more susceptible to such problems than are frequentist approaches.

REFERENCES

Abelson, R. P. (1997). A retrospective on the Significance Test Ban of 1999 (If there were no significance tests, they would be invented). In L. L. Harlow, S. A. Mulaik, & J. H. Steiger (Eds.), *What if there were no significance tests?* (pp. 117–141). Mahwah, NJ: Erlbaum.

Albert, J. (1996). *Bayesian computation using Minitab.* Belmont, CA: Wadsworth.

Baril, G. L., & Cannon, J. T. (1995).What is the probability that null hypothesis testing is meaningless? *American Psychologist, 50,* 1098–1099.

Berry, D. (1996). *Statistics: A Bayesian perspective.* Belmont, CA: Duxbury Press.

Borenstein, M. (1994). A note on the use of confidence intervals in psychiatric research. *Psychopharmacology Bulletin, 30,* 235–238.

Cervantes, M. (1986). *Don Quixote de la Mancha*. New York: Farrar, Straus & Giroux. (Original work published 1615)

Cohen, J. (1988). *Statistical power analysis for the behavioral sciences* (2nd ed.). Hillsdale, NJ: Erlbaum.

Cohen, J. (1994). The earth is round (p < .05). *American Psychologist, 49*, 997–1003.

Cook, T. D., & Campbell, D. T. (1979). *Quasi-experimentation: Design and analysis issues for field settings*. Chicago: Rand McNally.

Cooper, H. M. (1998). *Synthesizing research: A guide for literature reviews*. Newbury Park, CA: Sage.

Cooper, H., & Hedges, L. (Eds.). (1994). *The handbook of research synthesis*. New York: Russell Sage Foundation.

Frick, R. W. (1996). The appropriate use of null hypothesis testing. *Psychological Methods, 1*, 379–390.

Gelman, A., Carlin, J. B., Stern, H. S., & Rubin, D. B. (1995). *Bayesian data analysis*. New York: Chapman & Hall.

Gigerenzer, G. (1993). The superego, the ego, and the id in statistical reasoning. In G. Keren & C. Lewis (Eds.), *A handbook for data analysis in the behavioral sciences* (pp. 311–339). Hillsdale, NJ: Erlbaum.

Gigerenzer, G., Swijtink, Z., Porter, T., Daston, L., Beatty, J., & Kruger, L. (1989). *The empire of chance: How probability changed science and everyday life*. Cambridge, England: Cambridge University Press.

Hagan, R. L. (1997). In praise of the null hypothesis statistical test. *American Psychologist, 52*, 15–24.

Harlow, L. L. (1997). Significance testing introduction and overview. In L. L. Harlow, S. A. Mulaik, & J. H. Steiger (Eds.), *What if there were no significance tests?* (pp. 1–17). Mahwah, NJ: Erlbaum.

Hedges, L. V. (1998). Bayesian meta-analysis. In B. S. Everitt & G. Dunn (Eds.), *Statistical analysis of medical data: New developments* (pp. 251–275). New York: Oxford University Press.

Hedges, L. V., & Olkin, I. (1980). Vote-counting methods in research synthesis. *Psychological Bulletin, 88*, 359–369.

Kadane, J. B., & Wolfson, L. J. (1996). Priors for the design and analysis of clinical trials. In D. A. Berry & D. K. Stangl (Eds.), *Bayesian biostatistics* (pp. 157–184). New York: Marcel Dekker.

Kirk, R. (1996). Practical significance: A concept whose time has come. *Educational and Psychological Measurement, 56*, 746–759.

Lee, P. (1997). *Bayesian statistics*. New York: Wiley.

Loftus, G., & Masson, M. (1996). Using confidence intervals in within-subject designs. *Psychonomic Bulletin and Review, 1*, 476–490.

Louis, T. A., & Zelterman, D. (1994). Bayesian approaches to research synthesis. In H. Cooper & L. V. Hedges (Eds.), *The handbook of research synthesis* (pp. 411–422). New York: Russell Sage Foundation.

McGrath, R. E. (1998). Significance testing: Is there something better? *American Psychologist, 53*, 796–797.

Meehl, P. E. (1978). Theoretical risks and tabular asterisks: Sir Karl, Sir Ronald, and the slow progress of soft psychology. *Journal of Consulting and Clinical Psychology, 46*, 806–834.

Mulaik, S. A., Raju, N. S., & Harshman, R. A. (1997). There is a time and a place for significance testing. In L. L. Harlow, S. A. Mulaik, & J. H. Steiger (Eds.), *What if there were no significance tests?* (pp. 65–115). Mahwah, NJ: Erlbaum.

Pressley, C.A., Harrold, R., Scouten, E., Lyerla, R., & Wmeilman, P. (1994). *Core alcohol and drug survey: User's manual* (5th ed.).Carbondale, IL: Core Institute.

Pruzek, R. M. (1997). An introduction to Bayesian inference and its applications. In L. L. Harlow, S. A. Mulaik, & J. H. Steiger (Eds.), *What if there were no significance tests?* (pp. 287–318). Mahwah, NJ: Erlbaum.

Rosnow, R. L., & Rosenthal, R. (1989). Statistical procedures and the justification of knowledge in psychological science. *American Psychologist, 44*, 1276–1284.

Rozeboom, W.W. (1997). Good science is abductive, nothypothetico–deductive. In L. L. Harlow, S. A. Mulaik, & J. H. Steiger (Eds.), *What if there were no significance tests?* (pp. 335–391). Mahwah, NJ: Erlbaum.

Schmidt, F. L. (1992). What do data really mean? Research findings, meta-analysis, and cumulative knowledge in psychology. *American Psychologist, 47*, 1173–1181.

Schmidt, F. L. (1996). Statistical significance testing and cumulative knowledge in psychology: Implications for training of researchers. *Psychological Methods, 1*, 115–129.

Steiger, J. H., & Fouladi, R. (1997). Noncentrality interval estimation and the evaluation of statistical models. In L. L. Harlow, S. A. Mulaik, & J. H. Steiger (Eds.), *What if there were no significance tests?* (pp. 221–257). Mahwah, NJ: Erlbaum.

Sterling, T.D. (1959). Publication decisions and their possible effects on inferences drawn from tests of significance — or vice versa. *Journal of the American Statistical Association, 54*, 30–34.

Sterling, T.D., Rosenbaum, W.L., & Weinkam, J. J. (1995). Publication decisions revisited: The effect of the outcome of statistical tests on the decision to publish and vice versa. *The American Statistician, 49*, 108–112.

Tryon, W. W. (1998). The inscrutable null hypothesis. *American Psychologist, 53*, 796.

Wilkinson, L., & Task Force on Statistical Inference. (1999). Statistical methods in psychology journals: Guidelines and explanations. *American Psychologist, 54*, 594–604.

Winer, B. J. (1971). *Statistical principles in experimental design* (2nd ed.). New York: McGraw-Hill.

VI

SPECIAL TOPICS IN CLINICAL RESEARCH

A variety of special circumstances, methods, and problems emerge in clinical research. Three broad and interrelated areas of clinical research and the methodological issues they raise are highlighted in this selection of chapters. The first section pertains to the evaluation of psychotherapy and the relation of methodological issues to extension of findings from research to clinical practice. The second section pertains to evaluation in clinical work and methods that can be used to improve clinical care and the inferences that can be drawn about patient progress. The third section includes expansion of outcome assessment of interventions to address criteria that may be particularly important to patients and society at large.

TREATMENT EVALUATION: EFFICACY AND EFFECTIVENESS

Psychotherapy research has advanced considerably. There are now many interventions with strong empirical evidence in their behalf. Efforts have been made to delineate and distinguish them from a sea of unevaluated interventions. The treatments are referred to as *evidence-based treatments*, but many other terms have been used as well, including *empirically validated treatments*, *empirically supported treatments*, *evidence-based practice*, and *treatments that work* (e.g., Chambless et al., 1998; *Evidence Based Mental Health*, 1998; Nathan & Gorman, 2002; Roth & Fonagy, 1996). The different terms have emerged from somewhat independent attempts to identify such treatments spanning disciplines, various organizations or professional groups, and countries. Typically, the criteria for delineating such treatments include evidence in behalf of the treatment from studies that randomly assign participants to conditions, carefully specify the client population, use treatment manuals, and evaluate treatment outcome with multiple measures. Also, replication of treatment effects beyond an initial study is often required, especially replication by an investigator different from the one that originally demonstrated the effects.

All of this sounds wonderful and certainly objection free. After all, if there are evidence-based treatments, would anyone use any other kind of treatment? Actually, there are all sorts of reasons one might not use an evidence-based treatment. Most obviously, not every problem seen clinically has an evidence-based treatment that is available. Also, training is an issue. Most therapists in practice, most graduate students enrolled in clinical or counseling psychology, and most psychiatrists in residency training are not exposed to, yet trained in, evidence-based treatments. Research is slow to diffuse to application and also very slow to alter clinical training. There are methodological issues too that raise important concerns about evidence-based treatments and could explain why someone might want to use a treatment that is not evidence-based. Let us take up the methodological issues related to this literature.

For a treatment to be designated as an evidence-based treatment, it must be evaluated in well-controlled treatment outcome studies. Well-controlled studies often include practices that may restrict the generality of the findings. A natural tension exists in research in which meticulous control of the conditions for purposes of experimentation can compete with the extent to which the results may apply to less well-controlled settings (i.e., clinical work in everyday life). This is not an argument for loose or uncontrolled studies, but rather an argument for matching the design and conditions of experimentation to the goals of the study.

In contemporary research, the distinction between efficacy and effectiveness research has been proposed to capture the issue (Hoagwood & Hibbs, 1995). *Efficacy research* refers to treatment outcomes obtained in controlled psychotherapy studies that are conducted under laboratory and quasi-laboratory conditions (e.g., participants are recruited, they may show a narrow range of problems to achieve a fairly homogenous sample, treatment is specified in manual form, and treatment delivery is closely supervised and monitored). *Effectiveness research* refers to treatment outcomes obtained in clinic settings where the usual control procedures are not implemented (e.g., patients seek treatment, many present multiple clinical problems, treatment is delivered and varied at the discretion of the therapist, there is no formal monitoring of quality of treatment delivery). Efficacy and effectiveness studies can be conceived as a continuum or multiple continua because several dimensions can vary across clinic and laboratory settings that affect generality of the results (Kazdin, 2003). A key question is whether the treatments demonstrated in controlled studies (efficacy trials) will be effective when extended to clinical settings (effectiveness trials). The issue is an important place to see how interlocked substantive (the effects of psychotherapy) and methodological issues (generalization of the results) can be.

Chapter 22 by Peter E. Nathan, Scott P. Stuart, and Sara L. Dolan discusses efficacy and effectiveness research and the role of different types of studies in building the knowledge base. The chapter covers many topics that pertain to psychotherapy research methodology, including the use of various control and comparison conditions, the benefits and liabilities of random assignment, and the use of treatment manuals. The issue of efficacy versus effectiveness has been of concern for 40 to 50 years, as this chapter conveys, although the terms have varied (e.g., *analogue* vs. *applied research*, *laboratory* vs. *applied research*). In the process of describing the issues and concerns, the chapter provides an informative overview of several years of adult psychotherapy research and a few key studies that have had a special role in contemporary treatment literature.

In chapter 23, Jacqueline B. Persons and George Silberschatz provide two points of view on the utility of randomized controlled trials for therapists in clinical practice. *Randomized controlled trials* (RCTs), sometimes also referred to as *randomized controlled clinical trials*, are recognized in intervention research in medicine, psychology, and other disciplines as being the best and most definitive way to test the effects of a treatment. RCT has come to refer to a *true experiment* in which participants are assigned to conditions randomly and the investigator controls administration of the treatment. The *clinical trial portion* of RCT refers to the fact that the experiment focuses on treating a clinical problem (e.g., cancer, posttraumatic stress disorder). In this chapter, the authors provide opposing views about the utility of RCTs for clinical work. It is important for researchers interested in intervention research to be conversant with strengths and limitations of RCTs and their role in developing treatments for clinical work. Also, in this chapter, the role of other types of designs than RCTs (e.g., quasi experiments, single-case studies) is mentioned as well.

In chapter 24, Gregory N. Clarke discusses how one might bridge the differences in efficacy and effectiveness research. Critical dimensions of treatment research are presented including sampling of patients, therapist training, variations of treatment dose, and the study of treatment processes. Evaluation of these and other facets of treatment may improve generality of treatment results. Another lesson can be drawn from this chapter. In psychotherapy research, a concern is whether the effects of the treatment can be generalized to clinical practice. Perhaps as or even more important would be the extension of some methodological practices used in research, even in diluted form, to clinical practice. Most clinical practice, for example, does not systematically evaluate patient progress (no formal or systematic assessment) or follow a prescribed treatment regimen. These facets, if extended to treatment, may actually improve patient care (Kazdin, 2003). Systematic observation and evaluation ought not to be restricted to research. Many options exist for using such observations in clinical work, as discussed in a later section.

Chapter 25 by David B. Wilson and Mark W. Lipsey moves beyond efficacy and effectiveness. A central issue for research is the extent to which the *way* something is studied can influence the findings. As they discuss, the source of information, assessment of treatment outcome, comparison groups, and other design features can influence the findings. The chapter uses meta-analysis as a way to demonstrate the influence of methodological factors on treatment outcome. Meta-analysis is used very often as a way of reviewing a literature and testing hypotheses. This chapter nicely illustrates how such an analysis is accomplished.

I have mentioned earlier that methodology (e.g., participant-sampling techniques, measures, data-analytic techniques) is sometimes taught as a tool merely to elaborate a phenomenon of interest. Yet, methodology is more than a neutral means to achieve some end. What we see, find, and conclude can be directly influenced by how we go about conducting the study. Once this is understood, there can be a liberating effect on researchers and reviewers. Multiple ways of studying a phenomenon are essential to ensure that no single method is perhaps giving a narrow or biased picture. This is a theme that began the book with the two chapters of the introduction.

EVALUATION IN CLINICAL WORK

A distinction that one grows up with in clinical psychology is between research and clinical practice. The distinction often emphasizes interests of students in training and career paths, that is, some individuals emphasize and prefer to work in research and others in clinical practice. We say in graduate training that we combine these by training scientist–practitioners, that is, individuals who have an appreciation of both and perhaps even engage in both after they complete their degree. However, this is rarely the case. That is, very few clinical psychologists engage in both the science part (research) and practice (clinical work) or keep up on the research and integrate findings in their practice. In research, students learn to operationalize, test, and evaluate ideas and predictions. In clinical work, emphasis is on helping a particular client.

In clinical practice, there is usually little or no systematic assessment and evaluation of client progress, either through the use of measures of client change or documentation that treatment is responsible for change. Instead of systematic assessment, clinical judgment is used as the basis of measurement. Indeed, clinical judgment is usually the basis to decide what the client "needs," what treatment ought to be applied, whether therapeutic changes have been achieved, and when to stop or alter treatment. Clinical judgment has been roundly criticized because it has not fared very well when compared with the use of more systematic data to make decisions (see Dawes, 1994). It is important to move beyond the criticism. A few generations of researchers and clinicians have now lobbed cogent polemics at each other, and the price has continued to be quality of research (e.g., clinical research is often not clinically helpful) and quality of patient care (e.g., much of what is known is not used in clinical practice). It would be better perhaps to focus on issues a little differently and ask, "How can we extend knowledge from research to aid clinical care, and how can clinical care be conducted in a way that is systematic and of optimal benefit to the client?" Occasionally, innovative practitioners develop means of systematic evaluation in clinical practice to assess patient progress and to make decisions about treatment (e.g., Clement, 1999), but they are stark exceptions.

Evaluation in clinical practice is important in relation to the prior discussions of efficacy and effectiveness of therapy and whether findings in well-controlled studies generalize to clinical practice. Even if findings did generalize from research to practice, one would not necessarily expect an effective treatment to work with all or most patients all of the time. This is true of treatment whether it is medical or psychological. For example, medications for depression are effective (lead to recovery, significantly reduce symptoms) in approximately 50–60 percent of the adult patients (Agency for Health Care Policy and Research, 1999). This means that even with an effective treatment, many individuals may not be affected or improved with treatment. This is not an indictment of medication; any treatment is likely to have exceptions. Indeed, two agenda items for intervention research are to reduce the proportion of individuals who do not respond or who cannot be treated and to understand moderators of responsiveness to treatment. The fact that treatment does not always work means that evaluation of any particular application, for example, clinical work, is rather important.

A critical issue for clinical work is evaluation of patient progress during the course of treatment to ensure that progress is being made and to assist in decision making (e.g., when to alter treatment, add other treatments, or end treatment). Another reason for evaluating clinical work is that systematic collection of information might be used to draw inferences about what treatments work and for whom. That is, through the accumulation of data in clinical practice, one might be able to draw conclusions that would help patients in the future.

In this section, chapters discuss evaluation in clinical work. Chapter 26 by Michael J. Lambert, John C. Okiishi, Lynn D. Johnson and Arthur E. Finch provides a method of assessment that can be used in clinical work and illustrate how it can be applied. The chapter conveys how systematic evaluation in clinical work can yield important insights about therapy. The specific measure included in the chapter might be useful in many contexts and treatment settings. However, the purpose of including this chapter is not to advocate for a particular measure. Indeed, other types of measures are mentioned that might be used, and other sources could be cited that sample a range of measures for clinical work (Clement, 1999; Cone, 2000; Kazdin, 1993). The key point is that evaluation in clinical work is not an enemy or something that interferes with treatment. Just the opposite, clinical care demands assessment to ensure that progress in treatment and therapist decision making have a better basis than subjective judgment and opinion.

Research training for behavioral scientists usually focuses on group research designs, that is, studies in which two or more groups are compared in some way and, of course, the results are evaluated statistically. The many other types of research methodologies are not usually taught. Single-case experimental designs form one such category. These designs can be used to study phenomena in individuals but also in large groups. The methodology includes true experiments, that is, arrangements in which strong causal relations can be inferred. In terms of experimental validity and controlling sources of bias and artifact, single-case research meet the same criteria of rigor as the more familiar group studies.

There is knee-jerk skepticism about studying the individual and what can be learned in many areas within psychology. This is unfortunate. In the history of psychology and psychiatry, the "case study" has meant anecdotal cases in which unsystematic impressions of clinicians are provided. This is nothing like single-case experiments. Indeed, perhaps we have been unwittingly misled about the potential yield from studying individuals. Other authors have carefully elaborated the conditions of studying cases that permit one to draw causal inferences (Sechrest, Stewart, Stickle, & Sidani, 1996). It is important to mention single-case experiments and variations of them because of their special utility in clinical work.

In chapter 27, David L. Morgan and Robin K. Morgan provide an overview of single-case research and convey key characteristics. The methodology is compared with group research with which we are more familiar. Among the key characteristics are repeated (continuous) assessment and replication of intervention effects. Single-case research is a legitimate way of conducting experiments. However, the reason for mentioning the approach here is to provide methods of evaluation that might help patient care and inferences drawn about treatment in the context of clinical work.

In chapter 28, I discuss ways to improve the quality of inferences that can be drawn from case studies over traditional anecdotal methods. Assessment of the case over time, that is, on multiple occasions, was discussed in the previous chapter. Use of such assessments greatly enhances the conclusions one can reach about treatment. Patterns in the data can be used to evaluate change and to help rule out or make implausible rival hypotheses about what factors are responsible for change. A critical priority of case studies is patient care, that is, improvement of the case. The challenge is ensuring that this priority is maintained and that inferences can be drawn about change. Several case examples are provided that vary in the strength of conclusions that can be drawn about the intervention effects without sacrificing clinical care.

Although the chapter focuses on specific strategies of drawing inferences, there is a broader issue that led to its inclusion here. The goals of methodology are to permit one to draw valid inferences. The challenge is not to impose a rigid design on all situations, but to ask what information can be brought to bear to improve the quality of inferences. Methodology is a way of approaching situations to obtain better information than would otherwise be available, to overcome limits of unsystematic information and human perception, and to pose and test hypotheses. This applies equally to research and clinical practice.

The previous chapters suggest that a variety of assessments and design variations to evaluate clinical work. In chapter 29, Karla Moras, Leslie A. Telfer, and David H. Barlow use single-case designs to evaluate treatments for two patients with anxiety and mood disorders. The cases are treated and evaluated individually using varied design and assessment strategies. The chapter includes other excellent methodological practices, such as using multiple measures of outcome, evaluating treatment integrity, and using a manual to guide the therapy. The chapter nicely conveys the applicability of theory, hypothesis testing, and questions about the effectiveness of different treatments with the individual case. Also, this chapter shows that methodological features of research (e.g., using treatment manuals, monitoring treatment integrity) may be very applicable to clinical work.

EXPANDING OUTCOME ASSESSMENT AND DOMAINS

Treatment research, by definition, focuses on producing improvements in clients over the course of treatment. Evaluation of the change is usually based on statistical criteria (statistical significance). In clinical psychology and other areas with applied interests, interventions are intended to have impact that is important and makes a difference. Of course, this statement is obvious. Yet, if one canvasses treatment outcome studies, it is not clear in most instances that patients were helped in palpable ways.

Research focuses on statistically significant changes on one or more measures, and such changes do not necessarily reflect important differences in terms of client functioning in daily life. Consider a hypothetical example of a treatment study in which we provide treatment and show that those who receive treatment (as opposed to no treatment) improve significantly on a measure or few measures of adjustment. Let us say we use one of the most well developed and validated measures (e.g., Minnesota Multiphasic Personality Inventory) as part of our outcome assessment battery. Does improvement on the scale have any bearing to how the client is functioning in everyday life? Is the change made on the measure(s) one that signals an important change in day-to-day functioning? Statistically significant change may have no bearing on this question because the criteria for change have to do with means, standard deviations, effect sizes, sample sizes, and nothing really about the importance of the change (e.g., whether the clients' symptoms are reduced so they feel better and can go to work, whether their marriages were notably improved). The concept of clinical significance has been introduced as a supplement to statistical significance to address these concerns.

Clinical significance reflects the extent to which changes make a difference to the individual in everyday life. In chapter 30, I discuss the meaning of clinical significance and the main indices that are used in treatment research to define improvement that is important. Ambiguities exist regarding the utility of various ways of operationalizing clinical significance. Nevertheless, the chapter encourages the use of one or more measures in intervention research.

Changes or improvements in clients are clearly the priority foci of treatment research. At the same time, there are other measures of great interest that focus on characteristics of the treatment. For example, the extent to which clients and therapists find the treatment as acceptable or palatable with their views and expectations and the extent to which treatment is easily disseminable are two such criteria. An investigator may develop two treatments that are equally effective in treating a clinical problem. However, one may be much more acceptable to clients so they are more likely to adhere to treatment or remain in treatment. Also, one of the treatments may be more readily transmitted to clinicians who then could implement treatment. That is, the training required to administer treatment may be relatively minor and hence the treatment could be more easily disseminated.

A key measure of treatment that is of great concern is the cost of providing or delivering an intervention. Cost is related to other characteristics. For example, whether a treatment will be adopted or used at all may be related to cost. Insurance and third-party payers often cover the cost of treatment. A treatment that is expensive may not be covered or covered only under very restricted circumstances and hence not one that can be used very much by the public. Thus, researchers must not only be sensitive to the effects of treatment but also to the costs of achieving these effects. Cost of an intervention is also pertinent in relation to the benefits that treatment produces. Sometimes treatment and prevention programs are said to be not very costly at all (or even have no cost) in relation to the cost savings that will occur. For example, drug abuse, sexually transmitted diseases, and crime are major clinical and social problems; they are also extremely expensive in terms of actual costs (i.e., patient care, hospital contacts, morbidity, and mortality). If one of these could be reduced even a little, the cost savings to society might be large. These and related cost issues are not routinely covered in training and perhaps consequently in research on treatment evaluation. This is unfortunate because cost decisions often drive what treatments can or will be used.

Chapter 31 by Brian T. Yates conveys the importance of measuring costs in clinical research. Cost is an important dimension for evaluating treatment in part because it sensitizes us to other features of research (e.g., who is providing treatment, what are the relevant or most important outcomes, what are suitable control or comparison conditions). Key concepts and their measurement such as cost-effectiveness and cost–benefit analyses are presented. Recommendations are provided on ways to assess, report, and evaluate data on cost.

REFERENCES

Agency for Health Care Policy and Research. (1999). *Treatment of depression— Newer pharmacotherapies* (Publication No. 99-E014, Evidence Report / Technology Assessment No. 7). Rockville, MD: Author.

Chambless, D. L., Baker, M. J., Baucom, D. H., Beutler, L. E., Calhoun, K. S., Crits-Cristoph, P., et al. (1998). Update on empirically validated therapies, II. *The Clinical Psychologist, 51,* 3–16.

Clement, P. W. (1999). *Outcomes and incomes: How to evaluate, improve, and market your practice by measuring outcomes in psychotherapy.* New York: Guilford Press.

Cone, J. D. (2000). *Evaluating outcomes: Empirical tools for effective practice.* Washington, DC: American Psychological Association.

Dawes, R. M. (1994). *House of cards: Psychology and psychotherapy built on myth.* New York: Free Press.

Evidence-Based Mental Health. (1998). [Journal devoted to evidence-based treatments and linking research to practice]. *1*(1).

Hoagwood, K., & Hibbs, E. (Eds.). (1995). Special section: Efficacy and effectiveness in studies of child and adolescent psychotherapy. *Journal of Consulting and Clinical Psychology, 63,* 683–725.

Kazdin, A. E. (1993). Evaluation in clinical practice: Clinically sensitive and systematic methods of treatment delivery. *Behavior Therapy, 24,* 11–45.

Kazdin, A. E. (2003). *Research design in clinical psychology* (3rd ed.). Needham Heights, MA: Allyn & Bacon.

Nathan, P. E., &. Gorman, J. M. (Eds.). (2002). *Treatments that work* (2nd ed.). New York: Oxford University Press.

Roth, A., & Fonagy, P. (1996). *What works for whom: A critical review of psychotherapy research.* New York: Guilford Press.

Sechrest, L., Stewart, M., Stickle, T. R., & Sidani, S. (1996). *Effective and persuasive case studies.* Cambridge, MA: Human Services Research Institute.

TREATMENT EVALUATION: EFFICACY AND EFFECTIVENESS

22

RESEARCH ON PSYCHOTHERAPY EFFICACY AND EFFECTIVENESS: BETWEEN SCYLLA AND CHARYBDIS?

PETER E. NATHAN, SCOTT P. STUART, AND SARA L. DOLAN

Psychotherapy 50 years ago and psychotherapy today share very little. Available then only to a privileged few patients, psychotherapy was offered by the few psychiatrists and fewer psychologists and others trained at the minute number of available training centers. Fifty years ago, psychotherapy came in only one variety, heavily flavored by Freudian theory and practice. As a result, psychotherapy patients had to make a substantial investment in both time and money, so they were most often members of the elite financially and psychologically.

Psychotherapy training today is offered by virtually every clinical and counseling psychology training program, most psychiatric residencies, and many training programs in clinical social work and psychiatric nursing. It is the object, moreover, of many other pre- and postdoctoral training programs designed for core mental health professionals or for other helping profes-

Reprinted from *Psychological Bulletin*, *126*, 964–981. Copyright 2000 by the American Psychological Association.

sionals. Although managed care has succeeded in recent years in reducing access to long-term psychotherapy, it remains widely available in some form to most strata of society. Because the drug revolution has led many psychiatric residency programs to deemphasize training and research in psychotherapy in favor of psychopharmacology, it is largely in clinical and counseling psychology training programs and laboratories that today's most significant efforts to explore and develop psychotherapy further are taking place. Much of this research focuses on behavior therapy and cognitive–behavioral therapy (CBT), which have succeeded psychodynamic therapy as the psychotherapeutic treatments of choice for many conditions, primarily because of the strong empirical support they have garnered for their efficacy.

This review of 50 years of psychotherapy research ultimately highlights a distinction in psychotherapy research tactics that has attracted increasing attention in recent years. The distinction is between research on efficacy (e.g., outcome assessment under conditions of high internal validity) and research on effectiveness (e.g., outcome assessment under conditions of high external validity). Some researchers claim that only outcome research that takes place under laboratory conditions and follows the efficacy model provides meaningful psychotherapy outcome data, others swear by the real-world effectiveness model, and still others believe that only integration of the two will yield valid data on efficacy. This comprehensive historical review of the literature on this issue seeks to determine whether this question can be answered by research to date on the differential utility of psychotherapy efficacy and effectiveness research.

PSYCHOTHERAPY EFFICACY AND EFFECTIVENESS RESEARCH

Efficacy research focuses on the measurable effects of specific interventions. The clinical trial represents the prototypic efficacy study; it compares one or more experimental treatments with one or more control or comparison treatments that can be standard treatment, placebo, or waiting list. To maximize the likelihood of detecting treatment effects, factors that might obscure them are eliminated in efficacy studies to the extent possible. To reduce the impact of outcome expectations that participants might hold, clinical trials of psychotherapy are often single-blinded, meaning that patients do not know whether they have been assigned to an experimental, comparison, or control condition. (Double-blinding, in which the therapist or experimenter is also unaware of the identity of the active treatment, is generally a feature only of outcome studies of pharmacological treatment because of the near impossibility of disguising the intent of a psychotherapeutic intervention.) Efficacy studies also tend to use restrictive inclusion and exclusion criteria to create the homogeneous groupings of participants that make it possible to link a specific efficacious treatment to a particular diagnostic entity.

Because not all potentially confounding factors can be identified or controlled, participants in efficacy studies are commonly randomly assigned to experimental and control or comparison conditions to reduce the likelihood that those conditions will differ in unanticipated ways. Efficacy trials also typically use clinicians who are rigorously trained in the treatment they are to provide (it might also be incorporated in a treatment manual) to ensure that the treatment provided is the treatment intended. Treatment in efficacy studies is often provided at no cost to patients. Outcomes of treatment in efficacy studies are most often assessed on a short-term, targeted basis, typically focused on changes in symptoms rather than on more global changes in personality or quality of life.

Effectiveness research aims to determine whether treatments are feasible and have measurable beneficial effects across broad populations and in real-world settings. Typically included in effectiveness studies are persons in need of treatment, regardless of specific diagnoses, comorbid psychopathology, or length of illness. Clinicians in these studies are generally not trained specifically in the research protocol. Moreover, clinical circumstances rather than research design most often dictate choice of treatment method, frequency, duration, and outcome assessment. Although effectiveness studies may randomize assignment of patients to treatments, disguising the treatment to which a patient has been assigned is often not feasible. Outcome measures are often broadly defined as changes in degree of disability, quality of life, or personality, for instance, rather than targeted evaluations of clinical status.

Barlow (1996) has provided succinct definitions of efficacy and effectiveness research. Efficacy refers to "the results of a systematic evaluation of the intervention in a controlled clinical research context. Considerations relevant to the internal validity of these conclusions are usually highlighted" (p. 1051). Effectiveness has to do with "the applicability and feasibility of the intervention in the local setting where the treatment is delivered" and is designed to "determine the generalizability of an intervention with established efficacy" (p. 1055). Efficacy studies emphasize internal validity and replicability; effectiveness studies emphasize external validity and generalizability.

FACTORS THAT DISTINGUISH EFFICACY AND EFFECTIVENESS STUDIES

A range of differences in research methodology differentiates efficacy and effectiveness studies. For the most part, as the historical review of psychotherapy research that follows indicates, the specific factors that differentiate efficacy and effectiveness studies have been studied intensively only during the past decade, reflecting the maturation in research methodology that has taken place during that time.

Efficacy studies are concerned above all with replication. They are designed so that other researchers can conduct similar studies in similar settings to test the same hypotheses. This focus leads naturally to a number of research design issues that are of much less importance to those conducting effectiveness studies. Primary among these is the need to construct an *appropriate control condition* with which the experimental condition can be compared. As a corollary, the emphasis on internal validity dictates the need for *random assignment of participants* to either an active or a control condition. Efficacy studies must also define the type of treatment being provided, so that the therapy can be replicated as closely as possible in subsequent studies. This consideration has led to the widespread use of *treatment manuals* in efficacy studies, as well as procedures to ensure that the therapists conducting the intervention adhere reliably to the dictates of the manual. As well, priority is given in efficacy studies to *well-defined groups of patients* whose problems are specified using objective measures of pathology.

Appropriate Control Conditions

The inclusion of a control condition in psychotherapy studies raises two fundamental questions. The first involves the theoretical issue of whether a control condition is needed to draw valid conclusions about whether a treatment is beneficial. The second is the nature of the control condition when one is used. Theorists have long debated whether a placebo control is even possible in psychotherapy studies, given that the nonspecific factors present in almost any credible psychotherapy placebo have been identified by many experts to be powerful agents of change (J. D. Frank, 1971; Greenberg, 1994; Orlinsky & Howard, 1975).

There is little debate on the need for control conditions in outcome studies designed to maximize internal validity. In their discussion of efficacy and effectiveness studies, Mintz, Drake, and Crits-Cristoph (1996) concluded that both should include well-specified control conditions. Several theoretical objections to the inclusion of control conditions have been raised, however. These include an ethical objection to subjecting clients to a treatment presumed to be inert (or relatively less effective than the treatment being investigated) and a concern about the biases in treatment that may be introduced by the inclusion of a control group. The ethical objections have been addressed most recently with the general acknowledgment that placebo or presumed inert control conditions are not needed if the experimental treatment can be compared with a treatment of known effectiveness. In part because of these concerns, both Parloff (1986) and P. Horvath (1988), among others, have strongly suggested that psychotherapy outcome studies compare a treatment of known benefit with the experimental treatment, reserving placebo controls for studies in which purported mechanisms and processes of change are under investigation.

The second objection to the inclusion of control conditions is that they introduce bias in the patient population. For example, Seligman (1995) has criticized use of randomized control conditions. His point is that patients in community settings enter treatment in an active fashion to seek treatment for self-perceived problems, as opposed to research patients who enter treatment passively and must accept the possibility that they may be assigned to an ineffective treatment. Though internally consistent across studies, the passive entrance of research patients quite likely biases efficacy studies toward patients who are fundamentally different from those who seek treatment in effectiveness studies in naturalistic clinical settings.

Psychotherapy placebos can be divided into three broad categories, with the caveats that they may be used differently across studies and that the conceptualizations of each may vary across paradigms as well. Placebos may be characterized as completely inert, theoretically inert, or intentionally including nonspecific factors (discussed in the next section of this article) that may influence outcome but are missing the therapeutic elements hypothesized to affect outcome in the experimental treatment.

Those conceptualized as inert are typically designed to provide a treatment that has no therapeutic benefit but retains a reasonable degree of plausibility. To serve as a placebo, the control condition must be plausible to both the patient and the clinician, and thus, it must contain some elements of optimism for improvement, offering patients at least the possibility that they might improve. Psychotherapy placebos must meet more stringent requirements in this regard than medication placebos, as the therapist cannot be blinded to treatment. To create conditions in which the therapist is invested in the treatment, a rigorous rationale must be provided for the intervention. In this case, psychotherapy placebos presumed to be inert contain, in fact, many of the nonspecific factors believed to influence outcome, such as the provision of hope (J. D. Frank, 1973) and positive regard from the therapist providing the treatment (Rogers, 1957). Thus, despite the inert status accorded to some placebo controls, most are in fact active, if not specific, treatments. Those that are truly inactive typically lack plausibility and are therefore given questionable status as placebos.

Studies that use theoretically inert placebos include control interventions thought to be ineffective treatments for the disorder being studied. The National Institute of Mental Health Treatment of Depression Collaborative Research Program (NIMH-TDCRP; Elkin et al., 1989), detailed later in this article, is a classic example of such a study. Besides constituting a control for the pharmacological effects of medication, the placebo medication condition was designed to lack any of the hypothesized mechanisms of action of either interpersonal psychotherapy (IPT; Klerman, Weissman, Rounsaville, & Chevron, 1984) or CBT (Beck, Rush, Shaw, & Emery, 1979). Great care was taken to ensure that the clinicians who provided the placebo treatment did not use the techniques of either IPT or CBT and that they avoided such interventions reliably (Elkin, Parloff, Hadley, & Autry, 1985). Nonetheless, patients in the placebo medication condition reported symptom improvement comparable to that experienced by patients in the active treatment groups.

The NIMH-TDCRP exemplifies a problem inherent in this particular type of placebo design, in that some critics of the study have interpreted its findings to reflect, in substantial part, the impact of nonspecific effects. Many authors believe that nonspecific effects, irrespective of the presumed mechanism of action of an active treatment, are responsible for a great deal of the outcome variance in psychotherapy studies. Such factors as the provision of hope for change (J. D. Frank, 1971), the effects of persuasion (J. D. Frank, 1973), the opportunity to interact with a caring clinician (Rogers, 1957), and the demand characteristics of therapy (P. Horvath, 1988) are all potential agents for change in any credible placebo intervention. It has also recently been suggested that elements intrinsic to efficacy studies, such as the increased amount of contact with research personnel that typically occurs (Thase, 1999a) and the influence of the questionnaires used in the study on its outcomes, may also effect change.

Concerns over control of these influences have led researchers to adopt a third type of control condition. In it, the control or comparison treatment is acknowledged to contain nonspecific elements and is specifically constructed to emulate the active treatment in question, with the exception that it is designed not to include the active elements being tested in the active treatment. This type of deconstructed or dismantled comparison treatment has been used most frequently in psychotherapy research. A typical paradigm might involve the test of a behavior therapy intervention for panic disorder such as relaxation. In this situation, the comparison treatment would mimic all of the elements of the experimental treatment, including amount and frequency of contact, and would include even nonrelaxation elements such as exposure and desensitization; it would not include the relaxation induction. Although such a control condition might resolve questions about mechanisms of change, it is not likely to shed much light on the efficacy of the experimental treatment.

Two other types of nonplacebo control conditions have also been used in both efficacy and effectiveness studies. In some research, comparison of an active treatment with a treatment-as-usual condition is conducted. This type of control condition may be very appropriate for determining whether the treatment being evaluated is better than what is currently provided in the community—a question often asked by effectiveness researchers. Such a comparison may not, however, meet the criteria noted above for demonstrating efficacy of a treatment—namely, that the experimental treatment is equal to or better than a known efficacious treatment, as usual treatment may not be of proven efficacy and thus an invalid comparator. The treatment-as-usual paradigm, however, is frequently used as a placebo treatment in efficacy studies rather than as an active effectiveness comparator. In this situation, it would appear to be a very poor placebo, as it contains all of the nonspecific elements found in psychotherapeutic treatments, may include elements of the presumed active treatment, and is of questionable internal consistency.

Some authors have also used waiting list controls for psychotherapy studies. In these types of designs, no attempt is made to provide patients with a plausible placebo treatment. In fact, patients are advised that the waiting list is likely not to be effective. Although elements such as increased contact with other research personnel may be present, researchers conceptualize the waiting list as nonpsychotherapeutic. The drawback to this approach is that it may produce the type of patient bias noted above by Seligman (1995): Patients who enroll in psychotherapy studies in which they may be randomized to a waiting list control condition may be very different from those who seek treatment in community clinics.

Random Assignment of Participants

Random assignment to treatment is typically done whether the experimental treatment is being compared with a placebo or with another active treatment. Prospective, randomized assignment is considered an essential element of methodologically rigorous efficacy research (Mintz et al., 1996) because it provides statistically unbiased estimates of treatment effects. Effectiveness studies, on the other hand, may use post hoc comparisons of disaggregated groups, such as a retrospective comparison of depressed patients who received psychotherapy with those who received medication.

Random assignment to treatment has been heavily criticized for introducing a selection bias, in that clients may self-select for these types of efficacy studies (Seligman, 1995). However, although it is theoretically appealing to assume that patients who seek treatment actively in community settings are different from those who enter research protocols and face the prospect of randomization, there are no data to date that have substantiated this view. Hence, a more compelling critique is the argument that community-based effectiveness research may not allow for prospective randomization because particular clinic sites may be required to provide an active intervention, chosen by the patient in consultation with his or her clinician, to all who seek treatment. Moreover, if the goal of the effectiveness research is service oriented, that is, designed to quantify the effects of a given treatment for those patients who actively seek it, use of random assignment is obviously not desirable.

Random assignment to treatment does, however, appear to have an impact on outcome in research studies. In a meta-analysis of studies of marital and family psychotherapy, Shadish and Ragsdale (1996) reported that studies using random assignments to treatment had consistently higher mean posttest effects and less variable posttest effects than studies using nonrandom assignment. Although the authors found that the differences between the two groups of studies could be reduced somewhat by considering various covariables, the differences persisted, leading the authors to conclude that random assignment should continue to be considered the gold standard in psychotherapy efficacy studies.

Treatment Manuals

Psychotherapy manuals have become an essential part of most efficacy studies, in large part because it is generally agreed that efficacy studies should include at least the following three components: (a) a definitive description of the techniques specific to the therapy being tested, (b) a clear statement in concrete terms of the operations the therapist is to perform, and (c) a measure of the degree to which the therapist adheres to the prescribed techniques (Kiesler, 1994). Many therapy manuals describe the therapeutic stance to be taken by the clinician and also specify what types of techniques are not permissible. These measures facilitate a more objective comparison of differing psychotherapies and improved training of therapists in the manualized therapy (Kiesler, 1994).

Eifert, Schulte, Zvolensky, Lejuez, and Lau (1997) cited a number of advantages of manualized research paradigms, prominently including that they increase internal validity and standardization. In addition, Eifert et al. noted that manuals are helpful for clinical practice because they enable clinicians to administer efficacious treatments more effectively, reduce idiosyncrasy in therapeutic methods, and increase the clinician's focus on specific treatment goals and techniques. Detractors of manualized therapies have focused on theoretical weaknesses of the manual approach and on concerns that manuals prevent clinicians from fully practicing their therapeutic skills by constricting their possible responses and making it more difficult for them to use client feedback. To this end, when Crits-Christoph (1996) reexamined the results of his earlier meta-analysis of therapist effects in psychotherapy outcome studies (Crits-Christoph et al., 1991), he reported that manuals did "reduce therapist differences to a rather low level" (p. 260), specifically, to 4% of outcome variance due to therapist differences, as against 13% in studies that did not use treatment manuals.

The principal theoretical objection to therapy manuals is that they are nearly always disorder based (Eifert et al., 1997) rather than theory driven, because they typically use *Diagnostic and Statistical Manual (DSM)* classification to determine criteria for the disorder being treated. Both CBT and IPT are excellent examples of this trend, with a proliferation of modified therapies being developed for a wide variety of *DSM–IV* (American Psychiatric Association, 1994a) disorders once efficacy for the treatment of major depression was established.

Another theoretical argument against manual-based research is that it fails to inform clinicians about how to effectively treat specific patients. Two variations of the argument have been proposed. The first is that empirical findings are based on group means, and the average patient for whom such findings apply is simply a statistical abstraction that does not conform to the individual patients actually treated (Maling & Howard, 1994). The second avers that having to adhere to treatment manuals prevents therapists and patients from working together in a self-correcting way to improve outcome (Seligman, 1995). It is true that typical efficacy studies require that therapists follow a strictly defined protocol, with little or no allowance for the exercise of clinical judgment. Although most studies allow some flexibility in what can be done within a given session, therapists are not allowed to change the scheduling or frequency of sessions prescribed by the protocol (except to schedule well-defined emergency sessions when indicated).

A final objection to therapy manuals is the art versus science argument. It is well articulated by Edelson (1994), who argued that psychotherapy is an art based on relativistic observations. Rather than emphasizing reliability, the clinician strives to make meaningful observations uniquely based on the therapeutic dyad. The practice of psychotherapy, in his view, is concerned with the particulars of a given client as an individual, whereas psychotherapy research is concerned with generalities drawn from a population.

There is some evidence that the use of treatment manuals in efficacy studies does lead to differences in outcome. In a meta-analysis of short-term psychotherapies, Anderson and Lambert (1995) found that studies using treatment manuals had larger effect sizes than those that did not. This conclusion, however, may have been biased. The efficacy studies in question emphasized adherence to a treatment manual; studies allowing therapists to choose either to use their clinical judgment in a naturalistic treatment setting or to adhere to a treatment manual might have provided more objective data on outcomes.

Most efficacy studies use some measure of therapist adherence to the treatment manual as a means of preventing therapist drift. There is some evidence that adherence is correlated with greater therapy effects. E. Frank, Kupfer, Wagner, McEachran, and Cornes (1992) found that therapist adherence to IPT was directly correlated with improved outcome. However, when Jacobson and his colleagues (1989) compared the results of two versions of behavioral marital therapy delivered by therapists whose therapeutic flexibility was either constrained or encouraged, outcomes did not differ, although a trend for less relapse at follow-up in the flexibly treated couples was reported.

As a practical consequence of the need to maintain therapy integrity, manual-driven therapies tend to be short term, given that therapeutic drift becomes more problematic with the passage of time. As a consequence, and with some notable exceptions (e.g., E. Frank, Kupfer, & Perel, 1990; Kernberg, Selzer, Koenigsberg, Carr, & Appelbaum, 1989; Linehan, 1993), most efficacy studies are designed to test time-limited treatments for acute disorders. Coincidentally, the time-limited nature of efficacy studies parallels changes in clinical practice under managed care. Today's limited insurance benefits frequently constrain number of therapy sessions and may require therapist and client to negotiate ways to stretch a limited number of sessions over a lengthy period of time.

Well-Defined Groups of Patients

Efficacy studies require the reliable evaluation of patients and the use of reliable measures of symptoms over time (Mintz et al., 1996). Typically, potential patients are screened using standardized diagnostic instruments, generating disorder-based groups to whom the intervention can be provided. Replicability and internal validity requirements also dictate that patients selected for treatment be as homogeneous as possible in their diagnoses. The goal, which is not always realized because comorbid conditions are not always identified, is the generation of treatment and control groups with few or no confounding diagnoses. As many as 5 to 10 potential participants may be screened for every 1 enrolled in more rigorous studies (Thase, 1999a), both because of potentially confounding comorbidity and because their disorders may not be sufficiently severe.

Great care is also taken in efficacy studies to ensure that measures of symptomatology are valid and reliable. The ideal study combines measures from three observation points. These include patient self-reports, ratings from blinded and objective observers, and psychophysiological measures, if available. Although ratings from treating therapists may also used, they have a distinct bias potential. All assessments are cast in quantifiable terms so that comparisons can be made. Several different measures of a given pathological construct, such as depression, are also used. The measurement of longitudinal change requires multiple assessments over time, with careful consideration of the times at which the measures are obtained (Gottman & Rushe, 1993).

Critics have noted several concerns about these assessment provisions. First, measures of psychopathology are usually chosen because of their conformation to hypothesized mechanisms of change or active ingredients (Elkin, Pilkonis, Docherty, & Sotsky, 1988); some measures may also be chosen to reflect a theoretical conceptualization of the disorder being studied. In either case, the information gleaned from the treatment trial is limited by the assessment instruments used; instruments that are more restricted conceptually may miss changes in other domains because they do not measure them. Each school of psychotherapy may have its own unique instruments, making comparisons across studies very difficult.

Moreover, the measures used in a study may create bias in the response of patients to the interventions under investigation. In most cases, this demand bias is equivalent across the interventions being tested in a given study. However, there are some cases in which a treatment being assessed may be compromised by assessment questionnaires. For example, the effectiveness of a psychological treatment designed to treat somatization disorder and specifically constructed to avoid discussion of somatic symptoms by redirecting the patient away from discussion of physical problems may be impaired when patients are asked to respond in detail to repeated questions about physical symptoms. Others have questioned the limitation imposed by objective measures of outcome on the range of possible outcomes. To this end, attempts have been made to expand the constructs that are measured, including such elusive concepts as quality of life and life satisfaction. Many clinicians, however, continue to be dissatisfied with these efforts. They argue that research measures assess illness rather than suffering, do not capture the subjective reality of the patient, and do not address issues important to more psychodynamically inclined therapists, such as ego functioning and defense mechanisms (Edelson, 1994; Greenberg, 1994; Spence, 1994).

RESEARCH ON COMMON FACTORS

Are differences in psychotherapy outcomes strongly associated with specific types or schools of psychotherapy, as the historical overview of psychotherapy research that follows suggests? Or do variables common to all psychological treatments have the greatest influence on outcomes, as the not infrequent report of no differences in outcomes among treatments (called by some the "dodo bird effect") implies? In fact, through the years, a number of well-respected investigators have concluded that the so-called common variables may carry a very substantial amount of the treatment outcome variance. That research is reviewed briefly here.

Lambert and Bergin (1994) located common factors in the therapist, the client, and the therapeutic process. Within each of the three, they added, are three subfactors: support factors, such as therapeutic alliance, catharsis, and therapist warmth; learning factors, including corrective emotional experience, insight, and feedback; and action factors, which include cognitive mastery, modeling, and behavioral regulation. Many of these variables, these authors claimed, affect outcomes independent of specific therapeutic techniques used.

According to Beutler, Machado, and Neufeldt (1994), the therapist variables examined for their impact on outcomes extend across a broad continuum from objective demographic characteristics and sociocultural background factors of psychotherapists to subjective factors like therapist values, attitudes, and beliefs. They include factors quite specific to therapy (e.g., the therapist's role in the therapeutic relationship and his or her expectations for its success) as well as those well removed from it, such as cross-situational variables (e.g., therapists' cultural attitudes and emotional well-being). Therapist variables reflecting therapy-specific states, including the therapist's professional background (see, e.g., Berman & Norton, 1985) and his or her style and choice of interventions (Robinson, Berman, & Neimeyer, 1990), appear to exert the most powerful effects on therapy outcomes. Therapist-specific variables such as age and gender (see, e.g., Zlotnick, Elkin, & Shea, 1998) seem to affect therapy outcomes the least.

With occasional exceptions (see, e.g., Luborsky & Diguer, 1995), patient variables have not shown a consistent, robust relationship to therapeutic outcomes. Although the NIMH-TDCRP (Elkin et al., 1989) carefully screened potential participants for specific defined characteristics both to maximize diagnostic homogeneity and to facilitate treatment effectiveness, no single patient variable correlated robustly with outcome. In the same vein, although the YAVIS variables (patient youth, attractiveness, verbal ability, intelligence, and success in other domains) were once thought to be robust predictors of psychotherapy treatment success (see, e.g., Stoler, 1963), they have since been largely discounted. Other kinds of patient variables have attracted more recent empirical interest, including initial level of disorder severity and degree of psychiatric comorbidity (Elkin, 1995). It is largely from patient variables like these that empirical support is now sought for the hypothesis that matching patients to specific treatments on the basis of patient attributes may produce more robust treatment effects (see, e.g., Project MATCH Research Group, 1993, 1997).

Hans Strupp (1973) reported that therapeutic process variables—factors influencing therapists' reactions to patients' behavior and attitudes and vice versa—directly affect therapeutic outcomes. In a 1986 review of process–outcome research, Orlinsky and Howard (1986) concluded that process variables, including the strength of the therapeutic bond, the skillfulness with which interventions are performed, and the duration of the treatment relationship, all had a positive impact on outcomes. Nonetheless, critics of process research have continued to emphasize the difficulties of studying relationships between therapeutic process and outcome. Many (e.g., Butler & Strupp, 1986; Elkin, 1995; Stiles & Shapiro, 1989) have lamented the recent trend to design therapy outcome studies like drug trials (the so-called drug trial metaphor), given the problem in trying to isolate the active (process) ingredients of psychotherapy.

Following an extensive review of outcome studies, Lambert (1992) suggested that about 30% of psychotherapy outcome variance is attributable to therapist variables affecting the relationship with the patient, such as empathy, warmth, and acceptance of the patient. Svartberg, Seltzer, and Stiles (1998), A. O. Horvath and Symonds (1991), and Eaton, Abeles, and Gutfreund (1988) have concluded that the therapeutic alliance is the most important factor in determining positive therapeutic outcomes. Much earlier, Carl Rogers (1961) came to the same conclusion when he identified the necessary and sufficient conditions for a productive helping relationship as being therapist's unconditional positive regard for the patient, empathy, and genuineness. Ten years later, Hans Strupp (1973) also observed that the therapist's attitudes and feelings toward the patient have the potential powerfully to affect therapeutic outcome.

A recent resurgence in research on therapists' comfort with and belief in the therapy they practice has taken place. In comparative studies of psychotherapies, for example, the therapist's allegiance to a particular brand of psychotherapy has turned out to be a potent predictor of positive outcome. Luborsky et al. (1999) reviewed 29 treatment comparison studies, assessing researchers' allegiance to a compared treatment three ways: assessment of allegiance to a specific treatment as expressed in published studies (reprint-based assessment), Likert-type ratings of allegiance by close colleagues, and Likert-type self-ratings. The three methods were moderately intercorrelated, and all three positively related to treatment success. Overall, a composite measure of allegiance was found to correlate significantly with outcome, explaining 69% of its variance. Some observers, however, believe that this effect is inflated by researchers' commitment to a specific treatment modality (Hollon, 1999; Thase, 1999b). Others urge caution in interpreting these results lest the original goal of comparative studies be lost sight of: to find out what treatments work, for what people, under what conditions (Klein, 1999; Lambert, 1999; Shoham & Rohrbaugh, 1999).

OVERVIEW OF PSYCHOTHERAPY OUTCOME RESEARCH FROM THE 1950S TO THE 1980S

The 1950s and 1960s: Inadequate Research Methods, Disappointing Efficacy, Significant but Meaningless Psychotherapy Effects

Although Hans Eysenck's 1952 evaluation of the effects of psychotherapy, elaborated in a 1960 review (Eysenck, 1952, 1960), was not the first to assess psychotherapy outcomes, its emphasis on the primacy of data and its willingness to reach an unpopular conclusion distinguish it from other early evaluations of psychotherapy. The review's two most notable conclusions were (a) approximately two thirds of so-called neurotic patients recover or improve markedly within 2 years of the onset of their disorder, in the absence of treatment; and (b) there appears to be an inverse correlation between recovery and psychotherapy. Eysenck's controversial 1952 bottom line, elaborated in 1960, was that the psychotherapies in widest use at mid-century were largely ineffective.

Of specific relevance to the focus of this review was Eysenck's acknowledgment in both the 1952 and 1960 reviews, in response to numerous critics, that the inadequate methodology of the outcome studies on which he based his conclusions required qualification of his most provocative conclusions. Few of the studies included in Eysenck's (1952) review were controlled; the nature and severity of patients' illnesses were inadequately described, in part because of the unreliability of *DSM–I* (American Psychiatric Association, 1952); the length and precise nature of the treatments provided were insufficiently detailed; and treatment follow-ups were generally inadequate. In other words, virtually all the research on psychotherapy that Eysenck reviewed in 1952 failed to meet the methodological criteria today considered minimally necessary before including a study in a review of efficacy or effectiveness research. Accordingly, the methodological limitations of the studies on which Eysenck based his 1952 conclusions render its findings of little or no utility by current standards.

Eysenck's (1960) reexamination of the psychotherapy outcome literature 8 years later was based on data from research that was somewhat more adequate methodologically. He examined psychotherapy outcomes from the Cambridge–Somerville delinquency prevention project (Powers & Witmer, 1951; Teuber & Powers, 1953), for its time a state-of-the-art prevention/treatment study, and Rogers and Dymond's (1954) investigation of nondirective therapy, which broke new ground by using a control group and multiple, newly developed outcome measures. Nonetheless, Eysenck's conclusions in 1960 differed little from those in 1952: "With the single exception of psychotherapeutic methods based on learning theory, results of published research with military and civilian neurotics, and with both adults and children, suggest that the therapeutic effects of psychotherapy are small or non-existent" (Eysenck, 1960, p. 245).

Initiating our historical review of the psychotherapy outcome literature with Eysenck's 1952 and 1960 evaluations is intended to emphasize both the primitive state of psychotherapy research at mid-century and its discouraging findings on therapeutic outcomes. The design shortcomings ensured that the methodological subtleties on which current distinctions between efficacy and effectiveness research are based, as outlined above, were simply unavailable to the researchers of the time. Nonetheless, the broader problem that the efficacy/effectiveness distinction epitomizes—the real-world irrelevance of much psychological research, including research on psychotherapy outcomes—was very much on the minds of psychologists very early.

In his well-known presidential address to the American Psychological Association describing the "two disciplines of scientific psychology," for example, Cronbach (1957) distinguished between correlational methodologies (often used in clinical research) and experimental methods (more easily used in laboratory settings), concluding that only the latter detect causal agency. A few years later, writing in an influential statistics text, Hays (1963) affirmed that all significant results do not imply the same degree of true association between independent and dependent variables. Virtually any study can be made to show significant results if one uses enough subjects, regardless of how nonsensical the content may be. (p. 326)

Two years afterward, elaborating on Hays's observation from the clinical perspective, Cohen (1965) made one of the earliest references to an often-repeated truism about significant yet meaningless psychotherapy outcome research: Findings that are statistically significant may nonetheless be insignificant clinically.

Taking a distinctly contrary position for this era, Bergin (1966) identified six notable findings from psychotherapy research that he felt had clear relevance to clinical practice. They comprised the following: (a) Psychotherapy changes behavior, attitudes, and adjustment; (b) controls may improve over time as a result of "informal therapeutic encounters" (p. 235); (c) progress in therapy is a function of therapeutic warmth, empathy, adjustment, and experience; (d) only client-centered therapy has been validated empirically; (e) the psychodynamic therapies are of limited effectiveness and affect only a small number of conditions; and (f) behavior therapies show considerable promise.

The 1970s: Improved Research Methods, Enhanced Efficacy, Not Much More Help for Practitioners

A series of comprehensive reviews of the psychotherapy research literature in the early 1970s reflected two themes: hard-won advances in psychotherapy research methodology and encouraging data on the efficacy of new therapies, especially the behavior therapies and CBTs. Surprisingly, however, a number of these reviews, including Bergin and Suinn (1975), Gomes-Schwartz, Hadley, and Strupp (1978), and Howard and Orlinsky (1972), failed to raise the issue of the clinical relevance of psychotherapy research findings.

Reviewing research on psychotherapeutic processes reported in the late 1960s, Gendlin and Rychlak (1970) echoed two of Eysenck's earlier themes, lamenting the continuing inadequacy of psychotherapy research methodology—specifically, the paucity of control groups and "properly blind ratings" (p. 156)—and lauding the promise of behavior therapy. Given Cohen's (1965) then recent comments on significant but meaningless psychotherapy research findings, it is a bit surprising that this review, like later ones during this decade, failed to raise this issue even though most of the research reviewed consists of what would today be called *efficacy* studies. Moreover, no distinction was drawn in this review between psychotherapy research models analogous to the present-day distinction between efficacy and effectiveness studies; this distinction appeared only later in the decade, presumably because maturation of psychotherapy research methods only then made it meaningful.

In an early review of emerging findings on behavior therapy, Krasner (1971) emphasized repeatedly that behavior therapy, though derived from the experimental psychology laboratory, had nonetheless evolved clinically effective procedures for behavior change. Krasner (1971) also informed his readers, most of whom were presumably not behavior therapists, that

> the behavior therapy researcher uses a number of procedures and designs to go about acquiring information. These are: extrapolation from the experimental lab to clinical application; the use of the clinic as a source of hypotheses for laboratory research; the use of research as treatment; the single case as an experimental model; and the individual as his own control. (p. 515)

Here, Krasner was speaking of the fluidity with which behavior therapy traverses the divide between laboratory and consulting room, making clear that although he recognized a potential distinction between the two, the distinction was moot with regard to the evolving behavior therapies. The same theme is echoed by critics of current efforts to identify empirically supported treatments (see, e.g., Beutler, 1998; Goldfried & Wolfe, 1998), who emphasize the ease with which CBT fits the research model used to identify most of the treatments considered empirically supported.

The 1980s: Continued Advances in Methodology and Efficacy; "Clinical Research Has Little or No Influence on Clinical Practice"

Early in the 1980s, however, researchers began to take up the issue of the clinical utility of psychotherapy research with vigor. Likely reasons include acceptance by many of the meta-analytic concept of effect size as a reflection of the comparative impact of different therapies, as well as other methodological advances in psychotherapy research that heightened its apparent worth. When these advances were coupled with the continuing paradox of the paucity of clinicians consulting the journals when planning interventions, the issue was joined.

One of the earliest of those who commented on this paradox was Barlow (1981), writing in a special section of an issue of the *Journal of Consulting and Clinical Psychology* titled "Empirical Practice and Realistic Research: New Opportunities for Clinicians." Barlow's (1981) comments began provocatively:

> At present, clinical research has little or no influence on clinical practice. This state of affairs should be particularly distressing to a discipline whose goal over the last 30 years has been to produce professionals who would integrate the methods of science with clinical practice to produce new knowledge. (p. 147)

Reacting to Barlow's 1981 call for action, Sargent and Cohen (1983) designed a survey of psychologists to determine the variables associated with the persuasiveness of psychotherapy research strategies for psychologists interested in psychotherapy, strongly suggesting that psychology had finally begun to attend seriously to the issue. Responding to some of the same issues, Shapiro and Shapiro (1982, 1983) undertook a meta-analysis of 143 psychotherapy outcome studies published during the previous 5 years in which two or more treatments were compared with a control group. Although the statistical conclusions and internal validity of these studies were found to be "generally satisfactory," their construct and external validity were "severely limited by . . . unrepresentativeness of clinical practice" (Shapiro & Shapiro, 1983, p. 42).

The same year, Rosenthal (1983) reiterated the distinction between the statistical and social importance of the effects of psychotherapy and commented explicitly on discussions of effect sizes derived from recently published meta-analyses by Glass, Smith, and their colleagues (Glass, 1980; Smith, 1980; Smith, Glass, & Miller, 1980). He reintroduced an earlier metric by Rosenthal and Rubin (1979, 1982) for "an intuitively appealing general-purpose effect-size display whose interpretation is perfectly transparent, the binomial effect-size display (BESD)" (Rosenthal, 1983, p. 11). The BESD was designed to heighten the real-world clinical utility of psychotherapy research findings. Rosenthal (1983) described it as follows:

> The following question is addressed by the BESD: What is the effect on the success rate (e.g., survival rate, cure rate, improvement rate, selection rate, etc.) of the institution of a new treatment procedure? It therefore displays the change in success rate (e.g., survival rate, cure rate, improvement rate, selection rate, etc.) attributable to the new treatment procedure. (p. 11)

Rosenthal (1983) went on to demonstrate that substituting the BESD for the traditional variance estimate makes much more clear than the latter did the extent to which a significant change in outcomes has actually taken place. His compelling example showed that a modest change accounted for by only 10 percent of the variance can actually correspond to a marked increase in success rate from 34 percent to 66 percent or a dramatic decrease in death rate from 66 percent to 34 percent.

Kazdin (1986), Koss, Butcher, and Strupp (1986), and Parloff (1984) also commented on an emerging consensus: The psychotherapy outcome studies of the 1980s and before did not adequately reflect — or test — psychotherapy as it is described in textbooks or practiced in the real world. Nonetheless, at exceptional variance to this consensus, in a review of psychotherapy research published in the late 1980s, Goldfried, Greenberg, and Marmar (1990) concluded that "the development of methods for demonstrating clinical (in addition to statistical) significance has been one of the major advances in outcome research" (p. 661).

In a summary of efforts during the 1980s to extend empirical findings on psychotherapy to the consulting room, Hans Strupp (1989) asked rhetorically, "Can the practitioner learn from the researcher?" Strupp described the nub of the problem as follows: "Although research has flourished over the past several decades, there appears to be little evidence that clinicians have adopted a more positive view concerning the practical value of psychotherapy research" (p. 717). He went on to remind his readers that although psychotherapy has generally been found to be helpful, specific techniques have less often been identified as uniquely effective in treating specific disorders. As a consequence, many clinicians have concluded that what they do and how they do it may be less important than the therapeutic relationship they share with the patient. Strupp's (1989) suggested solution: "Instead of focusing on disembodied techniques, we must study and seek a better understanding of the human relationship between a particular patient and a particular therapist and of the transactions occurring between them" (p. 717).

Overview of 40 Years of Psychotherapy Research

This section of the review has traced the emerging recognition, over 40 years, of the infrequency with which psychotherapists relied on the work of psychotherapy researchers. During the decades of the 1950s and 1960s, the problem, largely unrecognized, appeared mainly to reflect the inadequacies of clinical research methodologies. Ironically, though, as these methods improved over the decades of the 1970s and 1980s, their clinical utility became even more of an issue (Nathan, 1998). During these 2 decades, attributions of responsibility shifted to the lack of correspondence between the therapies and patients chosen for empirical research and those typically involved in real-world clinical practice. These concerns, of course, are products of an essential feature of the efficacy model, which would be clearly labeled and thoroughly discussed only later.

THE 1990S: MOVEMENT TOWARD AND ELABORATION OF THE DISTINCTION BETWEEN EFFICACY AND EFFECTIVENESS

Concerns about the usefulness of psychotherapy research for clinicians coalesced in the 1990s as a focus on the distinction between psychotherapy outcome studies that focus on efficacy and those that focus on effectiveness. As detailed earlier, efficacy studies maximize internal validity; they are typically carefully controlled psychotherapy outcome inquiries that use diagnostically homogeneous, randomly assigned patient groups, and, often, manualized, time-limited treatments. By contrast, effectiveness studies aim to maximize external validity; generally taking place in real-world clinical settings, they often lack controls, diagnostic homogeneity, and random assignment of patients, in the effort faithfully to reflect real-world clinical realities. This section briefly reviews a few articles that anticipate the efficacy/effectiveness distinction, then considers in greater detail the outpouring of more recent discussions of the distinction.

The Case Formulation Approach (Persons, 1991)

Persons (1991) reviewed much of the recent literature in this area, emphasizing the field's growing concerns about the external validity of psychotherapy research and concluding that designs of earlier psychotherapy outcome studies were conceptually incompatible with the models of psychotherapy they were designed to evaluate. Persons blamed this situation on assignment of patients to standardized treatments on the basis of diagnosis rather than on assignment of patients to individualized treatments on the basis of theory-driven psychological assessment of each individual. In so doing, she recalled earlier criticisms of nomothetic approaches and advocacy for idiographic ones, including those of Luborsky (1984), Horowitz and his colleagues (1984), Strupp and Binder (1984), and Weiss, Sampson, and the Mount Zion Psychotherapy Research Group (1986).

Persons's (1991) solution to this longstanding problem: "the case formulation approach to psychotherapy research" (p. 102), which requires development of an "assessment-plus-treatment protocol" (p. 102) based directly on the psychotherapeutic model itself. Outcomes of the case formulation approach are to be cast ideographically because assessments are individualized and outcomes of treatment are to be assessed according to each patient's unique set of problems. Although the existence of treatment manuals that scrupulously reflect their therapeutic models and ideographically assess patients' outcomes would resolve the conceptual incompatibility problems of which Persons despaired, she acknowledged that they have their own problems. Manuals interfere with ongoing therapy and therapist spontaneity and make comparisons across outcomes difficult when they are based on different sets of evaluative criteria. Nonetheless, in this thoughtful review, Persons cogently identified the problem at the outset of the 1990s and considered the pros and cons of an intriguing solution.

Clarifying Clinically Significant Change (Jacobson & Truax, 1991)

Jacobson and Truax (1991) proposed to solve another common outcome research problem affecting clinical validity: statistically significant pre- and posttherapy behavior change scores with little apparent meaning clinically. This problem had been identified more than 25 years earlier by Cohen (1965). Although acknowledging that the effect size statistic derived from meta-analysis is an improvement over standard inferential statistics because it reflects the size of the treatment effect, Jacobson and Truax nonetheless lamented the frequent independence of the size of the effect from its clinical significance. To confront the problem, these authors harkened back to their earlier definition of clinically significant change: movement of someone outside the range of the dysfunctional population or into the range of the functional population (Jacobson, Follette, & Revenstorf, 1984). They then proposed three ways to operationalize this definition:

(a) The level of functioning subsequent to therapy should fall outside the range of the dysfunctional population where range is defined as extending to two standard deviations beyond (in the direction of functionality) the mean for that population.

(b) The level of functioning subsequent to therapy should fall within the range of the functional or normal population, where range is defined as within two standard deviations of the mean of that population.

(c) The level of functioning subsequent to therapy places that client closer to the mean of the functional population than it does to the mean of the dysfunctional population. (Jacobson & Truax, 1991, p. 13)

Reanalysis of NIMH-TDCRP Findings (Ogles, Lambert, & Sawyer, 1995)

Because of its sample size, diagnostic homogeneity, and rigorous treatment standards, the NIMH-TDCRP (Elkin, 1994; Elkin et al., 1985, 1989) represented an extremely important comparative study of mental health treatments. The first of its two primary goals was to test the feasibility and usefulness of the collaborative clinical trial model for psychotherapy research. The second was to test the effectiveness of two brief psychotherapies for the treatment of outpatient depression. Outcomes of treatment for 239 clinically depressed patients randomly assigned to one of four treatments at three sites were compared. The treatments included CBT, IPT, imipramine plus clinical management (CM), and placebo plus CM (PLA-CM). Although all four groups, including the PLA-CM group, reported significant improvements in symptoms, the magnitude of differences among the four immediately and 18 months after treatment was small. Accordingly, the clinical significance of the few statistically significant differences among groups was questioned.

Ogles, Lambert, and Sawyer (1995) reanalyzed these outcome data, using Jacobson and Truax's (1991) criteria for assessing clinical significance. The initial analysis (Elkin et al., 1989) had failed to consider either the reliability of pre- to posttreatment symptom changes or the clinical significance of multiple measures simultaneously. Accordingly, Ogles and his colleagues hypothesized that reanalysis according to the Jacobson and Truax criteria might be more revealing of clinically significant differences across conditions. In fact, the reanalysis yielded the following findings confirming clinical significance:

> A relatively large number of clients receiving treatment for depression make reliable improvements from pretreatment to posttreatment. These changes are not limited to client's self-report of current symptoms of depression but are also evident to clinical judges and on a self-report measure of diverse physical and psychological symptoms. (Ogles et al., 1995, p. 324)

Finding that three diverse outcome measures in this instance were consonant convinced Ogles and his colleagues of the validity of this method of assessing clinical significance, even though significant differences among the treatment groups were not found overall.

The *Consumer Reports* Survey: Effectiveness Study or Consumer Satisfaction Survey?

In 1994, 180,000 subscribers to *Consumer Reports* were asked to respond to a series of questions about their experiences with mental health professionals, physicians, medications, and self-help groups in the largest survey to date of consumers' views on psychotherapy and other mental health treatments ("Mental Health," 1995). Of the more than 7,000 readers who responded with detailed information about the persons from whom they sought help, about 3,000 reported having talked only to friends, family, or clergy, whereas about 4,100 said they had sought out mental health professionals, family doctors, and/or self-help groups. Thirty-seven percent of those who consulted a mental health professional saw a psychologist, 22 percent a psychiatrist, 14 percent a social worker, and 9 percent a marriage counselor. The 4,100 questionnaire respondents were in clear emotional need: Forty-three percent admitted they were in a "very poor" or "fairly poor" emotional state when they sought help.

The survey's principal findings included the following:

1. Level of satisfaction with therapy was equivalent whether respondents saw a social worker, psychologist, or psychiatrist; those who saw a marriage counselor were somewhat less likely to report having benefited from therapy.
2. Respondents who sought therapy from a family doctor reported doing well, but those who saw a mental health professional for more than 6 months reported doing much better.
3. Psychotherapy alone worked as well as combined psychotherapy and pharmacotherapy; while most persons who took prescribed medication found it helpful, many reported side effects.
4. The longer psychotherapy lasted, the more it helped.

5. Respondents who had tried self-help groups, especially Alcoholics Anonymous, felt especially good about the experience.

These findings painted an extremely encouraging picture of the impact of psychotherapy on this group of respondents. However, the study had important limitations. A mail survey of matters of this sensitivity and complexity, a substantially undefined and essentially undiagnosed group of respondents, and outcome questions that focused on generalized improvement rather than specific outcomes targeted to symptoms all raised concerns about the meaning of these findings. Troubling as well was the absence of an untreated control or comparison group. In the absence of such a group, it is impossible to say whether respondents who reported having benefited from treatment actually had done so or whether instead they had simply experienced a spontaneous remission of their symptoms with the passage of time.

Another shortcoming of the study was its minimal response rate: Only 4,100 respondents of the 180,000 subscribers to the magazine who had been sent the survey reported seeking professional help or joining groups; only 2,900 reported actually consulting a mental health professional. These numbers are low enough to raise the possibility that substantially more subscribers who had benefited from psychotherapy chose to respond to the questionnaire than those who did not, thereby skewing the findings in a positive direction. In the absence of data on the universe of *Consumer Reports* subscribers who sought professional help for their emotional problems, this serious design problem cannot be dismissed.

Martin Seligman (1995), a consultant to the project, acknowledged the gap between its methodology and that of other contemporary psychotherapy outcome studies. Nonetheless, he concluded that the *Consumer Reports* survey "complements the (more traditional) efficacy method, and that the best features of these two methods can be combined into a more ideal method that will best provide empirical validation of psychotherapy" (p. 965). Seligman urged his readers to appreciate the difference between efficacy studies (the traditional gold standard for judging psychotherapy outcomes) and effectiveness studies (feasibility and clinical utility in the real world, as epitomized by the *Consumer Reports* survey).

We believe, to the contrary, that the *Consumer Reports* study constituted a survey of consumer satisfaction rather than a psychotherapy effectiveness study. In our view, too many essential elements of both efficacy and effectiveness research—including information on the nature and severity of patients' diagnoses; therapists' training and experience; form, length, and nature of outcomes of the treatment; and a reliable metric for reflecting therapeutic change—were lacking to justify considering the study one of effectiveness research. The absence of an untreated comparison group and concerns over possible sampling bias add to our conviction that this study ought not to be held up as an exemplar of effectiveness research.

In 1996, the *American Psychologist* published a series of commentaries on Seligman's 1995 article and the *Consumer Reports* survey. Three articles focused on distinctions between efficacy and effectiveness research.

Hollon (1996) compared the standards to which research on psychopharmacologic agents and on psychotherapy is held, as well as the methods by which their effectiveness is typically assessed. He concluded that although efficacy studies "leave much to be desired," effectiveness designs are not a panacea, in large part because they cannot substitute "for the randomized controlled clinical trial when it comes to drawing causal inferences about whether psychotherapy (or any other treatment) actually works" (pp. 1029–1030).

Jacobson and Christensen (1996) questioned Seligman's assessment of the value of the *Consumer Reports* study on both conceptual and methodological grounds, concluding that the study is so seriously flawed that few conclusions can be drawn from it. Like Hollon (1996), they believed that despite the limitations of clinical trials,

> the randomized clinical trial is as good a method for answering questions of effectiveness as it is for answering questions of efficacy [so] the clinical trial, or group experiment, should usually be the methodology of choice for confirming the effectiveness of a treatment. (Jacobson & Christensen, 1996, p. 1031).

Howard, Moras, Brill, Martinovich, and Lutz (1996) suggested moving away from treatment-focused research, concerned as it is with establishing the comparative efficacy and effectiveness of clinical interventions aggregated over groups of patients, altogether. In its place, they favored patient-focused research, which attempts to monitor an individual's progress over the course of treatment and to provide feedback of this information to the practitioner, supervisor, or case manager. Patient-focused research focuses on both the actual and estimated progress of the patient, on the basis of his or her clinical characteristics, to provide information on the expected effectiveness of treatment as well as on the characteristics of patients whose response to treatment deviates from expectation.

In the final analysis, the *Consumer Reports* study has to be assessed as an ambitious failure. At the same time, the response it generated, both pro and con, did illuminate some meaningful new distinctions between efficacy and effectiveness research, largely by forcing both supporters and critics of the study to justify their positions more fully.

Development of Practice Guidelines (1993–Present)

The development of practice guidelines by the American Psychiatric Association (1993, 1994b, 1995, 1996, 1997) and the Division of Clinical Psychology of the American Psychological Association (Chambless et al.,

1996, 1998; Task Force on Promotion and Dissemination of Psychological Procedures, 1995) has predictably generated strong reactions from those who question the premises of the psychotherapy outcome research on which the guidelines rest. Strong exception, for example, was taken by Sol Garfield (1996), a well-known psychotherapy researcher, to the list of empirically validated treatments first published in 1995 by the Division 12 Task Force. A number of his concerns reflect the efficacy—effectiveness distinction, including the distortion to the psychotherapy process he believed the manuals typically used in efficacy studies cause, as well as the incomparability of psychotherapy patients in efficacy studies and those in real-world psychotherapy settings. Others have expressed similar concerns (see, e.g., Fensterheim & Raw, 1996; Goldfried & Wolfe, 1998).

Template for Developing Guidelines: Interventions for Mental Disorders and Psychosocial Aspects of Physical Disorders (1995)

In 1995, the same year the Division 12 Task Force published its initial list of empirically validated treatments, the *Template for Developing Guidelines: Interventions for Mental Disorders and Psychosocial Aspects of Physical Disorders* (American Psychological Association Task Force, 1995) was proposed by an American Psychological Association task force and subsequently adopted as official association policy by the American Psychological Association Council. Developed "to assure comprehensiveness and consistency" (p. 7) of practice guidelines, the *Template* has two features of relevance to our discussion.

The *Template* sought to ensure that the efficacy of a treatment included in a practice guideline is established not only by randomized clinical trials (RCTs), the gold standard for this purpose, but also in terms of the treatment comparisons made in those trials. Adding the outcome comparison—to no treatment, to nonspecific treatment variables, or to treatments known to be effective—provides an additional powerful evaluative dimension. RCTs that compare an experimental treatment with established, effective treatments clearly offer a more powerful test than those that compare it with nonrobust comparison treatments or with no treatment at all.

The *Template* also explicitly distinguished between therapeutic efficacy and effectiveness; it used the term *clinical utility* to describe the latter construct:

> Clinical practice guidelines for behavioral health care (should) be constructed on the basis of two simultaneous considerations or "axes." The first is that guidelines take into consideration a rigorous assessment of scientific evidence with the goal of measuring the efficacy of any given intervention (efficacy). The second axis specifies that guidelines consider the applicability and feasibility of the intervention in the local set-

ting where it is to be proffered (clinical utility). (American Psychological Association Task Force, 1995, p. i)

Although a series of well-designed studies might establish the efficacy of an intervention, unless it is effective in real-life clinical settings, it will not be useful:

> The clinical utility axis refers to the ability (and willingness) of practitioners to use, and of patients to accept, the treatment in question, and to the range of applicability of that treatment. It reflects the extent to which the intervention, regardless of the efficacy that may or may not have been demonstrated in the clinical research setting, will be effective in the practice setting in which it is to be applied. (American Psychological Association Task Force, 1995, p. 13)

Despite its commonsense substance and balanced tone, the *Template* has also been strongly criticized for many of the same reasons cited by opponents of empirically supported treatments and practice guidelines (as enumerated by Barlow, 1996, and Stricker, 1997).

Another Confirmation of the Dodo Bird Effect (Wampold et al., 1997)

In 1997, Bruce Wampold and his colleagues (Wampold et al., 1997) reported the results of a meta-analysis reexamining the dodo bird effect first proposed by Rosenzweig (1936). Previously reaffirmed by Luborsky, Singer, and Luborsky (1975), Smith and Glass (1977), Stiles, Shapiro, and Elliott (1986), and a number of others but disputed by Krasner (1971), Bergin and Suinn (1975), Rachman and Wilson (1980), and many others (most of them cognitive–behavioral therapists), the dodo bird effect is named for the well-known race in *Alice in Wonderland* (Carroll, 1865/1962). The *dodo bird effect* refers to efficacy comparisons among psychotherapies, usually by meta-analysis, that find no differences among them. The meta-analysis by Wampold and his colleagues revealed no differences in efficacy when 277 comparisons among diverse treatments were made, leading these researchers to conclude that there are no meaningful differences in effectiveness among credible ("bona fide") therapies.

The relevance of the dodo bird effect to the aims of this review is substantial. If there really are no differences in efficacy among psychotherapies, then little purpose is served in seeking to determine whether efficacy or effectiveness studies of psychotherapy provide the clearer picture of the ultimate value of a treatment.

Crits-Christoph (1997) and Howard, Krause, Saunders, and Kopta (1997) criticized the Wampold et al. (1997) meta-analysis on grounds similar to those chosen by earlier critics of earlier meta-analyses of psychotherapy outcomes affirming the dodo bird effect. Above all, they questioned the appropriateness of meta-analysis as a means of exploring differences in psychotherapy outcome and expressed serious concerns about the heterogeneity in design and methodology of the studies chosen for inclusion in the meta-analysis.

So far as we are concerned, the question of whether there are differences in effectiveness among psychotherapies remains open. Despite many efforts through the years to confirm or deny the dodo bird effect once and for all, it has neither been confirmed nor denied. Substantial questions have been raised through the years about meta-analyses of psychotherapy outcomes that found no differences in efficacy and, thus, affirmed the dodo bird effect. A growing number of sophisticated RCTs of psychotherapies have in recent years reported differences in psychotherapy effectiveness and, thus, denied the dodo bird effect. Hence, we conclude there is ample justification for trying to determine whether efficacy or effectiveness studies give the truest picture of psychotherapy outcomes, both for its own sake and as a possible alternative means of examining the dodo bird effect from a different perspective.

Review of Contemporary Research on Efficacy and Effectiveness (Kopta, Lueger, Saunders, & Howard, 1999)

Commencing a four-page discussion of efficacy and effectiveness research in a lengthy review of contemporary psychotherapy research, Kopta, Lueger, Saunders, and Howard (1999) acknowledged the continuing gap between clinical research and clinical practice. They suggested that part of the problem might lie in RCTs, proposing instead "that this approach should be replaced by naturalistic designs, which can provide results more applicable to real clinical practice, therefore strengthening external validity" (p. 449).

Like Seligman (1996), Howard et al. (1996), and Wampold (1997), Kopta et al. (1999) endorsed effectiveness studies as the best means of understanding psychotherapy's impact in real-world clinical settings. This position derives in part from research on Howard's dosage model (Howard, Kopta, Krause, & Orlinsky, 1986). However, because dose–effect designs, including RCTs, use grouped data and provide information about average patients, they are not as useful to the psychotherapist as they could be. Accordingly, Howard, Orlinsky, and Lueger (1995) and Tingey, Lambert, Burlinhame, and Hansen (1996) proposed a dose–outcome design, a single-case application of the dosage model, which tracks therapeutic progress across sessions. Howard et al. (1996) also proposed patient profiling, which would track improvement from pretreatment clinical status by means of hierarchical linear modeling. The aim of both is to increase the utility of data from effectiveness studies by enhancing the reliability of their measurement systems.

Kopta et al. (1999) also noted the increasing emphasis psychotherapy researchers have recently put on the development of new approaches to assessment. To this end, they described creative RCTs that have been used or proposed that can distinguish active ingredients if indeed they exist, dose – effect studies (that) can discover lawful outcome relationships across sessions for patients treated by different therapies as practiced in real clinical settings, using dose – outcome designs to group individual patients by treatment type and similar dose – response patterns . . . to answer Paul's patient-focused question, (and) outcome studies . . . to distinguish which psychotherapies are more efficient in addition to which ones are simply effective. (p. 453)

CURRENT EFFORTS TO INTEGRATE EFFICACY AND EFFECTIVENESS STUDIES

As the foregoing indicates, the evolution of concerns about the usefulness of psychotherapy research for clinical practice has progressed substantially from Eysenck's time. For the most part, these changes have occurred in step with advances in psychotherapy research methodology and the robustness of psychotherapy interventions.

During the 1950s and 1960s, although some psychologists spoke and wrote of their concerns that statistical significance is not always associated with clinical worth, little was said about the impact of psychotherapy research on the practice of psychotherapy, perhaps because of the primitive state of the methodology of psychotherapy research. Although the 1970s witnessed marked advances in research methodology that paralleled the emergence of a variety of promising behavioral and cognitive – behavioral techniques, surprisingly little was written about how these advances might affect clinical practice.

Early in the 1980s, however, researchers began to dwell in earnest on the usefulness of psychotherapy research to clinicians. The developments in research methodology of the 1970s played a role in the emergence of these concerns, both because they enabled researchers to evaluate the comparative impact of different therapies and because the worth of psychotherapy research increasingly began to be appreciated. The solutions proposed to resolve the problem during this time generally focused on efforts to make efficacy studies more relevant to clinical practice, though a few commentators systematically weighed the respective contributions of what today is called efficacy and effectiveness research. Some researchers also refocused the issue by suggesting that research on psychotherapy effectiveness might have a less substantial ultimate payoff than a focus on common variables.

These more general concerns about the usefulness of psychotherapy research coalesced early in the decade of the 1990s around the meaning and significance of distinctions between psychotherapy outcome studies that focus on efficacy and those that focus on effectiveness. Some researchers have claimed that improvements in efficacy research would be sufficient to fix the problem, others have emphasized effectiveness studies as an exclusive answer, and still others have recommended simultaneous attention to both. This brings us to the most recent period in this evolution, the latter half of the decade of the 1990s, a period characterized by initial efforts to integrate efficacy and effectiveness research into a coherent whole. A recent issue of the American Psychological Association's new electronic journal *Prevention and Treatment* featured three articles proposing two different approaches to this end.

The NIMH Integration Initiative

Norquist, Lebowitz, and Hyman (1999) (the last being the current director of NIMH) began their article by acknowledging that "the intrinsic efficacy of an intervention (either pharmacological or psychotherapeutic) . . . is not usually informative for treatment practice in the community" (abstract). The problem lies in the difference in the yield of research that follows a regulatory model (based on the requirements of the federal Food and Drug Administration) and research that adheres to a public health model (in which research is designed to evaluate the effectiveness of clinical interventions as they are likely to be delivered in community and specialized practice). The article's bottom line is a proposal for how the NIMH, in consultation with basic scientists, advocates, and other federal agencies, might bridge the gap between the regulatory (efficacy) and the public health (effectiveness) models.

Norquist et al. (1999) proposed a new paradigm. It would incorporate both experimental and observational work, albeit after changes in methods for both. Although their ideas are clearly in the process of evolution, Norquist and his colleagues suggested the following:

> Research designs must permit a loosening of exclusion criteria to allow for enrollment of people with different levels of disease severity and comorbid conditions. In addition, treatment settings must be more diversified to allow for a range of providers from primary care, managed care settings to tertiary care, academic centers. Outcome measures will need to incorporate domains that are important to consumers, families and policy makers (e.g., performance, disability, cost, resource use, etc.). . . . In addition, specific areas of treatment intervention research need to be launched (e.g., rehabilitation research) and reinvigorated (e.g., psychosocial intervention research). (¶ 16–17)

Research according to this new paradigm must "combine the designs of traditional clinical and services research studies" (Norquist et al., 1999, ¶ 18). Doing so requires compromises between the strict randomized designs of traditional clinical research and the more flexible observational designs of services research. Merging these designs requires NIMH to bring together methodologists with expertise across these fields to delineate what we currently know and what we don't [because it is] quite likely that new methods and statistical analytic approaches will need to be developed to address studies in the mental health area. (¶ 18)

To achieve these ambitious goals, a new paradigm, new methods, and new statistical approaches are all required. New methods of grant review and a new research infrastructure to facilitate submission, review, and funding of research within this new paradigm are also envisioned. It is clear that the entire enterprise must founder unless the new methods and new statistical procedures, which remain to be developed, can in fact be produced.

A companion article, written by Niederehe, Street, and Lebowitz (1999), detailed the new organizational entities that would facilitate NIHM's new research emphasis on the public health model and briefly described design changes researchers would be expected to incorporate in grant proposals that address the new research paradigm. Unfortunately, as the authors themselves observed,

at the present time, it is easier to recognize when a proposed design presents a good fit for the particular questions addressed in a given study than to specify in advance or in the abstract the desired features for any and all public health model studies. (¶ 10)

In other words, specific advice for researchers wishing to focus their research on this new paradigm is not yet available. Nonetheless, plans for several large-scale, multisite clinical trials that incorporate numerous features typically identified with effectiveness research are described. Both psychosocial and psychopharmacological treatments for specific target disorders will be compared in these trials, the first two of which will investigate treatments for bipolar disorder in adults and depression in children.

As noted in the article by Norquist et al. (1999), the Clinical Treatment and Services Research Workgroup of the National Advisory Mental Health Council recently published *Bridging Science and Service* (National Advisory Mental Health Council Workgroup, 1999). This document contains "a number of recommendations about methods development that NIMH should foster in this area of research, including some that relate to innovative combinations of research designs" (p. 4). Predictably, the report recommended that NIMH continue its support of efficacy, effectiveness, practice, and service systems research and expend additional effort to build bridges across these research foci. Examples of bridge building across these domains include loosening restrictive exclusion criteria and increasing the range of outcome measures in efficacy studies, seeking cost-effectiveness data and studying commonly practiced but not commonly studied interventions in effectiveness studies, and putting more resources into clinical epidemiology and dissemination research.

The report (National Advisory Mental Health Council Workgroup, 1999) also recommended that "NIMH should explore new methods for analysis of data from studies that incorporate innovative combinations of research designs" (p. 46) and "NIMH should encourage development of methods to explicitly evaluate trade-offs in alternate design features that differ in their implications for internal and external validity" (p. 47). In the first instance, the report envisioned studies that combine both experimental and observational designs or analytic features to address questions about treatment in a community context. These studies would be of longer duration, larger sample sizes, and broader domains of outcome than at present. As a result, a reduction in the intensity (or depth) of data collection may be required for such a study to be feasible. Such alternative approaches might entail a trade-off between breadth and depth of information collected and analyzed, on the one hand, and the ability of studies to inform either clinical or policy audiences, on the other. "Methodologists should develop approaches to model those trade-offs in breadth and depth for given study purposes and to maintain reasonable costs for the study" (p. 46).

In the second instance, innovative methods, otherwise unspecified, need to be fostered:

> Pursuit of the goals of methodological development requires integration of clinical and social science, particularly incorporation of statistical and econometric expertise. Expertise in qualitative analyses also is likely to be needed to generate new approaches to studying systems, treatments, and adherence with treatment. (National Advisory Mental Health Council Workgroup, 1999, p. 47)

In summary, the NIMH proposal embraced a dual strategy of modifying efficacy and effectiveness research on specific issues to maximize real-world payoff and developing new research designs and statistical procedures to avoid or minimize the well-known problems associated with efforts to adjust internal and external validity simultaneously. "When studies involve multiple design decisions that favor external or internal validity, rarely are both improved simultaneously" (National Advisory Mental Health Council Workgroup, 1999, p. 46). Whether these ambitious goals will be realized, of course, is anyone's guess at the present time.

Multisite Efficacy/Effectiveness Clinics

Klein and Smith (1999) proposed the development of "dedicated, multisite efficacy/effectiveness clinics" (abstract) to address the problems posed by the conflicting demands of internal and external validity in efficacy and effectiveness studies. These special clinics would also be structured to examine such understudied treatment issues as compliance, comorbidity, refractory illness, and withdrawal syndromes, as well as adjunctive and maintenance treatments. The clinics would emphasize careful, reliable, documented studies on process and outcome. They would also promote development of outcome norms for well-defined populations on such variables as diagnosis, economic status, history, and comorbidity. The proximate goal would be to generate, across cooperating clinics, "a large volume of well-delineated patients [who] could be treated and studied who may have high comorbidity with medical, psychiatric, and substance abuse conditions" (¶ 19). The distal goals would be both to develop benchmarks for expected treatment outcomes for these distinct groups of patients by means of normative sampling and to serve as hypothesis-generating therapeutic endeavors.

As with NIMH's new paradigm, however, Klein and Smith's (1999) proposal for efficacy/effectiveness clinics is long on enthusiasm, problem identification, and aspirations for change, but a good deal shorter on concrete details of design, methodology, and statistical analysis. Although understandable at this stage in the development of the concept, the relative lack of substance leaves the reader who appreciates some of the problems attendant on integrating efficacy and effectiveness studies uncertain to what extent integration can actually be effected. Instead, one is left to wonder whether these clinics would function largely as a more efficient means of meeting an older goal, strengthening the sequence linking initial hypothesis testing in efficacy studies and confirmation of these hypotheses by effectiveness studies.

Meta-Analyses of Psychotherapy in Clinically Representative Conditions

The NIMH effort to integrate efficacy and effectiveness research (National Advisory Mental Health Council Workgroup, 1999; Niederehe, Street, & Lebowitz, 1999; Norquist et al., 1999) assumed that these two research models, separately and jointly, ultimately lack the capacity to optimize internal and external validity. The Klein and Smith (1999) model of multisite efficacy/effectiveness clinics appears to draw the same conclusion, even though the proposal for solving the problem by this means differs somewhat from the NIMH proposal.

Recent analyses of the psychotherapy outcome literature by Shadish and his colleagues (Shadish, Navarro, Matt, & Phillips, 2000; Shadish et al., 1993, 1997) have taken a very different starting point but addressed a closely related set of issues. Using sophisticated random effects regression analyses and secondary analyses of prior meta-analyses, Shadish and his associates asked whether psychotherapy outcome studies ranging from less to more clinically representative differ in effectiveness, as reflected by a large array of outcome variables. In other words, they asked whether there are outcome differences in psychotherapy completed for efficacy research purposes and psychotherapy completed for effectiveness research purposes, thereby searching for substantive differences in results as a function of substantive differences in research methods.

Shadish and his colleagues consistently failed to find differences in efficacy/effectiveness as a function of where on the efficacy/effectiveness (clinically representative) continuum a study falls. Although this finding does not reduce the real methodological differences between the efficacy/ effectiveness research models to semantic ones, it does suggest that in terms of one very important factor, clinical usefulness, the distinction may be more apparent than real. This research also confirms prior findings indicating that therapy is more effective in larger doses when outcome measures are highly tailored to treatment and, less consistently, when behaviorally oriented therapies are used. These latter results buttress the view that the innovative data-analytic procedures used by this research team are sensitive to crucial variables affecting outcome.

In the first of these articles, Shadish and his colleagues (1997) asked 15 meta-analysts to provide effect sizes from 56 studies included in previous reviews that met one of three increasingly stringent levels of clinical representativeness. Effect sizes were then synthesized and compared with results from the original meta-analyses. Results indicated that the effect sizes of the more and the less clinically representative studies were essentially the same at all three criteria levels. Shadish et al. (2000) subsequently confronted some of the methodological problems of the 1997 study by synthesizing results from 90 psychotherapy outcomes that ranged widely in clinical representativeness. Random effects regression analyses indicated that the psychotherapies were equally effective across the clinical representativeness continuum, thereby confirming the 1997 findings.

Shadish's research calls into question the implicit assumption that efficacy and effectiveness studies of the same treatment modality yield incomparable outcomes as a function of their design differences. They suggest that these differences in design may be more apparent than real, at least in terms of their capacity to test the robustness of a treatment.

IN CONCLUSION

The discordant literature on efficacy and effectiveness research reviewed here parallels the continuing lack of consensus among psychotherapy researchers themselves and between them and clinicians on how best to add value to research findings on psychotherapy for practitioners. Some investigators continue to believe that the designs of clinical trials and other efficacy studies require neither substantial change nor enhancement with data from effectiveness studies. Others as strongly believe that there is a problem with exclusive reliance on the efficacy model. Of this group, some would rely almost exclusively on effectiveness studies, whereas others would work to bring efficacy and effectiveness research models into greater harmony with one another. Still others conclude that regardless of novel adjustments and new configurations, effectiveness and efficacy studies will never provide clinicians the information they require to do their jobs better; these individuals opt for continuing to seek a new paradigm altogether. Despite almost a decade of research on the efficacy/effectiveness distinction, a metric permitting rational choice between these alternatives has not yet been developed. Adding to the problem is the absence of agreement on the essential components of either efficacy or effectiveness trials: Seligman (1995, 1996) has been severely criticized for proclaiming the *Consumer Reports* survey a model effectiveness study rather than, as many have seen it, an equivocal survey of consumer satisfaction.

As troublesome as the continuing lack of consensus on an optimal therapy outcome research model after more than 50 years of efforts to develop such a model is the continuing gap in understanding between psychotherapy researchers and psychotherapists. A rift that has existed since Eysenck's (1952) initial review of psychotherapy outcomes so incensed the clinicians of his time, the inability of researchers to generate findings of value to clinicians continues to have a serious impact on the credibility of research findings on outcomes (Nathan, 1999). A substantial part of the problem, of course, is the inability of researchers to agree on either a most appropriate research model or the meaning of data from existing models. An apt illustration is the continuing inability of researchers to resolve the dodo bird conjecture, epitomized by the 1997 meta-analysis of psychotherapy outcomes by Wampold et al. (1997) and its accompanying critiques. If behavioral scientists cannot reliably document differences in effectiveness among treatments that clinicians are convinced do exist, why should clinicians put any faith in the efforts of researchers?

If this half-century dilemma is to be resolved anytime soon, it will require agreement on definitions of and the best means for using both efficacy and effectiveness studies. The APA *Template for Developing Guidelines* (American Psychological Association Task Force, 1995) might be a model for such an effort, despite the decidedly cool reception it has received from the practice community thus far. Despite their appeal to the quantitative mind, meta-analyses of psychotherapy outcomes seem likely to continue to generate irresolvable disagreement, as they have for more than a quarter of a century. Pending outcomes from the massive NIMH effort to integrate efficacy and effectiveness studies by means of new methodologies and statistics that have yet to be developed, continued efforts to improve the designs of efficacy and effectiveness research must be made. Ground rules for moving from efficacy studies to effectiveness studies need to be developed: When do practitioners know enough about a treatment's worth in the ideal environment of the efficacy study to determine its effectiveness with larger, more diverse populations in real-world settings? We are encouraged to believe that a focus on efficacy and effectiveness research may well resolve this problem of 50 years standing, given how far we have come in the development of these approaches in less than a decade.

REFERENCES

American Psychiatric Association. (1952). *Diagnostic and statistical manual of mental disorders*. Washington, DC: Author.

American Psychiatric Association. (1993). Practice guidelines for the treatment of major depressive disorder in adults. *American Journal of Psychiatry, 150*(Suppl.), 4126.

American Psychiatric Association. (1994a). *Diagnostic and statistical manual of mental disorders* (4th ed.). Washington, DC: Author.

American Psychiatric Association. (1994b). Practice guideline for the treatment of patients with bipolar disorder. *American Journal of Psychiatry, 151*(Suppl.), 12136.

American Psychiatric Association. (1995). Practice guideline for the treatment of patients with substance use disorders: Alcohol, cocaine, opioids. *American Journal of Psychiatry, 152*(Suppl.), 11159.

American Psychiatric Association. (1996). Practice guideline for the treatment of patients with nicotine dependence. *American Journal of Psychiatry, 153*(Suppl.), 10131.

American Psychiatric Association. (1997). Practice guideline for the treatment of patients with schizophrenia. *American Journal of Psychiatry, 154*(Suppl.), 4163.

American Psychological Association Task Force. (1995). *Template for developing guidelines: Interventions for mental disorders and psychosocial aspects of physical disorders*. Washington, DC: American Psychological Association.

Anderson, E., & Lambert, M. (1995). Short-term dynamically oriented psychotherapy: a review and meta-analysis. *Clinical Psychology Review, 15,* 503–514.

Barlow, D. H. (1981). On the relation of clinical research to clinical practice: Current issues. *Journal of Consulting and Clinical Psychology, 49,* 147–155.

Barlow, D. H. (1996). Health care policy, psychotherapy research, and the future of psychotherapy. *American Psychologist, 51,* 1050–1058.

Beck, A. T., Rush, A. J., Shaw, B. F., & Emery, G. (1979). *Cognitive therapy of depression.* New York: Guilford Press.

Bergin, A. E. (1966). Some implications of psychotherapy research for therapeutic practice. *Journal of Abnormal Psychology, 71,* 235–246.

Bergin, A. E., & Suinn, R. M. (1975). Individual psychotherapy and behavior therapy. In M. R. Rosenzweig & L. W. Porter (Eds.), *Annual review of psychology* (Vol. 26, pp. 509–556). Palo Alto, CA: Annual Reviews.

Berman, J. S., & Norton, N. C. (1985). Does professional training make a therapist more effective? *Psychological Bulletin, 98,* 401–407.

Beutler, L. E. (1998). Identifying empirically supported treatments: What if we didn't? *Journal of Consulting and Clinical Psychology, 66*, 113–120.

Beutler, L. E., Machado, P. P. P., & Neufeldt, S. A. (1994). Therapist variables. In A. E. Bergin & S. L. Garfield (Eds.), *Handbook of psychotherapy and behavior change* (4th ed., pp. 229–269). New York: Wiley.

Butler, S. F., & Strupp, H. H. (1986). Specific and nonspecific factors in psychotherapy: A problematic paradigm for psychotherapy research. *Psychotherapy, 23*, 30–40.

Carroll, L. (1962). *Alice's adventures in Wonderland*. Harmondsworth, Middlesex, England: Penguin Books. (Original work published in 1865)

Chambless, D. L., Baker, M. J., Baucom, D. H., Beutler, L. E., Calhoun, K. S., Crits-Christoph, P., et al. (1998). Update on empirically validated therapies, II. *Clinical Psychologist, 5*, 13–16.

Chambless, D. L., Sanderson, W. C., Shoham, V., Johnson, S. B., Pope, K. S., Crits-Christoph, P., et al. (1996). An update on empirically validated therapies. *Clinical Psychologist, 49*, 5–18.

Cohen, J. (1965). Some statistical issues in psychological research. In B. Wolman (Ed.), *Handbook of clinical psychology* (pp. 95–121). New York: McGraw-Hill.

Crits-Christoph, P. (1996). The dissemination of efficacious psychological treatments. *Clinical Psychology: Science and Practice, 3*, 260–263.

Crits-Christoph, P. (1997). Limitations of the dodo bird verdict and the role of clinical trials in psychotherapy research: Comment on Wampold et al. (1997). *Psychological Bulletin, 122*, 216–220.

Crits-Christoph, P., Baranacki, K., Kurcias, J. S., Beck, A. T., Carroll, K., Perry, K., et al. (1991). Meta-analysis of therapist effects in psychotherapy outcome studies. *Psychotherapy Research, 1*, 81–91.

Cronbach, L. J. (1957). Two disciplines of scientific psychology. *American Psychologist, 12*, 671–684.

Eaton, T. T., Abeles, N., & Gutfreund, M. J. (1988). Therapeutic alliance and outcome: Impact of treatment length and pretreatment symptomatology. *Psychotherapy, 25*, 536–542.

Edelson, M. (1994). Can psychotherapy research answer this psychotherapist's questions? In P. F. Talley, H. H. Strupp, & S. F. Butler (Eds.), *Psychotherapy research and practice: Bridging the gap* (pp. 60–87). New York: Basic Books.

Eifert, G. H., Schulte, D., Zvolensky, M. J., Lejuez, C. W., & Lau, A. W. (1997). Manualized behavior therapy: Merits and challenges. *Behavior Therapy, 28*, 499–509.

Elkin, I. (1994). The NIMH Treatment of Depression Collaborative Research Program: Where we began and where we are. In A. E. Bergin & S. L. Garfield (Eds.), *Handbook of psychotherapy and behavior change* (pp. 114–139). New York: Wiley.

Elkin, I. (1995). Further differentiation of common factors. *Clinical Psychology: Science and Practice, 2*, 75–78.

Elkin, I., Parloff, M. B., Hadley, S. W., & Autry, J. H. (1985). NIMH Treatment of Depression Collaborative Research Program: Background and research plan. *Archives of General Psychiatry, 42,* 305–316.

Elkin, I., Pilkonis, P. A., Docherty, J. P., & Sotsky, S. M. (1988). Conceptual and methodological issues in the comparative studies of psychotherapy and pharmacotherapy: II. Nature and timing of treatment effects. *American Journal of Psychiatry, 145,* 1070–1076.

Elkin, I., Shea, M. T., Watkins, J. T., Imber, S. D., Sotsky, S. M., Collins, J. F., et al. (1989). National Institute of Mental Health Treatment of Depression Collaborative Research Program: General effectiveness of treatments. *Archives of General Psychiatry, 46,* 971–982.

Eysenck, H. J. (1952). The effects of psychotherapy: An evaluation. *Journal of Consulting Psychology, 16,* 319–324.

Eysenck, H. J. (1960). *Behavior therapy and the neuroses.* Oxford, England: Pergamon Press.

Fensterheim, H., & Raw, S. D. (1996). Empirically validated treatments, psychotherapy integration, and the politics of psychotherapy. *Journal of Psychotherapy Integration, 6,* 207–215.

Frank, E., Kupfer, D. J., & Perel, J. M. (1990). Three-year outcomes for maintenance therapies in recurrent depression. *Archives of General Psychiatry, 47,* 1093–1099.

Frank, E., Kupfer, D. J., Wagner, E. F., McEachran, A. B., & Cornes, C. (1992). Efficacy of interpersonal psychotherapy as a maintenance treatment of recurrent depression: Contributing factors. *Archives of General Psychiatry, 48,* 1053–1059.

Frank, J. D. (1971). Therapeutic factors in psychotherapy. *American Journal of Psychotherapy, 25,* 350–361.

Frank, J. D. (1973). *Persuasion and healing: A comparative study of psychotherapy* (Rev. ed.). Baltimore: Johns Hopkins University Press.

Garfield, S. L. (1996). Some problems associated with "validated" forms of psychotherapy. *Clinical Psychology: Science and Practice, 3,* 218–229.

Gendlin, E. T., & Rychlak, J. F. (1970). Psychotherapeutic processes. In P. H. Mussen & M. R. Rosenzweig (Eds.), *Annual review of psychology* (Vol. 21, pp. 148–190). Palo Alto, CA: Annual Reviews.

Glass, G. V. (1980). Summarizing effect sizes. In R. Rosenthal (Ed.), *New directions for methodology of social and behavioral science: Quantitative assessment of research domains* (pp. 13–31). San Francisco: Jossey-Bass.

Goldfried, M. R., Greenberg, L., & Marmar, C. (1990). Individual psychotherapy: Process and outcome. In M. R. Rosenzweig & L. W. Porter (Eds.), *Annual review of psychology* (Vol. 41, pp. 659–688). Palo Alto, CA: Annual Reviews.

Goldfried, M. R., & Wolfe, B. E. (1998). Toward a more clinically valid approach to therapy research. *Journal of Consulting and Clinical Psychology, 66,* 143–150.

Gomes-Schwartz, B., Hadley, S. W., & Strupp, H. H. (1978). Individual psychotherapy and behavior therapy. In M. R. Rosenzweig & L. W. Porter (Eds.), *Annual review of psychology* (Vol. 29, pp. 435–472). Palo Alto, CA: Annual Reviews.

Gottman, J. M., & Rushe, R. H. (1993). The analysis of change: Issues, fallacies, and new ideas. *Journal of Consulting and Clinical Psychology, 61,* 907–910.

Greenberg, J. (1994). Psychotherapy research: A clinician's view. In P. F. Talley, H. H. Strupp, & S. F. Butler (Eds.), *Psychotherapy research and practice: Bridging the gap* (pp. 1–18). New York: Basic Books.

Hays, W. L. (1963). *Statistics.* New York: Holt, Rinehart & Winston.

Hollon, S. D. (1996). The efficacy and effectiveness of psychotherapy relative to medications. *American Psychologist, 51,* 1025–1030.

Hollon, S. D. (1999). Allegiance effects in treatment research: A commentary. *Clinical Psychology: Science and Practice, 6,* 107–112.

Horowitz, M. J., Marmar, C., Krupnick, K., Wilner, N., Kaltreider, N., & Wallerstein, R. (1984). *Personality styles and brief psychotherapy.* New York: Basic Books.

Horvath, A. O., & Symonds, D. B. (1991). Relationship between working alliance and outcome in psychotherapy: A meta-analysis. *Journal of Counseling Psychology, 38,* 139–149.

Horvath, P. (1988). Placebos and common factors in two decades of psychotherapy research. *Psychological Bulletin, 104,* 214–225.

Howard, K. I., Kopta, S. M., Krause, M. S., & Orlinsky, D. E. (1986). The dose–effect relationship in psychotherapy. *American Psychologist, 41,* 159–164.

Howard, K. I., Krause, M. S., Saunders, S. M., & Kopta, S. M. (1997). Trials and tribulations in the meta-analysis of treatment differences: Comments on Wampold et al. (1997). *Psychological Bulletin, 122,* 221–225.

Howard, K. I., Moras, K., Brill, P. L., Martinovich, Z., & Lutz, W. (1996). Evaluation of psychotherapy: Efficacy, effectiveness, and patient progress. *American Psychologist, 51,* 1059–1064.

Howard, K. I., & Orlinsky, D. E. (1972). Psychotherapeutic processes. In P. H. Mussen & M. R. Rosenzweig (Eds.), *Annual review of psychology* (Vol. 23, pp. 615–668). Palo Alto, CA: Annual Reviews.

Howard, K. I., Orlinsky, D. E., & Lueger, R. J. (1995). The design of clinically relevant outcome research: Some considerations and an example. In M. Aveline & D. A. Shapiro (Eds.), *Research foundations for psychotherapy practice* (pp. 3–47). Sussex, England: Wiley.

Jacobson, N. S., & Christensen, A. (1996). Studying the effectiveness of psychotherapy: How well can clinical trials do the job? *American Psychologist, 51,* 1031–1039.

Jacobson, N. S., Follette, W. C., & Revenstorf, D. (1984). Psychotherapy outcome research: Methods for reporting variability and evaluating clinical significance. *Behavior Therapy, 15,* 336–352.

Jacobson, N. S., Schmaling, K. B., Holtzworth-Munroe, A., Karr, J. L., Wood, L. R.,

& Follette, V. M. (1989). Research-structured vs. clinically flexible versions of social learning based marital therapy. *Behaviour Research and Therapy, 27,* 173–180.

Jacobson, N. S., & Truax, P. (1991). Clinical significance: A statistical approach to defining meaningful change in psychotherapy research. *Journal of Consulting and Clinical Psychology, 59,* 12–19.

Kazdin A. E. (1986). Comparative outcome studies of psychotherapy: Methodological issues and strategies. *Journal of Consulting and Clinical Psychology, 54,* 95–105.

Kernberg, O., Selzer, M., Koenigsberg, H., Carr, A., & Appelbaum, A. (1989). *Psychodynamic psychotherapy of borderline patients.* New York: Basic Books.

Kiesler, D. J.(1994). Standardization of intervention: The tie that binds psychotherapy research and practice. In P. F. Talley, H. H. Strupp, & S. F. Butler (Eds.), *Psychotherapy research and practice: Bridging the gap* (pp. 143–153). New York: Basic Books.

Klein, D. F. (1999). Dealing with the effects of therapy allegiances. *Clinical Psychology: Science and Practice, 6,* 124–126.

Klein, D. F., & Smith, L. B. (1999). Organizational requirements for effective clinical effectiveness studies. *Prevention and Treatment,* Article 0002a. Retrieved August 21, 2000, from http://;journals.apa.org/prevention/volume/pre0020002a.html

Klerman, G. L., Weissman, M. M., Rounsaville, B. J., & Chevron, E. S. (1984). *Interpersonal psychotherapy of depression.* New York: Basic Books.

Kopta, S. M., Lueger, R. J., Saunders, S. M., & Howard, K. I. (1999). Individual psychotherapy outcome and process research: Challenges leading to greater turmoil or a positive transition? In J. T. Spence, J. M. Darley, & D. J. Foss (Eds.), *Annual review of psychology* (Vol. 50, pp. 441–470). Palo Alto, CA: Annual Reviews.

Koss, M. P., Butcher, J. N., & Strupp, H. H. (1986). Brief psychotherapy methods in clinical research. *Journal of Consulting and Clinical Psychology, 54,* 60–67.

Krasner, L. (1971). Behavior therapy. In P. H. Mussen & M. R. Rosenzweig (Eds.), *Annual review of psychology* (Vol. 22, pp. 483–532). Palo Alto, CA: Annual Reviews.

Lambert, M. J. (1992). Psychotherapy outcome research: Implications for integrative and eclectic therapies. In J. C. Norcross & M. R. Goldfried (Eds.), *Handbook of psychotherapy integration* (pp. 94–129). New York: Basic Books.

Lambert, M. J. (1999). Are differential treatment effects inflated by researcher therapy allegiance? Could Clever Hans count? *Clinical Psychology: Science and Practice, 6,* 127–130.

Lambert, M. J., & Bergin, A. E. (1994). The effectiveness of psychotherapy. In S. L. Garfield & A. E. Bergin (Eds.), *Handbook of psychotherapy and behavior change* (4th ed., pp. 143–189). New York: Wiley.

Linehan, M. M. (1993). *Skills training manual for treating borderline personality disorder.* New York: Guilford Press.

Luborsky, L. (1984). *Principles of psychoanalytic psychotherapy: A manual for supportive – expressive (SE) treatment.* New York: Basic Books.

Luborsky, L., & Diguer, L. (1995, June). *The psychotherapist as a neglected variable: The therapist's treatment effectiveness.* Paper presented at the meeting of the Society for Psychotherapy Research, Vancouver, British Columbia, Canada.

Luborsky, L., Diguer, L., Seligman, D. A., Rosenthal, R., Krause, E. D., Johnson, S., et al. (1999). The researcher's own therapy allegiances: A "wild card" in comparisons of treatment efficacy. *Clinical Psychology: Science and Practice, 6,* 95–106.

Luborsky, L., Singer, B., & Luborsky, L. (1975). Comparative studies of psychotherapies: Is it true that "everybody has won and all must have prizes?" *Archives of General Psychiatry, 32,* 995–1008.

Maling, M. S., & Howard, K. I. (1994). From research to practice to research to. . . . In P. F. Talley, H. H. Strupp, & S. F. Butler (Eds.), *Psychotherapy research and practice: Bridging the gap* (pp. 246–253). New York: Basic Books.

Mental health: Does therapy help? (1995, November). *Consumer Reports,* 734–739.

Mintz, J., Drake, R. E., & Crits-Cristoph, P. (1996). Efficacy and effectiveness of psychotherapy: Two paradigms, one science. *American Psychologist, 51,* 1084–1085.

Nathan, P. E. (1998). Practice guidelines: Not yet ideal. *American Psychologist, 53,* 290–299.

Nathan, P. E. (1999, August). *And the dodo bird asked: "Well, what about studies of psychotherapy effectiveness?"* Invited address at the 107th Annual Convention of the American Psychological Association, Boston, MA.

National Advisory Mental Health Council Workgroup. (1999). *Bridging science and service.* Washington, DC: National Institute of Mental Health.

Niederehe, G., Street, L. L., & Lebowitz, B. D. (1999). NIMH support for psychotherapy research: Opportunities and questions. *Prevention and Treatment, 2,* Article0003a.

Norquist, G., Lebowitz, B., & Hyman, S. (1999). Expanding the frontier of treatment research. *Prevention and Treatment, 2,* Article 0001a. Retrieved August 21, 2000, from http://journals.apa.org/prevention/volume2/pre0020001a.html

Ogles, B. M., Lambert, M. J., & Sawyer, J. D. (1995). Clinical significance of the National Institute of Mental Health Treatment of Depression Collaborative Research Program data. *Journal of Consulting and Clinical Psychology, 63,* 321–326.

Orlinsky, D. E., & Howard, K. I. (1975). *Varieties of psychotherapeutic experience.* New York: Teachers College Press.

Orlinsky, D. E., & Howard, K. I. (1986). Process and outcome in psychotherapy. In S. L. Garfield & A. E. Bergin (Eds.), *Handbook of psychotherapy and behavior change* (3rd ed., pp. 311–381). New York: Wiley.

Parloff, M. B. (1984). Psychotherapy research and its incredible credibility crisis. *Clinical Psychology Review, 4,* 95–109.

Parloff, M. B. (1986). Placebo controls in psychotherapy research a sine qua non or a placebo for research problems? *Journal of Consulting and Clinical Psychology, 54*, 79–87.

Persons, J. B. (1991). Psychotherapy outcome studies do not accurately represent current models of psychotherapy: A proposed remedy. *American Psychologist, 46*, 99–106.

Powers, E., & Witmer, H. (1951). *An experiment in the prevention of delinquency: The Cambridge–Somerville youth study.* New York: Columbia University Press.

Project MATCH Research Group. (1993). Project MATCH: Rationale and methods for a multisite clinical trial matching patients to alcoholism treatment. *Alcoholism: Clinical and Experimental Research, 17*, 1130–1145.

Project MATCH Research Group. (1997). Matching alcoholism treatment to client heterogeneity: Project MATCH post-treatment drinking outcomes. *Journal of Studies on Alcohol, 58*, 7–29.

Rachman, S., & Wilson, G. T. (1980). *The effects of the psychological therapies.* Oxford, England: Pergamon Press.

Robinson, L. A., Berman, J. S., & Neimeyer, R. A. (1990). Psychotherapy for the treatment of depression: A comprehensive review of controlled outcome research. *Psychological Bulletin, 108*, 30–49.

Rogers, C. R. (1957). The necessary and sufficient conditions of therapeutic personality change. *Journal of Consulting Psychology, 21*, 95–103.

Rogers, C. R. (1961). *On becoming a person.* Boston: Houghton-Mifflin.

Rogers, C. R., & Dymond, R. (1954). *Psychotherapy and personality change.* Chicago: University of Chicago Press.

Rosenthal, R. (1983). Assessing the statistical and social importance of the effects of psychotherapy. *Journal of Consulting and Clinical Psychology, 51*, 4–13.

Rosenthal, R., & Rubin, D. B. (1979). A note on percent variance explained as a measure of the importance of effects. *Journal of Applied Social Psychology, 9*, 395–396.

Rosenthal, R., & Rubin, D. B. (1982). A simple, general purpose display of magnitude of experimental effect. *Journal of Educational Psychology, 74*, 166–169.

Rosenzweig, S. (1936). Some implicit common factors in diverse methods in psychotherapy. *American Journal of Orthopsychiatry, 6*, 412–415.

Sargent, M., & Cohen, L. H. (1983). Influence of psychotherapy research on clinical practice: An experimental survey. *Journal of Consulting and Clinical Psychology, 51*, 718–720.

Seligman, M. E. P. (1995). The effectiveness of psychotherapy: The *Consumer Reports* study. *American Psychologist, 50*, 965–974.

Seligman, M. E. P. (1996). Science as an ally of practice. *American Psychologist, 51*, 1072–1079.

Shadish, W. R., Navarro, A. M., Matt, G. E., & Phillips, G. (2000). The effects of psychological therapies in clinically representative conditions: A meta-analysis. *Psychological Bulletin, 126*, 512–529.

Shadish, W. R., Matt, G. E., Navarro, A. M., Siegle, G., Crits-Christoph, P., Hazel-rigg, M. D., et al. (1997). Evidence that therapy works in clinically representative conditions. *Journal of Consulting and Clinical Psychology, 65*, 355–365.

Shadish, W. R., Montgomery, L. M., Wilson, D., Wilson, M. R., Bright, I., & Okwumabua, T. (1993). Effects of family and marital psychotherapies: A meta-analysis. *Journal of Consulting and Clinical Psychology, 61*, 992–1002.

Shadish, W. R., & Ragsdale, K. (1996). Random versus nonrandom assignment in controlled experiments: Do you get the same answer? *Journal of Consulting and Clinical Psychology, 64*, 1290–1305.

Shapiro, D. A., & Shapiro, D. (1982). Meta-analysis of comparative therapy outcome studies: A replication and refinement. *Psychological Bulletin, 92*, 581–604.

Shapiro, D. A., & Shapiro, D. (1983). Comparative therapy outcome research: Methodological implications of meta-analysis. *Journal of Consulting and Clinical Psychology, 51*, 42–53.

Shoham, V., & Rohrbaugh, M. J. (1999). Beyond allegiance to comparative outcome studies. *Clinical Psychology: Science and Practice, 6*, 120–123.

Smith, M. L. (1980). Integrating studies of psychotherapy outcomes. In R. Rosenthal (Ed.), *New directions for methodology of social and behavioral science: Quantitative assessment of research domains* (pp. 47–61). San Francisco: Jossey-Bass.

Smith, M. L., & Glass, G. V. (1977). Meta-analysis of psychotherapy outcome studies. *American Psychologist, 32*, 752–760.

Smith, M. L., Glass, G. V., & Miller, T. I. (1980). *Benefits of psychotherapy*. Baltimore: Johns Hopkins University Press.

Spence, D. P. (1994). The failure to ask the hard questions. In P. F. Talley, H. H. Strupp, & S. F. Butler (Eds.), *Psychotherapy research and practice: Bridging the gap* (pp. 19–38). New York: Basic Books.

Stiles, W. B., & Shapiro, D. A. (1989). Abuse of the drug metaphor in psychotherapy process–outcome research. *Clinical Psychology Review, 9*, 521–543.

Stiles, W. B., Shapiro, D. A., & Elliott, R. (1986). "Are all psychotherapies equivalent?" *American Psychologist, 41*, 165–180.

Stoler, N. (1963). Client likeability: A variable in the study of psychotherapy. *Journal of Consulting Psychology, 27*, 175–178.

Stricker, G. (1997). Are science and practice commensurable? *American Psychologist, 52*, 442–448.

Strupp, H. H. (1973). *Psychotherapy: Clinical, research, and theoretical issues*. New York: Jason Aronson.

Strupp, H. H. (1989). Psychotherapy: Can the practitioner learn from the researcher? *American Psychologist, 44*, 717–724.

Strupp, H. H., & Binder, J. L. (1984). *Psychotherapy in a new key: A guide to time-limited psychotherapy*. New York: Basic Books.

Svartberg, M., Seltzer, M. H., & Stiles, T. C. (1998). The effects of common and specific factors in short-term anxiety-provoking psychotherapy. *Journal of Nervous and Mental Disease, 186*, 691–696.

Task Force on Promotion and Dissemination of Psychological Procedures. (1995). Training in and dissemination of empirically-validated psychological treatments: Report and recommendations. *Clinical Psychologist, 4*, 83–23.

Teuber, N., & Powers, E. (1953). Evaluating therapy in a delinquency prevention program. *Proceedings of the Association of Nervous and Mental Disease, 3*, 138–147.

Thase, M. E. (1999a). How should efficacy be evaluated in randomized clinical trials of treatments for depression? *Journal of Clinical Psychiatry, 60*(Suppl. 4), 23–32.

Thase, M. E. (1999b). What is the investigator allegiance effect and what should we do about it? *Clinical Psychology: Science and Practice, 6*, 113–115.

Tingey, R. C., Lambert, M. J., Burlinhame, G. M., & Hansen, N. B. (1996). Assessing clinical significance: Proposed extensions to method. *Psychotherapy Research, 6*, 109–123.

Wampold, B. E. (1997). Methodological problems in identifying efficacious psychotherapies. *Psychotherapy Research, 7*, 21–43.

Wampold, B. E., Mondin, G. W., Moody, M., Stich, F., Benson, K., & Ahn, H.-N. (1997). A meta-analysis of outcome studies comparing bona fide psychotherapies: Empirically, "all must have prizes." *Psychotherapy Bulletin, 122*, 203–215.

Weiss, J., & Sampson, H., & the Mount Zion Psychotherapy Research Group. (1986). *The psychoanalytic process: Theory, clinical observations, and empirical research*. New York: Guilford Press.

Zlotnick, C., Elkin, I., & Shea, M. T. (1998). Does the gender of a patient or the gender of a therapist affect the treatment of patients with major depression? *Journal of Consulting and Clinical Psychology, 66*, 655–659.

23

ARE RESULTS OF RANDOMIZED CONTROLLED TRIALS USEFUL TO PSYCHOTHERAPISTS?

JACQUELINE B. PERSONS AND GEORGE SILBERSCHATZ

The question of whether the results of randomized controlled trials (RCTs) are useful to practicing clinicians is a controversial one in the field of the psychological therapies. We present the two sides of the argument, with Persons arguing that information from RCTs is vital to clinicians and Silberschatz arguing that information from RCTs is irrelevant. After presenting each of our points of view, each author rebuts the other's position. We conclude with a brief review of our key points of agreement and disagreement.

Reprinted from the *Journal of Consulting and Clinical Psychology*, 66, 126–135. Copyright 1998 by the American Psychological Association.

Jacqueline B. Persons thanks Gerald Davison, Hanna Levenson, and Michael Tompkins for their helpful discussions. George Silberschatz acknowledges the helpful contributions of John Curtis, Nnamdi Pole, and Harold Sampson.

TWO POINTS OF VIEW

Results of RCTs Are Vital to Clinicians (Jacqueline B. Persons)

Clinicians must attend to the results of RCTs for clinical, ethical, and legal reasons. I present examples of clinically useful information provided by RCTs. I also describe factors that make it difficult to export RCT-supported protocols from research to clinical settings, and I propose strategies for alleviating some of those difficulties.

Importance of RCTs to Clinicians

Practitioners need information from RCTs for clinical, ethical, and legal reasons. I discuss each in turn.

Clinicians are routinely called upon to make decisions about alternative treatments. The RCT is designed specifically to assist in these decisions, because the RCT addresses questions of the form, Are Treatment A and Treatment B equally effective in the treatment of disorder X? Other types of studies, including naturalistic studies, can also address this question. However, a naturalistic comparison of Treatments A and B is a weaker design than the RCT because clinicians cannot be certain that the patients receiving Treatment A do not differ in some systematic way from the patients receiving Treatment B. RCTs (through random assignment, hence the name *RCT*) overcome this weakness (see Chambless & Hollon, 1998). Because clinicians need information about comparative treatment efficacy and because the RCT is one of the strongest designs to answer this question, I believe that unless psychotherapists attend to RCTs, they cannot offer their patients the best quality care.

Evidence from clinical trials is currently widely accepted by the scientific community as the gold standard of evidence about treatment efficacy. It is also generally accepted by the lay public; articles reporting results of clinical trials appear daily in the popular press. Because the RCT is the standard method of evaluating treatment efficacy, I believe that clinicians have an ethical responsibility to use RCTs to guide their work; this argument has also been made by others, including the Agency for Health Care Policy and Research, U.S. Public Health Service ([AHCPR], 1993; Klerman, 1990; McFall, 1991). Practicing without regard to the results of the RCTs can also have legal consequences (Klerman, 1990). Furthermore, because RCTs are the gold standard method for comparing treatments, I believe that in this debate the burden of proof falls on clinicians who assert that RCTs are not relevant to their work.

What Useful Information Do RCTs Provide to Therapists?

The RCT can answer the question, All else the same, what treatment is best for disorder X? RCTs can tell us which therapies are superior to other active therapies, which new therapies appear equal to older therapies of known efficacy, and which therapies are superior to placebo or to no treatment. I discuss each of these points here.

Numerous RCTs comparing active treatments for a particular clinical problem show superior outcomes for one or another treatment modality. For example, exposure to somatic cues plus cognitive therapy has been shown to be more effective than relaxation in treating panic (Barlow, Craske, Cerny, & Klosko, 1989); cognitive–behavior therapy has been shown to be more effective than nondirective therapy, short-term psychodynamic therapy, and pharmacotherapy in treating bulimia nervosa (Leitenberg, 1993); behavioral interventions have been shown to be superior to insight-oriented psychotherapy in treating nocturnal enuresis in children (Kaplan & Busner, 1993); stress innoculation training has been shown to be more effective than supportive counseling in treating symptoms of posttraumatic stress disorder (Foa, Rothbaum, Riggs, & Murdock, 1991); cognitive–behavior therapy and applied relaxation have both been shown to be more effective than nondirective psychotherapy in treating generalized anxiety (Borkovec & Costello, 1993); dialectical behavior therapy has been shown to be more effective than treatment as usual in reducing parasuicidal behavior and hospital days in women with borderline personality disorder (Linehan, Armstrong, Suarez, Allmon, & Heard, 1991); behavior therapy has been shown to be superior to pharmacotherapy in treating obsessive–compulsive disorder (Stanley & Turner, 1995); and two different treatments (social skills training plus chemotherapy and family psychoeducation plus chemotherapy) have each been shown to be superior to chemotherapy alone in the aftercare treatment of schizophrenic patients living in high-expressed-emotion households (Hogarty et al., 1986). These are only a few examples of randomized trials showing superior outcomes for a particular treatment for a particular problem.

RCTs also provide useful information when they show that a new treatment is equal in efficacy to a treatment that has repeatedly been shown to be superior to placebo or wait-list conditions. This type of evidence adds to our confidence in the efficacy of a new therapy. For example, RCTs have shown that interpersonal therapy and cognitive therapy do not differ in efficacy from pharmacotherapy for treatment of major depression (AHCPR, 1993; Clarkin, Pilkonis, & Magruder, 1996). This example demonstrates that therapists must be familiar with results of RCTs of pharmacotherapy as well as psychological therapies—in fact, they must be familiar with clinical trials of any therapy for the disorders they treat.

Clinicians can also make use of RCTs showing that a therapy is superior to no treatment or to a placebo, even if the therapy has not been compared with other active therapies. In fact, much of what we know about effective therapies stems not from demonstrations that these therapies are superior to other active therapies, but from demonstrations that they are superior to placebo or to no treatment. Therapies demonstrated effective in this way include interventions to treat social phobia (Hope, Holt, & Heimberg, 1993), major depression (Persons, 1993), and anxiety disorders in children (Kendall, 1994), among others.

I also believe that clinicians have an ethical and professional responsibility to recommend therapies that have been shown in RCTs to be superior to a no-treatment condition before they recommend therapies that have not been evaluated in an RCT. This view entails a distinction between therapies that have not been shown in controlled studies to be effective and ineffective therapies. The fact that a therapy has not been demonstrated effective in a controlled study does not mean that it is ineffective—in fact, it may be quite helpful. However, unless it has been studied in a controlled study, we have no compelling evidence that it is effective and we cannot be certain it is not harmful.

What Information Do RCTs Not Provide Clinicians?
When Do RCT-Supported Treatment Protocols Fall Short?

Although RCTs are invaluable, they frequently fail to meet clinicians' needs, for several reasons. First, RCTs provide information about the average case, whereas clinicians make treatment decisions about specific, unique cases (Howard, Krause, & Vessey, 1994). Second, RCT-supported protocols are difficult to use in clinical practice because most currently available protocols guide treatment of single disorders and problems, whereas most patients have multiple disorders and problems. Third, even when patients seek treatment for single disorders for which empirically supported protocols exist, the protocols often provide clinicians with little assistance in overcoming common obstacles—such as noncompliance and patient–therapist relationship difficulties—to following the protocols.

Difficulties using the results of RCTs are counterbalanced by the clinician's obligation to do evidence-based practice, that is, practice that relies on empirical evidence and methods, including evidence from RCTs. A model of evidence-based practice that attends to RCTs while accommodating some of the difficulties clinicians encounter when using the RCTs is presented in the next section.

Essential Components of Evidence-Based Practice

Evidence-based practice has (at least) three components: formally informing patients about treatment options and making treatment recommendations, providing RCT-supported treatments, and conducting the treatment as a scientific experiment.

Formally Informing the Patient About Treatment Options and Making Treatment Recommendations

In an evidence-based approach to treatment, the therapist makes treatment decisions collaboratively with the patient and his or her family. In contrast, in a non-evidence-based approach to treatment, the clinician makes treatment decisions unilaterally and may even begin treatment without discussing options! The process of informing the patient about treatment options and offering treatment recommendations is elegantly described in the practice guideline for treatment of depression in primary care written by AHCPR (1993).

I believe that clinicians have an ethical responsibility to inform patients about the findings from RCTs that are relevant to the patient's condition. Clinicians, in my view, also have an ethical responsibility to recommend treatments supported by evidence from RCTs before recommending treatments that are not supported by evidence from RCTs or that are not evaluated in RCTs. I also argue that because RCTs are widely accepted as the gold standard of evidence about treatment efficacy, even clinicians who do not view RCTs as useful to clinical practice have an ethical responsibility to rely on RCTs when providing information about treatment options and making treatment recommendations to their patients.

Providing RCT-Supported Treatments

I believe that clinicians have an ethical and professional responsibility to provide, as first-line treatment, interventions that have been shown superior or efficacious in RCTs before providing interventions that have been shown to be inferior or ineffective in RCTs, or that have not been studied in RCTs. However, as described above, it may be difficult to adapt an RCT-supported protocol designed for the average patient to the needs of the particular patient in the clinician's office. To do this, the evidence-based practitioner can rely on an idiographic (individualized) case formulation. Viewing the protocol as a nomothetic application of a nomothetic theory, the therapist can adapt the protocol to a particular case by using the nomothetic theory underpinning the RCT-supported protocol to develop an idiographic theory of the case at hand; this is an idiographic case formulation.

The idiographic formulation can guide all of the tasks of the therapy: developing a treatment plan, determining the type and order of interventions to be selected from the nomothetic protocol, managing treatment failure, handling noncompliance, and responding to patient–therapist interpersonal difficulties (see Persons, 1989). This method borrows from many, including Eifert, Evans, and McKendrick (1990), who used the term *principle-driven* therapy to describe this idea; it also relies on notions of idiographic conceptualization and treatment planning described in psychodynamic, behavioral, and other treatment modalities.

Treatment-as-Experiment

The clinician using this strategy conducts the treatment of each patient as a scientific experiment with a sample size of 1. This stance toward clinical work is well described by many (Barlow, Hayes, & Nelson, 1984; Hersen & Barlow, 1976; Kazdin, 1993; Stricker & Trierweiler, 1995). As much as possible, all of the steps described here are carried out collaboratively with the patient. The therapist begins by conducting a comprehensive assessment, developing a problem list, specifying the goals of treatment, and choosing strategies for measuring progress toward the goals. Next, the therapist constructs an idiographic hypothesis about the mechanisms causing, controlling, or maintaining the patient's problems, or both; this is the case formulation. The formulation is used to develop a treatment plan. As treatment proceeds, patient and therapist monitor its outcome; if results are poor, the therapist reformulates the case in an attempt to generate an alternative treatment plan. This hypothesis-testing approach to therapy is orientation neutral; in fact, it is illustrated in Silberschatz, Fretter, and Curtis (1986; see also Fretter, 1984, who use a cognitive–psychoanalytic approach to treatment).

Results of RCTs Are Useless to Clinicians (George Silberschatz)

For the past several years, whenever I have lectured on psychotherapy research or made clinical presentations to practicing psychotherapists, I have made it a point to ask my audience whether they were familiar with the findings of the National Institute of Mental Health Treatment of Depression Collaborative Research Program (NIMH Depression Study; Elkin et al., 1989). Typically, a number of people have heard of the study or have read about it; however, I have never heard anyone say that the way she or he practiced psychotherapy was influenced by the NIMH research or by any other RCT. The problem is not that clinicians are ignorant about or indifferent toward research; most clinicians are well informed and keep abreast of the clinical and research literature (see, e.g., recent surveys by Beutler, Williams, & Wakefield, 1993; Beutler, Williams, Wakefield, & Entwistle, 1995). I believe that RCTs have minimal impact on the practice of psychotherapy because the method and findings do not address the issues and concerns of the practicing clinician (Goldfried & Wolfe, 1996; Howard, Moras, Brill, Martinovich, & Lutz, 1996).

When a patient seeks therapy, the therapist must try to answer several basic questions: What is bothering the patient? What does the patient hope to accomplish in treatment? What has impeded the patient from achieving his or her goals? How can the therapist best help this patient? I believe that certain kinds of research studies are capable of providing useful data to answer these fundamental clinical questions (e.g., Crits-Christoph, Cooper, & Luborsky, 1988; Howard et al., 1996; Rice & Greenberg, 1984; Silberschatz, 1986; Silberschatz & Curtis, 1993). However, RCTs do not provide any meaningful help in addressing these questions, and consequently, they have had very little impact on clinicians and on the practice of psychotherapy. Goldfried and Wolfe (1996) have similarly suggested that RCTs have had minimal impact on the practice of therapy because they simply do not address issues that are most pertinent to the practicing therapist: how to treat patients who suffer from multiple disorders, how to treat underlying personality problems, how to resolve clinical impasses, and how or why do treatments work—that is, what are the actual mechanisms and processes of therapeutic change?

Research on the effective ingredients in psychotherapy is in its infancy. Empirical studies of psychotherapy change processes are rare, and consequently relatively little is known about basic mechanisms of change in psychotherapy. In RCTs, therapeutic approaches, and the implicit or explicit theories of change embedded within them, are codified in treatment manuals. However, therapy manuals tend to be oriented toward specific therapy techniques, rather than effective therapy ingredients or other variables that may supersede techniques (e.g., empathy, the therapeutic relationship, and therapeutic alliance). Goldfried and Wolfe (1996) pointed to the dangers of treatment manuals functioning "as more of a straightjacket than a set of guidelines" (p. 1014). They reviewed research suggesting that therapists who adhere too closely to treatment manuals compromise their clinical effectiveness. Moreover, therapies that easily lend themselves to manualization, and hence to the RCT method, are not necessarily those that are widely practiced (Parloff, 1979).

From the clinician's point of view, RCTs lack external or ecological validity. In the effort to optimize internal validity in RCTs (i.e., to assure that differences between groups are attributable only to treatment conditions), external validity is severely compromised if not totally sacrificed (Howard et al., 1996; Seligman, 1995, 1996). RCTs do not focus on the types of patients seen in practice, nor do they focus on the types of therapies that therapists actually do in their offices (Parloff, 1979; Persons, 1991). This point was vividly driven home at an NIMH psychotherapy research conference when a participant reminded the audience (ostensibly in jest) not to overlook "the first law of research: Don't use real patients" (Goldfried & Wolfe, 1996, p. 1011). Similarly, in an article titled "Psychotherapy Research Is Not Psychotherapy Practice," Fensterheim and Raw (1996) argued that controlled research studies use participants not patients; and even though they are drawn from a clinical population, research participants differ markedly from psychotherapy patients. RCTs usually focus on patients with a single diagnosis; large numbers of patients are screened out of these studies to achieve a homogenous diagnostic sample. Clinicians frequently treat complex cases suffering from multiple problems and diagnoses. Indeed, the type of patient most likely to be screened out of the RCT is the patient seen by the typical practicing therapist. Fensterheim and Raw (1996) questioned the validity of applying results from this narrowly defined population of research participants to therapy patients: "Considering the complexity of many of the patients 'typically seen by therapists in practice', the comorbidities, and the myriad life problems, there is the question of whether it is possible or ethical to use these protocols with such patients" (p. 169).

In addition to marked differences in patients seen in research and practice settings, the kinds of treatments carried out in most therapists' offices differ markedly from the kinds of treatments studied in RCTs. In most RCTs, treatment is highly specified with regard to number of sessions, techniques to be used, and timing of interventions, and treatment must be administered as uniformly as possible to the entire patient sample. In good clinical practice, it is flexibility, rather than uniformity or strict adherence to treatment manuals, that is required (Goldfried & Wolfe, 1996; Howard et al., 1996). Indeed, effective therapists tailor therapy to the problems and needs of the individual patient (for research bearing on this issue, see Silberschatz & Curtis, 1993; Silberschatz et al., 1986). Nezu (1996) has argued that even among the most homogeneous groups of patients, therapists, and patient–therapist dyads, "a therapy cookbook does not and probably cannot exist. As Hersen (1981) noted over 15 years ago, complex problems require complex solutions" (p. 162).

Seligman (1995) has argued that the very properties that make the RCT scientifically rigorous make it "the wrong method for empirically validating psychotherapy as it is actually done, because it omits too many crucial elements of what is done in the field" (p. 966). He delineated five properties that characterize psychotherapy as it is typically practiced and argued that each of these properties are absent from controlled clinical trial studies. (a) Psychotherapy, as practiced in the field, is not of fixed duration; therapy continues until the patient improves or terminates treatment. (b) In clinical practice, psychotherapy is self-correcting; if a particular strategy or technique appears not to be working, the clinician adopts a different approach. (c) Psychotherapy patients in the field frequently enter treatment by actively seeking a therapist of their choosing (as opposed to a passive process of random assignment). (d) Patients seen in therapists' offices typically have multiple problems rather than a single diagnosis. (e) Psychotherapy in the field is aimed at improving patients' general level of functioning, not just symptomatic improvement.

RCTs can be a powerful tool for assessing circumscribed, highly specified procedures (e.g., agricultural methods, pharmacotherapy, and certain medical procedures). I do not believe that psychotherapy, as practiced in the field by experienced practitioners, lends itself to the RCT methodology. Indeed, Howard et al. (1996) succinctly and cogently pointed out that there are three different questions that can be asked about any treatment and that the answers to these questions require fundamentally different research methods: Does a treatment work under controlled experimental conditions? Does it work in clinical practice? And does it work for this particular patient? RCTs are the standard method for addressing the first (efficacy) question; however, RCTs are the wrong method for studying psychotherapy as practiced in the field by experienced practitioners. To assess how therapy works in practice or whether it works for any given patient requires quasi-experimental procedures and a more case-specific research approach (Howard et al., 1996).

In arguing that RCTs are useless to clinicians, I am not saying that psychotherapy research is useless. In fact, I have been a strong advocate for scientific rigor in psychotherapy research (Silberschatz, 1994) as well as in training (Silberschatz, 1990), but scientific rigor is not synonymous with the RCT method. Goldfried and Wolfe (1996) argued that an alternative to the RCT is needed in psychotherapy outcome research: "What needs to be specified and replicated is not brand name therapies but identifiable processes of patient change and therapist behaviors that bring these about" (p. 1013; see also Howard et al., 1996). I briefly review two psychotherapy research strategies that are likely to be more clinically useful and productive than the RCT.

The *events paradigm* (Rice & Greenberg, 1984; Stiles, Shapiro, & Elliott, 1986) is a research approach that focuses on critical incidents between patient and therapist. The intensive analysis of such incidents is used to identify, describe, and empirically evaluate effective ingredients and therapeutic change processes in psychotherapy. Many researchers have productively used this paradigm; I shall give one brief illustration based on the work of the San Francisco Psychotherapy Research Group (formerly known as the Mount Zion Research Group; see Silberschatz, Curtis, Sampson & Weiss, 1991, for a review). Weiss (1993) developed a cognitive psychoanalytic theory of psychotherapy that includes explicit hypotheses about how therapy works. According to this theory, patients work in psychotherapy to disconfirm pathogenic beliefs either by testing them in the therapeutic relationship or by using the therapist's interpretations to disconfirm these beliefs. Thus, in Weiss's model, one critical change process in psychotherapy is the disconfirmation of pathogenic beliefs. Empirical studies have shown that when pathogenic beliefs are disconfirmed, patients show immediate progress within sessions (Silberschatz & Curtis, 1993; Silberschatz et al., 1986) as well as improvement at outcome (Norville, Sampson, & Weiss, 1996).

A second research strategy that has more direct relevance to clinicians and to the practice of psychotherapy is the effectiveness study. Unlike an RCT, which attempts to show that one manualized treatment stringently implemented under tightly controlled conditions to a narrowly specified sample of patients is more effective than a contrasting treatment, the effectiveness study is designed to evaluate how well psychotherapy works in the field; that is, how effective is psychotherapy as practiced by clinicians with patients seeking treatment? One recent example of such a study is the *Consumer Reports (CR)* study ("Mental Health," 1995). With a sample of 2,900 participants, the *CR* study is the largest single psychotherapy study in the literature. The sample consisted of a clinical population with diverse and multiple problems; it is representative of the patients clinicians tend to see in their practices rather than the selected patients (suffering from a single disorder) seen in RCTs. Also representative of clinical practice was the fact that the type and duration of treatment were not specified or fixed in advance. "Because the *CR* study was naturalistic, it informs us of how treatment works as it is actually performed—without manuals and with self-correction when a technique falters" (Seligman, 1995, p. 970). Although the *CR* study is not without methodological shortcomings (for a thorough review, see the October 1996, special issue of the *American Psychologist*; VandenBos, 1996), its ecological validity makes its findings comprehensible and useful to the practicing clinician. Seligman (1996) outlined a number of methodological refinements that would enhance the scientific rigor of future effectiveness studies.

RCT and horse race studies of psychotherapy are a waste of valuable resources, energy, and time. Although results from individual studies have suggested that one form of treatment is superior to another (some reviewers have suggested that these differences may be attributed to allegiance effects; Luborsky, Singer, & Luborsky, 1975; Robinson, Berman, & Neimeyer, 1990; Smith, Glass, & Miller, 1980), results from meta-analyses and literature reviews consistently show that no one school of therapy is superior to another (Lambert & Bergin, 1994; Lipsey & Wilson, 1993; Smith et al., 1980; Stiles et al., 1986). My interpretation of this consistent finding is that there are certain effective ingredients that cut across different schools of therapy. Expert therapists, regardless of their particular theoretical orientation, have some intuitive understanding of what these ingredients are and use them effectively in their clinical work. The disconfirmation of irrational or pathogenic beliefs is an example of an effective ingredient in psychotherapy (Weiss, 1993). An RCT comparing cognitive, experiential, and interpersonal therapy would most likely find no significant differences among treatments, because therapists in each condition were disconfirming patients' pathogenic beliefs, albeit through the use of very different techniques. This effective ingredient hypothesis may explain the lack of differences between psychological treatments. For example, the so-called placebo–clinical management condition in the NIMH Depression Study was essentially supportive therapy (Elkin et al., 1989).

I believe that research and knowledge in our field would be further advanced by focusing more on basic change mechanisms and less on which technique or school of therapy should win the biggest prize. We need to identify what the effective ingredients of psychotherapy are, how they can be maximized to improve the overall effectiveness of therapy, and how therapists can be trained to use them most effectively.

REBUTTAL: JACQUELINE B. PERSONS

Silberschatz raises three objections to RCTs; I address each in turn.

First, RCTs do not address the fundamental clinical questions that are most pertinent to practitioners, such as questions about the mechanisms of change in effective therapy and the nature of the therapeutic alliance. Instead, RCTs focus on outcome and on technique.

This objection reflects a value difference between Silberschatz and me (cf. Messer & Winokur, 1984). Silberschatz places a high value on process, whereas I place a high value on outcome (as do RCTs). Once this discrepancy is seen as a value difference, it is not meaningful to ask, Which is best? We can ask only which value is superior at guiding research or clinical work toward a certain goal (and even the choice of goals is likely to be based on values).

I argue that placing a high value on outcome (as RCTs do) enhances therapists' abilities to relieve patients' symptoms and improve their quality of life. Without controlled outcome studies to examine the efficacy of the treatments they provide, therapists may be providing treatments that do not alleviate suffering and may cause harm. Moreover, unless a therapy has been shown in controlled studies to be effective, I do not place a high value on studies of its mechanisms.

Therapists who emphasize the types of questions Silberschatz poses seem to me to be assuming that the therapy they do is effective. The effectiveness assumption is a risky one; the history of medicine is filled with reports of physicians who believed they were offering effective treatment but later learned (from RCTs) that their therapy was ineffective or even harmful (Frazier & Mosteller, 1995).

Silberschatz states that RCTs do not address topics that seem pertinent to practicing clinicians. This may be true. However, I speculate that RCTs do address topics of interest to patients. Second, RCTs lack ecological validity. They do not capture five properties of psychotherapy as it is usually practiced: (a) open-ended (vs. fixed duration in RCTs), (b) self-correcting (vs.

specified in advance in RCTs), (c) treatment and therapist actively chosen by the patient (vs. randomly assigned in RCTs), (d) patients have multiple problems (vs. single problems in RCTs), and (e) therapy is intended to improve general functioning (vs. symptom relief in RCTs).

I agree with Silberschatz that RCTs frequently study phenomena that are distant from the phenomena of clinical practice. However, there is nothing inherent in the RCT that requires this (Jacobson & Christensen, 1996). All five phenomena listed as characteristic of clinical practice can readily be studied in an RCT. RCTs can study open-ended treatment (e.g., Jacobson, Dobson, Fruzzetti, Schmaling, & Salusky, 1991), self-correcting and non-manualized treatment, multiple-problem patients (e.g., Linehan et al., 1991), and patients' general level of functioning (e.g., Elkin et al., 1989, and many others). To capture clinical practice as it actually happens, many RCTs randomly assign patients to receive treatment as usual in the community (cf. Linehan et al., 1991). It is even possible in an RCT to examine whether patients do better when they receive the therapy or therapist they prefer than when they are assigned to therapy or therapist. To address this question, an RCT could be conducted to compare outcomes for patients who are or are not assigned to their preferred therapy and therapist.

Although RCTs need not study homogeneous patient samples with manualized treatments, Silberschatz does correctly note that currently this is what usually happens. As a result, findings from RCTs are not easily generalized to clinical practice. However, I disagree with Silberschatz that, therefore, RCTs are irrelevant to clinical practice. Consider the following.

The patient in the clinician's office seeks treatment for depression. The patient meets criteria for major depressive disorder, which has been studied in dozens of RCTs. However, the patient does not meet the usual selection criteria of those RCTs because in addition to major depression this patient has coronary artery disease, irritable bowel syndrome, and panic disorder. The therapist in this situation has two choices: She or he can offer the patient one of the treatments shown to be effective in the RCTs, adapting it to the patient's circumstances, or she or he can ignore the results of the RCTs and provide his or her usual or preferred mode of treatment. An evidence-based practitioner will choose the first option.

Similarly, imagine that you have been diagnosed with bladder cancer. Suppose that treatments for bladder cancer have been studied in RCTs, but your case does not meet the typical selection criteria used in the RCTs. Would you like your physician to treat your cancer by extrapolating from the findings in the RCTs to the specifics of your case, or would you rather she or he treat you with whatever methods she or he is familiar and has found helpful in his or her clinical experience, without regard to the results of the latest RCTs? I would like my physician to be guided by the results of the latest RCTs, and I speculate that many readers would agree.

Silberschatz argues that RCTs are not useful because they do not study the therapies that most clinicians do. This statement does not make sense to me. It is not sensible to argue that a RCT studying new therapies is irrelevant to clinicians because they are not currently using those therapies.

I agree with Silberschatz that the treatments conducted by most therapists bear little resemblance to the treatments that have been shown in RCTs to be effective. However, this does not mean that RCTs are useless to practitioners. Instead, I conclude that most therapists are conducting therapies of undemonstrated efficacy, and I recommend that they begin doing the therapies shown effective in RCTs.

I agree with Silberschatz that the discrepancy between treatment provided in RCTs and that provided in routine practice suggests that the money spent on RCTs is wasted; money spent on RCTs is wasted if their findings are not used by the professional community. However, unlike Silberschatz, I do not conclude that we ought to stop spending money on RCTs; instead, I conclude that we need to do a better job of disseminating the findings of RCTs to the professional community. I also recommend that we begin conducting RCTs that incorporate many of the features of psychotherapy as it is practiced, so that results would be more directly relevant to practicing clinicians.

Third, most RCTs have found no significant differences between treatments and those that have may be due to allegiance effects.

This argument seems to me to conflict with some of Silberschatz's earlier ones. It suggests that if RCTs did frequently show differences between treatments, RCTs would be relevant to clinicians, but that because they frequently do not, they are not relevant. Wouldn't the clinician who accepted this argument need to keep abreast of the results of RCTs?

Although many RCTs of psychological therapies fail to find significant differences between active treatments, many do find differences (for some examples, see studies listed in the earlier section, "What Useful Information Do RCTs Provide to Psychotherapists?"). Several writers have recently argued that "the dodo bird" verdict ("Everyone has won and all must have prizes") is no longer true, although perhaps it once was (Chambless, 1996; Giles, 1993). I agree.

The common finding of tie results in RCTs pitting active treatments against one another does not support the conclusion that, therefore, all treatments are equal in efficacy and RCTs do not provide useful information. For example, exposure and response prevention (ERP) is widely considered the psychosocial treatment of choice for obsessive–compulsive disorder (OCD; Steketee & Lam, 1993).Thus, it is considered superior to psychodynamic psychotherapy, for example. However, the view of ERP as superior to psychodynamic psychotherapy is not based on the results of any RCT showing that ERP is superior to psychodynamic psychotherapy in the treatment of OCD. Instead, it is based on the fact that numerous RCTs examining hundreds of patients have uniformly shown ERP to be superior to wait-list, placebo, and alternative behavioral and cognitive–behavior treatments, and on the fact that psychodynamic psychotherapy for OCD has not been studied in a single RCT (see the review by Steketee & Lam, 1993).

Silberschatz argues that when RCTs do show differences between treatments, these differences may be due to allegiance effects. I agree with Silberschatz that allegiance effects may underlie some findings showing one therapy superior to another. However, I believe that the concern about allegiance effects demonstrates the importance of RCTs. We cannot assume that therapies work in the way we think they work—or even that they work at all—without careful measurement free of bias. It is for this reason that RCTs are essential. In fact, it is an RCT that would provide the most compelling test of the allegiance effects hypothesis. To test for allegiance effects, patients would be randomly assigned to therapists with high versus low allegiance to the therapy they were providing.

REBUTTAL: GEORGE SILBERSCHATZ

Persons argues that clinicians typically must decide whether one form of treatment is more effective than another for a particular patient and that the RCT is the strongest available method for answering this question. It is not. RCTs address efficacy issues in terms of mean responses for average patients; they do not address questions of central importance to the practicing clinician: Will the treatment work for a particular patient? As I discussed earlier, this question can be answered in a scientifically rigorous manner but not with the RCT method.

Persons acknowledges the difficulties of applying RCT results to specific patients, and as one solution, she advocates using the nomothetic RCT data in an idiographic way. There are two problems with this position. First, psychotherapy RCTs have very poor external validity; generalizing from the experimental condition to clinical practice is very risky. As Howard et al. (1996) pointed out,

> There is no logical connection between showing that a treatment can work and showing that a treatment does work. That is, a treatment that cannot be shown to produce statistically significant mean group differences in a carefully conducted clinical trial may still be demonstrably beneficial as actually practiced. Similarly, a treatment that has been shown to be effective in a clinical trial may not be effective as practiced. (p. 1060)

The second problem with extrapolating from RCTs to clinical practice is the assumption of patient homogeneity. RCT advocates believe that by selecting a circumscribed group of patients (e.g., major depressive disorder) using highly specific inclusion–exclusion criteria, one can then generalize treatment results to a comparable homogeneous group in practice. Kiesler (1966) referred to this assumption as "the uniformity myth" in psychotherapy research. It is a myth that does not fit clinical reality. In my own work, for instance, I find substantial differences among my educated, intelligent, middle-aged dysthymic patients and would therefore find it difficult to evaluate a study that found that treatment X is superior for this group of supposedly homogeneous patients. It is not surprising that uniformity assumptions do not hold up for psychotherapy research participants any better than they do for patients. Blatt (1992) identified two different types of depression and found that responsiveness to psychoanalytic therapy differed as a function of the two types. In an analysis of data from the NIMH Depression Study, Blatt, Quinlan, Pilkonis, and Shea (1995) found that one type of depression (perfectionistic self-criticism) predicted a poor level of therapeutic response across all treatment conditions.

Persons seems to discount alternative research designs such as repeated measures single-case studies because of difficulties with generalizability. Solutions for the problem of generalizability in small-sample studies have been discussed in the literature (e.g., Hersen & Barlow, 1976; Kazdin, 1982; see also Goldfried & Wolfe, 1996), for instance, serial replication of findings across different patients, therapists, and treatments. In my view, RCT advocates have sacrificed clinical validity in the effort to maximize experimental control (internal validity); I don't see the value of generalizing clinically meaningless findings. Persons states that RCTs address the question "*All else the same* [emphasis added], what treatment is best for disorder X?" (p. 549). But in phenomena as complex and multidimensional as psychopathology and psychotherapy, all else is not the same, and no amount of experimental manipulation can force all other things to be equal. Patients are not equal, therapists are not equal, and the therapeutic interactions between them are not equal, regardless of how meticulously manualized the treatments may be (for further discussion, see Davison & Lazarus, 1994; Fensterheim & Raw, 1996; Goldfried & Wolfe, 1996; Nezu, 1996; Stiles et al., 1986). In designing studies that assume that all other things are equal (or can be equalized), RCT advocates end up studying a phenomenon that is unfamiliar to most practicing clinicians. There are other scientifically rigorous approaches to studying psychotherapy that do not require such simplistic and false assumptions.

RCTs, according to Persons, provide therapists with useful information for they tell us which treatments are scientifically proven to be superior. If the data were so unequivocal, I doubt there would be much of a basis for debate. In fact, most large-scale reviews and meta-analyses of psychotherapy outcome studies have consistently shown that psychotherapy is effective but that no one treatment is superior (Lambert & Bergin, 1994; Lipsey & Wilson, 1993; Smith et al., 1980; Stiles et al., 1986). One can point to individual studies in which one treatment is found to be superior to another; however, such results must be viewed cautiously because (a) randomization (the bedrock of RCTs) can rarely be achieved in a single experiment and thus requires replication,[1] and (b) individual studies are vulnerable to allegiance effects — that is, the treatment found to be superior is typically the one that is practiced or advocated by the investigator (Luborsky et al., 1975; Robinson et al., 1990; Smith et al., 1980).

The crux of my disagreement with staunch RCT advocates is that they zealously overvalue the RCT as the scientific gold standard. Persons, for instance, states that most therapists are conducting treatments of undemonstrated efficacy or value, suggesting that the only demonstration of value is the RCT. Seligman (1996) persuasively argued that efficacy studies (RCTs) do not "have a unique claim on the empirical validation of psychotherapy" (p. 1077). He made the case that effectiveness studies, which rely on observational methods with causal modeling, and efficacy studies, which rely on randomization and experimental controls, are both scientifically rigorous methods for assessing psychotherapy. They each have their flaws as well as their strengths:

> They both narrow in on causation by eliminating alternative causes; the experimental method does this by random assignment of participants to control or experimental groups, and the observational method does this by measuring specified alternative causes and partialing them out. The experimental method has an edge in eliminating many unmeasured possible causes in one fell swoop, whereas the observational method has an edge in being able to generalize immediately to reality. (pp. 1075–1076)

I urge Persons and other psychotherapy research colleagues to guard against equating empirical validation with the RCT method. Seligman (1996; see also Fox, 1996, especially pp. 780–782) showed the perils of this false equation.

Persons and I disagree about many issues regarding psychotherapy practice and research, but there is one fundamental issue about which we agree wholeheartedly: the value of what she calls theory-driven idiographic treatment (see also Persons, 1991). I believe that most good clinicians rely (either implicitly or explicitly) on a model or theory to guide their understanding of human behavior and then apply their theory in a case-specific fashion. In fact, the therapist's ability to tailor interventions to the problems and needs of specific patients is, in my judgment, one of the key effective ingredients of psychotherapy. I believe that a theory-driven idiographic approach is essen-

---

[1] Investigators rely on random assignment in an effort to achieve comparable experimental and control groups. However, Howard, Krause, and Lyons (1993) have shown that randomization almost never perfectly equates groups in any single study (because of attrition, treatment confounds and high within-group variance on dependent variables).

tial to the scientific study of psychotherapy and that the results of such efforts are far more compelling than the results of RCTs.

DISCUSSION

Two very different points of view are presented here. Silberschatz argues that the phenomena studied in RCTs diverge so sharply from clinical practice that no generalization from the research to the clinical setting is possible. Persons agrees that the phenomena studied in RCTs often differ from clinical practice but argues that the clinician can—and has an ethical responsibility to—generalize from RCTs.

Silberschatz and Persons agree that more studies of psychotherapy as it exists in the clinical setting are needed. However, they disagree about the details of the particular studies each would recommend.

Persons recommends that steps be taken to increase the ecological validity of RCTs, with the hope that this will make them more acceptable and useful to practicing clinicians. She recommends that researchers conduct RCTs that study heterogeneous populations and the characteristics of therapy as it occurs in nature, including idiographic treatment (cf. Persons, 1991). She suggests that reporting of results of RCTs focuses more on individual cases and on clinical significance (cf. Jacobson & Truax, 1991) than is usually done. She also recommends that naturalistic outcome studies examine empirically the degree to which results of RCTs generalize to routine clinical practice (cf. Persons, Burns, & Perloff, 1988).

In contrast, Silberschatz views RCTs, even of naturally occuring clinical phenomena, as scientifically unproductive and clinically useless. Instead, he argues that process-outcome studies, effectiveness studies, and single-case research provide more valuable information to clinicians and contribute to understanding how therapy works (cf. Barlow et al., 1984; Crits-Christoph et al., 1988; Davison & Lazarus, 1994; Norville et al., 1996; Rice & Greenberg, 1984; Seligman, 1995; Silberschatz & Curtis, 1993; Silberschatz et al., 1986). Silberschatz agrees with Seligman (1996) that well-designed observational methods (with multiple regression analysis) can be used to test and rule out alternative explanations. Indeed, much of the work of the San Francisco Psychotherapy Research Group has used such methods to empirically evaluate competing hypotheses about how patients work in psychotherapy (for review, see Silberschatz, Curtis, Fretter, & Kelly, 1988; Silberschatz et al., 1991). Persons agrees that these types of studies are useful but does not see them as supplanting the RCTs because they do not address the same questions the RCTs address.

We agree that it is useful to study therapy as it occurs in nature. Thus, we agree that studies such as the CR study are quite useful, and we recommend that more studies of this sort be undertaken. We also agree that the CR study could be improved in many ways (by collecting data prospectively rather than retrospectively and by using better measures that assess patients' functioning, rather than satisfaction with treatment, for example).

Because the difference between our two positions is so sharp, we believe it is noteworthy that we can agree on the importance of studies of therapy as it occurs in nature. We also agree on the value of single-case studies; this methodology has been underused and has much to contribute. We believe that our agreement about the value of naturalistic studies of psychological therapies and single-case studies deserves particular note. These are areas in which therapists who otherwise differ considerably can agree and those in which clinicians and researchers, often divided, can join.

REFERENCES

Agency for Health Care Policy and Research, U.S. Public Health Service. (1993). *Depression in primary care: Vol. 2. Treatment of major depression* (Clinical Practice Guideline No. 5). Rockville, MD: Author.

Barlow, D. H., Craske, M. G., Cerny, J. A., & Klosko, J. S. (1989). Behavioral treatment of panic disorder. *Behavior Therapy, 20,* 261–282.

Barlow, D. H., Hayes, S. C., & Nelson, R. O. (1984). *The scientist–practitioner: Research and accountability in clinical and educational settings.* New York: Pergamon.

Beck, A. T., Rush, A. J., Shaw, B. F., & Emery, G. (1979). *Cognitive therapy of depression.* New York: Guilford Press.

Beutler, L. E., Williams, R. E., & Wakefield, P. J. (1993). Obstacles to disseminating applied psychological science. *Journal of Applied and Preventive Psychology, 2,* 53–58.

Beutler, L. E., Williams, R. E., Wakefield, P. J., & Entwistle, S. R. (1995). Bridging scientist and practitioner perspectives in clinical psychology. *American Psychologist, 50,* 984–994.

Blatt, S. J. (1992). The differential effect of psychotherapy and psychoanalysis on anaclitic and introjective patients: The Meninger Psychotherapy Research Project revisited. *Journal of the American Psychoanalytic Association, 40,* 691–724.

Blatt, S. J., Quinlan, D. M., Pilkonis, P., & Shea, T. (1995). The effects of need for approval and perfectionism on the brief treatment of depression. *Journal of Consulting and Clinical Psychology, 63,* 125–132.

Borkovec, T. D., & Costello, E. (1993). Efficacy of applied relaxation and cognitive–behavioral therapy in the treatment of generalized anxiety disorder. *Journal of Consulting and Clinical Psychology, 61,* 611–619.

Chambless, D. L. (1996). In defense of dissemination of empirically supported psychological interventions. *Clinical Psychology: Science and Practice, 3,* 230–235.

Chambless, D. L., & Hollon, S. D. (1998). Defining empirically supported therapies. *Journal of Consulting and Clinical Psychology, 66,* 7–18.

Clarkin, J. F., Pilkonis, P. A., & Magruder, K. M. (1996). Psychotherapy of depression: Implications for reform of the health care system. *Archives of General Psychiatry, 53*, 717–723.

Crits-Christoph, P., Cooper, A., & Luborsky, L. (1988). The accuracy of therapist's interpretations and the outcome of dynamic psychotherapy. *Journal of Consulting and Clinical Psychology, 56*, 490–495.

Davison, G. C., & Lazarus, A. A. (1994). Clinical innovation and evaluation: Integrating practice with inquiry. *Clinical Psychology: Science and Practice, 1*, 157–168.

Eifert, G. H., Evans, I. M., & McKendrick, V. G. (1990). Matching treatments to client problems not diagnostic labels: A case for paradigmatic behavior therapy. *Journal of Behavior Therapy and Experimental Psychiatry, 21*, 163–172.

Elkin, I., Shea, M. T., Watkins, J. T., Imber, S. D., Sotsky, S. M., & Collins, J. F. (1989). NIMH Treatment of Depression Collaborative Research Program: General effectiveness of treatments. *Archives of General Psychiatry, 46*, 971–982.

Fensterheim, H., & Raw, S. D. (1996). Psychotherapy research is not psychotherapy practice. *Clinical Psychology: Science and Practice, 3*, 168–171.

Foa, E. B., Rothbaum, B. O., Riggs, D. S., & Murdock, T. B. (1991). Treatment of posttraumatic stress disorder in rape victims: A comparison between cognitive–behavioral procedures and counseling. *Journal of Consulting and Clinical Psychology, 59*, 715–723.

Fox, R. E. (1996). Charlatanism, scientism, and psychology's social contract. *American Psychologist, 51*, 777–784.

Frazier, H. S., & Mosteller, F. (Eds.). (1995). *Medicine worth paying for: Assessing medical innovations.* Cambridge, MA: Harvard University Press.

Fretter, P. B. (1984). The immediate effects of transference interpretations on patients' progress in brief, psychodynamic psychotherapy. *Dissertation Abstracts International, 46* (6). (UMI No. 8512112)

Giles, T. R. (Ed.). (1993). *Handbook of effective psychotherapy.* New York: Plenum.

Goldfried, M. R., & Wolfe, B. (1996). Psychotherapy practice and research: Repairing a strained alliance. *American Psychologist, 51*, 1007–1016.

Hersen, M. (1981). Complex problems require complex solutions. *Behavior Therapy, 12*, 15–29.

Hersen, M., & Barlow, D. H. (1976). *Single-case experimental designs: Strategies for studying behavior change.* New York: Pergamon Press.

Hogarty, G. E., Anderson, C. M., Reiss, D. J., Kornblith, S. J., Greenwald, D. P., Javna, C. D., et al. (1986). Family psychoeducation, social skills training, and maintenance chemotherapy in the aftercare treatment of schizophrenia. *Archives of General Psychiatry, 43*, 633–642.

Hope, D. A., Holt, C. S., & Heimberg, R. G. (1993). Social phobia. In T. R. Giles (Ed.), *Handbook of effective psychotherapy* (pp. 227–251). New York: Plenum.

Howard, K. I., Krause, M. S., & Lyons, J. (1993). When clinical trials fail: A guide to disaggregation. In L. S. Onken, J. D. Blaine, & J. J. Boren (Eds.), *Behavioral treatments for drug abuse and dependence* (NIDA Research Monograph No. 137, pp. 291–302). Washington, DC: National Institute for Drug Abuse.

Howard, K. I., Krause, M. S., & Vessey, J. T. (1994). Analysis of clinical trial data: The problem of outcome overlap. *Psychotherapy, 31*, 302–307.

Howard, K. I., Moras, K., Brill, P. L., Martinovich, Z., & Lutz, W. (1996). Evaluation of psychotherapy: Efficacy, effectiveness, and patient progress. *American Psychologist, 51*, 1059–1064.

Jacobson, N. S., & Christensen, A. (1996). Studying the effectiveness of psychotherapy: How well can clinical trials do the job? *American Psychologist, 51*, 1031–1039.

Jacobson, N. S., Dobson, K., Fruzzetti, A. E., Schmaling, K. B., & Salusky, S. (1991). Marital therapy as a treatment for depression. *Journal of Consulting and Clinical Psychology, 59*, 547–557.

Jacobson, N. S., & Truax, P. (1991). Clinical significance: A statistical approach to defining meaningful change in psychotherapy research. *Journal of Consulting and Clinical Psychology, 59*, 12–19.

Kaplan, S. L., & Busner, J. (1993). Treatment of nocturnal enuresis. In T. R. Giles (Ed.), *Handbook of effective psychotherapy* (pp. 135–150). New York: Plenum.

Kazdin, A. E. (1982). *Single-case research designs: Methods for clinical and applied settings*. New York: Oxford University Press.

Kazdin, A. E. (1993). Evaluation in clinical practice: Clinically sensitive and systematic methods of treatment delivery. *Behavior Therapy, 24*, 11–45.

Kendall, P. C. (1994). Treating anxiety disorders in children: Results of a randomized clinical trial. *Journal of Consulting and Clinical Psychology, 62*, 100–110.

Kiesler, D. J. (1966). Some myths of psychotherapy research and the search for a paradigm. *Psychological Bulletin, 65*, 110–136.

Klerman, G. L. (1990). The psychiatric patient's right to effective treatment: Implications of Osheroff v. Chestnut Lodge. *Journal of Psychiatry, 147*, 409–418.

Lambert, M. J., & Bergin, A. E. (1994). The effectiveness of psychotherapy. In A. E. Bergin & S. L. Garfield (Eds.), *Handbook of psychotherapy and behavior change* (4th ed., pp. 143–189). New York: Wiley.

Leitenberg, H. (1993). Treatment of bulimia nervosa. In T. R. Giles (Ed.), *Handbook of effective psychotherapy* (pp. 279–303). New York: Plenum.

Linehan, M. M., Armstrong, H. E., Suarez, A., Allmon, D., & Heard, H. L. (1991). Cognitive–behavioral treatment of chronically parasuicidal borderline patients. *Archives of General Psychiatry, 48*, 1060–1064.

Lipsey, M. W., & Wilson, D. B. (1993). The efficacy of psychological, educational, and behavioral treatment: Confirmation from meta-analyses. *American Psychologist, 48*, 1181–1209.

Luborsky, L., Singer, B., & Luborsky, L. (1975). Comparative studies of psychotherapy: Is it true that "everyone has won and all must have prizes"? *Archives of General Psychiatry, 32*, 995–1008.

McFall, R. M. (1991). Manifesto for a science of clinical psychology. *The Clinical Psychologist, 44*, 75–88.

Mental health: Does therapy help? (1995, November). *Consumer Reports*, 734–739.

Messer, S. B., & Winokur, M. (1984). Ways of knowing and visions of reality in psychoanalytic therapy and behavior therapy. In H. Arkowitz & S. B. Messer (Eds.), *Psychoanalytic therapy and behavior therapy: Is integration possible?* (pp. 63–106). New York: Plenum.

Nezu, A. M. (1996). What are we doing to our patients and should we care if anyone else knows? *Clinical Psychology: Science and Practice, 3*, 160–163

Norville, R., Sampson, H., & Weiss, J. (1996). Accurate interpretations and brief psychotherapy outcome. *Psychotherapy Research, 6*, 16–29.

Parloff, M. B. (1979). Can psychotherapy research guide the policymaker? A little knowledge may be a dangerous thing. *American Psychologist, 34*, 296–306.

Persons, J. B. (1989). *Cognitive therapy in practice: A case formulation approach.* New York: Norton.

Persons, J. B. (1991). Psychotherapy outcome studies do not accurately represent current models of psychotherapy: A proposed remedy. *American Psychologist, 46*, 99–106.

Persons, J. B. (1993). Outcome of psychotherapy for unipolar depression. In T. R. Giles (Ed.), *Handbook of effective psychotherapy* (pp. 305–323). New York: Plenum.

Persons, J. B., Burns, D. D., & Perloff, J. M. (1988). Predictors of dropout and outcome in private practice patients treated with cognitive therapy for depression. *Cognitive Therapy and Research, 12*, 557–575.

Rice, L. N., & Greenberg, L. S. (1984). *Patterns of change.* New York: Guilford Press.

Robinson, L. A., Berman, J. S., & Neimeyer, R. A. (1990). Psychotherapy for the treatment of depression: A comprehensive review of controlled outcome research. *Psychological Bulletin, 108*, 30–49.

Seligman, M. E. P. (1995). The effectiveness of psychotherapy: The *Consumer Reports* Study. *American Psychologist, 50*, 965–974.

Seligman, M. E. P. (1996). Science as an ally of practice. *American Psychologist, 51*, 1072–1079.

Silberschatz, G. (1986). Testing pathogenic beliefs. In J. Weiss, H. Sampson, & the Mount Zion Psychotherapy Research Group (Eds.), *The psychoanalytic process: Theory, clinical observation, and empirical research* (pp. 256–266). New York: Guilford Press.

Silberschatz, G. (1990). Psychology's contribution to the future of psychoanalysis: A scientific attitude. In M. Meisels & E. R. Shapiro (Eds.), *Tradition and innovation in psychoanalytic education: Clark conference on psychoanalytic training for psychologists* (pp. 181–191). Hillsdale, NJ: Erlbaum.

Silberschatz, G. (1994). Abuse and disabuse of the drug metaphor in psychotherapy research: Hold on to the baby as you throw out the bath. *Journal of Consulting and Clinical Psychology, 62*, 949–951.

Silberschatz, G., & Curtis, J. T. (1993). Measuring the therapist's impact on the patient's therapeutic progress. *Journal of Consulting and Clinical Psychology, 61,* 403–411.

Silberschatz, G., Curtis, J. T., Fretter, P. B., & Kelly, T. J. (1988). Testing hypotheses of psychotherapeutic change processes. In H. Dahl, H. Kachele, & H. Thoma (Eds.), *Psychoanalytic process research strategies* (pp. 129–145). Berlin: Springer-Verlag.

Silberschatz, G., Curtis, J. T., Sampson, H., & Weiss, J. (1991). Mount Zion Hospital and Medical Center: Research on the process of change in psychotherapy. In L. E. Beutler & M. Crago (Eds.), *Psychotherapy research: An international review of programmatic studies* (pp. 56–64). Washington, DC: American Psychological Association.

Silberschatz, G., Fretter, P. B., & Curtis, J. T. (1986). How do interpretations influence the process of psychotherapy? *Journal of Consulting and Clinical Psychology, 54,* 646–652.

Smith, M. L., Glass, G. V., & Miller, T. L. (1980). *The benefits of psychotherapy.* Baltimore: Johns Hopkins University Press.

Stanley, M. A., & Turner, S. M. (1995). Current status of pharmacological and behavioral treatment of obsessive–compulsive disorder. *Behavior Therapy, 26,* 163–186.

Steketee, G., & Lam, J. (1993). Obsessive–compulsive disorder. In T. R. Giles (Ed.), *Handbook of effective psychotherapy* (pp. 253–278). New York: Plenum.

Stiles, W. B., Shapiro, D. A., & Elliott, R. (1986). Are all psychotherapies equivalent? *American Psychologist, 41,* 165–180.

Stricker, G., & Trierweiler, S. J. (1995). The local clinical scientist: A bridge between science and practice. *American Psychologist, 50,* 995–1002.

VandenBos, G. R. (Ed.). (1996). Outcome assessment of psychotherapy [Special issue]. *American Psychologist, 51*(10).

Weiss, J. (1993). *How psychotherapy works.* New York: Guilford Press.

24

IMPROVING THE TRANSITION FROM BASIC EFFICACY RESEARCH TO EFFECTIVENESS STUDIES: METHODOLOGICAL ISSUES AND PROCEDURES

GREGORY N. CLARKE

Recent proposed changes in the financing and organization of health service systems provide a compelling background for discussion of the relevance and applicability of findings from controlled laboratory studies (efficacy investigations) to broader mental health services systems (effectiveness research). If certain interventions prove effective in both laboratories and clinics, this may result in meaningful health care reforms with potentially improved services for consumers. Brook and Lohr (1985) advocate this perspective, noting that health care systems are improved not just by data from a single perspective but from an integration of data from efficacy, effectiveness, and quality-of-care perspectives.

Reprinted from the *Journal of Consulting and Clinical Psychology, 63*, 718–725. Copyright 1995 by the American Psychological Association.

However, several barriers limit consensus on the effectiveness and usefulness of mental health treatments in service system settings. First, empirical treatment outcome information is often incomplete and, for many disorders, all but unavailable. This lack of advanced treatment efficacy data is particularly true in child and adolescent mental health. Lacking controlled outcome research for a given disorder or problem area, it is difficult to resolve whether a given intervention will work as well in the clinical setting as it may in the laboratory. This should not be seen as a call to exhaust all avenues of efficacy research before initiating treatment effectiveness trials. Instead, the goal of this article is to encourage concurrent advances in both efficacy and effectiveness research, even to the point of addressing both perspectives within the same investigation.

Moving beyond the availability of research, however, there are several design and methodological shortcomings in the existing literature that limit the integration of efficacy methods within effectiveness trials. These shortcomings exist, in large part, because mental health outcome research is often designed to answer efficacy or theoretical questions. Scant attention is generally paid to generalization beyond the research paradigm (e.g., how well could this intervention be carried out in a clinical setting?).

This article attempts to address this issue by proposing methodological strategies that, if used in treatment outcome research, may help shift efficacy research findings and methods into effectiveness trials conducted in clinical and service delivery settings. Whenever possible, these issues are examined in the context of our own research in school- and clinic-based interventions for adolescent depression (Clarke, Hawkins, Murphy, Sheeber, Lewinsohn, & Seeley, 1995; Lewinsohn, Clarke, Hops, & Andrews, 1990), with examples of how the generalization of these studies may be improved.

Periodic reviews of methodological design and strategy in psychotherapy outcome research are nothing new (e.g., Kazdin, 1986). However, most previous discussions have been in the efficacy research literature, often weighted in favor of greater experimental control at the expense of generalization to real-world settings. This article revisits these same issues, but with the perspective of stretching research designs to encompass effectiveness issues. Bear in mind that this is not meant to preclude scientific rigor. Instead, I advocate retaining as much experimental control as possible while using greater creativity in the methodology and issues studied in treatment outcome research.

This article was inspired by Weisz, Weiss, and Donenberg's (1992) examination of the positive child psychotherapy effects in research studies, compared with the general absence of such effects in clinic-based studies. In their conclusion, Weisz et al. suggested that "a key task for researchers [is] . . . identifying those proper conditions under which effects of child therapy may be optimized." The present article responds to this issue by considering how study design features might help identify these optimizing conditions.

TABLE 24.1
Potential Mediating Factors

Factor	Description
1	Therapist training; degree of treatment structure; monitoring, protocol compliance
2	Combined or multiple treatments (e.g., pharmacotherapy and psychotherapy)
3	Multiple roles vs. single role for therapist
4	Participant selection (homogeneity vs. heterogeneity; comorbidity)
5	Control group (no treatment vs. attention placebo vs. usual care)
6	Treatment parameters (duration, dose, modality, location)

METHODOLOGICAL ISSUES

Weisz and Weiss (1989) provide a detailed review of aspects of controlled experimental methodology that differ enough between research and clinical settings to limit the generalization of positive findings from the former to the latter. A circumscribed set of these issues is summarized in Table 24.1. Each of these is briefly reviewed in turn, followed by suggestions for methodological changes to enhance generalizability.

Other issues identified by these and other authors (Kazdin, 1978), but not addressed here, include participant recruitment methods; professional versus nonprofessional therapists; measurement technology; participant, therapist, and assessor masking to therapy condition; service setting; and participant assignment. This article does not attempt to exhaustively catalog method variants to address each of these parameters. Instead, a sampler of design features is proposed to motivate investigators to broaden the scope of treatment outcome paradigms under consideration or in the planning stages.

DEGREE OF THERAPY STRUCTURE

Increasingly, controlled outcome trials of psychotherapy treatments provide intensive, specialized training in the specific research intervention protocol (Luborsky & DeRubeis, 1984). To simplify replication of the intervention across studies, researchers often "manualize" treatments by providing scripted therapist guidebooks (e.g., Clarke, Lewinsohn, & Hops, 1990; Moreau, Mufson, Weissman, & Klerman, 1991; see also Lambert & Ogles, 1988). Close compliance with these treatment manuals is often encouraged by audio- or videotaping therapy sessions for later compliance review by research staff (Clarke et al., 1995; Lewinsohn et al., 1990; Hollon, 1988).

These training and implementation methods result in interventions that are highly regimented and very reproducible, with high adherence to a predefined protocol. From a pure efficacy perspective, these are desirable features because they control for extraneous contributors to treatment outcome. However, these controls are unlikely to be used in nonresearch settings because of the increased effort and burden they require, as well as a lack of interest in enforcing a reproducible treatment regime in many clinical or service settings.

These therapy structure methodologies impede effectiveness trials of research treatments because, in my experience, real-world therapists often resist following rigid or uni-modality interventions. Many clinicians prefer to be responsive to client session-by-session presentations with a blended or "eclectic" therapy model, borrowing pieces of interventions as they seem relevant rather than using a scripted but potentially more cohesive protocol. Research interventions are often viewed as too regimented, leading clinicians (the interventionists in effectiveness trials) to resist using them out of concern that they may reduce psychotherapy to an automated "cookbook" approach, lacking responsiveness to individual client presentation.

How might outcome researchers design their studies differently to address this issue? One approach, which elaborates on a suggestion by Kendall and Lipman (1991), is to conduct treatment efficacy studies with several levels of experimental control over the implementation of therapy protocols to examine the effect on treatment outcome. Experimental conditions with less structured therapy content and implementation would resemble real-life clinical settings, although in a limited fashion. Of course, this does not mean that therapists would be allowed to deliver interventions completely unobserved or without limits. It is important to measure how much and in what way therapists deviate from a planned intervention (e.g., by using expert raters, a therapy content coding system, and videotaped intervention sessions).

An illustration of this proposal may examine the hypothetical effects of several potential mediators in the research on adolescent depression prevention. In a previous investigation (Clarke et al., 1995), my colleagues and I provided high school counselors with 40 hr of supervised training in the use of a scripted manual of cognitive intervention to prevent depression in at-risk youths. These counselors were strongly discouraged from deviating from the intervention protocol. Audiotaped reliability checks revealed that they were very compliant (94%) with the scripted protocol. Although satisfactory effects were obtained with the manual-specified intervention, it would be interesting to conduct this study again with the intent of exploring "therapy structure" issues. For example, a semi-factorial design may be used to examine the extent to which planned and measured variations in (a) therapist deviation from a regimented treatment protocol and (b) the use of structured intervention manuals and specialized training had an effect on outcome.

Three different implementation versions of the same cognitive therapy intervention could be used: [1]

1. Rigorous therapist training with a structured manual and minimal protocol deviation (enforced by means of video-taped monitoring). This is essentially the study as it was originally conducted, and it represents typical efficacy research design.
2. Similar therapist training with a structured manual but with minor to moderate protocol deviation permitted on the basis of therapists' clinical judgment. For example, anger management, although not part of the original protocol, might be offered to a depressed adolescent with comorbid conduct disorder. Therapists would be monitored by means of videotaped sessions, and deviations would be assessed and coded, but not corrected through supervision.
3. General therapist training in the same theoretical approach as espoused in the manual, but with no structured manual provided. Treatment course and planning would be based on the therapists' best clinical judgment. Similar to the second condition, therapist deviations would be assessed but not corrected.

Measuring how experienced clinicians elect to deviate from protocols is a difficult task but necessary in this design. If certain so-called deviations from protocol are associated with good client outcome, structured research interventions may be improved by the incorporation of these techniques or activities in the protocol. In this way, unstructured clinical practices might more systematically influence the development of effective structured research interventions, contributing to a two-way exchange of information between researchers and clinicians. At the very least, researchers may better understand which components of psychotherapy approaches are fairly robust and tolerant of individual therapist deviations, and which aspects are relatively fragile and should be carried out in a fairly uniform manner.

One may argue that this design introduces too many opportunities for unexplained results. For example, what if the least structured condition was associated with the best outcome? How would one know what aspects of the treatment accounted for this finding? Furthermore, can these positive findings be replicated, or were they just a function of unique therapist characteristics? Certainly therapy content data (from coded videotaped sessions)

---

[1] Note that the remaining cell in this design (no manual, but no deviation permitted) cannot be implemented, because where a manual is not provided it is not possible to ascertain whether protocol has been followed.

must be examined to determine whether systematic therapist deviations from established protocol were associated with better outcome. If so, subsequent studies could be conducted with controlled variations of these deviations to further test their impact on outcome. Regarding replication, a single study of this type is not meant to answer all questions. Replication is still as important to this type of design as it is in efficacy research, and failure to replicate would indeed raise questions as to whether uncontrolled therapy implementation is best.

Too few controlled psychotherapy studies have specifically tested these issues to predict what results would be obtained. However, Weiss and Weisz's (1990) meta-analysis of methodological factor effects on child psychotherapy outcome research suggests that increased methodological rigor is generally (although not uniformly) associated with more beneficial treatment outcome across unrelated studies. Although Weiss and Weisz (1990) did not specifically examine the mediating effects of intervention implementation rigor, extrapolating from their data suggests that more positive results may be obtained when treatment protocol is carefully carried out.

Although studies examining treatment implementation issues in a controlled paradigm are virtually unavailable in psychotherapy outcome research, these issues are an increasing focus of school-based prevention and health promotion research (Felner, Phillips, DuBois, & Lease, 1991). For example, Rohrbach, Graham, and Hansen (1993) examined the relationship between integrity of program delivery and outcomes of a school-based, psychosocial substance abuse prevention program. School districts were randomly assigned to either intensive or brief teacher training in the program: schools within districts were randomly assigned to have the principal involved or not involved in the intervention. Not only was program implementation highly variable but it also faded from the first to the second year. Delivery of the program in a rigorous manner was predictive of positive student outcomes. These results are similar to those reported in other studies of school-based substance abuse prevention programs (e.g., Botvin et al., 1989; Pentz et al., 1990). Although these findings are not directly applicable to traditional psychotherapy, many design and hypothesis issues examined by Rohrbach et al. (1993) are relevant to effectiveness studies that examine the implementation and real-life usefulness of psychotherapy services.

If future studies find that greater adherence to psychotherapy protocols predicts better client outcome, what implications would this have? Such a conclusion might be unpopular with clinicians, especially those who favor therapist autonomy. This likely fallout is an effect that researchers should acknowledge, because concerns regarding this use of effectiveness data is a major contributor to clinician resistance to the adoption of research interventions.

INTEGRATED VERSUS ISOLATED SERVICES

Efficacy studies typically offer their treatments in isolation, often to focus on the disorder of interest or to remove or control extraneous mediating factors (e.g., other treatments). This isolation is often twofold; first, research treatments often target only one disorder, diagnosis, or problem domain, without addressing psychiatric or general medical comorbidity in individuals. A second and related form of treatment isolation arises when efficacy studies provide only the research intervention, without the frequent clinical requirement to offer an integrated array of multiple different assessment, intervention, referral, and advocacy services in addition to the single research focus. This insularity means that research projects have a generally greater capacity to devote more time, resources, and follow-up to their limited number of participants. In contrast, effectiveness trials conducted at sites such as schools and community mental health programs can typically provide only a limited number of visits and contact hours to each client.

Although for theory testing it is often desirable to pare interventions down to a single, internally cohesive treatment component, this may not reflect mental health services as often provided in the community. For at least some populations and settings, services are often provided in an integrated intervention "package," consisting of several interconnected parts. For example, community-based services for individuals with chronic mental illnesses such as schizophrenia often include a physical examination, psychotropic medications, psychological services, case management, housing support, and social welfare services, with other components added as required (e.g., Solomon, 1992). Researchers must acknowledge that mental health interventions are often embedded in a larger context of general health and social services, and intervention trials of "atomized" psychotherapy components may have little external validity. Initial outcome studies of psychotherapy services may be geared toward testing the larger, integrated intervention package, with subsequent "component analyses" conducted only after the composite intervention is associated with beneficial outcome.

How could methodological variations in outcome research address this issue? Although daunting, one obvious solution is to develop an integrated intervention regime that offers research-based intervention tracks for a variety of common disorders, with clear triage rules regarding assignment to intervention (or interventions) on the basis of assessment findings. Furthermore, interventions must be integrated to address those instances in which participants have more than one disorder, and thus, they must enroll in more than one intervention track. The control condition for this design may be the locally evolved intervention standards for addressing the heterogeneous clinical presentation seen in the community. Defining these local standards for the purposes of an effectiveness trial requires substantial preliminary meetings with representative local providers to clarify and codify the usual and customary services provided for a given client population.

Such a protocol might also introduce realistic personnel and fiscal budgets to both research and control conditions, within which both conditions must provide all services required by the client sample. Budgetary caps of this sort simulate service system limits and may address the perception that research interventions are overly enriched. Caseloads and service burden would be comparable, increasing confidence in the generalizability of outcome findings.

Examples of research-based treatment parameters for psychiatric disorders are rare, but becoming less so. For example, the *Journal of the American Academy of Child and Adolescent Psychiatry* recently published practice parameters for several common child mental health disorders, including anxiety disorders (Bernstein & Shaw, 1993), attention-deficit hyperactivity disorders (Jaffe, 1991), schizophrenia (McClellan & Werry, 1994), and conduct disorder (Jaffe, 1992). Similarly, this journal has recently published several articles on the treatment of common combinations of comorbid disorders (e.g., Mueser, Bellack, & Blanchard, 1992; Shea, Widiger, & Klein, 1992). Parameters such as these may form the basis for developing the "integrated intervention regime" advocated earlier.

Of course, mounting a comprehensive study of this type might prove so costly that it would quickly exceed traditional research budget limits. Although easier said than done, the only realistic solution is to forge an alliance between traditional research funding bodies such as the National Institute of Mental Health and the public and private agencies that already provide some version of these services to the general population. This cooperation is the essence of successful services research, and readers interested in developing these unlikely yet necessary alliances will find that much has already been written about the process (e.g., Attkisson et al., 1992).

A less ambitious option would be to select participants with predefined comorbidity combinations (e.g., depression and substance abuse) and require research therapists to address the treatment and associated clinical issues important to both problem areas. Developing an assessment, triage, and intervention protocol for this circumscribed sample would be considerably easier. Although less realistic and less integrated than the totally comprehensive approach described first, this nonetheless represents a significant advance over existing efficacy studies.

Despite the difficulty of mounting an integrated research protocol, some investigators have made initial inroads toward developing such a model. For instance, the FAST (Families and Schools Together) Track Program (Conduct Problems Prevention Research Group, 1992) provides a research-based intervention model for the prevention of conduct disorder in youths by integrating family, school, peer group, and child intervention components. However, even this model is limited in terms of encompassing other disorders that may be comorbid with conduct disorder (e.g., depression).

Historically, my own investigations of adolescent depression treatment and prevention (see Clarke et al., 1995) have similarly taken a relatively narrow focus. However, future investigations could broaden both the sample and the intervention to address common comorbid diagnosis combinations, following the less ambitious of the two paradigms suggested earlier. Because alcohol and drug abuse–dependence is the most common comorbid *DSM–III–R* (*Diagnostic and Statistical Manual of Mental Disorders* [3rd ed., rev.; American Psychiatric Association, 1987]) diagnosis for adolescent depression (Rohde, Lewinsohn, & Seeley, 1991), focusing on this combination is a reasonable starting point. An omnibus, school-based, adolescent depression and substance abuse preventive intervention might combine the best features of the depression prevention program (Clarke et al., 1995) with aspects of successful substance abuse prevention programs such as the Midwestern Prevention Project (Pentz et al., 1990). One interesting study design among many possibilities is the implementation of both the separate and the combined prevention programs in the high school setting, with at-risk youths randomly assigned to depression-only, substance abuse-only, or the combined program. This design could be crossed with an "implementation" independent variable, with the programs administered either by school counselors (who would be obliged to provide all other services required by these youths) or by "single-purpose" research therapists (with no obligation to provide associated services). This design would contribute to the theoretical question of shared versus separate etiologies and treatments of depression and substance abuse, as well as address pragmatic issues of outcome as a function of therapist treatment obligations and their degree of integration in the service setting.

As stated earlier, this design example is not meant to capture all elements related to the issue of integrated versus isolated interventions but provides just one concrete example of how efficacy trials could extend their methodology to address effectiveness issues. Rather than representing a relaxing of research standards, this design is meant to be an example of extending efficacy research rigor to topics that previously have been studied (if at all) with less careful and controlled methods.

USUAL CARE VERSUS NO-TREATMENT OR PLACEBO-ATTENTION CONTROLS

The sine qua non (Parloff, 1986) of psychotherapy efficacy research is the randomly assigned control condition. Several variations exist, but the most common are the enforced no-treatment control, the waiting-list control, and the placebo-attention control. In the no-treatment and waiting-list control conditions, participants are prohibited from obtaining an active intervention altogether or for some predefined period, respectively. Participants enrolled in a placebo-attention control condition are provided with some structured activity believed to be therapeutically neutral (at least with respect to the theoretical model underlying the experimental treatment), in an attempt to control for the nonspecific aspects of interpersonal contact and the number of service hours provided in the experimental condition.

Although these control conditions help resolve theoretical issues and control threats to internal validity, they are usually untenable in clinical settings appropriate for effectiveness trials (Weisz, Weiss, & Donenberg, 1992). Furthermore, they do not provide outcome information specifically applicable to the extension of the treatment to a clinical care setting; that is, none of these control conditions represent what typically happens to clients who seek treatment but are not provided with it. If the problem is severe and chronic enough, these individuals often go elsewhere to obtain meaningful treatment.

These control conditions generate other problems. Participant dropout from enforced no-treatment and waiting-list control conditions can often be more pronounced than dropout from the active intervention, contributing to potential bias in comparisons of the retained control sample and the experimental condition. The placebo-attention control condition is also problematic in that it may not be as therapeutically neutral as advertised. Elkin et al. (Elkin, Parloff, Hadley, & Autry, 1985), Strupp (1977), and Parloff (1986) argued that most placebo-attention conditions include elements (e.g., a feeling of being understood, an opportunity for social contacts) which would be considered therapeutically active by at least some intervention modalities (e.g., client-centered therapies).

In our recent outcome studies (Clarke et al., 1995; Clarke & Hornbrook, 1994) we have shifted away from these traditional control conditions to a randomized usual-care control condition, identified as a "minimal-treatment" control by Weiss and Weisz (1990). In this condition, subjects are provided with mental health services typically offered in the service setting.[2] A similar control condition, the "best alternative treatment," compares the experimental therapy against the best available treatment, if such exists (O'Leary & Borkovec, 1978). These designs are all subsumed under the comparative outcome study design, the relative advantages and disadvantages of which are discussed by Basham (1986) and Kazdin (1986).

---

[2] This differs somewhat in our prevention trials (Clarke et al., 1995), where participants not yet meeting a clinical diagnosis are less likely to seek enrollment in treatment. Under these circumstances, usual-care participants are free to continue with any preexisting intervention or to seek any new assistance during the study period if they so desire. To equate the base level of nonexperimental intervention across both conditions, participants enrolled in the active prevention program are also permitted to continue any preexisting treatment and to seek out any additional treatment.

What impact would the use of this control condition have on outcome research? Weiss and Weisz (1990) reported in their meta-analysis of child psychotherapy studies that the outcome effect sizes associated with the minimal-treatment control group is indistinguishable from that associated with other, more traditional control conditions. From this data at least, using this type of control condition appears to neither endanger the internal validity of controlled outcome studies nor alter estimates of beneficial effect associated with the experimental intervention.

Given these cautions, what (if any) benefits are associated with a usual-care control condition that make it superior to traditional controls in effectiveness trials? I believe that the most important benefit of a usual-care control condition is that it represents a more generalizable test of the intervention. It has the greatest ecological validity of all common control conditions, with the greatest likelihood of corresponding to a real-world counterpart. Although a waiting-list control seems realistic, in my experience substantial numbers of these participants may surreptitiously seek other treatment and eventually drop out of the study. Enforced no-treatment and attention-placebo controls also have limited real-life counterparts.

More pragmatically, I agree with Weisz et al. (1992) that a comparative treatment design is more likely to be tolerated in clinical settings and, thus, overcome clinic staff resistance to effectiveness studies on their premises. Providentially, a usual-care control provides a more conservative test of the experimental intervention, as the new intervention must exceed the benefits associated with usual mental health care to emerge as successful, with the presumption, of course, that usual care imparts at least a minimum benefit. However, a control or comparison condition of this type should not be used uncritically. For example, the usual-care condition makes it much more difficult to characterize the services received by control participants, and in many situations this is important to assess. Kazdin (1986) provides a thorough review of the advantages and disadvantages of each type of control condition, and investigators should carefully examine these issues during planning for any outcome trial.

SAMPLE REPRESENTATIVENESS, HETEROGENEITY VERSUS HOMOGENEITY

As noted by Weisz and Weiss (1989), controlled outcome research studies typically use very strict participant inclusion criteria, resulting in a sample that may have only a limited resemblance to the usual cases of that disorder served in the community. For example, in previous adolescent depression treatment research (Lewinsohn et al., 1990) my colleagues and I limited the sample by restricting (but not eliminating) psychiatric comorbidity, requiring minimum reading levels, placing a moratorium on all other mental health treatment (or treatments), and placing other restrictions on sample characteristics.

Although there are compelling conceptual reasons to select a highly homogeneous patient sample (see Kendall & Lipman, 1991), the downside of homogeneity is that it yields patients that may be very different from their nonresearch counterparts, making generalization of results suspect. Pragmatically, overselection may also make participant recruitment more difficult. For example, local referral sources reported having many depressed adolescents to send to depression treatment studies, but only a few that met the stringent selection criteria.

In contrast, effectiveness studies must deal with the viscidities of the clinical world, where comorbidity is common, connection with multiple providers of therapy or social services (or both) is the norm among certain populations (e.g., children; severely mentally ill individuals), placing limits on other treatments is usually neither possible nor ethical, and participant characteristics are generally much more heterogeneous.

How might researchers design different studies to satisfy the goal of a homogeneous sample and also examine the intervention for effects among a more realistic and heterogeneous population? Although it is hardly the only approach, I recommend broadening recruitment for most all intervention outcome studies with a two-tiered participant recruitment strategy; I call this the "donut" model. A highly selected, homogeneous core sample (the "donut hole") could be recruited for testing basic theoretical issues regarding outcome, not dissimilar from efficacy study recruitment as presently practiced. However, to this I recommend adding a relatively unselected, comorbid, and heterogeneous sample (the donut ring) that would be recruited to examine generalizability and real-world effectiveness. Participant heterogeneity or homogeneity could be used as a dichotomous blocking variable in a factorial design, crossed with experimental condition, or it could be examined in the full sample by means of post hoc multivariate analyses of the mediating effects of several client and environment variables that differ across the two subsamples.

Increasing the heterogeneity of samples may be justified by the increased generalizability of the results; it also rests on the acknowledgment that many psychotherapies are potentially applicable with more than just one diagnosis. For example, cognitive therapy has been successfully used with depression (Beck, 1991), anxiety disorders (Butler, Fennell, Robson, & Gelder, 1991; Chambless & Gillis, 1993), and eating disorders (Fairburn et al., 1991; Wilson & Fairburn, 1993). Effectiveness studies of cognitive therapy may justifiably recruit more broadly within the broadband categorizations of overcontrolled or internalizing diagnoses, such as those listed earlier, and still hypothesize successful outcomes. The same approach could be used with the undercontrolled or externalizing disorders.[3] This strategy not only eases recruitment, a stumbling block to developing the large samples required in outcome studies, but simultaneously broadens sample heterogeneity. As long as diagnostic and other participant characteristic data is carefully assessed and recorded, post hoc regression analyses can be used to examine the effects of these characteristics on outcome.

Sample heterogeneity may also be increased by including different severity levels within the same problem area or symptom constellation, including individuals who may not meet a *DSM–III–R* diagnostic category but who have some subdiagnostic syndrome consisting of a reduced set of symptoms within the same category. Expanding samples in this manner may be important, as many individuals seeking service for mental health problems do not appear to qualify for a full *DSM–III–R* diagnosis yet may still be clearly impaired. For instance, Johnson, Weissman, and Klerman (1992) reported that in the general adult population, as much service burden and health impairment (or more) was associated with subdiagnostic depressive symptoms as with the clinical diagnoses of major depression or dysthymia. These data suggest that it is important to collect outcome data for these individuals as well as those who qualify for the full diagnostic categories.

Mark Hornbrook and I (Clarke & Hornbrook, 1994) are currently conducting just such a study. Adolescents at risk for depression by virtue of having a parent being treated for depression (see review by Downey & Coyne, 1990) are carefully assessed and then triaged to one of three severity levels: (a) clinically depressed adolescents (major depression, dysthymia, or both); (b) at-risk adolescents (elevated but subdiagnostic depressive symptom levels, past depressive episodes, or both); and (c) resilient adolescents (no current depressive symptoms or history). Randomized outcome trials are conducted at each severity level, with increasingly more intensive psychotherapeutic interventions (corresponding to clinical severity) contrasted against a usual-care control condition. Because this study is conducted within a large health maintenance organization (HMO), the costs of delivering experimental interventions are relatively easily measured and compared with the costs of all health care services consumed by the control group. Although the aims of the study go beyond the issues raised in the present article, the participant recruitment and triage methodology has been influenced by a broadened perspective of whom might benefit from psychotherapeutic interventions.

My experience working with schools and public agencies in psychotherapy outcome trials suggests that a broadening of the eligible pool of participants would simplify and enhance recruitment rather than complicate it.

---

[3] Child and adolescent examples of overcontrolled disorders include depression, anxiety, and eating disorders; examples of undercontrolled conditions include attention-deficit hyperactivity disorder, conduct disorder, and oppositional defiant disorders.

Because referring agencies do not have to cull out just the "pure" cases, the referral process is a less time-consuming and frustrating task. Another advantage of extending the sample in this way is that client and psychopathological characteristics, process variables, and other potential outcome mediators may have greater variability than is typically the case with a more homogeneous sample. Up to a point, this increased variability may potentiate multivariate analyses examining the effect of these mediators on treatment outcome across the combined sample, an often desirable post hoc analytical strategy to help identify important therapy issues and directions for future research.

TREATMENT PARAMETERS: DOSAGE, MODALITY, LOCATION, IMPLEMENTATION

This may be the most neglected yet potentially most important area of effectiveness research. After posing the general question "Does psychotherapy work?" most legislators and policy makers in the current national health care debate focus on the effectiveness of multiple variations in the delivery of efficacious intervention. For example, are patients with severe major depression better treated in inpatient or outpatient facilities, and at what costs? For how long? In groups or individual therapy, or both? Delivered by professionals or paraprofessionals? At present, there are few clear answers to these questions.

These are not just pragmatic (read "nonscientific") issues; they represent exciting questions that can have important and fundamental theoretical implications. For example, the relative benefit of group versus individual psychotherapy is obviously relevant from an effectiveness perspective; in service systems such as HMOs such a finding could have major implications for mental health service delivery (see Budman, 1992). However, studies examining this seemingly pragmatic issue can also address numerous theoretical issues related to therapeutic change. For instance, in several models of therapeutic process and change (Orlinsky & Howard, 1986) it is hypothesized that working through the dynamics of a developing therapist–client relationship is a significant contributor to positive treatment outcome. This relationship is presumably optimized in individual therapy and could be argued to be proportionally much weaker in group therapy, in which the therapist's attention is divided across many group participants.

However, suppose that future research were to find that individual and group versions of the same treatment approach produce roughly equivalent beneficial outcome (Tillitski [1990] and Weisz, Weiss, Alicke, & Klotz [1987] review these issues in child and adolescent psychotherapy). This hypothetical finding might suggest that a combination of client-to-client relationships in combination with a weaker therapist–client relationship is equivalent to an intensive therapist – client relationship, at least as far as psychotherapeutic benefit is concerned.

The key issue here is not whether this is a correct interpretation (this is, after all, only an example based on hypothetical findings), but that investigations of these more pragmatic implementation issues may also lead to a more thorough understanding of theoretical treatment models. In short, studies need not address only basic research or pragmatic issues; they may be designed to address both.

CONCLUSION

In summary, this article calls for the inclusion of methodological features to transfer desirable aspects of efficacy research (e.g., greater independent variable control) into combined efficacy – effectiveness trials. This message parallels several earlier calls for accelerated study of psychotherapy process variables (summarized by Marmar, 1990). However, the articles in this special section are proposing a different set of variables than those that have been the major focus of process researchers such as Orlinsky and Howard (1986). Traditionally, psychotherapy process research has focused on client and therapist characteristics and interactions, which is reasonable given the focus on how psychotherapy works. In contrast, the blending of psychotherapy efficacy and effectiveness approaches is better served by detailed study of the mediating effects of variables such as the setting in which services are delivered (e.g., school vs. clinic vs. home), the type of clinician who delivers these services, and other issues addressed earlier.

Marmar (1990), in a review of psychotherapy process research, argued for the value of embedding substudies of process variables within larger clinical (efficacy) trials. I agree with this position, but I argue that investigators must look beyond traditional therapeutic relationship variables and include what Kazdin (1986) calls treatment parameter variables, such as the frequency and duration of sessions, the setting in which the treatment is offered, therapist training and profession, and other parameters discussed in this article.

Such studies may manipulate these factors as independent variables or allow them to vary naturally and examine their effect on outcome with post hoc multivariate analyses. The first, more controlled approach is more likely to appeal to efficacy researchers, whereas the latter approach may be more acceptable to confirmed effectiveness investigators. Regardless, both groups (if researchers do self-identify into one or the other group) should be encouraged to generate hybrid studies, broadening the sample and issues under study to address effectiveness concerns while still maintaining as much rigor and experimental control as possible to eliminate or minimize competing explanatory hypotheses. In short, efficacy versus effectiveness is a somewhat artificial distinction, an unnatural dichotomy that a new generation of hybrid studies may help to break down.

REFERENCES

American Psychiatric Association. (1987). *Diagnostic and statistical manual of mental disorders* (3rd ed., rev.). Washington, DC: Author.

Attkisson, C., Cook, J., Karno, M., Lehman, A., McGlashan, T. H., Meltzer, H. Y., O'Connor, M., Richardson, D., Rosenblatt, A., Wells, K., et al. (1992). Clinical services research. *Schizophrenia Bulletin, 18*, 561–626.

Basham, R. B. (1986). Scientific and practical advantages of comparative design in psychotherapy outcome research. *Journal of Consulting and Clinical Psychology, 54*, 88–94.

Beck, A. T. (1991). Cognitive therapy: A 30-year retrospective. *American Psychologist, 46*, 368–375.

Bernstein, G. A., & Shaw, K. (1993). Practice parameters for the assessment and treatment of anxiety disorders. *Journal of the American Academy of Child and Adolescent Psychiatry, 32*, 1089–1098.

Botvin, G. J., Batson, H. W., Witts-Vitale, S., Bess, V., Baker, E., & Dusenbury, L. (1989). A psychosocial approach for smoking prevention for urban black youth. *Public Health Report, 104*, 573–582.

Brook, R. H., & Lohr, K. N. (1985). Efficacy, effectiveness, variations, and quality. *Medical Care, 23*, 710–722.

Budman, S. H. (1992). Models of brief individual and group psychotherapy. In J. L. Feldman & R. J. Fitzpatrick (Eds.), *Managed mental health care: Administrative and clinical issues* (pp. 231–248). Washington, DC: American Psychiatric Press.

Butler, G., Fennell, M., Robson, P., & Gelder, M. (1991). Comparison of behavior therapy and cognitive behavior therapy in the treatment of generalized anxiety disorder. *Journal of Consulting and Clinical Psychology, 59*, 167–175.

Chambless, D. L., & Gillis, M. M. (1993). Cognitive therapy of anxiety disorders. *Journal of Consulting and Clinical Psychology, 61*, 248–260.

Clarke, G. N., Hawkins, W., Murphy, M., Sheeber, L., Lewinsohn, P. M., & Seeley, J. R. (1995). Targeted prevention of unipolar depressive disorder in an at-risk sample of high school adolescents: A randomized trial of a group cognitive intervention. *Journal of the American Academy of Child and Adolescent Psychiatry, 34*, 312–321.

Clarke, G. N., & Hornbrook, M. (1994). *Prevention of depression in adolescent offspring of parents enrolled in a HMO.* (Grant application funded by the Services Research Branch of the National Institute of Mental Health [R01-MH51318-01A1])

Clarke, G. N., Lewinsohn, P. M., & Hops, H. (1990). *Instructor's manual for the Adolescent Coping with Depression Course.* Eugene, OR: Castalia Press.

Conduct Problems Prevention Research Group. (1992). A developmental and clinical model for the prevention of conduct disorder: The FAST Track Program. *Development and Psychopathology, 4,* 509–527.

Downey, G., & Coyne, J. C. (1990). Children of depressed parents: An integrative review. *Psychological Bulletin, 108,* 50–76.

Elkin, I., Parloff, M. B., Hadley, S. W., & Autry, J. H. (1985). NIMH Treatment of Depression Collaborative Research Program: Background and research plan. *Archives of General Psychiatry, 42,* 305–316.

Fairburn, C. G., Jones, R., Peveler, R. C., Carr, S. J., Solomon, R. A., O'Connor, M. E., Burton, J., & Hope, R. A. (1991). Three psychological treatments for bulimia nervosa: A comparative trial. *Archives of General Psychiatry, 48,* 463–469.

Felner, R. D., Phillips, R. S., DuBois, D., & Lease, A. M. (1991). Ecological interventions and the process of change for prevention: Wedding theory and research to implementation in real world settings. *American Journal of Community Psychology, 19,* 379–387.

Hollon, S. D. (1988, June). *Rating therapies for depression: Final report on the CSPRS.* Paper presented at the annual meeting of the Society for Psychotherapy Research, Santa Fe, NM.

Hopkins, K. D. (1982). The unit of analysis: Group means versus individual observation. *American Educational Research Journal, 19,* 5–18.

Jaffe, S. (1991). Practice parameters for the assessment and treatment of attention deficit hyperactivity disorder. Work Group on Quality Issues. *Journal of the American Academy of Child and Adolescent Psychiatry, 30,* i–iii.

Jaffe, S. (1992). Practice parameters for the assessment and treatment of conduct disorders. Work Group on Quality Issues. *Journal of the American Academy of Child and Adolescent Psychiatry, 31,* iv–vii.

Johnson, J., Weissman, M. M., & Klerman, G. L. (1992). Service utilization and social morbidity associated with depressive symptoms in the community. *Journal of the American Medical Association, 267,* 1478–1483.

Kazdin, A. E. (1978). Evaluating the generality of findings in analogue therapy research. *Journal of Consulting and Clinical Psychology, 46,* 673–686.

Kazdin, A. E. (1986). Comparative outcome studies of psychotherapy: Methodological issues and strategies. *Journal of Consulting and Clinical Psychology, 54,* 95–105.

Kendall, P. C., & Lipman, A. J. (1991). Psychological and pharmacological therapy: Methods and modes for comparative outcome research. *Journal of Consulting and Clinical Psychology, 59,* 78–87.

Lambert, M. J., & Ogles, B. M. (1988). Treatment manuals: Problems and promise. *Journal of Integrative and Eclectic Psychotherapy, 7,* 187–204.

Lewinsohn, P. M., Clarke, G. N., Hops, H., & Andrews, J. (1990). Cognitive-behavioral group treatment of depression in adolescents. *Behavior Therapy, 21,* 385–401.

Luborsky, L., & DeRubeis, R. J. (1984). The use of psychotherapy treatment manuals: A small revolution in psychotherapy research studies. *Clinical Psychology Review, 4,* 5–14.

Marmar, C. R. (1990). Psychotherapy process research: Progress, dilemmas, and future directions. *Journal of Consulting and Clinical Psychology, 58,* 265–272.

McClellan, J., & Werry, J. (1994). Practice parameters for the assessment and treatment of children and adolescents with schizophrenia. Work Group on Quality Issues. *Journal of the American Academy of Child and Adolescent Psychiatry, 33,* 616–635.

Moreau, D., Mufson, L., Weissman, M. M., & Klerman, G. L. (1991). Interpersonal psychotherapy for adolescent depression: Description of modification and preliminary application. *Journal of the American Academy of Child and Adolescent Psychiatry, 30,* 642–651.

Mueser, K. T., Bellack, A. S., & Blanchard, J. J. (1992). Comorbidity of schizophrenia and substance abuse: Implications for treatment. *Journal of Consulting and Clinical Psychology, 60,* 845–856.

O'Leary, K. D., & Borkovec, T. D. (1978). Conceptual, methodological, and ethical problems of placebo groups in psychotherapy research. *American Psychologist, 33,* 821–830.

Orlinsky, D. E., & Howard, K. I. (1986). Process and outcome in psychotherapy. In S. L. Garfield & A. E. Bergin (Eds.), *Handbook of psychotherapy and behavior change* (3rd ed., pp. 311–384). New York: Wiley.

Parloff, M. B. (1986). Placebo controls in psychotherapy research: A sine qua non or a placebo for research problems? *Journal of Consulting and Clinical Psychology, 54,* 79–87.

Pentz, M. A., Trebow, E. A., Hansen, W. B., MacKinnon, D. P., Dwyer, J. H., Johnson, C. A., Flay, B., Daniels, S., & Cormack, C. (1990). Effects of program implementation on adolescent drug use behavior: The Midwestern Prevention Project (MPP). *Evaluation Research, 14,* 264–289.

Rohde, P., Lewinsohn, P. M., & Seeley, J. R. (1991). Comorbidity with unipolar depression: II. Comorbidity with other mental disorders in adolescents and adults. *Journal of Abnormal Psychology, 100,* 214–222.

Rohrbach, L. A., Graham, J. W., & Hansen, W. B. (1993). Diffusion of a school-based substance abuse prevention program: Predictors of program implementation. *Preventive Medicine, 22,* 237–260.

Shea, M. T., Widiger, T. A., & Klein, M. H. (1992). Comorbidity of personality disorders and depression: Implications for treatment. *Journal of Consulting and Clinical Psychology, 60,* 857–868.

Solomon, P. (1992). The efficacy of case management services for severely mentally disabled adults. *Community Mental Health Journal, 28,* 163–180.

Strupp, H. (1977). A reformulation of the dynamics of the therapist's contribution. In A. S. Gurman & A. M. Razin (Eds.), *Effective psychotherapy: A handbook of research* (pp. 3–22). New York: Pergamon.

Tillitski, C. J. (1990). A meta-analysis of estimated effect sizes for group versus individual versus control treatments. *International Journal of Group Psychotherapy*, *40*, 215–224.

Weiss, B., & Weisz, J. R. (1990). The impact of methodological factors on child psychotherapy outcome research: A meta-analysis for researchers. *Journal of Abnormal Child Psychology*, *18*, 639–670.

Weisz, J. R., & Weiss, B. (1989). Assessing the effects of clinic-based psychotherapy with children. *Journal of Consulting and Clinical Psychology*, *57*, 741–746.

Weisz, J. R., Weiss, B., Alicke, M. D., & Klotz, M. L. (1987). Effectiveness of psychotherapy with children and adolescents: A meta-analysis for clinicians. *Journal of Consulting and Clinical Psychology*, *55*, 542–549.

Weisz, J. R., Weiss, B., & Donenberg, G. R. (1992). The lab versus the clinic: Effects of child and adolescent psychotherapy. *American Psychologist*, *47*, 1578–1585.

Wilson, G. T., & Fairburn, C. G. (1993). Cognitive treatments for eating disorders. *Journal of Consulting and Clinical Psychology*, *61*, 261–269.

25

THE ROLE OF METHOD IN TREATMENT EFFECTIVENESS RESEARCH: EVIDENCE FROM META-ANALYSIS

DAVID B. WILSON AND MARK W. LIPSEY

Systematic knowledge about the effectiveness of psychological and behavioral intervention depends almost exclusively on studies using experimental or quasi-experimental research designs. Among such designs, the well-executed randomized experiment is widely considered the gold standard because it is expected to produce an estimate of the mean treatment effect on a given dependent variable that deviates from the true value only by random error, which is kept small when statistical power is adequate. Unfortunately, when conducting treatment effectiveness research in real-world settings, ideal experimental design often cannot be attained: Randomization is incomplete, is undone by attrition, or is unethical or impractical; sample sizes are not sufficient to keep sampling error small relative to treatment effects; experimental control of conditions is lax or impossible; dependent variables are limited by low reliability or do not represent the outcome construct well;

Reprinted from *Psychological Methods*, 6, 413–429. Copyright 2001 by the American Psychological Association.

This work was supported in part by National Institute of Mental Health Grant RO1-MH51701.

and so forth (Conrad, 1994; Cook & Shadish, 1994; Dennis, 1990; Kazdin, 1992; Lipsey & Cordray, 2000).

Each such departure from the ideal potentially degrades the treatment effect estimate. But by how much? In what direction? Under what circumstances? The statistical and epistemological theory that underlies experimental design supports the claim that ideal design will yield valid estimates but provides little basis for appraising the consequences of various departures from the ideal. Indeed, the nature and magnitude of those consequences are largely empirical matters, but they can be investigated directly only with the results of ideal designs in hand as a standard of comparison, a difficult condition to fulfill. An alternative way to conceptualize the empirical question is in signal-detection terms. Research in a typical intervention domain investigates the effects of different treatment variants on different outcome constructs for different respondent samples using different methods and procedures. Some of the variation in observed effects across these studies stems from differences in substantive aspects of the intervention being investigated (treatment, outcome construct, respondents); this variation represents the "signal" the researcher wishes to detect. The remaining variation stems from differences in method or from randomly distributed sampling and measurement error; this variation represents the "noise" that potentially distorts or obscures the signal the researcher is attempting to detect. Over the typical range of substantive and method differences in a body of research, it would be informative to know that the proportion of variance in the observed effect sizes associated with the signal was large relative to that associated with the noise. This would tell us whether estimates of treatment effects are robust in the face of method variation and random error of the sort typical in the treatment domain examined; that is, how threatening are departures from ideal design to the resulting conclusions about treatment effects?

Obtaining a good empirical estimate of this signal-to-noise ratio would require an experiment on experiments. In this experiment, there would be a factor for each design feature of interest (e.g., type of assignment to conditions, treatment variant, type of outcome measure), each varied over a range typical of actual practice. Researchers would then be randomly assigned to these various factor levels and would be required to conduct a study using the stipulated configuration of substantive and method features. Each observation within this factorial design would thus reflect the results of an entire outcome study conducted using the research methods specified by the grand experiment.

It would be especially informative if the experiment on experiments identified the specific method features with the greatest potential to distort estimates of treatment effects and the circumstances in which those distortions were most likely. Designing treatment effectiveness studies often involves making trade-offs with respect to ideal design, and such information would give useful guidance to researchers about which compromises were likely to introduce serious error.

Of course, the experiment on experiments is not practical, but the issue it would address can be examined, albeit less definitively, by analyzing the results of multiple studies within a treatment domain in relation to the naturally occurring method and substantive variation across those studies. Meta-analysis does just this (Cook et al., 1992; Cooper & Hedges, 1994; Hunter & Schmidt, 1990; Rosenthal, 1991). A meta-analysis of a particular treatment domain, therefore, can be viewed as a quasi-experimental alternative to the experiment on experiments. Typically, method and substantive features vary across studies within a specific treatment research context, and the differences in the mean effect sizes associated with the method and substantive dimensions indicate their relative contribution to that variation. Analysis of such data can provide an assessment of the potential biases associated with different method features within the respective treatment domain (for similar approaches, see Heinsman & Shadish, 1996; Shadish & Ragsdale, 1996).

The findings resulting from this procedure, however, would be limited to the particular treatment domain for which the meta-analysis was done. Greater generality would be possible if multiple treatment domains were examined. This can be accomplished through a synthesis of the substantive and method effect size breakouts across multiple meta-analyses.

The current study uses the body of meta-analyses identified by Lipsey and Wilson (1993) to construct a meta-analysis of meta-analyses analogue to the experiment on experiments described previously. This body of 319 meta-analyses encompasses 16,525 separate studies of the effects of psychologically based treatments, predominately mental health and educational interventions but with considerable diversity within those categories. This diversity provides the basis for a broad examination of the role of method factors relative to substantive factors in accounting for the effects observed in studies of psychological intervention. Thus, the research question addressed by this study is, what is the role of method in treatment effect estimates? More specifically, what is the influence of method features relative to substantive intervention features on observed study outcomes?

METHOD

Identification and Retrieval of Meta-Analyses

A variety of search strategies were used to identify meta-analyses of psychologically based interventions reported between 1976, the year of Glass's pioneering work (Glass, 1976; Smith & Glass, 1977), and mid-1991. Potential meta-analyses were identified mainly through a computerized search of the following databases: Academic Index, Ageline, British Education Index, Child Abuse and Neglect, Criminal Justice Periodical Index, Dissertation

Abstracts, ECER/EXCEP Child, ERIC, Family Resources, Mental Health Abstracts, NCJRS, PAIS International, Population Bibliography, PsycINFO, Public Opinion Online, Religion Index, Social Scisearch, Sociological Abstracts, and U.S. Political Science Documents. Search terms included variations on meta-analysis (e.g., *meta-analysis, metaanalysis, meta-analytic*) and variations on quantitative review (e.g., *quantitative review, quantitative synthesis*). Meta-analyses were also identified through the references in articles reporting or discussing meta-analysis and through contact with other meta-analysts.

Selection Criteria

To be eligible for inclusion, a meta-analysis had to meet three criteria. First, it had to provide standardized mean difference effect sizes for treatment-control contrasts or statistics from which such effect sizes could be derived. Second, the studies meta-analyzed had to present research on the effects of treatments that manipulated psychological variables to produce psychological change. Third, those treatments had to represent types of interventions that are currently applied in practical domains (e.g., psychotherapy, parent effectiveness training, programs for juvenile delinquents, smoking cessation programs, pain management interventions, computer-based instruction, mastery learning). The search and selection procedure yielded 332 reports of 319 distinct meta-analyses: 181 for educational interventions, 123 for mental health interventions, and 15 for industrial/ organizational interventions of a psychosocial nature. Lipsey and Wilson (1993) briefly described the intervention area covered by each of these meta-analyses, and a bibliography of those meta-analyses not listed in Lipsey and Wilson (1993) is provided in the reference list.

Coding of Meta-Analysis Reports

Two types of data were extracted from each meta-analysis. First, the total effect size variance around the grand mean effect size was coded. When a total variance or standard deviation was not reported directly, variance was estimated from other reported statistics (e.g., the standard error). Second, information related to the effect size variance associated with selected study features was coded when available. Most of the meta-analyses reported breakouts of the mean effect sizes for such variables as type of research design (e.g., random and nonrandom), type of treatment (e.g., behavioral self-management, cognitive–behavioral, and biofeedback/relaxation therapy), different outcomes (e.g., depression and anxiety), and different samples (e.g., males and females).

The breakout dimensions were divided into those involving the intervention (e.g., treatment types, respondent characteristics, outcome constructs), referred to as *substantive* features, and those involving the methods and procedures used to study the intervention (e.g., design types, method quality, operationalization of dependent variables), referred to as *method* features. The specific categories into which breakouts of substantive and method features were sorted are described in the Results section. Effect size data associated with each breakout of interest were coded, including the mean effect sizes, number of effect sizes, number of studies, standard deviation (or variance or standard error), number of respondents, and any correlations between a breakout variable and effect size.

Estimating Variance Components

To represent the proportion of effect size variance associated with the study features of interest, eta-squared was computed for each breakout on a relevant study feature in each meta-analysis (Winer, Brown, & Michels, 1991, pp. 123–126). For the respective breakdown groups, eta-squared is the ratio of the between-groups sum of squares to the total sum of squares (Hays, 1988). The between-groups sum of squares was estimated as the weighted sum of the squared deviations of the mean effect size for each category of the breakout from the grand mean effect size, as follows, where j is the number of categories, k_j is the number of effect sizes per category, SS is the sum of squares, and ES is the effect size:

$$SS_{between} = \sigma k_j (\overline{ES}_j \, \overline{ES})._2$$

Estimation of the total sum of squares depended on the data available. When the variance or standard deviation around each mean effect in a breakout was reported, the total sum of squares was the sum of the SS between groups and the SS within groups, with the latter computed as

$$SS_{within} = \sigma k_j v_j,$$

where j is the number of categories, k_j is the number of effect sizes per category, and v_j is the variance of the effect sizes within each category. When variances for each breakout category were not provided, the total sum of squares was estimated from the total variance multiplied by the total number of effect sizes used in the breakout, which may not always have exactly equaled the k on which the original variance estimate was computed.

The resulting eta-square values provide an estimate of the proportion of the total variance in observed effect sizes associated with a study feature in each meta-analysis, as appropriate to the signal-to-noise framework for this investigation, but they do not carry information about the direction of the relationship involved. In many instances, it is informative to also know which category of a breakout variable is associated with larger or smaller effect sizes (e.g., whether the effect size variance associated with random vs. nonrandom assignment to conditions represents a tendency for randomized studies to yield larger or smaller effect sizes than nonrandomized ones). To describe further the direction and pattern of the relationship with study features for which this was meaningful, two additional indices were computed.

The simplest of these two indices was the arithmetic difference between the mean effect sizes for two-way comparisons of interest. For instance, we subtracted the mean effect size for nonrandomized comparison studies from the mean for randomized studies within each meta-analysis reporting this breakout. Assuming that randomized designs yield less bias, a positive difference (other things equal) indicates that nonrandom designs underestimate treatment effects and a negative difference indicates overestimation. This index not only describes the direction of the relationship between the study feature and effect size but indicates the magnitude of the associated difference directly.

The other directional index computed, when applicable, was the product–moment correlation coefficient (r). The correlation provides information in familiar form on both the direction and strength of the relationships by representing the linear relationship between ordered categories of a breakout variable and effect size. Because r^2 is the portion of the total variance of the dependent variable predictable from the least squares regression line, r can be defined as the square root of the ratio of the linear component of the between sum of squares to the total sum of squares (McNemar, 1966). The sum of squares for the linear component was computed using standard analysis of variance methods (e.g., Ferguson, 1966, pp. 343–344).

Statistical Analysis

The major forms of analysis for this project were description and comparison of the mean eta-squared values and, when appropriate, the mean difference and r indices for different categories of breakout variables. For such analyses, the values included should be statistically independent and weighted to reflect the precision with which they were estimated. In a typical meta-analysis, this is accomplished by using only a single effect size from each study in any given analysis and by weighting each by the inverse of its sampling variance (Hedges & Olkin, 1985). In the current instance, this approach was modified to accommodate the meta-analysis as the unit of analysis.

Independence of Indices

Two sources of dependencies among the index values required attention. First, multiple values relating to a category of breakout variables often were generated from a single meta-analysis. These dependencies were handled by averaging the values within a meta-analysis related to the same category or breakout variable so that each meta-analysis contributed only a single value to a given analysis. This was done separately for each analysis because both broad and narrow groupings of breakout variables were examined.

A second source of dependencies was overlap in studies included in related meta-analyses, such as two meta-analyses on cognitive–behavioral therapy or several meta-analyses on computer-aided instruction. The degree of statistical dependency in these cases is a function of the proportion of studies common to any two meta-analyses. This source of dependency was addressed by selectively eliminating one of any pair of meta-analyses with 25% or more studies in common. When the bibliography of studies included in a meta-analysis was unavailable, a judgment was made about the likely degree of overlap based on the topic. When two or more meta-analyses overlapped, the one based on the largest number of studies was selected except when exclusion of that one allowed for inclusion of smaller meta-analyses with a greater combined size. Few pairs of meta-analyses with any overlap were included in any analysis, and of those, the amount of overlap was generally less than 10%.

The Weighted-Bootstrap Mean and Confidence Interval

The central tendencies of the eta-square values across the meta-analyses, and those for the other indices, were computed as bootstrap means weighted by the harmonic means of the number of effect sizes contributing to each level of the breakout. The bootstrap resampling approach (Efron, 1982; Lunneborg, 1985; Mooney & Duval, 1993; Stine, 1990) was selected because it provided a method for estimating confidence intervals around the mean for each index without requiring assumptions about its underlying distributional properties.

RESULTS

The analysis focused on the portion of variability in effect sizes between studies within meta-analyses associated with various study features. An important initial question was, How much variability is there to be explained? If the effect sizes for the studies in a particular treatment domain show little variation, indicating substantial agreement on the outcome, then there is little variation to be explained by study features, methodological or substantive. For the 250 meta-analyses that provided pertinent data, the average variance across effect sizes within a meta-analysis was .52, which translates to a standard deviation of .72. J. Cohen's (1988) well-known guidelines identify .20 as a "small" effect size and .80 as a "large" one. Moreover, the grand mean effect size in this collection of meta-analyses has a standard deviation of only .29 across all the diverse interventions represented in it. Relative to these ranges, it is clear that the effect size variability within the typical meta-analysis in this set is quite substantial.

A relatively small proportion of the total variance associated with a study feature can represent meaningful differences among the associated effect sizes. For example, 4% of a total variance of .50 (i.e., an η^2 of .04) associated with a two-category breakout on a study feature (e.g., random vs. nonrandom assignment) represents a difference of .28 between the subgroup effect size means. Relative to the grand mean effect size for the meta-analysis in this example (.50), a .28 difference between the means for two subgroups of studies is substantial.

As mentioned earlier, the effect size breakouts of interest in relation to the effect size variance were those in one of four broad categories representing the features of the treatment, respondents, measurement, and design. Each of these is discussed in turn and then summarized in an overall model for observed treatment effect sizes. An assumption of these analyses is that there is little covariation in the eta-square between distinct breakout categories across meta-analyses. Study features are unlikely, however, to be truly independent. Of greatest concern is disproportionate covariation between breakout pairs because the driving research question is the relative effect of these breakout categories on effect size variability.

Treatment Features

Treatment features were differentiated into three subcategories: treatment types, treatment components (i.e., elements of treatments such as relaxation or empathetic reflection), and treatment dosage (i.e., intensity or duration). The categorization of pertinent breakouts as representing treatment types or treatment components distinguished general treatment approaches or protocols from their constituent elements or techniques. The heuristic used in making this distinction was that a treatment type was a relatively freestanding intervention, whereas a treatment component could be added to or subtracted from a treatment but would not generally stand alone as a complete intervention.

The mean eta-square values for effect size breakouts within each of these categories are shown in Table 25.1. Different treatment types were associated with the largest proportion of effect size variability, with treatment components and treatment intensity or duration, in turn, associated with roughly half as much. This indicates that within many of the treatment domains represented, as would be expected, different treatment configurations show differential effects. For all the treatment characteristics, however, the range in the mean eta-square values across meta-analyses was large, thus indicating greater differentials in some intervention areas than in others.

The mean eta-square value for differences in treatment intensity or duration (usually defined as the number of weeks of treatment) indicates that

TABLE 25.1
Mean Eta-Square Values for Selected Study Features

Study feature	M[a]	95%CI[b]	Range	Median	N[c]
Treatment features					
Treatment type	.08	.06–.10	.00.–.50	.08	116
Treatment component	.04	.03–.05	.00.–.43	.03	64
Intensity or duration	.05	.03–.07	.00–.49	.05	81
Respondent features					
Age	.04	.02–.06	.00–.10	.03	90
Gender	.02	.01–03	.00–.73	.01	34
Ethnicity	—	—	.01–.25	.09	7
Socioeconomic status	.05	.01–.09	.00–.14	.06	15
Diagnosis	.06	.03–.09	.00–.30	.04	26
Ability group	.05	.03–.07	.00–.63	.01	38
Measurement features					
Construct	.07	.05–.09	.00–.87	.06	107
Operationalization	.08	.02–.14	.00–.29	.05	11
Source of information	.05	.03–.07	.00–.21	.04	13
Researcher-developed measure	.02	.01–.03	.00–.48	.02	27
Design features					
Comparison group type	.05	.02–.08	.00–.52	.04	33
No treatment vs. placebo	.04	.02–.06	.00–.75	.03	23
No treatment vs. alternative treatment	.12	.00–.24	.00–.50	.14	16
Design type	.04	.02–.06	.00–.62	.02	93
Random vs. nonrandom	.02	.01–.03	.00–.59	.01	76
Comparison vs. pre–post	.06	.00–.12	.00–.62	.02	41
Methodological quality	.03	.02–.04	.00–.23	.02	65
Sample size	.04	.03–.05	.00–.68	.04	69

Note: Dashes indicate insufficient sample size for bootstrap procedure.
[a]Bootstrap mean, weighted by the harmonic mean of the number of studies contributing effect sizes to each level of the breakout. [b]Confidence interval based on standard deviation of bootstrap distribution. [c]Number of independent meta-analyses contributing to each mean eta-square.

this feature is associated with roughly 5% of the effect size variance. Recall that eta-squared is a nondirectional and nonlinear index. Different patterns of mean effects across categories of a study feature could each produce an equivalent eta-square. Study features such as treatment intensity have an ordinal nature, and as such it is meaningful also to assess whether there is a linear relationship between the study feature and effect size. This was assessed by the linear correlations between treatment dosage and effect size (Table 25.2). The mean correlation was slightly negative, although not significantly different from zero, and has a very wide range across meta-analyses. Examination of the meta-analyses yielding the largest negative and positive correlations did not reveal any obvious characteristics of the respective treatment domains that would explain this finding. It seems likely, however, that dose is confounded with other study features that offset its expected relationship to effect size. One candidate is the diagnostic severity of the re-

TABLE 25.2
Mean Linear Correlation Between Effect Size
and Study Features That Break Out Into Ordered Categories

Study feature	M[a]	Range	N[b]
Treatment feature			
Intensity or duration	−.02	−.44–.56	81
Respondent features			
Age	−.02	−.65–.35	90
Gender[c]	.00	−.30–.32	34
Measurement feature			
Researcher-developed measure	.10*	−.69–.36	27
Design features			
Comparison group type			
No treatment vs. placebo	.06	−.87–.66	23
No treatment vs. alternative treatment	.18*	−.53–.71	16
Design type			
Random vs. nonrandom	.04*	−.60–.77	76
Comparison vs. pre–post	−.08	−.78–.25	41
Methodological quality	−.06	−.48–.39	65
Sample size	−.08	−.59–.44	69

[a]Bootstrap mean, weighted by the harmonic mean of the number of studies contributing effect sizes to each level of the breakout. [b]Number of independent meta-analyses contributing to each mean eta-square. [c]A positive correlation indicates that larger average effects were observed for males.
*$p < .05$, based on a confidence interval derived from the standard deviation of a bootstrap distribution.

spondent population: A study involving a seriously impaired client group may have longer average treatment duration and poorer outcomes.

Respondent Features

The breakouts of respondent groups commonly reported in the meta-analyses were divided into those reflecting age, gender, ethnicity, socio-economic status, diagnosis (psychological meta-analyses), and ability (educational meta-analyses). The mean eta-square for these various categories of respondent breakouts ranged from .02 for gender to .06 for diagnosis (see Table 25.1). A large eta-squared median value for ethnicity (.09) was also observed but must be interpreted with caution given the small number of meta-analyses on which it is based (7; insufficient to compute a bootstrap mean).

It was possible to estimate the mean linear correlation for the breakouts of age and gender with effect size (see Table 25.2). Neither showed any clear directional relationship with effect size, and the means were not significantly different from zero. This finding indicates that across the treatment domains examined, the mean effect sizes for males and females and for older and younger respondents were roughly comparable on average, although they varied widely across intervention areas. The majority of the gender and age breakouts were from educational meta-analyses. The relationship of respondent features to program effects is likely to be domain specific; as such, the prior finding has limited generalizability. In a research domain in which respondent features are related to program effects, the failure to take into account the relevant respondent characteristics in the design would reduce the effect size and statistical power (Lipsey, 1990).

Outcome Constructs and Measurement Features

Outcome Constructs

The importance of the various dependent variable constructs that represent the expected outcomes of an intervention is reflected in the number of meta-analyses that reported breakouts of effect size by outcome construct. Different outcome constructs were associated with roughly 7%, on average, of the variance in effect sizes, almost the same amount as for treatment type (see Table 25.1). Within an intervention domain, therefore, effects on some of the outcome constructs measured were typically much larger than others. It is not, of course, especially surprising that treatments would have larger effects on some outcome variables than others. However, it is interesting that the amount of differentiation is so great given that researchers presumably measure all these outcomes in expectation of potential effects.

Measurement Operationalization

How an outcome construct is measured may matter as much as what is measured. To examine this possibility, the effect size breakouts for different measurement operationalizations were examined. Unfortunately, only 11 independent meta-analyses reported such breakouts, ranging from narrow to broad differences in how the constructs were operationalized. An example from the narrow end of the continuum is a breakout of the different versions of achievement tests used in studies of programs for teaching biology as inquiry (El-Nemr, 1980). At the broader end of the continuum is a breakout of different indices of recidivism (e.g., official arrest, self-report) in studies of delinquency interventions (Kaufman, 1985).

As shown in Table 25.1, these breakouts were associated with about the same proportion of variance in outcomes as differences in the constructs measured. The small number of meta-analyses contributing to this analysis and the correspondingly large confidence interval for the bootstrap-weighted mean limit any conclusion that can be drawn regarding this matter. However, this indication that different operationalizations of what is presumed to be the same outcome construct within the same treatment domain can lead to quite different results is disconcerting. This finding may be due in part to differential measurement reliability and validity. Hunter and Schmidt (1990) clearly showed the degradation in effect size attributable to measurement unreliability and invalidity.

Source of Information

Related to how an outcome construct is operationalized is the source of the information for the measure, independent of the construct. Several meta-analyses, mostly in mental health, grouped measures by who provided the information, such as self-report, therapist observation, or physiological measurement. These breakouts did not control for the construct measured and, as such, may be confounded. To the degree present, such a confound would inflate the eta-squared. As shown in Table 25.1, the source of the information accounts for slightly less variability in effect size than either the construct or the operationalization of the construct. Given the smaller average magnitude of the eta-squared and its smaller variability relative to that for constructs and operationalizations, it appears that the "who" may be less important than the "what" and "how" of measurement.

Origin of Measure

A final measurement feature examined in many meta-analyses was the origin of the outcome measure, that is, whether it was developed by the researcher or was a preexisting standardized or published instrument. These breakouts were found almost exclusively in meta-analyses of educational interventions and, on average, accounted for slightly less than half as much effect size variance as that associated with different constructs or measurement operationalizations (see Table 25.1). Because these breakouts involved only two categories (researcher developed vs. standardized or published), it was also possible to examine the direction of the effect (see Table 25.2). Researcher-developed measures generally yielded higher effect sizes within a given treatment domain than standardized or published measures. The direction of this effect was as anticipated, favoring tests developed specifically for the research study. Such measures may be more likely to tap the relevant aspects of the construct being changed by the intervention than a published measure that is not necessarily well adapted to the circumstances of a particular intervention.

The range of the mean effect size difference between researcher-developed versus standardized or published measures was quite large (Table 25.3), suggesting that the nature of this relationship is very different indifferent treatment domains. Closer inspection, however, revealed that only 4 of the 27 mean differences were negative, with one outlier of 1.3. The next

TABLE 25.3
Difference Between Mean Effect Sizes
for Study Features That Break Out Into Two Categories

Study feature	M^a	Range	N^b
Measurement feature			
Researcher-developed measure	.13*	−1.3–0.8	27
Design features			
Comparison group type			
No treatment vs. placebo	.13*	−1.0–1.6	23
No treatment vs.	.26*	−1.0–1.6	18
alternative treatment			
Design type			
Random vs. nonrandom	.03	1.1–0.8	80
Comparison vs. pre−post	−.13*	−1.6–0.5	47
Methodological quality	−.06	−.70–.64	41
Sample size	−.18*	−1.0–0.7	65

[a] Bootstrap mean, weighted by the harmonic mean of the number of studies contributing effect sizes to each level of the breakout.
[b] Number of independent meta-analyses contributing an eta-square.
*$p < .05$, based on a confidence interval derived from the standard deviation of a bootstrap distribution.

largest negative value was much less extreme (.36). Thus, the balance of evidence suggests that researcher-developed measures yield larger effects.

Design Features

Effect size breakouts related to study design most often described one of four different study features: type of comparison group, design type, sample size, and methodological quality. Each of these accounted for an average of roughly 2% to 5% of the effect size variance (see Table 25.1).

Type of Comparison Group

One set of breakouts contrasted the mean effect size for studies comparing treatment versus a no-treatment control group with that for studies comparing treatment versus a placebo control group. Another set contrasted the mean effect size for studies comparing treatment versus an alternative treatment. The eta-square value (see Table 25.1) showed that overall, the proportion of effect size variance associated with type of comparison group averaged about 5%; much more variance was associated with treatment-alternative treatment comparisons in the cases in which this breakdown was reported. The direction and magnitude of the relationships, as indexed by the average correlations and mean effect size differences for these breakouts (Tables 25.2 and 25.3), indicate, as expected, that studies contrasting treatment with no treatment yielded higher effect sizes than those that used either a placebo or alternative treatment as the control condition.

Design Type

Breakouts were examined for randomized versus nonrandomized assignment to experimental groups and for comparison group versus one-group pre–post designs. Comparison group designs were either randomized or nonrandomized and are distinguished from one-group pre–post designs in that the latter do not have a control condition. The mean eta-squared for comparison group designs (randomized and nonrandomized) versus the one-group pre–post design was three times that for the randomized versus nonrandomized designs (.06 vs. .02; see Table 25.1). Although the confidence intervals for these two estimates overlapped slightly, the finding suggests that the effect size estimates produced by randomized and nonrandomized comparison group designs are more similar to each other within an intervention area than estimates from either compared with those of one-group pre–post designs.

The mean correlation between randomized (coded 1) versus nonrandomized (coded 0) design type and effect size was .04 (Table 25.2), showing that randomized designs tended to yield slightly higher effect sizes. The magnitude of this effect can be seen in the overall mean effect size difference of .03 (Table 25.3), which was not significantly different from zero. It does not appear, therefore, that nonrandom comparison group type designs are greatly biased on average relative to randomized designs. However, it is important to recognize that the contrast here is between randomized and nonrandomized designs as they occur in typical intervention research. In practice, randomized designs often fall short of the ideal because of differential attrition, contamination of the control group, and other validity threats that degrade the initial randomization. The contrast between studies that were initially randomized versus studies that were initially nonrandomized, therefore, may not represent a large difference in the internal validity actually obtained at the conclusion of the studies. In addition, examination of the ranges for the correlations and the mean effect size differences (see Tables 25.2 and 25.3) shows that there was often substantial bias associated with nonrandomized designs within specific treatment domains. Thus, nonrandomized designs may yield quite different observed effects relative to randomized designs, but the difference is almost as likely to represent an upward as a downward bias.

The bias of one-group pre–post designs relative to comparison group designs was examined by combining the effect sizes from the randomized and nonrandomized designs, when reported separately, into a single category and contrasting it with the mean effect size for the one-group pre–post designs. The correlation between these two categories and effect size was .08 (see Table 25.2), and the mean magnitude of the effect size difference was about

.13 (see Table 25.3). The one-group pre–post design, therefore, generally overestimates treatment effects relative to comparison designs, and in some treatment domains, the bias is quite large.

Methodological Quality

Breakouts on the quality of study methods as rated by the meta-analysts in their coding were also examined, but these focused heavily on internal validity and, hence, overlapped the issue of type of design. Features that were coded in those ratings included type of assignment (e.g., P. A. Cohen, 1980), degree of differential attrition (e.g., Samson, Borger, Weinstein, & Walberg, 1984), and equivalence of groups at pretest (Sweitzer & Anderson, 1983). The effect size breakouts by method quality accounted for roughly 2% of the variability in study outcome (see Table 25.1). The direction and magnitude of bias associated with poorer quality studies represented in the correlation between method quality ratings and effect size (see Table 25.2) were slightly negative but nonsignificant; higher quality studies tended to have smaller effect sizes. The mean effect size difference between the high- and low-quality categories (see Table 25.3) showed the same pattern, also nonsignificant. This null finding is counter to the general belief that low method quality leads to biased results. It appears that low method quality functions more as error than as bias, reducing the confidence that can be placed in the findings but neither consistently over- nor underestimating program effects.

Sample Size

Beyond the small sample bias for effect size statistics demonstrated by Hedges (1981), we would not expect studies that varied in sample size, other things equal, to produce different effect sizes, only a difference in the precision with which those effect sizes were estimated. However, Table 25.1 shows that sample size was associated with about 4% of the effect size variability across studies within a treatment domain. Furthermore, the correlation and mean effect size difference (Tables 25.2 and 25.3) indicated that larger samples tended to yield smaller effects. The small sample bias demonstrated by Hedges cannot account for this difference; it is negligible in sample sizes above 20, and the great majority of studies in the sample size breakouts used larger samples than that.

A plausible explanation is that smaller studies may represent more tightly controlled implementations and evaluations of interventions and thus are more homogeneous with regard to both respondent populations and treatment delivery (Yeaton & Sechrest, 1981). This homogeneity would mean less variability on the dependent variable within a study and possibly stronger effects, with a corresponding increase in observed effect sizes. It is also possible that the differences associated with sample size reflect publication bias. Larger studies have greater power to detect small effects, and statistically significant findings may have greater likelihood of being submitted and accepted for publication. Published studies, in turn, are easier to locate and thus likely to be overrepresented in meta-analyses (Begg, 1994; Kraemer, Gardner, Brooks, & Yesavage, 1998; Lipsey & Wilson, 1993).

A Composite Model of Treatment Effect Estimates

Early in this article, a simple model was proposed in which observed intervention effects were viewed as a function of (a) substantive features of the intervention under study (e.g., treatment type, respondent characteristics), (b) features of the study methods (e.g., research design), and (c) stochastic error, particularly sampling error. The analyses reported here provide rough estimates of the proportions of observed effect size variance contributed by various specific substantive and methodological study features. We turn now to the task of combining that information to generate an order-of-magnitude estimate of the overall proportion of effect size variance associated with the interventions being studied relative to that stemming from other sources.

To accomplish this, we first identified those variance sources from the prior analysis that involved substantial conceptual overlap and selected the one with the broader scope. For instance, under measurement features (see Table 25.1), "source of information" and "researcher-developed measure" are not likely to be orthogonal study features, and both, in turn, are likely to be related to "operationalization." In this case, we judged measurement operationalization to cover the broadest range of measurement variations and dropped the other two categories from consideration. Similarly, under treatment features, we dropped the "treatment component" category in favor of the more global representation in "treatment type." For respondent features, no single category is more encompassing than the others, so, for this case, we simply averaged the eta-square values across all of them.

For summary purposes, we assume, rather generously, that there is little covariation among the eta-square indices for the conceptually distinct categories or, at least, that any covariation is not highly disproportionate across pairs of categories. On that basis, we can construct a rough estimate of the relative proportions of variance associated with substantive and methodological study features by adding together, within these respective groupings, the mean proportion of variance associated with each of the selected study features (Figure 25.1).

An overall estimate of the proportion of effect size variance attributable to subject-level sampling error was derived from 117 meta-analyses that reported sample size information for the studies included in the analysis. Across these meta-analyses, sampling error accounted for as little as 1% of the variance and as much as 100%. The mean was 26%, with the 25th and 75th percentiles at 7% and 39%, respectively. Thus, within the typical treat-

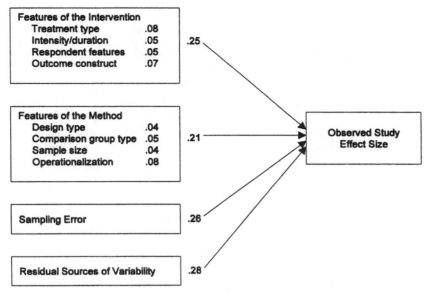

Features of the Intervention
Treatment type   .08
Intensity/duration   .05
Respondent features   .05
Outcome construct   .07

Features of the Method
Design type   .04
Comparison group type   .05
Sample size   .04
Operationalization   .08

Sampling Error

Residual Sources of Variability

.25

.21

.26

.28

Observed Study Effect Size

Figure 25.1. Proportion of variance in observed study effect size explained by selected study features.

ment domain represented in this sample, about 25% of the observed variability in effect sizes can be attributed to sampling error associated with the study-level subject samples.

With the different average proportion of variance estimates grouped according to whether they are related to substantive features of the intervention, methods, or sampling error, more than 70% of the effect size variance was represented in the composite model. The remainder constituted a residual category and was included as such for completeness. The resulting composite model is presented in Figure 25.1. As an initial estimate of the relative influence of various study features on observed outcomes, we believe this model has heuristic value, but of course, it is necessarily approximate. The inclusion of additional study features and better estimation of the statistically independent contribution of each feature to the variance in observed effects would almost certainly change the model to some unknown extent.

Some credibility is lent to the estimates in Figure 25.1 by virtue of their surprising similarity to the results from a very thorough partitioning of the effect size variance within a single meta-analysis of more than 400 studies of intervention with juvenile delinquents (Lipsey, 1992, 1997). Using multiple regression analysis to estimate the independent contribution of different groups of study features, Lipsey found that characteristics of the treatments, such as treatment type, dosage, and client type, accounted for only 22% of effect size variability. About 25% of the variance was associated with method features (e.g., group equivalence, control type, attrition, and measurement characteristics), and sampling error accounted for 27%. These results have less generality than those shown in Figure 25.1, because they are based on 1 meta-analysis rather than 319. On the other hand, they provide a more complete accounting of study features and better estimates of their independent contributions to effect size variance. The relatively close agreement between these two attempts to partition across-study effect size variance provides some assurance that the model presented in Figure 25.1 provides a reasonable, albeit approximate, summary of the relative influence of different groups of study features on the observed outcomes.

Perhaps the most striking aspect of the summary constructed in Figure 25.1 is the rough parity between the proportion of effect size variance associated with substantive features of the intervention and that associated with features of the study methods. This suggests that methodological choices made by the researcher have nearly as much influence on observed effect sizes as the features of the intervention phenomena under study. Moreover, although the residual category is unlikely to entirely represent variance associated with undocumented substantive study features, even if a large portion of it did, the total would still be surprisingly modest; only about half the variation in observed outcome would then be associated with differences in substantive intervention characteristics.

The rather large role of sampling error in observed study effects is also notable. It accounts for roughly 25% of the total variability, which is quite large relative to the portion associated with substantive features of the intervention. This indicates that for any substantive study feature to influence an observed effect, it must compete not only with distortions associated with study method but with considerable noise from sampling error.

DISCUSSION

This study started with the question, What is the role of method in treatment effect estimates? More specifically, what is the influence of method features relative to substantive features on observed study outcomes? Ideally, we would have found that the typical range of methods used by researchers was associated with little variation in observed effect sizes relative to that associated with substantive features of the intervention. Although the effect size variability attributable to specific methodological and measurement features was small to modest on average (e.g., eta-squares ranging from .02 to .10), that attributable to substantive features was of similar magnitude. Thus, the effect sizes observed in a typical treatment effectiveness study are in large part a function of method and sampling error. Viewed as a signal-to-noise ratio, the signal is relatively small and the random and nonrandom noise is relatively large.

Implications for Treatment Effectiveness Research

The indications of substantial instability in observed treatment effects found in the analyses presented here have particular importance for the interpretation of the findings from a single study. If the magnitude of the effect observed in the study is mainly a reflection of specific design and measurement choices, plus a substantial random component, different findings between studies are as likely to be the result of method differences or random variation as the result of substantive differences. Thus, a single study will not typically provide a trustworthy indication of the effectiveness of a particular treatment (Schmidt, 1992, 1996). Until the stability and generalizability of an effect across acceptable study methods and samples are established, evidence about a treatment effect is weak.

Within the inherent limits of a single study, one important design element is the procedure for assigning participants to experimental conditions. The benefits of random assignment for ensuring internal validity are well known, and the randomized clinical trial is generally viewed as the ideal design for assessing the effectiveness of an intervention (e.g., Boruch, 1997; Cook & Campbell, 1979). It was, therefore, surprising to find virtually no difference, on average, between the results from nonrandomized comparison group designs and those from randomized designs. Nonetheless, this finding cannot be interpreted as evidence for the equivalence of randomized and nonrandomized designs for providing estimates of treatment effects. A more likely explanation is that within some treatment domains the selection bias in one nonrandomized comparison is offset by an opposite bias in another such comparison. Cook and Leviton (1980) argued that it is plausible that selection bias acts as error rather than bias in many treatment domains, neither consistently over- nor underestimating effect sizes. A balanced distribution of selection biases across studies is by no means assured in any treatment domain, however, and large differences between random and nonrandom comparison group designs were found in some of the meta-analyses examined here. Similar differences were found by Heinsman and Shadish (1996) in four selected treatment domains they analyzed very closely. They found that randomized designs produced larger average effects than nonrandomized designs, although this difference was substantially reduced when they controlled for other study differences.

In a similar spirit, LaLonde and Maynard (1987) and Fraker and Maynard (1987) compared effect estimates from an experimental study of an employment training program with that from a quasi-experimental study. They found that not only did the quasi-experimental study produce different results but the results varied with the statistical model used. Thus, within the employment training domain, a quasi-experimental design produced results inconsistent with the findings from a randomized study even when using sophisticated statistical methods. On the other hand, in the classic case of the field trials for the Salk polio vaccine, a randomized clinical trial and a quasi-experimental design component found similar positive effects (Francis et al., 1955; Meldrum, 1998). A nonrandomized design will be vulnerable to selection bias, but whether significant bias typically occurs is an empirical question. The meta-analytic evidence currently available on this point is far from conclusive but does suggest that selection bias need not be large relative to the many other influences on the magnitude of a treatment effect estimate.

In any event, it is worth noting that although the proportion of variance associated with design type is smaller than that associated with most of the substantive features of the intervention (Table 25.1 and Figure 25.1), it is not a great deal smaller. Design type, therefore, generally contributes a significant amount of "noise" relative to the "signals" the researcher is attempting to detect. What is perhaps more interesting is that the way outcome measures are operationalized appears to be associated with at least as much variation in observed effects as type of design. Indeed, the estimates in Table 25.1 and Figure 25.1 show that the operationalization has a larger relationship with effect size than either of the two design features examined (design type and comparison group type). The number of meta-analyses reporting effect size breakouts according to how the outcome measure was operationalized, however, was much smaller than the number reporting about design type, so the resulting mean eta-squares estimate has a more limited empirical basis.

Nonetheless, the suggestion that the operationalization of the outcome variable may have as much influence on the study findings as the method of assignment to conditions raises important questions that warrant further investigation. Issues related to the quality and appropriateness of outcome measurement are not extensively discussed in the literature on experimental methods for studying treatment effectiveness. Correspondingly, the selection of the operationalization for the dependent variable is generally not discussed or explained in any depth in reports of treatment research. These practices are consistent with the assumption that this matter is not especially problematic and, hence, need not receive great attention in the design of the research. The findings presented here from those meta-analyses that break out effect sizes for different operationalizations of an outcome variable give a contrary indication; this matter may be quite problematic and could well deserve considerably more attention from researchers and methodologists.

Implications for Meta-Analysis

The findings presented here suggest that outcomes observed in a treatment study are, to a considerable extent, a function of specific features of the study methods and often of rather specific features of the intervention itself. Under these circumstances, meta-analysis is not only a relatively precise and effective way to summarize the findings of a body of treatment research and, in the process, gain the statistical power advantages of the combined sample size of the constituent studies but also the means by which the generalizability and stability of those findings are investigated and the respective influence of method, substance, and stochastic error is disentangled in the assessment of treatment effects (Cook, 1993).

One straightforward implication of this situation is the importance of meta-analysts attending to between-study differences and using appropriate analytic frameworks to assess them (e.g., Hedges & Olkin, 1985; Hunter & Schmidt, 1990). Mean effect size values, or breakouts only for major treatment types and outcome constructs, without examination of the amount and sources of variation in the effect sizes contributing to those means, may be very misleading if interpreted as treatment effects. Moreover, this task must be approached in a sophisticated way using multivariate analysis to help disentangle the relationship of different study features, especially method features, with effect sizes. This is critical given the correlational nature of meta-analytic data. Design features and outcome operationalizations are often related to treatment type, duration, respondent characteristics, and other such substantive features of the intervention. Differences in mean effect size that are observed between, for example, different treatment types may actually result from differences in method that are confounded with those treatment types.

Meta-analysis allows for statistical techniques to be used to control for the influence of study method features so that less confounded estimates can be derived for treatment effects. Such controls do not eliminate the possibility that observed differences are a function of unmeasured nuisance variables, but they do reduce the plausibility that the observed effects are the result of confounds with readily identifiable features of study method. Two examples of meta-analyses that applied such techniques to modeled or adjusted-for-method effects before interpreting substantive differences reinforce the conclusion just presented. Lipsey and Wilson (1998) and Shadish (1992) used different approaches to controlling for method features before interpreting substantive differences between mean effect sizes, and both found substantial method effects.

Limitations of This Study

The principal limitation of this study is that of necessity, the study features of interest could be represented only in broad categories. For example, the distinction between randomized and nonrandomized comparison group designs includes a broad range of design types (e.g., randomization with matching, nonrandomization with post hoc matching), and any of these may have greater or lesser attrition subsequent to the assignment. A more differentiated coding and reporting of study features by the meta-analysts whose results were examined here would have permitted a fuller and more detailed accounting of variance sources. This, in turn, might have increased the proportion of variance found to be associated with study features and reduced the unexplained residual variance.

Increased detail and precision could have been attained, of course, if we had coded the contributing studies de novo rather than relying on what was coded and reported in meta-analyses of those studies. As a practical matter, such an effort would have narrower coverage than the 16,525 studies included in the 319 meta-analyses we examined. The broad scope of our approach has the advantages of efficiency and generality but at the cost of less detail.

A second limitation of this study, implicit in the nature of the research process, is that it is correlational and, therefore, unable to test directly the causal influence of study features on observed outcomes. The experiment on experiments described early in this article would be required to support such causal inferences. Using the natural variation of study features within a treatment domain as an analogue to the experiment on experiments is the only practical approach to the research question we have attempted to address, but it has inherent problems. For instance, features of study methods within a treatment domain may well be confounded with substantive differences between studies and may either inflate or deflate the observed relationship between study features and effect size. Because of this possible confounding, a clean partitioning of the effect size variance was not attainable, even for the broad categories of study features we examined. What we have been able to present, therefore, represents a first approximation to the partitioning of effect size variance. More refined estimates will be possible when the practice of meta-analysis gives greater attention to coding and reporting study features and uses more sophisticated techniques for estimating their independent contributions to effect size.

These limitations must also be addressed through better reporting of research methods at the primary study level. Too often the descriptions of methods reported in treatment studies are vague and thus do not allow for careful description and differentiation in meta-analysis coding. Better reporting would enable meta-analysts to code studies into more tightly defined design categories, providing more useful information on the potential biases of specific design choices within that treatment domain. We believe these efforts are justified by the findings presented here. Within the limitations of the current state of study reporting and meta-analysis coding and analysis, these findings give empirical support to the view that the particulars of study method can have as large an influence on the findings as the particulars of the intervention under study and, moreover, that the latter may have far less influence than generally assumed. Better understanding of the nature and magnitude of these influences is essential to improving our methods for studying the effects of psychological, educational, and behavioral interventions.

REFERENCES

References marked with an asterisk indicate studies included in the meta-analysis that were not listed in the Lipsey and Wilson (1993) study.

*Angert, J. F., & Clark, F. E. (1982, May). *Finding the rose among the thorns: Some thoughts on integrating media research*. Paper presented at the meeting of the Association for Educational Communications and Technology, Dallas, TX. (ERIC Document Reproduction Service No. 223-192)

Begg, C. B. (1994). Publication bias. In H. Cooper & L. V. Hedges (Eds.), *The handbook of research synthesis* (pp. 399–409). New York: Russell Sage Foundation.

Boruch, R. F. (1997). *Randomized experiments for planning and evaluation: A practical guide*. Thousand Oaks, CA: Sage.

*Chidester, T. R., & Grigsby, W. C. (1984). A meta-analysis of the goal setting-performance literature. In *Academy of Management Proceedings* (pp. 202–206). Briarcliff Manor, NY: Academy of Management.

Cohen, J. (1988). *Statistical power analysis for the behavioral sciences* (2nd ed.). Hillsdale, NJ: Erlbaum.

Cohen, P. A. (1980). Effectiveness of student-rating feedback for improving college instruction: A meta-analysis of findings. *Research in Higher Education, 13*, 321–341.

Conrad, K. J. (Ed.). (1994). Critically evaluating the role of experiments. *New Directions for Program Evaluation, 63*.

Cook, T. D. (1993). A theory of the generalization of causal relationships. *New Directions for Program Evaluation, 57*, 39–82.

Cook, T. D., & Campbell, D. T. (1979). *Quasi-experimentation: Design and analysis issues for field settings*. Boston: Houghton-Mifflin.

Cook, T. D., Cooper, H., Cordray, D. S., Hartmann, H., Hedges, L. V., Light, R. J., et al. (1992). *Meta-analysis for explanation: A casebook*. New York: Russell Sage Foundation.

Cook, T. D., & Leviton, L. C. (1980). Reviewing the literature: A comparison of traditional methods with meta-analysis. *Journal of Personality, 48*, 449–472.

Cook, T. D., & Shadish, W. R. (1994). Social experiments: Some developments over the past fifteen years. *Annual Review of Psychology, 45*, 545–580.

Cooper, H., & Hedges, L. V. (Eds.). (1994). *The handbook of research synthesis*. New York: Russell Sage Foundation.

Dennis, M. L. (1990). Assessing the validity of randomized field experiments: An example from drug abuse treatment research. *Evaluation Review, 14*, 347–373.

Efron, B. (1982). *The jackknife, the bootstrap, and other resampling plans*. Philadelphia, PA: Society for Industrial and Applied Mathematics.

El-Nemr, M. A. (1980). A meta-analysis of the outcomes of teaching biology as inquiry (Doctoral dissertation, University of Colorado, 1979). *Dissertation Abstracts International, 40*, 5813A. (UMI No. 8011274)

Ferguson, G. A. (1966). *Statistical analysis in psychology and education* (2nd ed.). New York: McGraw-Hill.

Fraker, T., & Maynard, R. (1987). The adequacy of comparison group designs for evaluations of employment-related programs. *Journal of Human Resources, 22*, 194–227.

Francis, T., Jr., Korns, R., Voight, R., Boisen, M., Memphill, F., Napier, J., et al. (1955). An evaluation of the 1954 polio myclitis vaccine trials: Summary report. *American Journal of Public Health, 45*(Suppl.), 150.

Glass, G. V. (1976). *Primary, secondary and meta-analysis of research*. Educational Researcher, 538.

Hays, W. L. (1988). *Statistics* (4th ed.). Fort Worth, TX: Holt, Rinehart & Winston.

Hedges, L. V. (1981). Distribution theory for Glass's estimator of effect size and related estimators. *Journal of Educational Statistics, 6*, 107–128.

Hedges, L. V., & Olkin, I. (1985). *Statistical methods for meta-analysis*. Orlando, FL: Academic Press.

Heinsman, D. T., & Shadish, W. R. (1996). Assignment methods in experimentation: When do nonrandomized experiments approximate the answers from randomized experiments? *Psychological Methods, 1*, 154–169.

*Hembree, R. (1985). Model for meta-analysis of research in education with a demonstration in mathematics education. Effects of hand held calculators (Doctoral dissertation, University of Tennessee, 1984). *Dissertation Abstracts International, 45*, 3087A. (UMI No. 8429597)

*Henk, W. A., & Stahl, N. A. (1984, November). *A meta-analysis of the effect of notetaking on learning from lecture*. Paper presented at the meeting of the National Reading Conference, St. Petersburg Beach, FL. (ERIC Document Reproduction Service No. 258533)

*Horak, W. J. (1985, April). *A meta-analysis of learning science concepts from textual materials*. Paper presented at the meeting of the National Association for Research in Science Teaching, French Lick Springs, IN. (ERIC Document Reproduction Service No. 256629)

*Horonm, P. F., & Lynn, D. D. (1980). Learning hierarchies research. *Evaluation in Education, 4*, 8283.

Hunter, J. E., & Schmidt, F. L. (1990). *Methods of meta-analysis: Correcting error and bias in research findings*. Newbury Park, CA: Sage.

Kaufman, P. (1985). *Meta-analysis of juvenile delinquency prevention programs*. Unpublished master's thesis, Claremont Graduate School, Claremont, CA.

Kazdin, A. E. (Ed.). (1992). *Methodological issues and strategies in clinical research*. Washington, DC: American Psychological Association.

*Klauer, K. J. (1984). Intentional and incidental learning with instructional texts: A meta-analysis for 1970–1980. *American Educational Research Journal, 21*, 323–339.

Kraemer, H. C., Gardner, C., Brooks, J. O., III, & Yesavage, J. A. (1998). Advantages of excluding underpowered studies in meta-analysis: Inclusionist versus exclusionist viewpoints. *Psychological Methods, 3*, 23–31.

LaLonde, R., & Maynard, R. (1987). How precise are evaluations of employment and training programs: Evidence from a field experiment. *Evaluation Review, 11*, 428–451.

Lipsey, M. W. (1990). *Design sensitivity: Statistical power for experimental research.* Newbury Park, CA: Sage.

Lipsey, M. W. (1992). Juvenile delinquency treatment: A meta-analytic inquiry into the variability of effects. In T. D. Cook, H. Cooper, D. S. Cordray, H. Hartmann, L. V. Hedges, R. J. Light, et al. (Eds.), *Meta-analysis for explanation: A casebook* (pp. 83–127). New York: Russell Sage Foundation.

Lipsey, M. W. (1997). What can you build with thousands of bricks? Musings on the cumulation of knowledge in program evaluation. *New Directions for Evaluation, 76*, 7–24.

Lipsey, M. W., & Cordray, D. S. (2000). Evaluation methods for social intervention. *Annual Review of Psychology, 51*, 345–375.

Lipsey, M. W.& Wilson, D. B. (1993). The efficacy of psychological, educational, and behavioral treatment: Confirmation from meta-analysis. *American Psychologist, 48*, 1181–1209.

Lipsey, M. W., & Wilson, D. B. (1998). Effective intervention for serious juvenile offenders: A synthesis of research. In R. Loeber & D. Farrington (Eds.), *Serious and violent juvenile offenders: Risk factors and successful interventions* (pp. 313–395). Thousand Oaks, CA: Sage.

*Luiten, J., Ames, W., & Ackerson, G. (1980). A meta-analysis of the effects of advance organizers on learning and retention. *American Educational Research Journal, 4*, 211–218.

*Luiten, J. W. (1980). Advance organizers in learning. *Evaluation in Education, 4*, 4950.

Lunneborg, C. E. (1985). Estimating the correlation coefficient: The bootstrap approach. *Psychological Bulletin, 98*, 209–215.

*Lyday, N. L. (1984). A meta-analysis of the adjunct question literature (Doctoral dissertation, Pennsylvania State University, 1983). *Dissertation Abstracts International, 45*, 129A. (UMI No. 8409065)

McNemar, Q. (1966). *Psychological statistics* (3rd ed.). New York: Wiley.

Meldrum, M. (1998). "A calculated risk": The Salk polio vaccine fields trials of 1954. *British Medical Journal, 317*, 1233–1236.

*Mento, A. J., Steel, R. P., & Karren, R. J. (1987). A meta-analytic study of the effects of goal setting on task performance: 1966–1984. *Organizational Behavior and Human Decision Processes, 39*, 52–83.

Mooney, C. Z., & Duval, R. D. (1993). *Bootstrapping: A nonparametric approach to statistical inference*. Newbury Park, CA: Sage.

*Moore, D. W., & Readence, J. H. (1984). A quantitative and qualitative review of graphic organizer research. *Journal of Educational Research, 7*, 81–117.

*Ogles, B. M., Lambert, M. J., Weight, D. G., & Payne, I. R. (1990). Agoraphobia outcome measurement: A review and meta-analysis. *Psychological Assessment, 2*, 317–325.

*Parham, J. L. (1983). A meta-analysis of the use of manipulative materials and student achievement in elementary school mathematics (Doctoral dissertation, Auburn University, 1983). *Dissertation Abstracts International, 44*, 96A. (UMI No. 8312477)

*Powell, G. (1980, December). *A meta-analysis of the effects of "imposed" and "induced" imagery upon word recall*. Paper presented at the meeting of the National Reading Conference, San Diego, CA. (ERIC Document Reproduction Service No. 199 644)

*Readence, J., & Moore, D. W. (1981). A meta-analytic review of the effect of adjunct pictures on reading comprehension. *Psychology in the Schools, 18*, 218–224.

*Redfield, D. L., & Rousseau, E. W. (1981). A meta-analysis of experimental research on teacher questioning behavior. *Review of Educational Research, 51*, 237–245.

*Roberts, A. R., & Camasso, M. J. (1991). The effect of juvenile offender treatment programs on recidivism: A meta-analysis. *Notre Dame Journal of Law, Ethics and Public Policy, 5*, 421–441.

Rosenthal, R. (1991). *Meta-analytic procedures for social research* (2nd ed.). Newbury Park, CA: Sage.

Samson, G. E., Borger, J. B., Weinstein, T., & Walberg, H. J. (1984). Pre-teaching experiences and attitudes: A quantitative synthesis. *Journal of Research and Development in Education, 17*, 52–56.

Schmidt, F. L. (1992). What do data really mean? Research findings, meta-analysis, and cumulative knowledge in psychology. *American Psychologist, 47*, 1173–1181.

Schmidt, F. L. (1996). Statistical significance testing and cumulative knowledge in psychology: Implications for training of researchers. *Psychological Method, 1*, 115–129.

Shadish, W. R., Jr. (1992). Do family and martial psychotherapies change what people do? A meta-analysis of behavioral outcomes. In T. D. Cook, H. Cooper, D. S. Cordray, H. Hartmann, L. V. Hedges, R. J. Light, et al. (Eds.), *Meta-analysis for explanation: A casebook* (pp. 129–208). New York: Russell Sage Foundation.

Shadish, W. R., & Ragsdale, K. (1996). Random versus nonrandom assignment in psychotherapy experiments: Do you get the same answer? *Journal of Consulting and Clinical Psychology, 64*, 1290–1305.

Smith, M. L., & Glass, G. V. (1977). Meta-analysis of psychotherapy outcome studies. *American Psychologist, 32*, 752–760.

Stine, R. (1990). An introduction to bootstrap methods: Examples and ideas. In J. Fox & J. S. Long (Eds.), *Modern methods of data analysis* (pp. 325–373). Newbury Park, CA: Sage.

*Stone, C. L. (1983). A meta-analysis of advance organizer studies. Journal of *Experimental Education, 51*, 194–199.

Sweitzer, G. L., & Anderson, R. D. (1983). A meta-analysis of research on science teacher education practices associated with inquiry strategy. *Journal of Research in Science Teaching, 20*, 453–466.

*Tubbs, M. E. (1986). Goal setting: A meta-analytic examination of the empirical evidence. *Journal of Applied Psychology, 71*, 474–483.

Winer, B. J., Brown, D. R., & Michels, K. M. (1991). *Statistical principles in experimental design* (3rd ed.). New York: McGraw-Hill.

*Wood, R. E., Mento, A. J., & Locke, E. A. (1987). Task complexity as a moderator of goal effects: A meta-analysis. *Journal of Applied Psychology, 72*, 416–425.

Yeaton, W. H., & Sechrest, L. (1981). Critical dimensions in the choice and maintenance of successful treatments: Strength, integrity, and effectiveness. *Journal of Consulting and Clinical Psychology, 49*, 156–167.

EVALUATION
IN CLINICAL WORK

26

OUTCOME ASSESSMENT: FROM CONCEPTUALIZATION TO IMPLEMENTATION

MICHAEL J. LAMBERT, JOHN C. OKIISHI,
ARTHUR E. FINCH, AND LYNN D. JOHNSON

Clinicians have remained rather skeptical about the relevance and value of psychotherapy process and outcome research, looking elsewhere for guidance in directing their clinical practice (Talley, Strupp, & Butler, 1994). Although there is a rich database supporting the efficacy of many psychotherapies (summarized by Lambert & Bergin, 1994), health delivery providers in general, and psychotherapists in particular, are being challenged to document the outcome of the treatments they provide to given patients. Much of this documentation is focused on demonstrating that more expensive, time-intensive treatments produce better outcomes than less expensive interventions. Andrews (1995) has argued that the push for outcome research is a worldwide phenomenon independent of any specific payment system. It appears that psychotherapists will be involved in outcome assessment either by choice or by default. Professional psychologists are seemingly well suited to

Reprinted from *Professional Psychology: Research and Practice, 29*, 63–70. Copyright 1998 by the American Psychological Association.

the task of being practitioner–scientists and using outcome assessment to the advantage of their patients.

Outcome assessment has a long history, dating back to the 1930s (see Lambert, 1983, for a review). Early efforts at outcome assessment represented by small, well-controlled studies were driven by psychological theories and scientific considerations (e.g., comparing the effectiveness of behavioral vs. psychodynamic treatment). Outside of clinical trials research, current outcome assessment efforts are driven more by the practical constraints of applied practice and the need for accountability. This typically centers on the administration of standardized rating scales of the self-report variety. Froyd, Lambert, and Froyd (1996) identified the most frequently used scales and procedures in published studies of psychotherapy outcome. Many of these scales have excellent psychometric properties and an abundance of normative data, and many are well suited for measuring patient change (Ogles, Lambert, & Masters, 1996). However, most of these scales are designed for use with specific disorders, such as phobias, eating disorders, and major depression. Unfortunately, the use of many scales, each suitable for only a few patients within a clinician's caseload (e.g., depression scales and anxiety scales), is cumbersome at best. In addition, the cost of using scales on a routine basis can significantly increase health care costs. This is particularly true when outcome assessment is implemented by large managed care companies.

In response to the requests of government agencies, insurance purchasers, and consumers, managed care companies have seized on outcome assessment as a means of dealing with external pressures and have been able to implement outcome assessment processes on a large scale. Because of technological advances, it is now possible to implement computer-based information systems at a reasonable cost with clinical outcomes as the central component (Brown, Fraser, & Bendoraitis, 1995). Such technologically based outcome assessment can play a key role in enhancing patient care. It is our belief that by the turn of the century, clinicians will routinely collect outcome data on their clients, thus adding a bit more science to their art.

DEVELOPMENT OF A LOW-COST, EASY-TO-USE INSTRUMENT

In response to the need for a brief and cost-effective means of assessing patient outcome, we developed an instrument—the Outcome Questionnaire (OQ; Lambert, Hansen, et al., 1996)—that can be used for assessing patient change. This scale was developed in a university-based research program in collaboration with two large-scale managed care corporations. It is similar in format to many existing scales but is distinct in item content in that we sought to measure aspects of patient functioning that had been conceptualized from the point of view of outcome research (Lambert & Hill, 1994). Outcome researchers are consistent in suggesting the need to examine changes in patients' emotional states as well as their level of functioning in society (Strupp, Horowitz, & Lambert, 1997). Patient emotional state is usually conceptualized as the presence or absence of symptoms. Level of functioning is typically conceptualized as adequacy in social role functioning and satisfaction with interpersonal relations. The OQ was designed to measure three areas of patient functioning: symptomatic distress, interpersonal problems, and social role adjustment. It includes not only items assessing the intensity of symptomatic complaints (mainly anxiety and depression), poor interpersonal relations, and dysfunction in social roles but also items measuring positive mental health or quality of life (well-being). The content of the OQ items is consistent with the nature of symptoms found in a broad spectrum of employee assistance program, outpatient, and inpatient client samples. Once the final item pool was reduced to 45 items, the usual reliability and validity studies were conducted.

The data collected supported the idea that the OQ is reliable; test–retest coefficients were in the .70s and .80s and internal consistency in the low .90s. Validity studies suggest high correlations with other measures of symptomatic distress (e.g., Symptom Checklist–90–R; General Severity Index [Derogatis, 1977], $r = .72$; Beck Depression Inventory [Beck, Steer, & Garbin, 1988], $r = .80$) and moderate correlations with measures of interpersonal difficulties and social role adjustment (Inventory of Interpersonal Problems [Horowitz, Rosenberg, Baer, Ureno, & Villasenor, 1988], $r = .60$; Social Adjustment Rating Scale, [Weissman & Bothwell, 1976], $r = .62$; Lambert, Burlingame, et al., 1996; Umphress, Lambert, Smart, Barlow, & Clouse, 1997). Most important, the OQ was found to be relatively stable in nontreated individuals while being sensitive to change in patients undergoing psychotherapy (Lambert, Thompson, Andrews, Kadera, & Eriksen, 1996).

As a means of making use of the OQ easier, the OQ manual and a copy of the questionnaire can be obtained for a nominal fee, and once the user signs a licensing agreement, unlimited copies of the instrument may be made. Patient progress profile sheets are also provided to help clinicians track and display patient progress (see Figure 26.1 for a copy of the OQ and Figure 26.2 for profile sheets). Software solutions for administration and scoring of the OQ have been developed.[1] These programs provide rapid methods for scoring, graphing, and storing patient information, which may then be built into comprehensive clinical information systems (Brown et al., 1995). The advantages of computer-based administration and scoring are many, not the least of which is the time and expense that can be saved when large patient samples are studied. The OQ can be hand-scored without a key and graphed in less than 2 min if necessary.

---

[1] A software package that can be used for administration, scoring, graphing, and storing data may be obtained from Geof Gray, Algorithms for Behavioral Care, 44 Roosevelt Road, Westport, CT 06880; (800) 357-1200.

Outcome Questionnaire (OQ™-45.2)

Instructions: Looking back over the last week, including today, help us understand how you have been feeling. Read each item carefully and mark the box under the category which best describes your current situation. For this questionnaire, work is defined as employment, school, housework, volunteer work, and so forth. Please do not make any marks in the shaded areas.

Name:_____ Age:____yrs.

ID#_____ Sex M☐ F☐

Session #_____ Date___/___/___

	Never	Rarely	Sometimes	Frequently	Almost Always
1. I get along well with others.	4	3	2	1	0
2. I tire quickly.	0	1	2	3	4
3. I feel no interest in things.	0	1	2	3	4
4. I feel stressed at work/school.	0	1	2	3	4
5. I blame myself for things.	0	1	2	3	4
6. I feel irritated.	0	1	2	3	4
7. I feel unhappy in my marriage/significant relationship.	0	1	2	3	4
8. I have thoughts of ending my life.	0	1	2	3	4
9. I feel weak.	0	1	2	3	4
10. I feel fearful.	0	1	2	3	4
11. After heavy drinking, I need a drink the next morning to get going. (If you do not drink, mark "never")	0	1	2	3	4
12. I find my work/school satisfying.	4	3	2	1	0
13. I am a happy person.	4	3	2	1	0
14. I work/study too much.	0	1	2	3	4
15. I feel worthless.	0	1	2	3	4
16. I am concerned about family troubles.	0	1	2	3	4
17. I have an unfulfilling sex life.	0	1	2	3	4
18. I feel lonely.	0	1	2	3	4
19. I have frequent arguments.	0	1	2	3	4
20. I feel loved and wanted.	4	3	2	1	0
21. I enjoy my spare time.	4	3	2	1	0
22. I have difficulty concentrating.	0	1	2	3	4
23. I feel hopeless about the future.	0	1	2	3	4
24. I like myself.	4	3	2	1	0
25. Disturbing thoughts come into my mind that I cannot get rid of.	0	1	2	3	4
26. I feel annoyed by people who criticize my drinking (or drug use). (If not applicable, mark "never")	0	1	2	3	4
27. I have an upset stomach.	0	1	2	3	4
28. I am not working/studying as well as I used to.	0	1	2	3	4
29. My heart pounds too much.	0	1	2	3	4
30. I have trouble getting along with friends and close acquaintances.	0	1	2	3	4
31. I am satisfied with my life.	4	3	2	1	0
32. I have trouble at work/school because of drinking or drug use. (If not applicable, mark "never")	0	1	2	3	4
33. I feel that something bad is going to happen.	0	1	2	3	4
34. I have sore muscles.	0	1	2	3	4
35. I feel afraid of open spaces, of driving, or being on buses, subways, and so forth.	0	1	2	3	4
36. I feel nervous.	0	1	2	3	4
37. I feel my love relationships are full and complete.	4	3	2	1	0
38. I feel that I am not doing well at work/school.	0	1	2	3	4
39. I have too many disagreements at work/school.	0	1	2	3	4
40. I feel something is wrong with my mind.	0	1	2	3	4
41. I have trouble falling asleep or staying asleep.	0	1	2	3	4
42. I feel blue.	0	1	2	3	4
43. I am satisfied with my relationships with others.	4	3	2	1	0
44. I feel angry enough at work/school to do something I might regret.	0	1	2	3	4
45. I have headaches.	0	1	2	3	4

SD IR SR

Total=

Figure 26.1. The Outcome Questionnaire. (Copyright 1996 by American Professional Credentialing Services. Reprinted with permission.)

At this point in scale development, we believe that the OQ is an acceptable self-report measure of patient functioning. It has the advantage of being (a) brief (45 items) and suitable for repeated measurement on a weekly basis, (b) solid psychometrically, (c) sensitive to change over short time periods, and (d) inexpensive (approximately $0.03 per administration).

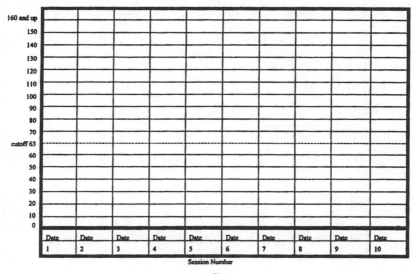

OQ™-45.2
TOTAL SCORE GRAPH WITH NORMATIVE CUTOFF

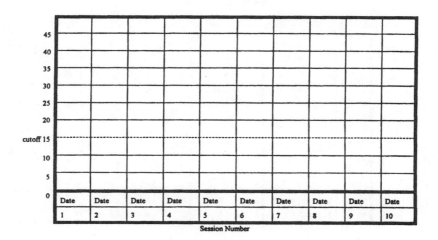

OQ™-45.2
SCALE 2: INTERPERSONAL RELATIONSHIPS (IR) GRAPH
WITH NORMATIVE CUTOFF

American Professional Credentialing Services 1996

Figure 26.2. Outcome Questionnaire profile sheet. (Copyright 1996 by American Professional Credentialing Services. Reprinted with permission.)   (*continued*)

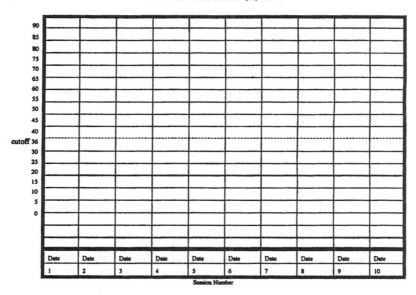

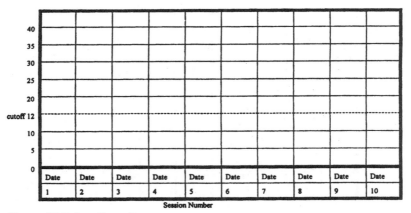

Figure 26.2. (continued)

SETTING A CUTOFF SCORE TO
DENOTE PATIENT IMPROVEMENT

In addition to scale development, it was deemed essential to develop a way of referencing patient status to markers of healthy functioning (cf. Tingey, Lambert, Burlingame, & Hansen, 1996). On the basis of the concepts of social validation (Kazdin, 1977; Wolf, 1978) and statistically derived clinical significance (Jacobson, Follette, & Revenstorf, 1986; Jacobson & Truax, 1991; Jacobson, Wilson, & Tupper, 1988), methods have been developed to set standards for clinically meaningful patient change. The clinical significance methodology allows for the calculation of two specific statistical indexes (a cutoff point between normal and dysfunctional samples and an evaluation of the reliability of the change score) that provide specific guidelines for interpreting patient change. Once a suitable measure appropriate for a wide range of patients was developed, the cutoff point for demarking the dysfunctional range of functioning from the functional range was calculated. Normative functioning was identified by taking the scores of a sample of community volunteers (normals) and patient samples (community mental health center and various outpatient groups) and then applying the Jacobson et al. (1984) formulas for clinically significant change cutoffs and for estimating the reliable change index.

The indexes are provided in the OQ manual and can be used to categorize a patient at any time a posttest is administered (Lambert, Hansen, et al., 1996). The cutoff score for movement into the functional range on the OQ was estimated to be 63. Most patients enter therapy with a raw score of 75 or above. The reliable change index was estimated to be 15. Patients who enter therapy in the dysfunctional range, move below 63 by the end of therapy, and improve by at least 15 points are considered "recovered." Patients who begin therapy in the dysfunctional range and improve by at least 15 points but do not enter the functional distribution are considered "improved." Patients who begin therapy in the functional range (less than 63) and improve by 15 points are also considered improved. All other patients are classified as exhibiting "no change" unless they increase (worsen) by 15 points, in which case they are classified as "deteriorated."

Patient progress can be monitored by referencing scores on the OQ as markers for decision making and patient feedback. An evaluation of patient progress, as made explicit by change from intake OQ score, may assist the clinician in modifying treatment plans and ultimately making decisions regarding termination of treatment. In summary, a satisfactory outcome is defined as clinically significant improvement (i.e., symptomatic recovery, improved intimate relationships, and social role performance) in which the patient has moved from a state of functioning characteristic of people who have a diagnosable disorder to that of the population at large.

In routine clinical practice, the clinician assumes responsibility for data collection. Patients are generally asked to come 10 min early for all appointments to complete the testing. In some health systems, OQ data are collected at intake and after every third or fifth session. However, this procedure necessitates keeping track of the date when the OQ should be readministered and often results in missing data, including possible loss of posttest data for patients who prematurely (or unilaterally) withdraw from treatment before the third session.

AN EXAMPLE OF THE OQ IN CLINICAL PRACTICE

Data from a group practice provider are presented to illustrate the use of this methodology. This psychologist's practice is based on solution-focused brief therapy (Johnson & Miller, 1994), an approach that emphasizes the identification of a problem, collaborative efforts to maintain a focus on the problem, and the limiting of therapy to finding a solution to the problem while maintaining a positive working alliance.

The data presented were derived from 27 consecutive private patients (14 men and 13 women) over the first few months of the therapist's implementation of the OQ for tracking patient progress. The patients' diagnoses were of a wide variety, including dysthymia, anxiety disorders, adjustment disorders, major depression, and substance abuse. Patients ranged in age from 22 to 45 years. They had between two and seven sessions of treatment, completing the OQ before each session. Patients received the OQ from the clinic secretary, who scored it and placed it in the patient's file before each session. Sometimes the scores were discussed with patients, and at other times they were not a part of the treatment sessions, depending on therapist and patient preference.

Table 26.1 contains the pretest, posttest, and final change score for each patient, along with the number of treatment sessions completed and the patient's classification according to the OQ manual protocol previously mentioned. Patients had a mean of 3.1 sessions and a mode of 2 sessions. Patients began therapy with a mean OQ score of 82.1 and ended therapy with a mean score of 60.4; as a group, they began treatment in a score range typical of outpatients in the original normative sample ($M = 83.1$, $SD = 22.2$, $N = 342$; Lambert, Hansen, et al., 1996). Of the 27 patients, 22 (82 percent) began treatment in the dysfunctional range. Of these 22 patients, 10 (46 percent) were considered recovered. An additional 14 percent were considered improved. None of the patients were classified as deteriorated, despite an expected base rate of 5 percent (Lambert & Bergin, 1994).

To facilitate comparison with other clinicians and expectations for recovery, we compared the outcomes of these patients with data reported in a prior study. These data, in combination, allowed us to compare the speed

TABLE 26.1.
Outcome Status for 27 Patients Receiving Psychotherapy

| Patient | Outcome Questionnaire score | | | No. sessions | Outcome |
	Pretest	Posttest	Change		
1	84	82	−2	2	No change
2	67	50	−17	2	Recovered
3	58	34	−24	4	Improved
4	96	99	+3	2	No change
5	90	47	−43	2	Recovered
6	112	26	−86	3	Recovered
7	93	66	−27	3	Recovered
8	94	70	−24	3	Improved
9	103	66	−37	3	Recovered
10	102	91	−11	4	No change
11	66	59	−7	4	No change
12	84	75	−9	7	No change
13	87	16	−71	2	Recovered
14	118	91	−27	3	Improved
15	81	24	−57	2	Recovered
16	88	91	+3	2	No change
17	68	57	−11	5	No change
18	76	79	+3	2	No change
19	83	44	−39	7	Recovered
20	87	86	−1	4	No change
21	90	80	−10	3	No change
22	91	73	−18	3	Improved
23	66	69	+3	2	No change
24	30	21	−9	2	No change
25	79	58	−21	2	Recovered
26	73	41	−32	2	Recovered
27	50	47	−3	4	No change
M	82.1	60.4	−21.3	3.1	
SD	18.8	24.7	22.8	1.4	
Mode				2	

with which this psychologist's patients returned to a state of normal functioning with that of a larger sample of patients treated by 36 clinicians in training who were studied by Kadera, Lambert, and Andrews (1996). The data are presented in Figure 26.3. The horizontal axis is based on the number of sessions completed by a patient. The vertical axis represents the percentage of patients who met criteria for recovery (i.e., they crossed the cutoff and improved by at least 15 points) after the specified number of sessions. If a patient passed the cutoff but then worsened enough to enter the dysfunctional sample, the first session after reentrance into the functional distribution was used as the session recovery point. Patients were considered recovered only if they terminated therapy in the functional range.

Percentage recovered figures were calculated for a sample size of 22 rather than 27, because 5 of the patients treated by the private practitioner

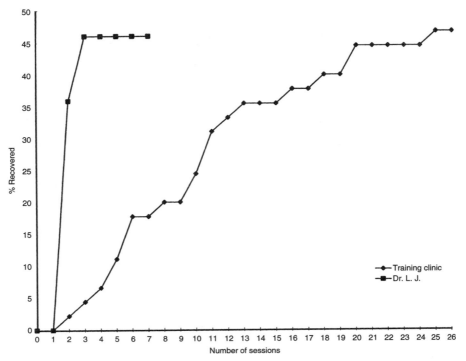

Figure 26.3. Comparison of dose−response curves for 22 patients seen by a specialist in brief therapy and 45 patients seen by a group of 36 trainee therapists. Dr. L. J. = Lynn D. Johnson.

started within the normal range of functioning. Because these 5 patients could not pass the cutoff, they could not meet our criteria for clinically significant change. Kadera et al. (1996) used similar methods for their sample of 45 patients who began in the dysfunctional range (from an original group of 67 patients).

As can be seen, the change noted in the 22 private practice patients treated showed a more rapid recovery curve than the curve produced from patients ($N = 45$) treated by the 36 student clinicians in the Kadera et al. (1996) study. In both studies, no patient met criteria for recovery after a single session of treatment. After two sessions, 36 percent of the private practice patients had met criteria, whereas only 2 percent of the Kadera et al. sample had achieved the same outcome. After seven sessions of treatment, 46 percent of the patients treated in private practice had met criteria, whereas the percentage of patients treated by the students in training had increased to about 18 percent. In fact, the patients treated by student therapists needed almost three times the sessions (21) to reach the final outcome attained by those treated by the private practice therapist.

Of course, the limited number of patients examined in both studies and the lack of random assignment preclude definitive conclusions about the differences that are apparent in these curves. Nevertheless, these data raise interesting questions about the causal factors that produce differences in the speed with which positive outcomes are attained by patients. Although the patients seem to have been equivalent at the beginning of treatment, as measured by OQ pretest scores and diagnostic classifications, there were notable differences between the treatments received by the groups that are worth pursuing in future research. For example, the private practice psychologist was committed to a brief therapy format, gearing his interventions toward immediate problem resolution. The Kadera et al. (1996) therapists offered treatment in a training clinic that exerted no time pressure for completion of treatment. The outpatient university training clinic emphasized an eclectic, time-unlimited treatment approach with individuals who did not have insurance coverage placing a limit on number of sessions. The clinic fees were in the range of $5 to $10 per session; as a result, few clients felt motivated to end treatment because of financial concerns.

In addition, the private practitioner had more than 20 years of experience and was the author of a book on the treatment approach he was offering. The Kadera et al. (1996) therapists, on the other hand, were typically in their 2nd or 3rd year of training in a PhD program. In Figure 26.3 , it appears that the patients in the Kadera et al. sample were approaching the recovery rates found in the private practice sample. And, in fact, by Session 26, the percentage of patients in the Kadera et al. sample who were categorized as recovered had just surpassed 46%. These data suggest that experience may play a primary role in determining the "efficiency" of the outcome rather than the ultimate success of treatment, a finding that has not been explored in the literature on experience, training, and outcome (Stein & Lambert, 1995) and needs considerably more documentation before it can be accepted.

Finally, a majority of the private practice patients received feedback about their improvement on the OQ, whereas none of the Kadera et al. (1996) patients or therapists received any information about OQ scores. The effects of feedback itself have not been studied, making it difficult to know about the kinds of processes feedback sets in motion and their impact on therapist behaviors, patient expectancies, and the like. Future research is clearly needed to explore the consequences of providing and withholding such data from patients as well as therapists. Will providing feedback to patients about their progress enhance therapeutic outcomes? Are there expectancy effects associated with providing feedback (e.g., therapist expectancy for positive changes) that may cause patients to report fewer symptoms than they are, in fact, experiencing?

Among other interesting findings, it is noteworthy that more than half of the patients treated in the private practice setting did not meet the criteria for recovery during treatment, even though they terminated treatment. Would more patients have met criteria for recovery if more sessions had been provided? On average, the private practice patients who recovered had

0.60 sessions after meeting criteria. Did they maintain their gains? Did those who did not meet criteria during treatment eventually "recover" because of the therapeutic contact? What would the costs and benefits be for extending treatment? These and many more questions could be answered or at least investigated if clinicians implemented outcome assessment as part of their routine practice.

Aside from research issues that may affect the practices of clinicians and even theoretical notions about personality and behavior change, there are several issues that have implications for clinical practice. Among these issues is the impact evaluation has for practice in managed care settings. Collecting outcome data enhances clinicians' ability to provide quality assurance data, possibly eliminating routine case review by managed health care organizations. Some clinicians, for example, use the OQ or a similar outcome measure along with satisfaction, utilization, and cost-effectiveness data to reduce or even eliminate outpatient review. Under this practice, when patients return to normal functioning, termination or spacing out of sessions follows; lack of progress results in consultation and revision of the treatment plan; and progress but failure to achieve criteria results in continued treatment.

Of course, use of a single, brief self-report questionnaire is hardly a sufficient method for understanding something as complex as patient change, and many other methods exist for indexing change. Recognizing the limitations and weaknesses inherent in the use of a single, brief self-report scale, we nonetheless recommend this procedure as a place to begin assessing patient improvement. Once this procedure becomes routine, other, more elaborate methods of documenting improvement can be used. A variety of suitable measures have been summarized by Ogles et al. (1996) as well as Sederer and Dickey (1996). Still, the question of balancing data from questionnaires with interviews and individualized goals is a difficult one to answer. What does one do when a patient has obvious problems and meets diagnostic criteria for a disorder but produces a normal score on a brief symptomatic measure? What procedure should be followed when the patient improves on a measure such as the OQ but fails to achieve specific therapeutic goals? Obviously, clinicians should not rely solely on the findings of a single test or single data source.

It may be necessary to emphasize goal attainment or problem solution as primary indicators of progress, rather than self-report measures, with patients who enter treatment with scores that fall within the normal range of functioning but have problems that are clearly in need of treatment. Our own research experience suggests that approximately 15 percent of patients in outpatient treatment, along with 5 percent in community health center populations and 20 percent–25 percent in employee assistance program settings, report functioning in the normal range on standardized tests at intake. Patients may be the best candidates for establishing specific treatment goals for the purpose of evaluating their progress. Although individualized goal may help the clinician index change for a particular patient, this method of measuring outcomes makes comparisons across patients, treatment methods, and clinicians difficult at best (Lambert & Brown, 1996).

CONCLUSIONS

We have identified what needs to be measured, established standards for a "medically sufficient recovery" (clinically significant change), discussed implementation of outcome assessment, and provided an example of use in practice, alluding to some of the limitations in the methodology. If clinicians make the effort to carefully collect and report outcome data that can be compared across clinicians and clinics, we believe that several positive benefits will result: (a) improvement in patient posttreatment status; (b) greater efficiency in treatment effects, with commensurate financial savings; (c) greater autonomy in providing services (both in the short and long term); (d) more input into national, local, and company-based policy decisions; and (e) greater ability to modify intervention strategies in the long run (e.g., having an impact on psychotherapeutic practices and theories). The time is right for grassroots cooperative and collaborative efforts that contribute to the common good. The professional psychologist is ideally skilled and situated to be the central contributor to such efforts.

REFERENCES

Andrews, G. (1995). Best practices in implementing outcome management: More science, more art, worldwide. *Behavioral Healthcare Tomorrow, 4*(3), 19–24.

Beck, A. T., Steer, R. A., & Garbin, M. G. (1988). Psychometric properties of the Beck Depression Inventory: Twenty-five years later. *Clinical Psychology Review, 8,* 77–100.

Brown, G. S., Fraser, J. B., & Bendoraitis, T. M. (1995). Transforming the future — The coming impact of CIS. *Behavioral Health Management, 14*(5), 8–12.

Derogatis, L. R. (1977). *The SCL–90 manual: Scoring, administration, and procedures for the SCL–90.* Baltimore: Johns Hopkins University School of Medicine, Clinical Psychometrics Unit.

Froyd, J. E., Lambert, M. J., & Froyd, J. D. (1996). A review of practices of psychotherapy outcome measurement. *Journal of Mental Health, 5,* 11–15.

Horowitz, L. M., Rosenberg, S. E., Baer, B. A., Ureno, G., & Villasenor, V. S. (1988). Inventory of Interpersonal Problems: Psychometric properties and clinical applications. *Journal of Consulting and Clinical Psychology, 56,* 885–892.

Jacobson, N. S., Follette, W. C., & Revenstorf, D. (1986). Toward a standard definition of clinically significant change. *Behavior Therapy, 17,* 308–311.

Jacobson, N. S., Follette, W. C., Revenstorf, D., Baucom, D. H., Hahlweg, K., &

Margolin, G. (1984). Variability in outcome and clinical significance of behavioral marital therapy: A reanalysis of outcome data. *Journal of Consulting and Clinical Psychology, 52,* 497–504.

Jacobson N. S., & Truax P. (1991). Clinical significance: A statistical approach to defining meaningful change in psychotherapy research. *Journal of Consulting and Clinical Psychology, 59,* 12–19.

Jacobson, N. S., Wilson, L., & Tupper, C. (1988). The clinical significance of treatment gains resulting from exposure-based interventions for agoraphobia: A reanalysis of outcome data. *Behavior Therapy, 19,* 539–552.

Johnson, L. D., & Miller, S. D. (1994). Modification of depression risk factors: A solution-focused approach. *Psychotherapy, 23,* 493–506.

Kadera, S. W., Lambert, M. J., & Andrews, A. A. (1996). How much therapy is really enough? A session-by-session analysis of the psychotherapy dose–effect relationship. *Psychotherapy: Research and Practice 5*(2), 1–21.

Kazdin, A. E. (1977). Assessing the clinical or applied importance of behavior change through social validation. *Behavior Modification, 1,* 427–452.

Lambert, M. J. (1983). Introduction to assessment of psychotherapy outcome: Historical perspective and current issues. In M. J. Lambert, E. R. Christensen, & S. S. DeJulio (Eds.), *The assessment of psychotherapy outcome* (pp. 3–32). New York: Wiley.

Lambert, M. J., & Bergin, A. E. (1994). The effectiveness of psychotherapy. In A. E. Bergin & S. L. Garfield (Eds.), *Handbook of psychotherapy and behavior change* (4th ed., pp. 143–189). New York: Wiley.

Lambert, M. J., & Brown G. S. (1996). Data-based management for tracking outcome in private practice. *Clinical Psychology, 32,* 172–178.

Lambert, M. J., Burlingame, G. M., Umphress, V. J., Hansen, N. B., Vermeersch, D., Clouse, G. C., et al. (1996). The reliability and validity of the Outcome Questionnaire. *Clinical Psychology and Psychotherapy, 3,* 249–258.

Lambert, M. J., Hansen, N. B., Umphress,V., Lunnen, K., Okiishi, J., Burlingame, G. M., et al. (1996). *Administration and scoring manual for the Outcome Questionnaire (OQ-45.2).* Stevenson, MD: American Professional Credentialing Services.

Lambert, M. J., & Hill, C. E. (1994). Assessing psychotherapy outcomes and processes. In A. E. Bergin & S. L. Garfield (Eds.), *Handbook of psychotherapy and behavior change* (pp. 72–113). New York: Wiley.

Lambert, M. J., Thompson, K., Andrews, A., Kadera, S., & Eriksen, K. (1996, June). *The test–retest artifact in estimates of psychotherapy dose–response estimates.* Paper presented at the annual meeting of the Society for Psychotherapy Research, Amelia Island, FL.

Ogles, B. M., Lambert, M. J., & Masters, K. (1996). *Assessing outcome in clinical practice.* New York: Allyn & Bacon.

Sederer, L. I., & Dickey, B. (1996). *Outcomes assessment in clinical practice.* Baltimore: Williams & Wilkins.

Stein, D. M., & Lambert, M. J. (1995). Graduate training in psychotherapy: Are therapy outcomes enhanced? *Journal of Consulting and Clinical Psychology, 63,* 182–196.

Strupp, H. H., Horowitz, L. M., & Lambert, M. J. (1997). *Measuring patient changes in mood, anxiety, and personality disorders: Toward a core battery.* Washington, DC: American Psychological Association.

Talley, P. F., Strupp, H. H., & Butler, S. F. (1994). *Psychotherapy research and practice: Bridging the gap.* New York: Basic Books.

Tingey, R., Lambert, M. J., Burlingame, G. M., & Hansen, N. (1996). Clinically significant change: Practical indicators for evaluating psychotherapy outcome. *Psychotherapy Research, 6,* 109–123.

Umphress, V. J., Lambert, M. J., Smart, D. W., Barlow, S. H., & Clouse, G. C. (1997). Concurrent and construct validity of the Outcome Questionnaire. *Journal of Psychoeducational Assessment, 15,* 40–45.

Weissman, M. M., & Bothwell, S. (1976). Assessment of social adjustment by patient self-report. *Archives of General Psychiatry, 33,* 1111–1115.

Wolf, W. M. (1978). Social validity: The case for subjective measurement, or how applied behavior analysis is finding its heart. *Journal of Applied Behavior Analysis, 11,* 203–214

27

SINGLE-PARTICIPANT RESEARCH DESIGN: BRINGING SCIENCE TO MANAGED CARE

DAVID L. MORGAN AND ROBIN K. MORGAN

During the 1980s and 1990s, health care costs skyrocketed because of advances in technology, an abundance of health care providers in metropolitan regions, and traditional fee-for-service reimbursement mechanisms. Managed care programs were developed as a way to curb these costs. In the process, freedoms historically enjoyed by health care providers have been curtailed. In addition, greater demands have been placed on health care providers to deliver interventions that possess documented effectiveness and to do so in a cost-effective manner (Berman, 2000).

That the managed care revolution has changed the way professional health care providers operate is hardly contestable. The practices of mental health professionals have come under particular scrutiny in a contemporary climate characterized by conflict on many fronts, from confidentiality issues (Acuff et al., 1999, to disputes about treatment duration and reimbursement (Dean, 1998, to fundamental questions about accountability. To a considerable extent, many of the disputes about health care provision hinge on the concept of accountability, or whether the health care provider can document or attest to the clinical usefulness of a particular treatment regimen. Doing so necessarily requires that health care providers be knowledgeable about and make contact with research literature bearing specific relevance to their practice. Historically, this requirement has seldom been met. Although many reasons for this lack of documentation exist, chief among them is the often insurmountable chasm that separates basic research from applied practice (Hayes, 1981; Hilliard, 1993; Marten & Heimberg, 1995; Seligman & Levant, 1998). One concrete example of this dilemma was provided by Sanavio (1998), who argued that behavior therapy (in the form of exposure and response prevention) is a highly effective treatment for obsessive–compulsive disorder. Despite this treatment effectiveness research, research demonstrating the cost-effectiveness of this intervention is virtually nonexistent, and unless behavior therapy can be shown to be as cost-effective and as easily delivered as medication, reimbursement for behavioral treatments by managed care companies may disappear.

It is interesting that just as clinicians have long lamented the inaccessibility or irrelevance of basic research to clinical practice, so too have the basic logic and machinery of psychological research come under scrutiny. A burgeoning contemporary literature attests to a growing disposition on the part of methodologists to place time-honored research designs under the microscope (Abelson, 1997; Cohen, 1990, 1994; Estes, 1997; Harris, 1997; Loftus, 1993, 1996). The results often prove to be less than flattering, particularly in matters of data analysis. Indeed, at a symposium held during the 1996 convention of the American Psychological Association (APA), a group of methodologists and statisticians actually discussed the notion of banning significance tests from APA journals (Shrout et al., 1996)! APA subsequently convened a task force on statistical inference (Wilkinson & the Task Force on Statistical Inference, 1999) to assess and offer recommendations concerning the use of statistical methods in psychological research. The matter is, of course, not resolved, and the dialogue continues in earnest, as most recently manifested in the open peer commentary format of the journal *Behavioral and Brain Sciences* (Chow, 1998). Regardless of the eventual outcome of this debate, the APA meeting and its subsequent fallout would seem, at the very least, to reflect some systematic unrest among researchers concerning psychology's version of the scientific method.

In joining the current dialogue concerning research methodology, in this article we argue that both basic and applied behavioral scientists have at their disposal a richer inventory of data collection and analysis techniques than circumscribed by the null hypothesis testing tradition. Among these techniques, single-participant experimentation boasts both a storied history and a largely unappreciated potential for basic science and professional practice. The single-participant alternative has produced solid and replicable empirical findings across a number of behavioral domains yet remains relatively obscure because of its disavowal of the statistical machinery that defines psychological research in the 21st century. At a time when psychology seems invested in examining how it conducts itself as a science, a critical evaluation of alternative research strategies seems prudent. This article demonstrates the unique epistemology and experimental strategies that distinguish single-participant research and the kinds of contributions that this research tradition can continue to make to the science and practice of psychology, especially for those professionals most affected by the exigencies of managed care.

A BRIEF HISTORY OF SINGLE-PARTICIPANT RESEARCH

Single-participant research is hardly a newcomer to psychology. Indeed, early experimental psychology, borrowing heavily from physiological laboratory methods, usually entailed manipulations of independent variables at the level of the individual participant (Boring, 1929). The subject matter of interest, and the sometimes invasive independent variables manipulated, often mitigated against the use of large numbers of participants. Consequently, data were collected from and presented not in aggregate form, but at the level of the individual participant. Of course, multiple participants actually took part in these studies, although this was done primarily as an exercise in interparticipant replication, not to enhance statistical power.

Even when experimentation turned to more psychological matters, the single-participant strategy served researchers well. Ebbinghaus (1885/1913), as the sole participant in his own research program, conducted the first systematic and thorough analysis of human memory. In doing so, he uncovered fundamental memory principles that remain, for the most part, unchallenged even today. In a similar manner, both classic and contemporary research in psychophysics has relied heavily on the intensive examination of individual perceptual processes, as represented, for example, in the receiver operating characteristics of signal-detection theory (Green & Swets, 1966; Swets, 1973). Finally, Pavlov's (1927) seminal research on the conditional reflex involved intrasubject comparisons of the dependent variable both before and after conditioning.

Perhaps the most ardent support for single-participant research has come from the operant research tradition, referred to by Skinner (1969) as the experimental analysis of behavior. To the behavior analyst, however, the method is more than a collection of experimental practices. Indeed, within the operant literature can be found a sizable and compelling epistemology supporting the single-participant method as a frequently superior alternative to the large-group hypothesis-testing designs familiar to psychologists (Michael, 1974; Sidman, 1960; Skinner, 1953, 1956, 1966). In his autobiography, Skinner (1979) made no bones about his early intentions to reshape both the conceptual and methodological practices of scientific psychology. His revisions left little of the discipline untouched, and his rejection of group designs and inferential statistics was particularly notable for its intransigence. In addition to Skinner's writings, Sidman's (1960) groundbreaking text, *Tactics of Scientific Research*, still considered the bible of operant methodology, served both as a model for conducting research and as a convincing argument for the advantages of single-participant methodology. Finally, in 1958, operant researchers at Columbia University and Harvard University contemplated establishing a journal that would be more appropriate for their manuscripts:

> We had trouble getting our reports published in the regular journals. We used very small numbers of subjects, we did not "design our experiments" with matched groups, our cumulative records did not look like learning curves, and we were asking questions (for example, about schedules) that were not found in the "literature." (Skinner, 1987 p. 447)

Despite the unprecedented control that these researchers had shown over the behavior of their participants, journal editors were reluctant to accept the research, most often because the designs were not standard group designs and because the data analysis was not informed by inferential statistics. Thus, in 1958, in an effort spearheaded by Charles Ferster, this fledgling group of scientists founded *The Journal of the Experimental Analysis of Behavior*, a forum devoted exclusively to presenting experimental data from individual organisms. It is interesting that this focus on individual-organism research remains the distinguishing feature of the journal today, regardless of the conceptual or theoretical framework characterizing the research.

The single-participant research design, then, has a rather lengthy history in the behavioral sciences, certainly more substantial than would be gleaned by perusing many contemporary textbooks on research methods in psychology. Moreover, the method was used by many of psychology's pioneers and across a rather diverse collection of research programs. Nevertheless, if one takes today's research design textbooks as reflective of the field, the single-participant method remains a relatively obscure option possessing little of the scientific rigor inherent in the more conventional group designs (Dermer & Hoch, 1999).

There are undoubtedly various reasons why single-participant methodology receives scant attention in serious discussions or writings on method in psychology. Perhaps paramount among these reasons is the uneasy fit between conventional inferential statistics and the data generated by single-participant studies. The issue is a complicated one, and little consensus has emerged regarding the appropriate method of analyzing sequential response data that, when obtained from a single organism, contain substantial serial dependency or autocorrelation (Bengali & Ottenbacher, 1997; Huitema, 1986). This serial dependency can increase the probability of both Type I and Type II errors in the interpretation of single-participant data (Sharpley & Alavosius, 1988). It is fortunate that researchers are aware of the problems inherent in analyzing such data, and a sizable literature has been devoted to exploring the role of both traditional and nontraditional inferential statistics in single-participant research (Franklin, Allison, & Gorman, 1997; R. R. Jones, Vaught, & Weinrott, 1977), including contemporary discussions of effect size estimation (Kromrey & Foster-Johnson, 1996) and meta-analysis (Baron & Derenne, 2000; Faith, Allison, & Gorman, 1997; Kollins, Newland, & Critchfield, 1999). In fact, at least one past associate editor of *The Journal of the Experimental Analysis of Behavior* reported an increase in the percentage of submitted manuscripts in which inferential statistics were used (Ator, 1999). At the very least, this may be interpreted as an increased awareness among researchers that inferential statistics may prove useful to single-participant researchers.

However, many single-participant researchers continue to justify the graphic display and visual analysis of such data, with little interest in formal null hypothesis testing (Hopkins, Cole, & Mason, 1998; Michael, 1974; Parsonson & Baer, 1986; Perone, 1999). These scholars argue that the data from an individual participant behaving under well-specified conditions should provide unequivocal evidence of an independent variable's effect and that such an effect should be visible to the naked eye. For Skinner (1969) the matter was hardly a contentious one:

> Unlike hypotheses, theories, and models, together with the statistical manipulations of data which support them, a smooth curve showing a change in probability of response as a function of a controlled variable is a fact in the bag, and there is no need to worry about it as one goes in search of others. (p. 84)

But it is not only the analysis and interpretation of data in single-participant studies that differ from traditional group designs. The method of data collection is similarly unorthodox and foreign to psychologists who have cut their methodological teeth on standard group designs. In an engaging and informative account of his development as a scientist, Skinner (1956) traced his growing frustration with large-*N* studies driven by statistical inference. Not only did group means obscure the orderly and systematic development of a behavioral repertoire in an experimental animal but the requirement of manipulating variables in dozens of separate experimental cubicles proved impractical and stifled attempts at following up on interesting functional processes as they were identified. "No matter how significant might be the relations we actually demonstrated, our statistical Leviathan had swum aground. The art of the method had stuck at a particular stage of its development" (Skinner, 1956, p. 228).

Perhaps also because Skinner reported to graduate school at Harvard University without prior schooling in psychology, he was lacking any formal indoctrination in the discipline's growing enchantment with Fisherian designs. In fact, his early years were spent in William Crozier's physiology laboratory, where he came to appreciate the experimental control and precise measurement strategies common to the natural sciences. Skinner was generally unimpressed with psychology at Harvard, prompting the following proclamation in a letter to a close friend: "I have almost gone over to physiology, which I find fascinating. But my fundamental interests lie in the field of Psychology, and I shall probably continue therein, even, if necessary, by making over the entire field to suit myself" (Skinner, 1979, p. 38). Nor would he waste much time redesigning the methods of experimental psychology that he found so wanting, in the process borrowing from Pavlov, whose impressive experimental achievements stemmed from a rigorous control over his subject matter and the observation of lawful behavioral principles in individual organisms. Pavlov's experimental method seemed to Skinner to be not only applicable to behavior as a subject matter but also consistent with his conceptual position that psychology was, in fact, a natural science.

Other sciences provided additional contributions to Skinner's developing methodology. From physical chemistry, he incorporated the concept of a steady state, which would prove invaluable to the experimental analysis of behavior. Skinner (1956) chose response rate as his primary dependent measure, and when behavior was observed repeatedly over long experimental sessions, it became possible to ascertain a steady state, as reflected in minimal variability and no discernible upward or downward trend in response rate. This strategy allowed for sensitive comparisons of steady-state responding under a preintervention or "baseline" phase and response rates during subsequent treatment phases. The steady-state strategy would eventually prove itself a powerful design feature not only in the context of both basic conditioning and psychophysical research but also in the then embryonic fields of behavioral pharmacology (Boren, 1966; Dews & Morse, 1961) and behavior therapy (M. C. Jones, 1924; Lindsley, Skinner, & Soloman, 1953; Wolpe, 1958). Of course, the strategy requires nearly continuous contact with one's subject matter and repeated measurement of dependent variables. Although this may at times be a tall order, the subject matter calls for nothing less. Both Skinner (1956) and Sidman (1960) were adamant about the importance of using research strategies that adequately captured the natural dimensions of the subject matter, and discrete group means seemed poorly suited to capturing the continuity of behavioral processes.

As a variant in research methodology, single-participant designs possess unambiguous advantages, if one is interested in the development of behavior in a single organism over time. Although this is not the explicit aim of all research in psychology, or the behavioral sciences in general, such a goal would seem to be endorsed, if perhaps unwittingly, more than might be acknowledged. In fact, at an applied level, it is seldom the case that treatment objectives center on how group averages respond to manipulated variables and interventions. For parents, teachers, therapists, and others charged with changing behavior, the individual ordinarily constitutes the unit of analysis, and change makes itself known only through multiple measures taken over prolonged observational periods. The single-participant design evolved because it allowed for a sensitive assessment of developing behavioral repertoires, which remains its primary advantage, whether realized in the basic laboratory or in clinical settings.

FEATURES OF SINGLE-PARTICIPANT DESIGNS

The phrase *single participant* is, of course, misleading if it is interpreted to mean that such an experiment involves only one participant. The essence of single-participant experimentation is simply that all dependent measures are collected repeatedly over the course of the experiment, and these data are not combined with those from other participants to produce group averages for data analysis. In most such experiments, data are collected from a handful of participants, although the numbers clearly do not begin to approach the large sample sizes expected of group designs. With proper controls and experimental manipulations, numerous intra- and interparticipant replications can be conducted with a small number of participants, allowing for strong inferences concerning functional relationships between behavior and its controlling variables.

Repeated Measures

Loftus (1996) has argued that psychology's slow progress as a science can be traced in large measure to the way we analyze and interpret data:

> What we do, I sometimes think, is akin to trying to build a violin using a stone mallet and a chain saw. The tool-to-task fit is not very good, and, as a result, we wind up building a lot of poor quality violins. (p. 161)

It is not, however, the data-analytic process alone that differentiates psychology from other sciences but the very conditions under which data are collected in the first place. Many observational strategies in psychology rely on a single observation of the dependent variable. The poor "goodness of fit" between this discrete measurement practice and a temporally dynamic subject matter is equivalent to underusing the resolving power of a microscope. In contrast, the single-participant design epitomizes the concept of repeated measures and, in so doing, inverts the measurement practices of group designs. Whereas the strategy in group research usually involves one or two dependent measures from a large sample of participants, single-participant research uses frequent and continuous measurement of the dependent variable from individual participants. This strategy is justified on two grounds. First, numerous measures of a participant's behavior increase the experimenter's confidence that the sample of behavior being measured is representative of that participant under those experimental conditions. This logic is not entirely unlike that attached to sampling issues in group designs, although the referents of such terms as sample and population are clearly markedly different in single-participant research. Second, repeated measures are considered a natural consequence of an epistemology that conceptualizes behavior as a continuously unfolding phenomenon. Behavior exhibits considerable serial dependence, and to be scientifically viable, observational and measurement schemes must make sufficient contact with this dimension of the subject matter. Computing measures of central tendency on dependent variables obtained from a single, discrete observation may be logistically convenient, but it compromises unnecessarily the natural dimensions of the subject matter.

Participants Serving as Their Own Controls

Similar to participants in within-participant group designs, participants in single-participant designs serve as their own controls, with comparisons being made across experimental conditions. But individual differences make no contribution to the variance in single-participant designs because no comparisons are made across participants. A participant's behavior in one phase of the experiment is compared with his or her own behavior under other phases, not with the behavior of other participants. This is viewed as the only relevant comparison, because in most natural settings, the question will be whether an individual's behavior has changed relative to his or her own baseline, not relative to that of another person. Indeed, the phrase *behavior change* assumes little meaning at the group level. In evaluating, for instance, whether a speech therapy intervention has been effective for a child, one needs to know how the child's speech after therapy compares with his or her speech before therapy, not how much the child's speech deviates from a statistically derived group average. It is difficult to envision a clinical application, at least within psychology, medicine, or other service-oriented disciplines, for which the purported goal is the alteration of group means. As a result, professionals in applied disciplines have come to recognize the limitations of standard group designs and the inherent logic and meaningfulness of single-participant designs to health science research (Elder, 1997; Ottenbacher, 1992; Perrin, 1998). This point was particularly well made by Lundervold and Bellwood (2000):

> Group experimental design methodology by definition is insensitive to the exigencies of everyday practice. Although group experimental design methodology is appropriate for technique testing, counseling practice is primarily concerned with the development of techniques that are effective for the individual case or technique building. Consequently, it is ironic that a research methodology, single-case ($N = 1$) design, developed for use in practice settings and capable of evaluating counseling process, evaluating counseling intervention outcomes, and demonstrat-

ing experimental control, continues to be the "best kept secret" in counseling. (p. 78)

Emphasis on Experimental Replication

The role of replication in scientific endeavors can hardly be overestimated. The self-corrective nature of science, often lauded as being one of the
advantages of science as a method of inquiry, depends on the ability to establish the reliability of discovered functional relationships, and replication
plays a crucial part in this agenda. Replication studies, however, are often hard to come by in the behavioral sciences, particularly certain areas of
"soft psychology" (Meehl, 1978). The practical exigencies of repeating a
study requiring large samples of participants may often preclude such work.
Without substantial resources, including monetary support, a replication involving hundreds, or perhaps thousands, of participants is an unlikely event.
This is unfortunate because it is precisely in such research areas, in which experimental controls are often lacking and variable definition and measurement exhibit considerable interstudy variability, that replication serves its
most useful purpose.

Single-participant research, in contrast, not only allows for but also
is in fact defined in part by its reliance on replication. The reliability of an
independent variable manipulation often can be evaluated through simple
intraparticipant replication across several phase changes in a single experiment. Replication is ordinarily done by alternating baseline (nontreatment) and treatment conditions. Of course, such reversal, or ABA, designs
are not always feasible for ethical or logistical reasons. Many kinds of behavior, particularly changes produced through learning, do not simply go away
or reverse once treatment is removed. When this is the case, interparticipant
replication becomes a viable option, most commonly through a multiple-
baseline strategy. Although there are several versions of the multiple-baseline
design (see, e.g., Kazdin, 1994), perhaps the most common entails repeated
implementation of treatment across several participants but after differing
baseline durations. The staggered manner in which treatment is implemented
controls for the kinds of threats to internal validity that are otherwise common in pretest–posttest designs. Thus, as a means of demonstrating interparticipant replication, the multiple-baseline design allows for strong causal
inferences, especially as the number of replications increases. Moreover,
such interparticipant replications are often quite manageable at little additional cost or effort when they are conducted within the context of single-
participant research.

The programmatic manipulation of independent variables, both within
and across participants, has long been the hallmark of research in the experimental analysis of behavior (Skinner, 1966). Moreover, when research is

conducted at the level of an individual participant, replication can be flexible and maximally sensitive to previous experimental findings. Problems that arise, be they methodological or technical, can often be promptly dealt with, and serendipitous discoveries that lead in different directions can be expeditiously pursued. The method is unabashedly inductive and resembles logically the research strategy of the natural scientist. Moreover, the single-participant design is compatible with the idiographic decision making of what Stricker and Trierweiler (1995) called the "local clinical scientist." This flexibility of method is unheard of in large-group designs in which hypothetico–deductive logic places substantial restraints on what will be observed during experimentation and what sorts of inferences can be drawn from the results. As Skinner (1956) suggested, this research mentality necessarily creates a kind of observational myopia whereby results that appear irrelevant to the experimental hypothesis garner little attention, despite the fact that they may bear substantial theoretical or empirical implications.

Graphic Presentation and Visual Analysis of Data

As we mentioned previously, data presentation and analysis in single-participant research differ markedly from data treatment in traditional group designs. The most conspicuous difference is, of course, the presentation of data from individual participants rather than summarized aggregate measures. Moreover, the conventional vehicle for data presentation in single-participant research is the real-time graph, in which dependent variable measures typically appear on the ordinate, and independent variable conditions (often depicted across time) typically appear on the abscissa. Individual data points on such graphs usually depict such measures as response rate and percentage of correct responding.

As we previously discussed, interpretation of single-participant data is seldom informed by the statistical criteria associated with the Fisherian tradition, and the question of how best to fit such data into the Fisherian protocol remains quite contentious (Ator, 1999; Baron, 1999; Branch, 1999; Huitema, 1986; Michael, 1974; Perone, 1999). Single-participant researchers argue that meaningful effects of an independent variable ought to be noticeable on visual inspection, particularly when the full power of the steady-state strategy is used. Thus, visual inspection of dependent measures during independent variable conditions, relative to baseline measures, represents the standard treatment of single-participant data. Rather than endorsing the formal decision criteria of null hypothesis testing designs, single-participant research evaluates behavior change relative to benchmarks provided by participants themselves. In addition, the very process of data presentation and analysis is an ongoing effort in single-participant studies, as opposed to a process that "kicks in" only once the data have been collected, as is more common in group studies. Perone (1999) has argued that the single-participant researcher retains more intimate and continuous contact with the subject matter of interest because of this style of data presentation:

> Skinner, the consummate tinkerer, was quite willing to scout about for new ways to conduct experiments. He rejected group-statistical methods not because they collided with his radical behaviorist epistemology, but rather because his experience revealed that they insulated the investigator from the behavior of the subject. (p. 111)

Treatment of Variability in Single-Participant Research

All scientific pursuits can be conceptualized as attempts to account for variability in the phenomenon of interest. The manner in which this is done differs across disciplinary boundaries, and in its treatment of variability, the single-participant method both methodologically and epistemologically distinguishes itself from group designs in psychology. Among the functions of statistical techniques in group research is the "neutralization" of error variance, a significant portion of which is contributed by individual differences. The fact that such variance is often described in our textbooks as "noise" or "nuisance" variability does much to capture the spirit of the Fisherian approach. Indeed, many statistical procedures, such as analysis of covariance, have been developed for the express purpose of statistically managing variables not targeted for primary analysis. In addition, the very use of measures of central tendency, such as the mean, illustrate a certain discomfort or lack of patience with the variability inherent in natural phenomena.

There is ample justification, however, to be suspicious of attempts to represent complex natural phenomena by means of convenient mathematical abstractions. Gould (1996) offered a compelling argument that in reducing our subject matter to single aggregate measures, we end up neglecting the one irreducible property of all natural phenomena, variability:

> What can be more discombobulating than a full inversion, or "grand flip," in our concept of reality: in Plato's world, variation is accidental, while essences record a higher reality; in Darwin's reversal, we value variation as a defining (and concrete earthly) reality, while averages (our closest operational approach to "essences") become mental abstractions. (p. 41)

Gould's (1996) position is articulated within the context of a discussion of evolution, whose status as science's grand unifying theory emerged only when it was acknowledged that genetic variation served as the raw material on which selective pressures could operate over time. Much of his provocative *Full House: The Spread of Excellence From Plato to Darwin* (Gould, 1996) is a timely scolding of all researchers who forget that variability is nature's originally dealt hand and that mathematical summarization is simply an effort to impose some sense of order, albeit arbitrary, on our observations.

If one begins with the assumption that variability represents the core subject matter of science, rather than an inevitable nuisance to be sidestepped, certain consequences for methodology follow. For the single-participant researcher, variability, as evidenced in the data of a single participant during the course of an experimental phase, is pivotal information about the impact of independent variables over time. The ongoing measurement of dependent variables allows for a sensitive metric of the participant's behavior, often in response to prolonged exposure to experimental conditions. Moreover, such refined assessment may frequently reveal the unintentional effects of extraneous factors when, for instance, behavior shows abrupt and marked deviations from a steady state in the absence of independent variable manipulations. Such deviations from steady-state behavior are always informative about functional relationships and can, in applied settings, prove especially useful in the development and modification of a treatment program. The question of why such variability occurs is an empirical one, which is best pursued through refinements in experimental procedure and, if need be, observational strategies, not through statistical maneuverings that discourage further inquiry.

When one has statistically controlled for a variable, more powerful data analysis may result, but little has been learned about that variable's impact on the subject matter. Experimentally controlling for variables, when possible, requires the researcher to come into direct contact with the relationships that occur between extraneous variables and the behavior of interest. Because these variables do exist and often exert influence outside the confines of a formal study, much can be gained in the process of attempting to control or eliminate such factors. What may be viewed as nuisance factors by the researcher may in fact be variables of unparalleled importance in the participant's natural setting. The single-participant method, owing largely to its flexible nature, renders assessment and control of such variables more feasible than is true of group designs.

The General Applicability of the Single-Participant Method

Perhaps because single-participant research received its most ardent endorsement from Sidman (1960) and Skinner (1966, 1969), the method and its supporting epistemology are viewed as idiosyncratic to the operant tradition. This is unfortunate, however, because the approach is theoretically neutral. Observing moment-to-moment interactions between an organism and its local environment does not commit one to any particular brand of theorizing or conceptual interpretation. Rather, it simply puts one in contact with a different dimension of the subject matter than offered by group designs and summarized measures.

A case in point is Newell and Simon's (1972) groundbreaking text titled *Human Problem Solving*, which details a research program for which rich and informative data could not have been generated by standard group methods. In a manner remarkably similar to Skinner's rejection of group designs, Newell and Simon adopted a research strategy that logically addressed the inherent parameters of their subject matter. Their approach was to ask participants to verbalize every step taken in a problem-solving task—a sort of dialogue or self-narration describing the details of their ongoing strategy. The development of protocol analysis (Ericsson & Simon, 1984) was in fact an important milestone in the study of problem solving, and the data presented in *Human Problem Solving* are culled exclusively from this idiographic process. Curiously absent, however, are the statistical tests and hypothesis-testing conventions long thought necessary to research in the behavioral sciences. It is in fact remarkable how many of psychology's classic empirical contributions were derived from methodological approaches bearing no resemblance to the null hypothesis testing tradition. A veritable "Who's Who" of psychology's luminaries, including Pavlov, Piaget, Ebbinghaus, and Skinner, conducted their very substantial research programs with alarmingly little concern for sample size or alpha levels (Morgan, 1998).

The relevance of research designs targeting development and change in individual behavior has clearly not been lost on professionals who deliver one-on-one services to their clients. Among those currently singing the praises of single-participant methodology are nursing and occupational and physical therapy practitioners (e.g., Backman, Harris, Chisholm, & Monette, 1997; Blair, 1986; Bryson-Brockman & Roll, 1996; Elder, 1997; Ottenbacher, 1992; Sterling & McNally, 1992). For instance, Holm, Santangelo, Brown, and Walter (2000) implemented a single-participant design to investigate the impact of three occupation-based interventions for reducing the frequency of disruptive vocalizations, distraction of others, and withdrawal from appropriate social interaction. The study involved 2 participants, a 17-year-old woman diagnosed with bipolar disorder, intermittent explosive disorder, and mild mental retardation and a 19-year-old woman diagnosed with major depression with psychiatric features, borderline personality disorder, and moderate mental retardation. The occupation-based interventions were implemented across three separate settings (school, a sheltered workshop, and two variations of a community living arrangement) in a multiple-baseline design. Dysfunctional behaviors occurred with less frequency in the school and sheltered-workshop settings than in the community setting.

In a similar manner, Linderman and Stewart (1999) used a single-participant approach to examine the effects of sensory integrative-based occupational therapy on the functional behaviors of two 3-year-old boys with pervasive developmental disorder. Repeated measures were taken during both a two-week baseline and a subsequent treatment phase. Both boys displayed substantial improvement in the areas of social interaction, approach toward new activities, and response to holding or hugging. Conversely, disruptive behaviors decreased in frequency and duration. Both of these studies highlight the unique advantages of the single-participant method. Because behavioral disorders invariably manifest themselves in an idiosyncratic manner, the processes of reliable assessment, treatment development and implementation, and treatment evaluation take on similarly individualistic dimensions. Moreover, group designs intended to identify effective interventions necessarily produce "conditional" knowledge, in that treatment efficacy will ultimately depend on several separate factors, some of which pertain to idiosyncratic client features. These idiosyncratic features, ordinarily beyond the scope of a large group study, are the heart and soul of single-participant designs.

LIMITATIONS OF SINGLE-PARTICIPANT RESEARCH DESIGNS

There is, of course, no reason to suppose that all questions about human experience can be pursued efficaciously only through single-participant methods. The nature of one's subject matter and the particular goals of the research project must inform all design and measurement issues. As we mentioned previously, single-participant designs are most suited to projects in which the unfolding behavioral repertoire of an individual organism is of primary interest. When, instead, one is interested in population parameters for the purpose of establishing social policies or regulations affecting educational, political, or social institutions, then group designs may have considerable usefulness.

Single-participant research is decidedly experimental in its approach. That is, the most powerful use of the method is when independent variables can be manipulated and conspicuous extraneous variables can be effectively controlled. Although such design features are more easily realized in laboratory settings, the method is capable of surprisingly effective exportation to natural settings. In fact, the flexible nature of the strategy and its capacity for rapid adaptation to changes in participants' behavior or setting features make single-participant research especially well suited to applied settings. In addition, the emphasis on ongoing dependent variable observation offers substantial benefits even when, for ethical or practical reasons, variables cannot be purposefully manipulated. The systematic collection of behavioral data under properly specified environmental conditions can provide invaluable information about a participant's behavior and its controlling variables, even in the absence of explicit interventions. Perhaps the most frequently mentioned shortcoming of single-participant (often called small-N) designs is their presumably minimal external validity. Their resemblance to clinical case studies in this regard is seldom ignored by methodology textbook authors who question the usefulness of data generated by a single participant. But the issue of generality is a complicated one, and the full measure of an experimental design cannot be adequately evaluated without a proper stock-taking of the phenomenon in question and the domains across which generality is being evaluated. Nor is the issue conveniently put to rest by the size of one's sample:

> We cannot dispose of the problem of subject generality by employing large groups of subjects and using statistical measures, such as the mean and variance of the groups. It is not true that the larger the group, the greater is the generality of the data. Representativeness is an actuarial problem to which the currently prevalent statistical design is not applicable. (Sidman, 1960 p. 47)

Ottenbacher (1990) has also argued that the formal statistical and probability requirements that are ordinarily considered necessary to ensure external validity almost never eventuate in clinical research. "Given the empirical exigencies associated with most clinical research in rehabilitation, generalizability judgments based on a statistical model are simply not possible or statistically legitimate" (p. 290).

As we previously described, single-participant designs are distinguished by their reliance on both intra- and interparticipant replications. The latter, in particular, serve not only as a reliability check on the particular functional relationship being pursued but also as an assessment of individual differences in its expression. Such replications, a staple feature of the method, are made possible by the ease with which changes in experimental conditions can be made across participants and on short notice. Thus, the generality of a behavioral phenomenon is seen not so much as an exercise in statistical inference but as an experimental practice in which replication allows for a thorough evaluation of generality across independent variable parameters, stimulus conditions, and participant variables.

CONCLUSION

The advent of managed care has led to significant changes in the landscape of health care practice, including a forceful mandate that practitioners be able to document the effectiveness of their clinical interventions. This emphasis on accountability places a premium on the conduct of research in applied settings. Yet the conventional null hypothesis machinery of psychological science is embarrassingly unwieldy in a practice environment, and health care providers consequently perceive themselves as disenfranchised from the business of demonstrating treatment effectiveness. Recently, however, both practitioners and methodologists representing divergent training and theoretical persuasions have questioned the continued uncritical acceptance of the Fisherian strategy within the behavioral sciences. If no alternative methods existed, such criticism would ring hollow. Alternatives, however, do exist, and among them single-participant research has enjoyed documented success in contributing to the empirical database of psychology. The method, rich in history, epistemology, and design power, has remained largely unappreciated because of its poor fit with the logic of statistical inference and deductive hypothesis testing. Its features include an unabashed interest in the development of behavioral repertoires, a staunch declaration that such development is obscured by group measures, and a flexibility of method reminiscent of the natural sciences. These features should be especially appealing to practicing clinicians who are delivering services to individual clients and whose professional responsibilities increasingly include documentation of treatment efficacy.

REFERENCES

Abelson, R. P. (1997). On the surprising longevity of flogged horses: Why there is a case for the significance test. *Psychological Science, 8,* 12–15.

Acuff, C., Bennett, B. E., Bricklin, P. M. Canter, M. B., Knapp, S. J., Moldawsky, S., & Phelps, R. (1999). Considerations for ethical practice in managed care. *Professional Psychology: Research and Practice, 30,* 563–575.

Ator, N. A. (1999). Statistical inference in behavior analysis: Environmental determinants? *The Behavior Analyst, 22,* 93–97.

Backman, C. L., Harris, S. R., Chisholm, J. M., & Monette, A. D. (1997). Single subject research in rehabilitation: A review of studies using AB, withdrawal, multiple baseline, and alternating treatments designs. *Archives of Physical Medicine and Rehabilitation, 78,* 1145–1153.

Baron, A. (1999). Statistical inference in behavior analysis: Friend or foe? *The Behavior Analyst, 22,* 83–85.

Baron, A., & Derenne, A. (2000). Quantitative summaries of single-subject studies: What do group comparisons tell us about individual performances? *The Behavior Analyst, 23,* 101–106.

Bengali, M. K., & Ottenbacher, K. J. (1997). The effect of autocorrelation on the results of visually analyzing data from single-subject designs. *American Journal of Occupational Therapy, 52,* 650–655.

Berman, B. (2000). The academic children's hospital primary care clinic: Responding to the challenge of a changing health care environment. *Clinical Pediatrics, 39,* 473–478.

Blair, C. E. (1986, May). A case for single-subject research in nursing. *AARN Newsletter, 42,* 15–16.

Boren, J. J. (1966). The study of drugs with operant techniques. In W. K. Honig (Ed.), *Operant behavior: Areas of research and application* (pp. 531–564). Englewood Cliffs, NJ: Prentice Hall.

Boring, E. G. (1929). A history of experimental psychology. New York: Appleton-Century-Crofts.

Branch, M. N. (1999). Statistical inference in behavior analysis: Some things significance testing does and does not do. The Behavior Analyst, 22, 87–92.

Bryson-Brockman, W., & Roll, D. (1996). Single-case experimental designs in medical education: An innovative research method. Academic Medicine, 71, 78–85.

Chow, S. L. (1998). Precis of statistical significance: Rationale, validity, and utility. Behavioral and Brain Sciences, 21, 169–194.

Cohen, J. (1990). Some things I have learned (so far). American Psychologist, 45, 1304–1312.

Cohen, J. (1994). The earth is round (p<.05). American Psychologist, 49, 997–1003.

Dean, R. G. (1998). Postmodernism and brief treatment: A more inclusive model. Crisis Intervention and Time-Limited Treatment, 4, 101–112.

Dermer, M. L., & Hoch, T. A. (1999). Improving descriptions of single-subject experiments in research texts written for undergraduates. The Psychological Record, 49, 49–66.

Dews, P. B., & Morse, W. H. (1961). Behavioral pharmacology. Annual Review of Pharmacology, 1, 145–174.

Ebbinghaus, H. (1913). Memory (H. A. Reuger & C. E. Bussenius, Trans). New York: Teachers College. (Original work published 1885)

Elder, J. H. (1997). Single-subject experimentation for psychiatric nursing. Archives of Psychiatric Nursing, 11, 133–138.

Ericsson, K. A., & Simon, H. A. (1984). Protocol analysis: Verbal reports as data. Cambridge, MA: MIT Press.

Estes, W. K. (1997). Significance testing in psychological research: Some persisting issues. Psychological Science, 8, 18–20.

Faith, M. S., Allison, D. B., & Gorman, B. S. (1997). Meta-analysis of single-case research. In R. D. Franklin, D. B. Allison, & B. S. Gorman (Eds.) Design and analysis of single-case research (pp. 245–277). Mahwah, NJ: Erlbaum.

Franklin, R. D., Allison, D. B., & Gorman, B. S. (Eds.). (1997). Design and analysis of single-case research. Mahwah, NJ: Erlbaum.

Gould, S. J. (1996). Full house: The spread of excellence from Plato to Darwin. New York: Three Rivers Press.

Green, D. M., & Swets, J. A. (1966). Signal detection theory and psychophysics. New York: Wiley.

Harris, R. J. (1997). Significance tests have their place. Psychological Science, 8, 8–11.

Hayes, S. C. (1981). Single-case experimental design and empirical clinical practice. Journal of Consulting and Clinical Psychology, 49, 193–211.

Hilliard, R. B. (1993). Single-case methodology in psychotherapy process and outcome research. Journal of Consulting and Clinical Psychology, 61, 373–380.

Holm, M. B., Santangelo, M. A., Brown, S. O., & Walter, H. (2000). Effectiveness of everyday occupations for changing client behaviors in a community living arrangement. *American Journal of Occupational Therapy, 54*, 361–371.

Hopkins, B. L., Cole, B. L., & Mason, T. L. (1998). A criticism of the usefulness of inferential statistics in applied behavior analysis. *The Behavior Analyst, 21*, 125–137.

Huitema, B. E. (1986). Autocorrelation in behavioral research: Wherefore art thou? In A. Poling & R. W. Fuqua (Eds.), *Research methods in applied behavior analysis: Issues and advances* (pp. 187–208). New York: Plenum.

Jones, M. C. (1924). The elimination of children's fears. *Journal of Experimental Psychology, 7*, 383–390.

Jones, R. R., Vaught, R. S., & Weinrott, M. (1977). Time-series analysis in operant research. *Journal of Applied Behavior Analysis, 4*, 45–49.

Kazdin, A. E. (1994). *Behavior modification in applied settings* (5th ed.). Pacific Grove, CA: Brooks/Cole.

Kollins, S. H., Newland, M. C., & Critchfield, T. S. (1999). Quantitative integration of single-subject studies: Methods and misinterpretations. *The Behavior Analyst, 22*, 149–157.

Kromrey, J. D., & Foster-Johnson, L. (1996). Determining the efficacy of intervention: The use of effect sizes for data analysis in single-subject research. *Journal of Experimental Education, 65*, 73–93.

Linderman, T. M., & Stewart, K. B. (1999). Sensory integrative-based occupational therapy and functional outcomes in young children with pervasive developmental disorders: A single-subject study. *American Journal of Occupational Therapy, 53*, 207–213.

Lindsley, O. R., Skinner, B. F., & Soloman, H. C. (1953). *Studies in behavior therapy: Status Report 1.* Waltham, MA: Metropolitan State Hospital.

Loftus, G. R. (1993). A picture is worth a thousand *p* values: On the irrelevance of hypothesis testing in the microcomputer age. *Behavior Research Methods, Instruments, & Computers, 25*, 250–256.

Loftus, G. R. (1996). Psychology will be a much better science when we change the way we analyze data. *Current Directions in Psychological Science, 5*, 161–171.

Lundervold, D. A., & Bellwood, M. F. (2000). The best kept secret in counseling: Single-case (large $N = 1$) experimental designs. In M. R. Jalongo, G. J. Gerlach, & W. Yan (Eds.), *Annual editions: Research methods* (pp. 78–90). Guilford, CT: McGraw-Hill/Dushkin.

Marten, P. A., & Heimberg, R. G. (1995). Toward an integration of independent practice and clinical research. *Professional Psychology: Research and Practice, 26*, 48–53.

Meehl, P. E. (1978). Theoretical risks and tabular asterisks: Sir Karl, Sir Ronald, and the slow progress of soft psychology. *Journal of Consulting and Clinical Psychology, 46*, 806–834.

Michael, J. (1974). Statistical inference for individual organism research: Mixed blessing or curse? *Journal of Applied Behavior Analysis, 7*, 647–653.

Morgan, D. L. (1998). Selectionist thought and methodological orthodoxy in psychological science. *The Psychological Record, 48,* 439–456.

Newell, A., & Simon, H. A. (1972). *Human problem solving.* Englewood Cliffs, NJ: Prentice Hall.

Ottenbacher, K. J. (1990). Clinically relevant designs for rehabilitation research: The idiographic model. *American Journal of Physical Medicine and Rehabilitation, 71,* 286–292.

Ottenbacher, K. J. (1992). Analysis of data in idiographic research: Issues and Methods. *American Journal of Physical Medicine and Rehabilitation, 71,* 202–208.

Parsonson, B. S., & Baer, D. M. (1986). The graphic analysis of data. In A. Poling & R. W. Fuqua (Eds.), *Research methods in applied behavior analysis: Issues and advances* (pp. 157–186). New York: Plenum.

Pavlov, I. P. (1927). *Conditioned reflexes.* London: Clarendon Press.

Perone, M. (1999). Statistical inference in behavior analysis: Experimental control is better. *The Behavior Analyst, 22,* 109–116.

Perrin, T. (1998). Single-system methodology: A way forward in dementia care. *British Journal of Occupational Therapy, 61,* 448–452.

Sanavio, E. (1998). *Behavior and cognitive therapy today: Essays in honor of Hans J. Eysenck.* Oxford, England: Elsevier Science.

Seligman, M. E. P., & Levant, R. F. (1998). Managed care policies rely on inadequate science. *Professional Psychology: Research and Practice, 29,* 211–212.

Sharpley, C. F., & Alavosius, M. P. (1988). Autocorrelation in behavioral data: An update. *Behaviour Change, 4,* 40–45.

Shrout, P. E. (Chair), Hunter, J. E., Harris, R. J., Wilkinson, L., Strouss, M. E., Applebaum, M. I., Hunt, E., & Levin, J. R. (1996, August). *Significance tests—Should they be banned from APA journals?* Symposium conducted at the 104th Annual Convention of the American Psychological Association, Toronto, Ontario, Canada.

Sidman, M. (1960). *Tactics of scientific research.* New York: Basic Books.

Skinner, B. F. (1953). *Science and human behavior.* New York: Macmillan.

Skinner, B. F. (1956). A case history in scientific method. *American Psychologist, 11,* 221–233.

Skinner, B. F. (1966). What is the experimental analysis of behavior? *Journal of the Experimental Analysis of Behavior, 9,* 213–218.

Skinner, B. F. (1969). *Contingencies of reinforcement: A theoretical analysis.* Englewood Cliffs, NJ: Prentice Hall.

Skinner, B. F. (1979). *The shaping of a behaviorist: Part two of an autobiography.* New York: Knopf.

Skinner, B. F. (1987). Antecedents. *Journal of the Experimental Analysis of Behavior, 48,* 447–493.

Sterling, Y. M., & McNally, J. A. (1992). Single-subject research for nursing practice. *Clinical Nurse Specialist, 6,* 21–26.

Stricker, G., & Trierweiler, S. J. (1995). The local clinical scientist: A bridge between science and practice. *American Psychologist, 50,* 995–1002.

Swets, J. A. (1973, December 7). The relative operating characteristics in psychology. *Science, 182,* 990–1000.

Wilkinson, L., & The Task Force on Statistical Inference. (1999). Statistical methods in psychology: Guidelines and explanations. *American Psychologist, 54,* 594–604.

Wolpe, J. (1958). *Psychotherapy by reciprocal inhibition.* Stanford, CA: Stanford University Press.

28

DRAWING VALID INFERENCES
FROM CASE STUDIES

ALAN E. KAZDIN

The case study has played a central role in clinical psychology. Indeed, understanding the individual person is occasionally considered to be a distinguishing characteristic of clinical psychology relative to other branches of the field (Korchin, 1976; Watson, 1951). The intensive study of the individual has contributed to clinical research and practice by providing a rich source of hypothesis about the bases of personality and behavior and by serving as a place to develop and apply intervention techniques (Bolgar, 1965; Garfield, 1974; Kazdin, 1980; Lazarus & Davison, 1971).

Despite its recognized heuristic value, the case study is usually considered to be inadequate as a basis for drawing valid scientific inferences. Relationships between independent and dependent variables are difficult to discern in a typical case study because of the ambiguity of the factor(s) responsible for performance. For example, treatment for a particular clinical case may be associated with therapeutic change. However, the basis for the

Reprinted from the *Journal of Consulting and Clinical Psychology*, 49, 183–192. Copyright 1981 by the American Psychological Association.

Preparation of this manuscript was facilitated by Grant MH31047 from the National Institute of Mental Health.

change cannot be determined from an uncontrolled case study. Even if treatment were responsible for change, several alternative interpretations of the case might be proposed. These alternative interpretations have been catalogued under the rubric of "threats to internal validity" (Campbell & Stanley, 1963).[1]

The case study has been discounted as a potential source of scientifically validated inferences, because threats to internal validity cannot be ruled out in the manner achieved in experimentation. Even though the case study is not experimental research, under several circumstances it can lead to knowledge about treatment effects for a given client that approximates the information achieved in experimentation. The present article examines the case study and its variations as a research tool. Alternative ways in which case studies are conducted and reported have important implications for drawing scientifically validated information. The present article discusses what can be done with the clinical case to improve the scientific inferences that can be drawn.

The case study as a potential source of scientifically valid information warrants careful scrutiny for several reasons. First, the case study has had tremendous impact on psychotherapy. Individual cases (e.g., Little Hans, Anna O., Little Albert) and series of cases (e.g., Masters & Johnson, 1970; Wolpe, 1958) have exerted remarkable influence on subsequent research and practice. Second, the case study draws attention to the frequently lamented hiatus between clinical practice and research. Clinicians have access to the individual case as their most convenient and feasible investigative tool, but inadequacies of the case study as a research strategy limit the inferences that can be drawn. Researchers often rigorously investigate psychotherapy but may sacrifice clinical relevance in the populations, therapeutic conditions, and standardization of treatment that research may require. Hence, investigation of psychotherapy often obscures aspects of the phenomenon of interest (Strupp & Hadley, 1979), and even under the best conditions, treatment may only be an "analogue" of the clinical situation (Kazdin, 1978).

One suggestion to help bring research and practice of psychotherapy closer together is to encourage clinicians to utilize single case experimental designs (Hersen & Barlow, 1976). The designs permit experimental investigation of the single case. The designs have been applied successfully and often dramatically in case reports where the effects of treatment have been

---

[1] The threats to internal validity refer to classes of variables that might produce effects mistaken for the effects of treatment. The major threats include the influence of (a) history (specific events occurring in time), (b) maturation (processes within the person), (c) testing (repeated exposure to the assessment procedures), (d) instrumentation (changes in the scoring procedures or criteria over time), (e) statistical regression (reversion of scores toward the mean or toward less extreme scores), (f) selection (differential composition of subjects among the groups), (g) mortality (differential attrition among groups), and (h) selection-maturation (and other) interactions (where differential changes occur as a function of other threats with selection). For additional threats, see Cook and Campbell (1979) and Kazdin (1980).

carefully documented with complex clinical problems seen in individual treatment. However, single-case experimental designs often impose special requirements (e.g., withdrawing or withholding treatment at different points in the designs) that are not always feasible in the clinical situation. Hence, some authors have suggested that the designs have not really been applied as widely as they should (Barlow, 1980) and perhaps often cannot be applied, because of the ethical, methodological, and practical obstacles inherent in clinical settings (Kazdin & Wilson, 1978).

Apart from the merits of single-case experimentation, nonexperimental alternatives need to be examined carefully. Indeed, in other areas of psychology, experimentation is not always possible. In such instances, important alternatives have been provided by elaborating the requirements for quasi-experiments (Campbell & Stanley, 1963), which can achieve some if not all of the goals of experimentation. Similarly, in the context of clinical practice, experiments are to be encouraged when opportunities exist. However, it is very important to elaborate the conditions that can be invoked to achieve several goals of experiments when rigorous investigations are not possible. The uncontrolled case study is a widely available investigative tool, and its methodological limitations, advantages, and alternatives need to be elaborated.

CHARACTERISTICS OF THE CASE STUDY

The case study has been defined in many different ways. Traditionally, the case study has referred to intensive investigation of the individual client. Case reports often include detailed descriptions of individual clients. The descriptions rely heavily on anecdotal accounts of the therapist to draw inferences about factors that contributed to the client's plight and changes over the course of treatment. Aside from the focus on the individual, the case study has come to refer to a methodological approach in which a person or group is studied in such a fashion that inferences cannot be drawn about the factors that contribute to performance (Campbell & Stanley, 1963; Paul, 1969). Thus, even if several persons are studied, the approach may still be that of a case study. Often cases are treated on an individual basis, but the information that is reported is aggregated across cases, for example, as in reports about the efficacy of various treatments (e.g., Lazarus, 1963; Wolpe, 1958). Hence, there is some justification for not delimiting the case study merely to the report of an individual client.

In general, the case study has been defined heterogeneously to denote several different things, including the focus on the individual, reliance on anecdotal information, and the absence of experimental controls. A central feature of the diverse definitions is that case studies differ from experimental demonstrations. Texts on methodology usually discount the case study as a preexperimental design and use it as a point of departure to show that experimentation is the alternative means for obtaining scientifically validated knowledge (Campbell & Stanley, 1963; Hersen & Barlow, 1976; Kazdin, 1980). However, the purpose of the present article is to suggest that case studies and experiments fall on a continuum that reflects the degree to which scientifically adequate inferences can be drawn. More importantly, several types of uncontrolled case studies can be identified that vary in the extent to which they permit valid conclusions.

The purpose of experimentation is to rule out threats to internal validity, which serve as alternative rival hypotheses of the results. For example, in clinical treatment research, single-case or between-groups experimental designs are required to rule out the impact of extraneous factors that might account for the findings. Case studies do not provide the arrangements that permit conclusions that are as clear as those available from experimentation. However, many of the threats to internal validity can be ruled out in case studies so that conclusions can be reached about the impact of treatment.

DIMENSIONS FOR EVALUATING CASE STUDIES

Case studies have been loosely and heterogeneously defined to include a variety of uncontrolled demonstrations aimed at showing that treatment produces therapeutic change. However, case studies may vary in how they are conducted and reported. The distinctions that can be made among case studies have important implications for drawing unambiguous conclusions. Major dimensions that can distinguish case studies insofar as they relate to internal validity, are presented below.

Type of Data

The main criterion that distinguishes case studies is the basis for claiming that a change has been achieved. At one extreme, anecdotal information may be relied on and include narrative accounts by the client and/or therapist regarding how client functioning has improved. Anecdotal reports are subject to a variety of limitations and sources of bias that need not be elaborated here. Suffice it to say that the anecdotal reports usually are not sufficient to conclude that changes really occurred in client behavior.

Case studies can include objective information, which refers to the large category of measurement strategies in which systematic and quantitative data are obtained. The specific measures encompass the gamut of assessment modalities and techniques (e.g., self-reports, ratings by others, overt behavior). Depending on other dimensions discussed below, objective information is a basic condition of a case study that has important implications for drawing inferences about the effects of treatment. The type of data obtained in a case study, that is, anecdotal or objective information, perhaps is the most important precondition for drawing inferences from a case study. Without some systematic data collection, other dimensions that might be applied to evaluate the case become almost irrelevant. Scientific inferences are difficult if not impossible to draw from anecdotal information. Indeed, it is the anecdotal information that is the problem rather than the fact that an individual case is studied. Even a rigorously designed experiment would be completely uninterpretable if anecdotal reports rather than objective assessment procedures served as the dependent measures.[2]

Assessment Occasions

Other dimensions that can distinguish case studies are the number and timing of assessment occasions. The occasions in which this objective information is collected have extremely important implications for drawing inferences from the case. Major options consist of collecting information on a one- or two-shot basis (e.g., posttreatment only, pre- and posttreatment, respectively) or continuously over time (e.g., every day or a few times per week) for an extended period.

When information is collected on one or two occasions, say before or after treatment, difficulties arise in inferring that change has occurred as a result of treatment. Other interpretations of the change might be proposed (e.g., testing, instrumentation, statistical regression). With continuous assessment over time conducted before or after treatment, artifacts associated with the assessment procedures become less plausible. That is, changes as a function of the measurement instrument, if evident, normally would be detected prior to treatment and would not necessarily obscure the pattern of data relied on to infer changes associated with treatment.

Continuous assessment provides an additional advantage that can strengthen the internal validity of the case study. Data from continuous assessment prior to treatment can serve as a basis for making predictions about likely performance in the future. Extrapolations about the likely direction of performance provide implicit predictions about what performance would be like. The effects of treatment can be judged by the extent to which departures in the data are evident from the previously projected performance.

---

[2] The absence of quantitative information may not necessarily rule out drawing causal inferences. Occasionally, intervention effects are so powerful that qualitative changes appear to be produced, and the certainty of change and the reason for this change are relatively unambiguous. These effects, occasionally referred to as "slam bang" effects (Gilbert, Light, & Mosteller, 1975), are evident throughout the history of medicine and psychology. For example, Shapiro (1963) described a case of a patient with terminal cancer who showed a dramatic remission of symptoms on separate occasions as a function of receiving inert substances (an inactive drug and water). In this case, the changes were so strong and immediate ("slam bang" effects) that the absence of careful measurement did not pose as serious a problem for drawing inferences that the administration of treatment led to change. Apart from occasional examples, in most instances, quantitative information is required to attest to the fact that changes have in fact occurred and that these changes can be assessed with procedures that are replicable.

Past and Future Projections

The extent to which valid inferences can be drawn about treatment effects is influenced by past and future projections of performance. The past and future projections may derive from continuous assessment which shows that the problem is stable and has not changed for an extended period. As noted above, continuous assessment can provide information extrapolated to the future that may serve as an implicit but testable prediction. If behavior appears stable for an extended period, changes that coincide with treatment suggest that the intervention may have led to change.

Past and future projections of performance also may be derived from understanding the course of a particular clinical problem. For some problems (e.g., obesity, social withdrawal), an extended history may be evident. The extended history is important from the standpoint of drawing inferences when change occurs. When change has occurred for a client whose problem has been evident for a long period, the plausibility that treatment caused the change is greatly increased. On the other hand, an acute clinical problem that has emerged relatively recently or is associated with a clear precipitating event may make evaluation of treatment slightly more difficult than it would be for a chronic problem. The acute or even episodic problem might be more amenable to the influence of extraneous (i.e., nontreatment) factors. Hence, it will be relatively difficult to rule out factors other than treatment that may account for the changes.

Projections of what the problems would be like in the future derived from understanding the particular clinical problem are also very relevant to drawing inferences about treatment. Research may suggest that a particular clinical problem is very likely to improve, worsen, or remain the same over a period of time. These alternative prognoses may be important when drawing inferences about treatment effects in a given case. For example, knowledge about the disorder may suggest that the problem will deteriorate over time (e.g., terminal cancer). The likely future for such a problem is highly relevant for evaluating whether treatment may be responsible for change. In the case of a patient with a terminal disease, improvements associated with a highly experimental treatment provide a strong inferential basis. Patient improvement strongly attests to the efficacy of treatment as the important intervention, because change in the disorder controverts the expected prediction.[3] Of course, with some clients and clinical problems, the future projections may

---

[3] This, of course, is not to say that the component the investigator believes to be important in the treatment was the one actually responsible for change, but only that the treatment and all that the treatment encompassed was the important event. The aspect(s) of treatment that caused change in experimentation is not a question of internal validity but rather one of construct validity (Cook & Campbell, 1976, 1979). In experimental research, the particular aspect of treatment may still be debated (construct validity), even though the experiment has ruled out the impact of extraneous influences (internal validity).

indicate that improvements are likely even if no treatments are provided. For example, in treatment of children who have specific fears, conclusions about the short-term or long-term effects of treatment in a clinical case may be difficult to reach, because the projection for the future is for improvement (Agras, Chapin, & Oliveau, 1972). In general, inferences about the effects of treatment in a given case are more easily made to the extent that predictions can be made on the basis of extraneous information that the problem, if untreated, will follow a particular course. The plausibility that the changes are a result of treatment depend in part on the extent to which changes in client performance depart from the expected and predicted pattern of performance.

Type of Effect

The degree to which inferences can be drawn about the causal agent in the treatment of a clinical case also depends on the kinds of changes that occur. The immediacy and magnitude of changes contribute to judgments that treatment may have caused the change. Usually, the more immediate the therapeutic changes after the onset of treatment, the stronger a case can be made that treatment was responsible for the change. Of course, as any other of the dimensions discussed, showing that the conditions are met, in this case an immediate change, does not by itself mean that treatment was responsible for the change. But the more immediate the change, the less likely alternative sources of influence coincident with treatment account for the change. Alternatively, when change is gradual or delayed rather than immediate, the plausibility of associating the change with a particular event in the past (i.e., treatment) decreases. As the latency between treatment administration and behavior change increases, the number of extraneous experiences that could account for the change increases as well.

Aside from the immediacy of change, the magnitude of change also contributes to the extent to which treatment can be accorded a causal role. More confidence might be placed in the causal role of treatment when relatively large changes are achieved. Of course, the magnitude and immediacy of change when combined increase the confidence that one can place in according treatment a causal role. Rapid and dramatic changes provide a strong basis for attributing the effects to treatment than more gradual and relatively small changes. A rapid and large change suggests that a particular intervention rather than randomly occurring extraneous influences accounts for the pattern of results.

Number and Heterogeneity of Subjects

Dimensions related to the subjects may influence the confidence that can be placed in conclusions about treatment effects. The number of cases included is important. Obviously, a stronger basis for inferring the effects of treatment stems from demonstrations with several cases rather than one case. The more cases that show changes associated with treatment, the more unlikely an extraneous event is responsible for change. An extraneous event that covaries with treatment and leads to therapeutic change is an unlikely rival hypothesis of the results, because the event must be common to all of the cases. The sheer number of cases obviously can contribute to the extent to which conclusions about treatment can be drawn by making implausible other explanations.

Aside from the number of cases, the heterogeneity of the cases may also contribute to drawing inferences about the cause of therapeutic change. If change is demonstrated across several clients who differ in various subject and demographic characteristics and the time that they are treated, the inferences that can be drawn are much stronger than if this diversity does not exist. Essentially, different persons have different histories and rates of maturation. As the diversity and heterogeneity of the clients and the conditions of treatment increase, it becomes increasingly implausible that the common experience shared by the clients (i.e., treatment) accounts for the changes.

APPLICATION OF THE DIMENSIONS

The above dimensions do not necessarily exhaust all of the factors that contribute to drawing firm conclusions from case studies. Also, each of the dimensions is discussed separately. Yet, any particular case can be examined in terms of where it lies on each of the dimensions. Precisely where a particular case falls on all of the dimensions determines the extent to which particular threats to internal validity or rival alternative hypotheses can be ruled out in interpreting the results.

All of the possible combinations of the dimensions would yield a large number of types of case studies that cannot be presented here. Many of the dimensions represent continua where an indefinite number of gradations are possible so a large set of types of cases could be enumerated. However, it is important to look at selected types of cases that vary on the dimensions mentioned earlier to show how internal validity can be addressed.

Table 28.1 illustrates a few types of cases that differ in their standing on the dimensions mentioned earlier. The extent to which each type of case rules out the specific threats to internal validity is also presented using a format that parallels similar analyses for true and quasi-experiments (Campbell & Stanley, 1963). For each case type, the collection of objective data was included. As noted earlier, the absence of objective or quantifiable data usually precludes drawing firm conclusions about whether change occurred. Drawing conclusions about the basis for change is premature, because the change

TABLE 28.1
Examples of Types of Cases and the Threats
to Internal Validity That They Address

Measure	Case example		
	1	2	3
Characteristic of Case			
Objective data	+	+	+
Continuous Assessment	−	+	+
Stability of problem	−	−	+
Immediate and marked effects	−	+	−
Multiple cases	−	−	+
Major threats to internal validity			
History	−	?	+
Maturation	−	?	+
Testing	−	+	+
Instrumentation	−	+	+
Statistical regression	−	+	+

Note: + indicates that the threat to internal validity is probably controlled, − indicates that the threat remains a problem, and ? indicates that the threat may remain uncontrolled. In preparation of the table, selected threats (mortality, selection, and others; see Footnote 1) were omitted because they arise primarily in the comparison of different groups in experiments and quasi-experiments. They are not usually a problem for a case study, which of course does not rely on group comparisons.

itself has not been carefully documented. In the case types illustrated in Table 28.1, the assumption will be made that some form of assessment was completed, even if only one or two occasions to measure performance before and after treatment.

Case Example Type 1: With Pre- and Postassessment

A case study where a client is treated may utilize pre- and posttreatment assessment. The inferences that can be drawn from a case with such assessment are not necessarily increased by the assessment alone. Whether specific threats to internal validity are ruled out depends on characteristics of the case with respect to the other dimensions. Table 28.1 illustrates a case with pre- and postassessment but without other optimal features that would address and rule out threats to internal validity.

If changes occur in the case from pre- to posttreatment assessment, one cannot draw valid inferences about whether the treatment led to change. It is quite possible that events occurring in time (history), processes of change within the individual (maturation), repeated exposure to assessment (testing), changes in the scoring criteria (instrumentation), or reversion of the score to the mean (regression) rather than treatment led to change. Hence, even though the case included objective assessment, the conclusion that can be drawn about the basis for change is not greatly improved over an anecdotal report.

Case Example Type 2: With Repeated Assessment and Marked Changes

If the case study includes assessment on several occasions before and after treatment, and the changes that occur at the time or over the course of treatment are relatively marked, then the inferences that can be drawn about treatment are vastly improved. Table 1 illustrates the characteristics of the case along with the extent to which specific threats to internal validity are addressed.

The fact that continuous assessment is included is important in ruling out the specific threats to internal validity that are related to assessment. First, the changes that coincide with treatment are not likely to result from exposure to repeated testing or changes in the instrument. When continuous assessment is utilized, changes due to testing or instrumentation could have been evident before treatment began. Similarly, regression to the mean from one data point to another, a special problem with assessment conducted only at two points in time, is eliminated. Repeated observation over time shows a pattern in the data. Extreme scores may be a problem for any particular assessment occasion in relation to the immediately prior occasion. However, these changes cannot account for the pattern of performance for an extended period.

Aside from continuous assessment, this case illustration was proposed to include relatively marked treatment effects, that is, changes that are relatively immediate and large. These types of changes produced in treatment help rule out the influence of history and maturation as plausible rival hypotheses. Maturation in particular may be relatively implausible, because maturational changes are not likely to be abrupt and large. However, a "?" was placed in the table, because maturation cannot be ruled out completely. In this case example, information on the stability of the problem in the past and future was not included. Hence, it is not known whether the clinical problem might ordinarily change on its own and whether maturational influences are plausible. Some problems that are episodic in nature conceivably could show marked changes that have little to do with treatment. With immediate and large changes in behavior, history is also not likely to account for the results. However, a "?" was placed in the table here too. Without a knowledge of the stability of the problem over time, one cannot be too confident about the impact of extraneous events.

For this case overall, much more can be said about the impact of treatment than in the previous case. Continuous assessment and marked changes help to rule out specific rival hypotheses. In a given instance, history and maturation may be ruled out too, although these are likely to depend on other dimensions in the table that specifically were not included in this case.

Case Example Type 3: With Multiple Cases, Continuous Assessment, and Stability Information

Several cases rather than only one may be studied where each includes continuous assessment. The cases may be treated one at a time and accumulated into a final summary statement of treatment effects or treated as a single group at the same time. In this illustration as characterized, assessment information is available on repeated occasions before and after treatment as in the last type of case. Also, the stability of the problem is known in this example. Stability refers to the dimension of past–future projections and denotes that information is available from other research that the problem does not usually change over time. When the problem is known to be highly stable or follows a particular course without treatment, the clinician has an implicit prediction of the effects of no treatment. The results can be compared to this predicted level of performance.

As evident in Table 1, the threats to internal validity are addressed by a case report meeting the specified characteristics. History and maturation are not likely to interfere with drawing conclusions about the causal role of treatment, because several different cases are included. All cases are not likely to have a single historical event or maturational process in common that could account for the results. Knowledge about the stability of the problem in the future also helps to rule out the influence of history and maturation. If the problem is known to be stable over time, this means that ordinary historical events and maturational processes do not provide a strong enough influence in their own right. Because of the use of multiple subjects and the knowledge about the stability of the problem, history and maturation are considered to be implausible explanations of therapeutic change.

The threats to internal validity related to testing are handled largely by the assessment over time. Repeated testing, changes in the instrument, and reversion of scores toward the mean may influence a comparison of performance from one occasion to another. Problems associated with testing are not likely to influence the pattern of data over a large number of occasions. Also, information about the stability of the problem helps to further make implausible changes due to testing. The fact that the problem is known to be stable means that it probably would not change merely as a function of assessment.

In general, the case study of the type illustrated in this example provides a strong basis for drawing valid inferences about the impact of treatment. The manner in which the multiple case report is designed does not constitute an experiment, as usually conceived, because each case represents an uncontrolled demonstration. However, characteristics of the type of case study can rule out specific threats to internal validity in a manner approaching that of true experiments.

General Comments

From the standpoint of experimentation, all of the above types of cases share a similar methodological status by being preexperimental and by not providing a sufficient basis for drawing scientifically valid inferences. The results that may emerge are usually rejected, because the data are from case studies. However, it is extremely important to shift the focus from the type of demonstration (i.e., case study versus experiment) to the specific threats to internal validity that interfere with drawing valid inferences. The focus on rival alternative hypotheses that may be proposed draws attention to characteristics of the case reports that can be altered to improve the scientific yield.

The purpose of experimentation is to make as implausible as possible alternative explanations of the results. At the end of an experimental investigation, the effects of the treatment should be the most plausible and parsimonious interpretation of the results. Case studies can also rule out alternative explanations that might compete with drawing inferences about the impact of treatment.

Specific procedures that can be controlled by the clinical investigator can influence the strength of the case demonstration. First, the investigator can collect objective data in place of anecdotal report information. Clear measures are needed to attest to the fact that change has actually occurred. Second, client performance can be assessed on several occasions, perhaps before, during, and after treatment. The continuous assessment helps rule out important rival hypotheses related to testing, which a simple pre- and post-treatment assessment strategy does not accomplish.

Third, the clinical investigator can accumulate cases that are treated and assessed in a similar fashion. Large groups are not necessarily needed but only the systematic accumulation of a number of clients. As the number and heterogeneity of clients increase and receive treatment at different points in time, history and maturation become less plausible as alternative rival hypotheses. If treatment is given to several clients on different occasions, one has to propose an intricate explanation showing how different historical events or maturational processes intervened to alter performance. As in ordinary experimentation, in such cases, treatment effects become the more likely interpretation.

Some features of the case study that can help rule out threats to internal validity are out of control of the clinical investigator. For example, knowledge about the stability of the problem over time comes from information extraneous to a particular client. Knowledge about the course of the disorder is required. However, even though this is not controllable by the clinical investigator, he or she can bring available information to bear when interpreting results. This is already implicit in some instances where, for example, the problem in treatment is known to have a high remission rate (e.g., childhood fears). Remission of the problem, which may normally occur over time, requires special care for interpreting the long-term effects of treatment with any particular case or intervention.

The clinical investigator cannot easily control whether the changes in treatment are immediate rather than marginal. However, the data pattern that does result should be examined specifically in light of other rival hypotheses that might explain the results. Could any historical events (e.g., family processes, job experiences) or maturational processes (e.g., decreased depression as a function of the passage of time since divorce or death of a relative) be brought to bear that might explain the pattern of results? Perhaps the pattern of the data can help rule out specific rival hypotheses.

It is not merely how we conduct case studies that might warrant reconsideration but how we conceptualize them as well. Much can be done in carrying out case studies to increase the strength of the inferences about causal events. The well-known criticism of case studies as research tools has fostered a methodological learned helplessness about what can be done. In fact, much can be done to rule out specific threats to internal validity within case studies, such as the use of assessment on multiple occasions and the accumulation of several cases.

Some of the dimensions that help rule out threats to internal validity are out of the control of the clinical investigator. For example, one cannot by fiat achieve immediate and marked therapeutic changes nor be sure of the stability of the problem over the past and future. However, the clinical investigator can bring to bear the available research on the nature of the problem and evaluate the likelihood that historical events and maturational processes could achieve the sorts of changes evident in treatment. It is not necessarily the lack of control over the clinical situation that is a problem. Within the limits of the situation, the clinical investigator might keep in mind some of the specific alternative rival hypotheses that need to be ruled out or made less plausible.

CONCLUSION

The case study occupies an extremely important place in clinical work both in inpatient and outpatient care. Case studies are widely recognized to serve as an important place to develop hypotheses about clinical problems and to explore innovative treatments. However, cases are usually considered to be completely inadequate as a basis for drawing scientifically validated inferences.

Case studies encompass several types of demonstrations that may differ in the extent to which inferences can be drawn. The issue is not whether a particular report is a case study. The focus on classifying reports on the basis of their lack of experimental design detracts from the more pertinent issue.

Drawing inferences, whether in case studies, quasi-experiments, or experiments, is a matter of ruling out rival hypotheses that could account for the results. In case studies, by definition, the number of rival hypotheses and their plausibility are likely to present greater problems than they would in experiments. However, it is possible to include features in the case study that help decrease the plausibility of specific rival hypotheses.

The present article discusses several possibilities for assessing performance that rule out selected threats to internal validity. The purpose in adopting this approach is not to legitimize the case study as a replacement for experimental research. Experiments based on intra- and intersubject methodology can uniquely rule out threats to internal validity and can provide relatively clear information about the impact of treatment. Although the case study is not a substitute for experimentation, it has and probably will continue to contribute greatly to the information available in the field. Hence, it is important to consider the case study as a potential source of scientifically useful information and to adopt procedures, where they exist, to increase the strength of case demonstrations in clinical situations when true or quasi-experiments are not viable options.

REFERENCES

Agras, W. S., Chapin, H. H., & Oliveau, D. C. (1972). The natural history of phobia. *Archives of General Psychiatry, 26*, 315–317.

Barlow, D. H. (1980). Behavior therapy: The next decade. *Behavior Therapy, 11*, 315–328.

Bolgar, H. (1965). The case study method. In B. B. Wolman (Ed.), *Handbook of clinical psychology.* New York: McGraw-Hill.

Campbell, D. T., & Stanley, J. C. (1963). *Experimental and quasi-experimental designs for research.* Chicago: Rand McNally.

Cook, T. D., & Campbell, D. T. (1976). The design and conduct of quasi-experiments and true experiments in field settings. In M. D. Dunnette (Ed.), *Handbook of industrial and organizational psychology.* Chicago: Rand McNally.

Cook, T. D., & Campbell, D. T. (Eds.). (1979). *Quasi-experimentation: Design and analysis issues for field settings.* Chicago: Rand McNally.

Garfield, S. L. (1974). *Clinical psychology: The study of personality and behavior.* Chicago: Aldine.

Gilbert, J. P., Light, R. J., & Mosteller, F. (1975). Assessing social innovations: An empirical base for policy. In C. A. Bennett & A. A. Lumsdaine (Eds.), *Evaluation and experiment.* New York: Academic Press.

Hersen, M., & Barlow, D. H. (1976). *Single-case experimental designs: Strategies for studying behavior change.* New York: Pergamon Press.

Kazdin, A. E. (1978). Evaluating the generality of findings in analogue therapy research. *Journal of Consulting and Clinical Psychology, 46,* 673–686.

Kazdin, A. E. (1980). *Research design in clinical psychology.* New York: Harper & Row.

Kazdin, A. E., & Wilson, G. T. (1978). *Evaluation of behavior therapy: Issues, evidence, and research strategies.* Cambridge, MA: Ballinger.

Korchin, S. J. (1976). *Modern clinical psychology.* New York: Basic Books.

Lazarus, A. A. (1963). The results of behaviour therapy in 126 cases of severe neurosis. *Behaviour Research and Therapy, 1,* 69–79.

Lazarus, A. A., & Davison, G. C. (1971). Clinical innovation in research and practice. In A. E. Bergin & S. L. Garfield (Eds.), *Handbook of psychotherapy and behavior change: An empirical analysis.* New York: Wiley.

Masters, W. H., & Johnson, V. E. (1970). *Human sexual inadequacy.* Boston: Little, Brown.

Paul, G. (1969). Behavior modification research: Design and tactics. In C. M. Franks (Ed.), *Behavior therapy: Appraisal and status.* New York: McGraw-Hill.

Shapiro, A. K. (1963). Psychological aspects of medication. In H. I. Lief, V. F. Lief, & N. R. Lief (Eds.), *The psychological basis of medical practice.* New York: Harper & Row.

Strupp, H. H., & Hadley, S. W. (1979). Specific vs. nonspecific factors in psychotherapy. *Archives of General Psychiatry, 36,* 1125–1137.

Watson, R. I. (1951). *The clinical method in psychology.* New York: Harper & Row.

Wolpe, J. (1958). *Psychotherapy by reciprocal inhibition.* Stanford, CA: Stanford University Press.

29

EFFICACY AND SPECIFIC EFFECTS DATA ON NEW TREATMENTS: A CASE STUDY STRATEGY WITH MIXED ANXIETY–DEPRESSION

KARLA MORAS, LESLIE A. TELFER, AND DAVID H. BARLOW

This article illustrates a case study research strategy that can yield preliminary efficacy data on psychotherapeutic treatments, as well as examine theorized mechanisms of action of treatments. Preliminary efficacy data on new treatments are a critical link to conducting controlled trials of potentially important psychotherapeutic interventions. However, as psychotherapy researchers have noted, a handicap to psychosocial treatment outcome research is that evidence for a treatment's efficacy is needed to support grant applications (e.g., to the National Institute of Mental Health [NIMH]) to study the treatment's efficacy. Furthermore, essentially no funding sources are

Reprinted from the *Journal of Consulting and Clinical Psychology, 61*, 412–420. Copyright 1993 by the American Psychological Association.

This work was supported in part by a National Alliance for Research on Schizophrenia and Depression Young Investigator Award to Karla Moras, Grant RO1 M-39096 from the National Institute of Mental Health (NIMH) to David H. Barlow, and by NIMH Clinical Research Center Grant P50 MH45178 to Paul Crits-Christoph.

available for preliminary efficacy studies of psychosocial treatments. The situation is a paradoxical one that differs from the circumstances affecting psychopharmacological treatment research, in which drug companies financially support and actively recruit investigators to do preliminary drug trials. The results of such trials are often subsequently used by investigators to support NIMH grant applications on drug treatments.

Using single-case designs to develop and study new treatments is not a novel idea. Wolpe's (1958) pioneering and broadly influential work on the technique of systematic desensitization, based on a series of 210 cases, is one notable example (Barlow, Hayes, & Nelson, 1984). Historically, however, single-case experimental designs have been used almost exclusively to study treatments derived from behavioral theories and principles, as illustrated by the examples used in major textbooks on single-case design (e.g., Barlow & Hersen, 1984; Hersen & Barlow, 1976; Kazdin, 1982). Thus, our goal in this article is to illustrate the application of single-case methodology to a treatment that is not primarily behavioral and to thereby attend investigators to the utility of such methods for preliminary studies of diverse forms of psychotherapy. In addition, one of our primary interests in conducting the case studies described here is to test a specific effects model of the therapeutic action of treatments for anxiety and for depression.

We used a single-case experimental design strategy to study a treatment for patients who have both an anxiety and a mood disorder as described in the *Diagnostic and Statistical Manual of Mental Disorders* (3rd ed., rev.; *DSM–III–R*; American Psychiatric Association, 1987). The strategy was developed to test the hypothesis that two existing treatment approaches, one for panic disorder (Barlow & Craske, 1989) and one for major depression (Klerman, Weissman, Rounsaville, & Chevron, 1984), could be modified and combined to create a useful treatment for patients with coexisting *DSM–III–R* generalized anxiety disorder (GAD) and major depression (MD). We further hypothesized that, because the combined treatment would focus on both anxiety and depression, it would be more effective for such patients than a treatment that targeted only one of the disorders. The foregoing hypothesis implied the additional hypothesis that each of the treatments would show some specific effect on the symptoms for which the treatment was developed; that is, the anxiety treatment component would have relatively more impact on symptoms of anxiety than depression, and the reverse would be true for the depression treatment component. The hypothesis is presented in schematic form in Figure 29.1.

The essence of our research strategy is to apply the same case study protocol in a replication series of cases, each of which is designed to provide data on outcome and on the pattern of symptom change associated with administration of each component of the treatment. The strategy was tailored to certain features of our situation, but it can be modified for other situations. A

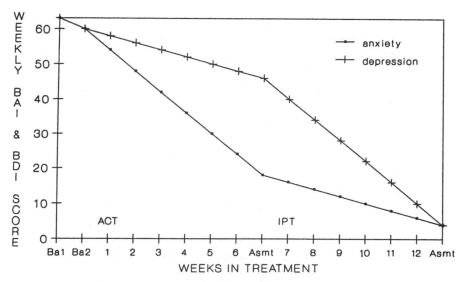

Figure 29.1. Hypothesized differential rates of change of symptoms of anxiety and depression during the anxiety control (ACT) component of the treatment and the Interpersonal Psychotherapy of Depression (IPT) component of the treatment. (BAI = Beck Anxiety Inventory; BDI = Beck Depression Inventory; Ba1 = Baseline Week 1; Ba2 = Baseline Week 2; Asmt = assessment week.)

"skeleton" strategy is presented that can be enhanced with more patients per therapist or with more therapists, when such resources are available. The elements of the strategy are listed next. References indicate where more extensive discussions of relevant aspects of case study methodology can be found.

1. Hypotheses were generated that the case study protocol was designed to examine, either statistically (e.g., by pooling data from a series of case studies) or by visual inspection (Barlow & Hersen, 1984; Kazdin, 1982). The hypotheses determined the design of the case study protocol.

2. An A/B/A/C/A/A single-case design was used in which A = assessment (2-week baseline); B = treatment for GAD; A = assessment (after six sessions of anxiety treatment); C = treatment for MD; A = assessment (after six sessions of depression treatment); and A = assessment (6-month and 1-year follow-ups). Depending on the hypotheses, when two treatments are administered, as they were in our cases, counterbalancing the order of the treatments across cases might be the optimal design because it controls for the influence of order effects on the dependent variables.

3. Patients were matched on intake diagnoses and on other potentially outcome-relevant demographic features. Patients in our case studies were required to meet *DSM–III–R* criteria for both GAD and MD; have about equally severe symptoms of GAD and MD; have no other clinically significant diagnoses; and be of similar age and marital, parental, and employment status.[1] The matching strategy is the "conservative approach" described by Barlow and Hersen (1984).

4. An assessment battery was used that included continuous self-report assessment (Kazdin, 1982) of dependent variables and diagnosticians' assessments of dependent variables by means of a structured interview. The main dependent variables in our cases were diagnostic and symptom measures of anxiety and depression. Patients made global ratings of their anxiety and depression daily, starting from the baseline assessment period. They also completed the Beck Anxiety Inventory (Beck, Epstein, & Brown, 1988) and the Beck Depression Inventory (Beck, Steer, & Garbin, 1988) weekly, starting from the baseline period. Therapist measures were not used because two of the investigators (Moras and Telfer) were the therapists and we assumed that measures we completed would be biased. Ideally, the therapists would be neither the investigators nor the developers of the treatment.

5. All assessments for a case were performed by the same diagnostician. To reduce error variance across the repeated clinical ratings on each case, the same diagnostician performed each assessment on any one patient, but different diagnosticians were used across cases.

6. Two therapists were used, each of whom treated an equal number of patients of each gender. A clinical replication strategy was used in which a series of case studies are completed, using the same design (Barlow et al., 1984; Barlow & Hersen, 1984; Hersen & Barlow, 1976). In a clinical replication strategy, more than one therapist participates, and an equal number of patients of each gender are treated by each therapist, to obtain data on the generalizability of findings. Two female therapists

---

[1] When a primary goal is to obtain generalizable outcome findings from a series of case studies, heterogeneity of cases on demographic variables is preferable to matching (Hersen & Barlow, 1976). Our interest in a process question (the relationship between changes in anxiety and depression over the course of treatment) led us to match on demographic variables. We thought that a person's typical environmental stressors caused by basic social responsibilities (e.g., employment, parenting, or marriage) would affect day-to-day fluctuations in anxiety and depression; therefore, we controlled for marital, parental, and employment status and for age group.

were a given in our situation. Ideally, with only two therapists available, one would have been male and one female, and each would treat an equal number of patients of each gender.

7. A treatment manual was created that specifies the conduct of the treatment. A treatment manual is required to teach the therapists how to conduct the treatment that is studied, help standardize each therapist's administration of the treatment across the case studies, and describe the treatment intervention to facilitate replication by other investigators.

8. Treatment sessions were audiotaped. Audiotapes are needed to evaluate the extent to which the designated treatment approach is adhered to by each therapist.

9. Outcome data from another treatment were compared with outcome data from the case studies to evaluate the efficacy of the new treatment. Case study outcome data were compared with outcome data on diagnostically similar cases who received only an anxiety-focused treatment for GAD (Barlow, Rapee, & Brown, 1992). The comparison was done to evaluate the efficacy of the new treatment, specifically its impact on anxiety and depression, compared with a treatment for anxiety only. This component of the research strategy is similar to Sidman's (1960) method of independent verification.

METHOD

This section describes how the foregoing strategy was applied in two completed case studies.

Patients

Patients were selected from those evaluated at an anxiety disorders specialty clinic. The main inclusion criterion was meeting diagnostic criteria for *DSM–III–R* GAD and MD, based on a structured diagnostic interview, the Anxiety Disorders Interview Schedule–Revised (ADIS–R; Di Nardo & Barlow, 1988). The ADIS–R includes a 9-point severity rating scale (0–8) that is used to indicate the clinical severity of each diagnosis assigned. Any case that had comorbid GAD and MD of approximately equal clinical severity and no other clinically significant disorder could be selected.

Two cases were selected and treated, each by a different therapist. The patients were well matched diagnostically as well as on potentially relevant sociodemographic characteristics (e.g., marital and parental status, age, and employment).

Case 1

The patient was a woman in her early 40s who had three children (ranging in age from 7 to 15). She held a medically oriented job. Her complaints were waking up and not feeling like getting out of bed, palpitations, poor appetite, and low energy level. She also reported symptoms consistent with excessive worry about financial matters and about inadvertently harming someone by making mistakes in her job. When asked about relationships in her life, she said that her husband was hard to live with and that she felt that she was suppressing anger, although he did not realize that anything was wrong. Her complaints had been going on for about 3 months, but she reported having experienced them intermittently for 10 years. Her *DSM–III–R* diagnoses and their clinical severity were Major Depressive Episode (single, moderate) 5 and Anxiety Disorder, Not Otherwise Specified 4.[2]

Case 2

The patient was a man in his mid-30s who had three children (ranging in age from 4 to 12). He worked full time in a semiskilled position. His complaints were "breaking down easy and crying a lot," a "no care attitude," feeling nervous, and feeling like running from his job. When asked about relationships in his life, he said that he and his wife "seemed to be going their own separate ways." However, he then quickly negated the statement by saying that they didn't seem to be growing apart; rather they seemed to be closer but more independent. The diagnosis based on two independent structured diagnostic interviews was co-principal Major Depression Episode (recurrent, moderate) 5 and GAD 5.

Therapists

Two therapists (Karla Moras and Leslie A. Telfer) conducted the treatments. The first is an experienced clinical psychologist; the other was, at the time of the study, a fourth-year graduate student in clinical psychology who had considerable clinical experience.

Instruments

Hamilton Anxiety Rating Scale (HARS)

The HARS (M. Hamilton, 1959) is a clinician-rated 13-item scale that is used in clinical research to assess symptoms conventionally accepted as

---

[2] The case was selected for the study although her anxiety diagnosis was *DSM-II¹-R* Anxiety Disorder Not Otherwise Specified, rather than GAD. She was accepted because although the diagnostic staff disagreed about whether she met the two spheres of worry criterion required for GAD, evidence for the criterion was presented.

signifiers of anxiety. The possible score range is 0 – 44. The HARS is included in the ADIS – R interview. HARS ratings were made at each assessment point by a diagnostic interviewer.

Hamilton Rating Scale for Depression (HRSD)

The HRSD (M. Hamilton, 1960) is a clinician-rated instrument that is commonly used to assess symptoms of depression. The 24-item version of the HRSD (Guy, 1976) was used in this study (the possible score range is 0 – 74). The HRSD is included in the ADIS – R interview. HRSD ratings were made at each assessment point by a diagnostician.

Beck Anxiety Inventory (BAI)

The BAI (Beck, Epstein, & Brown, 1988) is a 21-item self-report measure of somatic and cognitive symptoms of anxiety. The possible score range is 0 – 63. During treatment, patients completed the BAI weekly, immediately before each treatment session.

Beck Depression Inventory (BDI)

The BDI (Beck, Steer, & Garbin, 1988) is a 21-item, self-report measure of cognitive, mood, and neurovegetative symptoms of depression. The possible score range is 0 – 63. It was completed according to the same schedule as that used for the BAI.

Weekly Record of Anxiety and Depression (WRAD)

The WRAD (Barlow, 1988) is a self-report instrument that obtains a patient's daily global ratings of depression and average anxiety level, on a scale ranging from *none* (0) to *as much as you can imagine* (8). Patients completed the WRAD every day, starting from the baseline assessment through the posttreatment assessment (i.e., after the first 12 sessions of treatment).

Treatment

The treatment consisted of a modification of Barlow and Craske's (1989) cognitive – behavioral treatment for panic disorder and of Interpersonal Psychotherapy of Depression (IPT) as described by Klerman et al. (1984). The combined treatment included an anxiety control component for GAD and IPT for depression.

Anxiety Control Treatment (ACT) Component

ACT consisted of three modified components of Barlow and Craske's (1989) Panic Control Treatment (PCT), which includes cognitively and behaviorally focused interventions to reduce the frequency and intensity of panic attacks. PCT also is designed to teach skills and strategies for managing generalized anxiety and tension.

When used to treat panic disorder, the components of PCT are information about anxiety and panic attacks, breathing retraining, cognitive restructuring, and interoceptive exposure. Two components, breathing retraining and cognitive restructuring, are anxiety management strategies that can be readily applied to GAD, given that it is defined in the *DSM–III–R* primarily by cognitive (excessive worry and vigilance) and somatic symptoms. The interoceptive exposure component is theoretically more specific to panic disorder and was not used in ACT. We modified the information component of PCT slightly for use in ACT by eliminating sections that specifically explain the physiology of panic attacks.

The breathing retraining component of ACT essentially involved teaching the patient a way to (a) slow his or her breathing when experiencing symptoms of anxiety, and (b) refocus attention away from anxiety-provoking thoughts. Slowing breathing can reduce the intensity of somatic symptoms associated with anxiety, such as lightheadedness. The cognitive restructuring component involved teaching the patient how to identify habitual anxiety-provoking thoughts and then how to evaluate the validity of the negative predictions about future events that characterize anxiety-provoking thoughts.

IPT

A short-term treatment (recommended length is between 12 and 16 sessions) for outpatient depressive disorders such as MD, IPT (Klerman et al., 1984) is based on the premise that symptoms of clinical depression are either caused or maintained by various types of interpersonal problems. It is a very focused and problem-solving–oriented treatment.

The main techniques of IPT are (a) identifying an interpersonal problem area that seems to be most directly involved in a patient's current depressive episode and (b) using therapist interventions for that problem area as described in the IPT manual. The four IPT problem areas are grief, interpersonal role disputes, role transitions, and interpersonal skills deficits.

The problem area that seemed most appropriate for both cases was interpersonal role disputes, with the focal role dispute being within the marriage. In each case, the patient experienced dissatisfaction in the marital role but was unable or unwilling to express that dissatisfaction. Although Case 1 appreciated the opportunity to discuss her disappointments in her marriage with the therapist, she stopped short of actually renegotiating her role vis-à-vis her husband. It is unclear whether she would have eventually responded to encouragement to do so had the therapy gone on longer; however, she declined the offer of additional sessions. Case 2, on the other hand, was able to initiate direct discussions with his wife about his wishes for changes in their relationship. He had some increased satisfaction with the relationship, as well as reduced depression and increased hopefulness about change in their relationship.

Combined Treatment (ACT and IPT)

The standard protocol followed for each case study was six weekly sessions of ACT followed by 1 week with an assessment interview instead of a session, then six weekly sessions of IPT followed by an assessment interview 1 week after the sixth IPT session. Each case also had a follow-up assessment 1 year after the initial evaluation.

At the first treatment session, patients were told that their treatment would consist of two parts; one focused on the anxiety-related problems that they were experiencing, and one focused on depression. They were told that the anxiety-focused treatment would be first, that the depression-focused component would follow, and that the entire treatment was designed to be 12 weekly sessions. At Session 9 or 10, treatment termination was discussed, and patients were asked their opinion of their readiness to terminate. They were told that additional sessions were possible and that the upcoming assessment (after Session 12) could be used to help make a decision. The research plan allowed for 6 to 10 more sessions of IPT, although there was a 12-session "outcome" assessment after the 12th session, regardless of whether the patient wanted additional sessions.[3]

RESULTS

Pattern of Change in Anxiety and Depression Symptoms

Figures 29.2 and 29.3 show the weekly BAI and BDI scores of Cases 1 and 2, beginning at baseline and continuing to the post–Session-12 assessment. Figures 29.4 and 29.5 show the weekly mean of each patient's daily global ratings of depression and of their "average" level of anxiety. In general, the ratings on both measures show that symptoms of anxiety and depression were not differentially responsive to the anxiety- and the depression-focused components of the treatment; rather, in both cases the symptoms primarily changed in tandem.

---

[3] Up to 10 more sessions of IPT were offered to make the IPT component of the combined treatment comparable to the 12- to 16-session limit specified in the IPT manual and to explore the clinical speculation that more than 6 sessions for depression would be needed.

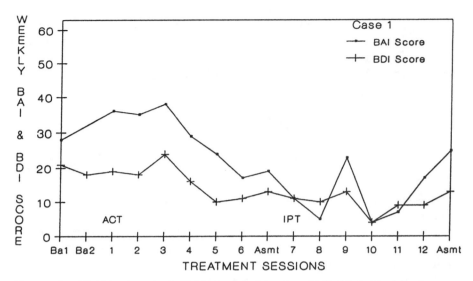

Figure 29.2. Weekly changes in Beck Anxiety Inventory (BAI; Beck, Epstein, & Brown, 1988) and Beck Depression Inventory (BDI; Beck, Steer, & Garbin, 1988) scores for Case 1. (Ba1 = Baseline Week 1; Ba2 = Baseline Week 2; ACT = anxiety control treatment; Asmt = assessment week; IPT = Interpersonal Psychotherapy of Depression treatment.)

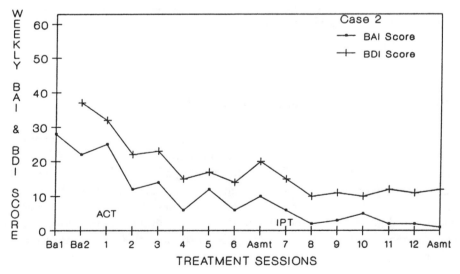

Figure 29.3. Weekly changes in Beck Anxiety Inventory (BAI; Beck, Epstein, & Brown, 1988) and Beck Depression Inventory (BDI; Beck, Steer, & Garbin, 1988) scores for Case 2. (Ba1 = Baseline Week 1; Ba2 = Baseline Week 2; ACT = anxiety control treatment; Asmt = assessment week; IPT = Interpersonal Psychotherapy of Depression treatment.)

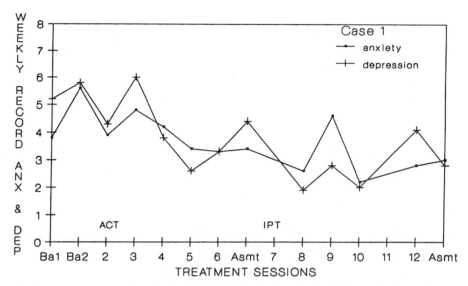

Figure 29.4. Weekly changes in self-reported anxiety and depression (Weekly Record of Anxiety and Depression; Barlow, 1988) for Case 1. (ANX = anxiety; DEP = depression; Ba1 = Baseline Week 1; Ba2 = Baseline Week 2, which also was the week preceding Session 1; ACT = anxiety control treatment; Asmt = assessment week; IPT = Interpersonal Psychotherapy of Depression treatment.)

Outcome

Efficacy

For the sake of brevity, only two outcome measures are reviewed here, the BDI and BAI scores and the HARS and HRSD scores. The BAI and BDI scores indicated that Case 2 showed remission of anxiety symptoms and mild depression at the end of treatment (see Beck & Steer, 1992a, 1992b, for severity guidelines for BAI and BDI scores) and clinically significant reduction in symptoms from pre- to posttreatment (Figure 29.3). The BDI and BAI scores for Case 1 were less positive. Although the patient showed remission of both anxiety and depression symptoms at Session 10, the symptoms began to increase again as termination approached. At the posttreatment assessment, anxiety was moderately severe and only slightly lower than at the pretreatment baseline period; depression was mild (Figure 29.2).

Table 29.1 shows pre- and posttreatment HARS and HRSD scores for Cases 1 and 2. Both cases showed small but comparable improvement in anxiety. Both showed comparable, slightly greater improvement in depression than in anxiety.

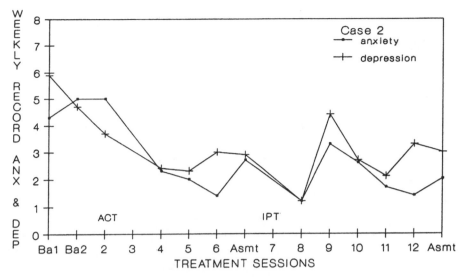

Figure 29.5. Weekly changes in self-reported anxiety and depression (Weekly Record of Anxiety and Depression; Barlow, 1988) for Case 2. (ANX = anxiety; DEP = depression; Ba1 = Baseline Week 1; Ba2 = Baseline Week 2, which also was the week preceding Session 1; ACT = anxiety control treatment; Asmt = assessment week; IPT = Interpersonal Psychotherapy of Depression treatment.)

Comparative Efficacy

The combined treatment was developed on the basis of the logical premise that if treatments have specific effects on anxiety and depression, then a treatment that combines anxiety-focused and depression-focused components will be associated with greater improvement in patients with comorbid anxiety and depressive disorders, compared with a treatment that focuses on anxiety or depression alone. We examined the premise by comparing the posttreatment HARS and HRSD scores of both cases to two diagnostically and symptomatically similar cases who received up to 15 sessions of an anxiety-focused, cognitive–behavioral treatment for GAD (Barlow et al., 1992). The anxiety treatment consisted of progressive muscle relaxation and cognitive restructuring; thus, it was similar to the ACT treatment used in the case studies that consisted of breathing retraining (which can facilitate relaxation) and cognitive restructuring.

As shown in Table 29.1, the two case studies, compared with two diagnostically similar cases who received only anxiety-focused treatment, showed small but comparable improvement in anxiety. However, inspection of the HRSD posttreatment scores suggests that the case study patients improved somewhat more in depression than did the comparison patients who were treated only for GAD (and for up to three sessions more than the two case studies). Thus, inspection of the pattern of posttreatment ratings sug-

TABLE 29.1
Outcome Comparison of Case Studies and Diagnostically Similar Cases Treated Only for GAD

Measure	Case studies[a]					
	Anxiety Tx only: GAD + MD or D + Marital[b] (n = 2)		Case 1 AnxNos + MD + Marital[b] (n = 1)		Case 2 GAD + MD + Marital[b] (n = 1)	
	Pre-Tx	Post-Tx	Pre-Tx	Post-Tx	Pre-Tx	Post-Tx
Hamilton Anxiety Rating Scale						
M	24.7	21.5	22	19	23	17
Range	22–27.5	19–24				
Hamilton Rating Scale for Depression[c]						
M	24.3	25	25	17	25	18
Range	22–26.5	20–30				

Note: Tx = Treatment; GAD = Generalized Anxiety Disorder as described in the *Diagnostic and Statistical Manual of Mental Disorders* (3rd ed., rev.; *DSM–III–R;* American Psychiatric Association, 1987); MD = *DSM–III–R* Major Depressive Episode; D = *DSM–III–R* Dysthymia; AnxNOS = *DSM–III–R* Anxiety Disorder Not Otherwise Specified (i.e., GAD with one sphere of worry). Cases from Barlow et al. (1992) who received up to 15 sessions of progressive muscle relaxation and cognitive restructuring for GAD.
[a] Patients treated for both GAD and MD.   [b] Marital = marital problems at intake.   [c] 24-item version (Guy, 1976).

gests the potential value of the combined treatment for patients with co-morbid GAD and MD, at least when an interpersonal problem such as marital distress is also present.

The posttreatment HARS and HRSD scores (see Table 29.1) also indicate that both case study patients still had clinically significant symptoms of anxiety and depression after 12 sessions of the combined treatment. The same was true of the diagnostically comparable patients from the GAD outcome study. The results suggest that such patients might need longer treatment of the types offered or alternative treatments.[4]

Some data were obtained on the preceding speculation. Case 2 accepted the offer for additional sessions after the posttreatment assessment that followed the depression component of the treatment. He attended 10 more sessions, for a total of 16 sessions of IPT. A termination assessment indicated that he no longer had clinically significant depression (he had an HRSD score of 6), and his HARS score (12) was also lower than his score at the prior 12-session assessment (17). At a follow-up assessment 6 months after treatment was terminated (and 1 year after the intake assessment), the patient's HRSD score was 1 and the HARS score was 6, indicating that

---

[4] Noting evidence such as this that existing cognitive-behavioral treatments for GAD yield less than optimal responses for some GAD patients, another treatment approach for GAD is being developed at the Center for Stress and Anxiety that incorporates several anxiety-focused interventions (Craske, Barlow, & O'Leary, 1992).

clinically significant symptoms were no longer present. Also, he no longer met criteria for any *DSM–III–R* disorder. Thus, for Case 2, the 6-month treatment period (22 weekly sessions) was associated with recovery 6 months later. However, Case 1, who had only 12 sessions (3 months) of treatment, was also recovered at her assessment 1 year after intake. Unfortunately, interpretation of her data in terms of length of treatment required for comorbid GAD and MD is complicated by the fact that she was taking Prozac at the 1-year assessment. However, the fact that she sought additional treatment is consistent with the conclusion that 12 weekly sessions of the treatments offered is not adequate for such patients.

DISCUSSION

We have presented a research strategy based on single-case methodology that can be used to generate preliminary efficacy data on new treatments as well as to examine theory-based hypotheses. The research strategy addresses one of the main impediments to preparing fundable grant applications for studies of the efficacy of promising new psychosocial treatments (i.e., the need for preliminary efficacy data). The problem is a serious one because no reliable source of funds currently is available for conducting needed developmental work on psychosocial treatments.

This report included no statistical tests of outcome differences between anxious and depressed patients who received the new combined treatment for GAD and MD (ACT and IPT) and those who received a cognitive–behavioral treatment focused only on GAD. Also, our case study methodology did not allow us to evaluate the effectiveness of the new treatment using the prevailing scientific standard that requires outcome comparisons between treated cases and diagnostically similar cases who receive no treatment, or a placebo treatment, for the same period of time.

One way to address both of the preceding limitations is to conduct a replication series of cases (i.e., "clinical replication"; see Barlow & Hersen, 1984), pool the data, and do statistical tests on those cases compared with (a) similar cases who were treated in a group outcome study and (b) no-treatment or placebo-treated controls. This approach was partially illustrated by our comparisons of the case study data with data from diagnostically similar patients who participated in a traditional treatment outcome study. Power analysis calculations (Kraemer & Thiemann, 1987) can be used to determine needed sample sizes for such statistical tests.

One strength of case study methodology was illustrated by the failure of the continuous self-report data to show the hypothesized differential impact of the anxiety-focused component of the treatment on anxiety symptoms and of the depression-focused component on symptoms of depression. It has been said that a single case can provide evidence that refutes a hypothesis by documenting a decisive counterexample to a generalization (Edelson, 1988). Although the statement might be arguable (i.e., reasons why a particular case study did not provide a valid test of a hypothesis can usually, perhaps always, be found), failure to support a hypothesis using a case study design that has high internal validity has an inherent persuasiveness that tends to prompt one to revise or refine theory. The foregoing phenomenon illustrates the unique efficiency of single-case methodology for treatment development research and for mechanisms of action studies.

What does the failure of our cases to demonstrate specific symptom effects of two symptom-specific treatments suggest? The finding was not surprising from at least two perspectives: (a) the general failure in the literature to detect hypothesized specific effects of treatments (e.g., Imber et al., 1990; Simons, Garfield, & Murphy, 1984), perhaps particularly with generalized emotional disorders involving negative affect (L. A. Clark & Watson, 1991) such as GAD (Barlow et al., 1992), and (b) evidence that self-reported anxiety and depression ratings are highly correlated (Gotlib & Cane, 1989). The failure to find the predicted specific effects opens the door to numerous speculations on possible reasons for the failure. We offer only two: One is a psychological hypothesis about mechanisms of action of symptom-focused psychotherapeutic interventions; the second posits a relationship between anxiety and depression based on emotion theory.

The psychological hypothesis accepts the premise that anxiety and depression have distinctive aspects, as well as overlapping features (e.g., D. A. Clark, Beck, & Stewart, 1990). The hypothesis also accepts the premise that the distinctive aspects of anxiety and depression can be specifically affected by specifically aimed interventions. The failure to find evidence for specific effects is hypothesized to be due to the impact of a person's psychological context on psychotherapeutic interventions. The construct of psychological context refers to features of psychological functioning that would affect any learning process, features such as verbal intelligence, ability to attend to verbal content, and spontaneous focus of attention (e.g., patients whose attention is predominantly drawn to interpersonal cues rather than to verbal cues and who might, therefore, attend more to how the therapist says something rather than to what the therapist says). The basic premise is that a person's psychological context is a very powerful filter through which our current methods of verbal dyadic intervention must pass. This filter can deflect, diffuse, and recode interventions that, in the therapist's mind, are clearly and precisely aimed at specific symptoms.

Alternatively, from the perspective of emotion theory, our failure to find evidence for specific effects of the anxiety-focused and depression-focused treatment components can be attributed to the underlying nature of depression (Barlow, 1988, 1991a, 1991b). In this theory, both anxiety and depression are characterized fundamentally by the activation of the sense of uncontrollability over negative life events. These negative affective states share similar cognitive and biological features. However, these stages may differ in terms of action tendencies. For example, the psychomotor slowing of depression may reflect "giving up" in the face of an onslaught of negative events, whereas a continuing response set of preparation and coping would be more characteristic of anxiety. Investigators working in the area of depression from a more cognitive perspective have arrived at a very similar formulation (Alloy, Kelly, Mineka, & Clements, 1990).

Inferring from the foregoing emotion theory, specific treatment effects were not found for one of two reasons: (a) the anxiety- and the depression-focused treatment components affected the shared features of anxiety and depression, not their different action tendencies or (b) our self-report measures tapped only the shared features of anxiety and depression (but see D. A. Clark et al., 1990), and measures of the different action tendencies would have shown specific responsiveness to the treatment components.

REFERENCES

Alloy, L. B., Kelly, K. A., Mineka, S., & Clements, C. M. (1990). Comorbidity of anxiety and depressive disorders: A helplessness–hopelessness perspective. In J. D. Maser & C. R. Cloninger (Eds.), *Comorbidity of mood and anxiety disorders* (pp. 499–543). Washington, DC: American Psychiatric Press.

American Psychiatric Association. (1987). *Diagnostic and statistical manual of mental disorders* (3rd ed., rev.). Washington, DC: Author.

Barlow, D. H. (1988). *Anxiety and its disorders*. New York: Guilford Press.

Barlow, D. H. (1991a). Disorders of emotion. *Psychological Inquiry, 2,* 58–71.

Barlow, D. H. (1991b). Disorders of emotion: Clarification, elaboration, and future directions. *Psychological Inquiry, 2,* 97–105.

Barlow, D. H., & Craske, M. G. (1989). *Mastery of your anxiety and panic*. Albany, NY: Graywind.

Barlow, D. H., Hayes, S. C., & Nelson, R. O. (1984). *The scientist practitioner: Research and accountability in clinical settings*. New York: Pergamon Press.

Barlow, D. H., & Hersen, M. (1984). *Single case experimental designs: Strategies for studying behavior change* (2nd ed.). New York: Pergamon Press.

Barlow, D. H., Rapee, R. L., & Brown, T. A. (1992). Behavioral treatment of generalized anxiety disorder. *Behavior Therapy, 23,* 551–570.

Beck, A. T., Epstein, N., & Brown, G. (1988). An inventory for measuring clinical anxiety. *Journal of Consulting and Clinical Psychology, 56,* 893–897.

Beck, A. T., & Steer, R. A. (1992a). *Beck Anxiety Inventory manual*. San Antonio, TX: The Psychological Corporation / Harcourt Brace Jovanovich.

Beck, A. T., & Steer, R. A. (1992b). *Beck Depression Inventory manual*. San Antonio, TX: The Psychological Corporation / Harcourt Brace Jovanovich.

Beck, A. T., Steer, R. A., & Garbin, M. G. (1988). Psychometric properties of the

Beck Depression Inventory: Twenty-five years later. *Clinical Psychology Review*, 8, 77–100.

Clark, D. A., Beck, A. T., & Stewart, B. (1990). Cognitive specificity and positive–negative affectivity: Complementary or contradictory views on anxiety and depression? *Journal of Abnormal Psychology*, 99, 148–155.

Clark, L. A., & Watson, D. (1991). Tripartite model of anxiety and depression: Psychometric evidence and taxonomic implications. *Journal of Abnormal Psychology*, 100, 316–336.

Craske, M. G., Barlow, D. H., & O'Leary, T. (1992). *Mastery of your anxiety and worry*. Albany, NY: Graywind.

Di Nardo, P. A., & Barlow, D. H. (1988). *Anxiety Disorders Interview Schedule–Revised* (ADIS-R). Albany: Phobia and Anxiety Disorders Clinic, State University of New York.

Edelson, M. (1988). *Psychoanalysis: A theory in crisis*. Chicago: University of Chicago Press.

Gotlib, I. H., & Cane, D. B. (1989). Self-report assessment of depression and anxiety. In P. C. Kendall & D. Watson (Eds.), *Anxiety and depression: Distinctive and overlapping features* (pp. 131–169). San Diego, CA: Academic Press.

Guy, W. (1976). *NCDEU assessment manual for psychopharmacology*. Washington, DC: U.S. Department of Health, Education, and Welfare.

Hamilton, M. (1959). The assessment of anxiety states by rating. *British Journal of Medical Psychology*, 32, 50–55.

Hamilton, M. (1960). A rating scale for depression. *Journal of Neurological and Neurosurgical Psychiatry*, 23, 56–62.

Hersen, M., & Barlow, D. H. (1976). *Single case experimental designs: Strategies for studying behavior change*. New York: Pergamon Press.

Imber, S. D., Pilkonis, P. A., Sotsky, S. M., Elkin, I., Watkins, J. T., Collins, J. F., Shear, M. T., Leber, W. R., & Glass, D. R. (1990). Mode-specific effects among three treatments for depression. *Journal of Consulting and Clinical Psychology*, 58, 352–359.

Kazdin, A. E. (1982). *Single-case research designs: Methods for clinical and applied settings*. New York: Oxford University Press.

Klerman, G. L., Weissman, M. M., Rounsaville, B. J., & Chevron, E. S. (1984). *Interpersonal psychotherapy for depression*. New York: Basic Books.

Kraemer, H. G., & Thiemann, S. (1987). *How many subjects? Statistical power analysis in research*. Beverly Hills, CA: Sage.

Sidman, M. (1960). *Tactics of scientific research*. New York: Basic Books.

Simons, A. D., Garfield, S. L., & Murphy, G. E. (1984). The process of change in cognitive therapy and pharmacotherapy for depression: Changes in mood and cognition. *Archives of General Psychiatry*, 41, 45–51.

Wolpe, J. (1958). *Psychotherapy by reciprocal inhibition*. Stanford, CA: Stanford University Press.

EXPANDING
OUTCOME ASSESSMENT
AND DOMAINS

30

CLINICAL SIGNIFICANCE: MEASURING WHETHER INTERVENTIONS MAKE A DIFFERENCE

ALAN E. KAZDIN

Clinical significance refers to the practical or applied value or importance of the effect of an intervention, that is, whether the intervention makes a real (e.g., genuine, palpable, practical, noticeable) difference in everyday life to the clients or to others with whom the clients interact. The assessment of clinical significance represents an important advance in the evaluation of intervention effects including treatment but extending to prevention, education, and rehabilitation as well. Apart from reliability of change or group differences (e.g., statistical significance) and the magnitude of experimental effects (e.g., effect size, correlation), the importance of the change and the impact on client functioning add critical dimensions. Treatments

The author is extremely grateful for research support from the Leon Lowenstein Foundation, the William T. Grant Foundation (98-1872-98), and the National Institute of Mental Health (MH59029) during the period in which this chapter was completed.

that produce reliable effects may be quite different in their impact on client functioning, and clinical significance brings this issue to light.

Consider for a moment that we complete a controlled psychotherapy outcome study and compare a treatment versus a no-treatment control group. At the end of treatment we evaluate the results. Standard methods of evaluation used in clinical trials include tests of statistical significance in the tradition of null hypothesis testing. Also, magnitude of effect might be computed (e.g., effect size, r) to convey how strong the effect was in statistical terms. Statistical significance and magnitude of effect provide important information. Yet, neither bears any necessary relation to clinical significance. Even extremely potent effects of treatment, as measured by effect size, for example, need not reflect improvements of any practical value to clients. Indeed, effect size might be computed on a measure that may bear little relation to everyday life (e.g., errors on a cognitive processing or laboratory task). Even if the measure is relevant (e.g., weight loss among obese patients), a large effect size might be obtained for small changes (e.g., 5 lb [2.3 kg] loss for most people in a treatment group and no weight change or a slight gain for most people in a control group). Clearly, clinical significance provides a pertinent dimension for evaluating treatment that is not captured by more commonly used evaluation methods.

Consider another example such as the treatment of anxiety, a relatively common focus of adult therapy. Assume we complete an outcome study comparing treatment versus no treatment for patients with severe anxiety. At the end of treatment, patients in the treatment group show decreases in anxiety and less anxiety do than patients in the no-treatment control group. Assume further that all differences are statistically significant. It is meaningful to ask whether the improvements on psychological measures (e.g., self-report questionnaires, direct observations in the lab) reflect or relate to impact on measures in everyday life. Now that the patients have been treated, can they go out of the house, participate in social situations, or enjoy life in ways that were somehow precluded by their anxiety? Changes on the usual psychological measures (e.g., self-report, interviews) do not directly answer these questions; it is possible to change on various inventories and questionnaires without any of these other benefits. Clinical significance raises the concern about changes in these other areas.

OVERVIEW OF CURRENT MEASURES

Treatment research has identified several ways of operationalizing clinical significance, and these continue to evolve (Kendall, 1999). Table 30.1 highlights several measures that have been used to measure clinical significance. Most intervention studies do not report the use of measures of clinical significance. Among studies that do report such measures, typically only

TABLE 30.1
Primary Means of Evaluating Clinical
Significance of Change in Intervention Studies

Type/Method	Defined	Criteria/Measures
Comparison method	Client performance is evaluated in relation to the performance of others (e.g., normative sample, patient sample)	1. Similarity to normative samples at the end of treatment 2. Dissimilarity (statistical departure from) to a dysfunctional sample
Absolute change	Amount of change the individual makes without comparison to other people or groups	1. Amount of change from pre- to posttreatment (e.g., a change of at least 2 standard deviations) 2. No longer meeting criteria for a psychiatric diagnosis 3. Complete elimination of the problems or symptoms
Subjective evaluation	Impressions, judgments, opinions of the client or those who interact with the client that a change is clearly important and makes a difference in everyday life	Ratings of 1. Current functioning 2. Whether the original problem continues to be evident or to affect functioning 3. Whether the change or changes produced in treatment make a difference
Social impact	Change on a measure that is recognized or considered to be critically important in everyday life; usually not a psychological inventory or standardized measure	Change reflected on such measures as arrest, truancy, days missed from work, hospitalization, survival, and cost

Note: This list is not intended to exhaust all possibilities. Other methods and variants and their strengths and limitations have been addressed in other sources (see Foster and Mash, 1999; Gladis, Gosch, Dishuk, and Crits-Cristoph, 1999; Jacobson, Roberts, Berns, and McGlinchy, 1999; Kazdin, 2003; Kendall, Marrs-Garcia, Nath, and Sheldrick, 1999; Lunnen and Ogles, 1998; Wolf, 1978).

one of the measures listed in Table 30.1 is used. The measures have been elaborated in several sources as noted in the table, and hence I do not review each of them here. It is worth commenting on a few measures to convey how they work and why it is reasonable to consider the measures as reflecting an important change.

Comparative methods dominate the measures of clinical significance currently in use. Among those in the table, the use of normative samples is the predominant measure. The question addressed by this method is to what extent do patients, after completing treatment (or some other intervention), fall within the normative range of performance? Before treatment, the clients presumably would depart considerably from their well-functioning peers (e.g., community samples of same age and sex) on the measures and in the domain that led to their selection (e.g., anxiety, depression, social withdrawal). Demonstrating that after treatment these same people are indistinguishable from or within the range of a normative, well-functioning sample on the measures of interest would be a reasonable definition of a clinically important change. Falling within the range of normative functioning has been used as a criterion for clinical significance for a few decades and across many problem domains (Kazdin, 1977; Kendall & Grove, 1988). To invoke this criterion, a comparison is made between treated patients and peers who are functioning well or without significant problems in everyday life. This requires that the measures used in the study have normative data available from community (nonpatient) samples. Also, some range is delineated (e.g., mean plus or minus a standard deviation) of the nonpatient sample to decide the range considered to be normative. The investigator identifies who among the treatment group falls within this range.

Clinical significance is also operationalized by diagnostic considerations. For example, one can show that patients met diagnostic criteria for a psychiatric disorder before treatment (e.g., anxiety, major depression). At the end of treatment, one can readminister diagnostic interviews. Presumably, a change that makes a difference would be evident if individuals no longer meet criteria for the disorder when treatment was completed. Of course, one can meet or not meet criteria for a diagnosis on the basis of the presence or absence or a small change in one symptom. Even so, this is not likely to explain an effect if a significant proportion of patients no longer meet criteria or even approach the criteria for the diagnosis.

Perhaps the clearest case of clinical significance among those listed in Table 30.1 pertains to the complete elimination of a problem. As an illustration, patients enter a treatment study that focuses on one of these problems: tics, panic attacks, alcohol abuse, or spouse abuse. At the end of treatment and perhaps over the course of follow-up, assessment reveals that the problem has been reduced to zero. This is a fairly clear case that the amount of change is very important and makes a difference.

The purpose of sampling a few indices of clinical significance is to raise critical issues in their use. These issues pertain to the conclusions that can be reached about the impact of treatment. In keeping with my writing style and dealings with people in everyday life, there are mixed messages in this chapter. First, measures of clinical significance ought to be used more to evaluate treatment outcome. Without such measures it is not at all clear that individuals have been helped in ways that make a difference in their lives. Second, current measures of clinical significance are quite difficult to interpret because they have been put into place without some of the basic conceptual and empirical work that underlies test validation and interpretation.

This chapter raises questions about the meaning and interpretation of measures of clinical significance, the importance of relating assessment of clinical significance to the goals of therapy, and evaluation of the constructs that clinical significance reflects. Recommended directions for research are also highlighted and include developing a typology of therapy goals, evaluating cutoff scores and thresholds for clinical significance, and attending to social as well as clinical impact of treatment.

MEANINGS OF CLINICAL SIGNIFICANCE

There are key issues that influence or determine whether a change is clinically significant. The issues reflect consideration of the question, What do we mean when we refer to change as *clinically significant*? The answers to which the question is directed are not of course the operational definitions in use but rather the concepts and constructs these definitions are designed to represent.

Amount or Degree of Change

The amount or degree of change is the most striking characteristic of the meaning of clinical significance. That is, a large change is one that is more likely to be clinically significant. However, scrutiny of the obvious raises significant issues about when to conclude that a clinically significant change exists. I suggest that a clinically significant change can occur when there is a large change in symptoms, a medium change in symptoms, and no change in symptoms. The suggestion that any amount of change might be clinically significant is not sophistry but rather conveys that clinical significance can and does mean many things, and these vary as a function of the type of problems and the goals of treatment.

Consider three situations and how the clinical significance of change might be demonstrated. First, consider the situation in which the client comes to treatment with many symptoms (e.g., of depression), and the goal is to reduce or eliminate these symptoms. After treatment, the client's symptoms have been reduced substantially. On standardized measures of depression and indeed on broader measures of psychopathology, this might be reflected in a statistically large change (e.g., 2 standard deviations) and symptom scores that fall within the normative range. (More is said later in this chapter about the meaning of a reduction of symptoms and entry into the normative range.) At this point, it is important to begin with the notion that clinical significance can mean a large change in symptoms.

Second, consider the same client but a slightly different outcome. Here the client improves, but at the end of treatment the client's behavior has not changed enough for it to fall within the normative range. From the researcher's standpoint, the criterion of clinical significance may not be met. Yet on a priori and perhaps even commonsense grounds, the change may be important and potentially clinically significant (i.e., in keeping with the definition of making a difference and having a practical value). After all from the standpoint of symptoms, one can be a little better or a lot better (e.g., fewer or less severe symptoms) without being all better or just like most people (e.g., no symptoms, normative range of symptoms, or recovered). If one is a little better or a lot better, that is important to identify for research and clinical purposes. Sometimes a little means a lot.

For example, a review of psychotherapy for depression suggests that treated cases change, but at the end of treatment clients are still more depressed than are those in the normative samples (Robinson, Berman, & Neimeyer, 1990). For severely depressed and suicidal patients, perhaps those who are hospitalized, an improvement might be sufficient to return them to everyday functioning even though their depressive symptoms are hardly near normative levels (cf. Tingey, Lambert, Burlingame, & Hansen, 1996). For less severely depressed patients, a small change in symptoms also may keep them out of the normative range. Yet, could it be that such individuals have made a clinically important change even though they do not fall within the normative range? The clients themselves might judge the changes to be quite significant, if we introduce the client's perspective on the matter. The perspective of the person judging clinical significance is relevant and raises a broader issue discussed later. Yet, it is conceivable that a little change goes a long way, could make a great difference to the client (i.e., be clinically significant), and affect his or her functioning in everyday life.

Finally, consider a different situation that arises in psychotherapy in which symptom change is not an issue. Several circumstances may make symptom change not relevant or not the main objective of therapy. It might be that the symptoms are deteriorating, and an effective treatment stops or postpones the deterioration. In another situation, perhaps the symptoms cannot be changed very much or at all (e.g., Tourette's syndrome, self-mutilation). The absence of effective treatments or the failure of ordinarily effective treatments that have been applied may lead us to consider that the symptoms are not likely to change. Alternatively, the impetus for seeking therapy may be a personality or character trait that one's dear friends and relatives find annoying. Many of these characteristics are stable and lifelong and might not be expected to change or to change very much. For each situation, we may not be able to do very much in terms of changing symptoms, but we may do a lot in terms of helping people cope with symptoms or improve the quality of life (Gladis et al., 1999).

Helping people cope is relevant to a wide range of issues brought to treatment, as reflected in coping with a personal disability (e.g., disfigurement, loss of mobility); with emergent and emotionally wrenching challenges (e.g., care of a child or spouse with an acute trauma or chronic disability); or with one's past (e.g., guilt, remorse in relation to a parent, abuse by a parent), present (e.g., diagnosis of a terminal disease, loss of a relative), or future (e.g., angst over a personal crossroads, impending major life event). For purposes of discussion, we might say that symptoms of the client are not the problem. Rather, the goals of therapy include coping with the situation, altering one's views, and taking action to manage the situation.

The three situations converge to make one point, namely, it is conceivable that therapeutic change can be important (i.e., clinically significant) when symptoms change a lot, when they change a little, and when they do not change at all, but the client is better able to cope with them. The determination of clinical significance in these situations is not arbitrary and does not challenge existing measures. Rather, the illustrations convey that clinical significance depends on the problems that are brought to treatment and the goals of treatment (Foster & Mash, 1999). The challenge is developing a method of connecting outcome measures and clinical significance on these measures to the goals of treatment.

Key Constructs

A marked change in symptoms could readily signal a clinically significant effect, but few would say that clinical significance is restricted to changes in symptoms. What are the constructs that underlie clinical significance, or what are the defining dimensions? To date, evaluation of clinical significance in treatment outcome research has emphasized symptom reduction. Symptoms are important, but it is interesting to consider their role in treatment referral and treatment more generally. The number of people with symptoms in everyday life (and not in treatment) is probably quite high. We know that approximately 18–20 percent of children, adolescents, and adults in the community meet criteria for a psychiatric disorder in a given year (e.g., Burke, Burke, Regier, & Rae, 1990; U.S. Congress, 1991). These refer to *diagnoses* (sets of multiple symptoms). The rates of people having one or two symptoms or as having subsyndromal disorders (sets of symptoms that fall below meeting diagnostic criteria) necessarily must be higher. Most people with symptoms and disorders are not referred for nor receive psychotherapy. Of course, just because individuals do not come to treatment does not mean they are functioning well. Seeking treatments depends on several factors, including the nature of the clinical problem, the availability of resources, and cultural views about seeking treatment. Yet, it is quite feasible that large numbers of individuals with disorders or sets of symptoms are managing or functioning adaptively, even if not optimally. Level of symptoms may not be the basis of receiving or evaluating treatment or the primary determinant of functioning adaptively or well.

Impairment may be much more critical than symptoms for entering treatment. Impairment includes difficulties in meeting role demands; interacting with others; and being restricted by what one can do in settings, situations, and activities in which one is involved. Impairment is related to but readily distinguishable from symptoms and disorders (Sanford, Offord, Boyle, Pearce, & Racine, 1992). Moreover, impairment is related to seeking treatment. In the case of child treatment, for example, impairment more than symptoms predicts the likelihood of being referred for treatment (Bird et al., 1990). Among adolescents, level of impairment at the end of treatment predicts the likelihood of relapse (Lewinsohn, Seeley, Hibbard, Rohde, & Sack, 1996). In adult therapy, many individuals who do come for therapy do not meet criteria for diagnoses, at least when assessed through standardized methods (e.g., Howard, Lueger, & Kolden, 1997). Quite possibly, functioning in everyday life, apart from or in combination with symptoms, is the basis for seeking treatment.

Clearly, symptoms and impairment can be related, and often both are core diagnostic features of various disorders (e.g., substance abuse, schizophrenia, to mention two; American Psychiatric Association, 1994). However, symptoms and impairment may not invariably be related or in any given case necessarily highly related. This is worth mentioning because we might reduce symptoms (e.g., to normative levels) and not necessarily affect impairment in important (clinically significant) ways or fail to reduce symptoms to a clinically significant degree but improve functioning in daily life.

Symptoms and symptom changes are important as indices of clinical significance. At the same time, there are reasons to be cautious because of the impetus for and conditions related to seeking treatment, the goals of treatment, and the possibility that important therapeutic changes may be unrelated to symptom change. It is meaningful to ask, What are the key constructs or dimensions along which clinical significance ought to be evaluated? There are likely to be many constructs and dimensions. Quality of life, impairment, and no doubt other indices might be proposed as viable alternatives.

Perspectives and Convergence of Measures

In psychotherapy research, there is long-standing recognition that evaluation of treatment effects entails many different perspectives, including those of the client, those in contact with the client (e.g., spouse, parents, coworkers), mental health professionals, and society at large (e.g., Kazdin & Wilson, 1978; Strupp & Hadley, 1977). Clinical significance invariably includes a frame of reference or perspective. It is quite appropriate for many treatment goals to ask, To *whom* is the treatment effect clinically significant?

Emphasis on symptom change may reflect the perspective of the investigator. The outcomes regarded as clinically significant are based on what we as researchers have decided are reasonable definitions and conventions

(Kazdin, 2001). Symptom change may not reflect what is actually important to the client from his or her perspective. Moreover, a large symptom change may not be reflected in other indices of practical or applied importance.

The perspective of the client has not been well attended to in the evaluation of clinical significance. Indeed, the client has been largely excluded from the process of defining a clinically significant change. Does the client, at the end of treatment, consider the change to be very important or one that has had palpable impact on his or her life? (Wolf, 1978). Of course, many cases exist in which one might not be able to use the opinion of the client (e.g., young child with autism, adolescent with conduct disorder, adult with borderline personality disorder). Also, client opinions (e.g., global ratings, judgments) can be influenced by a variety of factors and biases that could indicate significant change when in fact these changes are not reflected in other domains. Indeed, client satisfaction with treatment often shows only a weak relation to changes in symptoms (Lunnen & Ogles, 1998; Pekarik & Wolff, 1996). Thus, assessment and interpretation of the client's perspective raise their own challenges and, hence, cannot be considered as the singular or unambiguous criterion for whether treatment has had genuine impact on functioning. Even so, in outpatient treatment for adults, for example, it would seem that the client's perspective is absolutely critical.

It is worth distinguishing *actual* change and *perceived* change, no doubt an epistemological nightmare that I would like to gloss over for the moment. As an example of actual change, consider that the client has improved substantially in symptoms at the end of treatment. The actual changes in functioning, as reflected on objective and standardized tests, are obviously important. Perceived changes on the part of the client or those with whom the client interacts are critical as well. The difference between actual and perceived characteristics is readily evident and recognized as important in everyday life as, for example, reflected in *being* competent and *feeling* (perceiving oneself as) competent, in *being* in control and *feeling* in control, and in *being* attractive and *feeling* attractive. In the context of therapy, actual change or level of symptoms at the end of treatment (e.g., demonstrated on standardized measures) is distinguishable from perceived change (e.g., views about how much one has changed along the same dimension as the standardized measures). Actual and perceived change may be correlated. Whatever the correlation is, there may be no relation in a particular individual, and the relation might well be altered with therapy (e.g., because one changes and the other does not or the changes are in different directions). That is, clients may retain their symptoms, social ineptness, and rough demeanor but feel or perceive themselves as much better, as noticeably happier, and as having a better quality of life.

To simplify (and dichotomize) for purposes of presentation, envision a 2 × 2 matrix in which the rows are actual changes (clinically significant vs. not clinically significant) in the clients and the columns are perceived changes (clinically significant vs. not). Among the four cells that combine these, the cases in which discrepancies exist are perhaps especially interesting (e.g., the data show a clinically significant change but no change or modest change in client perceptions, and vice versa). The 2×2 matrix is simple because only two perspectives and a single construct (symptom change) are included. Even so, the illustration raises the issue of perspective and correspondence of measures of clinical significance, and both of these relate to the goals of treatment.

Ironically, much of psychotherapy research focuses on cognitively based treatments. These treatments underscore the importance of beliefs, attributions, and thought processes in relation to disorder or bases of therapeutic change. At the same time, there has been less appreciation of cognitive processes as a focus of treatment; changes in such processes are often an end in themselves rather than a means of reducing symptoms or changing disorders. How individuals view themselves, the world, and others is critical not only because it influences depression but also because it is related to the misery that many people bring to treatment, whether or not they are depressed.

In statistical evaluation, we recognize that a result may be statistically significant ($p < .05$) even though the null hypothesis (H_o) is true. That is, our results show that a difference exists even though there really is no difference in the world, a circumstance referred to as a *Type I error*. We also recognize that the results of our study may not be statistically significant even though H_o is false, that is, there really is a difference in the world, a circumstance called a *Type II error*. No doubt there are conceptually equivalent errors in relation to clinical significance, mutatis mutandis. These errors may be evident with a single index of clinical significance such as symptom scores falling in the normative range. For a given client whose scores fall within the normative range, there may be no real change or only a small change on some measure of functioning in everyday life. That is, there is a clinical Type I error in which we find a change and entry into normative range on our measure, but the symptoms these are designed to reflect in everyday life may not have changed for this individual or changed as much as the data suggest. The equivalent of Type I and Type II errors may also be evident when one compares different perspectives (e.g., client, mental health practitioner) and when one perspective reflects change and the other does not.

To call these *errors* is of course questionable, but Type I and Type II errors convey the concept of discrepancies among criteria and measures and the extent to which conclusions based on one measure of clinical significance correspond to those based on a criterion or another measure. The discrepancies could readily occur among different raters who are evaluating the clinical significance of the changes in the client (e.g., self- and other report) or evidence obtained that contrasts perceived change (e.g., self-ratings) and more objective or observational measures (e.g., return to work, engaging in activities).

MEASUREMENT VALIDATION

Interpretation of Current Indices

The meaning of current measures of clinical significance is not entirely clear, in part because there has been little validation of the measures (Kazdin, 2001). The reason for the paucity of validity studies may be because the measures of clinical significance are not really new or different measures. Rather, they are ways of using other measures, many of which are often well validated. Thus, clinical significance might be inferred by a change on a Minnesota Multiphasic Personality Inventory, Beck Depression Inventory, or Child Behavior Checklist. There seems to be no need to validate these measures anew because of the enormous amount of background research, including data on normative samples. Yet, problems remain in the use of clinical significance indices even when they are based on well-validated measures.

It might seem obvious that a client whose symptoms are outside the normal range before treatment and within that range after treatment has made a clinically significant change. Assume for the moment that the standardization and normative data for the measure have firmly established some normative range of functioning. At the end of treatment, what does a score in the normal range mean? First, the normative data from standardization samples are rarely based on the scores of individuals tested on two separate occasions. In contrast, when used to evaluate treatment, the measures are typically based on repeated assessment (pre- and posttreatment). The repetition of the measures combined with the context in which the measures are completed (treatment evaluation) makes the score at posttreatment for the clients not necessarily comparable to the data obtained in community samples. Simply stated, the assessment conditions of the normative sample and client sample at posttreatment are quite different.

Second, identical scores within the normative range from someone in a community sample and someone referred for treatment who has improved may not have the same meaning or correlates. For example, adolescents who met criteria for major depression before treatment may show a clinically significant change insofar as they achieve a cutoff that places them in the nonpsychiatric disorder range once treatment is completed. Yet, adolescents who no longer meet diagnostic criteria, but who once did, remain different from those who never met these criteria in terms of current impairment and long-term functioning (Gotlib, Lewinsohn, & Seeley, 1995; Lewinsohn et al., 1994).

In general, scores from community and clinical samples that fall within the same range (at the end of treatment) do not necessarily have the same meaning (e.g., concurrent and predictive validity). The quick reply to this concern is that in a treatment study, the use of a no-treatment control handles these ambiguities because clients in this group have repeated assessments and hence provide a basis of comparison. A control group is not relevant here. We wish to know if these clients (who fall within the normal range or who made a large change) function well or show palpable effects of treatment. It seems to me that even on the basis of scores on standardized and well-validated measures we cannot tell.

Interpretation of measures of clinical significance depends on the extent to which they relate to other criteria that reflect impact on a client's functioning in everyday life or perceived functioning, again, depending on the configuration of constructs that comprise clinical significance. Currently, we have operational definitions of clinical significance, many of which have been refined in remarkable ways. Yet, the operations to measure clinical significance ought not to be confused with the constructs they operationalize.

The question for any measure or index of clinical significance is the extent to which the measure in fact reflects a change that does have impact on the individual's functioning in every day life or a change that makes a difference. Validation is needed to attest to the fact that the measure relates to other indices of everyday functioning. Stated another way, clinical significance is not being measured merely because we say so or adopt some measure for purposes of convention. The measures must relate to the construct of interest. Measures of clinical significance require supporting evidence to establish that they actually do reflect important, practical, worthwhile, and genuine changes in functioning in every day life.

The Criterion Issue/Problem

It is easy to state that current measures ought to be validated, but there is no clear criterion against which to validate the measures. Indeed, there are likely to be multiple criteria, goals of therapy, and different perspectives, as raised earlier. Validation steps might begin by comparing treated cases who do show a clinically significant change and those who do not, as reflected on measures highlighted previously. We could show that those who have made a clinically significant change (e.g., fall into the normative range on symptoms) have higher mean scores on measures of marital adjustment, adaptive functioning, quality of life, and other such outcomes, when compared with those who have not made a clinically significant change. Yet this does not establish that the change or end of treatment made by those identified as showing a clinically significant effect are doing better in their everyday lives.

Among the alternatives for selection of criteria against which measures could be validated would be to identify the clients who state that they have made an important, worthwhile, and genuine change over the course of treatment. What are the predictors and correlates of these statements? A similar case might be made by asking others, people with whom the clients interact, whether differences in treatment are clear and important, and this too could be a criterion to help develop the construct or latent variable (clinically significant change) and then to see how various measures relate to that.

No single criterion may exist that can be used to validate existing measures of clinical significance. No doubt some treatment effects and clinical foci may be more easily validated than others. For example, therapy as applied to health domains may provide criteria that are more readily assessed. Treatment of obesity or cigarette smoking, as two examples, might be able to connect status at posttreatment (e.g., percentage overweight, number of cigarettes smoked) to other outcomes that can serve as validation for deciding if a clinically significant change or improvement has occurred. Falling within a range of 10 percent above normal body weight, as opposed to 50 percent above normal body weight at pretreatment, may greatly reduce the risk for all sorts of diseases and be used as a reasonable criterion for clinical significance. Here the use of normative data has validation evidence in its behalf because the data (10 percent above body weight) can be related to all sorts of other criteria (e.g., morbidity, mortality). Of course, just because health measures are available does not invariably provide a rock-solid criterion for clinically significant change, but the grounding is better if one can relate level of functioning to the likelihood (risk) of other outcomes.

In general, much more attention ought to be given to the criteria that are used to define clinical significance. Measures in current use warrant validation in relation to those criteria. Without such validation, it is unclear what our measures assess beyond the descriptive statement of an individual's score on that measure. We can say that the results of treatment produced clinically significant changes, but we must bear in mind that these changes may not have any impact on client functioning in everyday life.

General Comments

A standard assessment recommendation is to convey the need for multiple measures. This is intended to refer to multiple measures of a given construct, because no single measure can capture all of the components, and each measure has a method component (e.g., type of measure, reactivity of assessment) that can contribute to the score and its interpretation. These concerns are relevant to the assessment of clinical significance. Yet logically, prior concerns warrant assessment consideration. First, there are multiple constructs and meanings of clinical significance in the light of the various clinical problems and goals of therapy. These warrant elaboration at the conceptual level. Second, can we translate these meanings into criteria to validate measures or indices of clinical significance? What index can we use to reliably and validly reflect the likelihood that someone has made an important change? Also, we ought to ask the same questions about indices we can use to reflect the likelihood that the client or others affected by the client perceive that there has been an important change.

These questions are fundamental to assessment and evaluation of clinical significance. However, they raise broad issues about the multiple purposes and goals of treatment and the feasible, realistic, and ideal outcomes that may result. The implications are broad because they have bearing on such weighty topics as identifying evidence-based treatments. One may wish to judge treatments on the extent to which they change symptoms, but the results could be quite different if such other criteria were used as impairment, quality of life, or impact on others.

RESEARCH DIRECTIONS: BRIEFLY NOTED

Classification of Goals and Problems

Many reasons exist for seeking treatment, and no doubt these can vary widely over the course of childhood, adolescence, and adulthood. Clinically significant therapeutic change is probably quite different in meaning as a function of the different foci of treatment. Perhaps even when the focus is similar (e.g., anxiety, depression), the meaning and measure of clinical impact may vary over the course of development. A key question for research is whether the problems, goals, or foci of treatment can be categorized in some way to alert us to the most relevant means of assessing clinical significance.

Perhaps a typology of treatment goals or treatment foci can be developed. This is not a classification of clinical problems (e.g., such as disorders), but instead a typology at a higher level of abstraction to address the main goals of treatment. As an illustration, one might say that treatment goals include (a) reducing symptoms; (b) improving interpersonal relations and role functioning; (c) enhancing self-esteem and confidence; (d) enhancing the capacity to cope with or reconcile a particular situation, crisis, or problem; and (e) clarifying or addressing issues related to a past, current, or impending situation. These are not listed to propose a complete typology but rather to convey the broader issue that a typology of goals may be instructive. Needless to say, treatment may have many goals, goals are not independent, and goals can and do change.

The purpose of a typology would be to call forth those types of clinical significance that are most relevant. Making a large change in symptoms and falling into the normative range could be the primary or exclusive index of clinical significance but are not necessarily relevant when the primary goals of treatment are (b) through (e) above. Also, for some therapy, the outcome is not as critical as the process, that is, working on issues, clarifying meaning, soliciting someone else's perspective, and having a friend. The ride, as it were, may be as or more important than arriving at a destination. This may not be the focus of therapy in outcome research but addresses situations in which clients search for meaning and do so through psychotherapy. There is no reason to emphasize this latter focus here except to convey how the goals of therapy can vary. Perhaps we would profit from a way of identifying the primary domains of clinical significance to which we ought to attend and then a set of measures to operationalize these. Current measures of clinical significance do not begin with the view that there are multiple goals of therapy, and clinical significance is defined in relation to those goals. Measures also do not begin with the clients' views of what an important change would denote if treatment were helpful or wildly successful.

Perhaps insufficient appreciation of client views about the goals of treatment also contributes to some of the discrepancies in treatment outcomes more broadly. For example, among clients who drop out of treatment "prematurely" and against therapeutic advice, a rather significant proportion definitely improves (Kazdin & Wassell, 1998). It is likely that the goals of treatment of the clients were achieved even though the goals of the therapist may not have been. Lack of correspondence among client and therapist or other measures is not a methodological "problem" but rather a substantive and conceptual issue about the goals of treatment and the criteria for evaluating impact.

Cutoff Scores and Thresholds of Clinical Significance

There may be use in referring to clinical significance categorically (e.g., in or out of the normative range, recovered or not). This may be particularly useful or clear when symptoms are eliminated (e.g., no more panic attacks, tics, or encopresis). More often than not the changes are on a continuum. Any cutoff point to determine whether the change is clinically significant will raise the same issue. For example, some individuals who are considered to have changed to a clinically significant degree did not change on the criterion; others who did not change to a clinically significant degree on the measure did change on the criterion. One can investigate the classification of individuals at the end of treatment to determine which cutoff is the best at capturing those cases that made a significant (clinically) change. Using some cutoff based on normative data or a degree of change from pre- to posttreatment may not necessarily capture that.

Research is needed that evaluates alternative cutoff points and their utility in defining a clinically significant change. Central to this research is development of a criterion (or set of criteria) on which to judge the extent to which a particular cutoff in fact identifies individuals who have changed in marked ways, as discussed previously. On the measure of clinical significance (e.g., normative data), any particular cutoff score (or range) is likely to identify

- *true positives*—those who are correctly identified as having made a clinically significant change on the measure, such as falling within the normative range, and who show impact on the criterion measure from everyday life;
- *false positives*—those who are considered to have made a clinically significant change on the measure but not on the criterion measure;
- *true negatives*—those correctly identified as not having made a clinically significant change on the measure or on the criterion; and
- *false negatives*—those who did not show a clinically significant change on the measure when in fact on the criterion treatment clearly had important impact.

The cutoff point to maximize correct identification of cases that make a clinically significant change can be determined empirically.[1]

Insofar as clinical significance includes client report, there is a related matter of the threshold that individuals have for saying, perceiving, and believing that an important (clinically significant) change was made in treatment. It is readily conceivable that two clients coming to treatment with the same set of symptoms and who change equally (and fall within the normal range) will view their change quite differently. One might see the change as clinically important; the other as nugatory. This is why client perception (e.g., the person seeking treatment) may be critical in many applications of therapy.

The point about thresholds extends beyond the perception of the client. It is quite possible that a given change in symptoms or functioning for two clients may in fact have different impact on their lives. A reduction in marital conflict that is medium to large for two couples may be quite sufficient to improve and preserve the marriage for one couple but not enough to achieve these ends for another couple. The reason might be driven by variation between the families in other factors, including characteristics of the

---

[1] Tests of sensitivity and specificity are used to delineate different cutoff points to identify cases. In the present context, *sensitivity* is the probability of showing a clinically significant change on an outcome measure (e.g., falling within the normative range) among those individuals who have made a clinically significant change in everyday life (e.g., on another criterion). *Specificity* is the probability of *not* showing a clinically significant change on an outcome measure (e.g., not falling within the normative range) among those individuals who have *not* made a clinically significant change in everyday life. Methods for evaluating sensitivity and specificity, elaborated elsewhere (see Kraemer, 1992), are quite relevant to the evaluation and validation of measures of clinical significance.

parents (e.g., parent history of divorce, psychopathology) and family (e.g., socioeconomic disadvantage, strains of child rearing), and contextual influences (e.g., availability of social support, adequate day care), to mention a few. The larger point is that the value, significance, and impact of a therapeutic change of a given magnitude may vary considerably. Theory and research that elaborate the impact of diverse influences on clinically significant change could have rather important implications for therapy more generally.

CONCLUSIONS

Clinical significance has been intended to reflect the extent to which treatment makes a difference, one of practical or applied value in everyday life. Several measures of clinical significance are available, but we do not have a clear idea of the meaning of results that are clinically significant, that is, beyond meeting the criteria for the operational definition. Also, it is still quite possible that clients meet our operational definitions of clinically significant change but in fact are either not functioning much better, do not feel better, or are not seen as improved by significant others.

Some of the early controlled intervention (e.g., from the 1970s) using normative data to evaluate treatment outcome directly assessed how individuals were functioning at home, at school, and the community (see Kazdin, 1977, for a review). When clients returned to within normative ranges at the end of treatment, the effects were persuasive because functioning reflected performance in everyday settings. Direct assessment in daily life does not resolve all ambiguities because the measure may not relate to functioning outside of the assessment context (e.g., situation, setting, conditions of assessment). Yet, such observations appeared closer to the definition of clinical significance as a change that has impact on daily functioning. Any other type of measure can be just as or indeed more useful, valid, and meaningful, as long as evidence is provided showing that the measure or cutoff used to define clinical significance in fact relates to other criteria that more directly reflect real-world impact.

Enormous research opportunities exist for the assessment and evaluation of clinical significance (Kazdin, 2001). It would be valuable to begin with a definition and conceptual view of clinical significance and to derive and validate measures or indices in keeping with that conceptualization. What is in fact a clinically significant change, as defined by clients or consumers of treatment (e.g., through focus group, qualitative research)? A conceptual view is needed to organize the many facets (e.g., subjective evaluation, reports of others) and to permit tests that go beyond merely correlating measures with each other. Perhaps research ought to begin with the idea that clinical significance is multidimensional. The dimensions and their interrelations can be identified. The purpose in identifying multiple dimensions would be to evaluate clinical significance somewhat differently from current practices. Once key dimensions were identified and operationalized, we might use the data to obtain a profile of individual functioning, that is, the client's score on each dimension that defines clinical significance. Alternatively, it may be that the goals of treatment will prompt the relevant dimensions or prioritize the dimensions along which clinically significant change ought to be measured. Clearly, important questions wait to be addressed in relation to the meaning and measurement of clinical significance.

REFERENCES

American Psychiatric Association. (1994). *Diagnostic and statistical manual of mental disorders* (4th ed.). Washington, DC: Author.

Bird, H. R., Yager, T. J., Staghezza, B., Gould, M. S., Canino, G., & Rubio-Stipec, M. (1990). Impairment in the epidemiological measurement of psychopathology in the community. *Journal of the American Academy of Child and Adolescent Psychiatry, 29,* 796–803.

Burke, K. C., Burke, J. D., Regier, D. A., & Rae, D. S. (1990). Age at onset of selected mental disorders in five community populations. *Archives of General Psychiatry, 47,* 511–518.

Foster, S., & Mash, E. J. (1999). Assessing social validity in clinical treatment research: Issues and procedures. *Journal of Consulting and Clinical Psychology, 67,* 308–319.

Gladis, M. M., Gosch, E. A., Dishuk, N. M., & Crits-Cristoph, P. (1999). Quality of life: Expanding the scope of clinical significance. *Journal of Consulting and Clinical Psychology, 67,* 320–331.

Gotlib, I. H., Lewinsohn, P. M., & Seeley, J. R. (1995). Symptoms versus a diagnosis of depression: Differences in psychosocial functioning. *Journal of Consulting and Clinical Psychology, 63,* 90–100.

Howard, K. I., Lueger, R. J., & Kolden, G. G. (1997). Measuring progress and outcome in the treatment of affective disorders. In H. H. Strupp, L. M. Horowitz, & M. J. Lambert (Eds.), *Measuring patient changes in mood, anxiety, and personality disorders: Toward a core battery* (pp. 263–282). Washington, DC: American Psychological Association.

Jacobson, N. S., Roberts, L. J., Berns, S. B., & McGlinchey, J. B. (1999). Methods for defining and determining the clinical significance of treatment effects: Description, application, and alternatives. *Journal of Consulting and Clinical Psychology, 67,* 300–307.

Kazdin, A. E. (1977). Assessing the clinical or applied importance of behavior change through social validation. *Behavior Modification, 1,* 427–452.

Kazdin, A. E. (1999). The meanings and measurement of clinical significance. *Journal of Consulting and Clinical Psychology, 67,* 332–339.

Kazdin, A. E. (2001). Almost clinically significant ($p < .10$): Current measures may only approach clinical significance. *Clinical Psychology: Science and Practice*, 8, 455–462.

Kazdin, A. E. (2003). *Research design in clinical psychology* (4th ed.). Needham Heights, MA: Allyn & Bacon.

Kazdin, A. E., & Wassell, G. (1998). Treatment completion and therapeutic change among children referred for outpatient therapy. *Professional Psychology: Research and Practice*, 29, 332–340.

Kazdin, A. E., & Wilson, G. T. (1978). Criteria for evaluating psychotherapy. *Archives of General Psychiatry*, 35, 407–416.

Kendall, P. C. (Ed.). (1999). Clinical significance [Special section]. *Journal of Consulting and Clinical Psychology*, 67, 283–339.

Kendall, P. C., & Grove, W. M. (1988). Normative comparisons in therapy outcome. *Behavioral Assessment*, 10, 147–158.

Kendall, P. C., Marrs-Garcia, A., Nath, S. R., & Sheldrick, R. C. (1999). Normative comparisons for the evaluation of clinical significance. *Journal of Consulting and Clinical Psychology*, 67, 285–299.

Kraemer, H. C. (1992). *Evaluating medical tests: Objective and quantitative guidelines.* Newbury Park, CA: Sage.

Lewinsohn, P. M., Roberts, R. E., Seeley, J. R., Rohde, P., Gotlib, I. H., & Hops, H. (1994). Adolescent psychopathology: II. Psychosocial risk factors for depression. *Journal of Abnormal Psychology*, 103, 302–315.

Lewinsohn, P. M., Seeley, J. R., Hibbard, J., Rohde, P., & Sack, W. H. (1996). Cross-sectional and prospective relationships between physical morbidities and depression in older adolescents. *Journal of the American Academy of Child and Adolescent Psychiatry*, 35, 1120–1129.

Lunnen, K. M., & Ogles, B. M. (1998). A multiperspective, multivariable evaluation of reliable change. *Journal of Consulting and Clinical Psychology*, 66, 400–410.

Pekarik, G., & Wolff, C. B. (1996). Relationship of satisfaction to symptom change, follow-up adjustment, and clinical significance. *Professional Psychology: Research and Practice*, 27, 202–208.

Robinson, L. A., Berman, J. S., & Neimeyer, R. A. (1990). Psychotherapy for the treatment of depression: A comprehensive review of controlled outcome research. *Psychological Bulletin*, 108, 30–49.

Sanford, M. N., Offord, D. R., Boyle, M. H., Peace, A., & Racine, Y. A. (1992). Ontario Child Health Study: Social and school impairments in children aged 6–16 years. *Journal of the American Academy of Child and Adolescent Psychiatry*, 31, 60–67.

Strupp, H. H., & Hadley, S. W. (1977). A tripartite model of mental health and therapeutic outcomes. *American Psychologist*, 32, 187–196.

Tingey, R. C., Lambert, M. J., Burlingame, G. M., & Hansen, N. B. (1996). Assessing clinical significance: Proposed extensions to method. *Psychotherapy Research*, 6, 109–123.

U.S. Congress, Office of Technology Assessment. (1991). *Adolescent health* (OTA-H-468). Washington, DC: U.S. Government Printing Office.

Wolf, M. M. (1978). Social validity: The case of subjective measurement or how applied behavior analysis is finding its heart. *Journal of Applied Behavior Analysis, 11*, 203–214.

31

TOWARD THE INCORPORATION OF COSTS, COST-EFFECTIVENESS ANALYSIS, AND COST–BENEFIT ANALYSIS INTO CLINICAL RESEARCH

BRIAN T. YATES

I believe that we can understand, in a scientific manner, not only the techniques of treatment and their potential outcomes but also how treatment systems can deliver those techniques in ways that better realize their full potential effectiveness and that cost less. In clinical research, we devote most of our resources to the development and testing of new psychological techniques. The effectiveness of these technologies is our paramount concern in grant proposals, experimental designs, instrumentation, procedures, statistical analyses, and discussions of findings. The costs of psychological technologies can be measured too, but they seldom are. These costs may include the value of temporal and other personnel resources; spatial resources such as offices, supplies, and transportation; and particularly the time spent

Reprinted from the *Journal of Consulting and Clinical Psychology, 62,* 729–736. Copyright 1994 by the American Psychological Association.

by clients and others in treatment. I hope to show that the costs of clinical efforts are not mundane, unimportant, irrelevant, or too predictable to be of interest. Furthermore, once costs have been accurately and comprehensively assessed, we can empirically explore the entire system of linkages among the specific resources consumed in treatment, the therapeutic procedures that those resources make possible, the psychological and other processes produced by those procedures, and the outcomes achieved.

OUR INCOMPLETE RESEARCH AGENDA

By focusing scientific scrutiny on only the outcomes of treatment, investigators may be making mistakes that could become serious as budgets dwindle and clients become more sophisticated consumers of health services. The research methods that have been used for decades have generated a literature that now allows researchers to say much about which treatments are effective and why but little about how much treatments cost and hardly anything about which treatments deliver the best outcomes for the least money. Methods for assessing costs and for contrasting costs to effectiveness and benefits have been available for a decade or two, but they have not been used (e.g., Carter & Newman, 1976; Fishman, 1975; Levin, 1975; Newman & Sorensen, 1985; Rufener, Rachal, & Cruze, 1977; Weisbrod, 1983; Yates, 1980, 1985; cf. Yates & Newman, 1980a, 1980b). As pressure for cost containment evolves into pressure for cost cuts, investigators risk being unable to provide scientific answers to the questions that potential clients or funders may ask even before they inquire as to effectiveness (i.e., "What does it cost?" and "Is it really worth it?"; cf. McGuire, 1989). Essentially, I am saying our current approach to research in clinical psychology is incomplete. Assessing costs as well as outcomes also would allow researchers to construct a more complete theoretical and empirical model of psychological treatment. To these ends, I propose that we pay as much attention to the resources consumed in treatment as we do to the outcomes made possible by expenditure of those resources.

Furthermore, investigators need to focus beyond the comparison of treatments in terms of their outcomes and their costs, to analyze and really understand their cost-effectiveness and cost–benefit. Simple ratios of cost to effectiveness or monetary benefit only provide a limited and possibly mistaken understanding of how to squeeze the most effectiveness out of mental health technologies at the lowest possible costs. What researchers need to do is to go beyond a tabular comparison of costs and outcomes to the point where it is possible not only to measure costs, processes, and outcomes but also to discover and quantify the strength of the relationships among (a) resources consumed, (b) treatment procedures funded, (c) psychological and biological processes engendered by those procedures, and (d) interim and long-term outcomes produced.

This article considers several beliefs that may have impeded the measurement and analysis of relationships among the resources that make treatment possible, the procedures conducted in treatment, and the changes that therapists hope to make in clients' lives. Discussed briefly here are several of the more important beliefs regarding (a) the assessment of costs, (b) the degree to which psychological techniques, as opposed to treatment delivery systems, determine the outcome of services, and (c) what cost-effectiveness analysis and cost–benefit analysis are and can do for psychological treatment.

BELIEFS ABOUT COSTS AND COST-OUTCOME RELATIONSHIPS

"Cost is Directly Related to Outcome (or You Get What You Pay For)"

Howard, Kopta, Krause, and Orlinsky (1986) and Newman and Howard (1986) have shown with meta-analysis that there often is a direct relationship between the "dose" of a specific therapy procedure (e.g., number of sessions) and its effectiveness. This important, familiar relationship may be different from the relationship between the expense of a therapy session and the benefits one obtains from it. More expensive therapy is not necessarily better therapy, although spending more money for more sessions of an effective form of therapy may increase the likelihood of positive outcomes. When this is suggested, most people acknowledge the possibility of an indirect relationship between the resources expended in therapy and the outcomes attained. Most, however, maintain the position that more expensive therapy must be better therapy because, if it were not, then why would people pay so much for it? The laws of supply and demand may not, however, be operating in the mental health marketplace. The adjustment of price to reflect quality would likely occur if mental health services were provided in an open market with widely advertised prices and well-informed, rational consumers, but this is seldom the case in the mental health sector (McGuire, 1980, 1989).

Many studies could be cited to describe the position that more costly treatment is not necessarily more effective treatment (cf. Yates & Newman, 1980b). Karon and VandenBos (1976), for example, found that psychologists were as effective as psychiatrists in treating schizophrenics but were less expensive. Weisbrod (1983), among others, showed that inpatient treatment of schizophrenics is more expensive, but not more effective, than community care. Siegert and Yates (1980) found that therapy delivered by the most expensive delivery system for child management training was not more effective than therapy delivered by their least expensive delivery system. Hayashida et al. (1989) found that a drug abuse treatment that required more

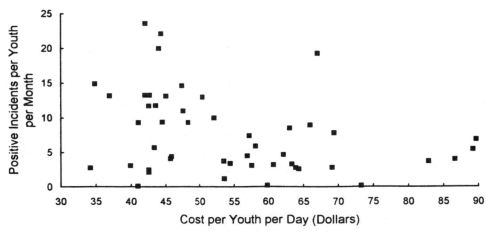

Figure 31.1. Desired outcomes may be inversely related to costs: Positive incidents in youth residential programs as a function of cost per youth ($r = -.33$, $N = 48$, $p < .05$).

time of clients, as well as more funds, was not more effective than another treatment that was considerably less expensive for clients and funders.

It even appears that outcomes can be inversely related to costs. I found that positive incidents reported in four residential treatment facilities for dependent and neglected urban youths were negatively correlated with monthly expenditures. As shown in Figure 31.1, the average number of positive incidents per youth per month had a correlation of $-.33$ with the average cost per youth per day ($p < .05$, two-tailed). the N for this Pearson r was 48, corresponding to one data point per month per home for 1 year.

The possibility of an occasional negative relationship between outcome and cost has been demonstrated in other areas of treatment as well. For example, in a study of clients with a phobia for snakes, Bandura, Blanchard, and Ritter (1969) not only contrasted the increase in clients' approaching a snake produced by (a) participant modeling, (b) symbolic modeling, and (c) systematic desensitization but also measured the minutes spent by therapists and clients in sessions. (Similar delivery systems were used in all treatment conditions [i.e., individual sessions in a clinic].) An analysis of variance showed that participant modeling was the most effective treatment procedure. Ninety-two percent of clients receiving the participant modeling procedure attained the terminal step in a "snake-approach" continuum of being able to sit with a 3-foot snake in their lap for 2 min. Systematic desensitization allowed only 25% of clients to reach the same terminal step. Bandura et al. also reported that participant modeling required the least time of clients: only 2 hr, 10 min on the average. Systematic desensitization required a significantly greater mean of 4 hr, 33 min. The amount of time required by the film modeling was an average 2 hr, 46 min. Film modeling was conducted by the client after the therapist had a brief discussion of the procedure with the client and after the client was shown how to operate the film projector.

For snake phobias, it seems possible that effectiveness may be maximized and costs minimized with the use of the participant modeling procedure. (This statement could not, of course, be made for any other simple phobia or any more general avoidance problem without careful replication of the Bandura et al. [1969] procedure with clients who have these different disorders.) These findings run contrary to the commonly encountered wisdom that "you get what you pay for." That adage most likely applies in economic situations in which outcomes and costs are accurately measured and widely known, so that supply and demand forces a positive price–outcome relationship.

"Money Spent Reflects Resources Used"

A primary reason for the dearth of cost data in clinical research may be the supposition that costs are trivial to measure (i.e., that they are simply the money spent on treatment). However, when costs are assessed carefully and thoroughly, as the value of resources consumed in treatment, it becomes evident that the crucial resource expenditures may be measured best in units not commonly associated with costs. For example, Yates, Haven, and Thoresen (1979) found that the assessment of staff resources expended in a residential treatment for predelinquent youths was most complete when the units of measurement were not dollars of salary paid to staff but minutes of time spent by staff in treatment-related activities. As shown in Table 31.1, valuation of the time actually spent by staff in treatment-related activities resulted in cost figures that varied considerably from the salary paid.

Generally, Yates et al. found that, during the month in which costs were assessed, individuals who received the highest rates of pay expended the exact amount of time for which they received payment: the doctoral staff, however, actually worked fewer hours than they should have to justify their salary. The majority of staff, who held lower degrees, expended far more resources than they were paid for. For instance, individuals with undergraduate degrees worked enough hours to have received a total of $13,675 if they had been paid for the hours they worked. They were paid only $2,972, however. This difference between resources expended and resources reimbursed was justified as being reimbursed by a barter of services (i.e., by the extensive training opportunities and supervision received by the BA-level staff). Nevertheless, the finding that the salaries of BA-level staff reflected only 21.7% of the time that the staff devoted to treatment suggests that relying on accounting records may underestimate treatment costs. This finding may not be limited to the settings that use volunteers and trainees to deliver much of the direct services.

TABLE 31.1

Differences Between Dollars Paid and the Value of Time Spent
in Treatment-Related Activities for Different Staff Groupings

Personnel Category	Salary Paid ($)	Hourly pay rate ($) (from local mental health pay scales)	Hours spent in treatment-related activities per month	Value of staff time (Hourly Pay Rate × Hours Spent)
MD, JD, CPA	1,462	45.00	32.5	1,462
PhD	849	15.67	50.9	798
MA	2,706	7.78	829.3	6,452
BA	2,972	7.66	1,785.2	13,675
Paraprofessional	0	5.53	532.3	2,943
Undergraduate	0	1.70	699.4	1,189
Other (includes clients' parents)	0	2.00	297.0	594
Total	7,988			27,112

Note: From *Improving Effectiveness and Reducing Costs in Mental Health* (p. 52) by B. T. Yates. 1980. Springfield, IL: Charles C Thomas. Copyright 1980 by Charles C Thomas. Reprinted with permission. MD = doctor of medicine (medical degree); JD = doctor of law (law degree); CPA = certified public accountant; PhD = doctor of philosophy; MA = master of arts; BA = bachelor of arts.

BELIEFS ABOUT TREATMENT TECHNIQUES VERSUS TREATMENT DELIVERY SYSTEMS

"It's Not the Medium; It's the Message"

We all too often hope that the innovative psychological techniques that are developed and, it is hoped, that others adopt will be so powerful that they can overcome barriers to the delivery of the techniques. Little research has been conducted on either (a) the way in which the procedures for applying those techniques to specific individuals transmit the full impact of these well-investigated techniques or (b) how much these different delivery systems cost. Research on how different delivery media may affect the costs and effectiveness of therapeutic "messages" can be revealing. For example, Yates (1978) contrasted a rigorously structured treatment program that used state-of-the-art techniques for obesity reduction to an eclectic commercial weight loss program. Both programs generated approximately the same outcomes: an average 30% reduction in excess adipose tissue. The average cost per percent reduction in obesity was $44.60 in the state-of-the-art program and $3 in the commercial program.

It can be argued that the state-of-the-art program spared no expense in implementing what had been hoped to be techniques of superior effectiveness and that this is justified when trying to translate basic research and theory into clinical practice. Certainly, more highly paid personnel were involved in the more expensive program. Also, the incentives under which the commercial program functioned were different from those governing the state-of-the-art program: Cost was something to be minimized in the commercial program, whereas superior effectiveness was the goal in the other program. Nonetheless, this study points out the impact that delivery systems can have on treatment effectiveness and costs. It illustrates what may be the case in much of psychology: There may be little or no substantial difference in effectiveness when different treatment technologies are delivered in clinical settings, but the systems used to deliver the new or old technology certainly can make a difference in the costs of treatment.

"More is Better"

A major assumption about the delivery of treatment services that probably creates unnecessary expenditures of time and energy by therapists and clients alike is that adding another technique to the treatment "stew" will improve outcome. It is understood, of course, that those techniques must be compatible with others used in treatment and that they have to be part of a coherent program of treatment. However, enthusiasm to provide the best treatment to the client may not only lead to unnecessary expense but also evoke psychology processes that actually diminish treatment outcomes.

For example, in a nine-condition treatment outcome study on a program developed by Yates (1987), it was found that adding a cognitive component or an exercise component to a diet component produced no more weight loss than the diet component alone. Exercise and cognitive components alone and in combination produced no significant weight loss. If these findings are considered generalizable, the common inclusion of cognitive and exercise components in weight loss programs seems unjustified. In fact, Yates' clients in the (a) diet + cognitive, (b) diet + exercise, and (c) diet + cognitive + exercise conditions spent substantially more time in program-related activities than did diet-only clients (see Table 31.2) to no apparent effect. A bibliotherapy condition, which involved no therapist contact, produced weight loss that was slightly but not significantly greater than the weight loss produced by the diet condition.

"Clients Have to Pay for Therapy for It to Work"

It is commonly believed that the more clients pay for treatment, the more benefit they will gain from it, although empirical investigations provide little support for this assumption (e.g., DeMuth & Kamis, 1980). It still can be maintained, however, that the outcomes of therapy may be better if clients struggle with treatment or if they devote more time or other personal resources to it. This also does not seem to be the case always.

Returning to the Yates (1987) study, an analysis of client perceptions of

TABLE 31.2
Cost and Effectiveness of Alternative Combinations
of Obesity Treatments

Treatment Component Combination	n	Median Weight Reduction Index (essentially % excess weight lost)[a]	Median no. of minutes spent by clients per day in treatment-related activities
Cognitive therapy	10	1.7	40
Diet	12	15.9[b]	13
Exercise	11	0.0	104
Cognitive therapy + diet	13	17.1[b]	36
Cognitive therapy + exercise	14	2.6	93
Diet + exercise	14	2.7	73
Cognitive therapy + diet + exercise	12	10.2[b]	128
Bibliotherapy + self-monitoring only[c]	12	4.5	51
Bibliotherapy only[d]	10	20.0[b]	70

Note: Adapted from "Cognitive vs. Diet vs. Exercise Components in Obesity Bibliotherapy: Effectiveness as a Function of Psychological Benefits Versus Psychological Costs" by B. T. Yates, 1987, *The Southern Psychologist, 3*, p. 38. Adapted with permission. Clients in all but the bibliotherapy + self-monitoring only condition and bibliotherapy only condition were reinforced by deposit return for the attainment of (a) self-monitoring goals and (b) change goals for the component or combination listed.
[a] Compare with the findings of Wilson (1978). [b] Percentages from weight-loss-producing conditions that Mann-Whitney U tests showed to differ significantly as a group from all other conditions. However, these conditions did not differ significantly among themselves. Dropouts were included in analyses and were given the last weight reported. [c] Clients in this condition were not reinforced by deposit return to achieving goals for completion of changes in diet, exercise, and analyses of cognitive self-statements. Only attainment of self-monitoring goals and attendance at mid- and posttreatment weighings were required for deposit return. [d] Clients in this condition were reinforced by deposit return solely for attending mid-and posttreatment weighings.

the costs of treatment to clients showed that the treatment for which clients reported spending the least amount of time (diet, with an average of 13 min / week) was not significantly different in outcome from conditions that inspired clients to devote significantly more time to treatment (see Table 31.2). Additional analyses showed that outcomes were highest in conditions that clients perceived to be cost beneficial (i.e., for which psychological benefits exceeded psychological costs).

Throughout the 10-week program, clients reported two costs (ratings of treatment difficulty on 10-point Likert scales and minutes spent in treatment-related activities) and two benefits (usefulness of and satisfaction with treatment, each rated on 10-point scales). Subjects seemed to carry out the suggested activities more in treatment conditions that seemed to offer more value, in terms of outcomes, than they required in terms of resources from the client.

Subject compliance with the treatment regimen may be related to subjects' perceptions of the benefits of treatment *relative* to the "hassle" and time costs required. Ratios were calculated for each subject to contrast psychological benefits to psychological costs. *Each* of the four possible benefit/cost ratios were significantly higher for the weight loss producing conditions . . . for ratios of satisfaction/difficulty, usefulness/difficulty, satisfaction/time, and usefulness/time. (Yates, 1987, p. 39)

Conditions that did not produce weight loss were viewed as having psychological costs that were not exceeded by psychological benefits: "The median benefit/cost ratios for all other [non-weight-loss producing] conditions were 1.0 for both satisfaction and usefulness versus difficulty" (Yates, 1987, p. 39).

These findings suggest another observation about the importance of considering costs as well as outcomes in treatment. It is possible that most psychological treatments would achieve respectable outcomes if clients complied with the suggested regimen. Compliance is, however, a function of many variables. Among these may be the cost–benefit of the treatment as perceived by the client. Evaluations of psychological treatments may find that substantial amounts of previously unexplained variance in treatment outcomes can be explained by treatment costs and benefits, as they were seen by treatment recipients.

BELIEFS AND CONCERNS ABOUT COST-EFFECTIVENESS ANALYSIS AND COST–BENEFIT ANALYSIS

The study discussed earlier illustrates a simple, even simplistic, method of analyzing the relationships between outcomes achieved (benefits, as perceived by the client, in this case) and resources consumed (costs, again as perceived by the client). Just dividing outcome by cost does not a cost–benefit or cost-effectiveness analysis make, however. The methodologies of cost-effectiveness analysis and cost–benefit analysis are complex (cf. Apsler & Harding, 1991). A description of these methods is beyond the scope of this article, and a variety of sources exist for more information (e.g., Levin, 1975, 1980; Newman & Sorensen, 1985; Rufener et al., 1977; Thompson, 1980; Warner, Luce, & Hellinger, 1983; Yates, 1980, 1985). There is, or at least can be, more to cost-effectiveness analysis and cost–benefit analysis than a few ratios or net benefit figures, also.

"Cost–Benefit Analysis Reduces Everything to the Lowest Common Denominator: Money"

Cost–benefit analysis does not require the use of any monetary figures. All that it requires is that the outcomes of services provided and the resources consumed to make those services possible be measured in the same units. The benefit/cost ratios computed earlier for client ratings of the usefulness of treatment versus its difficulty used no monetary units. Monetary units are simply the most common units in which resource data are available in most psychological service systems, and they allow resource expenditure information about staff, space, supplies, and equipment to be pooled for more global analyses.

"Cost–Benefit Analysis of Psychological Services Ignores the Most Important Outcomes"

Benefit is often interpreted as implying that one must show a profit or some other type of positive income flow. Although many psychologists seem adverse to placing a dollar sign on the results of their services, substantial increases in client income and corporate earnings have been shown to result from many types of psychological service (Jones & Vischi, 1979; Manuso, 1978; Silkman, Kelley, & Wolf, 1983). Furthermore, some of the most powerful arguments in favor of including psychological treatments in corporate health care packages have been the savings produced in health care costs. Cummings (1977) showed that one to four sessions of therapy returned $2.59, on the average, for every dollar spent on therapy. In general, many outcomes of psychological services are indeed nonmonetary, but those that are can be shown to often exceed the monetary value of resources consumed at levels of profit attractive to government agencies and most businesses (cf. Cummings & Follette, 1968; Jones & Vischi, 1979; Rufener et al., 1977; Yates, 1984). These findings also may allay the fears of those who were opposed to cost–benefit analysis largely because they feared that psychological therapies would not be cost beneficial according to quantitative analyses.

"To Be Meaningful, Cost-Effectiveness Analysis Requires Comparisons to Other Treatments"

Treatments that produce outcomes that are difficult to measure in the same units as those used to value resources (e.g., money) still can be assessed for the amount of resources consumed in cost-effectiveness analysis. In cost-effectiveness analysis, the outcomes of treatment are measured in whatever units are appropriate, whereas the value of resources consumed can be measured in different (e.g., monetary) units. Although a single cost-effectiveness ratio does not provide quite as much information about the potential return on investment as that yielded by a ratio of benefits to costs, the cost per outcome can be compared between treatments. Moreover, some people perceive some value in single ratios of cost to effectiveness with no explicit comparison (e.g., the cost per pound lost or average cost per former drug abuser not receded for 10 years).

"Cost–Benefit Analysis and Cost-Effectiveness Analysis Are Just Rationalizations for Funding Cuts"

In general, program evaluation can be either summative or formative (Scriven, 1967). *Summative* evaluations are designed to yield judgments about the worth of programs, and any evaluation—including cost–benefit analysis and cost-effectiveness analysis—can be summative. Inclusion of cost data in an evaluation may indeed increase the attention that a summative evaluation receives. *Formative* evaluations are attempts to understand the program as it currently operates, so that it can be improved. Formative cost-effectiveness analysis and cost–benefit analysis are just as possible as other forms of program evaluation that ignore costs. They may contribute more to program development than other forms of program evaluation because they consider financial and other resource-oriented aspects of the context in which the program functions.

I and other researchers have attempted to conduct cost-effectiveness and cost–benefit analyses that go beyond descriptions of cost/effectiveness ratios to more complex descriptions of relationships between costs and outcomes. Even simple graphs of the outcomes of one or more programs against costs can describe some of the complexity of cost–outcome relationships (cf. Siegert & Yates, 1980; Yates, 1978, 1985). More complex, mathematical models can be constructed to depict relationships between costs and outcomes and among resources spent, treatment procedures implemented, psychological changes achieved, and significant behavioral and lifestyle goals attained (cf. Yates, 1980). By incorporating information on budgets and other resource constraints into these models, researchers may be able to systematically determine how to maximize treatment outcomes while keeping within budgets. The more complete treatment models that are possible when cost data are combined with process and outcome data may increase the ability to deliver the best services to the most clients within the limits imposed by society and economy.

POSSIBLE IMPEDIMENTS TO COST-EFFECTIVENESS ANALYSIS AND COST–BENEFIT ANALYSIS

Assessing, analyzing, reporting, and using data on costs, cost-effectiveness, and cost–benefit can be seen as four stages of incorporating information about the resources consumed in clinical efforts into research on those efforts. Some studies already report or discuss costs along with effectiveness or benefits, but growth of this literature seems to have stalled. A search was conducted of the American Psychological Association's Psychological Abstracts Information Services (PsycINFO) database from 1967 through 1991 (the last full year accessible at the time this article was written). The search

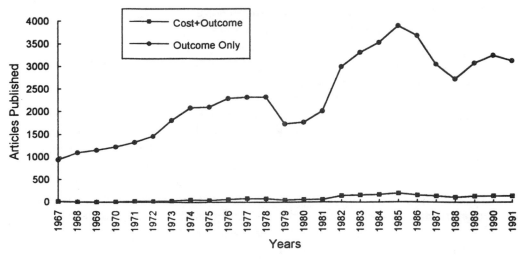

Figure 31.2. Change over a quarter of a century in articles in the *PsycINFO* database that include data on or discussion of cost, as well as effectiveness or benefit.

terms used were "((cost and effective$) or (cost and benefi$)) and 19___.yr.," where "$" was the wildcard used by the database service for one or more characters. The search for "effectiveness" or "benefits" articles simply omitted the "cost and" phrases. The terms *cost-effectiveness* and *cost–benefit analysis* could not be used directly, as these do not seem to be recognized search terms in PsycINFO. Figure 31.2 shows how few even these increased publications are, in relation to publications concerned with treatment effectiveness or benefits. Following a marked increase in both outcome-only publications and cost-plus-outcome publications in the mid-1980s, there has been a decline and subsequent plateauing of the number of both types. Figure 31.3 shows that this percentage has grown slowly but steadily over a quarter of a century from less than 1% in the late 1960s to slightly over 5% in the mid-1980s, settling in at about 4.5% for the past few years.

Of course, a variety of topics other than the outcome and cost outcome of therapy are addressed in some of the articles entered into these counts. Also, the introduction of keywords related to cost, cost-effectiveness, and cost–benefit in the abstracting process also may affect the number of citations retrieved in literature searches such as this. Nevertheless, the proportion of such articles is likely to be constant across years. These data suggest that interest in cost, cost-effectiveness analysis, and cost–benefit analysis continues, but that only a small portion of the research and discussion on treatment outcome includes any mention of treatment cost or the relationship between outcome and cost. The inclusion of cost and related information in research and discussion articles occurs in a small and no longer growing percent of those articles.

Why? Perhaps a cost-outcome analysis of these findings about cost- and outcome-oriented publications would be illuminating. Any effort requires the expenditure of resources: Research and article preparation certainly consume time and money. Adding to therapy outcome studies another class of variables to assess (i.e., costs and several more stages of analysis such as cost-effectiveness and cost–benefit analyses) requires additional time from researchers and support staff. In addition, many researchers would need to be familiar with the nuances of cost assessment, cost-effectiveness analysis, and cost–benefit analysis to routinely use these in addition to standard analyses. The costs of these new endeavors are considerable, at least relative to a lack of increment in understanding or increased possibility of publication or funding that many researchers perceive. In this article, I have tried to change these perceptions; it is not enough.

One way in which cost-effectiveness and cost–benefit analyses could be encouraged is for reviewers and editors to make some reporting of costs and of these analyses a recommended part of articles to be submitted to journals. Government funders use similar or more absolute contingencies to promote research into specific topics, on certain subject populations, or using particular methods, when announcing grant or contract programs. A similar call for inclusion of cost–benefit analysis was made in the public health arena several decades ago by Deniston, Rosenstock, and Getting (1968). Another important strategy for encouraging these analyses is to include these topics in training programs in clinical research and texts (e.g., see Kazdin, 1980, 1992).

Finally, economic and political disincentives for cost-effectiveness analysis, cost–benefit analysis, and program evaluation in general need to be

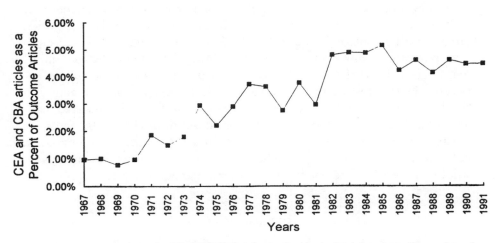

Figure 31.3. Articles in the PsycINFO database that include data on or discussion of cost as well as effectiveness of benefit. CEA = cost-effectiveness analysis. CBA = cost-benefit analysis.

eliminated from the arena of funding policy and decision making. Mental health administrators who may otherwise conduct or support cost-effectiveness analysis and cost–benefit analysis may not do so because they believe, based on previous personal or vicarious experience, that (a) data collected on program costs, procedures, and outcomes will be used against the program; (b) devoting resources to data collection, analysis, and feedback will result in funding cuts because "if your program can afford to do research, we can trim it and not hurt treatment"; and (c) programs that reduce their cost per client will have their funding reduced in proportion to their efficiency. To researchers, these beliefs may seem outlandish, but for many administrators and evaluators, these statements are all too real too often.

TOWARD DISCUSSIONS, DEBATES, AND DEVELOPMENT OF A NEW MODEL OF CLINICAL RESEARCH

There are many more misconceptions of research that considers costs as well as outcomes. I am certain that I still have much to learn about the possible negative consequences of examining costs as closely as outcomes (cf. Book, 1991). I hope that this article fosters an active dialogue among scientists, managers, and practitioners regarding how information about resources consumed, as well as outcomes produced, is used in formulating policy and making administrative and therapeutic decisions. The tensions that occasionally have pushed such discussions into the foreground in the past have not dissipated. Financial crises and limits on (and decrements in) public spending are, if anything, more common now. Competition among the mental health professions is considerable and will grow as funding diminishes. Divisions between scientists and practitioners may be widening further. My personal hope is that out of the vigorous discussions that usually occur when costs as well as outcomes are evaluated will come a revision of the scientist–practitioner model of practice and training. This much-debated model may fail too often because there is too strained and meager a connection between scientific research and clinical practice. Perhaps what's missing is a third component: the research-oriented as well as clinically sensitive management of the provision of psychological services (DeMuth, Yates, & Coates, 1984). By examining, discussing, and better understanding costs, cost-effectiveness, and cost–benefit in addition to effectiveness, perhaps we will find it easier to become better scientist–manager–practitioners.

REFERENCES

Apsler, R., & Harding, W. M. (1991). Cost-effectiveness analysis of drug abuse treatment: Current status and recommendations for future research. *NIDA Drug*

Abuse Services Research Series No. 1, 58 – 81 (DHHS Publication No. ADM 91-17777). Washington, DC: National Institute on Drug Abuse.

Bandura, A., Blanchard, E. B., & Ritter, B. (1969). Relative efficacy of desensitization and modeling approaches for inducing behavioral, affective, and attitudinal changes. *Journal of Personality and Social Psychology, 13*, 173 – 199.

Book, H. E. (1991). Is empathy cost efficient? *American Journal of Psychotherapy, 45*, 21 – 30.

Carter, D. E., & Newman, F. L. (1976). *A client-oriented system of mental health service delivery and program management: A workbook and guide* (DHEW Publication No. ADM 76-307). Rockville, MD: National Institute of Mental Health.

Cummings, N. A. (1977). Prolonged (ideal) versus short-term (realistic) psychotherapy. *Professional Psychology: Research and Practice, 8*, 491 – 501.

Cummings, N. A., & Follette, W. T. (1968). Psychiatric services and medical utilization in a prepaid health plan setting. *Medical Care, 5*, 31 – 41.

DeMuth, N. M., & Kamis, E. (1980). Fees and therapy: Clarification of the relationship of payment source to service utilization. *Journal of Consulting and Clinical Psychology, 48*, 793 – 795.

DeMuth, N. M., Yates, B. T., & Coates, T. C. (1984). Psychologists as managers: Overcoming old guilts and accessing innovative pathways for enhanced skills. *Professional Psychology: Research and Practice, 15*, 758 – 768.

Deniston, O. L., Rosenstock, I. M., & Getting, V. A. (1968). Evaluation of program effectiveness. *Public Health Reports, 83*, 323 – 335.

Fishman, D. B. (1975). Development of a generic cost-effectiveness methodology for evaluating patient services of a community mental health center. In J. Zusman & C. R. Wurster (Eds.), *Evaluation in alcohol, drug abuse, and mental health service programs* (pp. 139 – 159). Lexington, MA: Heath.

Hayashida, M., Alterman, A. I., McLellan, A. T., O'Brien, C. P., Purtill, J. J., Volricelli, J. R., Raphaelson, A. H., & Hall, C. P. (1989). Comparative effectiveness and costs of inpatient and outpatient detoxification of patients with mild-to-moderate alcohol withdrawal syndrome. *New England Journal of Medicine, 320*, 358 – 365.

Howard, K. I., Kopta, S. M., Krause, M. S., & Orlinsky, D. E. (1986). The dose – effect relationship in psychotherapy. *American Psychologist, 41*, 159 – 164.

Jones, K. R., & Vischi, T. R. (1979). Impact of alcohol, drug abuse, and mental health treatment on medical care utilization: A review of the research literature. *Medical Care, 17*, (Suppl.).

Karon, B. P., & VandenBos, G. R. (1976). Cost/benefit analysis: Psychologist versus psychiatrist for schizophrenics. *Professional Psychology: Research and Practice, 7*, 107 – 111.

Kazdin, A. E. (1980). *Research design in clinical psychology*. New York: Harper & Row.

Kazdin, A. E. (1992). *Research design in clinical psychology*. (2nd ed.). New York: Macmillan.

Levin, H. M. (1975). Cost-effectiveness analysis in evaluation research. In M. Guttentag & E. L. Struening (Eds.), *Handbook of evaluation research* (Vol. 2, pp. 89–122). Beverly Hills, CA: Sage.

Levin, H. M. (1980). *Cost-effectiveness: A primer.* Beverly Hills, CA: Sage.

Manuso, J. (1978). Testimony to the President's Commission on Mental Health, Panel on Cost and Financing. *Report of the President's Commission on Mental Health: Appendix* (Vol. 2, p. 512). Washington, DC: U.S. Government Printing Office.

McGuire, T. G. (1980). Markets for psychotherapy. In G. VandenBos (Ed.), *Psychotherapy: Practice, research, and policy* (pp. 187–245). Beverly Hills, CA: Sage.

McGuire, T. (1989). Outpatient benefits for mental health services in Medicare: Alignment with the private sector? *American Psychologist, 44,* 818–824.

Newman, F. L., & Howard, K. I. (1986). Therapeutic effort, treatment outcome, and national health policy. *American Psychologist, 41,* 181–187.

Newman, F. L., & Sorensen, J. E. (1985). *Integrated clinical and fiscal management in mental health: A guidebook.* Norwood, NJ: Ablex.

Rufener, B. L., Rachal, J. V., & Cruze, A. M. (1977). *Management effectiveness measures for NIDA drug abuse treatment programs* (GPO Stock No. 017-024-00577-1). Washington, DC: U.S. Government Printing Office.

Scriven, M. (1967). The methodology of evaluation. In R. W. Tyler, R. M. Gagne, & M. Scriven (Eds.), *Perspectives of curriculum evaluation* (pp. 39–83). Chicago: Rand-McNally.

Siegert, F. E., & Yates, B. T. (1980). Behavioral child-management cost-effectiveness: A comparison of individual in-office, individual in-home, and group delivery systems. *Evaluation & the Health Professions, 3,* 123–152.

Silkman, R., Kelley, J. M., & Wolf, W. C. (1983). An evaluation of two preemployment services: Impact on employment and earnings of disadvantaged youths. *Evaluation Review, 7,* 467–496.

Thompson, M. S. (1980). *Benefit–cost analysis for program evaluation.* Beverly Hills, CA: Sage.

Warner, K. E., Luce, B. R., & Hellinger, F. J. (1983). Cost–benefit and cost-effectiveness analysis in health care. *Inquiry, 20,* 193.

Weisbrod, B. A. (1983). A guide to benefit–cost analysis, as seen through a controlled experiment in treating the mentally ill. *Journal of Health Politics, Policy and Law, 6,* 808–845.

Wilson, G. T. (1978). Methodological considerations in treatment outcome research on obesity. *Journal of Consulting and Clinical Psychology, 46,* 687–702.

Yates, B. T. (1978). Improving the cost-effectiveness of obesity programs: Reducing the cost per pound. *International Journal of Obesity, 2,* 377–387.

Yates, B. T. (1980). *Improving effectiveness and reducing costs in mental health.* Springfield, IL: Charles C. Thomas.

Yates, B. T. (1984). How psychology can improve the effectiveness and reduce the costs of health services. *Psychotherapy, 21,* 439–451.

Yates, B. T. (1985). Cost-effectiveness analysis and cost–benefit analysis: An introduction. *Behavioral Assessment, 7*, 207–234.

Yates, B. T. (1987). Cognitive vs. diet vs. exercise components in obesity bibliotherapy: Effectiveness as a function of psychological benefits versus psychological costs. *The Southern Psychologist, 3*, 35–40.

Yates, B. T., Haven, W. G., & Thoresen, C. E. (1979). Cost-effectiveness analysis at Learning House: How much change for how much money? In J. S. Stumphauzer (Ed.), *Progress in behavior therapy with delinquents* (pp. 186–222). Springfield, IL: Charles C. Thomas.

Yates, B. T., & Newman, F. L. (1980a). Approaches to cost-effectiveness and cost–benefit analysis of psychotherapy. In G. VandenBos (Ed.), *Psychotherapy: Practice, research, and policy* (p. 103–162). Beverly Hills, CA: Sage.

Yates, B. T., & Newman, F. L. (1980b). Findings of cost-effectiveness and cost–benefit analysis of psychotherapy. In G. VandenBos (Ed.), *Psychotherapy: Practice, research, and policy* (pp. 163–185). Beverly Hills, CA: Sage.

VII

ETHICS IN RESEARCH

Psychological research raises several ethical issues and dilemmas. Two broad domains capture the range of issues and responsibilities of the investigator. First are the multiple responsibilities of the investigator in relation to the participants in research. Key among these are practices that are designed to protect participants' rights, privacy, and confidentiality of the information. Conditions to which participants are exposed (e.g., measures, interventions, experimental manipulations), information that may be presented or withheld, and use of the results all reflect domains in which research participants are in some way vulnerable. Apart from the procedures that are used within the investigation, how the information is used also can have adverse consequences for groups of participants. Scientific findings, particularly those that study human functioning in context (e.g., different cultural groups), are not ethically neutral, and many studies may have adverse consequences if they are considered to reflect deficiencies or untoward characteristics of groups of individuals (e.g., as a function of age, sex, ethnicity). These are some of the salient ethical issues raised in relation to participants, their treatment, and use of the information that they provide.

Second are multiple responsibilities of the investigator to the profession, science, and society at large. These pertain to obligations about maintaining the integrity of the research, reporting information accurately and honestly, sharing information, and ensuring that one's work is open to scrutiny.

Violations of these obligations have been evident in cases of conflict of interest, fraud, fabrication of data, and plagiarism that undermine the integrity of scientific research and public confidence (see Kazdin, 2003; Koocher & Keith-Spiegel, 1998; Miller & Hersen, 1992; National Academy of Sciences, 1989; Sales & Folkman, 2000). Addressing these matters explicitly in training of researchers is an important priority. Indeed, for universities that receive federal grants, researchers must document that they have received some training in the ethics of research to serve as an investigator, staff member, or research assistant in the research project.

There are many roles in which psychologists perform their professional activities (e.g., consultant to the courts, psychotherapist, teacher and mentor), and these roles raise diverse ethical issues and responsibilities. The chapters in this part pertain primarily to those ethical issues and considerations that arise in the context of research with human participants. Ethical issues in other contexts (e.g., animal research, clinical practice, consultation with the courts) are no less significant in terms of professional responsibilities but are beyond the purview of this book.

GUIDELINES AND CODES

Chapter 32 consists of the Ethical Principles of Psychologists and Code of Conduct developed by the American Psychological Association (APA). It is a set of professional standards, principles, and recommendations to guide research, practice, consultation, and other activities related to execution of the profession. The guidelines are revised periodically to make refinements, to address emergent issues, and to handle expanding roles of psychologists in daily life (e.g., litigation, consultation). The guidelines are formulated in such a way as to emphasize the investigator's responsibilities toward individuals who participate in research as well as to the scientific enterprise. The full set of professional guidelines are provided here, rather than those specific to research, because they are critically important in defining what it means to be a psychologist and the types of activities that are required. Although we can identify issues that tend to be specific to research (e.g., informed consent, use of deception), the ethical responsibilities associated with research cannot be divorced from more general principles and practices having to do with integrity and responsibility of the investigator and concern for the welfare of others. Thus, mastery of the letter and spirit of the ethical principles and codes is important.

General principles to guide behavior are presented at the beginning of the ethical code and serve as an overarching context to address a broad set of circumstances that may not be easily anticipated. Critical to the ethical codes is attention to the decision-making process. An investigator cannot be expected to be the arbiter of critical issues in which he or she may have a vested interest. Thus, he or she is encouraged to seek the input of colleagues to address ethically sensitive issues. In addition, more formal procedures for evaluating one's research are used to supplement ethical codes. Review committees in universities and research institutions are intended to evaluate research from the perspective of ethical issues and participant rights.

In chapter 33, M. Brewster Smith discusses five moral principles underlying ethical codes. The principles include: 1) respect for others, 2) beneficence and nonmaleficence, 3) justice, 4) trust, and 5) fidelity and scientific integrity. These are discussed in the context of religious and philosophical traditions, ethical codes, and legal regulations. The broad principles are important to convey because they provide a context for ethical codes more generally as well as practices that govern the review of research (e.g., in universities). It is critical for researchers to know both the ethical codes and the broader principles they are designed to reflect. Decision making in the design and evaluation of research may require considering, weighing, and balacing of key principles.

SPECIAL TOPICS AND ISSUES

Several ethical issues pertain to responsibilities of the investigator to one's colleagues, the profession, and science more generally. Included are issues such as fraud, deception, allocation of credit for ideas and research efforts of one's collaborators, sharing of materials, conflict of interest, and others, as mentioned previously. Any one of these is enormously important and has major implications for the conduct of science and integrity of the entire enterprise. For example, fraud in science, including the fabrication and misreporting of data, is the most flagrant abridgment of ethical responsibilities of the investigator.

Fraud can have multiple consequences by misrepresenting the findings in a particular area, jeopardizing public safety, and undermining confidence in research. Public safety is potentially jeopardized when the results of studies of the cause or treatment of disease (e.g., leukemia, heart disease) are fabricated, and decisions may follow that affect the care of individuals. Fraud in the context of findings that may have implications for public safety are the ones that are most likely to be considered newsworthy, but newsworthiness and public attention are not the issues. The core of the sciences is the accumulation of replicable knowledge—fraud directly interferes with this in principle and practice. There are of course other professions and careers in which saying things that are blatantly untrue is fine and making things up that others could not replicate even if they tried are fine, and indeed, may even earn accolades of one's peers (e.g., writing fiction and composing music, respectively). This is not the case in science.

In this section, a few ethical issues are taken up in more detail to increase sensitivity to the range of issues and the contexts in which they can emerge. In chapter 34, Barbara J. Fly, William P. van Bark, Laura Weinman, Karen Strohm Kitchener, and Patrick R. Lang focus on ethical transgressions of psychology graduate students. Inclusion of this chapter ought not to imply that graduate students, when compared with faculty or investigators at various research institutes, are more or less prone to ethical dilemmas, issues, or transgressions. Indeed, this is a valuable chapter because it conveys that ethical issues are not reserved for established investigators or large-scale programs of research. Ethical issues emerge when one designs and conducts psychological research. In this chapter, several issues are mentioned, including failure to maintain confidentiality, plagiarism, and falsification of data.

The chapter is designed to increase sensitivity to many ethical issues that can emerge and the implications for improving graduate training. The training component is critically important because much of ethics training in graduate school is making students aware of the codes. "Awareness" is not a very strong intervention in the scheme of psychological research. That is, awareness is likely to influence some people, but it is also likely to be ineffective with many and highly variable in its impact. So, for example, making people aware that special dieting and exercise regimens can increase longevity or that flossing is really important for health of one's gums and teeth helps change some people, but this is weak and highly variable as an intervention. Most people who are aware do not engage in the practices, and most people who engage in the undesired practices are probably aware that it may be unwise to do so.

Perhaps, similarly with ethical issues, we definitely want to make all researchers (and participants) aware of the codes and issues. Yet, is there more we can do to increase adherence to ethical codes, to make protection of rights more salient, and to improve the ethical treatment of human participants and animal subjects? This chapter addresses some of the challenges and how they might translate to improvements in training researchers.

Allocation of credit in research is one area of scientific misconduct and raises significant ethical issues and occasionally serves as a source of misery among investigators. Allocation of credit includes two major issues: (a) the failure to acknowledge one's sources or the direct use and copying of material of someone else without providing credit or acknowledgment (plagiarism) and (b) the division of credit among collaborators in research and published reports of that research. The misconduct that plagiarism represents is generally brought to the attention of students early in their education; the lesson is clear, namely, one is to acknowledge all sources of information and as a general guideline, when in doubt, recognize the sources of one's ideas and prior work. In general, few cases of plagiarism emerge, and sanctions can be severe.

There is another issue related to allocation of credit in which guidelines are less clear and sanctions are rarely invoked. Research projects are often collaborative; they involve multiple investigators and a team of people who have responsibility of varying types and in varying degrees for completion of the study. The different components of research and responsibilities from idea to the final published report are numerous. Allocation of credit emerges in deciding whom to include and list as authors on a research article, the order in which they are to appear, the relation between junior and senior scientists or faculty and students, and how the different roles and contributions affect authorship. When stated in its most abstract way, allocation of credit seems devoid of the massively intense emotions one often encounters in the issue. The issue takes on significance because publications are pertinent to careers, promotion, and income. Also, being included or not in an article and being recognized appropriately invoke personal views of justice. Thus, allocation of credit, important in its own right, can take on major significance to the individuals involved in the matter. The problems of allocation of credit are exacerbated by differences in status and power among the collaborators working on a project. No clear guidelines exist regarding authorship, and in all likelihood the topic remains undiscussed in most training programs.

In chapter 35 by Mark A. Fine and Lawrence A. Kurdek, the issues related to allocation of authorship credit and order are elaborated. The context is in collaborations between faculty and student, which are special in the sense that students can be involved in all facets of the study. Graduate students are often full collaborators, colleagues, or the primary investigator for a given project in their advisor's laboratory. In this chapter, the authors convey how allocation of credit and authorship relate specifically to the Ethical Principles of Psychologists and Code of Conduct. Hypothetical cases are provided to convey different scenarios in which allocation of credit and authorship raise problems. The chapter provides recommendations for determining authorship and order of authorship. It discusses authorship in the context of ethical issues. The topic of publishing and communication of research findings is taken up in Part VIII.

REFERENCES

Kazdin, A. E. (2003). *Research design in clinical psychology* (3rd ed.). Needham Heights, MA: Allyn & Bacon.

Koocher, G. P., & Keith-Spiegel, P. (1998). *Ethics in psychology: Professional standards and cases* (2nd ed.). New York: Oxford University Press.

Miller, D. J., & Hersen, M. (Eds.). (1992). *Research fraud in the behavioral and biomedical sciences.* New York: Wiley.

National Academy of Sciences, Committee on the Conduct of Science. (1989). *On being a scientist.* Washington, DC: National Academy Press.

Sales, B. D., & Folkman, S. (Eds.) (2000). *Ethics in research with human participants.* Washington, DC: American Psychological Association.

GUIDELINES AND CODES

32

ETHICAL PRINCIPLES
OF PSYCHOLOGISTS AND
CODE OF CONDUCT

AMERICAN PSYCHOLOGICAL ASSOCIATION

CONTENTS

Reprinted from the *American Psychologist, 57*. Copyright 2002 by the American Psychological Association.

737

ETHICAL STANDARDS

1. Resolving Ethical Issues

1.01 Misuse of Psychologists' Work
1.02 Conflicts Between Ethics and Law, Regulations, or Other Governing Legal Authority
1.03 Conflicts Between Ethics and Organizational Demands
1.04 Informal Resolution of Ethical Violations
1.05 Reporting Ethical Violations
1.06 Cooperating With Ethics Committees
1.07 Improper Complaints
1.08 Unfair Discrimination Against Complainants and Respondents

2. Competence

2.01 Boundaries of Competence
2.02 Providing Services in Emergencies
2.03 Maintaining Competence
2.04 Bases for Scientific and Professional Judgments
2.05 Delegation of Work to Others
2.06 Personal Problems and Conflicts

3. Human Relations

3.01 Unfair Discrimination
3.02 Sexual Harassment
3.03 Other Harassment
3.04 Avoiding Harm
3.05 Multiple Relationships
3.06 Conflict of Interest
3.07 Third-Party Requests for Services
3.08 Exploitative Relationships
3.09 Cooperation With Other Professionals
3.10 Informed Consent
3.11 Psychological Services Delivered to or Through Organizations
3.12 Interruption of Psychological Services

4. Privacy and Confidentiality

4.01 Maintaining Confidentiality
4.02 Discussing the Limits of Confidentiality
4.03 Recording
4.04 Minimizing Intrusions on Privacy
4.05 Disclosures
4.06 Consultations

INTRODUCTION AND APPLICABILITY

The American Psychological Association's (APA's) Ethical Principles of Psychologists and Code of Conduct (hereinafter referred to as the Ethics Code) consists of an introduction, a Preamble, five General Principles (A–E), and specific Ethical Standards. The Introduction discusses the intent, organization, procedural considerations, and scope of application of the Ethics Code. The Preamble and General Principles are aspirational goals to guide psychologists toward the highest ideals of psychology. Although the Preamble and General Principles are not themselves enforceable rules, they should be considered by psychologists in arriving at an ethical course of action. The Ethical Standards set forth enforceable rules for conduct as psychologists. Most of the Ethical Standards are written broadly, in order to apply to psychologists in varied roles, although the application of an Ethical Standard may vary depending on the context. The Ethical Standards are not exhaustive. The fact that a given conduct is not specifically addressed by an Ethical Standard does not mean that it is necessarily either ethical or unethical.

This Ethics Code applies only to psychologists' activities that are part of their scientific, educational, or professional roles as psychologists. Areas covered include but are not limited to the clinical, counseling, and school practice of psychology; research; teaching; supervision of trainees; public service; policy development; social intervention; development of assessment instruments; conducting assessments; educational counseling; organizational consulting; forensic activities; program design and evaluation; and administration. This Ethics Code applies to these activities across a variety of contexts, such as in person, postal, telephone, Internet, and other electronic transmissions. These activities shall be distinguished from the purely private conduct of psychologists, which is not within the purview of the Ethics Code.

Membership in the APA commits members and student affiliates to comply with the standards of the APA Ethics Code and to the rules and

This version of the APA Ethics Code was adopted by the American Psychological Association's Council of Representatives during its meeting, August 21, 2002, and is effective beginning June 1, 2003. Inquiries concerning the substance or interpretation of the APA Ethics Code should be addressed to the Director, Office of Ethics, American Psychological Association, 750 First Street, NE, Washington, DC 20002-4242. The Ethics Code and information regarding the Code can be found on the APA Web site, http://www.apa.org/ethics. The standards in this Ethics Code will be used to adjudicate complaints brought concerning alleged conduct occurring on or after the effective date. Complaints regarding conduct occurring prior to the effective date will be adjudicated on the basis of the version of the Ethics Code that was in effect at the time the conduct occurred.

The APA has previously published its Ethics Code as follows:

American Psychological Association. (1953). *Ethical standards of psychologists.* Washington, DC: Author.
American Psychological Association. (1959). Ethical standards of psychologists. *American Psychologist, 14,* 279–282.
American Psychological Association. (1963). Ethical standards of psychologists. *American Psychologist, 18,* 56–60.
American Psychological Association. (1968). Ethical standards of psychologists. *American Psychologist, 23,* 357–361.
American Psychological Association. (1977, March). Ethical standards of psychologists. APA *Monitor, 22–23.*
American Psychological Association. (1979). *Ethical standards of psychologists.* Washington, DC: Author.
American Psychological Association. (1981). Ethical principles of psychologists. *American Psychologist, 36,* 633–638.
American Psychological Association. (1990). Ethical principles of psychologists (Amended June 2, 1989). *American Psychologist, 45,* 390–395.
American Psychological Association. (1992). Ethical principles of psychologists and code of conduct. *American Psychologist, 47,* 1597–1611.

Request copies of the APA's Ethical Principles of Psychologists and Code of Conduct from the APA Order Department, 750 First Street, NE, Washington, DC 20002-4242, or phone (202) 336-5510.

procedures used to enforce them. Lack of awareness or misunderstanding of an Ethical Standard is not itself a defense to a charge of unethical conduct.

The procedures for filing, investigating, and resolving complaints of unethical conduct are described in the current Rules and Procedures of the APA Ethics Committee. APA may impose sanctions on its members for violations of the standards of the Ethics Code, including termination of APA membership, and may notify other bodies and individuals of its actions. Actions that violate the standards of the Ethics Code may also lead to the imposition of sanctions on psychologists or students whether or not they are APA members by bodies other than APA, including state psychological associations, other professional groups, psychology boards, other state or federal agencies, and payors for health services. In addition, APA may take action against a member after his or her conviction of a felony, expulsion or suspension from an affiliated state psychological association, or suspension or loss of licensure. When the sanction to be imposed by APA is less than expulsion, the 2001 Rules and Procedures do not guarantee an opportunity for an in-person hearing, but generally provide that complaints will be resolved only on the basis of a submitted record.

The Ethics Code is intended to provide guidance for psychologists and standards of professional conduct that can be applied by the APA and by other bodies that choose to adopt them. The Ethics Code is not intended to be a basis of civil liability. Whether a psychologist has violated the Ethics Code standards does not by itself determine whether the psychologist is legally liable in a court action, whether a contract is enforceable, or whether other legal consequences occur.

The modifiers used in some of the standards of this Ethics Code (e.g., *reasonably*, *appropriate*, *potentially*) are included in the standards when they would (1) allow professional judgment on the part of psychologists, (2) eliminate injustice or inequality that would occur without the modifier, (3) ensure applicability across the broad range of activities conducted by psychologists, or (4) guard against a set of rigid rules that might be quickly outdated. As used in this Ethics Code, the term *reasonable* means the prevailing professional judgment of psychologists engaged in similar activities in similar circumstances, given the knowledge the psychologist had or should have had at the time.

In the process of making decisions regarding their professional behavior, psychologists must consider this Ethics Code in addition to applicable laws and psychology board regulations. In applying the Ethics Code to their professional work, psychologists may consider other materials and guidelines that have been adopted or endorsed by scientific and professional psychological organizations and the dictates of their own conscience, as well as consult with others within the field. If this Ethics Code establishes a higher standard of conduct than is required by law, psychologists must meet the higher ethical standard. If psychologists' ethical responsibilities conflict with law, regulations, or other governing legal authority, psychologists make known their commitment to this Ethics Code and take steps to resolve the conflict in a responsible manner. If the conflict is unresolvable via such means, psychologists may adhere to the requirements of the law, regulations, or other governing authority in keeping with basic principles of human rights.

PREAMBLE

Psychologists are committed to increasing scientific and professional knowledge of behavior and people's understanding of themselves and others and to the use of such knowledge to improve the condition of individuals, organizations, and society. Psychologists respect and protect civil and human rights and the central importance of freedom of inquiry and expression in research, teaching, and publication. They strive to help the public in developing informed judgments and choices concerning human behavior. In doing so, they perform many roles, such as researcher, educator, diagnostician, therapist, supervisor, consultant, administrator, social interventionist, and expert witness. This Ethics Code provides a common set of principles and standards upon which psychologists build their professional and scientific work.

This Ethics Code is intended to provide specific standards to cover most situations encountered by psychologists. It has as its goals the welfare and protection of the individuals and groups with whom psychologists work and the education of members, students, and the public regarding ethical standards of the discipline.

The development of a dynamic set of ethical standards for psychologists' work-related conduct requires a personal commitment and lifelong effort to act ethically; to encourage ethical behavior by students, supervisees, employees, and colleagues; and to consult with others concerning ethical problems.

GENERAL PRINCIPLES

This section consists of General Principles. General Principles, as opposed to Ethical Standards, are aspirational in nature. Their intent is to guide and inspire psychologists toward the very highest ethical ideals of the profession. General Principles, in contrast to Ethical Standards, do not represent obligations and should not form the basis for imposing sanctions. Relying upon General Principles for either of these reasons distorts both their meaning and purpose.

Principle A: Beneficence and Nonmaleficence

Psychologists strive to benefit those with whom they work and take care to do no harm. In their professional actions, psychologists seek to safeguard the welfare and rights of those with whom they interact professionally and other affected persons, and the welfare of animal subjects of research. When conflicts occur among psychologists' obligations or concerns, they attempt to resolve these conflicts in a responsible fashion that avoids or minimizes harm. Because psychologists' scientific and professional judgments and actions may affect the lives of others, they are alert to and guard against personal, financial, social, organizational, or political factors that might lead to misuse of their influence. Psychologists strive to be aware of the possible effect of their own physical and mental health on their ability to help those with whom they work.

Principle B: Fidelity and Responsibility

Psychologists establish relationships of trust with those with whom they work. They are aware of their professional and scientific responsibilities to society and to the specific communities in which they work. Psychologists uphold professional standards of conduct, clarify their professional roles and obligations, accept appropriate responsibility for their behavior, and seek to manage conflicts of interest that could lead to exploitation or harm. Psychologists consult with, refer to, or cooperate with other professionals and institutions to the extent needed to serve the best interests of those with whom they work. They are concerned about the ethical compliance of their colleagues' scientific and professional conduct. Psychologists strive to contribute a portion of their professional time for little or no compensation or personal advantage.

Principle C: Integrity

Psychologists seek to promote accuracy, honesty, and truthfulness in the science, teaching, and practice of psychology. In these activities psychologists do not steal, cheat, or engage in fraud, subterfuge, or intentional misrepresentation of fact. Psychologists strive to keep their promises and to avoid unwise or unclear commitments. In situations in which deception may be ethically justifiable to maximize benefits and minimize harm, psychologists have a serious obligation to consider the need for, the possible consequences of, and their responsibility to correct any resulting mistrust or other harmful effects that arise from the use of such techniques.

Principle D: Justice

Psychologists recognize that fairness and justice entitle all persons to access to and benefit from the contributions of psychology and to equal quality in the processes, procedures, and services being conducted by psychologists. Psychologists exercise reasonable judgment and take precautions to ensure that their potential biases, the boundaries of their competence, and the limitations of their expertise do not lead to or condone unjust practices.

Principle E: Respect for People's Rights and Dignity

Psychologists respect the dignity and worth of all people, and the rights of individuals to privacy, confidentiality, and self-determination. Psychologists are aware that special safeguards may be necessary to protect the rights and welfare of persons or communities whose vulnerabilities impair autonomous decision making. Psychologists are aware of and respect cultural, individual, and role differences, including those based on age, gender, gender identity, race, ethnicity, culture, national origin, religion, sexual orientation, disability, language, and socioeconomic status, and consider these factors when working with members of such groups. Psychologists try to eliminate the effect on their work of biases based on those factors, and they do not knowingly participate in or condone activities of others based upon such prejudices.

ETHICAL STANDARDS

1. Resolving Ethical Issues

1.01 Misuse of Psychologists' Work

If psychologists learn of misuse or misrepresentation of their work, they take reasonable steps to correct or minimize the misuse or misrepresentation.

1.02 Conflicts Between Ethics and Law, Regulations, or Other Governing Legal Authority

If psychologists' ethical responsibilities conflict with law, regulations, or other governing legal authority, psychologists make known their commitment to the Ethics Code and take steps to resolve the conflict. If the conflict is unresolvable via such means, psychologists may adhere to the requirements of the law, regulations, or other governing legal authority.

1.03 Conflicts Between Ethics and Organizational Demands

If the demands of an organization with which psychologists are affiliated or for whom they are working conflict with this Ethics Code, psychologists clarify the nature of the conflict, make known their commitment to the Ethics Code, and to the extent feasible, resolve the conflict in a way that permits adherence to the Ethics Code.

1.04 Informal Resolution of Ethical Violations

When psychologists believe that there may have been an ethical violation by another psychologist, they attempt to resolve the issue by bringing it to the attention of that individual, if an informal resolution appears appropriate and the intervention does not violate any confidentiality rights that may be involved. (See also Standards 1.02, Conflicts Between Ethics and Law, Regulations, or Other Governing Legal Authority, and 1.03, Conflicts Between Ethics and Organizational Demands.)

1.05 Reporting Ethical Violations

If an apparent ethical violation has substantially harmed or is likely to substantially harm a person or organization and is not appropriate for informal resolution under Standard 1.04, Informal Resolution of Ethical Violations, or is not resolved properly in that fashion, psychologists take further action appropriate to the situation. Such action might include referral to state or national committees on professional ethics, to state licensing boards, or to the appropriate institutional authorities. This standard does not apply when an intervention would violate confidentiality rights or when psychologists have been retained to review the work of another psychologist whose professional conduct is in question. (See also Standard 1.02, Conflicts Between Ethics and Law, Regulations, or Other Governing Legal Authority.)

1.06 Cooperating With Ethics Committees

Psychologists cooperate in ethics investigations, proceedings, and resulting requirements of the APA or any affiliated state psychological association to which they belong. In doing so, they address any confidentiality issues. Failure to cooperate is itself an ethics violation. However, making a request for deferment of adjudication of an ethics complaint pending the outcome of litigation does not alone constitute noncooperation.

1.07 Improper Complaints

Psychologists do not file or encourage the filing of ethics complaints that are made with reckless disregard for or willful ignorance of facts that would disprove the allegation.

1.08 Unfair Discrimination Against Complainants and Respondents

Psychologists do not deny persons employment, advancement, admissions to academic or other programs, tenure, or promotion, based solely upon their having made or their being the subject of an ethics complaint. This does not preclude taking action based upon the outcome of such proceedings or considering other appropriate information.

2. Competence

2.01 Boundaries of Competence

(a) Psychologists provide services, teach, and conduct research with populations and in areas only within the boundaries of their competence, based on their education, training, supervised experience, consultation, study, or professional experience.

(b) Where scientific or professional knowledge in the discipline of psychology establishes that an understanding of factors associated with age, gender, gender identity, race, ethnicity, culture, national origin, religion, sexual orientation, disability, language, or socioeconomic status is essential for effective implementation of their services or research, psychologists have or obtain the training, experience, consultation, or supervision necessary to ensure the competence of their services, or they make appropriate referrals, except as provided in Standard 2.02, Providing Services in Emergencies.

(c) Psychologists planning to provide services, teach, or conduct research involving populations, areas, techniques, or technologies new to them undertake relevant education, training, supervised experience, consultation, or study.

(d) When psychologists are asked to provide services to individuals for whom appropriate mental health services are not available and for which psychologists have not obtained the competence necessary, psychologists with closely related prior training or experience may provide such services in order to ensure that services are not denied if they make a reasonable effort to obtain the competence required by using relevant research, training, consultation, or study.

(e) In those emerging areas in which generally recognized standards for preparatory training do not yet exist, psychologists nevertheless take reasonable steps to ensure the competence of their work and to protect clients/patients, students, supervisees, research participants, organizational clients, and others from harm.

(f) When assuming forensic roles, psychologists are or become reasonably familiar with the judicial or administrative rules governing their roles.

2.02 Providing Services in Emergencies

In emergencies, when psychologists provide services to individuals for whom other mental health services are not available and for which psychologists have not obtained the necessary training, psychologists may provide such services in order to ensure that services are not denied. The services are discontinued as soon as the emergency has ended or appropriate services are available.

2.03 Maintaining Competence

Psychologists undertake ongoing efforts to develop and maintain their competence.

2.04 Bases for Scientific and Professional Judgments

Psychologists' work is based upon established scientific and professional knowledge of the discipline. (See also Standards 2.01e, Boundaries of Competence, and 10.01b, Informed Consent to Therapy.)

2.05 Delegation of Work to Others

Psychologists who delegate work to employees, supervisees, or research or teaching assistants or who use the services of others, such as interpreters, take reasonable steps to (1) avoid delegating such work to persons who have a multiple relationship with those being served that would likely lead to exploitation or loss of objectivity; (2) authorize only those responsibilities that such persons can be expected to perform competently on the basis of their education, training, or experience, either independently or with the level of supervision being provided; and (3) see that such persons perform these services competently. (See also Standards 2.02, Providing Services in Emergencies; 3.05, Multiple Relationships; 4.01, Maintaining Confidentiality; 9.01, Bases for Assessments; 9.02, Use of Assessments; 9.03, Informed Consent in Assessments; and 9.07, Assessment by Unqualified Persons.)

2.06 Personal Problems and Conflicts

(a) Psychologists refrain from initiating an activity when they know or should know that there is a substantial likelihood that their personal problems will prevent them from performing their work-related activities in a competent manner.

(b) When psychologists become aware of personal problems that may interfere with their performing work-related duties adequately, they take appropriate measures, such as obtaining professional consultation or assistance, and determine whether they should limit, suspend, or terminate their work-related duties. (See also Standard 10.10, Terminating Therapy.)

3. *Human Relations*

3.01 Unfair Discrimination

In their work-related activities, psychologists do not engage in unfair discrimination based on age, gender, gender identity, race, ethnicity, culture, national origin, religion, sexual orientation, disability, socioeconomic status, or any basis proscribed by law.

3.02 Sexual Harassment

Psychologists do not engage in sexual harassment. Sexual harassment is sexual solicitation, physical advances, or verbal or nonverbal conduct that is sexual in nature, that occurs in connection with the psychologist's activities or roles as a psychologist, and that either (1) is unwelcome, is offensive, or creates a hostile workplace or educational environment, and the psychologist knows or is told this or (2) is sufficiently severe or intense to be abusive to a reasonable person in the context. Sexual harassment can consist of a single intense or severe act or of multiple persistent or pervasive acts. (See also Standard 1.08, Unfair Discrimination Against Complainants and Respondents.)

3.03 Other Harassment

Psychologists do not knowingly engage in behavior that is harassing or demeaning to persons with whom they interact in their work based on factors such as those persons' age, gender, gender identity, race, ethnicity, culture, national origin, religion, sexual orientation, disability, language, or socioeconomic status.

3.04 Avoiding Harm

Psychologists take reasonable steps to avoid harming their clients/patients, students, supervisees, research participants, organizational clients, and others with whom they work, and to minimize harm where it is foreseeable and unavoidable.

3.05 Multiple Relationships

(a) A multiple relationship occurs when a psychologist is in a professional role with a person and (1) at the same time is in another role with the same person, (2) at the same time is in a relationship with a person closely associated with or related to the person with whom the psychologist has the professional relationship, or (3) promises to enter into another relationship in the future with the person or a person closely associated with or related to the person.

A psychologist refrains from entering into a multiple relationship if the multiple relationship could reasonably be expected to impair the psychologist's objectivity, competence, or effectiveness in performing his or her functions as a psychologist, or otherwise risks exploitation or harm to the person with whom the professional relationship exists.

Multiple relationships that would not reasonably be expected to cause impairment or risk exploitation or harm are not unethical.

(b) If a psychologist finds that, due to unforeseen factors, a potentially harmful multiple relationship has arisen, the psychologist takes reasonable steps to resolve it with due regard for the best interests of the affected person and maximal compliance with the Ethics Code.

(c) When psychologists are required by law, institutional policy, or extraordinary circumstances to serve in more than one role in judicial or administrative proceedings, at the outset they clarify role expectations and the extent of confidentiality and thereafter as changes occur. (See also Standards 3.04, Avoiding Harm, and 3.07, Third-Party Requests for Services.)

3.06 Conflict of Interest

Psychologists refrain from taking on a professional role when personal, scientific, professional, legal, financial, or other interests or relationships could reasonably be expected to (1) impair their objectivity, competence, or effectiveness in performing their functions as psychologists or (2) expose the person or organization with whom the professional relationship exists to harm or exploitation.

3.07 Third-Party Requests for Services

When psychologists agree to provide services to a person or entity at the request of a third party, psychologists attempt to clarify at the outset of the service the nature of the relationship with all individuals or organizations involved. This clarification includes the role of the psychologist (e.g., therapist, consultant, diagnostician, or expert witness), an identification of who is the client, the probable uses of the services provided or the information obtained, and the fact that there may be limits to confidentiality. (See also Standards 3.05, Multiple Relationships, and 4.02, Discussing the Limits of Confidentiality.)

3.08 Exploitative Relationships

Psychologists do not exploit persons over whom they have supervisory, evaluative, or other authority such as clients/patients, students, supervisees, research participants, and employees. (See also Standards 3.05, Multiple Relationships; 6.04, Fees and Financial Arrangements; 6.05, Barter With Clients/Patients; 7.07, Sexual Relationships With Students and Supervisees; 10.05, Sexual Intimacies With Current Therapy Clients/Patients; 10.06, Sexual Intimacies With Relatives or Significant Others of Current Therapy Clients/Patients; 10.07, Therapy With Former Sexual Partners; and 10.08, Sexual Intimacies With Former Therapy Clients/Patients.)

3.09 Cooperation With Other Professionals

When indicated and professionally appropriate, psychologists cooperate with other professionals in order to serve their clients/patients effectively and appropriately. (See also Standard 4.05, Disclosures.)

3.10 Informed Consent

(a) When psychologists conduct research or provide assessment, therapy, counseling, or consulting services in person or via electronic transmission or other forms of communication, they obtain the informed consent of the individual or individuals using language that is reasonably understandable to that person or persons except when conducting such activities without consent is mandated by law or governmental regulation or as otherwise provided in this Ethics Code. (See also Standards 8.02, Informed Consent to Research; 9.03, Informed Consent in Assessments; and 10.01, Informed Consent to Therapy.)

(b) For persons who are legally incapable of giving informed consent, psychologists nevertheless (1) provide an appropriate explanation, (2) seek the individual's assent, (3) consider such persons' preferences and best interests, and (4) obtain appropriate permission from a legally authorized person, if such substitute consent is permitted or required by law. When consent by a legally authorized person is not permitted or required by law, psychologists take reasonable steps to protect the individual's rights and welfare.

(c) When psychological services are court ordered or otherwise mandated, psychologists inform the individual of the nature of the anticipated services, including whether the services are court ordered or mandated and any limits of confidentiality, before proceeding.

(d) Psychologists appropriately document written or oral consent, permission, and assent. (See also Standards 8.02, Informed Consent to Research; 9.03, Informed Consent in Assessments; and 10.01, Informed Consent to Therapy.)

3.11 Psychological Services Delivered to or Through Organizations

(a) Psychologists delivering services to or through organizations provide information beforehand to clients and when appropriate those directly affected by the services about (1) the nature and objectives of the services, (2) the intended recipients, (3) which of the individuals are clients, (4) the relationship the psychologist will have with each person and the organization, (5) the probable uses of services provided and information obtained, (6) who will have access to the information, and (7) limits of confidentiality. As soon as feasible, they provide information about the results and conclusions of such services to appropriate persons.

(b) If psychologists will be precluded by law or by organizational roles from providing such information to particular individuals or groups, they so inform those individuals or groups at the outset of the service.

3.12 Interruption of Psychological Services

Unless otherwise covered by contract, psychologists make reasonable efforts to plan for facilitating services in the event that psychological services are interrupted by factors such as the psychologist's illness, death, unavailability, relocation, or retirement or by the client's/patient's relocation or financial limitations. (See also Standard 6.02c, Maintenance, Dissemination, and Disposal of Confidential Records of Professional and Scientific Work.)

4.   *Privacy and Confidentiality*
4.01 Maintaining Confidentiality

Psychologists have a primary obligation and take reasonable precautions to protect confidential information obtained through or stored in any medium, recognizing that the extent and limits of confidentiality may be regulated by law or established by institutional rules or professional or scientific relationship. (See also Standard 2.05, Delegation of Work to Others.)

4.02 Discussing the Limits of Confidentiality

(a) Psychologists discuss with persons (including, to the extent feasible, persons who are legally incapable of giving informed consent and their legal representatives) and organizations with whom they establish a scientific or professional relationship (1) the relevant limits of confidentiality and (2) the foreseeable uses of the information generated through their psychological activities. (See also Standard 3.10, Informed Consent.)

(b) Unless it is not feasible or is contraindicated, the discussion of confidentiality occurs at the outset of the relationship and thereafter as new circumstances may warrant.

(c) Psychologists who offer services, products, or information via electronic transmission inform clients/patients of the risks to privacy and limits of confidentiality.

4.03 Recording

Before recording the voices or images of individuals to whom they provide services, psychologists obtain permission from all such persons or their legal representatives. (See also Standards 8.03, Informed Consent for Recording Voices and Images in Research; 8.05, Dispensing With Informed Consent for Research; and 8.07, Deception in Research.)

4.04 Minimizing Intrusions on Privacy

(a) Psychologists include in written and oral reports and consultations, only information germane to the purpose for which the communication is made.

(b) Psychologists discuss confidential information obtained in their work only for appropriate scientific or professional purposes and only with persons clearly concerned with such matters.

4.05 Disclosures

(a) Psychologists may disclose confidential information with the appropriate consent of the organizational client, the individual client/patient, or another legally authorized person on behalf of the client/patient unless prohibited by law.

(b) Psychologists disclose confidential information without the consent of the individual only as mandated by law, or where permitted by law for a valid purpose such as to (1) provide needed professional services; (2) obtain appropriate professional consultations; (3) protect the client/patient, psychologist, or others from harm; or (4) obtain payment for services from a client/patient, in which instance disclosure is limited to the minimum that is necessary to achieve the purpose. (See also Standard 6.04e, Fees and Financial Arrangements.)

4.06 Consultations

When consulting with colleagues, (1) psychologists do not disclose confidential information that reasonably could lead to the identification of a client/patient, research participant, or other person or organization with whom they have a confidential relationship unless they have obtained the prior consent of the person or organization or the disclosure cannot be avoided, and (2) they disclose information only to the extent necessary to achieve the purposes of the consultation. (See also Standard 4.01, Maintaining Confidentiality.)

4.07 Use of Confidential Information for Didactic or Other Purposes

Psychologists do not disclose in their writings, lectures, or other public media, confidential, personally identifiable information concerning their clients/patients, students, research participants, organizational clients, or other recipients of their services that they obtained during the course of their work, unless (1) they take reasonable steps to disguise the person or organization, (2) the person or organization has consented in writing, or (3) there is legal authorization for doing so.

5. Advertising and Other Public Statements

5.01 Avoidance of False or Deceptive Statements

(a) Public statements include but are not limited to paid or unpaid advertising, product endorsements, grant applications, licensing applications, other credentialing applications, brochures, printed matter, directory listings, personal resumes or curricula vitae, or comments for use in media such as print or electronic transmission, statements in legal proceedings, lectures and public oral presentations, and published materials. Psychologists do not knowingly make public statements that are false, deceptive, or fraudulent concerning their research, practice, or other work activities or those of persons or organizations with which they are affiliated.

(b) Psychologists do not make false, deceptive, or fraudulent statements concerning (1) their training, experience, or competence; (2) their academic degrees; (3) their credentials; (4) their institutional or association affiliations; (5) their services; (6) the scientific or clinical basis for, or results or degree of success of, their services; (7) their fees; or (8) their publications or research findings.

(c) Psychologists claim degrees as credentials for their health services only if those degrees (1) were earned from a regionally accredited educational institution or (2) were the basis for psychology licensure by the state in which they practice.

5.02 Statements by Others

(a) Psychologists who engage others to create or place public statements that promote their professional practice, products, or activities retain professional responsibility for such statements.

(b) Psychologists do not compensate employees of press, radio, television, or other communication media in return for publicity in a news item. (See also Standard 1.01, Misuse of Psychologists' Work.)

(c) A paid advertisement relating to psychologists' activities must be identified or clearly recognizable as such.

5.03 Descriptions of Workshops and Non-Degree-Granting Educational Programs

To the degree to which they exercise control, psychologists responsible for announcements, catalogs, brochures, or advertisements describing workshops, seminars, or other non-degree-granting educational programs ensure that they accurately describe the audience for which the program is intended, the educational objectives, the presenters, and the fees involved.

5.04 Media Presentations

When psychologists provide public advice or comment via print, Internet, or other electronic transmission, they take precautions to ensure that statements (1) are based on their professional knowledge, training, or experience in accord with appropriate psychological literature and practice; (2) are otherwise consistent with this Ethics Code; and (3) do not indicate that a professional relationship has been established with the recipient. (See also Standard 2.04, Bases for Scientific and Professional Judgments.)

5.05 Testimonials

Psychologists do not solicit testimonials from current therapy clients/patients or other persons who because of their particular circumstances are vulnerable to undue influence.

5.06 In-Person Solicitation

Psychologists do not engage, directly or through agents, in uninvited in-person solicitation of business from actual or potential therapy clients/patients or other persons who because of their particular circumstances are vulnerable to undue influence. However, this prohibition does not preclude (1) attempting to implement appropriate collateral contacts for the purpose of benefiting an already engaged therapy client/patient or (2) providing disaster or community outreach services.

6.   Record Keeping and Fees

6.01 Documentation of Professional and Scientific Work and Maintenance of Records

Psychologists create, and to the extent the records are under their control, maintain, disseminate, store, retain, and dispose of records and data relating to their professional and scientific work in order to (1) facilitate provision of services later by them or by other professionals, (2) allow for replication of research design and analyses, (3) meet institutional requirements, (4) ensure accuracy of billing and payments, and (5) ensure compliance with law. (See also Standard 4.01, Maintaining Confidentiality.)

6.02 Maintenance, Dissemination, and Disposal of Confidential Records of Professional and Scientific Work

(a) Psychologists maintain confidentiality in creating, storing, accessing, transferring, and disposing of records under their control, whether these are written, automated, or in any other medium. (See also Standards 4.01, Maintaining Confidentiality, and 6.01, Documentation of Professional and Scientific Work and Maintenance of Records.)

(b) If confidential information concerning recipients of psychological services is entered into databases or systems of records available to persons whose access has not been consented to by the recipient, psychologists use coding or other techniques to avoid the inclusion of personal identifiers.

(c) Psychologists make plans in advance to facilitate the appropriate transfer and to protect the confidentiality of records and data in the event of psychologists' withdrawal from positions or practice. (See also Standards 3.12, Interruption of Psychological Services, and 10.09, Interruption of Therapy.)

6.03 Withholding Records for Nonpayment

Psychologists may not withhold records under their control that are requested and needed for a client's/patient's emergency treatment solely because payment has not been received.

6.04 Fees and Financial Arrangements

(a) As early as is feasible in a professional or scientific relationship, psychologists and recipients of psychological services reach an agreement specifying compensation and billing arrangements.

(b) Psychologists' fee practices are consistent with law.

(c) Psychologists do not misrepresent their fees.

(d) If limitations to services can be anticipated because of limitations in financing, this is discussed with the recipient of services as early as is feasible. (See also Standards 10.09, Interruption of Therapy, and 10.10, Terminating Therapy.)

(e) If the recipient of services does not pay for services as agreed, and if psychologists intend to use collection agencies or legal measures to collect the fees, psychologists first inform the person that such measures will be taken and provide that person an opportunity to make prompt payment. (See also Standards 4.05, Disclosures; 6.03, Withholding Records for Nonpayment; and 10.01, Informed Consent to Therapy.)

6.05 Barter With Clients/Patients

Barter is the acceptance of goods, services, or other nonmonetary remuneration from clients/patients in return for psychological services. Psychologists may barter only if (1) it is not clinically contraindicated, and (2) the resulting arrangement is not exploitative. (See also Standards 3.05, Multiple Relationships, and 6.04, Fees and Financial Arrangements.)

6.06 Accuracy in Reports to Payors and Funding Sources

In their reports to payors for services or sources of research funding, psychologists take reasonable steps to ensure the accurate reporting of the nature of the service provided or research conducted, the fees, charges, or payments, and where applicable, the identity of the provider, the findings, and the diagnosis. (See also Standards 4.01, Maintaining Confidentiality; 4.04, Minimizing Intrusions on Privacy; and 4.05, Disclosures.)

6.07 Referrals and Fees

When psychologists pay, receive payment from, or divide fees with another professional, other than in an employer–employee relationship, the payment to each is based on the services provided (clinical, consultative, administrative, or other) and is not based on the referral itself. (See also Standard 3.09, Cooperation With Other Professionals.)

7. Education and Training

7.01 Design of Education and Training Programs

Psychologists responsible for education and training programs take reasonable steps to ensure that the programs are designed to provide the appropriate knowledge and proper experiences, and to meet the requirements for licensure, certification, or other goals for which claims are made by the program. (See also Standard 5.03, Descriptions of Workshops and Non-Degree-Granting Educational Programs.)

7.02 Descriptions of Education and Training Programs

Psychologists responsible for education and training programs take reasonable steps to ensure that there is a current and accurate description of the program content (including participation in required course- or program-related counseling, psychotherapy, experiential groups, consulting projects, or community service), training goals and objectives, stipends and benefits, and requirements that must be met for satisfactory completion of the program. This information must be made readily available to all interested parties.

7.03 Accuracy in Teaching

(a) Psychologists take reasonable steps to ensure that course syllabi are accurate regarding the subject matter to be covered, bases for evaluating progress, and the nature of course experiences. This standard does not preclude an instructor from modifying course content or requirements when the instructor considers it pedagogically necessary or desirable, so long as students are made aware of these modifications in a manner that enables them to fulfill course requirements. (See also Standard 5.01, Avoidance of False or Deceptive Statements.)

(b) When engaged in teaching or training, psychologists present psychological information accurately. (See also Standard 2.03, Maintaining Competence.)

7.04 Student Disclosure of Personal Information

Psychologists do not require students or supervisees to disclose personal information in course- or program-related activities, either orally or in writing, regarding sexual history, history of abuse and neglect, psychological treatment, and relationships with parents, peers, and spouses or significant others except if (1) the program or training facility has clearly identified this requirement in its admissions and program materials or (2) the information is necessary to evaluate or obtain assistance for students whose personal problems could reasonably be judged to be preventing them from performing their training- or professionally related activities in a competent manner or posing a threat to the students or others.

7.05 Mandatory Individual or Group Therapy

(a) When individual or group therapy is a program or course requirement, psychologists responsible for that program allow students in undergraduate and graduate programs the option of selecting such therapy from practitioners unaffiliated with the program. (See also Standard 7.02, Descriptions of Education and Training Programs.)

(b) Faculty who are or are likely to be responsible for evaluating students' academic performance do not themselves provide that therapy. (See also Standard 3.05, Multiple Relationships.)

7.06 Assessing Student and Supervisee Performance

(a) In academic and supervisory relationships, psychologists establish a timely and specific process for providing feedback to students and supervisees. Information regarding the process is provided to the student at the beginning of supervision.

(b) Psychologists evaluate students and supervisees on the basis of their actual performance on relevant and established program requirements.

7.07 Sexual Relationships With Students and Supervisees

Psychologists do not engage in sexual relationships with students or supervisees who are in their department, agency, or training center or over whom psychologists have or are likely to have evaluative authority. (See also Standard 3.05, Multiple Relationships.)

8.   *Research and Publication*

8.01 Institutional Approval

When institutional approval is required, psychologists provide accurate information about their research proposals and obtain approval prior to conducting the research. They conduct the research in accordance with the approved research protocol.

8.02 Informed Consent to Research

(a) When obtaining informed consent as required in Standard 3.10, Informed Consent, psychologists inform participants about (1) the purpose of the research, expected duration, and procedures; (2) their right to decline to participate and to withdraw from the research once participation has begun; (3) the foreseeable consequences of declining or withdrawing; (4) reasonably foreseeable factors that may be expected to influence their willingness to participate such as potential risks, discomfort, or adverse effects; (5) any prospective research benefits; (6) limits of confidentiality; (7) incentives for participation; and (8) whom to contact for questions about the research and research participants' rights. They provide opportunity for the prospective participants to ask questions and receive answers. (See also Standards 8.03, Informed Consent for Recording Voices and Images in Research; 8.05, Dispensing With Informed Consent for Research; and 8.07, Deception in Research.)

(b) Psychologists conducting intervention research involving the use of experimental treatments clarify to participants at the outset of the research (1) the experimental nature of the treatment; (2) the services that will or will not be available to the control group(s) if appropriate; (3) the means by which assignment to treatment and control groups will be made; (4) available treatment alternatives if an individual does not wish to participate in the research or wishes to withdraw once a study has begun; and (5) compensation for or monetary costs of participating including, if appropriate, whether reimbursement from the participant or a third-party payor will be sought. (See also Standard 8.02a, Informed Consent to Research.)

8.03 Informed Consent for Recording Voices and Images in Research

Psychologists obtain informed consent from research participants prior to recording their voices or images for data collection unless (1) the research consists solely of naturalistic observations in public places, and it is not anticipated that the recording will be used in a manner that could cause personal identification or harm, or (2) the research design includes deception, and consent for the use of the recording is obtained during debriefing. (See also Standard 8.07, Deception in Research.)

8.04 Client/Patient, Student, and Subordinate Research Participants

(a) When psychologists conduct research with clients/patients, students, or subordinates as participants, psychologists take steps to protect the prospective participants from adverse consequences of declining or withdrawing from participation.

(b) When research participation is a course requirement or an opportunity for extra credit, the prospective participant is given the choice of equitable alternative activities.

8.05 Dispensing With Informed Consent for Research

Psychologists may dispense with informed consent only (1) where research would not reasonably be assumed to create distress or harm and involves (a) the study of normal educational practices, curricula, or classroom management methods conducted in educational settings; (b) only anonymous questionnaires, naturalistic observations, or archival research for which disclosure of responses would not place participants at risk of criminal or civil liability or damage their financial standing, employability, or reputation, and confidentiality is protected; or (c) the study of factors related to job or organization effectiveness conducted in organizational settings for which there is no risk to participants' employability, and confidentiality is protected or (2) where otherwise permitted by law or federal or institutional regulations.

8.06 Offering Inducements for Research Participation

(a) Psychologists make reasonable efforts to avoid offering excessive or inappropriate financial or other inducements for research participation when such inducements are likely to coerce participation.

(b) When offering professional services as an inducement for research participation, psychologists clarify the nature of the services, as well as the risks, obligations, and limitations. (See also Standard 6.05, Barter With Clients/Patients.)

8.07 Deception in Research

(a) Psychologists do not conduct a study involving deception unless they have determined that the use of deceptive techniques is justified by the study's significant prospective scientific, educational, or applied value and that effective nondeceptive alternative procedures are not feasible.

(b) Psychologists do not deceive prospective participants about research that is reasonably expected to cause physical pain or severe emotional distress.

(c) Psychologists explain any deception that is an integral feature of the design and conduct of an experiment to participants as early as is feasible, preferably at the conclusion of their participation, but no later than at the conclusion of the data collection, and permit participants to withdraw their data. (See also Standard 8.08, Debriefing.)

8.08 Debriefing

(a) Psychologists provide a prompt opportunity for participants to obtain appropriate information about the nature, results, and conclusions of the research, and they take reasonable steps to correct any misconceptions that participants may have of which the psychologists are aware.

(b) If scientific or humane values justify delaying or withholding this information, psychologists take reasonable measures to reduce the risk of harm.

(c) When psychologists become aware that research procedures have harmed a participant, they take reasonable steps to minimize the harm.

8.09 Humane Care and Use of Animals in Research

(a) Psychologists acquire, care for, use, and dispose of animals in compliance with current federal, state, and local laws and regulations, and with professional standards.

(b) Psychologists trained in research methods and experienced in the care of laboratory animals supervise all procedures involving animals and are responsible for ensuring appropriate consideration of their comfort, health, and humane treatment.

(c) Psychologists ensure that all individuals under their supervision who are using animals have received instruction in research methods and in the care, maintenance, and handling of the species being used, to the extent appropriate to their role. (See also Standard 2.05, Delegation of Work to Others.)

(d) Psychologists make reasonable efforts to minimize the discomfort, infection, illness, and pain of animal subjects.

(e) Psychologists use a procedure subjecting animals to pain, stress, or privation only when an alternative procedure is unavailable and the goal is justified by its prospective scientific, educational, or applied value.

(f) Psychologists perform surgical procedures under appropriate anesthesia and follow techniques to avoid infection and minimize pain during and after surgery.

(g) When it is appropriate that an animal's life be terminated, psychologists proceed rapidly, with an effort to minimize pain and in accordance with accepted procedures.

8.10 Reporting Research Results

(a) Psychologists do not fabricate data. (See also Standard 5.01a, Avoidance of False or Deceptive Statements.)

(b) If psychologists discover significant errors in their published data, they take reasonable steps to correct such errors in a correction, retraction, erratum, or other appropriate publication means.

8.11 Plagiarism

Psychologists do not present portions of another's work or data as their own, even if the other work or data source is cited occasionally.

8.12 Publication Credit

(a) Psychologists take responsibility and credit, including authorship credit, only for work they have actually performed or to which they have substantially contributed. (See also Standard 8.12b, Publication Credit.)

(b) Principal authorship and other publication credits accurately reflect the relative scientific or professional contributions of the individuals involved, regardless of their relative status. Mere possession of an institutional position, such as department chair, does not justify authorship credit. Minor contributions to the research or to the writing for publications are acknowledged appropriately, such as in footnotes or in an introductory statement.

(c) Except under exceptional circumstances, a student is listed as principal author on any multiple-authored article that is substantially based on the student's doctoral dissertation. Faculty advisors discuss publication credit with students as early as feasible and throughout the research and publication process as appropriate. (See also Standard 8.12b, Publication Credit.)

8.13 Duplicate Publication of Data

Psychologists do not publish, as original data, data that have been previously published. This does not preclude republishing data when they are accompanied by proper acknowledgment.

8.14 Sharing Research Data for Verification

(a) After research results are published, psychologists do not withhold the data on which their conclusions are based from other competent professionals who seek to verify the substantive claims through reanalysis and who intend to use such data only for that purpose, provided that the confidentiality of the participants can be protected and unless legal rights concerning proprietary data preclude their release. This does not preclude psychologists from requiring that such individuals or groups be responsible for costs associated with the provision of such information.

(b) Psychologists who request data from other psychologists to verify the substantive claims through reanalysis may use shared data only for the declared purpose. Requesting psychologists obtain prior written agreement for all other uses of the data.

8.15 Reviewers

Psychologists who review material submitted for presentation, publication, grant, or research proposal review respect the confidentiality of and the proprietary rights in such information of those who submitted it.

9. *Assessment*

9.01 Bases for Assessments

(a) Psychologists base the opinions contained in their recommendations, reports, and diagnostic or evaluative statements, including forensic testimony, on information and techniques sufficient to substantiate their findings. (See also Standard 2.04, Bases for Scientific and Professional Judgments.)

(b) Except as noted in 9.01c, psychologists provide opinions of the psychological characteristics of individuals only after they have conducted an examination of the individuals adequate to support their statements or conclusions. When, despite reasonable efforts, such an examination is not practical, psychologists document the efforts they made and the result of those efforts, clarify the probable impact of their limited information on the reliability and validity of their opinions, and appropriately limit the nature and extent of their conclusions or recommendations. (See also Standards 2.01, Boundaries of Competence, and 9.06, Interpreting Assessment Results.)

(c) When psychologists conduct a record review or provide consultation or supervision and an individual examination is not warranted or necessary for the opinion, psychologists explain this and the sources of information on which they based their conclusions and recommendations.

9.02 Use of Assessments

(a) Psychologists administer, adapt, score, interpret, or use assessment techniques, interviews, tests, or instruments in a manner and for purposes that are appropriate in light of the research on or evidence of the usefulness and proper application of the techniques.

(b) Psychologists use assessment instruments whose validity and reliability have been established for use with members of the population tested. When such validity or reliability has not been established, psychologists describe the strengths and limitations of test results and interpretation.

(c) Psychologists use assessment methods that are appropriate to an individual's language preference and competence, unless the use of an alternative language is relevant to the assessment issues.

9.03 Informed Consent in Assessments

(a) Psychologists obtain informed consent for assessments, evaluations, or diagnostic services, as described in Standard 3.10, Informed Consent, except when (1) testing is mandated by law or governmental regulations; (2) informed consent is implied because testing is conducted as a routine educational, institutional, or organizational activity (e.g., when participants voluntarily agree to assessment when applying for a job); or (3) one purpose of the testing is to evaluate decisional capacity. Informed consent includes an explanation of the nature and purpose of the assessment, fees, involvement of third parties, and limits of confidentiality and sufficient opportunity for the client/patient to ask questions and receive answers.

(b) Psychologists inform persons with questionable capacity to consent or for whom testing is mandated by law or governmental regulations about the nature and purpose of the proposed assessment services, using language that is reasonably understandable to the person being assessed.

(c) Psychologists using the services of an interpreter obtain informed consent from the client/patient to use that interpreter, ensure that confidentiality of test results and test security are maintained, and include in their recommendations, reports, and diagnostic or evaluative statements, including forensic testimony, discussion of any limitations on the data obtained. (See also Standards 2.05, Delegation of Work to Others; 4.01, Maintaining Confidentiality; 9.01, Bases for Assessments; 9.06, Interpreting Assessment Results; and 9.07, Assessment by Unqualified Persons.)

9.04 Release of Test Data

(a) The term *test data* refers to raw and scaled scores, client/patient responses to test questions or stimuli, and psychologists' notes and recordings concerning client/patient statements and behavior during an examination. Those portions of test materials that include client/patient responses are included in the definition of *test data*. Pursuant to a client/patient release, psychologists provide test data to the client/patient or other persons identified in the release. Psychologists may refrain from releasing test data to protect a client/patient or others from substantial harm or misuse or misrepresentation of the data or the test, recognizing that in many instances release of confidential information under these circumstances is regulated by law. (See also Standard 9.11, Maintaining Test Security.)

(b) In the absence of a client/patient release, psychologists provide test data only as required by law or court order.

9.05 Test Construction

Psychologists who develop tests and other assessment techniques use appropriate psychometric procedures and current scientific or professional knowledge for test design, standardization, validation, reduction or elimination of bias, and recommendations for use.

9.06 Interpreting Assessment Results

When interpreting assessment results, including automated interpretations, psychologists take into account the purpose of the assessment as well as the various test factors, test-taking abilities, and other characteristics of the person being assessed, such as situational, personal, linguistic, and cultural differences, that might affect psychologists' judgments or reduce the accuracy of their interpretations. They indicate any significant limitations of their interpretations. (See also Standards 2.01b and c, Boundaries of Competence, and 3.01, Unfair Discrimination.)

9.07 Assessment by Unqualified Persons

Psychologists do not promote the use of psychological assessment techniques by unqualified persons, except when such use is conducted for training purposes with appropriate supervision. (See also Standard 2.05, Delegation of Work to Others.)

9.08 Obsolete Tests and Outdated Test Results

(a) Psychologists do not base their assessment or intervention decisions or recommendations on data or test results that are outdated for the current purpose.

(b) Psychologists do not base such decisions or recommendations on tests and measures that are obsolete and not useful for the current purpose.

9.09 Test Scoring and Interpretation Services

(a) Psychologists who offer assessment or scoring services to other professionals accurately describe the purpose, norms, validity, reliability, and applications of the procedures and any special qualifications applicable to their use.

(b) Psychologists select scoring and interpretation services (including automated services) on the basis of evidence of the validity of the program and procedures as well as on other appropriate considerations. (See also Standard 2.01b and c, Boundaries of Competence.)

(c) Psychologists retain responsibility for the appropriate application, interpretation, and use of assessment instruments, whether they score and interpret such tests themselves or use automated or other services.

9.10 Explaining Assessment Results

Regardless of whether the scoring and interpretation are done by psychologists, by employees or assistants, or by automated or other outside services, psychologists take reasonable steps to ensure that explanations of results are given to the individual or designated representative unless the nature of the relationship precludes provision of an explanation of results (such as in some organizational consulting, preemployment or security screenings, and forensic evaluations), and this fact has been clearly explained to the person being assessed in advance.

9.11. Maintaining Test Security

The term *test materials* refers to manuals, instruments, protocols, and test questions or stimuli and does not include *test data* as defined in Standard 9.04, Release of Test Data. Psychologists make reasonable efforts to maintain the integrity and security of test materials and other assessment techniques consistent with law and contractual obligations, and in a manner that permits adherence to this Ethics Code.

10. *Therapy*

10.01 Informed Consent to Therapy

(a) When obtaining informed consent to therapy as required in Standard 3.10, Informed Consent, psychologists inform clients/patients as early as is feasible in the therapeutic relationship about the nature and anticipated course of therapy, fees, involvement of third parties, and limits of confidentiality and provide sufficient opportunity for the client/patient to ask questions and receive answers. (See also Standards 4.02, Discussing the Limits of Confidentiality, and 6.04, Fees and Financial Arrangements.)

(b) When obtaining informed consent for treatment for which generally recognized techniques and procedures have not been established, psychologists inform their clients/patients of the developing nature of the treatment, the potential risks involved, alternative treatments that may be available, and the voluntary nature of their participation. (See also Standards 2.01e, Boundaries of Competence, and 3.10, Informed Consent.)

(c) When the therapist is a trainee and the legal responsibility for the treatment provided resides with the supervisor, the client/patient, as part of the informed consent procedure, is informed that the therapist is in training and is being supervised and is given the name of the supervisor.

10.02 Therapy Involving Couples or Families

(a) When psychologists agree to provide services to several persons who have a relationship (such as spouses, significant others, or parents and children), they take reasonable steps to clarify at the outset (1) which of the individuals are clients/patients and (2) the relationship the psychologist will have with each person. This clarification includes the psychologist's role and the probable uses of the services provided or the information obtained. (See also Standard 4.02, Discussing the Limits of Confidentiality.)

(b) If it becomes apparent that psychologists may be called on to perform potentially conflicting roles (such as family therapist and then witness for one party in divorce proceedings), psychologists take reasonable steps to clarify and modify, or withdraw from, roles appropriately. (See also Standard 3.05c, Multiple Relationships.)

10.03 Group Therapy

When psychologists provide services to several persons in a group setting, they describe at the outset the roles and responsibilities of all parties and the limits of confidentiality.

10.04 Providing Therapy to Those Served by Others

In deciding whether to offer or provide services to those already receiving mental health services elsewhere, psychologists carefully consider the treatment issues and the potential client's/patient's welfare. Psychologists discuss these issues with the client/patient or another legally authorized person on behalf of the client/patient in order to minimize the risk of confusion and conflict, consult with the other service providers when appropriate, and proceed with caution and sensitivity to the therapeutic issues.

10.05 Sexual Intimacies With Current Therapy Clients/Patients

Psychologists do not engage in sexual intimacies with current therapy clients/patients.

10.06 Sexual Intimacies With Relatives or Significant Others of Current Therapy Clients/Patients

Psychologists do not engage in sexual intimacies with individuals they know to be close relatives, guardians, or significant others of current clients/patients. Psychologists do not terminate therapy to circumvent this standard.

10.07 Therapy With Former Sexual Partners

Psychologists do not accept as therapy clients/patients persons with whom they have engaged in sexual intimacies.

10.08 Sexual Intimacies With Former Therapy Clients/Patients

(a) Psychologists do not engage in sexual intimacies with former clients/patients for at least two years after cessation or termination of therapy.

(b) Psychologists do not engage in sexual intimacies with former clients/patients even after a two-year interval except in the most unusual circumstances. Psychologists who engage in such activity after the two years following cessation or termination of therapy and of having no sexual contact with the former client/patient bear the burden of demonstrating that there has been no exploitation, in light of all relevant factors, including (1) the amount of time that has passed since therapy terminated; (2) the nature, duration, and intensity of the therapy; (3) the circumstances of termination; (4) the client's/patient's personal history; (5) the client's/patient's current mental status; (6) the likelihood of adverse impact on the client/patient; and (7) any statements or actions made by the therapist during the course of therapy suggesting or inviting the possibility of a posttermination sexual or romantic relationship with the client/patient. (See also Standard 3.05, Multiple Relationships.)

10.09 Interruption of Therapy

When entering into employment or contractual relationships, psychologists make reasonable efforts to provide for orderly and appropriate resolution of responsibility for client/patient care in the event that the employment or contractual relationship ends, with paramount consideration given to the welfare of the client/patient. (See also Standard 3.12, Interruption of Psychological Services.)

10.10 Terminating Therapy

(a) Psychologists terminate therapy when it becomes reasonably clear that the client/patient no longer needs the service, is not likely to benefit, or is being harmed by continued service.

(b) Psychologists may terminate therapy when threatened or otherwise endangered by the client/patient or another person with whom the client/patient has a relationship.

(c) Except where precluded by the actions of clients/patients or third-party payors, prior to termination psychologists provide pretermination counseling and suggest alternative service providers as appropriate.

33

MORAL FOUNDATIONS IN RESEARCH WITH HUMAN PARTICIPANTS

M. BREWSTER SMITH

All scientific inquiry with human research participants necessarily involves ethical issues. For example, the pursuit of psychological knowledge about people is itself an ethical goal in the scientist's scheme of values. Psychological research that deals with central and sensitive personal issues, such as people's inner conflicts and their private victories and defeats, aspirations and regrets, inherently risks harming or offending the people that it studies. Researchers who seek to contribute to the understanding and amelioration of serious social problems like AIDS, youth or family violence, or substance abuse need to consider the rights and interests of the vulnerable people being studied.

An ethical perspective on research decisions inherently involves tension between responsible judgment and the rigid application of rules. The

From *Ethics in Research With Human Participants* (pp. 3–10), edited by B. D. Sales and S. Folkman, 2000, Washington, DC: American Psychological Association. Copyright 2000 by the American Psychological Association. Adapted with permission.

requirements of the law may conflict with ethical ideals, as may be conspicuously the case with some issues concerning confidentiality. The methodological requirements of solid research may conflict with the rights of individuals or with competing conceptions of the public good. Principles and guidelines can identify what is ethically desirable and what is clearly unacceptable, but there is a large area in which researchers are left to make their own decisions. These decisions can be ethically responsible when made on the basis of an ethically sensitized appreciation of the relevant considerations.

But what should be taught to engender such an appreciation? When the American Psychological Association (APA) took the lead in 1973 in promulgating *Ethical Principles in the Conduct of Research With Human Participants* (see APA, 1982), primary concern focused on problems such as the use of deceptive procedures in psychological research, the potentially coercive implications of departmental participant pools, and threats to confidentiality in academic investigations. Although these ethical issues remain important, they are no longer representative of the range of issues that many psychologists face in their research today, especially in biomedical and community contexts. In addition, with many behavioral scientists increasingly involved in biomedical research, guidelines for behavioral research also need to be compatible with guidelines developed in the biomedical areas.

Federal regulation has elaborated a legal and bureaucratic framework centering on institutional review boards (IRBs) that provides a salient context for the researcher's ethical responsibility, although it does not absolve researchers from making their own difficult ethical decisions (Office for Protection From Research Risks; OPRR, 1991). This admonition is important because some IRBs may lack appropriate behavioral and social science expertise. Further, the *Ethical Principles of Psychologists and Code of Conduct* (APA, 2002) includes principles and standards enforceable for APA members concerning the ethical conduct of human research that are found in Section 7 (Training) and elsewhere in the document.

This chapter is intended to introduce the reader to the broader moral considerations and ethical principles that underlie ethical decision-making for researchers studying human behavior. (Note that ethical considerations in research with nonhuman animals are dealt with in the *Guidelines for Ethical Conduct in the Care and Use of Animals*, APA, 1996.)

HOW IS THIS ETHICAL APPROACH DIFFERENT FROM OTHERS?

Moral or ethical judgment is a human universal, but systematic treatments of ethical principles obviously vary across religious traditions and schools of philosophical thought. Among Western schools of thought, for example, different ethical priorities are highlighted by the Kantian or "deontological" approach that emphasizes respect for individual autonomy and the "utilitarian" approach linked with John Stuart Mill that emphasizes the balance of harms and benefits to people. The deontological approach holds that the morality of an action is directly related to its intrinsic nature: Actions are right or wrong regardless of their consequences.

The many variants of this approach share a common imperative: One's actions should strive to treat every person as an end and never as a means (Beauchamp & Childress, 1989; Bersoff & Koeppl, 1993). Respect for the dignity of the individual necessarily involves respect for individual autonomy. Conversely, utilitarianism, or consequentialist ethical theory, holds that the morality of an action is to be judged by its consequences, a perspective that highlights the balancing of costs and benefits.

Different religious and philosophical traditions propose different priorities and modes of analysis for determining what is the morally right course of action in a given situation. For example, most would agree that one should not take a life, but the determination of what comprises taking a life (e.g., abortion issues) or whether there are still higher principles (e.g., keeping society safe) differs among the traditions. Federal regulations (OPRR, 1991)[1] are legally binding to those conducting research in this country; ethical standards such as those in the APA's 2002 code are obligatory for members of the professional associations that promulgate them. In contrast, the analysis and recommendations contained in this chapter are not binding. They are offered, rather, with the aim of raising the level of ethical awareness and practice of researchers.

The responsibilities of researchers can be sorted into four sets: responsibilities (a) to science; (b) to society; (c) to students, apprentices, or trainees in research; and (d) to the participants in the research. The primary focus will be on responsibilities to the participants in research. This focus will be balanced with the other three sets of responsibilities: to science—to do research that indeed extends knowledge or deepens understanding; to society—as in the case of determining how the results of research are used or publicized; to students, apprentices, or trainees—to contribute to their education in regard to ethical issues in the conduct of research.

---

[1] Federal agencies that have adopted the 45 CFR Part 46 as the Common Rule include the U.S. Department of Agriculture, 7 CFR Part 1C; the U.S. Department of Energy, 10 CFR Part 745; the National Aeronautics and Space Administration, 14 CFR Part 1230; the U.S. Department of Commerce, 15 CFR Part 27; the Consumer Product Safety Commission, 16 CFR Part 1028; the International Development Cooperation Agency/Agency for International Development, 22 CFR Part 225; the U.S. Department of Housing and Urban Development, 24 CFR Part 60; the U.S. Department of Justice, 28 CFR Part 46; the U.S. Department of Defense, 32 CFR Part 219; the U.S. Department of Education, 34 CFR Part 97; the Department of Veterans Affairs, 38 CFR Part 16; the Environmental Protection Agency, 40 CFR Part 26; the U.S. Department of Health and Human Services, 45 CFR Part 46; the National Science Foundation, 45 CFR Part 690; and the U.S. Department of Transportation, 49 CFR Part 11. The Office of Science and Technology Policy and the Central Intelligence Agency (CIA) accepted the common rule but did not publish it separately—the CIA having done so in response to an Executive Order.

Efforts in the biomedical and psychological research community to meet these responsibilities have involved both the utilitarian and deontological traditions as well as more concrete guidelines, such as the Belmont Report, *Ethical Principles and Guidelines for the Protection of Human Subjects of Research* (OPRR, 1979), the report of the National Commission for the Protection of Human Subjects of Biomedical and Behavioral Research that set the framework for federal regulation.

Attention is also directed to the general principles included in the 2002 APA code (see chapter 32).

Five basic moral principles underlie the ethical guidance provided in this chapter:

    I.   Respect for Persons and Their Autonomy
    II.   Beneficence and Nonmaleficence
    III.   Justice
    IV.   Trust
    V.   Fidelity and Scientific Integrity.

These moral principles cover essentially the same ground as Ethical Principles A–E of the 2002 APA code, but as ethical principles, they are cast in terms especially relevant to research practice. Thus, Moral Principles I, II, and III are drawn from the Belmont Report. The relation of these moral principles to the aspirational ethical principles of the APA code is noted throughout the rest of this chapter. Because Ethical Standard 2, Competence, of the code responds to a characteristic of the researcher and his or her work, judgments about competence precede review of ethical responsibility. Although competence is not listed as one of the basic moral principles, it is assumed to be essential for the design and conduct of responsible research. For example, decisions about risks and benefits of a specific research study are often best informed by expertise in the subject matter of the research. Competence of the researcher would imply expertise in the domain of the research.

Moral Principle I. Respect for Persons and Their Autonomy

Researchers respect the human participants in their investigations as persons of worth whose participation is a matter of their autonomous choice. Insofar as persons have diminished autonomy, whether because of immaturity, incapacitation, or circumstances that severely restrict their liberty, they require special concern. Guidance provided in subsequent chapters relating to informed consent, coercion, deception, confidentiality, and privacy relate to this principle, which corresponds to Ethical Principle E in the APA code, Respect for People's Rights and Dignity.

There is an intrinsic relation between Moral Principle I and Moral Principle II, Beneficence and Nonmaleficence. The interests of proposed participants who have diminished capacity or opportunity for autonomous choice need to be appropriately represented and assurance provided that they will not be at risk for harmful consequences. In many cases for such persons, informed consent should involve proxies (e.g., parents or spouse). Conversely, federal regulations do not require informed consent in connection with some categories of research that involve essentially no risk. The judgment of "no risk" may of course be problematic, and researchers should strive to ensure that such decisions are not self-serving. It is best to seek external validation for such decisions through consultation with colleagues or institutional resources (e.g., IRBs).

Moral Principle II. Beneficence and Nonmaleficence

In the planning and conduct of research with human participants, the researcher should maximize the possible benefits and minimize the possible harms from the research. Whereas Moral Principle I represents the deontological tradition, Moral Principle II represents the utilitarian tradition. In the APA code, it corresponds to Ethical Principle A, Beneficence and Nonmaleficence.

This seemingly straightforward principle becomes complex and ambiguous in application. Costs and benefits can seldom be estimated accurately in advance, and they can rarely be balanced against each other. In much psychological research, the conceivable benefit is to the science, and through the science, potentially to society at large. One cannot balance costs to the participants against benefits to the science, although psychologists should keep both in view in deciding whether to do the research. Because no simple summation of costs and benefits is possible, the researcher cannot avoid moral responsibility for the decision.

As already noted, the relation between Moral Principles I and II is critical. Because it is impossible to balance costs to the individual against uncertain gains to the science and to society, the imposition of any appreciable cost, risk, or harm from participation in research increases the ethical priority for obtaining the participant's autonomous informed consent or its equivalent from the participant's appropriately designated advocate or representative. Special considerations apply when a scientifically required research design is incompatible with fully informed consent (as in the case of research involving placebo controls or deceptive instructions).

A further complication in research concerns possible costs or harm to groups or categories of people or to social institutions. The question arises about whether official or unofficial representatives can or should give or withhold consent on behalf of such collective entities. Although there is little consensus on this issue, sensitivity to it is ethically desirable. Again, it is recommended that researchers seek consultation when making decisions about research risks.

Moral Principle III. Justice

The principle of justice states an ideal for research that is unlikely to be fully achieved in actual human societies that are never fully just. In the APA code, it relates most closely to Ethical Principle D, Justice.

Considerations of *distributive justice* (the proper distribution of benefits and burdens) arose saliently in medical research, in which risky new procedures were traditionally tried on ward patients, with benefits reaped largely by patients in private care. Threats to justice in research often arise from the almost inherent power differential between experimenter and research participant. For example, in some field studies, participants could be those who are weak and marginal rather than those who are socially and politically powerful and who thus can more readily guard their own interests. Members of ethnic minority groups may be especially vulnerable and likewise find their special concerns neglected. Traditional assumptions about gender have led to the underinclusion of women and their concerns in research. Such power differentials necessitate safeguards against exploitation, lack of representation or under-representation in scientific studies.

Concerns with *procedural justice* (the adequacy of procedures to ensure fairness) are relevant at every stage of the research process. For example, appropriate procedures need to be established in advance of the research to ensure that research assistants and participants alike have adequate access to mechanisms to address their possible concerns about the research (e.g., issues relating to co-authorship by the research assistant or the adequacy of compensation offered to the participants).

Moral Principle IV. Trust

Researchers establish and maintain a relationship of trust with the participants in their research. Participation is based on explicit agreement about what the participant will experience and its consequences and about the researcher's obligations—for example, with respect to confidentiality. Such agreements anticipate relevant exceptions such as legally imposed exceptions to confidentiality.

This principle is closely related to Ethical Principle 1, Respect for Persons and Their Autonomy of the Belmont Report, and to Ethical Principle B of the APA code, Fidelity and Responsibility. Ethical concerns arise when informing the prospective participant of the purpose of the research or the details of the procedure when such disclosure compromises the validity of the research.

The relationship of trust between experimenter and participant ought to be reciprocal. In contemporary society, unfortunately, there is widespread mistrust of science and of public institutions, which fosters an unfavorable climate for the support and conduct of research. Overcoming initial distrust is a frequent problem in the planning and conduct of research. Researchers therefore should exercise great care to avoid giving occasion for increase in public distrust of behavioral and social research.

Moral Principle Versus Fidelity and Scientific Integrity

The researcher is committed to the discovery and promulgation of truth.

Recent criticism of "positivist" scientific epistemology that has challenged the objective status of scientific truth in no way relieves researchers from the obligation to do good science as that is understood in the research community. Scientific integrity — truthfulness — is not open to compromise. This principle corresponds to APA Ethical Principle C, Integrity.

RESOLVING ETHICAL CONFLICTS

Most research raises the potential for ethical conflicts. The approval of a research proposal by an IRB does not absolve the researcher from this ethical responsibility. IRBs differ in their composition, disciplinary expertise, institutional context, and interpretation of federal regulations. It may become part of the researcher's role to educate the IRB to relevant ethical considerations. Conversely, the IRB should alert researchers to ethical problems in their proposed research, and federal regulations require the researcher to defer to the IRB in matters of dispute.

In making ethical decisions about research, researchers should take into account the probable self-serving bias that can lead them to overestimate the scientific value of a proposed study and underestimate its ethical liabilities. Consultation with others less vulnerable to this bias, such as with colleagues experienced in the research area, is essential in compensating for it.

CONCLUSION

Five widely accepted general moral principles underlying the ethical conduct of research with human participants have been introduced in this chapter. Knowledge of these moral principles and consideration of the guidance provided here is important to researchers because merely following the requirements of law, federal regulators, and IRBs does not absolve the researcher from personal responsibility for resolving possible ethical conflicts that may arise in the conduct of their work. Finally, because the maintenance of high ethical standards is the shared responsibility of the research community, researchers typically communicate the substance of these principles' guidance through their roles as instructors, mentors, supervisors, reviewers, IRB members, and colleagues.

REFERENCES

American Psychological Association. (1982). *Ethical principles in the conduct of research with human participants*. Washington, DC: Author.

American Psychological Association. (2002). Ethical principles of psychologists and code of conduct. *American Psychologist, 57*.

American Psychological Association. (1996). *Guidelines for ethical conduct in the care and use of animals*. Washington, DC: Author.

Beauchamp, T. L., & Childress, J. F. (1989). *Principles of biomedical ethics*. New York: Oxford University Press.

Bersoff, D. N., & Koeppl, P. M. (1993). The relation between ethical codes and moral principles. *Ethics and Behavior, 3*, 345–357.

Office for Protection From Research Risks, Protection of Human Subjects. National Commission for the Protection of Human Subjects of Biomedical and Behavioral Research. (1979). *The Belmont Report: Ethical principles and guidelines for the protection of human subjects of research* (GPO 887-809). Washington, DC: U.S. Government Printing Office.

Office for Protection From Research Risks, Protection of Human Subjects. (1991, June 18).

Protection of human subjects: Title 45, Code of Federal Regulations, Part 46 (GPO 1992 O-307-551). OPRR Reports, pp. 4–17.

SPECIAL TOPICS
AND ISSUES

34

ETHICAL TRANSGRESSIONS OF PSYCHOLOGY GRADUATE STUDENTS: CRITICAL INCIDENTS WITH IMPLICATIONS FOR TRAINING

BARBARA J. FLY, WILLIAM P. VAN BARK, LAURA WEINMAN,
KAREN STROHM KITCHENER, AND PATRICK R. LANG

Although the annual reports of the Ethics Committee of the American Psychological Association (APA, 1994, 1995) document the fact that some psychologists violate the ethics code (APA, 1992) of the profession, little is known about similar ethical transgressions among graduate students (Mearns & Allen, 1991). Results of one such study indicated that 95 percent of responding students had dealt with at least one issue of impairment or ethical impropriety with a peer during their graduate training. Of the faculty

Reprinted from *Professional Psychology: Research and Practice*, 28, 492–495. Copyright 1997 by the American Psychological Association.

Barbara J. Fly and William P. van Bark are the joint first authors of this chapter.

We wish to thank Chuck Dennison, Alma Margeson, Sharon Anderson, and Tom Wilkens for their assistance in developing the questionnaire.

respondents, 93 percent reported being aware of a serious impairment in a student within the last 5 years (Mearns & Allen, 1991).

THE EXPLORATORY PROJECT

In our investigation, we used the critical incident technique (CIT) procedure, which was developed by Flanagan (1954) to study human behavior in a systematic manner. The CIT was used to generate the initial ethical problems for the first APA code of ethics (Pope & Vetter, 1992). The CIT is not a rigid set of rules for data collection but, rather, is a flexible set of principles that can be modified to fit a specific setting. The procedure involves gathering incidents of extreme behavior in defined situations (Flanagan, 1954). Extreme behaviors are used because they can be more accurately identified than routine behaviors, and situations are clearly defined to analyze the general aims of the activity. In addition, the CIT uses reports from qualified observers who are able to evaluate observations on the basis of defined objectives. In our investigation, the observers were the clinical and counseling psychology program training directors.

The CIT questionnaire first requested basic demographic information of the respondents and then requested respondents to recount up to three incidents of ethical transgressions made by students enrolled in their training programs. Respondents were told to define transgressions broadly as any error considered to be ethical in nature, not just ones that violated the APA ethics code. They were asked to describe the incident; state how they learned of the situation; describe what action, if any, was taken in response to the transgression; and provide enough detail (e.g., student year and gender) that a reader could form a relatively clear picture of the situation. The training directors were also asked to explain why they believed the incident involved an ethical issue.

In the fall of 1992, we sent questionnaires to all 243 training directors of APA-accredited clinical and counseling programs in the United States and Canada. A total of 75 questionnaires were returned, for a response rate of 31 percent. Eighty-nine incidents were reported by 47 respondents. Others reported no ethical transgressions ($n = 18$), discussed ethical issues rather than transgressions ($n = 4$), or chose not to respond ($n = 6$). Although the response rate was low, it was not atypical for this type of exploratory research (Anderson & Kitchener, 1996; Goodyear, Crego, & Johnson, 1992). Furthermore, the purposes of the study were not to obtain a random sample in order to make generalizations. Rather, because this was as an exploratory study, our purposes were (a) to describe and classify the kinds of ethical transgressions faculty report students make while in graduate school and (b) to identify how faculty responded to the transgressions when they were identified. As a consequence, the figures reported herein represent the proportion of reported transgressions and do not necessarily reflect the percentage of students who have difficulty with these issues.

The critical incidents were typed on cards and then sorted by two teams of readers. The result of the incident-sorting process identified eight major categories. The categories, definitions, percentages of ethical transgressions within the categories, and examples of responses are provided below. Identifying information in the examples has been changed to protect the anonymity of the respondents and the students.

Confidentiality (25 Percent)

This category was composed of incidents in which students failed to maintain confidentiality of clients, fellow students, colleagues, or faculty, either verbally or in the storage, transportation, or dissemination of material. Examples included the following:

1. A student in a practicum discussed a client (without using the client's name) in a social setting. Another person present in the social setting was able to identify the client and told the client about the fact that he or she was discussed outside of therapy.
2. A student on internship took home a report (with identifying data) in his or her vehicle. The report dropped out of the vehicle near the internship site. A person who was not connected to the internship site found the report and returned it to the training director.

Professional Boundaries, Sexual and Nonsexual (20 Percent)

In this category were incidents in which the student initiated, accepted, or engaged in a conversation or behavior of an intimate, romantic, or harassing nature with clients, fellow students, supervisors, or faculty. Such actions exceeded appropriate professional boundaries. Examples of these types of incidents included the following:

1. A practicum student invited a client, who was ostensibly depressed and lonely, to the student's apartment on the weekend if the client became depressed or lonely. (The client did not take the student up on the offer.)
2. A practicum student did an intake evaluation, including a sexual history, of a prospective client of the opposite gender. The student later called the client to say he or she would not be assigned as the client's therapist but was available to see the client socially.

Plagiarism or Falsification of Data (15 Percent)

Incidents in this category involved a student using elements of another's work or data without obtaining permission or citing the source appropriately. Examples of such incidents included the following:

1. A student plagiarized an article, almost in its entirety, and submitted it to an instructor with no reference to the source. The instructor was familiar with the article.
2. Two students had identical, unusual errors on their departmental comprehensive examinations.

Welfare (10 Percent)

This category was composed of incidents in which a student's conduct had the potential to place a client at risk for harm because of incomplete documentation; questionable judgment; inadequate consultation, supervision, or referral; or personal problems. Examples of incidents in this category included the following:

1. A student at a practicum site used new equipment as a treatment for pain. This student misused the equipment, keeping the client in a painful position for almost an hour. The client reported the incident to the supervisor, but the student denied it had happened. Equipment printouts were consulted that indicated the client was right. The student admitted he or she had lied out of fear of being removed from the program.
2. A student at a practicum site gathered information on a child sufficient to warrant suspicion of sexual abuse by the child's parent. However, the student failed to report the suspicion, even though his or her supervisor instructed the student to do so. The student revealed that the information obtained from the child was audiotaped without the parental consent and without the child's knowledge.

Procedural Breach With Ethical Implications (10 Percent)

This category included incidents in which the student failed to comply with department, placement, clinic, or other institutional policies, rules, or standards of conduct. Examples included the following:

1. A practicum student at an inpatient facility permitted a patient to leave the facility on a pass without the required authorization from a supervising psychiatrist.

2. A student took a client's chart home to work on progress notes. It was against facility policy to remove charts from the site.

Competency (9 Percent)

Incidents involving competency were characterized by a student providing or terminating services without proper training or with inadequate knowledge of laws, testing procedures, therapeutic techniques, or other elements of appropriate practice. Examples of these types of incidents included the following:

1. A student used a therapeutic technique with a client without having had training or supervision and without having researched the procedure.
2. A practicum student administered the Minnesota Multiphasic Personality Inventory to a foreign-born client for whom English was a weak second language. The student then interpreted test items for the client that the client had not understood. The test was scored and interpreted to the client as a valid profile.

Integrity–Dishonesty (8 Percent)

This category included those incidents in which a student lied to protect himself or herself, to avoid work, or to advance himself or herself. One example of such an incident involved a student who led a supervisor to believe he or she was counseling a client when, in fact, the student was not appearing for appointments.

Misrepresentation of Credentials (3 Percent)

This final category was composed of incidents in which the student made public statements about credentials that were false, fraudulent, or misleading. One example of such an incident is the following: A student who was enrolled in a training program was seeing clients privately for hypnotherapy. The student saw a client for several months before it came to the training director's attention. This student had a business card calling himself or herself a psychologist (which was illegal in the state where the incident occurred) and was clearly conducting psychotherapy in addition to hypnosis.

STUDENTS WHO MADE ETHICAL TRANSGRESSIONS

Training directors reported that 54 percent of the students who made these ethical transgressions had already had an ethics course. In addition, they reported that they most frequently learned of the incidents from a third party (36 percent), such as a friend or relative of the client, coworkers, practicum site staff, or peers. The second most prevalent way transgressions came to the training directors' attention was when faculty members or the training director witnessed the incident (25 percent). Other categories used to describe how training directors learned of transgressions included intentional and unintentional self-reports (15 percent), faculty recognized plagiarism (10 percent), reports made by clients or victims (7 percent), and unknown (7 percent).

The two most common actions taken in response to ethical transgressions were confrontation with a stipulation for some kind of remedial action, such as restitution, probation, or reimbursement (44 percent), and dismissal from the program (22 percent). Other categories of responses included no consequence (6 percent), referral for additional review (5 percent), counseling the student to drop out of the program (3 percent), dismissal of the student from the practicum (3 percent), course of action unknown (3 percent), and voluntary withdrawal from the program (2 percent).

IMPLICATIONS FOR TRAINING AND PRACTICE

Dual-role relationships and confidentiality are clearly problem areas for graduate students in professional psychology, similar to Pope and Vetter's (1992) observations that trained professionals most often encounter ethical dilemmas in the same two areas. In other words, the transgressions students make on the graduate level may be in the same areas where they will encounter the most frequent ethical dilemmas in professional practice. On the other hand, because training directors were not asked to describe the behaviors that occur most often, it may also be that dual-role relationships and confidentiality were described more frequently because they were considered most important or most potentially harmful. Other transgressions may in fact occur more frequently.

The incidents training directors described in the areas of dual-role relationships and confidentiality were serious. They, along with the transgressions in the competency category, could have had harmful effects on clients and seemed to reflect a failure to understand or abide by the core ethical values of the profession. In a similar manner, the categories of plagiarism or falsification of data, integrity – dishonesty, and misrepresentation of credentials all reflect some kind of dishonesty. These transgressions seemed to suggest that the students involved either did not value or did not understand the importance of honesty and integrity in maintaining trusting human relationships, a central value in psychology training.

The fact that most of the incidents occurred even after the student had training in ethics suggests the importance of focusing more attention in ethics education on these areas. It is possible that some of these problems, like those involving boundary issues and confidentiality, are more difficult for students to identify and confront because they potentially occur under so many conditions. Other incidents, such as plagiarism, were more blatant and may indicate the importance of attending to character issues in student selection.

TEACHING MORAL BEHAVIOR

The fact that most of these incidents occurred after ethics couse work may suggest that as a profession, we are not thinking broadly enough about how to help students develop ethical behavior. Although there is no formula for teaching new professionals how to avoid ethical transgressions, the psychological literature on moral behavior (Rest, 1983, 1986) provides some direction. On the basis of a review of the literature on morality, Rest identified four components that are involved in producing moral behavior. Ethics curricula that address all of these components may be more successful in preparing new professionals to appropriately negotiate ethical situations than those that do not.

Component 1, which Rest called *interpreting the situation*, involves being sensitized to the moral aspect of the event, considering the consequences of different choices made by the people involved, and trying to sort out one's feelings about the issue. Faculty can address this component by providing students with multiple examples of ethical situations that involve issues like confidentiality or multiple-role relationships, having students identify their feelings about the situations, and then suggesting what they would do or say. The ensuing discussions could provide opportunities for students to consider alternatives other than their own, to talk about the potential consequences for the different people involved, and to stimulate their moral empathy (Kitchener, 1986). Role-playing cases involving potential or actual transgressions and the use of vignettes, such as those developed by Steres (1992), to help students deal with sexual feelings in therapy also can achieve the same goals.

Rest called Component 2 *formulating the morally ideal course of action*. Using Component 2 processes, the individual chooses between possible courses of action and decides one is more ethical than another. Rest pointed to the moral development literature suggesting conceptions of justice and social cooperation develop over time with changes in cognitive capacity. Although age and education play major roles in promoting complex thinking about moral problems, one's level of moral judgement reflects more basic moral growth (Rest, 1983). Thus, ethics education that ignores students' ability to conceptualize ethical issues will likely have little impact on students' core thinking about moral issues. If students with an inadequate ability to conceptualize moral issues are selected into graduate programs, ethics education may be doomed to fail. On the other hand, even those who have the capacity to make complex moral judgments may still not have the tools to do so. Introducing students to general ethical decision-making models, like those suggested by Haas and Malouf (1989) or Kitchener (1984), or specific models regarding multiple-role relationships, such as suggested by Gottlieb (1993), may help.

The processes involved in Component 3, *deciding what one actually intends to do*, focus on deciding between moral values and other competing values. Values like self-interest, financial reward, or friendship may interfere with what one knows to be the right moral course of action. In this case, educators can help students recognize the human dimensions and weaknesses involved in making ethical mistakes. To do so, Borys and Pope (1989) suggested that ethics classes and training programs in general need to provide a safe atmosphere in which students can examine those impulses that might lead them to unwittingly break client confidence, stumble into harmful dual-role relationships, and so on.

Furthermore, faculty have to model the importance of being ethical (Kitchener, 1986) as well as the values of honesty that they expect their students to exhibit. As psychologists, we know that modeling is a powerful tool for learning. If faculty model disrespectful, dishonest, or exploitive relationships, the implicit message is that these attitudes are acceptable. If students received this implicit message, it would not be surprising if they did not place a high value on the ethical models and rules they learned in their ethics class about avoiding multiple-role relationships or being competent and honest.

The last component Rest identified sometimes comes under the rubric of ego strength or character. He refered to it as *executing or implementing a course of action*. It is basically the willingness (a) to do the right thing, sometimes even by sacrificing one's self or (b) to risk being different. Here, it might be helpful to suggest to students that they develop a moral community to provide them with consultation and support when they are faced with tough moral decisions. At the same time, faculty can address the real professional consequences of acting unethically for the student (e.g., loss of insurance, loss of status, loss of career) as well as the consequences for the consumer (Borys & Pope, 1989).

Issues of character are related to a question raised by one respondent regarding the possible relationship between underlying characterological features or disorders among some graduate students and the prevalence of ethical transgressions. The question seemed important because so many of the reported ethical transgressions were quite blatant. It may also be the case that the profession needs to distinguish between problematic behavior and underlying impairment (Lamb, Cochran, & Jackson, 1991). The question of whether this distinction enlightens psychology's understanding of ethical transgressions may also be an important topic for future investigation. Considering that ethical transgressions often harm those whom psychologists have promised to help, it is important for the profession to further investigate the frequency and causes of ethical transgressions in addition to helping students avoid them.

REFERENCES

American Psychological Association. (1992). Ethical principles of psychologists. *American Psychologist, 47,* 1597–1611.

American Psychological Association. *(1994).* Report of the Ethics Committee 1993. *American Psychologist, 40,* 659–666.

American Psychological Association. (1995). Report of the Ethics Committee 1994. *American Psychologist, 50,* 706–713.

Anderson, S. A., & Kitchener, K. S. (1996). Nonromantic, nonsexual relationships between psychologists and former clients: An exploratory study of critical incidents. *Professional Psychology: Research and Practice, 27,* 59–66.

Borys, D. S., & Pope, K. S. (1989). Dual relationships between therapist and client: A national study of psychologists, psychiatrists, and social workers. *Professional Psychology: Research and Practice, 20,* 283–293.

Flanagan, J. C. (1954). The critical incident technique. *Psychological Bulletin, 51,* 327–359.

Goodyear, R. K., Crego, C. A., & Johnson, M. W. (1992). Ethical issues in the supervision of student research: A study of critical incidents. *Professional Psychology: Research and Practice, 23,* 203–210.

Gottlieb, M. C. (1993). Avoiding exploitive dual relationships: A decision making model. *Psychotherapy, 30,* 41–47.

Haas, L. J., & Malouf, J. L. (1989). *Keeping up the good work.* Sarasota, FL: Professional Resource Exchange.

Kitchener, K. S. (1984). Intuition, critical evaluation and ethical principles. *The Counseling Psychologist, 12,* 43–55.

Kitchener, K. S. (1986). Teaching applied ethics in counselor education: An integration of psychological processes and philosophical analysis. *Journal of Counseling and Development, 64,* 306–310.

Lamb, D. H., Cochran, D. J., & Jackson, V. R. (1991). Training and organizational issues associated with identifying and responding to intern impairment. *Professional Psychology: Research and Practice, 22,* 291–296.

Mearns, J., & Allen, G. J. (1991). Graduate students' experiences in dealing with impaired peers, compared with faculty predictions: An exploratory study. *Ethics and Behavior, 1,* 191–202.

Pope, K. S., & Vetter, V. A. (1992). Ethical dilemmas encountered by members of the American Psychological Association: A national survey. *American Psychologist, 47,* 297–411.

Rest, J. R. (1983). Morality. In P. Mussen (Ed.), *Manual of child psychology: Vol. 3. Cognitive development* (pp. 556–629). New York: Wiley.

Rest, J. R. (1986). *Moral development: Advances in research and theory*. New York: Praeger.

Steres, L. M. (1992). *Sexual attraction in psychotherapy: A professional training intervention for clinical psychology graduate students*. Unpublished doctoral dissertation, California School of Professional Psychology.

35

REFLECTIONS ON DETERMINING AUTHORSHIP CREDIT AND AUTHORSHIP ORDER ON FACULTY–STUDENT COLLABORATIONS

MARK A. FINE AND LAWRENCE A. KURDEK

Scholarly activity is an expected and rewarded enterprise for many professionals (Keith-Spiegel & Koocher, 1985). In academic settings, decisions regarding promotion, tenure, and salary are heavily influenced not only by the number of publications in peer-reviewed journals but also by the number of first-authored publications (Costa & Gatz, 1992). Similarly, in applied settings, professionals with strong publication records are often considered to have more competence and expertise than their less published counterparts.

Clearly, authorship credit and authorship order are not trivial matters. Because of the importance of authorship credit, dilemmas may arise when more than one person is involved in a scholarly project. In this article, we

Reprinted from the *American Psychologist, 48*, 1141–1147. Copyright 1993 by the American Psychological Association.

specifically address collaborative efforts between faculty and undergraduate or graduate students. The importance of authorship in the faculty–student research context was underscored by Goodyear, Crego, and Johnston (1992), who found that authorship issues were among the "critical incidents" identified by experienced researchers in faculty–student research collaborations.

The purpose of this article is to contribute to the discussions regarding the determination of authorship credit and order of authorship—in the faculty–student research context. There are six parts to the article. To provide a context for the discussions, the first part presents four hypothetical cases. Because the final authorship decisions in these cases are based on considerations reviewed later in the article, the cases end before the final decisions were determined. The second part reviews available guidelines for determining authorship credit and order. The third part describes ethical issues related to authorship credit and authorship order when faculty and students collaborate. The fourth part of the article highlights several ethical principles that may provide assistance in resolving authorship dilemmas. The fifth part provides tentative recommendations for faculty who collaborate with students on scholarly projects. The final part revisits the four hypothetical cases with our opinions regarding what authorship decisions would have been appropriate.

HYPOTHETICAL CASES

Case 1

A student in a clinical psychology doctoral program conducted dissertation research at a practicum site. The initial idea for the study was developed between the practicum supervisor (a psychologist) and the student. The dissertation committee was composed of the chair, who was a psychology faculty member in the student's graduate department; the practicum supervisor; and another psychology faculty member in the same department. After the dissertation was approved, the chair of the committee raised the possibility of writing a journal article based on the dissertation. The student agreed to write the first and subsequent drafts of the manuscript, the committee chair agreed to supervise the writing process, and the practicum supervisor agreed to review drafts of the paper. On initial drafts, the student, practicum supervisor, and committee chair were first, second, and third authors, respectively. However, after numerous drafts, the student acknowledged losing interest in the writing process. The committee chair finished the manuscript after extensively reanalyzing the data.

Case 2

An undergraduate student asked a psychology member to supervise an honors thesis. The student proposed a topic, the faculty member primarily developed the research methodology, the student collected and entered the data, the faculty member conducted the statistical analyses, and the student used part of the analyses for the thesis. The student wrote the thesis under very close supervision by the faculty member. After the honors thesis was completed, the faculty member decided that data from the entire project were sufficiently interesting to warrant publication as a unit. Because the student did not have the skills necessary to write the entire study for a scientific journal, the faculty member did so. The student's thesis contained approximately one third of the material presented in the article.

Case 3

A psychologist and psychiatrist collaborated on a study. A student who was seeking an empirical project for a master's thesis was brought into the investigation after the design was developed. The student was given several articles in the content area, found additional relevant literature, collected and analyzed some of the data, and wrote the thesis under the supervision of the psychologist. After the thesis was completed, certain portions of the study, which required additional data analyses, were written for publication by the psychologist and the psychiatrist. The student was not asked to contribute to writing the journal article.

Case 4

An undergraduate student completed an honors thesis under the supervision of a psychology faculty member. The student chose the thesis topic and took initiative in exploring extant measures. Because no suitable instruments were found, the student and the faculty member jointly developed a measure. The student collected and entered the data. The faculty member conducted the statistical analyses. The student wrote the thesis with the faculty member's guidance, and few revisions were required. Because the student lacked the skills to rewrite the thesis as a journal article, the faculty member wrote the article and the student was listed as first author. Based on reviewers' comments to the first draft of the manuscript, aspects of the study not included in the thesis needed to be integrated into a major revision of the manuscript.

AVAILABLE GUIDELINES FOR DETERMINING
AUTHORSHIP CREDIT AND ORDER

In each of the four hypothetical cases described above, decisions regarding the authorship credit and order were required. Until the last decade, there were few published guidelines that provided assistance in this decision-making process.

As an initial guideline, the American Psychological Association's (APA's) Ethics Committee (1983) issued a policy statement on authorship of articles based on dissertations. The statement indicated that dissertation supervisors should be included as authors on such articles only when they made "substantial contributions" to the study. In such instances, only second authorship was appropriate for the supervisor because first authorship was reserved for the student. The policy also suggested that agreements regarding authorship be made before the article was written.

This policy statement was important because it recognized that dissertations, by definition, represent original and independent work by the student. Given the creative nature of the student's dissertation, an article that he or she writes based on that dissertation should have the student identified as first author. The faculty supervisor, at most, deserves second authorship.

Although this policy statement was helpful, it did not clearly define the key term *substantial contributions*. Furthermore, because the policy statement applied only to dissertation research, it did not provide guidance for faculty who engaged in collaborative projects with students outside of dissertations.

Current guidelines for making decisions regarding authorship credit and order are presented in the APA *Ethical Principles of Psychologists and Code of Conduct* (1992), which supersedes the 1983 policy. The APA code has a section relevant to the determination of authorship on scholarly publications. Section 6.23, Publication Credit, states

> (a) Psychologists take responsibility and credit, including authorship credit, only for work they have actually performed or to which they have contributed.
>
> (b) Principal authorship and other publication credits accurately reflect the relative scientific or professional contributions of the individuals involved, regardless of their relative status. Mere possession of an institutional position, such as Department Chair, does not justify authorship credit. Minor contributions to the research or to the writing for publication are appropriately acknowledged, such as in footnotes or in an introductory statement.
>
> (c) A student is usually listed as principal author on any multiple-authored article that is based primarily on the student's dissertation or thesis.

Although this section is clearer and more detailed that the comparable section in previous versions of the *Ethical Principles of Psychologists*, it fails to provide comprehensive guidance to faculty who publish with students. In particular, terms such as *professional contribution* and *minor contribution* are unclear and, as a result, are open to different interpretations (Keith-Spiegel & Koocher, 1985). In the absence of clear guidelines regarding authorship credit and authorship order on faculty – student collaborative publications, disagreements may occur, and one or both parties may feel exploited.

ETHICAL ISSUES INVOLVED IN DETERMINING AUTHORSHIP CREDIT AND ORDER ON FACULTY–STUDENT COLLABORATIVE PROJECTS

The ethical dilemmas that arise when faculty collaborate with students on work worthy of publication stem from the unique nature of the faculty – student relationship. Although collaboration between two professionals can occur on an egalitarian basis, collaboration between faculty and their students is inherently unequal. By nature of their degrees, credentials, expertise, and experience, many faculty supervise students. Supervisors are responsible not only for facilitating the growth and development of supervisees but also for portraying supervisees' abilities accurately to others. For example, faculty may write letters of recommendation for their supervisees, evaluate their work, assign grades, or give critical feedback to representatives of their undergraduate or graduate programs. Thus, faculty who function as supervisors must balance the potentially competing duties of fostering the growth of their trainees and presenting them to others in a fair and accurate manner.

We believe that there are two potential ethical dilemmas in faculty – student collaborations. The first dilemma arises when faculty take authorship credit that was earned by the student. Many of the authorship-related critical incidents identified in the Goodyear et al. (1992) and Costa and Gatz (1992) studies concerned faculty taking a level of authorship credit that was not deserved and not giving students appropriate credit. As one might expect, Tabachnick, Keith-Spiegel, and Pope (1991) found that faculty respondents perceived "accepting undeserved authorship on a student's published paper" as unethical.

The second dilemma occurs when students are granted undeserved authorship credit. There are three reasons why this dilemma is an ethical one. First, a publication on one's record that is not legitimately earned may falsely represent the individual's scholarly expertise. Second, if, because he or she is now a published author, the student is perceived as being more skilled than a peer who is not published, the student is given an unfair advantage professionally. Finally, if the student is perceived to have a level of competence that he or she does not actually have, he or she will be expected to accomplish tasks that may be outside the student's range of expertise.

How often do faculty give students the benefit of the doubt with respect to authorship on collaborative publications? Although we are aware of many instances when supervisors engaged in this practice, systematic empirical evidence related to the prevalence of this practice is rare. Twenty years ago, Over and Smallman (1973) found that "distinguished psychologists" had reduced rates of first-authored papers in the years following receipt of APA Scientific Contribution Awards. Zuckerman (1968) had similar findings in a study of Nobel laureates. Recently, Costa and Gatz (1992), in a survey of faculty and students asked to assign publication credit in hypothetical dissertation scenarios, found that higher academic rank and more teaching experience were positively related to faculty giving students more authorship credit.

One explanation of this positive relation between faculty experience and granting students high levels of authorship credit is that senior faculty are more likely than junior faculty to be sought after for research consultation by students and new faculty. However, it is also possible that they may be more generous — perhaps overly so — in granting students authorship because publication pressures have lessened for them. Interestingly, Costa and Gatz found that faculty were more likely than students to give the student authorship credit in the hypothetical scenarios.

ETHICAL PRINCIPLES IN DETERMINING AUTHORSHIP CREDIT AND ORDER ON FACULTY–STUDENT COLLABORATIVE PROJECTS

Three ethical principles are relevant to ethical dilemmas that arise with regard to authorship on faculty – student collaborative projects: beneficence, justice, and parentalism. These principles, from which ethical codes (e.g., the *Ethical Principles of Psychologists and Code of Conduct*) are developed, may provide guidance when the codes themselves are inadequate (Kitchener, 1984).

To be beneficent is "to abstain from injuring others and to help others further their important and legitimate interests, largely by preventing or removing possible harms" (Beauchamp & Walters, 1982, p. 28). In the context of the authorship issue, *beneficence* implies that supervisors should help students further their careers by including them as authors when their contributions are professional in nature. In our opinion, to avoid harming students and others in the long run, beneficence implies that faculty should grant students authorship credit and first author status only when they are deserved.

Justice — the second ethical principle — refers to the ethical duty to treat others fairly and to give them what they deserve: "An individual has been treated justly when he has been given what he or she is due or owed, what he or she deserves or can legitimately claim" (Beauchamp & Walters, 1982, p. 30). The principle of justice is often interpreted to infer that one should treat another unequally only if there is a morally relevant difference between them (Beauchamp & Walters, 1982). In the authorship setting, if students are not considered to be meaningfully different from professional colleagues, then they should be awarded authorship credit and order on the same basis as those of nonstudent colleagues. However, if one makes the contrasting assumption that students have less power and competence than nonstudent collaborators, then justice would be served by giving students differential treatment.

Parentalism — the final ethical principal — refers to "treatment that restricts the liberty of individuals, without their consent, where the justification for such action is either the prevention of some harm they might do to themselves or the production of some benefit they might not otherwise secure" (Beauchamp & Walters, 1982, p. 38). Parentalistic actions are generally considered to be most appropriate when they are directed toward persons who are nonautonomous (i.e., lack the capacity for self-determination; Beauchamp & Walters, 1982). Thus, the appropriateness of parentalistic behavior in the authorship context depends on the student's level of autonomy.

A supervisor who is acting parentistically might alone decide the level of authorship credit a student receives. Even if students are consulted in the decision-making process, supervisors may use their power to influence the nature of the decision and discount student input. Parentalism is also relevant to the issue of when authorship credit is decided. When the supervisor makes the decision after the work is completed, the student makes his or her contributions without knowing the extent of authorship that he or she will receive. Thus, even when the supervisor does not consult the student in the decision-making process, later decisions are more parentalistic than those rendered before the work has been completed.

RECOMMENDATIONS FOR DETERMINING
AUTHORSHIP CREDIT AND ORDER

How do the principles of beneficence, justice, and parentalism, in aggregate, provide guidance in determining authorship credit and order? To answer this question, we argue that two separate aspects of the authorship determination procedure need to be considered: (a) the process of how collaborators decide who will receive a given level of authorship credit for specified professional contributions and (b) the outcome resulting from the decision-making process. In this section, recommendations in each of these two areas are proposed.

Process Recommendations

As noted earlier, the principle of justice dictates that supervisors should treat students unequally only if there is a meaningful difference between them. With particular reference to the authorship decision-making process, we argue that faculty and students are not meaningfully different because faculty and students — particularly graduate students — have the autonomy, rationality, problem-solving ability, and fairness to mutually decide on authorship credit. Therefore, we propose that both faculty and students should have the opportunity to participate in the process of determining authorship credit. In addition, we argue that it is inappropriate for supervisors to assume a parentalistic stance in this process.

Our position should not be misinterpreted to indicate that faculty and students are equals in power, status, competence, and expertise. There are typically substantial differences between them in these areas. Rather, we believe that faculty and students are both sufficiently autonomous to mutually decide on what level of authorship credit will be awarded to each collaborator for specified professional contributions.

Several specific recommendations follow from the proposition that both faculty and students should meaningfully participate in the authorship decision-making process:

1. Early in the collaborative endeavor, the supervisor should provide the student with information related to how authorship decisions are made, the nature of professional and nonprofessional contributions to publications, the meaning of authorship credit and order, and the importance of both parties agreeing on what contributions will be expected of each collaborator for a given level of authorship credit. This information will provide the student with the knowledge necessary to exercise his or her autonomy and to choose whether to participate in the authorship determination process.

2. The supervisor and student should assess the specific abilities of each party, the tasks required to complete the scholarly publication, the extent of supervision required, and appropriate expectations for what each collaborator can reasonably contribute to the project.

3. On the basis of this assessment, the collaborators should discuss and agree on what tasks, contributions, and efforts are required of both parties to warrant authorship and to determine the order of authorship (Shawchuck, Fatis, & Breitenstein, 1986). Although they will not prevent disagreements from arising, such discussions may reduce their likelihood.

This recommendation is consistent with the notion of informed consent, which governs the development of agreements between psychologists and clients and between researchers and participants (Keith-Spiegel & Koocher, 1985). If authorship expectations are clearly established and agreed on early in the collaborative process, both the supervisor and the student have given their informed consent to participate in the project (Goodyear et al., 1992).

Although we are not necessarily advocating the use of signed informed consent forms, we see nothing in principle that would argue against their use. After all, written consent agreements are often developed by therapists and clients, researchers and subjects, and professors and students engaged in independent studies. In fact, in a similar vein, APA has considered requiring authors of submitted papers to include an "authorship paper," which would require authors to agree in writing to the use of their name on the paper and to the placement of their name in the listing of authors (Landers, 1988). If such forms are not used, we advocate making the agreement as clear as possible.

It should be recognized that some students may choose not to participate in the authorship decision-making process and may defer to the supervisor. As long as the student has been provided with sufficient information regarding authorship-related issues and has been encouraged to participate in this process, we believe that the student's choice should be respected. In such cases, the supervisor may appropriately make decisions regarding authorship credit and order without student input.

4. Agreements regarding authorship credit and order may need to be renegotiated for two reasons. First, scholarly projects often take unexpected turns that necessitate changes in initial agreements made in good faith. Second, many manuscripts need to be revised substantially before they are accepted for publication. These revisions may require additional professional contributions beyond those necessary for the completion of the initial draft of the manuscript. Thus, when such revisions are required, the supervisor and student should reexamine their original agreement and determine whether it needs to be modified.

Outcome Recommendations

We argue that the principles of beneficence and justice justify the use of a "relative standard" for determining authorship credit. According to this stance, there should be a varying standard for the level of professional contribution that is requried to attain a given level of authorship credit. Because collaborators differ in their scholarly expertise, their competence to contribute professionally to scholarly publications should be viewed as lying along a continuum. On one end of the continuum are collaborators who have limited competence in scholarly activities and who require intensive supervision. On the other end are collaborators who have considerable competence in scholarly endeavors and who function independently.

On the basis of the principle of justice, we advance the potentially controversial position that the level of contribution expected of a collaborator should depend on where he or she falls on this competence continuum. For the same level of authorship credit, one should expect greater professional contributions from collaborators who have more competence than from those who have less competence. When those who initially had less competence increase their levels of expertise, they should be expected to make more substantial professional contributions for the same level of authorship credit. This is consistent with the generative aspect of faculty – student collaboration — to provide students with experiences that will eventually allow them to conduct independent scholarship and to assist future students.

Where do students fall on the competence continuum? Of course students, as a group, are less competent in scholarly endeavors than faculty are. However, there are important individual differences in students' abilities. Some students function quite independently and have considerable talent in one or more areas related to scholarly activity. Others have less expertise and require intensive supervision. The key implication of this position is that, for the same level of authorship credit, justice is served by expecting relatively less of less competent collaborators than of more competent ones.

For example, a senior faculty member engaged in a collaborative project with an undergraduate psychology major should be expected to make more complex data analysis decisions than the student. However, if the student participated in the development of the research design, in the process of making data analysis decisions, and in the interpretation of the findings, within the limits of the student's limited expertise, his or her contributions should be considered professional and should be recognized with authorship credit. As the student's competence grows with increased coursework and experience, he or she should be expected to make greater contributions for the same level of authorship credit.

Therefore, we propose that faculty and students use a relative standard to determine authorship credit and order. However, we underscore the important point that in all cases when students are granted authorship, their contributions must be professional in nature. Our operational definition of *professional* is discussed below.

Several specific recommendations follow from the use of a relative standard for determining authorship credit and order:

1. To be included as an author on a scholarly publication, a student should, in a cumulative sense, make a professional contribution that is creative and intellectual in nature, that is integral to completion of the paper, and that requires an overarching perspective of the project. Examples of professional contributions include developing the research design, writing portions of the manuscript, integrating diverse theoretical perspectives, developing new conceptual models, designing assessments, contributing to data analysis decisions, and interpreting results (Bridgewater, Bornstein, & Walkenbach, 1981; Spiegel & Keith-Speigel, 1970). Such tasks as inputting data, carrying out data analyses specified by the supervisor, and typing are not considered professional contributions and may be acknowledged by footnotes to the manuscript (Shawchuck et al., 1986).

Fulfillment of one or two of the professional tasks essential to the completion of a collaborative publication does not necessarily justify authorship. Rather, the supervisor and student — in their discussions early in the collaborative process — must jointly decide what combination of professional activities warrants a given level of authorship credit for both parties. By necessity, there will be some variation in which tasks warrant authorship credit across differing research projects.

Particularly in complex cases, Winston's (1985) weighting schema procedure may be useful in determining which tasks are required for a given level of authorship credit. In this procedure, points are earned for various professional contributions to the scholarly publication. The number of points for each contribution varies depending on its scholarly importance, with research design and report writing assigned the most points. A contributor must earn a certain number of points to earn authorship credit, and the individual with the highest number of points is granted first authorship. This procedure has the advantage of helping all parties involved to carefully examine their respective responsibilities and contributions. However, in our opinion, it cannot be used in all cases because of collaborator differences in scholarly ability and because the importance of various professional tasks differs across projects. With modification (i.e., a weighting of points earned based on each collaborator's level of scholarly competence), it could be appropriate for the relative standard position that we advocate.

2. Authorship decisions should be based on the scholarly importance of the professional contribution and not just the time and effort made (Bridgewater et al., 1981). In our opinion, even if considerable time and effort are spent on a scholarly project, if the aggregate contribution is not judged to be professional by the criteria stated above, authorship should not be granted.

3. Although this may be another controversial position, we believe that authorship decisions should not be affected by whether students or supervisors were paid for their contributions or by their employment status (Bridgewater et al., 1981). In our opinion, it is the nature of the contribution that is made to the article that determines whether authorship credit is warranted and not whether participants received compensation for their efforts. We believe that financial remuneration is not a resource that can serve as a substitute for authorship credit.

4. As is often advocated when psychologists are confronted with ethical dilemmas (Keith-Spiegel & Koocher, 1985), we advise supervisors to consult with colleagues when authorship concerns arise. Furthermore, supervisors should encourage their students to do the same, whether with faculty or with student peers. With the informal input generated from such consultations, it is possible that new light will be shed on the issues involved and that reasonable and fair authorship agreements will result.

5. If the supervisor and student cannot agree, even after consultations with peers, on their authorship-related decisions, we recommend, as do Goodyear et al. (1992), the establishment of an ad hoc third party arbitration process. Whether this mechanism should be established at the local, state, or national level is unclear. Ethics committees, institutional review boards (IRBs), unbiased professionals (Shawchuck et al., 1986), or departmental

committees composed of faculty and students (Goodyear et al., 1992) are possible candidates for such an arbitration mechanism. The important point is that, given that both parties are considered to be equal contributors to this aspect of their work together, disputes need to be settled by outside parties. In such cases, arbitrators may find Winston's (1985) method helpful, because it requires as systematic review of all contributors' scholarly contributions (Shawchuck et al., 1986).

THE FOUR CASES REVISITED

In this final section, we return to the four hypothetical cases described at the outset of the article. First, we present our views on when authorship discussions should take place and then we offer our opinions regarding what authorship decisions are defensible in each case.

In Case 1, the discussion regarding authorship credit and order should ideally have taken place during the development of the thesis proposal but should certainly have occurred after the decision was made to attempt to publish the results. The clinical supervisor should also have been included in these deliberations. Similarly, in Cases 2 and 4, the discussion should have occurred during the initial stages of planning the honors project and no later than when the decision was made to submit a version of the thesis to a peer-reviewed journal. In Case 3, in addition to there being a need for the psychiatrist and supervisor to form an agreement regarding authorship credit, the student should have been a part of further authorship deliberations when brought into the project. Finally, in Case 4, the student should have been consulted when the revisions recommended by the reviewers were received by the faculty member.

Given the ethical considerations discussed in this article, what authorship decisions seem defensible in these cases? In Case 1, the student deserved authorship given the professional nature of his contribution: He participated in generating the idea, developing the research design, writing the proposal, collecting data, and producing several drafts of manuscript. The more difficult decision is whether the student deserved first authorship, given that he lost motivation toward the end of the writing process and the paper was finished by the faculty member who served as dissertation committee chair. In our opinion, the appropriateness of the student receiving first authorship depends on whether the collaborators believed that first authorship would be retained by the student if he did not fulfill the agreed-upon responsibilities. Similarly, the level of authorship credit received by the clinical supervisor depends on the extent to which he made professional contributions to the article as specified in the original agreement.

In Case 2, the student deserved authorship credit given that she generated the topic, participated somewhat in the design of the study, and wrote the paper for her honors project. Does she deserve first authorship? In our opinion, the ethical appropriateness of the student being first author revolves around whether she had the interest, motivation, and skill to expand her honors thesis so as to incorporate the complexity of the entire project. If she had the desire and commitment to do so, and therefore assumed responsibility for most components of the writing task, the supervisor had the ethical obligation to help her through this process and she would be listed as first author. If she had neither the interest nor the inclination to participate in this additional writing task, then it would be ethically appropriate for the supervisor to be identified as first author and the student as second author. In this latter instance, a footnote to the manuscript might be included that indicated that part of the article was based on the student's undergraduate honors thesis.

Case 3 presents a somewhat different dilemma. Did the student's contribution warrant authorship credit? The student did not participate in the generation of the research idea or design, he was given a great deal of assistance in conducting a literature review, and he did not participate in writing the manuscript for possible publication. Therefore, he was lacking in these areas of professional contribution. On the other hand, he gathered some additional literature, participated in some data analysis decisions, and wrote drafts of his thesis. These efforts were professional in nature.

Although further data analyses were conducted by the supervisor and the writing of the manuscript was completed by the supervisor and the psychiatrist, our position is that the student deserved third authorship. Although his participation was minimal, his contributions were, in a cumulative sense, professional. Furthermore, he functioned up to his relatively low level of scholarly competence.

Case 4 underscores the need for supervisors and students to recognize that their agreement may need to be reevaluated as the review process unfolds. The student clearly deserved authorship because she generated the research topic, participated in the design of the study and the development of assessments, and — given her relative inexperience — required surprisingly little supervision. We believe that the student should have been contacted when the reviews were available and should have been given an opportunity to participate in the revision process. If she did so, our position is that she would still deserve first authorship.

CONCLUSION

Collectively, these cases illustrate the potential complexities involved in determining authorship credit and order on faculty – student collaborative publications. In addition, they highlight our position that supervisors cannot expect as much from students as from experienced professional colleagues.

We hope that the issues raised, principles reviewed, and recommendations made in this article will help faculty engage in the process of making — in conjunction with their students — appropriate authorship decisions. We encourage faculty to give the appropriate amount of attention to the important issue of authorship through early, thorough, and systematic discussions leading to explicit agreements with their students.

REFERENCES

American Psychological Association Ethics Committee. (1983, February). *Authorship guidelines for dissertation supervision*. Washington, DC: Author.

Beauchamp, T., & Walters, L. (1982). *Contemporary issues in bioethics* (2nd ed.). Belmont, CA: Wadsworth.

Bridgewater, C. A., Bornstein, P. H., & Walkenbach, J. (1981). Ethical issues in the assignment of publication credit. *American Psychologist, 36,* 524 – 525.

Costa, M. M., & Gatz, M. (1992). Determination of authorship credit in published dissertations. *Psychological Science, 3,* 354 – 357.

Ethical principles of psychologists and code of conduct. (1992). *American Psychologist, 47,* 1597 – 1611.

Goodyear, R. K., Crego, C. A., & Johnston, M. W. (1992). Ethical issues in the supervision of student research: A study of critical incidents. *Professional Psychology: Research and Practice, 23,* 203 – 210.

Keith-Spiegel, P., & Koocher, G. P. (1985). *Ethics in psychology: Professional standards and cases*. New York: Random House.

Kitchener, K. S. (1984). Intuition, critical evaluation and ethical principles: The foundation for ethical decisions in counseling psychology. *The Counseling Psychologist, 12,* 43 – 55.

Landers, S. (1988, December). Should editors be detectives, too? *APA Monitor,* p. 15.

Over, R., & Smallman, S. (1973). Maintenance of individual visibility in publication of collaborative research by psychologists. *American Psychologist, 28,* 161 – 166.

Shawchuck, C. R., Fatis, M., & Breitenstein, J. L. (1986). A practical guide to the assignment of authorship credit. *The Behavior Therapist, 9,* 216 – 217.

Spiegel, D., & Keith-Spiegel, P. (1970). Assignment of publication credits: Ethics and practices of psychologists. *American Psychologist, 25,* 738 – 747.

Tabachnick, B. G., Keith-Spiegel, P., & Pope, K. S. (1991). Ethics of teaching: Beliefs and behaviors of psychologists as educators. *American Psychologist, 46,* 506 – 515.

Winston, R. B., Jr. (1985). A suggested procedure for determining order of authorship in research publications. *Journal of Counseling and Development, 63,*
515 – 518.

Zuckerman, H. A. (1968). Patterns of name ordering among authors of scientific papers: A study of social symbolism and its ambiguity. *American Journal of Sociology, 74,* 276 – 291.

VIII

PUBLICATION AND COMMUNICATION OF RESEARCH

Publication and communication of research findings are essential to progress in science. The written report of research findings adds to the cumulative record of what has been learned. Although many avenues exist for communicating research findings (e.g., convention presentations, books and book chapters, technical or working reports), journal publication is the most valued outlet. Journals serve as an archival base for accumulated knowledge and usually are disseminated to libraries and individuals and through electronic media on a much larger scale than other outlets. The tasks of preparing reports of empirical studies are similar across many formats, even though journal publication has its own special challenges (e.g., the review process, squeezing massive amounts of details within a limited page range, enrolling in psychotherapy after reading the comments reviewers have provided regarding one's write-up). These tasks consist of addressing substantive issues that served as impetus for the investigation and conveying the rationale and decision-making process underlying the methodology and design.

It is important to underscore the central role of methodology and methodological issues in preparing the research report. Decisions pertaining to who served as participants; what constructs and measures were selected; and why various comparison, control, or other conditions were or were not included are central to the report. The study might have been designed and executed in any number of ways, each of which is likely to have strengths and weaknesses. The rationale for methods that were selected and the consequences that various decisions have on the results are important to elaborate within the report. Readers of the article will want to know what the findings are but also what limits might be placed on their interpretation. There may be sampling issues (e.g., special characteristics of the sample), measurement issues (e.g., poor reliability of observational measures, no evidence for validity of critical measures, only one measure to operationalize a particular construct), data evaluation issues (e.g., insufficient power, failure to control for a confounding factor), and others (e.g., no evidence for reliability of diagnoses if delineation of patients is important, absence of measures of treatment integrity) that require the researcher to qualify what was said.

The written report will be evaluated by multiple criteria, including (a) Does this report make an important substantive contribution to the area of research? (b) Does the methodology (design and its execution) permit one to draw the conclusions the author wishes to make? and (c) Is the report well organized and complete in explaining what was done, why it was done, and how it was done? In addition to presentation of the research, the written report is an opportunity to influence the direction of the field. The author is in a special position to comment on the next steps in research, any lacunae in theory, and methodological obstacles that need to be resolved. The contribution of the study is not only in what questions were addressed but also in the questions, advances in theory, and changes in methods that the study will provoke.

Chapters in this part are designed to facilitate preparation of research reports. The chapters focus on the questions to be answered by the report, the integration of the study into a broader context of existing theory and research, and recommendations for presenting the material clearly. The chapters are not about good writing, although they include many recommendations about writing; rather, they are about ways of thinking about one's own research and research in the field. Thus, publication and communication of results extend beyond describing the study and include all of the critical issues about methodology raised in prior parts of this book.

CONNECTING ASSESSMENT, RESEARCH DESIGN, AND CONCLUSIONS

Chapter 36 by Leland Wilkinson and the Task Force on Statistical Inference of the American Psychological Association addresses issues related to statistical evaluation of the data. The focus of the work of the committee and the title suggest that this chapter belongs in a prior section on data evaluation and is out of place in a section on publication. For the moment, please ignore the title. The chapter covers many issues that need to be addressed directly in designing a study and preparing the write-up. It provides concrete guidelines that are enormously useful, as reflected in the italicized passages throughout the chapter. Most journals articles would be improved even if the author only attended to the points italicized in this report. The chapter does address statistical issues, but here too the guidelines convey concretely what is useful, essential, and beneficial to include when presenting the results. Finally, interpretation and discussion of the results are also covered. In short, the title might suggest a narrow focus, but the chapter is broad and provides a rich source of recommendations for preparing articles for publication.

JOURNAL PUBLICATION

The two chapters in this section are directed more explicitly on publishing papers in journals. In chapter 37, I discuss preparation of research reports for journal publication. The chapter discusses the task of the author in broad terms, that is, what is expected by readers and reviewers for journal publication. Also, each section of the manuscript (e.g., Introduction, Method, Results) is presented to convey the specific questions that the author ought to address. The chapter presents guidelines in the context of preparing reports of empirical studies related to assessment (e.g., measurement development and validation). Consequently, assessment issues are discussed as well.

Authors often prepare and publish review articles. Indeed, in graduate training, completion of a review paper may be a requirement or used as the basis for formulating an empirical study. The task presented to the student for the masters or doctoral degree is to develop a study that contributes significantly to the literature. Obviously this task is enhanced by knowing the current status of that literature, including strengths and limitations of substantive findings and methodological approaches of previous research. In chapter 38, Daryl J. Bem provides guidelines for writing a review article, including recommendations for writing clearly, organizing the review, and obtaining the necessary feedback to make revisions. There are many helpful hints. In passing, Bem comments on what many of us have experienced in writing, namely, we feel particularly elated about a phrase or passage that we consider to be clever, pithy, or otherwise brilliant. Such phrases are often the last to be deleted as we revise the paper; indeed through various revisions we might even build paragraphs around them. The sooner one can treat one's writing with less attachment to individual phrases and sections, the easier the writing and revision process becomes.

The literature review, however well organized and written, will be evaluated for its contribution. A summary of the relevant research is not enough; as Bem notes, a substantive contribution is needed as well. Consequently, the quality and contribution of review papers often are evaluated on the basis of what comes *after* the review portion, that is, what the author says about theory, new lines of research, and future directions. The review of existing studies is valuable insofar as this helps the author move to these other topics.

CONNECTING ASSESSMENT, RESEARCH DESIGN, AND CONCLUSIONS

36

STATISTICAL METHODS IN PSYCHOLOGY JOURNALS: GUIDELINES AND EXPLANATIONS

LELAND WILKINSON AND THE
TASK FORCE ON STATISTICAL INFERENCE

In the light of continuing debate over the applications of significance testing in psychology journals and after the publication of Cohen's (1994) article, the Board of Scientific Affairs (BSA) of the American Psychological Association (APA) convened a committee called the Task Force on Statistical Inference (TFSI) whose charge was "to elucidate some of the controversial issues surrounding applications of statistics including significance testing and its alternatives; alternative underlying models and data transformation; and newer methods made possible by powerful computers" (BSA, personal communication, February 28, 1996). Robert Rosenthal, Robert Abelson, and Jacob Cohen (cochairs) met initially and agreed on the desirability of having several types of specialists on the task force: statisticians, teachers of statistics,

Reprinted from the *American Psychologist, 54,* 594–604. Copyright 1999 by the American Psychological Association.

Jacob Cohen died on January 20, 1998. Without his initiative and gentle persistance, this report most likely would not have appeared. Grant Blank provided Kahn and Udry's (1986) reference. Gerard Dallal and Paul Velleman offered helpful comments.

journal editors, authors of statistics books, computer experts, and wise elders. Nine individuals were subsequently invited to join, and all agreed. These were Leona Aiken, Mark Appelbaum, Gwyneth Boodoo, David A. Kenny, Helena Kraemer, Donald Rubin, Bruce Thompson, Howard Wainer, and Leland Wilkinson. In addition, Lee Cronbach, Paul Meehl, Frederick Mosteller, and John Tukey served as Senior Advisors to the Task Force and commented on written materials.

The TFSI met twice in two years and corresponded throughout that period. After the first meeting, the task force circulated a preliminary report indicating its intention to examine issues beyond null hypothesis significance testing. The task force invited comments and used this feedback in the deliberations during its second meeting.

After the second meeting, the task force recommended several possibilities for further action, chief of which would be to revise the statistical sections of the *Publication Manual of the American Psychological Association* (APA, 1994). After extensive discussion, the BSA recommended that "before the TFSI undertook a revision of the *APA Publication Manual*, it might want to consider publishing an article in *American Psychologist*, as a way to initiate discussion in the field about changes in current practices of data analysis and reporting" (BSA, personal communication, November 17, 1997).

This report follows that request. The sections in italics are proposed guidelines that the TFSI recommends could be used for revising the APA publication manual or for developing other BSA supporting materials. Following each guideline are comments, explanations, or elaborations assembled by Leland Wilkinson for the task force and under its review. This report is concerned with the use of statistical methods only and is not meant as an assessment of research methods in general. Psychology is a broad science. Methods appropriate in one area may be inappropriate in another.

The title and format of this report are adapted from a similar article by Bailar and Mosteller (1988). That article should be consulted, because it overlaps somewhat with this one and discusses some issues relevant to research in psychology. Further detail can also be found in the publications on this topic by several committee members (Abelson, 1995, 1997; Rosenthal, 1994; Thompson, 1996; Wainer, in press; see also chapters in Harlow, Mulaik, & Steiger, 1997).

METHOD

Design

Make clear at the outset what type of study you are doing. Do not cloak a study in one guise to try to give it the assumed reputation of another. For studies that have multiple goals, be sure to define and prioritize those goals.

There are many forms of empirical studies in psychology, including case reports, controlled experiments, quasi-experiments, statistical simulations, surveys, observational studies, and studies of studies (meta-analyses). Some are hypothesis generating: They explore data to form or sharpen hypotheses about a population for assessing future hypotheses. Some are hypothesis testing: They assess specific a priori hypotheses or estimate parameters by random sampling from that population. Some are meta-analytic: They assess specific a priori hypotheses or estimate parameters (or both) by synthesizing the results of available studies.

Some researchers have the impression or have been taught to believe that some of these forms yield information that is more valuable or credible than others (see Cronbach, 1975, for a discussion). Occasionally, proponents of some research methods disparage others. In fact, each form of research has its own strengths, weaknesses, and standards of practice.

Population

The interpretation of the results of any study depends on the characteristics of the population intended for analysis. Define the population (participants, stimuli, or studies) clearly. If control or comparison groups are part of the design, present how they are defined.

Psychology students sometimes think that a statistical population is the human race or, at least, college sophomores. They also have some difficulty distinguishing a class of objects versus a statistical population—that sometimes we make inferences about a population through statistical methods, and other times we make inferences about a class through logical or other nonstatistical methods. Populations may be sets of potential observations on people, adjectives, or even research articles. How a population is defined in an article affects almost every conclusion in that article.

Sample

Describe the sampling procedures and emphasize any inclusion or exclusion criteria. If the sample is stratified (e.g., by site or gender) describe fully the method and rationale. Note the proposed sample size for each subgroup.

Interval estimates for clustered and stratified random samples differ from those for simple random samples. Statistical software is now becoming available for these purposes. If you are using a convenience sample (whose members are not selected at random), be sure to make that procedure clear to your readers. Using a convenience sample does not automatically disqualify a study from publication, but it harms your objectivity to try to conceal this by implying that you used a random sample. Sometimes the case for the representativeness of a convenience sample can be strengthened by explicit comparison of sample characteristics with those of a defined population across a wide range of variables.

Assignment

Random Assignment

For research involving causal inferences, the assignment of units to levels of the causal variable is critical. Random assignment (not to be confused with random selection) allows for the strongest possible causal inferences free of extraneous assumptions. If random assignment is planned, provide enough information to show that the process for making the actual assignments is random.

There are a strong research tradition and many exemplars for random assignment in various fields of psychology. Even those who have elucidated quasi-experimental designs in psychological research (e.g., Cook & Campbell, 1979) have repeatedly emphasized the superiority of random assignment as a method for controlling bias and lurking variables. *Random* does not mean "haphazard." Randomization is a fragile condition, easily corrupted deliberately, as we see when a skilled magician flips a fair coin repeatedly to heads, or innocently, as we saw when the drum was not turned sufficiently to randomize the picks in the Vietnam draft lottery. As psychologists, we also know that human participants are incapable of producing a random process (digits, spatial arrangements, etc.) or of recognizing one. It is best not to trust the random behavior of a physical device unless you are an expert in these matters. It is safer to use the pseudorandom sequence from a well-designed computer generator or from published tables of random numbers. The added benefit of such a procedure is that you can supply a random number seed or starting number in a table that other researchers can use to check your methods later.

Nonrandom Assignment

For some research questions, random assignment is not feasible. In such cases, we need to minimize effects of variables that affect the observed relationship between a causal variable and an outcome. Such variables are commonly called confounds or covariates. The researcher needs to attempt to determine the relevant covariates, measure them adequately, and adjust for their effects either by design or by analysis. If the effects of covariates are adjusted by analysis, the strong assumptions that are made must be explicitly stated and, to the extent possible, tested and justified. Describe methods used to attenuate sources of bias, including plans for minimizing dropouts, noncompliance, and missing data.

Authors have used the term *control group* to describe, among other things, (a) a comparison group, (b) members of pairs matched or blocked on one or more nuisance variables, (c) a group not receiving a particular treatment, (d) a statistical sample whose values are adjusted post hoc by the use

of one or more covariates, or (e) a group for which the experimenter acknowledges bias exists and perhaps hopes that this admission will allow the
reader to make appropriate discounts or other mental adjustments. None of
these is an instance of a fully adequate control group.

If we can neither implement randomization nor approach total control
of variables that modify effects (outcomes), then we should use the term *control group* cautiously. In most of these cases, it would be better to forgo the
term and use *contrast group* instead. In any case, we should describe exactly
which confounding variables have been explicitly controlled and speculate
about which unmeasured ones could lead to incorrect inferences. In the absence of randomization, we should do our best to investigate sensitivity to
various untestable assumptions.

Measurement

Variables

*Explicitly define the variables in the study, show how they are related to the
goals of the study, and explain how they are measured. The units of measurement
of all variables, causal and outcome, should fit the language you use in the introduction and discussion sections of your report.*

A variable is a method for assigning to a set of observations a value from
a set of possible outcomes. For example, a variable called *gender* might assign
each of 50 observations to one of the values male or female. When we define
a variable, we are declaring what we are prepared to represent as a valid observation and what we must consider as invalid. If we define the range of a
particular variable (the set of possible outcomes) to be from 1 to 7 on a Likert scale, for example, then a value of 9 is not an outlier (an unusually extreme value). It is an illegal value. If we declare the range of a variable to be
positive real numbers and the domain to be observations of reaction time (in
milliseconds) to an administration of electric shock, then a value of 3,000 is
not illegal; it is an outlier.

Naming a variable is almost as important as measuring it. We do well
to select a name that reflects how a variable is measured. On this basis, the name *IQ test score* is preferable to *intelligence* and *retrospective self-
report of childhood sexual abuse* is preferable to *childhood sexual abuse*. Without such precision, ambiguity in defining variables can give a theory an
unfortunate resistance to empirical falsification. Being precise does not
make us operationalists. It simply means that we try to avoid excessive
generalization.

Editors and reviewers should be suspicious when they notice authors
changing definitions or names of variables, failing to make clear what would
be contrary evidence, or using measures with no history and thus no known
properties. Researchers should be suspicious when codebooks and scoring

systems are inscrutable or more voluminous than the research articles on which they are based. Everyone should worry when a system offers to code a specific observation in two or more ways for the same variable.

Instruments

If a questionnaire is used to collect data, summarize the psychometric properties of its scores with specific regard to the way the instrument is used in a population. Psychometric properties include measures of validity, reliability, and any other qualities affecting conclusions. If a physical apparatus is used, provide enough information (brand, model, design specifications) to allow another experimenter to replicate your measurement process.

There are many methods for constructing instruments and psychometrically validating scores from such measures. Traditional true-score theory and item–response test theory provide appropriate frameworks for assessing reliability and internal validity. Signal-detection theory and various coefficients of association can be used to assess external validity. Messick (1989) has provided a comprehensive guide to validity.

It is important to remember that a test is not reliable or unreliable. Reliability is a property of the scores on a test for a particular population of examinees (Feldt & Brennan, 1989). Thus, authors should provide reliability coefficients of the scores for the data being analyzed even when the focus of their research is not psychometric. Interpreting the size of observed effects requires an assessment of the reliability of the scores.

Besides showing that an instrument is reliable, we need to show that it does not correlate strongly with other key constructs. It is just as important to establish that a measure does *not* measure what it should not measure as it is to show that it *does* measure what it should.

Researchers occasionally encounter a measurement problem that has no obvious solution. This happens when they decide to explore a new and rapidly growing research area that is based on a previous researcher's well-defined construct implemented with a poorly developed psychometric instrument. Innovators, in the excitement of their discovery, sometimes give insufficient attention to the quality of their instruments. Once a defective measure enters the literature, subsequent researchers are reluctant to change it. In these cases, editors and reviewers should pay special attention to the psychometric properties of the instruments used, and they might want to encourage revisions (even if not by the scale's author) to prevent the accumulation of results based on relatively invalid or unreliable measures.

Procedure

Describe any anticipated sources of attrition due to noncompliance, dropout, death, or other factors. Indicate how such attrition may affect the generalizability of the results. *Clearly describe the conditions under which measurements are taken (e.g., format, time, place, personnel who collected data). Describe the specific methods used to deal with experimenter bias, especially if you collected the data yourself.*

Despite the long-established findings of the effects of experimenter bias (Rosenthal, 1966), many published studies appear to ignore or discount these problems. For example, some authors or their assistants with knowledge of hypotheses or study goals screen participants (through personal interviews or telephone conversations) for inclusion in their studies. Some authors administer questionnaires. Some authors give instructions to participants. Some authors perform experimental manipulations. Some tally or code responses. Some rate videotapes.

An author's self-awareness, experience, or resolve does not eliminate experimenter bias. In short, there are no valid excuses, financial or otherwise, for avoiding an opportunity to double-blind. Researchers looking for guidance on this matter should consult the classic book of Webb, Campbell, Schwartz, and Sechrest (1966) and an exemplary dissertation (performed on a modest budget) by Baker (1969).

Power and Sample Size

Provide information on sample size and the process that led to sample size decisions. Document the effect sizes, sampling and measurement assumptions, as well as analytic procedures used in power calculations. Because power computations are most meaningful when done before data are collected and examined, it is important to show how effect size estimates have been derived from previous research and theory to dispel suspicions that they might have been taken from data used in the study or, even worse, constructed to justify a particular sample size. Once the study is analyzed, confidence intervals replace calculated power in describing results.

Largely because of the work of Cohen (1969, 1988), psychologists have become aware of the need to consider power in the design of their studies, before they collect data. The intellectual exercise required to do this stimulates authors to take seriously prior research and theory in their field, and it gives an opportunity, with incumbent risk, for a few to offer the challenge that there is no applicable research behind a given study. If exploration were not disguised in hypothetico–deductive language, then it might have the opportunity to influence subsequent research constructively.

Computer programs that calculate power for various designs and distributions are now available. One can use them to conduct power analyses for a range of reasonable alpha values and effect sizes. Doing so reveals how power changes across this range and overcomes a tendency to regard a single power estimate as being absolutely definitive.

Many of us encounter power issues when applying for grants. Even when not asking for money, think about power. Statistical power does not corrupt.

RESULTS

Complications

Before presenting results, report complications, protocol violations, and other unanticipated events in data collection. These include missing data, attrition, and nonresponse. Discuss analytic techniques devised to ameliorate these problems. Describe nonrepresentativeness statistically by reporting patterns and distributions of missing data and contaminations. Document how the actual analysis differs from the analysis planned before complications arose. The use of techniques to ensure that the reported results are not produced by anomalies in the data (e.g., outliers, points of high influence, nonrandom missing data, selection bias, attrition problems) should be a standard component of all analyses.

As soon as you have collected your data, before you compute *any* statistics, *look at your data*. Data screening is not data snooping. It is not an opportunity to discard data or change values to favor your hypotheses. However, if you assess hypotheses without examining your data, you risk publishing nonsense.

Computer malfunctions tend to be catastrophic: A system crashes; a file fails to import; data are lost. Less well known are more subtle bugs that can be more catastrophic in the long run. For example, a single value in a file may be corrupted in reading or writing (often in the first or last record). This circumstance usually produces a major value error, the kind of singleton that can make large correlations change sign and small correlations become large.

Graphical inspection of data offers an excellent possibility for detecting serious compromises to data integrity. The reason is simple: Graphics broadcast; statistics narrowcast. Indeed, some international corporations that must defend themselves against rapidly evolving fraudulent schemes use real-time graphic displays as their first line of defense and statistical analyses as a distant second. The following example shows why.

Figure 36.1 shows a scatter-plot matrix (SPLOM) of three variables from a national survey of approximately 3,000 counseling clients (Chartrand, 1997). This display, consisting of pairwise scatter plots arranged in a matrix, is found in most modern statistical packages. The diagonal cells contain dot plots of each variable (with the dots stacked like a histogram) and scales used for each variable. The three variables shown are questionnaire measures of respondent's age *(AGE)*, gender *(SEX)*, and number of years together in current relationship *(TOGETHER)*. The graphic in Figure 36.1 is not intended for final presentation of results; we use it instead to locate

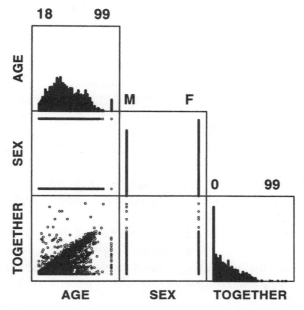

Figure 36.1. Scatter-plot matrix.
Note: M = male; F = female.

coding errors and other anomalies before we analyze our data. Figure 36.1 is a selected portion of a computer screen display that offers tools for zooming in and out, examining points, and linking to information in other graphical displays and data editors. SPLOM displays can be used to recognize unusual patterns in 20 or more variables simultaneously. We focus on these 3 only.

There are several anomalies in this graphic. The AGE histogram shows a spike at the right end, which corresponds to the value 99 in the data. This coded value most likely signifies a missing value, because it is unlikely that this many people in a sample of 3,000 would have an age of 99 or greater. Using numerical values for missing value codes is a risky practice (Kahn & Udry, 1986). The histogram for SEX shows an unremarkable division into two values. The histogram for TOGETHER is highly skewed, with a spike at the lower end presumably signifying no relationship. The most remarkable pattern is the triangular joint distribution of TOGETHER and AGE. Triangular joint distributions often (but not necessarily) signal an implication or a relation rather than a linear function with error. In this case, it makes sense that the span of a relationship should not exceed a person's age. Closer examination shows that something is wrong here, however. We find some respondents (in the upper left triangular area of the TOGETHER–AGE panel) claiming that they have been in a significant relationship longer than they have been alive! Had we computed statistics or fit models before examining the raw data, we would likely have missed these reporting errors. There is little reason to expect that *TOGETHER* would show any anomalous behavior with other variables, and even if *AGE* and *TOGETHER* appeared jointly in certain models, we may not have known anything was amiss, regardless of our care in examining residual or other diagnostic plots.

The main point of this example is that the type of "atheoretical" search for patterns that we are sometimes warned against in graduate school can save us from the humiliation of having to retract conclusions we might ultimately make on the basis of contaminated data. We are warned against fishing expeditions for understandable reasons, but blind application of models without screening our data is a far graver error.

Graphics cannot solve all our problems. Special issues arise in modeling when we have missing data. The two popular methods for dealing with missing data that are found in basic statistics packages—listwise and pairwise deletion of missing values—are among the worst methods available for practical applications. Little and Rubin (1987) have discussed these issues in more detail and offer alternative approaches.

Analysis

Choosing a Minimally Sufficient Analysis

The enormous variety of modern quantitative methods leaves researchers with the nontrivial task of matching analysis and design to the research question. Although complex designs and state-of-the-art methods are sometimes necessary to address research questions effectively, simpler classical approaches often can provide elegant and sufficient answers to important questions. Do not choose an analytic method to impress your readers or to deflect criticism. If the assumptions and strength of a simpler method are reasonable for your data and research problem, use it. Occam's razor applies to methods as well as to theories.

We should follow the advice of Fisher (1935):

> Experimenters should remember that they and their colleagues usually know more about the kind of material they are dealing with than do the authors of text-books written without such personal experience, and that a more complex, or less intelligible, test is not likely to serve their purpose better, in any sense, than those of proved value in their own subject. (p. 49)

There is nothing wrong with using state-of-the-art methods, as long as you and your readers understand how they work and what they are doing. On the other hand, don't cling to obsolete methods (e.g., Newman–Keuls or Duncan post hoc tests) out of fear of learning the new. In any case, listen to Fisher. Begin with an idea. Then pick a method.

Computer Programs

There are many good computer programs for analyzing data. More important than choosing a specific statistical package is verifying your results, understanding what they mean, and knowing how they are computed. If you cannot verify your results by intelligent "guesstimates," you should check them against the output of another program. You will not be happy if a vendor reports a bug after your data are in print (not an infrequent event). Do not report statistics found on a printout without understanding how they are computed or what they mean. Do not report statistics to a greater precision than is supported by your data simply because they are printed that way by the program. Using the computer is an opportunity for you to control your analysis and design. If a computer program does not provide the analysis you need, use another program rather than let the computer shape your thinking.

There is no substitute for common sense. If you cannot use rules of thumb to detect whether the result of a computation makes sense to you, then you should ask yourself whether the procedure you are using is appropriate for your research. Graphics can help you to make some of these determinations; theory can help in other cases. But never assume that using a highly regarded program absolves you of the responsibility for judging whether your results are plausible. Finally, when documenting the use of a statistical procedure, refer to the statistical literature rather than a computer manual; when documenting the use of a program, refer to the computer manual rather than the statistical literature.

Assumptions

You should take efforts to assure that the underlying assumptions required for the analysis are reasonable given the data. Examine residuals carefully. Do not use distributional tests and statistical indexes of shape (e.g., skewness, kurtosis) as a substitute for examining your residuals graphically.

Using a statistical test to diagnose problems in model fitting has several shortcomings. First, diagnostic significance tests based on summary statistics (such as tests for homogeneity of variance) are often impractically sensitive; our statistical tests of models are often more robust than our statistical tests of assumptions. Second, statistics such as skewness and kurtosis often fail to detect distributional irregularities in the residuals. Third, statistical tests depend on sample size, and as sample size increases, the tests often will reject innocuous assumptions. In general, there is no substitute for graphical analysis of assumptions.

Modern statistical packages offer graphical diagnostics for helping to determine whether a model appears to fit data appropriately. Most users are familiar with residual plots for linear regression modeling. Fewer are aware that John Tukey's paradigmatic equation, *data = fit + residual*, applies to a more general class of models and has broad implications for graphical analysis of assumptions. Stem-and-leaf plots, box plots, histograms, dot plots, spread/level plots, probability plots, spectral plots, autocorrelation and cross-correlation plots, coplots, and trellises (Chambers, Cleveland, Kleiner, & Tukey, 1983; Cleveland, 1995; Tukey, 1977) all serve at various times for displaying residuals, whether they arise from analysis of variance (ANOVA), nonlinear modeling, factor analysis, latent variable modeling, multidimensional scaling, hierarchical linear modeling, or other procedures.

Hypothesis Tests

It is hard to imagine a situation in which a dichotomous accept–reject decision is better than reporting an actual p value or, better still, a confidence interval. Never use the unfortunate expression "accept the null hypothesis." Always provide some effect size estimate when reporting a p value. Cohen (1994) has written on this subject in *American Psychologist*. All psychologists would benefit from reading his insightful article.

Effect Sizes

Always present effect sizes for primary outcomes. If the units of measurement are meaningful on a practical level (e.g., number of cigarettes smoked per day), then we usually prefer an unstandardized measure (regression coefficient or mean difference) to a standardized measure (r or d). It helps to add brief comments that place these effect sizes in a practical and theoretical context.

APA's (1994) publication manual included an important new "encouragement" (p. 18) to report effect sizes. Unfortunately, empirical studies of various journals indicate that the effect size of this encouragement has been negligible (Keselman et al., 1998; Kirk, 1996; Thompson & Snyder, 1998). We must stress again that reporting and interpreting effect sizes in the context of previously reported effects are essential to good research. They enable readers to evaluate the stability of results across samples, designs, and analyses. Reporting effect sizes also informs power analyses and meta-analyses needed in future research.

Fleiss (1994), Kirk (1996), Rosenthal (1994), and Snyder and Lawson (1993) have summarized various measures of effect sizes used in psychological research. Consult these articles for information on computing them. For a simple, general-purpose display of the practical meaning of an effect size, see Rosenthal and Rubin (1982). Consult Rosenthal and Rubin (1994) for information on the use of "counternull intervals" for effect sizes, as alternatives to confidence intervals.

Interval Estimates

Interval estimates should be given for any effect sizes involving principal outcomes. Provide intervals for correlations and other coefficients of association or variation whenever possible.

Confidence intervals are usually available in statistical software; otherwise, confidence intervals for basic statistics can be computed from typical output. Comparing confidence intervals from a current study with intervals from previous, related studies helps focus attention on stability across studies (Schmidt, 1996). Collecting intervals across studies also helps in constructing plausible regions for population parameters. This practice should help prevent the common mistake of assuming a parameter is contained in a confidence interval.

Multiplicities

Multiple outcomes require special handling. There are many ways to conduct reasonable inference when faced with multiplicity (e.g., Bonferroni correction of p values, multivariate test statistics, empirical Bayes methods). It is your responsibility to define and justify the methods used.

Statisticians speak of the curse of dimensionality. To paraphrase, multiplicities are the curse of the social sciences. In many areas of psychology, we cannot do research on important problems without encountering multiplicity. We often encounter many variables and many relationships.

One of the most prevalent strategies psychologists use to handle multiplicity is to follow an ANOVA with pairwise multiple-comparison tests. This approach is usually wrong for several reasons. First, pairwise methods such as Tukey's honestly significant difference procedure were designed to control a familywise error rate based on the sample size and number of comparisons. Preceding them with an omnibus F test in a stagewise testing procedure defeats this design, making it unnecessarily conservative. Second, researchers rarely need to compare all possible means to understand their results or assess their theory; by setting their sights large, they sacrifice their power to see small. Third, the lattice of all possible pairs is a straightjacket; forcing themselves to wear it often restricts researchers to uninteresting hypotheses and induces them to ignore more fruitful ones.

As an antidote to the temptation to explore all pairs, imagine yourself restricted to mentioning only pairwise comparisons in the introduction and discussion sections of your article. Higher order concepts such as trends, structures, or clusters of effects would be forbidden. Your theory would be restricted to first-order associations. This scenario brings to mind the illogic of the converse, popular practice of theorizing about higher order concepts in the introduction and discussion sections and then supporting that theorizing in the results section with atomistic pairwise comparisons. If a specific contrast interests you, examine it. If all interest you, ask yourself why. For a detailed treatment of the use of contrasts, see Rosenthal, Rosnow, and Rubin (2000).

There is a variant of this preoccupation with all possible pairs that comes with the widespread practice of printing p values or asterisks next to every correlation in a correlation matrix. Methodologists frequently point out that these p values should be adjusted through Bonferroni or other corrections. One should ask instead why any reader would want this information. The possibilities are as follows:

1. All the correlations are "significant." If so, this can be noted in a single footnote.
2. None of the correlations are "significant." Again, this can be noted once. We need to be reminded that this situation does not rule out the possibility that combinations or subsets of the correlations may be "significant." The definition of the null hypothesis for the global test may not include other potential null hypotheses that might be rejected if they were tested.
3. A subset of the correlations is "significant." If so, our purpose in appending asterisks would seem to be to mark this subset. Using "significance" tests in this way is really a highlighting technique to facilitate pattern recognition. If this is your goal in presenting results, then it is better served by calling attention to the pattern (perhaps by sorting the rows and columns of the correlation matrix) and assessing it directly. This would force you, as well, to provide a plausible explanation.

There is a close relative of all possible pairs called *all possible combinations*. We see this occasionally in the publishing of higher way factorial ANOVAs that include all possible main effects and interactions. One should not imagine that placing asterisks next to conventionally significant effects in a five-way ANOVA, for example, skirts the multiplicity problem. A typical five-way fully factorial design applied to a reasonably large sample of random data has about an 80 percent chance of producing at least one significant effect by conventional F tests at the .05 critical level (Hurlburt & Spiegel, 1976).

Underlying the widespread use of all-possible-pairs methodology is the legitimate fear among editors and reviewers that some researchers would indulge in fishing expeditions without the restraint of simultaneous test procedures. We should indeed fear the well-intentioned, indiscriminate search for structure more than the deliberate falsification of results, if only for the prevalence of wishful thinking over nefariousness. There are Bonferroni and recent related methods (e.g., Benjamini & Hochberg, 1995) for controlling this problem statistically. Nevertheless, there is an alternative institutional restraint. Reviewers should require writers to articulate their expectations well enough to reduce the likelihood of post hoc rationalizations. Fishing expeditions are often recognizable by the promiscuity of their explanations. They mix ideas from scattered sources, rely heavily on common sense, and cite fragments rather than trends.

If, on the other hand, a researcher fools us with an intriguing result caught while indiscriminately fishing, we might want to fear this possibility less than we do now. The enforcing of rules to prevent chance results in our journals may at times distract us from noticing the more harmful possibility of publishing bogus theories and methods (ill-defined variables, lack of parsimony, experimenter bias, logical errors, artifacts) that are buttressed by evidently impeccable statistics. There are enough good ideas behind fortuitous results to make us wary of restricting them. This is especially true in those areas of psychology where lives and major budgets are not at stake. Let replications promote reputations.

Causality

Inferring causality from nonrandomized designs is a risky enterprise. Researchers using nonrandomized designs have an extra obligation to explain the logic behind covariates included in their designs and to alert the reader to plausible rival hypotheses that might explain their results. Even in randomized experiments, attributing causal effects to any one aspect of the treatment condition requires support from additional experimentation.

It is sometimes thought that correlation does not prove causation but "causal modeling" does. Despite the admonitions of experts in this field, researchers sometimes use goodness-of-fit indices to hunt through thickets of competing models and settle on a plausible substantive explanation only in retrospect. McDonald (1997), in an analysis of a historical data set, showed the dangers of this practice and the importance of substantive theory. Scheines, Spirites, Glymour, Meek, and Richardson (1998; discussions following) offer similar cautions from a theoretical standpoint.

A generally accepted framework for formulating questions concerning the estimation of causal effects in social and biomedical science involves the use of "potential outcomes," with one outcome for each treatment condition. Although the perspective has old roots, including use by Fisher and Neyman in the context of completely randomized experiments analyzed by randomization-based inference (Rubin, 1990b), it is typically referred to as "Rubin's causal model" or RCM (Holland, 1986). For extensions to observational studies and other forms of inference, see Rubin (1974, 1977, 1978). This approach is now relatively standard, even for settings with instrumental variables and multistage models or simultaneous equations.

The crucial idea is to set up the causal inference problem as one of missing data, as defined in Rubin's (1976) article, where the missing data are the values of the potential outcomes under the treatment *not* received and the observed data include the values of the potential outcomes under the received treatments. Causal effects are defined on a unit level as the comparison of the potential outcomes under the different treatments, only one of which can ever be observed (we cannot go back in time to expose the unit to a different treatment). The essence of the RCM is to formulate causal questions in this way and to use formal statistical methods to draw probabilistic causal inferences, whether based on Fisherian randomization-based (permutation) distributions, Neymanian repeated-sampling randomization-based distributions, frequentist superpopulation sampling distributions, or Bayesian posterior distributions (Rubin, 1990a).

If a problem of causal inference cannot be formulated in this manner (as the comparison of potential outcomes under different treatment assignments), it is not a problem of inference for causal effects, and the use of "causal" should be avoided. To see the confusion that can be created by ignoring this requirement, see the classic Lord's paradox and its resolution by the use of the RCM in Holland and Rubin's (1983) chapter.

The critical assumptions needed for causal inference are essentially always beyond testing from the data at hand because they involve the missing data. Thus, especially when formulating causal questions from nonrandomized data, the underlying assumptions needed to justify any causal conclusions should be carefully and explicitly argued, not in terms of technical properties like "uncorrelated error terms," but in terms of real-world properties, such as how the units received the different treatments.

The use of complicated causal-modeling software rarely yields any results that have any interpretation as causal effects. If such software is used to produce anything beyond an exploratory description of a data set, the bases for such extended conclusions must be carefully presented and not just asserted on the basis of imprecise labeling conventions of the software.

Tables and Figures

Although tables are commonly used to show exact values, well-drawn figures need not sacrifice precision. Figures attract the reader's eye and help convey global results. Because individuals have different preferences for processing complex information, it often helps to provide both tables and figures. This works best when figures are kept small enough to allow space for both formats. Avoid complex figures when simpler ones will do. In all figures, include graphical representations of interval estimates whenever possible.

Bailar and Mosteller (1988) offer helpful information on improving tables in publications. Many of their recommendations (e.g., sorting rows and columns by marginal averages, rounding to a few significant digits, avoiding decimals when possible) are based on the clearly written tutorials of Ehrenberg (1975, 1981).

A common deficiency of graphics in psychological publications is their lack of essential information. In most cases, this information is the shape or distribution of the data. Whether from a negative motivation to conceal irregularities or from a positive belief that less is more, omitting shape infor-

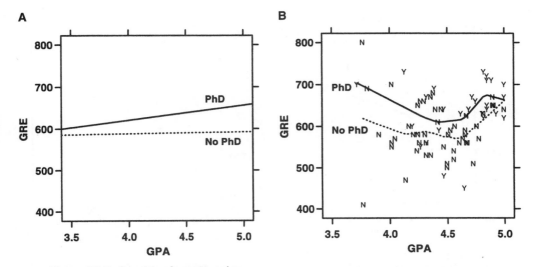

Figure 36.2. Graphics for regression.
Note: GRE = Graduate Record Examination; GPA = grade point average; PhD and No PhD = completed and did not complete the doctoral degree; Y = yes; N = no.

mation from graphics often hinders scientific evaluation. Chambers et al. (1983) and Cleveland (1995) offer specific ways to address these problems. The examples in Figure 36.2 do this using two of the most frequent graphical forms in psychology publications.

Figure 36.2 shows plots based on data from 80 graduate students in a Midwestern university psychology department, collected from 1969 through 1978. The variables are scores on the psychology advanced test of the Graduate Record Examination (GRE), the undergraduate grade point average (GPA), and whether a student completed a doctoral degree in the department (PhD). Figure 36.2A shows a format appearing frequently in psychology journal articles: two regression lines, one for each group of students. This graphic conveys nothing more than four numbers: the slopes and intercepts of the regression lines. Because the scales have no physical meaning, seeing the slopes of lines (as opposed to reading the numbers) adds nothing to our understanding of the relationship.

Figure 36.2B shows a scatter plot of the same data with a locally weighted scatter plot smoother for each PhD group (Cleveland & Devlin, 1988). This robust curvilinear regression smoother (called LOESS) is available in modern statistics packages. Now we can see some curvature in the relationships. (When a model that includes a linear and quadratic term for GPA is computed, the apparent interaction involving the PhD and no PhD groups depicted in Figure 36.2A disappears.) The graphic in Figure 36.2B tells us many things. We note the unusual student with a GPA of less than 4.0 and a psychology GRE score of 800; we note the less surprising student

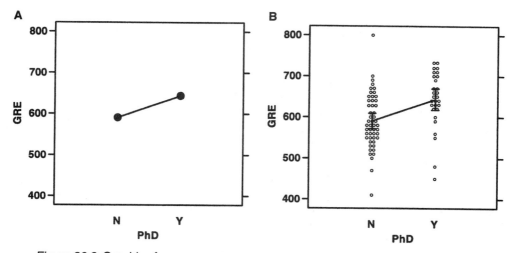

Figure 36.3. Graphics for groups.
Note: GRE = Graduate Record Examination; N = no; Y = yes.

with a similar GPA but a low GRE score (both of whom failed to earn doctoral degrees); we note the several students who had among the lowest GRE scores but earned doctorates, and so on. We might imagine these kinds of cases in Figure 36.2A (as we should in any data set containing error), but their location and distribution in Figure 36.2B tell us something about this specific data set.

Figure 36.3A shows another popular format for displaying data in psychology journals. It is based on the data set used for Figure 36.2. Authors frequently use this format to display the results of *t* tests or ANOVAs. For factorial ANOVAs, this format gives authors an opportunity to represent interactions by using a legend with separate symbols for each line. In more laboratory-oriented psychology journals (e.g., animal behavior, neuroscience), authors sometimes add error bars to the dots representing the means.

Figure 36.3B adds to the line graphic a dot plot representing the data and 95% confidence intervals on the means of the two groups (using the *t* distribution). The graphic reveals a left skewness of GRE scores in the PhD group. Although this skewness may not be severe enough to affect our statistical conclusions, it is nevertheless noteworthy. It may be due to ceiling effects (although note the 800 score in the no PhD group) or to some other factor. At the least, the reader has a right to be able to evaluate this kind of information.

There are other ways to include data or distributions in graphics, including box plots and stem-and-leaf plots (Tukey, 1977) and kernel density estimates (Scott, 1992; Silverman, 1986). Many of these procedures are found in modern statistical packages. It is time for authors to take advantage of them and for editors and reviewers to urge authors to do so.

DISCUSSION

Interpretation

When you interpret effects, think of credibility, generalizability, and robustness. Are the effects credible, given the results of previous studies and theory? Do the features of the design and analysis (e.g., sample quality, similarity of the design to designs of previous studies, similarity of the effects to those in previous studies) suggest the results are generalizable? Are the design and analytic methods robust enough to support strong conclusions?

Novice researchers err either by overgeneralizing their results or, equally unfortunately, by overparticularizing. Explicitly compare the effects detected in your inquiry with the effect sizes reported in related previous studies. Do not be afraid to extend your interpretations to a general class or population if you have reasons to assume that your results apply. This general class may consist of populations you have studied at your site, other populations at other sites, or even more general populations. Providing these reasons in your discussion will help you stimulate future research for yourself and others.

Conclusions

Speculation may be appropriate, but use it sparingly and explicitly. Note the shortcomings of your study. Remember, however, that acknowledging limitations is for the purpose of qualifying results and avoiding pitfalls in future research. Confession should not have the goal of disarming criticism. Recommendations for future research should be thoughtful and grounded in present and previous findings. Gratuitous suggestions ("further research needs to be done . . . ") waste space. Do not interpret a single study's results as having importance independent of the effects reported elsewhere in the relevant literature. The thinking presented in a single study may turn the movement of the literature, but the results in a single study are important primarily as one contribution to a mosaic of study effects.

Some had hoped that this task force would vote to recommend an outright ban on the use of significance tests in psychology journals. Although this might eliminate some abuses, the committee thought that there were enough counterexamples (e.g., Abelson, 1997) to justify forbearance. Furthermore, the committee believed that the problems raised in its charge went beyond the simple question of whether to ban significance tests.

The task force hopes instead that this report will induce editors, reviewers, and authors to recognize practices that institutionalize the thoughtless application of statistical methods. Distinguishing statistical significance from theoretical significance (Kirk, 1996) will help the entire research community publish more substantial results. Encouraging good design and logic will help improve the quality of conclusions. And promoting modern statistical graphics will improve the assessment of assumptions and the display of results.

More than 50 years ago, Hotelling, Bartky, Deming, Friedman, and Hoel (1948) wrote, "Unfortunately, too many people like to do their statistical work as they say their prayers—merely substitute in a formula found in a highly respected book written a long time ago" (p. 103). Good theories and intelligent interpretation advance a discipline more than rigid methodological orthodoxy. If editors keep in mind Fisher's (1935) words quoted in the Analysis section, then there is less danger of methodology substituting for thought. Statistical methods should guide and discipline our thinking but should not determine it.

REFERENCES

Abelson, R. P. (1995). *Statistics as principled argument*. Hillsdale, NJ: Erlbaum.

Abelson, R. P. (1997). On the surprising longevity of flogged horses: Why there is a case for the significance test. *Psychological Science, 23*, 12–15.

American Psychological Association. (1994). *Publication manual of the American Psychological Association* (4th ed.). Washington, DC: Author.

Bailar, J. C., & Mosteller, F. (1988). Guidelines for statistical reporting in articles for medical journals: Amplifications and explanations. *Annals of Internal Medicine, 108*, 266–273.

Baker, B. L. (1969). Symptom treatment and symptom substitution in enuresis. *Journal of Abnormal Psychology, 74*, 42–49.

Benjamini, Y., & Hochberg, Y. (1995). Controlling the false discovery rate: A practical and powerful approach to multiple testing. *Journal of the Royal Statistical Society, 57* (Series B), 289–300.

Chambers, J., Cleveland, W., Kleiner, B., & Tukey, P. (1983). *Graphical methods for data analysis*. Monterey, CA: Wadsworth.

Chartrand, J. M. (1997). [National sample survey]. Unpublished raw data.

Cleveland, W. S. (1995). *Visualizing data*. Summit, NJ: Hobart Press.

Cleveland, W. S., & Devlin, S. (1988). Locally weighted regression analysis by local fitting. *Journal of the American Statistical Association, 83*, 596–640.

Cohen, J. (1969). *Statistical power analysis for the behavioral sciences*. New York: Academic Press.

Cohen, J. (1988). *Statistical power analysis for the behavioral sciences* (2nd ed.). Hillsdale, NJ: Erlbaum.

Cohen, J. (1994). The earth is round ($p < .05$). *American Psychologist, 49*, 997–1003.

Cook, T. D., & Campbell, D. T. (1979). *Quasi-experimentation: Design and analysis issues for field settings*. Chicago: Rand McNally.

Cronbach, L. J. (1975). Beyond the two disciplines of psychology. *American Psychologist, 30*, 116–127.

Ehrenberg, A. S. C. (1975). *Data reduction: Analyzing and interpreting statistical data*. New York: Wiley.

Ehrenberg, A. S. C. (1981). The problem of numeracy. *American Statistician, 35*, 67–71.

Feldt, L. S., & Brennan, R. L. (1989). Reliability. In R. L. Linn (Ed.), *Educational measurement* (3rd ed., pp. 105–146). Washington, DC: American Council on Education.

Fisher, R. A. (1935). *The design of experiments*. Edinburgh, Scotland: Oliver & Boyd.

Fleiss, J. L. (1994). Measures of effect size for categorical data. In H. Cooper & L. V. Hedges (Eds.), *The handbook of research synthesis* (pp. 245–260). New York: Sage.

Harlow, L. L., Mulaik, S. A., & Steiger, J. H. (1997). *What if there were no significance tests?* Hillsdale, NJ: Erlbaum.

Holland, P. W. (1986). Statistics and causal inference. *Journal of the American Statistical Association, 81*, 945–960.

Holland, P. W., & Rubin, D. B. (1983). On Lord's paradox. In H. Wainer & S. Messick (Eds.), *Principals of modern psychological measurement* (pp. 3–25). Hillsdale, NJ: Erlbaum.

Hotelling, H., Bartky, W., Deming, W. E., Friedman, M., & Hoel, P. (1948). The teaching of statistics. *Annals of Mathematical Statistics, 19*, 95–115.

Hurlburt, R. T., & Spiegel, D. K. (1976). Dependence of F ratios sharing a common denominator mean square. *American Statistician, 20*, 74–78.

Kahn, J. R., & Udry, J. R. (1986). Marital coital frequency: Unnoticed outliers and unspecified interactions lead to erroneous conclusions. *American Sociological Review, 51*, 734–737.

Keselman, H. J., Huberty, C. J., Lix, L. M., Olejnik, S., Cribbie, R., Donahue, B., et al. (1998). Statistical practices of educational researchers: An analysis of their ANOVA, MANOVA, and ANCOVA analyses. *Review of Educational Research, 68*, 350–386.

Kirk, R. E. (1996). Practical significance: A concept whose time has come. *Educational and Psychological Measurement, 56*, 746–759.

Little, R. J. A., & Rubin, D. B. (1987). *Statistical analysis with missing data*. New York: Wiley.

McDonald, R. P. (1997). Haldane's lungs: A case study in path analysis. *Multivariate Behavioral Research, 3*, 21–38.

Messick, S. (1989). Validity. In R. L. Linn (Ed.), *Educational measurement* (3rd ed., pp. 13–103). Washington, DC: American Council on Education.

Rosenthal, R. (1966). *Experimenter effects in behavioral research*. New York: Appleton-Century-Crofts.

Rosenthal, R. (1994). *Parametric measures of effect size*. In H. Cooper & L. V. Hedges (Eds.), *The handbook of research synthesis* (pp. 231–244). New York: Sage.

Rosenthal, R., Rosnow, R. L., & Rubin, D. B. (2000). *Contrasts and effect sizes in behavioral research: A correlational approach*. New York: Cambridge University Press.

Rosenthal, R., & Rubin, D. B. (1982). A simple general purpose display of magnitude of experimental effect. *Journal of Educational Psychology, 74,* 166–169.

Rosenthal, R., & Rubin, D. B. (1994). The counternull value of an effect size: A new statistic. *Psychological Science, 5,* 329–334.

Rubin, D. B. (1974). Estimating causal effects of treatments in randomized and nonrandomized studies. *Journal of Educational Psychology, 66,* 688–701.

Rubin, D. B. (1976). Inference and missing data. *Biometrika, 63,* 581–592.

Rubin, D. B. (1977). Assignment of treatment group on the basis of a covariate. *Journal of Educational Statistics, 2,* 1–26.

Rubin, D. B. (1978). Bayesian inference for causal effects: The role of randomization. *Annals of Statistics, 6,* 34–58.

Rubin, D. B. (1990a). Formal modes of statistical inference for causal effects. *Journal of Statistical Planning and Inference. 25,* 279–292.

Rubin, D. B. (1990b). Neyman (1923) and causal inference in experiments and observational studies. *Statistical Science, 5,* 472–480.

Scheines, R., Spirites, P., Glymour, C., Meek, C., & Richardson, T. (1998). The TETRAD project: Constraint based aids to causal model specification. *Multivariate Behavioral Research, 33,* 65–117.

Schmidt, F. (1996). Statistical significance testing and cumulative knowledge in psychology: Implications for the training of researchers. *Psychological Methods, 1,* 115–129.

Scott, D. W. (1992). *Multivariate density estimation: Theory, practice, and visualization.* New York: Wiley.

Silverman, B. W. (1986). *Density estimation for statistics and data analysis.* New York: Chapman & Hall.

Snyder, P., & Lawson, S. (1993). Evaluating results using corrected and uncorrected effect size estimates. *Journal of Experimental Education, 61,* 334–349.

Thompson, B. (1996). AERA editorial policies regarding statistical significance testing: Three suggested reforms. *Educational Researcher, 2,* 522–630.

Thompson, B., & Snyder, P. A. (1998). Statistical significance and reliability analyses in recent JCD research articles. *Journal of Counseling and Development, 76,* 436–441.

Tukey, J. W. (1977). *Exploratory data analysis.* Reading, MA: Addison-Wesley.

Wainer, H. (2000). One cheer for null hypothesis significance testing. *Psychological Methods, 4,* 212–213.

Webb, E. J., Campbell, D. T., Schwartz, R. D., & Sechrest, L. (1966). *Unobtrusive measures: Nonreactive research in the social sciences.* Chicago: Rand McNally.

JOURNAL PUBLICATION

37

PREPARING AND EVALUATING RESEARCH REPORTS

ALAN E. KAZDIN

The research process consists of the design and execution of the study, analysis of the results, and preparation of the report (e.g., journal article). The final step seems straightforward and relatively easy, given the nature and scope of the other steps. In fact, one often refers to preparation of the article as merely "writing up the results." Yet the implied simplicity of the task belies the significance of the product in the research process. The article is not the final step in the process. Rather, it is an important beginning. The article is often a launching platform for the next study for the authors themselves or for others in the field who are interested in pursuing the findings. Thus, the report is central to the research process.

The article itself is not only a description of what was accomplished, but it also conveys the extent to which the design, execution, and analyses were well conceived and appropriate. Recognition of this facet of the report is the reason why faculty require students in training to write a proposal of

Reprinted from *Psychological Assessment, 7,* 228–237. Copyright 1995 by the American Psychological Association.

Completion of this research was supported by Research Scientist Award MH00353 and Grant MH35408 from the National Institute of Mental Health.

the study in advance of its execution. At the proposal stage, faculty can examine the thought processes, design, planned execution, and data analyses and make the necessary changes in advance. Even so, writing the full article at the completion of the study raises special issues. At that point, the authors evaluate critical issues, see shortcomings of the design, and struggle with any clashes or ambiguities of the findings in light of the hypotheses.

The purpose of this article is to discuss the preparation and evaluation of research reports (articles) for publication.[1] Guidelines are presented to facilitate preparation of research articles. The guidelines cover the types of details that are to be included, but more important, the rationale, logic, and flow of the article to facilitate communication and to advance the next stage of the research process. Thus, preparation of a research report involves many of the same considerations that underlie the design and plan of the research.

Reports of empirical studies have many characteristics in common, whether or not they focus on assessment. Even so, the present focus will emphasize studies that are designed to evaluate assessment devices, constructs that the measures are intended to reflect, and studies of test validation. Issues that commonly emerge in articles of assessment and hence the design of assessment studies are highlighted as well.

GUIDELINES FOR PREPARING REPORTS FOR PUBLICATION

Preparation of the report for publication involves three interrelated tasks, which I shall refer to as description, explanation, and contextualization. Failure to appreciate or to accomplish these tasks serves as a main source of frustration for authors, as their articles traverse the process of manuscript review toward publication. *Description* is the most straightforward task and includes providing details of the study. Even though this is an obvious requirement of the report, basic details often are omitted in published articles (e.g., the gender and race of the participants, means, and standard deviation; see Shapiro & Shapiro, 1983; Weiss & Weisz, 1990). *Explanation* is slightly more complex insofar as this task refers to presenting the rationale of several facets of the study. The justification, decision-making process, and the connections between the decisions and the goals of the study move well beyond description. There are numerous decision points in any given study, most of which can be questioned. The author is obliged to make the case to

---

[1] Preparation of manuscripts for publication can be discussed from the perspective of authors and the perspective of reviewers (i.e., those persons who evaluate the manuscript for publication). This article emphasizes the perspective of authors and the task of preparing an article for publication. The review process raises its own issues, which this article does not address. Excellent readings are available to prepare the author for the journal review process (Kafka, *The Trial*, The Myth of Sisyphus, and Dante's *Inferno*).

explain why the specific options elected are well suited to the hypotheses or the goals of the study. Finally, *contextualization* moves one step further away from description of the details of the study and addresses how the study fits in the context of other studies and in the knowledge base more generally. This latter facet of article preparation reflects such lofty notions as scholarship and perspective, because the author places the descriptive and explanatory material into a broader context.

The extent to which description, explanation, and contextualization are accomplished increases the likelihood that the report will be viewed as a publishable article and facilitates integration of the report into the knowledge base. Guidelines follow that emphasize these tasks in the preparation and evaluation of research reports. The guidelines focus on the logic to the study; the interrelations of the different sections; the rationale for specific procedures and analyses; and the strengths, limitations, and place of the study in the knowledge base. It may be helpful to convey how these components can be addressed by focusing on the main sections of manuscripts that are prepared for journal publication.

Main Sections of the Article

Abstract

At first glance, the abstract certainly may not seem to be an important section or core feature of the article. Yet, two features of the abstract make this section quite critical. First, the abstract is likely to be read by many more people than is the article. The abstract probably will be entered into various databases that are available internationally. Consequently, this is the only information that most readers will have about the study. Second, for reviewers of the manuscript and readers of the journal article, the abstract sometimes is the first impression of what the author studied and found. Ambiguity, illogic, and fuzziness here is ominous. Thus, the abstract is sometimes the only impression or first impression one may have about the study. What is said is critically important.

Obviously, the purpose of the abstract is to provide a relatively brief statement of purpose, methods, findings, and conclusions of the study. Critical methodological descriptors pertain to the participants and their characteristics, experimental and control groups or conditions, design, and major findings. Often space is quite limited; indeed, a word limit (e.g., 100- or 120-word maximum) may be placed on the abstract by the journals. It is useful to make substantive statements about the characteristics of the study and the findings rather than to provide general and minimally informative comments. Similarly, vacuous statements (e.g., "Implications of the results are discussed" or "Future directions for research are suggested") should be replaced with comments about the findings or one or two specific implications and research directions (e.g., "The findings raise the prospect that there is a Big One rather than a Big Five set of personality characteristics").

Introduction

The introduction is designed to convey the overall rationale and objective of the research. The task of the author is to convey in a clear and concise fashion why this particular study is needed and the current questions, void, or deficiency the study is designed to address. The section should not review the literature in a study-by-study fashion, but rather convey issues and evaluative comments that set the stage for the study that is to follow. The task of contextualization is critically important in this section. Placing the study in the context of what is and is not known and conveying the essential next step in research in the field require mastery of the pertinent literatures and reasonable communication skills. Saying that the study is important (without systematically establishing the context) or noting that no one else has studied this phenomenon often are viewed as feeble attempts to circumvent the contextualization of the study

Limitations of previous work and how those limitations can be overcome may be important to consider. These statements build the critical transition from an existing literature to the present study and establish the rationale for design improvements or additions in relation to those studies. Alternatively or in addition, the study may build along new dimensions to advance the theory, hypotheses, and constructs to a broader range of domains of performance, samples, settings, and so on. The rationale for the specific study must be very clearly established. If a new measure is being presented, then the need for the measure and how it supplements or improves on existing measures, if any are available, are important to include. If a frequently used measure is presented, the rationale needs to be firmly established what precisely this study will add.

In general, the introduction will move from the very general to the specific. The very general refers to the opening of the introduction, which conveys the area of research, general topic, and significance of a problem. For example, if an article is on the assessment of alcohol abuse or marital bliss (or their interrelation), a brief opening statement noting the current state of the topic and its implications outside of the context of measurement is very helpful. Although reviewers are likely to be specialists in the assessment domain, many potential readers would profit from clarification of the broader context.

The introduction does not usually permit authors to convey all of the information they wish to present. In fact, the limit is usually two to four manuscript pages. A reasonable use of this space involves brief paragraphs or implicit sections that describe the nature of the problem, the current status of the literature, the extension that this study is designed to provide, and how the methods to be used are warranted. To the extent that the author conveys a grasp of the issues in the area and can identify the lacunae that the study is designed to fill greatly improves the quality of the report and the chances of acceptance for journal publication.

Method

This section of the article encompasses several points related to who was studied, why, how, and so on. The section not only describes critical procedures, but also provides the rationale for methodological decisions. Initially, the research participants (or subjects) are described, including several basic descriptors (e.g., age, genders, ethnicity, education, occupation, and income). From a method and design standpoint, information beyond basic descriptors can be helpful to encompass factors that plausibly could affect generality or replication of the results or that might influence comparison of the data with information obtained from normative or standardization samples.

The rationale for the sample should be provided. Why was this sample included and how is it appropriate to the substantive area and question of interest? In some cases, the sample is obviously relevant because participants have the characteristic or disorder of interest (e.g., parents accused of child abuse) or are in a setting of interest (e.g., nursing home residents). In other cases, samples are included merely because they are available (college students or a clinic population recruited for some other purpose than the study). Such samples of convenience often count against the investigator. If characteristics of the sample are potentially objectionable in relation to the goals of the study, the rationale may require full elaboration to convey why the sample was included and how features of the sample may or may not be relevant to the conclusions the author wishes to draw. A sample of convenience is not invariable a problem for drawing valid inferences. Yet, invariably, a thoughtful discussion will be required regarding its use. More generally, participant selection, recruitment, screening, and other features warrant comment. The issue for the author and reviewer is whether features of the participant selection process could restrict the conclusions in some unique fashion or, worse, in some way represent a poor test of the hypotheses.

Assessment studies may be experimental studies in which groups vary in whether they receive an intervention or experimental manipulation. More commonly, assessment studies focus on intact groups without a particular manipulation. The studies form groups based on subject selection criteria (e.g., one type of patient vs. another, men vs. women) for analyses. The rationale for selecting the sample is obviously important. If the sample is divided into subgroups, it is as critical to convey how the groups will provide a test of the hypotheses and to show that characteristics incidental to the hypotheses do not differ or do not obscure interpretation of the results (see Kazdin, 1992). Also, the selection procedure and any risks of misclassification based on the operational criteria used (e.g., false positives and negatives) warrant comment. Reliability of the assessment procedures used to select cases, especially when human judgment is required, is very important because of the direct implications for interpretation and replication of the findings. A common example for which this arises in clinical research is in invoking psychiatric diagnoses using interview techniques.

Several measures are usually included in the study. Why the constructs were selected for study should be clarified in the introduction. The specific measures and why they were selected to operationalize the constructs should be presented in the method section. Information about the psychometric characteristics of the measures is often summarized. This information relates directly to the credibility of the results. Apart from individual assessment devices, the rationale for including or omitting areas that might be regarded as crucial (e.g., multiple measures, informants, and settings) deserves comment. The principle here is similar to other sections, namely, the rationale for the author's decisions ought to be explicit.

Occasionally, ambiguous statements may enter into descriptions of measures. For example, measures may be referred to as "reliable" or "valid" in previous research, as part of the rationale for use in the present study. There are, of course, many different types of reliability and validity. It is important to identity those characteristics of the measure found in prior research that are relevant to the present study. For example, high internal consistency (reliability) in a prior study may not be a strong argument for use of the measure in a longitudinal design in which the author hopes for test–retest reliability. Even previous data on test–retest reliability (e.g., over 2 weeks) may not provide a sound basis for test–retest reliability over annual intervals. The information conveys the suitability of the measure for the study and the rationale of the author for selecting the measure in light of available strategies.

Results

It is important to convey why specific analyses were selected and how a particular test or comparison addresses the hypotheses or purposes presented earlier in the article. It is often the case that analyses are reported in a rote fashion in which, for example, the main effects are presented first, followed by the interactions for each measure. The author presents the analyses in very much the same way as the computer printout that provided multiple runs of the data. Similarly, if several dependent measures are available, a particular set for analyses is automatically run (e.g., omnibus tests of multivariate analyses of variance followed by univariate analyses of variance for individual measures). These are not the ways to present the data.

In the presentation of the results, it is important to convey why specific tests were selected and how these tests serve the specific goals of the study. Knowledge of statistics is critical for selecting the analysis to address the hypotheses of interest and conditions met by the data. The tests ought to relate to the hypotheses, predictions, or expectations outlined at the beginning of the article (Wampold, Davis, & Good, 1990). Presumably, the original hypotheses were presented in a special (nonrandom) order, based on importance or level of specificity. It is very useful to retain this order when the statistics are presented to test these hypotheses. As a general rule, it is important to emphasize the hypotheses or relations of interest in the results; the statistics are only tools in the service of these hypotheses.

It is often useful to begin the results by presenting basic descriptors of the data (e.g., means and standard deviation for each group or condition) so the readers have access to the numbers themselves. If there are patterns in the descriptors, it is useful to point them out. Almost-significant results might be noted here to err on the side of conservatism regarding group equivalence on some domain that might affect interpretation of the results, particularly if power (or sample size) was weak to detect such differences.

The main body of the results presents tests of the hypotheses or predictions. Organization of the results (subheadings) or brief statements of hypotheses before the specific analyses are often helpful to prompt the author to clarify how the statistical test relates to the substantive questions. As a step towards that goal, the rationale for the statistical tests chosen or the variations within a particular type of test ought to be noted. For example, within factor analyses or multiple regression, the options selected (e.g., method of extracting factors, rotation, and method of entering variables) should be described along with the rationale of why these particular options are appropriate. The rationales are important as a general rule, but may take on even greater urgency because of the easy use of software programs that can run the analyses. Default criteria on many software programs are not necessarily related to the author's conceptualization of the data, that is, the hypotheses. (Such information is referred to as "default criteria" because if the results do not come out with thoughtless analyses, it is partially "de fault of the criteria de investigator used.") Statistical decisions, whether or not explicit, often bear conceptual implications regarding the phenomena under investigation and the relations of variables to each other and to other variables.

Several additional or ancillary analyses may be presented to elaborate the primary hypotheses. For example, one might be able to reduce the plausibility that certain biases may have accounted for group differences based on supplementary or ancillary data analyses. Ancillary analyses may be more exploratory and diffuse than tests of the primary hypotheses. Manifold variables can be selected for these analyses (e.g., gender, race, and height differences) that are not necessarily conceptually interesting in relation to the goals of the study. The author may wish to present data and data analyses that were unexpected, were not of initial interest, and were not the focus of the study. The rationale for these excursions and the limitations of interpretation are worth noting. From the standpoint of the reviewer and reader, the results should make clear what the main hypotheses were, how the analyses provide appropriate and pointed tests, and what conclusions can be reached as a result. In addition, thoughtful excursions (i.e., with the rationale guiding the reader) in the analyses are usually an advantage.

Discussion

The discussion consists of the conclusions and interpretations of the study and hence is the final resting place of all issues and concerns. Typically, the discussion includes an overview of the major findings, integration or relation of these findings to theory and prior research, limitations and ambiguities and their implications for interpretation, and future directions. The extent that this can be accomplished in a brief space (e.g., two to five manuscript pages) is to the author's advantage.

Description and interpretation of the findings may raise a tension between what the author wishes to say about the findings and their meaning versus what can be said in light of how the study was designed and evaluated. Thus, the discussion shows the reader the interplay of the introduction, method, and results sections. For example, the author might draw conclusions that are not quite appropriate given the method and findings. The discussion conveys flaws, problems, or questionable methodological decisions within the design that were not previously evident. However, they are flaws only in relation to the introduction and discussion. That is, the reader of the article can now recognize that if these are the types of statements the author wishes to make, the present study (design, measures, and sample) is not well suited for making them. The slight mismatch of interpretive statements in the discussion and the methodology is a common, albeit tacit basis for not considering a study as well conceived and well executed. A slightly different study may be required to support the specific statements the author makes in the discussion; alternatively, the discussion might be more circumscribed in the statements that are made.

It is usually to the author's credit to examine potential sources of ambiguity given that he or she is in an excellent position because of familiarity with procedures and expertise to understand the area. A candid, nondefensive appraisal of the study is very helpful. Here, too, contextualization may be helpful because limitations of a study are also related to prior research, trade-offs inherent in the exigencies of design and execution, what other studies have and have not accomplished, and whether a finding is robust across different methods of investigation. Although it is to the author's credit to acknowledge limitations of the study, there are limits on the extent to which reviewers grant a pardon for true confessions. At some point, the flaw is sufficient to preclude publication, whether or not it is acknowledged by the author. At other points, acknowledging potential limitations conveys critical understanding of the issues and directs the field to future work. This latter use of acknowledgment augments the contribution of the study and the likelihood of favorable evaluation by readers.

Finally, it is useful in the discussion to contextualize the results by continuing the story line that began in the introduction. With the present findings, what puzzle piece has been added to the knowledge base, what new questions or ambiguities were raised, what other substantive areas might be relevant for this line of research, and what new studies are needed? From the standpoint of contextualization, the new studies referred to here are not merely those that overcome methodological limitations of the present study, but rather those that focus on the substantive foci of the next steps for research.

Guiding Questions

The section-by-section discussion of the content of an article is designed to convey the flow or logic of the study and the interplay of description, explanation, and contextualization. The study ought to have a thematic line throughout, and all sections ought to reflect that thematic line in a logical way. The thematic line consists of the substantive issues guiding the hypotheses and the decisions of the investigator (e.g., with regard to procedures and analyses) that are used to elaborate these hypotheses.

Another way to consider the tasks of preparing a report is to consider the many questions the article ought to answer. These are questions for the authors to ask themselves or, on the other hand, questions reviewers and consumers of the research are likely to want to ask. Table 37.1 contains questions that warrant consideration. They are presented according to the different sections of a manuscript. The questions emphasize the descriptive information, as well as the rationale for procedures, decisions, and practices in the design and execution. Needless to say, assessment studies can vary widely in their purpose, design, and methods of evaluation, so the questions are not necessarily appropriate to each study nor are they necessarily exhaustive. The set of questions is useful as a way of checking to see that many important facets of the study have not been overlooked.

General Comments

Preparation of an article is often viewed as a task of describing what was done. With this in mind, authors often are frustrated at the reactions of reviewers. In reading the reactions of reviewers, the authors usually recognize and acknowledge the value of providing more details that are required (e.g., further information about the participants or procedure). However, when the requests pertain to explanation and contextualization, authors are more likely to be baffled or defensive. This reaction may be reasonable because graduate training devotes much less attention to these facets of preparing

TABLE 37.1
Major Questions to Guide Journal Article Preparation

Abstract

What were the main purposes of the study?
Who was studied (sample, sample size, special characteristics)?
How were participants selected?
To what conditions, if any, were participants exposed?
What type of design was used?
What were the main findings and conclusions?

Introduction

What is the background and context for the study?
What in current theory, research, or clinical work makes this study useful, important, or of interest?
What is different or special about the study in focus, methods, or design to address a need in the area?
Is the rationale clear regarding the constructs to be assessed?
What specifically were the purposes, predictions, or hypotheses?

Method

Participants
  Who were the participants and how many of them were in this study?
  Why was this sample selected in light of the research goals?
  How was this sample obtained, recruited, and selected?
  What are the participant and demographic characteristics of the sample (e.g., gender, age, ethnicity, race, socioeconomic status)?
  What if any inclusion or exclusion criteria were invoked (i.e., selection rules to obtain participants)?
  How many of those participants eligible or recruited actually were selected and participated in the study?
  Was informed consent solicited? How and from whom, if special populations were used?

Design
  What is the design (i.e., longitudinal, cross-sectional) and how does the design related to the goals of the study?
  How were the participant assigned to groups or conditions?
  How many groups were included in the design?
  How were the groups similar and different in how they were treated in the study?
  Why were these groups critical to address the questions of interest?

Assessment
  What were the constructs of interest and how were they measured?
  What are the relevant reliability and validity data from previous research (and from the present study) that support the use of these measures for the present purposes?
  Were multiple measures and methods used to assess the constructs?
  Are response sets or styles relevant to the use and interpretation of the measures?
  How was the assessment conducted? By whom (as assessors/observers)? In what order were the measures administered?
  If judges (raters) were used in any facet of assessment, what is the reliability (inter- or intrajudge consistency) in rendering their judgments/ratings?

Procedures
  Where was the study conducted (setting)?
  What materials, equipment, or apparatuses were used in the study?
  What was the chronological sequence of events to which participants were exposed?

TABLE 37.1 (continued)

What intervals elapsed between different aspects of the study (e.g., assessment occasions)?

What procedural checks were completed to avert potential sources of bias in implementation of the manipulation and assessments?

What checks were made to ensure that the conditions were carried out as intended?

What other information does the reader need to know to understand how participants were treated and what conditions were provided?

Results

What were the primary measures and data on which the predictions depend?

What are the scores on the measures of interest for the different groups and sample as a whole (e.g., measures of central tendency and variability)?

How do the scores compare with those of other study, normative, or standardization samples?

Are groups of interest within the study similar on measures and variables that could interfere with interpretation of the hypotheses?

What analyses were used and how specifically did these address the original hypotheses and purposes?

Were the assumptions of the data analyses met?

If multiple tests were used, what means were provided to control error rates?

If more than one group was delineated, were they similar on variables that might otherwise explain the results (e.g., diagnosis, age)?

Were data missing due to incomplete measures (not filled out completely by the participants) or due to loss of participants? If so, how were these handled in the data analyses?

Are there ancillary analyses that might further inform the primary analyses or exploratory analyses that might stimulate further work?

Discussion

What were the major findings of the study?

How do these findings add to research and how do they support, refute, or inform current theory?

What alternative interpretations can be placed on the data?

What limitations or qualifiers must be placed on the study given methodology and design issues?

What research follows from the study to move the field forward?

Note: Further discussion of questions that guide the preparation of journal articles can be obtained in additional sources (Kazdin, 1992; Maher, 1978). Concrete guidelines on the format for preparing articles are provided by the American Psychological Association (1994).

research reports than to description. Also, reviewers' comments and editorial decision letters may not be explicit about the need for explanation and contextualization. For example, some of the more general reactions of reviewers are often reflected in comments such as "Nothing in the manuscript is new," "I fail to see the importance of the study," or "This study has already been done in a much better way by others."[2] In fact, such characterizations may be true.

---

[2] I am grateful to my dissertation committee for permitting me to quote their comments at my oral exam. In keeping with the spirit embodied in their use of pseudonyms in signing the dissertation, they wish not to be acknowledged by name here.

Alternatively, the comments could also reflect the extent to which the author has failed to contextualize the study to obviate these kinds of reactions.

The lesson for preparing and evaluation research reports is clear. Describing a study does not eo ipso establish its contribution to the field, no matter how strongly the author feels that the study is a first. Also, the methodological options for studying a particular question are enormous in terms of possible samples, constructs and measures, and data-analytic methods. The reasons for electing the particular set for options the author has chosen deserve elaboration.

In some cases, the author selects options because they were used in prior research. This criterion alone may be weak, because objections levied at the present study may also be appropriate to some of the prior work as well. The author will feel unjustly criticized for a more general flaw in the literature. Yet, arguing for a key methodological decision solely because "others have done this in the past" provides a very weak rationale, unless the purpose of the study is to address the value of the option as a goal of the study. Also, it may be that new evidence has emerged that makes the past practice more questionable in the present. For example, investigators may rely on retrospective assessment to obtain lifetime data regarding symptoms or early characteristics of family life, a seemingly reasonable assessment approach. Evidence suggests, however, that such retrospective information is very weak, inaccurate, and barely above chance when compared with the same information obtained prospectively (e.g., Henry, Moffitt, Caspi, Langley, & Silva, 1994; Robins et al., 1985). As evidence accumulates over time to make this point clear and as the domain of false memories becomes more well studied, the use of retrospective assessment methods is likely to be less acceptable among reviewers. In short, over time, the standards and permissible methods may change.

In general, it is beneficial to the author and to the field to convey the thought processes underlying methodological and design decision. This information will greatly influence the extent to which the research effort is appreciated and viewed as enhancing knowledge. Yet, it is useful to convey that decisions were thoughtful and that they represent reasonable choices among the alternatives for answering the questions that guide the study. The contextual issues are no less important. As authors, we often expect the latent Nobel Prize caliber of the study to be self-evident. It is better to be very clear about how and where the study fits in the literature, what it adds, and what questions and research the study prompts.

COMMON INTERPRETIVE ISSUES IN EVALUATING ASSESSMENT STUDIES

In conducting studies and preparing reports of assessment studies, a number of issues can be identified to which authors and readers are often sensitive. These issues have to do with the goals, interpretation, and generality of the results of studies. I highlight three issues here: test validation, the relations of constructs to measures, and sampling. Each of these is a weighty topic in its own right and will be considered in other articles in this issue. In this article, they are addressed in relation to interpretation and reporting of research findings.

Interpreting Correlations Among Test Scores

Test validation is a complex and ongoing process involving many stages and types of demonstrations. As part of that process, evidence often focuses on the extent to which a measure of interest (e.g., a newly developed measure) is correlated with other measures. Interpreting seemingly simple correlations between measures requires attention to multiple considerations.

Convergent Validation

Convergent validity refers to the extent to which a measure is correlated with other measures that are designed to assess the same or related constructs (Campell & Fiske, 1959). There are different ways in which convergent validity can be shown, such as demonstrating that a given measure correlates with related measures at a given point in time (e.g., concurrent validity) and that groups selected on some related criterion (e.g., history of being abused vs. no such history) differ on the measure, as expected (e.g., criterion or known-groups validity).[3] In convergent validity, the investigator may be interested in showing that a new measure of a construct correlates with other measures of that same construct or that the new measure correlates with measures of related constructs. With convergent validity, some level of agreement between measures is sought.

In one scenario, the investigator may wish to correlate a measure (e.g., depression) with measures of related constructs (e.g., negative cognitions and anxiety). In this case, the investigator may search for correlations that are in the moderate range (e.g., $r = .40-.60$) to be able to say that measure of interest was correlated in the positive direction, as predicted, with the other (criterion) measures. Very high correlations raise the prospect that the measure is assessing the "same" construct or adds no new information. In cases in which the investigator has developed a new measure, the correlations of that measure will be with other measures of the same construct. In this case, high correlations may be sought to show that the new measure in fact does assess the construct of interest.

Interpretation of convergent validation data requires caution. To begin

---

[3] There are of course many different types of validity, and often individual types are referred to inconsistently. For a discussion of different types of validity and their different uses, the reader is referred to other sources (Kline, 1986; Wainer & Braun, 1988).

with, the positive, moderate-to-high correlations between two measures could well be due to shared trait variance in the construct domains, as predicted between the two measures. For example, two characteristics (e.g., emotionality and anxiety) might overlap because of their common psychological, biological, or developmental underpinnings. This is usually what the investigator has in mind by searching for convergent validity. However, other interpretations are often as parsimonious or even more so. For example, shared method variance may be a viable alternative interpretation for the positive correlation. *Shared method variance* refers to similarity or identity in the procedure or format of assessment (e.g., both measures are self-report or both are paper-and-pencil measures). For example, if two measures are completed by the same informant, their common method variance might contribute to the magnitude of the correlation. The correlations reflect the shared method variance, rather than, or in addition to, the shared construct variance.

The correlation between two measures that is taken to be evidence for validity also could be due to shared items in the measures. For example, studies occasionally evaluate the interrelations (correlations) among measures of depression, self-esteem, hopelessness, and negative cognitive processes. Measures of these constructs often overlap slightly, so that items in one particular scale have items that very closely resemble items in another scale (e.g., how one views or feels about oneself). Item overlap is not an inherent problem because conceptualizations of the two domains may entail common features (i.e., share trait variance). However, in an effort of scale validation, it may provide little comfort to note that the two domains (e.g., hopelessness and negative cognitive processes) are moderately to highly correlated "as predicted." When there is item overlap, the correlation combines reliability (alternative form or test–retest) with validity (concurrent and predictive).

Low correlations between two measures that are predicted to correlate moderately to highly warrant comment. In this case, the magnitude of the correlation is much lower than the investigator expected and is considered not to support the validity of the measure that is being evaluated. Three considerations warrant mention here and perhaps analysis in the investigation. First, the absolute magnitude of the correlation between two measures is limited by the reliability of the individual measures. The low correlation may then underestimate the extent to which the reliable portion of variance within each measure is correlated. Second, it is possible that the sample and its scores on one or both of the measures represent a restricted range. The correlation between two measures, even if high in the population across the full range of scores, may be low in light of the restricted range. Third, it is quite possible that key moderators within the sample account for the low correlation. For example, it is possible that the correlation is high (and positive) for one subsample (men) and low (and negative) for another subsample. When these samples are treated as a single group, the correlation may be low or zero, and nonsignificant. A difficulty is scavenging for these moderators in a post hoc fashion. However, in an attempt to understand the relations between measures, it is useful to compute within-subsample correlations on key moderators such as gender, ethnicity, and patient status (patient vs. community) where relations between the measures are very likely to differ. Of course, the study is vastly superior when an influence moderating the relations between measures is theoretically derived and predicted.

Discriminant Validity

Discriminant validity refers to the extent to which measures not expected to correlate or not to correlate very highly in fact show this expected pattern.[4] By itself, discriminant validity may resemble support for the null hypothesis; namely, no relation exists between two measures. Yet, the meaning of discriminant validity derives from the context in which it is demonstrated. That context is a set of measures, some of which are predicted to relate to the measure of interest (convergent validity) and others predicted to relate less well or not at all (discriminant validity). Convergent and discriminant validity operate together insofar as they contribute to construct validity (i.e., identifying what the construct is and is not like). A difficulty in many validational studies is attention only to convergent validity.

With discriminant validity, one looks for little or no relation between two or more measures. As with convergent validity, discriminant validity also raises interpretive issues. Two measures may have no conceptual connection or relation but still show significant and moderate-to-high correlations because of common method variance. If method variance plays a significant role, as is often the case when different informants are used, then all the measures completed by the same informant may show a similar level of correlation. In such a case, discriminant validity may be difficult to demonstrate.

Discriminant validity raises another issue for test validation. There is an amazing array of measures and constructs in the field of psychology, with new measures being developed regularly. The question in relation to discriminant validity is whether the measures are all different and whether they reflect different or sufficiently different constructs. The problem has been recognized for some time. For example, in validating a new test, Campbell (1960) recommended that the measure be correlated with measures of social desirability, intelligence, and acquiescence and other response sets. A minimal criterion for discriminant validation, Campbell proposed, is to show that the new measure cannot be accounted for by these other constructs. These other constructs, and no doubt additional ones, have been shown to have a

---

[4] Discriminant validity is used here in the sense originally proposed by Campbell and Fiske (1959). Occasionally, discriminant validity is used to refer to cases in which a measure can differentiate groups (e.g., Trull, 1991). The different meanings of the term and the derivation of related terms such as *discriminate, discriminative,* and *divergent validity* reflect a well-known paradox of the field, namely, that there is little reliability in discussing validity.

pervasive influence across several domains, and their own construct validity is relatively well developed. It is likely that they contribute to and occasionally account for other new measures.

Few studies have adhered to Campbell's (1960) advice, albeit the recommendations remain quite sound. For example, a recent study validating the Sense of Coherence Scale showed that performance on the scale has a low and nonsignificant correlation with intelligence ($r = .11$) but a small-to-moderate correlation ($r = .39$) with social desirability (Frenz, Carey, & Jorgensen, 1993). Of course, convergent and discriminant validity depend on multiple sources of influence rather than two correlations. Even so, as the authors noted, the correlation with social desirability requires explanation and conceptual elaboration.

General Comments

Convergent and discriminant validity raise fundamental issues about validation efforts because they require specification of the nature of the construct and then tests to identify the connections and boundary conditions of the measure. Also, the two types of validity draw attention to patterns of correlations among measures in a given study and the basis of correlation. The importance of separating or examining the influence of shared method factors that contribute to this correlation pattern motivated the recommendation to use multitrait and multimethod matrices in test validation (Campbell & Fiske, 1959). In general, demonstration of convergent and discriminant validity and evaluation of the impact of common method variance are critical to test validation. In the design and reporting of assessment studies, interpretation of the results very much depends on what can and cannot be said about the measure. The interpretation is greatly facilitated by providing evidence for both convergent and discriminant validity.

Constructs and Measures

Assessment studies often vary in the extent to which they reflect interests in constructs or underlying characteristics of the measures and in specific assessment devices themselves. These emphases are a matter of degree, but worth distinguishing to convey the point and its implications for preparing and interpreting research reports. Usually researchers develop measures because they are interested in constructs (e.g., temperament, depression, or neuroticism). Even in cases in which measures are guided by immediately practical goals (e.g., screening and selection), there is an interest in the bases for the scale (i.e., the underlying constructs).

The focus on constructs is important to underscore. The emphasis on constructs draws attention to the need for multiple measures. Obviously, a self-report measure is important, but it is an incomplete sample of the construct. Perhaps less obvious is the fact that direct samples of behavior also are limited, because they are only a sample of the conditions as specified at a given time under the circumstances of the observations. Sometimes investigators do not wish to go beyond the measure or at least too much beyond the measure in relation to the inferences they draw. Self-report data on surveys (e.g., what people say about a social issue or political candidate or what therapists say they do in therapy with their clients) and direct observations of behavior (e.g., how parents interact with their children at home) may be the assessment focus. Even in these instances, the measure is used to represent broader domains (e.g., what people feel, think, or do) beyond the confines of the operational measure. In other words, the measure may still be a way of talking about a broader set for referents that is of interest besides test performance. Anytime an investigator wishes to say more than the specific items or contents of the measure, constructs are of interest.

Any one measure, however well established, samples only a part or facet of the construct of interest. This is the inherent nature of operational definitions. In preparing reports of assessment studies, the investigator ought to convey what constructs are underlying the study and present different assessment devices in relation to the sampling from the construct domain. A weakness of many studies is using a single measure to assess a central construct of interest. A single measure can sample a construct, but a demonstration is much better when multiple measures represent that construct.

The focus on constructs draws attention to the interrelation among different constructs. Although a researcher may wish to validate a given measure and evaluate his or her operational definition, her or she also wants to progress up the ladder of abstraction to understand how the construct behaves and how the construct relates to other constructs. These are not separate lines of work, because an excellent strategy for validating a measure is to examine the measure in the context of other measures of that construct and measures of other constructs. For example, a recent study examined the construct psychological stress by administering 27 self-report measures and identifying a model to account for the measures using latent-variable analyses (Scheier & Newcomb, 1993). Nine latent factors were identified through confirmatory factor analyses (e.g., emotional distress, self-derogation, purpose in life, hostility, anxiety, and others). Of special interest is that the study permitted evaluation of several scales to each other as well as to the latent variable and the relation of latent variables (as second-order factors) to each other. This level of analysis provides important information about individual measures and contributes to the understanding of different but related domains of functioning and their interrelations to each other. At this higher level of abstraction, one can move from assessment to understanding the underpinnings of the constructs or domains of functioning (e.g., in development), their course, and the many ways in which they may be manifested.

Although all assessment studies might be said to reflect interest in constructs, clearly many focus more concretely at a lower level of abstraction. This is evident in studies that focus on the development of a particular scale, as reflected in evaluation of psychometric properties on which the scale depends. Efforts to elaborate basic features of the scale are critically important. Later in the development of the scale, one looks to a measure to serve new purposes or to sort individuals in ways that elaborate one's understanding of the construct. It is still risky to rely on a single measure of a construct no matter how well that validational research has been. Thus, studies using an IQ test or an objective personality inventory still raise issues if only one test is used, as highlighted later. For a given purpose (e.g., prediction), a particular measure may do very well. Ultimately, the goal is understanding in addition to prediction, and that requires greater concern with the construct and multiple measures that capture different facets of the construct.

In designing studies that emphasize particular measures, it is important to draw on theory and analyses of the underlying constructs as much as possible. From the standpoint of psychology, interest usually extends to the theory, construct, and clinical phenomena that the measure was designed to elaborate. Also, research that is based on a single assessment device occasionally is met with ambivalence. The ambivalence often results from the view that a study of one measure is technical in nature, crassly empirical, and theoretically bereft. The focus on a single measure without addressing the broader construct in different ways is a basis for these concerns. And, at the level of interpretation of the results, the reliance on one measure, however well standardized, may be viewed as a limitation.

At the same time, there is a widespread recognition that the field needs valid, standardized, and well-understood measures. Programs of research that do the necessary groundwork are often relied on when selecting a measure or when justifying its use in a study or grant proposal. When preparing articles on assessment devices, it is important to be sensitive to the implications that the study has for understanding human functioning in general, in addition to understanding how this particular measure operates. Relating the results of assessment studies to conceptual issues, rather than merely characterizing a single measure, can greatly enhance a manuscript and the reactions of consumers regarding the contribution.

Sample Characteristics and Assessment Results

Sampling can refer to many issues related to the participants, conditions of the investigation, and other domains to which one wishes to generalize (Brunswik, 1955). In assessment studies, a special feature of sampling warrants comment because of its relevance for evaluating research reports. The issue pertains to the structure and meaning of a measure with respect to different population characteristics. Occasionally, the ways in which studies are framed suggest that the characteristics of a scale inhere in the measure in some fixed way, free from the sample to which the scale was applied.

It is quite possible that the measure and indeed the constructs that the measure assesses behave differently across samples, as a function of gender, age, race, and ethnicity (e.g., McDermott, 1995). Such differences have important implications for test standardization and interpretation beyond the scope of the present discussion. Sensitivity to such potential differences and evaluation of such differences in the design of research can be very helpful. Ideally, an assessment study will permit analyses of the influence of one or more sample characteristics that plausibly could influence conclusions about the measure. For example, in a recent evaluation of scales to study motives for drinking alcohol, analyses showed that the factor model that fit the measure was invariant across male and female. Black and White, and older and younger adolescents (Cooper, 1994). The inclusion of multiple samples and a sufficient sample size to permit these subsample analyses ($N > 2,000$) enabled the research to make a significant contribution to assessment and scale structure. From the study, it was learned that the structure of the measure is robust across samples. Apart from scale characteristics, the generality of the model may have important implications for adolescent functioning in general.

A more common research approach is to sift through separate studies, each representing an attempt to replicate the factor structure with a slightly different population (e.g., Derogatis & Cleary, 1977; Schwarzwald, Weisenberg, & Solomon, 1991; Takeuchi, Kuo, Kim, & Leaf, 1989). Such research often shows that the central features of the measure differ with different samples. One difficulty lies in bringing order to these sample difference, in large part because they are not tied to theoretical hypotheses about characteristics of the samples that might explain the differences (Betancourt & Lopez, 1993). Also, from the standpoint of subsequent research, guidelines for using the measure are difficult to cull from the available studies.

Evaluating assessment devices among samples with different characteristics is important. However, one critically important step before evaluating these assessment devices is the replication of the scale results with separate samples from the same population. Some studies include large standardization samples and hence provide within-sample replication opportunities. More common among assessment studies is the evaluation of the measure with smaller samples. It is important to replicate findings on the structure of the scale or the model used to account for the factors within the scale. Even when separate samples are drawn from the same population, the findings regarding scale characteristics may not be replicated (e.g., Parker, Endler, & Bagby, 1993). Evaluation of multiple samples is very important in guiding use of the measure in subsequent research.

Sampling extends beyond issues related to participants. Sampling refers to drawing from the range of characteristics or domains to which one wishes to generalize (Brunswik, 1955). In relation to assessment studies, the use of multiple measures to assess a construct is based in part on sampling considerations. Conclusions should not be limited to a single operation (measure or type of measure). There may be irrelevancies associated with any single measure that influences the obtained relation between the constructs of interest. A study is strengthened to the extent that is samples across different assessment methods and different sources of information.

The familiar finding of using multiple measures of a given construct is that the measures often reflect different conclusions. For example, two measures of family functioning may show that they are not very highly related to each other. One measure may show great differences between families selected because of a criterion variable, whereas the other measure may not. These results are often viewed as mixed or as partial support for an original hypothesis. The investigator usually has to prepare a good reason why different measures of seemingly similar constructs show different results. However, the study is stronger for the demonstration when compared with a study that did not operationalize family functioning in these different ways. An issue for the field is to make much further conceptual progress in handling different findings that follow from different methods of assessment.

CONCLUSION

Preparing reports for publication involves describing, explaining, and contextualizing the study. The descriptive feature of the study is essential for the usual goals such as facilitating interpretation and permitting replication of the procedures, at least in principle. However, the tasks of explaining the study by providing a well thought-out statement of the decisions and contextualizing the study by placing the demonstration into the field more generally are the challenges. The value of a study is derived from the author's ability to make the case that the study contributes to the literature, addresses an important issue, and generates important answers and questions.

In this article, I discussed some of the ways in which authors can make such a case when preparing a research article.[5] Generally, the task is to convey the theme or story line, bringing all of the sections of the study in line with that, and keeping irrelevancies to a minimum. In the context of assess-

---

[5] In closing, it is important to convey that recommendations in this article regarding manuscript preparation and journal publication derive from my experiences as an editor rather than as an author. As an author, the picture has not always been as pretty. For example, over the course of my career, such as it is, two journals went out of business within a few months after a manuscript of mine was accepted for publication and fowarded to production. Although this could be coincidence in the career of one author, in this case the result was significant ($p < .05$), using a chi round test and correcting for continuity, sphericity, and leptokurtosis.

ment studies, three issues were highlighted because they affect many studies and their interpretation. These include interpretation of correlations between measures, the relation of constructs and measures, and sampling. Each issue was discussed from the standpoint of ways of strengthening research. Test validation, development of assessment methods from constructs, and sampling raise multiple substantive and methodological issues that affect both the planning and reporting of research. Many of the articles that follow elaborate on the issues.

REFERENCES

American Psychological Association. (1994). *Publication manual of the American Psychological Association* (4th ed.). Washington, DC: Author.

Betancourt, H., & Lopez, S. R. (1993). The study of culture, ethnicity, and race in American psychology. *American Psychologist, 48,* 629–637.

Brunswik, E. (1955). Representative design and probabilistic theory in a functional psychology. *Psychological Review, 62,* 193–217.

Campbell, D. T. (1960). Recommendations for APA test standards regarding construct, trait, and discriminant validity. *American Psychologist, 15,* 546–553.

Campbell, D. T., & Fiske, D. (1959). Convergent and discriminant validation by the multitrait–multimethod matrix. *Psychological Bulletin, 56,* 81–105.

Cooper, M. L. (1994). Motivations for alcohol use among adolescents: Development and validation of a four-factor model. *Psychological Assessment, 6,* 117–128.

Derogatis, L. R., & Cleary, P. A. (1977). Factorial invariance across gender for the primary symptom dimensions of the SCL-90. *British Journal of Social and Clinical Psychology, 16,* 347–356.

Frenz, A. W., Carey, M. P., & Jorgensen, R. S. (1993). Psychometric evaluation of Antonovsky's Sense of Coherence Scale. *Psychological Assessment, 5,* 145–153.

Henry, B., Moffitt, T. E., Caspi, A., Langley, J., & Silva, P. A. (1994). On the "remembrance of things past": A longitudinal evaluation of the retrospective method. *Psychological Assessment, 6,* 92–101.

Kazdin, A. E. (1992). *Research design in clinical psychology* (2nd ed). Needham Heights, MA: Allyn & Bacon.

Kline, P. (1986). *A handbook of test construction: Introduction to psychometric design.* London: Methuen.

Maher, B. A. (1978). A reader's, writer's, and reviewer's guide to assessing research reports in clinical psychology. *Journal of Consulting and Clinical Psychology, 46,* 835–838.

McDermott, P. A. (1995). Sex, race, class, and other demographics as explanations for children's ability and adjustment: A national appraisal. *Journal of School Psychology, 33,* 75–91.

Parker, J. D. A., Endler, N. S., & Bagby, R. M. (1993). If it changes, it might be unstable: Examining the factor structure of the Ways of Coping Questionnaire. *Psychological Assessment, 5*, 361–368.

Robins, L. N., Schoenberg, S. P., Homes, S. J., Ratcliff, K. S., Benham, A., & Works, J. (1985). Early home environment and retrospective recall. *American Journal of Orthopsychiatry, 55*, 27–41.

Scheier, L. M., & Newcomb, M. D. (1993). Multiple dimensions of affective and cognitive disturbance: Latent-variable models in a community sample. *Psychological Assessment, 5*, 230–234.

Schwarzwald, J., Weisenberg, M., & Solomon, Z. (1991). Factor invariance of SCL-90-R: The case of combat stress reaction. *Psychological Assessment, 3*, 385–390.

Shapiro, D. A., & Shapiro, D. (1983). Comparative therapy outcome research: Methodological implications of meta-analysis. *Journal of Consulting and Clinical Psychology, 51*, 42–53.

Takeuchi, D. T., Kuo, H., Kim, K., & Leaf, P. J. (1989). Psychiatric symptom dimensions among Asian Americans and native Hawaiians: An analysis of the symptom checklist. *Journal of Community Psychology, 17*, 319–329.

Trull, T. J. (1991). Discriminant validity of the MMPI–Borderline Personality Disorder scale. *Psychological Assessment, 3*, 232–238.

Wainer, H., & Braun, H. I. (Eds.). (1988). *Test validity*. Hilldale, NJ: Erlbaum.

Wampold, B. E., Davis, B., & Good, R. H., III. (1990). Hypothesis validity of clinical research. *Journal of Consulting and Clinical Psychology, 58*, 360–367.

Weiss, B., & Weisz, J. R. (1990). The impact of methodological factors on child psychotherapy outcome research: A meta-analysis for researchers. *Journal of Abnormal Child Psychology, 18*, 639–670.

38

WRITING A REVIEW ARTICLE FOR *PSYCHOLOGICAL BULLETIN*

DARYL J. BEM

You have surveyed an experimental literature and arrived at conclusions you believe are worth sharing with the wider psychological community. Now it is time to write. To publish. To tell the world what you have learned. The purpose of this article is to enhance the chances that the editors of *Psychological Bulletin* will let you do so.

According to the recent revision of the *Publication Manual of the American Psychological Association*,

> **review articles,** including meta-analyses, are critical evaluations of material that has already been published. By organizing, integrating, and evaluating previously published material, the author of a review article considers the progress of current research toward clarifying a problem. In a sense, a review article is tutorial in that the author
>
> - defines and clarifies the problem;
> - summarizes previous investigations in order to inform the reader of the state of current research;

- identifies relations, contradictions, gaps, and inconsistencies in the literature; and
- suggests the next step or steps in solving the problem. (American Psychological Association [APA], 1994, p. 5)

The inside front cover of *Bulletin* further notes that reviews "may set forth major developments within a particular research area or provide a bridge between related specialized fields within psychology or between psychology and related fields."

As these statements imply, *Bulletin* review articles are directed to a much wider audience than articles appearing in more specialized journals. Indeed, the current editor asserted in his first editorial that "*every* psychologist should read *Psychological Bulletin* . . . [b]ecause there is no better way to stay up-to-date with the field of psychology as a whole. . . . The *Bulletin* [provides] the best single vehicle for a continuing education in psychology" (Sternberg, 1991, p. 3). Moreover, the journal is frequently consulted by journalists, attorneys, congressional aids, and other nonpsychologists.

This means that your review should be accessible to students in Psychology 101, your colleagues in the Art History department, and your grandmother. No matter how technical or abstruse a review is in its particulars, intelligent nonpsychologists with no expertise in statistics, meta-analysis, or experimental design should be able to comprehend the broad outlines of your topic, to understand what you think the accumulated evidence demonstrates, and, above all, to appreciate why someone — anyone — should give a damn.

Thus, many of the writing techniques described in this article are designed to make your review article comprehensible to the widest possible audience. They are also designed to remain invisible or transparent to readers, thereby infusing your prose with a "subliminal pedagogy." Good writing is good teaching.

BEFORE WRITING

Let me begin on a pessimistic note: The chances that your review will be accepted for publication in *Psychological Bulletin* are only about 1 in 5. According to the current editor, "the #1 source of immediate-rejection letters is narrowly conceived topics" (R. J. Sternberg, personal communication, August 2, 1994). Translation: Nobody will give a damn. So the first question to ask about your intended review is whether it is likely to be interesting to a general audience of psychologists. If not, can it at least be made interesting — perhaps by extending its reach or setting it in a broader context? If your answer is that you think so, then you have already improved your chances. Read on.

The second obstacle to publication arises from the nature of the genre itself: Authors of literature reviews are at risk for producing mind-numbing lists of citations and findings that resemble a phone book—impressive cast, lots of numbers, but not much plot. So the second question to ask about your intended review is whether it has a clear take-home message. Again, editor Sternberg (1991):

> Literature reviews are often frustrating because they offer neither a point of view nor a take-home message. One is left with a somewhat undigested scattering of facts but little with which to put them together. I encourage authors to take a point of view based on theory and to offer readers a take-home message that integrates the review. . . . [T]o be lively and maintain reader interest, they need to make a point, not simply to summarize all the points everyone else has made. (p. 3)

As an additional antidote to dullness, Sternberg (1991) also encouraged authors to *"take risks in choosing topics, writing articles, and making submissions"* and not to be deterred because "they represent too much of a departure from current conventions, whether in conceptualization or methodology." In return, he pledged to "make every effort to ensure that top-quality work is rewarded rather than punished" (p. 3). So if an off-beat topic genuinely excites you, try submitting a review of it. (As a consumer service to readers, I have pretested the editor's sincerity by submitting an article on extrasensory perception [ESP]. He published it [Bem & Honorton, 1994].)

WRITING

The primary criteria for good scientific writing are accuracy and clarity. If your manuscript is written with style and flair, great. But this is a subsidiary virtue. First strive for accuracy and clarity.

Achieving Clarity

The first step toward clarity is to write simply and directly. A review tells a straightforward tale of a circumscribed question in want of an answer. It is not a novel with subplots and flashbacks but a short story with a single, linear narrative line. Let this line stand out in bold relief. Clear any underbrush that entangles your prose by obeying Strunk and White's (1979) famous dictum, "omit needless words," and by extending the dictum to needless concepts, topics, anecdotes, asides, and footnotes. If a point seems tangential to your basic argument, remove it. If you can't bring yourself to do this, put it in a footnote. Then, when you revise your manuscript, remove the footnote. In short, don't make your voice struggle to be heard above the ambient noise of cluttered writing. Let your 90th percentile verbal aptitude nourish your prose, not glut it. Write simply and directly.

A corollary of this directive is not to confuse *Bulletin* reviews with the literature reviews found in doctoral dissertations (even though some *Bulletin* reviews derive therefrom). Typically, these *are* novels with subplots and flashbacks, designed to assure dissertation committees that the candidate has covered any and all literatures conceivably related to the topic. If a dissertation proposes that love relationships in human adults recapitulate infant attachment styles, the biopsychologist on the committee will want to see a review of imprinting and its mating consequences in zebra finches. *Bulletin* readers will not. Omit needless literatures.

Organization

The second step toward clarity is to organize the manuscript so that it tells a coherent story. A review is more difficult to organize than an empirical report (for which there is a standardized APA format). Unfortunately, the guidance given by the *Publication Manual* (APA, 1994) is not very helpful: "The components of review articles, unlike the sections of reports of empirical studies, are arranged by relationship rather than by chronology" (p. 5). The vague generality of this guidance reflects that a coherent review emerges only from a coherent conceptual structuring of the topic itself. For most reviews, this requires a guiding theory, a set of competing models, or a point of view about the phenomenon under discussion.

An example of a review organized around competing models is provided by a *Bulletin* article on the emergence of sex differences in depression during adolescence (Nolen-Hoeksema & Girgus, 1994). The relevant literature consists primarily of studies examining specific variables correlated with depression, a hodgepodge of findings that less creative authors might have been tempted to organize chronologically or alphabetically. These authors, however, organized the studies in terms of whether they supported one of three developmental models: (a) The causes of depression are the same for the two sexes, but these causes become more prevalent in girls than in boys in early adolescence; (b) the causes of depression are different for the two sexes, and the causes of girls' depression become more prevalent in early adolescence; or (c) girls are more likely than boys to carry risk factors for depression before early adolescence, but these lead to depression only in the face of challenges that increase in prevalence in early adolescence. With this guiding structure, the findings fell into a recognizable pattern supporting the last model.

An example of a review organized around a point of view is provided by any of several *Bulletin* articles designed to convince readers to accept—or at least to seriously entertain—a novel or controversial conclusion. In these, tactics of persuasive communication structure the review. First, the commonly accepted conclusion is stated along with the putative reasons for its current acceptance. Next, the supporting and nonsupporting data for the author's view are presented in order of descending probative weight, and counterarguments to that view are acknowledged and rebutted at the point where they would be likely to occur spontaneously to neutral or skeptical readers. Finally, the reasons for favoring the author's conclusion are summarized.

This organizational strategy was the basis for the *Bulletin* article in which Charles Honorton and I sought to persuade readers to take seriously new experimental evidence for ESP (Bem & Honorton, 1994). Similar organization characterizes a *Bulletin* article whose authors argued that left-handers die at earlier ages than do right-handers (Coren & Halpern, 1991), a subsequent rebuttal to that conclusion (Harris, 1993), and an article whose author argued that the cross-cultural evidence does not support the commonly held view that there is universal recognition of emotion from facial expression (Russell, 1994).

There are many other organizing strategies, and Sternberg's (1991) editorial emphasizes that there is no one right way to write a review. As noted earlier, a coherent review emerges from a coherent conceptual structuring of the domain being reviewed. And if you remember to organize your review "by relationship rather than by chronology," then, by Jove, I think you've got it.

Metacomments

It is often helpful to give readers of a review article an early overview of its structure and content. But beyond that, you should avoid making "metacomments" about the writing. Expository prose fails its mission if it diverts the reader's attention to itself and away from the topic; the process of writing should be invisible to the reader. In particular, the prose itself should direct the flow of the narrative without requiring you to play tour guide. Don't say, "now that the three theories of emotion have been discussed, we can turn to the empirical work on each of them. We begin with the psychoanalytic account of affect . . . ." Instead, move directly from your discussion of the theories into the review of the evidence with a simple transition sentence such as, "each of these three theories has been tested empirically. Thus, the psychoanalytic account of affect has received support in studies that . . . ." Any other guideposts needed can be supplied by using informative headings and by following the advice on repetition and parallel construction given in the next section.

If you feel the need to make metacomments to keep the reader on the narrative path, then your plot line is probably already too cluttered or pretzel shaped, the writing insufficiently linear. Metacomments only oppress the prose further. Instead, copy edit. Omit needless words—don't add them.

Repetition and Parallel Construction

Inexperienced writers often substitute synonyms for recurring words and vary their sentence structure in the mistaken belief that this is more creative and interesting. Instead of using repetition and parallel construction, as in "women may be more expressive than men in the domain of positive emotion, but they are not more expressive in the domain of negative emotion," they attempt to be more creative: "Women may be more expressive than men in the domain of positive emotion, but it is not the case that they are more prone than the opposite sex to display the less cheerful affects."

Such creativity is hardly more interesting, but it is certainly more confusing. In scientific communication, it can be deadly. When an author uses different words to refer to the same concept in a technical article—where accuracy is paramount—readers justifiably wonder if different meanings are implied. The example in the preceding paragraph is not disastrous, and most readers will be unaware that their understanding flickered momentarily when the prose hit a bump. But consider the cognitive burden carried by readers who must hack through this "creative" jungle:

> The low-dissonance participants were paid a large sum of money while not being given a free choice of whether or not to participate, whereas the individuals we randomly assigned to the small-incentive treatment (the high-dissonance condition) were offered the opportunity to refuse.

This (fictitious) writer should have written.

> Low-dissonance individuals were paid a large sum of money and were required to participate; high-dissonance individuals were paid a small sum of money and were not required to participate.

The wording and grammatical structure of the two clauses are held rigidly parallel; only the variables vary. Repetition and parallel construction are among the most effective servants of clarity. Don't be creative; be clear.

Repetition and parallel construction also serve clarity at a larger level of organization. By providing the reader with distinctive guideposts to the structure of the prose, they can diminish or eliminate the need for meta-comments on the writing. For example, here are some guidepost sentences from earlier in this section:

> The first step toward clarity is to write simply and directly. . . .
> The second step toward clarity is to organize the manuscript so that . . . .
> An example of a review organized around competing models is provided by . . . .
> An example of a review organized around a point of view is provided by . . . .

If I had substituted synonyms for the recurring words or varied the grammatical structure of these sentences, their guiding function would have been lost, the reader's sense of the section's organization blurred. (I try so hard to be helpful, and I bet you didn't even notice. That, of course, is the point.)

Terminology

The specialized terminology of a discipline is called jargon, and it serves a number of legitimate functions in scientific communication. A specialized term may be more general, more precise, or freer of surplus meaning that any natural language equivalent (e.g., the term *disposition* encompasses, and hence is more general than, beliefs, attitudes, moods, and personality attributes; *reinforcement* is more precise and freer of surplus meaning than *reward*). Also, the technical vocabulary often makes an important conceptual distinction not apprehended in the layperson's lexicon (e.g., genotype vs. phenotype).

But if a jargon term does not satisfy any of these criteria, opt for English. Much of our jargon has become second nature and serves only to muddy our prose. (As an editor, I once had to interrogate an author at length to learn that a prison program for "strengthening the executive functions of the ego" actually taught prisoners how to fill out job applications.) And unless the jargon term is extremely well known (e.g., reinforcement), it should be defined—explicitly, implicitly, or by context and example—the first time it is introduced.

For example, in our article on ESP, Honorton and I decided that we could not proceed beyond the opening paragraph until we had first explicitly defined and clarified the unfamiliar but central theoretical term:

> The term *psi* denotes anomalous processes of information or energy transfer, processes such as telepathy or other forms of extrasensory perception that are currently unexplained in terms of known physical or biological mechanisms. The term is purely descriptive: It neither implies that such anomalous phenomena are paranormal nor connotes anything about their underlying mechanisms. (Bem & Honorton, 1994, p. 4)

Here is how one might define a technical term (ego control) and identify its conceptual status (a personality variable) more implicitly:

> The need to delay gratification, control impulses, and modulate emotional expression is the earliest and most ubiquitous demand that society places on the developing child. Because success at so many of life's tasks depends critically on the individual's mastery of such ego control, evidence for life-course continuities in this central personality domain should be readily obtained.

And finally, here is a (made-up) example in which the technical terms are defined only by the context. Note, however, that the technical abbreviation, MAO, is still identified explicitly when it is first introduced.

> In the continuing search for the biological correlates of psychiatric disorder, blood platelets are now a prime target of investigation. In particular, reduced monoamine oxidase (MAO) activity in the platelets is sometimes correlated with paranoid symptomatology, auditory hallucinations

or delusions in chronic schizophrenia, and a tendency toward psycho-pathology in normal men. Unfortunately, these observations have not always replicated, casting doubt on the hypothesis that MAO activity is, in fact, a biological marker in psychiatric disorder. Even the general utility of the platelet model as a key to central nervous system abnormalities in schizophrenia remains controversial. The present review attempts to clarify the relation of MAO activity to symptomatology in chronic schizophrenia.

This kind of writing would not appear in *Newsweek*, and yet it is still accessible to a nonspecialist who may know nothing about blood platelets, MAO activity, or biological markers. The structure of the writing itself adequately defines the relationships among these things and provides enough context to make the basic rationale behind the review comprehensible. At the same time, this introduction is neither condescending nor boring to the technically sophisticated reader. The pedagogy that makes it accessible to the nonspecialist is not only invisible to the specialist but also enhances the clarity of the review for both readers.

Ending

Most *Bulletin* reviews end with a consideration of questions that remain unanswered along with suggestions for the kinds of research that would help to answer them. In fact, suggesting further research is probably the most common way of ending a review.

Common, but dull. Why not strive to end your review with broad general conclusions — or a final grand restatement of your take-home message — rather than precious details of interest only to specialists? Thus, the statement, "further research is needed before it is clear whether the androgyny scale should be scored as a single, continuous dimension or partitioned into a four-way typology," might be appropriate earlier in the review but please, not your final farewell. Only the French essayist, Michel de Montaigne (1580/1943), was clever enough to end a review with a refreshing statement about further research: "Because [the study of motivation] is a high and hazardous undertaking, I wish fewer people would meddle with it" (p. 126).

You may wish to settle for less imperious pronouncements. But in any case, end with a bang, not a whimper.

Discussing Previous Work

Summarizing Studies

One of the tasks most frequently encountered in writing a *Bulletin* review is summarizing the methods and results of previous studies. The *Publication Manual* (APA, 1994) warns writers not to let the goal of brevity mislead them into writing a statement intelligible only to the specialist. One technique for describing an entire study succinctly without sacrificing clarity is to describe one variation of the procedure in chronological sequence, letting it convey an overview of the study at the same time. For example, here is one way of describing a complicated but classic experiment on cognitive dissonance theory (Festinger & Carlsmith, 1959):

> Sixty male undergraduates were randomly assigned to one of three conditions. In the $1 condition, the participant was first required to perform long repetitive laboratory tasks in an individual experimental session. He was then hired by the experimenter as an "assistant" and paid $1 to tell a waiting fellow student (a confederate) that the tasks were fun and interesting. In the $20 condition, each participant was hired for $20 to do the same thing. In the control condition, participants simply engaged in the tasks. After the experiment, each participant indicated on a questionnaire how much he had enjoyed the tasks. The results showed that $1 participants rated the tasks as significantly more enjoyable than did the $20 participants, who, in turn, did not differ from the control participants.

This kind of condensed writing looks easy. It is not, and you will have to rewrite such summaries repeatedly before they are both clear and succinct. The preceding paragraph was my eighth draft.

Citations

Reviews typically contain many more citations than other kinds of articles. The standard journal format permits you to cite authors in the text either by enclosing their last names and the year of publication in parentheses, as in (a) below, or by using their names in the sentence itself, as in (b).

> (a) "MAO activity in some patients with schizophrenia is actually higher than normal" (Tse & Tung, 1949).
> (b) "Tse and Tung (1949) reported that MAO activity in some patients with schizophrenia is actually higher than normal."

In general, you should use the form of (a), consigning your colleagues to parentheses. Your narrative should be about MAO activity in patients with schizophrenia, not about Tse and Tung. Occasionally, however, you might want to focus specifically on the authors or researchers: "Theophrastus (280 B.C.) implies that persons are consistent across situations, but Montaigne (1580) insists that they are not. Only Mischel (1968), Peterson (1968), and Vernon (1964), however, have actually surveyed the evidence in detail." The point is that you have a deliberate choice to make. Don't just intermix the two formats randomly, paying no attention to your narrative structure.

Ad Verbum Not Ad Hominem

If you take a dim view of previous research or earlier articles in the domain you reviewed, feel free to criticize and complain as strongly as you feel is commensurate with the incompetence you have uncovered. But criticize the work, not the investigators or authors. Ad hominem attacks offend editors and reviewers; moreover, the person you attack is likely to be asked to serve as one of the reviewers. Consequently, your opportunity to address—let alone, offend—readers will be nipped in the bud. I could launch into a sermonette on communitarian values in science, but I shall assume that this pragmatic warning is sufficient.

Formatting and Further Guidance

Your manuscript should conform to the prescribed format for articles published in APA journals. If it diverges markedly from that format, it may be returned for rewriting before being sent out for review. If you are unfamiliar with this format, you should consult recent issues of *Bulletin* and the new edition of the *Publication Manual* (APA, 1994). Even experienced writers should probably check this revision for recent changes in formatting style, new information on formatting with word processors, and instructions for submitting final versions of manuscripts on computer disk for electronic typesetting.

In addition to describing the mechanics of preparing a manuscript for APA journals, the *Publication Manual* (APA, 1994) also has a chapter on the expression of ideas, including writing style, grammar, and avoiding language bias. Sternberg (1993) has also written an article on how to write for psychological journals. Finally, this article has borrowed heavily from my earlier chapter on how to write an empirical journal article (Bem, 1987).

REWRITING

For many writers revising a manuscript is unmitigated agony. Even proofreading is painful. And so they don't. So relieved to get a draft done, they run it through the spell checker—some don't even do that—and then send it off to the journal, thinking that they can clean up the writing after the article has been accepted. Alas, that day rarely comes. Some may find solace in the belief that the manuscript probably would have been rejected even if it had been extensively revised and polished; after all, most APA journals, including *Bulletin*, accept only 15–20% of all manuscripts submitted. But from my own experience as an editor of an APA journal, I believe that the difference between the articles accepted and the top 15–20% of those rejected is frequently the difference between good and less good writing. Moral: Don't expect journal reviewers to discern your brilliance through the smog of polluted writing. Revise your manuscript. Polish it. Proofread it. Then submit it.

Rewriting is difficult for several reasons. First, it is difficult to edit your own writing. You will not notice ambiguities and explanatory gaps because *you* know what you meant to say; *you* understand the omitted steps. One strategy for overcoming this difficulty is to lay your manuscript aside for awhile and then return to it later when it has become less familiar. Sometimes it helps to read it aloud. But there is no substitute for practicing the art of taking the role of the nonspecialist reader, for learning to role-play grandma. As you read, ask yourself, "Have I been told yet what this concept means? Has the logic of this step been demonstrated? Would I know at this point what the dependent variables of this study were?" This is precisely the skill of the good lecturer in Psychology 101, the ability to anticipate the audience's level of understanding at each point in the presentation. Good writing is good teaching.

But because this is not easy, you should probably give a copy of a fairly polished manuscript to a friend or colleague for a critical reading. If you get critiques from several colleagues, you will have simulated the journal's review process. The best readers are those who have themselves had articles published in psychological journals but who are unfamiliar with the subject of your manuscript.

If your colleagues find something unclear, do not argue with them. They are right: By definition, the writing is unclear. Their suggestions for correcting the unclarities may be wrongheaded; but as unclarity detectors, readers are never wrong. Also resist the temptation simply to clarify their confusion verbally. Your colleagues don't want to offend you or appear stupid, so they simply mumble "oh yes, of course, of course" and apologize for not having read carefully enough. As a consequence, you are pacified, and your next readers, *Bulletin*'s reviewers, will stumble over the same problem. They will not apologize; they will reject.

Rewriting is difficult for a second reason: It requires a high degree of compulsiveness and attention to detail. The probability of writing a sentence perfectly the first time is vanishingly small, and good writers rewrite nearly every sentence of a manuscript in the course of polishing successive drafts. But even good writers differ from one another in their approach to the first draft. Some spend a long time carefully choosing each word and reshaping each sentence and paragraph as they go. Others pound out a rough draft quickly and then go back to extensive revision. Although I personally prefer the former method, I think it wastes time. Most writers should probably get the first draft done as quickly as possible without agonizing over stylistic niceties. Once it is done, however, compulsiveness and attention to detail become the required virtues.

Finally, rewriting is difficult because it usually means restructuring. Sometimes it is necessary to discard whole sections of a manuscript, add new ones, and then totally reorganize the manuscript just to iron out a bump in the logic of the argument. Don't get so attached to your first draft that you are unwilling to tear it apart and rebuild it. (This is why the strategy of crafting each sentence of a first draft wastes time. A beautiful turn of phrase that took me 20 minutes to shape gets trashed when I have to restructure the manuscript. Worse, I get so attached to the phrase that I resist restructuring until I can find a new home for it.) A badly constructed building cannot be salvaged by brightening up the wallpaper. A badly constructed manuscript cannot be salvaged by changing words, inverting sentences, and shuffling paragraphs.

Which brings me to the word processor. Its very virtuosity at making these cosmetic changes will tempt you to tinker endlessly, encouraging you in the illusion that you are restructuring right there in front of the monitor. Do not be fooled. You are not. A word processor—even one with a fancy outline mode—is not an adequate restructuring tool for most writers. Moreover, it can produce flawless, physically beautiful drafts of wretched writing, encouraging you in the illusion that they are finished manuscripts ready to be submitted. Do not be fooled. They are not. If you are blessed with an excellent memory (or a very large monitor) and are confident that you can get away with a purely electronic process of restructuring, do it. But don't be ashamed to print out a complete draft of your manuscript; spread it out on table or floor; take pencil, scissors, and scotch tape in hand; and then, all by your low-tech self, have at it.

If, after all this, your manuscript still seems interesting and you still believe your conclusions, submit it.

REWRITING AGAIN

Long ago and far away, a journal editor allegedly accepted a manuscript that required no revision. I believe the author was William James. In other words, if your review is provisionally accepted for publication "pending revisions in accord with the reviewers' comments," you should be deliriously happy. Publication is now virtually under your control. If your review is rejected, but you are invited to resubmit a revised version, you should still be happy—if not deliriously so—because you still have a reasonable shot at getting it published.

But this is the point at which many writers give up. As an anonymous reviewer of this article noted,

> in my experience as an associate editor, I thought a good deal of variance in predicting eventual publication came from this phase of the process. Authors are often discouraged by negative feedback and miss the essential positive fact that they have been asked to revise! They may never resubmit at all or may let an inordinate amount of time pass before they do (during which editors and reviewers become unavailable, lose the thread of the project, and so forth). An opposite problem is that some authors become defensive and combative, and refuse to make needed changes for no reason.

So don't give up yet. Feel free to complain to your colleagues or rail at your poodle because the stupid reviewers failed to read your manuscript correctly. But then turn to the task of revising your manuscript with a dispassionate, problem-solving approach. First, pay special attention to criticisms or suggestions made by more than one reviewer or highlighted by the editor in the cover letter. These *must* be addressed in your revision—even if not in exactly the way the editor or reviewers suggest.

Next, look carefully at each of the reviewers' misreadings. I argued earlier that whenever readers of a manuscript find something unclear, they are right; by definition, the writing is unclear. The problem is that readers themselves do not always recognize or identify the unclarities explicitly. Instead, they misunderstand what you have written and then make a criticism or offer a suggestion that makes no sense. In other words, you should also interpret reviewers' misreadings as signals that your writing is unclear.

Think of your manuscript as a pilot experiment in which the participants (reviewers) didn't understand the instructions you gave them. Analyze the reasons for their misunderstanding and then rewrite the problematic sections so that subsequent readers will not be similarly misled. Reviewers are almost always more knowledgeable about your topic, more experienced in writing manuscripts themselves, and more conscientious about reading your review than the average journal reader. If they didn't understand, neither will that average reader.

When you send in your revised manuscript, tell the editor in a cover letter how you have responded to each of the criticisms or suggestions made by the reviewers. If you have decided not to adopt a particular suggestion, state your reasons, perhaps pointing out how you remedied the problem in some alternative way.

Here are three fictitious examples of cover-letter responses that also illustrate ways of responding to certain kinds of criticisms and suggestions within the revision itself.

1.   *Wrong:* "I have left the section on the animal studies unchanged. If Reviewers A and C can't even agree on whether the animal studies are relevant, I must be doing something right."

Right: "You will recall that Reviewer A thought that the animal studies should be described more fully, whereas Reviewer C thought they should be omitted. A biopsychologist in my department agreed with Reviewer C that the animal studies are not really valid analogs of the human studies. So I have dropped them from the text but cited Snarkle's review of them in an explanatory footnote on page 26."

2.   *Wrong:* "Reviewer A is obviously Melanie Grimes, who has never liked me or my work. If she really thinks that behaviorist principles solve all the problems of obsessive–compulsive disorders, then let her write her own review. Mine is about the cognitive processes involved."

Right: "As the critical remarks by Reviewer A indicate, this is a contentious area, with different theorists staking out strong positions. Apparently I did not make it clear that my review was intended only to cover the cognitive processes involved in obsessive – compulsive disorders and not to engage the debate between cognitive and behavioral approaches. To clarify this, I have now included the word 'cognitive' in both the title and abstract, taken note of the debate in my introduction, and stated explicitly that the review does not undertake a comparative review of the two approaches. I hope this satisfactory."

3. *Right:* "You will recall that two of the reviewers questioned the validity of the analysis of variance, with Reviewer B suggesting that I use multiple regression instead. I agree with their reservations regarding the ANOVA but believe that a multiple regression analysis is equally problematic because it makes the same assumptions about the underlying distributions. So I have retained the ANOVA, but summarized the results of a nonparametric analysis, which yields the same conclusions. If you think it preferable, I could simply substitute this nonparametric analysis for the original ANOVA, although it will be less familiar to *Bulletin* readers."

Above all, remember that the editor is your ally in trying to shape a manuscript that will be a credit to both you and the journal. So cooperate in the effort to turn your sow's ear into a vinyl purse. Be civil and make nice. You may not live longer, but you will publish more.

REFERENCES

American Psychological Association. (1994). *Publication manual of the American Psychological Association* (4th ed.). Washington, DC: Author.

Bem, D. J. (1987). Writing the empirical journal article. In M. P. Zanna & J. M. Darley (Eds.), *The compleat academic: A practical guide for the beginning social scientist* (pp. 171–120). New York: Random House.

Bem, D. J., & Honorton, C. (1994). Does psi exist? Replicable evidence for an anomalous process of information transfer. *Psychological Bulletin, 115,* 4–18.

Coren, S., & Halpern, D. F. (1991). Left-handedness: A marker for decreased survival fitness. *Psychological Bulletin, 109,* 90–106.

de Montaigne, M. (1943). Of the inconsistency of our actions. In D. M. Frame (Trans.), *Selected essays: Translated and with introduction and notes by Donald M. Frame* (pp. 119–126). Roslyn, NY: Walter J. Black. (Original work published 1580)

Festinger, L., & Carlsmith, J. M. (1959). Cognitive consequences of forced compliance. *Journal of Abnormal and Social Psychology, 58,* 203–210.

Harris, L. J. (1993). Do left-handers die sooner than right-handers? Commentary on Coren and Halpern's (1991) "Left-handedness: A marker for decreased survival fitness." *Psychological Bulletin, 114,* 203–234.

Nolen-Hoeksema, S., & Girgus, J. S. (1994). The emergence of gender differences in depression during adolescence. *Psychological Bulletin, 115*, 424–443.

Russell, J. A. (1994). Is there universal recognition of emotion from facial expression? A review of the cross-cultural studies. *Psychological Bulletin, 115*, 102–141.

Sternberg, R. J. (1991). Editorial. *Psychological Bulletin, 109*, 3–4.

Sternberg, R. J. (1993). How to win acceptance by psychology journals: Twenty-one tips for better writing. In R. J. Sternberg (Ed.), *The psychologist's companion* (3rd ed., pp. 174–180). New York: Cambridge University Press.

Strunk, W., & White, E. B. (1979). *The elements of style* (3rd ed.). New York: Macmillan.

IX

PERSPECTIVES ON METHODOLOGY

This book has covered several topics pertaining to the design, execution, and evaluation of research. The readings focused on key practices central to research. In the process of presenting specific practices, some of the more general lessons that methodology teaches were not explicitly made. More general points can be identified that emerge from the readings as a whole, and these points are as significant as a guide to research as are the specific practices from which they are derived. In closing, in chapter 39 I address some of the more general lessons of methodology and their implications for conducting research.

39

METHODOLOGY: GENERAL LESSONS TO GUIDE RESEARCH

ALAN E. KAZDIN

At the outset of one's career, it is critical to learn the basics of research and to become adept in their application. The difficulty is that becoming good at research can mean adherence to a narrow range of practices, paradigms, and procedures. In contemporary psychology (sciences more generally), the dominant paradigm consists of investigations in which groups are compared and the data are evaluated quantitatively, usually with statistical significance testing. Because this is the dominant paradigm, it is important for students to master as much of these methods as they can. This book was devoted almost exclusively to this paradigm to help such mastery. At the same time, many other methods are equally "scientific" and rigorous and follow the same tenets outlined at the beginning of the book. Single-case research and qualitative research, barely mentioned in this book, are two such paradigms and have quite different approaches and yields (see Kazdin, 2003).

In all of the methodological approaches one could identify, multiple practices are used to move from idea to hypothesis and empirical test. This book has been devoted to many practices and methodological approaches. There are broader characteristics of methodology and lessons derived from these practices. These are worth considering because they encourage flexibility in research and can increase the yield from individual investigations. This closing chapter is devoted to some of the broader lessons that one can draw from specific practices.

METHODOLOGY IS DYNAMIC

When we are first exposed to methodology in course work, we quickly learn many of the standard practices of research and their rationales. The practices cover selection of independent and dependent variables, the research design, the participants, various procedures, and statistical analyses. In the process of learning standard practices, we often leave with the lesson that methodology and the constituent practices used to design, conduct, and evaluate research are static. This is not true at all.

Methodology is a dynamic area with constant evolution and changes. Perhaps one sign of this is the updated editions of this book. There is a constant stream of articles on methodology, and these could not flourish and pass the journal peer-review process if they merely recycled old ideas. In addition, there are journals on methodology in which design, assessment, and data evaluation are core topics. Two prominent examples are *Psychological Methods* and *Psychological Assessment*, in which novel practices and ideas are constantly published. Many journals in other fields (e.g., epidemiology, medicine, statistics) are devoted to methodology as well. Within clinical psychology, journals that are devoted to research (e.g., *Journal of Consulting and Clinical Psychology*, *Journal of Abnormal Psychology*) or to reviews of research (e.g., *Clinical Psychology: Science and Practice*, *Clinical Psychology Review*) regularly publish articles on critical topics related to assessment, design, and evaluation. Methodological articles invariably follow from and contribute to advances in substantive areas. Advances in substantive areas of research require further developments in methodology as nuances and new complexities (e.g., sources of artifact, ethical issues) emerge. The influence is the other way as well; advances in methodology or new ways to address a topic can lead to new substantive findings. The role of methodology leading to and following advances is evident in science in general. For example, advances in assessment in cognitive neuroscience (e.g., neuroimaging) and astronomy (e.g., Hubble telescope) have generated quite new findings and newly discovered phenomena. Imaging and telescope development (both hardware and software) are advancing greatly at this time and are generating new kinds of information that prior techniques did not allow.

How does methodology change? Let me count, or at least illustrate, the ways. What constitutes an appropriate control group, one might think, is well worked out and resolved. However, in treatment research there has been a major change in whether placebo control groups can be used. In the context of evaluating medications for diseases (e.g., HIV), new treatments have been compared with no-treatment and placebo control conditions. This has raised obvious ethical issues, one of which is whether a placebo group ought to be used in any design. If there is any other intervention that is known to help alleviate or delay the effects of HIV, perhaps that ought to be the only comparison group for any new treatment. Is it ethical to use a placebo group for comparison? New international research guidelines suggest that such groups ought not to be used.[1] The matter is not yet resolved but obviously has broad implications for intervention research more generally.

Even when life-and-death issues are not involved, is the use of a control condition that provides a bogus treatment legitimate? Psychotherapy treatment trials occasionally use an attention placebo control group, that is, a condition that is not a real treatment but that is presented to clients as if it were. Is this legitimate or advisable? I have stated the matter here too simply because all sorts of arguments exist on each side. The point is that a central methodological issue, what control groups can and ought to be used, is still a topic before us. Ethical issues and the protection of human and animal participants are central to research design, and control groups are only one place in which these issues emerge. Advances in technology often raise new issues about protection of individual rights. For example, research on the Internet or monitoring of behavior of individuals in their daily routines (e.g., through cell phones, telemetry, tracking Web sites people visit) raises the prospect of new abuses (e.g., invasion of privacy). New or modified guidelines are needed to protect participants. Also, investigators often develop treatments, software, or novel techniques that may have commercial value. Conflict of interest among scientists and withholding information (for commercial gain) complicates the sharing of materials for replication.

Methodology encompasses assessment and statistical evaluation, and these areas also raise a plethora of issues that are constantly evolving and changing. For example, when novel assessments emerge or become in more frequent use (e.g., different neuroimaging techniques), methodological issues are raised and discussed. These issues include types of assessment bias or artifacts associated with the assessment modality, difficulties in measurement interpretation, and validity and reliability issues.

---

[1] The guidelines for research noted here are referred to as the Declaration of Helsinki. In 1964, these guidelines were developed to protect research particiants. They were originally prompted by the gruesome medical experiments by the German Nazis during World War II. Recent revisions of the declaration by the World Medical Association indicate that placebo control groups should not be used in medical research. Rather, the comparison ought to be the best current treatment method available (see Enserink, 2000). This recommendation grew out of recent medical research on such serious conditions as HIV in which efforts were made in Africa and Asia to evaluate new medications (e.g., to prevent pregnant HIV-positive mothers from passing HIV to their newborns). The use of placebos in such trials has been controversial to say the least. Citizens have lobbied against use of placebos when a reasonable basis exists for providing the drug or another treatment. Whether or not the research focus is life threatening, patients ought not to be subjected to placebo control conditions if any reasonable alternative conditions could be provided. There is no justification for unnecessary suffering. Arguments on the other side have focused on the need to establish the effects of treatment to ensure the greatest benefit, and the matter is not yet resolved (Vieira, 2002).

Similarly, when statistical techniques emerge, they too become a source of discussion, and these discussions often raise pivotal issues for conducting and interpreting research. For example, meta-analysis is a way of reviewing a literature and testing hypotheses based on the accumulation of several studies. This is a methodology that became actively used within the past 25 years. Many other statistical analyses (e.g., individual growth curves, structural equation modeling, receiver operating characteristics) emerge and provide new ways of looking at the data and ways of testing new conceptualizations. Most of these analyses are not necessarily "new," but they are applied to new areas or in novel ways, and these lead to weighty discussions about how they ought to be used and interpreted.

The constantly changing nature of methodology has important implications for the individual researcher. A given hypothesis or data set might be evaluated in new ways, and the yield can be quite informative. On the one hand, of course, a new data-analytic technique should not drive or dictate the substantive question. Just because one learns or knows a type of analysis (e.g., structural equation modeling, meta-analysis) does not mean that all of the data or one's questions ought to be forced into that. At the same time, a novel analysis for a research area can cast the relationships among variables of interest in ways that contribute to theoretical and empirical advances. For these reasons, as researchers, it is advisable for us to keep abreast of advances in methodology. This is often difficult because researchers usually cannot easily take time out to attend classes or read about the analyses in sufficient detail to integrate them into their research. However, collaborations with others who use different methodologies (within psychology but also related disciplines) and with others who are often keen to learn novel methodologies (e.g., graduate students) are ways to integrate new or not so new but innovative approaches into one's research.

QUESTION THE BASICS

Another lesson from methodology, illustrated in several of the chapters, pertains to basic research practices. We engage in many practices; we ought to challenge them because they have enormous implications. Among the easy examples, most psychological studies include samples of 20 to 30 participants per group and then analyze the results statistically to test the null hypotheses of the study. Some of the chapters in this book alert us to the problems of such small samples. Among the issues, with sample sizes within this range, equivalence of groups is difficult to achieve with random assignment of participants to conditions (Hsu, 1989). Thus, we may believe that our groups are equivalent based on random assignment, but they may not be, and we are not likely to be able to detect the differences (because of weak power). The small sample sizes greatly contribute to the problem. Also, with small sample sizes statistical power is likely to be weak unless the effect of the intervention is rather large (Cohen, 1992). In one's own research, one ought to question studies with small sample sizes and then take action to increase statistical power as necessary (see Kazdin, 2003). Alternatively, some designs might be used in cases in which strong causal statements can be drawn but sample size is not critical. For example, in single-case experimental designs, the strength of the demonstration depends more on repeated or continuous assessment on multiple occasions rather than on a large sample size.

In recommending that one question or challenging the basics, consider the notion of statistical significance. In all likelihood, no factor is as strongly indoctrinated into our research thinking as the value of $p < .05$ as a criterion of statistical significance. In my opinion, the importance of $p < .05$ becomes lodged in the brain exactly along the same circuits and paths where "one's parents" are cognitively and biochemically represented. I say this because early in our academic life we learn to love and worship $p < .05$. As we grow older we have little conflicts about this but eventually come to terms with the conflicts and realize that $p < .05$ is just trying to do its best. Finally, we realize we cannot not do much better and maybe should be grateful, gracious, and loving of $p < .05$. This sequence is so much like the way many people evaluate their parents.

All that said, $p < .05$ ought to be challenged in one's own research. There are many occasions in which one would want to depart from $p < .05$, as in the cases in which power is known to be small and different consequences are associated with reaching a decision in one direction rather than another, to mention a few of many such circumstances (see Kazdin, 2003). Related, apart from evaluation of statistical significance, the sole reliance on significance was an issue raised in a few of the chapters. Significance testing ought to be supplemented whenever possible with such other indices as effect size; confidence intervals; and, where relevant, indices of clinical significance.

Random assignment of participants to conditions is such a central feature of research that it is heresy to say this is another methodological tenet that ought to be questioned. The virtues of random assignment are so wonderful that this method of assignment has been elevated to a lofty status. Researchers are often reticent to evaluate many hypotheses and intervention programs because random assignment (e.g., in the schools, day care facilities) is not possible. Also, reviewers of manuscripts considered for journal publication and reviewers for agencies that provide research funds (grants) are among the most slavish adherents to traditional research methods and would be unlikely to approve (i.e., accept for publication, fund) such research. Yet evaluations without random assignment can have an enormously important yield. It is instructive to note, as was evident in one of the prior readings, that random assignment and nonrandom assignment often lead to quite similar conclusions (Shadish & Ragsdale, 1996; Wilson & Lipsey, 2001). This does not mean that randomization ought to be skipped or is unimportant. Randomized controlled trials are still considered the best way of establishing the effectiveness of an intervention. However, there are many studies with non-random assignment and many opportunities for such studies. Question the basics even here. Is randomization possible in this situation, and if not, is it essential to test the hypotheses?

When I suggest "question the basics," I only mean to note that at the design stage one ought to ask oneself, "Can I do better in how the groups are formed, in how the constructs are measured, and in how the data are presented and evaluated?" Also, one might ask, "Are the standard practices enhancing or restricting what I wish to learn from this study?" Students often look to a published article as a model for what measures to use and what statistical analyses to conduct. This is reasonable because one often wants a study to be integrated into the literature. Commonalities among studies in experimental design, measures, and sampling contribute to that integration. Even so, one should continue to question the basics because the research yield can be much greater by expanding on them.

METHODOLOGICAL PRACTICES
CONTRIBUTE TO THE RESULTS

Methodological practices (e.g., what measures, design features, statistics) are not given the credit (or blame) they deserve in research findings. We test a few hypotheses and often have an implicit view that how we test these hypotheses is not that important and relevant. After all, if our main hypotheses are as robust and brilliant as we think, perhaps they will be evident under almost any conditions in which we test them.

Actually, methodology teaches that the methods used in a study often contribute to the specific findings. In one of the chapters earlier in the book (David B. Wilson & Mark W. Lipsey, chapter 25), this was made clear in the context of treatment studies. Such factors as the type of design and measures influence the conclusions that are reached. The point can be made in other ways. I already mentioned meta-analysis as a valuable research tool for reviewing a body of research. The results from meta-analyses are influenced by how the meta-analysis is conducted. For example, there are different ways of weighing the studies, combining measures within a study, and computing effect size (the metric used to combine several studies). These different ways are not trivial. In fact, the same set of studies can yield somewhat different conclusions based on how the meta-analysis is conducted and the assumptions that are used (see Matt, 1989; Matt & Navarro, 1997; Weisz, Weiss, Han, Granger, & Morton, 1995).

Other facets of the design including the measures, setting, and sample (e.g., age, ethnicity) can greatly determine the results of a study. For example, self-report measures are assumed to provide a reasonably good measure of the characteristics of the individual that is being assessed. The accumulation of validity data over time can provide the needed support for a given measure. Even so, characteristics of the measures can influence the substantive findings. For example, the extent which individuals view themselves as successful in life varies as a function of whether they rate this on a scale from 1 to 10 or from -5 to 5 (people rate themselves as more successful with the -5 to 5 scale). Also, the extent to which individuals report that they experience psychological symptoms depends on how the response alternatives are worded and the other alternatives in which they are embedded (see Schwarz, 1999). These are not minor matters. Indeed, one of the reasons we use multiple measures in a study is to overcome the limits of any single measure.

As another facet of methodology, characteristics of the investigator too can contribute to the findings. For example, in the context of psychotherapy research, the allegiance of the investigator can influence the results. The *allegiance* refers to the conceptual view or position (e.g., cognitive−behavioral, psychodynamic) to which the investigator subscribes. Investigators are more likely to find that the therapy associated with their conceptual view is more effective than another treatment or comparison condition that departs from their conceptual view (Luborsky et al., 1999). This finding is subject to many interpretations, but the main point here is to note that who studies what can also exert influence on the results.

In short, design, sample, measures, statistics, and other facets of the study can influence the findings. This does not call for an extreme view of methodological relativism or nihilism, that is, that all findings depend on all of the facets of the study or that nothing can be known because every finding is completely dependent on the specific circumstances and time in which it is obtained. Rather, the influence of methodology is a caution to the investigator not to become too wedded to a rigid paradigm or single way of demonstrating the phenomena of interest. In one of the chapters in the book (Brendan A. Maher, chapter 8), we were cautioned to vary the stimulus conditions (experimenter, procedures, materials presented to the participant) within an experiment. The point can be extended to many features of the study. Two recommendations to convey this point would be (a) to operationalize (measure) constructs in more than one way and (b) over time study the phenomenon of interest (hypotheses, predictions) in different ways. The yield is likely to be different and that alone may generate important theoretical and research leads.

BE CAUTIOUS IN MOVING FROM FINDINGS TO CONCLUSIONS

Methodology draws attention to the distinction between findings and conclusions. The *findings* refer to the results that are obtained. This is the descriptive feature of the study or what was found. A statement of a finding might be that one group was better or worse than another. The *conclusions* refer to the statements the investigator makes that move slightly beyond mere description. The conclusions might include an explanation of the findings and the likelihood that the findings were due to the intervention or to various artifacts, biases, or special conditions of the study.

Methodology is about designing a study so we can reach the conclusions we wish with a minimum of ambiguity. What groups and measures are used, how carefully the procedures are conducted, and how the data are collected and analyzed have implications for the findings and the conclusions. The quality of the methodology of a study determines what the investigator is entitled to say. For example, let us say that one is interested in replicating the frequently obtained finding that cognitive therapy reduces depression in adults. We design a randomized controlled trial and show that in fact patients who receive cognitive therapy are greatly improved. Their changes are greater than those achieved in a no-treatment control group. Statistical significance, effect size, and clinical significance all show wondrous differences. What are the findings and conclusions?

The findings of course are the group differences and that treatment was effective. The conclusions might be that cognitive therapy is effective and that changing one's cognitions leads to reductions in depression. Actually, on the basis of the findings, we are not entitled to speak about cognitions and their role in therapeutic change. By the design of this study, we do not know why patients improved. Change could be due to merely participating in treatment—any treatment might be better than no treatment, and we know only that treatment was better, not why it was better. Let us say, in the next study, we include three groups: cognitive therapy, standard clinic counseling (chatting about depression and putative psychodynamic underpinnings of depression), and no treatment. Cognitive therapy, let us say, is better than the other two groups, and these other groups do not differ from each other. We can say more and especially that cognitive therapy probably is not due to merely participating in treatment per se. We still cannot say anything about whether cognitions are important; we have not shown that cognitive processes are the agent responsible for change (i.e., mediate change). Conclusions need to be based on what is studied. This sounds obvious, but methodology sensitizes us to be careful about what we conclude from our own studies and what we allow authors to conclude from their studies. In passing, this example of cognitive therapy is interesting because this is a well-developed and replicated therapy for major depression. To date, no evidence exists (that I could find) that changes in cognitions are responsible for (i.e., mediate, cause, lead to) treatment effects.

The relation of findings and conclusions is not minor. In fact, a major reason for rejecting articles for publication is the discrepancy between what *can* be said in light of the design (findings) and what *is* said about the demonstration (conclusion). The lesson for our own research is to decide before doing the study what one would like to conclude when the study is completed. This conclusion is worth writing down and discussing with others. Then at the design stage consider if the study were completed, would it be possible to reach this on the basis of who, how, and what was studied.

CLOSING COMMENTS

Methodology for many researchers consists of a course or two—more if statistical courses are included. Understandably, students are interested in moving on to the stimulating substantive topics and issues that drive their work. This is how it should be. At the same time, there are some side effects of viewing methodology as fixed or remaining fixed in the methods one uses. A formulaic rigidity exists in much of the research in a given area. This can be conceived as well-placed convention. For example, ensuring that one uses reliable and valid measures cannot be cast aside as merely slavish adherence to convention. Also, one would not want to recommend that more people use measures that are *un*reliable and *in*valid.[2] That said, a rigidity is executed and enforced in research. It is executed insofar as within a given area of research often the designs, measures, and methods of evaluating treatment remain fixed or reflect a narrow range of options. Novel departures can have a novel yield given the points made previously about the ways in which methods can contribute to and partially dictate the results.

Rigidity exists in how research methods are "enforced." There are some probably benign ways in which this is evident. For example, amazing rigidity is enforced in preparing articles for publication. Publication "guidelines" are provided to psychologists, and these are followed among many disciplines (see, e.g., American Psychological Association, 2001). The guidelines dictate with extreme specificity precisely how to describe each component of a study, the language that can and cannot be used, how numbers are presented, and so on. Of course, much of this is useful in standardizing information that is presented, but much also has no bearing on the quality of the study or consistency of information provided. Indeed, it is still the case that studies that meet such guidelines leave out many critical issues of a study. Such issues were discussed in chapter 27 by Wilkinson and the Task Force on Statistical Inference.

---

[2] I hope that readers do not accept this statement too quickly. Personally, I strongly advocate the use of possibly unreliable and possibly invalid measures. For example, in therapy research we evaluate whether patients improve on all sorts of psychological measures (e.g., rating scales completed by patients, therapists). It would be valuable to supplement these with measures of functioning in everyday life to see if the patients have really changed. Indeed, the standardized measures do not really tell us if the patients have improved according to their criteria or whether changes have made a genuine difference (Kazdin, 2001). Inserting novel measures on an exploratory basis, even if their validity is not established, might lead to improved measures. These measures eventually would become valid through refinements in the measures and validity studies.

In short, the way we learn research methods and how to communicate the results of these can foster somewhat fixed thinking. There is comfort in adopting and then adhering to conventions. This chapter does not suggest beginning science anew or discarding everything we have used to this point in time. However, given the constant development of novel methods for research and the dependence of conclusions on methods of research, it is wise to invest in a broad portfolio of research practices. This chapter and many of the others in this book lobby for expanded methods of assessment, design, and evaluation.

REFERENCES

American Psychological Association. (2001). *Publication manual of the American Psychological Association* (5th ed.). Washington, DC: American Psychological Association.

Cohen, J. (1992). A power primer. *Psychological Bulletin, 112,* 155–159.

Enserink, M. (2000). Helsinki's new clinical rules: Fewer placebos, more disclosure? *Science, 290,* 418–419.

Hsu, L. M. (1989). Random sampling, randomization, and equivalence of contrasted groups in psychotherapy outcome research. *Journal of Consulting and Clinical Psychology, 57,* 131–137.

Kazdin, A. E. (2001). Almost clinically significant ($p < .10$): Current measures may only approach clinical significance. *Clinical Psychology: Science and Practice, 8,* 455–462.

Kazdin, A. E. (2003). *Research design in clinical psychology* (4th ed.). Needham Heights, MA: Allyn & Bacon.

Luborsky, L., Diguer, L., Seligman, D. A., Rosenthal, R., Krause, E. D., Johnson, S., et al. (1999). The researcher's own therapy allegiances: A "wild card" in comparisons of treatment efficacy. *Clinical Psychology: Science and Practice, 6,* 95–106.

Matt, G. E. (1989). Decision rules for selecting effect sizes in meta-analysis: A review and reanalysis of psychotherapy outcome studies. *Psychological Bulletin, 105,* 106–115.

Matt, G. E., & Navarro, A. M. (1997). What meta-analyses have and have not taught us about psychotherapy effects: A review and future directions. *Clinical Psychology Review, 17,* 1–32.

Schwarz, N. (1999). Self-reports: How the questions shape the answers. *American Psychologist, 54,* 93–105.

Shadish, W. R., & Ragsdale, K. (1996). Random versus nonrandom assignment in controlled experiments. Do you get the same answer? *Journal of Consulting and Clinical Psychology, 64,* 1290–1305.

Vieira, C. L. (2002). Tough placebo rules leave scientists out in the cold. *Science, 295,* 264.

Weisz, J. R., Weiss, B., Han, S. S., Granger, D. A., & Morton, T. (1995). Effects of psychotherapy with children and adolescents revisited: A meta-analysis of treatment outcome studies. *Psychological Bulletin, 117,* 450–468.

Wilson, D. B., & Lipsey, M. W. (2001). The role of method in treatment effectiveness research: Evidence from meta-analysis. *Psychological Methods, 6,* 413–429.

INDEX

as research component, 63
Behavior sampling, 245
Behavior therapy
　　for obsessive—compulsive disorder,
　　　　636
　　research on, 506
Bellwood, M. F., 642–643
Belmont Report, 774, 776
Beneficence, 744, 775, 796
Benefit (as term), 720
Bernoulli, Jacques, 381
Bessel, F. W., 383
Beta errors. *See* Type II errors
Beta weights, 411–412
Between-groups sum of squares, 593
Between-study differences, 609
Beutler, Larry, 189
Bias
　　in Harlow's "mother love" experi-
　　　　ments, 112–113
　　monomethod/monooperation, 304
　　observers', 245
　　selection, 607, 608
　　and Simpson's paradox, 154–157
　　sources of, 12–14
Bilingualism, 359
Biomedical research, ethical issues in, 772,
　　　774
Biometric school, 383, 384
Board of Ethnic Minority Affairs, 364–365
Board of Professional Affairs (BPA), 266
Board of Scientific Affairs (BSA), 813, 814
Bonferroni maneuver, 408–409
Bootstrap resampling approach, 595
Boundaries, professional, 747, 783
BPA (Board of Professional Affairs), 266
Bridging Science and Service (National Ad-
　　　visory Mental Health Council
　　　Workgroup), 533–534
Brown, R., 117–119
Brunswik, Egon, 163, 169
BSA. *See* Board of Scientific Affairs

Campbell, D. T., 112–113, 389–390,
　　　851–852
Capaldi, D. M., 86
Career counseling, 463
Carver, R. P., 438
Case formulation approach, 523
Case studies, 498, 655–668
　　assessment occasions, timing number
　　　of, 659

central role of, in clinical psychology,
　　　655
characteristics of, 657–658
continuous assessment with stability
　　　in multiple, 665
definition of, 657
internal validity of, 655–668
limitations of, 655–656
of mixed anxiety—depression,
　　　671–686
past/future projections of perfor-
　　　mance from, 660–661
pre- and postassessment in, 663
repeated assessment with marked
　　　changes in, 664
role of clinical investigator in,
　　　666–667
single case experimental designs vs.,
　　　656–657
subjects, number/heterogeneity of,
　　　661–662
type of data obtained from, 658–
　　　659
types of changes observed in, 661
value of, 656
Causality, 176–177, 827–828
Cause, 8, 386
Caution (in thinking), 8–9
CBT (cognitive—behavioral therapy),
　　　506
Center for Epidemiological Studies-
　　　Depression scale (CES-D), 356
Centering a variable, 82
CES-D (Center for Epidemiological
　　　Studies-Depression scale), 356
Chance, 386
Change(s)
　　actual vs. perceived, 699
　　clinical significance of, 625, 695–
　　　697
　　in scale, 61
Checklist format, 215
Child and adolescent mental health,
　　　570–577, 579–581
Child-clinical psychology, moderating/
　　　mediating effects in, 96
Children
　　acquisition of speech by, 117–119
　　relationship of height/intelligence/
　　　achievement in, 418–419
Chi-square test, 438
Christensen, A., 527

in research with human participants, 772

standards for, in APA Ethics Code, 752–754

Conflicts
  ethical, 745–746
  of interest, 750
Conformity to group pressure, 132
Consent, informed. *See* Informed consent
Consequent, affirming the, 391
Consistency, 201. *See also* Internal consistency
Construct precision specification, 245
Constructs, assessment of, 199, 852–854
Construct validity, 208–209, 239
Consultations, standards for, 754
Consumer Reports, 525–527, 556
Content validity, 238, 239, 241–244, 252
Context effects, 245
Context(s)
  and process examination, 65, 66
  of psychological events, 62–67
  as research component, 63
Contextualization (of reports), 839
Continuous assessment (case studies), 659, 665
Contrast effects, 245
Contrastive strategy, 68
Contributions, substantial, 794
Control group, 816–817
Controls
  definition of, 150
  in efficacy studies, 508–511
  in efficacy vs. effectiveness studies, 577–579
  no-treatment, 577–578
  participants serving as own, 642–643
  for study method features in meta-analysis, 609
  waiting-list, 511, 577–578
Convergence, 11
Convergent validation, 849–851
Convergent validity, 239, 247
Converging operations, 27–31
Convincingness, 176
Cook, T. D., 389–390
Cookie studies, 130–131
Cooperation, professional, 751
Copernicus, Nicolas, 6
Corporate health care packages, 720
Correlation coefficient (r), 128, 270–276
Correlation(s), 8

among test scores, 849–852
artifactual variation in, 445
confidence intervals for, 446–447
observed, as index of effect size, 446
set, 423
in statistical significance testing
  vs. meta-analysis, 443–445
unit vs. beta weights for, 411–412
Corroborated theories, 391–392
Cosmology, 462
Cost-benefit analyses, 456, 712, 719–724, 775
Cost-effectiveness, 239, 253–255, 712, 720–724
Cost factors, 711–724
  cost-effectiveness and cost-benefit analyses, beliefs about, 719–724
  cost-outcome relationships, beliefs about, 713–716
  impediments to analysis of, 721–724
  with interventions, 500–501
  need for focus on, 712–713, 724
  treatment techniques vs. delivery systems, beliefs about, 716–719
Cost-outcome relationships, 713–716
Couples, therapy involving, 768
Cramer, H., 380
Credentials, misrepresentation of, 785
Credibility, 176
Credit, allocation of. *See* Allocation of credit
Criterion-based test construction, 217–218
Critical incident technique (CIT), 782–785
Critical ratio, 385
Cross-method agreement, 295–308
Cross-validated multiple correlation, 412
Cuban Missile Crisis, 68
Curvilinear regression smoother (LOESS), 829
Cutoff points, 705–706

d. See Standardized mean difference
Dark adaptation, 119–120
Data
  from case studies, 658–659
  duplicate publication of, 763
  sharing, for verification, 763–764

Multivariate planned comparison, 400–401

National Adult Reading Test (NART), 311
National Advisory Mental Health Council Workgroup, 533–534
National Institute of Mental Health (NIMH), 189, 532–535
National Institute of Mental Health Treatment of Depression Collaborative Research Program (NIMH-TDCRP), 509–510, 524–525, 552
National Institutes of Health (NIH), 192
Native Americans, 195
Negative predictive power, 258
Neural imaging, 30
Newell, A., 646–647
Neyman, Jerzy, 414–416
NHST. *See* Null hypothesis statistical tests
NHT. *See* Null hypothesis significance testing
NIH (National Institutes of Health), 192
NIMH. *See* National Institute of Mental Health
NIMH-TDCRP. *See* National Institute of Mental Health Treatment of Depression Collaborative Research Program
Nonmaleficence, 744, 775
Nonpayment, withholding records for, 756
Nonrandom assignment, 816–817
"No risk" judgments, 775
Normal distribution(s), 382–383
Normative functioning, range of, 694
Norms, as impediment to unified psychology, 30
Norquist, G., 532–533
No-treatment control, 577–578
Nuisance variables, 148, 153–154, 159
Null hypotheses, 413–419
    and falsification, 390, 391
    proving, 417
    rejection/acceptance of, 454–455
    rejection of multivariate vs. univariate, 401
    in statistical power analysis, 429–432
Null hypothesis significance testing (NHT), 439, 448, 461–464
Null hypothesis statistical tests (NHST), 466–468, 484–486

alternatives to, 468
Bayesian analysis vs., 475–476, 480, 481
continued popularity of, 466
criticisms of, 466–468
example of, 470–472
meta-analysis vs., 472–475
Null hypothesis testing, 373, 374, 636–637, 639
Numerical results, reporting of, 409
Nunnally, J. C., 453

Oakes, M. L., 438, 452
Obesity programs, 716–719
Objectivity, significance testing and illusion of, 452
Observational studies, experiments vs., 140
Obsessive—compulsive disorder, 636
Ogles, B. M., 524–525
Omnibus *(F)* tests, 399–402, 438
Operant research, single-participant research in, 637–638
Operationalization (of outcome measures), 608
Optimists, 478–483
OQ. *See* Outcome Questionnaire
Organization (of writing), 862–863
Organizations
    assumptions applicable to, 69, 70
    ethical conflicts with demands of, 746
    psychological services delivered to/through, 752
Outcome assessment, 619–620, 631. *See also* Outcome Questionnaire
    drivers of, 619–620
    early efforts at, 620
    technologically based, 620
Outcome constructs, measurement of, 599
Outcome measures, operationalization of, 608
Outcome Questionnaire (OQ), 620–631
    design of, 621
    development of, 620–621
    example of, in clinical practice, 626–631
    features of, 621–622
    profile sheet of, 623–624
    and referencing of patient status, 625–626
    reliability of, 621
Outcomes

Psychological Abstracts Information
Services (PsycINFO), 276,
721–723
Psychological assessment. *See* Assessment(s)
Psychological Assessment (journal),
207–208, 210, 213, 217, 218, 227
Psychological Assessment Work Group
(PAWG), 266
Psychological Bulletin, review articles in. *See*
Review articles
Psychological phenomena
as basis of unified psychology, 35
divisions of psychology by, 38, 39
fields studying only parts of, 34–35
outside of core fields, 32–33
Psychological testing. *See also under* Test . . .
batteries, test, 304
contextual factors in, 309–312
evidence supporting goals of,
276–292
psychological assessment vs.,
292–293
validity of, 268–276
Psychology of Healthy Lifestyles (PHL),
469
The Psychology of Interpersonal Relations
(F. Heider), 67
Psychometric evaluation, in scale development, 221–228. *See also* Analogue
behavioral observation
Psychometric properties (of an instrument), 201
Psychopathology, measures of, 514
Psychopharmacology, 506
Psychosocial treatment outcome research,
671–672
Psychotherapy placebos, 509–510
PsycINFO database. *See* Psychological
Abstracts Information Services
Ptolemy, Claudius, 6
Publication and communication of research, 139, 807–808
and reliance on significance testing,
452
standards for, in APA Ethics Code,
759–764
Public statements, standards for, 754–756
Publishing/publications
authorship credit in. *See* Authorship
credit and order
multicultural content in, 190–196

research reports. *See* Research reports
review articles. *See* Review articles
statistical methods in. *See* Statistical methods in psychology
journals
p value, 414, 415, 420–421

Quetelet, Lambert Adolphe, 382, 383

r. *See* Correlation coefficient; Product-
moment correlation coefficient
Racism, 173–174
Random assignment, 577–578, 881–882
in efficacy studies, 508, 511–512
and statistical methods in psychology
journals, 816–817
Randomization, 147–154, 158, 159
Randomized controlled trials (RCTs), 495,
547–564
difficulties in application of, 550
and evidence-based practice, 551–552
useful information derived from,
548–550, 557–560
uselessness of results derived from,
552–557, 560–563
Randomized designs
limitations of, in treatment effectiveness research, 589–590
results from nonrandomized designs
vs., 607–608
Random sampling, 147–149, 151–154,
158, 159
Rating scales, standardized self-report, 620,
622
RCM. *See* Rubin's causal model
RCTs. *See* Randomized controlled trials
Reactive effects, 245
Real-time graphs, 644
"Reasonable" (as term in Ethics Code), 742
Recasting theoretical statements, 69
Recording methods, 245
Recording (of clients), 753, 760
Record keeping, standards for, 756–757
Recruitment of research participants,
356–357
Recurrence of ideas, 57–58
Referrals, standards for, 757
Regression
in ethnic minority assessment studies,
360
for testing mediated effects, 84–86
for testing moderated effects, 81–83

ABOUT THE EDITOR

Alan E. Kazdin is professor and director of the Child Study Center and John M. Musser Professor of Psychology at the Yale University School of Medicine and is director of the Child Conduct Clinic, an outpatient treatment service for children and their families. He received his PhD in clinical psychology from Northwestern University. Prior to coming to Yale, he was on the faculty of The Pennsylvania State University and the University of Pittsburgh School of Medicine. His research focuses on therapy for children and adolescents, including the treatment of aggressive and antisocial behavior, processes involved in therapeutic change, and barriers to participation in treatment. He has been a fellow of the Center for Advanced Study in the Behavioral Sciences, president of the Association for Advancement of Behavior Therapy, and chairman of the Department of Psychology at Yale University. He has received the Distinguished Scientific Contribution and Distinguished Professional Contribution Awards in Clinical Psychology from the American Psychological Association. He has been editor of various journals (*Journal of Consulting and Clinical Psychology*, *Behavior Therapy*, *Psychological Assessment*, and *Clinical Psychology: Science and Practice*). Currently, he is editor of *Current Directions in Psychological Science*. He has authored or edited more than 35 books on treatment, child and adolescent disorders, and methodology and research design, including *The Encyclopedia of Psychology* (Oxford University Press/American Psychological Association, 2000); *Psychotherapy for Children and Adolescents: Directions for Research and Practice*; *Behavior Modification in Applied Settings* (6th ed.); and *Research Design in Clinical Psychology* (4th ed.).